CONSUMER BEHAVIOUR

A European Perspective

PEARSON
Education

We work with leading authors to develop the strongest educational materials in marketing, bringing cutting-edge thinking and best learning practice to a global market.

Under a range of well-known imprints, including Financial Times Prentice Hall, we craft high quality print and electronic publications which help readers to understand and apply their content, whether studying or at work.

To find out more about the complete range of our publishing, please visit us on the World Wide Web at: **www.pearsoned.co.uk**

CONSUMER BEHAVIOUR

A European Perspective

Michael Solomon

Gary Bamossy

Søren Askegaard

Margaret K. Hogg

Prentice Hall

FINANCIAL TIMES

An imprint of **Pearson Education**

Harlow, England • London • New York • Boston • San Francisco • Toronto • Sydney • Singapore • Hong Kong
Tokyo • Seoul • Taipei • New Delhi • Cape Town • Madrid • Mexico City • Amsterdam • Munich • Paris • Milan

Pearson Education Limited

Edinburgh Gate
Harlow
Essex CM20 2JE
England

and Associated Companies throughout the world

Visit us on the World Wide Web at:
www.pearsoned.co.uk

First published by Prentice Hall Europe 1999
Second edition published 2002
Third edition published 2006

ISBN: 978-0-273-71472-9

British Library Cataloguing-in-Publication Data
A catalogue record for this book is available from the British Library

Library of Congress Cataloging-in-Publication Data
A catalog record for this book is available from the Library of Congress

10 9 8 7 6 5 4 3 2 1
11 10 09 08 07

Typeset in 9.5/12pt Palatino by 35
Printed and bound by Mateu Cromo, Madrid, Spain

The publisher's policy is to use paper manufactured from sustainable forests.

BRIEF CONTENTS

CONTENTS

Part A
CONSUMERS IN THE MARKETPLACE

Chapter 1
An introduction to consumer behaviour   3

Part B
CONSUMERS AS INDIVIDUALS

Chapter 2
Perception   35

Chapter 3
Learning and memory   61

Part C
CONSUMERS AS DECISION-MAKERS

Part D
A PORTRAIT OF EUROPEAN CONSUMERS

Chapter 11
European family structures and household decision-making   401

Chapter 12
Income and social class   427

Chapter 13
Age subcultures   455

Part E
CULTURE AND EUROPEAN LIFESTYLES

Chapter 17
New times, new consumers

Supporting resources

Visit **www.pearsoned.co.uk/solomon** to find valuable online resources

For instructors
- Instructor's Manual with suggested teaching tips
- Case study solutions
- PowerPoint slides that can be downloaded and used as OHTs

For more information please contact your local Pearson Education sales representative or visit **www.pearsoned.co.uk/solomon**

OneKey: All you and your students need to succeed

Convenience. Simplicity. Success.

OneKey is an exclusive new resource for instructors and students, giving you access to the best online teaching and learning tools 24 hours a day, 7 days a week.

OneKey means all your resources are in one place for maximum convenience, simplicity and success.

A OneKey product is available for *Consumer Behaviour: A European Perspective, third edition* for use with Blackboard™, WebCT and CourseCompass. It contains:

- Online Study Guide with up to 30 hours of enrichment material to reinforce learning

For more information about the OneKey product please contact your local Pearson Education sales representative or visit **www.pearsoned.co.uk/onekey**

PREFACE

We wrote this book because we're fascinated by the everyday activities of people. The field of consumer behaviour is, to us, the study of how the world is influenced by the action of marketers. We're fortunate enough to be teachers and researchers (and occasionally consultants) whose work allows us to study consumers. Given that we're also consumers, we can find both professional and personal interest in learning more about how this process works. As consumers and future managers, we hope you find this study to be fascinating as well. Whether you're a student, manager, or professor, we're sure you can relate to the trials and tribulations associated with last-minute shopping, preparing for a big night out, agonizing over a purchase decision, fantasizing about a week skiing in the Swiss Alps, celebrating a holiday on the Cote d'Azur, or commemorating a landmark event, such as graduating from university, getting a driver's licence, or (dreaming about) winning the lottery.

Buying, having and being

Our understanding of this field goes beyond looking at the act of *buying* only, but to both *having* and *being* as well. Consumer behaviour is much more than buying things; it also embraces the study about how having (or not having) things affects our lives, and how our possessions influence the way we feel about ourselves and about each other – our state of being. In addition to understanding why people buy things, we also try to appreciate how products, services and consumption activities contribute to the broader social world we experience. Whether shopping, cooking, cleaning, playing football or hockey, lying on the beach, emailing or texting friends, or even looking at ourselves in the mirror, our lives are touched by the marketing system.

The field of consumer behaviour is young, dynamic and in flux. It is constantly being cross-fertilized by perspectives from many different disciplines. We have tried to express the field's staggering diversity in this text. Consumer researchers represent virtually every social science discipline, plus a few represent the physical sciences and the arts for good measure. From this melting pot has come a healthy debate among research perspectives, viewpoints regarding appropriate research methods, and even deeply held beliefs about what are and what are not appropriate issues for consumer researchers to study in the first place.

A European perspective on consumers and marketing strategy

The main objective for this adaptation has been to significantly increase its relevance for European students and scholars, while retaining the accessibility, contemporary approach, and the level of excellence in the discussions of consumer behaviour theory and applications established over the last six editions of Michael Solomon's *Consumer Behavior*. Based on the 6th American edition, we have tried to satisfy the need for a comprehensive consumer behaviour textbook with a significant European content. Hence, we have added illustrative examples and cases which are analysed and discussed in a European consumer context, as well as numerous European scholarly references. The text also includes a number of advertisements of European origin to visualize various elements in the marketing applications of consumer behaviour theory. These changes, which focus on European consumers and research, have been made throughout the book. However, the most substantial changes have been made in the chapters dealing with demographic groups, subcultures and lifestyles, where the American perspective provided in earlier editions of Solomon's text has been replaced with a European one. EU enlargement to 25 Member States has increased the population by 20 per cent, to more than 450 million people. At the same time, this significant increase in population has only raised EU Gross Domestic Production by 4.5 per cent. This 3rd edition examines the demographics and social changes inherent in the structure of the new EU-25, and offers readers a variety of perspectives on European consumer desires and aspirations. The new edition also offers many examples of the new opportunities and challenges in this marketplace, as well as discussing the implications and challenges of carrying out business strategies and tactics.

The internationalization of market structures makes its increasingly necessary for business people to acquire a clear perspective and understanding of cultural differences and similarities among consumers from various countries. One of the challenges of writing this book has been to develop materials which illustrate *local* as well as *pan-European* and *global* aspects of consumer behaviour. In this spirit, we have kept a number of American and other non-European examples to illustrate various similarities and differences on the global consumer scene. The book also emphasizes the importance of understanding consumers in formulating marketing strategy. Many (if not most) of the fundamental concepts of marketing are based on the practitioner's ability to understand people. To illustrate the potential of consumer research to inform marketing strategy, the text contains numerous examples of specific applications of consumer behaviour concepts by marketing practitioners.

Pedagogical features

Throughout the text there are numerous boxed illustrative examples which highlight particular aspects of the impact and informing role that consumer behaviour has on marketing activities. These colour-coded boxes are called:

- **Multicultural dimensions**,
- **Marketing opportunity**, and
- **Marketing pitfall**,

and represent examples from several European and global markets. There are several other features within each chapter to assist you in learning and reviewing this text, and to check and critically review your understanding of topics; these include:

- an opening illustrative **vignette**,
- highlighted **Key terms**,
- a **Chapter summary**, and
- **Consumer behaviour challenge** questions.

To familiarize yourself with these features and how they will benefit your study from this text, they are reproduced and described in the Guided Tour on pages xviii–xxi.

Case study problems

The 3rd edition has 20 new cases! These cases were written by our European colleagues who teach and research consumer behaviour. The case material covers various companies, industries (e.g. the Greek wine industry, the Portuguese port wine industry, and the UK funeral industry) and countries (e.g. Austria, Belgium, Denmark, Eire, France, Germany, Greece, Portugal, Scotland, Sweden, Spain, Turkey and the UK). The cases integrate the topics covered in the preceding chapters, and appear at the end of each section. The questions at the end of each case study are designed to allow you to apply your understanding to real-life events and consumer behaviour activities; to develop your analytical skills; and to facilitate understanding of the different markets and cultural contexts across Europe. The questions often invite you to draw cross-cultural comparisons with your own consumer society.

Structure of the text

The structure of this textbook is simple: it goes from micro to macro. Think of the book as a sort of photograph album of consumer behaviour: each chapter provides a 'snapshot' of consumers, but the lens used to take each picture gets successively wider. The book begins with issues related to the individual consumer and expands its focus until it eventually considers the behaviours of large groups of people in their social settings. The topics to be covered correspond to the Wheel of Consumer Behaviour presented in the following figure.

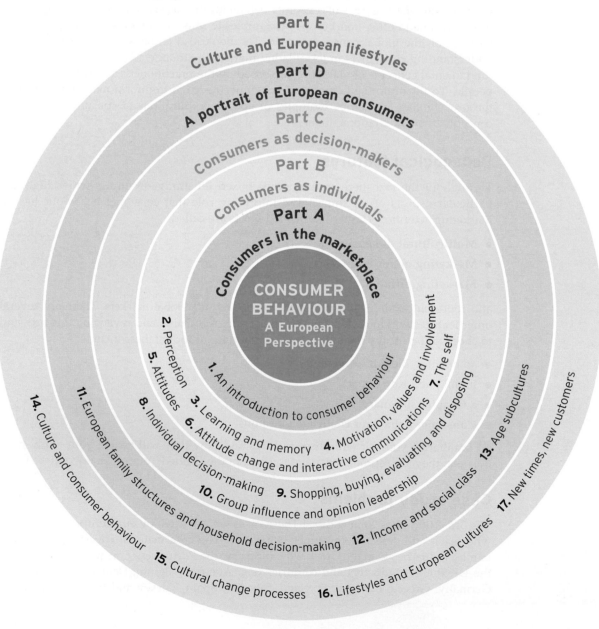

Following the Introductory chapter, Part B 'Consumers as individuals', considers the consumer at the most micro level. It examines how the individual receives information from his or her immediate environment and how this material is learned, stored in memory, and used to form and modify individual attitudes – both about products and about oneself. Part C, 'Consumers as decision-makers', explores the ways in which consumers use the information they have acquired to make decisions about consumption activities, both as individuals and as group members. Part D, 'A portrait of European consumers', further expands the focus by considering how the consumer functions as a part of a larger social structure. No other consumer behaviour textbook offers as complete and up-to-date materials on the consumers of the EU-25. This structure includes the influence of different social groups to which the consumer belongs and/or identifies with, featuring social class and age groups. Finally, Part E, 'Culture and European lifestyles', completes the picture as it examines marketing's impact on mass culture. This discussion focuses on the relationship of marketing to the expression of cultural values and lifestyles, how products and services are related to rituals and cultural myths, and the interface between marketing efforts and the creation of art, music, and other forms of popular culture that are so much a part of our daily lives. It also includes a section on major cultural change processes, analyzed from the perspectives of globalization and postmodernism.

GUIDED TOUR OF THE BOOK

ATTITUDES

It's a lazy Wednesday night, and Leah, Lynn and Nicki are hanging out at Nicki's flat in Manchester doing some channel-surfing. Leah clicks to the sports cable and the three friends see there's a women's soccer game on, being televised from America. Leah has been a fan for as long as she can remember – perhaps as a result of having three older brothers and growing up in a house which had Manchester United souvenirs in every room. She loves the subtle intensity of the game – the traps, the moves, the way players make it look easy to move a ball around a huge field as if it were a small patch of grass. Further, she's proud of Manchester United's rich history as a club, and its success as a business operation. But don't ask her opinion of having her beloved team's ownership taken over by some American businessman who doesn't even understand the game! Nicki's a glutton for thrills and chills: she converted to soccer after seeing Mick Jagger singing along with the British crowd in the stadium as the English team battled the Argentinians in an exciting, dramatic match in the 1998 World Cup. Lynn, on the other hand, doesn't know a corner kick from a penalty kick. For her, the most interesting part of the match was the footage being shown over and over of the US player Brandi Chastain's celebrating her successful penalty kick which won the match by taking her shirt off to reveal her sports bra. Lynn even bought one a few weeks later. Still, soccer doesn't really ring her chimes – but as long as she gets to hang out with her girlfriends she doesn't really care if they watch non-contact sports like soccer or contact sports like *The Jerry Springer Show* or *Big Brother*!

Opening vignette
Each chapter opens with a short, country-specific illustrative scenario, setting the scene for the chapter material and highlighting the interrelationships between the individual and his or her social realities.

---

138 CHAPTER 5 ATTITUDES

■ THE POWER OF ATTITUDES

Leah is just the kind of fan sponsoring companies like Nike, Gatorade and Adidas hope will turn women's soccer into an ongoing source of sports fanaticism. In America, attitudes towards the game have changed dramatically since the US women's team lost in the 1996 semi-finals in Sweden before a crowd of less than 3,000. The 1999 World Cup was won before an audience of over 90,000 screaming fans, many of whom were soccer mums who saw the players as important role models for their young daughters. In 1998 a record 7.5 million women and girls enrolled for soccer teams in the United States. There, women now represent just under half of all soccer player registrations.[2] These kinds of growth figures are not to be found in Europe. Soccer has a much richer, longer tradition here, and has been a sport dominated by male patronage at the stadiums and male viewership on the television. While amateur soccer clubs for women can be found in the UK and on the Continent, they are not nearly as popular as in the United States, and have to compete with other sports which attract female participants, such as field hockey.

On the other hand, following Chastain's exuberant show of skin there has been much written in the United States over the so-called 'babe factor' as some critics wonder whether women's athletics will ever be taken seriously by male fans. Others feel that attitudes towards the game are more complex than that; they argue that sex appeal does not have to be sacrificed for professionalism. The big question is whether these positive feelings will endure. The goal of the Women's World Cup is to establish a women's professional league over the next few years. Time will tell if this ambitious project will score big or be red-carded and left to dwindle on the sidelines in the United States.[3] To score big in professional sports in the United States, or in Europe, is all a question of attitudes, and the dominant attitude among European fans is that women's soccer just isn't that important, at least so far. As you'll see throughout this book, attitudes can vary significantly along gender lines, and from one culture to another.

The term attitude is widely used in popular culture. You might be asked, 'What is your attitude towards abortion?' A parent might scold, 'Young man, I don't like your attitude.' Some bars even euphemistically refer to Happy Hour as 'an attitude adjustment period'. For our purposes, though, an attitude is a lasting, general evaluation of people (including oneself), objects, advertisements or issues.[4] Anything towards which one has an attitude is called an attitude object (A_o).

This chapter will consider the contents of an attitude, how attitudes are formed, how they can be measured, and review some of the surprisingly complex relationships between attitudes and behaviour. Both as a theoretical concept, and as a tool to be used in the marketplace, the notion and dynamics of attitudes remain one of the most studied and applied of all behavioural constructs.[5] In the next chapter, we'll take a closer look at how attitudes can be changed – certainly an issue of prime importance to marketers.

■ THE CONTENT OF ATTITUDES

An attitude is *lasting* because it tends to endure over time. It is *general* because it applies to more than a momentary event, like hearing a loud noise (though over time you might develop a negative attitude towards all loud noises). Consumers have attitudes towards very product-specific behaviours (such as using Mentodent rather than Colgate toothpaste), as well as towards more general consumption-related behaviours (for example, how often you should brush your teeth). Attitudes help to determine who a person goes out with, what music he or she listens to, whether he or she will recycle or discard cans, or whether he or she chooses to become a consumer researcher for a living.

Key terms
Colour-highlighted within the text where they first appear, and with an icon (▶) in the margin to assist rapid navigation, key terms aid in reinforcing important points.

Marketing pitfalls

Marketing pitfall boxes bring to life possible marketing situations or dilemmas that might arise due to cultural differences or lack of knowledge.

Multicultural dimensions

These boxes highlight cultural differences in consumer behaviour across countries and continents to drive home diversity across the globe.

Marketing opportunities

These boxes show how consumer research informs marketing strategy, and the actual or potential application of consumer behaviour concepts by marketing practitioners.

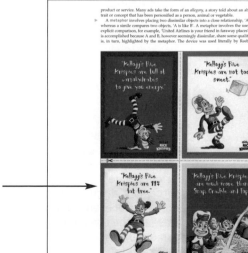
Colour photographs

Over 80 colour photographs and company advertisements are integrated throughout the text to help bring consumer behaviour topics to life.

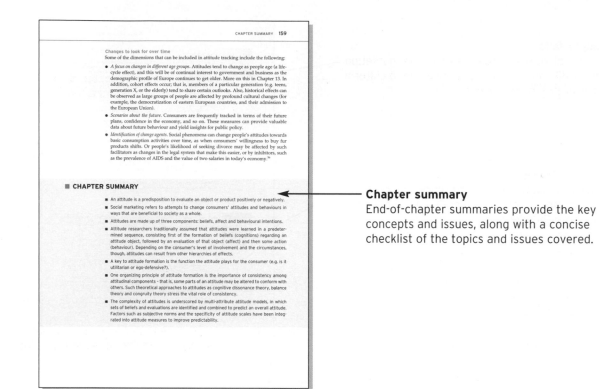

Chapter summary
End-of-chapter summaries provide the key concepts and issues, along with a concise checklist of the topics and issues covered.

Key terms
A list of key terms in the chapter, including a page reference where each term is first introduced, serves as a convenient revision tool.

Consumer behaviour challenge
Each chapter ends with short, discursive-style questions to encourage critical examination of topics and issues. These can be used individually or as a part of a group discussion.

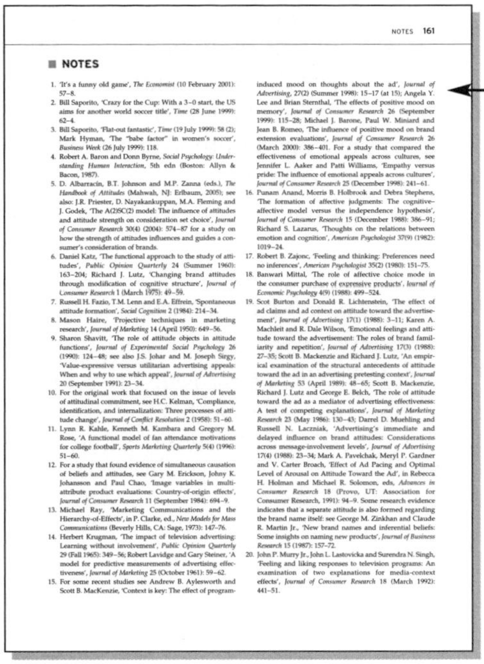

NOTES 161

■ NOTES

1. 'It's a funny old game', The Economist (10 February 2001): 57–8.
2. Bill Saporito, 'Crazy for the Cup: With a 3–0 start, the US aims for another world soccer title', Time (28 June 1999): 62–4.
3. Bill Saporito, 'Flat-out fantastic', Time (19 July 1999): 58 (2); Mark Hyman, 'The "babe factor" in women's soccer', Business Week (26 July 1999): 118.
4. Robert A. Baron and Donn Byrne, Social Psychology: Understanding Human Interaction, 5th edn (Boston: Allyn & Bacon, 1987).
5. D. Albarracin, B.T. Johnson and M.P. Zanna (eds.), The Handbook of Attitudes (Mahwah, NJ: Erlbaum, 2005); see also: J.R. Priester, D. Nayakankuppan, M.A. Fleming and J. Godek, 'The A(2)SC(2) model: The influence of attitudes and attitude strength on consideration set choice', Journal of Consumer Research 30(4) (2004): 574–87 for a study on how the strength of attitudes influences and guides a consumer's consideration of brands.
6. Daniel Katz, 'The functional approach to the study of attitudes', Public Opinion Quarterly 24 (Summer 1960): 163–204; Richard J. Lutz, 'Changing brand attitudes through modification of cognitive structure', Journal of Consumer Research 1 (March 1975): 49–59.
7. Russell H. Fazio, T.M. Lenn and E.A. Effrein, 'Spontaneous attitude formation', Social Cognition 2 (1984): 214–34.
8. Mason Haire, 'Projective techniques in marketing research', Journal of Marketing 14 (April 1950): 649–56.
9. Sharon Shavitt, 'The role of attitude objects in attitude functions', Journal of Experimental Social Psychology 26 (1990): 124–48; see also J.S. Johar and M. Joseph Sirgy, 'Value-expressive versus utilitarian advertising appeals: When and why to use which appeal', Journal of Advertising 20 (September 1991): 23–34.
10. For the original work that focused on the issue of levels of attitudinal commitment, see H.C. Kelman, 'Compliance, identification, and internalization: Three processes of attitude change', Journal of Conflict Resolution 2 (1958): 51–60.
11. Lynn R. Kahle, Kenneth M. Kambara and Gregory M. Rose, 'A functional model of fan attendance motivations for college football', Sports Marketing Quarterly 5(4) (1996): 51–60.
12. For a study that found evidence of simultaneous causation of beliefs and attitudes, see Gary M. Erickson, Johny K. Johansson and Paul Chao, 'Image variables in multi-attribute product evaluations: Country-of-origin effects', Journal of Consumer Research 11 (September 1984): 694–9.
13. Michael Ray, 'Marketing Communications and the Hierarchy-of-Effects', in P. Clarke, ed., New Models for Mass Communications (Beverly Hills, CA: Sage, 1973): 147–76.
14. Herbert Krugman, 'The impact of television advertising: Learning without involvement', Public Opinion Quarterly 29 (Fall 1965): 349–56; Robert Lavidge and Gary Steiner, 'A model for predictive measurements of advertising effectiveness', Journal of Marketing 25 (October 1961): 59–62.
15. For some recent studies see Andrew B. Aylesworth and Scott B. MacKenzie, 'Context is key: The effect of program-induced mood on thoughts about the ad', Journal of Advertising 27(2) (Summer 1998): 15–17 (at 15); Angela Y. Lee and Brian Sternthal, 'The effects of positive mood on memory', Journal of Consumer Research 26 (September 1999): 115–28; Michael J. Barone, Paul W. Miniard and Jean B. Romeo, 'The influence of positive mood on brand extension evaluations', Journal of Consumer Research 26 (March 2000): 386–401. For a study that compared the effectiveness of emotional appeals across cultures, see Jennifer L. Aaker and Patti Williams, 'Empathy versus pride: The influence of emotional appeals across cultures', Journal of Consumer Research 25 (December 1998): 241–61.
16. Punam Anand, Morris B. Holbrook and Debra Stephens, 'The formation of affective judgments: The cognitive-affective model versus the independence hypothesis', Journal of Consumer Research 15 (December 1988): 386–91; Richard S. Lazarus, 'Thoughts on the relations between emotion and cognition', American Psychologist 37(9) (1982): 1019–24.
17. Robert B. Zajonc, 'Feeling and thinking: Preferences need no inferences', American Psychologist 35(2) (1980): 151–75.
18. Banwari Mittal, 'The role of affective choice mode in the consumer purchase of expressive products', Journal of Economic Psychology 4(9) (1988): 499–524.
19. Scot Burton and Donald R. Lichtenstein, 'The effect of ad claims and ad context on attitude toward the advertisement', Journal of Advertising 17(1) (1988): 3–11; Karen A. Machleit and R. Dale Wilson, 'Emotional feelings and attitude toward the advertisement: The roles of brand familiarity and repetition', Journal of Advertising 17(3) (1988): 27–35; Scott B. Mackenzie and Richard J. Lutz, 'An empirical examination of the structural antecedents of attitude toward the ad in an advertising pretesting context', Journal of Marketing 53 (April 1989): 48–65; Scott B. Mackenzie, Richard J. Lutz and George E. Belch, 'The role of attitude toward the ad as a mediator of advertising effectiveness: A test of competing explanations', Journal of Marketing Research 23 (May 1986): 130–43; Darrel D. Muehling and Russell N. Laczniak, 'Advertising's immediate and delayed influence on brand attitudes: Considerations across message-involvement levels', Journal of Advertising 17(4) (1988): 23–34; Mark A. Pavelchak, Meryl P. Gardner and V. Carter Broach, 'Effect of Ad Pacing and Optimal Level of Arousal on Attitude Toward the Ad', in Rebecca H. Holman and Michael R. Solomon, eds, Advances in Consumer Research 18 (Provo, UT: Association for Consumer Research, 1991): 94–9. Some research evidence indicates that a separate attitude is also formed regarding the brand name itself: see George M. Zinkhan and Claude R. Martin Jr., 'New brand names and inferential beliefs: Some insights on naming new products', Journal of Business Research 15 (1987): 157–72.
20. John P. Murry Jr., John L. Lastovicka and Surendra N. Singh, 'Feeling and liking responses to television programs: An examination of two explanations for media-context effects', Journal of Consumer Research 18 (March 1992): 441–51.

Notes

Fully updated notes at the end of each chapter allow readers to find more sources to learn about a topic.

Case studies

At the end of each major section case studies cover various companies, industries and countries, and integrate the topics from the preceding chapters. Questions then allow the reader to test his or her understanding to real-life events and consumer behaviour activities, thus helping develop analytical skills.

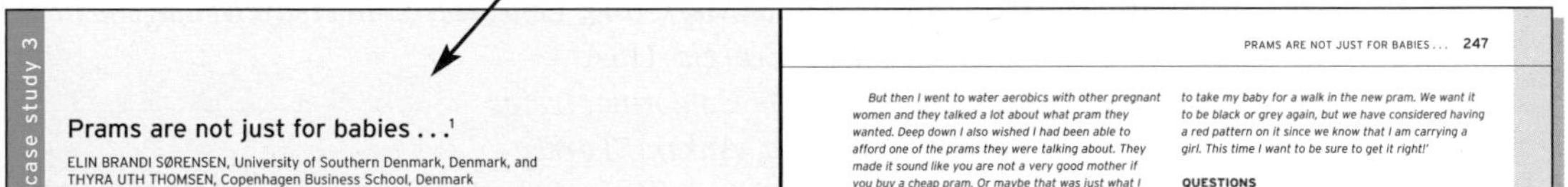

case study 3

Prams are not just for babies . . .[1]

ELIN BRANDI SØRENSEN, University of Southern Denmark, Denmark, and THYRA UTH THOMSEN, Copenhagen Business School, Denmark

PRAMS IN DENMARK

Many foreigners in Denmark have noticed the high prevalence of prams on the streets and have expressed surprise about their large size and their solid and practical appearance. And just as many have reacted with disbelief when they learn that most Danish children up to the age of two or three, sleep out of doors during the day in their prams, regardless of the time of year. It is assumed that sleeping outside will improve the immune defence system of the child. Many parents also find that their children sleep better, and for longer, when they sleep outside. Guidelines from the Danish health authorities confirm that if the mattress, the cover, and the child's clothing is appropriate it is safe to let the child sleep outside at temperatures as low as minus 10 degrees Celsius.

In the eyes of most Danish parents and parents-to-be, a pram is considered a necessity, a necessity that they will need within the first week or two of the child's birth. Therefore, the acquisition of a pram is typically organized before the birth of the child and thus becomes part of the preparations for the forthcoming addition to the family. However, even though the pram is considered a necessity, its acquisition is rarely considered a trivial matter.

In many cases the purchase of a pram represents the most expensive single item among the acquisitions made before the birth. And it is likely that the vehicle will stay with the family for at least five or six years, as it will probably be used by more than one child. It is also a very visible consumer good, that is, a consumer good that when used as a means of transportation is consumed in the public space – and is subject to the public gaze.

And, certainly, it appears to be a common experience that a pram has a clear potential to signal 'what kind of people we are', so that a pram potentially has a high symbolic value, very much in the same way as a car can have. This symbolic potential is a feature that most parents-to-be seem to be aware of – at one level or another. And this awareness may indeed spur speculations about 'what kind of parents would we like to be' – and maybe also 'what kind of parents would we not like to be'.

Thus, as Dorthe's case below will illustrate, the acquisition and usage of a pram is not just a practical matter. It may also include speculations about one's current identity and values, as well as one's future identity as a parent – a whole range of possible selves.

DORTHE

Dorthe is 25 years old and is currently training to become a pre-school teacher. She lives in a flat with her husband Jesper, and her two-year-old son Matias, in Ishøj, a suburb of Copenhagen, in a lower-income bracket neighbourhood inhabited by people of various ethnic origins. Compared with most other Danish first-time mothers, Dorthe was fairly young when she gave birth to her first child. She is now seven months pregnant with her second child and she is telling the story of the prams she has had.

'We bought our first pram in a sale about three months before Matias was born. Back then money meant a lot. At that time we were both students. Now Jesper has a well-paid job as a production engineer. But back then the price was an important issue. Jesper knew all about certain quality standards that he wanted to be fulfilled, while all I cared for was that I wanted it to be black or grey in order for it to be able match my clothes, no matter what colours I decided to wear. You know, it's a bit silly, but I wanted the pram and me to be a unified whole. I was very self-conscious at the time, because I had gained a lot of weight. So at least I wanted to look the best I could. Well, I also liked the kind of sporty design of the pram. We both used to do a lot of sports, so the design appealed to me somehow. Not that I have felt very sporty ever since, for sure, but at the time, it was still something that was kind of important for me.

I remember we had browsed around quite a few stores, and we felt lucky to find a model that fulfilled our criteria at a price that we could afford. It was a no-name brand bought at a discount retailer. But I loved it, and we took it home. I remember just sitting next to the pram and looking at it. It was the first time I really tried to imagine what it was going to be like . . . I tried to stand in front of the pram and to hold on to it to see how it felt. Well, I would rather not have anyone see how silly I was!

PRAMS ARE NOT JUST FOR BABIES . . . 247

But then I went to water aerobics with other pregnant women and they talked a lot about what pram they wanted. Deep down I also wished I had been able to afford one of the prams they were talking about. They made it sound like you are not a very good mother if you buy a cheap pram. Or maybe that was just what I thought to myself. I felt like they did not want to talk to me anymore, because I was someone who was not interested enough in my child, since I hadn't bought an expensive pram. Even though, deep down you know that your child doesn't care at all if it's in an "Odder" pram or a no-name pram. The child is completely indifferent as long as it is content and warm, which it will be in both prams. In fact this is not about the child – it's all about the mother.

After the birth of my child I started using my pram. I went for long walks in the neighbourhood. And that's when I finally decided to get rid of it. You know, a lot of the people in my neighbourhood are unemployed and a lot of them are of a different ethnic origin. And after a while I realized that they had all bought the same pram that I had. Consequently I was mistaken for one of them. They approached me and spoke to me in some foreign language that I didn't understand. I felt very uncomfortable. Also, I felt that other people looked at me as if I was some young, poor, unemployed loser who was never going to get any education.

I guess I realized that it is with prams as it is with a lot of other things: they say a lot about who you are as a person. Just like clothes do. So I told my husband that for this baby we would have to get another pram. He couldn't quite understand why, but he supported me. I talked to friends who had bought a high-end pram to figure out which one to buy and studied a lot of brochures. So now we have saved enough money to buy the 'Rolls Royce' of prams: an "Odder" pram. It's 1,000 euros but it's worth it! It looks classy and stylish in a discrete way. I cannot wait. It will make me feel so good to take my baby for a walk in the new pram. We want it to be black or grey again, but we have considered having a red pattern on it since we know that I am carrying a girl. This time I want to be sure to get it right!'

QUESTIONS

1. How can the symbolic self-completion theory discussed in Chapter 7 help us to understand the way Dorthe relates herself to her pram(s)? What does the pram mean to her in her role as a mother? What does it mean to her in her role as a citizen in her neighbourhood?
2. Discuss the idea of 'the ideal mother' that Dorthe is confronted with in her water aerobics class. How does she relate/react to this ideal? How does it make her feel? Could she have reacted/related differently to this ideal? If yes, how?
3. Consider the symbolic interactionism perspective discussed in Chapter 7. How is the meaning of Dorthe's first pram negotiated? You could construct a chart and/or time line containing the different influencers and their associated meanings.
4. Consider other life role transitions that may comprise major changes of the self (becoming an adult, leaving home, going to university, entering the job market, marriage, children leaving home, divorce, retirement, death of a spouse . . .). What generalizations could be drawn from Dorthe's case about these transitions, concerning the role of and meanings around the consumption of goods?

Note

1. This case is partly fictitious and partly based on interview material, which is reported in Thomsen, T.U. and E. Sørensen (2006) 'The first four-wheeled status symbol: Pram consumption as a vehicle for the construction of motherhood identity' (Journal of Marketing Management: Special Issue on Consuming Families, forthcoming).

ACKNOWLEDGEMENTS

Many of our colleagues from the business world as well as from universities throughout Europe have made significant contributions to both the first and second editions of this book by helping us identify important issues, and helping us think through them more clearly. We are grateful for their support, enthusiasm, and their willingness to share their knowledge with us. In addition, numerous colleagues developed European case materials and chapter-opening vignettes for this text, or provided valuable comments and feedback in the market research process and reviewing of manuscript drafts. To them, our special thanks:

Haya Al-Dajani, *Department of Marketing, University of Strathclyde, Scotland*
Carlos Ballesteros, *Universidad Pontificia Comillas, Madrid, Spain*
Suzanne C. Beckmann, *Copenhagen Business School, Denmark*
Russell W. Belk, *University of Utah, USA*
Carlos Brito, *University of Porto, Portugal*
Stephen Brown, *University of Ulster, Northern Ireland*
George Chryssohoidis, *Agricultural University of Athens, Greece*
Janeen Arnold Costa, *University of Utah, USA*
Alain Decrop, *University of Namur, Belgium*
Christian Derbaix, *Consumer Behaviour Analysis Laboratory, Catholic University of Mons, Belgium*
Kamaldeep Dhillon, *Institute of Psychiatry, Kings College London, UK*
Susan Eccles, *Department of Marketing, Lancaster University Management School, Lancaster, UK*
Karin M. Ekström, *Centre For Consumer Science (CFK), Goteborg University, Sweden*
Jonathan Elms, *Department of Marketing, Lancaster University Management School, UK*
Basil Englis, *Berry College, Georgia, USA*
Burçak Ertimur, *University of California, Irvine*
Güliz Ger, *Bilkent University, Ankara, Turkey*
Andrea Groeppel-Klein, *European University of Viadrina, Frankfurt (Oder), Germany*
Patrick Hetzel, *Académie de Limoges, France*
Sally Hibbert, *Nottingham University Business School, UK*
Robert J.W. Hogg, *Leeds University, UK*
Kalipso M. Karantinou, *Manchester Business School, UK and American College of Greece, Athens, Greece*
Ronan De Kervenoael, *Graduate School of Management, Sabanci University, Istanbul, Turkey*
Athanassios Krystallis, *Agricultural University of Athens, Greece*
Andrew Lindridge, *Manchester Business School, UK*
Pauline Maclaran, *De Montfort University, Leicester, UK*
Damien McLoughlin, *University College, Dublin, Ireland*
Gabriele Morello, *ISIDA, Palermo, Italy*
Stephanie O'Donohoe, *University of Edinburgh, Scotland*
Aphrodite Panagiotalides, *Evangelos Tsantalis S.A., Halkidiki, Greece*
Claude Pecheux, *Consumer Behaviour Analysis Laboratory, Catholic University of Mons, Belgium*
Elfriede Penz, *International Marketing and Management, Vienna University of Economics and Business Administration, Vienna, Austria*

Maria G. Piacentini, *Department of Marketing, Lancaster University, UK*
Dominique Roux, *Université Paris 12, France*
Özlem Sandikci, *Bilkent University, Ankara, Turkey*
Laura Sierra, *Universidad Pontificia Comillas, Madrid, Spain*
Elin Brandi Sørensen, *University of Southern Denmark, Odense, Denmark*
Diana Storm, *University of Southern Denmark, Odense, Denmark*
Carolyn Strong, *University of Wales, Cardiff, UK*
Thyra Uth Thomsen, *Copenhagen Business School, Denmark*
Darach Turley, *Dublin City University, Eire*
Carmelina Vela, *Universidad Pontificia Comillas, Madrid, Spain*

We'd also like to express our sincere thanks to our students in Denmark, the Netherlands and the UK who have proved to be valuable sources of ideas and examples throughout our work on this text. Special thanks, as well, to our Research Assistant, Laura Vallance (Lancaster University) who provided sterling and superb help in collecting material for the book and in reviewing our work-in-progress. We also thank her for her contributions to the supplementary materials. Thanks also to our friends and colleagues at Syddansk Universitet, Odense Universitet, the Vrije Universiteit, Amsterdam, the University of Utah, Lancaster University Management School and Manchester Business School for their support and inspiration throughout this project.

Gary, Søren and Margaret want to offer a special and personal word of thanks to Mike Solomon. While we were busy getting together the materials for this third European edition, Mike was already working hard on the manuscript for the 7th edition of *Consumer Behavior*. He shared materials with us as soon as they were ready, providing us with a pace and structure which kept us focused and on schedule! Mike was the perfect senior author – there when we needed something from him, and otherwise a positive source of energy and enthusiasm, coming from a comfortable distance. Ultimately, a great deal of synergy developed in our work together. We ended up sharing new materials, sources of research, and ideas in a mutual process of give and take. Thanks for giving us this opportunity to work with you, Mike.

Gary Bamossy would like to thank Anne Marie Parlevliet in Amsterdam for her excellent desk research on developments in The Netherlands and the EU. A special thanks to Janeen, Joost, Lieke and Jason – there are many time demands in taking on a book project, and as it develops, you recognize that you get an extra amount of support from the people you love. Søren Askegaard would like to thank Steen and Niels, his favourite fellow consumers, who perpetually tempted him to engage in a variety of leisurely consumption activities instead of revising this book. Margaret Hogg would like to say a very sincere 'thank you' to Richard, Daniel and Robert for their generous, unstinting and loving support throughout this project.

Finally, we would like to thank Thomas Sigel, Senior Acquisitions Editor, and Karen Mclaren, Senior Editor, and the rest of the Pearson Education team for their understanding, support and guidance during this revision.

PUBLISHER'S ACKNOWLEDGEMENTS

The publishers are grateful to the following for permission to reproduce copyright material:

Table 4.4 from Kahle, L. *et al.*, 'Implications of Social Values for Consumer Communications' in B. English, ed., *Global and Multinational Advertising*, Lawrence Erlbaum Associates, used with permission; Elsevier Science for Figure 4.5 from Nielsen, N.A., Bech-Larsen, T. and Grunert, K.G. (1998) 'Consumer Purchase Motives and Product Perceptions: A Laddering Study on Vegetable Oil in Three Countries', *Food Quality and Preference* 9(6) 455–66 and Figure 15.1 from Solomon, M. (1988) 'Building Up and Breaking Down: The Impact of Cultural Sorting on Symbolic Consumption' in J. Sheth and E.C. Hirschman, eds, *Research in Consumer Behaviour* 325–51; Routledge for Figure 4.6 adapted from Ratneshwar, S., Mick, D.G. and Huffman, C. (2000) 'Introduction', *The Why of Consumption*: 1–8; Table 5.2 reprinted by permission of FEVE (European Container Glass Federation); The University of Chicago Press for Figure 6.3 from Mitchell, A.A. (1986) 'The Effect of Verbal & Visual Components', *Journal of Consumer Research* 13 (June): 21, Figure 10.2 from Bearden, W.O. and Etzel, M.J. (1982) 'Reference Group Influence on Product and Brand Purchase Decisions', *Journal of Consumer Research* (September): 185, Figure 14.1 from McCracken, G. (1986) 'Culture and Consumption: A Theoretical Account of the Structure and Movement of the Cultural Meaning of Consumer Goods', *Journal of Consumer Research* 13 (June): 72, Figure 16.12 adapted from Peñalosa, L. (1994) *Atravesando Fronteras*/Border Crossings: A Critical Ethnographic Exploration of the Consumer Acculturation of Mexican Immigrants, *Journal of Consumer Research* 21 (June): 32–54, Table 4.7 from Richens, M.L. and Dawson, S. (1992) 'A Consumer Values Orientation for Materialism and its Measurement', *Journal of Consumer Research* 20 (December), Table 6.3 from McQuarrie, E.F. and Mick, D.G. (1992) 'On Resonance: A Critical Pluralistic Inquiry', *Journal of Consumer Research* 19 (September): 182, Table 8.2 from Bloch, P.H., Sherell, D.L. and Ridgway, N. (1986) 'Consumer Search: An Extended Framework', *Journal of Consumer Research* 13 (June): 120, Table 10.1 adapted from Whan Park, C. and Parker Lessig, V. (1977) 'Students and Housewives: Differences in Susceptibility to Reference Group Influence' *Journal of Consumer Research* 4 (September): 102, Table 14.1 from Rook, D.W. (1985) 'The Ritual Dimension of Consumer Behaviour', *Journal of Consumer Research* 12 (December): 251–64 and Table 14.2 from Ruth, J.A., Otnes, C.C. and Brunel, F.F. (1999) 'Gift Receipt and the reformulation of interpersonal relationships' *Journal of Consumer Research* 25 (March): 385–402; The American Marketing Association for Figure 6.4 adapted from Rathans, A.J., Swasy, J.L. and Marks, L. (1986) 'Effects of Television Commercial Repetition: Receiver Knowledge', *Journal of Marketing Research* 23 (February): 50–61, Figure 9.8 adapted from Jacoby, J., Berning, C.K. and Dietvorst, T.F. (1977) 'What about disposition?', *Journal of Marketing* 41 (April): 23, Figure 10.5 adapted from Feick, L. and Price, L. (1987) 'The Market Maven: A Diffuser of Marketplace Information', *Journal of Marketing* 51 (January): 83–7, Table 4.3 from Laurent, G. and Kapferer, J-N. (1985) 'Measuring Consumer Involvement Profiles', *Journal of Marketing Research* 22 (February): 45 and Table 13.1 from Holbrook, M.B. and Schindler, R.M. (1994) 'Age, Sex and Attitude Toward the Past as Predicters of Consumers'

Aesthetic Tastes for Cultural Products', *Journal of Marketing Research* 31 (August): 416; Figure 7.1 from the *Salt Lake City Tribune*, 11 March 1997, used with permission; Table 9.2 from Wolfinbarger, M. and Gilly, M.C. (2003) eTailQ: Dimensionalizing, measuring and predicting eTail quality, *Journal of Retailing* 79: Table 4, p. 191; Figure 9.2 from *Journal of Personality and Social Psychology*, 1980, 38, 311–22. Copyright © 1980 by the American Pyschological Association. Adapted with permission; The University of Miami for Figure 9.3 from Page-Wood, E.S., Kaufman, C.J. and Lane, P.M. (1990) 'The Art of Time', *Proceedings of the Academy of Marketing Science* © Academy of Marketing Science; Figure 9.4 from Venkatesh, A. (1998) 'Cybermarketscapes and Consumer Freedoms and Identities', *European Journal of Marketing* 32(7/8): 664–76, used with permission; Figure 9.5 from Rook, D. (1990) 'Is Impulse Buying (Yet) a Useful Marketing Concept?' unpublished manuscript, University of Southern California, used with permission; Figure 9.7 reprinted by permission of QFD Institute, © QFD Institute, www.qfdi.org. Supporting case study *Bagel Sales Double at Host Marriott* by Steve Lampa and Glenn Mazur. Copyright © 1996 by Steve Lampa and Glenn Mazur. All Rights Reserved. Available for free download at http://www.mazur.net/publishe.htm; Cambridge University Press for Figure 10.3 from Gergen, K.J. and Gergen, M., *Social Psychology* (New York: Harcourt Brace Jovanovich, 1981), adapted from F.C. Barlett (1932) *Remembering*; Figure 11.2 redrawn from *European Union Labour Force Survey*, reprinted by permission of the European Communities (Eurostat 2002); Figure 11.3 adapted from McNeal, J. and Chyon-Hwa Yeh, 'Born to Shop', *American Demographics*, June 1993, 36 and Table 13.3 from Mischis, G.P., 'Life Stages of the Mature Market', *American Demographics*, September 1996, used with permission from Media Central; The European Communities for Figure 12.1 redrawn from *Harmonised Statistics on Earnings*, Figure 41, (Eurostat 2004), Figure 12.2 redrawn from *Statistics in Focus*, Theme 3-7/2003 (Eurostat 2004), Figure 12.3 redrawn from *Statistics in Focus*, Theme 3-24/2003 (Eurostat 2004) and Figure 13.1 redrawn from *Demographic Statistics*, reprinted by permission of the European Communities; Figure 14.2 from Venkatesh, A., 'Ethnoconsumerism: A New Pardigm to Study Cultural and Cross-Cultural Consumer Behavior', in J.A. Costa and G. Bamossy, eds, *Marketing in a Multicultural World*, copyright © 1995 by Sage Publications. Reprinted by permission of Sage Publications; The University of Florida for Figure 14.4 based on Mick, D.G., DeMoss, M. and Faber, R.J. (1990) *Latent Motivations and Meanings of Self-Gifts*, research report, Centre of Retailing Education and Research; Figure 16.7 © 2001 by SRI Consulting Business Intelligence. All rights reserved; The Association for Consumer Research for Table 7.1 adapted from Debevec, K. and Iyer, E. (1986) 'Sex Roles and Consumer Perceptions of Promotions, Products, and Self: What Do We Know and Where Should We Be Headed', *Advances in Consumer Research* 13, Table 8.3 adapted from Duncan, C.P. (1990) 'Consumer Market Beliefs: A Review of the Literature and an Agenda for Future Research', *Advances in Consumer Research* 17: 729–735, Table 11.1 adapted from Gilly, M.C. and Enis, B.M. (1982) 'Recycling the Family Life Cycle: A Proposal for Redefinition' in A.A. Mitchell, (ed.) *Advances in Consumer Research* 9: 274 and Table 16.3 adapted from Smith, D. and Skalnik, J. (1995) 'Changing Patterns in the Consumption of

Alcoholic Beverages in Europe and the United States' in Flemming Hansen, (ed.), *European Advances in Consumer Research* 2; Sheffield Publishing Company for Table 15.3 from Berger, A.A. (1984) *Signs in Contemporary Culture: An Introduction to Semiotics*, © 1984, 1999 Sheffield Publishing Company, reprinted with permission of the publisher; MCB UP Ltd. for Table 15.4 from Foxall, G.R. and Bhate, S. (1993) 'Cognitive Style and Personal Involvement as Explicators of Innovative Purchasing of Health Food Brands', *European Journal of Marketing*, 27(2): 5–16; Table 16.2 adapted from Brunø, K., *et al.*, 'An Analysis of National and Cross-National Consumer Segments Using the Food-Related Lifestyle Instrument in Denmark, France, Germany and Great Britain', MAPP Working Paper no.35, Aarhus School of Business, January 1996. Used with permission; GfK AG Germany for Table 16.4 from Davison, J.A. and Grab, E. (1993) 'The Contributions of Advertising Testing to the Development of Effective International Adverising: The KitKat Case Study' *Marketing and Research Today* (February): 15–24; Thomson Learning for Table 17.1 from Brown, S. (1995) *Postmodern Marketing*, Table 4.2 on p. 120 (London: Routledge); Chapter 17, Figure 1 on p. 631 redrawn from *Evolución de los extranjeros residentes. España en Cifras 2003–04*, www.ine.es, on-line publications, date of publication 02.04 (May 20, 2004), reprinted by permission of Instituto Nacional de Estadistica (INE 2004); Chapter 17, Table 1 on p. 631 from *Explotación estadística del Padrón*. January 1, 2003, reprinted by permission of Instituto Nacional de Estadistica (INE 2003).

We are grateful to the following for permission to reproduce photographs and advertisements:
p. 16 The Jupiter Drawing Room (South Africa); pp. 17, 45, 55, 68 courtesy of the Advertising Archives; p. 20 by Jan Burwick, the German National Committee for UNICEF and Springer & Jacoby Fuenfte Werbeagentur GmbH & Co. KG; p. 22 American Association of Advertising Agencies; p. 37 by Oliviero Toscani, Benetton Group S.p.A.; p. 40 courtesy of Lexus and Team One Advertising; p. 41 Procter and Gamble Nederland B.V.; p. 42 courtesy of Campbell Soup Company; p. 44 Sunkist Growers, Inc. Sunkist is a registered trademark of © 2005 Sunkist Growers, Inc., Sherman Oaks, CA 91923, USA. All rights reserved; p. 69 Toyota Singapore and Saatchi & Saatchi Ltd.; p. 52 BooneOakley Advertising; p. 107 Swisspatat; pp. 71, 80, 82, 91 (both images), 93, 95, 97, 115, 178, 183, 187, 189, 193, 194, 220, 224, 226, 231, 273, 278, 286, 302, 303, 308 courtesy of the Advertising Archives; Screenshot on p. 108 Jones Soda Co. Screenshot frame reprinted with permission from Microsoft Corporation; p. 116 Crunch Fitness advertisement, DiMassimo, Inc.; p. 127 photographs courtesy of Professor Robert Kozinets; p. 180 noDNA GmbH; p. 142 Gary Bamossy; p. 185 Kessels Kramer; p. 198 from Effects of Involvement, Argument, Strength, and Source Characteristics on Central and Peripheral Processing in Advertising, *Psychology & Marketing*, 7, Fall, reprinted by permission of John Wiley & Sons, Inc. (Craig Andrews, J. and Shrimp, T.A. 1990); p. 211 Bianco Footwear Danmark A/S; p. 215 by Ilan Rubin, D'Adda, Lorenzini, Vigorelli, BBDO S.p.A.; p. 218 Goldsmith/Jeffrey and Bodyslimmers; p. 260 from the United States Postal Service. USPS Corporate Signature is a trademark owned by the United States Postal Service. Used with permission. All rights reserved; p. 266 Church & Dwight Co., Inc.; Screenshot on p. 280 Ask Jeeves, Inc. Screenshot frame reprinted with permission from Microsoft Corporation; p. 281 iParty Corp.; p. 283 Sopexa USA, © ONIVINS and Isabelle Dervaux; p. 286 (top) by Jacek Wolowski, Grey Worldwide Warszawa; p. 304 Volkswagen of South Africa; p. 305 courtesy of Qantas Airlines and M&C Saatchi; p. 310 Hewlett-Packard Development Company, L.P.; Screenshot on p. 317 Tesco Stores Limited. Screenshot frame reprinted with permission from Microsoft Corporation; p. 322 © SIME/Corbis; pp. 329, 333 Images Courtesy of the Advertising Archives; p. 335 Volkswagen of

The Netherlands; p. 336 Alamy/Stockfolio; pp. 352, 360, 364 courtesy of the Advertising Archives; p. 355 © Susan Goldman, The Image Works, Inc.; p. 365 Alamy/Martin Dalton; p. 373 used with permission from Google, Inc. Screenshot frame reprinted with permission from Microsoft Corporation; p. 414 Gary Bamossy; pp. 416, 449, courtesy of the Advertising Archives; p. 417 Søren Askegaard; pp. 456, 459, 461 Gary Bamossy; p. 467 Courtesy of Saga Magazine; p. 501 Corbis/Sygma; p. 507 Getty Images/Taxi/Gen Nishino; p. 517 Corbis/Neal Preston; p. 533 used with permission of Robson Brown Advertising, Newcastle upon Tyne, England; p. 535 courtesy of the Advertising Archives; p. 542 Corbis/R. Gates; p. 544 Maidenform, Inc.; p. 546 Diesel S.p.A.; p. 561 by Biel Capllonch, S,C,P,F . . . , Patricia Luján, Carlitos; p. 574 Corbis/Michael S Yamashinka; p. 602 Corbis/Mike R. Whittle; Ecoscene; p. 605 courtesy of the Advertising Archives; p. 607 courtesy www.adbusters.org; pp. 608, 610, 614 courtesy of the Advertising Archives; p. 616 Getty Images/M.N. Chan; p. 623 Søren Askegaard; p. 625 courtesy of the Advertising Archives; p. 632 Junta Islamica, info@institutohalal.com.

In some instances we have been unable to trace the owners of copyright material, and we would appreciate any information that would enable us to do so.

We are also grateful to the following for permission to reproduce textual material:
The New York Times for extracts from 'Marketing with Double Entendres' by Stuart Elliott published in *The New York Times* 4th October 2004 © The New York Times 2004, 'Wal-Mart is upgrading Its Vast In-Store Television Network: the fifth largest television network in the United States' by Constance L. Hays published in *The New York Times* 21st February 2005 © The New York Times 2005, and 'U.S. eating habits, and Europeans, are spreading visibly' by Lizette Alvarez published in *The New York Times* 31st October 2003 © The New York Times 2003; Dow Jones & Co Inc for extracts from 'Why custom-made shirts are a cut above' by Ernest Beck published in *Wall Street Journal Europe* 4–5th April 1997 © Dow Jones & Co Inc 1997, 'Cabin fever swirls around posh cottages on Norwegian coast' by Ernest Beck published in *Wall Street Journal Europe* 6th August 1997 © Dow Jones & Co Inc 1997, 'Cooler heads prevail as Britain loses lust for warm, cloudy ales' by James Hagerty published in *Wall Street Journal* 29th August 2000 © Dow Jones & Co Inc 2000, 'Marketers to Chinese women offer more room to be vain' by Cris Prystay published in *Wall Street Journal* 30th May 2002 © Dow Jones & Co Inc 2002, and 'Sex and the City singles out Asian women for marketers' by Cris Prystay and Montira Narkvichien published in *Wall Street Journal* 8th August 2002 © Dow Jones & Co Inc 2002; and Guardian Newspapers Limited for an extract from 'She's young, gifted and ahead of you at the till' by Amelia Hill and Anushka Asthana published in *The Observer* 2nd January 2005 © Guardian Newspapers Limited 2005; Out with curry and Bollywood from *The Financial Times Limited*, 25 November 2004, © Aditya Chakrabortty; Bigger not always better: size of cars no longer a reflection of social status, by Erica Bulman, from *The Financial Times Limited*, 3 March 2005, © AP Worldstream.

We are also grateful to the Financial Times Limited for permission to reprint the following material:
Such stuff as dreams are made on, © *Financial Times*, 28 October 2004; Advertiser's funny business, © *Financial Times*, 17 February 2004; Is the world falling out of love with US brands?, © *Financial Times*, 30 December 2004; Whisky taste designed for a youthful palate, © *Financial Times*, 22 January 2004; Product recalls rise sharply, © *Financial Times*, 21 March 2005; Companies that use basic instinct, © *Financial Times*, 25 February 2005; Figure 16.9 How to be happy, © *Financial Times*, 27/28 December 2003.

CONSUMERS IN THE MARKETPLACE

This introductory part comprises one chapter, which previews much of what this book is about and gives an overview of the field of consumer behaviour. The chapter examines how the field of marketing is influenced by the actions of consumers, and also how we as consumers are influenced by marketers. It also overviews consumer behaviour as a discipline of enquiry, and describes some of the different approaches that researchers use in order better to understand what makes consumers behave as they do.

1
An introduction to consumer behaviour

AN INTRODUCTION TO CONSUMER BEHAVIOUR

Nathalie is working at her computer. It is early autumn and the beginning of a new term at her Danish university. Time for getting new books and study materials. As a second-year student, she's not surprised to find that several of the required books are still unavailable at the campus bookshop.

She goes online to check if she can get her books from one of the internet bookshops. She uses her favourite portal (**www.jubii.dk**) to check out the Scandinavian bookshops, which she thinks might be able to deliver the books faster than their international competitors. None of them have all of the books in stock that she needs, and she really feels that she should get all of the books from the same store. On an impulse, Nathalie visits a student shop which sells used books and provides search facilities for Barnes & Noble. She searches for a couple of the titles she is looking for, but the search facility does not seem to work. For a moment, she considers putting some of her used books up for sale, then decides not to let herself be distracted, and moves on to the UK version of **Amazon.com**. She has heard from friends that prices are a little steeper here (relative to the other internet bookshops), but she knows this site well by now. Besides, the books she wants are in stock and can be delivered in about a week, maybe less. Considering that the chances of the books she needs appearing in the campus bookshop on time seem pretty slim, Nathalie decides to go ahead and buy them now online.

While she fills out the order form, she tries to plan where to go next. She and her friend are looking for an interesting topic for a course project and she wants to look in the social science section of **www.yahoo.com** for some inspiration. Also, she wants to visit a few of her favourite sites for news, music and travel. 'A little information update before meeting the girls this afternoon for coffee,' she thinks to herself. She clicks 'OK' to her order confirmation and is glad to have that out of the way. She navigates her way to **yahoo.com** and starts her search. All the while, she is thinking to herself that it would be nice to spend a little time checking out the latest in fashion and beauty tips; a little treat to herself while she still has some time on her hands. Suddenly Nathalie remembers that there were a couple of study plans to print out from the university website – and a few emails to answer. She checks her email account and is a little surprised to see that she has received so much mail today – seems like everybody just realized that summer is over and wants to get started on new projects. It makes her feel joyful, even sort of invigorated . . .

DIANA STORM, University of Southern Denmark, Odense, Denmark

■ CONSUMPTION IN EUROPE? THE EUROPEAN CONSUMER?

This is a book about consumer behaviour, written from a European perspective. But what does that mean exactly? Obviously, to write about a 'European' consumer or a 'European's consumer behaviour' is problematic. Some of the general theory about the psychological or sociological influences on consumer behaviour may be common to all Western cultures. On the one hand, some theories may be culturally specific. Certain groups of consumers do show similar kinds of behaviour across national borders, and research on consumers in Europe suggests that we even use our understanding of the consumption environment to make sense of the foreign cultures we are visiting.[1] On the other hand, the ways in which people live their consumption life vary greatly from one European country to another, and sometimes even within different regions of the same country. As a student of consumer behaviour, you might want to ask yourself: 'In which consumption situations do I seem to have a great deal in common with fellow students from other European countries? And in what ways do I seem to resemble more closely my compatriots? In what ways do subcultures in my country exert a strong influence on my consumption patterns, and how international are these subcultures?' To add to the complexity of all this, ten countries, incorporating 75 million people, 740,000 sq km and nine languages, have joined the European Union in 2005. These 'new' European consumers come from vastly different economic and political circumstances, and each has their own unique historical and cultural development. Much more on these consumers' aspirations and consumption behaviours will be reviewed in chapters in Part D of this text, A Portrait of European Consumers.

This book is about consumer behaviour theory in general, and we will illustrate our points with examples from various European markets as well as from the United States and other countries. Each chapter features 'Multicultural dimensions' boxes which spotlight international aspects of consumer behaviour. From both a global and a pan-European perspective, these issues will be explored in depth in Chapters 15 and 16.

Consumer behaviour: people in the marketplace

You can probably relate to at least some general aspects of Nathalie's behaviour. This book is about people like Nathalie. It concerns the products and services they buy and use, and the ways these fit into their lives. This introductory chapter briefly describes some important aspects of the field of consumer behaviour, including the topics studied, who studies them, and some of the ways these issues are approached by consumer researchers.

But first, let's return to Nathalie: the sketch which started the chapter allows us to highlight some aspects of consumer behaviour that will be covered in the rest of the book.

- As a consumer, Nathalie can be described and compared to other individuals in a number of ways. For some purposes, marketers might find it useful to categorize Nathalie in terms of her age, gender, income or occupation. These are some examples of descriptive characteristics of a population, or *demographics*. In other cases, marketers would rather know something about Nathalie's interests in fashion or music, or the way she spends her leisure time. This sort of information often comes under the category *psychographics*, which refers to aspects of a person's lifestyle and personality. Knowledge of consumer characteristics plays an extremely important role in many marketing applications, such as defining the market for a product or deciding on the appropriate techniques to employ when targeting a certain group of consumers.

- Nathalie's purchase decisions are heavily influenced by the opinions and behaviours of her friends. A lot of product information, as well as recommendations to use or avoid particular brands, is picked up in conversations among real people, rather than by way of television commercials, magazines or advertising messages. The bonds among Nathalie's group of friends are in part cemented by the products they all use. There is also pressure on each group member to buy things that will meet with the group's approval, and often a price to pay in the form of group rejection or embarrassment when one does not conform to others' conceptions of what is good or bad, 'in' or 'out'.

- As a member of a large society, people share certain cultural values or strongly held beliefs about the way the world should be structured. Other values are shared by members of *subcultures*, or smaller groups within the culture, such as ethnic groups, teens, people from certain parts of the country, or even 'Hell's Angels'. The people who matter to Nathalie – her *reference group* – value the idea that women in their early twenties should be innovative, style-conscious, independent and up front (at least a little). While many marketers focus on either very young targets or the thirty-somethings, some are recognizing that another segment which ought to be attracting marketers' interest is the rapidly growing segment of older (50+) people.[2]

- When browsing through the websites, Nathalie is exposed to many competing 'brands'. Many offerings did not grab her attention at all; others were noticed but rejected because they did not fit the 'image' with which she identified or to which she aspired. The use of *market segmentation strategies* means targeting a brand only to specific groups of consumers rather than to everybody – even if that means that other consumers will not be interested or may choose to avoid that brand.

- Brands often have clearly defined *images* or 'personalities' created by product advertising, packaging, branding and other marketing strategies that focus on positioning a product a certain way or by certain groups of consumers adopting the product. One's leisure activities in particular are very much lifestyle statements: it says a lot about what a person is interested in, as well as something about the type of person he or she would like to be. People often choose a product offering, a service or a place, or subscribe to a particular idea, because they like its image, or because they feel its 'personality' somehow corresponds to their own. Moreover, a consumer may believe that by buying and using the product, its desirable qualities will somehow magically 'rub off'.

- When a product succeeds in satisfying a consumer's specific needs or desires, as **http://www.amazon.co.uk** did for Nathalie, it may be rewarded with many years of *brand* or *store loyalty*, a bond between product or outlet and consumer that may be very difficult for competitors to break. Often a change in one's life situation or self-concept is required to weaken this bond and thus create opportunities for competitors.

- Consumers' evaluations of products are affected by their appearance, taste, texture or smell. We may be influenced by the shape and colour of a package, as well as by more subtle factors, such as the symbolism used in a brand name, in an advertisement, or even in the choice of a cover model for a magazine. These judgements are affected by – and often reflect – how a society feels that people should define themselves at that point in time. Nathalie's choice of a new hairstyle, for example, says something about the type of image women like her want to project. If asked, Nathalie might not be able to say exactly why she considered some websites and rejected others. Many product meanings are hidden below the surface of the packaging, the design and advertising, and this book will discuss some of the methods used by marketers and social scientists to discover or apply these meanings.

- **Amazon.co.uk** has a combined American and international image that appeals to Nathalie. A product's image is often influenced by its *country of origin*, which helps to determine its 'brand personality'. In addition, our opinions and desires are increasingly shaped by input from around the world, thanks to rapid advancements in communications and transportation systems (witness the internet!). In today's global culture, consumers often prize products and services that 'transport' them to different locations and allow them to experience the diversity of other cultures. Clearly, the internet has changed many young Europeans' consumer behaviours. Global music sales continues to fall, with Germany, Denmark, France, Sweden, Belgium, Greece and Ireland all having double digit decreases in sales of recorded music. While music sales fall, young European consumers seem to be searching the internet for another form of 'shopping', with 50 per cent of 'singles' reporting visiting a dating website at least once in the past year.[3]

▶ The field of **consumer behaviour** covers a lot of ground: it is the study of the processes involved when individuals or groups select, purchase, use or dispose of products, services, ideas or experiences to satisfy needs and desires. Consumers take many forms, ranging from a 6-year-old child pleading with her mother for wine gums to an executive in a large corporation deciding on an extremely expensive computer system. The items that are consumed can include anything from tinned beans to a massage, democracy, rap music, and even other people (the images of rock stars, for example). Needs and desires to be satisfied range from hunger and thirst to love, status or even spiritual fulfilment. There is a growing interest in consumer behaviour, not only in the field of marketing but from the social sciences in general. This follows a growing awareness of the increasing importance of consumption in our daily lives, in our organization of daily activities, in our identity formation, in politics and economic development, and in the flows of global culture, where consumer culture seems to spread, albeit in new forms, from North America and Europe to other parts of the world. This spread of consumer culture via marketing is not always well received by social critics and consumers, as we shall see in subsequent chapters.[4] Indeed, consumption can be regarded as playing such an important role in our social, psychological, economic, political and cultural lives that today it has become the 'vanguard of history'.[5]

Consumers are actors on the marketplace stage

▶ The perspective of **role theory**, which this book emphasizes, takes the view that much of consumer behaviour resembles actions in a play,[6] where each consumer has lines, props and costumes that are necessary to a good performance. Since people act out many different roles, they may modify their consumption decisions according to the particular 'play' they are in at the time. The criteria that they use to evaluate products and services in one of their roles may be quite different from those used in another role.

Another way of thinking about consumer roles is to consider the various 'plays' that the consumer may engage in. One classical role here is the consumer as a 'chooser' – somebody who, as we have seen with Nathalie, can choose between different alternatives and explores various criteria for making this choice. But the consumer can have many other things at stake than just 'making the right choice'. We are all involved in a communication system through our consumption activities, whereby we communicate our roles and statuses. We are also sometimes searching to construct our identity, our 'real selves', through various consumption activities. Or the main purpose of our consumption might be an exploration of a few of the many possibilities the market has to offer us, maybe in search of a 'real kick of pleasure'. On the more serious side, we might feel victimized by fraudulent or harmful offerings, and we may decide to take action against such risks from the marketplace by becoming active in consumer movements. Or we may react against the authority of the producers by co-opting their products, and turning them into something else, as when military boots all of a sudden became 'normal' footwear for peaceful girls. We may decide to take action as 'political consumers' and boycott products from companies or countries whose behaviour does not meet our ethical or environmental standards. Hence, as consumers we can be choosers, communicators, identity-seekers, pleasure-seekers, victims, rebels and activists – sometimes simultaneously.[7]

Figure 1.1 Some issues that arise during stages in the consumption process

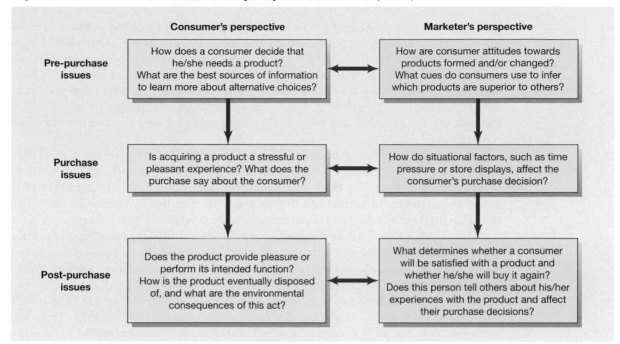

	Consumer's perspective	Marketer's perspective
Pre-purchase issues	How does a consumer decide that he/she needs a product? What are the best sources of information to learn more about alternative choices?	How are consumer attitudes towards products formed and/or changed? What cues do consumers use to infer which products are superior to others?
Purchase issues	Is acquiring a product a stressful or pleasant experience? What does the purchase say about the consumer?	How do situational factors, such as time pressure or store displays, affect the consumer's purchase decision?
Post-purchase issues	Does the product provide pleasure or perform its intended function? How is the product eventually disposed of, and what are the environmental consequences of this act?	What determines whether a consumer will be satisfied with a product and whether he/she will buy it again? Does this person tell others about his/her experiences with the product and affect their purchase decisions?

Consumer behaviour is a process

In its early stages of development, the field was often referred to as *buyer behaviour*, reflecting an emphasis on the interaction between consumers and producers at the time of purchase. Marketers now recognize that consumer behaviour is an ongoing *process*, not merely what happens at the moment a consumer hands over money or a credit card and in turn receives some good or service.

The **exchange**, in which two or more organizations or people give and receive something of value, is an integral part of marketing.[8] While exchange remains an important part of consumer behaviour, the expanded view emphasizes the entire consumption process, which includes the issues that influence the consumer before, during and after a purchase. Figure 1.1 illustrates some of the issues that are addressed during each stage of the consumption process.

Consumer behaviour involves many different actors

A consumer is generally thought of as a person who identifies a need or desire, makes a purchase and then disposes of the product during the three stages in the consumption process. In many cases, however, different people may be involved in the process. The *purchaser* and *user* of a product may not be the same person, as when a parent chooses clothes for a teenager (and makes selections that can result in 'fashion suicide' from the teenager's point of view). In other cases, another person may act as an *influencer*, providing recommendations for (or against) certain products without actually buying or using them. For example, a friend, rather than a parent, accompanying a teenager on a shopping trip may pick out the clothes that he or she decides to purchase.

Finally, consumers may be organizations or groups in which one person may make the decisions involved in purchasing products that will be used by many, as when a purchasing agent orders the company's office supplies. In other organizational situations, purchase decisions may be made by a large group of people – for example, company accountants, designers, engineers, sales personnel and others – all of whom will have a say in the various stages of the consumption process. As we'll see in a later chapter, one important organization is the family, where different family members play pivotal roles in decision-making regarding products and services used by all.

■ CONSUMERS' IMPACT ON MARKETING STRATEGY

Surfing websites or discussing products and brands can be a lot of fun – almost as much fun as actually making the purchases! But, on the more serious side, why should managers, advertisers and other marketing professionals bother to learn about this field?

The answer is simple: understanding consumer behaviour is good business. A basic marketing concept states that firms exist to satisfy consumers' needs. These needs can only be satisfied to the extent that marketers understand the people or organizations that will use the products and services they offer, and that they do so *better* than their competitors.

Consumer response may often be the ultimate test of whether or not a marketing strategy will succeed. Thus, knowledge about consumers is incorporated into virtually every facet of a successful marketing plan. Data about consumers help marketers to define the market and to identify threats and opportunities in their own and other countries that will affect how consumers receive the product. In every chapter, we'll see how developments in consumer behaviour can be used as input to marketing strategies. Boxes headed 'Marketing opportunity' will highlight some of these possibilities. Sony's introduction of the Walkman is one good example of how consumers initially turned down the product when the concept was tested in the market.[9] The product was launched anyway and the Walkman was an immense success – Sony revolutionized the mobile music experience and sold almost 300 million Walkmans in the process. This does not mean that Sony now eschews consumer research, as is demonstrated by these few examples of marketing actions that resulted from studies focused on understanding consumers:

- Recent research found that today's teens see portable cassette players as dinosaurs. Sony's advertising agency followed 125 teens to see how they use products in their day-to-day lives. Now, even portable CD players seem obsolete and not cool – with the consumer movement to removable 'memory sticks' instead of a CD player that can work with MP3 files. The Walkman also needed a fresh message, so Sony's agency decided to use an alien named Plato to appeal to teens. This character was chosen to appeal to today's culturally ethnically diverse marketplace. As the account director explained, 'An alien is no one, so an alien is everyone.'[10] In addition to the memory stick players, the Apple iPod has also greatly changed the consumer music scene. The designer of the iPod, Jonathan Ives, has himself become part of popular culture, and in a recent poll was voted Most Influential Person in British Culture, beating author J.K. Rowling and Ricky Gervais, star and creator of the popular television programme *The Office*.[11]

- A woman in a consumer group which was discussing dental hygiene commented that tartar felt 'like a wall' on her teeth. This imagery was used in ads for Colgate Tartar Control, in which room-sized teeth were shown covered by walls of tartar.[12]

- Researchers for a manufacturer of Swiss chocolate found that many chocolate lovers hide secret 'stashes' around their house. One respondent confessed to hiding chocolate bars inside her lingerie drawer. The result was an ad campaign theme of 'The True Confessions of Chocaholics'.[13]

Market segmentation: to whom are we marketing?

▶ Whether within or across national boundaries, effective **market segmentation** delineates segments whose members are similar to one another in one or more characteristics and different from members of other segments. Depending on its goals and resources, a company may choose to focus on just one segment or several, or it may ignore differences among segments by pursuing a mass market strategy. In the internet-based market,

Table 1.1 Variables for market segmentation

Category	Variables	Location of discussion
Demographics	Age	Chapter 13
	Gender	Chapter 7
	Social class, occupation, income	Chapter 12
	Ethnic group, religion	Chapter 16
	Stage in life	Chapter 11
	Purchaser vs. user	Chapter 11
Geographic	Region	Chapter 16
	Country differences	Chapter 16
Psychographic	Self-concept, personality	Chapter 7
	Lifestyle	Chapter 16
Behavioural	Brand loyalty, extent of usage	Chapter 8
	Usage situation	Chapter 9
	Benefits desired	Chapter 4

Amazon.com tries to reach multiple segments at the same time, while Google News UK focuses on being a search engine for information and news for consumers in the United Kingdom.[14]

In many cases, it makes a lot of sense to target a number of market segments. The likelihood is that no one will fit any given segment description exactly, and the issue is whether or not consumers differ from our profile in ways that will affect the chances of their adopting the products we are offering.

Many segmentation variables form the basis for slicing up a larger market, and a great deal of this book is devoted to exploring the ways marketers describe and characterize different segments. The segmentation variables listed in Table 1.1 are grouped into four categories, which also indicate where in the book these categories are considered in more depth.

While consumers can be described in many ways, the segmentation process is valid only when the following criteria are met:

● Consumers within the segment are similar to one another in terms of product needs, and these needs are different from consumers in other segments.

● Important differences among segments can be identified.

● The segment is large enough to be profitable.

● Consumers in the segment can be reached by an appropriate marketing mix.

● The consumers in the segment will respond in the desired way to the marketing mix designed for them.

▶   **Demographics** are statistics that measure observable aspects of a population, such as birth rate, age distribution or income. The national statistical agencies of European countries and pan-European agencies such as EuroStat[15] are major sources of demographic data on families, but many private firms gather additional data on specific population groups. The changes and trends revealed in demographic studies are of great interest to marketers, because the data can be used to locate and predict the size of markets for many products, ranging from mortgages to baby food.

In this book, we'll explore many of the important demographic variables that make consumers the same as, or different from, others. We'll also consider other important
▶   characteristics that are not so easy to measure, such as **psychographics** – differences in

consumers' personalities and tastes which can't be measured objectively. For now, let's summarize a few of the most important demographic dimensions, each of which will be developed in more detail in later chapters. However, a word of caution is needed here. The last couple of decades have witnessed the growth of new consumer segments that are less dependent on demographics and more likely to borrow behavioural patterns and fashions across what were formerly more significant borders or barriers. It is now not so uncommon to see men and women, or grandmothers and granddaughters, having similar tastes. Hence, useful as they might be, marketers should beware of using only demographic variables to predict consumer tastes.

Age

Consumers in different age groups have very different needs and wants, and a better understanding of the ageing process of European consumers will continue to be of great importance to marketers as well as public policy decision-makers.[16] While people who belong to the same age group differ in many other ways, they do tend to share a set of values and common cultural experiences that they carry throughout life.[17] *Marie Claire*, the French magazine that is published in 25 editions and 14 languages, has noticed that its circulation and readership has fallen in past years, due primarily to not keeping pace with its younger readers and their reading habits. In the past, article length was typically nine to ten pages, and what is now desired is two to five pages. Rather than concentrating on serious articles on contemporary women's issues, the newer and younger readership is looking for something more fun and entertaining. Finding the balance of 'fun' (e.g. 'Four Celebs secrets to fabulous legs') and 'serious' (e.g. 'The role of the veil in Islamic dress') has been the challenge in bridging women readers of different age groups.[18]

Gender

Many products, from fragrances to footwear, are targeted at men or women. Differentiating by sex starts at a very early age – even nappies are sold in pink-trimmed versions for girls and blue for boys. As proof that consumers take these differences seriously, market research has revealed that many parents refuse to put baby boys in pink nappies![19]

One dimension that makes segmenting by gender so interesting is that the behaviours and tastes of men and women are constantly evolving. In the past most marketers assumed that men were the primary decision-makers for car purchases, but this perspective is changing with the times.

Sometimes, the gender segmentation can be an unintended product of an advertising strategy. Wranglers launched a European campaign featuring macho Wild West values such as rodeo riding, after an earlier campaign, featuring a supermodel, had made their sales of jeans to women grow 400 per cent but put men off their brand.[20]

marketing opportunity

Websites for women

Segmenting by gender is alive and well in cyberspace.[21] In France, for example, a group of women started the country's first women's electronic magazine and web portal called **Newsfam.com.** These entrepreneurs are hoping to reproduce the success of American sites like **iVillage.com** and **Women.com.**[22] To underscore the idea that men and women differ in their tastes and preferences (the French would say *vive la différence!*), a website for high-tech products called **Hifi.com** opened a sister site just for women called **herhifi.com.** It avoids jargon, offers friendly advice and finds ways to make home entertainment systems relevant to women.[23] Probably a sound strategy, considering that six out of every ten new internet users are female.[24]

Marketers are paying increasing attention to demographic changes throughout Europe, and particularly with respect to changing income levels in Eastern Europe.

Mitsubishi

Family structure

A person's family and marital status is yet another important demographic variable, since this has such a big effect on consumers' spending priorities. Young bachelors and newly-weds are the most likely to take exercise, go to wine bars and pubs, concerts and the cinema and to consume alcohol. Families with young children are big purchasers of health foods and fruit juices, while single-parent households and those with older children buy more junk food. Home maintenance services are most likely to be used by older couples and bachelors.[25]

Social class and income

People in the same social class are approximately equal in terms of their incomes and social status. They work in roughly similar occupations and tend to have similar tastes in music, clothing and so on. They also tend to socialize with one another and share many ideas and values.[26] The distribution of wealth is of great interest to marketers, since it determines which groups have the greatest buying power and market potential.

Race and ethnicity

Immigrants from various countries in Africa and Asia are among the fastest-growing ethnic groups in Europe. As our societies grow increasingly multicultural, new opportunities develop to deliver specialized products to racial and ethnic groups, and to introduce other groups to these offerings.

Sometimes, this adaptation is a matter of putting an existing product or service into a different context. For example, in Great Britain there is a motorway service station and cafeteria targeted at the Muslim population. It has prayer facilities, no pork menus and serves *halal* meat.[27] And now, Turks in Berlin do not have to rely solely on the small immigrants' greengroceries and kiosks known from so many other European cities. A Turkish chain has opened the first department store in Berlin, carrying Turkish and Middle Eastern goods only, catering to both the large Turkish population as well as to other immigrant groups and Germans longing for culinary holiday memories.[28]

multicultural dimensions

As we will discuss shortly, people can express their self and their cultural and religious belonging through consumption patterns. At times, this has led to cultural clashes, as in an example involving France or Denmark, where young Muslim women's wearing of headscarves either in school or at work has been debated for several years, and has even led to legislation prohibiting the wearing of 'conspicuous religious symbols' in French public schools.[29] Wearing a headscarf is criticized for being a religious statement, which should not be allowed in the explicitly secular French public schools, as a sign of oppression of women or as incompatible with the 'modern' image of the employing company. However, a headscarf is not just a headscarf. There are at least four culturally bound ways of displaying this controversial textile: the 'Italian way', known from stars of the 1950s and 1960s such as Sophia Loren, Claudia Cardinale or Gina Lollobrigida on the back seats of scooters and revived by nostalgia movements; the 'women's lib' way with the knot in the back as displayed by many Scandinavian women in the 1970s; the 'German Hausfrau' version with a bow in the front; and the much-disputed Muslim version. In Turkey, one may see a lot of women wearing headscarves, but one can tell from the way they are tied whether this is a religious expression from a religious woman or rather an expression of a cultural tradition, and as such more a rural than a religious reference.[30]

Geography

In Europe, most of the evidence points to the fact that cultural differences persist in playing a decisive role in forming our consumption patterns and our unique expressions of consumption. At the same time, global competition tends to have a homogenizing effect in some markets such as music, sports, clothing and entertainment, and multinational companies such as Sony, Pepsi, Nintendo, Nike and Levi Strauss continue to dominate or play important roles in shaping markets.[31] With the creation of the single European market, many companies have begun to consider even more the possibilities of standardized marketing across national boundaries in Europe. The increasing similarity of the brands and products available in Europe does not mean that the consumers are the same, however! Variables such as personal motivation, cultural context, family relation patterns and rhythms of everyday life, all vary substantially from country to country and from region to region. And consumption of various product categories is still very different: in 1995 the per capita consumption of cheese per annum was 16.9 kg in France and 6.1 kg in Ireland; consumption of potatoes was 13.8 kg in Italy and 59.9 kg in Finland.[32] In marketing research, the possibility of operating with standard criteria for something as 'simple' as demographics for market segmentation is constantly under discussion. But to date the results have not always been encouraging.[33]

To sum up, a European segmentation must be able to take into consideration:

● consumption which is common across cultures (the global or regional, trends, lifestyles and cultural patterns that cross borders); and

● consumption which is specific between different cultural groups (differences in values, lifestyles, behavioural patterns, etc. among different cultures and subcultures).

marketing opportunity

New segments

Marketers have come up with so many ways to segment consumers – from the overweight to overachievers – that you might think they had run out of segments. Hardly. Changes in lifestyle and other characteristics of the population are constantly creating new opportunities. The following are some 'hot' market segments.

The gay community: In more and more societies, the gay minority is becoming increasingly visible. New media featuring homosexual lifestyles and the consumption patterns attached to them flourish and marketers claim that the gay community is as attractive a marketing niche as many other subcultures and that this group forms a 'hungry target'.[34] For example, in the marketing of Copenhagen as a tourist destination, the gay community has been explicitly chosen as one of the target markets. The gay segment tends to be economically upmarket and is frequently involved in travelling and short holidays to metropolitan areas. So the tourist board has tried to reach it through specific marketing activities targeted at gay environments in Europe. Recently, London has emerged as 'more than a destination' tourist spot for gays, based on the city's overall welcome to gays, which is not focused on just one specific area or neighbourhood. The government-funded 'visitbrittain' website targets gay visitors, touting Britain as the 'United Queendom'.[35]

Single females: A worldwide study by Young and Rubicam has discovered a new and interesting market segment, that of well-educated, intelligent women who choose to stay single and pursue their life and career goals without husband or children. Furthermore, they represent heavy-spending consumers. They are reportedly brand-loyal and highly influenced by their friends in terms of consumption choices. The way to reach this attractive consumer group is to speak to their feelings of independence and self-respect.[36]

Disabled people: In the wake of legislation on the rights of disabled people, some marketers are starting to take notice of the estimated 10–15 per cent of the population who have some kind of disability. Initiatives include special phone numbers for hearing-impaired customers and assistance services for disabled people. IBM and Nissan have also used disabled actors in their advertising campaigns.[37] Mattel Inc., which produces Barbie, launched a sister doll, Becky, in a wheelchair – a reflection of the growing awareness of the disabled population in society.

Even then, the problem of specifying the relevant borders arises. Cultural borders do not always follow national borders. Although national borders are still very important for distinguishing between cultures, there may be important regional differences within a country, as well as cultural overlap between two countries.[38] Add to this immigration and the import of foreign (often American) cultural phenomena, and you begin to understand why it is very difficult to talk about European countries as being culturally homogeneous. For example, it is important to distinguish between, say, Dutch *society* with all its multicultural traits and Dutch *culture*, which may be one, albeit dominant, cultural element in Dutch society. Furthermore, Dutch culture (as is the case with all cultures) is not a *static* but a *dynamic* phenomenon, which changes over time and from contact, interaction and integration with other cultures.

Relationship marketing: building bonds with consumers

Marketers are carefully defining customer segments and listening to people as never before. Many of them have realized that the key to success is building lifetime relationships between brands and customers. Marketers who believe in this philosophy – so-called **relationship marketing** – are making an effort to keep in touch with their customers on a regular basis, and are giving them reasons to maintain a bond with the company over time. Various types of membership of retail outlets, petrol companies and co-operative movements illustrate this. One co-operative chain offers reductions to its members on such diverse goods as travelling, clothing, home appliances, electronics and garden furniture.[39] A new trend is to form consortia of diverse companies from different sectors, such as supermarkets, banks, petrol retailers, telecommunications and the entertainment and leisure industry. The consortium then issues a loyalty card to help secure a stable clientele.[40]

Some companies establish these ties by offering services that are appreciated by their customers. Many companies donate a small percentage of the purchase price to a charity such as the Red Cross or the World Wildlife Fund, or for the care of the poor and marginalized in society. This cements the relationship by giving customers an additional reason to continue buying the company's products year after year.

Another revolution in relationship building is being brought to us by courtesy of ▶ **database marketing**. This involves tracking consumers' buying habits by computer and crafting products and information tailored precisely to people's wants and needs.

Keeping close tabs on their customers allows database marketers to monitor their preferences and communicate with those who show an interest in their products or services. Information is passed to the appropriate division for follow-up. DVD online rental companies such as ScreenSelect in the UK and Web.DE in Germany are testing a system that makes recommendations based on a consumer's prior rentals and offers special promotions based on these choices.[41] However, some consumers feel threatened by this kind of surveillance and resist such marketing efforts. Hence, attempts have been made to ensure that database marketing conforms to the requirements of respondent confidentiality.[42]

■ MARKETING'S IMPACT ON CONSUMERS

For better or worse, we live in a world that is significantly influenced by marketers. We are surrounded by marketing stimuli in the form of advertisements, shops and products competing for our attention and our cash. Much of what we learn about the world is filtered by marketers, whether through conspicuous consumption depicted in glamorous magazine advertising or via the roles played by family figures in TV commercials. Ads show us how we ought to act with regard to recycling, alcohol consumption and even the types of house or car we aspire to. In many ways we are at the mercy of marketers, since we rely on them to sell us products that are safe and perform as promised, to tell us the truth about what they are selling, and to price and distribute these products fairly.

Popular culture

▶ **Popular culture**, the music, films, sports, books and other forms of entertainment consumed by the mass market, is both a product of and an inspiration for marketers. Our lives are also affected in more fundamental ways, ranging from how we acknowledge social events such as marriages, deaths or holidays to how we view societal issues such as air pollution, gambling and addiction. The football World Cup, Christmas shopping, tourism, newspaper recycling, cigarette smoking and Barbie dolls are all examples of products and activities that touch many of us in our lives.

Marketing's role in the creation and communication of popular culture is especially emphasized in this book. This cultural influence is hard to ignore, although many people fail to appreciate the extent to which their view of the world – their film and music icons, the latest fashions in clothing, food and interior design, and even the physical features that they find attractive or not in sexual partners – is influenced by the marketing system. Product placement, whereby products and brands are exposed in popular films or TV series, or sponsorships of various mediated or live events such as concerts or quizzes, are examples of companies' new ways to command our attention. How about sleeping in your own culture, even when you're travelling abroad? Holland International's travel catalogue offers Dutch tourists the opportunity to sleep in 'Amsterdam canal houses' or 'farm village cottages' complete with Dutch traditional foods, and they can even register for their room at the reception desk using the Dutch language. All the comforts of home . . . in Turkey![43]

Consider the product characters that marketers use to create a personality for their products. From the Michelin Man to Ronald McDonald, popular culture is peopled with fictional heroes. In fact, it is likely that more consumers will recognize characters such as these than can identify former prime ministers, captains of industry or artists. They may not exist, but many of us feel that we 'know' them, and they certainly are effective *spokes-characters* for the products they promote. If you don't believe it, visit **www.toymuseum.com**.

The meaning of consumption

One of the fundamental premises of consumer behaviour is that people often buy products not for what they do, but for what they *mean*.[44] This principle does not imply that a product's primary function is unimportant, but rather that the roles products play and the **meaning** that they have in our lives go well beyond the tasks they perform. The deeper meanings of a product may help it to stand out from other, similar goods and services – all things being equal, a person will choose the brand that has an image (or even a personality!) consistent with his or her underlying ideas.

For example, although most people probably can't run faster or jump higher if they are wearing Nikes rather than Reeboks, many diehard loyalists swear by their favourite brand. These arch-rivals are marketed in terms of their image – meanings that have been carefully crafted with the help of legions of rock stars, athletes, slickly produced commercials – and many millions of dollars. So, when you buy a Nike 'swoosh' you may be doing more than choosing footwear – you may also be making a lifestyle statement about the type of person you are, or want to be. For a relatively simple item made of leather and laces, that's quite a feat!

As we have already seen, the hallmark of marketing strategies at the beginning of the twenty-first century is an emphasis on building relationships with customers. The nature of these relationships can vary, and these bonds help us to understand some of the possible meanings products have for us. Here are some of the types of relationship a person may have with a product:[45]

- *Self-concept attachment* – the product helps to establish the user's identity.
- *Nostalgic attachment* – the product serves as a link with a past self.
- *Interdependence* – the product is a part of the user's daily routine.
- *Love* – the product elicits bonds of warmth, passion or other strong emotion.

One American consumer researcher has developed a classification scheme in an attempt to explore the different ways that products and experiences can provide meaning to people.[46] This consumption typology was derived from a two-year analysis of supporters of a baseball team, but it is easily transferable to the European context. This perspective views consumption as a type of action in which people make use of consumption objects in a variety of ways. Focusing on an event such as a football match is a useful reminder that when we refer to consumption, we are talking about intangible experiences, ideas and services (the thrill of a goal or the antics of a team mascot) in addition to tangible objects (like the food and drink consumed at the stadium). This analysis identified four distinct types of consumption activities:

1 *Consuming as experience* – when the consumption is a personal emotional or aesthetic goal in itself. This would include activities like the pleasure derived from learning

IT'S OKAY TO STARE.
It's hard not to when you're looking at a world record holder.

PROUD SPONSOR OF THE SA PARALYMPIC TEAM
A NIKE CARES TRUST INITIATIVE

People with disabilities are beginning to be a more common focus of advertising messages, as exemplified by this South African ad for Nike.
© The Jupiter Drawing Room (South Africa)

how to interpret the offside rule, or appreciating the athletic ability of a favourite player.

2 *Consuming as integration* – using and manipulating consumption objects to express aspects of the self. For example, some fans express their solidarity with the team by identifying with, say, the mascot and adopting some of its characteristic traits. Attending matches in person rather than watching them on TV allows the fan to integrate his or her experience more completely with his/her self – the feeling of 'having been there'.

3 *Consuming as classification* – the activities that consumers engage in to communicate their association with objects, both to self and to others. For example, spectators might dress up in the team's colours and buy souvenirs to demonstrate to others that they are diehard fans. Unfortunately, the more hard core express their contempt for opponents' supporters violently. There is a profound 'us' and 'them' dichotomy present here.

4 *Consuming as play* – consumers use objects to participate in a mutual experience and merge their identities with that of a group. For example, happy fans might scream in unison and engage in an orgy of jumping and hugging when their team scores a goal – this is a different dimension of shared experience compared with watching the game at home.

The global consumer

By 2006, the majority of people on earth will live in urban centres – the number of megacities, defined as urban centres of 10 million or more, is projected to grow to 26 in 2015.[47] One highly visible – and controversial – by-product of sophisticated marketing strategies is the movement towards a **global consumer culture**, in which people are united by their common devotion to brand-name consumer goods, film stars and rock stars.[48] Some products in particular have become so associated with an American lifestyle that they are prized possessions around the world. In Chapters 16 and 17 we will pay special attention to the good and bad aspects of this cultural homogenization.[49]

On the other hand, popular culture continues to evolve as products and styles from different cultures mix and merge in new and interesting ways. For example, although superstars from the USA and the UK dominate the worldwide music industry, there is a movement afoot to include more diverse styles and performers. In Europe, local music acts are grabbing a larger share of the market and pushing international (that is, English-speaking) acts down the charts. Revenue from Spanish-language music has quadrupled in five years.

A 'cousin' of the global consumer is the much debated Euro-consumer. Marketing researchers are heavily involved in a debate about the possibilities of finding market segments that are European rather than national in character. In a study on the consumption of luxury goods, it was concluded that one could draw a demographic portrait of the average European consumer of luxury goods. However, important differences between the countries were also detected. Consumers who expressed more positive attitudes towards cultural change were also more likely to consume luxury goods, independent of their demographics and social class.[50] Given these findings, it is questionable how much is gained from working with the concept of the Euro-consumer in terms of segment description. For a product such as cars, which intuitively and in terms of functionality would seem relatively easy to market as a European-wide product, the models still appear in a variety of versions to suit particular national needs and wants. The Euro-consumer will be discussed in detail in Chapter 16.

The Burberry brand ties the traditional with the modern by placing a Rolls Royce in the background, with fashion model Stella Tennant in the foreground, showing the Burberry plaids.
The Advertising Archives

Marketing ethics

In business, conflicts often arise between the goal to succeed in the marketplace and the desire to conduct business honestly and maximize the well-being of consumers by providing them with safe and effective products and services. Some people argue that by the time people reach university, secondary school or are actually employed by companies, it is a little late to start teaching them ethics! Still, many universities and corporations are now focusing very intently on teaching and reinforcing ethical behaviour.

Prescribing ethical standards of conduct

Professional organizations often devise a code of ethics for their members. For example, European or national consumer protection laws or various national marketing associations' codes of ethics provide guidelines for conduct in many areas of marketing practice. These include:

- Disclosure of all substantial risks associated with a product or service.
- Identification of added features that will increase the cost.
- Avoidance of false or misleading advertising.
- Rejection of high-pressure or misleading sales tactics.
- Prohibition of selling or fund-raising under the guise of conducting market research.

Socially responsible behaviour

Whether intentionally or not, some marketers do violate their bond of trust with consumers. In some cases these actions are illegal, as when a manufacturer deliberately mislabels the contents of a package or a retailer adopts a 'bait-and-switch' selling strategy, whereby consumers are lured into the store with promises of inexpensive products with the sole intention of getting them to switch to higher-priced goods. A similar problematic issue of the luring of consumers is the case of misleading claims, for instance on food product labels.[51] For example, what about a label such as '100 per cent fat-free strawberry jam'?

In other cases, marketing practices have detrimental effects on society even though they are not explicitly illegal. The introduction of so-called alcopops, a mix of alcohol and soda or lemonade, targeted more or less explicitly at the teen market, has caused considerable debate in various European countries. Following negative press coverage, sales have gone down in Sweden and the UK, and the two largest retail chains in Denmark withdrew these drinks from their product range.[52] Others have run into difficulties by sponsoring commercials depicting groups of people in an unfavourable light to get the attention of a target market. One may recall the heated debate as to whether Benetton's advertising campaigns are attempts to sensitize consumers to the world's real problems, as the company contends, or to exploit unfortunate people – as in the ads depicting an AIDS victim, a dead Croat soldier or a ship packed with Albanian refugees – in order to sell more Benetton clothing.[53]

A crucial barometer of ethical behaviour is what actions a marketer takes once a company is made aware of a problem with its advertising or products. In 1996 a Danish hypermarket chain, which for years had run a campaign guaranteeing the lowest prices compared to competitors, was involved in a scandal when it was discovered that employees were under instruction to change price tags just before a newspaper journalist checked them.[54]

In contrast, Procter & Gamble voluntarily withdrew its Rely tampons following reports of women who had suffered toxic shock syndrome (TSS) after using them. Although scientists did not claim a causal link between Rely and the onset of TSS, the company agreed to undertake extensive advertising notifying women of the symptoms of TSS and asking them to return their boxes of Rely for a refund. The company took a

$75 million loss and sacrificed an unusually successful new product which had already captured about 25 per cent of the huge sanitary product market.[55]

Faced with the rising phenomenon of the 'political consumer' – a consumer who expresses his or her political and ethical viewpoints by selecting and avoiding products from companies which are antithetical to these viewpoints – the industry is increasingly coming to realize that ethical behaviour is also good business in the long run, since the trust and satisfaction of consumers translates into years of loyalty from customers. However, many problems remain. Throughout this book, ethical issues related to the practice of marketing are highlighted. Special boxes headed 'Marketing pitfall' feature dubious marketing practices or the possible adverse effects on consumers of certain marketing strategies.

marketing pitfall

Women for s@le! The charge against abuse of marketing techniques has taken on new dimensions with the rise of the internet. Would you like to buy a Latvian girl for escort service? Or a Russian bride by mail order? The trade in women from eastern Europe, Asia or Latin America has reached new heights with the easier contact made possible by the internet. Obvious problems are created by the difficulty of distinguishing between serious marriage bureaus or au pair agencies on the one side and organized traders of women for various kinds of prostitution services on the other. According to human rights organizations, many women who believe that they are going to marry the prince of their lives end up as 'sexual services workers', sometimes under slavery-like conditions.[56]

Public policy and consumerism

Public concern for the welfare of consumers has been an issue since at least the beginning of the twentieth century. This is normally referred to as **consumer policy**. Partly as a result of consumers' efforts, many national and international agencies have been established to oversee consumer-related activities. Consumers themselves continue to have a lively interest in consumer-related issues, ranging from environmental concerns, such as pollution caused by oil spills or toxic waste, the use of additives and genetically manipulated material in food and so on, to excessive violence and sex on television.

Consumer research and consumer welfare

The field of consumer behaviour can play an important role in improving our lives as consumers.[57] Many researchers play a role in formulating or evaluating public policies, such as ensuring that products are labelled accurately, that people can comprehend important information presented in advertising, or that children are not exploited by programme-length toy commercials masquerading as television shows.

Of course, to a large degree consumers are dependent on their governments to regulate and police safety and environmental standards. The extent of supervision may depend on such factors as the national political and cultural climate. Debates within the EU concerning regulation of the use of pesticides and food additives are examples here. In addition, a country's traditions and beliefs may make it more sympathetic to one or the other point of view expressed by consumers or producers. For example, the cross-Atlantic debate concerning market acceptance of genetically modified food products has also given rise to research about consumers' attitudes toward the acceptability and labelling of such products.[58]

There is also a growing movement to develop knowledge about **social marketing**, which attempts to encourage such positive behaviours as increased literacy and to discourage negative activities such as drink-driving.[59] A project in Sweden aimed at curbing adolescent drinking illustrates social marketing at work. The Swedish Brewers'

Table 1.2 EU priorities for consumer policy

Ten major priorities for the future development of consumer policy have been defined by the European Commission:

- Major improvement in the education and information of consumers
- Completion, review and updating of the legislative framework to protect consumer interests in the internal market
- Review of the consumer aspects of financial services
- Review of the protection of consumer interests in the supply of essential public utility services
- Helping consumers to benefit from the information society
- Improving consumer confidence in foodstuffs
- Practical encouragement of sustainable consumption
- Strengthening and increasing consumer representation
- Helping the development of consumer policies in central and eastern Europe
- Review of consumer policy in developing countries.

Source: European Commission, www.cec.org.uk (accessed 25 July 2005).

Association is investing 10 million Skr (about $7.5 million) in a cooperative effort with the Swedish Non-Violence Project to change teens' attitudes to alcohol consumption. Consumer researchers working on the project discovered that Swedish adolescents freely admit that they 'drink in order to get drunk' and enjoy the feeling of being intoxicated, so persuading them to give up alcohol is a formidable task. However, the teens reported that they are also afraid of losing control over their own behaviour, especially if there is a risk of their being exposed to violence. And while worries about the long-term health effects of drinking don't concern this group (after all, at this age many believe they will live forever), female adolescents reported a fear of becoming less attractive as a result of prolonged alcohol consumption.

This German ad for Unicef makes a statement about the problem of child labour.

© German National Committee for UNICEF and Springer & Jacoby Fuenfte Werbeagentur GmbH & Co. KG. Photo: Jan Burwick

Based on these findings, the group commissioned to execute this project decided to stress a more realistic message of 'drink if you want to, but within a safe limit. Don't lose control, because if you do, you might get yourself into violent situations.' They made up the motto 'Alco-hole in your head' to stress the importance of knowing one's limits. This message is being emphasized along with strong visual images that appear on billboards, in video spots that depict situations involving young drinkers getting out of control, and in school presentations given by young people who will be credible role models for teens.[60]

■ DO MARKETERS MANIPULATE CONSUMERS?

One of the most common and stinging criticisms of marketing is that marketing techniques (especially advertising) are responsible for convincing consumers that they 'need' many material goods and that they will be unhappy and somehow inferior if they do not have these 'necessities'. The issue is complex, and one that is certainly worth considering: do marketers give people what they want, or do they tell people what they ought to want?

Philosophers have approached this issue when considering the concept of free will. It has been argued that in order to claim that consumers are acting autonomously in response to ads, the capacity for free will and free action must be present. That is, the consumer must be capable of deciding *independently* what to do, and not be prevented from carrying out that decision. This, it has been argued, is probably true for purely informative advertising, where only the product or store information required to make a rational decision is provided, whereas the case for advertising where imagery or underlying motivations are tapped is not as clear.[61] Such a view presupposes that informative advertising is somehow more objective than imagery-based advertising. But functionality and utility are also important images of a specific cultural context that uses references to our reason to seduce us.[62] Three issues related to the complex relationship between marketing practices and consumers' needs are considered here.

Do marketers create artificial needs?

The marketing system has come under fire from both ends of the political spectrum. On the one hand, some conservative traditionalists believe that advertising contributes to the moral breakdown of society by presenting images of hedonistic pleasure. On the other hand, some leftists argue that the same misleading promises of material pleasure function to buy off people who would otherwise be revolutionaries working to change the system.[63] Through advertising, then, the system creates demand that only its products can satisfy.

One possible response to such criticism is that a need is a basic biological motive, while a want represents one way that society has taught us that the need can be satisfied. For example, while thirst is biologically based, we are taught to want Coca-Cola to satisfy that thirst rather than, say, goat's milk. Thus, the need is already there: marketers simply recommend ways to satisfy it. A basic objective of advertising is to create awareness that these needs exist, rather than to create them.

However, marketers are important engineers of our environment. And beyond the level of banality, needs are always formed by the social environment. Thus, in a sense, needs are always 'artificial' because we are interested in needs only in their social form. Alternatively, needs are never artificial because they are always 'real' to the people who feel them. 'Needs' are something we are socialized to have. In the case of the Coca-Cola vs. goat's milk example, it should be remembered that we do not eat and drink solely to satisfy a biological need. We eat and drink for a number of reasons, all of them embedded in our cultural context. What is the need of a sofa? A TV? A car? A textbook

This ad was created by the American Association of Advertising Agencies to counter charges that ads create artificial needs. Compare this message with the Marketing opportunity on page 23. What is your conclusion?

American Association of Advertising Agencies

on consumer behaviour? Thus, a better response would be that marketers do not create artificial needs, but they do contribute heavily to the socialization of people in contemporary society and thus to the establishment of the *social* system of needs. Consequently, marketers must take a share of responsibility for the development of society.

Is advertising necessary?

As the social commentator Vance Packard wrote nearly 50 years ago, 'Large-scale efforts are being made, often with impressive success, to channel our unthinking habits, our purchasing decisions, and our thought processes by the use of insights gleaned from psychiatry and the social sciences.'[64] The economist John Kenneth Galbraith believed that radio and television are important tools to accomplish this manipulation of the masses. Since virtually no literacy is required to use these media, they allow repetitive and compelling communications to reach almost everyone.

Goods are arbitrarily linked to desirable social attributes. One influential critic even argued that the problem is that we are not materialistic enough – that is, we do not sufficiently value goods for the utilitarian functions they deliver, but instead focus on the irrational value of goods for what they symbolize. According to this view, 'Beer would be enough for us, without the additional promise that in drinking it we show ourselves to be manly, young at heart, or neighbourly. A washing machine would be a useful machine to wash clothes, rather than an indication that we are forward-looking or an object of envy to our neighbours.'[65]

Such arguments seem somewhat outdated at the beginning of the twenty-first century, when advertising has been embraced as an art form in itself. Today, children are brought up to be both consumers and readers of advertising. A predominantly functional approach to consumption, as in the former planned economies of eastern Europe, did not make people happier, nor did it prevent them from establishing mythologies about other goods, such as the scarce and expensive ones from the West. Advertisers, just like marketers, are important communicators. Their importance must be accompanied by a sense of responsibility concerning the social and individual effect of their messages.

marketing opportunity

As eastern European countries turn into market economies, some fear that consumers are being exploited as Western advertisements bombard them with products they didn't know they needed. In Poland, for example, previously taboo items like women's sanitary towels are being advertised for the first time, and new markets are being created for products such as pet food. The actions of one Polish entrepreneur illustrate how a consumer's search for social approval can be channelled into a want for a product.

Beginning with an ad campaign featuring Miss Poland, he single-handedly created a market for electronic hair removers (Polish women usually did not shave their legs). He also persuaded a leading Polish fashion designer to announce that hairy legs were out of fashion in Europe, and he organized local beauty contests to find the best legs. At the last report, he was selling 30,000 hair removers a month.[66]

Do marketers promise miracles?

Consumers are led to believe via advertising that products have magical properties; they will do special and mysterious things for them that will transform their lives. They will be beautiful, have power over others' feelings, be successful, be relieved of all ills, and so on. In this respect, advertising functions as mythology does in primitive societies: it provides simple, anxiety-reducing answers to complex problems. Is this a problem in itself?

Yes and no. The consumer is not an automaton that will react in a predefined way to certain stimuli. On the other hand, we are all partly socialized by the market and its messages. So, whereas the manipulative effectiveness of advertising is often overstated, there is little doubt that advertising creates and changes patterns of consumption. This is especially so in the new market economies, where the population does not maintain the same distance from and critical attitude to advertising messages and imagery.

But the effect is in general more subtle than simple manipulative persuasion. In most cases, advertisers simply do not know enough about people to manipulate them directly. Consider that the failure rate for new products ranges from 40 to 80 per cent. The main effect of advertising may often be found on the more general level, in the promotion of the idea that your self and your personal relationships, your success and your image all depend on your consumer choices.

■ CONSUMER BEHAVIOUR AS A FIELD OF STUDY

Although people have been consumers for a very long time, it is only recently that consumption per se has been the focus of formal study. In fact, while many business schools now require that marketing students take a consumer behaviour course, most universities and business schools did not even offer such a course until the 1970s. Much of the impetus for the attention now being given to consumer behaviour was the realization by many business people that the consumer really *is* the boss.

Interdisciplinary influences on the study of consumer behaviour

Consumer behaviour is a very new field and, as it grows, it is being influenced by many different perspectives. Indeed, it is hard to think of a field that is more interdisciplinary. People with a background in a very wide range of fields – from psychophysiology to literature – can now be found doing consumer research. Consumer researchers are employed by universities, manufacturers, museums, advertising agencies and governments. Professional groups, such as the Association for Consumer Research, have been formed since the mid-1970s, and European academics and practitioners are major contributors to the growing literature on consumer behaviour.

Researchers approach consumer issues from different perspectives. You might remember a fable about blind men and an elephant. The gist of the story is that each man touched a different part of the animal, and, as a result, the descriptions each gave of the elephant were quite different. This analogy applies to consumer research as well. A similar consumer phenomenon can be studied in different ways and at different levels depending on the training and interests of the researchers studying it.

Figure 1.2 covers some of the disciplines in the field and the level at which each approaches research issues. These disciplines can be loosely characterized in terms of their focus on micro vs. macro consumer behaviour topics. The fields closer to the top of the pyramid concentrate on the individual consumer (micro issues), while those towards the base are more interested in the aggregate activities that occur among larger groups of people, such as consumption patterns shared by members of a culture or subculture (macro issues).

Figure 1.2 The pyramid of consumer behaviour

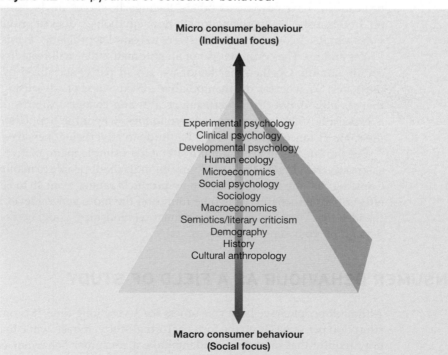

The issue of strategic focus

Many people regard the field of consumer behaviour as an applied social science. Accordingly, the value of the knowledge generated has traditionally been measured in terms of its ability to improve the effectiveness of marketing practice. Recently, though, some researchers have argued that consumer behaviour should not have a strategic focus at all; the field should not be a 'handmaiden to business'. It should instead focus on understanding consumption for its own sake, rather than because the knowledge can be applied by marketers.[67] This view is probably not held by most consumer researchers, but it has encouraged many to expand the scope of their work beyond the field's traditional focus on the purchase of consumer goods. And it has certainly led to some fierce debates among people working in the field! In fact, it can also be argued that business gets better research from non-strategic research projects because they are unbiased by strategic goals. Take a relatively simple and common consumer object like the women's magazine, found in every culture in a variety of versions. How much is there to say about the 'simple' act of buying such a magazine? Well, quite a lot. Table 1.3 lists some potential issues relevant for the marketing of or advertising in women's

Table 1.3 Interdisciplinary research issues in consumer behaviour

Disciplinary focus	Magazine usage sample research issues
Experimental Psychology: product role in perception, learning and memory processes	How specific aspects of magazines, such as their design or layout, are recognized and interpreted; which parts of a magazine are most likely to be read
Clinical Psychology: product role in psychological adjustment	How magazines affect readers' body images (e.g. do thin models make the average woman feel overweight?)
Microeconomics/Human Ecology: product role in allocation of individual or family resources	Factors influencing the amount of money spent on magazines in a household
Social Psychology: product role in the behaviours of individuals as members of social groups	Ways that ads in a magazine affect readers' attitudes towards the products depicted; how peer pressure influences a person's readership decisions
Sociology: product role in social institutions and group relationships	Pattern by which magazine preferences spread through a social group
Macroeconomics: product role in consumers' relations with the marketplace	Effects of the price of fashion magazines and expense of items advertised during periods of high unemployment
Semiotics/Literary Criticism: product role in the verbal and visual communication of meaning	Ways in which underlying messages communicated by models and ads in a magazine are interpreted
Demography: product role in the measurable characteristics of a population	Effects of age, income and marital status of a magazine's readers
History: product role in societal changes over time	Ways in which our culture's depictions of 'femininity' in magazines have changed over time
Cultural Anthropology: product role in a society's beliefs and practices	Ways in which fashions and models in a magazine affect readers' definitions of masculine vs. feminine behaviour (e.g. the role of working women, sexual taboos)

magazines which can be researched based on the variety of disciplines influencing consumer research.

This more critical view of consumer research has led to the recognition that not all consumer behaviour and/or marketing activity is necessarily beneficial to individuals or to society. As a result, current consumer research is likely to include attention to the 'dark side' of consumer behaviour, such as addiction, prostitution, homelessness, shoplifting or environmental waste. This activity builds upon the earlier work of researchers who, as we have seen, have studied consumer issues related to public policy, ethics and consumerism.

The issue of two perspectives on consumer research

One general way to classify consumer research is in terms of the fundamental assumptions the researchers make about what they are studying and how to study it. This set of beliefs is known as a **paradigm**. Like other fields of study, consumer behaviour is dominated by a paradigm, but some believe it is in the middle of a *paradigm shift*, which occurs when a competing paradigm challenges the dominant set of assumptions.

The basic set of assumptions underlying the dominant paradigm at this point in time is called **positivism**. This perspective has significantly influenced Western art and science since the late sixteenth century. It emphasizes that human reason is supreme and that there is a single, objective truth that can be discovered by science. Positivism encourages us to stress the function of objects, to celebrate technology and to regard the world as a rational, ordered place with a clearly defined past, present and future. Some feel that positivism puts too much emphasis on material well-being, and that its logical outlook is dominated by an ideology that stresses the homogeneous views of a predominantly Western and male culture.

The newer paradigm of **interpretivism** questions these assumptions. Proponents of this perspective argue that our society places too much emphasis on science and technology, and that this ordered, rational view of consumers denies the complexity of the social and cultural world in which we live. Interpretivists stress the importance of symbolic, subjective experience, and the idea that meaning is in the mind – that is, we each construct our own meanings based on our unique and shared cultural experiences, so that there are no single right or wrong references. To the value we place on products, because they help us to create order in our lives, is added an appreciation of consumption as a set of diverse experiences.

The major differences between these two perspectives are summarized in Table 1.4.

Table 1.4 Positivist vs. interpretivist approaches to consumer behaviour

Assumptions	Positivist approach	Interpretivist approach
Nature of reality	Objective, tangible Single	Socially constructed Multiple
Goal	Prediction	Understanding
Knowledge generated	Time-free Context-independent	Time-bound Context-dependent
View of causality	Existence of real causes	Multiple, simultaneous shaping events
Research relationship	Separation between researcher and subject	Interactive, co-operative, with researcher being part of phenomenon under study

Source: Adapted from Laurel A. Hudson and Julie L. Ozanne, 'Alternative ways of seeking knowledge in consumer research', *Journal of Consumer Research* 14 (March 1988): 508-21. Reprinted with the permission of The University of Chicago Press.

In addition to the cross-cultural differences in consumer behaviour discussed earlier, it is also clear that research styles differ significantly between Europe and North America and also within European countries. For example, studies have shown that European researchers tend to consider the cultural dimension much more than their American counterparts.[68] Further, two special sessions at a European consumer research conference revealed that there seem to be important differences between the way consumer behaviour is conceived in Germany and Great Britain, for example.[69] A recent and more 'bridging' perspective on approaches to the study of consumer research argues that the study of particular consumption contexts are not an end in themselves, but rather that studying human behaviour in a consumption context is useful for generating new constructs and theoretical insights. This approach, consumer culture theory (CCT), embraces a variety of methodological approaches (used by both positivist and interpretivist), and recognizes that managers can make use of multiple methods to better understand trends in the marketplace, such as the complexities of lifestyle, multicultural marketing, and how consumers use media as part of their lives.[70]

Consumer research is still moving on. From its original emphasis on buying behaviour and the factors influencing the decision-making process, the field gradually widened to become a study of consumer behaviour in a more general sense, also taking into consideration what happened before and after the purchase. After the introduction of the interpretivist approach, a broader research perspective has included many new and non-psychological facets in the increasingly complex portraits of consumers. And it can be argued that the field increasingly looks beyond the single individual and his or her social background and environment to describe and analyse the complex relationships that have led us to start characterizing our present society as a **consumer society**.[71] The facts of living in a consumer society and being surrounded by consumer culture permeate this book but will be dealt with in more detail in Chapter 14.

■ CHAPTER SUMMARY

- ■ Consumer behaviour is the study of the processes involved when individuals or groups select, purchase, use or dispose of products, services, ideas or experiences to satisfy needs and desires.

- ■ A consumer may purchase, use and/or dispose of a product, but these functions may be performed by different people. In addition, consumers may be thought of as role players who need different products to help them play their various parts.

- ■ Market segmentation is an important aspect of consumer behaviour. Consumers can be segmented along many dimensions, including product usage, demographics (the objective aspects of a population, such as age and sex) and psychographics (psychological and lifestyle characteristics). Emerging developments, such as the new emphasis on relationship marketing and the practice of database marketing, mean that marketers are much more attuned to the wants and needs of different consumer groups.

- ■ Marketing activities exert an enormous impact on individuals. Consumer behaviour is relevant to our understanding of both public policy issues (e.g. ethical marketing practices) and of the dynamics of popular culture.

- ■ It is often said that marketers create artificial needs. Although this criticism is oversimplified, it is true that marketers must accept their share of the responsibility for how society develops and what is considered necessary to have and what is acceptable, nice and fun to do within society.

- The field of consumer behaviour is interdisciplinary: it is composed of researchers from many different fields who share an interest in how people interact with the marketplace. These disciplines can be categorized by the degree to which their focus is micro (the individual consumer) or macro (the consumer as a member of groups or of the larger society).

- There are many perspectives on consumer behaviour, but research orientations can roughly be divided into two approaches. The positivist perspective, which currently dominates the field, emphasizes the objectivity of science and the consumer as a rational decision-maker. The interpretivist perspective, in contrast, stresses the subjective meaning of the consumer's individual experience and the idea that any behaviour is subject to multiple interpretations rather than one single explanation.

▶ KEY TERMS

Consumer behaviour (p. 5)
Consumer policy (p. 19)
Consumer society (p. 27)
Database marketing (p. 14)
Demographics (p. 9)
Exchange (p. 7)
Global consumer culture (p. 17)
Interpretivism (p. 26)
Market segmentation (p. 8)

Meaning (p. 15)
Paradigm (p. 26)
Popular culture (p. 14)
Positivism (p. 26)
Psychographics (p. 9)
Relationship marketing (p. 13)
Role theory (p. 6)
Social marketing (p. 19)

CONSUMER BEHAVIOUR CHALLENGE

1 This chapter states that people play different roles and that their consumption behaviours may differ depending on the particular role they are playing. State whether you agree or disagree with this perspective, giving examples from your own life.

2 Some researchers believe that the field of consumer behaviour should be a pure, rather than an applied, science. That is, research issues should be framed in terms of their scientific interest rather than their applicability to immediate marketing problems. Do you agree?

3 In recent years, there has been a large debate about the influence that internet shopping will have on our consumer lives. Try listing the changes that you personally have made in your buying and consumption patterns due to e-commerce. Compare these changes with changes experienced by other people from various social groups, e.g. somebody from your parents' generation, an IT freak, or somebody with a lower educational background.

4 Name some products or services that are widely used by your social group. State whether you agree or disagree with the notion that these products help to form bonds within the group, and support your argument with examples from your list of products used by the group.

5 Although demographic information on large numbers of consumers is used in many marketing contexts, some people believe that the sale of data on customers' incomes, buying habits and so on constitutes an invasion of privacy and should be banned. Comment on this issue from both a consumer's and a marketer's point of view.

6 List the three stages in the consumption process. Describe the issues that you considered in each of these stages when you made a recent important purchase.

7 State the differences between the positivist and interpretivist approaches to consumer research. For each type of inquiry, give examples of product dimensions that would be more usefully explored using that type of research over the other.

8 What aspects of consumer behaviour are likely to be of interest to a financial planner? To a university administrator? To a graphic arts designer? To a social worker in a government agency? To a nursing instructor?

9 Select a product and brand that you use frequently and list what you consider to be the brand's determinant attributes. Without revealing your list, ask a friend who is approximately the same age but of the opposite sex to make a similar list for the same product (the brand may be different). Compare and contrast the identified attributes and report your findings.

10 Collect ads for five different brands of the same product. Report on the segmentation variables, target markets and emphasized product attributes in each ad.

■ NOTES

1. Andrea Davies, James Fitchett and Avi Shankar, 'An Ethnoconsumerist Enquiry into International Consumer Behaviour', in Darach Turley and Stephen Brown, eds, *European Advances in Consumer Research: All Changed, Changed Utterly?* 6 (Valdosta, GA: Association for Consumer Research, 2003): 102–7.

2. Christian Alsted, 'De unge, smukke og rige – oldies', *Markedsføring* 11 (1992): 30.

3. Kay Larsen, 'Global music sales fell in 2003, but 2nd half softened in the drop' *Wall Street Journal* (8 April 2003): B6; Gabi Ouwerkerk and Hotze Zijlstra, 'Vlinders op internet', *De Telegraaf* (4 January 2005), http://www2.telegraaf.nl/i-mail/16940401/Vlinders_op_internet.html.

4. Mike Featherstone, ed., *Global Culture. Nationalism, Globalization, and Modernity* (London: Sage, 1990). For a critical review of the effects and reception of (American style) marketing, see Johansson, Johny K., *In Your Face: How American Marketing Excess Fuels Anti-Americanism* (Upper Saddle River, NJ: Financial Times Prentice Hall, 2004).

5. Daniel Miller, 'Consumption as the Vanguard of History', in D. Miller, ed., *Acknowledging Consumption* (London: Routledge, 1995): 1–57.

6. Erving Goffman, *The Presentation of Self in Everyday Life* (Garden City, NY: Doubleday, 1959); George H. Mead, *Mind, Self, and Society* (Chicago: University of Chicago Press, 1934); Michael R. Solomon, 'The role of products as social stimuli: A symbolic interactionism perspective', *Journal of Consumer Research* 10 (December 1983): 319–29.

7. Yiannis Gabriel and Tim Lang, *The Unmanageable Consumer* (London: Sage, 1995).

8. Frank Bradley, *Marketing Management: Providing, Communicating and Delivering Value* (London: Prentice-Hall, 1995).

9. See the extremely interesting account of the history of the Sony Walkman in Paul du Gay et al., *Doing Cultural Studies: The Story of the Sony Walkman* (London: Sage/Open University, 1997).

10. Quoted in Evan Ramstad, 'Walkman's plan for reeling in the ears of wired youths', *Wall Street Journal Interactive Edition* (18 May 2000).

11. BBC News, 'iPod designer leads culture list', http://news.bbc.co.uk/1/hi/entertainment/arts/3481599.stm (accessed 11 February 2004).

12. Jeffrey F. Durgee, 'On Cézanne, hot buttons, and interpreting consumer storytelling', *Journal of Consumer Marketing* 5 (Fall 1988): 47–51.

13. Annetta Miller, 'You are what you buy', *Newsweek* (4 June 1990) 2: 59. If you're a chocaholic, or just interested in chocolate, have a look at http://www.chocolate.org/chocolatelink.html (accessed 25 July 2005).

14. http://news.google.com/news?ned=uk (accessed 25 July 2005).

15. http://epp.eurostat.cec.eu.int/portal/page?_pageid=1090,30070682,1090_30298591&_dad=portal&_schema=PORTAL (accessed 25 July 2005).

16. Päivi Munter and Norma Cohen, 'Ageing populations "will create crippling debt"', *Financial Times* (31 March 2004).

17. Natalie Perkins, 'Zeroing in on consumer values', *Ad Age* (22 March 1993): 23.

18. Charles Goldsmith and Anne-Michelle Morice, '*Marie Claire* wants to add some fun', *Wall Street Journal* (12 April 2004): B-1.

19. Jennifer Lawrence, 'Gender-specific works for diapers – almost too well', *Ad Age* (8 February 1993): S-10 (2).

20. 'Wrangler ad ropes in men', *Marketing* (27 March 1997).

21. 'Tech brands face a gender divide', *American Demographics* (February 2000): 16.

22. Amy Barrett, 'Site blends frivolous, serious to draw French women online', *Wall Street Journal Interactive Edition* (11 April 2000).

23. Erika Check, Walaika Haskins and Jennifer Tanaka, 'Different appeals', *Newsweek* (13 March 2000): 15.

24. Top 10 multi-category travel sites in Europe
    (1) Expedia: 4,448,000 (unique audience) of which 42.4 per cent were women.
    (2) Lastminute.com: 3,976,000 of which 50.6 per cent were women.
    (3) voyages-sncf.com: 3,304,000 of which 43.6 per cent were women.
    (4) Opodo: 2,193,000 of which 43.5 per cent were women.
    (5) Yahoo! Travel: 1,748,000 of which 46.4 per cent were women.
    (6) TUI: 1,726,000 of which 48.9 per cent were women.
    (7) ebookers: 1,276,000 of which 51.0 per cent were women.
    (8) eDreams: 1,217,000 of which 42.5 per cent were women.
    (9) Virgin Travel: 1,190,000 of which 46.2 per cent were women.
    (10) Hapag-Lloyd: 1,096,000 of which 43.6 per cent were women.
    Source: Nielsen//NetRatings NetView home and work data except CH and ES home only, Feb 04 & 05 (*Nielsen//NetRatings*, March 2005).

25. Charles M. Schaninger and William D. Danko, 'A conceptual and empirical comparison of alternative household life cycle models', *Journal of Consumer Research* 19 (March 1993): 580–94; Robert E. Wilkes, 'Household life-cycle stages, transitions, and product expenditures', *Journal of Consumer Research* 22(1) (June 1995): 27–42.

26. Richard P. Coleman, 'The continuing significance of social class to marketing', *Journal of Consumer Research* 10 (December 1983): 265–80.

27. BBS Radio (4 January 1997).

28. *Information* (26 September 2000): 11; see also: Kerstin Hilt, 'Mail order firm ships a taste of home', *Deutsche Welle* (29 December 2004), http://www.dw-world.de/dw/article/0,1564,1441829,00.html.

29. See http://en.wikipedia.org/wiki/French_law_to_ban_conspicuous_religious_symbols for an overview of conspicuous religious symbols in French schools (2005).

30. Özlem Sandikci and Güliz Ger, 'Fundamental Fashions: The Cultural Politics of the Turban and the Levi's', paper presented at the 2000 Association for Consumer Research Conference, Salt Lake City (19–22 October 2000).

31. Jean-Claude Usunier, *Marketing Across Cultures*, 3rd edn (London: Prentice-Hall, 2000).

32. Euromonitor, *European Marketing Data and Statistics*, 32nd edn (1997).

33. Rena Bartos, 'International demographic data? Incomparable!', *Marketing and Research Today* (November 1989): 205–12.

34. Søren Askegaard and Tage Koed Madsen, 'The local and the global: homogeneity and heterogeneity in food consumption in European regions', *International Business Review* 7(6) (1998): 549–68.

35. *Information* (4 February 1997); Vanessa Thorpe, 'London becomes Europe's pink capital', *The Observer* (9 January 2005), http://media.guardian.co.uk/site/story/0,14173,1386236,00.html.

36. *Markedsføring* 18 (7 September 2000): 16.

37. *Markedsføring* 17 (25 August 2000): 8.

38. Richard Vezina, Alain d'Astous and Sophie Deschamps, 'The Physically Disabled Consumer: Some Preliminary Findings and an Agenda for Future Research', in F. Hansen, ed., *European Advances in Consumer Research* 2 (Provo, UT: Association for Consumer Research, 1995): 277–81.

39. *Samvirke* 3 (March 1997).

40. 'Play your cards right', *Marketing* (17 April 1997): 32–3.

41. http://www.screenselect.co.uk/visitor/home.html and http://web.de/, 2005.

42. Barry Leventhal, 'An approach to fusing market research with database marketing', *Journal of the Market Research Society* 39(4) (1997): 545–58.

43. Peter van Erven-Dorens, 'Hollandse hap aan Turkse kust' (Dutch snacks on the Turkish Coast), *Reiskrant* (4 January 2005), http://reiskrant.nl/reiskrant/reisnieuws/16943671/Hollandse_hap_in_Turks_hotel.html.

44. Sidney J. Levy, 'Symbols for sale', *Harvard Business Review* 37 (July–August 1959): 117–24.

45. Susan Fournier, 'Consumers and their brands. Developing relationship theory in consumer research', *Journal of Consumer Research* 24 (March 1998): 343–73.

46. Douglas B. Holt, 'How consumers consume: a typology of consumption practices', *Journal of Consumer Research* 22(1) (June 1995): 1–16.

47. Brad Edmondson, 'The dawn of the megacity', *Marketing Tools* (March 1999): 64.

48. For a discussion of this trend, see Russell W. Belk, 'Hyperreality and globalization: Culture in the age of Ronald McDonald', *Journal of International Consumer Marketing* 8 (3/4) (1995): 23–37.

49. For a fully fledged study of this process, see Tom O'Dell, *Culture Unbound. Americanization and Everyday Life in Sweden* (Lund: Nordic Academic Press, 1997).

50. Bernard Dubois and Gilles Laurent, 'Is there a Euro Consumer for Luxury Goods?', in W.F. van Raaij and G. Bamossy, eds, *European Advances in Consumer Research* 1 (Provo, UT: Association for Consumer Research, 1993): 58–69.

51. R. Pearce, 'Social responsibility in the marketplace: assymetric information in food labelling', *Business Ethics: A European Review* 8(1) (1999): 26–36.

52. *Politiken* (14 November 1997): 13.

53. Pasi Falk, 'The Advertising Genealogy', in P. Sulkunen, J. Holmwood, H. Radner and G. Schulze, eds, *Constructing the New Consumer Society* (London: Macmillan, 1997): 81–107.

54. *Morgenavisen Jyllands-Posten* (22 November 1996): 1, 6, 7.

55. Larry Edwards, 'The decision was easy', *Advertising Age* 2 (26 August 1987): 106.

56. *Information* (2–3 September 2000): 11; Victor Malarek, *The Natashas: The New Global Sex Trade Book* (Viking Canada, 2003).

57. For scientific consumer research and discussions related to public policy issues, there is a special European journal, the *Journal of Consumer Policy* (available in university libraries).

58. G.K. Hadfield and D. Thompson, 'An information-based approach to labeling bio-technology consumer products', *Journal of Consumer Policy* 21 (1998): 551–78; H. Sheehy, M. Legault and D. Ireland, 'Consumers and biotechnology: A synopsis of survey and focus group research', *Journal of Consumer Policy* 21 (1998): 359–86.

59. See Philip Kotler and Alan R. Andreasen, *Strategic Marketing for Nonprofit Organizations*, 4th edn (Englewood Cliffs, NJ: Prentice Hall, 1991); Jeff B. Murray and Julie L. Ozanne, 'The critical imagination: Emancipatory interests in consumer research', *Journal of Consumer Research* 18 (September 1991): 192–44; William D. Wells, 'Discovery-oriented consumer research', *Journal of Consumer Research* 19 (March 1993): 489–504.

60. Bertil Swartz, '"Keep Control": The Swedish Brewers' Association Campaign to Foster Responsible Alcohol Consumption Among Adolescents', paper presented at the ACR Europe Conference, Stockholm, June 1997; Anna Oloffson, Ordpolen Informations AB, Sweden, personal communication, August 1997.

61. Roger Crisp, 'Persuasive advertising, autonomy, and the creation of desire', *Journal of Business Ethics* 6 (1987): 413–18.

62. Søren Askegaard and A. Fuat Firat, 'Towards a Critique of Material Culture, Consumption and Markets' in S. Pearce, ed., *Experiencing Material Culture in the Western World* (London: Leicester University Press, 1997): 114–39.

63. William Leiss, Stephen Kline and Sut Jhally, *Social Communication in Advertising: Persons, Products & Images of Well-Being* (Toronto: Methuen, 1986); Jerry Mander, *Four Arguments for the Elimination of Television* (New York: William Morrow, 1977).

64. Vance Packard, *The Hidden Persuaders* (London: Longmans Green, 1957).

65. Raymond Williams, 'Advertising: The Magic System', in *Problems in Materialism and Culture* (London: New Left Books, 1962).

66. Steven Engelberg, 'Advertising pervades Poland, turning propaganda to glitz', *New York Times* (26 May 1992) 2: A1.

67. Morris B. Holbrook, 'The Consumer Researcher Visits Radio City: Dancing in the Dark', in E.C. Hirschman and M.B. Holbrook, eds, *Advances in Consumer Research* 12 (Provo, UT: Association for Consumer Research, 1985): 28–31.

68. Jean-Claude Usunier, 'Integrating the Cultural Dimension into International Marketing', Proceedings of the Second Conference on the Cultural Dimension of International Marketing (Odense: Odense University, 1995): 1–23.

69. Hansen, ed., *European Advances in Consumer Research* 2.

70. Eric J. Arnould and Craig J. Thompson, 'Consumer culture theory (CCT): Twenty years of research', *Journal of Consumer Research* 31 (March 2005): 868–82.

71. Per Østergaard and Christian Jantzen, 'Shifting Perspectives in Consumer Research: From Buyer Behaviour to Consumption Studies' in S.C. Beckmann and R. Elliott, eds, *Interpretive Consumer Research* (Copenhagen: Copenhagen Business School Press, 2000): 9–23.

2
Perception

3
Learning
and
memory

CONSUMERS AS INDIVIDUALS

In this part, we focus on the internal dynamics of consumers. While 'no man is an island', each of us is to some degree a self-contained receptor for information from the outside world. We are constantly confronted with advertising messages, products, other people persuading us to buy, and reflections of ourselves. Each chapter in this part will consider a different aspect of the consumer – sensations, memories and attitudes – that is invisible to others.

Chapter 2 describes the process of perception, in which information from the outside world about products and other people is absorbed by the individual and interpreted. Chapter 3 focuses on the ways this information is stored mentally and how it adds to our existing knowledge about the world as it is learned. Chapter 4 discusses our reasons or motivations for absorbing this information and how particular needs and wants influence the way we think about products.

Chapters 5 and 6 discuss how attitudes – our evaluations of all these products, ad messages, and so on – are formed and (sometimes) changed by marketers. When all of these 'internal' parts are put together, the unique role of each individual consumer as a self-contained agent in the marketplace will become clear. The last chapter in this part, Chapter 7, further explores how our views about ourselves affect what we do, want and buy.

4	5	6	7	Case studies
Motivation, values and involvement	Attitudes	Attitude change and interactive communications	The self	1–4

PERCEPTION

Fabienne is a 35-year-old mother of two and works at the French National Railway Company's headquarters in Lyon Part Dieu. Twice a week she uses her two-hour lunch break to go to the nearby shopping centre, the biggest in Lyons. Today she had just two things in mind: a quick bite to eat and a present for her son, Georges-Hubert. As she enters the shopping centre she is immediately drawn to the appetizing aroma of pizza coming from a nearby fast-food restaurant. She decides to stop and buy a slice and a small bottle of mineral water. Next she decides to go to a shop called Nature et Découvertes, the French version of the Californian Nature Company. She has never been there before, but Catherine, her 14-year-old daughter, says that all her friends are talking about it. It seems to be the perfect place to buy a small microscope for Georges-Hubert's birthday.

On entering the shop she is very surprised. As in all shops her eyes are immediately and highly stimulated, but what makes this shop different is that there is more to it than that: all five of her senses are appealed to. The background music lets Fabienne discover birdsong, the sound of the forest, nature itself. As she is able to handle the products, Fabienne can familiarize herself with new shapes, new materials. An appeal is also made to her sense of taste when she is offered a cup of herbal tea. Finally, the natural aromas from the woods and plants combined with synthetic aromatics recreate the delicious atmosphere of the undergrowth to appeal to her sense of smell.

Fabienne likes the shop very much and for half an hour loses all sense of time. She wanders round as if in a trance. When she finally goes to the cash desk she realizes that not only does she have the little microscope in her hands, but a candle as well, and a book on trees.

PATRICK HETZEL, University of Paris II, Panthéon-Assas

■ INTRODUCTION

We live in a world overflowing with sensations. Wherever we turn, we are bombarded by a symphony of colours, sounds and odours. Some of the 'notes' in this symphony occur naturally, such as the barking of a dog, the shadows of the evening sky or the heady smell of a rose bush. Others come from people; the person sitting next to you might have dyed blonde hair, bright pink jeans, and be wearing enough perfume to make your eyes water.

Marketers certainly contribute to this commotion. Consumers are never far from advertisements, product packages, radio and television commercials, and advertising hoardings that clamour for their attention. Each of us copes with this bombardment by paying attention to some stimuli and screening out others. When we do make a decision to purchase, we are responding not only to these influences but to our interpretations of them. The aim of Nature et Découvertes is to open the doors to the emotions, to a sense of wonder, to get in touch with one's capacity for pleasure. Unlike many other sales outlets there is a determined motivation to create sensory effects to the utmost, to play on all five senses simultaneously. In a situation like this, the appeal is not so much to Fabienne's mind as to her perceptions, her emotions.

This chapter focuses on the process of perception, in which sensations are absorbed by the consumer and used to interpret the surrounding world. After discussing the stages of this process, the chapter examines how the five senses (sight, smell, sound, touch and taste) affect consumers. It also highlights some of the ways in which marketers develop products and communications that appeal to the senses.

The chapter emphasizes that the way in which a marketing stimulus is presented plays a role in determining whether the consumer will make sense of it or even notice it at all. The techniques and marketing practices that make messages more likely to be noticed are discussed. Finally, the chapter discusses the process of interpretation, in which the stimuli that are noticed by the consumer are organized and assigned meaning.

■ THE PERCEPTUAL PROCESS

As you sit in a lecture hall, you may find your attention shifting. One minute you are concentrating on the lecture, and in the next, you catch yourself daydreaming about the weekend ahead before you realize that you are missing some important points and tune back into the lecture.

People undergo stages of information processing in which stimuli are input and stored. However, we do not passively process whatever information happens to be present. Only a very small number of the stimuli in our environment are ever noticed. Of these, an even smaller number are attended to. And the stimuli that do enter our consciousness are not processed objectively. The meaning of a stimulus is interpreted by the individual, who is influenced by his or her unique biases, needs and experiences. These three stages of *exposure (or sensation)*, *attention* and *interpretation* make up the process of perception. The stages involved in selecting and interpreting stimuli are illustrated in Figure 2.1, which provides an overview of the perceptual process.

From sensation to perception

▶ **Sensation** refers to the immediate response of our sensory receptors (e.g. eyes, ears,
▶ nose, mouth, fingers) to such basic stimuli as light, colour and sound. **Perception** is the process by which these stimuli are selected, organized and interpreted. We process raw data (sensation); however, the study of perception focuses on what we add to or take away from these sensations as we assign meaning to them.

Figure 2.1 An overview of the perceptual process

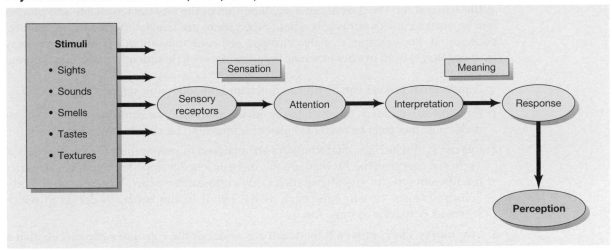

The subjective nature of perception is demonstrated by a controversial advertisement developed for Benetton. Because a black man and a white man were handcuffed together, the ad was the target of many complaints about racism after it appeared in magazines and on hoardings, even though the company has a reputation for promoting racial tolerance. People interpreted it to mean that the black man had been arrested by a white man.[1] Even though both men are dressed identically, people's prior assumptions shaped the ad's meaning. Of course, the company's goal was exactly that: to expose us to our own perceptual prejudice through the ambiguity of the photo.

▶ Such interpretations or assumptions stem from **schemas**, or organized collections of beliefs and feelings. That is, we tend to group the objects we see as having similar characteristics, and the schema to which an object is assigned is a crucial determinant of how we choose to evaluate this object at a later time.

The perceptual process can be illustrated by the purchase of a new aftershave. We have learned to equate aftershave with romantic appeal, so we search for cues that (we believe) will increase our attractiveness. We make our selection by considering such

One in a series of controversial ads from Benetton, trying to expose our prejudice to ourselves.

Handcuffs – © Copyright 1989 Benetton Group S.p.A. Photo: Oliviero Toscani factors as the image associated with each alternative and the design of the bottle, as well as the actual scent. We thus access a small portion of the raw data available and process it to be consistent with our wants. These expectations are largely affected by our cultural background. For example, a male consumer self-conscious about his masculinity may react negatively to an overtly feminine brand name, even though other men may respond differently.

A perceptual process can be broken down into the following stages:[2]

1 *Primitive categorization*, in which the basic characteristics of a stimulus are isolated: our male consumer feels he needs to bolster his image, so he chooses aftershave.

2 *Cue check*, in which the characteristics are analysed in preparation for the selection of a schema: everyone has his own unique, more or less developed schemas or categories for different types of aftershave, such as 'down-to-earth macho', 'mysterious' or 'fancy French'. We use certain cues, such as the colour of the bottle, to decide in which schema a particular cologne fits.

3 *Confirmation check*, in which the schema is selected: the consumer may decide that a brand falls into his 'mysterious' schema.

4 *Confirmation completion*, in which a decision is made as to what the stimulus is: the consumer decides he has made the right choice, and then reinforces this decision by considering the colour of the bottle and the interesting name of the aftershave.

Such experiences illustrate the importance of the perceptual process for product positioning. In many cases, consumers use a few basic dimensions to categorize competing products or services, and then evaluate each alternative in terms of its relative standing on these dimensions.

▶ This tendency has led to the use of a very useful positioning tool – a **perceptual map**. By identifying the important dimensions and then asking consumers to place competitors within this space, marketers can answer some crucial strategic questions, such as which product alternatives are seen by consumers as similar or dissimilar, and what opportunities exist for new products that possess attributes not represented by current brands. Figure 2.2 offers a perceptual map of the iconic Burberry brand, showing its 'old' position from the 1980s and 1990s, and the shift in perceptions of the brand in more recent years.

Figure 2.2 Perceptual map of the Burberry brand, relative to competitors

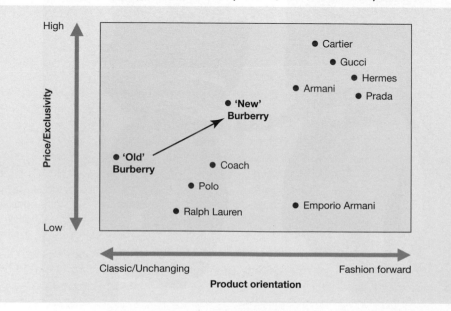

marketing opportunity

'When a British public official recently described one of the government's public relations issues as 'a complete Horlicks' – by which he is supposed to have meant a right mess – the incident surely counted as the lowest point in the 130-year history of GlaxoSmithKline's classic bedtime drink. A year later, however, things have started to look up. In an attempt to change the perceptions of the product, the veteran brand has revamped its appearance and has worked to convince sleep-deprived party-goers and stressed-out working mothers that Horlicks is a product that speaks to their needs.

Horlicks' attempt to draw in a new generation of drinkers highlights a dilemma faced by many so-called heritage brands, which have seen the average age of their customers creep up year by year. The first option for brand owners is to proceed gradually, updating the look and feel of the brand through fine adjustments to its imagery and tone. Such an approach aims to attract younger people to the brand without alienating existing customers. The other option is to reinterpret the traditional values of the brand in contemporary idiom to reach younger consumers.

The product was given a creamier taste and repackaged in an eye-catching carton, with a moon-shaped 'do-not-disturb sign' symbolising restful sleep. An aversion to taking risks with brands that consumers hold in affection – even if they are no longer buying them so heavily – may explain why companies often prefer to modernise gradually when sales start to slip. The danger, however, is that in a crowded marketplace changes that are subtly communicated risk being drowned out by the surrounding media cacophony.

No amount of clever marketing will restore the fortunes of a brand for which consumers no longer have a need, however. To avoid becoming irrelevant, says Jez Frampton, chief executive of Interbrand in the UK, companies must invest in their products as well as their image. Whether Horlicks can connect with a younger market remains to be seen. In the brand's favour is the fact that its central idea – offering people something that will help them to unwind at the end of a hectic day, and promote restful sleep – seems more relevant today than at any time in the past.'[3]

■ SENSORY SYSTEMS

External stimuli, or sensory inputs, can be received on a number of channels. We may see an advertising hoarding, hear a jingle, feel the softness of a cashmere sweater, taste a new flavour of ice cream or smell a leather jacket.

The inputs picked up by our five senses constitute the raw data that generate many types of responses. For example, sensory data emanating from the external environment (hearing a song on the radio) can generate internal sensory experiences when the song on the radio triggers a young man's memory of his first dance and brings to mind the smell of his date's perfume or the feel of her hair on his cheek.

Sensory inputs evoke historical imagery, in which events that actually occurred are recalled. Fantasy imagery results when an entirely new, imaginary experience is the response to sensory data. These responses are an important part of **hedonic consumption**, or the multi-sensory, fantasy and emotional aspects of consumers' interactions with products.[4] The data that we receive from our sensory systems determine how we respond to products.

Although we usually trust our sensory receptors to give us an accurate account of the external environment, new technology is making the linkage between our senses and reality more questionable. Computer-simulated environments, or *virtual reality*, allow surgeons to 'cut into' a person without drawing blood or an architect to see a building design from different perspectives. This technology, which creates a three-dimensional

This ad for a luxury car emphasizes the contribution of all our senses to the evaluation of a driving experience. Lexus use a lot of sensory imagery in their campaigns. In a recent British campaign, Lexus used the slogan 'The loudest sound you will hear inside the Lexus is yourself thinking', thereby alluding to a classic campaign for Rolls Royce, which in the 1950s stated: 'At sixty miles an hour, the loudest sound you'll hear is the electric clock'.

Courtesy of Lexus and Team One Advertising

perceptual environment which the viewer experiences as being virtually real, is already being adapted to everyday pursuits, such as virtual reality games.

Enterprising business people will no doubt continue to find new ways to adapt this technology for consumers' entertainment – perhaps by developing 'virtual catalogues' which allow a person to browse through a shop without leaving his or her armchair. Until that time, though, we are mostly affected by marketers' ability to manipulate real sensory inputs along five distinct channels. In this section, we'll take a brief look at some of the processes involved in the business applications of sensory stimuli.

Vision

Marketers rely heavily on visual elements in advertising, store design and packaging. Meanings are communicated on the visual channel through a product's size, styling, brightness and distinctiveness compared with competitors.

Colour in the marketplace

Colours are rich in symbolic value and cultural meanings. For example, the display of red, white and blue evokes feelings of patriotism for both British and French people. Such powerful cultural meanings make colour a central aspect of many marketing strategies. Colour choices are made with regard to packaging, advertising, and even shop fittings. Indeed, there is evidence to suggest that some colours (particularly red) are arousing while others (such as blue) are relaxing. The power of colours to evoke positive and negative feelings makes this an important consideration in advertising design. Like the colour of your teeth? Europeans have recently paid attention to a new route to pearly white teeth. Tooth whiteners (peroxide strips) in the European Union will soon be available with a 6 per cent solution (the current limit is .1 per cent), and this reworking of the European Community Cosmetic Directive will allow consumers to switch from

DANKZIJ DE UNIEKE VEZELBESCHERMER IS DREFT NOG VEILIGER VOOR GEKLEURDE KATOEN. JE FAVORIETE MODEKLEURE
KOMEN DUS STRALEND FRIS UIT DE MACHINE. IEDERE KEER WEER. OOK DEZE FEL ORANJE OUTFIT. DREFT, NIETS IS VEILIGE

The text in the ad reads: 'Where would the bright orange be without Dreft?' Orange is the national colour of the Netherlands, so the ad simultaneously underlines the colour-protecting qualities of the product and, through the national colour code, refers to the strength of the Dutch nation.
Procter and Gamble Nederland B.V.

costly dental treatments to off-the-shelf treatments. What does having white teeth suggest to you?[5]

A special use of colour was introduced in a TV commercial by the brand Circle Coffee. This showed an orange circle with a coffee bean inside while the voice-over told the viewer to stare at the bean for 30 seconds; then, when the screen went black, a blue circle 'magically' appeared on the screen. This illusion is created by the perceptual law of complementary colours – a fitting illusion, given that another of the company's coffee brands is Blue Circle.[6]

The ability of colours to 'colour' our expectations is frequently exploited by marketers. Recently, marketers of products from beer and soft drinks to deodorant and petrol have launched new 'clear' products, which are intended to convey such qualities as purity and simplicity as a counter to over-elaborate product claims.[7] Green, too, has been gaining in popularity as consumers' ecological consciousness has grown.

multicultural dimensions

Cultural differences in colour preferences create the need for marketing strategies tailored to different countries. While many northern European women now believe that heavy makeup is unprofessional and not very flattering, traditional femininity is still valued by Latin Americans. Mexican women, for example, are passionate in their love for vibrant lipsticks and nail varnish. Mexican girls are taught to be attentive to their appearance from early childhood. Baby girls have pierced ears, and housewives typically get dressed up in brightly coloured high heels to go to the supermarket. For these women, the 'natural look' is out. As one legal secretary in Mexico City explained, 'When you don't wear makeup, men look at you like you are sick or something.'[8]

Today colour is a key issue in package design. But the choice used to be made casually. The familiar Campbell's Soup can was produced in red and white because a company executive liked the football kit at a particular university! Now colour is a serious business, and companies frequently employ consultants to assist in these decisions. In Switzerland, an instant coffee container was redesigned with diagonal strips of mauve. The package won a design award, but sales dropped off significantly. Consumers did not associate the colour mauve with coffee.[9]

Some colour combinations come to be so strongly associated with a particular corporation that they become known as the company's livery, and the company may even be granted exclusive use of the colours. Eastman Kodak is one such company and has successfully protected its yellow, black and red in court. As a rule, however, this protection is granted only if there is the possibility that consumers might be confused about what they are buying if a competitor uses the same colour combination.[10]

Since the number of competing brands has proliferated for many types of products, colour can be a critical spur to sales. When introducing a white cheese as a 'sister product' to an existing blue Castello cheese, a Danish company launched it in a red package and under the name of Castello Bianco. The red package was chosen for maximum visibility and signal effect. Although taste tests were very positive, sales were disappointing. A semiotic analysis of consumer interpretations showed that the red packaging and the name gave the consumers the wrong association about the product type and its degree of sweetness (due to associations with the vermouth Martini Bianco). It was relaunched in a white packaging and with the name 'white Castello', and almost immediately sales figures more than doubled.[11]

In a given year, certain colours appear to be 'hot' and show up over and over again in clothing, home furnishings, cars, and so on. But favourite colours disappear as fast as they come, to be replaced by another set of 'hot' colours the next year or season.

Consumers' colour choices may be affected by these trends. One simple reason is that consumers' choices are largely limited by the colours available in the stores. Few people, however, realize the extent to which these 'hot' colours result from choices made by industry insiders, in a process known as colour forecasting. Colour experts in various consulting groups meet periodically to predict what colours will best reflect a season in

The slight changes in the design of Campbell's canned soups illustrate the company's efforts to keep the central, traditional features of the brand packaging while making sure that the product does not begin to look dated.

Campbell Soup Company

one year's, five years' and sometimes even ten years' time. Members make colour predictions based on cultural and social trends, and these recommendations are then used by manufacturers in production forecasting.

Smell

Odours can stir the emotions or have a calming effect. They can invoke memories or relieve stress. Some of our responses to scents result from early associations with other experiences. As one marketer noted, an example 'is a baby-powder scent that is frequently used in fragrances because the smell connotes comfort, warmth, and gratification'.[12]

Consumers' love of fragrances has contributed to a very large industry. Because this market is extremely competitive (30–40 new scents are introduced each year) and expensive (it costs an average of £30 million to introduce a new fragrance), manufacturers are scrambling to find new ways to expand the use of scents and odours in our daily lives. While traditional floral scents, such as rose and jasmine, are still widely used, newer fragrances feature such scents as melon peach (Elizabeth Arden's Sunflowers) and a blend of peach, mandarin orange, waterlily and white cloud rose (Sun Moon Stars by Karl Lagerfeld).[13] A later trend, supported by the marketing efforts of, among others, Calvin Klein, are perfumes positioned as unisex. In addition to the perfume market, home fragrance products, consisting primarily of potpourri, room sprays and atomizers, drawer liners, sachets and scented candles, represent important markets. But the use of smell goes further than that. An association of employers in the wood industry used a scratch'n'sniff card to convince potential apprentices of the advantages of smell in the wood industry compared with other professions.[14]

Sound

Music and sound are also important to marketers. Consumers spend vast amounts of money each year on compact discs and cassettes, advertising jingles maintain brand awareness and background music creates desired moods.[15] In a novel development, greetings card manufacturers are prospering by selling consumers the ability to send their own sounds to others: Hallmark Cards Inc. sells 'Recordable Greetings Cards' that allow the sender to record a personal 10-second message on a microchip. The message plays automatically when the card is opened.[16] There is also evidence that the literal sound that one makes when pronouncing a brand's name can influence perceptions of the product's attributes. English-language speaking consumers infer that brands containing the vowel sound of short 'i' are lighter than brands containing the vowel sound of 'a'.[17]

Many aspects of sound affect people's feelings and behaviours. One British company stresses the importance of the sound a packaging gives when opened, after having watched consumers open, close and reopen it several times during a test, clearly also listening to the right sound of the opening procedure.[18] Two areas of research that have widespread applications in consumer contexts are the effects of background music on mood and the influence of speaking rate on attitude change and message comprehension.

Muzak is heard by millions of people every day. This so-called 'functional music' is played in stores, shopping centres and offices either to relax or stimulate consumers. There is general agreement that muzak contributes to the well-being and buying activities of customers, but no scientific proof exists. *Time compression* is a technique used by broadcasters to manipulate perceptions of sound. It is a way to pack more information into a limited time by speeding up an announcer's voice in commercials. The speaking rate is typically accelerated to about 120–130 per cent of normal. Most people fail to notice this effect.

This ad metaphorically illustrates the natural quality and taste sensation of a lemon as a substitute for salt.
Sunkist Growers, Inc.

The evidence for the effectiveness of time compression is mixed. It has been shown to increase persuasion in some situations but to reduce it in others. One explanation for a positive effect is that the listener uses a person's speaking rate to infer whether the speaker is confident; people seem to think that fast talkers must know what they are talking about.

Another explanation is that the listener is given less time to elaborate on the assertions made in the commercial. The acceleration disrupts normal responses to the ad and changes the cues used to form judgements about its content. This change can either hinder or facilitate attitude change, depending on other conditions.[19]

Touch

Although relatively little research has been done on the effects of tactile stimulation on consumer behaviour,[20] common observation tells us that this sensory channel is important. Moods are stimulated or relaxed on the basis of sensations of the skin, whether from a luxurious massage or the bite of a winter wind.

Touch has even been shown to be a factor in sales interactions. There are considerable cultural differences in the world as well as within Europe concerning the appropriate amount and kind of touching in interpersonal interactions. In general, northern Europeans touch less than their southern European counterparts. Many British think the French shake hands excessively.[21]

Tactile cues have symbolic meaning. People associate the textures of fabrics and other products with underlying product qualities. The perceived richness or quality of the material in clothing, bedding or upholstery is linked to its 'feel', whether it is rough or smooth, soft or stiff. A smooth fabric such as silk is equated with luxury, while denim is considered practical and durable. The vibration of a mobile phone against the owner's body signals a personal telephone call coming in, as well as some degree of respect about not disturbing others in the area. Some of these tactile/quality associations are summarized in Table 2.1. Fabrics that are composed of rare materials or that require a high degree of processing to achieve their smoothness or fineness tend to be more expensive and thus are seen as being classier. Similarly, lighter, more delicate textures are assumed to be feminine. Roughness is often positively valued for men, while smoothness is sought by women.

Just as fabrics are prized for their texture, some drinks are presented as having a luxurious 'feel'. This ad for Velvet Hot Chocolate links the chocolate drink to a well known brand of chocolate, and ties them together as 'irresistible'.
The Advertising Archives

Table 2.1 Tactile oppositions to fabrics

Perception	Male	Female	
High-class	Wool	Silk	Fine
Low-class	Denim	Cotton	
	Heavy	Light	Coarse

Taste

Our taste receptors contribute to our experience of many products. Sensory analysis is used to account for the human perception of sensory product qualities. One study used sensory analysis to assess butter biscuits: the crispness, buttery-taste, rate of melt, density, 'molar packing' (the amount of biscuit that sticks to the teeth) and the 'notes' of the biscuit, such as sweetness, saltiness or bitterness.[22]

Food companies go to great lengths to ensure that their products taste as they should. Philips's highly successful Senseo coffee machine produces a creamy head of foam on the top of a cup of home-brewed coffee.[23] Companies may use a group of 'sensory panellists' as tasters. These consumers are recruited because they have superior sensory abilities, and are then given six months' training. Or they rely on lay people, i.e. ordinary consumers. In a blind taste test, panellists rate the products of a company and its competitors on a number of dimensions. The results of such studies are important to discover both different consumer preferences and, thus, different consumer segments, and the positioning of a company or a brand in terms of the most important sensory qualities of the product.[24]

Are blind taste tests worth their salt? While taste tests often provide valuable information, their results can be misleading when it is forgotten that objective taste is only one component of product evaluation. The most famous example of this mistake concerns New Coke, Coca-Cola's answer to the Pepsi Challenge.[25] The new formulation was preferred to Pepsi in blind taste tests (in which the products were not identified) by an average of 55 per cent to 45 per cent in 17 markets, yet New Coke ran into problems when it replaced the older version. People do not buy a cola for taste alone; they are buying intangibles like brand image as well.

Sometimes taste test failures can be overcome by repositioning the product. For example, Vernor's ginger ale did poorly in a taste test against leading ginger ales. When the research team introduced it as a new type of soft drink with a tangier taste, it won easily. As an executive noted, 'People hated it because it didn't meet the preconceived expectations of what a ginger ale should be.'[26]

■ SENSORY THRESHOLDS

If you have ever blown a dog whistle and watched pets respond to a sound you cannot hear, you will know that there are some stimuli that people simply are not capable of perceiving. And, of course, some people are better able to pick up sensory information than are others.

The science that focuses on how the physical environment is integrated into our personal, subjective world is known as **psychophysics**. By understanding some of the physical laws that govern what we are capable of responding to, this knowledge can be translated into marketing strategies.

The absolute threshold

When we define the lowest intensity of a stimulus that can be registered on a sensory channel, we speak of a threshold for that receptor. The **absolute threshold** refers to the minimum amount of stimulation that can be detected on a sensory channel. The sound emitted by a dog whistle is too high to be detected by human ears, so this stimulus is beyond our auditory absolute threshold. The absolute threshold is an important consideration in designing marketing stimuli. A hoarding might have the most entertaining story ever written, but this genius is wasted if the print is too small for passing motorists to read it.

The differential threshold

The **differential threshold** refers to the ability of a sensory system to detect changes or differences between two stimuli. A commercial that is intentionally produced in black and white might be noticed on a colour television because the intensity of colour differs from the programme that preceded it. The same commercial being watched on a black-and-white television would not be seen as different and might be ignored altogether.

The issue of when and if a change will be noticed is relevant to many marketing situations. Sometimes a marketer may want to ensure that a change is noticed, such as when merchandise is offered at a discount. In other situations, the fact that a change has been made is downplayed, as in the case of price increases or when the size of a product, such as a chocolate bar, is decreased.

A consumer's ability to detect a difference between two stimuli is relative. A whispered conversation that might be unintelligible on a noisy street can suddenly become public and embarrassing knowledge in a quiet library. It is the relative difference between the decibel level of the conversation and its surroundings, rather than the loudness of the conversation itself, that determines whether the stimulus will register.

The minimum change in a stimulus that can be detected is also known as the **JND**, which stands for just noticeable difference. In the nineteenth century, Ernst Weber, a

▶ psychophysicist, found that the amount of change that is necessary to be noticed is related to the original intensity of the stimulus. The stronger the initial stimulus, the greater the change must be for it to be noticed. This relationship is known as **Weber's Law**. Many companies choose to update their packages periodically, making small changes that will not necessarily be noticed at the time. When a product icon is updated, the manufacturer does not want people to lose their identification with a familiar symbol.

■ PERCEPTUAL SELECTION

Although we live in an 'information society', we can have too much of a good thing. Consumers are often in a state of sensory overload, exposed to far more information than they are capable of or willing to process. People in a noisy, crowded bar or party for several hours may feel the need to step outside periodically to take a break. A consumer can experience a similar feeling of being overwhelmed after being forced to sift through the claims made by hundreds of competing brands. Further, the competition for our attention is increasing steadily with the increasing number of exposures to television commercials and other types of advertising.

▶ Because the brain's capacity to process information is limited, consumers are very selective about what they pay attention to. **Perceptual selectivity** means that people attend to only a small portion of stimuli to which they are exposed. Consumers practise a form of psychic economy, picking and choosing among stimuli, to avoid being over-whelmed by *advertising clutter*. This over-abundance of advertising stimuli highlights two important aspects of perceptual selectivity as they relate to consumer behaviour: exposure and attention.

marketing pitfall

Consumers and marketers are increasingly annoyed by advertising clutter. Advertising professionals feel that the proliferation of ads in both traditional media as well as non-traditional locations, such as in cinemas and on TV monitors in doctors' waiting rooms, is threatening the quality of their work. They fear that consumers will be so bombarded by competing stimuli that they won't be in a receptive frame of mind when their messages are transmitted. Consumers are also fed up. More and more surveys reveal that it takes a very good ad to avoid consumer boredom and hold the attention: either a good joke, nice aesthetics – whatever these are – or some real information.

Exposure

▶ **Exposure** is the degree to which people notice a stimulus that is within range of their sensory receptors. Consumers concentrate on certain stimuli, are unaware of others, and even go out of their way to ignore some messages. An experiment by a bank illustrates consumers' tendencies to miss or ignore information in which they are not interested. After a law was passed in America requiring banks to explain details about money transfer in electronic banking, the Northwestern National Bank distributed a pamphlet to 120,000 of its customers at considerable cost to provide the required information – hardly exciting bedtime reading. In 100 of the leaflets, a phrase in the middle of the pamphlet offered the reader $10.00 just for finding that paragraph. Not a single person claimed it.[27]

Selective exposure
Experience, which is the result of acquiring stimulation, is one factor that determines how much exposure to a particular stimulus a person accepts. Perceptual filters based on consumers' past experiences influence what we decide to process.

Perceptual vigilance is a factor in selective exposure. Consumers are more likely to be aware of stimuli that relate to their current needs. These needs may be conscious or unconscious. A consumer who rarely notices car ads will become very much more conscious of them when he or she is in the market for a new car. A newspaper ad for a fast-food restaurant that would otherwise go unnoticed becomes significant when one glances at the paper during a five o'clock class.

The advent of the video recorder has allowed consumers armed with remote control fast-forward buttons to be much more selective about which TV messages they are exposed to. By 'zipping', viewers fast-forward through commercials when watching their favourite programmes. A video recorder marketed by Mitsubishi can remove the need for zipping. It distinguishes between the different types of TV signals used to broadcast programmes and commercials and automatically pauses during ads. Witness also the market success of TIVO in the United Kingdom, and other European markets.[28]

Zipping has enhanced the need for advertising creativity. Interesting commercials do not get zipped as frequently. Evidence indicates that viewers are willing to stop fast-forwarding to watch an appealing or novel commercial. In addition, longer commercials and those that keep a static figure on the screen (such as a brand name or a logo) appear to counteract the effects of zipping; they are unaffected by a speed increase, since the figure remains in place.[29]

Adaptation

▶ Another factor affecting exposure is **adaptation**, or the degree to which consumers continue to notice a stimulus over time. The process of adaptation occurs when consumers no longer pay attention to a stimulus because it is so familiar.[30] Almost like drug addiction, a consumer can become 'habituated' and require increasingly stronger 'doses' of a stimulus for it to continue to be noticed. For example, a consumer on the way to work might read a new advertising hoarding, but after a few days it becomes part of the passing scenery.

Several factors can lead to adaptation:

- *Intensity*: Less intense stimuli (e.g. soft sounds or dim colours) habituate because they have less of a sensory impact.
- *Duration*: Stimuli that require relatively lengthy exposure in order to be processed tend to habituate because they require a long attention span.
- *Discrimination*: Simple stimuli tend to habituate because they do not require attention to detail.
- *Exposure*: Frequently encountered stimuli tend to habituate as the rate of exposure increases.
- *Relevance*: Stimuli that are irrelevant or unimportant will habituate because they fail to attract attention.

Attention

▶ **Attention** is the degree to which consumers focus on stimuli within their range of exposure. Because consumers are exposed to so many advertising stimuli, marketers are becoming increasingly creative in their attempts to gain attention for their products. Some successful advertisers such as Apple, Nike, The Gap, and Dyson have created a visual identity with their television ads, and then deliver more detailed product information in other places, such as websites and newspaper stories in which third party experts provide independent reviews.[31]

A dynamic package is one way to gain this attention. Some consulting firms have established elaborate procedures to measure package effectiveness, using such instruments as an angle meter, which measures package visibility as a shopper moves down the aisle and views the package from different angles. Also, data from eye-tracking tests, in which consumers' eye movements as they look at packages and ads are followed and measured, can result in subtle but powerful changes that influence their impact. Eye-tracking tests are also used to evaluate in-store displays.[32]

Countering advertising clutter

Many marketers are attempting to counter the sensory overload caused by advertising clutter in order to call attention to their products. One expensive strategy involves buying large blocks of advertising space in order to dominate consumers' attention. IBM has experimented with buying two or three consecutive full-page newspaper ads. And Coca-Cola once bought a full five-minute block of TV commercial time on Danish television shortly before Christmas.

Other companies are using 'bookend ads', where a commercial for one product is split into parts that are separated by commercials for other products. The first part creates conflict, and the second resolves it. This technique motivates the viewer to keep watching in order to get the rest of the story. For example, a TV commercial for Tuborg's special Christmas brew beer showed a cartoon Santa Claus in his sleigh going from one side of the screen to the other. After a couple of other commercials, he reappears, this time meeting a Tuborg delivery van going in the opposite direction. He quickly turns his sleigh round and follows the van as Tuborg wishes everybody a merry Christmas and a happy new year.

Some advertisers have taken to printing part of their ads upside down to get the reader's attention. Perhaps reflecting differences in level of cultural involvement in advertising, the editor of the Starch-Tested Copy newsletter noted, 'I find people don't like to work at reading their ads! Americans don't like it. There's a disorienting aspect they find uncomfortable. The English, on the other hand, like it.'[33]

Another solution has been to put ads in unconventional places, where there will be less competition for attention. These include the backs of supermarket shopping trolleys, pedestrian underpasses, floors of sports stadiums and even films, as the growing interest in product placement has shown.[34] More obscure places where advertisements can be found are public toilets,[35] petrol pump handles and on the steps in the London Underground.[36] And, of course, runner Linford Christie's specially designed contact lenses with the Puma logo created a lot of publicity.[37] An executive at Campbell's Soup, commenting on the company's decision to place ads in church bulletins, noted, 'We have to shake consumers up these days in order to make them take notice ... Television alone won't do that. Now we have to hit them with our ads where they shop and play and on their way to work.'[38] Of course, such a policy may backfire if people are getting more and more weary of the difficulty of finding advertising-free moments in their life.

Creating contrast

When many stimuli are competing to be noticed, one will receive attention to the extent that it differs from those around it. Stimuli that fall into unpredictable patterns often command a lot of attention. Size and colour differences are also powerful ways to achieve contrast. A black-and-white object in a colour ad is quite noticeable, as is a block of printed type surrounded by large amounts of white space. The size of the stimulus itself in contrast to the competition is also important.

An increasingly frequent way of creating contrast is by using advertising clichés and then giving them a twist. A mortgage company used the cliché of a homecoming soldier and the young waiting wife to advertise new restoration loans. After seeing the woman gazing out of the window and the soldier in the troop transport, he is shown finally arriving – only to hit his head hard on a low-hanging tie beam.[39] In general, self-referential advertisements where sympathy and credibility are created by mocking advertising or other cultural stereotypes are becoming more common.[40]

■ INTERPRETATION: DECIDING WHAT THINGS MEAN

▶ Interpretation refers to the meaning that people assign to sensory stimuli. Just as people differ in terms of the stimuli that they perceive, the eventual assignment of meanings to these stimuli varies as well. Two people can see or hear the same event, but their interpretation of it may be completely different.

▶ Consumers assign meaning to stimuli based on the *schema*, or set of beliefs, to which the stimulus is assigned. During a process known as priming, certain properties of a stimulus are more likely to evoke a schema than others. As evidenced by the case of Castello cheese quoted earlier, a brand name can communicate expectations about product attributes and colour consumers' perceptions of product performance by activating a schema.

▶ Stimulus ambiguity occurs when a stimulus is not clearly perceived or when it conveys a number of meanings. In such cases, consumers tend to project their own wishes and desires to assign meaning. Although ambiguity in product advertisements is normally seen as undesirable to marketers, it is frequently used creatively to generate contrast, paradox, controversy or interest. For example, a popular ad for Benson & Hedges cigarettes featured a group of people sitting around a dinner table, while a man wearing only pyjama bottoms stands in the background. This ambiguous character yielded valuable publicity for the company as people competed to explain the meaning of the mysterious 'pyjama man'.

Stimulus organization

People do not perceive a single stimulus in isolation. Our brains tend to relate incoming sensations to imagery of other events or sensations already in memory based on some fundamental organizational principles. A number of perceptual principles describe how stimuli are perceived and organized.

marketing opportunity

Companies such as the Anglo-Dutch Unilever and France's Picard are attempting to change consumer perceptions of frozen foods. In supermarkets across the UK, it is the chiller cabinet rather than the freezer that increasing numbers of shoppers head for first. The chilled food section is where much of the innovation in convenience food is happening and where manufacturers compete most aggressively for space. Chilled food is perceived by the consumer as fresher and healthier. But, cry the champions of frozen food, it is food picked or prepared and immediately frozen that keeps its nutritional value, and does not rely on preservatives in the way that some chilled or ambient (tinned) food does. In the UK, frozen food already faces increasingly stiff competition from the chilled pretender, and suffers from stigma. 'In the UK, frozen food is seen as an inferior product, and consumer perception of freshness is warped. Frozen food is seen as the last resort, eaten when you can't get to the shops, or fed to the children.' This is less true in the other seven countries where ICF operates. 'Perception of frozen food in southern Europe is that it is modern, so they have fewer hang-ups,' says Andrew Beattie, Unilever's Rotterdam-based marketing director for frozen foods.[41] Critical to the development of new perceptions regarding frozen foods is newly designed logo and packaging, with a warmer, more contemporary design, which implies that the food is the product of natural sunlight rather than factory freezing, and more pleasant lighting in the freezer area. In France, the main reasons for the surge in 'surgelé' (as frozen food is called) are two-career couples, children with overcommitted activities, and the desire to avoid spending whatever leisure time there is chopping, dredging and sautéing. In 1960, the French consumed only 2 kg of frozen food products per year, while in 2001, this figure has gone up to over 30 kg. Shopping for frozen packages in an antiseptic, ultra-white Picard store or in similar aisles at France's national supermarket chains may lack romance, but it is reliable.[42]

Figure 2.3 Principles of stimulus organization derived from gestalt psychology

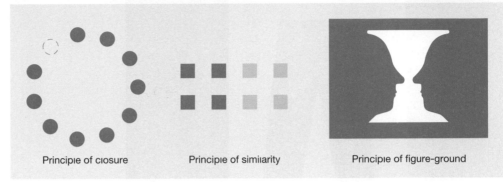

Principle of closure   Principle of similarity   Principle of figure-ground

The gestalt

▶ These principles are based on work in **gestalt psychology**, a school of thought maintaining that people derive meaning from the totality of a set of stimuli, rather than from any individual stimulus. The German word *Gestalt* roughly means whole, pattern or configuration, and this perspective is best summarized by the saying 'the whole is greater than the sum of its parts'. A piecemeal perspective that analyses each component of the stimulus separately will be unable to capture the total effect. The gestalt perspective provides several principles relating to the way stimuli are organized. Three of these principles, or perceptual tendencies, are illustrated in Figure 2.3.

▶ The gestalt **principle of closure** implies that consumers tend to perceive an incomplete picture as complete. That is, we tend to fill in the blanks based on our prior experience. This principle explains why most of us have no trouble reading a neon sign, even if one or two of its letters are burned out, or filling in the blanks in an incomplete message, as illustrated by the J&B ad shown here. The principle of closure is also at work when we hear only part of a jingle or theme. Utilization of the principle of closure in

This J&B ad illustrates the use of the principle of closure, in which people participate in the ad by mentally filling in the gaps.

The Paddington Corporation

This billboard for Wrangler jeans makes creative use of the figure-ground principle.
BooneOakley Advertising

marketing strategies encourages audience participation, which increases the chance that people will attend to the message.

▶   The **principle of similarity** tells us that consumers tend to group together objects that share similar physical characteristics. That is, they group like items into sets to form an integrated whole. This principle is used by companies who have extended product lines, but wish to keep certain features similar, such as the shape of a bottle, so that it is easy for the consumer to recognize that he or she is in fact buying a shampoo of brand X.

▶   Another important gestalt concept is the **figure-ground principle**, in which one part of a stimulus (the figure) will dominate while other parts recede into the background. This concept is easy to understand if one thinks of a photograph with a clear and sharply focused object (the figure) in the centre. The figure is dominant, and the eye goes straight to it. The parts of the configuration that will be perceived as figure or ground can vary depending on the individual consumer as well as other factors. Similarly, in marketing messages that use the figure-ground principle, a stimulus can be made the focal point of the message or merely the context that surrounds the focus.

The role of symbolism in interpretation

When we try to make sense of a marketing stimulus, whether a distinctive package, an elaborately staged television commercial or perhaps a model on the cover of a magazine, we do so by interpreting its meaning in the light of associations we have with these images. For this reason much of the meaning we take away is influenced by what we make of the symbolism we perceive. After all, on the surface many marketing images have virtually no literal connection to actual products. What does a cowboy have to do with a bit of tobacco rolled into a paper tube? How can a celebrity such as the football star Gary Lineker enhance the image of a potato crisp?[43]

    For assistance in understanding how consumers interpret the meanings of symbols, ▶ some marketers are turning to a field of study known as **semiotics**, which examines the correspondence between signs and symbols and their role in the assignment of meaning.[44] Semiotics is important to the understanding of consumer behaviour, since consumers use products to express their social identities. Products have learned meanings, and we rely on advertising to work out what those meanings are. As one set of researchers put it, 'advertising serves as a kind of culture/consumption dictionary; its entries are products, and their definitions are cultural meanings'.[45]

According to the semiotician Charles Sanders Peirce, every message has three basic components: an object, a sign and an interpretant. A marketing message such as a

▶ Marlboro ad can be read on different levels. On the lowest level of reading, the **object**
▶ would be the product that is the focus of the message (Marlboro cigarettes). The **sign** is the sensory imagery that represents the intended meanings of the object (the contents of
▶ the ad, in this case, the cowboy). The **interpretant** is the meaning derived (this man smokes these cigarettes). But this man is not any man. He is a cowboy – and not just any cowboy. The interpretant 'man (cowboy) smoking these cigarettes' in itself becomes a sign, especially since we have already seen many examples of these ads from this company. So, on the second, connotative level, this sign refers to the fictive personality of 'the Marlboro Man', and its interpretant consists of all the connotations attached to the Marlboro Man, for example his being a 'rugged, individualistic American'. On the third level, called the ideological level, the interpretant of the 'rugged, individualistic American' becomes a sign for what is stereotypically American. So its object is 'America', and the interpretant all the ideas and characteristics that we might consider as typically and quintessentially American. This semiotic relationship is shown in Figure 2.4. By means of such a chain of meanings, the Marlboro ad both borrows from and contributes to reinforcing a fundamental 'myth of America'. We will return to the discussion of myths and consumption in Chapter 14.

From the semiotic perspective of Peirce, signs are related to objects in one of three ways. They can resemble objects, be connected to them with some kind of causal or other
▶ relation, or be conventionally tied to them.[46] An **icon** is a sign that resembles the product in some way (e.g. Apple Computers uses the image of an apple to represent itself). An index is a sign that is connected to a product because they share some property (e.g. the pine tree on certain cleaning products conveys the shared property of fresh, natural scent). A symbol is a sign that is related to a product through purely conventional associations (e.g. the Mercedes star which in addition to the Mercedes-Benz company provides associations with German industrial quality and ingenuity).

The Glenfiddich ad on page 55 illustrates some of the subtle semiotic processes that convey meaning in advertising. The product, cognac, is a luxury alcoholic beverage associated with a soft, smooth taste, luxurious surroundings and a large price tag. The label is an icon – it literally represents the product.

The use of symbols provides a powerful means for marketers to convey product attributes to consumers. For example, expensive cars, designer fashions and diamond jewellery – all widely recognized symbols of success – frequently appear in ads to associate products with affluence or sophistication. The rhetoric of advertising is an additional field of analysis which has been useful for the discussion of how advertising communicates its messages.[47] Semiotic analysis of ads has been connected to product and brand life cycles in order to establish some guidelines about when to use the most complex advertising forms.[48]

One aspect of the semiotics of consumption, which used to be relatively neglected compared to the semiotics of advertising, is the semiotics of goods as such. In recent years, instead of studying messages about commodities there has been an increased number of studies of commodities as messages.[49] Semiotics of consumer goods, then, focus on the ability of goods to communicate either by themselves or in connection with other goods. A related field of study is symbolic consumption,[50] which focuses not so much on the good as sign per se, but rather on the meanings attached to the act of consuming the good. Here, in many cases, the good becomes an indexical sign for some

Figure 2.4 Relationship of components in semiotic analysis of meaning

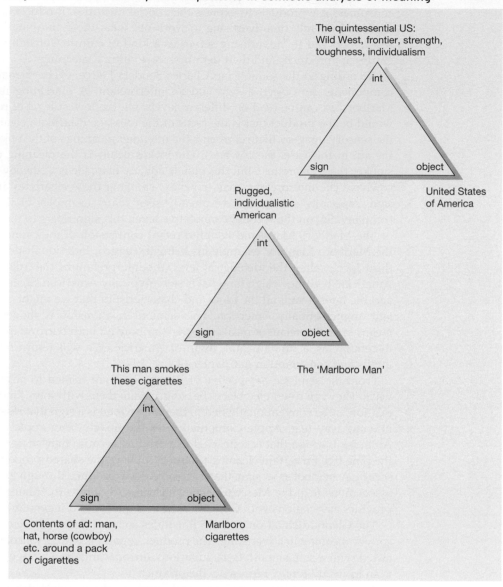

attributes that characterize the consumer, such as trendiness, wealth, femininity or others that place the consumer in some subcultural context.

Other uses of semiotics include industrial design[51] and design of distribution outlets. For example, in a semiotic study of the meanings and expectations consumers would attach to a new hypermarket, the researchers generated four different value profiles among potential customers. These profiles were linked to preferences for different designs of the hypermarket and its interior, thus helping the planners to conceive a type of hypermarket that was pleasing to most consumers.[52]

Semiotics plays a central role in much of the recent challenging consumer behaviour theory. The fact that consumers have become increasingly aware of how they communicate through their consumption as well as what they communicate has led to the designation of the present world as a 'semiotic world'.[53] Furthermore, it has been argued that we feel more confident in creating our own messages rather than just following what is proposed by marketing or fashion statements. This tendency to eclecticism means that we are increasingly likely to match things, such as articles of clothing, furniture or even lifestyles that traditionally have not been perceived as fitting together.

An illustration of how to read an advertisement semiotically. Note again the reference to smoothness, also found in some of the other beverage ads in this chapter.

The Advertising Archives

As we have already argued, one of the hallmarks of modern advertising is that it creates a condition where advertising is becoming self-referential. An increasing number of ads and commercials are referring, often ironically or tongue-in-cheek, to other advertisements, and thus creating a universe of their own, which in many ways is independent from the goods actually advertised. Advertising thus becomes an art in itself and is appreciated as such rather than as deceptive information about products.[54] **Hyperreality** refers to the becoming real of what is initially simulation or 'hype'.[55] Advertisers create new relationships between objects and interpretants by inventing new connections between products and benefits, such as equating Marlboro cigarettes with the American frontier spirit.[56] To a large extent, over time the relationship between the symbol and reality is increasingly difficult to discern, and the 'artificial' associations between advertisement symbols, product symbols and the real world may take on a life of their own.

For example, Tasters' Choice coffee perfected the concept of an ongoing series of 'soap opera' commercials where a romantic relationship is slowly cultivated between two actors, a commercial form later adopted by other coffee brands such as Nestlé's Gold Blend.

Hyperreality will be discussed again in the final chapter of the book, because it has been linked to the concept of postmodernism, the idea that we are living in a period of radical cultural change where certain hitherto dominant features and assumptions of modern societies are challenged.

■ CHAPTER SUMMARY

- Perception is the process by which physical sensations such as sights, sounds and smells are selected, organized and interpreted. The eventual interpretation of a stimulus allows it to be assigned meaning. A perceptual map is a widely used marketing tool which evaluates the relative standing of competing brands along relevant dimensions.

- Marketing stimuli have important sensory qualities. We rely on colours, odours, sounds, tastes and even the 'feel' of products when forming evaluations of them.

- Not all sensations successfully make their way through the perceptual process. Many stimuli compete for our attention, and the majority are not noticed or comprehended.

- People have different thresholds of perception. A stimulus must be presented at a certain level of intensity before it can be detected by sensory receptors. In addition, a consumer's ability to detect whether two stimuli are different (the differential threshold) is an important issue in many marketing contexts, such as changing a package design, altering the size of a product or reducing its price.

- Some of the factors that determine which stimuli (above the threshold level) do get perceived are the amount of exposure to the stimulus, how much attention it generates and how it is interpreted. In an increasingly crowded stimulus environment, advertising clutter occurs when too many marketing-related messages compete for attention.

- A stimulus that is attended to is not perceived in isolation. It is classified and organized according to principles of perceptual organization. These principles are guided by a gestalt, or overall, pattern. Specific grouping principles include closure, similarity and figure-ground relationships.

- The final step in the process of perception is interpretation. We make sense of the world through the interpretation of signs: icons, indexes and symbols. This interpretation is often shared by others, thus forming common languages and cultures. The degree to which the symbolism is consistent with our previous experience affects the meaning we assign to related objects. Every marketing message contains a relationship between the product, the sign or symbol, and the interpretation of meaning. A semiotic analysis involves the correspondence between message elements and the meaning of signs.

- Signs function on several levels. The intended meaning may be literal (e.g. an icon like a street sign with a picture of children playing). The meaning may be indexical; it relies on shared characteristics (e.g. the horizontal stripe in a stop sign means do not pass beyond this). Finally, meaning can be conveyed by a symbol, where an image is given meaning by convention or by agreement by members of a society (e.g. stop signs are octagonal, while yield signs are triangular).

▶ KEY TERMS

Absolute threshold (p. 46)
Adaptation (p. 48)
Attention (p. 48)
Differential threshold (p. 46)
Exposure (p. 47)
Figure-ground principle (p. 52)
Gestalt psychology (p. 51)
Hedonic consumption (p. 39)
Hyperreality (p. 55)
Icon (p. 53)
Interpretant (p. 53)
Interpretation (p. 50)
JND (p. 46)
Object (p. 53)

Perception (p. 36)
Perceptual map (p. 38)
Perceptual selectivity (p. 47)
Priming (p. 50)
Principle of closure (p. 51)
Principle of similarity (p. 52)
Psychophysics (p. 46)
Schema (p. 37)
Semiotics (p. 52)
Sensation (p. 36)
Sign (p. 53)
Stimulus ambiguity (p. 50)
Weber's Law (p. 47)

CONSUMER BEHAVIOUR CHALLENGE

1 Many studies have shown that our sensory detection abilities decline as we grow older. Discuss the implications of the absolute threshold for marketers attempting to appeal to the elderly.

2 Interview 3-5 male and 3-5 female friends regarding their perceptions of both men's and women's fragrances. Construct a perceptual map for each set of products. Based on your map of perfumes, do you see any areas that are not adequately served by current offerings? What (if any) gender differences did you obtain regarding both the relevant dimensions used by raters and the placement of specific brands along these dimensions?

3 Assume that you are a consultant for a marketer who wants to design a package for a new premium chocolate bar targeted to an affluent market. What recommendations would you provide in terms of such package elements as colour, symbolism and graphic design? Give the reasons for your suggestions.

4 Do you believe that marketers have the right to use any or all public spaces to deliver product messages? Where would you draw the line in terms of places and products that should be restricted?

5 Find one ad that is rich in symbolism and perform a semiotic analysis of it. Identify each type of sign used in the ad and the product qualities being communicated by each. Comment on the effectiveness of the signs that are used to communicate the intended message.

6 Using magazines archived in the library, track the packaging of a specific brand over time. Find an example of gradual changes in package design that may have been below the JND.

7 Collect a set of current ads for one type of product (e.g. personal computers, perfumes, laundry detergents or athletic shoes) from magazines, and analyse the colours employed. Describe the images conveyed by different colours, and try to identify any consistency across brands in terms of the colours used in product packaging or other aspects of the ads.

8 Look through a current magazine and select one ad that captures your attention over the others. Give the reasons why.

9 Find ads that utilize the techniques of contrast and novelty. Give your opinion of the effectiveness of each ad and whether the technique is likely to be appropriate for the consumers targeted by the ad.

■ NOTES

1. Kim Foltz, 'Campaign on harmony backfires for Benetton', *New York Times* (20 November 1989): D8.
2. Jerome S. Bruner, 'On perceptual readiness', *Psychological Review* 64 (March 1957): 123–52.
3. Alica Clegg, 'Such stuff as dreams are made of', *Financial Times* (28 October 2004), http://news.ft.com/cms/s/b30b7434-283b-11d9-9308-00000e2511c8.html.
4. Elizabeth C. Hirschman and Morris B. Holbrook, 'Hedonic consumption: Emerging concepts, methods, and propositions', *Journal of Marketing* 46 (Summer 1982): 92–101.
5. Clare Dowdy, 'Hollywood smiles spread across Europe', *Financial Times* (17 March 2004), http://news.ft.com/servlet/ContentServer?pagename=FT.com/StoryFT/FullStory&c=StoryFT&cid=1079419714360&p=1057562408029.
6. *Markedsføring* 1 (1995): 18.
7. 'Crystal clear persuasion', *Tufts University Diet and Nutrition Letter* (January 1993): 1.
8. Dianne Solis, 'Cost no object for Mexico's makeup junkies', *The Wall Street Journal* (7 June 1994): B1.
9. Maryon Tysoe, 'What's wrong with blue potatoes?', *Psychology Today* 19 (December 1985).
10. Meg Rosen and Frank Alpert, 'Protecting your business image: The Supreme Court rules on trade dress', *Journal of Consumer Marketing* 11(1) (1994): 50–5.
11. 'Ny emballage og nyt navn fordoblede salget', *Markedsføring* 12 (1992): 24.
12. Quoted in Cynthia Morris, 'The mystery of fragrance', *Essence* 71 (May 1988) 3: 71.
13. Suein L. Hwang, 'Seeking scents that no one has smelled', *The Wall Street Journal* (10 August 1994): B12.
14. 'En duft af træ', *Markedsføring* 13 (1996): 6.
15. Gail Tom, 'Marketing with music', *Journal of Consumer Marketing* 7 (Spring 1990): 49–53; J. Vail, 'Music as a marketing tool', *Advertising Age* (4 November 1985): 24.
16. Joan E. Rigdon, 'Hallmark cards can send a message that's a real earful for a loved one', *The Wall Street Journal* (5 November 1993): A5I.
17. N.T. Tavassoli and Y.H. Lee, 'The differential interaction of auditory and visual advertising elements within Chinese and English', *Journal of Marketing Research* 40(4) (November 2003): 468–80.
18. *Marketing* (3 April 1997).
19. For research in time compression, see James MacLachlan and Michael H. Siegel, 'Reducing the costs of television commercials by use of time compression', *Journal of Marketing Research* 17 (February 1980): 52–7; James MacLachlan, 'Listener perception of time compressed spokespersons', *Journal of Advertising Research* 2 (April/May 1982): 47–51; Danny L. Moore, Douglas Hausknecht and Kanchana Thamodaran, 'Time compression, response opportunity, and persuasion', *Journal of Consumer Research* 13 (June 1986): 85–99.
20. J. Peck and T.L. Childers, 'Individual differences in haptic information processing: The "need for touch" scale', *Journal of Consumer Research*, 30(3) (2003): 430–42.
21. Jean-Claude Usunier, *Marketing Across Cultures* (Hemel Hempstead: Prentice Hall, 1996).
22. Anne C. Bech, Erling Engelund, Hans Jørn Juhl, Kai Kristensen and Carsten Stig Poulsen, 'QFood. Optimal Design of Food Products', *MAPP Working Paper* no. 19 (Aarhus: The Aarhus School of Business, 1994); Hans Jørn Juhl, 'A Sensory Analysis of Butter Cookies – An Application of Generalized Procrustes Analysis', *MAPP Working Paper* no. 20 (Aarhus: The Aarhus School of Business, 1994).
23. Richard Tomkins, 'Products that aim for your heart', *Financial Times* (28 April 2005), http://news.ft.com/cms/s/d92c1660-b809-11d9-bc7c-00000e2511c8.html. Senseo has been so successful with this new product that they have a website for several European countries. See http://www.senseo.com/content/default.html.
24. Andreas Scharf, 'Positionierung neuer bzw. modifizierter Nahrungs- und Genußmittel durch integrierte Markt- und Sensorik-forschung', *Marketing ZFP* 1 (1st quarter 1995): 5–17.
25. See Tim Davis, 'Taste tests: Are the blind leading the blind?', *Beverage World* (April 1987) 3: 43.
26. Quoted in Davis, 'Taste tests', 44.
27. '$10 sure thing', *Time* (4 August 1980): 51.

28. David Kilburn, 'Japanese VCR edits out the ads', *Advertising Age* (20 August 1990): 16. For TIVO in the United Kingdom, go to http://archive.tivocommunity.com/tivo-vb/history/forum/14-1.html. TIVO's corporate website: http://www.tivo.com/0.0.asp (accessed 5 August 2005).

29. Craig Reiss, 'Fast-forward ads deliver', *Advertising Age* (27 October 1986) 2: 3; Steve Sternberg, 'VCR's: impact and implications', *Marketing and Media Decisions* 22 (December 1987) 5: 100.

30. Martin O'Neill and Adrian Palmer, 'The Effects of Survey Timing Upon Visitor Perceptions of Destination Service Quality', in Darach Turley and Stephen Brown, eds, *European Advances in Consumer Research: All Changed, Changed Utterly?* 6 (Valadosta, GA: Association for Consumer Research, 2003): 37–41.

31. Gary Silverman, 'Image is everything in attention wars', *Financial Times* (17 January 2005), http://news.ft.com/cms/s/23a18ba4-68b3-11d9-9183-00000e2511c8,ft_acl=ftalert_ftarc_ftcol_ftfree_ftindsum_ftmywap_ftprem_ftspecial_ftsurvey_ftworldsub_ftym.

32. 'It's all in the mind', *Marketing* (27 March 1997): 31–4.

33. Quoted in Stuart Elliott, 'When up is down, does it sell?', *New York Times* (21 February 1992) 2: D1.

34. 'Reklamer i det skjulte', *Markedsføring* 7 (1996): 28.

35. 'Toilet ads', *Marketing* (5 December 1996): 11.

36. 'Rare media well done', *Marketing* (16 January 1997): 31.

37. Christian Alsted and Hanne Hartvig Larsen, 'Toward a semiotic typology of advertising forms', *Marketing and Semiotics. Selected Papers from the Copenhagen Symposium*, ed. Hanne Hartvig Larsen, David Glen Mick and Christian Alsted (Copenhagen: Handelshøjskolens forlag, 1991): 75–103.

38. Kim Foltz, *New York Times* (23 October 1989): D11.

39. 'Realkredit for mennesker', *Markedsføring* 4 (1996): 10.

40. Stephen Brown, *Postmodern Marketing* (London: Routledge, 1995).

41. Clare Dowdy, 'A fresh look inside the shop freezer', *Financial Times* (24 March 2004), http://news.ft.com/servlet/ContentServer?pagename=FT.com/StoryFT/FullStory&c=StoryFT&cid=1079419893700&p=1059480266913.

42. Elaine Sciolino, 'Foie gras in the freezer? Just don't tell anyone!', *The New York Times* (19 December 2002), http://www.nytimes.com/2002/12/19/international/europe/19PARI.html?ex=1041353523&ei=1&en=4560794b5f85c27c.

43. Apparently, many consumers think the answer is 'he cannot!' See http://news.bbc.co.uk/2/hi/talking_point/3270473.stm for a discussion on whether celebrities should endorse 'junk food'.

44. See David Mick, 'Consumer research and semiotics: Exploring the morphology of signs, symbols, and significance', *Journal of Consumer Research* 13 (September 1986): 196–213.

45. Teresa J. Domzal and Jerome B. Kernan, 'Reading advertising: The what and how of product meaning', *Journal of Consumer Marketing* 9 (Summer 1992): 48–64, at 49.

46. Winfried Nöth, *Handbook of Semiotics* (London: Sage, 1994); David Mick, 'Consumer research and semiotics'; Charles Sanders Peirce, in Charles Hartshorne, Paul Weiss and Arthur W. Burks (eds.), *Collected Papers* (Cambridge, MA: Harvard University Press, 1931–58).

47. Jacques Durand, 'Rhetorical Figures in the Advertising Image', in Jean Umiker-Sebeok, ed. *Marketing and Semiotics. New Directions in the Study of Signs for Sale* (Berlin: Mouton de Gruyter, 1987): 295–318.

48. Alsted and Larsen, 'Toward a semiotic typology of advertising forms'.

49. Winfried Nöth, 'The language of commodities. Groundwork for a semiotics of consumer goods', *International Journal of Research in Marketing* 4 (1988): 173–86.

50. See the early introduction of the field: Elizabeth C. Hirschman and Morris B. Holbrook, eds, *Symbolic Consumer Behavior* (Ann Arbor, MI: Association for Consumer Research, 1981).

51. Odile Solomon, 'Semiotics and marketing. New directions in industrial design applications', *International Journal of Research in Marketing* 4 (1988): 201–15.

52. Ibid.

53. James Ogilvy, 'This postmodern business', *Marketing and Research Today* (February 1990): 4–22.

54. Chantal Cinquin, 'Homo Coca-Colens: From Marketing to Semiotics and Politics', in Umiker-Sebeok, ed. *Marketing and Semiotics*: 485–95.

55. A. Fuat Firat and Alladi Venkatesh, 'Postmodernity: The age of marketing', *International Journal of Research in Marketing*, 10(3) (1993): 227–49.

56. Jean Baudrillard, *Simulations* (New York: Semiotext(e), 1983).

57. Brown, *Postmodern Marketing*.

LEARNING AND MEMORY

Mario Rossi is a 60-year-old Italian insurance man, and still very active in his field. He is a pleasant, sociable and easygoing fellow, and has made a very good career for himself. Together with his wife and four children, he lives in a comfortable flat in the suburbs of Rome. Although Rome is full of historical sites to visit, Mario is a staunch nature-lover, and he prefers to 'get back to nature' in his free time.

Mario's dog, Raphael, recognizes the sound of his master's old Fiat drawing up outside as he arrives home late after work, and Raphael begins to get excited at the prospect of having his master back home. Mario's 'first love' was a Fiat 126, and in spite of his good income he keeps the old car running. Relaxing and sipping a glass of Chianti is just what he needs after a hard day's work. The pieces of furniture in his sitting room, and even his television set, are not the latest models, but he likes it that way – the old objects give him a sense of security. Slowly unwinding, he looks forward to spending the weekend with his family and friends at his house in the countryside. He grew up there, and is very attached to the old villa and everything in it.

He often imagines what it will be like when he retires, when he will be able to live there permanently, surrounded by his family. It will be like the good old days, when he was a boy and life was uncomplicated, less chaotic. He pictures them all sitting around the table enjoying a leisurely meal (with pasta, of course!) made from home-grown produce, and afterwards sitting together.

This peaceful fantasy is in stark contrast to the reality of last weekend! His two eldest sons had gone off to a football match. The youngest ones restlessly complained about the fact that there was still no internet connection in the house, and then went into another room to settle down in front of the television for what they called an afternoon's entertainment!

GABRIELE MORELLO, ISIDA, Palermo, Italy

■ INTRODUCTION

▶ **Learning** refers to a relatively permanent change in behaviour which comes with experience. This experience does not have to affect the learner directly: we can learn vicariously by observing events that affect others.[1] We also learn even when we are not trying to do so. Consumers, for example, recognize many brand names and can hum many product jingles, even for those product categories they themselves do not use. This casual, unintentional acquisition of knowledge is known as *incidental learning*. Like the concept of perception discussed in the last chapter, learning is an ongoing process. Our knowledge about the world is constantly being revised as we are exposed to new stimuli and receive feedback that allows us to modify behaviour in other, similar situations. The concept of learning covers a lot of ground, ranging from a consumer's simple association between a stimulus such as a product logo (such as Coca-Cola) and a response (e.g. 'refreshing soft drink') to a complex series of cognitive activities (like writing an essay on learning for a consumer behaviour exam). Psychologists who study learning have advanced several theories to explain the learning process. These range from those focusing on simple stimulus–response associations to perspectives that regard consumers as complex problem-solvers who learn abstract rules and concepts by observing others. Understanding these theories is important to marketers as well, because basic learning principles are at the heart of many consumer purchase decisions. In this chapter we'll explore how learned associations among feelings, events and products – and the memories they evoke – are an important aspect of consumer behaviour.

■ BEHAVIOURAL LEARNING THEORIES

▶ **Behavioural learning theories** assume that learning takes place as the result of responses to external events. Psychologists who subscribe to this viewpoint do not focus on internal thought processes. Instead, they approach the mind as a 'black box' and emphasize the observable aspects of behaviour, as depicted in Figure 3.1. The observable aspects consist of things that go into the box (the stimuli, or events perceived from the outside world) and things that come out of the box (the responses, or reactions to these stimuli).

This view is represented by two major approaches to learning: classical conditioning and instrumental conditioning. People's experiences are shaped by the feedback they receive as they go through life. Similarly, consumers respond to brand names, scents, jingles and other marketing stimuli based on the learned connections they have formed over time. People also learn that actions they take result in rewards and punishments, and this feedback influences the way they respond in similar situations in the future.

Figure 3.1 The consumer as a 'black box': a behaviourist perspective on learning

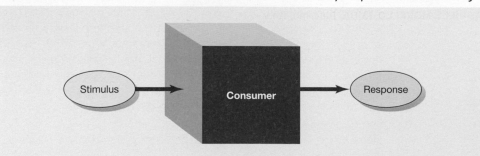

Consumers who are complimented on a product choice will be more likely to buy that brand again, while those who get food poisoning at a new restaurant will not be likely to patronize it in the future.

Classical conditioning

▶ **Classical conditioning** occurs when a stimulus that elicits a response is paired with another stimulus that initially does not elicit a response on its own. Over time, this second stimulus causes a similar response because it is associated with the first stimulus. This phenomenon was first demonstrated in dogs by Ivan Pavlov, a Russian physiologist doing research on digestion in animals.

Pavlov induced classically conditioned learning by pairing a neutral stimulus (a bell) with a stimulus known to cause a salivation response in dogs (he squirted dried meat powder into their mouths). The powder was an unconditioned stimulus (UCS) because it was naturally capable of causing the response. Over time, the bell became a conditioned stimulus (CS): it did not initially cause salivation, but the dogs learned to associate the bell with the meat powder and began to salivate at the sound of the bell only. The drooling of these canine consumers over a sound, now linked to feeding time, was a conditioned response (CR), just as Mario's dog Raphael begins to get excited hearing his master's Fiat 126 coming close to home.

This basic form of classical conditioning primarily applies to responses controlled by the autonomic (e.g. salivation) and nervous (e.g. eye blink) systems. That is, it focuses on visual and olfactory cues that induce hunger, thirst or sexual arousal. When these cues are consistently paired with conditioned stimuli, such as brand names, consumers may learn to feel hungry, thirsty or aroused when later exposed to the brand cues.

Classical conditioning can have similar effects for more complex reactions, too. Even a credit card becomes a conditioned cue that triggers greater spending, especially since it is a stimulus that is present only in situations where consumers are spending money. People learn that they can make larger purchases when using credit cards, and they also have been found to leave larger tips than they do when using cash.[2] Small wonder that American Express reminds us, 'Don't leave home without it.' Conditioning effects are more likely to occur after the conditioned and unconditioned stimuli have been paired a number of times.[3] Repeated exposures increase the strength of stimulus–response associations and prevent the decay of these associations in memory.

Conditioning will not occur or will take longer if the CS is only occasionally presented
▶ with the UCS. One result of this lack of association may be **extinction**, which occurs when the effects of prior conditioning are reduced and finally disappear. This can occur, for example, when a product is overexposed in the marketplace so that its original allure is lost. The Lacoste polo shirt, with its distinctive crocodile logo, is a good example of this effect. When the once-exclusive crocodile started to appear on baby clothes and many other items, it lost its cachet and was soon replaced by other contenders, such as the Lauren polo player.[4]

▶ **Stimulus generalization** refers to the tendency of stimuli similar to a CS to evoke similar, conditioned responses.[5] Pavlov noticed in subsequent studies that his dogs would sometimes salivate when they heard noises that only resembled a bell (e.g. keys jangling). People react to other, similar stimuli in much the same way that they responded to an original stimulus. A chemist shop's bottle of own-brand mouthwash deliberately packaged to resemble Listerine mouthwash may evoke a similar response among consumers who assume that this 'me-too' product shares other characteristics of the original. These 'lookalikes' tactics work, and companies have targeted well-known brands ranging from Unilever's Blue Band margarine, and Calvé peanut butter, to Hernes scarves. Similar colours, shapes and designs are all stimuli which consumers organize and interpret, and up to a point, these tactics are perfectly legal![6]

▶ **Stimulus discrimination** occurs when a stimulus similar to a CS is not followed by a UCS. In these situations, reactions are weakened and will soon disappear. Part of the learning process involves making a response to some stimuli but not to other, similar stimuli. Manufacturers of well-established brands commonly urge consumers not to buy 'cheap imitations' because the results will not be what they expect.

Operant conditioning

▶ **Operant conditioning**, also known as instrumental conditioning, occurs as the individual learns to perform behaviours that produce positive outcomes and to avoid those that yield negative outcomes. This learning process is most closely associated with the psychologist B.F. Skinner, who demonstrated the effects of instrumental conditioning by teaching animals to dance, pigeons to play ping-pong, and so on, by systematically rewarding them for desired behaviours.[7]

While responses in classical conditioning are involuntary and fairly simple, those in instrumental conditioning are made deliberately to obtain a goal and may be more complex. The desired behaviour may be learned over a period of time, as intermediate actions are rewarded in a process called *shaping*. For example, the owner of a new shop may award prizes to shoppers just for coming in, hoping that over time they will continue to drop in and eventually buy something.

Also, classical conditioning involves the close pairing of two stimuli. Instrumental learning occurs as a result of a reward received following the desired behaviour and takes place over a period in which a variety of other behaviours are attempted and abandoned because they are not reinforced. A good way to remember the difference is to keep in mind that in instrumental learning the response is performed because it is instrumental to gaining a reward or avoiding a punishment. Consumers over time come to associate with people who reward them and to choose products that make them feel good or satisfy some need.

Operant conditioning (instrumental learning) occurs in one of three ways. When the ▶ environment provides **positive reinforcement** in the form of a reward, the response is strengthened, and appropriate behaviour is learned. For example, a woman who is complimented after wearing Obsession perfume will learn that using this product has the ▶ desired effect, and she will be more likely to keep buying the product. **Negative reinforcement** also strengthens responses so that appropriate behaviour is learned. A perfume company, for example, might run an ad showing a woman sitting alone on a Saturday night because she did not use its fragrance. The message to be conveyed is that she could have avoided this negative outcome if only she had used the perfume. In contrast to situ- ▶ ations where we learn to do certain things in order to avoid unpleasantness, **punishment** occurs when a response is followed by unpleasant events (such as being ridiculed by friends for wearing an offensive-smelling perfume). We learn not to repeat these behaviours.

When trying to understand the differences between these mechanisms, keep in mind that reactions from a person's environment to behaviour can be either positive or negative and that these outcomes or anticipated outcomes can be applied or removed. That is, under conditions of both positive reinforcement and punishment, the person receives a reaction after doing something. In contrast, negative reinforcement occurs when a negative outcome is avoided: the removal of something negative is pleasurable and hence is rewarding. Finally, when a positive outcome is no longer received, extinction is likely to occur, and the learned stimulus–response connection will not be maintained (as when a woman no longer receives compliments on her perfume). Thus, positive and negative reinforcement strengthen the future linkage between a response and an outcome because of the pleasant experience. This tie is weakened under conditions of both punishment and extinction because of the unpleasant experience. The relationships among these four conditions are easier to understand by referring to Figure 3.2.

Figure 3.2 Four types of learning outcomes

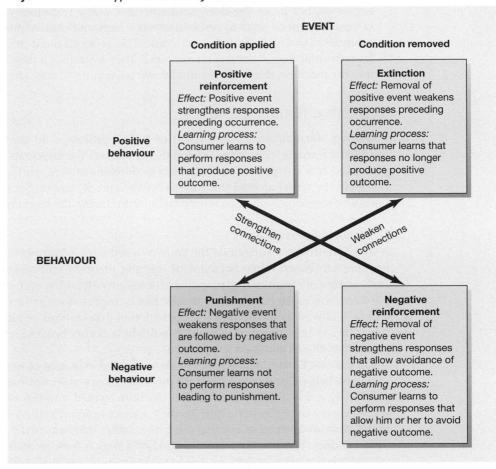

An important factor in operant conditioning is the set of rules by which appropriate reinforcements are given for a behaviour. The issue of what is the most effective reinforcement schedule to use is important to marketers, because it relates to the amount of effort and resources they must devote to rewarding consumers in order to condition desired behaviours.

- *Fixed-interval reinforcement.* After a specified period has passed, the first response that is made brings the reward. Under such conditions, people tend to respond slowly immediately after being reinforced, but their responses speed up as the time for the next reinforcement approaches. For example, consumers may crowd into a store for the last day of its seasonal sale and not reappear again until the next one.

- *Variable-interval reinforcement.* The time that must pass before reinforcement is delivered varies around some average. Since the person does not know exactly when to expect the reinforcement, responses must be performed at a consistent rate. This logic is behind retailers' use of so-called secret shoppers – people who periodically test for service quality by posing as customers at unannounced times. Since store employees never know exactly when to expect a visit, high quality must be constantly maintained.

- *Fixed-ratio reinforcement.* Reinforcement occurs only after a fixed number of responses. This schedule motivates people to continue performing the same behaviour over and over again. For example, a consumer might keep buying groceries at the same store in order to earn a gift after collecting 50 books of trading stamps.

- *Variable-ratio reinforcement.* The person is reinforced after a certain number of responses, but he or she does not know how many responses are required. People in such situations tend to respond at very high and steady rates, and this type of behaviour is very difficult to extinguish. This reinforcement schedule is responsible for consumers' attraction to slot machines. They learn that if they keep feeding money into the machine, they will eventually win something (if they don't go broke first).

Cognitive learning theory

▶ **Cognitive learning** occurs as a result of mental processes. In contrast to behavioural theories of learning, cognitive learning theory stresses the importance of internal mental processes. This perspective views people as problem-solvers who actively use information from the world around them to master their environment. Supporters of this viewpoint also stress the role of creativity and insight during the learning process.

The issue of consciousness

A lot of controversy surrounds the issue of whether or when people are aware of their learning processes. While behavioural learning theorists emphasize the routine, automatic nature of conditioning, proponents of cognitive learning argue that even these simple effects are based on cognitive factors: that is, expectations are created that a stimulus will be followed by a response (the formation of expectations requires mental activity). According to this school of thought, conditioning occurs because subjects develop conscious hypotheses and then act on them.

On the one hand, there is some evidence for the existence of non-conscious procedural knowledge. People apparently do process at least some information in an automatic, passive way, which is a condition that has been termed mindlessness.[8] When we meet someone new or encounter a new product, for example, we have a tendency to respond to the stimulus in terms of existing categories, rather than taking the trouble to formulate different ones. Our reactions are activated by a trigger feature, some stimulus that cues us towards a particular pattern. For example, men in one study rated a car in an ad as superior on a variety of characteristics if a seductive woman (the trigger feature) was present in the ad, despite the fact that the men did not believe the woman's presence actually had an influence.[9]

Nonetheless, many modern theorists are beginning to regard some instances of conditioning as cognitive processes, especially where expectations are formed about the linkages between stimuli and responses. Indeed, studies using masking effects, in which it is difficult for subjects to learn CS/UCS associations, show substantial reductions in conditioning.[10] For example, an adolescent girl may observe that women on television and in real life seem to be rewarded with compliments and attention when they smell nice and wear alluring clothing. She works out that the probability of these rewards occurring is greater when she wears perfume and deliberately wears a popular scent to obtain the pay-off of social acceptance.

Observational learning

▶ **Observational learning** occurs when people watch the actions of others and note the reinforcements they receive for their behaviours. This type of learning is a complex process: people store these observations in memory as they accumulate knowledge, perhaps using this information at a later point to guide their own behaviours. This process of imitating the behaviour of others is called modelling. For example, a woman shopping for a new kind of perfume may remember the reactions a friend received when wearing a certain brand several months earlier, and she will base her behaviour on her friend's actions. In order for observational learning in the form of modelling to occur, four conditions must be met.[11] (These factors are summarized in Figure 3.3.)

Figure 3.3 Components of observational learning

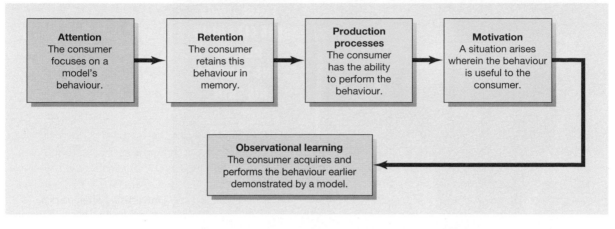

1 The consumer's attention must be directed to the appropriate model who, for reasons of attractiveness, competence, status or similarity, it is desirable to emulate.

2 The consumer must remember what is said or done by the model.

3 The consumer must convert this information into actions.

4 The consumer must be motivated to perform these actions.

■ MARKETING APPLICATIONS OF LEARNING PRINCIPLES

Understanding how consumers learn is very important to marketers. After all, many strategic decisions are based on the assumption that consumers are continually accumulating information about products and that people can be 'taught' to prefer some alternatives over others.

Behavioural learning applications

Many marketing strategies focus on the establishment of associations between stimuli and responses. Behavioural learning principles apply to many consumer phenomena, ranging from the creation of a distinctive brand image to the perceived linkage between a product and an underlying need.

How marketers take advantage of classical conditioning principles

The transfer of meaning from an unconditioned stimulus to a conditioned stimulus explains why 'made-up' brand names like Marlboro, Coca-Cola or IBM can exert such powerful effects on consumers. The association between the Marlboro Man and the cigarette is so strong that in some cases the company no longer even includes the brand name in its ad. When nonsense syllables (meaningless sets of letters) are paired with such evaluative words as beauty or success, the meaning is transferred to the nonsense syllables. This change in the symbolic significance of initially meaningless words shows that complex meanings can be conditioned. Recent studies have shown that attitudes formed through classical conditioning are enduring.[12]

These conditioned associations are crucial to many marketing strategies that rely on the creation and perpetuation of positive **brand equity**, in which a brand has strong positive associations in a consumer's memory and commands a lot of loyalty as a result.[13] As we will see in the next chapter, a product with brand equity holds a tremendous advantage in the marketplace.

FOUR TIMES
THE CLEANING
POWER
AND KIND TO
HIS SKIN.

NEW AJAX COMPACT HAS FOUR TIMES
THE POWER OF CONVENTIONAL LIQUIDS,
AND WITH ITS NEUTRAL pH LEVEL
IT'S STRONG ON DIRT BUT KIND TO
SURFACES AND SKIN.

AJAX COMPACT. OUR NEXT GENERATION CLEANER

Advertising often pairs a product with a positive stimulus (the attractive male model), or to a positive outcome (kind to his skin).
The Advertising Archives

Repetition One advertising researcher argues that more than three exposures are wasted. The first creates awareness of the product, the second demonstrates its relevance to the consumer, and the third serves as a reminder of the product's benefits.[14] However, even this bare-bones approach implies that repetition is needed to ensure that the consumer is actually exposed to (and processes) the ad at least three times. Marketers attempting to condition an association must ensure that the consumers they have targeted will be exposed to the stimulus a sufficient number of times.

On the other hand, it is possible to have too much of a good thing. Consumers can become so used to hearing or seeing a marketing stimulus that they cease to pay attention to it (see Chapter 2). This problem, known as advertising wear-out, can be reduced by varying the way in which the basic message is presented.

Conditioning product associations Advertisements often pair a product with a positive stimulus to create a desirable association. Various aspects of a marketing message, such as music, humour or imagery, can affect conditioning. In one study, subjects who viewed a slide of pens paired with either pleasant or unpleasant music were more likely later to select the pen that appeared with pleasant music.[15]

The order in which the conditioned stimulus and the unconditioned stimulus is presented can affect the likelihood that learning will occur. Generally speaking, the unconditioned stimulus should be presented prior to the conditioned stimulus. The technique of backward conditioning, such as showing a soft drink (the CS) and then playing a jingle (the UCS), is generally not effective.[16] Because sequential presentation is desirable for conditioning to occur, classical conditioning is not very effective in static situations, such as in magazine ads, where (in contrast to TV or radio) the marketer cannot control the order in which the CS and the UCS are perceived.

Just as product associations can be formed, so they can be extinguished. Because of the danger of extinction, a classical conditioning strategy may not be as effective for products that are frequently encountered, since there is no guarantee they will be accompanied by the CS. A bottle of Pepsi paired with the refreshing sound of a carbonated beverage being poured over ice may seem like a good example of conditioning. Unfortunately, the product would also be seen in many other contexts where this sound was absent, reducing the effectiveness of the conditioning.

By the same reasoning, a novel tune should be chosen over a popular one to pair with a product, since the popular song might also be heard in many situations in which the product is not present.[17] Music videos in particular may serve as effective UCSs because they often have an emotional impact on viewers and this effect may transfer to ads accompanying the video.[18]

Applications of stimulus generalization The process of stimulus generalization is often central to branding and packaging decisions that attempt to capitalize on consumers' positive associations with an existing brand or company name, as exemplified by a hairdressing establishment called United Hairlines.[19] In one 20-month period, Procter & Gamble introduced almost 90 new products. Not a single product carried a new brand name. In fact, roughly 80 per cent of all new products are actually extensions of existing brands or product lines.[20] Strategies based on stimulus generalization include the following:

- *Family branding*, in which a variety of products capitalize on the reputation of a company name. Companies such as Campbell's, Heinz, Philips and Sony rely on their positive corporate images to sell different product lines.

- *Product line extensions*, in which related products are added to an established brand. Dole, which is associated with fruit, was able to introduce refrigerated juices and juice bars, while Sun Maid went from raisins to raisin bread. Other recent extensions include Woolite rug cleaner, and the various models of Nike Air shoes.[21]

- *Licensing*, in which well-known names are 'rented' by others. This strategy is increasing in popularity as marketers try to link their products and services with well-established figures. Companies as diverse as McDonald's and Harley-Davidson have authorized the use of their names on products. Japan Airlines recently licensed the rights to use Disney characters, and, in addition to painting Mickey Mouse and Donald Duck on several of its planes, the carrier is requiring its flight attendants to wear mouse ears on some domestic flights![22]

- Marketers are increasingly capitalizing on the public's enthusiasm for films and popular TV programmes by developing numerous *product tie-ins*.

- *Lookalike packaging*, in which distinctive packaging designs create strong associations with a particular brand. This linkage is often exploited by makers of generic or

Many marketing strategies focus on the establishment of associations between stimuli and responses. Associating products with the imagery of riding in a Toyota with one's comfortable, modern living room is one example of this stimulus–response application.

Used with permission of Toyota Singapore and Saatchi & Saatchi Ltd.

private-label brands who wish to communicate a quality image by putting their products in very similar packages. As one chemist chain store executive commented, 'You want to tell the consumer that it's close to the national brand. You've got to make it look like, within the law, close to the national brand. They're at least attracted to the package.'[23]

Applications of stimulus discrimination An emphasis on communicating a product's distinctive attributes vis-à-vis its competitors is an important aspect of positioning, in which consumers learn to differentiate a brand from its competitors (see Chapter 2). This is not always an easy task, especially in product categories where the brand names of many of the alternatives look and sound alike. For example, one survey showed that many consumers have a great deal of trouble distinguishing between products sold by the top computer manufacturers. With a blur of names like OmniPlex, OptiPlex, Premmia, Premium, ProLinea, ProLiant, etc., this confusion is not surprising.[24]

Companies with a well-established brand image try to encourage stimulus discrimination by promoting the unique attributes of their brands: the constant reminders for American Express traveller's cheques: 'Ask for them by name . . .' On the other hand, a brand name that is used so widely that it is no longer distinctive becomes part of the public domain and can be used by competitors, as has been the case for such products as aspirin, cellophane, yo-yos and escalators.

How marketers take advantage of instrumental conditioning principles

Principles of instrumental conditioning are at work when a consumer is rewarded or punished for a purchase decision. Business people shape behaviour by gradually reinforcing consumers for taking appropriate actions. For example, a car dealer might encourage a reluctant buyer to try sitting in a showroom model, then suggest a test drive, and so on.

Marketers have many ways of reinforcing consumers, ranging from a simple thank you after a purchase to substantial rebates and follow-up phone calls. For example, a life insurance company obtained a much higher rate of policy renewal among a group of new customers who received a thank you letter after each payment compared to a control group that did not receive any reinforcement.[25]

▶ A popular technique known as **frequency marketing** reinforces regular purchasers by giving them prizes with values that increase along with the amount purchased. This operant learning strategy was pioneered by the airline industry, which introduced 'frequent-flyer' programmes in the early 1980s to reward loyal customers. Well over 20 per cent of food stores now offer trading stamps or some other frequent-buyer promotion. Manufacturers in the fast-moving consumer goods (FMCG) category also make use of this technique in food stores. For example, Douwe Egberts, the coffee manufacturer owned by Sara Lee, offers stamps which can be saved and redeemed for a whole range of coffee-related products such as espresso makers, service sets and coffee grinders, including their classic (and nostalgic) hand coffee grinder.

In some industries, these reinforcers take the form of clubs, including a Hilton Hotel Club. Club members usually earn bonus points to set against future purchases, and some get privileges such as magazines and free telephone numbers and sometimes even invitations to exclusive outings.

How marketers take advantage of cognitive learning principles

Consumers' ability to learn vicariously by observing how the behaviour of others is reinforced makes the lives of marketers much easier. Because people do not have to be directly reinforced for their actions, marketers do not necessarily have to reward or punish them for purchase behaviours. Instead, they can show what happens to desirable models who use or do not use their products and know that consumers will often be motivated to imitate these actions at a later time. For example, a perfume commercial may depict a woman surrounded by a throng of admirers who are providing her with positive reinforcement for using the product. Needless to say, this learning process is more practical than providing the same personal attention to each woman who actually buys the perfume!

Consumers' evaluations of models go beyond simple stimulus–response connections. For example, a celebrity's image is often more than a simple reflexive response of good or bad: it is a complex combination of many attributes.[26] In general, the degree to which a model will be emulated depends upon his or her social attractiveness. Attractiveness can be based upon several components, including physical appearance, expertise or similarity to the evaluator.

These factors will be addressed further in Chapter 6, which discusses personal characteristics that make a communication's source more or less effective in changing consumers' attitudes. In addition, many applications of consumer problem-solving are related to ways in which information is represented in memory and recalled at a later date. This aspect of cognitive learning is the focus of the next section.

This cereal ad illustrates the principle of vicarious reinforcement. The model uses the product and is shown reaping the reward - the approval of her boyfriend.

The Advertising Archives

Figure 3.4 The memory process

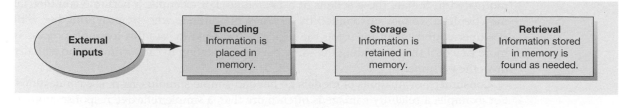

■ THE ROLE OF LEARNING IN MEMORY

▶ **Memory** involves a process of acquiring information and storing it over time so that it will be available when needed. Contemporary approaches to the study of memory employ an information-processing approach. They assume that the mind is in some ways like a computer: data are input, processed and output for later use in revised form. In
▶ the **encoding** stage, information is entered in a way the system will recognize. In the
▶ **storage** stage, this knowledge is integrated with what is already in memory and 'ware-
▶ housed' until needed. During **retrieval**, the person accesses the desired information.[27] The memory process is summarized in Figure 3.4.

As suggested by Mario's memories and musings at the beginning of the chapter, many of our experiences are locked inside our heads, and we maintain those memories and recall those experiences if prompted by the right cues. Marketers rely on consumers to retain information they have learned about products and services, trusting that it will later be applied in situations where purchase decisions must be made. During the consumer decision-making process, this internal memory is combined with external memory – which includes all the product details on packages in shopping lists, and through other marketing stimuli – to permit brand alternatives to be identified and evaluated.[28] Research supports the idea that marketers can distort a consumer's recall of a product experience. What we think we 'know' about products can be influenced by advertising messages to which we are exposed after using them. This *post-experience advertising* is more likely to alter actual memories when it is very similar or activates memories about the actual experience. For example, advertising can make a remembered product experience more favourable than it actually was.[29]

Encoding of information for later retrieval

The way information is encoded or mentally programmed helps to determine how it will be represented in memory. In general, incoming data that are associated with other information already in memory stand a better chance of being retained. For example, brand names that are linked to physical characteristics of a product category (such as Coffee-mate creamer or Sani-Flush toilet bowl cleaner) or that are easy to visualize (e.g. Tide, or Omo detergent) tend to be more easily retained in memory than more abstract brand names.[30]

Types of memory

A consumer may process a stimulus simply in terms of its sensory meaning, such as its colour or shape. When this occurs, the meaning may be activated when the person sees a picture of the stimulus. We may experience a sense of familiarity on seeing an ad for a new snack food we recently tasted, for example.

In many cases, though, meanings are encoded at a more abstract level. *Semantic meaning* refers to symbolic associations, such as the idea that rich people drink champagne or that fashionable men wear an earring.

Episodic memories are those that relate to events that are personally relevant, such as Mario's.[31] As a result, a person's motivation to retain these memories will be strong. Couples often have 'their song' that reminds them of their first date or wedding. The memories that might be triggered upon hearing this song would be quite different and unique for them.

Commercials sometimes attempt to activate episodic memories by focusing on experiences shared by many people. Recall of the past may have an effect on future behaviour. A university fund-raising campaign can get higher donations by evoking pleasant memories. Some especially vivid associations are called *flashbulb* memories. These are usually related to some highly significant event. One method of conveying product information is through a *narrative* or a story. Much of the social information that an individual acquires is represented in memory this way. Therefore, utilizing this method in product advertising can be an effective marketing technique. Narratives persuade people to construct a mental representation of the information they are viewing. Pictures aid in this construction and allow for a more developed and detailed mental representation.[32]

Memory systems

According to the information-processing perspective, there are three distinct memory systems: sensory memory, short-term memory (STM) and long-term memory (LTM). Each plays a role in processing brand-related information. The interrelationships of these memory systems are summarized in Figure 3.5.

▶ **Sensory memory** permits storage of the information we receive from our senses. This storage is very temporary: it lasts a couple of seconds at most. For example, a person might be walking past a bakery and get a brief, but enticing, whiff of bread baking inside. While this sensation would only last for a few seconds, it would be sufficient to allow the person to determine if he or she should investigate further. If the information is retained for further processing, it passes through an attentional gate and is transferred to short-term memory.

▶ **Short-term memory** also stores information for a limited period of time, and its capacity is limited. Similar to a computer, this system can be regarded as working memory: it holds the information we are currently processing. Verbal input may be stored acoustically (in terms of how it sounds) or semantically (in terms of its meaning).[33]

Figure 3.5 Relationships among memory systems

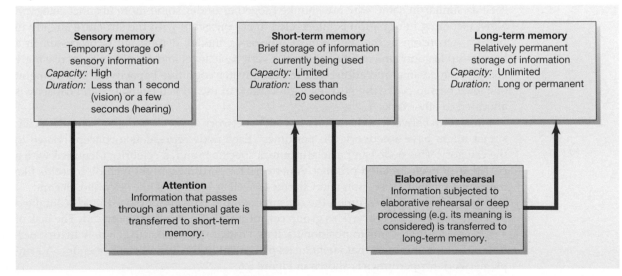

The information is stored by combining small pieces into larger ones in a process known as 'chunking'. A chunk is a configuration that is familiar to the person and can be manipulated as a unit. For example, a brand name can be a chunk that summarizes a great deal of detailed information about the brand.

Initially, it was believed that STM was capable of processing 5–9 chunks of information at a time, and for this reason phone numbers were designed to have seven digits.[34] It now appears that 3–4 chunks is the optimum size for efficient retrieval (seven-digit phone numbers can be remembered because the individual digits are chunked, so we may remember a three-digit exchange as one piece of information).[35]

▶ **Long-term memory** is the system that allows us to retain information for a long period of time. In order for information to enter into long-term memory from short-term memory, elaborative rehearsal is required. This process involves thinking about the meaning of a stimulus and relating it to other information already in memory. Marketers sometimes assist in the process by devising catchy slogans or jingles that consumers repeat on their own.

Storing of information in memory

Relationships among the types of memory are a source of some controversy. The traditional perspective, known as multiple-store, assumes that STM and LTM are separate systems. More recent research has moved away from the distinction between the two types of memory, instead emphasizing the interdependence of the systems. This work argues that, depending upon the nature of the processing task, different levels of processing occur that activate some aspects of memory rather than others. These approaches
▶ are called **activation models of memory**.[36] The more effort it takes to process information (so-called deep processing), the more likely it is that information will be placed in long-term memory.

Activation models propose that an incoming piece of information is stored in an associative network containing many bits of related information organized according to some set of relationships. The consumer has organized systems of concepts relating to brands, stores, and so on.

Knowledge structures

▶ These storage units, known as **knowledge structures**, can be thought of as complex spiders' webs filled with pieces of data. This information is placed into nodes, which are connected by associative links within these structures. Pieces of information that are seen as similar in some way are chunked together under some more abstract category. New, incoming information is interpreted to be consistent with the structure already in place.[37] According to the hierarchical processing model, a message is processed in a bottom-up fashion: processing begins at a very basic level and is subject to increasingly complex processing operations that require greater cognitive capacity. If processing at one level fails to evoke the next level, processing of the ad is terminated, and capacity is allocated to other tasks.[38]

Links form between nodes as an associative network is developed. For example, a consumer might have a network for 'perfumes'. Each node represents a concept related to the category. This node can be an attribute, a specific brand, a celebrity identified with a perfume, or even a related product. A network for perfumes might include concepts like the names Chanel, Obsession and Charlie, as well as attributes like sexy and elegant.

When asked to list perfumes, the consumer would recall only those brands contained
▶ in the appropriate category. This group constitutes that person's **evoked set**. The task of a new entrant that wants to position itself as a category member (e.g. a new luxury perfume) is to provide cues that facilitate its placement in the appropriate category. A sample network for perfumes is shown in Figure 3.6.

Figure 3.6 An associative network for perfumes

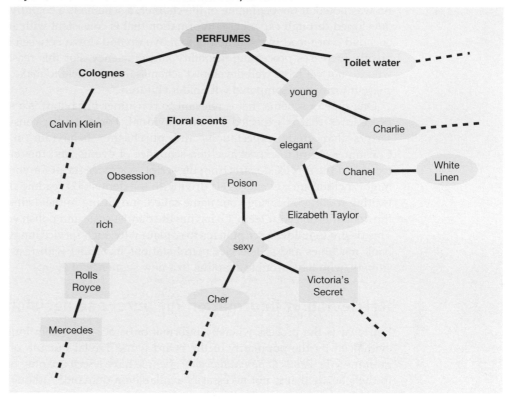

Spreading activation

A meaning can be activated indirectly: energy spreads across nodes at varying levels of abstraction. As one node is activated, other nodes associated with it also begin to be triggered. Meaning thus spreads across the network, bringing up concepts including competing brands and relevant attributes that are used to form attitudes towards the brand.

This process of spreading activation allows consumers to shift back and forth between levels of meaning. The way a piece of information is stored in memory depends upon the type of meaning assigned to it. This meaning type will, in turn, determine how and when the meaning is activated. For example, the memory trace for an ad could be stored in one or more of the following ways:

- *Brand-specific* – in terms of claims made for the brand.
- *Ad-specific* – in terms of the medium or content of the ad itself.
- *Brand identification* – in terms of the brand name.
- *Product category* – in terms of how the product works, where it should be used, or experiences with the product.
- *Evaluative reactions* – in terms of whether 'that looks like fun'.[39]

Levels of knowledge

Knowledge is coded at different levels of abstraction and complexity. Meaning concepts are individual nodes (e.g. elegant). These may be combined into a larger unit, called a *proposition* (also known as a belief). A proposition links two nodes together to form a more complex meaning, which can serve as a single chunk of information. For example, a proposition might be that 'Chanel is a perfume for elegant women'.

▶   Propositions are, in turn, integrated to produce a complex unit known as a **schema**. As was noted at the beginning of the chapter, a schema is a cognitive framework that is developed through experience. Information that is consistent with an existing schema is encoded more readily.[40] The ability to move up and down between levels of abstraction greatly increases processing flexibility and efficiency. For this reason, young children, who do not yet have well-developed schemas, are not able to make efficient use of purchase information compared with older children.[41]

One type of schema that is relevant to consumer behaviour is a script, a sequence of procedures that is expected by an individual. For example, consumers learn service scripts that guide expectations and purchasing behaviour in business settings. Consumers learn to expect a certain sequence of events, and they may become uncomfortable if the service departs from the script. A service script for your visit to the dentist might include such events as (1) driving to the dentist, (2) reading old magazines in the waiting room, (3) hearing your name called and sitting in the dentist's chair, (4) having the dentist probe your teeth, (5) having the dentist scale and polish your teeth, and so on. This desire to follow a script helps to explain why such service innovations as automatic bank machines and self-service petrol stations have met with resistance by some consumers, who have trouble adapting to a new sequence of events.[42]

Retrieving of information for purchase decisions

Retrieval is the process whereby information is accessed from long-term memory. As evidenced by the popularity of the board game Trivial Pursuit, or the television programme *Who Wants to Be a Millionaire?*, people have a vast quantity of information stored in their heads that is not necessarily available on demand. Although most of the information entered in long-term memory does not go away, it may be difficult or impossible to retrieve unless the appropriate cues are present.

Factors influencing retrieval

Some differences in retrieval ability are physiological. Older adults consistently display inferior recall ability for current items, such as prescription information, though events that happened to them when they were younger may be recalled with great clarity.[43]

Other factors are situational, relating to the environment in which the message is delivered. Not surprisingly, recall is enhanced when the consumer pays more attention to the message in the first place. Some evidence indicates that information about a pioneering brand (the first brand to enter a market) is more easily retrieved from memory than follower brands because the product's introduction is likely to be distinctive and, in the short term, no competitors divert the consumer's attention.[44] In addition, descriptive brand names are more likely to be recalled than are those that do not provide adequate cues as to what the product is.[45]

The viewing environment of a marketing message can also affect recall. For example, commercials shown during baseball games yield the lowest recall scores among sports programmes because the activity is stop-and-go rather than continuous. Unlike football or basketball, the pacing of baseball gives many opportunities for attention to wander even during play. Similarly, General Electric found that its commercials do better in television programmes with continuous activity, such as stories or dramas, compared with variety or talk shows, which are punctuated by a series of acts.[46] Finally, a large-scale analysis of TV commercials found that commercials shown first in a series of ads are recalled better than those shown last.[47]

State-dependent retrieval   In a process termed state-dependent retrieval, people are better able to access information if their internal state is the same at the time of recall as it was when the information was learned.

This phenomenon, called the *mood congruence effect*, underscores the desirability of matching a consumer's mood at the time of purchase when planning exposure to marketing communications. A consumer is more likely to recall an ad, for example, if his or her mood or level of arousal at the time of exposure is similar to that in the purchase environment. By recreating the cues that were present when the information was first presented, recall can be enhanced.[48]

Familiarity and recall As a general rule, prior familiarity with an item enhances its recall. Indeed, this is one of the basic goals of marketers who are trying to create and maintain awareness of their products. The more experience a consumer has with a product, the better use that person is able to make of product information.[49]

However, there is a possible fly in the ointment: as noted earlier in the chapter, some evidence indicates that overfamiliarity can result in inferior learning and/or recall. When consumers are highly familiar with a brand or an advertisement, they may attend to fewer attributes because they do not believe that any additional effort will yield a gain in knowledge.[50] For example, when consumers are exposed to the technique of radio replay, where the audio track from a television ad is replayed on the radio, they do very little critical, evaluative processing and instead mentally replay the video portion of the ad.[51]

Salience and recall The salience of a brand refers to its prominence or level of activation in memory. As noted in Chapter 2, stimuli that stand out in contrast to their environment are more likely to command attention, which, in turn, increases the likelihood that they will be recalled. Almost any technique that increases the novelty of a stimulus also improves recall (a result known as the von Restorff effect).[52] This effect explains why unusual advertising or distinctive packaging tends to facilitate brand recall.[53]

As we saw in Chapter 2, introducing a surprise element in an ad can be particularly effective. This strategy aids recall even if the stimulus is not relevant to the factual information being presented.[54] In addition, so-called mystery ads, where the brand is not identified until the end, are more effective at building associations in memory between the product category and that brand – especially in the case of novel brands.[55]

Pictorial vs. verbal cues There is some evidence for the superiority of visual memory over verbal memory, but this advantage is unclear because it is more difficult to measure recall of pictures.[56] However, the available data indicate that information presented in pictorial form is more likely to be recognized later.[57] Certainly, visual aspects of an ad are more likely to grab a consumer's attention. In fact, eye-movement studies indicate that about 90 per cent of viewers look at the dominant picture in an ad before they bother to view the copy.[58]

While pictorial ads may enhance recall, however, they do not necessarily improve comprehension. One study found that television news items presented with illustrations (still pictures) as a backdrop result in improved recall for details of the news story, even though understanding of the story's content does not improve.[59] Visual imagery can be especially effective when it includes verbal cues that relate to the consumer's existing knowledge.

Factors influencing forgetting

Marketers obviously hope that consumers will not forget their products. However, in a poll of more than 13,000 adults, over half were unable to remember any specific ad they had seen, heard or read in the previous 30 days.[60] Forgetting is obviously a problem for marketers.

Early memory theorists assumed that memories fade due to the simple passage of time. In a process of decay, the structural changes in the brain produced by learning

▶ simply go away. Forgetting also occurs due to **interference**: as additional information is learned, it displaces the earlier information.

Stimulus–response associations will be forgotten if the consumers subsequently learn new responses to the same or similar stimuli in a process known as *retroactive interference*. Or prior learning can interfere with new learning, a process termed *proactive interference*. Since pieces of information are stored in memory as nodes that are connected to one another by links, a meaning concept that is connected by a larger number of links is more likely to be retrieved. But, as new responses are learned, a stimulus loses its effectiveness in retrieving the old response.[61]

These interference effects help to explain problems in remembering brand information. Consumers tend to organize attribute information by brand.[62] Additional attribute information regarding a brand or similar brands may limit the person's ability to recall old brand information. Recall may also be inhibited if the brand name is composed of frequently used words. These words cue competing associations and result in less retention of brand information.[63]

In one study, brand evaluations deteriorated more rapidly when ads for the brand appeared with messages for 12 other brands in the same category than when the ad was shown with ads for 12 dissimilar products.[64] By increasing the salience of a brand, the recall of other brands can be impaired.[65] On the other hand, calling a competitor by name can result in poorer recall for one's own brand.[66]

Finally, a phenomenon known as the *part-list cueing effect* allows marketers to utilize the interference process strategically. When only a portion of the items in a category are presented to consumers, the omitted items are not as easily recalled. For example, comparative advertising that mentions only a subset of competitors (preferably those that the marketer is not very worried about) may inhibit recall of the unmentioned brands with which the product does not compare favourably.[67]

Products as memory markers

Products and ads can themselves serve as powerful retrieval cues. Indeed, the three types of possessions most valued by consumers are furniture, visual art and photos. The most common explanation for this attachment is the ability of these things to summon memories of the past.[68] Products are particularly important as markers when our sense of past is threatened, as when a consumer's current identity is challenged due to some change in role caused by divorce, moving, graduation, and so on.[69] Products have mnemonic qualities that serve as a form of external memory by prompting consumers to retrieve episodic memories. For example, family photography allows consumers to create their own retrieval cues, with the 11 billion amateur photos taken annually forming a kind of external memory bank for our culture.

Researchers are just beginning to probe the effects of autobiographical memories on buying behaviour. These memories appear to be one way that advertisements create emotional responses: ads that succeed in getting us to think about our own past also appear to get us to like these ads more – especially if the linkage between the nostalgia experience and the brand is strong.[70]

The power of nostalgia

▶ **Nostalgia** has been described as a bitter-sweet emotion, where the past is viewed with both sadness and longing. References to 'the good old days' are increasingly common, as advertisers call up memories of distant youth – feelings they hope will translate to what they're selling today. A stimulus is at times able to evoke a weakened response much later, an effect known as spontaneous recovery, and this re-established connection may explain consumers' powerful nostalgic reactions to songs or pictures they have not been exposed to in many years.

multicultural dimensions

Classic American TV shows are popular around the world, but few are as admired as *Dallas* is in Romania. In that eastern European country, the show's star, J.R. Ewing, is revered. Although many US viewers saw J.R. as a greedy, unprincipled villain they 'loved to hate', in Romania J.R. has become the symbol of American enterprise and a role model for the new capitalists who are trying to transform the country's economy. So, it's only fitting that J.R. was selected to endorse Lukoil, a brand of Russian motor oil. Advertisements in the Romanian market claim that the oil is 'the choice of a true Texan'![71] (Does Texan George W. Bush know where Romania is on the map?)

Many European companies are making use of nostalgic appeals, some of which are not based on the too distant past! Berlin's Humboldt University and City Museum have staged a fashion show of the 1960s, displaying clothes, appliances and posters from the communist era. The show, entitled *Ostalgie*, which is a play on words for 'East Nostalgia' in the German language, gave a nostalgic view of a time when goods might have been shoddy but when there was no unemployment or homelessness. There's growing interest in the Trabant (the joke used to be that you could double the value of a Trabant by filling it with sand) which has resulted in the Son of Trabant, built in the same factory where they used to build the original. Likewise, western European multinationals are relaunching local brands of east European origin in response to a backlash against the incursion of foreign products. From cigarettes to yogurt, multinationals are trying to lure consumers by combining yesteryear's product names with today's quality. Local brands like Nestlé's Chokito or Unilever's Flora margarine brands are now among the companies' best-selling products in eastern European markets.

Considerable care goes into the production values of campaigns which are intended to evoke nostalgia. Mulino Bianco, the Italian producer of cakes, biscuits and cereals, carefully developed a campaign depicting the quiet aspects of rural life to increase sales of cakes, which are typically served only on special occasions. The campaign showed a white farmhouse on a green hill, next to a watermill. Parents, children and friends are shown in a slow, relaxed, informal atmosphere, far from the hectic urban commitments of work. The object was to evoke a relationship between 'the good old days' and cakes, and to present cakes as genuine food to be eaten every day during normal meals. In Italy, where the tension to escape from the hectic urban life is high, the campaign was quite successful. In France, where eating habits are different, and the appeal to rural life is weaker, the same campaign was not successful.[72]

marketing opportunity

The rebirth of the Beetle

Hoping to win back former buyers – and to lure new ones – Volkswagen has in the past few years unveiled an updated version of the small, round-shouldered car that became a generational icon in the US in the 1960s and 1970s. Back in those days, the 'Bug' was cramped and noisy, but it was a hit because it was relatively cheap, fuel-efficient, and had symbolic value as a protest against Detroit's 'big boats'. In contrast to the Bug of old, the new one caters to consumers craving for space, with more headroom and legroom in front. Jens Neumann, the VW executive in charge of North America, feels 'The Beetle is the core of the VW soul. If we put it back in people's minds, they will think of our other products more.' The revised Beetle's resemblance to the old one is literally skin deep. Unlike the original, which had an air-cooled engine in the rear, the new Beetle is packed with the latest German technology, including an optional fuel-efficient turbo-diesel direct-injection motor. Otherwise the car is essentially a Golf with a number of Beetle-type characteristics to evoke nostalgia: curvy body panels; round dashboard dials and controls; circular sideview mirrors; side running boards; and indented door handles you grip to open. In the US, VW has deliberately priced the Bug above cars that appeal to most first-time buyers because it intends to attract far more than the college-age market. 'It is a classless car, and the Beetle will target a broad swathe of people who simply *love* the car, and aren't just looking for a utilitarian commuting box.' So far, the car boasts the youngest demographics in the US automobile industry. However, while the reintroduction of the Beetle has been successful in the US, its nostalgic appeal has not extended to Europe, where VW's Golf model is far more popular.[73]

Memory and aesthetic preferences

In addition to liking ads and products that remind us of our past, our prior experiences also help to determine what we like now. Some recent research indicates that people's tastes in such products as films and clothing are influenced by what was popular during certain critical periods of their youth. For example, liking for specific songs appears to be related to how old a person was when those songs were popular: on average, songs that were popular when an individual was 23–24-years-old are the most likely to be favoured.[74] In the United States, the Nickelodeon cable network programmes its *Nick at Nite* segment, which features repeats, by selecting the shows that were highly rated when its major audience was 12 years old.[75] Similar programming strategies are followed by several satellite stations throughout Europe. In addition, it seems that men form preferences for women's clothing styles that were in vogue when these men were in their early twenties.[76]

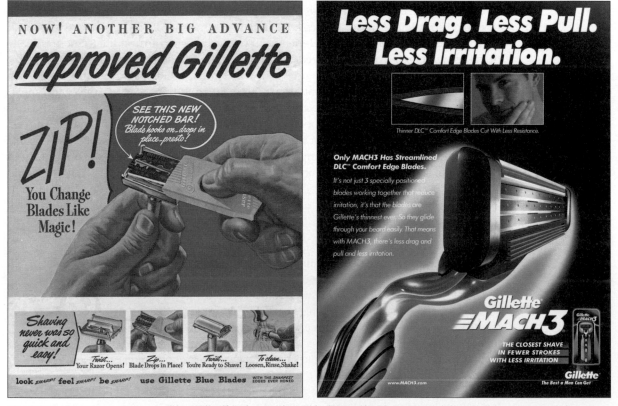

The Gillette brand has always positioned itself as innovative. This 'innovative' brand association is learned, and reinforced, over their customers' lifetime.

The Advertising Archives

More generally, many marketers understand that life-long brand loyalties are formed at a fairly early age: they view the battle for the hearts (and wallets) of students and young adults as a long-term investment. These age-related preferences will be further addressed in Chapter 13.

Measuring memory for advertising

Because advertisers pay so much money to place their messages in front of consumers, they are naturally concerned that people will actually remember these messages at a later point. It seems that they have good reason to be concerned. In one study, less than 40 per cent of television viewers made positive links between commercial messages and the corresponding products; only 65 per cent noticed the brand name in a commercial; and only 38 per cent recognized a connection to an important point.[77]

More worryingly, only 7 per cent of television viewers can recall the product or company featured in the most recent television commercial they watched. This figure represents less than half the recall rate recorded in 1965 and may be attributed to such factors as the increase of 30- and 15-second commercials and the practice of airing television commercials in clusters rather than in connection with single-sponsor programmes.[78]

Recognition vs. recall

One indicator of good advertising is, of course, the impression it makes on consumers. But how can this impact be defined and measured? Two basic measures of impact are recognition and recall. In the typical recognition test, subjects are shown ads one at a time and asked if they have seen them before. In contrast, free recall tests ask consumers to produce independently previously acquired information and then perform a recognition test on it.

Under some conditions, these two memory measures tend to yield the same results, especially when the researchers try to keep the viewers' interest in the ads constant.[79] Generally, though, recognition scores tend to be more reliable and do not decay over time in the way recall scores do.[80] Recognition scores are almost always better than recall scores because recognition is a simpler process and more retrieval cues are available to the consumer.

Both types of retrieval play important roles in purchase decisions. Recall tends to be more important in situations where consumers do not have product data at their disposal, and so they must rely upon memory to generate this information.[81] On the other hand, recognition is more likely to be an important factor in a store, where consumers are confronted with thousands of product options and information (i.e. where external memory is abundantly available) and where the task may simply be to recognize a familiar package. Unfortunately, package recognition and familiarity can have a negative consequence in that warning labels may be ignored, since their existence is taken for granted and not really noticed.[82]

The Starch Test

A widely used commercial measure of advertising recall for magazines is called the Starch Test, a syndicated service founded in 1932. This service provides scores on a number of aspects of consumers' familiarity with an ad, including such categories as 'noted', 'associated' and 'read most'. It also scores the impact of the component parts of an overall ad, giving such information as 'seen' for major illustrations and 'read some' for a major block of copy.[83] Such factors as the size of the ad, whether it appears towards the front or the back of the magazine, if it is on the right or left page, and the size of illustrations play an important role in affecting the amount of attention given to an ad as determined by Starch scores.

A picture is worth a thousand words. Product icons - like the Jolly Green Giant who has appeared in ads and on packaging for more than 30 years - are a significant factor in product recognition.
The Advertising Archives

Problems with memory measures

While the measurement of an ad's memorability is important, the ability of existing measures to assess these dimensions accurately has been criticized for several reasons.

Response biases Results obtained from a measuring instrument are not necessarily due to what is being measured, but rather to something else about the instrument or the respondent. This form of contamination is called a **response bias**. For example, people tend to give 'yes' responses to questions regardless of what is asked. In addition, consumers are often eager to be 'good subjects' by pleasing the experimenter. They will try to give the responses they think he or she is looking for. In some studies, the claimed recognition of bogus ads (ads that have not been seen before) is almost as high as the recognition rate of real ads.[84]

Memory lapses People are also prone to forgetting information unintentionally. Typical problems include omitting (the leaving out of facts), averaging (the tendency to 'normalize' things and not report extreme cases), and telescoping (the inaccurate recall of time).[85] These distortions call into question the accuracy of various product usage databases that rely upon consumers to recall their purchase and consumption of food and household items. In one study, for example, people were asked to describe what portion of various foods – small, medium or large – they ate in a normal meal; however, different definitions of 'medium' were used (e.g. 185 ml vs. 375 ml). Regardless of the measurement specified, about the same number of people claimed they normally ate medium portions.[86]

Memory for facts vs. feelings Although techniques are being developed to increase the accuracy of memory scores, these improvements do not address the more fundamental issue of whether recall is necessary for advertising to have an effect. In particular, some critics argue that these measures do not adequately tap the impact of 'feeling' ads where the objective is to arouse strong emotions rather than to convey concrete product benefits. Many ad campaigns, including those for Hallmark cards, Chevrolet and Pepsi, use this approach.[87] An effective strategy relies on a long-term build-up of feeling rather than on a one-shot attempt to convince consumers to buy the product.

Also, it is not clear that recall translates into preference. We may recall the benefits touted in an ad but not believe them. Or the ad may be memorable because it is so obnoxious, and the product becomes one we 'love to hate'. The bottom line is that while recall is important, especially for creating brand awareness, it is not necessarily sufficient to alter consumer preferences. To accomplish this, marketers need more sophisticated attitude-change strategies. These issues will be discussed in Chapters 5 and 6.

■ CHAPTER SUMMARY

- Learning is a change in behaviour that is caused by experience. Learning can occur through simple associations between a stimulus and a response or via a complex series of cognitive activities.

- Behavioural learning theories assume that learning occurs as a result of responses to external events. Classical conditioning occurs when a stimulus that naturally elicits a response (an unconditioned stimulus) is paired with another stimulus that does not initially elicit this response. Over time, the second stimulus (the conditioned stimulus) comes to elicit the response as well.

- This response can also extend to other, similar, stimuli in a process known as stimulus generalization. This process is the basis for such marketing strategies as licensing and family branding, in which a consumer's positive associations with a product are transferred to other contexts.

- Operant or instrumental conditioning occurs as the person learns to perform behaviours that produce positive outcomes and avoid those that result in negative outcomes. While classical conditioning involves the pairing of two stimuli, instrumental learning occurs when reinforcement is delivered following a response to a stimulus. Reinforcement is positive if a reward is delivered following a response. It is negative if a negative outcome is avoided by not performing a response. Punishment occurs when a response is followed by unpleasant events. Extinction of the behaviour will occur if reinforcement is no longer received.

- Cognitive learning occurs as the result of mental processes. For example, observational learning takes place when the consumer performs a behaviour as a result of seeing someone else performing it and being rewarded for it.

- Memory refers to the storage of learned information. The way information is encoded when it is perceived determines how it will be stored in memory. The memory systems known as sensory memory, short-term memory and long-term memory each play a role in retaining and processing information from the outside world.

- Information is not stored in isolation, it is incorporated into knowledge structures, where it is associated with other related data. The location of product information in associative networks and the level of abstraction at which it is coded help to determine when and how this information will be activated at a later time. Some factors that influence the likelihood of retrieval include the level of familiarity with an item, its salience (or prominence) in memory and whether the information was presented in pictorial or written form.

- Products also play a role as memory markers: they are used by consumers to retrieve memories about past experiences (autobiographical memories) and are often valued for their ability to do this. This function also contributes to the use of nostalgia in marketing strategies.

■ Memory for product information can be measured through either recognition or recall techniques. Consumers are more likely to recognize an advertisement if it is presented to them than to recall one without being given any cues.

▶ KEY TERMS

Activation models of memory (p. 74)	Negative reinforcement (p. 64)
Behavioural learning theories (p. 62)	Nostalgia (p. 78)
Brand equity (p. 67)	Observational learning (p. 66)
Classical conditioning (p. 63)	Operant conditioning (p. 64)
Cognitive learning (p. 66)	Positive reinforcement (p. 64)
Encoding (p. 72)	Punishment (p. 64)
Evoked set (p. 74)	Response bias (p. 82)
Extinction (p. 63)	Retrieval (p. 72)
Frequency marketing (p. 70)	Schema (p. 76)
Interference (p. 78)	Sensory memory (p. 73)
Knowledge structures (p. 74)	Short-term memory (p. 73)
Learning (p. 62)	Stimulus discrimination (p. 64)
Long-term memory (p. 74)	Stimulus generalization (p. 63)
Memory (p. 72)	Storage (p. 72)

CONSUMER BEHAVIOUR CHALLENGE

1 Identify three patterns of reinforcement and provide an example of how each is used in a marketing context.

2 Describe the functions of short-term and long-term memory. What is the apparent relationship between the two?

3 Devise a 'product jingle memory test'. Compile a list of brands that are or have been associated with memorable jingles, such as Opal Fruits or Heinz Baked Beans. Read this list to friends, and see how many jingles are remembered. You may be surprised at the level of recall.

4 Identify some important characteristics for a product with a well-known brand name. Based on these attributes, generate a list of possible brand extension or licensing opportunities, as well as some others that would be unlikely to be accepted by consumers.

5 Collect some pictures of 'classic' products that have high nostalgia value. Show these pictures to consumers and allow them to make free associations. Analyse the types of memories that are evoked, and think about how these associations might be employed in a product's promotional strategy.

■ NOTES

1. Robert A. Baron, *Psychology: The Essential Science* (Boston: Allyn & Bacon, 1989).
2. Richard A. Feinberg, 'Credit cards as spending facilitating stimuli: A conditioning interpretation', *Journal of Consumer Research* 13 (December 1986): 348–56.
3. R. A. Rescorla, 'Pavlovian conditioning: It's not what you think it is', *American Psychologist* 43 (1988): 151–60; Elnora W. Stuart, Terence A. Shimp and Randall W. Engle, 'Classical conditioning of consumer attitudes: Four experiments in an advertising context', *Journal of Consumer Research* 14 (December 1987): 334–9; Terence A. Shimp, Elnora W. Stuart and Randall W. Engle, 'A program of classical conditioning experiments testing variations in the conditioned stimulus and context', *Journal of Consumer Research* 18(1) (June 1991): 1–12.
4. 'Anemic crocodile', *Forbes* (15 August 1994): 116.
5. Baron, *Psychology*.
6. Caitlin Ingrassia, 'Counterfeiter, imitators: fine line, *The Wall Street Journal* (16 January 2004), http://online.wsj.com/article/0,,SB107421653820930400,00.html?mod=article-outset-box; see also: 'AH moet twee verpakkingen aanpassingen' (video), *RTL Nieuws* (28 April 2005), http://www.rtl.nl/actueel/rtlnieuws/video/.
7. For a comprehensive approach to consumer behaviour based on operant conditioning principles, see Gordon R. Foxall, 'Behavior analysis and consumer psychology', *Journal of Economic Psychology* 15 (March 1994): 5–91. Foxall also sets out some consumer behaviour based on a neo-behaviourist perspective. By identifying environmental determinants, he develops four classes of consumer behaviour: *accomplishment, pleasure, accumulation* and *maintenance*. For an extensive discussion on this approach, see the entire special issue of Gordon R. Foxall, 'Science and interpretation in consumer behavior: a radical behaviourist perspective', *European Journal of Marketing* 29(9) (1995): 3–99.
8. Ellen J. Langer, *The Psychology of Control* (Beverly Hills, CA: Sage, 1983); Klaus G. Grunert, 'Automatic and strategic processes in advertising effects', *Journal of Marketing* 60 (1996): 88–91.
9. Robert B. Cialdini, *Influence: Science and Practice*, 2nd edn (New York: William Morrow, 1984).
10. Chris T. Allen and Thomas J. Madden, 'A closer look at classical conditioning', *Journal of Consumer Research* 12 (December 1985): 301–15.
11. Albert Bandura, *Social Foundations of Thought and Action: A Social Cognitive View* (Englewood Cliffs, NJ: Prentice Hall, 1986); Baron, *Psychology*.
12. Allen and Madden, 'A closer look at classical conditioning'; Chester A. Insko and William F. Oakes, 'Awareness and the conditioning of attitudes', *Journal of Personality and Social Psychology* 4 (November 1966): 487–96; Carolyn K. Staats and Arthur W. Staats, 'Meaning established by classical conditioning', *Journal of Experimental Psychology* 54 (July 1957): 74–80; Randi Priluck Grossman and Brian D. Till, 'The persistence of classically conditioned brand attitudes', *Journal of Advertising* 21(1) (Spring 1998): 23–31.
13. Stijn M.J. van Osselaer and Joseph W. Alba, 'Consumer learning and brand equity', *Journal of Consumer Research* 27(1) (June 2000): 1–16; Kevin Lane Keller, 'Conceptualizing, measuring, and managing customer-based brand equity', *Journal of Marketing* 57 (January 1993): 1–22; Patrick Bawise, 'Brand equity: Snark or boojum?', *International Journal of Research in Marketing* 10 (1993): 93–104; W. Fred van Raaij and Wim Schoonderbeer, 'Meaning Structure of Brand Names and Extensions', in W. Fred van Raaij and Gary J. Bamossy, eds, *European Advances in Consumer Research* 1 (Provo, UT: Association for Consumer Research, 1993): 479–84; Gil McWilliam, 'The Effect of Brand Typology on Brand Extension Fit: Commercial and Academic Research Findings', in van Raaij and Bamossy, eds, *European Advances in Association for Consumer Research* 1: 485–91; Elyette Roux and Frederic Lorange, 'Brand Extension Research: A Review', in van Raaij and Bamossy, eds, *European Advances in Consumer Research* 1: 492–500; 'The art of perception', *Marketing* (28 November 1996): 25–9.
14. Herbert Krugman, 'Low recall and high recognition of advertising', *Journal of Advertising Research* (February/March 1986): 79–86.
15. Gerald J. Gorn, 'The effects of music in advertising on choice behavior: A classical conditioning approach', *Journal of Marketing* 46 (Winter 1982): 94–101.
16. Calvin Bierley, Frances K. McSweeney and Renee Vannieuwkerk, 'Classical conditioning of preferences for stimuli', *Journal of Consumer Research* 12 (December 1985): 316–23; James J. Kellaris and Anthony D. Cox, 'The effects of background music in advertising: A reassessment', *Journal of Consumer Research* 16 (June 1989): 113–18.
17. Frances K. McSweeney and Calvin Bierley, 'Recent developments in classical conditioning', *Journal of Consumer Research* 11 (September 1984): 619–31.
18. Basil G. Englis, 'The Reinforcement Properties of Music Videos: "I Want My . . . I Want My . . . I Want My . . . MTV" ' (paper presented at the meetings of the Association for Consumer Research, New Orleans, 1989).
19. 'Giving bad puns the business', *Newsweek* (11 December 1989): 71.
20. Bernice Kanner, 'Growing pains – and gains: Brand names branch out', *New York* (13 March 1989): 22.
21. Peter H. Farquhar, 'Brand equity', *Marketing Insights* (Summer 1989): 59.
22. John Marchese, 'Forever harley', *New York Times* (17 October 1993): 10; 'Spamming the globe', *Newsweek* (29 August 1994): 8.
23. Quoted in 'Look-alikes mimic familiar packages', *New York Times* (9 August 1986): D1; 'Action fails to match spirit of lookalike law', *Marketing* (27 March 1997): 19.
24. Laurie Hays, 'Too many computer names confuse too many buyers', *Wall Street Journal* (29 June 1994): B1 (2 pp).
25. Blaise J. Bergiel and Christine Trosclair, 'Instrumental learning: Its application to customer satisfaction', *Journal of Consumer Marketing* 2 (Fall 1985): 23–8.
26. Terence A. Shimp, 'Neo-Pavlovian Conditioning and Its Implications for Consumer Theory and Research', in Thomas S. Robertson and Harold H. Kassarjian, eds, *Handbook of Consumer Behavior* (Englewood Cliffs, NJ: Prentice Hall, 1991).
27. K.K. Desai and Wayne Hoyer, 'Descriptive characteristics of memory-based consideration sets: Influence of usage occasion frequency and usage location familiarity', *Journal of Consumer Research* 27(3) (December 2000): 309–23;

R.C. Atkinson and R.M. Shiffrin, 'Human Memory: A Proposed System and Its Control Processes', in K.W. Spence and J.T. Spence, eds, *The Psychology of Learning and Motivation: Advances in Research and Theory* (New York: Academic Press, 1968): 89–195.

28. James R. Bettman, 'Memory factors in consumer choice: a review', *Journal of Marketing* (Spring 1979): 37–53. For a study that explored the relative impact of internal versus external memory on brand choice, see Joseph W. Alba, Howard Marmorstein and Amitava Chattopadhyay, 'Transitions in preference over time: The effects of memory on message persuasiveness', *Journal of Marketing Research* 29 (November 1992): 406–17. For other research on memory and advertising, see H. Shanker Krishnan and Dipankar Chakravarti, 'Varieties of Brand Memory Induced by Advertising: Determinants, Measures, and Relationships', in David A. Aaker and Alexander L. Biel, eds, *Brand Equity and Advertising: Advertising's Role in Building Strong Brands* (Hillsdale, NJ: Lawrence Erlbaum Associates, 1993): 213–31; Bernd H. Schmitt, Nader T. Tavassoli and Robert T. Millard, 'Memory for print ads: Understanding relations among brand name, copy, and picture', *Journal of Consumer Psychology* 2(1) (1993): 55–81; Marian Friestad and Esther Thorson, 'Remembering ads: The effects of encoding strategies, retrieval cues, and emotional response', *Journal of Consumer Psychology* 2(1) (1993): 1–23; Surendra N. Singh, Sanjay Mishra, Neeli Bendapudi and Denise Linville, 'Enhancing memory of television commercials through message spacing', *Journal of Marketing Research* 31 (August 1994): 384–92.

29. Kathryn R. Braun, 'Postexperience advertising effects on consumer memory', *Journal of Consumer Research* 25 (March 1999): 319–34.

30. Kim Robertson, 'Recall and recognition effects of brand name imagery', *Psychology and Marketing* 4 (Spring 1987): 3–15.

31. Endel Tulving, 'Remembering and knowing the past', *American Scientist* 77 (July/August 1989): 361.

32. Rashmi Adaval and Robert S. Wyer, Jr., 'The role of narratives in consumer information processing', *Journal of Consumer Psychology* 7(3) (1998): 207–46.

33. Baron, *Psychology*.

34. George A. Miller, 'The magical number seven, plus or minus two: Some limits on our capacity for processing information', *Psychological Review* 63 (1956): 81–97.

35. James N. MacGregor, 'Short-term memory capacity: Limitation or optimization?', *Psychological Review* 94 (1987): 107–8.

36. See Catherine A. Cole and Michael J. Houston, 'Encoding and media effects on consumer learning deficiencies in the elderly', *Journal of Marketing Research* 24 (February 1987): 55–64; A.M. Collins and E.F. Loftus, 'A spreading activation theory of semantic processing', *Psychological Review* 82 (1975): 407–28; Fergus I.M. Craik and Robert S. Lockhart, 'Levels of processing: A framework for memory research', *Journal of Verbal Learning and Verbal Behavior* 11 (1972): 671–84.

37. Walter A. Henry, 'The effect of information-processing ability on processing accuracy', *Journal of Consumer Research* 7 (June 1980): 42–8.

38. Anthony G. Greenwald and Clark Leavitt, 'Audience involvement in advertising: Four levels', *Journal of Consumer Research* 11 (June 1984): 581–92.

39. Kevin Lane Keller, 'Memory factors in advertising: The effect of advertising retrieval cues on brand evaluations', *Journal of Consumer Research* 14 (December 1987): 316–33. For a discussion of processing operations that occur during brand choice, see Gabriel Biehal and Dipankar Chakravarti, 'Consumers' use of memory and external information in choice: Macro and micro perspectives', *Journal of Consumer Research* 12 (March 1986): 382–405.

40. Susan T. Fiske and Shelley E. Taylor, *Social Cognition* (Reading, MA: Addison-Wesley, 1984).

41. Deborah Roedder John and John C. Whitney Jr., 'The development of consumer knowledge in children: A cognitive structure approach', *Journal of Consumer Research* 12 (March 1986): 406–17.

42. Michael R. Solomon, Carol Surprenant, John A. Czepiel and Evelyn G. Gutman, 'A role theory perspective on dyadic interactions: The service encounter', *Journal of Marketing* 49 (Winter 1985): 99–111.

43. Roger W. Morrell, Denise C. Park and Leonard W. Poon, 'Quality of instructions on prescription drug labels: Effects on memory and comprehension in young and old adults', *The Gerontologist* 29 (1989): 345–54.

44. Frank R. Kardes, Gurumurthy Kalyanaram, Murali Chandrashekaran and Ronald J. Dornoff, 'Brand Retrieval, Consideration Set Composition, Consumer Choice, and the Pioneering Advantage' (unpublished manuscript, University of Cincinnati, OH, 1992).

45. Nijar Dawar and Philip Parket, 'Marketing universals: Consumers' use of brand name, price, physical appearance, and retailer reputation as signals of product quality', *Journal of Marketing* 58 (1994): 81–95; Judith Lynne Zaichkowsky and Padma Vipat, 'Inferences from Brand Names', in van Raaij and Bamossy, eds, *European Advances in Consumer Research* 1: 534–40.

46. Krugman, 'Low recall and high recognition of advertising'.

47. Rik G.M. Pieters and Tammo H.A. Bijmolt, 'Consumer memory for television advertising: A field study of duration, serial position, and competition effects', *Journal of Consumer Research* 23 (March 1997): 362–72.

48. Margaret G. Meloy, 'Mood-driven distortion of product information', *Journal of Consumer Research* 27(3) (December 2000): 345–59.

49. Eric J. Johnson and J. Edward Russo, 'Product familiarity and learning new information', *Journal of Consumer Research* 11 (June 1984): 542–50.

50. Eric J. Johnson and J. Edward Russo, 'Product Familiarity and Learning New Information', in Kent Monroe, ed., *Advances in Consumer Research* 8 (Ann Arbor, MI: Association for Consumer Research, 1981): 151–5; John G. Lynch and Thomas K. Srull, 'Memory and attentional factors in consumer choice: Concepts and research methods', *Journal of Consumer Research* 9 (June 1982): 18–37.

51. Julie A. Edell and Kevin Lane Keller, 'The information processing of coordinated media campaigns', *Journal of Marketing Research* 26 (May 1989): 149–64.

52. Lynch and Srull, 'Memory and attentional factors in consumer choice'.

53. Joseph W. Alba and Amitava Chattopadhyay, 'Salience effects in brand recall', *Journal of Marketing Research* 23 (November 1986): 363–70; Elizabeth C. Hirschman and Michael R. Solomon, 'Utilitarian, Aesthetic, and Familiarity

Responses to Verbal Versus Visual Advertisements', in Thomas C. Kinnear, ed., *Advances in Consumer Research* 11 (Provo, UT: Association for Consumer Research, 1984): 426–31.

54. Susan E. Heckler and Terry L. Childers, 'The role of expectancy and relevancy in memory for verbal and visual information: What is incongruency?', *Journal of Consumer Research* 18 (March 1992): 475–92.

55. Russell H. Fazio, Paul M. Herr and Martha C. Powell, 'On the development and strength of category-brand associations in memory: The case of mystery ads', *Journal of Consumer Psychology* 1(1) (1992): 1–13.

56. Hirschman and Solomon, 'Utilitarian, aesthetic, and familiarity responses to verbal versus visual advertisements'.

57. Terry Childers and Michael Houston, 'Conditions for a picture-superiority effect on consumer memory', *Journal of Consumer Research* 11 (September 1984): 643–54; Terry Childers, Susan Heckler and Michael Houston, 'Memory for the visual and verbal components of print advertisements', *Psychology and Marketing* 3 (Fall 1986): 147–50.

58. Werner Krober-Riel, 'Effects of Emotional Pictorial Elements in Ads Analyzed by Means of Eye Movement Monitoring', in Kinnear, ed., *Advances in Consumer Research* 11: 591–6.

59. Hans-Bernd Brosius, 'Influence of presentation features and news context on learning from television news', *Journal of Broadcasting and Electronic Media* 33 (Winter 1989): 1–14.

60. Raymond R. Burke and Thomas K. Srull, 'Competitive interference and consumer memory for advertising', *Journal of Consumer Research* 15 (June 1988): 55–68.

61. Ibid.

62. Johnson and Russo, 'Product Familiarity and Learning New Information'.

63. Joan Meyers-Levy, 'The influence of brand names association set size and word frequency on brand memory', *Journal of Consumer Research* 16 (September 1989): 197–208.

64. Michael H. Baumgardner, Michael R. Leippe, David L. Ronis and Anthony G. Greenwald, 'In search of reliable persuasion effects: II. Associative interference and persistence of persuasion in a message-dense environment', *Journal of Personality and Social Psychology* 45 (September 1983): 524–37.

65. Alba and Chattopadhyay, 'Salience effects in brand recall'.

66. Margaret Henderson Blair, Allan R. Kuse, David H. Furse and David W. Stewart, 'Advertising in a new and competitive environment: persuading consumers to buy', *Business Horizons* 30 (November/December 1987): 20.

67. Lynch and Srull, 'Memory and attentional factors in consumer choice'.

68. Russell W. Belk, 'Possessions and the extended self', *Journal of Consumer Research* 15 (September 1988): 139–68.

69. Russell W. Belk, 'The Role of Possessions in Constructing and Maintaining a Sense of Past', in Marvin E. Goldberg, Gerald Gorn and Richard W. Pollay, eds, *Advances in Consumer Research* 16 (Provo, UT: Association for Consumer Research, 1990): 669–78.

70. Hans Baumgartner, Mita Sujan and James R. Bettman, 'Autobiographical memories, affect and consumer information processing', *Journal of Consumer Psychology* 1 (January 1992): 53–82; Mita Sujan, James R. Bettman and Hans Baumgartner, 'Influencing consumer judgments using autobiographical memories: A self-referencing perspective', *Journal of Marketing Research* 30 (November 1993): 422–36.

71. Roger Thurow, 'Bucharest is plastered with J.R. Ewing in an ad push by Russian oil company', *Wall Street Journal Interactive Edition* (21 December 1999).

72. Gabriella Stern, 'VW hopes nostalgia will spur sales of retooled Beetle, fuel US comeback', *Wall Street Journal, Europe* (7 May 1997): 4; 'Ostalgie for the day when they'd never had it so good', *The Independent* (10 February 1997); Almar Latour, 'Shelf wars', *Central European Economic Review* 4 (Dow Jones, May 1997); G. Morello, *The Hidden Dimensions of Marketing* (Amsterdam: Vrije Universiteit, 1993): 13.

73. Kevin Goldman, 'New campaigns tip the hat to nostalgia', *Wall Street Journal* (9 August 1994): B4; Jean Halliday, 'VW Beetle: Liz Vanzura', *Advertising Age* 70 (1999): 4; Daniel Howes, 'VW Beetle is a bust in Europe, where Golf is car of choice', *Detroit News* (13 April 1999): B1.

74. Morris B. Holbrook and Robert M. Schindler, 'Some exploratory findings on the development of musical tastes', *Journal of Consumer Research* 16 (June 1989): 119–24.

75. Randall Rothenberg, 'The past is now the latest craze', *New York Times* (29 November 1989): D1.

76. See Morris B. Holbrook, 'Nostalgia and consumption preferences: Some emerging patterns of consumer tastes', *Journal of Consumer Research* 20 (September 1993): 245–56; Robert M. Schindler and Morris B. Holbrook, 'Critical periods in the development of men's and women's tastes in personal appearance', *Psychology and Marketing* 10(6) (November/December 1993): 549–64; Morris B. Holbrook and Robert M. Schindler, 'Age, sex, and attitude toward the past as predictors of consumers' aesthetic tastes for cultural products', *Journal of Marketing Research* 31 (August 1994): 412–22.

77. 'Only 38% of T.V. audience links brands with ads', *Marketing News* (6 January 1984): 10.

78. 'Terminal television', *American Demographics* (January 1987): 15.

79. Richard P. Bagozzi and Alvin J. Silk, 'Recall, recognition, and the measurement of memory for print advertisements', *Marketing Science* (1983): 95–134.

80. Adam Finn, 'Print ad recognition readership scores: An information processing perspective', *Journal of Marketing Research* 25 (May 1988): 168–77.

81. Bettman, 'Memory factors in consumer choice'.

82. Mark A. deTurck and Gerald M. Goldhaber, 'Effectiveness of product warning labels: effects of consumers' information processing objectives', *Journal of Consumer Affairs* 23(1) (1989): 111–25.

83. Finn, 'Print ad recognition readership scores'.

84. Surendra N. Singh and Gilbert A. Churchill Jr., 'Response-bias-free recognition tests to measure advertising effects', *Journal of Advertising Research* 29 (June/July 1987): 23–36.

85. William A. Cook, 'Telescoping and memory's other tricks', *Journal of Advertising Research* 27 (February/March 1987): 5–8.

86. 'On a diet? Don't trust your memory', *Psychology Today* (October 1989): 12.

87. Hubert A. Zielske and Walter A. Henry, 'Remembering and forgetting television ads', *Journal of Advertising Research* 20 (April 1980): 7–13.

MOTIVATION, VALUES AND INVOLVEMENT

Jez looks at the menu in the trendy Edinburgh health food restaurant that Tessel (his Dutch girlfriend of six months' standing) has dragged him to for her birthday celebration. Tessel is really surprised by how much less emphasis Jez and his friends put on birthdays, compared with the Netherlands where birthday celebrations are really important – regardless of how old you are. Jez, meanwhile, is reflecting on what a man will give up for love. Now that Tessel has converted to vegetarianism, she's slowly but surely persuading him to give up burgers and pizzas for healthier, preferably organic, fare. He can't even hide from tofu and other vegan delights in the Edinburgh University Refectory; and the café in the student union has just started offering 'veggie' alternatives to its usual full Scottish breakfast (a calorie-laden fry-up of eggs, bacon, sausages, tomatoes, mushrooms, black pudding, haggis and potatoes).

Tessel is totally into vegetarianism (she had not become a total vegan yet, as she still loves pickled herring and smoked eel, real Dutch delicacies); she claims that eating this way not only cuts out unwanted fat, but is also good for the environment. Just his luck to fall head-over-heels for a Green, organic-food-eating environmentalist. As Jez gamely tries to decide between the stuffed artichokes with red pepper vinaigrette and the grilled marinated zucchini, fantasies of a tuna steak shimmer before his eyes – he wonders if that would be allowed, maybe for his birthday celebration next month?

■ INTRODUCTION

As a vegetarian, Tessel certainly is not alone in believing that eating organic foods is good for the body, the soul and the planet.[1] It is estimated that 7 per cent of the general population is vegetarian, and women and younger people are even more likely to adopt a meatless diet. An additional 10–20 per cent of consumers are interested in vegetarian options in addition to their normal fare of dead animals. In a 2003 survey of 12–19-year-olds, 20 per cent of respondents (and close to one in three of the females) said vegetarianism is 'in'. There has been a lively debate in Europe about genetically modified foods as well, although genetic modification for medical purposes has not met with such widespread hostility in Europe. Consumers see 'functional foods as placed midway on the combined "naturalness–healthiness continuum" from organically processed to genetically modified'[2] but tend to remain unconvinced that genetically modified foods can offer any significant health benefits.[3] However, concerns about adult, and more especially childhood, obesity means that diet has become a burning issue for many European governments.[4] It's obvious our menu choices have deep-seated consequences.

The forces that drive people to buy and use products are generally straightforward, as when a person chooses what to have for lunch. As hard-core vegans demonstrate, however, even the consumption of basic food products may also be related to wide-ranging beliefs regarding what is appropriate or desirable. Among the more general population there are strong beliefs about genetically modified foods, which have proved difficult to alter via information campaigns.[5] In some cases, these emotional responses create a deep commitment to the product. Sometimes people are not even fully aware of the forces that drive them towards some products and away from others. Often a person's *values* – his or her priorities and beliefs about the world – influence these choices.

To understand motivation is to understand *why* consumers do what they do. Why do some people choose to bungee jump off a bridge or go white-water rafting, whereas others spend their leisure time playing chess or gardening?[6] Whether to quench a thirst, kill boredom, or to attain some deep spiritual experience, we do everything for a reason, even if we can't articulate what that reason is. Marketing students are taught from Day One that the goal of marketing is to satisfy consumers' needs. However, this insight is useless unless we can discover *what* those needs are and *why* they exist.

■ THE MOTIVATION PROCESS: A PSYCHOLOGICAL PERSPECTIVE

▶ **Motivation** refers to the processes that cause people to behave as they do. From a *psy-*
▶ *chological perspective* motivation occurs when a **need** is aroused that the consumer wishes to satisfy. Once a need has been activated, a state of tension exists that drives the consumer to attempt to reduce or eliminate the need. This need may be *utilitarian* (a desire to achieve some functional or practical benefit, as when a person eats green vegetables for nutritional reasons) or it may be *hedonic* (an experiential need, involving emotional responses or fantasies, as when Jez thinks longingly about a juicy steak). The distinction between the two is, however, a matter of degree. The desired end-state is the consumer's
▶ **goal**. Marketers try to create products and services that will provide the desired benefits and permit the consumer to reduce this tension.

Whether the need is utilitarian or hedonic, a discrepancy exists between the consumer's present state and some ideal state. This gulf creates a state of tension. The magnitude of this tension determines the urgency the consumer feels to reduce the tension.
▶ This degree of arousal is called a **drive**. A basic need can be satisfied in any number of ways, and the specific path a person chooses is influenced both by his or her unique set of experiences and by the values instilled by cultural, religious, ethnic or national background.

Above: Pirelli uses the sport metaphor of world-class competition to emphasize motivation and top performance.

This ad for health clubs and exercise regimes shows men an undesired state (lack of muscle tone and fitness, as dictated by contemporary Western culture), and suggests a solution to the problem of spare inches around the waist (purchase of health club membership in order to attain a fit and healthy body).

▶   These personal and cultural factors combine to create a **want**, which is one manifestation of a need. For example, hunger is a basic need that must be satisfied by all; the lack of food creates a tension state that can be reduced by the intake of such products as paella, pizzas, spaghetti, chocolate biscuits, raw fish or bean sprouts. The specific route to drive reduction is culturally and individually determined. Once the goal is attained, tension is reduced and the motivation recedes (for the time being). Motivation can be described in terms of its *strength*, or the pull it exerts on the consumer, and its *direction*, or the particular way the consumer attempts to reduce motivational tension.

■ MOTIVATIONAL STRENGTH

The degree to which a person is willing to expend energy to reach one goal as opposed to another reflects his or her underlying motivation to attain that goal. Many theories have been advanced to explain why people behave the way they do. Most share the basic idea that people have some finite amount of energy that must be directed towards certain goals.

Biological vs. learned needs

Early work on motivation ascribed behaviour to *instinct*, the innate patterns of behaviour that are universal in a species. This view is now largely discredited. For one thing, the existence of an instinct is difficult to prove or disprove. The instinct is inferred from the behaviour it is supposed to explain (this type of circular explanation is called a *tautology*).[7] It is like saying that a consumer buys products that are status symbols because he or she is motivated to attain status, which is hardly a satisfying explanation.

Drive theory

▶ **Drive theory** focuses on biological needs that produce unpleasant states of arousal (e.g. your stomach grumbles during the first lecture of the day – you missed breakfast). We are motivated to reduce the tension caused by this arousal. Tension reduction has been proposed as a basic mechanism governing human behaviour.

In a marketing context, tension refers to the unpleasant state that exists if a person's consumption needs are not fulfilled. A person may be grumpy or unable to concentrate very well if she hasn't eaten, or someone may be dejected or angry if he cannot afford that new car he wants. This state activates goal-oriented behaviour, which attempts to reduce or eliminate this unpleasant state and return to a balanced one called
▶ **homeostasis**.

Those behaviours that are successful in reducing the drive by satisfying the underlying need are strengthened and tend to be repeated. (This aspect of the learning process was discussed in Chapter 3.) Your motivation to leave class early to grab a snack would be greater if you hadn't eaten in 24 hours than if you had eaten breakfast only two hours earlier. If you did sneak out and got indigestion after, say, wolfing down a packet of crisps, you would be less likely to repeat this behaviour the next time you wanted a snack. One's degree of motivation, then, depends on the distance between one's present state and the goal.

Drive theory, however, runs into difficulties when it tries to explain some facets of human behaviour that run counter to its predictions. People often do things that *increase* a drive state rather than decrease it. For example, people may delay gratification. If you know you are going out for a five-course dinner, you might decide to forgo a snack earlier in the day even though you are hungry at that time. And, as we shall see in the discussion of desire, the most rewarding thing may often be the tension of the drive state itself rather than its satisfaction. It's not the kill, it's the thrill of the chase.

Expectancy theory

▶ Most current explanations of motivation focus on cognitive factors rather than biological ones to understand what drives behaviour. **Expectancy theory** suggests that behaviour is largely pulled by expectations of achieving desirable outcomes – *positive incentives* – rather than pushed from within. We choose one product over another because we expect this choice to have more positive consequences for us. Thus the term *drive* is used here more loosely to refer to both physical and cognitive, i.e. learned, processes.

■ MOTIVATIONAL DIRECTION

Motives have direction as well as strength. They are goal oriented in that they drive us to satisfy a specific need. Most goals can be reached by a number of routes, and the objective of a company is to convince consumers that the alternative it offers provides the best chance to attain the goal. For example, a consumer who decides that she needs a pair of jeans to help her reach her goal of being accepted by others can choose among Levi's, Wranglers, Diesel, Calvin Klein and many other alternatives, each of which promises to deliver certain benefits.

A technical product can satisfy hedonic desires.

The Advertising Archives

Needs vs. wants

The specific way a need is satisfied depends on the individual's unique history, learning experiences and his or her cultural environment. The particular form of consumption used to satisfy a need is termed a want. For example, two classmates may feel their stomachs rumbling during a lunchtime lecture. If neither person has eaten since the night before, the strength of their respective needs (hunger) would be about the same. However, the way each person goes about satisfying this need might be quite different. The first person may be a vegetarian like Tessel who fantasizes about gulping down a big bowl of salad, whereas the second person like Jez might be equally aroused by the prospect of a large plateful of bacon and eggs.

Types of needs

A start to the discussion of needs and wants can best be illustrated by considering two basic types of need. People are born with a need for certain elements necessary to maintain life, such as food, water, air and shelter. These are called *biogenic needs*. People have many other needs, however, that are not innate. We acquire *psychogenic needs* as we become members of a specific culture. These include the need for status, power, affiliation, and so on. Psychogenic needs reflect the priorities of a culture, and their effect on behaviour will vary in different environments. For example, an Italian consumer may be driven to devote a good chunk of his income to products that permit him to display his individuality, whereas his Scandinavian counterpart may work equally hard to ensure that he does not stand out from his group. These cultural differences in the expression of consumer values will be discussed more fully in Chapter 16.

This distinction is revealing because it shows how difficult it is to distinguish needs from wants. How can we tell what part of the motivation is a psychogenic need and what part is a want? Both are profoundly formed by culture, so the distinction is problematic at best. As for the biogenic needs, we know from anthropology that satisfaction of these needs leads to some of the most symbolically rich and culturally based activities of humankind. The ways we want to eat, dress, drink and provide shelter are far more interesting to marketers than our need to do so. And, in fact, human beings need very little in the strict sense of the word. Charles Darwin was astonished to see the native Americans of Tierra del Fuego sleep naked in the snow. Hence, the idea of satisfaction of biogenic needs is more or less a given thing for marketing and consumer research because it is on the most basic level nothing more than a simple prerequisite for us to be here. Beyond that level, and of much greater interest (and challenge!) to marketers, is a concept embedded in culture such as wants.[8]

As we have seen, another traditional distinction is between the motivation to satisfy either utilitarian or hedonic needs. The satisfaction of *utilitarian needs* implies that consumers will emphasize the objective, tangible attributes of products, such as fuel economy in a car; the amount of fat, calories, and protein in a cheeseburger; and the durability of a pair of blue jeans. *Hedonic needs* are subjective and experiential. Here, consumers might rely on a product to meet their needs for excitement, self-confidence, fantasy, and so on. Of course, consumers can be motivated to purchase a product because it provides *both* types of benefits. For example, a mink coat might be bought because it feels soft against the skin, because it keeps one warm through the long cold winters of Northern Europe, and because it has a luxurious image. But again the distinction tends to hide more than it reveals, because functionality can bring great pleasure to people and is an important value in the modern world.[9]

We expect today's technical products to satisfy our needs – instantly.
The Advertising Archives

MOTIVATIONAL CONFLICTS

A goal has *valence*, which means that it can be positive or negative. A positively valued goal is one towards which consumers direct their behaviour; they are motivated to *approach* the goal and will seek out products that will help them to reach it. However, not all behaviour is motivated by the desire to approach a goal. As we saw in the previous chapter's discussion of negative reinforcement, consumers may instead be motivated to *avoid* a negative outcome.[10] They will structure their purchases or consumption activities to reduce the chances of attaining this end result. For example, many consumers work hard to avoid rejection, a negative goal. They will stay away from products that they associate with social disapproval. Products such as deodorants and mouthwash frequently rely on consumers' negative motivation by depicting the onerous social consequences of underarm odour or bad breath.

Because a purchase decision can involve more than one source of motivation, consumers often find themselves in situations where different motives, both positive and negative, conflict with one another. Because marketers are attempting to satisfy consumers' needs, they can also be helpful by providing possible solutions to these dilemmas. As shown in Figure 4.1, three general types of conflicts can occur: approach–approach; approach–avoidance and avoidance–avoidance.

Approach-approach conflict

▶ In an **approach-approach conflict**, a person must choose between two desirable alternatives. A student might be torn between going home for the holidays or going on a skiing trip with friends. Or, she might have to choose between two CDs.

▶ The **theory of cognitive dissonance** is based on the premise that people have a need for order and consistency in their lives and that a state of tension is created when beliefs or behaviours conflict with one another. The conflict that arises when choosing between two alternatives may be resolved through a process of *cognitive dissonance reduction*, where people are motivated to reduce this inconsistency (or dissonance) and thus eliminate unpleasant tension.[11]

Figure 4.1 Three types of motivational conflict

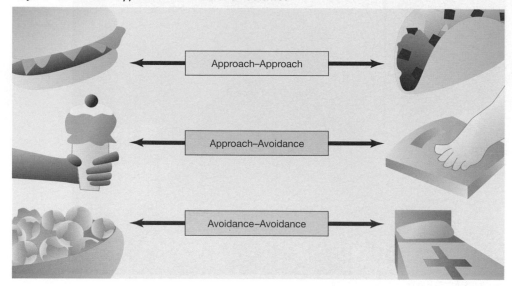

A state of dissonance occurs when there is a psychological inconsistency between two or more beliefs or behaviours. It often occurs when a consumer must make a choice between two products, where both alternatives usually possess both good and bad qualities. By choosing one product and not the other, the person gets the bad qualities of the chosen product and loses out on the good qualities of the one not chosen.

This loss creates an unpleasant, dissonant state that the person is motivated to reduce. People tend to convince themselves, after the fact, that the choice they made was the right one by finding additional reasons to support the alternative they chose, or perhaps by 'discovering' flaws with the option they did not choose. A marketer can resolve an approach–approach conflict by bundling several benefits together. For example, many low calorie products claim that they have 'all the taste' *and* 'half the calories', allowing the consumer to avoid having to choose between better taste and fewer calories.

Approach-avoidance conflict

Many of the products and services we desire have negative consequences attached to them as well. We may feel guilty or ostentatious when buying a status-laden product such as a fur coat, or we might feel like a glutton when contemplating a box of chocolates. When we desire a goal but wish to avoid it at the same time, an **approach-avoidance conflict** exists. Some solutions to these conflicts include the proliferation of fake furs, which eliminate guilt about harming animals to make a fashion statement, and the success of low calorie and diet foods, such as those produced by Weight Watchers, that promise good food without the calories (**weight-watchers.com**). Some marketers counter consumer resistance to overconsumption and spending by promising more (benefits) from less, as in an Audi advertisement (in 2000), whereas other marketers try to overcome guilt by convincing consumers that they deserve luxuries (such as when the model for L'Oréal cosmetics claims 'Because I'm worth it!'). Sometimes consumers go outside the conventional marketplace to satisfy their needs, wants and desires, for instance drag-racing in Moscow where young Russian car fanatics fulfil their drive for thrill-seeking outside the law.[12]

The Partnership for a Drug-Free America points out the negative consequences of drug addiction for those who are tempted to start.

The Advertising Archives

Avoidance-avoidance conflict

Sometimes consumers find themselves 'caught between a rock and a hard place'. They may face a choice with two undesirable alternatives, for instance the option of either throwing more money into an old car or buying a new one. Marketers frequently address an **avoidance-avoidance conflict** with messages that stress the unforeseen benefits of choosing one option (e.g. by emphasizing special credit plans to ease the pain of new car payments).

■ CLASSIFYING CONSUMER NEEDS

Much research has been done on classifying human needs. On the one hand, some psychologists have tried to define a universal inventory of needs that could be traced systematically to explain virtually all behaviour. One such effort, developed by Henry Murray, delineates a set of 20 psychogenic needs that (sometimes in combination) result in specific behaviours. These needs include such dimensions as *autonomy* (being independent), *defendance* (defending the self against criticism), and even *play* (engaging in pleasurable activities).[13]

Murray's needs structure serves as the basis for a number of widely used personality tests such as the Thematic Apperception Technique (TAT) and the Edwards' Personal Preference Schedule (EPPS). In the TAT, test subjects are shown four to six ambiguous pictures and are asked to write answers to four questions about the pictures. These questions are: (1) What is happening? (2) What has led up to this situation? (3) What is being thought? (4) What will happen? Each answer is then analysed for references to certain needs and scored whenever that need is mentioned. The theory behind the test is that people will freely project their own subconscious needs to the stimulus. By getting their responses to the picture, you are really getting at the person's true needs for achievement or affiliation or whatever other need may be dominant. Murray believed that everyone has the same basic set of needs, but that individuals differ in their priority ranking of these needs.[14]

Specific needs and buying behaviour

Other motivational approaches have focused on specific needs and their ramifications for behaviour. For example, individuals with a high *need for achievement* strongly value personal accomplishment.[15] They place a premium on products and services that signify success because these consumption items provide feedback about the realization of their goals. These consumers are good prospects for products that provide evidence of their achievement. One study of working women found that those who were high in achievement motivation were more likely to choose clothing they considered businesslike, and less likely to be interested in apparel that accentuated their femininity.[16] Some other important needs that are relevant to consumer behaviour include the following:

Need for affiliation (to be in the company of other people):[17] This need is relevant to products and services that are 'consumed' in groups and alleviate loneliness, such as team sports, bars and shopping centres.

Need for power (to control one's environment):[18] Many products and services allow consumers to feel that they have mastery over their surroundings, ranging from cars with 'souped up' engines and loud sound systems that impose the driver's musical tastes on others to luxury resorts that promise to respond to every whim of their pampered guests.

Need for uniqueness (to assert one's individual identity):[19] Products can satisfy this need by pledging to accentuate a consumer's distinctive qualities. For example, Cachet perfume claims to be 'as individual as you are'.

Maslow's hierarchy of needs

One influential approach to motivation was proposed by the psychologist Abraham Maslow. Maslow's approach is a general one, originally developed to understand personal growth and the attainment of 'peak experiences'.[20] Maslow formulated a hierarchy of biogenic and psychogenic needs, in which certain levels of motives are specified. This *hierarchical* approach implies that the order of development is fixed – that is, a certain level must be attained before the next, higher one is activated. Marketers have embraced this perspective because it (indirectly) specifies certain types of product benefits people might be looking for, depending on the different stages in their development and/or their environmental conditions.[21] However, as we shall see it contains many problems, and we shall devote space to it here because it is a 'standard' in marketing knowledge rather than because we believe in its theoretical and practical value.

Maslow's levels are summarized in Figure 4.2. At each level, different priorities exist in terms of the product benefits a consumer is looking for. Ideally, an individual progresses up the hierarchy until his or her dominant motivation is a focus on 'ultimate' goals, such as justice and beauty. Unfortunately, this state is difficult to achieve (at least on a regular basis); most of us have to be satisfied with occasional glimpses, or *peak experiences*.

Figure 4.2 Levels of need in the Maslow hierarchy

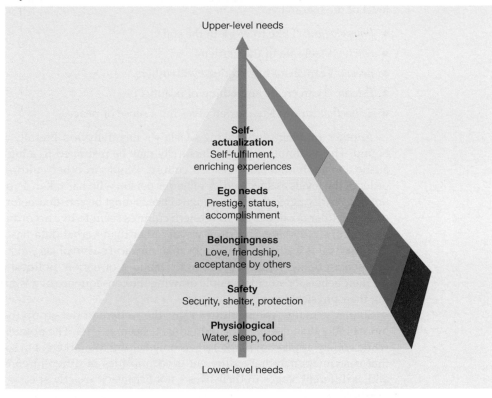

The implication of Maslow's hierarchy is that one must first satisfy basic needs before progressing up the ladder (i.e. a starving man is not interested in status symbols, friendship or self-fulfilment).[22] This suggests that consumers value different product attributes depending upon what is currently available to them. For example, consumers in the emerging economies of the former Eastern bloc are now bombarded with images of luxury goods, yet may still have trouble obtaining basic necessities.[23] In one study, Romanian students named the products they hoped to acquire. Their wish lists included not only the expected items such as sports cars and the latest model televisions, but also staples like water, soap, furniture and food.[24]

The application of this hierarchy by marketers has been somewhat simplistic, especially as the same product or activity can satisfy a number of different needs. Sex, for example, is characterized as a basic biological drive. While this observation is true throughout most of the animal kingdom, it is obviously a more complicated phenomenon for humans. Indeed, this activity could conceivably fit into every level of Maslow's hierarchy. A sociobiologist, who approaches human behaviour in terms of its biological origins, might argue that reproductive behaviour provides security because it ensures continuation of a person's gene pool and the provision of children to care for the person in old age. Sex can also express love and affiliation at the belongingness level. In addition, sex is often used as a vehicle to attain status, domination over another and to satisfy ego needs; it can be a significant determinant of self-respect. Finally, a sexual experience can be self-actualizing in that it may provide an ecstatic, transcendental experience. The same thing could be said for almost any kind of consumer experience. While eating certainly is necessary for our survival, it also is very much a social act (belongingness), a status act as in the consumption of champagne or other expensive wines, and an act through which the gourmet or the caring, cooking mother or father can obtain self-actualization. The house gives us shelter, but is also a security device, a home for the family, a status object and a field for actualizing our personal aspirations.

Another example would be gardening that has been found to satisfy needs at every level of the hierarchy:[25]

- *Physiological:* 'I like to work in the soil.'
- *Safety:* 'I feel safe in the garden.'
- *Social:* 'I can share my produce with others.'
- *Esteem:* 'I can create something of beauty.'
- *Self-actualization:* 'My garden gives me a sense of peace.'

Another problem with taking Maslow's hierarchy too literally is that it is culture-bound. The assumptions of the hierarchy may be restricted to a highly rational, materialistic and individualistic Western culture. People in other cultures may question the order of the levels as specified. A religious person who has taken a vow of celibacy would not necessarily agree that physiological needs must be satisfied before self-fulfilment can occur. Neither do all people in Western cultures seem to live according to Maslow's hierarchy. In fact, research based on visual rather than verbal data has indicated that spiritual survival is a stronger motivator than physical survival, as can be seen from patriots or freedom fighters giving their life for the idea of nation, political or religious fanatics for their beliefs, or suicidal people drawing the consequence of a 'spiritual death' by ending their physical lives.[26]

Similarly, many Asian cultures value the welfare of the group (belongingness needs) more highly than needs of the individual (esteem needs). The point is that this hierarchy, while widely applied in marketing, is only helpful to marketers in so far as it reminds us that consumers may have different need priorities in different consumption situations and at different stages in their lives – not because it exactly specifies a consumer's progression up the ladder of needs. It also does not take account of the cultural formation of needs. It provides a picture of a jungle law society, an economy of survival, where the culture-(re)producing and self-actualizing aspects of human activities are not taken into account.

■ HIDDEN MOTIVES: THE PSYCHOANALYTICAL PERSPECTIVE

A motive is an underlying reason for behaviour and not something researchers can see or easily measure. Furthermore, the same behaviour can be caused by a configuration of different motives. To compound the problem of identifying motives, the consumer may be unaware of the actual need/want he or she is attempting to satisfy, or alternatively he or she may not be willing to admit that this need exists. Because of these difficulties, motives must often be *inferred* by the analyst. Although some consumer needs undoubtedly are utilitarian and fairly straightforward, some researchers feel that a great many purchase decisions are not the result of deliberate, logical decisions. On the contrary, people may do things to satisfy motives of which they are not even aware.

Sigmund Freud had a profound, if controversial, impact on many basic assumptions about human behaviour. His work changed the way we view such topics as adult sexuality, dreams and psychological adjustment. Freudian theory developed the idea that much of human behaviour stems from a fundamental conflict between a person's desire to gratify his or her physical needs and the necessity to function as a responsible member of society. This struggle is carried out in the mind among three systems. (Note that these systems do not refer to physical parts of the brain.)

The *id* is entirely oriented towards immediate gratification – it is the 'party animal' of the mind. It operates according to the pleasure principle: behaviour is guided by the primary desire to maximize pleasure and avoid pain. The id is selfish and illogical. It directs a person's psychic energy towards pleasurable acts without regard for the consequences.

The *superego* is the counterweight to the id. This system is essentially the person's conscience. It internalizes society's rules (especially as communicated by parents) and works to prevent the id from seeking selfish gratification.

Finally, the *ego* is the system that mediates between the id and the superego. It is in a way a referee in the fight between temptation and virtue. The ego tries to balance these two opposing forces according to the reality principle. It finds ways to gratify the id that will be acceptable to the outside world. These conflicts occur on an unconscious level, so the person is not necessarily aware of the underlying reasons for his or her behaviour.

Some of Freud's ideas have also been adapted by consumer researchers. In particular, his work highlights the potential importance of unconscious motives underlying purchases. The implication is that consumers cannot necessarily tell us their true motivation for choosing a product, even if we can devise a sensitive way to ask them directly.

Motivational research

The first attempts to apply Freudian ideas to understand the deeper meanings of products and advertisements were made in the 1950s as a perspective known as **motivational research** was developed. This approach was largely based on psychoanalytic (Freudian) interpretations, with a heavy emphasis on unconscious motives. A basic assumption is that socially unacceptable needs are channelled into acceptable outlets. Product use or avoidance is motivated by unconscious forces which are often determined in childhood.

This form of research relies on *depth interviews* probing deeply into each person's purchase motivations. These can be derived only after questioning and interpretation on the part of a carefully trained interviewer. This work was pioneered by Ernest Dichter, a psychoanalyst who was trained in Vienna in the early part of the twentieth century. Dichter conducted in-depth interview studies on over 230 different products, and many of his findings have been incorporated into marketing campaigns.[27] For example, Esso (or Exxon) for many years reminded consumers to 'Put a Tiger in Your Tank' after Dichter found that people responded well to powerful animal symbolism containing vaguely suggestive overtones.

Criticisms of motivational research

Motivational research has been attacked for two quite different reasons. Some feel it does not work, while others feel it works *too* well. On the one hand, social critics attacked this school of thought for giving advertisers the power to manipulate consumers.[28] On the other hand, many consumer researchers felt the research lacked sufficient rigour and validity, since interpretations were subjective and indirect.[29] Because conclusions are based on the analyst's own judgement and are derived from discussions with a small number of people, some researchers are doubtful about the degree to which these results can be generalized to a large market. In addition, because the original motivational researchers were heavily influenced by orthodox Freudian theory, their interpretations usually carried strong sexual overtones. This emphasis tends to overlook other plausible causes for behaviour. It is worth noting that it has been argued that such over-interpretations and disregard of the more mundane and obvious were more common in the American market than in the British leading, for example, to a greater discrediting in the USA than in Europe of qualitative research in general and motivational research in particular.[30]

The positive side of motivational research

Motivational research had great appeal at least to some marketers for several reasons, some of which are detailed here. Motivational research tends to be less expensive than large-scale, quantitative survey data because interviewing and data processing costs are relatively small.

The knowledge derived from motivational research may help in the development of marketing communications that appeal to deep-seated needs and thus provide a more powerful hook to relate a product to consumers. Even if they are not necessarily valid for all consumers in a target market, these insights can be valuable when used in an exploratory way. For example, the rich imagery that may be associated with a product can be used creatively when developing advertising copy.

Some of the findings seem intuitively plausible after the fact. For example, motivational studies concluded that coffee is associated with companionship, that people avoid prunes because they remind them of old age, and that men fondly equate the first car they owned as a young man with the onset of their sexual freedom.

Table 4.1 Major motives for consumption as identified by Ernest Dichter

Motive	
Power – masculinity-virility	Power: Sugary products and large breakfasts (to charge oneself up), bowling, electric trains, hot rods, power tools Masculinity-virility: Coffee, red meat, heavy shoes, toy guns, buying fur coats for women, shaving with a razor
Security	Ice cream (to feel like a loved child again), full drawer of neatly ironed shirts, real plaster walls (to feel sheltered), home baking, hospital care
Eroticism	Sweets (to lick), gloves (to be removed by woman as a form of undressing), a man lighting a woman's cigarette (to create a tension-filled moment culminating in pressure, then relaxation)
Moral purity – cleanliness	White bread, cotton fabrics (to connote chastity), harsh household cleaning chemicals (to make housewives feel moral after using), bathing (to be equated with Pontius Pilate, who washed blood from his hands), oatmeal (sacrifice, virtue)
Social acceptance	Companionship: Ice cream (to share fun), coffee Love and affection: Toys (to express love for children), sugar and honey (to express terms of affection) Acceptance: Soap, beauty products
Individuality	Gourmet foods, foreign cars, cigarette holders, vodka, perfume, fountain pens
Status	Scotch, ulcers, heart attacks, indigestion (to show one has a high-stress, important job!); carpets (to show one does not live on bare earth like peasants)
Femininity	Cakes and cookies, dolls, silk, tea, household curios
Reward	Cigarettes, candy, alcohol, ice cream, cookies
Mastery over environment	Kitchen appliances, boats, sporting goods, cigarette lighters
Disalienation (a desire to feel connectedness to things)	Home decorating, skiing, morning radio broadcasts (to feel 'in touch' with the world)
Magic – mystery	Soups (having healing powers), paints (change the mood of a room), carbonated drinks (magical effervescent property), vodka (romantic history), unwrapping of gifts

Source: Adapted from Jeffrey F. Durgee, 'Interpreting Dichter's Interpretations: An Analysis of Consumption Symbolism in *The Handbook of Consumer Motivation*', *Marketing and Semiotics: Selected Papers from the Copenhagen Symposium*, ed. Hanne Hartvig-Larsen, David Glen Mick and Christian Alsted (Copenhagen: Handelshøjskolens forlag, 1991).

Other interpretations were harder for some people to accept, such as the observation that a woman baking a cake symbolizes giving birth, or that men are reluctant to give blood because they feel that their vital fluids are being drained. On the other hand, some people do refer to a pregnant woman as 'having a bun in the oven'.[31] Motivational research for the Red Cross did find that men (but not women) tend to overestimate drastically the amount of blood that is taken during a donation. This group counteracted the fear of loss of virility by symbolically equating the act of giving blood with fertilization: 'Give the gift of life.' Despite its drawbacks, motivational research continues to be employed as a useful diagnostic tool. Its validity is enhanced, however, when it is used in conjunction with other research techniques available to the consumer researcher.

■ CONSUMER DESIRE

▶ More recently, researchers have begun to discuss the importance of the concept of **desire** for understanding consumer behaviour. Desire as a motivational construct is quite revolutionary, since it turns the attention away from satisfaction and over to the thrills of the process of desiring.[32] This potentially opens up a better understanding of consumer insatiability than can be provided by needs and wants. Desire, furthermore, better captures the seductive spirit of the positioning of many contemporary brands and the

An example of a collage used to explore consumer desire.

deep feelings involved in consumer goods' contribution to the formation of consumers' self-images. Because emotions, unruly passions and bodily cravings and pleasures are so central to the experience of desiring, desire reintroduces the bodily aspect of motivation without reducing it to biogenic needs.[33] On the contrary, the concept of desire also emphasizes that, even though desires, needs and wants are felt psychologically, the concept of society (often called 'the Other' in the literature on desire) is very central to the understanding of desire. Thus, desire would refer to the *sociogenic* nature of needs.[34]

One study of consumer desires in Denmark, Turkey and the United States concluded that desires were much more profound than wants, that desire is cyclical and basically insatiable, and that what is desired is more often various kinds of social relationship mediated by consumption experiences than consumption in itself. Finally, desire has an interesting relationship with control. On the one hand, control kills desire, as expressed in many consumers' antonyms to desire being an overly routinized lifestyle with the same repetitive patterns day in and day out – what the French call 'metro – boulot – dodo' (the cycle of metro – work – sleep). On the other hand, it is potentially harmful because it contains an important element of excess and lack of control over oneself.[35] The study used collages among other techniques to explore consumer desire, and the collage on p. 103 illustrates some of the featured findings: that desire is positive but potentially harmful if out of control (the balance, the fight with one's own shadow) and can lead to impossible dreams (the ugly man and the model) or to excess and violation of norms (Hugh Grant and the prostitute).

Desire is one way of dealing with very passionate consumers, stressing the very emotional and sometimes irrational side of consumer behaviour. If consumer desire is investigated from a more rationalizing and cognitive psychological perspective, it tends to be dealt with under the term consumer *involvement*.

multicultural dimensions

Paradise: satisfying needs?

Presumably, a person who has had all of his or her needs satisfied lives in 'paradise'. Conceptualizations of paradise have implications for the marketing and consumption of any products, such as vacation travel, that seek to invoke an ideal state. However, the definition of just what constitutes paradise appears to differ across cultures. To pursue this idea further, the concept of paradise was compared between groups of American and Dutch college students. Informants in both cultures constructed a collage of images to illustrate their overall concept of paradise, and they wrote an essay to accompany and explain this collage. Some similarities were evident in the two societies: both Americans and Dutch emphasized the personal, experiential aspects of paradise, saying 'paradise is different for everyone . . . a feeling . . . a state of being'. In addition, individuals in both societies said that paradise must include family, friends and significant others.

However, the Dutch and Americans differed in important and interesting ways. The Americans consistently emphasized hedonism, materialism, individuality, creativity, and issues of time and space consistent with a society in which time is segmented and viewed almost as a commodity (more on this in Chapter 10). Conversely, the Dutch respondents showed a concern for social and environmental responsibility, collective societal order and equality, and a balance between work and play as part of paradise. For instance, one Dutch student said that 'Respect for animals, flowers, and plants . . . regenerating energy sources, such as wind, water, and sun' are all important parts of paradise. Marketers should expect that, because concepts of paradise differ somewhat, different images and behaviours may be evoked when Americans and Dutch are confronted with marketing messages such as 'Hawaii is Paradise', or 'you can experience paradise when you drive this car'.[36]

A Dutch respondent's collage emphasises this person's conception of paradise as a place where there is interpersonal harmony and concern for the environment.

■ CONSUMER INVOLVEMENT

Do consumers form strong relationships with products and services? If you don't believe so, consider these recent events:

- A consumer in Brighton, England loves a local restaurant called the All In One so much, he had its name and phone number tattooed on his forehead. The owner remarked, '. . . whenever he comes in, he'll go straight to the front of the queue'.[37]

- *Lucky* is a magazine devoted to shopping for shoes and other fashion accessories. The centrefold of the first issue featured rows of make-up sponges. The editor observes, 'It's the same way that you might look at a golf magazine and see a spread of nine irons. *Lucky* is addressing one interest in women's lives, in a really obsessive, specific way.'[38]

These examples illustrate that people can get pretty attached to products. As we have seen, a consumer's motivation to attain a goal increases his or her desire to expend the effort necessary to acquire the products or services he or she believes will be instrumental in satisfying that goal. However, not everyone is motivated to the same extent – one person might be convinced he or she can't live without the latest style or modern convenience, whereas another is not interested in this item at all.

▶ Involvement is defined as 'a person's perceived relevance of the object based on their inherent needs, values, and interests'.[39] The word *object* is used in the generic sense and refers to a product (or a brand), an advertisement, or a purchase situation. Consumers can find involvement in all these *objects*. Figure 4.3 shows that because involvement is a motivational construct, different antecedents can trigger it. These factors can be something about the person, something about the object, or something about the situation, which can combine to determine the consumer's motivation to process product-related information at a given point in time. When consumers are intent on doing what they can to satisfy a need, they will be motivated to pay attention and process any information felt to be relevant to achieving their goals.

On the other hand, a person may not bother to pay any attention to the same information if it is not seen as relevant to satisfying some need. Tessel, for instance, who prides herself on her knowledge of the environment and green issues, may read everything she can find about the subject, while another person may skip over this information without giving it a second thought.

Figure 4.3 Conceptualizing components of involvement

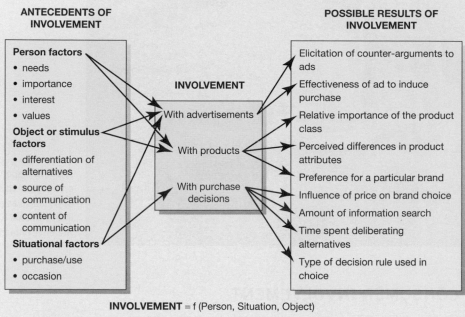

INVOLVEMENT = f (Person, Situation, Object)

The level of involvement may be influenced by one or more of these factors. Interactions among persons, situation, and object factors are likely to occur.

Involvement can be viewed as the motivation to process information.[40] To the degree that there is a perceived linkage between a consumer's needs, goals or values and product knowledge, the consumer will be motivated to pay attention to product information. When relevant knowledge is activated in memory, a motivational state is created that drives behaviour (e.g. shopping). As felt involvement with a product increases, the consumer devotes more attention to ads related to the product, exerts more cognitive effort to understand these ads, and focuses more attention on the product-related information in them.[41] However, this kind of 'rational' involvement may be the exception rather than the rule, even for such products as stereos, TVs and VCRs, as a company executive from Philips once argued.[42]

Levels of involvement: from inertia to passion

The type of information processing that will occur thus depends on the consumer's level of involvement. It can range from *simple processing*, where only the basic features of a message are considered, all the way to *elaboration*, where the incoming information is linked to one's pre-existing knowledge system.[43]

Inertia

We can think of a person's degree of involvement as a continuum, ranging from absolute lack of interest in a marketing stimulus at one end to obsession at the other. Consumption at the low end of involvement is characterized by **inertia**, where decisions are made out of habit because the consumer lacks the motivation to consider alternatives. At the high end of involvement, we can expect to find the type of passionate intensity reserved for people and objects that carry great meaning for the individual. Celebrity worship is evident in activities ranging from autograph collections to the sky-high prices fetched at auctions by possessions that used to belong to stars such as John Lennon, Elton

Lang Gysi Knoll

Rezepte gegen die Langeweile: www.kartoffel.ch

The Swiss Potato Board is trying to increase involvement with its product. The ad reads, 'Recipes against boredom'.
Swisspatat

John or Jimi Hendrix. For the most part, however, a consumer's involvement level with products falls somewhere in the middle, and the marketing strategist must determine the relative level of importance to understand how much elaboration of product information will occur.

▶ When consumers are truly involved with a product, an ad or a website, they enter what has been called a **flow state**. This state is the Holy Grail of web designers who want to create sites that are so entrancing that the surfer loses all track of time as he or she becomes engrossed in the site's contents (and hopefully buys things in the process!). Flow is an optimal experience characterized by:

● a sense of playfulness;

● a feeling of being in control;

● concentration and highly focused attention;

● mental enjoyment of the activity for its own sake;

● a distorted sense of time;

● a match between the challenge at hand and one's skills.[44]

Cult products

▶ **Cult products** command fierce consumer loyalty, devotion – and maybe even worship by consumers who are very highly involved with a brand. These items take many forms, from Apple computers and Harley-Davidson motorcycles to Barbie dolls and Manchester United football strips. What else explains a willingness to pay up to $3,400 for a pair of shoes designed by Manolo Blahnik?

Loyal users can log in and hang out at the Jones Soda Web site.
http://www.jonessoda.com/index.html.
Courtesy of Jones Soda Co.

marketing opportunity

Anyone who can create a cult brand goes straight to marketing heaven, but this is very difficult to do from scratch. One entrepreneur is well on his way. In 1996 Peter van Stolk was barely getting shelf space for his Jones Soda brand. He started putting his colourful drinks in unconventional places like record stores, hair salons, tattoo parlors, even sex shops. After a buzz started around Jones, van Stolk stoked it by asking fans to send him their photographs, which he plastered on his labels. The company's website (**www.jonessoda.com**) has become a forum for Jones fans to chat about school, life or soda.[45]

The many faces of involvement

As previously defined, involvement can take many forms. It can be cognitive, as when a 'webhead' is motivated to learn all she can about the latest spec of a new multimedia PC, or emotional, as when the thought of a new Armani suit gives a clotheshorse goose pimples.[46] Further, the very act of buying the Armani may be very involving for people who are passionately devoted to shopping. To complicate matters further, advertisements, such as those produced for Nike or Adidas, may themselves be involving for some reason (for example, because they make us laugh, cry, or inspire us to work harder). It seems that involvement is a fuzzy concept, because it overlaps with other things and means different things to different people. Indeed, the consensus is that there are actually several broad types of involvement related to the product, the message, or the perceiver.[47]

Product involvement is related to a consumer's level of interest in a particular product. Many sales promotions are designed to increase this type of involvement.

Message–response involvement (also known as *advertising involvement*), refers to the consumer's interest in processing marketing communications.[48] Television is considered a low-involvement medium because it requires a passive viewer who exerts relatively little control (remote control 'zapping' notwithstanding) over content. In contrast, print is often seen as a high-involvement medium. The reader is actively involved in processing the information and is able to pause and reflect on what he or she has read before moving on.[49] We'll discuss the role of message characteristics in changing attitudes in Chapter 6.

nc2
by Nu Colour

WILD AT EMOTIONS

Many marketing messages, such as this ad for a cosmetics company in Taiwan, focus on emotions rather than cognitions.
Pao&Paws Ad Agency

marketing opportunity

Quick Burger, France's second largest fast-food chain, discovered a route to increasing customers' involvement. The company became a partner in a marketing programme called Multipoints, an interactive service which allowed consumers to collect points that could then be redeemed for discounts and prizes. More than 70,000 French consumers signed up for the service. Using a device that resembled a calculator, participants entered codes they found in print ads and advertising hoardings or heard on radio programmes. They could even hold the device against their TV screens during programming that was specially encoded to dispense credits. People could win points for playing along with certain game shows and answering questions correctly. They could then redeem their points for merchandise at Quick Burger restaurants and other locations (including selected travel agencies and news-stands) by plugging their device into a computer terminal. The hamburger chain awarded consumers 500 free points per week just for visiting, which gave them additional motivation to patronize Quick Burger instead of its arch-rival, McDonald's.[50]

Purchase situation involvement refers to differences that may occur when buying the same object for different contexts. Here the person may perceive a great deal of social risk or none at all. For example, when you want to impress someone you may try to buy a brand or a product with a certain image that you think reflects good taste. When you have to buy a gift for someone in an obligatory situation, like a wedding gift for a cousin you do not really like, you may not care what image the gift portrays. Or you may actually pick something cheap that reflects your desire to distance yourself from that cousin.

Ego involvement (sometimes described as *enduring involvement*) refers to the importance of a product to a consumer's self-concept. This concept implies a high level of social risk: the prospect of the product not performing its desired function may result in embarrassment or damage to the consumer's self-concept (Chapter 7 is devoted to the importance

Table 4.2 A scale to measure product involvement

To me (object to be judged) is		
1 Important	_:_:_:_:_:_:_	Unimportant*
2 Boring	_:_:_:_:_:_:_	Interesting
3 Relevant	_:_:_:_:_:_:_	Irrelevant*
4 Exciting	_:_:_:_:_:_:_	Unexciting*
5 Means nothing	_:_:_:_:_:_:_	Means a lot to me
6 Appealing	_:_:_:_:_:_:_	Unappealing*
7 Fascinating	_:_:_:_:_:_:_	Mundane*
8 Worthless	_:_:_:_:_:_:_	Valuable
9 Involving	_:_:_:_:_:_:_	Uninvolving*
10 Not needed	_:_:_:_:_:_:_	Needed

Note: Totalling the ten items gives a score from a low of 10 to a high of 70.
*Indicates item is reverse scored. For example, a score of 7 for item no. 1 (important/unimportant) would actually be scored as 1.

Source: Judith Lynne Zaichkowsky, 'The Personal Involvement Inventory: Reduction, revision, and application to advertising', *Journal of Advertising* 23(4) (December 1994): 59-70.

of the self-concept for consumer behaviour issues). For example, Tessel's vegetarianism and interest in green issues are clearly an important part of her self-identity (her choice of organic foods are said to have high sign value). This type of involvement is independent of particular purchase situations. It is an ongoing concern related to the self and often hedonic or experiential experiences (the emotions felt as a result of using products).[51]

Measuring involvement

The measurement of involvement is important for many marketing applications. For example, research evidence indicates that a viewer who is more involved with a television show will also respond more positively to commercials contained in that show, and that these spots will have a greater chance of influencing his or her purchase intentions.[52] The many conceptualizations of involvement have led to some confusion about the best way to measure the concept. One of the most widely used measures of the state of involvement is the scale shown in Table 4.2.

Teasing out the dimensions of involvement

Two French researchers devised a scale to measure the antecedents of product involvement, arguing that no single component of involvement is predominant. Recognizing that consumers can be involved with a product because it is a risky purchase and/or its use reflects on or affects the self, they advocate the development of an *involvement profile* containing five components:[53]

1 The personal interest a consumer has in a product category, its personal meaning or importance.

2 The perceived importance of the potential negative consequences associated with a poor choice of product (risk importance).

3 The probability of making a bad purchase.

4 The pleasure value of the product category.

5 The sign value of the product category (how closely it's related to the self).

Table 4.3 Involvement profiles for a set of French consumer products

	Importance of negative consequences	Subjective probability of mispurchase	Pleasure value	Sign value
Dresses	121	112	147	181
Bras	117	115	106	130
Washing machines	118	109	106	111
TV sets	112	100	122	95
Vacuum cleaners	110	112	70	78
Irons	103	95	72	76
Champagne	109	120	125	125
Oil	89	97	65	92
Yogurt	86	83	106	78
Chocolate	80	89	123	75
Shampoo	96	103	90	81
Toothpaste	95	95	94	105
Toilet soap	82	90	114	118
Detergents	79	82	56	63

Average product score = 100.

Source: Gilles Laurent and Jean-Noël Kapferer, 'Measuring consumer involvement profiles', *Journal of Marketing Research* 22 (February 1985): 45, Table 3.

These researchers asked a sample of homemakers to rate a set of 14 product categories on each of the facets of involvement. The results are shown in Table 4.3. These data indicate that no single component captures consumer involvement. For example, the purchase of a durable product such as a vacuum cleaner is seen as risky, because one is stuck with a bad choice for many years. However, the vacuum cleaner does not provide pleasure (hedonic value), nor is it high in sign value (i.e. its use is not related to the person's self-concept).[54] In contrast, chocolate is high in pleasure value but is not seen as risky or closely related to the self. Dresses and bras, on the other hand, appear to be involving for a combination of reasons.

Segmenting by involvement levels

A measurement approach of this nature allows consumer researchers to capture the diversity of the involvement construct, and it also provides the potential to use involvement as a basis for market segmentation. For example, a yogurt manufacturer might find that even though its product is low in sign value for one group of consumers, it might be highly related to the self-concept of another market segment, such as health food enthusiasts or avid dieters. The company could adapt its strategy to account for the motivation of different segments to process information about the product. These variations are discussed in Chapter 6. Note also that involvement with a product class may vary across cultures. While this sample of French consumers rated champagne high in both sign value and personal value, the ability of champagne to provide pleasure or be central to self-definition might not transfer to other countries. For example, whereas a typical French family would find champagne an absolutely essential part of the celebration of a marriage, a Danish family, especially from a rural area, might find consumption of champagne an excessive luxury and perhaps also to some extent a sign of decadence.[55]

Strategies to increase involvement

Although consumers differ in their level of involvement with respect to a product message, marketers do not just have to sit back and hope for the best. By being aware of some basic factors that increase or decrease attention, they can take steps to increase the likelihood that product information will get through. A marketer can boost consumers' motivations to process relevant information by using one or more of the following techniques:[56]

- *Appeal to the consumers' hedonic needs.* For example, ads using sensory appeals generate higher levels of attention.[57]

- *Use novel stimuli, such as unusual cinematography, sudden silences, or unexpected movements in commercials.* When a British firm called Egg Banking introduced a credit card to the French market in 2002, its advertising agency created unusual commercials to make people question their assumptions. One ad stated 'Cats always land on their paws', and then two researchers in white lab coats dropped a kitten off a rooftop – never to see it again (animal rights activists were not amused).[58]

- *Use prominent stimuli, such as loud music and fast action, to capture attention in commercials.* In print formats, larger ads increase attention. Also, viewers look longer at coloured pictures as opposed to black and white.

- *Include celebrity endorsers to generate higher interest in commercials.* (We'll discuss this strategy in Chapter 6.)

- *Build a bond with consumers by maintaining an ongoing relationship with them.* The routes to cultivating brand loyalty will be discussed further in Chapter 8.

- *The internet has provided companies with new possibilities for creating loyalty bonds with customers.* For example, girls can customize their own doll at Mattel's My Design website, located at **www.barbie.com/mydesign**. They can specify her skin tone, hair and eye colour and outfits. They can also name the doll, and she comes with a personality profile they can tailor from choices on the website.[59]

net profit

It's human nature to be more involved with a product that's directly relevant to your individual wants and needs. One of the exciting advantages of the internet is the ability to *personalize* content, so that a website offers unique information or products tailored to each web surfer. Consider these different approaches to personalization that build the different kinds of involvement we've been discussing:

- *Product involvement*: A recent survey found that 75 per cent of American adults want more customized products and – more importantly – 70 per cent are willing to pay extra for them. This desire is even more acute among young people; 85 per cent of 18-24-year-olds want more customized products, particularly in such domains as clothing, shoes, electronics and travel services.[60] **Venturoma.com** lets the shopper create her own blend of massage oils, skin creams or body washes, while **Customatix.com** lets you design your own sports and casual shoes. In Asia, Coca-Cola is testing its 'Style-A-Coke' shrink-wrap system that lets consumers customize their Coke bottles with different sleeve designs.[61]

- *Message-response involvement*: An advertising campaign in the Netherlands directs teens to a Web-design site where they can create their own Coca-Cola commercials. At the end of the month, about 10 to 15 finalists will appear on a website, where people can view them and vote for their favourite.[62] In a more powerful application of this idea, a British ad for a homeless charity lets viewers create their own message by selecting different story lines. The ad traces the story of Paul, a teenager from a troubled family. Viewers can click to make different choices for Paul as his fortunes decline, such as whether to report his bullying stepfather to the police, or whether to prostitute himself ('To have sex for money press Green now').[63] Or, how about film posters that talk back to you? ThinkPix Smart Displays are part of a new wave of posters that will enable a celebrity on the wall to wink at you as you pass by. And, to personalize the process, film-goers will insert a card indicating their tastes in order to see posters that show trailers featuring stars they like.[64]

● *Purchase situation involvement*: To a denizen of the online world, a *skin* is a graphical interface that acts as both the face and the control panel of a computer program. Rather than settling for the boring skins that come with most programs, many people prefer to make and trade their own unique ones. According to the product manager for RealPlayer, 'This kind of customization is a huge factor in driving product use . . . We're getting into a world where one size doesn't fit all, and one of the great benefits of technology is having the experience tailored to you'. In addition to the more than 15 million skins that have been created for RealPlayer, many other games, including The Sims and the multiplayer Unreal Tournament have websites devoted to user-created skins. Players swap skins of the Incredible Hulk or Rambo or even playable skins of themselves. Film companies and record labels now routinely commission artists to create promotional skins for films like *Blow* and *Frequency* and for music artists like U2, Britney Spears and 'N Sync.[65]

■ VALUES

▶ Generally speaking, a **value** can be defined as a belief about some desirable end-state that transcends specific situations and guides selection of behaviour.[66] Thus, values are general and different from attitudes in that they do not apply to specific situations only. A person's set of values plays a very important role in his or her consumption activities, since many products and services are purchased because (it is believed) they will help us to attain a value-related goal. Two people can believe in the same behaviours (for example, vegetarianism) but their underlying belief systems may be quite different (animal activism vs. health concerns). The extent to which people share a belief system is a function of individual, social and cultural forces. Advocates of a belief system often seek out others with similar beliefs, so that social networks overlap and as a result believers tend to be exposed to information that supports their beliefs (e.g. environmentalists rarely socialize with factory farmers).[67]

As we'll see in Chapters 16 and 17, the specific values that motivate people vary across cultures, yet within each culture there is usually a set of underlying goals that most members of that culture agree are important. One comparison of management practices concerning industrial buying behaviour in Europe and North America concluded that, in Europe, development of relationships is seen as more important, whereas in North America, rigour and competitiveness are the key issues.[68] Such differences may be interpreted as pointing to fundamental differences in values in the business worlds of the two continents. But large differences can also be detected within Europe, for example between the Anglo-Saxon approach, which is closer to the American model described above, and the Germanic-Alpine (including Scandinavia) model, which is more oriented towards the relationship approach.[69]

Core values

▶ Every culture has a set of **core values** that it imparts to its members.[70] For example, people in one culture might feel that being a unique individual is preferable to subordinating one's identity to the group, while another group may emphasize the virtues of group membership. In many cases, values are universal. Who does not desire health, wisdom or world peace? But on the other hand, values do change over time. In Japan young people are working hard to adopt Western values and behaviours – which explains why the current fashion for young people is bleached, blond hair, chalky make-up and a deep tan. Government policies have encouraged this type of consumer spending. However, changing patterns of consumption have increased feelings of personal liberation among the younger generation. They are now challenging many of the values of the past as shown, for instance, by the increasing school drop-out rate, which has grown by 20 per cent.[71] Similar concerns about the consequences of what is often called a value crisis are also discussed in European societies. Likewise, one may wonder what happened to the traditional Scandinavian modesty – in both Denmark and Sweden people are now showing more willingness to share their private lives with thousands of others in either talk shows or docu-soaps of the *Big Brother* variety.

Sometimes, one must be careful of interpreting social events in terms of values. For example, a hugely successful advertisement in Japan promoted breast cancer awareness by showing an attractive woman in a sundress drawing stares from men on the street as a voice-over said, 'If only women paid as much attention to their breasts as men do'. The same ad flopped in France – according to the *Wall Street Journal* because the use of humour to talk about a serious disease offended the French.[72] Does this seem like a plausible explanation to you?

Value systems

One perspective on the study of values stresses that what sets cultures apart is the *relative importance*, or ranking, of these universal values. This set of rankings constitutes a culture's **value system**.[73] To illustrate the difference in value systems, consider the results of a comparison between the adherence to a set of values in a variety of countries (see Table 4.4).[74] What can one draw from such a table? In one of the studies that constituted this table, Norway, Germany and the USA were compared.[75] The value of sense of belonging is very important in Germany and Norway, but much less so in the United States, which is consistent with many other studies underlining the individualistic character of the American culture. Likewise, the value of security is very important in Germany and the United States but much less so in Norway. The results seem to indicate that the value of security in the United States is understood in terms of social security, whereas in Germany it is understood more in terms of social relationships. In Norway it is interpreted much as in the United States but it does not represent the same importance due to the elaborate social security of the Norwegian welfare state: they are simply inclined to take security for granted. Thus, it is obvious that unless one understands the context, one may draw very erroneous conclusions from this kind of research, for instance that security is not very important.

Table 4.4 Distribution of LOV (List of Values) values in different countries (% rating as most important value)

	Germany	USA	Norway	France	Denmark	USSR	Japan
Self-fulfilment	4.8	9.6	7.7	30.9	7.1	8.8	36.7
Sense of belonging	28.6	7.9	33.4	1.7	13.0	23.9	2.3
Security	24.1	20.6	10.0	6.3	6.3	5.7	10.9
Self-respect	12.9	21.1	16.6	7.4	29.7	10.1	4.7
Warm relationships with others	7.9	16.2	13.4	17.7	11.3	23.3	27.6
Fun and enjoyment in life/Excitement*	10.1	4.5	3.6	16.6	16.8	9.7	7.5
Being well respected	6.1	8.8	8.4	4.0	5.0	8.5	2.1
Sense of accomplishment	5.4	11.4	6.8	15.4	10.9	10.1	8.3

*The value 'excitement' was collapsed into 'fun and enjoyment' because just a negligible percentage in certain samples selected this as the most important value.

Source: Reprinted from Lynn Kahle, Sharon Beatty and John Mager, 'Implications of Social Values for Consumer Communications: The Case of the European Community', in B. Englis, ed., *Global and Multinational Advertising* (Hillsdale, NJ: Lawrence Erlbaum Ass.): 47-64.

Many advertisements appeal to people's values to persuade them to change or modify their behaviours. This ad, sponsored by the city of Paris, says to dog owners: 'you are quite right not to clean up after your dog. After all, he'll take care of that for you'.

The Advertising Archives

Every culture is characterized by its members' endorsement of a value system. These end-states may not be equally endorsed by everyone, and in some cases values may even seem to contradict one another (e.g. westerners in general appear to value both conformity and individuality and seek to find some accommodation between the two). Nonetheless, it is usually possible to identify a general set of *core values* which uniquely define a culture. These beliefs are taught to us by *socialization agents*, including parents, friends and teachers. The process of learning the beliefs and behaviours endorsed by one's own culture is termed **enculturation**. In contrast, the process of learning the value system and behaviours of another culture (often a priority for those who wish to understand consumers and markets in foreign countries) is called **acculturation**.[76]

As we saw in the example above, such core values must be understood in the local context – that is, the meaning of the values changes when the cultural context shifts. 'Security' is *not* the same for English, Scandinavian, German and Italian consumers. This is a serious challenge to the idea that it is possible to compare value systems by studying the rankings of universal sets of values across countries.

Applications of values to consumer behaviour

Despite their importance, values have not been as widely applied to direct examinations of consumer behaviour as might be expected. One reason is that broad-based concepts such as freedom, security, or inner harmony are more likely to affect general purchasing patterns than to differentiate between brands within a product category. For this reason, some researchers have found it convenient to make distinctions among broad-based *cultural values* such as security or happiness, *consumption-specific values* such as convenient shopping or prompt service, and *product-specific values* such as ease of use or durability, that affect the relative importance people in different cultures place on possessions.[77] However, such a distinction may border on abusing the value concept, since it is normally taken to represent the most general and profound level in the social psychological hierarchy.

While some aspects of brand image such as sophistication tend to be common across cultures, others are more likely to be relevant in specific places. The characteristic of peacefulness is valued to a larger extent in Japan, while the same holds true for passion in Spain and ruggedness in the USA.[78] Because values drive much of consumer behaviour (at least in a very general sense), we might say that virtually all consumer research ultimately is related to the identification and measurement of values. This

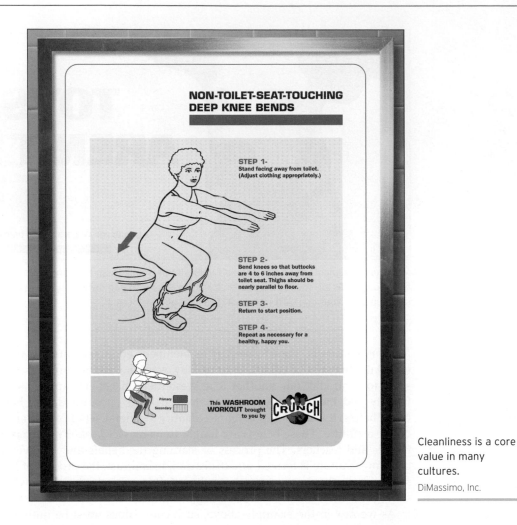

Cleanliness is a core value in many cultures.

DiMassimo, Inc.

process can take many forms, ranging from qualitative research techniques such as ethnography to quantitative techniques such as laboratory experiments and large-scale surveys. This section will describe some specific attempts by researchers to measure cultural values and apply this knowledge to marketing strategy.

A number of companies track changes in values through large-scale surveys. For instance, one Young and Rubicam study tracked the new segment of single, professional career women without any ambitions of creating a family. They are among the highest consuming segments and are characterized by central values such as freedom and independence.[79] Some of these services are discussed in Chapter 15. Many companies use value inventories in order to adapt their strategies. SAS, the airline, which for a long time addressed 'hard values' of their key segment, business travellers, realized that this segment had started to express more informal and 'softer' values, and they changed their communication profile accordingly.[80]

Such ideas are reflected in a recent theory of consumer value. According to this theory, value for a consumer is the consumer's evaluation of a consumer object in terms of which general benefit the consumer might get from consuming it.[81] As such, the value at stake in consumption is tied much more to the consumption experience than to general existential values of the person. Thus, it is suggested that the consumer experience may generate eight distinct types of consumer value:

● *Efficiency* – referring to all products aimed at providing various kinds of convenience for the consumer.

- *Excellence* – addressing situations where the experience of quality is the prime motivation.
- *Status* – when the consumer pursues success and engages in impression management and conspicuous consumption.
- *(Self-)Esteem* – situations where the satisfaction of possessing is in focus, as is the case with materialism.
- *Play* – the value of having fun in consuming.
- *Aesthetics* – searching for beauty in one's consumption of, e.g., designer products, fashion or art.
- *Ethics* – referring to motivations behind, e.g., morally or politically correct consumption choices.
- *Spirituality* – experiencing magical transformations or sacredness in the consumption, as known from devoted collectors.[82]

marketing pitfall

Sometimes companies may overestimate the change in values. This could be the case for the discussion about the 'rudest poster advertisement of the summer' in 2000, an ad for Organics Colour Active Shampoo featuring a young woman on the beach peering down her own bikini bottoms juxtaposed with the declaration 'keeps hair colour so long, you'll forget your natural one'. However, maybe the provocation was deliberate – at least, no plans were announced to withdraw the campaign voluntarily.[83]

marketing opportunity

The values treasured by a culture create opportunities for new products that might seem strange or a bit excessive to foreigners. Consider the 'toilet wars' now under way in Japan, as companies vie with each other to produce the most sophisticated and luxurious bathroom fixture.

Why the commotion over commodes? As one marketing executive explains, in a Japanese house 'the only place you can be alone and sit quietly is likely to be the toilet'. Take cramped living conditions, and then factor in a love of new technology. Now, add a strong cultural emphasis on cleanliness: Many Japanese wear gloves to protect themselves from strangers' germs and some ATM machines dispense cash that's been sanitized (yes, banks literally 'launder' their money!). Nearly half of Japanese homes already have toilets with a water jet spray used to wash and massage the buttocks. Let the games begin:

- It all started when Matsushita unveiled a toilet seat equipped with electrodes that send a mild electric charge through the user's buttocks, yielding a digital measurement of body-fat ratio.
- Engineers from Inax counterattacked with a toilet that glows in the dark. When in use, the toilet plays any of six soundtracks, including chirping birds, rushing water, tinkling wind chimes, or the strumming of a traditional Japanese harp.
- Matsushita retaliated with a $3,000 throne that greets a user by flipping its lid, and by blasting its twin air nozzles that provide air-conditioning in the summer and heat in the winter.
- Toto weighed in with the WellyouII model that automatically measures the user's urine sugar levels by making a collection with a little spoon held by a retractable, mechanical arm.
- What's next? Matsushita is working on devices to measure weight, heartbeat, blood pressure and other health indicators; the toilet will send results to a doctor via a built in Internet-capable cell phone. Also in the works are talking toilets equipped with microchips that will greet each user with a personalized message such as words of encouragement from Mom, and soon people will be able to give their toilets simple verbal commands.[84]

Table 4.5 Two types of values in the Rokeach Value Survey

Instrumental values	Terminal values
Ambitious	A comfortable life
Broadminded	An exciting life
Capable	A sense of accomplishment
Cheerful	A world at peace
Clean	A world of beauty
Courageous	Equality
Forgiving	Family security
Helpful	Freedom
Honest	Happiness
Imaginative	Inner harmony
Independent	Mature love
Intellectual	National security
Logical	Pleasure
Loving	Salvation
Obedient	Self-respect
Polite	Social recognition
Responsible	True friendship
Self-controlled	Wisdom

Source: Richard W. Pollay, 'Measuring the cultural values manifest in advertising', *Current Issues and Research in Advertising* (1983): 71–92.

The Rokeach Value Survey

▶ The psychologist Milton Rokeach identified a set of **terminal values**, or desired end-states, that apply (to various degrees) to many different cultures. The *Rokeach Value*
▶ *Survey*, a scale used to measure these values, also includes a set of **instrumental values**, which are composed of actions needed to achieve these terminal values.[85] Table 4.5 lists these two sets of values. These sets of values have been used in many studies, for example to investigate the changes in the value system of post-Soviet Russia.[86]

The List of Values (LOV)

Although some evidence indicates that differences in these global values do translate into product-specific preferences and differences in media usage, the Rokeach Value Survey has not been widely applied to consumer behaviour issues.[87] One reason is that many societies are evolving into smaller and smaller sets of *consumption microcultures* within the larger culture, each with its own set of core values. As an alternative, the *List of Values (LOV) scale* was developed to isolate values with more direct marketing applications.[88]

This instrument identifies nine consumer values which can be related to differences in consumption behaviours. It includes the following values: sense of belonging, fun and enjoyment in life, excitement, warm relationships with others, self-fulfilment, being well respected, sense of accomplishment, self-respect and security. This was the instrument used in the studies summarized in Table 4.4 on page 114. Likewise, in a comparative study of French and German consumers, the values of sense of belonging and self-respect were much more popular in Germany, whereas the values of fun and enjoyment in life, self-fulfilment and self-accomplishment were chosen as the most important values in France significantly more often.[89]

However, it should be noted that the cross-cultural validity of such value instruments is, at best, difficult to obtain since, as we have already said, the meaning of values may differ significantly in different cultural contexts.[90] For example, the LOV did not do very well in a test of its cross-cultural validity.[91,92]

Figure 4.4 The motivational domains of Schwartz value survey

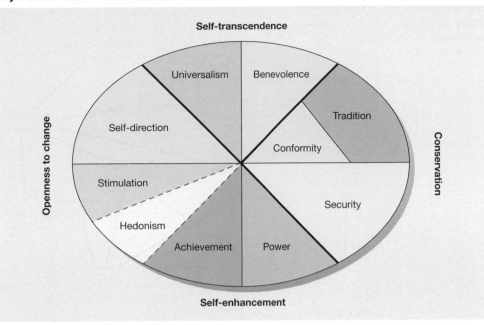

Schwartz value survey

This very elaborate set of values, containing 56 different values organized in ten so-called motivational domains, has been demonstrated to be among the more cross-culturally valid instruments.[93] The structuring of values in interrelated motivational domains provides a theoretical framework for this approach to values which many researchers find satisfactory compared to other value inventories. More specifically, it has been demonstrated to distinguish between cultures[94] and types of media consumption behaviour[95] better than the traditional dichotomy of individualism and collectivism. The values are located in a space demarcated by the poles 'openness to change' vs. 'conservation' and 'self-transcendence' vs. 'self-enhancement'. These dimensions seem relatively universal for a lot of syndicated lifestyle and value surveys (see also Chapter 16). A mapping of the motivational domains can be seen in Figure 4.4. The Schwartz value survey was used to profile Danish consumers with environmentally friendly attitudes and behaviour, where it turned out that such values as 'protecting the environment' and 'unity with nature' but also 'mature love', 'broadminded' and 'social justice' characterized the 'green' segment, whereas values such as 'authority', 'social power', 'national security' and 'politeness' were the most characteristic of the non-green segment.[96] (See also Chapter 9.)

■ THE MEANS-END CHAIN MODEL

▶ Another research approach that incorporates values is termed a **means-end chain model**. This approach assumes that very specific product attributes are linked at levels of increasing abstraction to terminal values. The person has valued end-states, and he or she chooses among alternative means to attain these goals. Products are thus valued as the

▶ means to an end. Through a technique called **laddering**, consumers' associations between specific attributes and general consequences are uncovered. Consumers are helped to climb up the 'ladder' of abstraction that connects functional product attributes with desired end-states.[97] Based upon consumer feedback, researchers create *hierarchical value maps* that show how specific product attributes get linked to end-states (see Figure 4.5).

Figure 4.5
Hierarchical value maps for vegetable oil in three countries

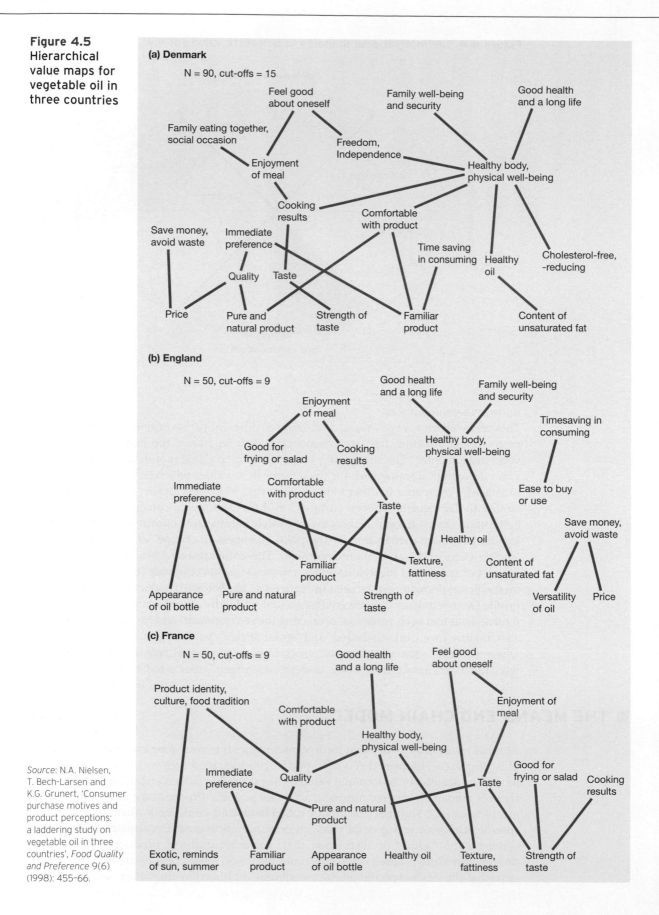

Source: N.A. Nielsen, T. Bech-Larsen and K.G. Grunert, 'Consumer purchase motives and product perceptions: a laddering study on vegetable oil in three countries', *Food Quality and Preference* 9(6) (1998): 455–66.

To understand how laddering works, consider somebody who expresses a liking for a light beer. Probing might reveal that this attribute is linked to the consequence of not getting drunk. A consequence of not getting drunk is that he or she will be able to enjoy more interesting conversations, which in turn means that he or she will be more sociable. Finally, better sociability results in better friendship, a terminal value for this person.[98]

Laddering is not without problems, however, since the laddering technique might generate invalid answers if the respondent is pushed up the ladder by too strong an emphasis on the sequence in the means–end chain. Consumers should be allowed to jump back and forth, to make loops and forks and take blind alleys, which requires more skill of the interviewer but is also a more accurate representation of the respondent's thought processes.[99] Furthermore, it has been argued that in researching the demand for status goods, using laddering techniques can be problematic since motivations for conspicuous consumption are difficult for consumers to express or reveal.[100]

MECCAs

The notion that products are consumed because they are instrumental in attaining more abstract values is central to one application of this technique, called the Means–End Conceptualization of the Components of Advertising Strategy (MECCAs). In this approach, researchers first generate a map depicting relationships between functional product or service attributes and terminal values. This information is then used to develop advertising strategy by identifying elements such as the following:[101]

- *Message elements:* the specific attributes or product features to be depicted.
- *Consumer benefit:* the positive consequences of using the product or service.
- *Executional framework:* the overall style and tone of the advertisement.
- *Leverage point*: the way the message will activate the terminal value by linking it with specific product features.
- *Driving force:* the end value on which the advertising will focus.

This technique was used to develop an advertising strategy for the Danish fish trade organization.[102] In spite of the country's huge fishing industry and ample supply of fresh fish, the Danish consumption of fish per capita was considerably lower than in several other European countries. Researchers used a means–end approach to investigate Danish consumers' attitudes to eating fish. They concluded that some of the main problems were found in the lack of ideas for preparation and variation of fished-based meals among Danish housewives. This was in sharp contrast to the traditional driving force used by the organization, stressing that fish is healthy.[103]

Based on these results, an advertising campaign was created. Instead of its usual emphasis on fish as a healthy food, this time message elements emphasized convenience and good taste. The consumer benefit was quick and easy preparation, which made dinner or lunch an easy task to accomplish. The executional framework was a humorous one. Two middle-aged, traditional-looking people are portrayed in various situations, where the male is sceptical about the idea of eating fish for lunch or dinner. In one of the TV spots, the wife is talking to somebody else over the telephone. Her remarks lead the TV viewers (and the husband listening in the background) to think that they are talking about the other family's sex life ('You do it TWICE a week!' 'It takes FIFTEEN minutes!!!' 'So HE likes that?'). In fact, a friend is telling the wife how she prepares fish for dinner. The leverage point is that these recipes allow the wife to prepare delicious meals very quickly, which in turn provides for a happy family life, the driving force (terminal value). Almost immediately after the campaign, the trade organization registered an increase in the consumption of fresh fish.

Figure 4.5 shows three different hierarchical value maps, or sets of ladders, from a study of consumers' perceptions and motivations with regard to cooking oils. The three ladders demonstrate some important differences between the three markets. Health is the central concept most often referred to for the Danes and is linked to several personal values. The British also focus on health but the links to personal values are fewer and less differentiated, indicating a lower product involvement. Saving money and avoiding waste is more important to the British than to the other samples. The French focus a lot on previous knowledge of the product, indicating more routine with buying oils. Theirs is also the only culture that links oil (especially olive oil) with cultural identity and fundamental food culture.[104] These ladders illustrate the central importance of cultural and contextual differences for consumers' motivation structures.

Syndicated surveys

A number of companies who track changes in values through large-scale surveys sell the results of these studies to marketers, who often also pay a fee to receive regular updates on changes and trends. This approach originated in the mid-1960s. As we'll see in later chapters, it's often useful to go beyond simple demographics like a person's age to understand the values and preferences a group of people might have in common. This philosophy applies to understanding the youth market – as much as adults would like to lump all young people together, in fact there are important differences among them in terms of what they value and these priorities may mean that they have more in common with a young person halfway around the globe than with the person next door.

The *New World Teen Study* surveyed over 27,000 teenagers in 44 countries and identified six values segments that characterize young people from Cairo to Caracas. Companies like Coca-Cola and Royal Philips Electronics have used the results of this massive segmentation exercise to develop ads that appeal to youth around the world. Table 4.6 summarizes some of the findings from this study.

marketing pitfall

Strongly held values can make life very difficult for marketers who sell personal-care products. This is the case with tampons; 70 per cent of American women use them, but only 100 million out of a potential market of 1.7 billion eligible women around the world do. Resistance to using this product posed a major problem for Tambrands. This company makes only one product, so it needs to sell tampons in as many countries as possible to continue growing. But, Tambrands has trouble selling its feminine hygiene products in some cultures such as Brazil, where many young women fear they will lose their virginity if they use a tampon. A commercial developed for this market included an actress who says in a reassuring voice, 'Of course, you're not going to lose your virginity'.

Prior to launching a new global advertising campaign for Tampax in 26 countries, the firm's advertising agency conducted research and divided the world into three clusters based on residents' resistance to using tampons. Resistance was so intense in Muslim countries that the agency didn't even try to sell there.

In Cluster One (including the United States, the United Kingdom, and Australia), women felt comfortable with the idea and offered little resistance. A teaser ad was developed to encourage more frequency of use: 'Should I sleep with it, or not?'

In Cluster Two (including France, Israel, and South Africa), about 50 per cent of women use the product, but some concerns about the loss of virginity remain. To counteract these objections, the marketing strategy focused on obtaining the endorsements of gynaecologists within each country.

In Cluster Three (including Brazil, China, and Russia), Tambrands encountered the greatest resistance. To try to make inroads in these countries, the researchers found that the first priority is simply to explain how to use the product without making women feel squeamish - a challenge they still are trying to puzzle out. If they do - and that's a big if - Tambrands will have changed the consumer behaviour of millions of women and added huge new markets to its customer base in the process.[105]

Table 4.6 New World Teen Study

Segment	Key countries	Driving principles	Overview	Marketing approach
Thrills and Chills	Germany, England, Lithuania, Greece, Netherlands, South Africa, United States, Belgium, Canada, Turkey, France, Poland, Japan, Italy, Denmark, Argentina, and Norway	Fun, friends, irreverance, and sensation	Stereotype of the devil-may-care, trying-to-become-independent hedonist. For the most part, they come from affluent or middle-class parents, live mainly in developed countries, and have allowance money to spend.	Respond to sensory stimulation. Tend to get bored easily so stale advertising messages will escape their notice. They want action ads with bells and whistles, humour, novelty, colour, and sound. Edgier than their peers. Constantly seek out the new. First ones to hear of the newest technology or the hippest Web site. Experimenting is second nature. Wear all sorts of body rings and wear their hair in different shades.
Resigned	Denmark, Sweden, Korea, Japan, Norway, Germany, Belgium, Netherlands, Argentina, Canada, Turkey, England, Spain, France, and Taiwan	Friends, fun, family, and low expectations	Resemble the thrills-and-chills teens, often decorating their bodies with rings and dye. However, they are alienated from society and very pessimistic about their chances for economic success. The punk rockers of the world, who sometimes take drugs and drink to excess. Respond to heavy metal and grunge music that emphasizes the negative and angry side of society.	Do not have as much discretionary income to spend as teens in other segments. Infrequent consumers save for some fast-food, low-ticket clothes items, tobacco, and alcohol. They are drawn to irony and to ads that make fun of the pomposity of society.
World Savers	Hungary, Philippines, Venezuela, Brazil, Spain, Colombia, Belgium, Argentina, Russia, Singapore, France, Poland, Ukraine, Italy, South Africa, Mexico, and England	Environment, humanism, fun, and friends	A long list of do-good global and local causes that spark their interest. The intelligentsia in most countries who do well in school. They are the class and club leaders who join many organizations. They attend the same parties as the thrills-and-chills kids. But, they are more into romance, relationships, and strong friendships. Eagerly attend concerts, operas, and plays. They exhibit a *joie de vivre* about life and enjoy dancing or drinking at bars and cafés with friends. They love the outdoors as well, including camping, hiking, and other sports activities.	Attracted by honest and sincere messages that tell the truth. Offended by any ad that puts people down or makes fun of another group. Piggyback a promotion with a worthwhile cause.
Quiet Achievers	Thailand, China, Hong Kong, Ukraine, Korea, Lithuania, Russia, and Peru	Success, anonymity, anti-individualism, and social optimism	Value anonymity and prefer to rest in the shadows. They are the least rebellious of all the groups, avoid the limelight and do not ever want to stand out in the crowd. These are the bookish and straight kids who study long hours, are fiercely ambitious and highly goal-directed. Their top priority is to make good grades in school and use higher education to further their career advancement. Most of the quiet achievers live in Asia, especially	Love to purchase stuff. Part of the reward for working diligently is being able to buy products. Their parents will defer to their children's needs when it comes to computers and other technological products that will aid in homework. This group is also keen on music; they are inner directed and adept at creating their own good times. Prefer ads that address the benefits

Table 4.6 (cont'd)

Segment	Key countries	Driving principles	Overview	Marketing approach
			Thailand and China. But these somewhat stereotypical studious types also exist in the United States, where they are sometimes regarded as being techies or nerds.	of a product. They are embarrassed by ads that display rampant sexuality. And they do not respond to the sarcastic or the irreverent.
Boot-strappers	Nigeria, Mexico, United States, India, Chile, Puerto Rico, Peru, Venezuela, Colombia, and South Africa	Achievement, individualism, optimism, determination, and power	Most dreamy and childlike of the six segments. They live sheltered and ordered lives that seem bereft of many forms of typical teen fun and wild adult-emulating teen behavior. Spend a lot of time at home, doing homework and helping around the house. Eager for power; they are the politicians in every high school who covet the class offices. They view the use of authority as a means for securing rewards, and they are constantly seeking out recognition. Geographically many of these teens come from emerging nations such as Nigeria and India. In the United States, bootstrappers represent one in every four teens. Moreover, they represent 40% of young African Americans. A major error of U.S. marketers is to misread the size and purchasing power of this ambitious African American segment.	Young yuppies in training. They want premium brands and luxury goods. Bootstrappers are also on the lookout for goods and services that will help them get ahead. They want to dress for success, have access to technology and software, and stay plugged into the world of media and culture to give them a competitive edge. They are attracted by messages that portray aspirations and possibilities for products and their users.
Upholders	Vietnam, Indonesia, Taiwan, China, Italy, Peru, Venezuela, Puerto Rico, India, Philippines, and Singapore	Family, custom, tradition, and respect for individuals	Traditions act as a rigid guideline, and these teens would be hard-pressed to rebel or confront authority. They are content to rest comfortably in the mainstream of life, remaining unnoticed. The girls seek mostly to get married and have families. The boys perceive that they are fated to have jobs similar to their fathers'. Predominate in Asian countries, such as Indonesia and Vietnam that value old traditions and extended family relationships. Teens in these countries are helpful around the home and protective of their siblings. Moreover, many upholders are in Catholic countries where the Church and tradition guide schooling, attitudes, and values.	Advertisers and marketers have had success selling to upholders using youthful, almost childlike communication and fun messages. These are teens that still watch cartoons and are avid media consumers. They are highly involved in both watching and playing sports, particularly basketball and soccer. More than any other group, they plan to live in their country of birth throughout adulthood. Essentially upholders are homebodies. They are deeply rooted in family and community and they like to make purchase decisions that are safe and conform to their parents' values. Brands that take a leadership stance will attract upholders for their risk-free quality value and reliability.

Source: Adapted from 'The six value segments of global youth', *Bandweek* 11, no. 21 (May 22, 2000), 38, based on data initially presented in *The $100 Billion Allowance: How to Get Your Share of the Global Teen Market* by Elissa Moses (New York: John Wiley & Sons, 2000).

■ MATERIALISM: THE ULTIMATE 'WHY' OF CONSUMPTION?

Materialism may be considered a more general value underlying other consumer values, thus reassuring us that an obvious way of realizing one's values is through consumption.

Consumption as a goal

Members of 'cargo cults' in the South Pacific literally worshipped cargo that was salvaged from crashed aircraft or washed ashore from ships. These people believed that the ships and planes passing near their islands were piloted by their ancestors, and they tried to attract them to their villages. During the Second World War, they went so far as to construct fake planes from straw in the hope of luring real ones.[106]

▶ While not everyone literally worships material goods in this way, things do play a central role in many people's lives. Materialism refers to the importance people attach to worldly possessions. Westerners in general (and Americans in particular) are often stereotyped as being members of a highly materialistic society where people often gauge their worth and that of others in terms of how much they own. Materialists are more likely to value possessions for their status and appearance-related meanings, whereas those who do not emphasize this value tend to prize products that connect them to other people or that provide them with pleasure in using them.[107] As a result, products valued by high materialists are more likely to be publicly consumed and to be more expensive. A study that compared specific items valued by both types of people found that products associated with high materialists include jewellery, china, or a holiday home, whereas those linked to low materialists included a mother's wedding gown, picture albums, a rocking chair from childhood, or a garden.[108] The priorities of materialism tend to emphasize the well-being of the individual versus the group, which may conflict with family or religious values. That conflict may help to explain why people with highly material values tend to be less happy.[109]

In Europe, we often take the existence of an abundance of products and services for granted, until we remember how recent many of these developments are. The commonness of ownership of cars, freezers, telephones and televisions is all a post-1950s' phenomenon. In fact, one way to think about marketing is as a system that provides a certain standard of living to consumers. To some extent, then, our lifestyles are influenced by the standard of living we have come to expect and desire. However, there is evidence that how much money we have does not relate directly to happiness: 'as long as people are not battling poverty, they tend to rate their happiness in the range of 6 or 7, or higher, on a 10-point scale'.[110]

The living standard of consumers in many countries, particularly in Asia, has also increased considerably in recent years. And new products are steadily becoming 'necessities'. A Gallup study of 22,500 adults in 17 European countries found that ownership of such items as microwave ovens, VCRs and mobile phones has 'exploded' in recent years.[111] The mobile phone has become the symbol of the mass market in China where average income remains about $1,000 per annum. 'China is now the world's largest market for cellphone subscriptions, but is not the largest for handsets because frugal Chinese buyers hold on to them for an average of 29 months, longer than in many other markets'.[112] Advertising encourages this emphasis on consumption and increasingly portrays consumption as an end in itself, rather than as a means to attain well-being.[113]

Of course, not everyone stresses the value of materialism to the same degree. Individual differences have been found among consumers in terms of this emphasis. One approach partitions the value of materialism into three categories: success, centrality and happiness.[114] The scale items used to measure these categories are shown in Table 4.7.

Cross-cultural differences have also been analysed. One study of 12 countries resulted in the following ranking in degree of materialism from highest to lowest: Romania,

Table 4.7 A scale to measure categories of materialism

Category	Scale items
Success	• 'I admire people who own expensive homes, cars and clothes.'
	• 'Some of the most important achievements in life include acquiring material possessions.'
	• 'I don't put much emphasis on the amount of material objects people own as a sign of success.'*
	• 'The things I own say a lot about how well I'm doing in life.'
	• 'I like to own things that impress people.'
	• 'I don't pay much attention to the material objects other people own.'*
	• 'I usually buy only the things I need.'*
Centrality	• 'I try to keep my life simple, as far as possessions are concerned.'*
	• 'The things I own aren't all that important to me.'*
	• 'I enjoy spending money on things that aren't practical.'
	• 'Buying things gives me a lot of pleasure.'
	• 'I like a lot of luxury in my life.'
	• 'I put less emphasis on material things than most people I know.'*
	• 'I have all the things I really need to enjoy life.'*
Happiness	• 'My life would be better if I owned certain things I don't have.'
	• 'I wouldn't be any happier if I owned nicer things.'*
	• 'I'd be happier if I could afford to buy more things.'
	• 'It sometimes bothers me quite a bit that I can't afford to buy all the things I'd like.'

Note: Respondents indicate whether they agree or disagree with each item on a five-point scale.
*Items with an asterisk are reverse scored.

Source: Adapted from Marsha L. Richins and Scott Dawson, 'A consumer values orientation for materialism and its measurement: Scale development and validation', *Journal of Consumer Research* 20 (December 1992), Table 3. Reprinted with permission of The University of Chicago Press.

USA, New Zealand, Ukraine, Germany, Turkey, Israel, Thailand, India, UK, France and Sweden.[115] From these results, several conclusions can be drawn. First of all, materialism is not directly linked to affluence, as has often been proposed. On the contrary, some of the most materialistic cultures are the ones where most consumers (feel that they) lack a lot of things. But this obviously is not the only explanation, since the United States, New Zealand and Germany score relatively high as well, and India scores low. Since neither wealth, 'Westernness', nor any other single variable can explain these differences, it must be concluded that materialism is a consequence of several factors, including such things as social stability, access to information, reference models, as well as historical developments and cultural values.

This study was followed up by another based on qualitative depth interviews, adding more insight into consumers' different ways of coping with their own materialism, which was generally perceived as something negative. Basically, two ways of dealing with materialism were found: either you condemn materialism and provide an explanation why your personal materialism is a particularly good one, or you admit to being a 'bad' materialist but provide an excuse for being so. The different kinds of attitudes towards materialism are listed below:

- *Justifying materialism (my materialism is a good materialism)*
  - 'I am a passionate connoisseur, not a vulgar materialist – I have passion for and knowledge about the things I collect, it is not just a matter of having as much as possible.'
  - 'Terminal materialism is bad, but instrumental materialism is good, for instance to provide security for my family.'
  - 'I spend my money so that I can share my goods with others and give them pleasure'.
- *Excusing (materialism is bad, but . . .)*
  - 'Society (or the media, or the environment) made me do it.'
  - 'It's just the way of the modern world – everybody is like that.'
  - 'I deserve it since I have been deprived of opportunities for so long' (e.g. people in newly marketized economies).[116]

The disenchantment among some people with a culture dominated by big corporations shows up in events that promote uniqueness and anti-corporate statements. Probably the most prominent movement in the USA is the annual Burning Man project. This is a week-long annual anti-market event, where thousands of people gather at Black Rock Desert in Nevada to express themselves and proclaim their emancipation from Corporate America. The highlight of the festival involves the burning of a huge figure of a man made out of wood that symbolizes the freedom from market domination. Ironically, some critics point out that even this high-profile anti-market event is being commercialized as it becomes more popular each year.[117]

Participants at the anti-corporate Burning Man Festival find novel ways to express their individuality.
Courtesy of Professor Robert Kozinets

Figure 4.6 Contextualizing the 'why' of consumption

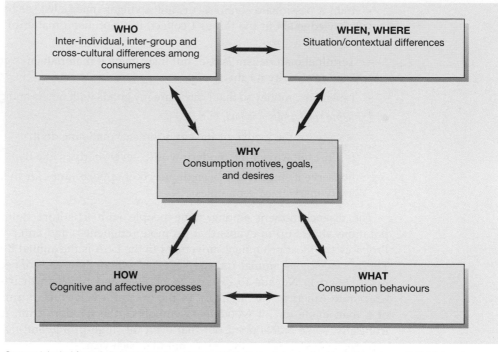

Source: Adapted from S. Ratneshwar, D. G. Mick and C. Huffman, 'Introduction', in S. Ratneshwar, D. G. Mick and C. Huffman, eds, *The Why of Consumption* (London: Routledge, 2000): 1–8.

The 'why' of consumption

As we have seen in this chapter, there are many reasons why we want to engage in consumption activities. One of the main lessons to retain is probably that the 'why?' question cannot stand alone, but must be asked with reference to a number of other questions such as 'who?', indicating personal, group and cultural differences; 'when?' and 'where?', indicating situational and contextual differences; 'how?', pointing to the reflexive and emotional processes involved; and finally 'what?' kind of consumption items and consumer behaviour are we talking about. These dimensions, which are all to some extent addressed later in this book, are illustrated in Figure 4.6.

■ CHAPTER SUMMARY

- Marketers have claimed that they try to satisfy consumer needs, but the reasons why any product is purchased can vary widely. The identification of consumer motives is an important step in ensuring that the appropriate needs and wants will be met by a product.

- Traditional approaches to consumer behaviour have focused on the abilities of products to satisfy rational needs (utilitarian motives), but hedonic motives (e.g. the need for exploration or for fun) also play a key role in many purchase decisions. Hence there has been a shift away from talking about needs and towards talking about goals, wants and desires.

- As demonstrated by Maslow's hierarchy of needs, the same product can satisfy different needs (as well as different goals, wants and desires), depending on the consumer's state at the time. In addition to his or her objective situation (have basic physiological needs already been satisfied?), the consumer's degree of involvement with the product must be considered.

■ Product involvement can range from very low where purchase decisions are made via inertia to very high where consumers form very strong bonds with what they buy. In addition to considering the degree to which consumers are involved with a product, marketing strategists also need to assess the extent of their involvement with marketing messages and with the purchase situation.

■ Since consumers are not necessarily able or willing to communicate their underlying desires to marketers, various techniques such as projective tests can be employed to assess desires indirectly.

■ Consumer motivations are often driven by underlying values. In this context, products take on meaning because they are seen as being instrumental in helping the person to achieve some goal that is linked to a value, such as individuality or freedom.

■ Values are basic, general principles used to judge the desirability of end-states. All cultures form a value system which sets them apart from other cultures. Some researchers have developed lists to account for such value systems and used them in cross-cultural comparisons.

■ One approach to the study of values is the means-end chain, which tries to link product attributes to consumer values via the consequences that usage of the product will have for the consumer.

■ *Materialism* refers to the importance people attach to worldly possessions. Materialism may be considered a more general value underlying other consumer values, thus reassuring us that an obvious way of realizing one's values is through consumption.

▶ KEY TERMS

Acculturation (p. 115)

Approach-approach conflict (p. 95)

Approach-avoidance conflict (p. 96)

Avoidance-avoidance conflict (p. 97)

Core values (p. 113)

Cult products (p. 107)

Desire (p. 103)

Drive (p. 90)

Drive theory (p. 92)

Enculturation (p. 115)

Expectancy theory (p. 93)

Flow state (p. 107)

Freudian theory (p. 100)

Goal (p. 90)

Homeostasis (p. 92)

Inertia (p. 106)

Instrumental values (p. 118)

Involvement (p. 105)

Laddering (p. 119)

Materialism (p. 125)

Means-end chain (p. 119)

MECCAs (p. 121)

Motivation (p. 90)

Motivational research (p. 101)

Need (p. 90)

Terminal values (p. 118)

Theory of cognitive dissonance (p. 95)

Value (p. 113)

Value system (p. 114)

Want (p. 92)

CONSUMER BEHAVIOUR CHALLENGE

1 Describe three types of motivational conflicts, citing an example of each from current marketing campaigns.

2 Should consumer researchers have the right to probe into the consumer's unconscious? Is this a violation of privacy, or just another way to gather deep knowledge of purchase motivations?

3 What is the difference between a want and a desire? Think about your own feelings and try to describe the differences.

4 Devise separate promotional strategies for an article of clothing, each of which stresses one of the levels of Maslow's hierarchy of needs.

5 Collect a sample of ads that appeals to consumers' values. What value is being communicated in each ad, and how is this done? Is this an effective approach to designing a marketing communication?

6 What is your conception of paradise? Construct a collage consisting of images you personally associate with paradise, and compare the results with those of your classmates. Do you detect any common themes?

7 Construct a hypothetical means–end chain model for the purchase of a bouquet of roses. How might a florist use this approach to construct a promotional strategy?

8 Describe how a man's level of involvement with his car would affect how he is influenced by different marketing stimuli. How might you design a strategy for a line of car batteries for a segment of low-involvement consumers, and how would this strategy differ from your attempts to reach a segment of men who are very involved in working on their cars?

9 Interview members of a celebrity fan club. Describe their level of involvement with the 'product' and devise some marketing opportunities to reach this group.

10 'High involvement is just a fancy term for expensive.' Do you agree?

11 'University students' concerns about ethics, the environment and vegetarianism are just a passing fad; a way to look "cool".' Do you agree?

12 Think about some of the excuses or explanations you have used towards yourself or towards others for materialistic wants. How do they correspond to the explanations and excuses accounted for here?

13 'Although more money delivers big increases in happiness when you are poor, each extra dollar makes less difference once your basic needs have been met.'[118] Debate this viewpoint in class.

14 Some market analysts see a shift in values among young people. They claim that this generation has not had a lot of stability in their lives. They are fed up with superficial relationships, and are yearning for a return to tradition. This change is reflected in attitudes toward marriage and family. One survey of 22–24-year-old women found that 82 per cent thought motherhood was the most important job in

the world. *Brides* magazine reports a swing towards traditional weddings – 80 per cent of brides today are tossing their garters. Daddy walks 78 per cent of them down the aisle.[119] So, what do you think about this? Are young people indeed returning to the values of their parents (or even their grandparents)? How have these changes influenced your perspective on marriage and family?

■ NOTES

1. See Susan Baker, Keith E. Thompson and Julia Engelken, 'Mapping the values driving organic food choice: Germany vs the UK', *European Journal of Marketing* 38 (2004): 995ff. Their study showed that although there were similarities between German and UK consumers of organic products in terms of values related to health, well-being and enjoyment, there were differences in terms of product attributes linked to achieving these values. A major difference was that UK consumers did not necessarily link organic food with the environment.

2. Tino Bech-Larsen and Klaus G. Grunert, 'The Influence of Tasting Experience and Health Benefits on Nordic Consumers' Rejection of Genetically Modified Foods', in Andrea Groppel-Klein and Franz-Rudolf Esch, eds, *European Advances in Consumer Research* 5 (Valdosta, GA: Association for Consumer Research, 2001): 11–14.

3. Ibid.

4. Laura Smith, 'Childhood obesity fuelled by cartoons', *The Guardian* (24 February 2005): 5.

5. Bech-Larsen and Grunert, 'The Influence of Tasting Experience and Health Benefits': 11–14.

6. Paul Hewer, 'Consuming Gardens: Representations of Paradise, Nostalgia and Postmodernism', in Darach Turley and Stephen Brown, eds, *European Advances in Consumer Research* 6 (Valdosta, GA: Association for Consumer Research, 2003): 327–31.

7. Robert A. Baron, *Psychology: The Essential Science* (Needham, MA: Allyn & Bacon, 1989).

8. Jean Baudrillard, 'La genèse idéologique des besoins', *Cahiers internationaux de sociologie* 47 (1969): 45–68.

9. Søren Askegaard and A. Fuat Firat, 'Towards a Critique of Material Culture, Consumption, and Markets', in S. Pearce, ed., *Experiencing Material Culture in the Western World* (London: Leicester University Press, 1997): 114–39.

10. See for instance the discussion in Emma N. Banister and Margaret K. Hogg, 'Negative symbolic consumption and consumers' drive for self-esteem: the case of the fashion industry', *European Journal of Marketing* 38(7) (2004): 850–68.

11. Leon Festinger, *A Theory of Cognitive Dissonance* (Stanford, CA: Stanford University Press, 1957).

12. Jeannie Whalen, 'Meet the leader of the pack: Moscow's drag-racing queen Katya Karenina organizes illicit matches under the nose of the city police force', *The Wall Street Journal* (9 December 2002) jeanne.whalen@wsj.com.

13. See Paul T. Costa and Robert R. McCrae, 'From catalog to classification: Murray's needs and the five-factor model', *Journal of Personality and Social Psychology* 55 (1988): 258–65; Calvin S. Hall and Gardner Lindzey, *Theories of Personality*, 2nd edn (New York: Wiley, 1970); James U. McNeal and Stephen W. McDaniel, 'An analysis of need-appeals in television advertising', *Journal of the Academy of Marketing Science* 12 (Spring 1984): 176–90.

14. Michael R. Solomon, Judith L. Zaichkowsky, and Rosemary Polegato, *Consumer Behaviour: Buying, Having, and Being – Canadian Edition* (Scarborough, Ontario: Prentice Hall Canada, 1999).

15. See David C. McClelland, *Studies in Motivation* (New York: Appleton-Century-Crofts, 1955).

16. Mary Kay Ericksen and M. Joseph Sirgy, 'Achievement Motivation and Clothing Preferences of White-Collar Working Women', in Michael R. Solomon, ed., *The Psychology of Fashion* (Lexington, MA: Lexington Books, 1985): 357–69.

17. See Stanley Schachter, *The Psychology of Affiliation* (Stanford, CA: Stanford University Press, 1959).

18. Eugene M. Fodor and Terry Smith, 'The power motive as an influence on group decision making', *Journal of Personality and Social Psychology* 42 (1982): 178–85.

19. C. R. Snyder and Howard L. Fromkin, *Uniqueness: The Human Pursuit of Difference* (New York: Plenum, 1980).

20. Abraham H. Maslow, *Motivation and Personality*, 2nd edn (New York: Harper & Row, 1970).

21. A more recent integrative view of consumer goal structures and goal-determination processes proposes six discrete levels of goals wherein higher-level (vs. lower-level) goals are more abstract, more inclusive and less mutable. In descending order of abstraction, these goal levels are life themes and values, life projects, current concerns, consumption intentions, benefits sought and feature preferences. See Cynthia Huffman, S. Ratneshwar and David Glen Mick, 'Consumer Goal Structures and Goal-Determination Processes, An Integrative Framework', in S. Ratneshwar, David Glen Mick and Cynthia Huffman, eds, *The Why of Consumption* (London: Routledge, 2000): 9–35.

22. See, however, Primo Levi, *If This Is A Man* (London: Abacus by Sphere Books, 1987); his discussion of the importance of friendship for surviving extreme conditions of deprivation; and his description of the loss of his concentration camp friend and companion Alberto (p. 161).

23. See also Karin M. Ekstrom, Marianne P. Ekstrom and Helena Shanahan, 'Families in the Transforming Russian Society: Observations from Visits to Families in Novgorod the Great', in Groeppel-Klein and Esch, eds, *European Advances in Consumer Research* 5: 145–54.

24. Quoted in Russell W. Belk, 'Romanian Consumer Desires and Feelings of Deservingness', in Lavinia Stan, ed., *Romania in Transition* (Hanover, NH: Dartmouth Press, 1997): 191–208, quoted on p. 193.

25. Study conducted in the Horticulture Department at Kansas State University, cited in 'Survey tells why gardening's good', *Vancouver Sun* (12 April 1997): B12.

26. Richard Maddock, 'A Theoretical and Empirical Substructure of Consumer Motivation and Behaviour', in Flemming Hansen, ed., *European Advances in Consumer Research* 2 (Provo, UT: Association for Consumer Research, 1995): 29–37.

27. Ernest Dichter, *A Strategy of Desire* (Garden City, NY: Doubleday, 1960); Ernest Dichter, *The Handbook of Consumer Motivations* (New York: McGraw-Hill, 1964); Jeffrey J. Durgee, 'Interpreting Dichter's Interpretations: An Analysis of Consumption Symbolism in *The Handbook of Consumer Motivations*', *Marketing and Semiotics. Selected Papers from the Copenhagen Symposium*, ed. Hanne Hartvig Larsen, David G. Mick and Christian Alsted (Copenhagen: Handelshøjskolens forlag 1991): 52–74; Pierre Martineau, *Motivation in Advertising* (New York: McGraw-Hill, 1957).

28. Vance Packard, *The Hidden Persuaders* (New York: D. McKay, 1957).

29. Harold Kassarjian, 'Personality and consumer behavior: A review', *Journal of Marketing Research* 8 (November 1971): 409–18.

30. Bill Schlackman, 'An Historical Perspective', in Sue Robson and Angela Foster, *Qualitative Research in Action* (London: Edward Arnold, 1988): 15–23.

31. See also Russell W. Belk, Güliz Ger and Søren Askegaard, 'Metaphors of Consumer Desire', in Kim P. Corfman and John Lynch, Jr., eds, *Advances in Consumer Research* 23 (Provo, UT: Association for Consumer Research, 1996): 368–73.

32. Richard Elliott, 'Existential consumption and irrational desire', *European Journal of Marketing* 31(3/4) (1997): 285–96.

33. Russell W. Belk, Güliz Ger and Søren Askegaard, 'The Missing Streetcar Named Desire', in Ratneshwar, Mick and Huffman, eds, *The Why of Consumption*: 98–119.

34. Robert Bocock, *Consumption* (London: Routledge 1993).

35. Russell W. Belk, Güliz Ger and Søren Askegaard, 'Consumer Desire in Three Cultures', in D. MacInnis and M. Brucks, eds, *Advances in Consumer Research* 14 (Provo, UT: Association for Consumer Research, 1997): 24–8.

36. Gary J. Bamossy and Janeen Costa, 'Consuming Paradise: A Cultural Construction' (paper presented at the Association for Consumer Research Conference, June 1997, Stockholm).

37. Quoted in 'Forehead advertisement pays off', *Montgomery Advertiser* (4 May 2000): 7A.

38. Quoted in Alex Kuczynski, 'A new magazine celebrates the rites of shopping', *The New York Times on the Web* (8 May 2000).

39. Judith Lynne Zaichkowsky, 'Measuring the involvement construct in marketing', *Journal of Consumer Research* 12 (December 1985): 341–52.

40. Andrew Mitchell, 'Involvement: A Potentially Important Mediator of Consumer Behaviour', in William L. Wilkie, ed., *Advances in Consumer Research* 6 (Provo, UT: Association for Consumer Research, 1979): 191–6.

41. Richard L. Celsi and Jerry C. Olson, 'The role of involvement in attention and comprehension processes', *Journal of Consumer Research* 15 (September 1988): 210–24.

42. Ton Otker, 'The highly involved consumer: A marketing myth?', *Marketing and Research Today* (February 1990): 30–6.

43. Anthony G. Greenwald and Clark Leavitt, 'Audience involvement in advertising: Four levels', *Journal of Consumer Research* 11 (June 1984): 581–92.

44. Mihaly Csikszentmihalyi, *Flow: The Psychology of Optimal Experience* (New York: HarperCollins, 1991); Donna L. Hoffman and Thomas P. Novak, 'Marketing in hypermedia computer-mediated environments: Conceptual foundations', *Journal of Marketing* (July 1996), 60, 50–68.

45. Melanie Wells, 'Cult brands', *Forbes* (16 April 2001): 198–205.

46. Judith Lynne Zaichkowsky, 'The Emotional Side of Product Involvement', in Paul Anderson and Melanie Wallendorf, eds, *Advances in Consumer Research* 14 (Provo, UT: Association for Consumer Research): 32–35.

47. For a recent discussion of interrelationship between situational and enduring involvement, see Marsha L. Richins, Peter H. Bloch and Edward F. McQuarrie, 'How enduring and situational involvement combine to create involvement responses', *Journal of Consumer Psychology* 1(2) (1992): 143–53. For more information on the involvement construct see 'Special issue on involvement' *Psychology and Marketing* 10(4) (July/August 1993).

48. Rajeev Batra and Michael L. Ray, 'Operationalizing Involvement as Depth and Quality of Cognitive Responses', in Alice Tybout and Richard Bagozzi, eds, *Advances in Consumer Research* 10 (Ann Arbor, MI: Association for Consumer Research, 1983): 309–13.

49. Herbert E. Krugman, 'The impact of television advertising: Learning without involvement', *Public Opinion Quarterly* 29 (Fall 1965): 349–56.

50. Bruce Crumley, 'Multipoints add up for quick burger', *Advertising Age* (29 November 1993): 14; http://lescahiersduburger.free.fr/Fast-food/quick-france.htm (accessed 10 January 2004).

51. Marsha L. Richins and Peter H. Bloch, 'After the new wears off: The temporal context of product involvement', *Journal of Consumer Research* 13 (September 1986): 280–5.

52. Kevin J. Clancy, 'CPMs must bow to "involvement" measurement', *Advertising Age* (20 January 1992): 26.

53. Gilles Laurent and Jean-Noël Kapferer, 'Measuring consumer involvement profiles', *Journal of Marketing Research* 22 (February 1985): 41–53; this scale was validated on an American sample as well, see William C. Rodgers and Kenneth C. Schneider, 'An empirical evaluation of the Kapferer–Laurent consumer involvement profile scale', *Psychology & Marketing* 10 (July/August 1993): 333–45. For an English translation of this scale see Jean-Noël Kapferer and Gilles Laurent, 'Further evidence on the consumer involvement profile: Five antecedents of involvement', *Psychology and Marketing* 10 (July/August 1993): 347–56.

54. Note though that the marketing of the Dyson cleaner has involved appeals about revolutionary technological design and thus indirectly to status issues. Note the successful launch of Dyson in the USA where it was priced at three times more than many of its rival vacuum cleaners: Terry Macalister 'Dyson evokes Beatles as cleaner sweeps to No 1 in America', *The Guardian* (23 February 2005) http://www.guardian.co.uk/uk_news/story/0,,1423127,00.html

55. Culture clash experienced by one of the authors.

56. David W. Stewart and David H. Furse, 'Analysis of the impact of executional factors in advertising performance', *Journal of Advertising Research* 24 (1984): 23–26; Deborah J. MacInnis, Christine Moorman and Bernard J. Jaworski, 'Enhancing and measuring consumers' motivation, opportunity, and ability to process brand information from ads', *Journal of Marketing* 55 (October 1991): 332–53.

57. Morris B. Holbrook and Elizabeth C. Hirschman, 'The experiential aspects of consumption: Consumer fantasies, feelings, and fun', *Journal of Consumer Research* 9 (September 1982): 132–40.

58. Elaine Sciolino, 'Disproving notions, raising a fury', *The New York Times on the Web* (21 January 2003).

59. K. Oanh Ha, 'Have it your way', *Montgomery Advertiser* (9 November 1998): 2D.

60. Rebecca Gardyn, 'Swap meet', *American Demographics* (July 2001): 51–6.

61. Lawrence Speer and Magz Osborne, 'Coke tests custom bottles', *Advertising Age* (4 November 2002): 16.

62. Erin White, 'Coke moves to let teens pitch soda to themselves', *The Wall Street Journal Interactive Edition* (10 January 2003).

63. Erin White, 'Interactive commercials face one big challenge: Laziness', *The Wall Street Journal Interactive Edition* (2 August 2002).

64. Michel Marriot, 'Movie posters that talk back', *The New York Times on the Web* (12 December 2002).

65. David Kushner, 'From the skin artist, always a free makeover', *The New York Times on the Web* (21 March 2002).

66. Shalom H. Schwartz and Warren Bilsky, 'Toward a universal psychological structure of human values', *Journal of Personality and Social Psychology* 53 (1987): 550–62.

67. Ajay K. Sirsi, James C. Ward and Peter H. Reingen, 'Microcultural analysis of variation in sharing of causal reasoning about behavior', *Journal of Consumer Research* 22 (March 1996): 345–72.

68. Bernard Cova and Robert Salle, 'Buying behaviour in European and American Industry: Contrasts', *European Management Journal* 9(4) (1991): 433–6.

69. Christian Dussart, 'Capitalism against Capitalism: Political and Economic Implications of Marketing Practice in Europe', in M. J. Baker, ed., *Perspectives on Marketing Management* 4 (London: John Wiley & Sons, 1994): 119–34.

70. Richard W. Pollay, 'Measuring the cultural values manifest in advertising', *Current Issues and Research in Advertising* (1983): 71–92.

71. Howard W. French, 'Vocation for dropouts is painting Tokyo red', *New York Times on the Web* (5 March 2000).

72. Sarah Ellison, 'Sexy-ad reel shows what tickles in Tokyo can fade fast in France', *Wall Street Journal Interactive Edition* (31 March 2000).

73. Milton Rokeach, *The Nature of Human Values* (New York: Free Press, 1973).

74. Lynn Kahle, Sharon Beatty and John Mager, 'Implications of Social Values for Consumer Communications: The Case of the European Community', in B. Englis, ed., *Global and Multinational Advertising* (Hillsdale, NJ: Lawrence Erlbaum Ass.): 47–64.

75. Suzanne C. Grunert and Gerhard Scherhorn, 'Consumer values in West Germany: Underlying dimensions and cross cultural comparison with North America', *Journal of Business Research* 20 (1990): 97–107.

76. See for instance the discussion of acculturation issues and British South East Asian women in A.M. Lindridge, M.K. Hogg and M. Shah, 'Imagined multiple worlds: How South Asian women in Britain use family and friends to navigate the "border crossings" between household and societal contexts', *Consumption, Markets and Culture* 7(3) (September 2004): 211–38.

77. Donald E. Vinson, Jerome E. Scott and Lawrence R. Lamont, 'The role of personal values in marketing and consumer behaviour', *Journal of Marketing* 41 (April 1977): 44–50; John Watson, Steven Lysonski, Tamara Gillan and Leslie Raymore, 'Cultural values and important possessions: A cross-cultural analysis', *Journal of Business Research* 55 (2002): 923–31.

78. Jennifer Aaker, Veronica Benet-Martinez and Jordi Garolera 'Consumption symbols as carriers of culture: A study of Japanese and Spanish brand personality constructs', *Journal of Personality and Social Psychology* (2001).

79. *Markedsføring* (25 August 2000): 8. See also Amelia Hill and Anushka Asthana, 'She's young, gifted and ahead of you at the till', *Observer* (2 January 2005): 7, http://observer.guardian.co.uk/uk_news/story/0,6903,1382042,00.html which describes 10 million twenty-to-thirty somethings in UK 'who are the new darlings of the retailers and politicians want their vote'. They are key decision makers and spenders in homeware stores.

80. *Markedsføring* (12 November 1999): 2.

81. Morris B. Holbrook, *Consumer Value* (London: Routledge, 1999).

82. Ibid. This book contains a chapter by various consumer researchers on each of the value types.

83. *Marketing* (24 August 2000): 2.

84. James Brooke, 'Japanese masters get closer to the toilet nirvana', *The New York Times on the Web* (8 October 2002).

85. Milton Rokeach, *Understanding Human Values* (New York: The Free Press, 1979); see also J. Michael Munson and Edward McQuarrie, 'Shortening the Rokeach Value Survey for Use in Consumer Research', in Michael J. Houston, ed., *Advances in Consumer Research* 15 (Provo, UT: Association for Consumer Research, 1988): 381–86.

86. Jacques-Marie Aurifeille, 'Value Changes and Their Marketing Implications: A Russian Survey', in W.F. van Raaij and G. Bamossy, eds, *European Advances in Consumer Research* 1 (Provo, UT: Association for Consumer Research, 1993): 249–61.

87. B.W. Becker and P.E. Conner, 'Personal values of the heavy user of mass media', *Journal of Advertising Research* 21 (1981): 37–43; Vinson, Scott and Lamont, 'The Role of Personal Values in Marketing and Consumer Behaviour': 44–50.

88. Sharon E. Beatty, Lynn R. Kahle, Pamela Homer and Shekhar Misra, 'Alternative measurement approaches to consumer values: The List of Values and the Rokeach Value Survey', *Psychology and Marketing* 2 (1985): 181–200.

89. Pierre Valette-Florence, Suzanne C. Grunert, Klaus G. Grunert and Sharon Beatty, 'Une comparaison franco-allemande de l'adhésion aux valeurs personnelles', *Recherche et Applications en Marketing* 6(3) (1991): 5–20.

90. Klaus G. Grunert, Suzanne C. Grunert and Sharon Beatty, 'Cross-cultural research on consumer values', *Marketing and Research Today* 17 (1989): 30–9.

91. Suzanne C. Grunert, Klaus G. Grunert and Kai Kristensen, 'Une méthode d'estimation de la validité interculturelle des instruments de mesure: Le cas de la mesure des valeurs des consommateurs par la liste des valeurs LOV', *Recherche et Applications en Marketing* 8(4) (1993): 5–28.

92. Beatty, Kahle, Homer and Misra, 'Alternative measurement approaches to consumer values': 181–200; Lynn R. Kahle and Patricia Kennedy, 'Using the List of Values (LOV) to understand consumers', *Journal of Consumer Marketing* 2 (Fall 1988): 49–56; Lynn Kahle, Basil Poulos and Ajay Sukhdial, 'Changes in social values in the United States during the past decade', *Journal of Advertising Research* 28 (February/March 1988): 35–41; see also Wagner A. Kamakura and Jose Alfonso Mazzon, 'Value segmentation: A model for the measurement of values and value systems', *Journal of Consumer Research* 18 (September 1991): 28; Jagdish N. Sheth, Bruce I. Newman and Barbara L. Gross, *Consumption Values and Market Choices: Theory and Applications* (Cincinnati: South-Western Publishing Co., 1991).

93. Shalom H. Schwartz and Warren Bilsky, 'Toward a theory of universal content and structure of values: Extensions and cross cultural replications', *Journal of Personality and Social Psychology* 58 (1990): 878–91; Shalom H. Schwartz, 'Universals in the Content and Structure of Values: Theoretical Advance and Empirical Test in 20 Countries', in M. Zanna, ed., *Advances in Experimental Social Psychology* 25 (San Diego, CA: Academic Press, 1992): 1–65.

94. Shalom H. Schwartz, 'Beyond Individualism/Collectivism: New Cultural Dimensions of Values' in U. Kim et al., eds, *Individualism and Collectivism* (Thousand Oaks, CA: Sage, 1994): 85–119.

95. Sarah Todd, Rob Lawson and Haydn Northover, 'Value Orientation and Media Consumption Behavior', in B. Englis and A. Olofsson, eds, *European Advances in Consumer Behaviour* 3 (Provo, UT: Association for Consumer Research): 328–32.

96. Suzanne C. Grunert and Hans Jørn Juhl, 'Values, environmental attitudes, and buying of organic foods', *Journal of Economic Psychology* 16 (1995): 39–62.

97. Thomas J. Reynolds and Jonathan Gutman, 'Laddering theory, method, analysis, and interpretation', *Journal of Advertising Research* (February/March 1988): 11–34; Beth Walker, Richard Celsi and Jerry Olson, 'Exploring the Structural Characteristics of Consumers' Knowledge', in Melanie Wallendorf and Paul Anderson, eds, *Advances in Consumer Research* 14 (Provo, UT: Association for Consumer Research, 1986): 17–21.

98. Andreas Hermann, 'Wertorientierte produkt- und werbegestaltung', *Marketing ZFP* 3 (3rd quarter 1996): 153–63.

99. Klaus G. Grunert and Suzanne C. Grunert, 'Measuring subjective meaning structures by the laddering method: Theoretical considerations and methodological problems', *International Journal of Research in Marketing* 12(3) (1995): 209–25. This volume of *IJRM* is a special issue on means–end chains and the laddering technique.

100. Roger Mason, 'Measuring the Demand for Status Goods: An Evaluation of Means–End Chains and Laddering', in Hansen, ed., *European Advances in Consumer Research* 2: 78–82.

101. Thomas J. Reynolds and Alyce Byrd Craddock, 'The application of the MECCAS model to the development and assessment of advertising strategy: A case study', *Journal of Advertising Research* (April/May 1988): 43–54.

102. This example was adapted from Michael R. Solomon, Gary Bamossy and Søren Askegaard, *Consumer Behaviour: A European Perspective*, 2nd edn (London: Pearson Education, 2002).

103. Elin Sørensen, Klaus G. Grunert and Niels Asger Nielsen, 'The Impact of Product Experience, Product Involvement and Verbal Processing Style on Consumers' Cognitive Structures with Regard to Fresh Fish', *MAPP Working Paper* 42 (Aarhus: The Aarhus School of Business, October 1996).

104. N.A. Nielsen, T. Bech-Larsen and K.G. Grunert, 'Consumer purchase motives and product perceptions: A laddering study on vegetable oil in three countries', *Food Quality and Preference* 9(6) (1998): 455–66.

105. Yumiko Ono, 'Tambrands ads try to scale cultural, religious obstacles', *The Wall Street Journal Interactive Edition* (17 March 1997), http://interactive4.wsj.com/archive

106. Russell W. Belk, 'Possessions and the extended self', *Journal of Consumer Research* 15 (September 1988): 139–68; Melanie Wallendorf and Eric J. Arnould, '"My favourite things": A cross-cultural inquiry into object attachment, possessiveness, and social linkage', *Journal of Consumer Research* 14 (March 1988): 531–47.

107. Marsha L. Richins, 'Special possessions and the expression of material values', *Journal of Consumer Research* 21 (December, 1994): 522–33.

108. Ibid.

109. James E. Burroughs and Aric Rindfleisch, 'Materialism and well-being: A conflicting values perspective', *Journal of Consumer Research* 29 (December 2002): 348ff.

110. Daniel Kahneman cited in Benedict Carey, 'TV time, unlike child care, ranks high in mood study', *NYTimes.com* (3 December 2004); see also Richard Tomkins, 'Materialism damages well-being,' *Financial Times* (27 November 2003) http://news.ft.com/servlet/ContentServer?pagename=FT.com/StoryFT/FullStory&c=StoryFT&cid=1069493548137&p=1012571727088.

111. 'Europeans more active as consumers', *Marketing News* (10 June 1994): 17.

112. Duncan Clark, Managing Director of Beijing consulting company, BDA China, quoted in Keith Bradsher, 'Consumerism grows in China, with Beijing's blessing', *NYT Online* (1 December 2003).

113. Russell W. Belk and Richard W. Pollay, 'Images of ourselves: The good life in twentieth century advertising', *Journal of Consumer Research* 11 (March 1985): 887–97.

114. Marsha L. Richins and Scott Dawson, 'A consumer values orientation for materialism and its measurement: Scale development and validation', *Journal of Consumer Research* 20 (December 1992).

115. Güliz Ger and Russell Belk, 'Cross-cultural differences in materialism', *Journal of Economic Psychology* 17 (1996): 55–77.

116. Güliz Ger and Russell Belk, 'Accounting for materialism in four cultures', *Journal of Material Culture* 4(2) (1999): 183–204.

117. Robert V. Kozinets, 'Can consumers escape the market? Emancipatory illuminations from burning man', *Journal of Consumer Research* 29 (June 2002): 20–38; see also Douglas B. Holt, 'Why do brands cause trouble? A dialectical theory of consumer culture and branding', *Journal of Consumer Research* 29 (June 2002): 70–90.

118. Tomkins, 'Materialism damages well-being'.

119. Helene Stapinski, 'Y Not Love?', *American Demographics* (February 1999): 62–8.

ATTITUDES

It's a lazy Wednesday night, and Leah, Lynn and Nicki are hanging out at Nicki's flat in Manchester doing some channel-surfing. Leah clicks to the sports cable and the three friends see there's a women's soccer game on, being televised from America. Leah has been a fan for as long as she can remember – perhaps as a result of having three older brothers and growing up in a house which had Manchester United souvenirs in every room. She loves the subtle intensity of the game – the traps, the moves, the way players make it look easy to move a ball around a huge field as if it were a small patch of grass. Further, she's proud of Manchester United's rich history as a club, and its success as a business operation. But don't ask her opinion of having her beloved team's ownership taken over by some American businessman who doesn't even understand the game![1] Nicki's a glutton for thrills and chills: she converted to soccer after seeing Mick Jagger singing along with the British crowd in the stadium as the English team battled the Argentinians in an exciting, dramatic match in the 1998 World Cup. Lynn, on the other hand, doesn't know a corner kick from a penalty kick. For her, the most interesting part of the match was the footage being shown over and over of the US player Brandi Chastain's celebrating her successful penalty kick which won the match by taking her shirt off to reveal her sports bra. Lynn even bought one a few weeks later. Still, soccer doesn't really ring her chimes – but as long as she gets to hang out with her girlfriends she doesn't really care if they watch non-contact sports like soccer or contact sports like *The Jerry Springer Show* or *Big Brother*!

■ THE POWER OF ATTITUDES

Leah is just the kind of fan sponsoring companies like Nike, Gatorade and Adidas hope will turn women's soccer into an ongoing source of sports fanaticism. In America, attitudes towards the game have changed dramatically since the US women's team lost in the 1996 semi-finals in Sweden before a crowd of less than 3,000. The 1999 World Cup was won before an audience of over 90,000 screaming fans, many of whom were soccer mums who saw the players as important role models for their young daughters. In 1998 a record 7.5 million women and girls enrolled for soccer teams in the United States. There, women now represent just under half of all soccer player registrations.[2] These kinds of growth figures are not to be found in Europe. Soccer has a much richer, longer tradition here, and has been a sport dominated by male patronage at the stadiums and male viewership on the television. While amateur soccer clubs for women can be found in the UK and on the Continent, they are not nearly as popular as in the United States, and have to compete with other sports which attract female participants, such as field hockey.

On the other hand, following Chastain's exuberant show of skin there has been much written in the United States over the so-called 'babe factor' as some critics wonder whether women's athletics will ever be taken seriously by male fans. Others feel that attitudes towards the game are more complex than that; they argue that sex appeal does not have to be sacrificed for professionalism. The big question is whether these positive feelings will endure. The goal of the Women's World Cup is to establish a women's professional league over the next few years. Time will tell if this ambitious project will score big or be red-carded and left to dwindle on the sidelines in the United States.[3] To score big in professional sports in the United States, or in Europe, is all a question of attitudes, and the dominant attitude among European fans is that women's soccer just isn't that important, at least so far. As you'll see throughout this book, attitudes can vary significantly along gender lines, and from one culture to another.

▶ The term **attitude** is widely used in popular culture. You might be asked, 'What is your attitude towards abortion?' A parent might scold, 'Young man, I don't like your attitude.' Some bars even euphemistically refer to Happy Hour as 'an attitude adjustment period'. For our purposes, though, an attitude is a lasting, general evaluation of people (including oneself), objects, advertisements or issues.[4] Anything towards which
▶ one has an attitude is called an **attitude object** (A_o).

This chapter will consider the contents of an attitude, how attitudes are formed, how they can be measured, and review some of the surprisingly complex relationships between attitudes and behaviour. Both as a theoretical concept, and as a tool to be used in the marketplace, the notion and dynamics of attitudes remain one of the most studied and applied of all behavioural constructs.[5] In the next chapter, we'll take a closer look at how attitudes can be changed – certainly an issue of prime importance to marketers.

■ THE CONTENT OF ATTITUDES

An attitude is *lasting* because it tends to endure over time. It is *general* because it applies to more than a momentary event, like hearing a loud noise (though over time you might develop a negative attitude towards all loud noises). Consumers have attitudes towards very product-specific behaviours (such as using Mentodent rather than Colgate toothpaste), as well as towards more general consumption-related behaviours (for example, how often you should brush your teeth). Attitudes help to determine who a person goes out with, what music he or she listens to, whether he or she will recycle or discard cans, or whether he or she chooses to become a consumer researcher for a living.

The functions of attitudes

▶ The **functional theory of attitudes** was initially developed by the psychologist Daniel Katz to explain how attitudes facilitate social behaviour.[6] According to this pragmatic approach, attitudes exist because they serve a function for the person. That is, they are determined by a person's motives. Consumers who expect that they will need to deal with similar information at a future time will be more likely to start forming attitudes in anticipation of this event.[7]

Two people can each have the same attitude towards an object for very different reasons. As a result, it can be helpful for a marketer to know why an attitude is held before attempting to change it. The following are attitude functions as identified by Katz:

- *Utilitarian function.* The utilitarian function is related to the basic principles of reward and punishment. We develop some of our attitudes towards products simply on the basis of whether these products provide pleasure or pain. If a person likes the taste of a cheeseburger, that person will develop a positive attitude towards cheeseburgers. Ads that stress straightforward product benefits (e.g. you should drink Diet Coke 'just for the taste of it') appeal to the utilitarian function.

- *Value-expressive function.* Attitudes that perform a value-expressive function express the consumer's central values or self-concept. A person forms a product attitude not because of its objective benefits, but because of what the product says about him or her as a person (e.g. 'What sort of woman reads *Elle*?'). Value-expressive attitudes are highly relevant to lifestyle analyses, where consumers cultivate a cluster of activities, interests and opinions to express a particular social identity.

- *Ego-defensive function.* Attitudes that are formed to protect the person, from either external threats or internal feelings, perform an ego-defensive function. An early marketing study indicated that housewives in the 1950s resisted the use of instant coffee because it threatened their conception of themselves as capable homemakers.[8] Products that promise to help a man project a 'macho' image (e.g. Marlboro cigarettes) may be appealing to his insecurities about his masculinity. Another example of this function is deodorant campaigns that stress the dire, embarrassing consequences of underarm odour.

- *Knowledge function.* Some attitudes are formed as the result of a need for order, structure or meaning. This need is often present when a person is in an ambiguous situation or is confronted with a new product (e.g. 'Bayer wants you to know about pain relievers').

An attitude can serve more than one function, but in many cases a particular one will be dominant. By identifying the dominant function a product serves for consumers (i.e. what benefits it provides), marketers can emphasize these benefits in their communications and packaging. Ads relevant to the function prompt more favourable thoughts about what is being marketed and can result in a heightened preference for both the ad and the product.

One American study determined that for most people coffee serves more of a utilitarian function than a value-expressive function. As a consequence, subjects responded more positively to copy for a fictitious brand of coffee that read, 'The delicious, hearty flavour and aroma of Sterling Blend coffee comes from a blend of the freshest coffee beans' (i.e. a utilitarian appeal) than they did to copy that read, 'The coffee you drink says something about the type of person you are. It can reveal your rare, discriminating taste' (i.e. the value-expressive function). In European countries with a strong 'coffee culture', such as Germany, the Benelux and Scandinavian countries, ads are more likely to stress the value-expressive function, in which the more social and ritualistic aspects of coffee consumption are expressed.[9]

As we saw in the experiences of the three Manchester women watching a soccer game, the importance of an attitude object may differ quite a bit for different people. Understanding the attitude's centrality to an individual and to others who share similar characteristics can be useful to marketers who are trying to devise strategies that will appeal to different customer segments. A study of football game attendance illustrates that varying levels of commitment result in different fan 'profiles'.[10] The study identified three distinct clusters of fans:[11]

- One cluster consisted of the real diehard fans like Leah who were highly committed to their team and who displayed an enduring love of the game. To reach these fans, the researchers recommended that sports marketers should focus on providing them with greater sports knowledge and relate their attendance to their personal goals and values.

- A second cluster was like Nicki – their attitudes were based on the unique, self-expressive experience provided by the game. They enjoyed the stimulation of cheering for a team and the drama of the competition itself. These people are more likely to be 'brand switchers', fair-weather fans who shift allegiances when the home team no longer provides the thrills they need. This segment can be appealed to by publicizing aspects of the visiting teams, such as advertising the appearance of stars who are likely to give the fans a game they will remember.

- A third cluster was like Lynn – they were looking for camaraderie above all. These consumers attend games primarily to take part in small-group activities such as a pre- or post-game party which may accompany the event. Marketers could appeal to this cluster by providing improved peripheral benefits, such as making it easier for groups to meet at the stadium, improving parking, and offering multiple-unit pricing.

The ABC model of attitudes and hierarchies of effects

Most researchers agree that an attitude has three components: affect, behaviour and cognition. **Affect** refers to the way a consumer feels about an attitude object. **Behaviour** involves the person's intentions to do something with regard to an attitude object (but, as will be discussed later, an intention does not always result in an actual behaviour). **Cognition** refers to the beliefs a consumer has about an attitude object. These three components of an attitude can be remembered as the ABC model of attitudes.

This model emphasizes the interrelationships between knowing, feeling and doing. Consumers' attitudes towards a product cannot be determined simply by identifying their beliefs about it. For example, a researcher may find that shoppers 'know' a particular digital camera has a 10X optical zoom lens, auto-focus and can also shoot *QuickTime Movies*, but such findings do not indicate whether they feel these attributes are good, bad or irrelevant, or whether they would actually buy the camera.

While all three components of an attitude are important, their relative importance will vary depending upon a consumer's level of motivation with regard to the attitude object. Attitude researchers have developed the concept of a **hierarchy of effects** to explain the relative impact of the three components. Each hierarchy specifies that a fixed sequence of steps occurs en route to an attitude. Three different hierarchies are summarized in Figure 5.1.

The standard learning hierarchy

Leah's positive attitude towards soccer closely resembles the process by which most attitudes have been assumed to be constructed. A consumer approaches a product decision as a problem-solving process. First, he or she forms beliefs about a product by accumulating knowledge (beliefs) regarding relevant attributes. Next, the consumer evaluates these beliefs and forms a feeling about the product (affect).[12] Over time, Leah assembled

Figure 5.1 Three hierarchies of effects

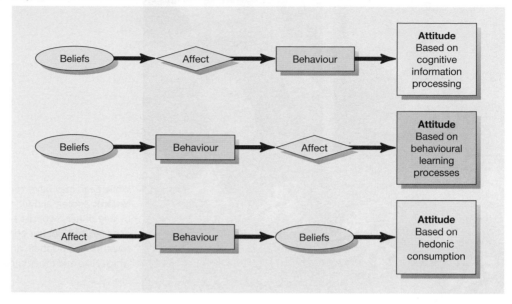

information about the sport, began to recognize the players, and learned which teams were superior to others. Finally, based on this evaluation, the consumer engages in a relevant behaviour, such as buying the product or supporting a particular team by wearing its shirt. This careful choice process often results in the type of loyalty displayed by Leah: the consumer 'bonds' with the product over time and is not easily persuaded to experiment with other brands. The standard learning hierarchy assumes that a consumer is highly involved in making a purchase decision.[13] The person is motivated to seek out a lot of information, carefully weigh alternatives, and come to a thoughtful decision. As we saw in Chapter 4, this process is likely to occur if the decision is important to the consumer or in some way central to the consumer's self-concept. If you understand the level of fan support for Manchester United, then you'll appreciate just how central Leah's attitudes about soccer (or, in this case, Manchester United) are for her.

While attitudes that Leah holds towards Manchester United may be well understood to be positive, it is not always an easy and straightforward task to assume that any related product purchases she makes will be consistent with her positive attitudes towards the team. Imagine that Leah is considering the purchase of some Nike soccer shoes for herself, and as part of gathering information about the shoes, she comes across an article on globalization, and Nike's use of outsourcing the labour for making soccer shoes to factories in low labour cost countries such as Vietnam. Leah's attitudes towards globalization, coupled with her own cognitive beliefs about the labour conditions in these factors may in fact lead her to have a negative affect towards the Nike shoes. At the same time, Leah's attitude towards buying a well-made soccer shoe at a very competitive price might be quite positive!

The low-involvement hierarchy

In contrast to Leah, Nicki's interest in the attitude object (soccer) is at best lukewarm. She is not particularly knowledgeable about the sport, and she may have an emotional response to an exciting game but not to a specific team. Nicki is typical of a consumer who forms an attitude via the *low-involvement hierarchy of effects*. In this sequence, the consumer does not initially have a strong preference for one brand over another, but instead

While Leah may have very positive attitudes towards soccer, and for the soccer boot made by one of her favourite brands, Nike, she still needs to sort out her conflicting attitudes towards globalization, and labour practices, which Nike and other shoe manufacturers use.
Photo: Gary Bamossy

acts on the basis of limited knowledge and then forms an evaluation only after the product has been purchased or used.[14] The attitude is likely to come about through behavioural learning, in which the consumer's choice is reinforced by good or bad experiences with the product after purchase. Nicki will probably be more likely to tune in to future games if they continue to have the same level of drama and excitement as the England–Argentina match.

The possibility that consumers simply don't care enough about many decisions to assemble a set of product beliefs carefully and then evaluate them is important, because it implies that all of the concern about influencing beliefs and carefully communicating information about product attributes may be largely wasted. Consumers aren't necessarily going to pay attention anyway; they are more likely to respond to simple stimulus–response connections when making purchase decisions. For example, a consumer choosing between paper towels might remember that 'Brand X absorbs more quickly than Brand Y', rather than bothering to compare systematically all of the brands on the shelf.

The notion of low involvement on the part of consumers is a bitter pill for some marketers to swallow. Who wants to admit that what they market is not very important or involving? A brand manager for, say, a brand of chewing gum or cat food may find it hard to believe that consumers don't put that much thought into purchasing her product because she herself spends many of her waking (and perhaps sleeping) hours thinking about it.

For marketers, the ironic silver lining to this low-involvement cloud is that, under these conditions, consumers are not motivated to process a lot of complex brand-related information. Instead, they will be swayed by principles of behavioural learning, such as the simple responses caused by conditioned brand names, point-of-purchase displays, and so on. This results in what we might call the *involvement paradox*: the less important the product is to consumers, the more important are many of the marketing stimuli (e.g. packages, jingles) that must be devised to sell it.

The experiential hierarchy

In recent years researchers have begun to stress the significance of emotional response as a central aspect of an attitude. According to the experiential hierarchy of effects,

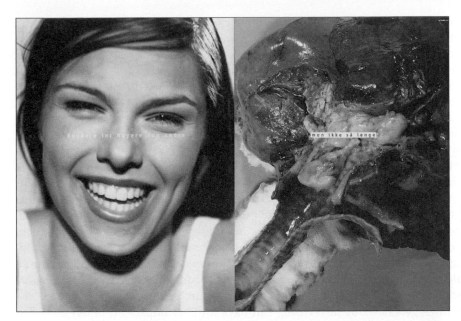

'Smokers are more sociable than others ... while it lasts.' This Norwegian ad represents the many anti-smoking campaigns running in European markets.

John Hopkins Bloomberg School of Public Health

consumers act on the basis of their emotional reactions (just as Lynn enjoys watching TV with her friends, regardless of what is on). Although the factors of beliefs and behaviour are recognized as playing a part, a consumer's overall evaluation of an attitude object is considered by many to be the core of an attitude.

This perspective highlights the idea that attitudes can be strongly influenced by intangible product attributes such as package design, and by consumers' reactions to accompanying stimuli such as advertising and even the brand name. As discussed in Chapter 4, resulting attitudes will be affected by consumers' hedonic motivations, such as how the product makes them feel or the fun its use will provide. Numerous studies indicate that the mood a person is in when exposed to a marketing message influences how the ad is processed, the likelihood that the information presented will be remembered, and how the person will feel about the advertised item and related products in the future.[15]

One important debate about the experiential hierarchy concerns the independence of cognition and affect. On the one hand, the *cognitive–affective model* argues that an affective judgement is the last step in a series of cognitive processes. Earlier steps include the sensory registration of stimuli and the retrieval of meaningful information from memory to categorize these stimuli.[16]

On the other hand, the *independence hypothesis* takes the position that affect and cognition involve two separate, partially independent systems; affective responses do not always require prior cognitions.[17] The number one song in the 'Top Ten' hit parade may possess the same attributes as many other songs (dominant bass guitar, raspy vocals, persistent downbeat), but beliefs about these attributes cannot explain why one song becomes a classic while another sharing the same characteristics ends up in the bargain bin at the local record shop. The independence hypothesis does not eliminate the role of cognition in experience. It simply balances this traditional, rational emphasis on calculated decision-making by paying more attention to the impact of aesthetic, subjective experience. This type of holistic processing is more likely to occur when the product is perceived as primarily expressive or delivers sensory pleasure rather than utilitarian benefits.[18]

There's more to marketing than product attitudes

Marketers who are concerned with understanding consumers' attitudes have to contend with an even more complex issue: in decision-making situations, people form attitudes towards objects other than the product itself that can influence their ultimate selections. One additional factor to consider is attitudes towards the act of buying in general. As we'll see later in the chapter, sometimes people are reluctant, embarrassed or just too lazy to expend the effort to obtain a desired product or service.

In addition, consumers' reactions to a product, over and above their feelings about the product itself, are influenced by their evaluations of its advertising. Our evaluation of a product can be determined solely by our appraisal of how it is depicted in marketing communications – that is, we don't hesitate to form attitudes about products we've never even seen personally, much less used.

▶ The **attitude towards the advertisement (A$_{ad}$)** is defined as a predisposition to respond in a favourable or unfavourable manner to a particular advertising stimulus during a particular exposure occasion. Determinants of A$_{ad}$ include the viewer's attitude towards the advertiser, evaluations of the ad execution itself, the mood evoked by the ad and the degree to which the ad affects viewers' arousal levels.[19] A viewer's feelings about the context in which an ad appears can also influence brand attitudes. For example, attitudes about an ad and the brand depicted will be influenced if the consumer sees the ad while watching a favourite TV programme.[20] The effects demonstrated by A$_{ad}$ emphasize the importance of an ad's entertainment value in the purchase process.[21]

The feelings generated by advertising can have a direct impact on brand attitudes. Commercials can evoke a wide range of emotional responses, from disgust to happiness. Further, there is evidence that emotional responses will vary from one group of consumers to another. In an empirical study of students and housewives in Belgium and Holland, the results showed that the Belgians were more positive towards the hedonic and sociocultural aspects of advertising than their Dutch counterparts. In the UK, Ford's ad campaign research on the Ford Ka, which is targeting an image-oriented market, showed it annoyed 41 per cent of 55–64-year-olds, compared with only 18 per cent of 25–34-year-olds. These feelings can be influenced both by the way the ad is done (i.e. the specific advertising execution) and by the consumer's reactions to the advertiser's motives. For example, many advertisers who are trying to craft messages for adolescents and young adults are encountering problems because this age group, having grown up in a 'marketing society', tends to be sceptical about attempts to persuade them to buy things.[22] These reactions can, in turn, influence memory for advertising content.[23] At least three emotional dimensions have been identified in commercials: pleasure, arousal and intimidation.[24] Specific types of feelings that can be generated by an ad include the following:[25]

- *Upbeat feelings* – amused, delighted, playful.
- *Warm feelings* – affectionate, contemplative, hopeful.
- *Negative feelings* – critical, defiant, offended.

marketing pitfall

Is there a European attitude towards humour in advertising?

'One of the reasons the use of humour is so widespread is that it is such a versatile tool. 'It has a surprisingly broad range of applications. It can act as a razor-sharp discriminator, allowing advertisers to address very tightly defined demographic and attitudinal segments, but because humour is universal it can also act as a catch-all, a way of appealing to everyone,' says advertising psychologist David Lewis.

Humour may be universal, but few nations use it to the extent it is used in the UK. Research carried out three years ago by the University of Luton into the devices used in beer advertising found that 88 per cent of British beer ads used humour, compared with a third of Dutch beer ads and only 10 per cent of German beer commercials. Brits' reliance on humour reflects historic and cultural factors peculiar to this country, say commentators. A major ingredient is our antipathy to 'the sell', argues writer and communications consultant Paul Twivy, who has written comedy scripts for television and run a major advertising agency. 'It's a feature of the British malaise. We are embarrassed about the hard sell. Germany for instance has a tradition of revering engineering, so they are quite happy to talk unironically about product quality. We on the other hand still look down on commerce and value amateurism and effortless success in a way that can be traced back to the nineteenth century. So humour which entertains is a way of selling, while not being seen to sell.' Others say that it reflects a narrow range of emotional responses and attitudes within the national culture. 'Other countries are much more open about expressing a wide range of attitudes. We tend to be repressed and self-deprecating and consider it rude to wear our emotions on our sleeve. So we use humour as a way of not expressing what we really feel,' says Andy Nairn, joint planning director at advertising agency Miles Calcraft Briginshaw Duffy. The upshot is that American advertising, for instance, has a much wider emotional repertoire than British, using joy, love, ambition and desire in a way that would simply make British audiences gag.'[26] How do you respond to humorous ads from different countries in Europe? Do they all strike you as 'funny', and does the approach improve your attitude towards the advertiser's sponsor?

■ FORMING ATTITUDES

We all have lots of attitudes, and we don't usually question how we got them. No one is born with the conviction that, say, Pepsi is better than Coke or that heavy metal music liberates the soul. Where do these attitudes come from?

An attitude can form in several different ways, depending on the particular hierarchy of effects in operation. It can occur because of classical conditioning, in which an attitude object, such as the name Pepsi, is repeatedly paired with a catchy jingle ('You're in the Pepsi Generation . . .'). Or it can be formed through instrumental conditioning, in which consumption of the attitude object is reinforced (Pepsi quenches the thirst). Alternatively, the learning of an attitude can be the outcome of a very complex cognitive process. For example, a teenager may come to model the behaviour of friends and media figures who drink Pepsi because she believes that this act will enable her to fit in with the desirable images of the Pepsi Generation.

It is thus important to distinguish between types of attitudes, since not all are formed the same way.[27] A highly brand-loyal consumer like Leah, the Manchester United fan, has an enduring, deeply held positive attitude towards an attitude object, and this involvement will be difficult to weaken. On the other hand, another consumer like Nicki, who likes the drama and excitement more than the subtle aspects of soccer, may have a mildly positive attitude towards a product but be quite willing to abandon it when something better comes along. This section will consider the differences between strongly and weakly held attitudes and briefly review some of the major theoretical perspectives that have been developed to explain how attitudes form and relate to one another in the minds of consumers.

Levels of commitment to an attitude

Consumers vary in their commitment to an attitude, and the degree of commitment is related to their level of involvement with the attitude object, as follows:[28]

- *Compliance.* At the lowest level of involvement, compliance, an attitude is formed because it helps in gaining rewards or avoiding punishments from others. This attitude is very superficial: it is likely to change when the person's behaviour is no longer monitored by others or when another option becomes available. A person may drink Pepsi because that is the brand the café sells and it is too much trouble to go elsewhere for a Coca-Cola.

- *Identification*. A process of identification occurs when attitudes are formed in order for the consumer to be similar to another person or group. Advertising that depicts the social consequences of choosing some products over others is relying on the tendency of consumers to imitate the behaviour of desirable models.

- *Internalization*. At a high level of involvement, deep-seated attitudes are internalized and become part of the person's value system. These attitudes are very difficult to change because they are so important to the individual. For example, many consumers had strong attitudes towards Coca-Cola and reacted quite negatively when the company attempted to switch to the New Coke formula. This allegiance to Coke was obviously more than a minor preference for these people: the brand had become intertwined with their social identities, taking on patriotic and nostalgic properties.

The consistency principle

Have you ever heard someone say, 'Pepsi is my favourite soft drink. It tastes terrible', or 'I love my husband. He's the biggest idiot I've ever met'? Perhaps not very often, because these beliefs or evaluations are not consistent with one another. According to the ▶ **principle of cognitive consistency**, consumers value harmony among their thoughts, feelings and behaviours, and they are motivated to maintain uniformity among these elements. This desire means that, if necessary, consumers will change their thoughts, feelings or behaviours to make them consistent with their other experiences. The consistency principle is an important reminder that attitudes are not formed in a vacuum. A significant determinant of the way an attitude object will be evaluated is how it fits with other, related attitudes already held by the consumer.

marketing pitfall

World falls out of love with US brands?

'It is no accident that 64 of the most valuable 100 global brands, as measured by Interbrand, are owned by US companies. For more than half a century, the US and its products have stood for progress, glamour and freedom in the minds of consumers around the world. Yet there seems to be a growing challenge for US companies in the attitudes of people such as John McInally, a Scottish management consultant living in Brussels, whose boycott of US products goes as far as asking that his four-year-old son not be given Coca-Cola at birthday parties. 'I used to have a lot of respect for America; now there is mostly fear,' says Mr McInally. 'You feel pretty powerless, but the one thing you can do is stop buying American products.'

There is little doubt that there are more Mr McInallys in the world today than there were before Abu Ghraib and Guantánamo Bay became household names. Poll after poll has shown that allegations of human rights abuses and the failure to find weapons of mass destruction in Iraq have tarnished the international reputation of the US.

Yet geopolitics seems to be easily left behind when shoppers get to the till. Those activists who express their anger at the US through conscious boycotts of its companies remain a small minority. The bigger question worrying the business world is whether the opinion poll data point to a more subtle tarnishing of US brands in the minds of millions of ordinary consumers. If the American dream played such an important role in the growth of iconic US brands, what happens if significant numbers of consumers begin to think of the US as a bit of a nightmare?'[29]

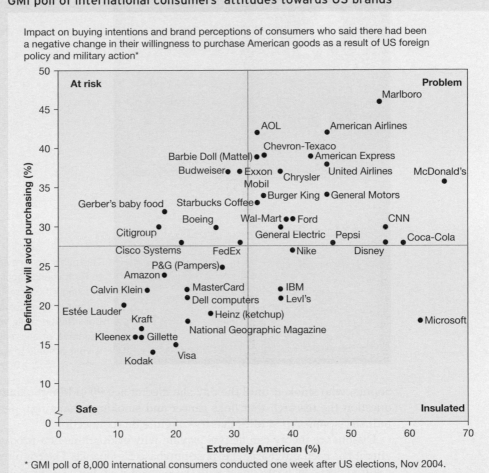

GMI poll of international consumers' attitudes towards US brands

Impact on buying intentions and brand perceptions of consumers who said there had been a negative change in their willingness to purchase American goods as a result of US foreign policy and military action*

* GMI poll of 8,000 international consumers conducted one week after US elections, Nov 2004.

Source: Interbrand, and Dan Roberts, 'Is the world falling out of love with US brands?', *Financial Times*, 30 December 2004.

Cognitive dissonance theory revisited

In the last chapter, we discussed the role played by cognitive dissonance when consumers are trying to choose between two desired products. Cognitive dissonance theory has other important ramifications for attitudes, since people are often confronted with situations in which there is some conflict between their attitudes and behaviours.[30]

The theory proposes that, much like hunger or thirst, people are motivated to reduce this negative state by making things fit with one another. The theory focuses on situations where two cognitive elements are inconsistent with one another.

A cognitive element can be something a person believes about himself, a behaviour he performs or an observation about his surroundings. For example, the two cognitive elements 'I know smoking cigarettes causes cancer' and 'I smoke cigarettes' are dissonant. This psychological inconsistency creates a feeling of discomfort that the smoker is motivated to reduce. The magnitude of dissonance depends upon both the importance and the number of dissonant elements.[31] In other words, the pressure to reduce dissonance is more likely to be observed in high-involvement situations in which the elements are more important to the individual.

Dissonance reduction can occur by either eliminating, adding or changing elements. For example, the person could stop smoking (eliminating) or remember Great-Aunt

This public service advertisement hopes to form young people's attitudes towards drinking. Of course, individuals will vary in their level of commitment to drinking. Does this ad strike you primarily at a cognitive, or an emotional, level? What is your attitude towards the ad?

Sophia, who smoked until the day she died at age 90 (adding). Alternatively, he might question the research that links cancer and smoking (changing), perhaps by believing industry-sponsored studies that try to refute this connection.

Dissonance theory can help to explain why evaluations of a product tend to increase after it has been purchased, i.e. post-purchase dissonance. The cognitive element 'I made a stupid decision' is dissonant with the element 'I am not a stupid person', so people tend to find even more reasons to like something after buying it.

A field study performed at a horse race demonstrates post-purchase dissonance. Gamblers evaluated their chosen horses more highly and were more confident of their success after they had placed a bet than before. Since the gambler is financially committed to the choice, he or she reduces dissonance by increasing the attractiveness of the chosen alternative relative to the unchosen ones.[32] One implication of this phenomenon is that consumers actively seek support for their purchase decisions, so marketers should supply them with additional reinforcement to build positive brand attitudes.

While the consistency principle works well in explaining our desire for harmony among thoughts, feelings and behaviours, and subsequently in helping marketers understand their target markets, it isn't a perfect predictor of the way in which we hold seemingly *related* attitudes, as we saw in the case of Leah's attitudes towards soccer, Nike and labour practices in our globalized economy.

Self-perception theory

Do attitudes necessarily change following behaviour because people are motivated to feel good about their decisions? **Self-perception theory** provides an alternative explanation of dissonance effects.[33] It assumes that people use observations of their own behaviour to determine what their attitudes are, just as we assume that we know the attitudes of others by watching what they do. The theory states that we maintain consistency by inferring that we must have a positive attitude towards an object if we have bought or consumed it (assuming that we freely made this choice).

Self-perception theory is relevant to the low-involvement hierarchy, since it involves situations in which behaviours are initially performed in the absence of a strong internal attitude. After the fact, the cognitive and affective components of attitude fall into line. Thus, buying a product out of habit may result in a positive attitude towards it after the fact – namely, why would I buy it if I didn't like it?

Self-perception theory helps to explain the effectiveness of a sales strategy called the ▶ **foot-in-the-door technique**, which is based on the observation that a consumer is more likely to comply with a request if he or she has first agreed to comply with a smaller request.[34] The name of this technique comes from the practice of door-to-door selling, when the salesperson was taught to plant his or her foot in a door so the prospect could not slam it shut. A good salesperson knows that he or she is more likely to get an order if the customer can be persuaded to open the door and talk. By agreeing to do so, the customer has established that he or she is willing to listen. Placing an order is consistent with this self-perception. This technique is especially useful for inducing consumers to answer surveys or to donate money to charity. Such factors as the time lag between the first and second requests, the similarity between the two requests, and whether the same person makes both requests have been found to influence their effectiveness.[35]

Social judgement theory

▶ **Social judgement theory** assumes that people assimilate new information about attitude objects in the light of what they already know or feel.[36] The initial attitude acts as a frame of reference, and new information is categorized in terms of this existing standard. Just as our decision that a box is heavy depends in part on other boxes we have lifted, so we develop a subjective standard when making judgements about attitude objects.

One important aspect of the theory is the notion that people differ in terms of the infor-▶ mation they will find acceptable or unacceptable. They form **latitudes of acceptance and rejection** around an attitude standard. Ideas that fall within a latitude will be favourably received, while those falling outside this zone will not. There are plenty of examples of how latitudes of acceptance and rejection are influencing marketing practices and consumers' behaviour in Europe: Recently, childhood obesity has become an alarming European issue, prompting the Belgian parliament's ban of Coca-Cola machines in Belgium's elementary schools.[37] Likewise, European attitudes towards smoking have clearly evolved towards a latitude of rejection – providing GlaxoSmithKline with the opportunity to launch new anti-smoking products such as nicotine replacement gums and patches, and giving many pubs and bars the opportunity to reposition themselves as non-smoking venues.[38]

Messages that fall within the latitude of acceptance tend to be seen as more consistent with one's position than they actually are. This process is called an *assimilation effect*. On the other hand, messages falling in the latitude of rejection tend to be seen as even further from one's position than they actually are, resulting in a *contrast effect*.[39]

As a person becomes more involved with an attitude object, his or her latitude of acceptance shrinks. In other words, the consumer accepts fewer ideas that are removed from his or her own position and tends to oppose even mildly divergent positions. This tendency is evident in ads that appeal to discriminating buyers, which claim that knowledgeable people will reject anything but the very best, for example, 'Choosy mothers choose Jif' (Jif is Unilever's brand of peanut butter in many countries, and is known as Cif in many other countries). On the other hand, relatively uninvolved consumers will consider a wider range of alternatives. They are less likely to be brand-loyal and will be more likely to be brand-switchers.[40]

Balance theory

▶ **Balance theory** considers relations among elements a person might perceive as belonging together.[41] This perspective involves relations (always from the perceiver's subjective point of view) among three elements, so the resulting attitude structures are called *triads*. Each triad contains (1) a person and his or her perceptions of (2) an attitude object and (3) some other person or object.

These perceptions can be positive or negative. More importantly, people *alter* these perceptions in order to make relations among them consistent. The theory specifies that people desire relations among elements in a triad to be harmonious, or balanced. If they are not, a state of tension will result until perceptions are changed and balance is restored.

Elements can be perceived as going together in one of two ways. They can have a *unit relation*, where one element is seen as belonging to or being a part of the other (something like a belief), or a *sentiment relation*, where the two elements are linked because one has expressed a preference (or dislike) for the other. A couple might be seen as having a positive sentiment relation. If they marry, they will have a positive unit relation. The process of divorce is an attempt to sever a unit relation.

To see how balance theory might work, consider the following scenario:

- Monica would like to go out with Anthony, who is in her consumer behaviour class. In balance theory terms, Monica has a positive sentiment relation with Anthony.

- One day, Anthony attends class wearing clothing that allows his fellow students to see his tattoo. Anthony has a positive unit relation with the tattoo. It belongs to him and is literally a part of him.

- Monica does not like tattooed men. She has a negative sentiment relation with tattoos.

According to balance theory, Monica faces an unbalanced triad, and she will experience pressure to restore balance by altering some aspect of the triad, as shown in Figure 5.2. She could, for example, decide that she does not like Anthony after all. Or her liking for Anthony could prompt a change in her attitude towards tattoos. Finally, she could

Figure 5.2 Alternative routes to restoring balance in a triad

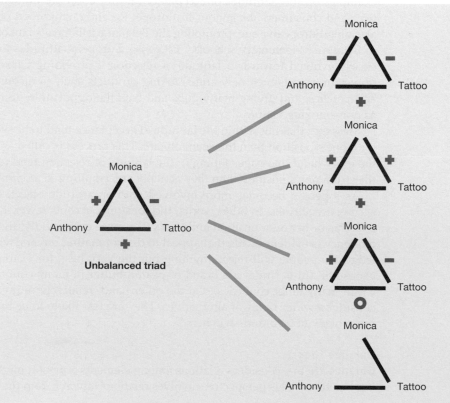

choose to 'leave the field' by thinking no more about Anthony and his controversial tattoo. Note that while the theory does not specify which of these routes will be taken, it does predict that one or more of Monica's perceptions will have to change in order to achieve balance. While this distortion is an oversimplified representation of most attitude processes, it helps to explain a number of consumer behaviour phenomena.

Balance theory reminds us that when perceptions are balanced, attitudes are likely to be stable. On the other hand, when inconsistencies are observed we are more likely to observe changes in attitudes. Balance theory also helps to explain why consumers like to be associated with positively valued objects. Forming a unit relation with a popular product (buying and wearing fashionable clothing or driving a high-performance car) may improve one's chances of being included as a positive sentiment relation in other people's triads.

Finally, balance theory is useful in accounting for the widespread use of celebrities to endorse products. In cases where a triad is not fully formed (that is, one involving perceptions about a new product or one about which the consumer does not yet have a well-defined attitude), the marketer can create a positive sentiment relation between the consumer and the product by depicting a positive unit relation between the product and a well-known personality. In other cases, behaviours are discouraged when admired people argue against them, as is the goal when athletes feature in government-sponsored anti-drug campaigns.

This 'balancing act' is at the heart of celebrity endorsements, in which it is hoped that the star's popularity will transfer to the product. This strategy will be considered at length in the next chapter.

■ ATTITUDE MODELS

A consumer's overall evaluation of a product sometimes accounts for the bulk of his or her *attitude* towards it. When market researchers want to assess attitudes, it can often be sufficient for them simply to ask the consumer, 'How do you feel about Heineken?', or 'How do you feel about the eventual acceptance of a European constitution?'

However, as we saw earlier, attitudes can be a lot more complex than that. One problem is that a product or service may be composed of many attributes or qualities – some of which may be more important than others to particular people. Another problem is that a person's decision to act on his or her attitude is affected by other factors, such as whether it is felt that buying a product will meet with approval of friends or family (if Leah's closest friends are strongly opposed to using cheap labour for the making of Nike soccer boots, this may be a key reason for her not to buy Nike). For these reasons, attitude models have been developed that try to specify the different elements that might work together to influence people's evaluations of attitude objects.

Multi-attribute attitude models

A simple response does not always tell us everything we need to know about why the consumer has certain feelings towards a product or about what marketers can do to ▶ change the consumer's attitude. For this reason, **multi-attribute attitude models** have been extremely popular among marketing researchers. This type of model assumes that a consumer's attitude (evaluation) of an attitude object (A_o) will depend on the beliefs he or she has about several or many attributes of the object. The use of a multi-attribute model implies that an attitude towards a product or brand can be predicted by identifying these specific beliefs and combining them to derive a measure of the consumer's overall attitude. We'll describe how these work, using the example of a consumer evaluating a complex attitude object that should be very familiar: a university.

Basic multi-attribute models specify three elements:[42]

- *Attributes* are characteristics of the A_o. Most models assume that the relevant characteristics can be identified. That is, the researcher can include those attributes that consumers take into consideration when evaluating the A_o. For example, scholarly reputation is an attribute of a university.

- *Beliefs* are cognitions about the specific A_o (usually relative to others like it). A belief measure assesses the extent to which the consumer perceives that a brand possesses a particular attribute. For example, a student might have a belief that Oxford colleges have a strong academic standing.

- *Importance weights* reflect the relative priority of an attribute to the consumer. Although an A_o can be considered on a number of attributes, some will be more important than others (i.e. they will be given greater weight), and these weights are likely to differ across consumers. In the case of universities, for example, one student might stress the school's library resources, while another might assign greater weight to the social environment in which the university is located.

Measuring attitude elements

Suppose a supermarket chain wanted to measure shoppers' attitudes towards its retail outlets. The firm might administer one of the following types of attitude scales to consumers by mail, phone or in person.[43]

Single-item scales One simple way to assess consumers' attitudes towards a store or product is to ask them for their general feelings about it. Such a global assessment does not provide much information about specific attributes, but it does give managers some sense of consumers' overall attitudes. This single-item approach often uses a Likert scale, which measures respondents' overall level of agreement or feelings about an attitude statement.

> How satisfied are you with your grocery store?
> Very satisfied   Somewhat satisfied   Satisfied   Not at all satisfied

Multiple-item batteries Attitude models go beyond such a simple measure, since they acknowledge that an overall attitude may often be composed of consumers' perceptions about multiple elements. For this reason, many attitude measures assess a set of beliefs about an issue and combine these reactions into an overall score. For example, the supermarket might ask customers to respond to a set of Likert scales and combine their responses into an overall measure of store satisfaction:

> 1 My supermarket has a good selection of produce.
> 2 My supermarket maintains sanitary conditions.
> 3 I never have trouble finding exotic foods at my supermarket.

> Agree   Agree   Neither agree   Disagree   Disagree
> strongly   somewhat   nor disagree   somewhat   strongly

The *semantic-differential scale* is useful for describing a person's set of beliefs about a company or brand, and it is also used to compare the images of competing brands. Respondents rate each attribute on a series of rating scales, where each end is anchored by adjectives or phrases, such as this one:

> My supermarket is
> Dirty 1–2–3–4–5–6–7 Clean

Semantic-differential scales can be used to construct a profile analysis of the competition, where the images of several stores or products can be compared visually by plotting the mean ratings for each object on several attributes of interest. This simple technique can help to pinpoint areas where the product or store diverges sharply from the

Figure 5.3 Hypothetical profiles of three types of cinema

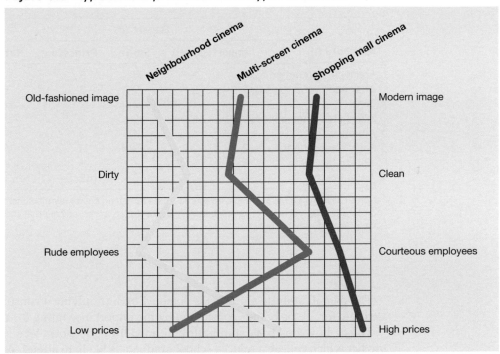

competitors (in either a positive or a negative way). The fictitious profiles of three different types of cinema are shown in Figure 5.3. Based on these findings, the management of a multi-screen cinema might want to emphasize its wide selection of films and/or try to improve its image as a modern cinema, or improve its cleanliness.

The Fishbein model

The most influential multi-attribute model is the Fishbein model, named after its primary developer.[44] The model measures three components of attitude.

1 *Salient beliefs* people have about an A_o (those beliefs about the object that are considered during evaluation).

2 *Object-attribute linkages*, or the probability that a particular object has an important attribute.

3 *Evaluation* of each of the important attributes.

Note, however, that the model makes some assumptions that may not always be warranted. It assumes that we have been able to specify adequately all the relevant attributes that, for example, a student will use in evaluating his or her choice about which college to attend. The model also assumes that he or she will go through the process (formally or informally) of identifying a set of relevant attributes, weighing them and summing them. Although this particular decision is likely to be highly involving, it is still possible that his or her attitude will be formed by an overall affective response (a process known as *affect-referral*).

By combining these three elements, a consumer's overall attitude towards an object can be computed. (We'll see later how this basic equation has been modified to increase its accuracy.) The basic formula is

$$A_{ijk} = \sum B_{ijk} I_{ik}$$

where i = attribute; j = brand; k = consumer; I = the importance weight given attribute i by consumer k; B = consumer k's belief regarding the extent to which brand j possesses attribute i; and A = a particular consumer k's attitude score for brand j.

Table 5.1 The basic multi-attribute model: Sandra's college decision

Attribute (i)	Importance (I)	Beliefs (b)			
		Smith	Princeton	Rutgers	Northland
Academic reputation	6	8	9	6	3
All women	7	9	3	3	3
Cost	4	2	2	6	9
Proximity to home	3	2	2	6	9
Athletics	1	1	2	5	1
Party atmosphere	2	1	3	7	9
Library facilities	5	7	9	7	2
Attitude score		163	142	153	131

Note: These hypothetical ratings are scored from 1 to 10, and higher numbers indicate 'better' standing on an attribute. For a negative attribute (e.g. cost), higher scores indicate that the school is believed to have 'less' of that attribute (i.e. to be cheaper).

The overall attitude score (A) is obtained by multiplying a consumer's rating of each attribute for all the brands considered by the importance rating for that attribute.

To see how this basic multi-attribute model might work, let's suppose we want to predict which college a middle-school graduate is likely to attend. After months of waiting, Sandra has been accepted at four colleges. Since she must now decide between these, we would first like to know which attributes Sandra will consider in forming an attitude towards each college. We can then ask Sandra to assign a rating regarding how well each college performs on each attribute and also determine the relative importance of the attributes to her. An overall attitude score for each college can then be computed by summing scores on each attribute (after weighing each by its relative importance). These hypothetical ratings are shown in Table 5.1. Based on this analysis, it seems that Sandra has the most favourable attitude towards Smith. She is clearly someone who would like to attend an all-women's college with a solid academic reputation rather than a college that offers a strong athletics programme or a party atmosphere.

Strategic applications of the multi-attribute model

Imagine you are the director of marketing for Northland University, another institution Sandra is considering. How might you use the data from this analysis to improve your image?

Capitalize on relative advantage If one's brand is viewed as being superior on a particular attribute, consumers like Sandra need to be convinced that this particular attribute is an important one. For example, while Sandra rates Northland's social atmosphere highly, she does not believe this attribute is a valued aspect for a college. As Northland's marketing director, you might emphasize the importance of an active social life, varied experiences or even the development of future business contacts forged through strong school friendships.

Strengthen perceived product/attribute linkages A marketer may discover that consumers do not equate his or her brand with a certain attribute. This problem is commonly addressed by campaigns that stress the product's qualities to consumers (e.g. 'new and improved'). Sandra apparently does not think much of Northland's academic quality, sports facilities or library. You might develop an informational campaign to improve these perceptions (e.g. 'Little-known facts about Northland').

Add a new attribute Product marketers frequently try to create a distinctive position from their competitors by adding a product feature. Northland might try to emphasize some unique aspect, such as a supervised work-experience programme for business graduates, which takes advantage of links with the local community.

Influence competitors' ratings Finally, you might try to decrease the positive rating of competitors. This type of action is the rationale for a strategy of comparative advertising. One tactic might be to publish an ad that lists the tuition fees of a number of local colleges, as well as their attributes with which Northland can be favourably compared, as the basis for emphasizing the value for money obtained at Northland.

■ USING ATTITUDES TO PREDICT BEHAVIOUR

Although multi-attribute models have been used by consumer researchers for many years, they have been plagued by a major problem: in many cases, knowledge of a person's attitude is not a very good predictor of behaviour. In a classic demonstration of 'do as I say, not as I do', many studies have obtained a very low correlation between a person's reported attitude towards something and his or her actual behaviour towards it. Some researchers have been so discouraged that they have questioned whether attitudes are of any use at all in understanding behaviour.[45] This questionable linkage can be a big headache for advertisers when consumers love a commercial yet fail to buy the product. A Norwegian charity won an award for a popular advertising campaign on which it spent 3 million Nkr (£300,000), only to find that it resulted in just 1.7 million Nkr in donations.[46]

The extended Fishbein model

The original Fishbein model, which focused on measuring a consumer's attitude towards a product, has been extended in a number of ways to improve its predictive ability. ▶ The revised version is called the **theory of reasoned action**.[47] The model is still not perfect, but its ability to predict relevant behaviour has been improved.[48] Some of the modifications to this model are considered here.

Intentions vs. behaviour

Many factors might interfere with actual behaviour, even if the consumer's intentions are sincere. He or she might save up with the intention of buying a stereo system. In the interim, though, any number of things – being made redundant or finding that the desired model is out of stock – could happen. It is not surprising, then, that in some instances past purchase behaviour has been found to be a better predictor of future behaviour than is a consumer's behavioural intention.[49] The theory of reasoned action aims to measure behavioural intentions, recognizing that certain uncontrollable factors inhibit prediction of actual behaviour.

Social pressure

The theory acknowledges the power of other people in influencing behaviour. Many of our behaviours are not determined in isolation. Much as we may hate to admit it, what we think others would like us to do may be more relevant than our own individual preferences.

In the case of Sandra's college choice, note that she is very positive about going to an all-female institution. However, if she feels that this choice would be unpopular (perhaps her friends will think she is mad), she might ignore or downgrade this preference when making her final decision. A new element, the subjective norm (SN), was thus added to include the effects of what we believe other people think we should do. The value of SN is arrived at by including two other factors: (1) the intensity of a normative belief

(NB) that others believe an action should be taken or not taken, and (2) the motivation to comply (MC) with that belief (i.e. the degree to which the consumer takes others' anticipated reactions into account when evaluating a course of action or a purchase).

Attitude towards buying

▶ The model now measures **attitude towards the act of buying (A_{act})**, rather than only the attitude towards the product itself. In other words, it focuses on the perceived consequences of a purchase. Knowing how someone feels about buying or using an object proves to be more valid than merely knowing the consumer's evaluation of the object itself.[50]

To understand this distinction, consider a problem that might arise when measuring attitudes towards condoms. Although a group of college students might have a positive attitude towards condom use, does this necessarily predict that they will buy and use them? A better prediction would be obtained by asking the students how likely they are to buy condoms. While a person might have a positive A_o towards condoms, A_{act} might be negative due to the embarrassment or the trouble involved.

Obstacles to predicting behaviour

Despite improvements to the Fishbein model, problems arise when it is misapplied. In many cases the model is used in ways for which it was not intended or where certain assumptions about human behaviour may not be warranted.[51] Other obstacles to predicting behaviour are as follows:

1 The model was developed to deal with actual behaviour (e.g. taking a slimming pill), not with the outcomes of behaviour (e.g. losing weight) which are assessed in some studies.

2 Some outcomes are beyond the consumer's control, such as when the purchase requires the cooperation of other people. For instance, a woman might seek a mortgage, but this intention will be worthless if she cannot find a banker to give her one.

3 The basic assumption that behaviour is intentional may be invalid in a variety of cases, including those involving impulsive acts, sudden changes in one's situation, novelty-seeking or even simple repeat-buying. One study found that such unexpected events as having guests, changes in the weather or reading articles about the health qualities of certain foods exerted a significant effect on actual behaviours.[52]

4 Measures of attitude often do not really correspond to the behaviour they are supposed to predict, either in terms of the A_o or when the act will occur. One common problem is a difference in the level of abstraction employed. For example, knowing a person's attitude towards sports cars may not predict whether he or she will purchase a Porsche 911. It is very important to match the level of specificity between the attitude and the behavioural intention.

5 A similar problem relates to the time-frame of the attitude measure. In general, the longer the time between the attitude measurement and the behaviour it is supposed to assess, the weaker the relationship will be. For example, predictability would improve markedly by asking consumers the likelihood that they would buy a house in the next week as opposed to within the next five years.

6 Attitudes formed by direct, personal experience with an A_o are stronger and more predictive of behaviour than those formed indirectly, such as through advertising.[53] According to the attitude accessibility perspective, behaviour is a function of the person's immediate perceptions of the A_o in the context of the situation in which it is encountered. An attitude will guide the evaluation of the object, but only if it is activated from memory when the object is observed. These findings underscore the importance of strategies that induce trial (e.g. by widespread product sampling to encourage the consumer to try the product at home, by taste tests, test drives, etc.) as well as those that maximize exposure to marketing communications.

**marketing
pitfall**

Free the carp?

For Joseph Vladsky, the insight came one December evening in Warsaw at a supermarket packed with Christmas shoppers. While walking past the fish department, he saw something that stopped him in his tracks. There, in white plastic tubs, were carp – more carp, it seemed, than water. Some were floating belly up. A group of shoppers peered eagerly into the tubs, selecting the main course for their holiday supper. Shop assistants in stained aprons fished out the chosen carp, tossed them onto scales, then dropped them, still flopping, into plastic bags. If asked, the shop assistants would kill the carp with a quick blow to the head from a thick wooden stick or metal pipe. 'Christmas is supposed to be a joyful time', Mr Vladsky recalls thinking. 'But then you go to the market, and there's a tank of fish, dying, being killed. How terrible.'

Carp have graced east European holiday tables since the seventeenth century, when Christian monks first recognized the Asian import as a substitute for meatless feasts. Hundreds of years later, having carp for Christmas came to symbolize defiance of Communist rule. Today, Polish consumers still buy their carp live, and deliver the fatal blow at home, letting the fish swim out their final days in the family bathtub. Lately, however, sales have been stagnant, even though the price has fallen more than 30 per cent over the past three years. Newly affluent Poles seem to prefer salmon or mahi-mahi. Others simply hate waiting for the carp to get out of the bathtub and into the oven (there is a lingering smell in the tub!), and then there are those like Mr Vladsky who object to the seasonal slaughter. Recent media coverage by the Animal Protection Society regarding the inhumane and insanitary conditions surrounding 'Christmas Carp' have slowed the consumption of carp. In Mr Vladsky's case, his children became so attached to the carp in their friend's bathtub that they gave them names, and started treating them as pets. Slowly, attitudes towards killing live carp for Christmas are changing . . .[54]

Question: *How would you apply Fishbein's (no pun intended) multi-attribute model to predict future behaviour of Polish consumption of carp, given the changing attitudes described above?*

**multicultural
dimensions**

The theory of reasoned action has primarily been applied in the West. Certain assumptions inherent in the model may not necessarily apply to consumers from other cultures. Several of the following diminish the universality of the theory of reasoned action:

● The model was developed to predict the performance of any voluntary act. Across cultures, however, many consumer activities, ranging from taking exams and entering military service to receiving an inoculation or even choosing a marriage partner, are not necessarily voluntary.

● The relative impact of subjective norms may vary across cultures. For example, Asian cultures tend to value conformity and face-saving, so it is possible that subjective norms involving the anticipated reactions of others to the choice will have an even greater impact on behaviour for many Asian consumers.

● The model measures behavioural intentions and thus presupposes that consumers are actively anticipating and planning future behaviours. The intention concept assumes that consumers have a linear time sense, i.e. they think in terms of past, present and future. As will be discussed in a later chapter, this time perspective is not held by all cultures.

● A consumer who forms an intention is (implicitly) claiming that he or she is in control of his or her actions. Some cultures tend to be fatalistic and do not necessarily believe in the concept of free will. Indeed, one study comparing students from the United States, Jordan and Thailand found evidence for cultural differences in assumptions about fatalism and control over the future.[55]

Table 5.2 Recycling rate of container glass (%)

Country	1990	1995	1996	1997	1998	1999	2000	2001	2002	2003	2004
Austria	60	n.a.	n.a.	88	86	84	84	83	87	86	88
Belgium	59	67	66	75	n.a.	n.a.	87	88	95	88	90
Denmark	40	63	66	70	63	63	65	65	76	71	75
Finland	46	50	63	62	69	78	89	91	92	73	72
France	41	70	50	52	55	55	55	55	55	58	58
Germany	54	75	79	79	81	81	83	87	90	88	91
Greece	16	35	29	26	27	25	26	27	27	30	24
Ireland	19	39	46	38	37	35	35	40	49	67	69
Italy	49	53	53	34	37	41	40	55	58	59	61
Netherlands	66	80	81	82	85	91	78	78	78	81	76
Norway	34	75	75	76	81	83	85	88	88	86	90
Portugal	23	42	42	44	42	42	40	34	35	38	39
Spain	27	32	35	37	41	40	31	33	36	38	41
Sweden	35	61	72	76	84	84	86	84	87	92	96
Switzerland	61	85	89	91	91	93	91	92	94	96	96
Turkey	30	12	13	20	31	25	24	24	23	22	24
United Kingdom	21	27	22	23	24	26	29	34	34	36	44

n.a. = Not available

Source: FEVE (European Container Glass Federation); *Consumers in Europe: Facts and Figures*, Eurostat, Theme 3: Population and Social Statistics (Luxembourg, 2001).

Tracking attitudes over time

An attitude survey is like a snapshot taken at a single point in time. It may tell us a lot about the position of a person, issue or object at that moment, but it does not permit many inferences about progress made over time or any predictions about possible future changes in consumer attitudes. To accomplish these tasks, it is necessary to develop an attitude-tracking programme. This activity helps to increase the predictability of behaviour by allowing researchers to analyse attitude trends over an extended period of time. It is more like a film than a snapshot. For example, a longitudinal survey conducted by Eurostat of Europeans' attitudes regarding recycling behaviour shows how attitudes can shift over a decade of time, and across countries. Table 5.2 shows the results of a large-scale study carried out in 15 countries. The percentage of respondents reporting that they recycle container glass tends to be growing over the past decade, but at uneven rates, and at very different starting points for each country in the EU.

These results would suggest that even as Europe moves towards a more integrated union with a common currency, consumers from individual countries vary in their recycling attitudes.

Tracking studies

Attitude tracking involves the administration of an attitude survey at regular intervals. Preferably, the same methodology will be used each time so that results can be reliably compared. Several services, such as Gallup, the Henley Centre or the Yankelovich Monitor, track consumer attitudes over time.

This activity can be extremely valuable for strategic decision-making. For example, one financial services firm monitored changes in consumer attitudes towards one-stop banking centres. Although a large number of consumers were enthusiastic about the idea when it was first introduced, the number of people who liked the concept did not increase over time despite the millions of dollars invested in advertising to promote the centres. This finding indicated some problems with the way the concept was being presented, and the company decided to 'go back to the drawing board', and eventually came up with a new way to communicate the advantages of this service.

Changes to look for over time

Some of the dimensions that can be included in attitude tracking include the following:

- *A focus on changes in different age groups.* Attitudes tend to change as people age (a life-cycle effect), and this will be of continual interest to government and business as the demographic profile of Europe continues to get older. More on this in Chapter 13. In addition, cohort effects occur; that is, members of a particular generation (e.g. teens, generation X, or the elderly) tend to share certain outlooks. Also, historical effects can be observed as large groups of people are affected by profound cultural changes (for example, the democratization of eastern European countries, and their admission to the European Union).

- *Scenarios about the future.* Consumers are frequently tracked in terms of their future plans, confidence in the economy, and so on. These measures can provide valuable data about future behaviour and yield insights for public policy.

- *Identification of change agents.* Social phenomena can change people's attitudes towards basic consumption activities over time, as when consumers' willingness to buy fur products shifts. Or people's likelihood of seeking divorce may be affected by such facilitators as changes in the legal system that make this easier, or by inhibitors, such as the prevalence of AIDS and the value of two salaries in today's economy.[56]

■ CHAPTER SUMMARY

- An attitude is a predisposition to evaluate an object or product positively or negatively.

- Social marketing refers to attempts to change consumers' attitudes and behaviours in ways that are beneficial to society as a whole.

- Attitudes are made up of three components: beliefs, affect and behavioural intentions.

- Attitude researchers traditionally assumed that attitudes were learned in a predetermined sequence, consisting first of the formation of beliefs (cognitions) regarding an attitude object, followed by an evaluation of that object (affect) and then some action (behaviour). Depending on the consumer's level of involvement and the circumstances, though, attitudes can result from other hierarchies of effects.

- A key to attitude formation is the function the attitude plays for the consumer (e.g. is it utilitarian or ego-defensive?).

- One organizing principle of attitude formation is the importance of consistency among attitudinal components - that is, some parts of an attitude may be altered to conform with others. Such theoretical approaches to attitudes as cognitive dissonance theory, balance theory and congruity theory stress the vital role of consistency.

- The complexity of attitudes is underscored by multi-attribute attitude models, in which sets of beliefs and evaluations are identified and combined to predict an overall attitude. Factors such as subjective norms and the specificity of attitude scales have been integrated into attitude measures to improve predictability.

► KEY TERMS

Affect (p. 140)

Attitude (p. 138)

Attitude object (A_o) (p. 138)

Attitude towards the act of buying (A_{act}) (p. 156)

Attitude towards the advertisement (A_{ad}) (p. 144)

Balance theory (p. 149)

Behaviour (p. 140)

Cognition (p. 140)

Foot-in-the-door technique (p. 149)

Functional theory of attitudes (p. 139)

Hierarchy of effects (p. 140)

Latitudes of acceptance and rejection (p. 149)

Multi-attribute attitude models (p. 151)

Principle of cognitive consistency (p. 146)

Self-perception theory (p. 148)

Social judgement theory (p. 149)

Theory of reasoned action (p. 155)

CONSUMER BEHAVIOUR CHALLENGE

1 Contrast the hierarchies of effects outlined in the chapter. How will strategic decisions related to the marketing mix be influenced by which hierarchy is operative among target consumers?

2 List three functions played by attitudes, giving an example of how each function is employed in a marketing situation. To examine European countries' attitudes towards a wide variety of issues, go to the website: **http://europa.eu.int/en/comm/dg10/ infcom/epo/eo.html**. Which sorts of attitudes expressed in different countries seem utilitarian, value-expressive or ego-defensive? Why?

3 Think of a behaviour exhibited by an individual that is inconsistent with his or her attitudes (e.g. attitudes towards cholesterol, drug use or even buying things to attain status or be noticed). Ask the person to elaborate on why he or she does the behaviour, and try to identify the way the person has resolved dissonant elements.

4 Using a series of semantic-differential scales, devise an attitude survey for a set of competing cars. Identify areas of competitive advantage or disadvantage for each model you incorporate.

5 Construct a multi-attribute model for a set of local restaurants. Based on your findings, suggest how restaurant managers can improve their establishments' image using the strategies described in the chapter.

NOTES

1. 'It's a funny old game', *The Economist* (10 February 2001): 57–8.
2. Bill Saporito, 'Crazy for the Cup: With a 3–0 start, the US aims for another world soccer title', *Time* (28 June 1999): 62–4.
3. Bill Saporito, 'Flat-out fantastic', *Time* (19 July 1999): 58 (2); Mark Hyman, 'The "babe factor" in women's soccer', *Business Week* (26 July 1999): 118.
4. Robert A. Baron and Donn Byrne, *Social Psychology: Understanding Human Interaction*, 5th edn (Boston: Allyn & Bacon, 1987).
5. D. Albarracín, B.T. Johnson and M.P. Zanna (eds.), *The Handbook of Attitudes* (Mahwah, NJ: Erlbaum, 2005); see also: J.R. Priester, D. Nayakankuppan, M.A. Fleming and J. Godek, 'The A(2)SC(2) model: The influence of attitudes and attitude strength on consideration set choice', *Journal of Consumer Research* 30(4) (2004): 574–87 for a study on how the strength of attitudes influences and guides a consumer's consideration of brands.
6. Daniel Katz, 'The functional approach to the study of attitudes', *Public Opinion Quarterly* 24 (Summer 1960): 163–204; Richard J. Lutz, 'Changing brand attitudes through modification of cognitive structure', *Journal of Consumer Research* 1 (March 1975): 49–59.
7. Russell H. Fazio, T.M. Lenn and E.A. Effrein, 'Spontaneous attitude formation', *Social Cognition* 2 (1984): 214–34.
8. Mason Haire, 'Projective techniques in marketing research', *Journal of Marketing* 14 (April 1950): 649–56.
9. Sharon Shavitt, 'The role of attitude objects in attitude functions', *Journal of Experimental Social Psychology* 26 (1990): 124–48; see also J.S. Johar and M. Joseph Sirgy, 'Value-expressive versus utilitarian advertising appeals: When and why to use which appeal', *Journal of Advertising* 20 (September 1991): 23–34.
10. For the original work that focused on the issue of levels of attitudinal commitment, see H.C. Kelman, 'Compliance, identification, and internalization: Three processes of attitude change', *Journal of Conflict Resolution* 2 (1958): 51–60.
11. Lynn R. Kahle, Kenneth M. Kambara and Gregory M. Rose, 'A functional model of fan attendance motivations for college football', *Sports Marketing Quarterly* 5(4) (1996): 51–60.
12. For a study that found evidence of simultaneous causation of beliefs and attitudes, see Gary M. Erickson, Johny K. Johansson and Paul Chao, 'Image variables in multi-attribute product evaluations: Country-of-origin effects', *Journal of Consumer Research* 11 (September 1984): 694–9.
13. Michael Ray, 'Marketing Communications and the Hierarchy-of-Effects', in P. Clarke, ed., *New Models for Mass Communications* (Beverly Hills, CA: Sage, 1973): 147–76.
14. Herbert Krugman, 'The impact of television advertising: Learning without involvement', *Public Opinion Quarterly* 29 (Fall 1965): 349–56; Robert Lavidge and Gary Steiner, 'A model for predictive measurements of advertising effectiveness', *Journal of Marketing* 25 (October 1961): 59–62.
15. For some recent studies see Andrew B. Aylesworth and Scott B. MacKenzie, 'Context is key: The effect of program-induced mood on thoughts about the ad', *Journal of Advertising*, 27(2) (Summer 1998): 15–17 (at 15); Angela Y. Lee and Brian Sternthal, 'The effects of positive mood on memory', *Journal of Consumer Research* 26 (September 1999): 115–28; Michael J. Barone, Paul W. Miniard and Jean B. Romeo, 'The influence of positive mood on brand extension evaluations', *Journal of Consumer Research* 26 (March 2000): 386–401. For a study that compared the effectiveness of emotional appeals across cultures, see Jennifer L. Aaker and Patti Williams, 'Empathy versus pride: The influence of emotional appeals across cultures', *Journal of Consumer Research* 25 (December 1998): 241–61.
16. Punam Anand, Morris B. Holbrook and Debra Stephens, 'The formation of affective judgments: The cognitive–affective model versus the independence hypothesis', *Journal of Consumer Research* 15 (December 1988): 386–91; Richard S. Lazarus, 'Thoughts on the relations between emotion and cognition', *American Psychologist* 37(9) (1982): 1019–24.
17. Robert B. Zajonc, 'Feeling and thinking: Preferences need no inferences', *American Psychologist* 35(2) (1980): 151–75.
18. Banwari Mittal, 'The role of affective choice mode in the consumer purchase of expressive products', *Journal of Economic Psychology* 4(9) (1988): 499–524.
19. Scot Burton and Donald R. Lichtenstein, 'The effect of ad claims and ad context on attitude toward the advertisement', *Journal of Advertising* 17(1) (1988): 3–11; Karen A. Machleit and R. Dale Wilson, 'Emotional feelings and attitude toward the advertisement: The roles of brand familiarity and repetition', *Journal of Advertising* 17(3) (1988): 27–35; Scott B. Mackenzie and Richard J. Lutz, 'An empirical examination of the structural antecedents of attitude toward the ad in an advertising pretesting context', *Journal of Marketing* 53 (April 1989): 48–65; Scott B. Mackenzie, Richard J. Lutz and George E. Belch, 'The role of attitude toward the ad as a mediator of advertising effectiveness: A test of competing explanations', *Journal of Marketing Research* 23 (May 1986): 130–43; Darrel D. Muehling and Russell N. Laczniak, 'Advertising's immediate and delayed influence on brand attitudes: Considerations across message-involvement levels', *Journal of Advertising* 17(4) (1988): 23–34; Mark A. Pavelchak, Meryl P. Gardner and V. Carter Broach, 'Effect of Ad Pacing and Optimal Level of Arousal on Attitude Toward the Ad', in Rebecca H. Holman and Michael R. Solomon, eds, *Advances in Consumer Research* 18 (Provo, UT: Association for Consumer Research, 1991): 94–9. Some research evidence indicates that a separate attitude is also formed regarding the brand name itself: see George M. Zinkhan and Claude R. Martin Jr., 'New brand names and inferential beliefs: Some insights on naming new products', *Journal of Business Research* 15 (1987): 157–72.
20. John P. Murry Jr., John L. Lastovicka and Surendra N. Singh, 'Feeling and liking responses to television programs: An examination of two explanations for media-context effects', *Journal of Consumer Research* 18 (March 1992): 441–51.

21. Barbara Stern and Judith Lynne Zaichkowsky, 'The impact of entertaining advertising on consumer responses', *Australian Marketing Researcher* 14 (August 1991): 68–80; Mark Ritson, 'Polysemy: The Multiple Meanings of Advertising' in Darach Turley and Stephen Brown, eds, *European Advances in Consumer Research: All Changed, Changed Utterly?* 6 (Valadosta, GA: Association for Consumer Research, 2003): 341; Stefano Puntoni, Mark Ritson and Lan Nguyen, 'The Multiple Meanings of a TV Ad' in Turley and Brown, eds, *European Advances in Consumer Research: All Changed, Changed Utterly?* 6: 432; Magnus Soderlund, 'The Smiling Female Model in Ads: Does She Really Make a Difference?' in Turley and Brown, eds, *European Advances in Consumer Research: All Changed, Changed Utterly?* 6: 343; Karolina Brodin and Mark Ritson, 'The Impact of Advertisign Interaction on Advertising Polsemy' in Turley and Brown, eds, *European Advances in Consumer Research: All Changed, Changed Utterly?* 6: 343.

22. For a recent study that examined the impact of scepticism on advertising issues, see David M. Boush, Marian Friestad and Gregory M. Rose, 'Adolescent skepticism toward TV advertising and knowledge of advertiser tactics', *Journal of Consumer Research* 21 (June 1994): 165–75; see also Lawrence Feick and Heribert Gierl, 'Skepticism about advertising: A comparison of East and West German consumers', *International Journal of Research in Marketing* 13 (1996): 227–35; Rik Pieters and Hans Baumgartner, 'The Attitude Toward Advertising of Advertising Practitioners, Homemakers and Students in The Netherlands and Belgium', in W. Fred van Raaij and Gary J. Bamossy, eds, *European Advances in Consumer Research* 1 (Provo, UT: Association for Consumer Research, 1993): 39–45.

23. Basil G. Englis, 'Consumer Emotional Reactions to Television Advertising and Their Effects on Message Recall', in S. Agres, J.A. Edell and T.M. Dubitsky, eds, *Emotion in Advertising: Theoretical and Practical Explorations* (Westport, CT: Quorum Books, 1990): 231–54.

24. Morris B. Holbrook and Rajeev Batra, 'Assessing the role of emotions as mediators of consumer responses to advertising', *Journal of Consumer Research* 14 (December 1987): 404–20.

25. Marian Burke and Julie Edell, 'Ad reactions over time: Capturing changes in the real world', *Journal of Consumer Research* 13 (June 1986): 114–18.

26. Alex Benady, 'Advertisers' funny business', *Financial Times* (17 February 2004), http://news.ft.com/servlet/ContentServer?pagename=FT.com/StoryFT/FullStory&c=StoryFT&cid=1075982574327&p=1012571727085.

27. Kelman, 'Compliance, identification, and internalization': 51–60.

28. See Sharon E. Beatty and Lynn R. Kahle, 'Alternative hierarchies of the attitude–behaviour relationship: The impact of brand commitment and habit', *Journal of the Academy of Marketing Science* 16 (Summer 1988): 1–10.

29. Dan Roberts, 'Is the world falling out of love with U.S. brands?', *Financial Times* (30 December 2004), http://news.ft.com/cms/s/502f6994-59d5-11d9-ba09-00000e2511c8.html.

30. Leon Festinger, *A Theory of Cognitive Dissonance* (Stanford, CA: Stanford University Press, 1957).

31. Chester A. Insko and John Schopler, *Experimental Social Psychology* (New York: Academic Press, 1972).

32. Robert E. Knox and James A. Inkster, 'Postdecision dissonance at post time', *Journal of Personality and Social Psychology* 8(4) (1968): 319–23.

33. Daryl J. Bem, 'Self-Perception Theory', in Leonard Berkowitz, ed., *Advances in Experimental Social Psychology* (New York: Academic Press, 1972): 1–62.

34. Jonathan L. Freedman and Scott C. Fraser, 'Compliance without pressure: the foot-in-the-door technique', *Journal of Personality and Social Psychology* 4 (August 1966): 195–202; for further consideration of possible explanations for this effect, see William DeJong, 'An examination of self-perception mediation of the foot-in-the-door effect', *Journal of Personality and Social Psychology* 37 (December 1979): 221–31; Alice M. Tybout, Brian Sternthal and Bobby J. Calder, 'Information availability as a determinant of multiple-request effectiveness', *Journal of Marketing Research* 20 (August 1988): 280–90.

35. David H. Furse, David W. Stewart and David L. Rados, 'Effects of foot-in-the-door, cash incentives and follow-ups on survey response', *Journal of Marketing Research* 18 (November 1981): 473–8; Carol A. Scott, 'The effects of trial and incentives on repeat purchase behavior', *Journal of Marketing Research* 13 (August 1976): 263–9.

36. Muzafer Sherif and Carl I. Hovland, *Social Judgment: Assimilation and Contrast Effects in Communication and Attitude Change* (New Haven, CT: Yale University Press, 1961).

37. 'Cola geweerd uit Belgische basisscholen', *De Telegraaf* (4 January 2005), http://www2.telegraaf.nl/buitenland/16939271/Cola_geweerd_uit_Belgische_basisscholen.html.

38. Andrew Jack, 'GSK launches €5 m NiQuitin marketing drive', *Financial Times* (10 January 2005), http://news.ft.com/cms/s/042bcb56-62ad-11d9-8e5d-00000e2511c8.html; Peter John, 'Wetherspoon to stub out smoking in its 650 pubs', *Financial Times* (25 January 2005), http://news.ft.com/cms/s/2b37e7d8-6e75-11d9-a60a-00000e2511c8.html.

39. Joan Meyers-Levy and Brian Sternthal, 'A two-factor explanation of assimilation and contrast effects', *Journal of Marketing Research* 30 (August 1993): 359–68.

40. Mark B. Traylor, 'Product involvement and brand commitment', *Journal of Advertising Research* (December 1981): 51–6.

41. Fritz Heider, *The Psychology of Interpersonal Relations* (New York: Wiley, 1958).

42. William L. Wilkie, *Consumer Behavior* (New York: Wiley, 1986).

43. A number of criteria beyond the scope of this book are important in evaluating methods of attitude measurement, including such issues as reliability, validity and sensitivity. For an excellent treatment of attitude-scaling techniques, see David S. Aaker and George S. Day, *Marketing Research*, 4th edn (New York: Wiley, 1990).

44. Martin Fishbein, 'An investigation of the relationships between beliefs about an object and the attitude toward that object', *Human Relations* 16 (1983): 233–40.

45. Allan Wicker, 'Attitudes versus actions: The relationship of verbal and overt behavioral responses to attitude objects', *Journal of Social Issues* 25 (Autumn 1969): 65.

46. Laura Bird, 'Loved the ad. May (or may not) buy the product', *Wall Street Journal* (7 April 1994): B1 (2 pp.); 'Which half?', *The Economist* (8 June 1996): 80.

47. Icek Ajzen and Martin Fishbein, 'Attitude–behavior relations: A theoretical analysis and review of empirical research', *Psychological Bulletin* 84 (September 1977): 888–918.

48. Morris B. Holbrook and William J. Havlena, 'Assessing the real-to-artificial generalizability of multi-attribute attitude models in tests of new product designs', *Journal of Marketing Research* 25 (February 1988): 25–35; Terence A. Shimp and Alican Kavas, 'The theory of reasoned action applied to coupon usage', *Journal of Consumer Research* 11 (December 1984): 795–809.

49. Richard P. Bagozzi, Hans Baumgartner and Youjae Yi, 'Coupon Usage and the Theory of Reasoned Action', in Holman and Solomon, eds, *Advances in Consumer Research* 18: 24–7; Edward F. McQuarrie, 'An alternative to purchase intentions: The role of prior behavior in consumer expenditure on computers', *Journal of the Market Research Society* 30 (October 1988): 407–37; Arch G. Woodside and William O. Bearden, 'Longitudinal Analysis of Consumer Attitude, Intention, and Behavior Toward Beer Brand Choice', in William D. Perrault Jr., ed., *Advances in Consumer Research* 4 (Ann Arbor, MI: Association for Consumer Research, 1977): 349–56.

50. Michael J. Ryan and Edward H. Bonfield, 'The Fishbein Extended Model and consumer behavior', *Journal of Consumer Research* 2 (1975): 118–36.

51. Blair H. Sheppard, Jon Hartwick and Paul R. Warshaw, 'The theory of reasoned action: A meta-analysis of past research with recommendations for modifications and future research', *Journal of Consumer Research* 15 (December 1988): 325–43.

52. Joseph A. Cote, James McCullough and Michael Reilly, 'Effects of unexpected situations on behavior–intention differences: A garbology analysis', *Journal of Consumer Research* 12 (September 1985): 188–94.

53. Russell H. Fazio, Martha C. Powell and Carol J. Williams, 'The role of attitude accessibility in the attitude-to-behavior process', *Journal of Consumer Research* 16 (December 1989): 280–8; Robert E. Smith and William R. Swinyard, 'Attitude–behavior consistency: The impact of product trial versus advertising', *Journal of Marketing Research* 20 (August 1983): 257–67.

54. Elizabeth Williamson, 'Free the carp? That's one way to get them out of the bathtub', *Wall Street Journal* (22 December 2000): A1.

55. Joseph A. Cote and Patriya S. Tansuhaj, 'Culture Bound Assumptions in Behavior Intention Models', in Thom Srull, ed., *Advances in Consumer Research* 16 (Provo, UT: Association for Consumer Research, 1989): 105–9.

56. Matthew Greenwald and John P. Katosh, 'How to track changes in attitudes', *American Demographics* (August 1987): 46.

ATTITUDE CHANGE AND INTERACTIVE COMMUNICATIONS

Jenny was delighted when she found out she was pregnant and, unusually for her, she loved all the attention and fuss that pregnancy entailed. However, she also found it quite stressful and focused her efforts on trying to ensure that she made the 'right' decisions along the way. Prior to Freddie's birth, Jenny tried to get hold of as much information about pregnancy and babies as possible. She read books, magazines, pamphlets in doctors' surgeries, in fact pretty much anything she could get her hands on to ensure that she had the most current and accurate information available. Armed with this information she made a series of decisions about how she would bring up her baby and the major consumption decisions associated with this.

In Jenny's attempts to be environmentally friendly she had made the decision to use cloth nappies rather than the more popular and convenient choice of disposable nappies. She considered the energy used when machine washing nappies – the focus of recent PR campaigns by the major producers of disposable nappies – but remained convinced that terry cotton nappies were a better bet for the environment. She also did lots of homework before choosing a pushchair. She tended to look at the *Which?* guides produced by the UK Consumers' Association before making important choices. On this occasion she also consulted various magazines and newspaper articles, which helped her to differentiate between the plethora of brand names and models such as Mamas and Papas 03 Sport, Silver Cross XT Pushchair, Bugaboo Frog, Maclaren Volo, Stokke Xplory and Britax Vista. With so much choice she had needed to read all the manufacturers' advertising very carefully; and the various consumer reports helped her to clarify what was really important (such as weight, size, tyres, foot rest). In the end she went for one of the more reasonably priced pushchairs, which as well as ranking highly in the various reports was recommended by her health visitor.

Jenny was determined to breastfeed. Her family, the midwives and the information she had read all convinced her that 'breast is best'. Breastfeeding would be fairly straightforward she thought – so that was one commitment she shouldn't have a problem with. But on Freddie's arrival breastfeeding proved extremely difficult for her. The more difficult it became the more guilty and frustrated Jenny felt – what was wrong with her? Why couldn't she do what was 'best' for her baby? Her difficulties culminated in the development of a breastfeeding infection, which necessitated supplementing her breast milk with formula milk.

Also, Jenny was determined that Freddie would not use a dummy – she considered them as the 'easy option' and 'lazy' parenting. Jenny's mother had never believed in the use of dummies and several of the parenting books she read also discouraged dummies. However, Jenny had been given a set of dummies as a 'Secret Santa' present* and had held on to them – 'just in case'. One day, following the advice of some women at the mother and baby group she attended, she found that Freddie could soon be calmed by the occasional use of a dummy when he was particularly upset. She said: 'Before I had a baby I thought "I am not having a dummy" but when they are crying you start to think about what you can do to make it work. But it is knowing that other people approve of it as well, that makes you think it is OK.' All the books and words from other parents were helpful but for some decisions Jenny found that, for her, motherhood is about flexibility and there is no 'best' way – except for what is best for you and your own child.

* Secret Santa is a Christmas work ritual whereby work colleagues draw a name at random and buy Christmas presents for each other (anonymously) for a specified amount (typically £5, about 8 euros).

EMMA N. BANISTER, Department of Marketing, Lancaster University Management School.

■ CHANGING ATTITUDES THROUGH COMMUNICATION

As consumers we are constantly bombarded by messages inducing us to change our attitudes. These persuasion attempts can range from logical arguments to graphic pictures, and from intimidation by peers to exhortations by celebrity spokespeople. And, communications flow both ways – the consumer may seek out information sources in order to learn more about these options, for instance by surfing the net. The increasing choice of ways to access marketing messages is changing the way we think about persuasion attempts. In Jenny's case, her attitudes towards motherhood had been influenced by health professionals (dietary advice from the doctor during pregnancy; midwives at the antenatal classes who showed videos about breastfeeding her new baby); other experts (authors of mother and baby books); by public policy statements (e.g. 'breast is best'); by her mother and peers (friends from the mother and baby group); and by her pre-existing political views (importance of environmentally responsible behaviour). However, some of her beliefs and attitudes moderated when she became a mother: the difficulties which she experienced in establishing breastfeeding made her more accepting of using formula milk; and when desperately seeking to comfort a crying baby, she discovered the relief that dummies could bring to both distressed baby *and* mother.

This chapter will review some of the factors that help to determine the effectiveness of marketing communications (the issues of peer influence and word-of-mouth are dealt with at greater length in Chapter 10). Our focus will be on some basic aspects of communication that specifically help to determine how and if attitudes will be created or modified. This objective relates to **persuasion**, which refers to an active attempt to change attitudes. Persuasion is, of course, the central goal of many marketing communications. We'll learn more about how marketers try to accomplish this throughout the chapter. However, marketers need to bear in mind that there is evidence of increasingly negative perceptions of advertising. Research reported by J. Walker Smith, President of Yankelovich and Partners, showed the 54 per cent of respondents to their survey 'avoid buying products that overwhelm them with advertising'; 60 per cent said their opinion of advertising 'is much more negative than just a few years ago'; 61 per cent said they agreed that the amount of advertising and marketing to which they are exposed 'is out of control'. Also, 65 per cent said they believed that they 'are constantly bombarded with too much' advertising; and 69 per cent said they 'are interested in products and services that would help them skip or block marketing.'[1]

We begin by setting the stage and listing some basic psychological principles that influence people to change their minds or comply with a request:[2]

- *Reciprocity*: People are more likely to give if they receive. That's why including money in a mail survey questionnaire increases the response rate by an average of 65 per cent over surveys that come in an empty envelope.

- *Scarcity*: Items become more attractive when they are less available. In one study that asked people to rate the quality of chocolate biscuits, participants who got only two biscuits liked them better than did those who got ten of the same kind of biscuit. That helps to explain why we tend to value 'limited edition' items.

- *Authority*: We'll talk more about the importance of who delivers the message. We tend to believe an authoritative source much more readily. That explains why public service broadcasters, who have hard-won reputations for impartiality and objectivity (e.g. the BBC in Great Britain) can be so influential in forming public attitudes; and also why they are so fiercely protective of their independence from government and politicians.

- *Consistency*: As we saw in the last chapter, people try not to contradict themselves in terms of what they say and do about an issue. In one study, students at an Israeli university who solicited donations to help people with disabilities doubled the amount they normally collected in a neighbourhood by first asking the residents to sign a petition supporting those with disabilities two weeks before asking for donations.

- *Liking*: As we'll see later, we tend to agree with those we like or admire. In one study good-looking fund-raisers raised almost twice as much as other volunteers who were not as attractive.

- *Consensus*: We often take into account what others are doing before we decide what to do. We'll talk more about the power of conformity in Chapter 10. This desire to fit in with what others are doing influences our actions – for example, people are more likely to donate to a charity if they first see a list of the names of their neighbours who have already done so.

Decisions, decisions: tactical communications options

Suppose a car company wants to create an advertising campaign for a new soft-top model targeted at young drivers. As it plans this campaign, it must develop a message that will create desire for the car by potential customers. To craft persuasive messages that might persuade someone to buy this car instead of the many others available, we must answer several questions:

- *Who will be shown driving the car in an ad?* A motor-racing ace? A career woman? A new mother like Jenny? A rock star? The source of a message helps to determine consumers' acceptance of it as well as their desire to try the product.

- *How should the message be constructed?* Should it emphasize the negative consequences of being left out when others are driving cool cars and you're still driving around in your old banger? Should it directly compare the car with others already on the market, or maybe present a fantasy in which a tough-minded female executive meets a dashing stranger while cruising down the highway with the soft top down? Should it emphasize the safety features which would appeal to parents with a new baby to consider?

- *What media should be used to transmit the message?* Should it be depicted in a print ad? On television? Sold door to door? On a website? If a print ad is produced, should it be run in the pages of *Good Housekeeping*? *Car and Driver*? *Mother and Baby*? Sometimes *where* something is said can be as important as what is said. Ideally, the attributes of the product should be matched to those of the medium. For example, magazines with high prestige are more effective at communicating messages about overall product image and quality, whereas specialized expert magazines do a better job at conveying factual information.[3]

● *What characteristics of the target market might influence the ad's acceptance?* If targeted users are frustrated in their daily lives, they might be more receptive to a fantasy appeal. If they're status oriented, perhaps a commercial should show bystanders swooning with admiration as the car glides by.

The elements of communication

Marketers and advertisers have traditionally tried to understand how marketing messages can change consumers' attitudes by thinking in terms of the **communications model**, which specifies that a number of elements are necessary for communication to be achieved. In this model, a *source* must choose and encode a message (i.e. initiate the transfer of meaning by choosing appropriate symbolic images which represent the meaning). The meaning must be put into the *message*. There are many ways to say something, and the structure of the message has a major effect on how it is perceived. The message must be transmitted via a *medium*, which could be television, radio, magazines, hoardings, personal contact, website, or even a matchbook cover. Toyota placed its message about the Spider in a sophisticated CD/ROM format for the US market that it knew would be accessed by young, cutting-edge consumers – just the ones it was trying to reach. One or more *receivers* then interpret the message in the light of their own experiences. Finally, *feedback* must be received by the source, which uses the reactions of receivers to modify aspects of the message. *Launch* uses the Web to collect such information from its subscribers. Figure 6.1 depicts the traditional communications process.

An updated view: interactive communications

While the traditional communications model is not entirely wrong, it also doesn't tell the whole story – especially in today's dynamic world of interactivity, in which consumers

Figure 6.1 The traditional communications model

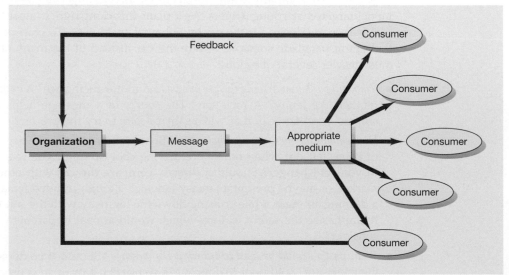

▶ have many more choices available to them and greater control over which messages they will choose to process.[4] In fact, a popular strategy known as **permission marketing** is based on the idea that a marketer will be much more successful trying to persuade consumers who have agreed to let him or her try – consumers who 'opt out' of listening to the message probably weren't good prospects in the first place.[5] On the other hand, those who say they are interested in learning more are likely to be receptive to marketing communications they have already chosen to see or hear. As the permission marketing concept reminds us, we don't have to just sit there and take it. We have a voice in deciding what messages we choose to see and when – and we exercise that option more and more.

The traditional model was developed to understand mass communications, where information is transferred from a producer (source) to many consumers (receivers) at one time – typically via print, television or radio. This perspective essentially views advertising as the process of transferring information to the buyer before a sale. A message is seen as perishable – it is repeated (perhaps frequently) for a fairly short period of time and then it 'vanishes' as a new campaign eventually takes its place.

This traditional communications model was strongly influenced by a group of theorists known as the *Frankfurt School*, which dominated mass communications research for most of the last century. In this view, the media exert direct and powerful effects on individuals, and are often used by those in power to brainwash and exploit the population. The receiver is basically passive – a 'couch potato' who is simply the receptacle for many messages – and may often be duped or persuaded to act based on the information he or she sees or hears (i.e. is 'fed' by the media).

Uses and gratifications

Is this an accurate picture of the way we relate to marketing communications? Proponents of **uses and gratifications theory** argue instead that consumers are an active, goal-directed audience who draw on mass media as a resource to satisfy needs. Instead of asking what media do *for* or *to* people, they ask what people do *with* the media.[6]

The uses and gratifications approach emphasizes that media compete with other sources to satisfy needs, and that these needs include diversion and entertainment as well as information. This also means that the line between marketing information and entertainment is continuing to blur – especially as companies are being forced to design more attractive retail outlets, catalogues and websites in order to attract consumers. Toyota's site (**www.toyota.com**) provides a lot more than the latest specifications about available car options: it includes interests like gardening, travel and sports.

Research with young people in Great Britain finds that they rely on advertising for many gratifications, including entertainment (some report that the 'adverts' are better than the programmes), escapism, play (some report singing along with jingles, others make posters out of magazine ads), and self-affirmation (ads can reinforce their own values or provide role models).[7] A new satellite network, the Advert Channel, recently started showing advertisements 24 hours a day in Great Britain.[8] It's important to note that this perspective is not arguing that media play a uniformly positive role in our lives, only that recipients are making use of the information in a number of ways. For example, marketing messages have the potential to undermine self-esteem as consumers use the media to establish unrealistic standards for behaviour, attitudes or even their own appearance.[9] A comment by one study participant illustrates this negative impact. She observed that when she watched TV with her boyfriend, 'really, it makes you think "oh no, what must I be like?" I mean you're sitting with your boyfriend and he's saying "oh, look at her. What a body!"'[10]

An interactionist perspective on communication

▶ The **interactionist** perspective on communication does not describe human communication as 'mechanistically' as does the classic communications model. Briefly, interactionism relies on three basic premises about communication, which focus on the meaning of objects, ideas and actions:[11]

1 Human beings act towards objects on the basis of the meanings that objects have for them.

2 The meaning of objects is derived from the social interaction that they provide.

3 These meanings are processed and modified through an interpretive process which a person uses in dealing with the object encountered.

The interactionist perspective tones down the importance of the external stimuli, and views consumers as 'interpreters', wherein meaning does not arise from the objects themselves, nor from the psyche, but from interaction patterns. This view argues that meanings are not given 'once and for all' and are readily retrievable from memory. Rather, they are recreated and interpreted anew in each communicative action. Hence, the central role of the 'communicating self' must be taken into consideration. The self is seen as an active participant in the creation of meaning from the various signs in the marketplace rather than as a passive decoder of meanings which may be inherent in the message. Thus, from an interactionist perspective, there is no sender and receiver as such, only *communicators* who are always engaged in mutual sending and receiving of messages. Here, the self is both an object (a 'me') and a subject ('I') of action. The 'me' contains the consciousness of the acting self seen in relation to past experiences of the self and of others. There is thus a constant interpretation of both the self and the other as objects, as well as the object of the communication (the 'message' in the traditional communication model) going on. Figure 6.2 provides an overview of this interactionist communication model.

The model comprises several components.[12] The first component is that of '*role and role taking*'. Here, the communicator performs a role, following some scripts of past experiences, interpreting the situation and acting accordingly. These are efforts at seeing the 'other' from the perspective of 'self'. But the role-playing also involves taking the role of the 'other' to see oneself or seeing the self from the perspective of the other (imagining the image that the other may have).

The second component is *orientation*, which suggests that these roles we carry out are oriented towards an object. This object might be one of the communicators but also any other idea, thing or person. To the extent that the interpretive orientations of the

Figure 6.2 Interactionist communications model

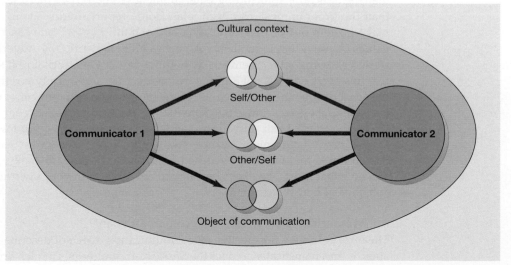

communicators are similar, we can say that there is agreement, or congruence, between them, and that the communicators share the meanings pertaining to themselves and the object. Congruence is typically a matter of degree, and neither total congruence nor total incongruence are possible. Finally, there is the component of *cultural embeddedness*, which suggests that the symbols and other communicative devices used in the communicative process occur in a cultural context.

As an example, consider a company and its advertising agency. As part of the creative process, the ways in which the advertising agency see themselves, the selected target market, the product and campaign in question and the cultural context of the country will play a role in how they interpret the message they are about to create and send out. Likewise, the consumer's past experiences with this company's products, the meanings that the consumer attaches, based on cultural background and present context (present aspirations), coupled with the campaign seen in relation to former campaigns, are all important to the interpretation of the campaign's elements and the subsequent interpretation of the whole message (see Question 5 at the end of this chapter to assess a global print and web campaign for encouraging young men to purchase a particular brand of cognac).

Who's in charge of the remote?

Technological and social developments are forcing us to rethink the picture of the passive consumer, as people are increasingly playing a proactive role in communications. In other words, they are to a greater extent becoming active partners in the communications process. Their input is helping to shape the messages they and others like them receive, and furthermore they may seek out these messages rather than sit at home and wait to see them on TV or in the newspaper.

One of the early signs of this communications revolution was the humble hand-held remote control device. As VCRs became commonplace in the home, consumers had more say in what they wanted to watch – and when. No longer were they at the mercy of the TV networks to decide when to see their favourite programmes; nor did they necessarily have to forsake one programme because it conflicted with another's time slot.

Since that time, of course, our ability to control our media environment has mushroomed. Just ask some of the people who are now using DVRs (digital video recorders) to watch TV shows whenever they wish – and who are skipping over the commercials.[13] Caller ID devices and answering machines allow us to decide if we will accept a phone call during dinner, and to know the source of the message before picking up the phone. A bit of surfing allows us to identify kindred spirits around the globe, to request information about products, and even to provide suggestions to product designers and market researchers.

Levels of interactive response

The key to understanding the dynamics of interactive marketing communications is to consider exactly what is meant by a response.[14] The early perspective on communications primarily regarded feedback in terms of behaviour – did the recipient go out and buy the soap powder after being exposed to an ad for it?

However, a variety of other responses are possible as well, including building awareness of the brand, informing us about product features, reminding us to buy a new package when we've run out, and – perhaps most importantly – building a long-term relationship. Therefore a transaction is *one* type of response, but forward-thinking marketers realize that customers can interact with them in other valuable ways as well. For this reason it is helpful to distinguish between two basic types of feedback.

First-order response Direct marketing vehicles such as catalogues and television infomercials are interactive – if successful, they result in an order, which is most definitely a response! So, let's think of a product offer that directly yields a transaction as a *first-order response*. In addition to providing revenue, sales data are a valuable source of feedback that allow marketers to gauge the effectiveness of their communications efforts.

Second-order response However, a marketing communication does not have to result in an immediate purchase to be an important component of interactive marketing. Messages can prompt useful responses from customers, even though these recipients do not necessarily place an order immediately after being exposed to the communication. Customer feedback in response to a marketing message that is not in the form of a transaction is a *second-order response*.

A second-order response programme, the Pepperidge Farm No Fuss Pastry Club in the United States, illustrates how a firm communicates directly with users without trying to make an immediate sale. The club boasted more than 30,000 members who had been generated through a combination of promotion efforts, including a magazine mail-in offer, an offer on packages of Pepperidge Farm products, publicity created by news reports about the club and a sign-up form available in supermarket outlets. Pepperidge Farm used surveys to determine members' attitudes towards issues related to its business, and the company also collected valuable information on how those people used frozen puff pastry products.[15] Though the company's immediate goal was not to generate the first-order response of selling frozen pastry, it knew that the second-order responses received from club members would result in loyal customers over time – and many more first-order responses as a result.

Another example of second-order response is feedback via freephone numbers. In a survey of caller logs Nestlé found that only 20 per cent represented complaints from customers. In a pilot study, they followed up consumers who had agreed to be contacted for further feedback. Some of the issues which came to light, which had not emerged via earlier market research such as focus groups, included the view that the standard 8 oz Coffee-mate jar was too small – Nestlé increased the standard size jar to 15 oz and saw a substantial increase in sales. The company also learnt that the flavours were difficult to identify from the pastel-coloured containers: in response, the company brightened the colours of the containers.[16]

■ THE SOURCE

Regardless of whether a message is received by 'snail mail' or email, common sense tells us that the same words uttered or written by different people can have very different effects. Research on *source effects* has been carried out for more than 50 years. By attributing the same message to different sources and measuring the degree of attitude change that occurs after listeners hear it, it is possible to determine which aspects of a communicator will induce attitude change.[17]

Under most conditions, the source of a message can have a big impact on the likelihood that the message will be accepted. The choice of a source to maximize attitude change can tap into several dimensions. The source can be chosen because he or she is an expert, attractive, famous, or even a 'typical' consumer who is both likeable and trustworthy. Two particularly important source characteristics are *credibility* and *attractiveness*.[18]

How do marketing specialists decide whether to stress credibility or attractiveness when choosing a message source? There should be a match between the needs of the recipient and the potential rewards offered by the source. When this match occurs, the recipient is more motivated to process the message. People who tend to be sensitive about social acceptance and the opinions of others, for example, are more persuaded by an attractive source, whereas those who are more internally oriented are swayed by a credible, expert source.[19]

The choice may also depend on the type of product. A positive source can help to reduce risk and increase message acceptance overall, but particular types of sources are more effective at reducing different kinds of risk. Experts are effective at changing attitudes towards utilitarian products that have *high performance risk*, such as vacuum cleaners (i.e. they may be complex and not work as expected). Celebrities are more effective when they focus on products such as jewellery and furniture that have high *social risk*: the user of such products is aware of their effect on the impression others have of him or her. Finally, 'typical' consumers, who are appealing sources because of their similarity to the recipient, tend to be most effective when providing real-life endorsements for everyday products that are low risk, such as biscuits.[20]

Source credibility

▶ **Source credibility** refers to a source's perceived expertise, objectivity or trustworthiness. This characteristic relates to consumers' beliefs that a communicator is competent, and is willing to provide the necessary information to evaluate competing products adequately. A credible source can be particularly persuasive when the consumer has not yet learned much about a product or formed an opinion of it.[21] The decision to pay an expert or a celebrity to promote a product can be a very costly one, but researchers have concluded that on average the investment is worth it simply because the announcement of an endorsement contract is often used by market analysts to evaluate a firm's potential profitability, thereby affecting its expected return. On average, then, the impact of endorsements appears to be so positive that it offsets the cost of hiring the spokesperson.[22]

The sleeper effect

Although in general more positive sources tend to increase attitude change, exceptions can occur. Sometimes a source can be obnoxious or disliked and still manage to be effective at getting the product's message across. In some instances the differences in attitude change between positive sources and less positive sources seem to get erased over time. After a while people appear to 'forget' about the negative source and end up changing
▶ their attitudes anyway. This process is known as the **sleeper effect**.[23]

The explanation for the sleeper effect is a subject of debate, as is the more basic question regarding whether and when it really exists. Initially, the *dissociative cue hypothesis* proposed that over time the message and the source become disassociated in the consumer's mind. The message remains on its own in memory, causing the delayed attitude change.[24]

Another explanation is the *availability-valence hypothesis*, which emphasizes the selectivity of memory owing to limited capacity.[25] If the associations linked to the negative source are less available than those linked to the message information, the residual impact of the message enhances persuasion. Consistent with this view, the sleeper effect has been obtained only when the message was encoded deeply; it had stronger associations in memory than did the source.[26]

Building credibility

Credibility can be enhanced if the source's qualifications are perceived as somehow relevant to the product being endorsed. For example, the footballer Gary Lineker is popularly known in the UK as 'Mr Nice' – a personality type which was a natural for the crisp manufacturer Walkers to tie in to their advertising campaign that Walkers Crisps are 'so nice that the nicest people would nick [steal] them'. Before the campaign unprompted awareness of Walkers ads was around 40 per cent. Following Lineker's antics of stealing packets of crisps from little boys, awareness never fell below 60 per cent, and sales have soared.[27] Similarly, Ronald Biggs, whose claim to fame was his 1963 role in 'The Great Train Robbery' in the UK, successfully served as a spokesman in Brazil for a company that makes door locks – a topic about which he is presumably knowledgeable![28] Tommy Hilfiger cultivated a rebellious, street-smart image by using rapper Snoop Doggy Dogg (who was acquitted of murder charges) to help launch his line and Coolio, a former crack addict and thief, as a runway model.[29] Parents may not be thrilled by these message sources – but isn't that the point?

Source biases

A consumer's beliefs about a product's attributes can be weakened if the source is perceived to be the victim of bias in presenting information.[30] *Knowledge bias* implies that a source's knowledge about a topic is not accurate. *Reporting bias* occurs when a source has the required knowledge, but his or her willingness to convey it accurately is compromised – as, for instance, when an expert endorses a product. While his or her credentials might be appropriate, the fact that the expert is perceived as a 'hired gun' compromises credibility.

Companies appreciate the value of having experts validate their products and sometimes their efforts to acquire these testimonials can get them into trouble. For example, Microsoft was criticized when the software company offered to pay 'travel costs' for academics if they presented papers at conferences and mentioned how Microsoft programs helped them in their work.[31]

Concerns are growing in the advertising world about the public's scepticism regarding celebrities who endorse products for money. It doesn't help matters when Britney Spears appears in lavish commercials for Pepsi-Cola but is caught on camera drinking Coca-Cola. Tiger Woods promoted Rolex's Tudor watches for five years, but then he abruptly switched to Swiss rival TAGHeuer. Although Tiger explained the defection simply by noting that 'My tastes have changed', it's possible that the estimated $2 million he's now getting for this new endorsement may have been a factor.[32]

What is a marketer to do? One increasingly popular solution is to involve celebrities in the actual design of the products they're pitching. Michael Jordan oversees the design of Nike's Jordan line of apparel and footwear, and actresses like Victoria Principal create skin-care products for home-shopping networks. Jennifer Lopez even had veto power over the design of the bottle for her new fragrance, Glow by J-Lo.[33]

marketing pitfall

For celebrity campaigns to be effective, the endorser must have a clear and popular image. In addition, the celebrity's image and that of the product he or she endorses should be similar - this effect is known as the **match-up hypothesis**.[34] Many promotional strategies employing stars fail because the endorser has not been selected very carefully - some marketers just assume that because a person is 'famous' he or she will serve as a successful spokesperson.

The images of celebrities can, however, be pre-tested to increase the probability of consumer acceptance. One widely used technique is the so-called '*Q*' *rating* (Q stands for quality) developed by a market research company. This rating considers two factors in surveys: consumers' level of familiarity with a name and the number of respondents who indicate that a person, programme or character is a favourite. While not the most sophisticated research technique, the Q rating acknowledges that familiarity with a celebrity's name in itself is not sufficient to gauge popularity since some widely known people are also widely disliked. Celebrities with a low Q rating include Michael Jackson, Madonna and Cyndi Lauper. Those with high ratings include Stevie Wonder, Billy Joel, Phil Collins, Whitney Houston, Cher and Dolly Parton.[35] In 2003 Michael Jordan had the highest SportsQ rating with 51 (in 2002 he had received 58); while Tiger Woods was the second placed athlete in the Q ratings with 44.[36] However, even a high Q rating does not guarantee success if the celebrity's specific image doesn't match up with the featured product.

Another potential problem is what to do about celebrity endorsers who 'misbehave'. Pepsi had to abandon its sponsorship of Michael Jackson after the singer was accused of child abuse. Madonna met a similar fate following the release of her controversial *Like a Prayer* music video. Then, of course, there's always O.J. Simpson . . . To avoid some of these problems, most endorsement contracts now contain a morality clause which allows the company to release the celebrity if so warranted.[37] Other advertisers are looking a lot more favourably at characters like Bugs Bunny, who tend to stay out of trouble!

However, some advertisers want something different. They often deliberately go for athletes with negative public reputations in order to attract attention, especially of those consumers who see themselves as rebels, and therefore who would be likely to identify with this aspect of the company's image. The best example of this is probably Allan Iverson who 'has been repeatedly in trouble with the law and the NBA, and he makes inappropriate public statements. In spite of this behaviour, the amount of money he gets paid in endorsement contracts is almost comparable to the figures Michael Jordan earned in his prime.'[38]

Hype vs. buzz: the corporate paradox

Obviously many marketers spend lavishly to create marketing messages that they hope will convince hordes of customers that they are the best. There's the rub – in many cases they may be trying too hard! We can think of this as the **corporate paradox** – the more involved a company appears to be in the dissemination of news about its products, the less credible it becomes.[39] As we'll see in Chapter 10, consumer word-of-mouth typically is the most convincing kind of message. As Table 6.1 shows, **buzz** is word-of-mouth that is viewed as authentic and generated by customers. In contrast, **hype** is dismissed as inauthentic – corporate propaganda planted by a company with an axe to grind. So, the challenge to marketers is to get the word out and about without it looking like they are trying too hard.

The now-famous *Blair Witch Project* that led many viewers to believe the fictional treatment was in fact a real documentary demonstrated the power of a brand that seems as if it's not one. Some marketers are trying to borrow the veneer of buzz by mounting 'stealth' campaigns that seem as if they are untouched by the corporate world. *Buzz building* has become the new mantra for many companies that recognize the power of underground word-of-mouth.[40] Indeed, a small cottage industry has sprung up as some firms begin to specialize in the corporate promotion business by planting comments on websites which are made to look as if they originated from actual consumers. Consider one example:

● When RCA records wanted to create a buzz around teen pop singer Christina Aguilera, they hired a team of young people to swarm the Web and chat about her on popular teen sites like **alloy.com**, **bolt.com** and **gurl.com**. Posing as fans, they posted entries raving about her new material. Just before one of her albums was launched,

Table 6.1 Hype versus buzz

Hype	Buzz
Advertising	Word-of-Mouth
Overt	Covert
Corporate	Grass-roots
Fake	Authentic
Skepticism	Credibility

RCA also hired a direct marketing company to email electronic postcards filled with song snippets and biographical information to 50,000 web addresses.[41] The album quickly went to No. 1 in the charts.

As powerful as these tactics are, they have the potential to poison the well in a big way. Web surfers, already sceptical about what they see and hear, may get to the point where they assume every 'authentic' site they find is really a corporate front. Until then, however, buzz building online is growing strongly. Still, there's no beating the impact of a marketing message that really does originate with product users.

Source attractiveness

▶ **Source attractiveness** refers to the source's perceived social value. This quality can emanate from the person's physical appearance, personality, social status, or his or her similarity to the receiver (we like to listen to people who are like us). A compelling source has great value and endorsement deals are constantly in the works. Even dead sources can be attractive: the great-grandson of the artist Renoir is putting his famous ancestor's name on bottled water, and the Picasso family licensed their name to the French car maker Citroën.[42]

Star power: celebrities as communications sources

The use of celebrity endorsers is an expensive but commonly used strategy. While a celebrity endorsement strategy is expensive, it can pay off handsomely.[43] Oasis soft drinks is a case in point. Oasis had a very successful soft drinks launch in 1995 and became market leader in the adult soft drinks sector of the UK. The drink capitalized on the vibrant nature of the TV personality and transvestite Lily Savage, who provided the voice-over for the ads. Ms Savage was seen as ideal for launching the Oasis brand because of her 'larger than life persona, memorable personality and appeal to young people. She is seen as very down-to-earth, very British and with a witty sense of humour – exactly the kind of attitude the brand wanted to own.'[44] There is a growing move to use openly gay and lesbian celebrities in advertising. 'The mainstreaming of gay and lesbian endorsers . . . comes after major advertisers like Ford and Procter and Gamble sponsored campaigns aimed at the gay and lesbian market.'[45] American Express, Audi, Cartier, Volkswagen and Wrigley are other companies who have followed this new advertising trend.

Celebrities increase awareness of a firm's advertising and enhance both company image and brand attitudes.[46] Tiger Woods is now the richest endorser in sports history, with an estimated income of $62 million per year (not counting the money he makes actually winning golf tournaments!).[47] Why do stars command this kind of money? One study found that famous faces capture attention and are processed more efficiently by the brain than are 'ordinary' faces.[48] When used properly, famous or expert spokespeople can be of great value in improving the fortunes of a product. A celebrity endorsement strategy can be an effective way to differentiate among similar products. One reason for this effectiveness is that consumers are better able to identify products that are associated with a spokesperson.[49] This is especially important when consumers do not perceive many actual differences among competitors, as often occurs when brands are in the mature stage of the product life cycle.

More generally, star power works because celebrities represent *cultural meanings* – they symbolize important categories such as status and social class (a 'working-class heroine' like Roseanne), gender (a 'manly man' like Sylvester Stallone or Paul Hogan, or a strong feminine character, such as Reebok's endorser, Venus Williams[50]), age (the boyish Michael J. Fox) and even personality types (the eccentric Kramer from *Seinfeld*). Ideally, the advertiser decides what meanings the product should convey (that is, how it should be positioned in the marketplace), and then chooses a celebrity who has come to evoke that meaning. The product's meaning thus moves from the manufacturer to the consumer, using the star as a vehicle.[51]

Famous people can be effective because they are credible, attractive, or both, depending on the reasons for their fame. The computer guru Bill Gates is unlikely to be a 'fashion symbol' to most Europeans, but he may be quite effective at influencing people's attitudes towards unrestricted access to the internet (and he's apparently a fashion symbol to the Koreans – see the 'Multicultural dimension'!). On the other hand, Elizabeth Hurley may not be perceived as an expert in cosmetics, but Estée Lauder expected her to be a persuasive source for a message about perfumes and cosmetics.

The effectiveness of celebrities as communications sources often depends upon their perceived credibility. Consumers may not trust a celebrity's motives for endorsing a product, or they may question the star's competence to evaluate the product's claims. This 'credibility gap' appears to be widening. In a recent one-year period, for example, the number of consumers who found celebrity advertising 'less than credible' jumped to 52 per cent. The greatest erosion of confidence was found in younger consumers, 64 per cent of whom thought that celebrities appeared in ads just for the money.[52] The lack of credibility is aggravated by incidences where celebrities endorse products that they do not really believe in, or in some cases do not use. After Pepsi paid over $5 million to singer Michael Jackson in an endorsement deal, the company was not pleased by his later confession that he doesn't drink cola – and cola fans weren't too impressed either.[53]

In spite of this 'credibility gap', there are some celebrities who endorse so many products that they can be seen as 'serial advertisers'. John Cleese, for example, endorses nine different organizations, promoting everything from soft drinks to telecommunications to anti-smoking campaigns (Schweppes, Sainsbury's, Talking Pages, American Express, Sony, Compaq, Cellnet, Norwich Union Direct and anti-smoking!). Here, the concept of interactive communications discussed earlier in the chapter comes into play: 'There is a complicity between the audience and someone like Cleese. He knows that we know that he knows he is selling something, but if he entertains, engages, or surprises us, then we'll forgive him.'[54]

multicultural dimensions

Does this work for you?

Park Jin Sung combs through a rack of button-down shirts at a clothes shop in Seoul. After close examination, he picks out one in light blue that has a stiff, narrow collar and buttons spaced just right, so that the top two can be left open without exposing too much chest. 'Bill would wear this. The collar on this other one is too floppy. Definitely not Bill's style,' Mr Park says. William H. Gates, Chairman of Microsoft Corp., may not be considered the epitome of chic in Europe, but in Seoul, Korea, he is a serious style icon. Young South Koreans believe that 'dressing for success' means copying Mr Gates's wardrobe, down to his round, tortoise-shell glasses, unpolished shoes and wrinkle-free trousers.[55] While Bill Gates doesn't even try to be an endorser of style in Korea, or elsewhere, some celebrities choose to maintain their credibility by endorsing products only in other countries. Many celebrities who do not do many American advertisements appear frequently in Japan. Mel Gibson endorses Asahi beer, Sly Stallone appears for Kirin beer, Sean Connery plugs Ito hams and the singer Sheena was featured in ads for Shochu liquor - dressed in a kimono and wig. Even the normally reclusive comedian and film director Woody Allen featured in a campaign for a large Tokyo department store.[56] **Japander.com** is a website where consumers can see Hollywood stars in Japanese commercials: George Clooney advertising Toyota cars (2001); Harrison Ford promoting Kirin beer (mid 1990s); and Brad Pitt selling blue jeans (late 1990s).[57]

Celebrity
endorsement in
advertising.
The Advertising
Archives

'What is beautiful is good'

Almost everywhere we turn, beautiful people are trying to persuade us to buy or do something. Our society places a very high premium on physical attractiveness, and we tend to assume that people who are good-looking are cleverer, more fashionable and so on. Such an assumption is called a *halo effect*, which occurs when persons who rank high on one dimension are assumed to excel on others as well. This effect can be explained in terms of the consistency principle discussed in Chapter 5, which states that people are more comfortable when all of their judgements about a person go together. This notion has been termed the 'what is beautiful is good' stereotype.[58] A physically attractive source tends to facilitate attitude change. His or her degree of attractiveness exerts at least modest effects on consumers' purchase intentions or product evaluation.[59] How does this happen?

One explanation is that physical attractiveness functions as a cue that facilitates or modifies information processing by directing consumers' attention to relevant marketing stimuli. Some evidence indicates that consumers pay more attention to ads that contain attractive models, though not necessarily to the ad copy.[60] In other words, an ad with a beautiful person may stand a better chance of getting noticed, but not necessarily read. While we may enjoy looking at a beautiful or handsome person, these positive feelings do not necessarily affect product attitudes or purchase intentions.[61]

Beauty can also function as a source of information. The effectiveness of highly attractive spokespeople in ads appears to be largely limited to those situations where the advertised product is overtly related to attractiveness or sexuality.[62] The *social adaptation perspective* assumes that information seen to be instrumental in forming an attitude will be more heavily weighted by the perceiver. We filter out irrelevant information to minimize cognitive effort.

Under the right circumstances, an endorser's level of attractiveness constitutes a source of information instrumental to the attitude change process and thus functions as a central, task-relevant cue.[63] An attractive spokesperson, for this reason, is more likely to be an effective source when the product is relevant to attractiveness. For example, attractiveness affects attitudes toward ads about perfume or aftershave (where attractiveness is relevant) but not toward coffee ads, where attractiveness is not. Finally, in the global marketplace the notions of what comprises 'beauty' and 'attractiveness' are certainly culturally based (see the 'Marketing opportunity' for Gillette).

marketing opportunity

'The best a man can get' each morning is a clean, close shave with a razor, shaving cream and same-brand toiletries, according to the global ad campaign of Gillette Co., the Boston-based shaving industry giant. But is a wet shave with a razor the best a European woman can get, too? That's the question facing Gillette and other companies as they pitch their new generation of designed-for-women shaving systems in Europe, hoping to entice women to wet shave. Currently, the world's biggest markets are the US, India and Russia. In eastern Europe, razor blades were in short supply during the Communist era. Today, sales of premium shaving systems are exploding in countries such as Russia and Poland.

The market potential in western Europe is huge. Only 30 per cent of European women wet shave, compared to 75 per cent in the United States. What's more, there is still a large number of European women who don't remove hair from their underarms and legs at all. If the percentage of women wet shaving in Europe were to reach American levels, the total sales of blades would increase by 500 million annually.

Unlike in the US, where women have been removing body hair for decades, attitudes differ in Europe, and are often deeply rooted in cultural traditions, economic conditions and varying perceptions of beauty. Many of these behaviours are learned from the family or from female role models, and changing culturally linked behaviour is difficult. In France and the UK, for example, most women share behaviours of their American counterparts and wet shave. Spanish women also remove body hair – a habit which can be traced back to the Moorish influence – but they usually go to waxing salons, or they wax at home. In Germany, shaving has more of a generational influence, with wet shaving being more common among younger women who have been influenced by the media, cinema, foreign travel and supermodels with sleek legs and underarms.

Due to the complex market structure, shaving companies confront two challenges: one is to convince women who wet shave (but usually grab a simple disposable razor for use in the shower) to switch to new shaving systems which include ergonomically designed razors, pastel colours, built-in lubricants and special blade design elements to avoid nicks and cuts. The other major goal is to introduce women to hair removal – and wet shaving as the preferred method.[64]

Non-human endorsers

Celebrities can be effective endorsers, but there are drawbacks to using them. As noted previously, their motives may be suspect if they promote products that don't fit their images or if they come to be seen as never having met a product they didn't like (for a fee). They may be involved in a scandal or upset customers, as when Madonna's controversial comments about the Catholic Church caused trouble for Coca-Cola. Or, they may be prima donnas who don't show up on time for a shoot or who are overly demanding.

For these reasons some marketers seek alternatives, including cartoon characters and mascots. After all, as the marketing director for a company that manufactures costumed characters for sports teams and businesses points out, 'You don't have to worry about your mascot checking into rehab.' Such characters were popular between the 1930s and

www.noDNA.com

A German firm called NoDNA offers
its own stable of cybermodels such
as Tyra, who is shown here.
noDNA GmbH

1960s, but then came to be seen as dated and frivolous. However, there is evidence that
advertising mascots such as E.B. the bunny (for Energizer batteries) are increasing in
popularity again.[65] Mars M&M's characters beat Tony the Tiger, Mr Peanut and the
Pillsbury Doughboy in a contest to find America's favourite advertising icon.[66]

▶   Increasingly popular these days is the use of virtual models. An **avatar** is the manifestation of a Hindu deity in superhuman or animal form. In the computing world it has
come to mean a cyberspace presence represented by a character that you can move
around inside a visual, graphical world. Many consumers became more aware of these
cybermodels following the film *Simone*, which starred Al Pacino as a washed-up director
who creates a virtual actress that the public believes is real. Although a flesh-and-blood
woman named Rachel Roberts played the title role, New Line Cinema kept her existence
a secret for almost two years as it tried to create a buzz that Simone really was a computer concoction.[67]

Avatars like Simone originated in computer games like *The Sims*, but now they are
starting to appear in online advertising and on e-commerce sites as a mechanism for
enhancing the online experience. Now, rock bands, soft drinks makers and other big-time
marketers are using avatars. Coca-Cola Co. launched an avatar-populated site for the
Hong Kong market where avatars mill around and chat in a Coke-sponsored world.
British Telecom also tested such products as avatar email, software that makes the
sender's face appear and speak the message aloud.[68]

The creation of avatars for commercial formats is evolving into a cottage industry as
demand for compelling figures begins to grow. For example, the German firm No DNA
GmbH (**www.nodna.com**) offers a variety of 'virtualstars'. These are computer-generated
figures that appear as caricatures, 'vuppets' (cartoon-type mascots and animals) and
'replicants' that are doubles of real people. Its models receive hundreds of love letters
and even a few marriage proposals.[69]

The advantages of virtual avatars compared to flesh-and-blood models include
the ability to change the avatar in real time to suit the needs of the target audience

or individual consumer. From an advertising perspective they are likely to be more cost-effective than hiring a real person. From a personal selling and customer service perspective they have the ability to handle multiple customers at any one time, they are not geographically limited, and they are operational 24/7, thus freeing up company employees and sales personnel to perform other activities.

Countries as product endorsers?

Do you take care to distinguish between Australian and Chilean wines, take pride in eating original Greek feta cheese, or go to some lengths to convince guests that they will like authentic Italian grappa? If so, then you're like most consumers, who *sometimes* pay real attention to the influence that country-of-origin information has on the process of evaluating and choosing products. The crucial word here is *sometimes*, since the effects of country-of-origin information can range from strong to weak to non-existent. At the cognitive level, there are many products for which the additional information of country of origin plays little or no role in our decision-making process. For example, most consumers would have no doubts about buying a pocket calculator made in China or the Philippines, because we believe that this 'simple' technology has diffused across borders, and that these less industrialized countries can make calculators as well as any other country.

Fashion and clothing manufacturing technology has also diffused around the world, but would you prefer to buy an Armani suit made in Italy or in the Philippines? Research has shown that a strong brand name can compensate for a product manufactured in a country with an unknown or weak image. Sony consumer electronics may be assembled in less industrialized countries, but as consumers we have beliefs about the quality that underlies Sony's name. A shirt with the sound-alike name Ralph Loren or LaCost may be made in the Maldives or Sri Lanka, but consumers believe that the fashion designing and quality controls will be consistent with their image of the brand name. Honda has even shipped cars produced in the USA back to Japan, as a statement of their belief in the quality of the 'American-made' Hondas!

Like brand names, country-of-origin information provides consumers with cognitive-based information, as well as prompting affective-based reactions. Although the research results on country-of-origin effects are mixed, it is clear that the 'made in' label can be important to us, depending on the consumption situation (Russian caviar might make a good impression on your boss, but how about picking her up in a Russian car?) and the level of involvement we feel towards the product or service. With the rise in patriotism, regionalism and ethnic identity around the world, multinational and regional countries, as well as country-sponsored export agencies, will continue to promote their country and its positive associations.[70] However, promoting products on the basis of country of origin can be problematic where these claims could be construed as 'racist';[71] or where there are laws against marketing campaigns based on country of origin which might discriminate against other imports, e.g. the EU.[72]

■ THE MESSAGE

A major study of more than 1,000 commercials identified factors that determine whether or not a commercial message will be persuasive. The single most important feature was whether the communications contained a brand-differentiating message. In other words, did the communication stress a unique attribute or benefit of the product?[73] Table 6.2 lists some other good and bad elements.

Recent research has also shown that heavy and light users of a brand respond differently to various types of messages, suggesting different communications strategy options for heavy and light users. In the case of heavy users cognitions, evaluations and intention

Table 6.2 Positive and negative effects of elements in television commercials

Positive effects	Negative effects
• Showing convenience of use	• Extensive information on components, ingredients or nutrition
• Showing new product or improved features	
• Casting background (i.e. people are incidental to message)	• Outdoor setting (message gets lost)
• Indirect comparison to other products	• Large number of on-screen characters
• Demonstration of the product in use	• Graphic displays
• Demonstration of tangible results (e.g. bouncy hair)	
• An actor playing the role of an ordinary person	
• No principal character (i.e. more time is devoted to the product)	

Source: Adapted from David W. Stewart and David H. Furse, 'The effects of television advertising execution on recall, comprehension, and persuasion', *Psychology & Marketing* 2 (Fall 1985): 135–60. Copyright © 1985, John Wiley & Sons, Inc.

to buy a brand all interact closely with each other; whereas for light users, cognitions, affect and evaluative attitude interact closely, but intention to buy the brand is less closely linked.[74]

Characteristics of the message itself help to determine its impact on attitudes. These variables include *how* the message is said as well as *what* is said. Some of the issues facing marketers include the following:

● Should the message be conveyed in words or pictures?

● How often should the message be repeated?

● Should a conclusion be drawn, or should this be left up to the listener?

● Should both sides of an argument be presented?

● Is it effective to make an explicit comparison with competitors' products?

● Should blatant sexual appeal be used?

● Should negative emotions, such as fear, ever be aroused?

● How concrete or vivid should the arguments and imagery be?

● Should the ad be funny?

Sending the message

The saying 'one picture is worth ten thousand words' captures the idea that visual stimuli can economically deliver big impact, especially when the communicator wants to influence receivers' emotional responses. For this reason, advertisers often place great emphasis on vivid and creative illustrations or photography.[75]

On the other hand, a picture is not always as effective at communicating factual information. Ads that contain the same information, presented in either visual or verbal form, have been found to elicit different reactions. The verbal version affects ratings on the utilitarian aspects of a product, whereas the visual version affects aesthetic evaluations. Verbal elements are more effective when reinforced by an accompanying picture, especially if the illustration is *framed* (the message in the picture is strongly related to the copy).[76]

Because it requires more effort to process, a verbal message is most appropriate for high-involvement situations, such as in print contexts in which the reader is motivated to pay real attention to the advertising. Because verbal material decays more rapidly in

The use of humour in advertising.
The Advertising Archives

memory, more frequent exposures are needed to obtain the desired effect. Visual images, in contrast, allow the receiver to *chunk* information at the time of encoding (see Chapter 3). Chunking results in a stronger memory trace that aids retrieval over time.[77]

Visual elements may affect brand attitudes in one of two ways. First, the consumer may form inferences about the brand and change his or her beliefs because of an illustration's imagery. For example, people in a study who saw an ad for a box of tissues accompanied by a photo of a sunset were more likely to believe that the brand came in attractive colours. Second, brand attitudes may be affected more directly; for example, a strong positive or negative reaction elicited by the visual elements will influence the consumer's attitude toward the ad (A_{ad}), which will then affect brand attitudes (A_b). Figure 6.3 illustrates this *dual component model* of brand attitudes.[78]

Vividness

Pictures and words may both differ in *vividness*. Powerful descriptions or graphics command attention and are more strongly embedded in memory. The reason may be because they tend to activate mental imagery, while abstract stimuli inhibit this process.[79] Two studies recently showed 'that stylistic properties of ad pictures can communicate descriptive concepts that affect perceptions. However, this appears to occur only when viewers engage in ample processing of the ad and the accessibility of an appropriate descriptive

Figure 6.3 Effects of visual and verbal components of advertisements on brand attitude

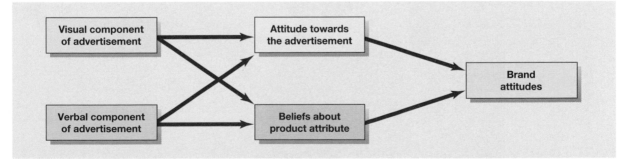

Source: Andrew A. Mitchell, 'The effect of verbal and visual components of advertisements on brand attitudes and attitude toward the advertisement', *Journal of Consumer Research* 13 (June 1986): 21. Reprinted by permission of The University of Chicago Press.

concept is heightened, independent of the stylistic property.'[80] This vividness effect can, of course, cut both ways: negative information presented in a vivid manner may result in more negative evaluations at a later time.[81]

The concrete discussion of a product attribute in ad copy also influences the importance of that attribute, because more attention is drawn to it. For example, the copy for a watch that read 'According to industry sources, three out of every four watch breakdowns are due to water getting into the case' was more effective than this version: 'According to industry sources, many watch breakdowns are due to water getting into the case.'[82]

Repetition

Repetition can be a two-edged sword for marketers. As noted in Chapter 3, multiple exposures to a stimulus are usually required for learning (especially conditioning) to occur. Contrary to the saying 'familiarity breeds contempt', people tend to like things that are more familiar to them, even if they were not that keen on them initially.[83] This is known as the *mere exposure* phenomenon. Positive effects for advertising repetition are found even in mature product categories – repeating product information has been shown to boost consumers' awareness of the brand, even though nothing new has been said.[84] On the other hand, as we saw in Chapter 2, too much repetition creates *habituation*, whereby the consumer no longer pays attention to the stimulus because of fatigue or boredom. Excessive exposure can cause *advertising wear-out*, which can result in negative reactions to an ad after seeing it too much.[85]

▶   The **two-factor theory** explains the fine line between familiarity and boredom by proposing that two separate psychological processes are operating when a person is repeatedly exposed to an ad. The positive side of repetition is that it increases familiarity

Figure 6.4 Two-factor theory and advertising wear-out

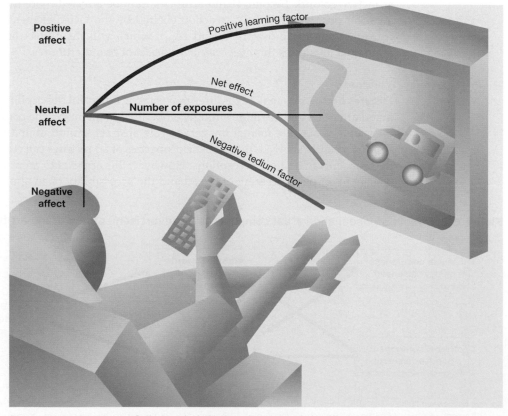

Source: Adapted from Arno J. Rethans, John L. Swasy and Lawrence Marks, 'Effects of television commercial repetition: receiver knowledge', *Journal of Marketing Research* 23 (February 1986): 50–61, Figure 1.

As this Dutch ad illustrates, the way something is said can be as significant as what is said.

Kessels Kramer

and thus reduces uncertainty about the product. The negative side is that over time boredom increases with each exposure. At some point the amount of boredom incurred begins to exceed the amount of uncertainty reduced, resulting in wear-out. Figure 6.4 depicts this pattern. Its effect is especially pronounced in cases where each exposure is of a fairly long duration (such as a 60-second commercial).[86]

The theory implies that advertisers can overcome this problem by limiting the amount of exposure per repetition (such as using 15-second spots). They can also maintain familiarity but alleviate boredom by slightly varying the content of ads over time through campaigns that revolve around a common theme, although each spot may be different. Recipients who are exposed to varied ads about the product absorb more information about product attributes and experience more positive thoughts about the brand than do those exposed to the same information repeatedly. This additional information allows the person to resist attempts to change his or her attitude in the face of a counter-attack by a competing brand.[87]

Constructing the argument

Many marketing messages are similar to debates or trials, where someone presents arguments and tries to convince the receiver to shift his or her opinion accordingly. The way the argument is presented may be as important as what is said.

One vs. two-sided arguments

Most messages merely present one or more positive attributes about the product or reasons to buy it. These are known as *supportive arguments*. An alternative is to use a *two-sided message*, where both positive and negative information is presented. Research has indicated that two-sided ads can be quite effective, yet they are not widely used.[88]

Why would a marketer want to devote advertising space to publicizing a product's negative attributes? Under the right circumstances, the use of *refutational arguments*, where a negative issue is raised and then dismissed, can be quite effective. This approach can increase source credibility by reducing reporting bias. Also, people who are sceptical about the product may be more receptive to a balanced argument instead of a 'white-wash'.[89] In one novel application, a Château Potelle winery ad included both positive and negative reviews of a wine by two experts. The ad suggested that consumers develop their own taste rather than relying on reviews in wine magazines.[90]

This is not to say that the marketer should go overboard in presenting major problems with the product. The typical refutational strategy discusses relatively minor attributes that may present a problem or fall short when compared with competitors. These draw-backs are then refuted by emphasizing positive, important attributes. For example, the car-hire firm Avis got a lot of mileage out of claiming to be only 'No. 2', while an ad for Volkswagen wocfully described one of its cars as a 'lemon' because there was a scratch on the glove compartment chrome strip.[91] A two-sided strategy appears to be the most effective when the audience is well educated (and presumably more impressed by a balanced argument).[92] It is also best to use when receivers are not already loyal to the product; 'preaching to the choir' about possible drawbacks may raise doubts unnecessarily.

Drawing conclusions

A related factor is whether the argument should draw conclusions, or whether the points should merely be presented, permitting the consumer to arrive at his or her own conclusion. Should the message say 'Our brand is superior', or should it add 'You should buy our brand'? On the one hand, consumers who make their own inferences instead of having them spoon-fed to them will form stronger, more accessible attitudes. On the other, leaving the conclusion ambiguous increases the chance that the desired attitude will not be formed.

The response to this issue depends on the consumers' motivation to process the ad and the complexity of the arguments. If the message is personally relevant, people will pay attention to it and spontaneously form inferences. However, if the arguments are hard to follow or consumers' motivation to follow them is absent, it is safer for the ad to draw conclusions.[93]

Types of message appeals

The *way* something is said can be as significant as *what* is said. A persuasive message can tug at the heartstrings or scare you, make you laugh, make you cry or leave you yearning to learn more. In this section, we'll review the major alternatives available to communicators who wish to *appeal* to a message recipient.

Emotional vs. rational appeals

The French firm L'Oréal persuades millions of women around the world to buy its personal care products by promising them Parisian chic, associating them with its sexy spokes-women, and using the self-assured slogan, 'Because I'm worth it.' Now the company is feeling pressure from an unlikely rival. Procter & Gamble is applying the no-nonsense ▶ **comparative advertising** strategy it's long used to sell soap and nappies to cosmetics as well. After P&G acquired Clairol in 2001, the company better known for Tide detergent and many other household products suddenly became the largest seller of cosmetics in supermarkets and club stores. A current P&G promotion for Pantene hair conditioner offers a '10-day challenge', promising hair that is 60 per cent healthier, 85 per cent shinier, 80 per cent less prone to breakage and 70 per cent less frizzy. In another case, after using 60 different methods to measure the size of pores, length of wrinkles and the colour and size of age spots, P&G researchers used results from one of the tests to proclaim that Olay Total Effects Night Firming Cream worked better than leading department-store brands (including those made by L'Oréal). Now P&G is trying to penetrate the high-end market, where L'Oréal rules. The head of L'Oréal discounts this factual approach by arguing that, when it comes to selling cosmetics, '. . . you have to both inform, convince but also seduce consumers . . . and not just ram facts down their throats'.[94]

So, which is better: to appeal to the head or to the heart? The answer often depends upon the nature of the product and the type of relationship consumers have with it.

Some years ago, both Toyota and Nissan introduced a large luxury car that sold for over £30,000. The two companies chose very different ways to communicate their product's attributes. Toyota's advertising for its Lexus model used a rational appeal, with ads concentrating on the large number of technical advancements incorporated in the car's design. Print ads were dominated by copy describing these engineering features.

In sharp contrast, Nissan's controversial campaign for its Infiniti used an emotional appeal, with a series of print and television ads that did not discuss the car at all. Instead the ads focused on the Zen-like experience of driving and featured long shots of serene landscapes. As one executive involved with the campaign explained, 'We're not selling the skin of the car; we're selling the spirit.'[95] While these ads were innovative, most American consumers had trouble grasping the Japanese conception of luxury. Later ads for the Infiniti emphasized functional features of the car to compensate for this initial confusion.

The goal of an emotional appeal is to establish a connection between the product and the consumer, a strategy known as *bonding*.[96] Emotional appeals have the potential to increase the chance that the message will be perceived, they may be more likely to be retained in memory and they can also increase the consumer's involvement with the product. Although Nissan's gamble on emphasizing the aesthetic aspects of its product did not pay off in this case, other emotional appeals are quite effective. Many companies turned to this strategy after realizing that consumers do not find many differences between brands, especially those in well-established, mature categories. Ads for products ranging from cars (Nissan) to cards (Hallmark) focus instead on emotional aspects. Mercury Vehicles' capitalization on emotional attachments to old rock songs succeeded in lowering the median age of their consumers for some models by ten years.[97]

This ad makes an emotional appeal (based on the softness of the bathroom tissue) rather than a rational appeal based on other performance criteria (for example, strength of the tissue paper; or value for money, such as unit cost)

The Advertising Archives

The precise effects of rational vs. emotional appeals are hard to gauge. Though recall of ad contents tends to be better for 'thinking' ads than for 'feeling' ads, conventional measures of advertising effectiveness (e.g. day-after recall) may not be adequate to assess cumulative effects of emotional ads. These open-ended measures are oriented towards cognitive responses, and feeling ads may be penalized because the reactions are not as easy to articulate.[98]

marketing pitfall

As the foot soldiers of Nike Inc. first set out to conquer foreign lands and win World War Shoe, they marched forth under this doctrine: *Speak loudly and carry a big shtick*. 'Europe, Asia, and Latin America: Barricade your stadiums. Hide your trophies. Invest in some deodorant', blared a Nike ad in *Soccer America* magazine. At least on Europe's hallowed football (or 'soccer') fields, the early results are not nearly as victorious as Nike would have liked. Their television ads throughout Europe have inspired controversy, frenzy and outrage – just the way that Nike typically likes it. A British TV ad featuring a French soccer player saying how his spitting at a fan and insulting his coach won him a Nike contract resulted in a scathing editorial against Nike in the sport's international federation newsletter. Nike has a tough task ahead of it: to win over European soccer fans where rival Adidas is king – in a game that traditionally doesn't have the glitz and packaging of basketball. Now a bit chastised, Nike is modifying its 'question authority' approach as it tries to win over the sports organizations in countries that don't appreciate its violent messages and antiestablishment themes.[99]

Nike is discovering that its iconoclastic culture is not as universal as it thought. With annual sales approaching $9 billion, Nike is pinning its future on the international sneaker (trainers) and sportswear markets. The company believes its domestic sales in America, which average an astounding $20 per person, may be peaking. By contrast, per capita Nike sales in Japan are $4, in Germany $3, and in China just over 2 cents. The trick will be for Nike to keep the cool edge that has appealed to America's sneaker-buying culture while recognizing that sometimes subtlety is better than shock tactics, and homage better than outrage, when dealing with tradition-bound European and Asian cultures.[100]

Sex appeals

Echoing the widely held belief that 'sex sells', many marketing communications – for everything from perfumes to cars – feature heavy doses of erotic suggestions that range from subtle hints to blatant displays of flesh. Of course, the prevalence of sex appeals varies from country to country. American firms run ads abroad that would not go down well in the United States. For example, a recent 'cheeky' ad campaign designed to boost the appeal of American-made Lee Jeans among Europeans features a series of bare buttocks. The messages are based on the concept that if bottoms could choose jeans, they would opt for Lee: 'Bottoms feel better in Lee Jeans'.[101]

Bare flesh is so much a part of French advertising that a minor backlash is brewing as some critics complain that the advertising industry is making sex boring![102] Perhaps not surprisingly, female nudity in print ads generates negative feelings and tension among female consumers, whereas men's reactions are more positive.[103] Another study found that males dislike nude males in ads, whereas females responded well to undressed males – but not totally nude ones.[104]

Does sex work? Although the use of sex does appear to draw attention to an ad, it may actually be counter-productive to the marketer. In one survey, an overwhelming 61 per cent of the respondents said that sexual imagery in a product's ad made them less likely to buy it.[105] There is some evidence that sexually suggestive subliminal advertising might influence consumers' feelings, rather than their cognitive responses, towards advertisements.[106] Ironically, a provocative picture can be *too* effective; it attracts so much attention that it hinders processing and recall of the ad's contents. Sexual appeals appear to be ineffective when used merely as an attention-grabber. They do, however, appear to work when the product is *itself* related to sex (e.g. lingerie or condoms). Overall, though, use of a strong sexual appeal is not very well received.[107]

**marketing
opportunity**

Marketing with double entendres – marketing opportunity or marketing pitfall?

'Virgin Atlantic Airways is hoping business travelers will say, 'Oh, behave!' after seeing a cheeky new commercial, which uses bawdy British humour to spoof soft-core pornography.

The jest even extends to the choice of media for the parody, which will appear where the intended audience watches actual soft-core pornography, on the sex-oriented entertainment channels of the closed-circuit television systems in hotel rooms. The spoof, almost 10 minutes long, promotes Virgin Atlantic's 'Upper Class Suite' service on flights between London and New York. Though there is no nudity or profanity, there is enough wink-wink, nudge-nudge japery to fill a fourth Austin Powers film. First, there is the title, 'Suite & Innocent', then come woodenly acted characters with names like Miles High, Big Ben and Summer Turbulence, who deliver dialogue replete with double entendres about 'your first time' on board and enjoying 'several inches more' of legroom.

The plot, such as it is, is centered on a buxom blonde, the chief executive of a lingerie company, who enjoys a business trip from New York to London in a Virgin Atlantic Upper Class Suite. In one scene, a venture capitalist she meets on board offers to invest in her company, and as he writes a cheque for $100 million, she recites aloud each zero by moaning, 'Oh, oh, oh, oh.''[108]

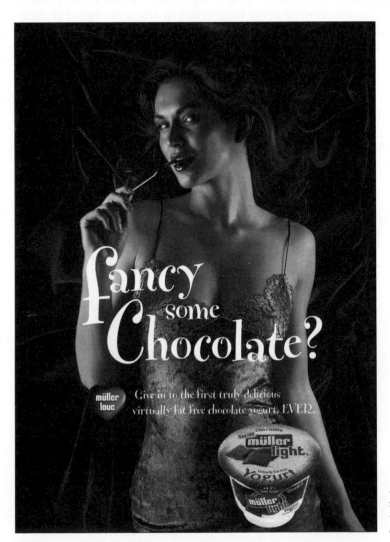

An ad employing a sexual appeal.
The Advertising Archives

Humorous appeals

The use of humour can be problematic, particularly because what is funny to one person may be offensive or incomprehensible to another. Views about the effectiveness of humour in advertising as part of a marketing communications strategy can vary even within companies. Within Coca-Cola, the 'Buddies' advertisement had a mixed reception. '"Buddies" features two friends taking a break from a game of hoops. The first guy to the fridge gulps his Coke, then uses his friend's can to cool off, pressing it to his forehead, neck and stomach before sticking it sideways in his armpit. When the friend arrives, he is handed the second Coke and starts swigging it with no clue where it had been.'[109] Senior executives (such as the former president Donald Keough) preferred the 1970s' hit ad 'I'd Like to Buy the World a Coke' and exerted their influence to achieve the withdrawal of this humorous ad, although the Buddies ad was seen to have a cooler image and to be more popular with younger consumers. Different cultures may have different senses of humour and use funny material in diverse ways. For example, commercials in the United Kingdom are more likely to use puns and satire than those in the United States.[110]

Does humour work? Overall, humorous advertisements do get attention. One study found that recognition scores for humorous alcohol ads were better than average. However, the verdict is mixed as to whether humour affects recall or product attitudes in a significant way.[111] One function it may play is to provide a source of *distraction*. A funny ad inhibits the consumer from *counter-arguing* (thinking of reasons why he or she doesn't agree with the message), thereby increasing the likelihood of message acceptance.[112]

Humour is more likely to be effective when the brand is clearly identified and the funny material does not 'swamp' the message. This danger is similar to that of beautiful models diverting attention from copy points. Subtle humour is usually better, as is humour that does not make fun of the potential consumer. Finally, humour should be appropriate to the product's image. An undertaker or a bank might want to avoid humour, while other products adapt to it quite well. Sales of Sunsweet pitted prunes improved dramatically based on the claim, 'Today the pits, tomorrow the wrinkles.'[113]

Humorous ads like this one from Budapest grab our attention.

McCann-Erickson, New York

**marketing
opportunity**

Advertiser's funny business

'Legendary Adman David Ogilvy used to encourage aspiring copywriters with the words: 'The best ideas come from jokes. Make your thinking as funny as possible.' But he also famously observed that 'nobody buys from a clown' . . .

If you look at any commercial break it soon becomes apparent that humour has become the dominant mode of commercial discourse . . . Some were brilliantly funny, such as the new campaign for Hellmann's mayonnaise . . . Others were toe-curlingly awful . . . Why should this be so? . . . Brands as well established as Audi, Nike, L'Oréal and Calvin Klein have spurned attempts to make us laugh.

One of the reasons the use of humour is so widespread is that it is such a versatile tool . . . Humour remains a legitimate marketing tool so powerful that our physiological response to it can be measured, says advertising psychologist David Lewis, who has researched the effects of humorous advertising using encephalograph equipment to measure how the brain responds to ads.

There are three main reasons why it is so powerful, he says. 'When we laugh or smile we compress the blood vessels and squeeze more blood to the brain which releases endorphins and makes us feel good.' These good feelings then have a halo effect. 'They put us in a good mood, which makes us see the product in a more positive light.'

His research also revealed that comic narratives have a very similar effect on the brain to hypnosis. 'Even very short stories put us into a trance-like state in which your attention becomes quite precise and intense. It switches off the critical analytical mind, which is why it is much easier to instil your brand message while people are in this state,' he says.

Well-judged humour can also have an important social function, argues writer and communications consultant Paul Twivy. 'It can be a source of social cohesion. Groups of people who laugh together are sharing the same values. It also says a lot about the advertiser. To be funny, you have to be observant and outwardly focused. The subtext of a good joke or genuinely funny ad is that the teller is responsive to and aware of his audience.'

Paradoxically, this may explain why when humour goes wrong it can be spectacularly damaging to brands. In 1998, the supermarket chain Sainsbury's aired a campaign starring John Cleese in which he abused the firm's staff through a megaphone, trumpeting the slogan 'Value to shout about'. The campaign did attract new customers – mostly value shoppers looking for special offers. But it also alienated existing customers and staff . . . This highlights one of the great dangers for advertisers: it is almost impossible to predict whether a comic idea will work as intended . . . Even if your ad is funny, there is still a danger that the campaign's humour is not sufficiently branded says Twivy. The result is that audiences often remember the joke in the slot, rather than the brand.

'Too often humour is used generically, using a celebrity, funny technique or twist in the tale, with the brand just tacked on. It is much harder to integrate the brand values and product features into the script. This actually turns the ad into a sophisticated version of the hard sell,' says Twivy.

Examples of this include the Walkers Crisps campaign with Gary Lineker, which is actually a vehicle for announcing promotions and line extensions, as well as promoting core brand values; Stella Artois, which uses wit and big production budgets to communicate the brand positioning as 'reassuringly expensive'; and Tesco's Dotty campaign, which uses the annoying biddy to express Tesco's pernickety attention to detail.

Clearly humour is more applicable in some sectors than others. 'By and large, humour works best for trivial low impact buys such as sweets, beer, children's products,' says Lewis.'[114]

Fear appeals

▶ **Fear appeals** highlight the negative consequences that can occur unless the consumer changes a behaviour or an attitude. This strategy is widespread: fear appeals are used in

Figure 6.5 The relationship between fear and attitude change

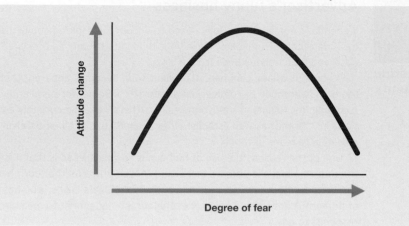

over 15 per cent of all television ads.[115] The arousal of fear is a common tactic for social policy issues, such as encouraging consumers to change to a healthier lifestyle by stopping smoking, using contraception, taking more exercise, eating a more balanced diet, drinking without driving (by relying on a designated driver in order to reduce physical risk to themselves or others). It can also be applied to social risk issues by threatening one's success with the opposite sex, career and so on. This tactic has been half-jokingly called 'slice of death'.

Does fear work? Fear appeals are usually most effective when only a moderate amount of fear is induced and when a solution to the problem is presented.[116] As shown in Figure 6.5, increasing levels of fear do not result in increased change: the relationship instead resembles an inverted U-shaped curve. If the threat is too great, the audience tends to deny that it exists as a way to rationalize the danger. Consumers will tune out of the ad because they can do nothing to solve the problem.[117] This approach also works better when source credibility is high.[118]

When a weak threat is ineffective, this may be because there is insufficient elaboration of the harmful consequences of engaging in the behaviour. When a strong threat doesn't work, it may be because *too much* elaboration interferes with the processing of the recommended change in behaviour – the receiver is too busy thinking of reasons why the message doesn't apply to him or her to pay attention to the offered solution.[119]

A study that manipulated subjects' degree of anxiety about AIDS, for example, found that condom ads were evaluated most positively when a moderate threat was used. In this context, copy that promoted the use of the condom because 'Sex is a risky business' (moderate threat) resulted in more attitude change than either a weaker threat that instead emphasized the product's sensitivity or a strong threat that discussed the certainty of death from AIDS.[120] Similarly, scare tactics have not been as effective as hoped in getting teenagers to decrease their use of alcohol or drugs. Teens simply tune out the message or deny its relevance to them.[121] On the other hand, a study of adolescent responses to social versus physical threat appeals in drug prevention messages found that social threat is a more effective strategy.[122]

Some of the research on fear appeals may be confusing a threat (the literal content of a message, such as saying 'engage in safe sex or die') with fear (an emotional response to the message). According to this argument, greater fear does result in greater persuasion – but not all threats are equally effective because different people will respond differently to the same threat. Therefore, the strongest threats are not always the most persuasive because they may not have the desired impact on the perceiver. For example, raising the spectre of AIDS is about the strongest threat that can be delivered to sexually active young people – but this tactic is only effective if they believe they will get the disease. Because many young people (especially those who live in fairly affluent areas) don't believe that 'people like them' will be exposed to the AIDS virus, this strong threat may not actually result in a high level of fear.[123] The bottom line is that more precise measures of actual fear responses are needed before definitive conclusions can be drawn about the impact of fear appeals on consumption decisions.

multicultural dimensions

American gun manufacturers are capitalizing on women's fears regarding self- and home defence. According to the National Rifle Association, 15-20 million American women own guns. At least three manufacturers have introduced guns for women. One company makes a .32 magnum model called a 'Bonnie', to go with a .38 'Clyde' for his-and-hers shooting. Smith & Wesson introduced the LadySmith, a revolver with a slimmed-down grip.[124] The company's ads have been criticized for preying on the fears of women. They include such copy as 'The world is different today than when you grew up' and 'Personal security is a very real issue'. A magazine called *Women & Guns* now has a readership of over 25,000.[125] In addition to gun safety, it features articles on firearm fashions. The cover of a recent issue featured an attractive woman wearing a pistol holder strapped above her knee with the caption 'Self-Defense Goes Thigh High'.

The message as artform: metaphors be with you

Marketers may be thought of as storytellers who supply visions of reality similar to those provided by authors, poets and artists. These communications take the form of stories because the product benefits they describe are intangible and must be given tangible meaning by expressing them in a form that is concrete and visible. Advertising creatives rely (consciously or not) on various literary devices to communicate these meanings. For example, a character like the Jolly Green Giant or the California Raisins may personify a

ELEMONATE.

There's a new, sharper way to stop bacteria breeding on your sponge. Fairy with Antibacterial Agents now comes in Lemon Zest.

Fairy uses the metaphor of 'lighting the fuse and blowing the germs away' in its sales pitch for Lemon Fairy with its antibacterial agents.
The Advertising Archives

product or service. Many ads take the form of an *allegory*, a story told about an abstract trait or concept that has been personified as a person, animal or vegetable.

▶ A **metaphor** involves placing two dissimilar objects into a close relationship, 'A is B', whereas a simile compares two objects, 'A is like B'. A metaphor involves the use of an explicit comparison, for example, 'United Airlines is your friend in faraway places'. This is accomplished because A and B, however seemingly dissimilar, share some quality that is, in turn, highlighted by the metaphor. The device was used literally by Reebok to

Kellogg's using cartoon characters to advertise to children.
The Advertising Archives

Table 6.3 Some examples of advertising resonance

Product/headline	Visual
Embassy Suites: 'This Year, We're Unwrapping Suites by the Dozen'	Chocolate kisses with hotel names underneath each
Toyota auto parts: 'Our Lifetime Guarantee May Come as a Shock'	Man holding a shock absorber
Bucks filter cigarettes: 'Herd of These?'	Cigarette pack with a picture of a stag
Bounce fabric softener: 'Is There Something Creeping Up Behind You?'	Woman's dress bunched up at the back of her due to static
Pepsi: 'This Year, Hit the Beach Topless'	Pepsi bottle cap lying on the sand
ASICS athletic shoes: 'We Believe Women Should Be Running the Country'	Woman jogging in a rural setting

Source: Adapted from Edward F. McQuarrie and David Glen Mick, 'On resonance: A critical pluralistic inquiry into advertising rhetoric', *Journal of Consumer Research* 19 (September 1992): 182, Table 1. Reprinted with permission of The University of Chicago Press.

equate its Metaphors line of shoes with comfort. Metaphors allow the marketer to activate meaningful images and apply them to everyday events.[126] In the stock market, 'white knights' battle 'hostile raiders' using 'poison pills', while Tony the Tiger allows us to equate Frosties cereal with strength, and Merrill Lynch's bull sends the message that the company is 'a breed apart'.[127]

▶ **Resonance** is another type of literary device that is frequently used in advertising. It is a form of presentation that combines a play on words with a relevant picture. Table 6.3 gives some examples of actual ads that rely on the principle of resonance. Whereas metaphor substitutes one meaning for another by connecting two things that are in some way similar, resonance uses an element that has a double meaning, such as a pun in which there is a similarity in the sound of a word but a difference in meaning. For example, an ad for a diet strawberry shortcake dessert might bear the copy 'berried treasure' so that the qualities associated with buried treasure – being rich, hidden and associated with adventurous pirates – are conveyed about the brand. Because the text departs from expectations, it creates a state of tension or uncertainty on the part of the viewer until he or she figures out the word play. Once the consumer 'gets it', he or she may prefer the ad to a more straightforward message.[128] Research into how consumers process complex advertising images which are mainly pictures with little or no accompanying text (i.e. 'copy-less' ads) is still in its early stages.[129]

Forms of story presentation

Just as a story can be told in words or pictures, the way the audience is addressed can also make a difference. Commercials are structured like other art forms, borrowing conventions from literature and art as they communicate their messages.[130] One important distinction is between a *drama* and a *lecture*.[131] A lecture is like a speech where the source speaks directly to the audience in an attempt to inform them about a product or persuade them to buy it. Because a lecture clearly implies an attempt at persuasion, the audience will regard it as such. Assuming listeners are motivated to do so, the merits of the message will be weighed, along with the credibility of the source. Cognitive responses, such as counter-arguments, will occur. The appeal will be accepted to the extent that it overcomes objections and is congruent with a person's beliefs.

In contrast, a drama is similar to a play or film. Whereas an argument holds the viewer at arm's length, a drama draws the viewer into the action. The characters only address the audience indirectly; they interact with each other about a product or service in an imaginary setting. Dramas attempt to be experiential – to involve the audience emotionally. In *transformational advertising*, the consumer associates the experience of product usage with some subjective sensation. Thus, ads for the Infiniti attempted to transform the 'driving experience' into a mystical, spiritual event.

■ THE SOURCE VS. THE MESSAGE: SELL THE STEAK OR THE SIZZLE?

Two major components of the communications model, the source and the message, have been reviewed. Which aspect has more impact in persuading consumers to change their attitudes? Should marketers worry more about *what* is said, or *how* it's said and *who* says it?

The answer is, it depends. Variations in a consumer's level of involvement, as discussed in Chapter 4, result in the activation of very different cognitive processes when a message is received. Research indicates that this level of involvement will determine which aspects of a communication are processed. The situation appears to resemble a traveller who comes to a fork in the road: one or the other path is chosen, and this choice has a big impact on the factors that will make a difference in persuasion attempts.

The elaboration likelihood model

▶ The **elaboration likelihood model (ELM)** assumes that once a consumer receives a message he or she begins to process it.[132] Depending on the personal relevance of this information, one of two routes to persuasion will be followed. Under conditions of high involvement, the consumer takes the *central route* to persuasion. Under conditions of low involvement, a *peripheral route* is taken instead. This model is shown in Figure 6.6.

The central route to persuasion
When the consumer finds the information in a persuasive message to be relevant or somehow interesting, he or she will carefully attend to the message content. The person is likely actively to think about the arguments presented and generate *cognitive responses* to these arguments. On hearing a radio message warning about drinking alcohol while

Figure 6.6 The elaboration likelihood model of persuasion

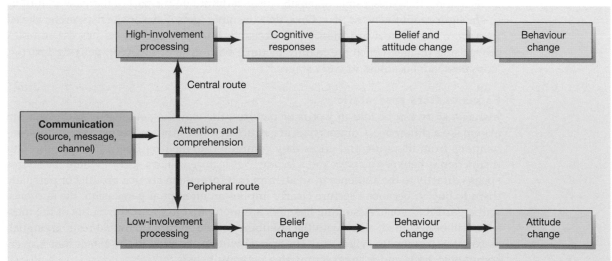

Source: From *Consumer Behavior*, 2nd edn, by John C. Mowen, Macmillan Publishing Company.

pregnant, an expectant mother might say to herself, 'She's right. I really should stop drinking alcohol now that I'm pregnant.' Or, she might offer counter-arguments, such as 'That's a load of nonsense. My mother had a cocktail every night when she was pregnant with me, and I turned out OK.' If a person generates counter-arguments in response to a message, it is less likely that he or she will yield to the message, whereas the generation of further supporting arguments by the consumer increases the probability of compliance.[133]

The central route to persuasion is likely to involve the traditional hierarchy of effects, as discussed in Chapter 5. Beliefs are carefully formed and evaluated, and the resulting strong attitudes will be likely to guide behaviour. The implication is that message factors, such as the quality of arguments presented, will be important in determining attitude change. Prior knowledge about a topic results in more thoughts about the message and also increases the number of counter-arguments.[134]

The peripheral route to persuasion

In contrast, the peripheral route is taken when the person is not motivated to think deeply about the arguments presented. Instead, the consumer is likely to use other cues in deciding on the suitability of the message. These cues might include the product's package, the attractiveness of the source, or the context in which the message is presented. Sources of information extraneous to the actual message content are called *peripheral cues* because they surround the actual message.

The peripheral route to persuasion highlights the paradox of low involvement discussed in Chapter 4: when consumers do not care about a product, the stimuli associated with it increase in importance. The implication here is that low-involvement products may be purchased chiefly because the marketer has done a good job in designing a 'sexy' package, choosing a popular spokesperson, or perhaps just creating a pleasant shopping environment.

Support for the ELM model

The ELM model has received a lot of research support.[135] In one study, undergraduates were exposed to one of several mock advertisements for Break, a new brand of low-alcohol beer. Using the technique of *thought listing*, they were asked to provide their thoughts about the ads, which were later analysed. Two versions of the ads are shown on p. 198.[136] Three independent variables crucial to the ELM model were manipulated.

1 *Message-processing involvement:* Some subjects were motivated to be highly involved with the ads. They were promised a gift of low-alcohol beer for participating in the study and were told that the brand would soon be available in their area. Low-involvement subjects were not promised a gift and were told that the brand would be introduced in a distant area.

2 *Argument strength:* One version of the ad used strong, compelling arguments to drink Break (e.g. 'Break contains one-half of the amount of alcohol of regular beers and, therefore, has less calories than regular beer.'), whereas the other listed only weak arguments (e.g. 'Break is just as good as any other regular beer.')

3 *Source characteristics:* Both ads contained a photo of a couple drinking the beer, but their relative social attractiveness was varied by their dress, their posture and non-verbal expressions, and the background information given about their educational achievements and occupations.

Consistent with the ELM model, high-involvement subjects had more thoughts related to the ad messages than did low-involvement subjects, who devoted more cognitive activity to the sources used in the ad. The attitudes of high-involvement subjects were more likely to be swayed by powerful arguments, whereas the attitudes of

Craig Andrews, J. and Shrimp, T.A. (1990) Effects of Involvement, Argument, Strength, and Source Characteristics on Central and Peripheral Processing in Advertising, *Psychology & Marketing*, 7, Fall, pp. 195–214. Copyright © 1990 John Wiley & Sons, Inc. Reprinted with permission of John Wiley & Sons, Inc.

low-involvement subjects were more likely to be influenced by the ad version using attractive sources. The results of this study, paired with numerous others, indicate that the relative effectiveness of a strong message and a favourable source depends on consumers' level of involvement with the product being advertised.

These results underscore the basic idea that highly involved consumers look for the 'steak' (strong, rational arguments). Those who are less involved are more affected by the 'sizzle' (the colours and images used in packaging or endorsements by famous people). It is important to remember, however, that the same communications variable can be both a central and a peripheral cue, depending on its relation to the attitude object. The physical attractiveness of a model might serve as a peripheral cue in a car commercial, but her beauty might be a central cue for a product such as shampoo, where the product's benefits are directly tied to enhancing attractiveness.[137]

■ CHAPTER SUMMARY

- *Persuasion* refers to an attempt to change consumers' attitudes.

- The *communications model* specifies the elements needed to transmit meaning. These include a source, message, medium, receiver, and feedback.

- The *traditional view of communications* tends to regard the perceiver as a passive element in the process. Proponents of the *uses and gratifications approach* instead regard the consumer as an active participant who uses media for a variety of reasons.

- New developments in *interactive communications* highlight the need to consider the active roles a consumer might play in obtaining product information and building a relationship with a company. Advocates of *permission marketing* argue that it's more effective to send messages to consumers who have already indicated an interest in learning about a product than trying to contact people 'cold' with these solicitations.

- A product-related communication that directly yields a transaction is a *first-order response*. Customer feedback in response to a marketing message that is not in the form of a transaction is a *second-order response*. This may take the form of a request for more information about a good, service or organization, or perhaps receipt of a 'wish list' from the customer that specifies the types of product information he or she would like to get in the future.

- Two important characteristics that determine the effectiveness of a source are its *attractiveness* and *credibility*. Although celebrities are often used with the purpose of enhancing these characteristics, their credibility is not always as strong as marketers hope. Marketing messages that consumers perceive as buzz (that are authentic and consumer-generated) tend to be more effective than those they categorize as hype (that are inauthentic, biased and company-generated).

- Some elements of a message that help to determine its effectiveness are whether it is conveyed in words or pictures, whether an emotional or a rational appeal is employed, the frequency with which it is repeated, whether a conclusion is drawn, whether both sides of the argument are presented, and whether the message includes fear, humour or sexual references.

- Advertising messages often incorporate elements from art or literature such as dramas, lectures, metaphors, allegories and resonance.

- The relative influence of the source versus the message depends on the receiver's level of involvement with the communication. The *elaboration likelihood model* specifies that a less involved consumer will more likely be swayed by source effects, whereas a more involved consumer will be more likely to attend to and process components of the actual message.

▶ KEY TERMS

Avatar (p. 180)
Buzz (p. 175)
Communications model (p. 168)
Comparative advertising (p. 186)
Corporate paradox (p. 175)
Elaboration likelihood model (ELM) (p. 196)
Fear appeals (p. 191)
Hype (p. 175)
Interactionist (p. 169)

Metaphor (p. 194)
Permission marketing (p. 169)
Persuasion (p. 166)
Resonance (p. 195)
Sleeper effect (p. 173)
Source attractiveness (p. 176)
Source credibility (p. 173)
Two-factor theory (p. 184)
Uses and gratifications theory (p. 169)

CONSUMER BEHAVIOUR CHALLENGE

1 Identify the theoretical and managerial issues in changing attitudes through communications as outlined in the vignette about Jenny, and her baby Freddie, at the beginning of the chapter. Identify and discuss the ethical issues of using marketing techniques to promote social behaviours (e.g. healthy eating during pregnancy; breast is best). Are these issues similar to the ethical issues in promoting 'wet shaving' among European women? Why or why not?

2 A government agency wants to encourage the use of designated drivers by people who have been drinking. What advice could you give the organization about constructing persuasive communications? Discuss some factors that might be important, including the structure of the communications, where they should appear, and who should deliver them. Should fear appeals be used, and if so, how?

3 Why would a marketer consider saying negative things about his or her product? When is this strategy feasible? Can you find examples of it?

4 Create a list of celebrities who match up with products in your country. What are the elements of the celebrities and products that make for a 'good match'? Why? Which celebrities have a global or European-wide appeal, and why?

5 Go to the Martell cognac website at **www.martell.com** and review the company's site. To attract more young men to the lagging spirits brand, the 'I am Martell' ad campaign and website aim to build a cult following around a French woman, synonymous with the brand. Martell's new global campaign relies heavily on sex appeal. How does this campaign seem to match up with your country's cultural values? Does the campaign seem persuasive to you? Why, or why not?

6 A marketer must decide whether to incorporate rational or emotional appeals in its communications strategy. Describe conditions that are more favourable for using one or the other.

7 Collect ads that rely on sex appeal to sell products. How often are the benefits of the actual product communicated to the reader?

8 'Too often humour is used generically, using a celebrity, funny technique or twist in the tale, with the brand just tacked on.'[138] Find humorous ads which are examples and counter-examples of this statement; and then critique this point of view.

9 Observe the process of counter-argumentation by asking a friend to talk out loud while watching a commercial. Ask him or her to respond to each point in the ad or to write down reactions to the claims made. How much scepticism regarding the claims can you detect?

10 Make a log of all the commercials shown on one television channel during a six-hour period. Categorize each according to product category, and whether they are presented as drama or argument. Describe the types of messages used (e.g. two-sided arguments), and keep track of the types of spokespeople (TV actors, famous people, animated characters). What can you conclude about the dominant forms of persuasive tactics currently employed by marketers?

11 Collect examples of ads that rely on the use of metaphors or resonance. Do you feel these ads are effective? If you were marketing the products, would you feel more comfortable with ads that use a more straightforward, 'hard-sell' approach? Why, or why not?

12 Create a list of current celebrities whom you feel typify cultural categories (clown, mother figure, etc.). What specific brands do you feel each could effectively endorse?

13 The American Medical Association encountered a firestorm of controversy when it agreed to sponsor a line of health care products manufactured by Sunbeam (a decision it later reversed). Should trade or professional organizations, health or legal professionals, journalists, professors and others endorse specific products at the expense of other offerings?

14 Conduct an 'avatar hunt' by going to e-commerce websites, online video game sites and online communities like The Sims or Cybertown that let people select what they want to look like in cyberspace. What seem to be the dominant figures people are choosing? Are they realistic or fantasy characters? Male or female? What types of avatars do you believe would be most effective for each of these different kinds of websites and why?

15 Many companies rely on celebrity endorsers as communications sources to persuade. Especially when targeting younger people, these spokespeople often are 'cool' musicians, athletes or film stars. In your opinion, who would be the most effective celebrity endorser today, and why? Who would be the least effective? Why?

■ NOTES

1. Stuart Elliott, 'New survey on ad effectiveness', *NYT Online* (14 April 2004).
2. Robert B. Cialdini and Kelton V.L. Rhoads, 'Human behavior and the marketplace', *Marketing Research* (Fall 2001).
3. Gert Assmus, 'An empirical investigation into the perception of vehicle source effects', *Journal of Advertising* 7 (Winter 1978): 4–10; for a more thorough discussion of the pros and cons of different media, see Stephen Baker, *Systematic Approach to Advertising Creativity* (New York: McGraw-Hill, 1979).
4. Alladi Venkatesh, Ruby Roy Dholakia and Nikhilesh Dholakia, 'New Visions of Information Technology and Postmodernism: Implications for Advertising and Marketing Communications', in Walter Brenner and Lutz Kolbe, eds, *The Information Superhighway and Private Households: Case Studies of Business Impacts* (Heidelberg: Physical-Verlag, 1996): 319–37; Donna L. Hoffman and Thomas P. Novak, 'Marketing in hypermedia computer-mediated environments: Conceptual foundations', *Journal of Marketing* 60(3) (July 1996): 50–68; for an early theoretical discussion of interactivity in communications paradigms, see R. Aubrey Fischer, *Perspectives on Human Communication* (New York: Macmillan, 1978).
5. Seth Godin, *Permission Marketing: Turning Strangers into Friends, and Friends into Customers* (New York: Simon & Schuster, 1999).
6. First proposed by Elihu Katz, 'Mass communication research and the study of popular culture: An editorial note on a possible future for this journal', *Studies in Public Communication* 2 (1959): 1–6. For a more recent discussion of this approach, see Stephanie O'Donohoe, 'Advertising uses and gratifications', *European Journal of Marketing* 28(8/9) (1994): 52–75.
7. Mark Ritson and Richard Elliott, 'The social uses of advertising: an ethnographic study of adolescent advertising audiences', *Journal of Consumer Research* 25(3) (December 1999): 260–78.
8. Nat Ives, 'All commercials, all the time', *NYT Online* (26 July 2004). There are various shows, e.g. *Ad Chat, Adverts for You* and *Advert Focus*, and viewers can also vote which commercials they want to see.
9. Lucy Ward, 'Doubt and depression burden teenage girls', *The Guardian* (24 February 2005): 11.
10. Quoted in O'Donohoe, 'Advertising uses and gratifications' (1994): 66.
11. Herbert Blumer, *Symbolic Interactionism: Perspective and Method* (Berkeley: University of California Press, 1969): 2.
12. Fischer, *Perspectives on Human Communication* (1978): 174–8.
13. Brad Stone, 'The war for your TV', *Newsweek* (29 July 2002): 46–7.
14. This section is adapted from a discussion in Michael R. Solomon and Elnora W. Stuart, *Marketing: Real People, Real Choices*, 3rd edn (Upper Saddle River, NJ: Prentice Hall, 2002).
15. Thomas L. Harris, 'PR gets personal', *Direct Marketing* (April 1994): 29–32.
16. Deborah Ball, 'Toll-free tips: Nestlé hotlines yield big ideas', *The Wall Street Journal* 3 (September 2004): A7.
17. Carl I. Hovland and W. Weiss, 'The influence of source credibility on communication effectiveness', *Public Opinion Quarterly* 15 (1952): 635–50.
18. Herbert Kelman, 'Processes of opinion change', *Public Opinion Quarterly* 25 (Spring 1961): 57–78; Susan M. Petroshuis and Kenneth E. Crocker, 'An empirical analysis of spokesperson characteristics on advertisement and product evaluations', *Journal of the Academy of Marketing Science* 17 (Summer 1989): 217–26.
19. Kenneth G. DeBono and Richard J. Harnish, 'Source expertise, source attractiveness, and the processing of persuasive information: A functional approach', *Journal of Personality and Social Psychology* 55(4) (1988): 541–6.
20. Hershey H. Friedman and Linda Friedman, 'Endorser effectiveness by product type', *Journal of Advertising Research* 19(5) (1979): 63–71; for a more recent study that

looked at *non-target market effects* – the effects of advertising intended for other market segments, see Jennifer L. Aaker, Anne M. Brumbaugh and Sonya A. Grier, 'Non-target markets and viewer distinctiveness: The impact of target marketing on advertising attitudes', *Journal of Consumer Psychology* 9(3) (2000): 127–40.

21. S. Ratneshwar and Shelly Chaiken, 'Comprehension's role in persuasion: The case of its moderating effect on the persuasive impact of source cues', *Journal of Consumer Research* 18 (June 1991): 52–62.

22. Jagdish Agrawal and Wagner A. Kamakura, 'The economic worth of celebrity endorsers: An event study analysis', *Journal of Marketing* 59 (July 1995): 56–62.

23. Anthony R. Pratkanis, Anthony G. Greenwald, Michael R. Leippe and Michael H. Baumgardner, 'In search of reliable persuasion effects: III. The sleeper effect is dead, long live the sleeper effect,' *Journal of Personality and Social Psychology* 54 (1988): 203–18.

24. Herbert C. Kelman and Carl I. Hovland, 'Reinstatement of the communication in delayed measurement of opinion change', *Journal of Abnormal Psychology* 48(3) (1953): 327–35.

25. Darlene Hannah and Brian Sternthal, 'Detecting and explaining the sleeper effect', *Journal of Consumer Research* 11 (September 1984): 632–42.

26. David Mazursky and Yaacov Schul, 'The effects of advertisment encoding on the failure to discount information: Implications for the sleeper effect', *Journal of Consumer Research* 15 (June 1988): 24–36.

27. 'Reach for the stars', *Marketing Today* (September 1996): 104–5.

28. 'Robber makes it Biggs in ad', *Advertising Age* (29 May 1989): 26.

29. Robert LaFranco, 'MTV conquers Madison Avenue', *Forbes* (3 June 1996): 138.

30. Alice H. Eagly, Andy Wood and Shelly Chaiken, 'Causal inferences about communicators and their effect in opinion change', *Journal of Personality and Social Psychology* 36(4) (1978): 424–35.

31. William Dowell, 'Microsoft offers tips to agreeable academics', *Time* (1 June 1998): 22.

32. Quoted in Suzanne Vranica and Sam Walker, 'Tiger Woods switches watches: Branding experts disapprove', *The Wall Street Journal Online* (7 October 2002).

33. Stuart Elliott, 'Celebrity promoter says the words and has her say', *The New York Times on the Web* (25 November 2002).

34. Michael A. Kamins, 'An investigation into the "match-up" hypothesis in celebrity advertising: When beauty may be only skin deep', *Journal of Advertising* 19(1) (1990): 4–13; Lynn R. Kahle and Pamela M. Homer, 'Physical attractiveness of the celebrity endorser: A social adaptation perspective', *Journal of Consumer Research* 11 (March 1985): 954–61.

35. Bruce Haring, 'Company totes up popularity quotients', *Billboard Magazine* 101 (1989): 12.

36. Kevin E. Kahle and Lynn R. Kahle 'Sports Celebrities' Image: A Critical Evaluation of the Utility of Q Scores', working paper (n.d.) University of Oregon.

37. Larry Armstrong, 'Still starstruck', *Business Week* (4 July 1994): 38; Jeff Giles, 'The risks of wishing upon a star', *Newsweek* (6 September 1993): 38.

38. Kahle and Kahle 'Sports celebrities' image'.

39. This section is based upon a discussion in Michael R. Solomon, *Conquering Consumerspace: Marketing Strategies for a Branded World* (New York: AMACOM, 2003); see also David Lewis and Darren Bridger, *The Soul of the New Consumer: Authenticity – What We Buy and Why in the New Economy* (London: Nicholas Brealey Publishing, 2000).

40. Jeff Neff, 'Pressure points at IPG', *Advertising Age* (December 2001): 4.

41. Wayne Friedman, 'Street marketing hits the internet', *Advertising Age* (May 2000): 32; Erin White, 'Online buzz helps album skyrocket to top of charts', *The Wall Street Journal Interactive Edition* (5 October 1999): available from www.wsj.com.

42. Kruti Trivedi, 'Great-grandson of artist Renoir uses his name for marketing blitz', *The Wall Street Journal Interactive Edition* (2 September 1999).

43. Judith Graham, 'Sponsors line up for rockin' role', *Advertising Age* (11 December 1989): 50.

44. Nicole Dickenson, 'Can celebrities ruin a launch?', *Campaign* (3 May 1996): 34.

45. Stuart Elliott, 'More gay celebrities in ads', *NYT Online* (10 March 2004).

46. Michael A. Kamins, 'Celebrity and noncelebrity advertising in a two-sided context', *Journal of Advertising Research* 29 (June–July 1989): 34; Joseph M. Kamen, A.C. Azhari and J.R. Kragh, 'What a spokesman does for a sponsor', *Journal of Advertising Research* 15(2) (1975): 17–24; Lynn Langmeyer and Mary Walker, 'A First Step to Identify the Meaning in Celebrity Endorsers', in Rebecca H. Holman and Michael R. Solomon, eds, *Advances in Consumer Research* 18 (Provo, UT: Association for Consumer Research, 1991): 364–71.

47. Vranica and Walker, 'Tiger Woods switches watches'.

48. Heather Buttle, Jane E. Raymond and Shai Danziger, 'Do Famous Faces Capture Attention', paper presented at Association for Consumer Research Conference Columbus, Ohio (October 1999).

49. Jeffrey Burroughs and Richard A. Feinberg, 'Using response latency to assess spokesperson effectiveness', *Journal of Consumer Research* 14 (September 1987): 295–9.

50. Joseph Pereira, 'Reebok serves up tennis star in new ads', *Wall Street Journal* (18 January 2001): B2.

51. Grant McCracken, 'Who is the celebrity endorser? Cultural foundations of the endorsement process', *Journal of Consumer Research* 16(3) (December 1989): 310–21.

52. Thomas R. King, 'Credibility gap: More consumers find celebrity ads unpersuasive', *Wall Street Journal* (5 July 1989): B5; Haring, 'Company totes up popularity quotients': 12.

53. Pamela G. Hollie, 'A rush for singers to promote goods', *New York Times* (14 May 1984): D1.

54. Dominique Midgely, 'Variety performers avoid overexposure', *Marketing* (February 1996): 9.

55. Choi Hae Won, 'Bill Gates, style icon? Oh yes – in Korea, where geek is chic', *Wall Street Journal* (4 January 2001): A1.

56. Marie Okabe, 'Fading yen for foreign stars in ads', *Singapore Straits-Times* (1986).

57. Erin White, 'Found in translation? Stars who make ads overseas recoil at internet exposure: Mr DiCaprio fights back' *The Wall Street Journal* (20 September 2004); Page B1.

58. Karen K. Dion, 'What is beautiful is good', *Journal of Personality and Social Psychology* 24 (December 1972): 285–90.

59. Michael J. Baker and Gilbert A. Churchill Jr., 'The impact of physically attractive models on advertising evaluations', *Journal of Marketing Research* 14 (November 1977): 538–55; Marjorie J. Caballero and William M. Pride, 'Selected effects of salesperson sex and attractiveness in direct mail advertisements', *Journal of Marketing* 48 (January 1984): 94–100; W. Benoy Joseph, 'The credibility of physically attractive communicators: A review,' *Journal of Advertising* 11(3) (1982): 15–24; Kahle and Homer, 'Physical attractiveness of the celebrity endorser'; Judson Mills and Eliot Aronson, 'Opinion change as a function of communicator's attractiveness and desire to influence', *Journal of Personality and Social Psychology* 1 (1965): 173–7.

60. Leonard N. Reid and Lawrence C. Soley, 'Decorative models and the readership of magazine ads', *Journal of Advertising Research* 23(2) (1983): 27–32.

61. Marjorie J. Caballero, James R. Lumpkin and Charles S. Madden, 'Using physical attractiveness as an advertising tool: an empirical test of the attraction phenomenon,' *Journal of Advertising Research* (August/September 1989): 16–22.

62. Baker and Churchill Jr., 'The impact of physically attractive models on advertising evaluations'; George E. Belch, Michael A. Belch and Angelina Villareal, 'Effects of Advertising Communications: Review of Research', in *Research in Marketing* 9 (Greenwich, CT: JAI Press, 1987): 59–117; A.E. Courtney and T.W. Whipple, *Sex Stereotyping in Advertising* (Lexington, MA: Lexington Books, 1983).

63. Kahle and Homer, 'Physical attractiveness of the celebrity endorser'.

64. Ernest Beck, 'Shaving industry targets European women', *Wall Street Journal Europe* (6 May 1977): 4.

65. Stuart Elliott, 'The media business: advertising; as marketers revive familiar brand characters, prepare to see more of a certain cat and bunny', *NYT Online* (27 August 2004).

66. Suzanne Vranica, 'M&Ms icons voted America's favorite', *The Wall Street Journal* (20 September 2004): B4.

67. David Germain, 'Simone leading lady is living and breathing model', *The New York Times* (26 August 2002): D1.

68. Tran T.L. Knanh and Regalado Antonio, 'Web sites bet on attracting viewers with humanlike presences of avatars', *The Wall Street Journal Interactive Edition* (24 January 2001).

69. Olaf Schirm, President, No DNA GmbH, personal internet communication, 13 August 2002.

70. For an excellent review of the country-of-origin literature, see Nicholas Papadopoulos and Louise Heslop, *Product and Country Images: Research and Strategy* (New York: The Haworth Press, 1993). See also Zeynep Gürhan-Canli and Durairaj Maheswaran, 'Determinants of country-of-origin

evaluations', *Journal of Consumer Research* 27(1) (June 2000): 96–108; Israel D. Nebenzahl, Eugene D. Jaffe and Shlomo I. Lampert, 'Towards a theory of country image effect on product evaluation', *Management International Review* 37 (1997): 27–49; Johny K. Johansson, 'Why country of origin effects are stronger than ever', in Basil Englis and Anna Olofsson, eds, *Association for Consumer Research*, European Conference, Stockholm (June 1997); Allan Jaeger, 'Crafting the image of the Netherlands abroad', *The Netherlander* (31 May 1997): 13.

71. Julian Baseley, Director of Earlex Group quoted in Paula Dear, 'Made in Britain', *BBC News Magazine* (13 April 2005) (http:news.bbc.co.uk/1/hi/magazine/4437467.stm)

72. Dear, 'Made in Britain'.

73. David W. Stewart and David H. Furse, 'The effects of television advertising execution on recall, comprehension, and persuasion', *Psychology and Marketing* 2 (Fall 1985): 135–60.

74. Robert D. Jewell and H. Rao Unnava, 'Exploring differences in attitudes between light and heavy brand users', *Journal of Consumer Psychology* 14(1&2) (2004): 75–80.

75. R.C. Grass and W.H. Wallace, 'Advertising communication: Print vs. TV', *Journal of Advertising Research* 14 (1974): 19–23.

76. Elizabeth C. Hirschman and Michael R. Solomon, 'Utilitarian, Aesthetic, and Familiarity Responses to Verbal Versus Visual Advertisements', in Thomas C. Kinnear, ed., *Advances in Consumer Research* 11 (Provo, UT: Association for Consumer Research, 1984): 426–31.

77. Terry L. Childers and Michael J. Houston, 'Conditions for a picture-superiority effect on consumer memory', *Journal of Consumer Research* 11 (September 1984): 643–54.

78. Andrew A. Mitchell, 'The effect of verbal and visual components of advertisements on brand attitudes and attitude toward the advertisement', *Journal of Consumer Research* 13 (June 1986): 12–24.

79. John R. Rossiter and Larry Percy, 'Attitude change through visual imagery in advertising', *Journal of Advertising Research* 9(2) (1980): 10–16.

80. Laura A. Peracchio and Joan Meyers-Levy, 'Using stylistic properties of ad pictures to communicate with consumers', *Journal of Consumer Research* 32(1) (2005): 29–41.

81. Jolita Kiselius and Brian Sternthal, 'Examining the vividness controversy: An availability-valence interpretation', *Journal of Consumer Research* 12 (March 1986): 418–31.

82. Scott B. Mackenzie, 'The role of attention in mediating the effect of advertising on attribute importance', *Journal of Consumer Research* 13 (September 1986): 174–95.

83. Robert B. Zajonc, 'Attitudinal effects of mere exposure', Monograph, *Journal of Personality and Social Psychology* 8 (1968): 1–29.

84. Giles D'Souza and Ram C. Rao, 'Can repeating an advertisement more frequently than the competition affect brand preference in a mature market?', *Journal of Marketing* 59 (April 1995): 32–42.

85. George E. Belch, 'The effects of television commercial repetition on cognitive response and message acceptance,' *Journal of Consumer Research* 9 (June 1982): 56–65; Marian Burke and Julie Edell, 'Ad reactions over time:

Capturing changes in the real world', *Journal of Consumer Research* 13 (June 1986): 114–18; Herbert Krugman, 'Why three exposures may be enough', *Journal of Advertising Research* 12 (December 1972): 11–14.

86. Robert F. Bornstein, 'Exposure and affect: Overview and meta-analysis of research, 1968–1987', *Psychological Bulletin* 106(2) (1989): 265–89; Arno Rethans, John Swasy and Lawrence Marks, 'Effects of television commercial repetition, receiver knowledge, and commercial length: A test of the two-factor model', *Journal of Marketing Research* 23 (February 1986): 50–61.

87. Curtis P. Haugtvedt, David W. Schumann, Wendy L. Schneier and Wendy L. Warren, 'Advertising repetition and variation strategies: Implications for understanding attitude strength', *Journal of Consumer Research* 21 (June 1994): 176–89.

88. Linda L. Golden and Mark I. Alpert, 'Comparative analysis of the relative effectiveness of one- and two-sided communication for contrasting products', *Journal of Advertising* 16 (1987): 18–25; Kamins, 'Celebrity and noncelebrity advertising in a two-sided context'; Robert B. Settle and Linda L. Golden, 'Attribution theory and advertiser credibility', *Journal of Marketing Research* 11 (May 1974): 181–5.

89. See Alan G. Sawyer, 'The effects of repetition of refutational and supportive advertising appeals', *Journal of Marketing Research* 10 (February 1973): 23–33; George J. Szybillo and Richard Heslin, 'Resistance to persuasion: Inoculation theory in a marketing context', *Journal of Marketing Research* 10 (November 1973): 396–403.

90. Lawrence M. Fisher, 'Winery's answer to critics: Print good and bad reviews', *New York Times* (9 January 1991): D5.

91. Golden and Alpert, 'Comparative analysis of the relative effectiveness of one- and two-sided communication for contrasting products'.

92. Belch et al., 'Effects of advertising communications'.

93. Frank R. Kardes, 'Spontaneous inference processes in advertising: the effects of conclusion omission and involvement on persuasion', *Journal of Consumer Research* 15 (September 1988): 225–33.

94. Quoted in Sarah Ellison and John Carreyrou, 'Beauty battle: giant L'Oréal faces off against rival P&G', *Wall Street Journal Interactive Edition* (9 January 2003).

95. Michael Lev, 'For car buyers, technology or Zen', *New York Times* (22 May 1989): D1.

96. 'Connecting consumer and product', *New York Times* (18 January 1990): D19.

97. Edward F. Cone, 'Image and reality', *Forbes* (14 December 1987): 226.

98. H. Zielske, 'Does day-after recall penalize "feeling" ads?', *Journal of Advertising Research* 22 (1982): 19–22.

99. Roger Thurow, 'As in-your-face ads backfire, Nike finds a new global tack', *Wall Street Journal Interactive Edition* (5 May 1997).

100. Roger Thurow, 'In global push, Nike finds its brash ways don't always pay off', *Wall Street Journal Europe* (6 May 1997): A1.

101. Allessandra Galloni, 'Lee's cheeky ads are central to new European campaign', *Wall Street Journal Online* (15 March 2002).

102. John Lichfield, 'French get bored with sex', *The Independent*, London (30 July 1997).

103. Belch et al., 'Effects of advertising communications'; Courtney and Whipple, *Sex Stereotyping in Advertising*; Michael S. LaTour, 'Female nudity in print advertising: An analysis of gender differences in arousal and ad response,' *Psychology and Marketing* 7(1) (1990): 65–81; B.G. Yovovich, 'Sex in advertising – the power and the perils', *Advertising Age* (2 May 1983): M4–M5; for an interesting interpretive analysis, see Richard Elliott and Mark Ritson, 'Practicing Existential Consumption: The Lived Meaning of Sexuality in Advertising,' in Frank R. Kardes and Mita Sujan, eds, *Advances in Consumer Research* 22 (Provo, UT: Association for Consumer Research, 1995): 740–5.

104. Penny M. Simpson, Steve Horton and Gene Brown, 'Male nudity in advertisements: A modified replication and extension of gender and product effects', *Journal of the Academy of Marketing Science* 24(3) (1996): 257–62.

105. Rebecca Gardyn, 'Where's the lovin'?', *American Demographics* (February 2001): 10.

106. Andrew B. Aylesworth, Ronald C. Goodstein and Ajay Kalra, 'Effect of archetypal embeds on feelings: An indirect route to affecting attitudes?', *Journal of Advertising* 28(3) (Fall 1999): 73–81.

107. Michael S. LaTour and Tony L. Henthorne, 'Ethical judgments of sexual appeals in print advertising', *Journal of Advertising* 23(3) (September 1994): 81–90.

108. Stuart Elliott, 'Marketing with double entendres', *NYT Online* (4 October 2004).

109. Betsy McKay and Chad Terhune, 'Coke pulls TV ad after some call it the pits', *The Wall Street Journal* (8 June 2004): B1.

110. Marc G. Weinberger and Harlan E. Spotts, 'Humor in U.S. versus U.K. TV commercials: A comparison', *Journal of Advertising* 18(2) (1989): 39–44.

111. Thomas J. Madden, 'Humor in Advertising: An Experimental Analysis' (working paper, no. 83–27, University of Massachusetts, 1984); Thomas J. Madden and Marc G. Weinberger, 'The effects of humor on attention in magazine advertising', *Journal of Advertising* 11(3) (1982): 8–14; Weinberger and Spotts, 'Humor in U.S. versus U.K. TV commercials;' see also Ashesh Mukherjee and Laurette Dubé, 'The Use of Humor in Threat-Related Advertising', unpublished manuscript, McGill University, June 2002.

112. David Gardner, 'The distraction hypothesis in marketing', *Journal of Advertising Research* 10 (1970): 25–30.

113. 'Funny ads provide welcome relief during these gloom and doom days', *Marketing News* (17 April 1981): 3.

114. Alex Benady, 'Advertiser's funny business', *Financial Times* (17 February 2004), http://news.ft.com/servlet/ContentServer?pagename=FT.com/StoryFT/FullStory&c=StoryFT&cid=1075982574327&p=1012571727085.

115. Lynette S. Unger and James M. Stearns, 'The Use of Fear and Guilt Messages in Television Advertising: Issues and Evidence', in Patrick E. Murphy et al., eds, *1983 AMA Educators' Proceedings* (Chicago: American Marketing Association, 1983): 16–20.

116. Michael L. Ray and William L. Wilkie, 'Fear: The potential of an appeal neglected by marketing', *Journal of Marketing* 34 (1970) 1: 54–62.

117. Ibid.

118. Brian Sternthal and C. Samuel Craig, 'Fear appeals: Revisited and revised', *Journal of Consumer Research* 1 (December 1974): 22–34.

119. Punam Anand Keller and Lauren Goldberg Block, 'Increasing the effectiveness of fear appeals: The effect of arousal and elaboration,' *Journal of Consumer Research* 22 (March 1996): 448–59.

120. Ronald Paul Hill, 'An exploration of the relationship between AIDS-related anxiety and the evaluation of condom advertisements', *Journal of Advertising* 17(4) (1988): 35–42.

121. Randall Rothenberg, 'Talking too tough on life's risks?', *New York Times* (16 February 1990): D1.

122. Denise D. Schoenbachler and Tommy E. Whittler, 'Adolescent processing of social and physical threat communications', *Journal of Advertising* 25(4) (Winter 1996): 37–54.

123. Prof. Herbert J. Rotfeld, Auburn University, personal communication, 9 December 1997; Herbert J. Rotfeld, 'Fear appeals and persuasion: assumptions and errors in advertising research', *Current Issues and Research in Advertising* 11(1) (1988): 21–40; Michael S. LaTour and Herbert J. Rotfeld, 'There are threats and (maybe) fear-caused arousal: Theory and confusions of appeals to fear and fear arousal itself', *Journal of Advertising* 26(3) (Fall 1997): 45–59.

124. 'A drive to woo women – and invigorate sales', *New York Times* (2 April 1989).

125. Carrie Goerne, 'Gun companies target women: Foes call it "Marketing to fear" ', *Marketing News* 2 (31 August 1992): 1.

126. For an initial discussion about classifying different types of visual imagery used in advertising metaphors see: Lampros Gkiouzepas and Margaret K. Hogg, 'Visual imagery and metaphors in advertising: towards an analytical framework', in *Proceedings of the Fourth Critical Management Studies Conference* (Cambridge, 2005): 34. See also http://www.mngt.waikato.ac.nz/ejrot.

127. Barbara Stern, 'Literary criticism and consumer research: Overview and illustrative analysis', *Journal of Consumer Research* 16 (1989): 322–34; see also Cynthia Crossen, 'A is to B as C is to . . .', *Wall Street Journal* (22 August 2000): A1; Mark Stefik, *Internet Dreams: Archetypes, Myths, and Metaphors* (Cambridge, MA: MIT Press, 1996).

128. Edward F. McQuarrie and David Glen Mick, 'On resonance: A critical pluralistic inquiry into advertising rhetoric', *Journal of Consumer Research* 19 (September 1992): 180–97.

129. See Tze Wee Chan and Margaret K. Hogg, 'Copyless ads: the impact of complex advertising images on attitude toward the advertisement', Proceedings of the European Marketing Academy Conference (EMAC) (Milan, 2005): 223.

130. See Linda M. Scott, 'The Troupe: Celebrities as Dramatis Personae in Advertisements', in Holman and Solomon, eds, *Advances in Consumer Research* 18: 355–63; Stern, 'Literary criticism and consumer research': Judith Williamson, *Decoding Advertisements* (Boston: Marion Boyars, 1978).

131. John Deighton, Daniel Romer, and Josh McQueen, 'Using drama to persuade', *Journal of Consumer Research* 16 (December 1989): 335–43.

132. Richard E. Petty, John T. Cacioppo and David Schumann, 'Central and peripheral routes to advertising effectiveness: The moderating role of involvement', *Journal of Consumer Research* 10(2) (1983): 135–46.

133. Jerry C. Olson, Daniel R. Toy and Philip A. Dover, 'Do cognitive responses mediate the effects of advertising content on cognitive structure?', *Journal of Consumer Research* 9(3) (1982): 245–62.

134. Julie A. Edell and Andrew A. Mitchell, 'An Information Processing Approach to Cognitive Responses,' in S.C. Jain, ed., *Research Frontiers in Marketing: Dialogues and Directions* (Chicago: American Marketing Association, 1978).

135. See Mary Jo Bitner and Carl Obermiller, 'The Elaboration Likelihood Model: Limitations and Extensions in Marketing,' in Elizabeth C. Hirschman and Morris B. Holbrook, eds, *Advances in Consumer Research* 12 (Provo, UT: Association for Consumer Research, 1985): 420–5; Meryl P. Gardner, 'Does attitude toward the ad affect brand attitude under a brand evaluation set?', *Journal of Marketing Research* 22 (1985): 192–98; C.W. Park and S.M. Young, 'Consumer response to television commercials: The impact of involvement and background music on brand attitude formation', *Journal of Marketing Research* 23 (1986): 11–24; Petty, Cacioppo and Schumann, 'Central and peripheral routes to advertising effectiveness'; for a discussion of how different kinds of involvement interact with the ELM, see Robin A. Higie, Lawrence F. Feick and Linda L. Price, 'The Importance of Peripheral Cues in Attitude Formation for Enduring and Task-Involved Individuals', in Holman and Solomon, eds, *Advances in Consumer Research* 18: 187–93.

136. J. Craig Andrews and Terence A. Shimp, 'Effects of involvement, argument strength, and source characteristics on central and peripheral processing in advertising', *Psychology and Marketing* 7 (Fall 1990): 195–214.

137. Richard E. Petty, John T. Cacioppo, Constantine Sedikides and Alan J. Strathman, 'Affect and persuasion: a contemporary perspective', *American Behavioral Scientist* 31(3) (1988): 355–71.

138. Benady, 'Advertiser's funny business'.

THE SELF

Gareth, a marketing director, is a happily married man, and his two children aged ten and nine provide immense joy in his life. However, at 42 he feels younger than his years, and somewhat anxious about his totally family-oriented life – he has a nice house, a magnificent garden and takes regular family holidays in rural France. But he has begun to feel the loss of his previous, extravagant, carefree life, one in which he perceived himself to be a well-dressed, admired individual of good taste and discernment who always turned heads when he entered the room. He is apprehensive that his 'Gareth the family man' role has totally taken over his life's spirit. It's a life he loves and one which has his complete commitment, but one which he also views as 'prudent and sensible'.

Some months into the development of these feelings, Gareth is contacted by his company's personnel department about replacing his company car. Three years earlier he had selected a sensible Audi 80 with the needs of the family in mind. In the meantime, his wife has bought a Volvo Estate, which is always used for family travel. He has an exorbitant budget allocated to car purchase, due to his long-term commitment and excellent contribution to company performance over the last 18 months. As a result he can select almost any car he desires. After a prolonged search and extensive thought he decides on a Porsche Boxster.

The Porsche Boxster, a well-designed and admired car for the driver of good taste and discernment, has the image of a sporty, confident, powerful individual. The current press campaign displays a successful 30-something man being admired at the traffic lights, in the office car parks *and* at the local school collecting his children. Whilst driving home Gareth plays his CD collection at full volume, exceeds the legal speed limit when he believes it is 'safe' to do so, and generally feels more like the much-revered Gareth who graduated some 20 years ago. Now to consider trying some of those men's cosmetics and moisturizers that he's read so much about lately in *Maxim*, *GQ*, *Esquire* and *FHM* magazines . . .

CAROLYN STRONG, University of Wales, Cardiff

■ PERSPECTIVES ON THE SELF

Gareth is not alone in feeling that his self-image and possessions affect his 'value' as a person. Consumers' insecurities about their appearance are rampant: it has been estimated that 72 per cent of men and 85 per cent of women are unhappy with at least one aspect of their appearance.[1] Reflecting this discontent, new cosmetics for men and new clinical 'beauty procedures' have grown rapidly in Europe in the past few years, and revenues for men's cosmetics are projected to approach 1 billion euros![2] Many products, from cars to aftershave, are bought because the person is trying to highlight or hide some aspect of the self. In this chapter, we'll focus on how consumers' feelings about themselves shape their consumption habits, particularly as they strive to fulfil their society's expectations about how a male or female should look and act.

Does the self exist?

The 1980s were called the 'Me Decade' because for many this time was marked by an absorption with the self. While it seems natural to think about each consumer having a self, this concept is actually a relatively new way of regarding people and their relationship to society. The idea that each human life is unique, rather than a part of a group, developed in late medieval times (between the eleventh and fifteenth centuries in Europe). The notion that the self is an object to be pampered is even more recent. In addition, the emphasis on the unique nature of the self is much greater in Western societies.[3] Many Eastern cultures by contrast stress the importance of a collective self, where the person's identity is derived in large measure from his or her social group.

Both Eastern and Western cultures see the self as divided into an inner, private self and an outer, public self. But where they differ is in terms of which part is seen as the 'real you'. The West tends to subscribe to an independent construal of the self which emphasizes the inherent separateness of each individual. Non-Western cultures, in contrast, tend to focus on an interdependent self where one's identity is largely defined by the relationships one has with others.[4]

For example, a Confucian perspective stresses the importance of 'face' – others' perceptions of the self and maintaining one's desired status in their eyes. One dimension of face is *mien-tzu* – reputation achieved through success and ostentation. Some Asian cultures developed explicit rules about the specific garments and even colours that certain social classes and occupations were allowed to display, and these live on today in Japanese style manuals which provide very detailed instructions for dressing and for addressing a particular individual.[5] That orientation is at odds with such Western practices as 'casual Fridays', which encourage employees to express their unique selves. To illustrate these cross-cultural differences further, a recent Roper Starch Worldwide survey compared consumers in 30 countries to see which were the most and least vain. Women living in Venezuela topped the charts: 65 per cent said they thought about their appearance all the time.[6] Other high-scoring countries included Russia and Mexico. The lowest scorers lived in the Philippines and Saudi Arabia (where only 28 per cent of consumers surveyed agreed with this statement).

The self can be understood from many different theoretical vantage points. As discussed in Chapter 4, a psychoanalytical or Freudian perspective regards the self as a system of competing forces riddled with conflict. In Chapter 3 we also noted that behaviourists tend to regard the self as a collection of conditioned responses. From a cognitive orientation, the self is an information-processing system, an organizing force that serves as a nucleus around which new information is processed.[7]

Self-concept

▶ The **self-concept** refers to the beliefs a person holds about his or her attributes, and how he or she evaluates these qualities. While one's overall self-concept may be positive, there are certainly parts of the self that are evaluated more positively than others. For example, Gareth felt better about his professional identity than he did about his pending 'middle age' identity.

Components of the self-concept

The self-concept is a very complex structure. It is composed of many attributes, some of which are given greater emphasis when the overall self is being evaluated. Attributes of self-concept can be described along such dimensions as their content (for example, facial attractiveness vs. mental aptitude), positivity or negativity (i.e. self-esteem), intensity, stability over time and accuracy (that is, the degree to which one's self-assessment corresponds to reality).[8] As we'll see later in the chapter, consumers' self-assessments can be quite distorted, especially with regard to their physical appearance.

Self-esteem

Self-esteem refers to the positivity of a person's self-concept. People with low self-esteem do not expect that they will perform very well, and they will try to avoid embarrassment, failure or rejection. In developing a new line of snack cakes, for example, Sara Lee found that consumers low in self-esteem preferred portion-controlled snack items because they felt they lacked self-control.[9] In contrast, people with high self-esteem expect to be successful, will take more risks and are more willing to be the centre of attention.[10] Self-esteem is often related to acceptance by others. As you probably remember, teenagers who are members of high-status groups have higher self-esteem than their excluded classmates.[11]

Marketing communications can influence a consumer's level of self-esteem. Exposure to ads can trigger a process of *social comparison*, where the person tries to evaluate his or her self by comparing it to the people depicted in these artificial images. This form of comparison appears to be a basic human motive, and many marketers have tapped into this need by supplying idealized images of happy, attractive people who just happen to be using their products.

The social comparison process was illustrated in a study which showed that female college students do tend to compare their physical appearance with advertising models. Furthermore, study participants who were exposed to beautiful women in advertisements afterwards expressed lowered satisfaction with their own appearance, as compared to controls.[12] Another study demonstrated that young women's perceptions of their own body shapes and sizes can be altered after being exposed to as little as 30 minutes of television programming.[13]

Self-esteem advertising attempts to change product attitudes by stimulating positive feelings about the self.[14] One strategy is to challenge the consumer's self-esteem and then show a linkage to a product that will provide a remedy. Sometimes compliments are derived by comparing the person to others. One recent European advertising campaign even took to comparing different European nationalities, with the focus on self-esteem. British women face a stereotype: they are the plump ones on the beaches of Europe. Until now, that image has been fodder for jokes – not an advertising campaign. Slim-Fast, the diet brand, is running ads that rally British women to lose weight or lose face to sexier Continental counterparts in France, Spain and Sweden. One Slim-Fast ad is a photo of a French model and reads, 'I love British women. They make me look great.' Another spot shows a gorgeous Spanish woman, 'Face it, British women, it's not last year's bikini getting smaller.' One proposed ad read: 'You've got to be brave to share the beach with me.' After focus groups found it too insulting, the advertising agency softened the copy by making it more collective. It became: 'British women are so brave sharing the beach with us.' They also dropped the line, 'I bet your boyfriend thinks I look great in this.'[15]

Real and ideal selves

Self-esteem is influenced by a process where the consumer compares his or her actual standing on some attribute to some ideal. A consumer might ask 'Am I as attractive as I

▶ would like to be?', 'Do I make as much money as I should?', and so on. The **ideal self** is
▶ a person's conception of how he or she would like to be, while the **actual self** refers to
our more realistic appraisal of the qualities we have or lack.

The ideal self is partly moulded by elements of the consumer's culture, such as heroes
or people depicted in advertising who serve as models of achievement or appearance.[16]
Products may be purchased because they are believed to be instrumental in helping us
achieve these goals. Some products are chosen because they are perceived to be consistent with the consumer's actual self, while others are used to help reach the standard set
by the ideal self.

Fantasy: bridging the gap between the selves

While most people experience a discrepancy between their real and ideal selves, for some
consumers this gap is larger than for others. These people are especially good targets for
▶ marketing communications that employ *fantasy* appeals.[17] A **fantasy** or daydream is a
self-induced shift in consciousness, which is sometimes a way of compensating for a lack
of external stimulation or of escaping from problems in the real world.[18] Many products
and services are successful because they appeal to consumers' tendency to fantasize.
These marketing strategies allow us to extend our vision of ourselves by placing us in
unfamiliar, exciting situations or by permitting us to try interesting or provocative roles.
And with today's technology, like Dove's Real Beauty campaign[19] or the virtual digitized
preview from the plastic surgeon's PC of how your new face lift will probably look, consumers can experiment before taking the plunge in the real world.

Multiple selves

In a way, each of us is really a number of different people – your mother probably would
not recognize the 'you' that emerges while you're on holiday with a group of friends! We
have as many selves as we do different social roles. Depending on the situation, we act
differently, use different products and services, and we even vary in terms of how much
we like ourselves. A person may require a different set of products to play a desired role:
she may choose a sedate, understated perfume when she is being her professional self,
but splash on something more provocative on Saturday night as she becomes her *femme
fatale* self. The dramaturgical perspective on consumer behaviour views people much like
actors who play different roles. We each play many roles, and each has its own script,
props and costumes.[20]

The self can be thought of as having different components, or *role identities*, and only
some of these are active at any given time. Some identities (e.g. husband, boss, student)
are more central to the self than others, but other identities (e.g. stamp collector, dancer
or advocate for greater equality in the workplace) may be dominant in specific situations.
For example, executives in a survey undertaken in the United States, the UK and some
Pacific Rim countries said that different aspects of their personalities come into play
depending on whether they are making purchase decisions at home or at work. Not surprisingly, they report being less time-conscious, more emotional and less disciplined in
their home roles.[21]

Symbolic interactionism

If each person potentially has many social selves, how does each develop and how do we
▶ decide which self to 'activate' at any point in time? The sociological tradition of **symbolic
interactionism** stresses that relationships with other people play a large part in forming
the self.[22] This perspective maintains that people exist in a symbolic environment, and the
meaning attached to any situation or object is determined by the interpretation of these
symbols. As members of society, we learn to agree on shared meanings. Thus, we 'know'
that a red light means stop, or that McDonald's 'golden arches' mean fast food.

While this Bianco Footwear ad is making a visually playful metaphor which likens the 'Stiletto Effect' of the model's legs to the stiletto heel of the shoes, an additional message to female consumers is also part of the ad - the message that thin is fashionable.

Bianco Footwear Danmark A/S

Like other social objects, the meanings of consumers themselves are defined by social consensus. The consumer interprets his or her own identity, and this assessment is continually evolving as he or she encounters new situations and people. In symbolic interactionist terms, we *negotiate* these meanings over time. Essentially the consumer poses the question: 'Who am I in this situation?' The answer to this question is greatly influenced by those around us: 'Who do *other people* think I am?' We tend to pattern our behaviour on the perceived expectations of others in a form of *self-fulfilling prophecy*. By acting the way we assume others expect us to act, we may confirm these perceptions. This pattern of self-fulfilling behaviour is often expressed in our 'gendered roles', as we will see later in this chapter.

The looking-glass self

This process of imagining the reactions of others towards us is known as 'taking the role of the other', or the **looking-glass self**.[23] According to this view, our desire to define ourselves operates as a sort of psychological sonar: we take readings of our own identity by 'bouncing' signals off others and trying to project what impression they have of us. The looking-glass image we receive will differ depending upon whose views we are considering.

Like the distorted mirrors in a funfair, our appraisal of who we are can vary, depending on whose perspective we are taking and how accurately we are able to predict their evaluations of us. A successful man like Gareth may have doubts about his role as a middle-aged 'family man' as it conflicts with his earlier self-image as dapper and carefree (whether these perceptions are true or not). A self-fulfilling prophecy may be at work here, since these 'signals' can influence Gareth's actual behaviour. If he doesn't believe he's dapper, he may choose clothing and behaviour that actually make him less dapper. On the other hand, his self-confidence in a professional setting may cause him to assume that others hold his 'executive self' in even higher regard than they actually do (we've all known people like that!).

Self-consciousness

There are times when people seem to be painfully aware of themselves. If you have ever walked into a class in the middle of a lecture and noticed that all eyes were on you, you can understand this feeling of *self-consciousness*. In contrast, consumers sometimes behave with shockingly little self-consciousness. For example, people may do things in a stadium, a riot or a student party that they would never do if they were highly conscious of their behaviour.[24]

Some people seem in general to be more sensitive to the image they communicate to others (on the other hand, we all know people who act as if they're oblivious to the impression they are making!). A heightened concern about the nature of one's public 'image' also results in more concern about the social appropriateness of products and consumption activities.

Several measures have been devised to measure this tendency. Consumers who score high on a scale of *public self-consciousness*, for example, are also more interested in clothing and are heavier users of cosmetics.[25] A similar measure is *self-monitoring*. High self-monitors are more attuned to how they present themselves in their social environments, and their product choices are influenced by their estimates of how these items will be perceived by others.[26] Self-monitoring is assessed by consumers' extent of agreement with such items as 'I suppose I put on a show to impress or entertain others', or 'I would probably make a good actor'.[27] High self-monitors are more likely than low self-monitors to evaluate products consumed in public in terms of the impressions they make on others.[28] Similarly, other research has looked at aspects of *vanity*, such as a fixation on physical appearance or on the achievement of personal goals. Perhaps not surprisingly, groups like body-builders and fashion models tend to score higher on this dimension.[29]

■ CONSUMPTION AND SELF-CONCEPT

By extending the dramaturgical perspective a bit further, it is easy to see how the consumption of products and services contributes to the definition of the self. For an actor to play a role convincingly, he or she needs the correct props, stage setting and so on. Consumers learn that different roles are accompanied by *constellations* of products and activities which help to define these roles.[30] Some 'props' are so important to the roles we play that they can be viewed as a part of the *extended self*, a concept to be discussed shortly.

Products that shape the self: you are what you consume

Recall that the reflected self helps to shape self-concept, which implies that people see themselves as they imagine others see them. Since what others see includes a person's clothing, jewellery, furniture, car and so on, it stands to reason that these products also help to determine the perceived self. A consumer's products place him or her in a social role, which helps to answer the question 'Who am I *now*?'

People use an individual's consumption behaviours to help them make judgements about that person's social identity. In addition to considering a person's clothes, grooming habits, and such like, we make inferences about personality based on a person's choice of leisure activities (squash vs. soccer), food preferences (vegetarians vs. 'steak and chips' people), cars or home decorating choices. People who are shown pictures of someone's sitting room, for example, are able to make surprisingly accurate guesses about his or her personality.[31] In the same way that a consumer's use of products influences others' perceptions, the same products can help to determine his or her *own* self-concept and social identity.[32]

A consumer exhibits *attachment* to an object to the extent that it is used by that person to maintain his or her self-concept.[33] Objects can act as a sort of security blanket by reinforcing our identities, especially in unfamiliar situations. For example, students who decorate their room or house with personal items are less likely to drop out. This coping process may protect the self from being diluted in an unfamiliar environment.[34]

The use of consumption information to define the self is especially important when an identity is yet to be adequately formed, something that occurs when a consumer plays a new or unfamiliar role. **Symbolic self-completion theory** predicts that people who have an incomplete self-definition tend to complete this identity by acquiring and displaying symbols associated with it.[35] Adolescent boys may use 'macho' products like cars and cigarettes to bolster their developing masculinity: these items act as a 'social crutch' to be leaned on during a period of uncertainty about identity.

Loss of self

The contribution of possessions to self-identity is perhaps most apparent when these treasured objects are lost or stolen. One of the first acts performed by institutions that want to repress individuality and encourage group identity, such as prisons or convents, is to confiscate personal possessions.[36] Victims of burglaries and natural disasters commonly report feelings of alienation, depression or of being 'violated'. One consumer's comment after being robbed is typical: 'It's the next worse thing to being bereaved; it's like being raped.'[37] Burglary victims exhibit a diminished sense of community, reduced sense of privacy and take less pride in their house's appearance than do their neighbours.[38]

The dramatic impact of product loss is highlighted by studying post-disaster conditions, when consumers may literally lose almost everything but the clothes on their backs following a fire, hurricane, flood or earthquake. Some people are reluctant to undergo the process of recreating their identity by acquiring all new possessions. Interviews with disaster victims reveal that some are reluctant to invest the self in new possessions and so become more detached about what they buy. This comment from a woman in her fifties is representative of this attitude: 'I had so much love tied up in my things. I can't go through that kind of loss again. What I'm buying now won't be as important to me.'[39]

Self/product congruence

Because many consumption activities are related to self-definition, it is not surprising to learn that consumers demonstrate consistency between their values (see Chapter 4) and the things they buy.[40] **Self-image congruence models** predict that products will be chosen when their attributes match some aspect of the self.[41] These models assume a process of cognitive matching between these attributes and the consumer's self-image.[42]

While results are somewhat mixed, the ideal self appears to be more relevant as a comparison standard for highly expressive social products such as perfume. In contrast, the actual self is more relevant for everyday, functional products. These standards are also likely to vary by usage situation. For example, a consumer might want a functional, reliable car to commute to work everyday, but a flashier model with more 'zing' when going out on a date in the evening. Sadly, there are examples of people using products by which the goal of enhancing the ideal self ends up conflicting with and damaging the actual self. The body-building craze that swept through the United States and the northeast of England resulted in an increasing number of young men using anabolic steroids for body-building. This steroid use may 'bulk up' the physique (and provide a faster attainment of the ideal self), but it also damages the actual self, since the steroids cause male infertility.[43]

Research tends to support the idea of congruence between product usage and self-image. One of the earliest studies to examine this process found that car owners' ratings of themselves tended to match their perceptions of their cars – drivers of the sporty Pontiac model saw themselves as more active and flashier than did Volkswagen drivers.[44] Congruity has also been found between consumers and their most preferred brands of beer, soap, toothpaste and cigarettes relative to their least preferred brands, as well as between consumers' self-images and their favourite shops.[45] Some specific attributes that have been found to be useful in describing some of the matches between consumers and products include rugged/delicate, excitable/calm, rational/emotional and formal/informal.[46]

While these findings make some intuitive sense, we cannot blithely assume that consumers will always buy products whose characteristics match their own. It is not clear that consumers really see aspects of themselves in down-to-earth, functional products that don't have very complex or human-like images. It is one thing to consider a brand personality for an expressive, image-oriented product like perfume and quite another to impute human characteristics to a toaster.

Another problem is the old 'chicken-and-egg' question: do people buy products because the products are seen as similar to the self, or do they *assume* that these products must be similar because they have bought them? The similarity between a person's self-image and the images of products purchased does tend to increase with ownership, so this explanation cannot be ruled out.

The extended self

As noted earlier, many of the props and settings consumers use to define their social roles in a sense become a part of their selves. Those external objects that we consider a part of us comprise the **extended self**. In some cultures, people literally incorporate objects into the self – they lick new possessions, take the names of conquered enemies (or in some cases eat them) or bury the dead with their possessions.[47] We don't usually go that far, but many people do cherish possessions as if they were a part of them. Many material objects, ranging from personal possessions and pets to national monuments or landmarks, help to form a consumer's identity. Just about everyone can name a valued possession that has a lot of the self 'wrapped up' in it, whether it is a treasured photograph, a trophy, an old shirt, a car or a cat. Indeed, it is often possible to construct a pretty accurate 'biography' of someone just by cataloguing the items on display in his or her bedroom or office.

In one study on the extended self, people were given a list of items that ranged from electronic equipment, facial tissues and television programmes to parents, body parts and favourite clothes. They were asked to rate each in terms of its closeness to the self. Objects were more likely to be considered a part of the extended self if 'psychic energy' was invested in them by expending effort to obtain them or because they were personalized and kept for a long time.[48]

In an important study on the self and possessions, four levels of the extended self were described. These range from very personal objects to places and things that allow people to feel like they are rooted in their larger social environments:[49]

- *Individual level.* Consumers include many of their personal possessions in self-definition. These products can include jewellery, cars, clothing and so on. The saying 'You are what you wear' reflects the belief that one's things are a part of what one is.
- *Family level.* This part of the extended self includes a consumer's residence and its furnishings. The house can be thought of as a symbolic body for the family and often is a central aspect of identity.

FRANCESCO**BIASIA**
HANDBAGS

This Italian ad demonstrates that our favourite products are part of the extended self.

D'Adda, Lorenzini, Vigorelli, BBDO S.p.A.
Photo: Ilan Rubin

- *Community level*. It is common for consumers to describe themselves in terms of the neighbourhood or town from which they come. For farming families or residents with close ties to a community, this sense of belonging is particularly important.
- *Group level*. Our attachments to certain social groups can be considered a part of self. A consumer may feel that landmarks, monuments or sports teams are a part of the extended self.

■ GENDER ROLES

Sexual identity is a very important component of a consumer's self-concept. People often conform to their culture's expectations about how those of their gender should act, dress, speak and so on. Of course, these guidelines change over time, and they can differ radically across societies. Some societies are highly dichotomized, with little tolerance for deviation from gender norms. In other societies this is not the case, and greater freedom in behaviour, including behaviour stemming from sexual orientation, is allowed. In certain societies, lip-service is paid to gender equality, but inequalities are just under the surface; in others, there is greater sharing of power, of resources and of decision-making. To the extent that our culture is everything that we learn, then virtually all aspects of the consumption process must be affected by culture. It is not always clear to what extent sex differences are innate rather than culturally shaped – but they're certainly evident in many consumption decisions![50]

Consider the gender differences market researchers have observed when comparing the food preferences of men and women. Women eat more fruit, men are more likely to eat meat. As one food writer put it, 'Boy food doesn't grow. It is hunted or killed.' Men are more likely to eat Frosted Flakes or Corn Flakes, while women prefer multigrain cereals. Men are more likely than women to consume soft drinks, while women account for the bulk of sales of bottled water. The sexes also differ sharply in the quantities of food they eat: when researchers at Hershey's discovered that women eat smaller amounts of sweets, the company created a white chocolate confection called Hugs, one of the most successful food launches of all time.

Gender differences in socialization

A society's assumptions about the proper roles of men and women are communicated in terms of the ideal behaviours that are stressed for each sex (in advertising, among other places). It is likely, for instance, that many women eat smaller quantities because they have been 'trained' to be more delicate and dainty.

Gender goals and expectations

▶ In many societies, males are controlled by **agentic goals**, which stress self-assertion and
▶ mastery. Females, on the other hand, are taught to value **communal goals**, such as affiliation and the fostering of harmonious relations.[51]

Every society creates a set of expectations regarding the behaviours appropriate for men and women, and finds ways to communicate these priorities. This training begins very young: even children's birthday stories reinforce sex roles. A recent analysis showed that while stereotypical depictions have decreased over time, female characters in children's books are still far more likely to take on nurturant roles such as baking and gift-giving. The adult who prepares the birthday celebration is almost always the mother – often no adult male is present at all. On the other hand, the male figure in these stories is often cast in the role of a miraculous provider of gifts.[52]

Macho marketers?

Marketing has historically been defined largely by men, so it still tends to be dominated by male values. Competition rather than cooperation is stressed, and the language of warfare and domination is often used. Strategists often use distinctly masculine concepts: 'market penetration' or 'competitive thrusts', for example. Marketing articles in academic journals also emphasize agentic rather than communal goals. The most pervasive theme is power and control over others. Other themes include instrumentality (manipulating people for the good of an organization) and competition.[53] This bias may diminish in years to come, as more marketing researchers begin to stress such factors as emotions and aesthetics in purchase decisions, and as increasing numbers of women graduate in marketing!

Gender vs. sexual identity

Sex role identity is a state of mind as well as body. A person's biological gender (i.e. male
▶ or female) does not totally determine whether he or she will exhibit **sex-typed traits**, or characteristics that are stereotypically associated with one sex or the other. A consumer's subjective feelings about his or her sexuality are crucial as well.[54]

Unlike maleness and femaleness, masculinity and femininity are *not* biological characteristics. A behaviour considered masculine in one culture may not be viewed as such in another. For example, the norm in northern Europe, and in Scandinavia in particular, is that men are stoic, while cultures in southern Europe and in Latin America allow men to show their emotions. Each society determines what 'real' men and women should and should not do.

Sex-typed products

Many products also are *sex-typed*: they take on masculine or feminine attributes, and consumers often associate them with one sex or another.[55] The sex-typing of products is often created or perpetuated by marketers (e.g. Princess telephones, boys' and girls' toys, and babies' colour-coded nappies). Even brand names appear to be sex-typed: those containing alphanumerics (e.g. Formula 409, 10W40, Clorox 2) are assumed to be technical and hence masculine.[56] Our gender also seems to influence the instrumentality of the products we buy. Studies have shown that men tend to buy instrumental and leisure items impulsively, projecting independence and activity, while women tend to buy symbolic and self-expressive goods concerned with appearance and emotional aspects of self. Other research has shown, for example, that men take a more self-oriented approach to buying clothing, stressing its use as expressive symbols of personality and functional benefits, whilst women have 'other-oriented' concerns, choosing to use clothes as symbols of their social and personal interrelatedness with others.[57]

Androgyny

▶ Masculinity and femininity are not opposite ends of the same dimension. **Androgyny** refers to the possession of both masculine and feminine traits.[58] Researchers make a distinction between *sex-typed people*, who are stereotypically masculine or feminine, and *androgynous people*, whose mixture of characteristics allows them to function well in a variety of social situations.

Differences in sex-role orientation can influence responses to marketing stimuli, at least under some circumstances.[59] For example, research evidence indicates that females are more likely to undergo elaborate processing of message content, so they tend to be more sensitive to specific pieces of information when forming a judgement, while males are more influenced by overall themes.[60] In addition, women with a relatively strong masculine component in their sex-role identity prefer ad portrayals that include non-traditional women.[61] Some research indicates that sex-typed people are more sensitive to the sex-role depictions of characters in advertising, although women appear to be more sensitive to gender role relationships than are men.

This French shoe ad pokes fun at ads that demean women by proclaiming: 'No woman's body was exploited in the making of this advertisement.'
Eram and Devarrieuxvillaret Ad Agency

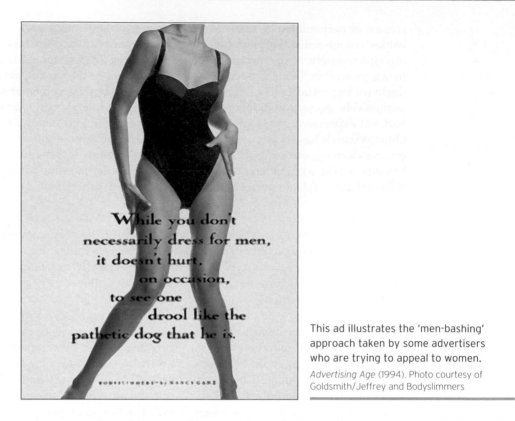

While you don't necessarily dress for men, it doesn't hurt, on occasion, to see one drool like the pathetic dog that he is.

BODYSLIMMERS by NANCY GANZ

This ad illustrates the 'men-bashing' approach taken by some advertisers who are trying to appeal to women.

Advertising Age (1994). Photo courtesy of Goldsmith/Jeffrey and Bodyslimmers

In one study, subjects read two versions of a beer advertisement, couched in either masculine or feminine terms. The masculine version contained phrases like 'X Beer has the strong aggressive flavour that really asserts itself with good food and good company . . .', while the feminine version made claims like 'Brewed with tender care, X Beer is a full-bodied beer that goes down smoothly and gently . . .' People who rated themselves as highly masculine or highly feminine preferred the version that was described in (respectively) very masculine or feminine terms.[62] Sex-typed people in general are more concerned with ensuring that their behaviour is consistent with their culture's definition of gender appropriateness.

Female gender roles

Gender roles for women are changing rapidly. Social changes, such as the dramatic increase in the proportion of women in waged work, have led to an upheaval in the way women are regarded by men, the way they regard themselves and in the products they choose to buy. Modern women now play a greater role in decisions regarding traditionally male purchases. For example, more than 60 per cent of new car buyers under the age of 50 are female, and women even buy almost half of all condoms sold.[63]

multicultural dimensions

One of the most marked changes in gender roles is occurring in Japan. Traditional Japanese wives stay at home and care for their children while their husbands work late and entertain clients. The good Japanese wife is expected to walk two paces behind her husband. However, these patterns are changing as women are less willing to live vicariously through their husbands. More than half of Japanese women aged between 25 and 29 are either working or looking for a job.[64] Japanese marketers and advertisers are beginning to depict women in professional situations (though still usually in subservient roles), and even to develop female market segments for such traditionally male products as cars.

Segmenting women

In the 1949 film *Adam's Rib*, Katharine Hepburn played a stylish and competent lawyer. This film was one of the first to show that a woman can have a successful career and still be happily married. Historically, married women have worked outside the home, especially during wartime. However, the presence of women in a position of authority is a fairly recent phenomenon. The evolution of a new managerial class of women has forced marketers to change their traditional assumptions about women as they target this growing market.

Ironically, it seems that in some cases marketers have overcompensated for their former emphasis on women as housewives. Many attempts to target the vast market of females employed outside the home tend to depict all these women in glamorous, executive positions. This portrayal ignores the fact that the majority of women do not hold such jobs, and that many work because they have to, rather than for self-fulfilment. This diversity means that not all women should be expected to respond to marketing campaigns that stress professional achievement or the glamour of the working life.

Whether or not they work outside the home, many women have come to value greater independence and respond positively to marketing campaigns that stress the freedom to make their own lifestyle decisions. American Express has been targeting women for a long time, but the company found that its 'Do you know me?' campaign did not appeal to women as much as to men. A campaign aimed specifically at women featured confident women using their American Express cards. By depicting women in active situations, the company greatly increased its share of the woman's credit card market.[65]

Cheesecake: the depiction of women in advertising

As implied by the ads for Virginia Slims cigarettes – 'You've come a long way, baby!' – attitudes about female sex roles changed remarkably during the twentieth century. Still, women continue to be depicted by advertisers and the media in stereotypical ways. Analyses of ads in such magazines as *Time*, *Newsweek*, *Playboy* and even *Ms.* have shown that the large majority of women included were presented as sex objects (so-called 'cheesecake' ads) or in traditional roles.[66] Similar findings have been obtained in both the UK and the United States.[67] One of the biggest culprits may be rock videos, which tend to reinforce traditional women's roles.

Ads may also reinforce negative stereotypes. Women are often portrayed as stupid, submissive, temperamental, or as sexual objects who exist solely for the pleasure of men. An ad for Newport cigarettes illustrated how the theme of female submission may be perpetuated. The copy 'Alive with pleasure!' was accompanied by a photo of a woman in the woods, playfully hanging from a pole being carried by two men. The underlying message may be interpreted as two men bringing home their captured prey.[68]

Although women continue to be depicted in traditional roles, this situation is changing as advertisers scramble to catch up with reality. For example, the highly successful Dove Real Beauty campaign has significantly changed women's perceptions of what is 'beautiful', particularly with respect to the notion of beauty and natural ageing. The campaign shows women in various roles, and at varying ages, and the notion of 'beauty' is central to the discussions.[69] Women are now as likely as men to be central characters in television commercials. But while males are increasingly depicted as spouses and parents, women are still more likely than men to be seen in domestic settings. Also, about 90 per cent of all narrators in commercials are male. The deeper male voice apparently is perceived as more authoritative and credible.[70]

Some ads now feature *role reversal*, where women occupy traditional men's roles. In other cases, women are portrayed in romantic situations, but they tend to be more sexually dominant. Ironically, current advertising is more free to emphasize traditional female traits now that sexual equality is becoming more of an accepted fact. This freedom is demonstrated in a German poster for a women's magazine. The caption reads 'Today's women can sometimes show weakness, because they are strong'.

marketing pitfall

Marketers continue to grapple with ways to entice female customers for traditionally male-oriented products, such as cars and computers, without offending them. One early effort by Tandy Corp. illustrates the potential for these efforts to backfire. When the company decided to market personal computers to women in 1990, it did so by packaging them with software for doing such 'feminine' tasks as making Christmas lists, taking inventories of silverware and china, and generating recipes. Women were not amused by the homemaker stereotype, and the campaign failed.[71]

Male sex roles

While the traditional conception of the ideal male as a tough, aggressive, muscular man who enjoys 'manly' sports and activities is not dead, society's definition of the male role is evolving. Men in the late 1990s were allowed to be more compassionate and to have close friendships with other men. In contrast to the depiction of macho men who do not show feelings, some marketers were promoting men's 'sensitive' side. An emphasis on male bonding was the centrepiece of many ad campaigns, especially for beers.[72]

The prototype of the 'new man' was expressed in the positioning statement for Paco Rabanne Pour Homme, an aftershave that attempted to focus on this new lifestyle: 'Paco Rabanne Pour Homme is a prestige men's fragrance for the male who is not a clichéd stereotype, the man who understands and accepts the fluidity of male/female relationships.' The ideal personality of the target consumer for the aftershave was described by the company with adjectives like confident, independent, romantic, tender and playful.

REO certainly has a clearly targeted market for their new cologne. Does this exclusive brand positioning make good business sense to you? Why or why not?
The Advertising Archives

In several European countries, the recent strong rise of sales of male cosmetics, moisturizers and beauty aids for men is all part of the rise of the 'male metro-sexual'. Having male celebrities like David Beckham, Brad Pitt and Tom Cruise (each approaching an 'older' age, and still looking great!) use cosmetics has been a real boost to sales. At Bumrungrad Hospital in Bangkok, the strongest growing cosmetic procedure comes from males in America and Europe, who come for face lifts and a series of shots to boost testosterone, a combination of procedures which makes for a younger appearance and more virile man.[73]

marketing opportunity

As sex roles for males evolve, formerly 'feminine' products such as fragrances and hair colouring are being marketed to men. Even nail polish is slowly making its way onto men's bathroom shelves – the Hard Candy line offers its Candy Man collection, which includes a metallic gold called Cowboy and a forest green shade named Oedipus. And, responding to pressures felt by many men to look younger, ads aimed at getting men to remove grey hair have tripled over the past decade. Roper Starch Worldwide reports that 36 per cent of men have either tried colouring their hair or were open to it. L'Oréal's new Feria line for men's hair includes new hues like Camel (brownish orange) and Cherry Cola. Other vanity products introduced in recent years include Bodyslimmers underwear that sucks in the waist, and Super Shaper Briefs that round out the buttocks (for an extra $5 the buyer can get an 'endowment pad' that slips in the front . . .).[74]

Men in Japan are taking it a step further: it's fashionable for everyone from high school students to professional baseball players to tweeze their eyebrows. Others are putting mud packs on their cheeks and using hairpins, and market researchers are starting to see an interest among men in wearing foundation make-up. These choices illustrate the lengths to which one sex will go to please the other: the men are apparently trying to compete with the large number of boyish, clean-cut actors and singers who are now the rage among young Japanese women.[75]

The joys of fatherhood

Males' lifestyles are changing to allow greater freedom of expression in clothing choices, hobbies such as cooking, and so on. Men are getting more involved in bringing up children, and advertising campaigns for such companies as Kodak, Omega watches and Pioneer electronics stress the theme of fatherhood.[76] Still, this change is coming slowly. A commercial for 7–11 stores (a corner shop chain in America and western Europe) showed two men out for a walk, each with a pushchair. As they neared a 7–11, they began to push faster until they were racing each other. The campaign's creative director explained, 'We showed them engaged in a competition to make it easier for men to accept the concept of taking care of children.'[77]

Beefcake: the depiction of men in advertising

Men as well as women are often depicted in a negative fashion in advertising. They frequently come across as helpless or bumbling. As one advertising executive put it, 'The woman's movement raised consciousness in the ad business as to how women can be depicted. The thought now is, if we can't have women in these old-fashioned traditional roles, at least we can have men being dummies.'[78]

Just as advertisers are criticized for depicting women as sex objects, so the same accusations can be made about how males are portrayed – a practice correspondingly known as 'beefcake'.[79] An advertising campaign for Sansabelt trousers featured the theme 'What women look for in men's pants.' Ads featured a woman who confides, 'I always lower my eyes when a man passes [pause] to see if he's worth following.' One female executive commented, 'turnabout is fair play . . . If we can't put a stop to sexism in advertising . . . at least we can have some fun with it and do a little leering of our own.'[80]

Gay and lesbian consumers

Gay and lesbian consumers are still largely ignored by marketers. This situation is starting to change, however, as some marketers are acknowledging the upmarket demographic profile of these consumers.[81] IKEA, the Swedish furniture retailer with outlets throughout Europe and in several major US cities, broke new ground by running a TV spot featuring a gay male couple purchasing a dining-room table at the shop.[82] Other major companies making an effort to market to homosexuals include AT&T, Anheuser-Busch, Apple Computers, Benetton, Philip Morris, Seagram and Sony.[83] Gay consumers can even get their own credit card – a Rainbow Visa card issued by Travelers Bank USA. Using tennis star Martina Navratilova as spokeswoman, such groups as the National Center for Lesbian Rights are benefited by users of the card. The card allows people who don't qualify based on income to apply with a same-sex partner.[84]

The percentage of the population that is gay and lesbian is difficult to determine, and efforts to measure this group have been controversial.[85] However, the respected research company Yankelovich Partners Inc., which has tracked consumer values and attitudes since 1971 in its annual Monitor survey, now includes a question about sexual identity in its survey. This study was virtually the first to use a sample that reflects the population as a whole instead of polling only smaller or biased groups (such as readers of gay publications) whose responses may not be representative of all consumers. About 6 per cent of respondents identified themselves as gay/homosexual/lesbian.

As civil rights gains are made by gay activists, the social climate is becoming more favourable for firms targeting this market segment.[86] In one of the first academic studies in this field, the conclusion was that gays and lesbians did not qualify as a market segment because they did not satisfy the traditional criteria of being identifiable, accessible and of sufficient size.[87] Subsequent studies have argued that the segmentation criteria rely on outdated assumptions regarding the nature of consumers, marketing activities and the ways in which media are used in the contemporary marketplace. Here, the argument is that identifiability is an unreliable construct for socially subordinated groups, and really isn't the issue anyway. How marketers segment (by race, ethnicity, gender or, in this case, sexuality) isn't as important as whether the group itself expresses consumption patterns in identifiable ways. Similarly, the accessibility criterion continues with the assumption of active marketers who contact passive consumers. This criterion also

As gays and lesbians continue to become more socially intergrated into the mainstream of European cultures, many companies (large and small) are also becoming more visible and open in their support of this social movement. This photo, taken at the Gay & Lesbian Parade in Berlin in June 2001, shows the involvement and support of Ford in the day's celebrations.

needs to take into account the dramatic changes in media over the past two decades, in particular the use of speciality media by marketers to access special-interest segments. Gay consumers are also active web surfers: the website **Gay.com** attracts 1 million consumers a month. As many as 65 per cent of gay and lesbian internet users go online more than once a day and over 70 per cent make purchases online.[88] Finally, sufficient size assumes separate campaigns are necessary to reach each segment, an assumption that ignores consumers' ability and willingness to explore multiple media.[89]

At least in some parts of the United States and Europe, homosexuality appears to be becoming more mainstream and accepted. Mattel even sells an Earring Magic Ken doll, complete with *faux*-leather vest, lavender mesh shirt and two-tone hair (though the product has become a favourite of gay men, the company denied it was targeted at that group).

marketing opportunity

Lesbian consumers have recently been in the cultural spotlight, perhaps due in part to the actions of such high-profile cultural figures as Martina Navratilova, singers k.d. lang and Melissa Etheridge, and actress Ellen deGeneres. Whatever the reason, American Express, Stolichnaya vodka, Atlantic Records and Naya bottled water are among those corporations now running ads in lesbian publications (an ad for American Express Travellers Cheques for Two shows two women's signatures on a cheque). Acting on research that showed that lesbians are four times as likely to own one of their cars, Subaru of America recently began to target this market as well.[90]

■ BODY IMAGE

▶ A person's physical appearance is a large part of his or her self-concept. **Body image** refers to a consumer's subjective evaluation of his or her physical self. As was the case with the overall self-concept, this image is not necessarily accurate. A man may think of himself as being more muscular than he really is, or a woman may think she is fatter than is the case. In fact, it is not uncommon to find marketing strategies that exploit consumers' tendencies to distort their body images by preying upon insecurities about appearance, thereby creating a gap between the real and the ideal physical self and, consequently, the desire to purchase products and services to narrow that gap.

Body cathexis

▶ A person's feelings about his or her body can be described in terms of **body cathexis**. Cathexis refers to the emotional significance of some object or idea to a person, and some parts of the body are more central to self-concept than others. One study of young adults' feelings about their bodies found that these respondents were most satisfied with their hair and eyes and had least positive feelings about their waists. These feelings were related to consumption of grooming products. Consumers who were more satisfied with their bodies were more frequent users of such 'preening' products as hair conditioner, hairdryers, aftershave, artificial tanning products, toothpaste and pumice soap.[91] In a large-scale study of older women in six European countries, the results showed that women would like to 'grow old beautifully', and that they were prepared to follow diets, exercise and use cosmetics to reach this goal. Wrinkles were the biggest concern, and Greek and Italian women were by far the most concerned about how to combat ageing, with northern European women expressing more agreement with the statement that ageing was natural and inevitable.[92]

As suggested by this Benetton ad, a global perspective on ideals of beauty is resulting in more ways to be considered attractive.

The Advertising Archives

Ideals of beauty

A person's satisfaction with the physical image he or she presents to others is affected by how closely that image corresponds to the image valued by his or her culture. In fact, infants as young as two months show a preference for attractive faces.[93] An **ideal of beauty** is a particular model, or exemplar, of appearance. Ideals of beauty for both men and women may include physical features (big breasts or small, bulging muscles or not) as well as clothing styles, cosmetics, hairstyles, skin tone (pale vs. tan) and body type (petite, athletic, voluptuous, etc.).

Is beauty universal?

Recent research indicates that preferences for some physical features over others are 'wired in' genetically, and that these reactions tend to be the same among people around the world. Specifically, people appear to favour features associated with good health and youth, attributes linked to reproductive ability and strength. Men are also more likely to use a woman's body shape as a sexual cue, and it has been theorized that this is because feminine curves provide evidence of reproductive potential. During puberty a typical female gains almost 15 kg of 'reproductive fat' around hips and thighs which supplies the approximately 80,000 extra calories needed for pregnancy. Most fertile women have waist : hip ratios of 0.6 : 0.8, an hourglass shape that happens to be the one men rank highest. Even though preferences for total weight change, waist : hip ratios tend to stay in this range – even the super-thin model Twiggy (who pioneered the 'waif' look decades before Kate Moss!) had a ratio of 0.73.[94] Other positively valued female characteristics include a higher forehead than average, fuller lips, a shorter jaw and a smaller chin and nose. Women, on the other hand, favour men with a heavy lower face, those who are slightly above average height and those with a prominent brow.

Of course, the way these faces are 'packaged' still varies enormously, and that's where marketers come in. Advertising and other forms of mass media play a significant role in determining which forms of beauty are considered desirable at any point in time. An ideal of beauty functions as a sort of cultural yardstick. Consumers compare themselves to some standard (often advocated by the fashion media) and are dissatisfied with their appearance to the extent that it doesn't match up to it. These mass media portrayals have been criticized not only on social grounds, but on issues of health as well. In a study of New Zealand print advertisements over the period 1958–88, the findings confirmed that advertising models became thinner and less curvaceous over the 30-year period, resulting in contemporary models being approximately 8.5 kg lighter than they would be if they had the same body shape as models of the late 1950s. To achieve the currently fashionable body shape, a young woman of average height would have to weigh approximately 42 kg, which is far below the recommended level for good health.[95] Clearly, what constitutes 'beauty' for women involves a number of complex relationships – a recent study in the Netherlands found that Dutch women consider friendliness, self-confidence, happiness and humour are the most important pillars of female beauty, while only 2 per cent found 'pretty' as a description for female beauty. A majority of the over 3,200 women in the study felt that the media's depiction of the 'ideal' female beauty was unrealistic. Most of the women in the study complained slightly over their weight and the shape of their body.[96]

Ideals of beauty over time

While beauty may be only skin deep, throughout history and across cultures women in particular have worked very hard to attain it. They have starved themselves, painfully bound their feet, inserted plates into their lips, spent countless hours under hairdryers, in front of mirrors and beneath ultraviolet lights, and have undergone breast reduction or enlargement operations to alter their appearance and meet their society's expectations of what a beautiful woman should look like.

Periods of history tend to be characterized by a specific 'look', or ideal of beauty. American history can be described in terms of a succession of dominant ideals. For example, in sharp contrast to today's emphasis on health and vigour, in the early 1800s it was fashionable to appear delicate to the point of looking ill. The poet John Keats described the ideal woman of that time as 'a milk white lamb that bleats for man's protection'. Other looks have included the voluptuous, lusty woman as epitomized by Lillian Russell, the athletic Gibson Girl of the 1890s, and the small, boyish flapper of the 1920s as exemplified by Clara Bow.[97]

Throughout much of the nineteenth century, the desirable waistline for American women was 18 inches, a circumference that required the use of corsets pulled so tight that they routinely caused headaches, fainting fits, and possibly even the uterine and spinal disorders common among women of the time. While modern women are not quite as 'strait-laced', many still endure such indignities as high heels, body waxing, eye-lifts and liposuction. In addition to the millions spent on cosmetics, clothing, health clubs and fashion magazines, these practices remind us that – rightly or wrongly – the desire to conform to current standards of beauty is alive and well.

The ideal body type of Western women has changed radically over time, and these changes have resulted in a realignment of *sexual dimorphic markers* – those aspects of the body that distinguish between the sexes. For example, analyses of the measurements of *Playboy* centrefolds over a 20-year period from 1958 to 1978 show that these ideals got thinner and more muscular. The average hip measurement went from 36 inches in 1958 to just over 34 inches in 1978. Average bust size shrank from almost 37 inches in 1958 to about 35 inches in 1978.[98]

The first part of the 1990s saw the emergence of the controversial 'waif' look, where successful models (notably Kate Moss) were likely to have bodies resembling those of young boys. More recently, the pendulum seems to be shifting back a bit, as the more buxom 'hourglass figure' popular in the 1950s (exemplified by the Marilyn Monroe ideal) has reappeared.[99] One factor leading to this change has been the opposition to the use of super-thin models by feminist groups, who charge that these role models encourage starvation diets and eating disorders among women who want to emulate the look.[100] These groups have advocated boycotts against companies like Coca-Cola and Calvin Klein who have used wafer-thin models in their advertising. Some protesters have even

☐ fat?
☐ fit?

Does true beauty only squeeze into size 8?

campaignforrealbeauty.co.uk ✈ | *Dove*

The Dove campaign emphasizes that our ideals about beauty, and what is beautiful, vary over time, place and age.

The Advertising Archives

taken to pasting stickers over these ads that read 'Feed this woman', or 'Give me a cheeseburger'.

We can also distinguish among ideals of beauty for men in terms of facial features, musculature and facial hair – who could confuse Tom Cruise with Mr Bean? In fact, one national survey which asked both men and women to comment on male aspects of appearance found that the dominant standard of beauty for men is a strongly masculine, muscled body – though women tend to prefer men with less muscle mass than men themselves strive to attain.[101] Advertisers appear to have the males' ideal in mind – a study of men appearing in advertisements found that most sport the strong and muscular physique of the male stereotype.[102]

Working on the body

Because many consumers are motivated to match up to an ideal appearance, they often go to great lengths to change aspects of their physical selves. From cosmetics to plastic surgery, tanning salons to diet drinks, a multitude of products and services are directed towards altering or maintaining aspects of the physical self in order to present a desirable appearance. It is difficult to overstate the importance of the physical self-concept (and the desire by consumers to improve their appearance) to many marketing activities.

Sizeism

As reflected in the expression 'you can never be too thin or too rich', many Western societies have an obsession with weight. Even primary school children perceive obesity as worse than being disabled.[103] The pressure to be slim is continually reinforced both by advertising and by peers. Americans in particular are preoccupied by what they weigh. They are continually bombarded by images of thin, happy people.

Could this really be your body? Physical self-concept and improving one's appearance are important motivations in consumer behaviour.
Soloflex, Inc.

How realistic are these appearance standards? In Europe, the public discourse on appearance and body weight is becoming more active and visible, particularly with respect to the weight of European children. Of the 77 million children in the European Union, 14 million are overweight. In 2005, the EU planned to launch a 'platform' on diet, physical activity and health as a public policy approach to the issue of weight. Obesity is especially acute in Mediterranean countries, underscoring concerns that people in the southern region are turning away from the traditional diet of fish, fruits and vegetables to fast food, high in fat and refined carbohydrates.[104] Still, many consumers focus on attaining an unrealistic ideal weight, sometimes by relying on height and weight charts which show what one should weigh. These expectations are communicated in subtle ways. Even fashion dolls, such as the ubiquitous Barbie, reinforce the ideal of thinness. The dimensions of these dolls, when extrapolated to average female body sizes, are unnaturally long and thin.[105] In spite of Americans' obsession about weight, as a country they continue to have a greater percentage of obesity in the general population relative to all European countries, as shown in Figure 7.1. Within Europe, Greek, Spanish, British and German men lead the European Union in measures of obesity.[106] Want to calculate your own body mass index? Go to **http://www.consumer.gov/weightloss/bmi.htm#BMI** and fill in your personal data.

Body image distortions

While many people perceive a strong link between self-esteem and appearance, some consumers unfortunately exaggerate this connection even more, and sacrifice greatly to attain what they consider to be a desirable body image. Women tend to be taught to a greater degree than men that the quality of their bodies reflects their self-worth, so it is not surprising that most major distortions of body image occur among females.

Men do not tend to differ in ratings of their current figure, their ideal figure and the figure they think is most attractive to women. In contrast, women rate both the figure

Figure 7.1 Body mass index for selected countries

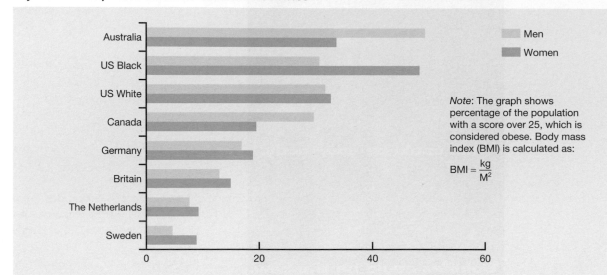

Source: Adapted from *Salt Lake City Tribune* (11 March 1997): A-1; see also *The Economist* (9 December 2000): 57.

they think is most attractive to men and their ideal figure as much thinner than their actual figure.[107] In one survey, two-thirds of college women admitted resorting to unhealthy behaviour to control weight. Advertising messages that convey an image of slimness help to reinforce these activities by arousing insecurities about weight.[108]

A distorted body image has been linked to the rise in ineating disorders, which are particularly prevalent among young women. People with anorexia regard themselves as fat, and starve themselves in the quest for thinness. This condition may be accompanied by bulimia, which involves two stages: first, binge eating occurs (usually in private), where more than 5,000 calories may be consumed at one time. The binge is then followed by induced vomiting, abuse of laxatives, fasting and/or overly strenuous exercise – a 'purging' process that reasserts the woman's sense of control.

Most eating disorders are found in white, teenaged girls and students. Victims often have brothers or fathers who are hypercritical of their weight. In addition, binge eating may be encouraged by one's peers. Groups such as athletic teams and social clubs at school may develop positive norms regarding binge eating. In one study of a female social club, members' popularity within the group increased the more they binged.[109]

Eating disorders do affect some men as well. They are common among male athletes who must also conform to various weight requirements, such as jockeys, boxers and male models.[110] In general, though, most men who have distorted body images consider themselves to be too light rather than too heavy: society has taught them that they must be muscular to be masculine. Men are more likely than women to express their insecurities about their bodies by becoming addicted to exercise. In fact, striking similarities have been found between male compulsive runners and female anorexics. These include a commitment to diet and exercise as a central part of one's identity and susceptibility to body image distortions.[111]

Cosmetic surgery

American consumers are increasingly electing to have cosmetic surgery to change a poor body image.[112] More than half a million cosmetic surgical procedures are performed in the US every year, and this number continues to grow.[113] There is no longer much (if any) psychological stigma associated with having this type of operation: it is commonplace and accepted among many segments of consumers.[114] In fact, men now account for as many as 20 per cent of plastic surgery patients. Popular operations include the implantation of silicon pectoral muscles (for the chest) and even calf implants to fill out 'chicken legs'.[115]

multicultural dimensions

Belly button reconstruction is now a popular form of cosmetic surgery in Japan, as women strive for the perfect navel they can show off as they wear the midriff fashions now popular there. The navel is an important part of Japanese culture, and mothers often save a baby's umbilical cord. In Japanese, a 'bent navel' is a grouch, and the phrase which would roughly mean 'give me a break' translates as 'yeah, and I brew tea in my belly button'. A popular insult among children: 'Your mother has an outie [protruding belly button].'[116]

Many women turn to surgery either to reduce weight or to increase sexual desirability. The use of liposuction, where fat is removed from the thighs with a vacuum-like device, has almost doubled since it was introduced in the United States in 1982.[117] Some women believe that larger breasts will increase their allure and undergo breast augmentation procedures. Although some of these procedures have generated controversy due to possible negative side effects, it is unclear whether potential medical problems will deter large numbers of women from choosing surgical options to enhance their (perceived) femininity. The importance of breast size to self-concept resulted in an interesting and successful marketing strategy undertaken by an underwear company. While conducting focus groups on bras, an analyst noted that small-chested women typically reacted with hostility when discussing the subject. They would unconsciously cover their chests with their arms as they spoke and felt that their needs were ignored by the fashion industry. To meet this overlooked need, the company introduced a line of A-cup bras called 'A-OK' and depicted wearers in a positive light. A new market segment was born. Other companies are going in the opposite direction by promoting bras that create the illusion of a larger cleavage. In Europe and the United States, both Gossard and Playtex are aggressively marketing specially designed bras offering 'cleavage enhancement' which use a combination of wires and internal pads to create the desired effect. Recently, the market for women's bras has had to contend with at least one natural development: unaugmented breasts (no surgery) are getting bigger by themselves, as a result of using the pill and changes in diet. The average cup size in Britain has grown from 34B to 36C over the past 30 years, and bra designers such as Bioform and Airotic, and retailers such as Knickerbox and Victoria's Secret, have all responded with new product offerings to meet what they consider to be a long-term market trend.[118]

Body decoration and mutilation

The body is adorned or altered in some way in every culture. Decorating the self serves a number of purposes.[119]

multicultural dimensions

Cosmetic surgeons often try to mould their patients into a standard ideal of beauty, using the features of such Caucasian classic beauties as Grace Kelly or Katharine Hepburn as a guide. The aesthetic standard used by surgeons is called the *classic canon*, which spells out the ideal relationships between facial features. For example, it states that the width of the base of the nose should be the same as the distance between the eyes.

However, this standard applies to the Caucasian ideal, and is being revised as people from other ethnic groups are demanding less rigidity in culture's definition of what is beautiful. Some consumers are rebelling against the need to conform to the Western ideal. For example, a rounded face is valued as a sign of beauty by many Asians, and thus giving cheek implants to an Asian patient would remove much of what makes her face attractive.

Some surgeons who work on African-Americans are trying to change the guidelines they use when sculpting features. For example, they argue that an ideal African-American nose is shorter and has a more rounded tip than does a Caucasian nose. Doctors are beginning to diversify their 'product lines', offering consumers a broader assortment of features that better reflect the diversity of cultural ideals of beauty in a heterogeneous society.[120]

Racial differences in beauty ideals also surfaced in a study of teenagers. White girls who were asked to describe the 'ideal' girl agreed she should be 5ft 7ins, weigh between 45 and 50 kg, and have blue eyes and long, flowing hair – in other words, she should look a lot like a Barbie doll. Almost 90 per cent of the girls in this study said they were dissatisfied with their weight.

In contrast, 70 per cent of the black girls in the same study responded that they were *satisfied* with their weight. They were much less likely to use physical characteristics to describe the ideal girl, instead emphasizing someone who has a personal sense of style and who gets along with others. It was only when prodded that they named such features as fuller hips, large thighs and a small waist, which, the authors of the study say, are attributes valued by black men.[121]

- *To separate group members from non-members*. The Chinook Indians of North America used to press the head of a newborn baby between two boards for a year, permanently altering its shape. In our society, teenagers go out of their way to adopt distinctive hair and clothing styles that will distinguish them from adults.

- *To place the individual in the social organization*. Many cultures engage in rites of passage at puberty when a boy symbolically becomes a man. Young men in Ghana paint their bodies with white stripes to resemble skeletons to symbolize the death of their child status. In Western culture, this rite may involve some form of mild self-mutilation or engaging in dangerous activities.

- *To place the person in a gender category*. The Tchikrin Indians of South America insert a string of beads in a boy's lip to enlarge it. Western women wear lipstick to enhance femininity. At the turn of the century, small lips were fashionable because they represented women's submissive role at that time.[122] Today, big, red lips are provocative and indicate an aggressive sexuality. Some women, including a number of famous actresses and models, have collagen injections or lip inserts to create large, pouting lips (known in the modelling industry as 'liver lips').[123]

- *To enhance sex-role identification*. Wearing high heels, which podiatrists agree are a prime cause of knee and hip problems, backaches and fatigue, can be compared with the traditional Oriental practice of foot-binding to enhance femininity. As one doctor observed, 'When they [women] get home, they can't get their high-heeled shoes off fast enough. But every doctor in the world could yell from now until Doomsday, and women would still wear them.'[124]

- *To indicate desired social conduct*. The Suya of South America wear ear ornaments to emphasize the importance placed in their culture on listening and obedience. In Western society gay men may wear an earring to signal how they expect to be treated.

- *To indicate high status or rank*. The Hidates Indians of North America wear feather ornaments that indicate how many people they have killed. In our society, some people wear glasses with clear lenses, even though they do not have eye problems, to increase their perceived status.

- *To provide a sense of security*. Consumers often wear lucky charms, amulets, rabbits' feet and so on to protect them from the 'evil eye'. Some modern women wear a 'mugger whistle' around their necks for a similar reason.

Tattoos

Tattoos – both temporary and permanent – are a popular form of body adornment. This body art can be used to communicate aspects of the self to onlookers and may serve some of the same functions that other kinds of body painting do in primitive cultures. In fact, much of the recent literature and discourse on tattoos centres on the theme of users as 'Modern Primitives'.[125] Tattoos (from the Tahitian *ta-tu*) have deep roots in folk art. Until recently, the images were crude and were primarily either death symbols (e.g. a skull), animals (especially panthers, eagles and snakes), pin-up women or military designs. More current influences include science fiction themes, Japanese symbolism and tribal designs.

A tattoo may be viewed as a fairly risk-free (?) way of expressing an adventurous side of the self. Tattoos have a long history of association with people who are social outcasts. For example, the faces and arms of criminals in sixth-century Japan were tattooed as a way of identifying them, as were Massachusetts prison inmates in the nineteenth century. These emblems are often used by marginal groups, such as bikers or Japanese *yakuze* (gang members), to express group identity and solidarity. In Europe today, the growth of tattoos on individuals of all ages and social classes can be seen both as a form of communication, and a growth in commodification. European consumers are more and more often using their own skin as part of their expression of consumer culture.[126]

Body piercing

Decorating the body with various kinds of metallic inserts has evolved from a practice associated with some fringe groups to become a popular fashion statement. Piercings can range from a hoop protruding from a navel to scalp implants, where metal posts are inserted in the skull (do not try this at home!). Publications such as *Piercing Fans International Quarterly* are seeing their circulations soar and websites featuring piercings

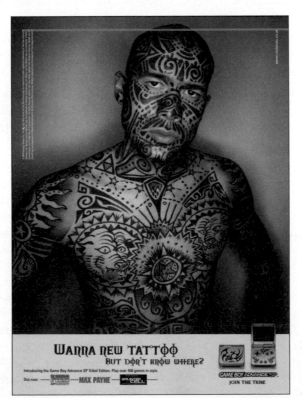

Body decoration can be permanent, or (hopefully!) temporary, in order to distinguish oneself, shock others, signify group membership, or express a particular mood or message.
The Advertising Archives

and piercing products are attracting numerous followers. This popularity is not pleasing to hard-core piercing fans, who view the practice as a sensual consciousness-raising ritual and are concerned that now people just do it because it's trendy. As one customer waiting for a piercing remarked, 'If your piercing doesn't mean anything, then it's just like buying a pair of platform shoes.'[127]

■ CHAPTER SUMMARY

- Consumers' *self-concepts* are reflections of their attitudes towards themselves. Whether these attitudes are positive or negative, they will help to guide many purchase decisions; products can be used to bolster self-esteem or to 'reward' the self.

- Many product choices are dictated by the similarity the consumer perceives between his or her personality and attributes of the product. The *symbolic interactionist perspective* on the self implies that each of us actually has many selves, and a different set of products is required as props to play each. Many things other than the body can also be viewed as part of the self. Valued objects, car, homes and even attachments to sports teams or national monuments are used to define the self, when these are incorporated into the extended self.

- A person's *sex-role identity* is a major component of self-definition. Conceptions about masculinity and femininity, largely shaped by society, guide the acquisition of 'sex-typed' products and services.

- Advertising and other media play an important role in socializing consumers to be male and female. While traditional women's roles have often been perpetuated in advertising depictions, this situation is changing somewhat. The media do not always portray men accurately either.

- Sometimes these activities are carried to an extreme, as people try too hard to live up to cultural ideals. One example is found in eating disorders, where women in particular become obsessed with thinness.

- A person's conception of his or her body also provides feedback to self-image. A culture communicates certain ideals of beauty, and consumers go to great lengths to attain these. Many consumer activities involve manipulating the body, whether through dieting, cosmetic surgery or tattooing.

► KEY TERMS

Actual self (p. 210)

Agentic goals (p. 216)

Androgyny (p. 217)

Body cathexis (p. 223)

Body image (p. 223)

Communal goals (p. 216)

Extended self (p. 214)

Fantasy (p. 210)

Ideal of beauty (p. 224)

Ideal self (p. 210)

Looking-glass self (p. 211)

Self-concept (p. 208)

Self-image congruence models (p. 213)

Sex-typed traits (p. 216)

Symbolic interactionism (p. 210)

Symbolic self-completion theory (p. 213)

CONSUMER BEHAVIOUR CHALLENGE

1 How might the creation of a self-conscious state be related to consumers who are trying on clothing in changing rooms? Does the act of preening in front of a mirror change the dynamics by which people evaluate their product choices? Why?

2 Is it ethical for marketers to encourage infatuation with the self?

3 List three dimensions by which the self-concept can be described.

4 Compare and contrast the real vs. the ideal self. List three products for which each type of self is likely to be used as a reference point when a purchase is considered.

5 Watch a series of ads featuring men and women on television. Try to imagine the characters with reversed roles (the male parts played by women, and vice versa). Can you see any differences in assumptions about sex-typed behaviour?

6 To date, the bulk of advertising targeted at gay consumers has been placed in exclusively gay media. If it was your decision, would you consider using mainstream media to reach gays, who constitute a significant proportion of the general population? Or, bearing in mind that members of some targeted segments have serious objections to this practice, especially when the product (e.g. alcohol, cigarettes) may be viewed as harmful in some way, do you think gays should be singled out at all by marketers?

7 Do you agree that marketing strategies tend to have a male-oriented bias? If so, what are some possible consequences for specific marketing activities?

8 Construct a 'consumption biography' of a friend or family member. Make a list and/or photograph his or her favourite possessions, and see if you or others can describe this person's personality just from the information provided by this catalogue.

9 Some consumer advocates have protested at the use of super-thin models in advertising, claiming that these women encourage others to starve themselves in order to attain the 'waif' look. Other critics respond that the media's power to shape behaviour has been overestimated, and that it is insulting to people to assume that they are unable to separate fantasy from reality. What do you think?

■ NOTES

1. Daniel Goleman, 'When ugliness is only in patient's eye, body image can reflect mental disorder', *New York Times* (2 October 1991): C13.

2. Tatiana Boncompagni, 'Newest wrinkle in the anti-ageing war', *Financial Times* (12 March 2004), http://news.ft.com/servlet/ContentServer?pagename=FT.com/StoryFT/FullStory&c=StoryFT&cid=1078381734673&p=1016625900932; Rhymer Rigby, 'Grooming the male market', *Financial Times* (3 February 2004), http://news.ft.com/servlet/ContentServer?pagename=FT.com/StoryFT/FullStory&c=StoryFT&cid=1073281521382&p=1059480266913.

3. Harry C. Triandis, 'The self and social behavior in differing cultural contexts', *Psychological Review* 96 (1989) 3: 506–20; H. Markus and S. Kitayama, 'Culture and the self: Implications for cognition, emotion, and motivation', *Psychological Review* 98 (1991): 224–53.

4. Markus and Kitayama, 'Culture and the self'.

5. Nancy Wong and Aaron Ahuvia, 'A Cross-Cultural Approach to Materialism and the Self', in Dominique Bouchet, ed., *Cultural Dimensions of International Marketing* (Denmark, Odense University, 1995): 68–89.

6. Lisa M. Keefe, 'You're so vain', *Marketing News* (28 February 2000): 8.

7. Anthony G. Greenwald and Mahzarin R. Banaji, 'The self as a memory system: Powerful, but ordinary', *Journal of Personality and Social Psychology* 57 (1989)1: 41–54; Hazel Markus, 'Self Schemata and Processing Information About the Self', *Journal of Personality and Social Psychology* 35 (1977): 63–78.

8. Morris Rosenberg, *Conceiving the Self* (New York: Basic Books, 1979); M. Joseph Sirgy, 'Self-concept in consumer behavior: A critical review', *Journal of Consumer Research* 9 (December 1982): 287–300.

9. Emily Yoffe, 'You are what you buy', *Newsweek* (4 June 1990): 59.

10. Roy F. Baumeister, Dianne M. Tice and Debra G. Hutton, 'Self-presentational motivations and personality differences in self-esteem', *Journal of Personality* 57 (September 1989): 547–75; Ronald J. Faber, 'Are Self-Esteem Appeals Appealing?', *Proceedings of the 1992 Conference of the American Academy of Advertising*, ed. Leonard N. Reid (1992): 230–5.

11. B. Bradford Brown and Mary Jane Lohr, 'Peer-group affiliation and adolescent self-esteem: An integration of ego identity and symbolic-interaction theories', *Journal of Personality and Social Psychology* 52 (1987) 1: 47–55.

12. Marsha L. Richins, 'Social comparison and the idealized images of advertising', *Journal of Consumer Research* 18 (June 1991): 71–83; Mary C. Martin and Patricia F. Kennedy, 'Advertising and social comparison: Consequences for female preadolescents and adolescents', *Psychology and Marketing* 10 (November/December 1993) 6: 513–30.

13. Philip N. Myers Jr. and Frank A. Biocca, 'The elastic body image: The effect of television advertising and programming on body image distortions in young women', *Journal of Communication* 42 (Summer 1992): 108–33.

14. Jeffrey F. Durgee, 'Self-esteem advertising', *Journal of Advertising* 14 (1986) 4: 21.

15. Erin White and Deborah Ball, 'Slim-Fast pounds home tough talk ads aimed at U.K. women offer steady diet of barbs to encourage weight loss', *The Wall Street Journal* (28 May 2004): B3.

16. Sigmund Freud, *New Introductory Lectures in Psycho-analysis* (New York: Norton, 1965).

17. Harrison G. Gough, Mario Fioravanti and Renato Lazzari, 'Some implications of self versus ideal-self congruence on the revised adjective check list', *Journal of Personality and Social Psychology* 44 (1983) 6: 1214–20.

18. Steven Jay Lynn and Judith W. Rhue, 'Daydream believers', *Psychology Today* (September 1985): 14.

19. http://campaignforrealbeauty.co.uk (accessed 5 August 2005).

20. Erving Goffman, *The Presentation of Self in Everyday Life* (Garden City, NY: Doubleday, 1959); Michael R. Solomon, 'The role of products as social stimuli: A symbolic interactionism perspective', *Journal of Consumer Research* 10 (December 1983): 319–29.

21. Julie Skur Hill, 'Purchasing habits shift for execs', *Advertising Age* (27 April 1992): 1–16.

22. George H. Mead, *Mind, Self and Society* (Chicago: University of Chicago Press, 1934).

23. Charles H. Cooley, *Human Nature and the Social Order* (New York: Scribner's, 1902).

24. J.G. Hull and A.S. Levy, 'The organizational functions of the self: An alternative to the Duval and Wicklund model of self-awareness', *Journal of Personality and Social Psychology* 37 (1979): 756–68; Jay G. Hull, Ronald R. Van Treuren, Susan J. Ashford, Pamela Propsom and Bruce W. Andrus, 'Self-consciousness and the processing of self-relevant information', *Journal of Personality and Social Psychology* 54 (1988) 3: 452–65.

25. Arnold W. Buss, *Self-Consciousness and Social Anxiety* (San Francisco: W.H. Freeman, 1980); Lynn Carol Miller and Cathryn Leigh Cox, 'Public self-consciousness and makeup use', *Personality and Social Psychology Bulletin* 8 (1982) 4: 748–51; Michael R. Solomon and John Schopler, 'Self-consciousness and clothing', *Personality and Social Psychology Bulletin* 8 (1982) 3: 508–14.

26. Morris B. Holbrook, Michael R. Solomon and Stephen Bell, 'A re-examination of self-monitoring and judgments of furniture designs', *Home Economics Research Journal* 19 (September 1990): 6–16; Mark Snyder and Steve Gangestad, 'On the nature of self-monitoring: matters of assessment, matters of validity', *Journal of Personality and Social Psychology* 51 (1986): 125–39.

27. Snyder and Gangestad, 'On the nature of self-monitoring'.

28. Timothy R. Graeff, 'Image congruence effects on product evaluations: The role of self-monitoring and public/private consumption', *Psychology and Marketing* 13(5) (August 1996): 481–99.

29. Richard G. Netemeyer, Scot Burton and Donald R. Lichtenstein, 'Trait aspects of vanity: Measurement and relevance to consumer behavior', *Journal of Consumer Research* 21 (March 1995): 612–26.

30. Michael R. Solomon and Henry Assael, 'The forest or the trees? A gestalt approach to symbolic consumption', in Jean Umiker-Sebeok, ed., *Marketing and Semiotics: New Directions in the Study of Signs for Sale* (Berlin: Mouton de Gruyter, 1987): 189–218.

31. Jack L. Nasar, 'Symbolic meanings of house styles', *Environment and Behavior* 21 (May 1989): 235–57; E.K. Sadalla, B. Verschure and J. Burroughs, 'Identity symbolism in housing', *Environment and Behavior* 19 (1987): 599–687.

32. Douglas B. Holt and Craig J. Thompson, 'Man-of-action heroes: The pursuit of heroic masculinity in everyday consumption', *Journal of Consumer Research* 31 (September 2004): 425–40; Michael R. Solomon, 'The role of products as social stimuli: A symbolic interactionism perspective', *Journal of Consumer Research* 10 (December 1983): 319–28; Robert E. Kleine III, Susan Schultz-Kleine and Jerome B. Kernan, 'Mundane consumption and the self: A social-identity perspective', *Journal of Consumer Psychology* 2 (1993) 3: 209–35; Newell D. Wright, C.B. Claiborne and M. Joseph Sirgy, 'The Effects of Product Symbolism on Consumer Self-Concept', in John F. Sherry Jr. and Brian Sternthal, eds, *Advances in Consumer Research*

19 (Provo, UT: Association for Consumer Research, 1992): 311–18; Susan Fournier, 'A Person-Based Relationship Framework for Strategic Brand Management', Ph.D. dissertation, University of Florida, 1994.

33. A. Dwayne Ball and Lori H. Tasaki, 'The role and measurement of attachment in consumer behavior', *Journal of Consumer Psychology* 1 (1992) 2: 155–72.

34. William B. Hansen and Irwin Altman, 'Decorating personal places: A descriptive analysis', *Environment and Behavior* 8 (December 1976): 491–504.

35. R.A. Wicklund and P.M. Gollwitzer, *Symbolic Self-Completion* (Hillsdale, NJ: Lawrence Erlbaum, 1982).

36. Erving Goffman, *Asylums* (New York: Doubleday, 1961).

37. Quoted in Floyd Rudmin, 'Property crime victimization impact on self, on attachment, and on territorial dominance', *CPA Highlights, Victims of Crime Supplement* 9 (1987) 2: 4–7.

38. Barbara B. Brown, 'House and Block as Territory', paper presented at the Conference of the Association for Consumer Research, San Francisco, 1982.

39. Quoted in Shay Sayre and David Horne, 'I Shop, Therefore I Am: The Role of Possessions for Self Definition', in Shay Sayre and David Horne, eds, *Earth, Wind, and Fire and Water: Perspectives on Natural Disaster* (Pasadena, CA: Open Door Publishers, 1996): 353–70; Recently in Germany, the 'loss of self' was taken to the ultimate extreme when a 43-year-old German from Berlin advertised on the internet that he would like to be eaten. His ad was answered and, with his consent, he was cut into pieces, frozen and placed in the freezer next to the takeaway pizza. See: 'Cannibal to face murder charge at re-trial', *The Guardian* (23 April 2005), http://www.guardian.co.uk/international/story/0,,1468373,00.html.

40. Deborah A. Prentice, 'Psychological correspondence of possessions, attitudes, and values', *Journal of Personality and Social Psychology* 53 (1987) 6: 993–1002.

41. Sak Onkvisit and John Shaw, 'Self-concept and image congruence: Some research and managerial implications', *Journal of Consumer Marketing* 4 (Winter 1987): 13–24. For a related treatment of congruence between advertising appeals and self-concept, see George M. Zinkhan and Jae W. Hong, 'Self-Concept and Advertising Effectiveness: A Conceptual Model of Congruency, Conspicuousness, and Response Mode', in Rebecca H. Holman and Michael R. Solomon, eds, *Advances in Consumer Research* 18 (Provo, UT: Association for Consumer Research, 1991): 348–54.

42. C.B. Claiborne and M. Joseph Sirgy, 'Self-Image Congruence as a Model of Consumer Attitude Formation and Behavior: A Conceptual Review and Guide for Further Research', paper presented at the Academy of Marketing Science Conference, New Orleans, 1990.

43. Liz Hunt, 'Rise in infertility linked to craze for body building', *The Independent* (12 July 1995): 12; Paul Kelso, Duncan Mackay and Matthew Taylor, 'From gym to club to school: the shock spread of steroid abuse', *The Guardian* (14 November 2003), http://www.guardian.co.uk/uk_news/story/0,,1084792,00.html.

44. Al E. Birdwell, 'A study of influence of image congruence on consumer choice', *Journal of Business* 41 (January 1964): 76–88; Edward L. Grubb and Gregg Hupp, 'Perception of self, generalized stereotypes, and brand selection', *Journal of Marketing Research* 5 (February 1986): 58–63.

45. Ira J. Dolich, 'Congruence relationship between self-image and product brands', *Journal of Marketing Research* 6 (February 1969): 80–4; Danny N. Bellenger, Earle Steinberg and Wilbur W. Stanton, 'The congruence of store image and self image as it relates to store loyalty', *Journal of Retailing* 52 (1976) 1: 17–32; Ronald J. Dornoff and Ronald L. Tatham, 'Congruence between personal image and store image', *Journal of the Market Research Society* 14 (1972) 1: 45–52.

46. Naresh K. Malhotra, 'A scale to measure self-concepts, person concepts, and product concepts', *Journal of Marketing Research* 18 (November 1981): 456–64.

47. Ernest Beaglehole, *Property: A Study in Social Psychology* (New York: Macmillan, 1932).

48. M. Csikszentmihalyi and Eugene Rochberg Halton, *The Meaning of Things: Domestic Symbols and the Self* (Cambridge, MA: Cambridge University Press, 1981).

49. Russell W. Belk, 'Possessions and the extended self', *Journal of Consumer Research* 15 (September 1988): 139–68.

50. Janeen Arnold Costa, 'Introduction', in J. A. Costa, ed., *Gender Issues and Consumer Behavior* (Thousand Oaks, CA: Sage, 1994).

51. Joan Meyers-Levy, 'The influence of sex roles on judgment', *Journal of Consumer Research* 14 (March 1988): 522–30.

52. Kimberly J. Dodson and Russell W. Belk, 'Gender in Children's Birthday Stories', in Janeen Costa, ed., *Gender, Marketing, and Consumer Behavior* (Salt Lake City, UT: Association for Consumer Research, 1996): 96–108.

53. Elizabeth C. Hirschman, 'A Feminist Critique of Marketing Theory: Toward Agentic-Communal Balance', working paper, School of Business, Rutgers University, New Brunswick, NJ, 1990.

54. Eileen Fischer and Stephen J. Arnold, 'Sex, gender identity, gender role attitudes, and consumer behavior', *Psychology and Marketing* 11 (March/April 1994) 2: 163–82.

55. Kathleen Debevec and Easwar Iyer, 'Sex Roles and Consumer Perceptions of Promotions, Products, and Self: What Do We Know and Where Should We Be Headed', in Richard J. Lutz, ed., *Advances in Consumer Research* 13 (Provo, UT: Association for Consumer Research, 1986): 210–14; Joseph A. Bellizzi and Laura Milner, 'Gender positioning of a traditionally male-dominant product', *Journal of Advertising Research* (June/July 1991): 72–9.

56. Janeen Arnold Costa and Teresa M. Pavia, 'Alphanumeric brand names and gender stereotypes', *Research in Consumer Behavior* 6 (1993): 85–112.

57. Helga Dittmar, Jane Beattie and Susanne Friese, 'Gender identity and material symbols: Objects and decision considerations in impulse purchases', *Journal of Economic Psychology* 16 (1995): 491–511; Jason Cox and Helga Dittmar, 'The functions of clothes and clothing (dis)satisfaction: A gender analysis among British students', *Journal of Consumer Policy* 18 (1995): 237–65.

58. Sandra L. Bem, 'The measurement of psychological androgyny', *Journal of Consulting and Clinical Psychology* 42 (1974): 155–62; Deborah E. S. Frable, 'Sex typing and gender ideology: Two facets of the individual's gender psychology that go together', *Journal of Personality and Social Psychology* 56 (1989) 1: 95–108.

59. See D. Bruce Carter and Gary D. Levy, 'Cognitive aspects of early sex-role development: The influence of gender schemas on preschoolers' memories and preferences for sex-typed toys and activities', *Child Development* 59 (1988): 782–92; Bernd H. Schmitt, France Le Clerc and Laurette Dube-Rioux, 'Sex typing and consumer behavior: A test of gender schema theory', *Journal of Consumer Research* 15 (June 1988): 122–7.

60. Carol Gilligan, *In a Different Voice: Psychological Theory and Women's Development* (Cambridge, MA: Harvard University Press, 1982); Joan Meyers-Levy and Durairaj Maheswaran, 'Exploring differences in males' and females' processing strategies', *Journal of Consumer Research* 18 (June 1991): 63–70.

61. Lynn J. Jaffe and Paul D. Berger, 'Impact on purchase intent of sex-role identity and product positioning', *Psychology and Marketing* (Fall 1988): 259–71; Lynn J. Jaffe, 'The unique predictive ability of sex-role identity in explaining women's response to advertising', *Psychology and Marketing* 11 (September/October 1994) 5: 467–82.

62. Leila T. Worth, Jeanne Smith and Diane M. Mackie, 'Gender schematicity and preference for gender-typed products', *Psychology and Marketing* 9 (January 1992): 17–30.

63. Julie Candler, 'Woman car buyer – don't call her a niche anymore', *Advertising Age* (21 January 1991): S-8; see also Robin Widgery and Jack McGaugh, 'Vehicle message appeals and the new generation woman', *Journal of Advertising Research* (September/October 1993): 36–42; Blayne Cutler, 'Condom mania', *American Demographics* (June 1989): 17.

64. Laurel Anderson and Marsha Wadkins, 'The New Breed in Japan: Consumer Culture', unpublished manuscript, Arizona State University, Tempe, 1990; Doris L. Walsh, 'A familiar story', *American Demographics* (June 1987): 64.

65. B. Abrams, 'American Express is gearing new ad campaign to women', *Wall Street Journal* (4 August 1983): 23.

66. 'Ads' portrayal of women today is hardly innovative', *Marketing News* (6 November 1989): 12; Jill Hicks Ferguson, Peggy J. Kreshel and Spencer F. Tinkham, 'In the pages of *Ms.*: Sex role portrayals of women in advertising', *Journal of Advertising* 19 (1990) 1: 40–51.

67. Richard Elliott, Abigail Jones, Andrew Benfield and Matt Barlow, 'Overt sexuality in advertising: A discourse analysis of gender responses', *Journal of Consumer Policy* 18 (1995): 187–217; Sonia Livingstone and Gloria Greene, 'Television advertisements and the portrayal of gender', *British Journal of Social Psychology* 25 (1986): 149–54; for one of the original articles on this topic, see L.Z. McArthur and B.G. Resko, 'The portrayal of men and women in American television commercials', *Journal of Social Psychology* 97 (1975): 209–20.

68. Richard Edel, 'American dream vendors', *Advertising Age* (9 November 1988): 153.

69. http://campaignforrealbeauty.co.uk (accessed 5 August 2005).

70. Daniel J. Brett and Joanne Cantor, 'The portrayal of men and women in U.S. television commercials: A recent content analysis and trends over 15 years', *Sex Roles* 18 (1988): 595–609.

71. Kyle Pope, 'High-tech marketers try to attract women without causing offense', *Wall Street Journal* (17 March 1994): B1 (2).

72. Gordon Sumner, 'Tribal rites of the American male', *Marketing Insights* (Summer 1989): 13.

73. Margaret G. Maples, 'Beefcake marketing: the sexy sell', *Marketing Communications* (April 1983): 21–5; Christina Passariello, 'New market for men's cosmetics gives beauty-product sales a lift', *Dow Jones Newswire* (7 April 2004); Rigby 'Grooming the male market'; author personal interview with Dr Peter Morley, Bumrungrad Hospital, Bangkok, 17 May 2005.

74. Jim Carlton, 'Hair-dye makers, sensing a shift, step up campaigns aimed at men', *Wall Street Journal Interactive Edition* (17 January 2000); Yochi Dreazen (no headline), *Wall Street Journal Interactive Edition* (8 June 1999); Cyndee Miller, 'Cosmetics makers to men: Paint those nails', *Marketing News* (12 May 1997): 14 (2).

75. Yumiko Ono (no headline), *Wall Street Journal Interactive Edition* (11 March 1999).

76. 'Changing conceptions of fatherhood', *USA Today* (May 1988): 10; see also Holt and Thompson, 'Man-of-action heroes'.

77. Quoted in Kim Foltz, 'In ads, men's image becomes softer', *New York Times* (26 March 1990): D12.

78. Quoted in Jennifer Foote, 'The ad world's new bimbos', *Newsweek* (25 January 1988): 44.

79. Maples, 'Beefcake marketing'.

80. Quoted in Lynn G. Coleman, 'What do people really lust after in ads?', *Marketing News* (6 November 1989): 12.

81. Riccardo A. Davis, 'Marketers game for gay events', *Advertising Age* (30 May 1994): S-1 (2); Cyndee Miller, 'Top marketers take bolder approach in targeting gays', *Marketing News* (4 July 1994): 1 (2); see also Douglas L. Fugate, 'Evaluating the US male homosexual and lesbian population as a viable target market segment', *Journal of Consumer Marketing* 10(4) (1993) 4: 46–57; Laura M. Milner, 'Marketing to Gays and Lesbians: A Review', unpublished manuscript, the University of Alaska, 1990.

82. Kate Fitzgerald, 'IKEA dares to reveal gays buy tables, too', *Advertising Age* (28 March 1994): 3(2); Miller, 'Top marketers take bolder approach in targeting gays': 1(2); Paula Span, 'ISO the gay consumer', *Washington Post* (19 May 1994): D1 (2).

83. Kate Fitzgerald, 'AT&T addresses gay market', *Advertising Age* (16 May 1994): 8.

84. James S. Hirsch, 'New credit cards base appeals on sexual orientation and race', *Wall Street Journal* (6 November 1995): B1 (2).

85. Projections of the incidence of homosexuality in the general population are often influenced by assumptions of the researchers, as well as the methodology they employ (e.g. self-report, behavioural measures, fantasy measures). For a discussion of these factors, see Edward O. Laumann,

John H. Gagnon, Robert T. Michael and Stuart Michaels, *The Social Organization of Homosexuality* (Chicago: University of Chicago Press, 1994).

86. Lisa Peñaloza, 'We're here, we're queer, and we're going shopping! A critical perspective on the accommodation of gays and lesbians in the U.S. marketplace', *Journal of Homosexuality* 31(1/2) (1966): 9–41.

87. Fugate, 'Evaluating the U.S. male homosexual and lesbian population as a viable target market segment'. See also Laumann, Gagnon, Michael and Michaels, *The Social Organization of Homosexuality*.

88. Laura Koss-Feder, 'Out and about', *Marketing News* (25 May 1998): 1(2); Rachel X. Weissman, 'Gay market power', *American Demographics* 21 (June 1999) 6: 32–3.

89. Peñaloza, 'We're here, we're queer, and we're going shopping!'.

90. Michael Wilke, 'Subaru adds lesbians to niche marketing drive', *Advertising Age* (4 March 1996): 8.

91. Dennis W. Rook, 'Body Cathexis and Market Segmentation', in Michael R. Solomon, ed., *The Psychology of Fashion* (Lexington, MA: Lexington Books, 1985): 233–41.

92. 'Nederlandse vrouw krijt lachend rimpels', *De Telegraaf* (26 April 1997): TA5.

93. Jane E. Brody, 'Notions of beauty transcend culture, new study suggests', *New York Times* (21 March 1994): A14.

94. Geoffrey Cowley, 'The biology of beauty', *Newsweek* (3 June 1996): 61–6.

95. Michael Fay and Christopher Price, 'Female body-shape in print advertisements and the increase in anorexia nervosa', *European Journal of Marketing* 28 (1994): 12.

96. 'Vrouwen hebben complexe relatie met schoonheid' ('Women have a complex relationship with beauty') *De Telegraaf* (31 January 2005), http://www2.telegraaf.nl/binnenland/17688091/_Vrouwen_hebben_complexe_relatie_met_schoonheid_.html.

97. Lois W. Banner, *American Beauty* (Chicago: The University of Chicago Press, 1980); for a philosophical perspective, see Barry Vacker and Wayne R. Key, 'Beauty *and* the beholder: The pursuit of beauty through commodities', *Psychology and Marketing* 10 (November/December 1993) 6: 471–94.

98. David M. Garner, Paul E. Garfinkel, Donald Schwartz and Michael Thompson, 'Cultural expectations of thinness in women', *Psychological Reports* 47 (1980): 483–91.

99. Kathleen Boyes, 'The new grip of girdles is lightened by lycra', *USA Today* (25 April 1991): 6D.

100. Stuart Elliott, 'Ultrathin models in Coca-Cola and Calvin Klein campaigns draw fire and a boycott call', *New York Times* (26 April 1994): D18; Cyndee Miller, 'Give them a cheeseburger', *Marketing News* (6 June 1994): 1 (2).

101. Jill Neimark, 'The beefcaking of America', *Psychology Today* (November/December 1994): 32 (11).

102. Richard H. Kolbe and Paul J. Albanese, 'Man to man: A content analysis of sole-male images in male-audience magazines', *Journal of Advertising* 25(4) (Winter 1996): 1–20.

103. 'Girls at 7 think thin, study finds', *New York Times* (11 February 1988): B9.

104. Beth Carney, 'In Europe, the fat is in the fire', *Business Week* (8 February 2005), http://www.businessweek.com/

bwdaily/dnflash/feb2005/nf2005028_5771_db016.htm?chan=gb. For a comprehensive report on obesity in the EU, go to http://www.iotf.org (accessed 5 August 2005).

105. Elaine L. Pedersen and Nancy L. Markee, 'Fashion Dolls: Communicators of Ideals of Beauty and Fashion', paper presented at the international Conference on Marketing Meaning, Indianapolis, 1989; Dalma Heyn, 'Body hate', *Ms.* (August 1989): 34; Mary C. Martin and James W. Gentry, 'Assessing the internalization of physical attractiveness norms', *Proceedings of the American Marketing Association Summer Educators' Conference* (Summer 1994): 59–65.

106. 'So Germans can be gourmets too', *The Economist* (9 December 2000): 57. See also The European Commission, Eurostat, and 'International survey: Teens fattest in the U.S.', CNN (6 January 2004), http://www.cnn.com/2004/HEALTH/parenting/01/05/obese.teens.ap/index.html.

107. Debra A. Zellner, Debra F. Harner and Robbie I. Adler, 'Effects of eating abnormalities and gender on perceptions of desirable body shape', *Journal of Abnormal Psychology* 98 (February 1989): 93–6.

108. Robin T. Peterson, 'Bulimia and anorexia in an advertising context', *Journal of Business Ethics* 6 (1987): 495–504.

109. Christian S. Crandall, 'Social contagion of binge eating', *Journal of Personality and Social Psychology* 55 (1988): 588–98.

110. Judy Folkenberg, 'Bulimia: Not for women only', *Psychology Today* (March 1984): 10.

111. Eleanor Grant, 'The exercise fix: What happens when fitness fanatics just can't say no?', *Psychology Today* 22 (February 1988): 24.

112. John W. Schouten, 'Selves in transition: Symbolic consumption in personal rites of passage and identity reconstruction', *Journal of Consumer Research* 17 (March 1991): 412–25.

113. Monica Gonzalez, 'Want a lift?', *American Demographics* (February 1988): 20.

114. Annette C. Hamburger and Holly Hall, 'Beauty quest', *Psychology Today* (May 1988): 28.

115. Emily Yoffe, 'Valley of the silicon dolls', *Newsweek* (26 November 1990): 72.

116. Norihiko Shirouzu, 'Reconstruction boom in Tokyo: Perfecting imperfect bellybuttons', *Wall Street Journal* (4 October 1995): B1.

117. Keith Greenberg, 'What's hot: Cosmetic surgery', *Public Relations Journal* (June 1988): 23.

118. 'Bra wars', *The Economist* (2 December 2000): 64.

119. Ruth P. Rubinstein, 'Color, Circumcision, Tattoos, and Scars', in Solomon, ed., *The Psychology of Fashion*: 243–54; Peter H. Bloch and Marsha L. Richins, 'You look "mahvelous": The pursuit of beauty and marketing concept', *Psychology and Marketing* 9 (January 1992): 3–16.

120. Kathy H. Merrell, 'Saving faces', *Allure* (January 1994): 66 (2).

121. 'White weight', *Psychology Today* (September/October 1994): 9.

122. Sondra Farganis, 'Lip service: The evolution of pouting, pursing, and painting lips red', *Health* (November 1988): 48–51.

123. Michael Gross, 'Those lips, those eyebrows: New face of 1989 (new look of fashion models)', *New York Times Magazine* (13 February 1989): 24.

124. Quoted in 'High heels: Ecstasy's worth the agony', *New York Post* (31 December 1981).

125. Mike Featherstone, ed., *Body Modification* (Thousand Oaks, CA: Sage, 2000); Anne M. Velliquette and Jeff B. Murray, 'The New Tattoo Subculture', in *Mapping the Social Landscape: Readings in Sociology*, ed. Susan Ferguson (Mountain View, CA: Mayfield, 1999): 56–68; Anne M. Velliquette, Jeff B. Murray and Elizabeth H. Creyer, 'The Tattoo Renaissance: An Ethnographic Account of Symbolic Consumer Behavior', in Joseph W. Alba and J. Wesley Hutchinson, eds, *Advances in Consumer Research* 25 (Provo, UT: Association for Consumer Research, 1998): 461–7; Anne M. Velliquette, 'Modern Primitives: The Role of Product Symbolism in Lifestyle Cultures and Identity', dissertation, University of Arkansas Press, 2000; Margo DeMello, *Bodies of Inscription: A Cultural History of the Modern Tattoo Community* (Durham, NC: Duke University Press, 2000); Anne Veliquette and Gary Bamossy, 'Modern Primitives: The Role of the Body and Product Symbolism in Lifestyle Cultures and Identity', in Andrea Groppel-Klein and Franz-Rudolf Esch, eds, *European Advances in Consumer Research* 5 (Valdosta, GA: Association for Consumer Research, 2001): 21–2.

126. Jonathan Schroeder, 'Branding the Body: Skin and Consumer Communication', in Darach Turley and Stephen Brown, eds, *European Advances in Consumer Research: All Changed, Changed Utterly?* 6 (Valdosta, GA: Association for Consumer Research 2003): 23; Maurice Patterson and Richard Elliott, 'Harsh Beauty: The Alternative Aesthetic of Tattooed Women', in Turley and Brown, eds, *European Advances in Consumer Research* 6: 23; Dannie Kjeldgaard and Anders Bengtsson, 'Acts, Images, and Meaning of Tattooing', in Turley and Brown, eds, *European Advances in Consumer Research* 6: 24; Jonathan Schroeder and Janet Borgerson, 'Skin Signs: The Epidermal Schema in Contemporary Marketing Communications', in Turley and Brown, eds, *European Advances in Consumer Research* 6: 26; Roy Langer, 'SKINTWO: (Un)-covering the Skin in Fetish Carnivals', in Turley and Brown, eds, *European Advances in Consumer Research* 6: 27.

127. Quoted in Wendy Bounds, 'Body-piercing gets under America's skin', *Wall Street Journal* (4 April 1994): B1 (2), B4.

Appealing to taste buds or healthy lifestyles? Marketing low-fat foods to consumers in Greece

ATHANASSIOS KRYSTALLIS and GEORGE CHRYSSOHOIDIS,
Agricultural University of Athens, Greece

THE SETTING

A number of health organizations, including the World Health Organization (WHO), have recommended consumers '. . . to reduce daily fat intake below 30 per cent of total calories'; '. . . to limit intake of saturated fatty acids, which should not exceed 10 per cent of total energy intake'; and '. . . to consume less than 300 mg of cholesterol daily'. The need to reduce fat and cholesterol-related consumption is gaining increasing public acceptance. Growing awareness of the link between diet and health has led to major changes in consumer habits. As a result, there is a growing demand for foods with health enhancing properties, such as 'low-fat' or 'light' products. For the past decade, world production of low-fat food has expanded and it is now a multi-billion dollar industry. In the UK, for example, sales of reduced calorie products amounted to more than US$800 million, with an estimated growth of 5 per cent per year; and in the United States sales since the mid 1990s have grown to US$40 billions.

The concept of low-fat products means that these products have a minimal level of fat. This level often requires some modifications to the composition and nature of the product. This modification can affect different aspects of these low-fat products, including their sensory properties and their healthiness. This means that claims such as 'low', 'reduced', 'less', 'lean', 'light', 'healthy' are not always supported by a clear definition of the changes in the composition of the product. This has led to considerable confusion among consumers. Besides being perceived as healthier, low-fat products must offer good quality and hedonic attributes, which should in principle be at least the same as those of the regular (full-fat) products to which consumers are accustomed, if these low-fat products are to be a commercial success. Thus, the conflict between 'health' and 'sensory appeal' (e.g. taste) is recognized as being influential in the choice of low-fat products by consumers.

Another important influential factor in the low-fat food market has been the drive for weight loss, i.e. the body's aesthetic appeal. Over the last decades, there has been a marked trend toward an increasingly thin, and yet physically fit, ideal of attractiveness in economically advanced societies, directly linked to the consumption of low-fat food products. However, cost is an equally important factor in this market. Higher lean-to-fat ratios and other non-food ingredients have tended to raise the cost of manufacturing low-fat products. It is estimated that these new low-fat products may be anywhere from 10 to 30 per cent dearer than their full-fat counterparts. This apparent drawback may be partially offset by the fact that growing numbers of consumers are interested in reducing fat intake and so may perceive low-fat products as better value for money.

THE SURVEY

A study in 2002 examined Greek consumers' attitudes towards low-fat food products. The research revolved around the potential conflict between the 'sensory appeal' (taste) and the 'healthiness' of low-fat products. The study aimed to segment the Greek market in terms of users' attitudes towards light products. All four consumer clusters identified in the survey paid particular attention to the hedonic factor when consuming food, and assigned less importance to price in their overall selection criteria when choosing foodstuffs. Additionally, the percentages of awareness of and use of low-fat products, by consumers, were approximately equal, while the market penetration of these low-fat products was fairly widespread.

Cluster 1 consisted of 'fervent supporters' of the low-fat food products. The large majority of this cluster (strongly) agreed that low-fat products met their expectations in terms of sensory characteristics, and that low-fat products are healthier due to their lower calorie content.

Cluster 2 comprised 'satisfied consumers with low-fat food products' healthiness'. Almost all these cluster members (strongly) agreed that low-fat products did not meet their expectations in terms of sensory appeal. However, the vast majority of the cluster believed that low-fat products are healthier when compared with their full-calorie counterparts.

Cluster 3 was defined as the 'opposed to the low-fat products'. In line with cluster 2, all cluster 3 members believed that low-fat products did not meet their expectations in terms of sensory characteristics.

Furthermore, they (strongly) disagreed with the view that low-fat products are healthier than their full-calorie equivalents. Cluster members were either occasional low-fat product users or they bought them for another reason, e.g. weight loss for aesthetic reasons, without consciously relating this to improved health.

Finally, cluster 4 comprised *'satisfied consumers with low-fat food products' sensory characteristics'*. Low-fat products met the sensory expectations of the large majority of this fourth cluster. They were occasional low-fat product buyers, for whom the taste of the low-fat products was not perceived to be a constraint, or, similar to cluster 3, they consumed low-fat products for aesthetic reasons.

Overall, the survey concluded that those consumers who considered low-fat products to be healthy tended to be young, a slightly higher ratio of male to female, mostly married, of average income, and their educational level did not appear to be related to their high degree of health awareness. Those who did not think that low-fat products were healthy tended to be middle-aged, of either sex, mostly married, of low to average income, and their educational level was not a significant discriminating factor. In general, the socio-demographic differences were not particularly remarkable.

THE LESSONS LEARNED

Greek consumers seemed to be willing to substitute specially manufactured low-fat foods in their diet. It appears that low-fat products constitute common food choices; and the purchase of low-fat foods cannot be taken as indicative of any kind of 'innovative' food purchase behaviour.

One of the most important findings was consumers' uncertainty about whether or not low-fat food products are superior to their full-calorie counterparts in terms of sensory appeal and healthiness. This uncertainty was shared by more than one type of low-fat product user. The motives behind the selection of low-fat foods differed for different consumer types, and are linked to different attitudes towards hedonism and healthiness. These two motives seem to function either as substitutes or in a complementary way, depending on the perceptions that consumers have of low-fat foods.

Furthermore, the main constraint Greek consumers are faced with when consuming light foods is their sensory appeal, especially when these low-fat foods are compared to 'common' food products. Healthiness seems to be much less important as a constraint on Greek consumer behaviour. While information which identifies products as low in fat generally lowers judgements of expected sensory quality, the magnitude of this effect was often found to be rather small, partly because it

differed markedly in strength and direction amongst various consumer sub-groups, in this particular case among the four clusters. On the contrary, low-fat foods were considered to be healthier by the majority (61.3 per cent) of the sample.

MARKETING IMPLICATIONS

A very popular misinterpretation of the 'low-fat' claim means that a large percentage of consumers perceive low caloric intake products as healthier products. Yet this equation is accurate only indirectly, through the beneficial results of a low-fat diet in terms of individual health and physical condition. Two important matters seem to be overlooked: (a) weight reduction as a selection motive for low-fat food is not, and should not be, directly related to one's health, although it constitutes a potential motive to buy light food products for a large percentage of consumers (clusters 3 and 4), and (b) the fact that these products possibly contain some unhealthy chemical additives such as fat substitutes.

Consequently, the degree of conscious purchasing of low-fat foods closely reflects consumers' underlying health consciousness, which thus turns out to be a central motive of low-fat preference. Clusters 1 and 2 which perceive low-fat products as being healthier can be considered to be conscious low-fat food 'buyers'. On the other hand, the remaining 40 per cent appear to purchase low-fat foods either occasionally ('opposed') or because of reasons not directly related to the health consciousness selection motive ('users').

Nevertheless, marketers need to recognize that willingness to purchase foods in order to be healthy is often combined with a willingness to pay premiums for purchasing low-fat food products. Culture, education, purchasing power and other factors (e.g. labelling, information) considerably influence consumer habits, and hence the percentage of income spent on food. Since all social groups do not purchase the same kind of food products, the extent to which price affects acceptance will vary according to the type of low-fat product and the type of consumer motivation.

Finally, two additional implications should be kept in mind: (1) hedonic responses to sensory characteristics of foods may be modified by extended sensory exposure. This should be encouraging for the low-fat food industry in the long run, because whereas dietary changes initially have had poor acceptance by clusters 2 and 3, these may over time achieve better levels of acceptance simply through repeated use; (2) when consumers have a negative opinion about the healthiness of low-fat food, as is the case with clusters 3 and 4, counter-arguments via marketing communications might be the only way in which these opinions can be challenged and changed.

QUESTIONS

1 Search for market data/reports about low-fat food products in your country. In your opinion, does the conflict between taste and healthiness also apply?

2 Identify the 4Ps for low-fat products (product, price, place, promotion) for each consumer cluster. Which of the four components should the relevant promotion strategy be based on?

3 Comment on consumers' tendency to misinterpret the low-fat claim to be a healthy claim. Do you believe that this applies to your country too? Can you think of examples from other product categories where consumers tend to misinterpret the different claims made about goods and services?

Should I – or shouldn't I? Consumers' motivational conflicts in purchase decisions for electronics

ELFRIEDE PENZ, International Marketing and Management, Vienna University of Economics and Business Administration, Vienna

Consumers are faced with decisions throughout their daily lives. Making choices in general, and deciding how to spend money on products in particular, often involves a psychological conflict. According to Miller, a motivational conflict arises due to 'competition between incompatible responses' within an individual (Miller 1944), because it often involves several positive (approach–approach), several negative (avoidance–avoidance), and also several positive as well as negative (approach–avoidance) consequences. Should I have a tomato pizza or sushi? Should I spend my money on a concert ticket or would it be better to save it for my holidays? Should I take the car and search for a parking space for half an hour or should I take the underground and lose an hour in travelling time?

THE GROWTH IN CONSUMER ELECTRONICS PURCHASING

A purchase decision which is of increasing importance for young Austrians involves spending money on electronics, and in particular on communications. According to Euromonitor, the strongest growth in consumer expenditure over the last few years, at 174.9 per cent, was on communications. This trend was driven particularly by mobile phones and the internet. Further growth is expected, and it is forecast that by 2015 around 5.4 billion euros will be spent on communications. In terms of PC ownership, an increase of 953.8 per cent between 1990 and 2003 resulted in a penetration of 34.7 per cent, compared to just 3.3 per cent in 1990. The number of people making online purchases as a percentage of the total number of online users was 47.5 per cent in 2003, up from 20.1 per cent in 2000.

Sales of consumer electronics, and in particular portable as well as digital equipment, including DVD players, MiniDisc players, MP3 players and portable computers are growing, in contrast to the downward trends which can be observed in many white and brown goods, which are characterised by saturation and extreme competition. Fascination with new equipment and increasing mobility are two factors which lure consumers into electronics stores, in order to purchase the technical equipment, such as mobile phones, MP3 players, DVD players and state-of-the-art computers which are central to their lifestyles. Furthermore, the different functionalities of the products – for instance, mobile phones with integrated fax and internet access, computers with built-in CD writers and/or DVD players – make consumer electronics appealing to the youth population. These items make it less necessary to invest in several appliances, which in turn saves money for consumers. Overall, new products like these generate new social trends at work and at home as they allow greater flexibility in lifestyles and make it possible for people to be more mobile.

RETAIL STRUCTURE IN AUSTRIA

The durable goods retail sector in Austria is extremely fragmented with a large number of small and medium-sized traders with one outlet. In general, the retail sector in Austria is gradually turning into a modern, consumer-oriented, market-driven environment with consumers favouring large retail outlets and specialist chain stores. Price competition in the retail sector is extremely aggressive and the retailer concentration in many retail sub-sectors is increasing. However, there is stringent legislation in Austria to protect the small and medium-sized retailers from the rapid expansion of larger retailers. This legislation includes, for example, stringent building regulations to stop the expansion of new megastores, shopping centres and large outlets; strict shop opening hours and regulations to stop retailers opening stores on Sundays; and strict requirements for the awarding of business licences. Labour laws are also strict and extensive, although minimum salaries are relatively low in the retail sector. However, paid holidays and other compulsory payments (sick leave and high social insurance costs) increase the cost of labour to around 200 per cent of the salary.

There has been some liberalization, for instance with seasonal sales. These rules were abolished in 1992. Before that, only two sales per year were allowed, in summer and winter, and their dates were fixed by law. The government also extended the shop opening hours in 1997 as, after joining the EU in 1995, many Austrians living in the border regions started to cross over to Germany, Italy and other neighbouring countries to go shopping on Saturdays and to get round the restricted shopping hours in Austria. To sum up, consumers' growing preference in Austria is for large outlets with a broader range of products at low prices and very little service, and with plenty of parking spaces.

The leading retailer in the durable goods sector in Austria is Media-Saturn. It has a market share of around 40 per cent among the sector specialists. It has two strong retail brands, Media Markt and Saturn, which have totally different outlet strategies to create maximum market exposure for Media-Saturn. Media Markt outlets are between 2,500 sq m and 3,000 sq m in size, located on the outskirts of cities in large shopping complexes and positioned as specialist retailers for the consumer electronics sector. Saturn outlets, on the other hand, have an average selling space of around 350 sq m, and are located in inner cities, in department stores or shopping centres. Both target the middle-market and lower-upper market segments in the durable goods sector with mass-market products. The unique selling point for both outlets is value for money. They sell well-known consumer electronics manufacturers' brands as well as some exclusive products at competitive prices. In 2003, Media-Saturn had 22 outlets with sales of 629.5 million euros and it is planning continued expansion in the future. Cosmos and Niedermeyer are the other two specialist multiples. In 2003, Cosmos had 20 outlets (sales 296.1 million euros) and Niedermeyer 120 (sales 226.2 million euros), spread throughout the country.

SCENARIO

Eva recently started studying psychology in Vienna and for that reason she moved from the very small town in which she grew up to the capital, Vienna. She rented a room in a nice flat which she shares with three other students, Viktoria, Franz and Dominik.

One afternoon after she got back from a lecture, Eva picked up the post and found a leaflet from a big electronics retailer, offering a notebook at a special price. She looked at it with particular interest because, since moving to Vienna, Eva had been looking for a notebook which she could use for studying and also for sending emails and chatting with friends all around the world. The Samsung P28 Series seemed to be perfect for her, because it provides a high degree of connectivity with USB ports for connecting peripherals such as printers and digital cameras. It also included the option of integrated wireless LAN to connect to public wireless 'hot spots'. Without knowing exactly how that works, Eva was sure she had seen adverts about hot spots before and thought she might well make use of that, too. She also wanted to send pictures to her friends with the

digital camera she had been given for her birthday and therefore thought that this particular feature would be perfect for her.

Eva must have been sitting in the kitchen reading the leaflet for about half an hour when Viktoria and Franz came home. Eva thought that this would a good opportunity to ask them for their opinions about the special offer. Franz as a student of informatics is very interested in technical applications, so perhaps he would be able explain to her what hot spots were and whether or not she needed USB ports. At that point a lively argument broke out about the best place to buy a laptop. Viktoria had recently been to one of the big electronics stores in Mariahilferstrasse, a busy shopping street, because she had wanted to buy a MiniDisc player. Franz knew most of the electronics stores because he was a real enthusiast, hanging around them whenever possible and trying out new products. By then Dominik had also come home so he joined in as well. He frequently visited Saturn or Cosmos because he could listen to new CDs as long as he wanted in the booths there.

However, Viktoria was very negative about the big retailers, because her last visit hadn't been very successful. Asked why, she said: 'It must be one of the largest and the most popular places in town! I visited it during working hours and it was so overcrowded! All those long shelves with no clear indication about where to find anything. It was really difficult for me to find the section where they sold MiniDisc players. Also I was so confused by all the adverts hanging up everywhere.' Franz interrupted. He laughed at her and scoffed that *this* was such a typical girlie-thing: women never find the right place because they lack any sense of spatial orientation; and they don't understand technical stuff anyway. *He* had never had any difficulties in finding what he wanted. 'So, then, why does it always take so long when you go to do the shopping?' she yelled at him. Everybody in the flat-share knew that he had negative feelings about shopping and often got lost around the supermarket.

'Viktoria is right,' Dominik said, trying to calm things down and take the heat out of the quarrel, 'and even worse is that it is almost impossible to get hold of one of the sales assistants to find out any information. The chances of finding one with accurate information are really low.' Once he had had to wait almost 40 minutes to find a sales assistant to ask about a particular mobile phone. The assistant was nice and friendly and tried to help, but he was not responsible for that particular product and could only give very general information. Even worse, the information on the price tag was wrong and when Dominik, after waiting another 20 minutes at the cash desk, wanted to pay, it turned out that it cost almost double what was shown on the ticket. 'Never mind,' Dominik said, 'at least the listening stations are okay there and nobody bothers you, because they have plenty of them.'

Viktoria didn't give up at this point. She was proud of her consumer skills. She said she usually visited several electronics stores to look at different brands and prices. She had found out about different offers by looking up information on the internet. If after all this she was still in some doubt, then she would find a salesperson to ask for advice. However, she admitted, that's the least preferred option, because she always got the feeling that they just wanted to persuade her to buy the most expensive product, although they knew that most people look for the cheapest price or at least the best price/value ratio. Eventually, she ordered her MiniDisc player online from a shop Franz recommended. She was attracted to buy online by the price, and also because it was an exciting experience purchasing online. She already knew what the MiniDisc player looked like from the electronics stores she had visited beforehand. However, Dominik held the opposite view about online shopping. 'I am definitely not a "sissy", but have you ever thought of how secure the payment procedure really is? I wouldn't give them my details that easily!'

The discussion went on for some time. Eva remained unsure about whether or not she should consider the advertised notebook in her purchase decision. She was also a little bit disappointed because she still had no exact idea of the technical features and didn't dare to ask Franz. The stories that her friends reported were not very persuasive and she didn't like to feel like a fool being alone in an overcrowded and disorganized shopping environment. So she decided to text her friend Silvia, who had recently bought a notebook. The next day they went together to Mariahilferstrasse, which Eva always enjoyed as she loved window shopping. When they entered the shop, the two young women headed towards the place where the special offers were displayed. It took about ten minutes before they found it and to their big surprise the counter, which was covered with point of sale material about 'Our recent advertising campaign' was more or less empty. Instead of notebooks, there were only empty boxes lying around.

They looked for somebody on the staff and asked a young guy if he had a clue where all the notebooks had gone. The answer they received was rather unsatisfactory. He declared himself not responsible for this section of the store and told them to look for somebody else. It took them some time to find an older man who was bustling around some TV sets so they

expected him to be responsible for electronics, which he immediately confirmed. When they told him that they wanted to buy the Samsung laptop which was advertised in the flyer, he responded that they had already run out of stock. Already very annoyed, they felt cheated and they asked him what the store offered as an alternative. They followed him into an area where lots of notebooks were displayed. Obviously he wasn't really happy at having to accompany them and to explain to them the advantages and disadvantages of the different models, so Eva and Silvia decided to look at them on their own, which they usually liked doing rather than talking to the sales assistants in these shops. They spent half an hour comparing models and Silvia's recent shopping experience. However, the range of laptops wasn't very impressive, two or three other models had also run out of stock, especially the cheaper ones. With feelings of disappointment Eva and Silvia left the store without having bought anything.

QUESTIONS

1 Discuss the motivational conflict Eva is experiencing. What are the approach aspects and what are the avoidance aspects in her situation? Which kind of conflict is she in?

2 What causes the motivational conflicts for the flat-mates in terms of
   (a) situational/environmental aspects?
   (b) social aspects?
   (c) personal/psychological aspects?

   Compare and discuss differences between them.

3 Eva is in a difficult situation and does not know how to resolve the conflict. She ended up not buying at that particular store but still did not succeed in purchasing a laptop. What other options does she have to resolve the uneasy and uncomfortable situation and at the same time get the desired product?

4 Viktoria bought her MiniDisc Player online. Discuss this kind of 'escape'. Should bricks-and-mortar companies try to avoid giving consumers such escapes? What strategies would you recommend to bricks-and-mortar companies?

5 Using your own experiences from similar situations, identify and evaluate potential conflict relievers.

Sources

Euromonitor (2005), http://www.euromonitor.com

Miller, N.E. (1944), 'Experimental Studies of Conflict', in Hunt, ed., *Personality and Behaviour Disorders* (New York: John Wiley & Sons): 431–65.

Further reading

Elliot, A.J. and T.M. Thrash (2002), 'Approach–avoidance motivation in personality: Approach and avoidance temperaments and goals', *Journal of Personality and Social Psychology* 82(5): 804-18.

Johnson, J.G. and J.R. Busemeyer (2001), 'Multiple-stage decision-making: The effect of planning horizon length on dynamic consistency', *Theory and Decision* 51: 217-46.

Maher, B.A. (1964), 'The application of the approach–avoidance conflict model to social behavior', *Conflict Resolution* 8(3): 287-91.

Smith, M. et al. (2002), 'Contemporary measures of approach and avoidance goal orientations: Similarities and differences', *British Journal of Educational Psychology* 72: 155-90.

Updegraff, J.A. et al. (2004), 'What makes experiences satisfying? The interaction of approach–avoidance motivations and emotions in well-being', *Journal of Personality and Social Psychology* 86(3): 496-504.

Prams are not just for babies . . .[1]

ELIN BRANDI SØRENSEN, University of Southern Denmark, Denmark, and
THYRA UTH THOMSEN, Copenhagen Business School, Denmark

PRAMS IN DENMARK

Many foreigners in Denmark have noticed the high prevalence of prams on the streets and have expressed surprise about their large size and their solid and practical appearance. And just as many have reacted with disbelief when they learn that most Danish children up to the age of two or three, sleep out of doors during the day in their prams, regardless of the time of year. It is assumed that sleeping outside will improve the immune defence system of the child. Many parents also find that their children sleep better, and for longer, when they sleep outside. Guidelines from the Danish health authorities confirm that if the mattress, the cover, and the child's clothing is appropriate it is safe to let the child sleep outside at temperatures as low as minus 10 degrees Celsius.

In the eyes of most Danish parents and parents-to-be, a pram is considered a necessity, a necessity that they will need within the first week or two of the child's birth. Therefore, the acquisition of a pram is typically organized before the birth of the child and thus becomes part of the preparations for the forthcoming addition to the family. However, even though the pram is considered a necessity, its acquisition is rarely considered a trivial matter.

In many cases the purchase of a pram represents the most expensive single item among the acquisitions made before the birth. And it is likely that the vehicle will stay with the family for at least five or six years, as it will probably be used by more than one child. It is also a very visible consumer good, that is, a consumer good that when used as a means of transportation is consumed in the public space – and is subject to the public gaze.

And, certainly, it appears to be a common experience that a pram has a clear potential to signal 'what kind of people we are', so that a pram potentially has a high symbolic value, very much in the same way as a car can have. This symbolic potential is a feature that most parents-to-be seem to be aware of – at one level or another. And this awareness may indeed spur speculations about 'what kind of parents would we like to be' – and maybe also 'what kind of parents would we *not* like to be'.

Thus, as Dorthe's case below will illustrate, the acquisition and usage of a pram is not just a practical matter. It may also include speculations about one's current identity and values, as well as one's future identity as a parent – a whole range of possible selves.

DORTHE

Dorthe is 25 years old and is currently training to become a pre-school teacher. She lives in a flat with her husband Jesper, and her two-year-old son Matias, in Ishøj, a suburb of Copenhagen, in a lower-income bracket neighbourhood inhabited by people of various ethnic origins. Compared with most other Danish first-time mothers, Dorthe was fairly young when she gave birth to her first child. She is now seven months pregnant with her second child and she is telling the story of the prams she has had.

'We bought our first pram in a sale about three months before Matias was born. Back then money meant a lot. At that time we were both students. Now Jesper has a well-paid job as a production engineer. But back then the price was an important issue. Jesper knew all about certain quality standards that he wanted to be fulfilled, while all I cared for was that I wanted it to be black or grey in order for it to be able match my clothes, no matter what colours I decided to wear. You know, it's a bit silly, but I wanted the pram and me to be a unified whole. I was very self-conscious at the time, because I had gained a lot of weight. So at least I wanted to look the best I could. Well, I also liked the kind of sporty design of the pram. We both used to do a lot of sports, so the design appealed to me somehow. Not that I have felt very sporty ever since, for sure, but at the time, it was still something that was kind of important for me.

I remember we had browsed around quite a few stores, and we felt lucky to find a model that fulfilled our criteria at a price that we could afford. It was a no-name brand bought at a discount retailer. But I loved it, and we took it home. I remember just sitting next to the pram and looking at it. It was the first time I really tried to imagine what it was going to be like . . . I tried to stand in front of the pram and to hold on to it to see how it felt. Well, I would rather not have anyone see how silly I was!

But then I went to water aerobics with other pregnant women and they talked a lot about what pram they wanted. Deep down I also wished I had been able to afford one of the prams they were talking about. They made it sound like you are not a very good mother if you buy a cheap pram. Or maybe that was just what I thought to myself. I felt like they did not want to talk to me anymore, because I was someone who was not interested enough in my child, since I hadn't bought an expensive pram. Even though, deep down you know that your child doesn't care at all if it's in an "Odder" pram or a no-name pram. The child is completely indifferent as long as it is content and warm, which it will be in both prams. In fact this is not about the child – it's all about the mother.

After the birth of my child I started using my pram. I went for long walks in the neighbourhood. And that's when I finally decided to get rid of it. You know, a lot of the people in my neighbourhood are unemployed and a lot of them are of a different ethnic origin. And after a while I realized that they had all bought the same pram that I had. Consequently I was mistaken for one of them. They approached me and spoke to me in some foreign language that I didn't understand. I felt very uncomfortable. Also, I felt that other people looked at me as if I was some young, poor, unemployed loser who was never going to get any education.

I guess I realized that it is with prams as it is with a lot of other things: they say a lot about who you are as a person. Just like clothes do. So I told my husband that for this baby we would have to get another pram. He couldn't quite understand why, but he supported me. I talked to friends who had bought a high-end pram to figure out which one to buy and studied a lot of brochures. So now we have saved enough money to buy the 'Rolls Royce' of prams: an "Odder" pram. It's 1,000 euros but it's worth it! It looks classy and stylish in a discrete way. I cannot wait. It will make me feel so good to take my baby for a walk in the new pram. We want it to be black or grey again, but we have considered having a red pattern on it since we know that I am carrying a girl. This time I want to be sure to get it right!'

QUESTIONS

1 How can the symbolic self-completion theory discussed in Chapter 7 help us to understand the way Dorthe relates herself to her pram(s)? What does the pram mean to her in her role as a mother? What does it mean to her in her role as a citizen in her neigbourhood?

2 Discuss the idea of 'the ideal mother' that Dorthe is confronted with in her water aerobics class. How does she relate/react to this ideal? How does it make her feel? Could she have reacted/related differently to this ideal? If yes, how?

3 Consider the symbolic interactionism perspective discussed in Chapter 7. How is the meaning of Dorthe's first pram negotiated? You could construct a chart and/or time line containing the different influencers and their associated meanings.

4 Consider other life role transitions that may comprise major changes of the self (becoming an adult, leaving home, going to university, entering the job market, marriage, children leaving home, divorce, retirement, death of a spouse . . .). What generalizations could be drawn from Dorthe's case about these transitions, concerning the role of and meanings around the consumption of goods?

Note

1. This case is partly fictitious and partly based on interview material, which is reported in Thomsen, T.U. and E. Sørensen (2006) 'The first four-wheeled status symbol: Pram consumption as a vehicle for the construction of motherhood identity' (*Journal of Marketing Management*: Special Issue on Consuming Families, forthcoming).

Hidden motives: is consumer behaviour shaped by fairy-tale archetypes?

ANDREA GROEPPEL-KLEIN, European University of Viadrina, Frankfurt (Oder), Germany

ARCHETYPES AND CONSUMER BEHAVIOUR

Ernest Dichter and Vance Packard were convinced that consumer behaviour is shaped by hidden motives, which can be detected by using psychoanalytical research. For instance, Ernest Dichter argued that whenever consumers eat ice cream, in fact what they are trying to do is to satisfy the innate need for 'security'. These psychoanalytical findings (derived from 'research on the couch' rather than from experimental research in a laboratory) have attracted controversy because they do not fit into 'exact' positivistic research paradigms with respect to inter-subjective perceived comprehensibility. This has meant that consumer behaviour researchers have tended to neglect these research findings. However, current progress in neuro(physio-)logical research and modern brain imaging technologies has started to allow us to shed some light on unconscious processes and instincts, thus offering the possibility of validating psychoanalytical research today which was originally undertaken by Sigmund Freud many decades ago.

Jung's archetypal psychology also belongs to this group of psychoanalytical research about consumer behaviour. Carl G. Jung (1875-1961) was influenced by his mentor Sigmund Freud, but developed his own ideas – and in contrast to Freud, Jung was not such a staunch supporter of experimental or neurological research. Using Jung's theory (1954/1959a, b), the psyche can be divided into three parts. Part one is the conscious mind termed the 'ego'. Closely related to the ego is the second part, the *personal unconscious* that includes anything not presently conscious. The personal unconscious includes both memories that can easily be brought to mind and those that have been suppressed for some reason. Jung's third part of the psyche is called the *collective unconscious*', and it is this element that makes his theory stand out from others.

Jung's collective unconscious can be characterized as the 'psychic inheritance' or as the kind of knowledge with which all human beings are born. The individual is never directly aware of this collective reservoir of experiences, but it can indirectly influence personal feelings and behaviour. Effects that illustrate the functioning of the collective unconscious are experiences of first love, of déjà vu and the immediate recognition and understanding of certain myths. The content of the collective unconscious is characterized by so-called 'archetypes' that represent inborn and universal ways of perceiving and comprehending the world, and which provide individuals with 'wisdom' about the past and predispose people to experience the world as their ancestors did. Thus, archetypes have an instinctive or biological function (Veen 1994) and act as regulators and stimulators. As inherent experiences of the human species, they are stable across time and societies, but can be culturally coded in typical iconic representations (Hirschman 2000).

The variety of archetypal images is substantial. In this study special attention is devoted to (1) the hero, who is characterized as a man who can master all challenges in life and is able to rescue an unhappy or threatened woman, and (2) the Cinderella archetype, the young, innocent and beautiful woman, who lives in distress or misery and is rescued by a gallant prince who promises her a wonderful life free of worry and care.

ARCHETYPES AND ADVERTISING CAMPAIGNS

Walle (1986: 22) argues that archetypes 'constitute valuable tools for practitioners such as strategic planners of promotional campaigns', because archetypal advertising resonates from innate human universals and focuses on innate needs. Indeed, a content analysis of advertisements in German magazines and newspapers shows that many brands (even prestigious credit institutions or sophisticated newspapers) use archetypal motives like brave heroes, innocent maidens like Sleeping Beauty, or pictures associated with such fairy tales as *Cinderella*, *The Frog Prince*, or animal archetypes like the faithful horse or the lion in their marketing communications.

Do advertising campaigns that are shaped by archetypal myths really appeal to all consumers? As a counter-argument, the feminist movement (e.g. Enns 1994: 73; Lauter and Rupprecht 1985) believes that, on the one hand, the greater the prevalence of fairy tales about heroic men and needy women, the more difficult it will be for women to change stereotypical role expectations. On the other hand, currently more and more students are female; they often achieve better examination results than their male colleagues and increasing numbers of women are gaining high career positions. Thus, the Cinderella archetype may be called into question by women's current experience, or may even be changing. The book *The Cinderella Complex* (Dowling 1981) questions the abdication of women's power to males and asks why, in the old fairy tales, we never hear about what happens to the young Cinderella after she marries the prince. Will she really be happy and satisfied with a spouse role or will there be a tendency to break out of the repressive castle existence? To summarize, we could question whether a modern young woman still believes that she needs to do no more with her life than find a gallant prince who will take care of her. In other words: do typical archetypes like Cinderella or Sleeping Beauty really reflect women's ideals and can they therefore be used successfully in advertising strategies?

In this context, a relationship between personality variables and preferred archetypes can be assumed. Holbrook and Olney (1995) found that people vary in the degree to which they are attracted either by romanticism or by classicism. These findings could lead to the assumption that individual levels of romanticism also influence the perceived appeal of different archetypes such as Cinderella-like figures, or Sleeping Beauty.

In our study (for details see Groeppel-Klein, Domke and Bartmann 2005), we investigated whether archetypes like Cinderella or Sleeping Beauty cause positive attitudes and unconscious responses. In order to gain insights into the more or less unconscious reactions of test participants, we measured *phasic arousal* evoked by archetypal stimuli. From a psycho-physiological perspective, arousal is a fundamental feature of behaviour. It can be defined as the basic neuro-physiological process underlying all activity in the human organism. Thus, arousal is the basis of emotions, motivation, information processing and behavioural reactions (Bagozzi, Gopinath and Nyer 1999). Basically, a distinction can be made between tonic and phasic arousal. Tonic arousal refers to a relatively long-term state of consciousness. Phasic arousal arises in response to specific stimuli, resulting in short-term variations in the arousal level. It indicates the body's ready state for reaction and is closely related to attention, that is, enhanced sensitivity of the organism to relevant stimuli and stimuli processing (Boucsein 1992).

Empirical studies emphasize the relevance of phasic arousal in marketing communication (Groeppel-Klein and Baun 2001). *Arousal* is an important factor in *predicting approach behaviour*. Furthermore, since consumers cannot willingly influence their arousal reactions, it is either a valid indicator of *unconscious reactions* or a detection mechanism for social desirability articulation biases – providing that arousal is measured accurately. In contrast to verbal methods, psycho-physiological measures such as heart rate, electroencephalogram (EEG), and electrodermal reaction (EDR) are the most valid indicators, since *deliberately influencing* the test results obtained from these methods is almost impossible. In addition, EDR (Boucsein 1992: 263) is considered to be the most sensitive indicator of arousal that could be relevant to behaviour and can be recorded *simultaneously* with the perception of a stimulus. Due to these advantages, we employed EDR as indicator. EDR is founded on the psycho-physiological fact that increasing arousal leads to increasing sweat gland activity of the palms of our hands, and even the very smallest psychological change can be detected (Boucsein 1992). The hydration depends on external and internal factors and leads to electric conductivity of the skin, thus making it possible to measure it by means of two electrodes attached to the skin. The amplitude (measured in η-Siemens) describes the strength of each phasic arousal reaction. The intensity of perceived arousal over a certain *period of time* can be arrived at by summing all single amplitudes so as to obtain the *total amplitude* that is the most important phasic arousal parameter in experiments.

EXPERIMENTAL STUDIES

Archetypal advertising focuses on innate needs. This would suggest that a message that is compatible with innate desires or desired behaviour will evoke higher arousal than one that is less focused on these innate drives. Thus, we can hypothesize whether a TV commercial or a film that uses a typical fairy-tale archetype (like Cinderella) will evoke higher phasic arousal reactions than films without this archetype. Furthermore, the question arises whether all people show similar responses, or whether different personalities are more or less attracted by Cinderella-archetypes.

We tested our hypotheses in two empirical studies. The first study was conducted in October and November 2004 in a lecture room at our university. First, students were chosen randomly and asked if they were interested in participating in an advertising experiment. Then, the participants completed a general questionnaire about their personal attitudes towards career, family, self-concept, self-esteem and romanticism. Students were told that we wanted to arrange a typical advertising situation, in which films are normally interrupted by TV commercials. Before being presented with different TV commercials, the test participant was attached to the

EDR electrodes and asked to relax and to watch the film just as in a cinema or at home. Only one commercial used an archetypal myth: the story taking place in a typical enchanted 'fairy-tale castle'. The prince wants to rescue and wake up Sleeping Beauty, but all kissing attempts fail. Only the aroma and flavour of a cookie (named Prinzenrolle) works, so that Sleeping Beauty is finally enraptured by her rescuer. During EDR registration, a marker was set on the registered data whenever a new commercial started, and another one when the scene from the film began. Thus, the arousal reaction of each commercial and of the film could be registered. After showing the TV commercials, half the sample (randomly chosen) was presented with the last scene of *Pretty Woman* whereas the other half watched a sequence from *Gone With The Wind*. We chose these two films, because, on the one hand, the Cinderella 'archetype has shaped movies such as *Pretty Woman*' (Waters 2003), whereas on the other, Scarlett O'Hara (as we established through an internet search) is characterized as a 'woman who fought with her sweat and blood to keep her family's plantation, a woman who overcame every war and obstacle' (unknown reviewer, www.target.com) and 'her incredible tenacity makes her a contender' (Isaacs 2004: 4). Thus, viewing the film was also part of the experiment though participants were not aware of it. Afterwards, EDR test participants were detached from the electrodes, and completed the second part of the questionnaire, including items measuring attitude towards the ad, the brand and the film.

The second study was conducted in February 2005, with an experimental design and questionnaire comparable to those of Study 1. In contrast to our first study, half the sample (randomly chosen) was exposed to the archetypal TV commercial Sleeping Beauty (Prinzenrolle), whereas the other half was exposed to a more informational TV commercial of Prinzenrolle that showed a group of cooks (called the 'cookie-experts') with white coats and long chef's hats preparing hot chocolate sauce for their delicious cookies. This experimental design was chosen in order to find out if the archetypal TV commercial of Prinzenrolle was indeed more effective than a more informational spot for the same brand. Furthermore, the Calgon water-softener spot of Study 1 was replaced by a spot also advertising cookies (with the brand name Hanuta). This clip showed a female fencer fighting with one of the famous three musketeers. She wins and gets the Hanuta. This commercial was chosen, on the one hand, to present a tough and fearless *female* actor and, on the other, to show an additional 'sweets' spot to examine whether arousal reactions were simply evoked by this special *product category*. After presenting the TV commercials,

half the sample viewed the last scene of *Pretty Woman* whereas the other half watched a sequence from *Erin Brockovich*. Scarlett O'Hara (Study 1) is probably one of the most prominent examples of a fearless female character. However, *Gone With The Wind* was shot before the Second World War and is set in the American Civil War, whereas *Pretty Woman* was produced in 1990 and features a modern *zeitgeist*. Furthermore, Julia Roberts is one of the most popular actresses in Hollywood, and the arousal reaction to *Pretty Woman* might simply be due to her charisma. Therefore, in the second study, we wanted to control a potential Julia Roberts effect, and compared *Pretty Woman* to another film starring Julia Roberts as Erin Brockovich who is characterized as 'an inspirational reminder of the power of the human spirit. Her passion, tenacity, and steadfast desire to fight for the rights of the underdog defied the odds' (www.erinbrockovich.com).

RESULTS

The first study compares the archetypal TV commercial (Prinzenrolle) with four other non-archetypal commercials, and demonstrates significantly higher arousal for the archetypal spot (Figure 1). In Study 2, we built in controls to test for whether the famous brand name or the product category might be responsible for the arousal reactions, with the result that the archetypal spot evokes a significantly higher level of arousal (Figure 2) and a more positive attitude towards the ad than both the informational spot for this brand and the Hanuta spot.

The film presenting a typical Cinderella archetype as character (*Pretty Woman*) was compared with

Figure 1 Study 1 – Arousal differences between commercials

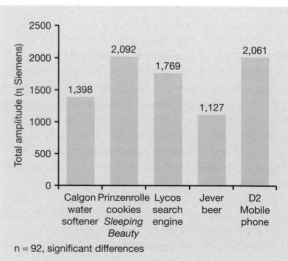

n = 92, significant differences

Figure 2 Study 2 – Arousal differences between cookie commercials

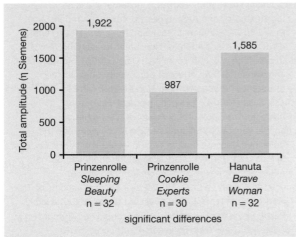

films presenting brave, aggressive and selfish female characters (Study 1: Scarlett O'Hara, *Gone With The Wind*; Study 2: *Erin Brockovich*). The results show significantly higher arousal (Figure 3) and a more favourable attitude towards the film featuring the Cinderella archetype.

In our first study, we also investigated the relationship between personality types and responses to the archetypal commercial and the different films. Using statements measuring attitudes towards career, family, romanticism, self-concept clarity and self-esteem, we found three personality groups among female test participants. Women in the first segment are characterized by romanticism (they enjoy daydreaming and believe in love at first sight), they want to be protected by their future husband and yearn for a life

Figure 3 Arousal differences between films

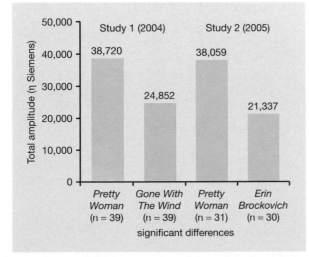

without worries. Though they are quite self-confident, they still have an unclear self-concept. This segment is called 'optimistic daydreamers'. The second group (called 'cool self-made women') considers it important to believe in facts rather than dreams, and always likes to keep a cool head. They have a clear self-concept and high self-esteem. The third cluster ('self-condemned losers') has an extremely negative score on 'high self-esteem'. These women perceive themselves as failures, and have no self-confidence at all. They are neither energetic nor career oriented, nor do they have any optimistic daydreams as to how they could change their lives. However, they want to be protected in life. Regarding the archetypal commercial, arousal and assessment of the commercial differ significantly between the three female groups ('optimistic daydreamers' showed very positive responses). The results of the arousal responses with respect to *Pretty Woman* yielded no significant differences between the three clusters. Does this mean that even 'cool-headed women' cannot avoid being affected unconsciously by the *Pretty Woman* story?

QUESTIONS

1 Explain the notion of 'archetypes'.

2 In our studies EDR was used as an indicator to measure 'phasic arousal'. Explain the 'arousal construct' and how EDR measurement works. Why was this method used?

3 Discuss the relationship between personality traits and preference for Cinderella archetypes from a female *and* a male perspective. Women's emancipation might also have changed men's expectations and philosophy about life. Analogously, we could question whether men are still attracted by the hero scheme. Does a man always feel capable of mastering all obstacles, and is he really keen on assuming responsibility for his wife and family, or does the hero claim rather lead to a feeling of being burdened? How would you measure gender differences?

4 Do you agree with Walle (1986: 22) who describes archetypes as constituting 'valuable tools for practitioners such as strategic planners of promotional campaigns'?

EXERCISES

1 Conduct a content analysis of current advertising campaigns in newspapers and magazines published in your country. Do you also find archetypal ads?

2 Imagine you were a researcher with the task of analysing the effects of archetypes in advertising campaigns, but you have no opportunity to use EDR measurement. Which alternative methods would you use to find out whether consumer behaviour is shaped by archetypes?

3 Discuss the relevance of new brain imaging technologies to consumer research. Do you think that psychoanalytical research may be validated one day by these new methods?

Sources

Bagozzi, Richard P., Mahesh Gopinath and Prashanth U. Nyer (1999), 'The role of emotions in marketing', *Journal of the Academy of Marketing Science* 27 (Spring): 184-206.

Boucsein, Wolfram (1992), *Electrodermal Activity* (New York, London: Plenum Press).

Dowling, Colette (1981), *The Cinderella Complex: Women's Hidden Fear of Independence* (New York: Summit Books).

Enns, Carolyn Zerbe (1994), 'Archetypes and gender: Goddesses, warriors, and psychological health', *Journal of Counseling and Development* 73 (November/December): 127-33.

Freud, Sigmund (1933), *New Introductory Lectures on Psychoanalysis* (New York: Norton).

Groeppel-Klein, Andrea and Dorothea Baun (2001), 'The Role of Customers' Arousal for Retail Stores - Results from An Experimental Pilot Study Using Electrodermal Activity as Indicator', in *Advances in Consumer Research* 28, Mary C. Gilly and Joan Meyers-Levy, eds (Provo, UT: Association for Consumer Research): 412-19.

Groeppel-Klein, Andrea, Anja Domke and Benedikt Bartmann (2005), 'Pretty Woman or Erin Brockovich? Unconscious and Conscious Reactions to Commercials and Movies Shaped by Fairy Tale Archetypes - Results From Two Experimental Studies', Working Paper, European University, Viadrina.

Hirschman, Elizabeth C. (2000), 'Consumers' Use of Intertextuality and Archetypes', in *Advances in Consumer Research* 27, Stephen J. Hoch and Robert J. Meyer, eds (Provo, UT: Association for Consumer Research): 57-63.

Holbrook, Morris B. and Thomas J. Olney (1995), 'Romanticism and wanderlust: An effect of personality on consumer preference', *Psychology and Marketing* 12 (3): 207-22.

Isaacs, Susan (2004), 'Brave dames and wimpettes', http://www.susanisaacs.com/bib/brave_dames.php.

Jung, Carl Gustav (1954/1959a), 'The Archetypes and the Collective Unconscious', in *The Collected Works of C.G. Jung*, 9, Part I, Sir Herbert Read, Michael Fordham and Gerhard Adler, eds (New York: Bollingen, Pantheon): 3-41.

Jung, Carl Gustav (1954/1959b), 'Psychological Aspects of The Mother Archetype', in *The Collected Works of C.G. Jung*, 9, Part I, Sir Herbert Read, Michael Fordham and Gerhard Adler eds (New York: Bollingen, Pantheon): 75-110.

Jung, Carl Gustav (1961), *Memories, dreams, reflections* (New York: Random House).

Lauter, Estella and Carol Schreier Rupprecht (1985), *Feminist Archetypal Theory* (Knoxville: University of Tennessee Press).

Veen, Steve Vander (1994), 'The Consumption of Heroes and the Hero Hierarchy of Effects', in *Advances in Consumer Research* 21, Chris T. Allen and Deborah Roedder John, eds (Provo, UT: Association for Consumer Research): 332-6.

Walle, Alf (1986), 'Archetypes, athletes and advertising', *Journal of Consumer Marketing* 3 (November): 21-9.

Waters, Jen (2003), 'Cinderella. A biography of an archetype', *Washington Times*, 31 May.

CONSUMERS AS DECISION-MAKERS

This part explores how we make consumption decisions and discusses the many influences exerted by others in this process. Chapter 8 focuses on the basic sequence of steps we undergo when making a decision. Chapter 9 considers how the particular situation we find ourselves in affects these decisions and how we go about evaluating what we've bought afterwards. Chapter 10 provides an overview of group processes and discusses the reasons why we are motivated to conform to the expectations of our fellow group members. It also considers how some individuals in particular (called 'opinion leaders') are likely to influence the consumption behaviour of others in a group.

INDIVIDUAL DECISION-MAKING

Daniel has had it up to here. There's no way he is going to go on watching TV on his tiny, antiquated black-and-white set. It was bad enough trying to see the graphics of the possible answers to questions on *Who Wants to Be a Millionaire?* The final straw was when he couldn't tell Arsenal from Ajax during last Wednesday night's football match. When he finally went next door – in total exasperation – to watch the second half on Michelle's big set, he really realized what he had been missing out on. Budget or not, it was time to act: a man has to get his priorities right.

Where to start looking? The Web, naturally. Daniel checks out a few comparison-shopping websites – there's no point in slogging around the high street shops at this early stage. After narrowing down his options, he ventures out to look at the possible sets which he has identified. He knows he will get some good advice at the small specialist high street retailer so he decides to start there; and then he can hunt around for the best buy. He figures he'll probably find the most affordable models at one of the out-of-town 'big shed' retailers. Arriving at the local specialist retailer, Daniel goes to the television section, where he can browse quietly away. Eventually, one of the sales assistants asks him if he wants any help. Daniel asks some questions, and gets some useful advice and tips about what features to think about when making his purchase; and one or two recommendations about current good buys. Before leaving the shop, Daniel asks the salesman to write down the model names and numbers (and prices) for him. Daniel then heads off to one of the out-of-town 'big shed' retailers. When he gets there he makes straight for the Video Zone at the back – barely noticing the rows of toasters, microwave ovens and stereos on his way. Within minutes, a smiling salesman in a cheap suit accosts him. Daniel reckons that these guys don't know what they're talking about, and they're just out to make a sale, no matter what. Anyway, he has already collected all the information he needs for making his decision.

Daniel starts to look at the 26-inch colour sets. He knew his friend Ruth had a set by Prime Wave that she really liked, and his fellow hockey player, Hannah, had warned him to stay away from the Kamashita. Although Daniel finds a Prime Wave model loaded with features such as a sleep timer, on-screen programming menu, cable compatible tuner, and picture-in-picture, he chooses the less-expensive Precision 2000X because it has one feature that really catches his fancy: stereo broadcast reception; and it had been highly recommended by the high street specialist retailer.

Later that day, Daniel is a happy man as he sits in his armchair, watching the Oxford and Cambridge Boat Race. If he's going to be a couch potato, he's going to do it in style . . . next up, the hockey championships.

■ CONSUMERS AS PROBLEM-SOLVERS

A consumer purchase is a response to a problem, which in Daniel's case is the perceived need for a new TV. His situation is similar to that encountered by consumers virtually every day of their lives. He realizes that he wants to make a purchase, and he goes through a series of steps in order to make it. These steps can be described as: (1) problem recognition, (2) information search, (3) evaluation of alternatives, and (4) product choice. After the decision is made, the quality of that decision affects the final step in the process, when learning occurs based on how well the choice worked out. This learning process, of course, influences the likelihood that the same choice will be made the next time the need for a similar decision occurs.

An overview of this decision-making process is shown in Figure 8.1. This chapter begins by considering various approaches consumers use when faced with a purchase decision. It then focuses on three of the steps in the decision process: how consumers recognize the problem, or need for a product; their search for information about product choices; and the ways in which they evaluate alternatives to arrive at a decision.

Figure 8.1 Stages in consumer decision-making

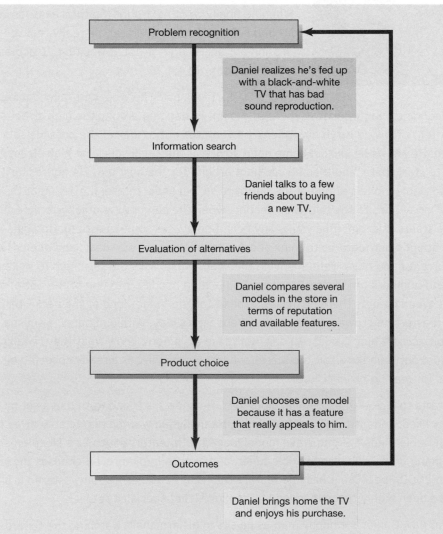

Chapter 9 considers influences in the actual purchase situation, as well as the person's satisfaction with the decision.

Since some purchase decisions are more important than others, the amount of effort we put into each one differs. Sometimes the decision-making process is done almost automatically; we seem to make snap judgements based on very little information. At other times, reaching a purchase decision begins to resemble a full-time job. A person may literally spend days or weeks thinking about an important purchase such as a new home, even to the point of obsession.

Perspectives on decision-making

▶ Traditionally, consumer researchers have approached decision-making from a **rational perspective**. In this view, people calmly and carefully integrate as much information as possible with what they already know about a product, painstakingly weighing the pluses and minuses of each alternative, and arriving at a satisfactory decision. This process implies that steps in decision-making should be carefully studied by marketing managers in order to understand how information is obtained, how beliefs are formed, and what product choice criteria are specified by consumers. Products then can be developed that emphasize appropriate attributes, and promotional strategies can be tailored to deliver the types of information most likely to be desired in the most effective formats.[1]

How valid is this perspective? While consumers do follow these decision-making steps when making some purchases, such a process is not an accurate portrayal of many of our purchase decisions.[2] Consumers simply do not go through this elaborate sequence every time they buy something. If they did, their entire lives would be spent making such decisior ~ leaving them with very little time to enjoy the things they eventually decide to buy. Some of our consumption behaviours simply don't seem 'rational' because they don't always seem to serve a logical purpose (e.g. people who break the law to collect the eggs of a rare bird in Scotland called an osprey even though the eggs have no monetary value[3]); other purchase behaviours are done with virtually no advance planning at all (e.g. impulsively grabbing that tempting bar of chocolate at the checkout till while waiting to pay for groceries in the supermarket). Still other actions are actually
▶ contrary to those predicted by rational models. For example, **purchase momentum** occurs when these initial impulses actually increase the likelihood that we will buy even more (instead of less as our needs are satisfied), almost as if we get caught up in a spending spree.[4]

Researchers are now beginning to realize that decision-makers actually possess a repertoire of strategies. A consumer evaluates the effort required to make a particular choice, and then he or she chooses a strategy best suited to the level of effort required. This sequence of events is known as *constructive processing*. Rather than using a big stick to kill an ant, consumers tailor their degree of cognitive 'effort' to the task at hand.[5] When a well-thought-out rational approach is necessary, we'll invest the brainpower required for the decision. Otherwise, we look for short cuts or fall back upon learned responses that 'automate' these choices. Researchers are also beginning to understand the role that controlling the information flow can have on consumers' decisions, as increased control leads to increased performance. These new insights promise to be particularly important in the new online environments where 'marketers have the potential to integrate interactive communication systems back into mass communication' (Deighton 1996)[6] where controlling the information flow can particularly influence the quality of consumers' decisions, memory, knowledge and confidence.[7] Research on information structure (the amount of information in a choice set) is also relevant in the new electronic marketplaces, where consumers are regularly faced with information overload when making decisions.[8] A recent study suggests that: 'consumers adapt their acquisition of information in

This ad for the US Postal Service presents a problem, illustrates the decision-making process and offers a solution.

response to changes in information structure. When a choice set contains more information per element, fewer acquisitions are made, more time is spent per acquisition, and customers are more selective in their information acquisition.'[9]

Some decisions are made under conditions of low involvement, as discussed in Chapter 4. In many of these situations, the consumer's decision is a learned response to environmental cues (see Chapter 3), as when he or she decides to buy something on impulse that is being promoted as a special offer in a shop. A concentration on these types of decisions can be described as the **behavioural influence perspective**. Under these circumstances, managers must concentrate on assessing the characteristics of the environment, such as the design of a retail outlet or whether a package is enticing, that influence members of a target market.[10]

In other cases, consumers are highly involved in a decision, but still the selections made cannot be explained entirely rationally. For example, the traditional approach is hard pressed to explain a person's choice of art, music, or even a partner. In these cases, no single quality may be the determining factor. Instead, the **experiential perspective** stresses the *Gestalt*, or totality, of the product or service.[11] Marketers in these areas focus on measuring consumers' affective responses to products or services and developing offerings that elicit appropriate subjective reactions.

Figure 8.2 A continuum of buying decision behaviour

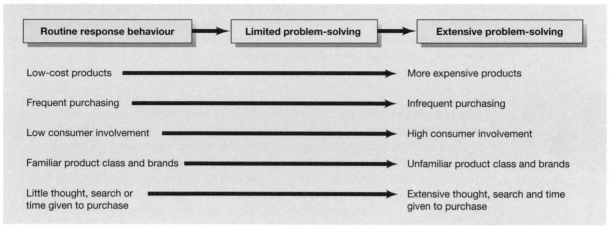

Types of consumer decisions

One helpful way to characterize the decision-making process is to consider the amount of effort that goes into the decision each time it must be made. Consumer researchers have found it convenient to think in terms of a continuum, which is anchored on one end by habitual decision-making and at the other extreme by extended problem-solving. Many decisions fall somewhere in the middle and are characterized by limited problem solving. This continuum is presented in Figure 8.2.

Extended problem-solving

▶ Decisions involving **extended problem-solving** correspond most closely to the traditional decision-making perspective. As indicated in Table 8.1, the extended problem-solving process is usually initiated by a motive that is fairly central to the self-concept (see Chapter 7), and the eventual decision is perceived to carry a fair degree of risk. The

Table 8.1 Characteristics of limited vs. extended problem-solving

	Limited problem-solving	Extended problem-solving
Motivation	Low risk and involvement	High risk and involvement
Information search	Little search Information processed passively In-store decision likely	Extensive search Information processed actively Multiple sources consulted prior to store visits
Alternative evaluation	Weakly held beliefs Only most prominent criteria used Alternatives perceived as basically similar Non-compensatory strategy used	Strongly held beliefs Many criteria used Significant differences perceived among alternatives Compensatory strategy used
Purchase	Limited shopping time; may prefer self-service Choice often influenced by store displays	Many outlets shopped if needed Communication with store personnel often desirable

consumer tries to collect as much information as possible, both from memory (internal search) and from outside sources (external search). Based on the importance of the decision, each product alternative is carefully evaluated. The evaluation is often done by considering the attributes of one brand at a time and seeing how each brand's attributes shape up to some set of desired characteristics.

net profit

Marketers continue to seek out strategies that enhance consumers' involvement with their messages and products in order to capture their attention and make it more likely that people will tune in to the information they are presenting. Interactive TV is one new route to achieving this goal. Cable companies, satellite TV, and software giants including Microsoft have made interactive TV a key part of their strategies, pouring billions into it. While Americans have been pretty apathetic about interactive, the concept is gaining critical mass in Europe, particularly in the UK. British consumers routinely use their TVs to place bets on races, change camera angles while watching sporting events (e.g. 'player-cams' that follow specific athletes during soccer games), and interact with game shows.[12]

Europeans also commonly use *teletext*, a one-way information service that lets them view news headlines, weather reports, schedules for film shows, flight times and other titbits on their TVs. Again, these services are not easily found in the United States, partly because of the higher usage of the internet there. As a result, these applications are less likely to rely upon coordinated efforts among broadcasters and more on individual pay television providers. In addition, American companies have focused more on technology than content, while European firms have done the opposite. As one American industry executive observed, 'Here we were focused on building a better mousetrap. In Europe they were figuring out what the mouse wanted to eat.'[13]

Limited problem-solving

▶ **Limited problem-solving** is usually more straightforward and simple. Buyers are not as motivated to search for information or to evaluate each alternative rigorously. People instead use simple *decision rules* to choose among alternatives. These cognitive short cuts (more about these later) enable consumers to fall back on general guidelines, instead of having to start from scratch every time a decision is to be made.

Habitual decision-making

Both extended and limited problem-solving modes involve some degree of information search and deliberation, though they vary in the degree to which these activities are
▶ undertaken. At the other end of the choice continuum, however, lies **habitual decision-making**; this refers to decisions that are made with little or no conscious effort. Many purchase decisions are so routinized that we may not realize we've made them until we look in our shopping trolleys. We make choices characterized by *automaticity* with minimal effort and without conscious control.[14]

While this kind of thoughtless activity may seem dangerous at worst or stupid at best, it is actually quite efficient in many cases. The development of habitual, repetitive behaviour allows consumers to minimize the time and energy spent on mundane purchase decisions. On the other hand, habitual decision-making poses a problem when a marketer tries to introduce a new way of doing an old task. In this case consumers must be convinced to 'unfreeze' their former habit and replace it with a new one – perhaps by using an ATM machine instead of a live bank teller, or switching to self-service petrol pumps instead of being served by an attendant.

marketing opportunity

Exciting advances in technology promise to automate our routine tasks even more. These new gadgets are part of a recent trend called **silent commerce** that enables transactions and information gathering to occur in the background without any direct intervention by consumers or managers. In Singapore, cars 'talk' to the streets they drive on. Retailers in the USA are testing a system that enables products to inform the store when they've been purchased so that stocks can be replenished quickly. In kitchens later on in this decade, ready-made frozen meals might automatically give cooking instructions to microwave ovens.[15]

Many of these new *smart products* will be possible because the items themselves will be embedded with a tiny plastic tag that holds a very inexpensive computer chip capable of storing a small amount of information along with a tiny antenna that lets the chip communicate with a computer network. Researchers predict that in time these tags will be on almost everything from egg cartons, that will alert a store manager when their contents have passed their expiry date, to roof tiles on houses that will email a roofing repair company when they fall off. A wine lover can check on the contents of her home wine cellar while browsing the new shipment of cabernets. You'll always know the location of your sunglasses – or maybe even those mysterious socks that always seem to 'vanish' in the tumble-dryer![16]

Or, how about a doll that buys her own clothes? A new concept doll devised by Accenture is being billed as 'an autonomous purchasing object' that does just that. The firm took an ordinary Barbie doll and gave it wireless implants that let it communicate with other wired dolls and accessories within range to determine if it 'wants' them. For example, this beefed-up Barbie detects the presence of clothing and compares it with her existing wardrobe to see if she already owns that fashionable pair of low-waisted jeans. If not, the toy can send a purchase order to a home PC or buy straight from the manufacturer via a wireless connection. Her owner can limit Barbie's expense account, but otherwise she's on her own.[17]

■ PROBLEM RECOGNITION

▶ **Problem recognition** occurs whenever the consumer sees a significant difference between his or her current state of affairs and some desired or ideal state. The consumer perceives there is a problem to be solved, which may be large or small, simple or complex. A person who unexpectedly runs out of petrol on the motorway has a problem, as does the person who becomes dissatisfied with the image of his or her car, even though there may be nothing mechanically wrong with it. Although the quality of Daniel's TV had not changed, for example, his *standard of comparison* was altered, and he was confronted with a desire he did not have prior to watching his friend's TV.

Problem creation

Figure 8.3 shows that a problem can arise in one of two ways. As in the case of the person running out of petrol, the quality of the consumer's *actual state* can move downward (*need recognition*). On the other hand, as in the case of the person who craves a high-performance car, the consumer's *ideal state* can move upward (*opportunity recognition*). Either way, a gulf occurs between the actual state and the ideal state.[18] In Daniel's case, a problem was perceived as a result of opportunity recognition; his ideal state in terms of television reception quality was altered.

Need recognition can occur in several ways. The quality of the person's actual state can be diminished simply by running out of a product, by buying a product that turns out not to satisfy needs adequately, or by creating new needs (e.g. buying a house can set off an avalanche of other choices, because many new things will be needed to furnish the house). Opportunity recognition occurs when a consumer is exposed to different or

Figure 8.3 Problem recognition: shifts in actual or ideal states

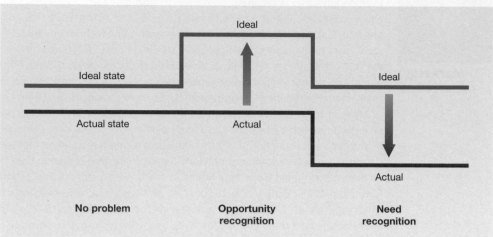

better quality products. This shift often occurs because the person's circumstances have somehow changed, as when an individual goes to university or gets a new job. As the person's frame of reference shifts, purchases are made to adapt to the new environment.

marketing pitfall

A common structure for advertisements has been to present a person who has a physical or social problem, and then 'miraculously' show how the product will resolve it. Some marketers have gone so far as to invent a problem and then offer a remedy for it. In the 1940s, for example, the Talon zipper was touted as a cure for 'gaposis', the horrifying condition that develops when puckers appear around the buttons on a woman's skirt. Listerine, a mouthwash, which was originally sold to fight dandruff, carried warnings about 'bottle bacillus', which caused 'infectious dandruff'. Geritol gave us a remedy for 'tired blood', and Wisk detergent drew our attention to the shame of 'ring around the collar'.[19]

Even when real problems are depicted in ads, the offered solutions are sometimes too simplistic, implying that the problem will disappear if the product is used. One analysis of over 1,000 television ads found that about 80 per cent suggest that the problem will be resolved within seconds or minutes of using the product. In addition, 75 per cent of the ads make definite claims that the product will solve the problem, and over 75 per cent imply that this solution is a one-step process – all the consumer needs to do is buy the product, and the problem will go away.[20] Consumers, however, are becoming more cynical and less susceptible to such claims. As many marketers are discovering, consumers of the new millennium are more receptive to realistic ads that provide solid information about the product. In addition, both the government and consumer groups are now taking a more active interest in product claims, and marketers are more cautious about the content of their ads.

Marketers' role in problem creation

While problem recognition can and does occur naturally, this process is often spurred by marketing efforts. In some cases, marketers attempt to create *primary demand*, where consumers are encouraged to use a product or service regardless of the brand they choose. Such needs are often encouraged in the early stages of a product's life cycle, as, for example, when microwave ovens were first introduced. *Secondary demand*, where consumers are prompted to prefer a specific brand instead of others, can occur only if primary demand already exists. At this point, marketers must convince consumers that a problem can be best solved by choosing their brand over others in the same category.

■ INFORMATION SEARCH

▶ Once a problem has been recognized, consumers need adequate information to resolve it. **Information search** is the process by which the consumer surveys his or her environment for appropriate data to make a reasonable decision. This section will review some of the factors involved in this search.

Types of information search

A consumer may recognize a need and then search the marketplace for specific information (a process called *pre-purchase search*). On the other hand, many consumers, especially veteran shoppers, enjoy browsing just for the fun of it, or because they like to stay up-to-date on what's happening in the marketplace. They are engaging in *ongoing search*.[21] Some differences between these two search modes are described in Table 8.2.

Table 8.2 A framework for consumer information search

	Pre-purchase search	Ongoing search
Determinants	Involvement in the purchase Market environment Situational factors	Involvement with the product Market environment Situational factors
Motives	Making better purchase decisions	Building a bank of information for future use Experiencing fun and pleasure
Outcomes	Increased product and market knowledge Better purchase decisions Increased satisfaction with the purchase outcome	Increased product and market knowledge, leading to • future buying efficiencies • personal influences Increased impulse buying Increased satisfaction from search and other outcomes

Source: Peter H. Bloch, Daniel L. Sherrell and Nancy M. Ridgway, 'Consumer search: An extended framework', *Journal of Consumer Research* 13 (June 1986): 120. Reprinted with permission by The University of Chicago Press.

tangled web

Following the dot.com bust of a few years ago, the Web has lost some of its original lustre. Yet most industry analysts still see a bright future for e-commerce – for example, while holiday retail sales overall were abysmal in 2002, online sales posted strong gains from the year before.[22] What is changing is what we'll see when we visit websites and what we do when we get there. Many website developers are cutting back on the glitzy 'bells and whistles' such as elaborate animations that take forever to load. A lot of web surfers are more goal-oriented than in the early days of the World Wide Web (that is, a few years ago).

Now many want to use the Web for information search rather than for entertainment (at least when they're not playing online video games). In March 2000, according to a survey by the Pew Internet & American Life Project in Washington, people averaged 90 minutes per online session. A year later, when the same people were polled, that number had dropped to 83 minutes. According to the report, those polled said that they were using the Web more to conduct business than to explore new areas, aiming to get offline as quickly as possible.[23] People are also seeking more control over what they see and what information they access.

Research on this process demonstrates that surfers who can provide input over what they see on a site remember more of the site's contents, exhibit superior knowledge about the domain and are more confident in their judgements.[24] Indeed, almost 80 per cent of internet users in a 2002 survey said they expect to find the product information they need on a website.[25] Web surfing isn't quite as much fun as it used to be, but it's becoming a lot more useful.

Internal vs. external search

Information sources can be roughly broken down into two kinds: internal and external. As a result of prior experience and simply living in a consumer culture, each of us often has some degree of knowledge about many products already in our memory. When confronted with a purchase decision, we may engage in *internal search* by scanning our own memory bank to assemble information about different product alternatives (see Chapter 3). Usually, though, even the most market-aware of us needs to supplement this knowledge with external search, where information is obtained from advertisements, friends, or just plain people-watching.

Deliberate vs. 'accidental' search

Our existing knowledge of a product may be the result of *directed learning*: on a previous occasion we had already searched for relevant information or experienced some of the alternatives. A parent who bought a birthday cake for one child last month, for example, probably has a good idea of the best kind to buy for another child this month.

Alternatively, we may acquire information in a more passive manner. Even though a product may not be of direct interest to us right now, exposure to advertising, packaging and sales promotion activities may result in *incidental learning*. Mere exposure over time to conditioned stimuli and observations of others results in the learning of much material that may not be needed for some time after the fact, if ever. For marketers, this result

This ad for Arm & Hammer demonstrates the strategy of identifying new problems an existing product can solve.

Church & Dwight Co., Inc.

is a benefit of steady, 'low-dose' advertising, as product associations are established and maintained until the time they are needed.[26]

In some cases, we may be so expert about a product category (or at least believe we are) that no additional search is undertaken. Frequently, however, our own existing state of knowledge is not satisfactory to make an adequate decision, and we must look elsewhere for more information. The sources we consult for advice vary. They may be impersonal and marketer-dominated sources, such as retailers and catalogues; they may be friends and family members; or they may be unbiased third parties such as *Which?* magazine or other consumer reports which are published in a number of European countries.[27]

marketing pitfall

Labels provide valuable information about the proper way to use products, but sometimes they can be . . . less than clear. Here are some examples of 'interesting' labels:[28]

- On a Conair Pro Style 1600 hair dryer: 'WARNING: Do not use in shower. Never use while sleeping.'
- Instructions for folding up a portable baby carriage: 'Step 1: Remove baby.'
- On Tesco's Tiramisu dessert (printed on bottom of box): 'Do not turn upside down.'
- On Marks & Spencer's bread pudding: 'Product will be hot after heating.'
- On packaging for a Rowenta iron: 'Do not iron clothes on body.'
- On Nytol sleeping aid: Warning: 'May cause drowsiness.'

The economics of information

The traditional decision-making perspective incorporates the *economics-of-information* approach to the search process: it assumes that consumers will gather as much data as needed to make an informed decision. Consumers form expectations of the value of additional information and continue to search to the extent that the rewards of doing so (what economists call the *utility*) exceed the costs. This utilitarian assumption also implies that the most valuable units of information will be collected first. Additional pieces will be absorbed only to the extent that they are seen to be adding to what is already known.[29] In other words, people will put themselves out to collect as much information as possible, as long as the process of gathering it is not too onerous or time-consuming.[30]

Variety seeking, the desire to choose new alternatives over more familiar ones, can influence consumers to switch from their favourite product to a less pleasurable item. This can occur even before an individual becomes satiated or tired of his or her favourite product. Explanations of this phenomenon stem from research that supports the idea that consumers are willing to trade enjoyment for variety because the unpredictability itself is rewarding; and variety seeking is a choice strategy that occurs as a result of pleasurable memories of ringing the changes.[31]

Do consumers always search rationally?

This assumption of rational search is not always supported. As we've seen, consumers don't necessarily engage in a rational search process where they carefully identify every alternative before choosing one they prefer. The amount of external search for most products is surprisingly small, even when additional information would most likely benefit the consumer. For example, lower-income shoppers, who have more to lose by making a bad purchase, actually search *less* prior to buying than do more affluent people.[32]

Like our friend Daniel, some consumers typically visit only one or two stores and rarely seek out unbiased information sources prior to making a purchase decision,

May cause drowsiness, dizzy spells, and vomiting. If affected, carry on. It's normal.

La Guillotine Beer 9·1% Proof. Have a nice coma.

This Singaporean beer ad reminds us that not all product decisions are made rationally.

especially when little time is available to do so.[33] This pattern is especially prevalent for decisions regarding durable goods such as appliances or cars, even when these products represent significant investments. One study of Australian car buyers found that more than a third had made only two or fewer trips to inspect cars prior to buying one.[34] Finally, there is some evidence that even having information available on the package does not necessarily mean that consumers make use of it. Environmentally friendly products in Finland are beginning to carry the Nordic Environmental Label to assist consumers in their choice of environmentally safe products. In a study which asked Finnish consumers to evaluate detergent and batteries choices, little use was made of and little trust was placed in the 'green label' on the packages, in spite of the positive attitudes that Finnish citizens have towards the environment. The results suggest that marketers have a long way to go in order to provide clear, easily comprehensible and unbiased information regarding 'green' products.[35]

This tendency to avoid external search is less prevalent when consumers consider the purchase of symbolic items, such as clothing. In those cases, not surprisingly, people tend to do a fair amount of external search, although most of it involves seeking the opinions of peers.[36] Although the stakes may be lower financially, these self-expressive decisions may be seen as having dire social consequences if the wrong choice is made. The level of perceived risk, a concept to be discussed shortly, is high.

In addition, consumers are often observed to engage in *brand switching*, even if their current brand satisfies their needs. For example, researchers for British brewer Bass Export who were studying the American beer market discovered a consumer trend towards having a repertoire of two to six favourite brands, rather than sticking to only one. This preference for brand switching led the firm to begin exporting their Tennent's 1885 lager to the United States, positioning the brew as an alternative to young drinkers' usual favourite brands.[37]

Sometimes, it seems that people simply like to try new things – they are interested in variety seeking, in which the priority is to vary one's product experiences, perhaps as a form of stimulation or to reduce boredom. Variety seeking is especially likely to occur when people are in a good mood, or when there is relatively little stimulation elsewhere in their environment.[38] In the case of foods and beverages, variety seeking can occur due to a phenomenon known as *sensory-specific satiety*. Put simply, this means the pleasant-ness of a food item just eaten drops while the pleasantness of uneaten foods remains unchanged.[39] So even though we have favourites, we still like to sample other possibil-ities. Ironically, consumers may actually switch to less-preferred options for variety's sake even though they enjoy the more familiar option more. On the other hand, when the decision situation is ambiguous or when there is little information about competing brands, consumers tend to opt for the safe choice by selecting familiar brands and main-taining the status quo.

Brand familiarity influences confidence about a brand, which in turn affects purchase intention.[40] Still, the tendency of consumers to shift brand choices over time means that marketers can never relax in the belief that once they have won a customer, he or she is necessarily theirs forever.[41]

Biases in the decision-making process

Consider the following scenario: You've been given a free ticket to an important football match. At the last minute, though, a sudden snowstorm makes getting to the football ground somewhat dangerous. Would you still go? Now, assume the same game and snowstorm, except this time you paid a lot of money for the ticket. Would you go?

Analyses of people's responses to this situation and to other similar puzzles illustrates principles of **mental accounting**, where decisions are influenced by the way a problem is posed (called *framing*), and by whether it is put in terms of gains or losses.[42] For exam-ple, people are more likely to risk their personal safety in the storm if they paid for the football ticket. Only the most diehard fan would fail to recognize that this is an irrational choice, as the risk to the person is the same regardless of whether he or she got a great bargain on the ticket. This decision-making bias is called the *sunk-cost fallacy* – having paid for something makes us reluctant to waste it.

Another bias is known as *loss aversion*. People place much more emphasis on loss than they do on gain. For example, for most people losing money is more unpleasant than gaining money is pleasant. **Prospect theory**, a descriptive model of how people make choices, finds that utility is a function of gains and losses, and risk differs when the con-sumer faces options involving gains versus those involving losses.[43]

To illustrate this bias, consider the following choices. For each, would you take the safe bet or choose to gamble?

- *Option 1*. You're given 100 euros and then offered a chance to flip a coin: heads you win 30 euros; tails you lose 30 euros.
- *Option 2*. You're given a choice of getting 100 euros outright, or accepting a coin flip that will win you either 115 euros or 85 euros.

In one study, 70 per cent of those given option 1 chose to gamble, compared to just 43 per cent of those offered option 2. Yet, the odds are the same for both options! The difference is that people prefer 'playing with the house money'; they are more willing to take risks when they perceive they're using someone else's resources. So, contrary to a rational decision-making perspective, we value money differently depending on its source. This explains why someone might choose to spend a big bonus on some frivolous purchase, but they would never consider taking that same amount out of their savings account for this purpose.

Finally, research in mental accounting demonstrates that extraneous characteristics of the choice situation can influence our selections, even though they wouldn't if we were totally rational decision-makers. As one example, participants in a survey were provided with one of two versions of this scenario:

> *You are lying on the beach on a hot day. All you have to drink is iced water. For the last hour you have been thinking about how much you would enjoy a nice cold bottle of your favorite brand of beer. A companion gets up to go and make a phone call and offers to bring back a beer from the only nearby place where beer is sold (either a fancy resort hotel or a small, run-down grocery store, depending on the version you're given). He says that the beer might be expensive and so asks how much you are willing to pay for it. . . . What price do you tell him?*

In this survey, the median price given by participants who were in the fancy resort version was $2.65, but those given the grocery store version were only willing to pay $1.50! In both versions the consumption act is the same, the beer is the same, and no 'atmosphere' is consumed because the beer is being brought back to the beach.[44] So much for rational decision-making!

How much search occurs?

As a general rule, search activity is greater when the purchase is important, when there is a need to learn more about the purchase, and/or when the relevant information is easily obtained and utilized.[45] Consumers differ in the amount of search they tend to undertake, regardless of the product category in question. All things being equal, younger, better-educated people who enjoy the shopping/fact-finding process tend to conduct more information search. Women are more inclined to search than men are, as are those who place greater value on style and the image they present.[46] A recent study of information search in high technology markets suggested that use of information channels can be segmented by age and education, with older consumers accessing information channels with less complex information compared with more highly educated consumers who tend to search all information channels. In addition, 'during each segment of the search consumers tend to use multiple sources of information'.[47]

The consumer's prior expertise

Should prior product knowledge make it more or less likely that consumers will engage in search? Product experts and novices use very different procedures during decision-making. Novices who know little about a product should be the most motivated to find out more about it. However, experts are more familiar with the product category, so they should be able to better understand the meaning of any new product information they might acquire.

So, who searches more? The answer is neither: search tends to be greatest among those consumers who are *moderately knowledgeable* about the product. There is an inverted-U relationship between knowledge and external search effort, as shown in Figure 8.4. People with very limited expertise may not feel they are capable of searching extensively. In fact, they may not even know where to start. Daniel, who did spend a lot of time researching his purchase, is only partly representative of this situation. He used the Web to do some research; visited a specialist store for advice and then went to one other store. However, he only looked at brands with which he was already familiar. In addition, he focused on only a small number of product features.[48]

The *type* of search undertaken by people with varying levels of expertise differs as well. Because experts have a better sense of what information is relevant to the decision, they tend to engage in *selective search*, which means their efforts are more focused and

Figure 8.4 The relationship between amount of information search and product knowledge

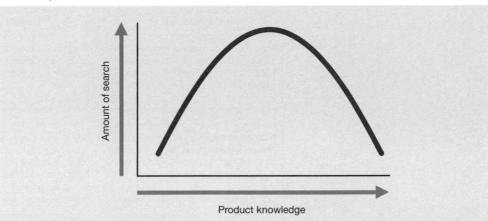

efficient. In contrast, novices are more likely to rely on the opinions of others and to rely on 'non-functional' attributes, such as brand name and price, to distinguish among alternatives. They may also process information in a 'top-down' rather than a 'bottom-up' manner, focusing less on details than on the big picture. For instance, they may be more impressed by the sheer amount of technical information presented in an ad than by the actual significance of the claims made.[49]

Perceived risk

As a rule, purchase decisions that involve extensive search also entail some kind of **perceived risk**, or the belief that the product has potentially negative consequences. Perceived risk may be present if the product is expensive or is complex and difficult to understand, or if the brand is unfamiliar. Mood effects on consumers' attitudes and perceptions about risk are stronger when brands are unfamiliar.[50] Perceived risk can also be a factor when a product choice is visible to others and we run the risk of embarrassment if the wrong choice is made.[51]

Figure 8.5 lists five kinds of risk – including objective (e.g. physical danger) and subjective factors (e.g. social embarrassment) – as well as the products that tend to be affected by each type. As this figure notes, consumers with greater 'risk capital' are less affected by perceived risks associated with the products. For example, a highly self-confident person would be less worried about the social risk inherent in a product, whereas a more vulnerable, insecure consumer might be reluctant to take a chance with a product that might not be accepted by peers.

marketing opportunity

The spread of the HIV virus has created a boom in home-testing kits which encourage people to find out if they have been infected in a less threatening environment than a clinic or a doctor's surgery. The typical kit allows the consumer to send a blood sample to a testing lab, and results are returned in 3-7 days. While high-risk groups such as adolescents and gay men are most likely to need the kits, some speculate that sales will come primarily from the 'worried well', those who are less likely to be infected in the first place. Companies are taking different approaches, ranging from humorous to provocative to serious, as they try to find the best way to reach people who are unlikely to go to a clinic to be tested. In one ad for Home Access, the copy (targeted at young, straight males) reads: 'Nothing arouses a woman like knowing you're responsible'.[52]

Figure 8.5 Five types of perceived risk

	Buyers most sensitive to risk	Purchases most subject to risk
Monetary risk	Risk capital consists of money and property. Those with relatively little income and wealth are most vulnerable.	High-price items that require substantial expenditures are most subject to this form of risk.
Functional risk	Risk capital consists of alternate means of performing the function or meeting the need. Practical consumers are most sensitive.	Products or services whose purchase and use requires the buyer's exclusive commitment and precludes redundancy are most sensitive.
Physical risk	Risk capital consists of physical vigour, health and vitality. Those who are elderly, frail, or in ill health are most vulnerable.	Mechanical or electrical goods (such as vehicles or flammables), drugs and medical treatment, and food and beverages are most sensitive.
Social risk	Risk capital consists of self-esteem and self-confidence. Those who are insecure and uncertain are most sensitive.	Socially visible or symbolic goods, such as clothes, jewellery, cars, homes, or sports equipment are most subject to it.
Psychological risk	Risk capital consists of affiliations and status. Those lacking self-respect or attractiveness to peers are most sensitive.	Expensive personal luxuries that may engender guilt; durables; and services whose use demands self-discipline or sacrifice are most sensitive.

■ EVALUATION OF ALTERNATIVES

Much of the effort that goes into a purchase decision occurs at the stage in which a choice must be made from the available alternatives. After all, modern consumer society abounds with choices. In some cases, there may be literally hundreds of different brands (as in cigarettes) or different variations of the same brand (as in shades of lipstick), each clamouring for our attention.

Just for fun, ask a friend to name all of the brands of perfume she can think of. The odds are she will reel off three to five names rather quickly, then stop and think awhile before coming up with a few more. It is likely that the first set of brands are those with which she is highly familiar, and she probably wears one or more of these. The list may also contain one or two brands that she does not like and would perhaps like to forget. Note also that there are many, many more brands on the market that she did not name at all.

If your friend were to go to a shop to buy perfume, it is likely that she would consider buying some or most of the brands she listed initially. She might also consider a few more possibilities if these were forcefully brought to her attention while at the shop counter – for example, if she was approached by a salesperson who was spraying scent samples on shoppers, which is a common occurrence in some department stores.

This BT Cellnet ad appeals to the need for social recognition and approbation from peer groups.

The Advertising Archives

Identifying alternatives

How do we decide which criteria are important, and how do we narrow down product alternatives to an acceptable number and eventually choose one instead of the others? The answer varies depending upon the decision-making process used. A consumer engaged in extended problem-solving may carefully evaluate several brands, whereas someone making a habitual decision may not consider any alternatives to their normal brand. Furthermore, some evidence indicates that more extended processing occurs in situations in which negative emotions are aroused due to conflicts among the choices available. This is most likely to occur where difficult trade-offs are involved, as when a person must choose between the risks involved in undergoing a bypass operation versus the potential improvement in his or her life if the operation is successful.[53]

The alternatives actively considered during a consumer's choice process are his or her **evoked set**. The evoked set comprises those products already in memory (the retrieval set), plus those prominent in the retail environment. For example, recall that Daniel did not know much about the technical aspects of television sets, and he had only a few major brands in memory. Of these, two were acceptable possibilities and one was not. The alternatives that the consumer is aware of but would not consider buying are his or

Figure 8.6 Identifying alternatives: getting in the game

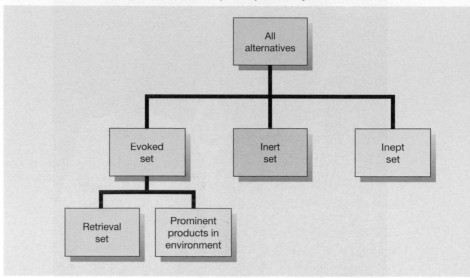

her *inept set*, while those not under consideration at all comprise the *inert set*. You can easily guess in which set a marketer wants its brand to appear! These categories are depicted in Figure 8.6.

Consumers often include a surprisingly small number of alternatives in their evoked set. One study combined results from several large-scale investigations of consumers' evoked sets and found that the number of products included in these sets was limited, although there were some marked variations by product category and across countries. For example, the average evoked set size for American beer consumers was fewer than three, whereas Canadian consumers typically considered seven brands. In contrast, while car buyers in Norway studied two alternatives, American consumers on average looked at more than eight models before making a decision.[54]

For obvious reasons, a marketer who finds that her or his brand is not in the evoked set of a target market has cause to worry. A product is not likely to be placed in the evoked set after it has previously been considered and rejected. Indeed, a new brand is more likely to be added to the evoked set than is an existing brand that was previously considered but passed over, even after additional positive information has been provided for that brand.[55] For marketers, consumers' unwillingness to give a rejected product a second chance underlines the importance of ensuring that it performs well from the time it is introduced.

Product categorization

Remember that when consumers process product information, they do not do so in a vacuum. Instead, a product stimulus is evaluated in terms of what people already know about a product or those things to which it is similar. A person evaluating a particular 35-mm camera will most likely compare it with other 35-mm cameras rather than to a Polaroid camera, and the consumer would certainly not compare it with a slide projector or DVD. Since the category in which a product is placed determines the other products it will be compared with, *categorization* is a crucial determinant of how a product is evaluated.

The products in a consumer's evoked set are likely to be those that share some similar features. This process can either help or hurt a product, depending on what people compare it with. When faced with a new product, consumers refer to their already existing knowledge in familiar product categories to form new knowledge.[56]

▶ It is important to understand how this knowledge is represented in a consumer's **cognitive structure**, which refers to a set of factual knowledge about products (beliefs) and the way these beliefs are organized in people's minds.[57] We discussed these knowledge structures in Chapter 4. One reason is that marketers want to ensure that their products are correctly grouped. For example, General Foods brought out a new line of Jell-O flavours, such as Cranberry Orange, that it called Jell-O Gelatin Flavors for Salads. Unfortunately, the company discovered that people would use it only for salad, because the name encouraged them to put the product in their 'salad' structure rather than in their 'dessert' structure. The product line was dropped.[58]

marketing pitfall

Kimberly-Clark Corp., the maker of successful paper products including Kleenex and Scott tissues, learned the hard way about the perils of product categorization and consumers' resistance to new categories. The company announced 'the most significant category innovation since toilet paper first appeared in roll form in 1890': Cottonelle Fresh Rollwipes, a roll of moist wipes in a plastic dispenser that clips onto a regular toilet-paper holder. To quiet skeptics who questioned whether Americans would change their habits so dramatically, Kimberly-Clark unveiled its research showing that 63% of adults were already in the habit of wetting toilet paper or using a wipe.

Although the company spent more than $100 million to develop the roll and dispenser and guards it with more than 30 patents, high hopes for the product have been disappointed. Part of the problem is that the company is dealing with a product most people don't even want to discuss in the first place, and its advertising failed to show consumers what the wipes even do. Its ad agency tried to create a fun image with TV ads showing shots of people splashing in the water from behind with the slogan, 'sometimes wetter is better.' A print ad with an extreme close-up of a sumo wrestler's derriere didn't go over much better. To make matters worse, the company didn't design a version in small product sizes so it couldn't give away free samples. And, the wipes are packaged in a container that is immediately visible in a bathroom - another 'own goal' for people already bashful about buying the product.[59]

Levels of categorization

Not only do people group things into categories, but these groupings occur at different levels of specificity. Typically, a product is represented in a cognitive structure at one of three levels. To understand this idea, consider how someone might respond to these questions about an ice-cream cone: What other products share similar characteristics, and which would be considered as alternatives to eating a cone?

These questions may be more complex than they first appear. At one level, a cone is similar to an apple, because both could be eaten as a dessert. At another level, a cone is similar to a slice of pie, because both are eaten for dessert and both are fattening. At still another level, a cone is similar to an ice-cream sundae – both are eaten for dessert, are made of ice cream and are fattening.

It is easy to see that the items a person associates with, say, the category 'fattening dessert' influence the choices he or she will make for what to eat after dinner. The middle level, known as a *basic level category*, is typically the most useful in classifying products, because items grouped together tend to have a lot in common with each other, but still permit a range of alternatives to be considered. The broader *superordinate category* is more abstract, whereas the more specific *subordinate category* often includes individual brands.[60] These three levels are depicted in Figure 8.7.

Figure 8.7 Levels of abstraction in categories of dessert

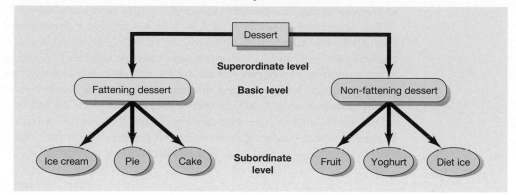

Of course, not all items fit equally well into a category. Apple pie is a better example of the subordinate category 'pie' than is rhubarb pie, even though both are types of pie. Apple pie is thus more *prototypical*, and would tend to be considered first, especially by category novices. In contrast, pie experts will tend to have knowledge about both typical and atypical category examples.[61]

Strategic implications of product categorization

Product categorization has many strategic implications. The way a product is grouped with others has very important ramifications for determining both its competitors for adoption and what criteria will be used to make this choice.

Product positioning

The success of a *positioning strategy* often hinges on the marketer's ability to convince the consumer that his or her product should be considered within a given category. For example, the orange juice industry tried to reposition orange juice as a drink that could be enjoyed all day long ('It's not just for breakfast anymore'). On the other hand, soft drinks companies are now attempting the opposite by portraying carbonated drinks as suitable for breakfast consumption. They are trying to make their way into consumers' 'breakfast drink' category, along with orange juice, grapefruit juice and coffee. Of course, this strategy can backfire, as PepsiCo discovered when it introduced Pepsi A.M. and positioned it as a coffee substitute. The company did such a good job of categorizing the drink as a morning beverage that customers wouldn't drink it at any other time, and the product failed.[62]

Identifying competitors

At the abstract, superordinate level, many different product forms compete for membership. The category 'entertainment' might comprise both bowling and the ballet, but not many people would consider the substitution of one of these activities for the other. Products and services that on the surface are quite different, however, actually compete with each other at a broad level for consumers' discretionary cash. While bowling or ballet may not be a likely trade-off for many people, it is feasible, for example, that a symphony orchestra might try to lure away season ticket-holders to the ballet by positioning itself as an equivalent member of the category 'cultural event'.[63]

Consumers are often faced with choices between non-comparable categories, in which a number of attributes exist that cannot be directly related to one another (the old problem of comparing apples and oranges). The comparison process is easier when consumers can derive an overlapping category that encompasses both items (for instance, entertainment, value, usefulness) and then rate each alternative in terms of that super-ordinate category.[64]

Exemplar products

As we saw with the case of apple pie versus rhubarb, if a product is a really good example of a category it is more familiar to consumers and is more easily recognized and recalled.[65] Judgements about category attributes tend to be disproportionately influenced by the characteristics of category exemplars.[66] In a sense, brands that are strongly associated with a category 'call the shots' by defining the evaluative criteria that should be used to evaluate all category members.

Being a bit less than prototypical is not necessarily a bad thing, however. Products that are moderately unusual within their product category may stimulate more information processing and positive evaluations, because they are neither so familiar that they will be taken for granted nor so discrepant that they will be dismissed.[67] A brand that is strongly discrepant may occupy a unique niche position, whereas those that are moderately discrepant remain in a distinct position within the general category.[68]

Locating products

Product categorization also can affect consumers' expectations regarding the places where they can locate a desired product. If products do not clearly fit into categories (is a carpet furniture?), consumers' ability to find them or make sense of them may be diminished. For instance, a frozen dog food that had to be thawed and cooked failed in the market, partly because people could not adapt to the idea of buying dog food in the 'frozen foods for people' section of their supermarkets.

■ PRODUCT CHOICE: SELECTING AMONG ALTERNATIVES

Once the relevant options from a category have been assembled and evaluated, a choice must be made among them.[69] Recall that the decision rules guiding choice can range from very simple and quick strategies to complicated processes requiring much attention and cognitive processing. The choice can be influenced by integrating information from sources such as prior experience with the product or a similar one, information present at the time of purchase, and beliefs about the brands that have been created by advertising.[70]

Evaluative criteria

When Daniel was looking at different television sets, he focused on one or two product features and completely ignored several others. He narrowed down his choices by only considering two specific brand names, and from the Prime Wave and Precision models, he chose one that featured stereo capability.

▶ **Evaluative criteria** are the dimensions used to judge the merits of competing options. In comparing alternative products, Daniel could have chosen from among any number of criteria, ranging from very functional attributes ('does this TV come with remote control?') to experiential ones ('does this TV's sound reproduction make me imagine I'm in a concert hall?').

Another important point is that criteria on which products *differ* from one another carry more weight in the decision process than do those where the alternatives are *similar*. If all brands being considered rate equally well on one attribute (e.g. if all TVs come with remote control), consumers will have to find other reasons to choose one over
▶ another. The attributes actually used to differentiate among choices are **determinant attributes**.

Marketers can play a role in educating consumers about which criteria should be used as determinant attributes. For example, research indicated that many consumers view the use of natural ingredients as a determinant attribute. The result was promotion of toothpaste made from baking soda, which the company, Church & Dwight, already manufactured for its Arm & Hammer brand.[71] Sometimes a company can even invent a determinant attribute: PepsiCo accomplished this by stamping freshness dates on soda cans. The company spent about $25 million on an advertising and promotional campaign to convince consumers that there's nothing quite as horrible as a stale can of soda – even though it has been estimated that 98 per cent of all cans are consumed well before this could be a problem. Six months after introducing the campaign, an independent survey found that 61 per cent of respondents felt that freshness dating is an important attribute for a soft drink.[72]

The decision about which attributes to use is the result of *procedural learning*, in which a person undergoes a series of cognitive steps before making a choice. These steps include identifying important attributes, remembering whether competing brands differ on those attributes, and so on. In order for a marketer to recommend a new decision criterion effectively, his or her communication should convey three pieces of information:[73]

This advert for Powerade uses a series of explicit appeals linked to different evaluation criteria such as endurance, speed, energy and co-ordination.

The Advertising Archives

- It should point out that there are significant differences among brands on the attribute.
- It should supply the consumer with a decision-making rule, such as *if* (deciding among competing brands), *then* . . . (use the attribute as a criterion).
- It should convey a rule that can be easily integrated with how the person has made this decision in the past. Otherwise, the recommendation is likely to be ignored because it requires too much mental work.

marketing opportunity

Cybermediaries

As anyone who's ever typed a phrase like 'home theatres' into a search engine like Google knows, the Web delivers enormous amounts of product and retailer information in seconds. In fact, the biggest problem Web surfers face these days is narrowing down their choices, not increasing them. In cyberspace, simplification is key. Some people even use web filters like **intermute.com** to remove soundtracks, pop-up frames and other distractions from the sites they find.

With the tremendous number of websites available, and the huge number of people surfing the Web each day, how can people organize information and decide where to click? One type of business that is growing to meet this demand is called a **cybermediary**. This is an intermediary that helps to filter and organize online market information so that customers can identify and evaluate alternatives more efficiently.[74] Cybermediaries take different forms.[75]

- *Directories* and *portals* such as Yahoo! or **fashionmall.com** are general services that tie together a large variety of different sites.
- *Website evaluators* reduce the risk to consumers by reviewing sites and recommending the best ones. For example, Point Communications selects sites that it designates as 'Top 5%' of the Web.
- *Forums*, *fan clubs* and *user groups* offer product-related discussions to help customers sift through options.
- *Intelligent agents* are sophisticated software programs that use *collaborative filtering* technologies to learn from past user behaviour in order to recommend new purchases. For example, when you let **Amazon.com** suggest a new book, it's using an intelligent agent to suggest novels based on what you and others like you have bought in the past. This approach was introduced in 1995 (the Stone Ages in web time!) by Firefly to make recommendations for taste-based products like music, books and films.[76] Now, a variety of 'shopping bots' are available to act as online purchasing shopping agents, including **clickthebutton.com**, **mysimon.com**, **dealtime.com** and Ask Jeeves. Collaborative filtering is still in its infancy. In the next few years, expect to see many new web-based methods developed to simplify the consumer decision-making process. Now if only someone could come up with an easier way to pay for all the great stuff you find courtesy of shopping bots!

Heuristics: mental short cuts

Do we actually perform complex mental calculations every time we make a purchase decision? Of course not! To simplify decisions, consumers often employ decision rules that allow them to use some dimensions as substitutes for others. For example, Daniel relied on certain assumptions as substitutes for prolonged information search. In particular, he assumed the selection at the out-of-town big shed retailer would be more than sufficient, so he did not bother to investigate any of its competitors. This assumption served as a short cut to more extended information processing.[77]

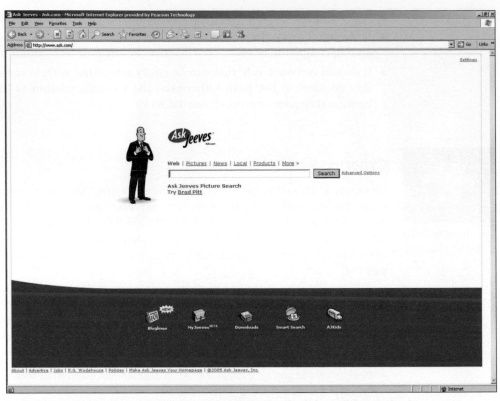

Search engines like Ask Jeeves simplify the process of online information search.

http://www.ask.com/. Courtesy of Ask Jeeves, Inc.

Especially where limited problem-solving occurs prior to making a choice, consumers often fall back on **heuristics**, or mental rules-of-thumb that lead to a speedy decision. These rules range from the very general ('Higher-priced products are higher-quality products' or 'Buy the same brand I bought last time') to the very specific ('Buy Silver Spoon, the brand of sugar my mother always bought').[78]

Sometimes these short cuts may not be in consumers' best interests. A consumer who personally knows one or two people who have had problems with a particular make of car, for example, might assume he or she would have similar trouble with it and thus overlook the model's overall excellent repair record.[79] The influence of such assumptions may be enhanced if the product has an unusual name, which makes it *and* the experiences with it more distinctive.[80]

Relying on a product signal

One frequently used short cut is the tendency to infer hidden dimensions of products from observable attributes. The aspect of the product that is visible acts as a **product signal** that communicates some underlying quality. Such inferences explain why someone trying to sell a used car takes great pains to be sure the car's exterior is clean and shiny: potential buyers often judge the vehicle's mechanical condition by its appearance, even though this means they may drive away in a shiny, clean death trap.[81]

i want everything at my party to be yellow.
i want yellow balloons, yellow cups, and yellow
icing on my cake because yellow is the prettiest
color ever. except for pink. i want everything at
my party to be pink.

www.iparty.com > birthdays > basics > **pink** > cups/plates/napkins/favors > order

i want. i click. iparty.com

aol keyword: iparty

Consumers often simplify choices by using heuristics such as automatically choosing a favourite colour or brand.
iParty Corp.

When product information is incomplete, judgements are often derived from beliefs about *covariation*, or perceived associations among events that may or may not actually influence one another.[82] For example, a consumer may form an association between product quality and the length of time a manufacturer has been in business. Other signals or attributes believed to co-exist with good or bad products include well-known brand names, country of origin, price and the retail outlets that carry the product.

Unfortunately, consumers tend to be poor estimators of covariation. Their beliefs persist despite evidence to the contrary. Similar to the consistency principle discussed in Chapter 5, people tend to see what they are looking for. They will look for product information that confirms their guesses. In one experiment, consumers sampled four sets of products to determine if price and quality were related. Those who believed in this relationship prior to the study elected to sample higher-priced products, thus creating a sort of self-fulfilling prophecy.[83]

Market beliefs: is it better if I have to pay more for it?

Consumers often form assumptions about companies, products and stores. These market beliefs then become the short cuts that guide their decisions – whether or not they are accurate.[84] Recall, for instance, that Daniel chose to shop at a large 'electronics supermarket' because he *assumed* the prices would be more competitive there than at a specialized shop. A large number of **market beliefs** have been identified. Some of these are listed in Table 8.3. How many do you share?

Table 8.3 Common market beliefs

Brand	All brands are basically the same.
	Generic products are just name brands sold under a different label at a lower price.
	The best brands are the ones that are purchased the most.
	When in doubt, a national brand is always a safe bet.
Store	Specialized shops are good places to familiarize yourself with the best brands; but once you know what you want, it's cheaper to buy it at a discount outlet.
	A store's character is reflected in its window displays.
	Sales people in specialized shops are more knowledgeable than other sales personnel.
	Larger stores offer better prices than small stores.
	Locally owned stores give the best service.
	A store that offers a good value on one of its products probably offers good values on all of its items.
	Credit and return policies are most lenient at large department stores.
	Stores that have just opened usually charge attractive prices.
Prices/Discounts/Sales	Sales are typically run to get rid of slow-moving merchandise.
	Stores that are constantly having sales don't really save you money.
	Within a given store, higher prices generally indicate higher quality.
Advertising and sales promotion	'Hard-sell' advertising is associated with low-quality products.
	Items tied to 'giveaways' are not good value (even with the freebie).
	Coupons represent real savings for customers because they are not offered by the store.
	When you buy heavily advertised products, you are paying for the label, not for higher quality.
Product/Packaging	Largest-sized containers are almost always cheaper per unit than smaller sizes.
	New products are more expensive when they're first introduced; prices tend to settle down as time goes by.
	When you are not sure what you need in a product, it's a good idea to invest in the extra features, because you'll probably wish you had them later.
	In general, synthetic goods are lower in quality than goods made of natural materials.
	It's advisable to stay away from products when they are new to the market; it usually takes the manufacturer a little time to sort out the bugs.

Source: Adapted from Calvin P. Duncan, 'Consumer Market Beliefs: A Review of the Literature and an Agenda for Future Research', in Marvin E. Goldberg, Gerald Gorn and Richard W. Pollay, eds, *Advances in Consumer Research* 17 (Provo, UT: Association for Consumer Research, 1990): 729-35.

Do higher prices mean higher quality? The assumption of a *price–quality relationship* is one of the most pervasive market beliefs.[85] Novice consumers may in fact consider price as the *only* relevant product attribute. Experts also consider this information, although in these cases price tends to be used for its informational value, especially for products (e.g. virgin wool) that are known to have wide quality variations in the marketplace. When this quality level is more standard or strictly regulated (e.g. Harris Tweed sports jackets), experts do not weigh price in their decisions. For the most part, this belief is justified; you do tend to get what you pay for. However, let the buyer beware: the price–quality relationship is not always justified.[86]

Country of origin as a product signal

Modern consumers choose among products made in many countries. European consumers may buy Portuguese, Italian or Brazilian shoes, Japanese cars, clothing imported from Taiwan, or microwave ovens built in South Korea. Consumers' reactions to these imports are mixed. In some cases, people have come to assume that a product made overseas is of better quality (cameras, cars), whereas in other cases the knowledge that a product has been imported tends to lower perceptions of product quality (apparel).[87] In general, people tend to rate their own country's products more favourably than do foreigners, and products from industrialized countries are rated better than are those from developing countries.

▶ As briefly discussed in Chapter 6 when we were talking about persuasive communication, a product's **country of origin** in some cases is an important piece of information in the decision-making process.[88] A product's origin, then, is often used as a signal of quality. Certain items are strongly associated with specific countries, and products from those countries often attempt to benefit from these linkages. Countries, in their turn, can be very protective of product names which potentially provide them with an important competitive advantage in winning customers. The European Union has been trying to achieve a global trade agreement to protect some of its product names such as champagne and wines like Beaujolais, chianti and Madeira; cheeses such as Roquefort, Feta and Gorgonzola; as well as meat products like Parma ham and Mortadella sausages. This has been opposed in some non-EU countries where these names are seen as

▶ generic.[89] Country of origin can function as a **stereotype** – a knowledge structure based

A product's country-of-origin in some cases is an important piece of information in the decision-making process. Certain items are strongly associated with specific countries, and products from those countries often attempt to benefit from these linkages.

Sopexa USA. © Copyright ONIVINS and Isabelle Dervaux

on inferences across products. These stereotypes may be biased or inaccurate, but they do play a constructive role in simplifying complex choice situations.[90] For example, a Brazilian soft drinks company is now trying to market a beverage it is calling Samba in the United States. Samba is made from the guaraná berry, and this sweet, flowery-tasting soft drink is extremely popular in Brazil. The company is capitalizing on the carefree, partying image that many Americans have of Brazilians to get them to try it. In its commercials, a scantily clad woman says, 'In Brazil we do things a little differently. We laugh a little more, wear a little less and dance the samba. Dance the dance. Drink the drink.'[91]

One study showed college students in Ireland, the USA and Australia photographs of 'Irish pubs' taken in each of those three countries and asked them to guess which were the authentic ones from Ireland. Most respondents were more likely to pick the bars that were not actually the Irish ones; the bars in the USA and Australia tended to contain more stereotypical Irish decorations like four-leaf clovers that you're not as likely to find in the original article.[92]

marketing opportunity

The growing popularity of *faux* Irish pubs around the world attests to the power of country stereotypes to influence consumers' preferences. About 800 Irish-themed pubs have been opened in countries including South Africa, Italy, Hong Kong and Russia. The Irish brewer Guinness PLC encourages the establishment of these outputs, since an Irish pub is mere blarney without Guinness on tap. The company helps owners design the pub and even assists in locating Irish bar staff to dispense its thick brew. As one Guinness executive explained, 'We created a mythology of an Irish ambience.'[93] Since Guinness launched its Irish Pub Concept in 1992 it has helped over 1,250 entrepreneurs in 36 countries establish their own Irish pubs. Aspiring publicans can choose from five pre-set designs: Victorian Dublin, Irish Brewery Pub, Irish Pub Shop, Irish County Cottage or Gaelic.

multicultural dimensions

Japanese consumers have a strong interest in European and American products, and other countries work hard to cultivate a favourable image in the discriminating Japanese market. Dentsu, the largest Japanese advertising agency, has conducted several studies for the Commission of the European Union to determine how Japanese consumers perceive European countries, the United States and some Asian countries, and how they evaluate products from those countries.

The study involved personal interviews with 1,600 consumers ranging in age from 15 to 59. Respondents rated countries on such overall dimensions as 'rich in history/tradition', 'abundant natural scenery' and 'would like to visit', as well as on product-related characteristics, such as 'high-quality, performance products' and 'well-designed, stylish products'. The results showed that the Japanese public associates Europe with history, tradition and well-designed products, while American advanced technology and agriculture are highly rated (products from South Korea and Taiwan tended to be rated lower than those from the United States or Europe).

Overall, respondents told the researchers that foreign products (i.e. non-Japanese) are well regarded in terms of style, but are assumed to be lower in technological sophistication than most Japanese products. There was also a widespread feeling that many non-Japanese products are not well suited to Japanese needs. These consumers felt that many foreign goods are too expensive and need more thorough after-sales service.

A perceptual map (these were described in Chapter 2) summarizing Japanese consumers' images of European countries and the United States is shown in Figure 8.8. The five countries in Group 1 have the most 'image wealth': they are strong in both overall appeal and in ratings

Figure 8.8 Perceptual positioning by country of origin among Japanese consumers

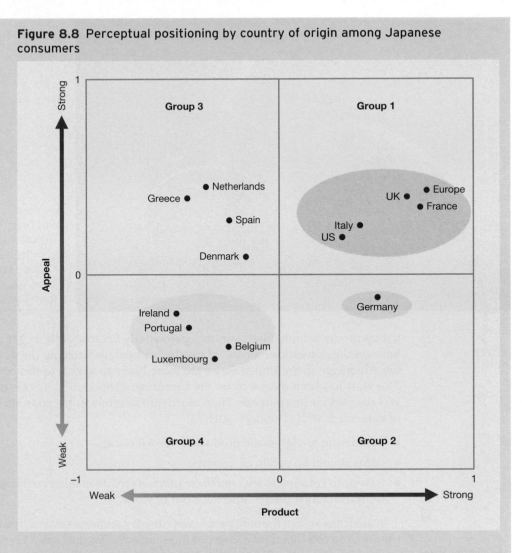

of product quality. Germany is the sole country in Group 2, indicating that its products are better regarded than is the country as a whole. The countries in Group 3 have positive images, but have yet to transfer these good feelings to their products. Finally, the countries in Group 4 appear to have their work cut out if they hope to win over the hearts and wallets of Japanese consumers.[94]

Recent evidence indicates that learning of a product's country of origin is not necessarily good or bad. Instead, it has the effect of stimulating the consumer's interest in the product to a greater degree. The purchaser thinks more extensively about the product and evaluates it more carefully.[95] The origin of the product can thus act as a product attribute that combines with other attributes to influence evaluations.[96] In addition, the consumer's own expertise with the product category moderates the effects of this attribute. When other information is available, experts tend to ignore country-of-origin information, whereas novices continue to rely on it. However, when other information is unavailable or ambiguous, both experts and novices will rely on this attribute to make a decision.[97]

The tendency to prefer products or people of one's own culture to those from other countries is called **ethnocentrism**. Ethnocentric consumers are likely to feel it is wrong

Potato, woman and song

Some countries are strongly associated with certain types of alcoholic products. This Polish ad plays on these stereotypes.
Grey Worldwide Warszawa. Photo: Jacek Wolowski

to buy products from other countries, particularly because of the negative effect this may have on the domestic economy. Marketing campaigns stressing the desirability of 'buying American' in the United States are more likely to appeal to this consumer segment. This trait has been measured on the Consumer Ethnocentrism Scale (CETSCALE) that was devised for this purpose. The scale identifies ethnocentric consumers by their extent of agreement with statements such as:

● purchasing foreign-made products is un-American,
● curbs should be put on all imports,
● American consumers who purchase products made in other countries are responsible for putting their fellow Americans out of work.[98]

Americans are not the only people who display ethnocentrism. Citizens of many countries tend to feel that their native products are superior (just ask a Frenchman to choose

AUSTRALIANS WOULDN'T GIVE A XXXX FOR ANYTHING ELSE.

This advertisement illustrates Australian ethnocentrism by emphasizing the importance placed by Australian consumers on drinking their own 'XXXX' beer, as opposed to any other beverage.
The Advertising Archives

between French or Californian wines!). Many Canadians are concerned about the dilution of their culture due to a strong US influence. In one poll, 25 per cent of the country's citizens identified 'life, liberty, and the pursuit of happiness' as a Canadian constitutional slogan rather than an American one.[99] Canadian nationalism was stoked by a commercial for Molson Canadian beer called 'The Rant' that almost overnight became an unofficial anthem in Canada. A flannel-shirted young Canadian walks onto a stage and calmly begins explaining away Canadian stereotypes: 'I'm not a lumberjack or a fur trader. I don't live in an igloo or eat blubber or own a dog sled . . . My name is Joe and I . . . AM . . . CANADIAN! . . .' In the six weeks after the ad started airing, the Molson brand gained almost two points in market share.[100] The scale for testing for ethnocentrism (CETSCALE) was originally developed in the USA, and its applicability in other cultural contexts such as Spain is currently being explored.[101]

Choosing familiar brand names: loyalty or habit?

Branding is a marketing strategy that often functions as a heuristic. People form preferences for a favourite brand, and then they literally may never change their minds in the course of a lifetime. In a study of the market leaders in 30 product categories by the Boston Consulting Group, it was found that 27 of the brands that were number one in 1930 in the United States remain at the top today. These include such perennial American favourites as Ivory Soap, Campbell's Soup and Gold Medal Flour.[102] A recent study has applied cultural theory to understanding how brands become icons over time.[103]

A brand that exhibits that kind of staying power is treasured by marketers, and for good reason. Brands that dominate their markets are as much as 50 per cent more profitable than their nearest competitors.[104] A survey on brand power in Asia, Australia, South Africa, Europe and the United States calculated brand scores to produce the list of the most positively regarded brand names around the world given in Table 8.4.[105]

In a survey of global brands, Interbrand and *BusinessWeek* identified the importance for companies of building 'communities around their products and services creating "cult brands" that enable customers to feel as if they own the brand. Cutting-edge technology companies did well as four of the top five biggest gainers in brand value are from the tech sector, while long-established brands such as Coca-Cola, Disney and Ford actually lost brand value . . . the overall number of American companies on the list dropped from 64 to 58.'[106]

Consumers' attachments to certain brands, such as Marlboro, Coca-Cola and Levi's, are so powerful that this loyalty is often considered as a positive product attribute in and of itself. Brand equity can actually be quantified in terms of *goodwill*, defined as

Table 8.4 The most positively regarded brand names around the world

	1990	1996
1	Coca-Cola	McDonald's
2	Kellogg's	Coca-Cola
3	McDonald's	Disney
4	Kodak	Kodak
5	Marlboro	Sony
6	IBM	Gillette
7	American Express	Mercedes-Benz
8	Sony	Levi's
9	Mercedes-Benz	Microsoft
10	Nescafé	Marlboro

the difference between the market value and the book value of a brand. The British company Grand Metropolitan recorded the brand names it had acquired on its balance sheets, including these intangible assets in its financial reports to shareholders.[107] In 1992, Marlboro was the most valuable brand name in the world, valued at $31.2 billion.[108] By 2004, Marlboro was the tenth most valuable brand name in the world, valued at $22.13 billion, with Coca-Cola leading the world's brands and valued at $67.39 billion.[109]

However, there are growing concerns about the impact of geopolitics on some of the iconic US brands in European markets (e.g. Germany and France) where Coca-Cola, Marlboro, McDonald's, Wal-Mart, Disney and Gap have all reported weak or falling sales, though the companies also point to local factors.[110] A recent survey of 8,000 consumers in eight countries showed strong evidence of the potential influence of politics on consumer behaviour, with 20 per cent of European and Canadian consumers saying that they would refrain from buying US brands because of US foreign policy.[111]

multicultural dimensions

'Is the world falling out of love with US brands?'

'For more than half a century, the US and its products have stood for progress, glamour and freedom in the minds of consumers around the world. However poll after poll has shown that allegations of human rights abuses and the failure to find weapons of mass destruction in Iraq have tarnished the international reputation of the US. But geopolitics is easily left behind when shoppers get to the till. Those activists who express their anger at the US through conscious boycotts of its companies remain a small minority . . .

The bigger question worrying the business world is whether the opinion poll data point to a more subtle tarnishing of US brands in the minds of millions of ordinary consumers. If the American dream played such an important role in the growth of iconic US brands, what happens if significant numbers of consumers begin to think of the US as a bit of a nightmare?

Mr Nye, a former dean of Harvard's Kennedy School of Government and assistant secretary of defence in the Clinton administration, is one of many who are certain of the connection. 'US brands have benefited from a sense that it is fashionable, chic and modern to be American,' he says. 'The other side of that coin is when US policies become unpopular, there is a cost.'

Earl Taylor, chief marketing officer of the Marketing Science Institute, a US think-tank, takes a different view: 'Consumers are able to compartmentalise the brands of a country from its foreign policy,' he says. 'If there was a simple relationship between US brands and foreign policy we would have seen it decades ago.' Could it be that it is the era of one-size-fits-all global brands, rather than US dominance of consumer markets, that is coming to an end?

But there is growing evidence that this is a problem that US companies cannot afford to ignore. In European markets such as Germany and France many iconic US names – Coca-Cola, Marlboro, McDonald's, Wal-Mart, Disney, Gap – have reported weak or falling sales, though each blames other local factors. Not all brands are treated the same, of course. Companies such as Kodak, Kleenex, Visa and Gillette are simply not perceived as American. Users of Microsoft software might know its heritage but have few alternatives. Technology companies also seem immune – as the worldwide success of Apple's iPod and the Chinese purchase of IBM's consumer PC business demonstrate.

But among those consumer companies perceived as American, and vulnerable to boycotts, there is a remarkably consistent set of problems in the countries that have seen the biggest swing in public opinion. Coca-Cola, which makes 80 per cent of its profits outside North America, sold 16 per cent less beverages to Germans in the third quarter of 2004 than a year previously. McDonald's blamed falling German sales for virtually eliminating growth across Europe. And Altria sold 24.5 per cent fewer Marlboro cigarettes in France and 18.7 per cent fewer in Germany during the third quarter.

In each instance other factors play a role. The falling dollar masks problems by inflating repatriated profits and lowering the cost of exports. Marlboro, for example, blames tax changes that encourage customers to trade down to cheaper brands. Coke says German bottling laws have a similar effect. But neither seems able to overcome such obstacles as well as it used to. Most importantly, some European companies such as Unilever and Nestlé have experienced their own problems with weak consumer spending.

Neville Isdell, new chief executive of Coca-Cola, is typical of many business leaders who work hard to stress local credentials with sports sponsorship and customised advertising. 'We are not an American brand,' he says. Starbucks, the coffee chain, has thrived by making more of its products' associations with the developing world than of its own Seattle heritage.

If nothing else, the trend reveals a declining confidence in the aspirational pull of the US. Simon Anholt, author of *Brand America*, sums up how far the US has slipped from its pedestal: 'The world's love affair with America isn't exactly over, but it has stopped being a blind and unquestioning kind of love.''[112]

Inertia: the fickle customer

▶ Many people tend to buy the same brand just about every time they go shopping. This consistent pattern is often due to **inertia** – a brand is bought out of habit merely because less effort is required. If another product is introduced that is for some reason easier to buy (for instance, it is cheaper or the original product is out of stock), the consumer will not hesitate to do so. A competitor who is trying to change a buying pattern based on inertia often can do so rather easily, because little resistance to brand switching will be encountered if the right incentive is offered. Since there is little to no underlying commitment to a particular brand, promotional tools such as point-of-purchase displays, extensive couponing, or noticeable price reductions may be sufficient to 'unfreeze' a consumer's habitual pattern.

Brand loyalty: a 'friend', tried and true

▶ This kind of fickleness will not occur if true **brand loyalty** exists. In contrast to inertia, brand loyalty is a form of repeat purchasing behaviour reflecting a *conscious* decision to continue buying the same brand.[113] For brand loyalty to exist, a pattern of repeat purchase must be accompanied by an underlying positive attitude towards the brand. Brand loyalty may be initiated by customer preference based on objective reasons, but after the brand has existed for a long time and is heavily advertised it can also create an emotional attachment, either by being incorporated into the consumer's self-image or because it is associated with prior experiences.[114] Purchase decisions based on brand loyalty also become habitual over time, though in these cases the underlying commitment to the product is much firmer.

Compared to an inertia situation in which the consumer passively accepts a brand, a brand-loyal consumer is actively (sometimes passionately) involved with his or her favourite. Because of the emotional bonds that can come about between brand-loyal consumers and products, 'true-blue' users react more vehemently when these products are altered, redesigned or withdrawn.[115] Recall, for example, when Coca-Cola replaced its tried-and-true formula with New Coke in the 1980s.

A decade ago, marketers struggled with the problem of *brand parity*, which refers to consumers' beliefs that there are no significant differences among brands. For example, one survey at that time found that more than 70 per cent of consumers worldwide believed that all paper towels, all soaps and all crisps are alike.[116] Some analysts even proclaimed the death of brand names, predicting that private label or generic products that offered the same value for less money would kill off the tried-and-true products.

However, the reports of this death appear to be premature – major brands are making a dramatic comeback. Some attribute this renaissance to information overload – with too many alternatives (many of them unfamiliar names) to choose from, people seem to be looking for a few clear signals of quality. Following a period in the late 1980s and early 1990s when people had strong doubts about the ability of large companies to produce quality products, more recent surveys indicate consumers are slowly beginning to trust major manufacturers again.[117] Brand names are very much alive.

net profit

Brand loyalty lives - online. Many brand fans create personal web pages that trumpet their allegiance to one or more favourite products. These pages may take the form of passionate essays or perhaps photo albums that show in vivid detail the ways the page creator uses the product. Many of them include external links that provide reams of additional details about the featured products. A study of these personal web pages found that the brands referenced range from common software and net application products to entertainment/entertainers (fan sites), clothing, financial/governmental/political organizations, restaurants and even household goods. In addition to providing a fascinating glimpse into how far people will go to express their allegiance to favourite products (yes, even to appliances!), these personal online 'shrines' to favourite products potentially are a great untapped resource for marketers that want to locate brand-loyal followers who will help them to spread the word in cyberspace.[118]

Decision rules

Consumers consider sets of product attributes by using different rules, depending on the complexity of the decision and the importance of the decision to them. As we have seen, in some cases these rules are quite simple: people simply rely on a short cut to make a choice. In other cases, though, more effort and thought is put into carefully weighing alternatives before coming to a decision.

One way to differentiate among decision rules is to divide them into those that are *compensatory* versus those that are *non-compensatory*. To aid the discussion of some of these rules, Table 8.5 summarizes the attributes of the TV sets Daniel considered. It is now possible to see how some of these rules result in different brand choices.

Non-compensatory decision rules

Simple decision rules are non-compensatory, meaning that a product with a low standing on one attribute cannot make up for this position by being better on another. Simple ► **non-compensatory decision rules** are therefore short cuts to making choices. This means that people simply eliminate all options that do not meet some basic standards. A consumer like Daniel who uses the decision rule, 'Only buy well-known brand names',

Table 8.5 Hypothetical alternatives for a television set

Attribute	Importance ranking	Brand ratings		
		Kamashita	Prime Wave	Precision
Size of screen	1	Excellent	Excellent	Excellent
Stereo broadcast capability	2	Good	Poor	Excellent
Brand reputation	3	Poor	Excellent	Excellent
On-screen programming	4	Poor	Excellent	Poor
Cable-ready capability	5	Good	Good	Good
Sleep timer	6	Good	Excellent	Poor

would not consider a new brand, even if it were equal or superior to existing ones. When people are less familiar with a product category or are not very motivated to process complex information, they tend to use simple, non-compensatory rules, which are summarized below:[119]

The Lexicographic Rule When the lexicographic rule is used, the brand that is the best on the most important attribute is selected. If two or more brands are seen as being equally good on that attribute, the consumer then compares them on the second most important attribute. This selection process goes on until the tie is broken. In Daniel's case, because both the Prime Wave and Precision models were tied on his most important attribute (a 26-inch screen), the Precision was chosen because of its rating on this second most important attribute – its stereo capability.

The Elimination-by-Aspects Rule Using the elimination-by-aspects rule, brands are also evaluated on the most important attribute. In this case, though, specific cut-offs are imposed. For example, if Daniel had been more interested in having a sleep timer on his TV (if that had had a higher importance ranking), he might have stipulated that his choice 'must have a sleep timer'. Because the Prime Wave model had one and the Precision did not, the Prime Wave would have been chosen.

The Conjunctive Rule Whereas the two former rules involve processing by attribute, the conjunctive rule entails processing by brand. As with the elimination-by-aspects procedure, cut-offs are established for each attribute. A brand is chosen if it meets all of the cut-offs, while failure to meet any one cut-off means it will be rejected. If none of the brands meet all of the cut-offs, the choice may be delayed, the decision rule may be changed, or the cut-offs may be modified.

If Daniel had stipulated that all attributes had to be rated 'good' or better, he would not have been able to choose any of the options. He might then have modified his decision rule, conceding that it was not possible to attain these high standards in the price range he was considering. In this case, Daniel might decide that he could live without on-screen programming, so the Precision model could again be considered.

Compensatory decision rules

▶ Unlike non-compensatory decision rules, **compensatory decision rules** give a product a chance to make up for its shortcomings. Consumers who employ these rules tend to be more involved in the purchase and thus are willing to exert the effort to consider the entire picture in a more exacting way. The willingness to offset good product qualities against bad ones can result in quite different choices. For example, if Daniel had not been concerned about having stereo reception, he might have chosen the Prime Wave model. But because this brand doesn't feature this highly ranked attribute, it doesn't stand a chance when he uses a non-compensatory rule.

Two basic types of compensatory rules have been identified. When using the *simple additive rule*, the consumer merely chooses the alternative that has the largest number of positive attributes. This choice is most likely to occur when his or her ability or motivation to process information is limited. One drawback to this approach for the consumer is that some of these attributes may not be very meaningful or important. An ad containing a long list of product benefits may be persuasive, despite the fact that many of the benefits included are actually standard within the product class and aren't determinant attributes at all.

The more complex version is known as the *weighted additive rule*.[120] When using this rule, the consumer also takes into account the relative importance of positively rated attributes, essentially multiplying brand ratings by importance weights. If this process sounds familiar, it should. The calculation process strongly resembles the multi-attribute attitude model described in Chapter 5.

■ CHAPTER SUMMARY

- Consumers are faced with the need to make decisions about products all of the time. Some of these decisions are very important and entail great effort, whereas others are made more or less automatically.

- Perspectives on decision-making range from a focus on habits that people develop over time to novel situations involving a great deal of risk where consumers must carefully collect and analyse information prior to making a choice. Many of our decisions are highly automated and made largely by habit. This trend is accelerating as marketers begin to introduce smart products that enable silent commerce where some purchases are made automatically by the products themselves (e.g. a malfunctioning appliance that contacts the repairer directly).

- A typical decision process involves several steps. The first is problem recognition, where the consumer first realizes that some action must be taken. This realization may be prompted in a variety of ways, ranging from the actual malfunction of a current purchase to a desire for new things based on exposure to different circumstances or advertising that provides a glimpse into what is needed to 'live the good life'.

- Once a problem has been recognized and is seen as sufficiently important to warrant some action, *information search* begins. This search may range from simply scanning memory to determine what has been done to resolve the problem in the past, to extensive fieldwork in which the consumer consults a variety of sources to amass as much information as possible. In many cases, people engage in surprisingly little search. Instead, they rely on various mental short cuts, such as brand names or price, or they may simply imitate others.

- In the *evaluation of alternatives* stage, the product alternatives that are considered comprise the individual's evoked set. Members of the *evoked set* usually share some characteristics; they are categorized similarly. The way products are mentally grouped influences which alternatives will be considered, and some brands are more strongly associated with these categories than are others (in other words, they are more prototypical).

- The World Wide Web has changed the way many consumers search for information. Today, the problem is often weeding out excess detail rather than searching for more. Comparative search sites and intelligent agents help to filter and guide the search process. Cybermediaries such as web portals may be relied upon to sort through massive amounts of information to simplify the decision-making process.

- Research in the field of behavioural economics illustrates that decision-making is not always strictly rational. Principles of mental accounting demonstrate that decisions can be influenced by the way a problem is posed (called framing) and whether it is put in terms of gains or losses.

- When the consumer eventually must make a product choice from among alternatives, a number of decision rules may be used. *Non-compensatory rules* eliminate alternatives that are deficient on any of the criteria the consumer has chosen to use. *Compensatory rules*, which are more likely to be applied in high-involvement situations, allow the decision maker to consider each alternative's good and bad points more carefully to arrive at the overall best choice.

- Very often, heuristics, or mental rules-of-thumb, are used to simplify decision-making. In particular, people develop many market beliefs over time. One of the most common beliefs is that price is positively related to quality. Other heuristics rely on well-known brand names or a product's country of origin as signals of product quality. When a brand is purchased consistently over time, this pattern may be due to true *brand loyalty*, or simply to *inertia* because it's the easiest thing to do.

▶ **KEY TERMS**

Behavioural influence perspective (p. 260)
Brand loyalty (p. 289)
Cognitive structure (p. 275)
Compensatory decision rules (p. 291)
Country of origin (p. 283)
Cybermediary (p. 279)
Determinant attributes (p. 277)
Ethnocentrism (p. 285)
Evaluative criteria (p. 277)
Evoked set (p. 273)
Experiential perspective (p. 260)
Extended problem-solving (p. 261)
Habitual decision-making (p. 262)
Heuristics (p. 280)
Inertia (p. 289)

Information search (p. 265)
Limited problem-solving (p. 262)
Market beliefs (p. 281)
Mental accounting (p. 269)
Non-compensatory decision rule (p. 290)
Perceived risk (p. 271)
Problem recognition (p. 263)
Product signal (p. 280)
Prospect theory (p. 269)
Purchase momentum (p. 259)
Rational perspective (p. 259)
Silent commerce (p. 263)
Stereotype (p. 283)
Variety seeking (p. 267)

CONSUMER BEHAVIOUR CHALLENGE

1 If people are not always rational decision-makers, is it worth the effort to study how purchasing decisions are made? What techniques might be employed to understand experiential consumption and to translate this knowledge into marketing strategy?

2 List three product attributes that can be used as quality signals and provide an example of each.

3 Explain the 'evoked set'. Why is it difficult to place a product in a consumer's evoked set after it has already been rejected? What strategies might a marketer use in an attempt to accomplish this goal?

4 Define the three levels of product categorization described in the chapter. Diagram these levels for a health club.

5 Discuss two different non-compensatory decision rules and highlight the difference(s) between them. How might the use of one rule versus another result in a different product choice?

6 Choose a friend or parent who shops for groceries on a regular basis and keep a log of their purchases of common consumer products during the term. Can you detect any evidence of brand loyalty in any categories based on consistency of purchases? If so, talk to the person about these purchases. Try to determine if his or her choices are based on true brand loyalty or on inertia. What techniques might you use to differentiate between the two?

7 Form a group of three. Pick a product and develop a marketing plan based on each of the three approaches to consumer decision-making: rational, experiential and behavioural influence. What are the major differences in emphasis among the three

perspectives? Which is the most likely type of problem-solving activity for the product you have selected? What characteristics of the product make this so?

8 Find a person who is about to make a major purchase. Ask that person to make a chronological list of all the information sources consulted prior to making a decision. How would you characterize the types of sources used (i.e. internal versus external, media versus personal, etc.)? Which sources appeared to have the most impact on the person's decision?

9 Perform a survey of country-of-origin stereotypes. Compile a list of five countries and ask people what products they associate with each. What are their evaluations of the products and likely attributes of these different products? The power of a country stereotype can also be demonstrated in another way. Prepare a brief description of a product, including a list of features, and ask people to rate it in terms of quality, likelihood of purchase, and so on. Make several versions of the description, varying only the country from which it comes. Do ratings change as a function of the country of origin?

10 Ask a friend to 'talk through' the process he or she used to choose one brand rather than others during a recent purchase. Based on this description, can you identify the decision rule that was most likely employed?

11 Technology has the potential to make our lives easier by reducing the amount of clutter we need to work through in order to access the information on the internet that really interests us. On the other hand, perhaps intelligent agents that make recommendations based only on what we and others like us have chosen in the past limit us - they reduce the chance that we will stumble upon something (e.g. a book on a topic we've never heard of, or a music group that's different from the style we usually listen to). Will the proliferation of shopping 'bots make our lives too predictable by only giving us more of the same? If so, is this a problem?

12 Give one of the scenarios described in the section on biases in decision-making to 10 to 20 people. How do the results you obtain compare with those reported in the chapter?

13 Think of a product you recently shopped for online. Describe your search process. How did you become aware you wanted/needed the product? How did you evaluate alternatives? Did you end up buying online? Why, or why not? What factors would make it more or less likely that you would buy something online rather than in a traditional store?

14 Consider the five types of perceived risk in Figure 8.5 of this chapter within the context of making a decision to purchase a new diamond. Review the following websites, and discuss the kinds of risk you would consider in buying a diamond on the Web: **www.diamond.com, www.mondera.com, www.bluenile.com**.

■ NOTES

1. John C. Mowen, 'Beyond consumer decision making', *Journal of Consumer Marketing* 5(1) (1988): 15–25.

2. Richard W. Olshavsky and Donald H. Granbois, 'Consumer decision making – fact or fiction', *Journal of Consumer Research* 6 (September 1989): 93–100.

3. Chris Marks, 'As two osprey nests are raided, fears that thieves see Scotland as a soft option', *Daily Mail* (14 May 2002).

4. Ravi Dhar, Joel Huber and Uzma Khan, 'The Shopping Momentum Effect', paper presented at the Association for Consumer Research Conference, Atlanta, October 2002.

5. James R. Bettman, 'The Decision Maker Who Came in from the Cold' (presidential address), in Leigh McAllister and Michael Rothschild, eds, *Advances in Consumer Research* 20 (Provo, UT: Association for Consumer Research, 1993): 7–11; John W. Payne, James R. Bettman and Eric J. Johnson, 'Behavioral decision research: A constructive processing perspective', *Annual Review of Psychology* 4 (1992): 87–131; J.R. Bettman, M.F. Luce and J.W. Payne 'Constructive consumer choice processes', *Journal of Consumer Research* 25(3) (December 1998): 187–217; for an overview of recent developments in individual choice models, see Robert J. Meyer and Barbara E. Kahn, 'Probabilistic Models of Consumer Choice Behavior', in Thomas S. Robertson and Harold H. Kassarjian, eds, *Handbook of Consumer Behavior* (Upper Saddle River, NJ: Prentice Hall, 1991): 85–123.

6. Dan Ariely, 'Controlling the information flow: Effects on consumers' decision making and preferences', *Journal of Consumer Research*, 27 (September 2000): 245; John Deighton, 'The future of interactive marketing', *Harvard Business Review* 74(6) (1996): 151–62.

7. Ariely, 'Controlling the information flow': 233–48.

8. Nicholas H. Lurie, 'Decision making in information-rich environments: The role of information structure', *Journal of Consumer Research*, 30 (March 2004): 473–86.

9. Ibid.: 484–5.

10. Mowen, 'Beyond consumer decision making'.

11. The Fits-Like-a-Glove (FLAG) framework is a new decision-making perspective that views consumer decisions as a holistic process shaped by the person's unique context: see Douglas E. Allen, 'Toward a theory of consumer choice as sociohistorically shaped practical experience: The fits-like-a-glove (FLAG) framework', *Journal of Consumer Research* 28 (March 2002): 515–32.

12. Jennifer Lee, 'In the U.S., interactive TV still awaits an audience', *New York Times* (31 December 2001): C1.

13. Quoted in ibid.: C8.

14. Joseph W. Alba and J. Wesley Hutchinson, 'Dimensions of consumer expertise', *Journal of Consumer Research* 13 (March 1988): 411–54.

15. Kevin Maney, 'Tag it: Tiny wireless wonders improve convenience', *Montgomery Advertiser* (6 May 2002): D1.

16. Ibid.

17. Thomas Maeder, 'What Barbie wants, Barbie gets', *Wired* (January 2002): 4.

18. Gordon C. Bruner III and Richard J. Pomazal, 'Problem recognition: The crucial first stage of the consumer decision process', *Journal of Consumer Marketing* 5(1) (1988): 53–63.

19. Ross K. Baker, 'Textually transmitted diseases', *American Demographics* (December 1987): 64.

20. Julia Marlowe, Gary Selnow and Lois Blosser, 'A content analysis of problem-resolution appeals in television commercials', *Journal of Consumer Affairs* 23(1) (1989): 175–94.

21. Peter H. Bloch, Daniel L. Sherrell and Nancy M. Ridgway, 'Consumer search: An extended framework', *Journal of Consumer Research* 13 (June 1986): 119–26.

22. 'Holidays look merry for online retailers', *Wall Street Journal Interactive Edition* (24 December 2002).

23. Lisa Guernsey, 'As the Web matures, fun is hard to find', *The New York Times on the Web* (28 March 2002).

24. Ariely, 'Controlling the information flow': 233–48.

25. 'Survey cites use of internet to gather data', *The New York Times on the Web* (30 December 2002).

26. Girish Punj, 'Presearch decision making in consumer durable purchases', *Journal of Consumer Marketing* 4 (Winter 1987): 71–82.

27. H. Beales, M.B. Jagis, S.C. Salop and R. Staelin, 'Consumer search and public policy', *Journal of Consumer Research* 8 (June 1981): 11–22.

28. Examples provided by Dr William Cohen, personal communication, October 1999.

29. Itamar Simonson, Joel Huber and John Payne, 'The relationship between prior brand knowledge and information acquisition order', *Journal of Consumer Research* 14 (March 1988): 566–78.

30. John R. Hauser, Glen L. Urban and Bruce D. Weinberg, 'How consumers allocate their time when searching for information', *Journal of Marketing Research* 30 (November 1993): 452–66; George J. Stigler, 'The economics of information', *Journal of Political Economy* 69 (June 1961): 213–25; for a set of studies focusing on online search costs see John G. Lynch Jr. and Dan Ariely, 'Wine Online: Search Costs and Competition on Price, Quality, and Distribution' (unpublished manuscript, Duke University).

31. Rebecca K. Ratner, Barbara E. Kahn and Daniel Kahneman, 'Choosing less-preferred experiences for the sake of variety', *Journal of Consumer Research* 26 (June 1999): 1–15.

32. Cathy J. Cobb and Wayne D. Hoyer, 'Direct observation of search behavior', *Psychology and Marketing* 2 (Fall 1985): 161–79.

33. Sharon E. Beatty and Scott M. Smith, 'External search effort: An investigation across several product categories', *Journal of Consumer Research* 14 (June 1987): 83–95; William L. Moore and Donald R. Lehmann, 'Individual differences in search behavior for a nondurable', *Journal of Consumer Research* 7 (December 1980): 296–307.

34. Geoffrey C. Kiel and Roger A. Layton, 'Dimensions of consumer information seeking behavior', *Journal of Marketing Research* 28 (May 1981): 233–9; see also Narasimhan Srinivasan and Brian T. Ratchford, 'An empirical test of a model of external search for automobiles', *Journal of Consumer Research* 18 (September 1991): 233–42.

35. Kiel and Layton, 'Dimensions of consumer information seeking behavior'; see also Srinivasan and Ratchford, 'An empirical test of a model of external search for automobiles'; Mari Niva, Eva Heiskanen and Päivi Timonen, 'Environmental information in consumer decision making', *National Consumer Research Centre* (Helsinki, July 1996).

36. David F. Midgley, 'Patterns of interpersonal information seeking for the purchase of a symbolic product', *Journal of Marketing Research* 20 (February 1983): 74–83.

37. Cyndee Miller, 'Scotland to U.S.: "This Tennent's for you"', *Marketing News* (29 August 1994): 26.

38. Satya Menon and Barbara E. Kahn, 'The impact of context on variety seeking in product choices', *Journal of Consumer Research* 22 (December 1995): 285–95; Barbara E. Kahn and Alice M. Isen, 'The influence of positive affect on variety seeking among safe, enjoyable products', *Journal of Consumer Research* 20 (September 1993): 257–70.

39. J. Jeffrey Inman, 'The Role of Sensory-Specific Satiety in Consumer Variety Seeking Among Flavors' (unpublished manuscript, A.C. Nielsen Center for Marketing Research, University of Wisconsin-Madison, July 1999).

40. Michael Laroche, Chankon Kim and Lianxi Zhou, 'Brand familiarity and confidence as determinants of purchase intention: An empirical test in a multiple brand context', *Journal of Business Research* 37 (1996): 115–20.

41. Barbara E. Kahn, 'Understanding Variety-Seeking Behavior From a Marketing Perspective', unpublished manuscript, University of Pennsylvania, University Park, 1991; Leigh McAlister and Edgar A. Pessemier, 'Variety-seeking behavior: An interdisciplinary review', *Journal of Consumer Research* 9 (December 1982): 311–22; Fred M. Feinberg, Barbara E. Kahn and Leigh McAlister, 'Market share response when consumers seek variety', *Journal of Marketing Research* 29 (May 1992): 228–37; Kahn and Isen, 'The influence of positive affect on variety seeking among safe, enjoyable products'.

42. Gary Belsky, 'Why smart people make major money mistakes', *Money* (July 1995): 76; Richard Thaler and Eric J. Johnson, 'Gambling with the house money or trying to break even: The effects of prior outcomes on risky choice', *Management Science* 36 (June 1990): 643–60; Richard Thaler, 'Mental accounting and consumer choice', *Marketing Science* 4 (Summer 1985): 199–214.

43. Daniel Kahneman and Amos Tversky, 'Prospect theory: An analysis of decision under risk,' *Econometrica* 47 (March 1979): 263–91; Timothy B. Heath, Subimal Chatterjee and Karen Russo France, 'Mental accounting and changes in price: The frame dependence of reference dependence', *Journal of Consumer Research* 22(1) (June 1995): 90–7.

44. Quoted in Thaler, 'Mental accounting and consumer choice': 206.

45. Girish N. Punj and Richard Staelin, 'A model of consumer search behavior for new automobiles', *Journal of Consumer Research* 9 (March 1983): 366–80.

46. Cobb and Hoyer, 'Direct observation of search behavior'; Moore and Lehmann, 'Individual differences in search behavior for a nondurable'; Punj and Staelin, 'A model of consumer search behavior for new automobiles'.

47. Judi Strebel, Tulin Erdem and Joffre Swait, 'Consumer search in high technology markets: Exploring the use of traditional information channels', *Journal of Consumer Psychology* 14(1&2) (2004): 96–104.

48. James R. Bettman and C. Whan Park, 'Effects of prior knowledge and experience and phase of the choice process on consumer decision processes: A protocol analysis', *Journal of Consumer Research* 7 (December 1980): 234–48.

49. Alba and Hutchinson, 'Dimensions of consumer expertise'; Bettman and Park, 'Effects of prior knowledge and experience and phase of the choice process on consumer decision processes'; Merrie Brucks, 'The effects of product class knowledge on information search behavior', *Journal of Consumer Research* 12 (June 1985): 1–16; Joel E. Urbany, Peter R. Dickson and William L. Wilkie, 'Buyer uncertainty and information search', *Journal of Consumer Research* 16 (September 1989): 208–15.

50. Alexander Fedorikhin and Catherine A. Cole, 'Mood effects on attitudes, perceived risk and choice: Moderators and mediators', *Journal of Consumer Psychology*, 14(1&2) (2004): 2–12.

51. For a discussion of 'collective risk', where consumers experience a reduction in perceived risk by sharing their exposure with others who are also using the product or service, see an analysis of Hotline, an online file-sharing community in Markus Geisler, 'Collective Risk', working paper, Northwestern University, March 2003.

52. Cyndee Miller, 'HIV kits target untested market', *Marketing News* (20 January 1997): 1, 11.

53. Mary Frances Luce, James R. Bettman and John W. Payne, 'Choice processing in emotionally difficult decisions', *Journal of Experimental Psychology: Learning, Memory, and Cognition* 23 (March 1997): 384–405; example provided by Prof. James Bettman, personal communication, 17 December 1997.

54. John R. Hauser and Birger Wernerfelt, 'An evaluation cost model of consideration sets', *Journal of Consumer Research* 16 (March 1990): 393–408.

55. Robert J. Sutton, 'Using empirical data to investigate the likelihood of brands being admitted or readmitted into an established evoked set', *Journal of the Academy of Marketing Science* 15 (Fall 1987): 82.

56. Cyndee Miller, 'Hemp is latest buzzword', *Marketing News* (17 March 1997): 1.

57. Alba and Hutchinson, 'Dimensions of consumer expertise'; Joel B. Cohen and Kunal Basu, 'Alternative models of categorization: Toward a contingent processing framework', *Journal of Consumer Research* 13 (March 1987): 455–72.

58. Robert M. McMath, 'The perils of typecasting', *American Demographics* (February 1997): 60.

59. Emily Nelson, 'Moistened toilet paper wipes out after launch for Kimberly-Clark', *The Wall Street Journal Interactive Edition* (15 April 2002).

60. Eleanor Rosch, 'Principles of Categorization', in E. Rosch and B.B. Lloyd, eds, *Recognition and Categorization* (Hillsdale, NJ: Erlbaum, 1978).

61. Michael R. Solomon, 'Mapping product constellations: A social categorization approach to symbolic consumption', *Psychology and Marketing* 5(3) (1988): 233–58.

62. McMath, 'The perils of typecasting'.
63. Elizabeth C. Hirschman and Michael R. Solomon, 'Competition and Cooperation Among Culture Production Systems', in Ronald F. Bush and Shelby D. Hunt, eds, *Marketing Theory: Philosophy of Science Perspectives* (Chicago: American Marketing Association, 1982): 269–72.
64. Michael D. Johnson, 'The differential processing of product category and noncomparable choice alternatives', *Journal of Consumer Research* 16 (December 1989): 300–9.
65. Mita Sujan, 'Consumer knowledge: Effects on evaluation strategies mediating consumer judgments', *Journal of Consumer Research* 12 (June 1985): 31–46.
66. Rosch, 'Principles of categorization'.
67. Joan Meyers-Levy and Alice M. Tybout, 'Schema congruity as a basis for product evaluation', *Journal of Consumer Research* 16 (June 1989): 39–55.
68. Mita Sujan and James R. Bettman, 'The effects of brand positioning strategies on consumers' brand and category perceptions: Some insights from schema research', *Journal of Marketing Research* 26 (November 1989): 454–67.
69. See William P. Putsis Jr. and Narasimhan Srinivasan, 'Buying or just browsing? The duration of purchase deliberation', *Journal of Marketing Research* 31 (August 1994): 393–402.
70. Robert E. Smith, 'Integrating information from advertising and trial: Processes and effects on consumer response to product information', *Journal of Marketing Research* 30 (May 1993): 204–19.
71. Jack Trout, 'Marketing in tough times', *Boardroom Reports* 2 (October 1992): 8.
72. Stuart Elliott, 'Pepsi-Cola to stamp dates for freshness on soda cans', *New York Times* (31 March 1994): D1; Emily DeNitto, 'Pepsi's gamble hits freshness dating jackpot', *Advertising Age* (19 September 1994): 50.
73. Amna Kirmani and Peter Wright, 'Procedural learning, consumer decision making and marketing communication', *Marketing Letters* 4(1) (1993): 39–48.
74. Michael Porter, *Competitive Advantage* (New York: Free Press, 1985).
75. Material in this section adapted from Michael R. Solomon and Elnora W. Stuart, *Welcome to Marketing.com: The Brave New World of E-Commerce* (Englewood Cliffs, NJ: Prentice Hall, 2001).
76. Phil Patton, 'Buy here, and we'll tell you what you like', *The New York Times on the Web* (22 September 1999).
77. Robert A. Baron, *Psychology: The Essential Science* (Boston: Allyn & Bacon, 1989); Valerie S. Folkes, 'The availability heuristic and perceived risk', *Journal of Consumer Research* 15 (June 1989): 13–23; Daniel Kahneman and Amos Tversky, 'Prospect theory: An analysis of decision under risk', *Econometrica* 47 (1979): 263–91.
78. Wayne D. Hoyer, 'An examination of consumer decision making for a common repeat purchase product', *Journal of Consumer Research* 11 (December 1984): 822–9; Calvin P. Duncan, 'Consumer Market Beliefs: A Review of the Literature and an Agenda for Future Research,' in Marvin E. Goldberg, Gerald Gorn and Richard W. Pollay, eds, *Advances in Consumer Research* 17 (Provo, UT: Association for Consumer Research, 1990): 729–35; Frank Alpert, 'Consumer market beliefs and their managerial implications: An empirical examination', *Journal of Consumer Marketing* 10(2) (1993): 56–70.
79. Michael R. Solomon, Sarah Drenan and Chester A. Insko, 'Popular induction: When is consensus information informative?', *Journal of Personality* 49(2) (1981): 212–24.
80. Folkes, 'The availability heuristic and perceived risk'.
81. Beales et al., 'Consumer search and public policy'.
82. Gary T. Ford and Ruth Ann Smith, 'Inferential beliefs in consumer evaluations: An assessment of alternative processing strategies', *Journal of Consumer Research* 14 (December 1987): 363–71; Deborah Roedder John, Carol A. Scott and James R. Bettman, 'Sampling data for covariation assessment: The effects of prior beliefs on search patterns', *Journal of Consumer Research* 13 (June 1986): 38–47; Gary L. Sullivan and Kenneth J. Berger, 'An investigation of the determinants of cue utilization', *Psychology and Marketing* 4 (Spring 1987): 63–74.
83. John et al., 'Sampling data for covariation assessment'.
84. Duncan, 'Consumer market beliefs'.
85. Chr. Hjorth-Andersen, 'Price as a risk indicator', *Journal of Consumer Policy* 10 (1987): 267–81.
86. David M. Gardner, 'Is there a generalized price–quality relationship?', *Journal of Marketing Research* 8 (May 1971): 241–3; Kent B. Monroe, 'Buyers' subjective perceptions of price', *Journal of Marketing Research* 10 (1973): 70–80.
87. Durairaj Maheswaran, 'Country of origin as a stereotype: Effects of consumer expertise and attribute strength on product evaluations', *Journal of Consumer Research* 21 (September 1994): 354–65; Ingrid M. Martin and Sevgin Eroglu, 'Measuring a multi-dimensional construct: Country image', *Journal of Business Research* 28 (1993): 191–210; Richard Ettenson, Janet Wagner and Gary Gaeth, 'Evaluating the effect of country of origin and the "Made in the U.S.A." Campaign: A conjoint approach', *Journal of Retailing* 64 (Spring 1988): 85–100; C. Min Han and Vern Terpstra, 'Country-of-origin effects for uni-national and bi-national products', *Journal of International Business* 19 (Summer 1988): 235–55; Michelle A. Morganosky and Michelle M. Lazarde, 'Foreign-made apparel: Influences on consumers' perceptions of brand and store quality', *International Journal of Advertising* 6 (Fall 1987): 339–48.
88. See Richard Jackson Harris, Bettina Garner-Earl, Sara J. Sprick and Collette Carroll, 'Effects of foreign product names and country-of-origin attributions on advertisement evaluations', *Psychology and Marketing* 11 (March/April 1994): 129–45; Terence A. Shimp, Saeed Samiee and Thomas J. Madden, 'Countries and their products: A cognitive structure perspective', *Journal of the Academy of Marketing Science* 21 (Fall 1993): 323–30.
89. 'EU steps up global battle over Parma ham, Roquefort cheese' *NYT online* (28 August 2003).
90. Durairaj Maheswaran, 'Country of origin as a stereotype: Effects of consumer expertise and attribute strength on product evaluations', *Journal of Consumer Research* 21 (September 1994): 354–65.
91. Joshua Levine, 'The dance drink', *Forbes* (12 September 1994): 232.
92. Caroline K. Lego, Natalie T. Wood, Stephanie L. McFee and Michael R. Solomon, 'A thirst for the real thing in

themed retail environments: Consuming authenticity in Irish pubs', *Journal of Foodservice Business Research* 5(2) (2003): 61–75.

93. Quoted in Howard Banks, 'We'll provide the shillelaghs', *Forbes* 68(2) (8 April 1996): 72; see also Brendan I. Koerner, 'Spreading the taste of Ireland', *U.S. News and World Report* (24 February 1997): 15. For an ethnographic study of the 'authenticity' of Irish pubs, see Michael R. Solomon, Caroline K. Lego, Natalie T. Quilty and Stephanie L. Wright, 'A thirst for the real thing in themed retail environments: Consuming authenticity in Irish pubs', *Proceedings of the Society for Marketing Advances* (2000).

94. *Images of Europe: A Survey of Japanese Attitudes Toward European Products*, Report prepared by Dentsu Inc. for the Commission of the European Communities, Brussels, 1994.

95. Sung-Tai Hong and Robert S. Wyer Jr., 'Effects of country-of-origin and product-attribute information on product evaluation: An information processing perspective', *Journal of Consumer Research* 16 (September 1989): 175–87; Marjorie Wall, John Liefeld and Louise A. Heslop, 'Impact of country-of-origin cues on consumer judgments in multi-cue situations: A covariance analysis', *Journal of the Academy of Marketing Science* 19(2) (1991): 105–13.

96. Wai-Kwan Li and Robert S. Wyer Jr., 'The role of country of origin in product evaluations: Informational and standard-of-comparison effects', *Journal of Consumer Psychology* 3(2) (1994): 187–212.

97. Maheswaran, 'Country of origin as a stereotype'.

98. Items excerpted from Terence A. Shimp and Subhash Sharma, 'Consumer ethnocentrism: Construction and validation of the CETSCALE', *Journal of Marketing Research* 24 (August 1987): 282.

99. Roger Ricklefs, 'Canada fights to fend off American tastes and tunes', *The Wall Street Journal Interactive Edition* (24 September 1998).

100. Adam Bryant, 'Message in a beer bottle', *Newsweek* (29 May 2000): 43.

101. Teodoro Luque-Martinez, Jose-Angel Ibanez-Zapata and Salvador del Barrio-Garcia, 'Consumer ethnocentrism measurement – an assessment of the reliability and validity of the CETSCALE in Spain', *European Journal of Marketing* 34(11/12) (2000): 1353ff.

102. Richard W. Stevenson, 'The brands with billion-dollar names', *New York Times* (28 October 1988): A1.

103. Douglas B. Holt, *How Brands Become Icons: The Principles of Cultural Branding* (Boston: Harvard Business School Press, 2004).

104. Ronald Alsop, 'Enduring brands hold their allure by sticking close to their roots', *The Wall Street Journal*, centennial edn (1989): B4.

105. 'Assessing brands: Broad, deep, long and heavy', *The Economist* (16 November 1996): 84–5.

106. *Business Week*/Interbrand's Annual Ranking of 'The best global brands', Press Release *BusinessWeekOnline* archive www.businessweek.com (22 July 2004).

107. 'What's in a name?', *The Economist* (27 August 1988): 62.

108. Stuart Elliott, 'What's in a name? Perhaps billions', *New York Times* (12 August 1992): D6.

109. Interbrand, cited in Dan Roberts, 'Is the world falling out of love with US brands?' *Financial Times* (30 December 2004) http://news.ft.com/cms/s/502f6994-59d5-11d9-ba09-00000e2511c8.html.

110. Roberts, 'Is the world falling out of love with US brands?'

111. Ibid.

112. Ibid.

113. Jacob Jacoby and Robert Chestnut, *Brand Loyalty: Measurement and Management* (New York: Wiley, 1978).

114. Anne B. Fisher, 'Coke's brand loyalty lesson', *Fortune* (5 August 1985): 44.

115. Jacoby and Chestnut, *Brand Loyalty*.

116. Ronald Alsop, 'Brand loyalty is rarely blind loyalty', *The Wall Street Journal* (October 19, 1989): B1.

117. Betsy Morris, 'The brand's the thing', *Fortune* (4 March 1996): 72 (8).

118. Hope Jensen Schau and Mary C. Gilly, 'We are what we post: The presentation of self in personal webspace', *Journal of Consumer Research* 30 (December 2003): 385–404; Hope Schau, Temple University, personal communication, March 2003.

119. C. Whan Park, 'The effect of individual and situation-related factors on consumer selection of judgmental models', *Journal of Marketing Research* 13 (May 1976): 144–51.

120. Joseph W. Alba and Howard Marmorstein, 'The effects of frequency knowledge on consumer decision making', *Journal of Consumer Research* 14 (June 1987): 14–25.

SHOPPING, BUYING, EVALUATING AND DISPOSING

Helmut's old VW barely resembled a car any more. His friends at the last Green Party meeting commented on the fading Greenpeace sticker on the windscreen and the growing oil spots on the road under his old car. They had also discussed with great enthusiasm the new ecologically sound hybrid cars soon to be introduced on the German market and suggested that Helmut ought to think about getting one. His colleagues at the bank where he worked joked about his car making theirs look bad in the staff car park. With the coming of spring Helmut's heart turned to love – and sports cars. After much encouragement from his work colleagues, he replaced his faithful old Beetle with a new BMW. Both he and his friends were elated. The staff car park was much improved and his problems were over – or so he thought. The old VW was still in his garage and he could not decide whether to sell it for a few hundred euros which he could use now, or have the car recycled at a significant cost. The next Green Party meeting was at hand and, recalling their advice, he wondered whether he should have opted for a less stylish, hybrid car. His anxiety was so high about being 'exposed' as a closet yuppie that he even considered driving the old VW to the meeting, if it would start. He could not help wondering whether he had done the right thing in buying the BMW, but it seemed like such a good idea at the time.

SUZANNE BECKMANN, Copenhagen Business School

■ INTRODUCTION

Helmut's dilemma highlights the importance of the purchase situation (it is spring, one wants to feel more 'seductive') and the post-purchase evaluation (was it the right choice?). On top of this, the experience of service linked to the act of purchasing and evaluating the purchase play central roles. In a British poll, 80 per cent of consumers said that they would change suppliers if they were unhappy with the service; and 86 per cent said that they expected better service currently than they did five years ago.[1] Furthermore, the issue of environmental friendliness is becoming more and more important for many purchase decisions, just as it was for Helmut, even though environmentalism in this case was overruled by other desires.

Helmut's experience illustrates some of the concepts to be discussed in this chapter. Making a purchase is often not a simple, routine matter of going to a shop and choosing something. As illustrated in Figure 9.1, a consumer's choices are affected by many personal factors, such as mood, time pressure and the particular situation or context for which the product is needed. In some situations, like the purchase of a car or a home, the salesperson or the reference group (which we will discuss in Chapter 10) play a pivotal role in the final choice. And today people are using the Web to arm themselves with product and price information before they even enter a car dealership or a shop (note Daniel's preliminary search for televisions via the internet in the opening vignette of Chapter 8), which puts added pressure on retailers to deliver the value they expect.

The store environment also exerts a major influence: shopping is like a stage performance, with the customer involved either as a member of the audience or as an active participant. The quality of the performance is affected by the other *cast members* (salespeople or other shoppers), as well as by the *setting* of the play (the image of a particular store and the 'feeling' it imparts) and *props* (store fittings and promotional material which try to influence the shopper's decisions).

In addition, the consumer activity per se occurs *after* a product has been purchased and brought home. After using a product, the consumer must decide whether he or she is satisfied with it. The satisfaction process is especially important to marketers, who realize that the key to success is not selling a product once, but rather forging a relationship with the consumer so that he or she will continue to buy in the future. Finally, just as Helmut thought about the resale of his car, we must also consider how consumers go about disposing of products and how secondary markets (e.g. second-hand car dealers) often play a pivotal role in product acquisition. This chapter considers many issues related to purchase and post-purchase phenomena.

Figure 9.1 Issues related to purchase and post-purchase activities

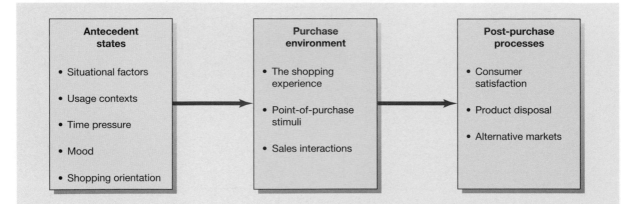

Antecedent states	Purchase environment	Post-purchase processes
• Situational factors	• The shopping experience	• Consumer satisfaction
• Usage contexts	• Point-of-purchase stimuli	• Product disposal
• Time pressure	• Sales interactions	• Alternative markets
• Mood		
• Shopping orientation		

■ ANTECEDENT STATES

A person's mood or physiological condition at the time of purchase can have a major impact on what is bought and can also affect how products are evaluated.[2] One reason is that behaviour is directed towards certain goal states, as was discussed in Chapter 3. In addition, the person's particular social identity, or the role that is being played at a given time, will be influential.[3]

Situational effects: mood and consumption situations

A consumer's mood will have an impact on purchase decisions. For example, stress can reduce a consumer's information-processing and problem-solving abilities.[4] Two dimensions determine whether a shopper will react positively or negatively to a store environment: *pleasure* and *arousal*. A person can enjoy or not enjoy a situation, and he or she can feel stimulated or not. As Figure 9.2 indicates, different combinations of pleasure and arousal levels result in a variety of emotional states. For example, an arousing situation can be either distressing or exciting, depending on whether the context is positive or negative (e.g. a street riot vs. a street festival). Maintaining an upbeat mood in a pleasant context is one factor behind the success of theme parks such as Disneyland, which try to provide consistent doses of carefully calculated stimulation to patrons.[5]

A specific mood is some combination of these two factors. For example, the state of happiness is high in pleasantness and moderate in arousal, while elation would be high on both dimensions.[6] In general, a mood state (either positive or negative) biases judgements of products and services in that direction.[7] Put simply, consumers like things better when they are in a good mood (this may explain the popularity of the business lunch!).

Moods can be affected by store design, the weather or other factors specific to the consumer. In addition, music and television programming can affect mood; this has important consequences for commercials.[8] When consumers hear happy music or watch happy programmes, they have more positive reactions to commercials and products, especially when the marketing appeals are aimed at arousing emotional reactions.[9]

Figure 9.2 Dimensions of emotional states

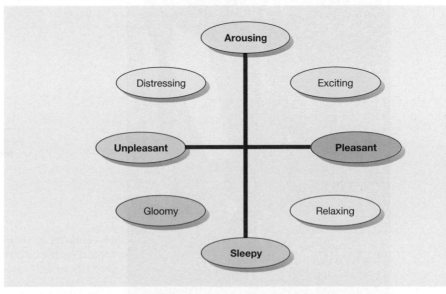

Source: James Russell and Geraldine Pratt, 'A description of the affective quality attributed to environment', *Journal of Personality and Social Psychology* 38 (August 1980): 311-22.

A *consumption situation* is defined by factors over and above characteristics of the person and of the product. Situational effects can be behavioural (such as entertaining friends) or perceptual (being depressed, or feeling pressed for time).[10] Common sense tells us that people tailor their purchases to specific occasions or that the way we feel at a specific time affects what we feel like buying or doing.

One reason for this variability is that the role a person plays at any time is partly determined by his or her *situational self-image*: 'Who am I right now?' (see also Chapter 7).[11] Someone trying to impress his girlfriend by playing the role of 'man about town' may spend more lavishly, ordering champagne rather than beer and buying flowers – purchases he would never consider when he is with his male friends in a pub and playing the role of 'one of the boys'. As this example demonstrates, knowledge of what consumers are doing at the time a product is consumed may improve predictions of product and brand choice.[12] As one renowned European consumer researcher has pointed out, the question '*where* is consumer behaviour?' has been surprisingly little investigated.[13]

marketing pitfall

Sometimes a marketing strategy can work too well. This was the case with Nabisco's Grey Poupon mustard brand, which the company has successfully positioned as a premium product in the USA. The problem was that consumers tend to save the brand for special occasions rather than spreading the mustard on just any old sandwich.

Grey Poupon's 'special' cachet was due to its long-running advertising campaign, in which toffee-nosed aristocrats passed the mustard through the windows of their limousines. The campaign is so well known that the familiar tag line 'Pardon me, would you have any Grey Poupon?' was even repeated in the film *Wayne's World*.

To dig themselves out of this situational hole, the brand's advertising agency developed a new advertising campaign, with magazine ads featuring simpler occasions, such as a picnic.[14]

This Burberry ad shows the situational context for the consumption of their products, notably in social settings and by upper class, young adult consumers.
The Advertising Archives

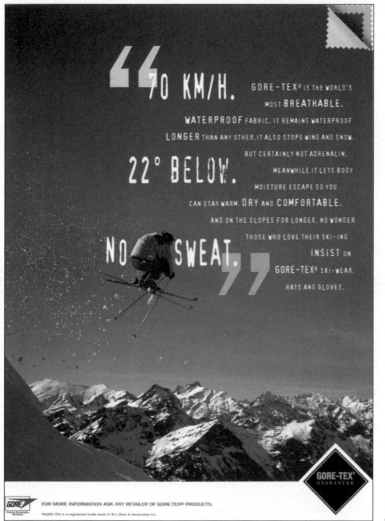

Clothing choices often are heavily influenced by the situation in which they need to be worn.

The Advertising Archives

Situational segmentation

By systematically identifying important usage situations, market segmentation strategies can be developed to position products that will meet the specific needs arising from these situations. Many product categories are amenable to this form of segmentation. For example, consumers' furniture choices are often tailored to specific settings. We prefer different styles for a town house, country cottage, or an executive suite. The South African ad for Volkswagen on p. 304 emphasizes the versatility of the Volkswagen people carrier bus for different situations.[15]

Table 9.1 gives one example of how situations can be used to fine-tune a segmentation strategy. By listing the major contexts in which a product is used (e.g. skiing and sunbathing for a suntan lotion) and the different users of the product, a matrix can be constructed that identifies specific product features that should be emphasized for each situation. For example, during the summer a lotion manufacturer might promote the fact that the bottle floats and is hard to lose, but promote its non-freezing formula during the winter season. Furthermore, our brand loyalty may be dependent on the situation. French research has demonstrated how our brand loyalty within product categories such as fruit juice, cheese or coffee depends on whether our situation is one of the following: shopping for a party for friends, running out of the product ourselves, or the shop having run out of stock.[16]

This South African ad for Volkswagen emphasizes that brand criteria can differ depending upon the situation in which the product will be used.

Courtesy of Volkswagen of South Africa

Table 9.1 A person-situation segmentation matrix for suntan lotion

Situation	Young children Fair skin Dark skin	Teenagers Fair skin Dark skin	Adult women Fair skin Dark skin	Adult men Fair skin Dark skin	Benefits/features
Beach/boat sunbathing	Combined insect repellent		Summer perfume		a. Product serves as windburn protection b. Formula and container can stand heat c. Container floats and is distinctive (not easily lost)
Home-poolside sunbathing			Combined moisturizer		a. Product has large pump dispenser b. Product won't stain wood, concrete, furnishings
Sunlamp bathing			Combined moisturizer and massage oil		a. Product is designed specifically for type of lamp b. Product has an artificial tanning ingredient
Snow skiing			Winter perfume		a. Product provides special protection from special light rays and weather b. Product has antifreeze formula
Person benefit/ features	Special protection a. Protection is critical b. Formula is non-poisonous	Special protection a. Product fits in jeans pocket b. Product used by opinion leaders	Special protection Female perfume	Special protection Male perfume	

Source: Adapted from Peter R. Dickson, 'Person-situation: Segmentation's missing link', *Journal of Marketing* 46 (Fall 1982): 62.

A recent study of 2,500 online customers[17] identified 'occasion-based segmentation'. Using variables such as length of session, time spent on each page of the website, and the user's familiarity with the site, seven different occasions were identified which could be classified into two groups. Firstly, Loitering, Information Please and Surfing – this group spent between 33 and 70 minutes online, and were more likely to purchase. The second group, Quickies, Just the Facts, Single Mission and Do It Again, remained online for much shorter periods. 'Depending on the occasion, some users will be far more open to a range of messages, while others will pay attention only to highly targeted messages. Others will simply whizz by and ignore anything unrelated to what they are doing. So it's only by decoding the type of occasion – such as gathering product information – that marketers can fully harness the web's interactive powers by aiming messages and offers at the right place at the right time.'[18]

■ SOCIAL AND PHYSICAL SURROUNDINGS

A consumer's physical and social environment can make a big difference in affecting his or her motives for product purchase and usage and also affect how he or she evaluates products. Important cues include the person's physical surroundings, as well as the amount and type of other consumers also present in that situation. Dimensions of the physical environment, such as decor, smells and even temperature can significantly influence consumption. One study found that the use of scents in the retail environment can increase the pleasure and hedonic values derived from shopping.[19]

Many stores and services (like airlines) try to differentiate themselves in terms of the physical environments they offer, touting such amenities as comfort and space.

Courtesy of Qantas Airlines and M&C Saatchi

▶ In addition to physical cues, many of a consumer's purchase decisions are significantly affected by the groups or social settings in which these occur (as we shall see in the next chapter). In some cases, the presence or absence of **co-consumers**, the other patrons in a setting, can be a determinant attribute (see the discussion in Chapter 8) and function as a product attribute, as when an exclusive resort or boutique promises to provide privacy to privileged customers. At other times, the presence of others can have positive value. A sparsely attended football match or an empty bar can be depressing sights.

The presence of large numbers of people in a consumer environment increases arousal levels, so a consumer's subjective experience of a setting tends to be more intense. This polarization, however, can be both positive and negative. While the experience of other people creates a state of arousal, the consumer's actual experience depends on his or her *interpretation of* and *reaction to* this arousal. Crowding may result in avoidance (leaving the store earlier), aggressiveness (rushing others), opportunism (using the extra time to find bargains) or self-blame (for coming into the store at the wrong hour).[20] It is important, therefore, to distinguish between *density* and *crowding* for this reason. Density refers to the actual number of people occupying a space, while the psychological state of crowding exists only if a negative affective state occurs as a result of this density.[21] For example, 100 students packed into a classroom designed for 75 may result in an unpleasant situation for all concerned, but the same number of people jammed together at a party occupying a room of the same size might just make for a great party.

In addition, the *type* of consumers who patronize a store or service can serve as a store attribute; and the *type* of consumers who use a product can influence evaluations. We may infer something about a store by examining its customers. For this reason, some restaurants require men to wear a jacket for dinner, and bouncers at some 'hot' nightspots hand-pick patrons from the queue based on whether they have the right 'look' for the club. To paraphrase the comedian Groucho Marx, 'I would never join a club that would have me for a member!'

Temporal factors

Time is one of consumers' most precious and limiting resources. We talk about 'making time' or 'spending time' and we are frequently reminded that 'time is money'. Our perspectives on time can affect many stages of decision-making and consumption, such as needs that are stimulated, the amount of information search we undertake and so on. Common sense tells us that more careful information search and deliberation occurs when we have the luxury of taking our time. A meticulous shopper who would normally price an item at three different stores before buying might be found sprinting through the shopping centre on Christmas Eve, just before closing time, frantically scooping up anything left on the shelves that might serve as a last-minute gift.

Economic time

Time is an economic variable; it is a resource that must be divided among activities.[22] Consumers try to maximize satisfaction by allocating time to the appropriate combination of tasks. Of course, people's allocation decisions differ; we all know people who seem to play all of the time, and others who are workaholics. An individual's priorities
▶ determine his or her **time style**.[23] Time style, it has been suggested, incorporates such dimensions as economic time, past orientation, future orientation, time submissiveness and time anxiety.[24] Recent research identified four dimensions of time: social, temporal, planning, and polychromic orientation. The social dimension refers to individuals' categorization of time as either 'time for me' or 'time with/for others'. The temporal orientation depicts the relative significance individuals attach to past, present or future. The planning orientation dimension alludes to different time management styles varying on a continuum from analytic to spontaneous. And lastly, polychromic orientation denotes

doing-one-thing-at-a-time versus multitasking time styles. By viewing time as a multi-dimensional construct, the richness and complexity of the nature and interactions of four different time style dimensions were revealed. These multiple dimensions of time style push and pull individuals in different directions, which ultimately leads to psychological conflicts. From these dimensions, five emergent symbolic metaphors of time were proposed,[25] which reflected US women participants' perspective on time and the process by which the perspective was created:

1 '*Time is a pressure cooker*: Women who personify this metaphor are usually analytic in their planning, other oriented, and monochronic in their time styles. They treat shopping in a methodical manner and they often feel under pressure and in conflict.

2 *Time is a map*: Women who exemplify this metaphor are usually analytic planners, have a future temporal orientation and a polychronic time style. They often engage in extensive information search and in comparison shopping.

3 *Time is a mirror*: Women who come under this metaphor are also analytic planners and have a polychromic orientation. However, they have a past temporal orientation. Due to their risk averseness in time use, these women are usually loyal to products and services they know and trust.

4 *Time is a river*: Women whose time styles can be described through this metaphor are usually spontaneous in their planning orientation and have a present focus. They go on unplanned, short and frequent shopping trips undertaken on impulse.

5 *Time is feast*: These women are analytic planners who have a present temporal orientation. They view time as something to be consumed in the pursuit of sensory pleasure and gratification and, hence, they are motivated by hedonic and variety seeking desires in their consumption behavior.'

Some of the implications for consumer behaviour which flowed from this research[26] included that:

1 'There are major differences in individuals' attitudes and behaviors in relation to shopping across the five temporal metaphors.

2 These symbolic metaphors are also associated with differences in individuals' consumption of leisure, food habits, expenditure of time and money on keeping up with appearances.

3 In the domain of food habits, women who exemplify time as a feast metaphor demonstrated preference for fresh and novel ingredients, while women that fit with the mirror metaphor were more inclined towards convenience food choices.

4 Individuals who placed emphasis on keeping up with their appearances coupled with their social orientation were found to spend more time and money on their presentation of self and their material possessions.'

Many consumers believe they are more pressed for time than ever before, a feeling called **time poverty**. This feeling may, however, be due more to perception than to fact. People may simply have more options for spending their time and feel pressured by the weight of it all. The average working day at the turn of the century was 10 hours (6 days per week), and women did 27 hours of housework per week, compared to under 5 hours now. Of course, one reason for this difference is that men are sharing these burdens more; and in some families maintaining an absolutely spotless home may not be as important as it used to be.[27]

This sense of *time poverty* has made consumers very responsive to marketing innovations that allow them to save time. More and more companies, and in Denmark even some kindergartens, offer to do the shopping and other daily chores for busy families during working hours, so that the whole evening can be devoted to family activities.

Time poverty is creating opportunities for many new products (like portable soups) that let people multitask.

The Advertising Archives

New online business concepts based on improved delivery are popping up all over the Web. Delivery of videos, groceries, dry cleaning or developed photos to customers' doors are a few of the new time-saving online possibilities.[28] In a British pilot project, the Safeway supermarket chain provided 200 consumers with personal organizers to create shopping lists. By using frequent shopper data, the device can suggest items to replenish based on past purchase patterns. A 'smart refrigerator' developed by Frigidaire comes with a bar-code scanner so that consumers can order a fresh bottle of salad dressing, ketchup or other frequently used items by scanning the used container across the door. The refrigerator picks up the bar code and automatically orders a fresh supply from the supermarket (see also the Electrolux refrigerator described in Chapter 15).[29] In Hong Kong rush-hour commuters no longer need to stand and queue to buy Underground tickets. Instead, a scanner automatically reads an Octopus card and automatically deducts the fare from their account. The card doesn't even require contact to be read, so women can just pass their entire handbag over the scanner and race to catch their trains.[30]

net profit

With the increase in time poverty, researchers are also noting a rise in *polychronic activity*, where consumers do more than one thing at a time.[31] One area where this type of activity is especially prevalent is eating. Many consumers often do not allocate a specific time to dining, but do something else while eating. As one food industry executive commented, 'We've moved beyond grazing and into gulping.'[32] On the other hand, counter-trends of slow food are also found among other segments. A new 'slow food movement' originating in Italy and spreading via France to several European countries and even the United States witnesses a cultural resistance to the disappearance of cooking and eating a meal as a social event.[33]

Psychological time

The psychological dimension of time, or how it is experienced, is an important actor in ▶ **queuing theory**. A consumer's experience of waiting can radically influence his or her perceptions of service quality. Although we assume that something must be good if we have to wait for it, the negative feelings aroused by long waits can quickly deter customers.[34] For example, it seems that the longer the wait, the more we like to wait alone rather than with others, presumably because for a short wait it is pleasant to have others to talk to, but the longer the waiting time, the more we perceive our fellow waiters as the main reason for the delay.[35] There are large cross-cultural differences in the acceptance of waiting time. Some 20 per cent of Sicilians consider a waiting time of 30 minutes for a dental appointment reasonable, and the average waiting time at a bank counter is 24 minutes.[36] What do you think?

Marketers have adopted a variety of 'tricks' to minimize psychological waiting time. These techniques range from altering customers' perceptions of a queue's length to providing distractions that divert attention away from waiting.[37] However, one study concluded that differences in queuing systems had only a minor effect on perceived waiting time compared to differences in waiting environment attractiveness and actual waiting time.[38]

- One hotel chain, after receiving numerous complaints about the wait for lifts, installed mirrors near the lift entrances. People's natural tendency to check their appearance reduced complaints, even though the actual waiting time was unchanged.

- Airline passengers often complain of the time they have to wait to claim their baggage. In one airport, it would take them one minute to walk from the plane to the baggage carousel where they would wait seven minutes for their luggage. By changing the layout so that the walk to the carousel took six minutes and bags arrived two minutes after that, complaints were almost entirely eliminated. More and more airlines are introducing 'ticket-less flights' and self-check-in procedures in order to cut costs but also to avoid the annoying queues at the check-in counter.

- Automated check-out cashier registers are being tested in a variety of countries and contexts. One Swedish study found that many customers in both a grocery store and a library embraced the new technique in spite of its 'impersonal character' because they found it easy and quicker to use (after a period of adaptation), even if the actual time saving was not that significant.[39]

multicultural dimensions

Even though the western time concept may become more and more dominant, at least in the international business world, this conception of time is far from universal. Large cultural differences exist in terms of people's time perspectives.[40] Some cultures run on procedural time and ignore the clock completely. People decide to do something 'when the time is right'. Much of the world appears to live on 'event time': for example, in Burundi people might arrange to meet when the cows return from the watering hole, while in Madagascar the response if someone asks how long it takes to get to the market might be 'the time it takes to cook rice'.[41]

Alternatively, in circular or cyclic time, people are governed by natural cycles, such as the regular occurrence of the seasons (a perspective found in many Latino cultures). To these consumers, the notion of the future does not make sense, because that time will be much like the present. Since the concept of future value does not exist, these consumers often prefer to buy an inferior product that is available now to waiting for a better one that will become available later. Also, it is hard to convince people who function on circular time to buy insurance or save for the future.

A social scientist recently compared the pace of life in 31 cities around the world as part of a study of time styles. He and his assistants timed how long it takes pedestrians to walk 60 feet and postal clerks to sell a stamp. Based on these responses, the fastest countries were claimed to be:

1. Switzerland, 2. Ireland, 3. Germany, 4. Japan, 5. Italy

and the slowest countries:

31. Mexico, 30. Indonesia, 29. Brazil, 28. El Salvador, 27. Syria.

Obviously, such national results depend on the actual place of measurement: consider, for example, the difference of Sicilian time compared with Milan time.[42]

Multitasking has become a way of life for many of us.
Hewlett-Packard Development Company, L.P.

The fluidity of time is important for marketers to understand, because we're more likely to be in a consuming mood at some times rather than others. We can identify time categories in terms of when people are likely to be receptive to marketing messages:[43]

- *Flow time*: In a flow state we become so absorbed in an activity we notice nothing else. Not a good time to be hitting people with ads.
- *Occasion time*: Special moments when something monumental occurs, such as a birth or an important job interview. Ads clearly relevant to the situation will be given our undivided attention.
- *Deadline time*: When we're working against the clock. This is the worst time to catch someone's attention.
- *Leisure time*: During down time, we are more likely to notice ads and perhaps try new things.
- *Time to kill*: Waiting for something to happen such as catching a plane or sitting in a waiting room. This is bonus time, where we feel we have the luxury to focus on extraneous things. As a result we are more receptive to commercial messages, even for products we don't normally use.

Social time

Social time has been proposed as an important but overlooked time dimension in consumer behaviour.[44] Social time refers to the time in relation to social processes and rhythms and schedules in society. It takes into account how determined our lives are by interrelated temporal phenomena, such as working hours, opening hours, eating hours and other institutionalized schedules.

To most Western consumers, time is something that is neatly compartmentalized: we wake up in the morning, go to school or work, come home, eat, go out, go to bed, then do it all over again. This perspective is called linear separable time (or Christian time): events proceed in an orderly sequence and different times are well defined: 'There's a time and a place for everything.' In this worldwide 'modernized' conception of time, there is a

Figure 9.3 Drawings of time

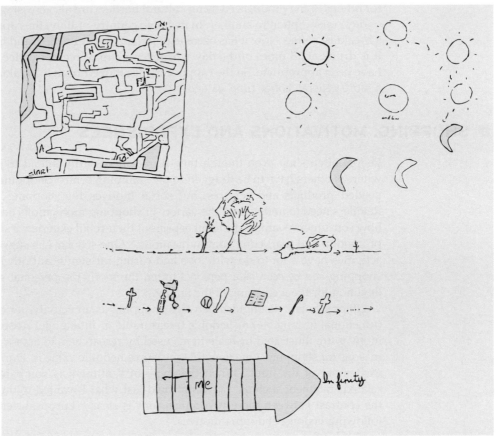

Source: Esther S. Page-Wood, Carol J. Kaufman and Paul M. Lane, 'The Art of Time', *Proceedings of the Academy of Marketing Science* (1990).

clear sense of past, present and future, and the present is preferred to the past, whereas the future is generally rated better than the present.[45] Many activities are performed as the means to an end that will occur at a future point, as when people 'save for a rainy day'.

But even in North European and American cultures, the very linear and compartmentalized chronological time is not hegemonic, as indicated by the above-mentioned psychological time patterns, which call for a more relativistic and complex approach to time structures in societies most influenced by economic time concepts.[46]

When groups of university students were asked to draw a picture of time, the resulting sketches (Figure 9.3) illustrated some of these different temporal perspectives.[47] The drawing at the top represents procedural time: there is a lack of direction from left to right and little sense of past, present and future. The two drawings in the middle denote cyclical time, with regular cycles designated by markers. The bottom drawing represents linear time, with a segmented time line moving from left to right in a well-defined sequence.

marketing pitfall

An emphasis on speed resulted in some serious public relations problems for the American pizza delivery company Domino's Pizza, which guarantees delivery within 30 minutes. Critics claimed that this policy encouraged reckless driving and backed up this charge with some damaging statistics. In 1989, more than a dozen lawsuits, stemming from death or serious injuries caused by delivery people rushing to make the half-hour deadline, were filed against the company. The employee death rate was 50 per 100,000, equal to that suffered in the mining industry.[48] Domino's no longer offers the guarantee.

Some products and services are believed to be appropriate for certain times and not for others. Some products crossing cultural borders are also crossing over from one time of day consumption to another. In its home country of Italy, the cappuccino is known as a breakfast coffee. Now it has become popular all over Europe, and in these new markets it is drunk at all times of the day whenever a cup of regular coffee would traditionally have been appropriate. So the cappuccino has moved from a 'breakfast time' category to a more general 'coffee time' category.[49]

■ SHOPPING: MOTIVATIONS AND EXPERIENCES

People often shop even though they do not necessarily intend to buy anything at all, whereas others have to be dragged to the shopping centre. Shopping is a way to acquire needed products and services, but social motives for shopping also are important. Retailers need to understand the variety of shopping motivations because these all affect how consumers evaluate different aspects of their retail experience such as atmospherics, promotion and marketing communications.[50] One scholar has suggested that shopping activities have a lot to do with love and caring for significant others, to the extent that shopping can be seen as a person's (often the mother's) personal sacrifice of time and devotion for the well-being of the family.[51]

Other scholars distinguish between shopping as an activity performed for utilitarian (functional or tangible) or hedonic (pleasurable or intangible) reasons.[52] These different motives are illustrated by scale items used by researchers to assess people's underlying reasons for shopping. One item that measures hedonic value is 'During the trip, I felt the excitement of the hunt.' When that type of sentiment is compared to a functionally related statement such as 'I accomplished just what I wanted to on this shopping trip', the contrast between these two dimensions is clear.[53] European research identified the following hedonic shopping motives:[54]

- *Anticipated utility*: Desire for innovative products, expectations of benefits or hedonistic states which will be provided by the product to be acquired.
- *Role enactment*: Taking on the culturally prescribed roles regarding the conduct of shopping activity, such as careful product and price comparisons, possibly discussed with other shoppers.
- *Choice optimization*: Desire to find the absolutely best buy.
- *Negotiation*: To seek economic advantages and sports-like pleasure through bargaining interactions with sellers in a 'bazaar atmosphere'.
- *Affiliation*: Shopping centres are a natural place to affiliate. The shopping arcade has become a central meeting place for teenagers. It also represents a controlled, secure environment for other groups, such as the elderly.
- *Power and authority*: Entering a power game with the sales personnel and maybe feeling superior to the personnel. As every salesperson knows, some people love the experience of being waited on, even though they may not necessarily buy anything. One men's clothing salesman offered this advice: 'remember their size, remember what you sold them last time. Make them feel important! If you can make people feel important, they are going to come back. Everybody likes to feel important!'[55]
- *Stimulation*: Searching for new and interesting things offered in the marketplace – shopping just for fun.

Recent US research[56] has identified six broad categories of hedonic shopping motivations:[57]

- '*Adventure shopping*: refers to shopping for stimulation, adventure and the feeling of being in another world.

- *Social shopping*: refers to the enjoyment of shopping with friends and family, socializing while shopping and bonding with others while shopping.
- *Gratification shopping*: involves shopping for stress relief, shopping to alleviate a negative mood and shopping as a special treat to oneself.
- *Idea shopping*: refers to shopping to keep up with trends and new fashions and to see new products and innovations.
- *Role shopping*: reflects the enjoyment that shoppers derive from shopping for others, the influence that this activity has on the shoppers' feelings and moods, and the excitement and intrinsic joy felt by shoppers when finding the perfect gift for others.
- *Value shopping*: refers to shopping for sales, looking for discounts and hunting for bargains.'

Shopping, therefore, is an activity that can be performed for either utilitarian (functional or tangible) or hedonic (pleasurable or intangible) reasons.[58] Women often find emotional fulfilment in the act of buying while men seek to demonstrate their expertise or ability to procure status items.[59] Obviously there are many exceptions to this viewpoint, but nonetheless it's clear that the reasons we shop are more complex than may appear on the surface.

Do people hate to shop or love it? It depends. From the six hedonic motivations above five shopper segments were identified:[60]

- '*Minimalists*: mainly middle-aged males who scored low on all the hedonic motivations apart from value shopping.
- *Gatherers*: mainly younger males who are enthusiastic about information gathering on new products and trends; they scored highly on idea and role shopping.
- *Providers*: mainly middle-aged women, who emphasized role and value shopping in their responses, and who scored low on non-generosity.
- *Enthusiasts*: largely younger women who scored highly across all the hedonic motivations.
- *Traditionalists*: women slightly outnumbered men in this group; and these respondents tended to be younger to middle-aged with moderate scores on most of the hedonic dimensions.'

▶ Consumers can also be segmented in terms of their **shopping orientation**, or general attitudes about shopping. These orientations may vary depending on the particular product categories and store types considered. Many people feel insecure about shopping for a car (many women, for instance, feel quite intimidated by car showrooms), but they may love to browse in record shops. Our feelings about shopping are also influenced by the culture in which we live. Several shopping types have been identified, although the following list does not cover the whole range of possibilities:[61]

- *The economic shopper*: a rational, goal-oriented shopper who is primarily interested in maximizing the value of his or her money.
- *The personalized shopper*: a shopper who tends to form strong attachments to store personnel ('I shop where they know my name').
- *The ethical shopper*: a shopper who likes to help out the underdog and will support local shops rather than chain stores.
- *The apathetic shopper*: one who does not like to shop and sees it as a necessary but unpleasant chore.
- *The recreational shopper*: a person who views shopping as a fun, social activity – a preferred way to spend leisure time.

Given what we said above, however, one type of shopper is missing from this list: *the hate-to-shop shopper*. He or she is emerging from research on a variety of examples of the aversive side of shopping, including the hassle of finding a parking space, shopping with a girl- or boyfriend with completely different shopping motivations, dealing with the fact that just when you've made a purchase you find something better or less expensive, or coping with intruding 'can-I-help-you' sales assistants.[62]

multicultural dimensions

Who loves to shop the most? In a survey of women around the world, over 60 per cent said they enjoy shopping for clothes in every country except Hong Kong, where only 39 per cent responded so positively. The 'Born to Shop' prize goes to Latin Americans: over 80 per cent of women in countries like Brazil and Colombia agree that clothes shopping is a favourite activity. Other high-scoring countries include France, Italy and Japan. In comparison, only 61 per cent of American women said they like or love to go clothes shopping. Reflecting the casual trend that's swept the country in recent years, the survey indicates that American women are more likely to say that they are not as interested in clothing as they used to be, are more willing to be slightly underdressed at a party rather than slightly overdressed, and are more willing to wear one comfortable outfit all day long than change clothes to fit each occasion. Almost everywhere in the world, women agreed that store displays are the most important source of information about clothing. Two exceptions are German women, who ranked fashion magazines highest, and Mexican women, who reported that their families are the best place to learn about what to wear.

Trends in the purchase environment

We see bumper stickers and T-shirts everywhere: 'Shop 'til you drop', 'When the going gets tough, the tough go shopping', 'Born to shop'. Like it or not, shopping is a major activity for many consumers. The competition for shoppers among retailers is getting tougher. Retailers must now offer something extra to lure shoppers, whether that something is excitement or just plain bargains.[63] One prominent trend is the tendency to blur the boundaries between types of outlet. For example, supermarket and hypermarket chains posed a serious threat to the petrol companies by taking larger and larger shares of their market from the mid 1990s onwards (in France, the supermarkets' share was about 50 per cent).[64] In Denmark and other countries, the petrol stations are striking back, increasing their share of the market for daily groceries.

Another European trend is the increase of trade from kiosks (for instance in Greece), and from smaller stores with extended opening hours carrying a small selection of daily goods as well as snack products, sweets, newspapers, etc., sometimes more or less like the 7–11 concept imported from the United States. In many countries, such kiosks are well established and are often run by Middle Eastern or North African immigrants. But in countries such as Finland, where the introduction of kiosks is more recent, it has created a whole new situation for a certain part of the retail system.[65]

In order to be able to compete in the European single market, many retail chains have undergone an internationalization process. For example, of the top 25 European retail chains of daily goods, only one (no. 25) is not internationalized or at least participating in an international network of cooperating chains. The ten biggest companies control 30 per cent of the turnover in daily goods in Europe, and the concentration is growing.[66]

Store loyalty

In this turbulent environment, store-loyal consumers are highly valued by retailers. They will routinely visit a small set of stores without considering others or doing much in the

way of comparative pre-purchase searching. However, consumers now have an abundance of choices regarding where to shop, including the electronic alternatives. For this
reason, people tend not to be as store-loyal as they once were.[67] In Great Britain, the retail
chain Tesco was the biggest spender on marketing among British retailers in 1990–4.
Together with the introduction of a customer loyalty's card, their marketing strategy helped
them to take over from their rival Sainsbury's as the biggest British retailer. Sainsbury's
finally gave up its initial resistance to the introduction of loyalty cards in 1996. Their new
card became an instant success: between June and August of that year they issued more
than 5 million loyalty cards and gained 1 per cent market share increase.[68]

■ E-COMMERCE: CLICKS VS. BRICKS

As more and more websites pop up to sell everything from fridge magnets to cars,
▶ marketers continue to debate how this cyberspace marketplace in the online world
will affect how they conduct business.[69] In particular, many are losing sleep wondering
whether e-commerce is destined to replace traditional retailing, work in concert with it,
or perhaps even fade away to become another fad your kids will laugh about some
day. That's unlikely, even though the predictions so far concerning the e-revolution
have tended grossly to overestimate the growth rapidity. Even in the most 'advanced' e-
commercial markets, like the USA, the share of turnover is still only a few per cent of the
total market exchanges taking place. And the largest proportion is still accounted for
by the business-to-business market. The European online buying population will be well
over 100 million in just a few years.[70] A Swedish survey indicates that searching for
product and service information are more important aspects of internet behaviour than
actual purchases (note Daniel's behaviour in the opening vignette for Chapter 8). Only
9 per cent of consumers want to buy food online (and a mere 1 per cent had actually tried
it), and even the highest scoring purchase types like travel and ticket purchase do not
exceed 30 per cent.[71] But there are obvious differences between the older and younger
segments concerning these matters. The e-market will become more and more important
– however, it will not come overnight and not to the same extent in all sectors. So far the

Many online shopping sites offer
time-saving convenience. This
French ad for a shopping/home
delivery website says, 'stop the
muscle training on Saturdays . . .
yes, this is total laziness. But
so what?'

Jean & Montmarin, Paris

obvious e-commerce failures in consumer markets have largely exceeded the number of successes.

For marketers, the growth of online commerce is a sword that cuts both ways: On the one hand, they can reach customers around the world even if they're physically located 100 miles from nowhere. On the other hand, their competition now comes not only from the shop across the street, but from thousands of websites spanning the globe. A second problem is that offering products directly to consumers has the potential to cut out the middleman – the loyal store-based retailers who carry the firm's products and who sell them at a marked-up price.[72] The 'clicks vs. bricks' dilemma is raging in the marketing world.

So, can you have your cake and eat it too? Coca-Cola thinks so, with its new 'think local, act local' strategy based on a philosophy of getting closer to the consumers. A Danish–Swedish–Norwegian–Finnish (probably as local as Coca-Cola gets!) campaign featuring an Indiana Jones-inspired adventure quiz has as its primary purpose to get teenagers to log on to the Coca-Cola website in order to participate in a quiz with adventurous travels as prizes. 'If we want to communicate on the teens premises, we have to make an active use of the internet and SMS media', says one executive.[73] This is also becoming true for US teenagers who have been slower than other teenagers to adopt mobile phones for text messaging.[74] Another possibility for reaching the youth markets is product placement in the chat rooms. For example, a virtual rose given to a fellow chatterer could be from a branded chain of florists. Or the chat environment can be constructed as a cruise ship with various branded services and games available for the chatterers.[75] But more serious organizations have also demonstrated their abilities to utilize the net. A Danish anti-cancer organization supporting research and cancer patients has a website where visitors can give a small gift by clicking on a button. Immediately 'thank you' appears with six banners referring to sponsoring companies who paid for the small gift, encouraging the visitor to visit the sponsors. This format has produced a much higher rate of banner-clicking than normal commercial banners.[76]

So, what makes e-commerce sites successful? According to a survey by NPD Online, 75 per cent of online shoppers surveyed said that good customer service would make them shop at the site again.[77] A study of how online grocery shoppers negotiated three different store layouts, freeform, grid and racetrack,[78] indicated that they found the freeform layout most useful for finding shopping list products within the store, and also by far the most entertaining to use. They also found the grid layout much easier to use than the other layouts.[79] Another recent study suggested that 'four factors were predictive of customer judgments about quality and satisfaction, customer loyalty and attitudes towards a website (see Table 9.2):

- *Website design*. This covers all elements of the customer's experience at the website including navigation, information search, order processing, appropriate personalization and product selection.
- *Fulfilment/reliability*. This involves, firstly, the accurate display and description of a product so that what customers receive is what they thought they ordered; and secondly, the delivery of the right product within the time frame promised.
- *Privacy/security*. This involves the security surrounding credit card payments and the privacy of shared information.
- *Customer service*. This needs to be responsive, helpful and willing service with a quick response time to customer enquiries.'[80]

Many successful e-tailers are learning that using technology to provide extra value for customers is attracting and keeping customers. A variety of online banking services are becoming very popular.[81] And estate agents can provide much more information, floor plans and more appealing photographs of homes for sale as well as virtual guided tours,

Table 9.2 eTailQ items: measuring customer satisfaction with websites

Factor	Customer judgement
Website design	1. The website provides in-depth information.
	2. The site doesn't waste my time.
	3. It is quick and easy to complete this transaction at this website.
	4. The level of personalization at this site is about right, not too much or too little.
	5. This website has good selection.
Fulfilment/reliability	6. The product that came was represented accurately by the website.
	7. You get what you ordered from this site.
	8. The product is delivered by the time promised by the company.
Security/privacy	9. I feel like my privacy is protected at this site.
	10. I feel safe in my transactions with this website.
	11. The website has adequate security features.
Customer service	12. The company is willing and ready to respond to customer needs.
	13. When you have a problem, the website shows a sincere interest in solving it.
	14. Inquiries are answered promptly.

Source: Based on Mary Wolfinbarger and Mary C. Gilly, 'eTailQ: Dimensionalizing, measuring and predicting etail quality', *Journal of Retailing* 79 (2003): Table 4. Reproduced by permission.

for example, than has been possible through the traditional print media. In a similar way companies such as Expedia have offered potential customers virtual tours of holiday destinations including pictures of hotel rooms and beaches.[82] Interactive TV is letting home viewers provide input to the videos played on MTV and to play along on *Who Wants to Be a Millionaire?* Soon MTV viewers will be able to use their remote controls to purchase the CDs that go with the music videos they are seeing. In Germany, the most successful application of interactive television (after home shopping) is the call-in quiz show, which combines television and telephone.[83]

E-commerce sites like Tesco give shoppers the option of shopping without leaving home. http://www.tesco.com. Courtesy of Tesco Stores Limited

Figure 9.4 Everyday life of a consumer in cyberspace

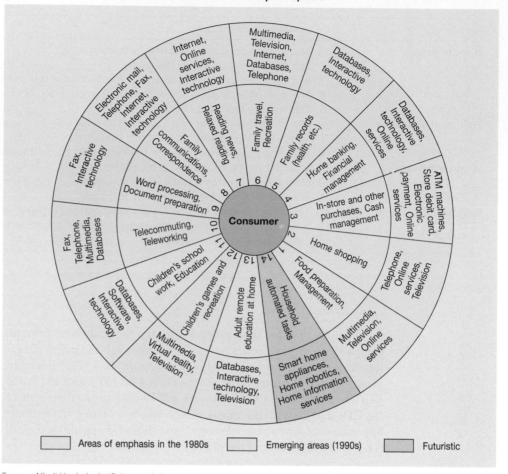

Areas of emphasis in the 1980s ☐   Emerging areas (1990s) ☐   Futuristic ▨

Source: Alladi Venkatesh, 'Cybermarketscapes and consumer freedoms and identities', *European Journal of Marketing* 32(7/8) (1998): 664–76. Used by permission.

From the consumer's perspective, electronic marketing has increased convenience by breaking down many of the barriers caused by time and location. You can shop 24 hours a day without leaving home, you can read today's newspaper without getting drenched picking up a hard copy when it is pouring with rain, and you don't have to wait for the 6 o'clock news to find out what the weather will be like tomorrow – at home or around the globe. And, with the increasing use of hand-held devices and wireless communications, you can get that same information – from stock quotes to the weather – even when you're away from your computer. In Figure 9.4, the major domains in the development of consumer possibilities in cyberspace are depicted.

Consumer experiences in cyberspace can be analysed according to two dimensions: *telepresence* and *bricolage*.[84] Telepresence expresses the degree to which the consumer feels immersed in the virtual environment, the time spent there and the positive feelings generated, whereas bricolage (a French word meaning getting by with whatever is at hand) is an indication of the interactive medium's possibilities for the consumer to be in control of the information gathered and used, presumably leading to a higher degree of involvement in and retention of the information.

However, all is not perfect in the virtual world. E-commerce does have its limitations. Security is one important concern. We hear horror stories of consumers whose credit cards and other identity information has been stolen. While an individual's financial liability in most theft cases is limited to approximately 60 euros or £40, the damage to one's credit rating can last for years. Some shady companies are making money by prying and then selling personal information to others – one company promotes itself as 'an amazing new tool that allows you to find out EVERYTHING you ever wanted to know about your friends, family, neighbours, employees, and even your boss!'[85] Pretty scary. Almost daily we hear of hackers getting into a business or even a government website and causing havoc. Businesses risk the loss of trade secrets and other proprietary information. Many must spend significant amounts to maintain security and conduct regular audits to ensure the integrity of their sites.

Other limitations of e-commerce relate to the actual shopping experience. While it may be satisfactory to buy a computer or a book on the internet, buying clothing and other items in which touching the item or trying it on is essential may be less attractive. Lack of tactile input (feeling material; smelling a bouquet) is one the major factors which deters consumers from using the internet for buying goods. A recent study established that consumers with a higher need for tactile inputs tended not to use the internet so much for product purchase; and men tend to exhibit less need for tactile input than women when evaluating products.[86] Even though most companies have very liberal returns policies, consumers can still get stuck with large delivery and return postal charges for items where the material does not hang properly, or they don't fit, or they simply aren't the right colour. However, a potentially interesting counter-example to this is the purchase of wedding dresses online, where customers have the opportunity to co-design their dresses. This was a particularly attractive opportunity for customers who were already comfortable with technology and already owned personal technological devices; have already bought formal clothes online; and regularly spend time online.[87] Some of the pros and cons of e-commerce are summarized in Table 9.3. It's clear that traditional shopping isn't quite dead yet.

Many of the winners in the future retail scene will be those who can create a high degree of synergy between their online and offline outlets.[88] There is already evidence of

Table 9.3 Pros and cons of e-commerce

Benefits of e-commerce	Limitations of e-commerce
For the consumer	**For the consumer**
Shop 24 hours a day	Lack of security
Less travelling	Fraud
Can receive relevant information in seconds	Can't touch items
from any location	Exact colours may not reproduce on
More choice of products	computer monitors
More products available to less-developed countries	Expensive to order and then return
Greater price information	Potential breakdown of human
Lower prices so that less affluent can purchase	relationships
Participate in virtual auctions	
Fast delivery	
Electronic communities	
For the marketer	**For the marketer**
The world is the marketplace	Lack of security
Decreases costs of doing business	Must maintain site to reap benefits
Very specialized businesses can be successful	Fierce price competition
Real-time pricing	Conflicts with conventional retailers
	Legal issues not resolved

Source: Adapted from Michael R. Solomon and Elnora W. Stuart, *Welcome to Marketing.Com: The Brave New World of E-Commerce* (Englewood Cliffs, NJ: Prentice Hall, 2001).

the rewards for retailers who successfully link offline with online because the fastest growing trend in consumer behaviour is combining patronage of offline company outlets (shops and/or mail order catalogues) with online company websites.[89]

Bricks-and-mortar retailers will need to work hard to give shoppers something they can't get (yet anyway) in the virtual world – a stimulating or pleasant environment in which to browse with sensory appeals not available online.[90] They will need to build emotional bonds with their customers through imaginative and entertaining retail design and merchandising strategies.[91] Now let's consider how they're doing that.

■ SERVICESCAPES: RETAILING AS THEATRE

Shopping can no longer be regarded as a simple act of purchasing.[92] A retail culture has arisen,[93] where the act of shopping has taken on new entertainment and/or experiential dimensions as retailers compete for customers' attention, not to speak of their loyalty. The act of shopping ties into a number of central existential aspects of human life such as sexuality.[94] Furthermore, the customer may be regarded not as a passive recipient of the offerings of the purchase environment but rather as an active co-creator of this very environment and the meanings attached to it,[95] in a situation analogous to the focus among 'marketing mavens' (see next chapter) on flexibility in the area of product supply and tailor-made marketing mixes for the individual consumer.[96] One of the most obvious trends in the retailing sector in Europe is the construction of shopping centres, often modelled on American prototypes. In the United States today, the shopping centre or mall is often a focal point in a community: 94 per cent of adults visit a mall at least once a month and more than half of all retail purchases (excluding cars and petrol) are made in a mall.[97] Shopping centres are also flourishing in Europe, where, once introduced into an area, they often bring with them a whole new combination of leisure activities, shopping and social encounters in safe environments.[98]

The competition for customers is becoming even more intense as non-store alternatives from websites and print catalogues to TV shopping networks and home shopping parties continue to multiply. With all of these shopping alternatives available, how can a traditional store compete?

Shopping centres are becoming giant entertainment centres, almost to the point that their traditional retail occupants seem like an afterthought. Shopping centres have tried to gain the loyalty of shoppers by appealing to their social motives as well as providing access to desired goods. It is now typical to find such features as children's rides, miniature golf, and batting cages in a suburban shopping centre. As one retailing executive put it, 'Malls are becoming the new mini-amusement parks.'[99] The importance of creating a positive, vibrant and interesting image has led innovative marketers to blur the line between shopping and the theatre. Shopping centres and individual stores have to create environments that stimulate people and allow them to shop and be entertained at the same time.[100] Themed shopping centres and stores bear witness to the multitude of styles that flourish in the attempt to attract consumers who seek more than just a distribution outlet.[101] The Hard Rock Café, established in London over 25 years ago, now has over 45 restaurants around the world, and has become a sort of pilgrimage place in itself. Some consumers make a point of collecting as many Hard Rock Café merchandise items (T-shirts, etc.) from as many HRCs in the world as possible.

The classic European counterpart to the American mall is the department store.[102] The first department stores can be seen as marking the introduction of a modern consumer culture, nourished by dreams of abundance.[103] Department stores often hold elaborate store-wide promotions based, for example, on the culture of a selected country (see also De Bijenkorf's promotions in Amsterdam). During these events the entire store is transformed, with each department featuring unusual merchandise from the country. These promotions are accompanied by lavish parties, food and entertainment associated with that country.

The following are a few examples of 'performers' in the retailing theatre:

- A Dutch internet bank, ING, has turned the ground floor of its office in Toronto, Canada, into a stylish café, complete with counter, armchairs, sofas and background music. But in addition to the variety of coffees, the chalkboard behind the counter announces interest rates in various savings accounts and other banking information.[104]

- The Powerscourt Townhouse Centre in Dublin succeeded in merging a variety of styles and features, including a grand piano on a stage in the central hall, to make a sort of new version of a Victorian marketplace atmosphere. Unlike the Mall of America, it does not appear as a carefully planned environment but rather a happy blend of many consumption opportunities including an Italian restaurant, a modern hairstylist, an antique shop, etc. in a stylish classical setting.[105]

- American malls, the new 'retail-entertainment complexes', have also attracted a lot of attention among European retail environment designers and academics in the last few years. Minneapolis's Mall of America, the largest one in the United States, is organized around a complete amusement park (Camp Snoopy) as well as a Lego playing/exhibition area. Furthermore, it comprises 400 stores, 45 restaurants, 9 discos and 14 cinemas and ranks among the foremost *tourist attractions* in the USA. It has a complete aquatic theme park (Underwater World) as well as a number of other featured themed environments including Planet Hollywood and Rainforest Café, and an Italian restaurant, Tutti Benucci, built upon the image of a classical 1950s' southern Italian restaurant by Mr Benucci himself, using his family photos as wall decoration and his grandmother's and mother's recipes in the kitchen. The only thing is, Mr Benucci never really existed but was created by a marketing department . . .[106]

The quest to entertain means that many stores are going all-out to create imaginative environments that transport shoppers to fantasy worlds or provide other kinds of stimulation. This strategy is called **retail theming**. Innovative merchants today use four basic kinds of theming techniques:

- *Landscape themes* rely upon associations with images of nature, earth, animals and the physical body. Bass Pro Shops, for example, create a simulated outdoor environment including pools stocked with fish.

- *Marketscape themes* build upon associations with man-made places. An example is The Venetian hotel in Las Vegas that lavishly recreates parts of the Italian city.

- *Cyberspace themes* are built around images of information and communications technology. eBay's retail interface instils a sense of community among its vendors and traders.

- *Mindscape themes* draw upon abstract ideas and concepts, introspection and fantasy, and often possess spiritual overtones. At the Seibu store in Tokyo, shoppers enter as neophytes at the first level. As they progress through the physical levels of the store each is themed to connote increasing levels of consciousness until they emerge at the summit as completed shoppers.[107]

multicultural dimensions

American retailers, including Blockbuster Video, Original Levi's stores, Foot Locker, Toys"Я"Us and The Gap, are exporting their version of the dynamic retail environment to Europe – with some adaptations. These 'invasions' often begin in Britain, since cultural differences seem smaller, bureaucratic hurdles lower and personnel costs reduced. The Gap found that it needed to stock smaller sizes than in the US, and that many of its European customers prefer darker colours. Also, some retailers have done away with the 'greeters' who stand at the entrance in many American stores – Europeans tend to find them intimidating.[108]

Hard Rock Café: one of the oldest and most well-established themed consumer environments.
© SIME/Corbis

Spectacular consumption environments represent another example of servicescapes, where the emphasis is on *play*, and the co-creation of the experience by the producer and the consumer. Recent research within a themed retail environment, the ESPN Zone Chicago, examined the agency of the consumer in this type of environment and how the use of technology affected consumers' sense of reality. Consumers seemed to exercise creative control over the spectacular environment by using technology and their bodies to produce parts of the spectacle, and to create and alter space, suggesting a dialectical relationship between producers and consumers. The researchers identified two ludic elements that help us understand the role of *play* in consumption environments:[109]

1 *'Liminoid Real Estate*: This refers to the creation of new worlds through consumer play, which consumers interpret as different realities. This notion of transcendent surrender provides a link between play and religion, ritual, sacrifice and the sacred.

2 *The Observe Panapticon*: This refers to physical structures that are designed in a way that appeals to exhibitionistic desires of consumers by enabling them to be observed by others.'

Store image

With so many stores competing for customers, how do consumers select one rather than another? Like products, we can think of stores as having 'personalities'. Some stores have very clearly defined images (either good or bad). Others tend to blend into the crowd. They may not have anything distinctive about them and may be overlooked for this reason. This personality, or **store image**, is composed of many different factors. The design and general image of the store is central to the perception of the goods displayed there, whether we are talking about fashion,[110] food products[111] or any other type of good. Store features, coupled with such consumer characteristics as shopping orientation, help to predict which shopping outlets people will prefer.[112] Some of the important dimensions of a store's profile are location, merchandise suitability and the knowledge and congeniality of the sales staff.[113]

These features typically work together to create an overall impression. When shoppers think about stores, they may not say, 'Well, that place is fairly good in terms of convenience, the salespeople are acceptable, and services are good.' They are more likely to say, 'That place gives me the creeps', or 'I always enjoy shopping there.' Consumers evaluate stores in terms of both their specific attributes *and* a global evaluation, or the

▶ **store gestalt** (see Chapter 2).[114] This overall feeling may have more to do with such intangibles as interior design and the types of people one finds in the store than with aspects such as returns policies or credit availability. As a result, some stores are likely to be consistently in consumers' evoked sets (see Chapter 8), whereas others will never be considered.[115]

A recent makeover of FedEx retail outlets illustrates the crucial role design can play in communicating a desirable store image. Consumer research conducted by Ziba Design for FedEx indicated that, compared to its main competitors, the firm's brand personality was more innovative, leading-edge and outgoing – but this impression was certainly not reinforced by its cluttered storefront locations where customers go to drop off packages for delivery. The designers used colours and shapes associated with these attributes to make over the stores.

Atmospherics

Because a store's image is now recognized as a very important aspect of the retailing mix,

▶ store designers pay a lot of attention to **atmospherics**, or the 'conscious designing of space and its various dimensions to evoke certain effects in buyers'.[116] These dimensions include colours, scents and sounds. For any store or any shopping centre, one may think of this process as a careful *orchestration* of the various elements, each playing its part to form a whole.[117]

Many elements of store design can be cleverly controlled to attract customers and produce desired effects on consumers. Light colours impart a feeling of spaciousness and serenity, and signs in bright colours create excitement. In one subtle but effective application, fashion designer Norma Kamali replaced fluorescent lights with pink ones in department store dressing rooms. The light had the effect of flattering the face and banishing wrinkles, making female customers more willing to try on (and buy) the company's bathing suits.[118] One study found that brighter in-store lighting influenced people to examine and handle more merchandise.[119]

In addition to visual stimuli, all sorts of cues can influence behaviours.[120] For example, music can affect eating habits. A study found that diners who listened to loud, fast music ate more food. In contrast, those who listened to Mozart or Brahms ate less and more slowly. The researchers concluded that diners who choose soothing music at mealtimes can increase weight loss by at least five pounds a month![121] Classical music can have a positive effect on consumers' evaluation of store atmosphere.[122]

In-store decision-making

Despite all their efforts to 'pre-sell' consumers through advertising, marketers are increasingly recognizing the significant degree to which many purchases are strongly influenced by the store environment. Women tell researchers, for example, that store displays are one of the major information sources they use to decide what clothing to buy.[123] A Danish survey indicated that nine out of ten customers did not plan the purchase of at least one-third of the goods they acquired.[124] The proportion of unplanned purchases is even higher for other product categories such as food – it's estimated that about two out of every three supermarket purchases are decided in the aisles. And people with lists are just as likely to make spontaneous purchases as those without them.[125] For the US market it is estimated that the purchase of 85 per cent of sweets and chewing gum, almost 70 per cent of cosmetics and 75 per cent of oral hygiene purchases are unplanned.[126]

Marketers are scrambling to engineer purchasing environments in order to increase the likelihood that they will be in contact with consumers at the exact time they make a decision. This strategy even applies to drinking behaviour: Diageo, the world's largest liquor company, discovered that 60 per cent of bar customers don't know what they will drink until seconds before they place their orders. To make it more likely that the customer's order will include Smirnoff vodka, Johnnie Walker Scotch or one of its other brands, Diageo launched its Drinks Invigoration Team to increase what it calls its 'share of throat'. The Dublin-based team experiments with bar 'environments', bottle-display techniques and how to match drinks to customers' moods. For example, the company researchers discovered that bubbles stimulate the desire for spirits, so it's developing bubble machines to put in the back of bars. Diageo has even categorized bars into types and is identifying the types of drinkers – and the drinkers they prefer – who frequent each. These include 'style bars', where cutting-edge patrons like to sip fancy fresh-fruit martinis, and 'buzz bars', where the clientele is receptive to a drink made of Smirnoff and energy brew Red Bull.[127]

Spontaneous shopping

When a shopper is prompted to buy something in a shop, one of two different processes may be at work: *unplanned buying* may occur when a person is unfamiliar with a store's layout or perhaps when under some time pressure; or, a person may be reminded to buy something by seeing it on a store shelf. About one-third of unplanned buying has been attributed to the recognition of new needs while within the store.[128]

Impulse buying

▷ In contrast, **impulse buying** occurs when the person experiences a sudden urge that he or she cannot resist. For this reason, so-called impulse items such as sweets and chewing gum are conveniently placed near the checkout. Similarly, many supermarkets have installed wider aisles to encourage browsing, and the widest tend to contain products with the highest margin. Low mark-up items that are purchased regularly tend to be stacked high in narrower aisles, to allow shopping trolleys to speed through.[129] A more recent high-tech tool has been added to encourage impulse buying: a device called 'The Portable Shopper', a personal scanning gun which allows customers to ring up their own purchases as they shop. The gun was initially developed for Albert Heijn, the Netherlands' largest grocery chain, to move customers through the store more quickly. It is now in use in over 150 supermarkets worldwide.[130]

One particular type of occasion where a lot of impulse buying goes on is the seasonal sales, which appeal especially to younger and price-conscious shoppers according to one British study.[131] In general, shoppers can be categorized in terms of how much advance planning they do. *Planners* tend to know what products and specific brands they will buy beforehand, *partial planners* know they need certain products, but do not decide on specific brands until they are in the store, and *impulse purchasers* do no advance planning whatsoever.[132] Figure 9.5 was drawn by a consumer who participated in a study on consumers' shopping experiences and who was asked to sketch a typical impulse purchaser.

Point-of-purchase stimuli

Because so much decision-making apparently occurs while the shopper is in the purchasing environment, retailers are beginning to pay more attention to the amount of information in their stores, as well as to the way it is presented. It has been estimated that impulse purchases increase by 10 per cent when appropriate displays are used. Consumers' images of a good-value-for-money purchase are in many cases not induced

Smart retailers recognize that many purchase decisions are made at the time the shopper is in the store. That's one reason why grocery carts sometimes resemble billboards on wheels.

Peter Byron/Photo Researchers, Inc.

Figure 9.5 One consumer's image of an impulse buyer

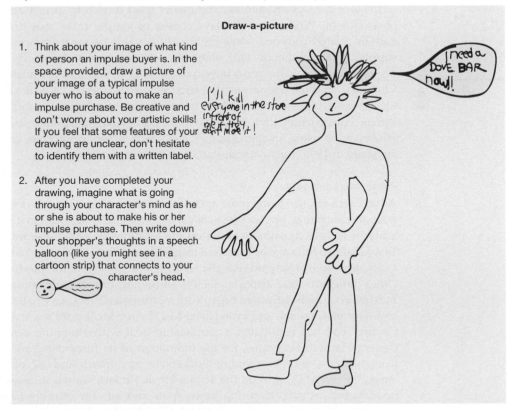

Source: Dennis Rook, 'Is Impulse Buying (Yet) a Useful Marketing Concept?', unpublished manuscript, University of Southern California, Los Angeles, 1990: Figure 7.A.

by careful price examinations but by powerful and striking in-store information.[133] That
▶ explains why US companies spend more than \$13 billion each year on **point-of-
purchase stimuli (POP)**. A POP can be an elaborate product display or demonstration,
a coupon-dispensing machine, or someone giving out free samples of a new perfume in
the cosmetics aisles. Recent research indicated that European consumers responded
more positively to spray samplers than to vials and plugs in the promotion campaign
for a fragrance. 'Both fragrance marketers and retailers confirm[ed] that spray samplers
successfully entice customers to try, experience and buy an upscale product. The sprays
are able to effectively communicate the feel, gesture and essence of a brand' and are now
being increasingly tried out in the U.S. as an effective way of getting consumers to try
a new fragrance.[134] Winning consumers in the store with packaging and displays is
regarded as 'the first moment of truth'.[135] P&G are now putting designers alongside R&D
and marketing managers because 'competitive advantage comes not just from patents,
but also from incorporating design into products, much like Apple, Sony or Dell'.[136]

Much of the growth in point-of-purchase activity has been in new electronic technologies.[137] Videotronic, a German hardware producer, has specialized in compact in-
store video displays. The newest feature is a touch-screen selection with various pieces
of information which eventually provoke scent to appear.[138] The Point-of-Purchase Radio
Corporation offers in-store radio networks which are now used by about 60 grocery
chains.[139] Some shopping trolleys have a small screen that displays advertising, which is
keyed to the specific areas of the store through which the trolley is wheeled.[140] New interactive possibilities seem to enhance the effectiveness of POP information systems,[141]
although the effect of in-store advertising and other POP continues to be difficult to
assess. High-tech solutions such as hand-held computers which will process filmed as
well as alphanumerical data are used by Reebok to show whether their in-store efforts
are used correctly and which type works best in comparison with competitors.[142]

In-store *displays* are another commonly used device to attract attention in the store
environment. While most displays consist of simple racks that dispense the product
and/or related coupons, some highlight the value of regarding retailing as theatre by
supplying the 'audience' with elaborate performances and scenery. For example, POP
displays are one of the most important tools in the annual toy acquisition peak before
Christmas, and the winners are the large and established brands like Barbie, Lego, etc. as
well as newcomers who know how to make an impressive visual impact. In the UK market for construction toys, Lego has long dominated, with Meccano a distant second.
However, by using an aggressive POP strategy, K'Nex came close to a 20 per cent market share in 1996 from a standing start that same year.[143]

Place-based media

Advertisers are also being more aggressive about hitting consumers with their messages,
wherever they may be. *Place-based media* is a specialized medium that is growing in popularity: it targets consumers based on the locations in which the message is delivered.
Tesco plans to follow Wal-Mart and install TV in 300 stores where 'in between news clips,
recipe tips and beauty advice, the screens will show ads for products in the aisles'.[144]
Other outlets include airports, doctors' surgeries, university campuses or health clubs.
Turner Broadcasting System began such ventures as Checkout Channel for supermarkets
and Airport Channel, and even tested McDTV for McDonald's restaurants.[145] Twentieth
Century Fox has negotiated a partnership deal with shopping centres owned by US
General Growth Properties for the promotion of its films using methods which range
from banners, posters, window stickers to tray liners and ad placements in eating
areas.[146] Even MTV is in on the act: its Music Report, shown in record stores, is a two-
hour 'video capsule' featuring video spots and ads for music retailers and corporate
sponsors. An MTV executive observed, 'They're already out there at the retail environment. They're ready to spend money.'[147] A Dutch CD retailer, Free Record Shop, has

installed a device that permits shoppers to compile and burn their own CD in-store. Consumers can select up to 74 minutes of music and are charged a per-song amount (up to 1.23 euros). The teens are delighted about this legal way of making personalized compilations. The company hopes to spread the system to their other stores in the Netherlands, Belgium, Norway and France.[148]

multicultural dimensions

Wal-Mart is upgrading its vast in-store television network: the fifth-largest television network in the United States

'Wal-Mart TV Network, a Web network of in-store programming that the company started in 1998. These days it shows previews of soon-to-be-released movies, snippets of sports events and rock concerts, and corporate messages from the world of Wal-Mart, including some intended to improve its battered public image. But the principal reason for Wal-Mart TV is to show a constant stream of consumer product ads purchased by companies like Kraft, Unilever, Hallmark and PepsiCo. And little wonder. According to Wal-Mart and to an agency that handles its ad sales, the TV operation captures some 130 million viewers every four weeks, making it the fifth-largest television network in the United States after NBC, CBS, ABC and Fox.'[149]

net profit

The ATM machine is slowly but surely being transformed into a high-tech point-of-purchase display as marketers find new ways to use it to deliver products and advertising. The Bank of America's machines show a brief ad while a customer waits for the cash to drop. But that's yesterday's news. State-of-the art web-enabled ATMs are being developed that will take the cash withdrawal experience to a new level. Soon users will have access to account updates and coupon printing while full motion videos play in the background. This new generation of ATMs will be able to scan a deposited cheque and print a copy of it on your receipt. These machines will do a lot more than your banking, however. They will offer such services as ticket purchasing, personalized stock market share quotes, sports scores, maps, directions, bill payment and the ability to call up an image of a cancelled cheque from your account.[150] Soon, you'll be able to spend your money before you even withdraw it!

The salesperson

One of the most important in-store factors is the salesperson, who attempts to influence the buying behaviour of the customer.[151] This influence can be understood in terms of ▶ **exchange theory**, which stresses that every interaction involves an exchange of value. Each participant gives something to the other and hopes to receive something in return.[152]

What 'value' does the customer look for in a sales interaction? There are a variety of resources a salesperson might offer. For example, they might offer expertise about the product to make the shopper's choice easier. Alternatively, the customer may be reassured because the salesperson is an admired or likeable person whose tastes are similar and who is seen as someone who can be trusted.[153] A long stream of research attests to the impact of a salesperson's appearance on sales effectiveness. In sales, as in much of life, attractive people appear to hold the upper hand.[154] In addition, it's not unusual for service personnel and customers to form fairly warm personal relationships; these have been termed *commercial* friendships (think of all those patient bartenders who double as therapists for many people). Researchers have found that commercial friendships are similar to other friendships in that they can involve affection, intimacy, social support, loyalty and reciprocal gift giving. They also work to support marketing objectives such as satisfaction, loyalty and positive word-of-mouth.[155]

A buyer/seller situation is like many other dyadic encounters (two-person groups); it is a relationship where some agreement must be reached about the roles of each participant, when a process of *identity negotiation* occurs.[156] For example, if the salesperson immediately establishes him- or herself as an expert, the salesperson is likely to have more influence over the customer through the course of the relationship. Some of the factors that help to determine a salesperson's role (and relative effectiveness) are their age, appearance, educational level and motivation to sell.[157]

In addition, more effective salespeople usually know their customers' traits and preferences better than do ineffective salespeople, since this knowledge allows them to adapt their approach to meet the needs of the specific customer.[158] The ability to be adaptable is especially vital when customers and salespeople differ in terms of their *interaction styles*.[159] Consumers, for example, vary in the degree of assertiveness they bring to interactions. At one extreme, non-assertive people believe that complaining is not socially acceptable and may be intimidated in sales situations. Assertive people are more likely to stand up for themselves in a firm but non-threatening way. Aggressives may resort to rudeness and threats if they do not get their way.[160]

■ POST-PURCHASE SATISFACTION

▶ **Consumer satisfaction/dissatisfaction (CS/D)** is determined by the overall feelings, or attitude, a person has about a product after it has been purchased. Consumers engage in a constant process of evaluating the things they buy as they integrate these products into their daily consumption activities.[161] Despite evidence that customer satisfaction is steadily declining in many industries, good marketers are constantly on the lookout for sources of dissatisfaction so that they can improve.[162] Customer satisfaction has a real impact on profitability: a recent study conducted among a large sample of Swedish consumers found that product quality affects customer satisfaction, which in turn results in increased profitability among firms who provide quality products.[163] Quality is more than a marketing 'buzzword'.

Perceptions of product quality

Just what do consumers look for in products? The answer's easy: they want quality and value. Especially because of foreign competition, claims of product quality have become strategically crucial to maintaining a competitive advantage.[164] Consumers use a number of cues to infer quality, including brand name, price, and even their own estimates of how much money has been put into a new product's advertising campaign.[165] These cues, as well as others such as product warranties and follow-up letters from the company, are often used by consumers to relieve perceived risk and assure themselves that they have made smart purchase decisions.[166]

What is quality?

Although everyone wants quality, it is not clear exactly what it means. In *Zen and the Art of Motorcycle Maintenance*, a cult book from the mid-1970s, the hero literally goes mad trying to work out the meaning of quality.[167] Marketers appear to use the word 'quality' as a catch-all term for 'good'. Because of its wide and imprecise usage, the attribute 'quality' threatens to become a meaningless claim. If everyone has it, what good is it?

One way to define quality is to establish uniform standards to which products from around the world must conform. This is the intention of the International Standards

This ad for Audi relies on a claim about quality based on technical excellence in engineering and design.
The Advertising Archives

Organization, a Geneva-based organization that does just that. A set of quality criteria was initially developed in 1987 to regulate product quality. The broad set of guidelines is known as **ISO standards**. These standards exist in different versions and cover issues related to the manufacture and installation of products and post-sale servicing, but also sustainability and environmentally friendly production processes.

The importance of expectations

Global standards for quality help to ensure that products work as promised, but consumers' evaluations of those products are a bit more complex. Satisfaction or dissatisfaction is more than a reaction to the actual performance quality of a product or service. First of all, satisfaction is not just a matter of functional but also of the hedonic performance of the product – something which may be more difficult for the producer to ensure beforehand. When we buy a book, we don't expect that the pages will come loose or fall out.[168]

Satisfaction, then, is highly influenced by prior expectations regarding all aspects of quality. According to the **expectancy disconfirmation model**, consumers form beliefs about product performance based on prior experience with the product and/or communications about the product that imply a certain level of quality.[169] When something performs the way we thought it would, we may not think much about it. If, on the other hand, it fails to live up to expectations, negative affect may result. Furthermore, if performance happens to exceed our expectations, we are satisfied and pleased.

To understand this perspective, think about different types of restaurants. People expect to be provided with sparkling clear glassware at high-class restaurants, and they might become upset if they discover a grimy glass. On the other hand, we may not be surprised to find fingerprints on our mug at a local 'greasy spoon'; we may even shrug it off because it contributes to the 'charm' of the place. An important lesson emerges for marketers from this perspective: don't overpromise if you can't deliver.[170]

marketing pitfall

Consumers are not the only ones who are angry. Many employees have an axe to grind as well. At a website put up by a disgruntled former employee of a certain fast-food franchise, we share the pain of this ex-burger cook: 'I have seen the creatures that live at the bottom of the dustbins. I have seen the rat by the carbonated drinks machine. I have seen dead frogs in the fresh salad lettuce.'[171] Chips with that?

A website called customerssuck.com gets 1,200 hits a day. This is a forum for restaurant and store workers who have to grin and bear it all day. Once off the clock, they can share their frustrations about the idiocy, slovenliness and insensitivity of their customers. Some contributors to the website share stupid questions their customers ask, such as 'How much is a 99 cent cheeseburger?' while others complain about working conditions and having to be nice to not-so-nice people. The slogan of the site is 'the customer is never right'.[172] Clearly, there are a lot of unhappy people on both sides of the cash till.

This perspective underscores the importance of *managing expectations* – customer dissatisfaction is usually due to expectations exceeding the company's ability to deliver. Figure 9.6 illustrates the alternative strategies a firm can choose in these situations. When confronted with unrealistic expectations about what it can do, the firm can either accommodate these demands by improving the range or quality of products it offers, alter the expectations, or perhaps even choose to abandon the customer if it is not feasible to meet his or her needs.[173] Expectations are altered, for example, when waiters tell patrons in advance that the portion size they have ordered will not be very big, or when new car buyers are warned of strange smells they will experience during the running-in period. A firm also can under-promise, as when Xerox inflates the time it will take for a service rep to visit. When the rep arrives a day earlier, the customer is impressed.

One approach to customer satisfaction, known as the *Kano-model*, operates with three kinds of expectation: basis, performance and enthusiasm expectations. The first includes the implicit and taken-for-granted qualities expected from a product. If these are not satisfied, the product will never be able to live up to the customer's requirements, but even if fulfilled, they do not profile the product because these qualities are taken for granted as a minimum. For the performance expectations satisfaction is proportional to how well the product lives up to the expectations. Such quality requirements are often specified and articulated by the customer. As for enthusiasm-related product features, it is wrong to call them expectations since their essential character is that they are *not* expected by the customer. Therefore, such positive surprises can lead to a very great feeling of satisfaction, since the product quality was even better than expected.[174] Furthermore, research evidence indicates that product experience is important for

Figure 9.6 Customer expectation zones: managing quality expectations

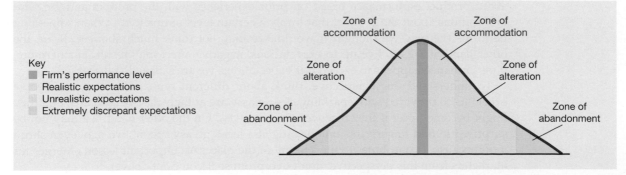

customer satisfaction. When people have no experiences they are relatively easy to satisfy, but with growing experience they become harder to satisfy. Then, when they reach a certain level of experience, satisfaction again becomes easier to obtain, since consumers are now 'experts' and this facilitates choice and generates more realistic expectations.[175]

Furthermore, satisfaction levels are determined not only by the product purchased but also by the expectations about the quality of alternatives that were *not* purchased. In other words, the higher the expectations about unselected alternatives, the lower the level of satisfaction with the chosen good.[176] A general conclusion which one should draw from such a discussion is that consumer goals may be multiple and the product or service offer so complex to evaluate that any measurement of satisfaction must be used with caution.[177]

Quality and product failures

The power of quality claims is most evident when a company's product fails. Here, consumers' expectations are dashed and dissatisfaction results. In these situations, marketers must immediately take steps to reassure customers. When the company confronts the problem truthfully, consumers are often willing to forgive and forget, as was the case with Perrier when traces of benzene were found in the water. When the company appears to be dragging its heels or covering up, on the other hand, consumer resentment will grow, as occurred during Union Carbide's chemical disaster in India, the massive Alaskan oil spill caused by the tanker *Exxon Valdez* or the recent corporate scandals such as the collapse of Enron.

Acting on dissatisfaction

If a person is not happy with a product or service, what can be done? Essentially, a consumer can take one or more possible courses of action:[178]

1 *Voice response*: The consumer can appeal directly to the retailer for redress (e.g. a refund).

2 *Private response*: Express dissatisfaction about the store or product to friends and/or boycott the store. As will be discussed in Chapter 10, negative word-of-mouth (WOM) can be very damaging to a retailer's reputation.

3 *Third-party response*: The consumer can take legal action against the merchant, register a complaint with the Ombudsman, or perhaps write a letter to a newspaper (e.g. the weekly consumer complaints page in *The Guardian*'s *G2* section).

A number of factors influence which route is taken. The consumer may in general be assertive or meek. Action is more likely to be taken for expensive products such as household durables, cars and clothing than for inexpensive products.[179] If the consumer does not believe that the store will respond positively to a complaint, the person will be more likely to switch brands than fight.[180] Ironically, marketers should *encourage* consumers to complain to them: people are more likely to spread the word about unresolved negative experiences to their friends than they are to boast about positive occurrences.[181] Consumers are more likely to spread negative information about a bad service than they are to spread information about a successful complaint handling. Complaint management is thus not as good an alternative as high-quality service in the first place.[182] In addition, consumers who are satisfied with a store are more likely to complain; they take the time to complain because they feel connected to the store. Older people are more likely to complain, and are much more likely to believe the store will actually resolve the problem. Shoppers who get their problems resolved feel even *better* about the store than if nothing went wrong.[183]

tangled web

Many dissatisfied customers and disgruntled former employees have been inspired to create their own websites just to share their tales of woe with others. For example, a website for people to complain about the Dunkin' Donuts chain became so popular that the company bought it in order to control the bad press it was getting. A customer initially created the site to express his outrage over the fact that he was unable to get skimmed milk for his coffee.[184] As a media lawyer observed, 'The person who, 20 years ago, was confined to walking up and down outside Chase Bank with a placard can now publish to millions of people with the click of a button.'[185] Indeed, a single individual can do a lot of damage in cyberspace. One famous hacker who went by the *nom de guerre* of Pimpshiz hacked into more than 200 websites to insert a message supporting Napster before he was finally arrested.[186]

The Web is a very efficient staging ground for mass demonstrations. Political activists protesting against corporate policies are able to mobilize large numbers of consumers by touting their causes online. Some websites like **fightback.com** maintained by consumer activist David Horowitz focus on a range of consumerism issues, while others like **mcspotlight.org** chronicle the ostensible misdeeds of a specific company like McDonald's. Indeed, while their life spans often are brief, at any one time there are a surprising number of web pages out there devoted to trashing specific companies, such as **walmartsucks.com**, **NorthWorstAir.org**, **chasebanksucks.com** and **starbucked.com**.

■ TQM: GOING BACK TO THE GEMBA

Many analysts who study consumer satisfaction or who are trying to design new products or services to increase it recognize that it is crucial to understand how people actually interact with their environment in order to identify potential problems. These investigations typically are done in focus groups where a small set of consumers try out a new item while being observed by company personnel. However, some researchers advocate a more up-close and personal approach that allows them to watch people in the actual environment where the item is consumed. The Japanese approach to Total Quality Management (TQM), a complex set of management and engineering procedures aimed at reducing errors and increasing quality, has influenced this perspective.

▶   To help attain this objective, researchers can *go to the gemba*. The **gemba** means the one true source of information. According to this philosophy, it's essential to send marketers and designers to the precise place where the product or service is being used rather than asking consumers to interact with it in a simulated environment. Figure 9.7 illustrates this idea in practice. Host Foods, which operates food concessions in major airports, sent a team to the *gemba* – in this case, an airport cafeteria – to identify problem areas. Employees watched as customers chose (or didn't) to enter the facility, then followed them as they inspected the menu, chose cutlery, paid and found a table. The findings were crucial to Host's redesign of the restaurant to make it easier to use. For example, the team hadn't realized the problem caused by having to put down one's luggage to enter the food line and not being able to keep an eye on valuables during the process.[187]

■ PRODUCT DISPOSAL

Because people often do form strong attachments to products, the decision to dispose of something can be a painful one. One function performed by possessions is to serve as anchors for our identities: our past lives on in our things.[188] This attachment is

Figure 9.7 Going to the gemba

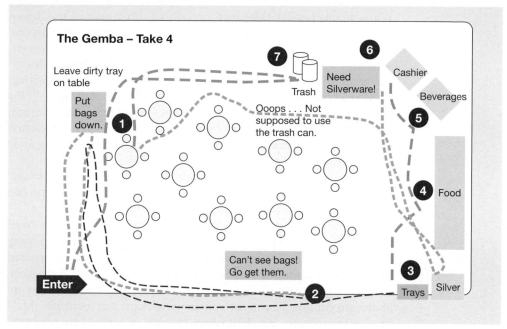

exemplified by the Japanese, who ritually 'retire' worn-out sewing needles, chopsticks and even computer chips by burning them as thanks for good service.[189]

Although some people have more trouble than others in discarding things, even a 'magpie' does not keep everything. Consumers must often dispose of things, either because they have fulfilled their designated functions, or possibly because they no longer fit with consumers' views of themselves. Concern about the environment coupled with a need for convenience has made ease of product disposal a key attribute in categories from razors to nappies. Since we will deal with recycling and environmentalism in a later chapter, we will only briefly address other aspects of product disposal here.

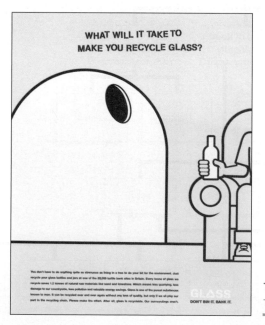

This British ad promotes the recycling of glass.
The Advertising Archives

Disposal options

When a consumer decides that a product is no longer of use, several choices are available. The person can either (1) keep the item, (2) temporarily dispose of it, or (3) permanently dispose of it. In many cases, a new product is acquired even though the old one still functions. Some reasons for this replacement include a desire for new features, a change in the person's environment (e.g. a refrigerator is the wrong colour for a freshly painted kitchen), or a change in the person's role or self-image.[190] Figure 9.8 provides an overview of consumers' disposal options. Compared with the original scheme, we have added the opportunity of 'to be recycled' in the lower left corner. This is interesting because it bears witness to the fact that thinking about recycling as a 'natural' thing to do is a rather recent occurrence.

The issue of product disposal is doubly vital because of its enormous public policy implications. We live in a throwaway society, which creates problems for the environment and also results in a great deal of unfortunate waste.

Training consumers to recycle has become a priority in many countries. Japan recycles about 40 per cent of its rubbish, and this relatively high rate of compliance is partly due to the social value the Japanese place on recycling: citizens are encouraged by dustbin lorries that periodically rumble through the streets playing classical music or children's songs.[191] Companies continue to search for ways to use resources more efficiently, often at the prompting of activist consumer groups. For example, McDonald's restaurants bowed to pressure by eliminating the use of styrofoam packages, and its outlets in Europe experimented with edible breakfast plates made of maize.[192]

A study examined the relevant goals consumers have in recycling. It used a means–end chain analysis of the type described in Chapter 4 to identify how specific

Figure 9.8 Consumers' disposal options

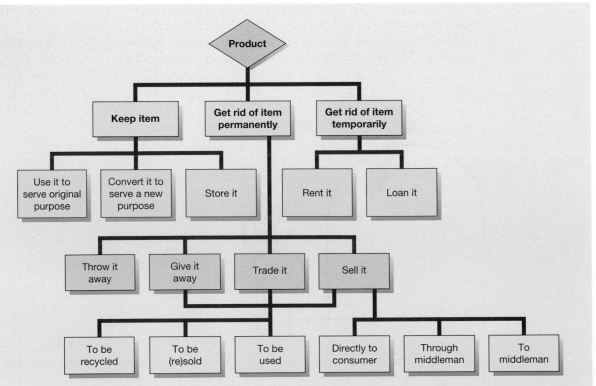

Source: Adapted from Jacob Jacoby, Carol K. Berning and Thomas F. Dietvorst, 'What about disposition?', *Journal of Marketing* 41 (April 1977): 23.

En als u erop uitgekeken bent,
ruimen we hem weer netjes op.

Volkswagen. Wie anders?

This Dutch ad says, 'and when you've had enough of it, we'll clear it away nicely'.
Courtesy of Volkswagen of The Netherlands

instrumental goals are linked to more abstract terminal values. The most important lower-order goals identified were 'avoid filling up landfills', 'reduce waste', 'reuse materials' and 'save the environment'. These were linked to the terminal values of 'promote health/avoid sickness', 'achieve life-sustaining ends' and 'provide for future generations'. Another study reported that the perceived effort involved in recycling was the best predictor of whether people would go to the trouble – this pragmatic dimension outweighed general attitudes toward recycling and the environment in predicting intention to recycle.[193] By applying such techniques to study recycling and other product disposal behaviours, it will be easier for social marketers to design advertising copy and other messages that tap into the underlying values that will motivate people to increase environmentally responsible behaviour.[194]

marketing pitfall

As if other kinds of waste weren't bad enough, one consequence of our infatuation with new technology is working out what to do with the things that quickly become obsolete. Now even discarded mobile phones are becoming a problem as customers rapidly switch among mobile services and upgrade to new models. One popular solution seems to be to ship unwanted electronic waste such as old computer monitors and circuit boards to the Third World. As much as 50 to 80 per cent of electronic waste collected for recycling in the United States is placed on container ships and sent to China, India, Pakistan or other developing countries, where it is reused or recycled under largely unregulated conditions. Recycling industries in these places often use young children to handle cathode ray tubes filled with lead and other toxic substances. The European Union is so concerned about the problem that it is moving toward requiring manufacturers to take cradle-to-grave responsibility for their products.[195]

marketing opportunity

Some enterprising entrepreneurs have found profitable ways to encourage recycling by creating fashion items out of recycled materials. Two young jewellery designers in New York created a fad by making necklaces out of old bottle caps. They even pay homeless people to collect the caps. A company called Little Earth Productions Inc. makes all its products from recycled materials. They sell backpacks decorated with old licence plates, a shoulder bag made from rubber and hubcaps, and even purses crafted from discarded tuna cans.[196]

Lateral cycling: junk vs. 'junque'

▶ Interesting consumer processes occur during lateral cycling, where already-purchased objects are sold to others or exchanged for yet other things. Many purchases are made second-hand, rather than new. The reuse of other people's things is especially important in our throwaway society because, as one researcher put it, 'there is no longer an "away" to throw things to'.[197]

Flea markets, garage sales, classified advertisements, bartering for services, hand-me-downs, car-boot sales, charity shops and the black market all represent important alternative marketing systems that operate alongside the formal marketplace. In the United States the number of used-merchandise retail establishments has grown at about ten times the rate of other stores;[198] and the number of flea markets has grown exponentially since 1990 when there were more than 3,500.[199] These outlets provide consumers with opportunities to buy and sell items related to popular cultural events and people to which they have long-term attachments. For example, demand for rock 'n' roll memorabilia from icons like The Beatles or Buddy Holly remains strong. A buyer recently paid $850,000 for a guitar that formerly belonged to the Grateful Dead's Jerry Garcia.[200] In the face of the changing economic environment, and the mounting costs of weddings, there is a growing market for second-hand wedding dresses. Second-hand retailers report that business is booming. 'In order to keep their stock fresh with the latest styles – strapless and spaghetti-strap dresses are currently "in" – most bridal consignment

Flea markets are an important form of lateral cycling.
Alamy/Stockfolio

shops have age limits on dresses, ranging from one to three years, with unusual sizes or styles the exception. The gowns are typically reduced by 25 per cent or more from the retail price and the bride receives half of the sale; gowns that were originally in the $3,000 to $5,000 range, and by name designers like Ms Wang or Badgley Mischka, sell best.'[201]

The internet has revolutionized the lateral cycling process, as millions of people flock to eBay to buy and sell their 'treasures'. This phenomenally successful online auction site started as a trading post for Beanie Babies and other collectibles. Now two-thirds of the site's sales are for practical goods. eBay expects to sell $2 billion worth of used cars and $1 billion worth of computers a year. Coming next are event tickets, food, industrial equipment and property.[202]

Ironically, an economic slowdown is good news for auction sites like eBay, because it's the kind of business that prospers when other businesses aren't doing well. As one analyst explained, 'The interesting thing about eBay is that it may benefit because some people may choose not to buy something new, like a computer or consumer electronics.' Hobbies and crafts also are selling strongly, which may be due to the number of people staying at home rather than travelling.

Free recycling – which already existed in a number of forms offline, for example, jumble sales and donations to charity shops and church institutions (such as the Salvation Army) – has also started to emerge online with the establishment of **www.freecycle.org** by a consumer in Tucson, Arizona, keen to give away a queen-size bed and some packing peanuts. What started as an email circular to friends turned into a website for the exchange of unwanted items. 'Free, legal and appropriate for all ages': these are the only constraints on what is offered via the site.[203]

Despite its success, there's sometimes a bittersweet quality to eBay. Some of the sellers are listing computers, fancy cars, jewellery and other luxury items because they desperately need the money. As one vendor explained when he described the classic convertible he wanted to sell, 'I am out of money and need to pay my rent, so my toys have to be sold.' The site witnessed a particularly strong surge in these kinds of messages following 9/11 when many people got laid off in the wake of a sluggish economy. In the words of an accountant who lost his job, 'Things were bad before, and then they got really bad after the bombings. Everything completely dried up.' Noting that he used to sell merchandise on eBay as a hobby but now he's forced to sell some of his own possessions, including his BMW and his wife's jewellery, he commented, 'If it weren't for eBay, I'm not sure what I'd be doing. We definitely would not be able to pay the bills.'[204]

While traditional marketers have paid little attention to the second-hand market,[205] factors such as concern about the environment, demands for quality and cost and fashion consciousness are conspiring to make these 'secondary' markets more important.[206] Economic estimates of this **underground economy** range from 3 per cent to 30 per cent of the GNP of the USA and up to 70 per cent of the GDP of other countries. Interest in antiques, period accessories and specialized magazines catering for this niche is increasing. Lassco (London Architectural Salvage and Supply Company) has many reclaimed items, ranging from padded green leather desks from the old British Library Reading Room (retailing for £6,500, about 9,500 euros), a red Gilbert Scott telephone box (for £750, or 1,100 euros), to stained-glass windows from churches (£10,000, or over 16,000 euros). '**Reclaimers** are not, strictly speaking, antique dealers, and very definitely not junk merchants . . . they are not in the business of plundering the past, they are in the business of rescuing large lumps of history from the wrecking ball . . . reclaiming is . . . part of the current craze for "collectables" (architectural salvage is big on eBay).'[207] Other growth areas include markets for used computers and ski swaps, where used ski equipment is exchanged. A new generation of second-hand shopkeepers is developing markets for everything from used office equipment to cast-off kitchen sinks. Many are non-profit ventures started with government funding. These efforts remind us that recycling is actually the last step in the familiar mantra of the environmental movement: reduce, reuse, recycle.[208] Only if no use is found for an item should it be shredded and made into something else.

■ CHAPTER SUMMARY

- *The act of purchase* can be affected by many factors. These include the consumer's antecedent state (his or her mood, time pressure, or disposition toward shopping). Time is an important resource that often determines how much effort and search will go into a decision. Mood can be affected by the degree of pleasure and arousal present in a store environment.

- *The usage context* of a product can be a basis for segmentation; consumers look for different product attributes depending on the use to which they intend to put their purchase. The presence or absence of other people (co-consumers) - and the types of people they are - can also affect a consumer's decisions.

- *The shopping experience* is a pivotal part of the purchase decision. In many cases, retailing is like theatre - the consumer's evaluation of stores and products may depend on the type of 'performance' he or she witnesses. This evaluation can be influenced by the actors (salespeople), the setting (the store environment), and props (store displays). A *store image*, like a brand personality, is determined by a number of factors such as perceived convenience, sophistication, expertise of salespeople, and so on. With increasing competition from non-store alternatives, the creation of a positive shopping experience has never been more important. Online shopping is growing in importance, and this new way to acquire products has both good (e.g. convenience) and bad (e.g. security) aspects.

- Since many purchase decisions are not made until the time the consumer is actually in the store, *point-of-purchase (POP)* stimuli are very important sales tools. These include product samples, elaborate package displays, place-based media, and in-store promotional materials such as 'shelf talkers'. POP stimuli are particularly useful in stimulating impulse buying, where a consumer yields to a sudden urge for a product.

- The consumer's encounter with a salesperson is a complex and important process. The outcome can be affected by such factors as the salesperson's similarity to the customer and his or her perceived credibility.

- *Consumer satisfaction* is determined by the person's overall feeling toward the product after purchase. Many factors influence perceptions of product quality, including price, brand name and product performance. Satisfaction is often determined by the degree to which a product's performance is consistent with the consumer's prior expectations of how well it will function.

- *Product disposal* is an increasingly important problem. Recycling is one option that will continue to be stressed as consumers' environmental awareness grows. Products may also be introduced by consumers into secondary markets during a process of *lateral cycling* which occurs when objects are bought and sold second-hand or bartered in an increasingly important underground economy.

► KEY TERMS

Atmospherics (p. 323)
Co-consumers (p. 306)
Consumer satisfaction/dissatisfaction (CS/D) (p. 328)
Cyberspace (p. 315)
Exchange theory (p. 327)
Expectancy disconfirmation model (p. 329)
Gemba (p. 332)
Impulse buying (p. 324)
ISO standards (p. 329)

Lateral cycling (p. 336)
Point-of-purchase stimuli (POP) (p. 326)
Queuing theory (p. 308)
Reclaimers (p. 337)
Retail theming (p. 321)
Shopping orientation (p. 313)
Store gestalt (p. 323)
Store image (p. 322)
Time poverty (p. 307)
Time style (p. 306)
Underground economy (p. 337)

CONSUMER BEHAVIOUR CHALLENGE

1 Discuss some of the motivations for shopping described in the chapter. How might a retailer adjust his or her strategy to accommodate these motivations?

2 Compare and contrast the two lists of hedonic shopping motives identified on pp. 312 and 313 in European and US research. How would you account for any differences? Why might shopping motives vary across cultures?

3 Do you think shopping motives might be different between online and offline shopping? If so, why?

4 What are some positive and negative aspects of requiring employees who interact with customers to wear some kind of uniform or to impose a dress code in the office?

5 Think about exceptionally good and bad salespeople you have encountered in the past. What qualities seem to differentiate them?

6 List the five stages of a long-term service relationship. How can a practitioner of relationship marketing incorporate each stage into his or her strategy?

7 The store environment is heating up as more and more companies put their promotional resources into point-of-purchase efforts. Shoppers are now confronted by videos at the checkout, computer monitors attached to their shopping trolleys, and so on. Place-based media expose us to ads in non-shopping environments. Do you feel that these innovations are unacceptably intrusive? At what point might shoppers rebel and demand some peace while shopping? Do you see any market potential in the future for stores that 'counter-market' by promising a 'hands-off' shopping environment?

8 Find a spectacular consumption environment and examine how consumers' play is encouraged and constrained by producers. How is technology used by producers and consumers in this environment to create and alter the sense of reality and

space in this spectacular environment? If you don't have a spectacular consumption environment near you, consider these questions (and the associated research findings) about the co-creation of meaning between producers and consumers within the context of the online world e.g. computer games.

9 Discuss the concept of 'time style'. Based on your own experiences, how might consumers be segmented in terms of their time styles?

10 Recent research (among American married and single women without children) has shown that there are major differences in individuals' attitudes and behaviours in relation to shopping across five metaphors of time as: pressure cooker; map; mirror; river; and feast. Consider how these temporal metaphors might vary across households (e.g. married with children); age (e.g. empty nest households); and culture.

11 Compare and contrast different cultures' conceptions of time. What are some implications for marketing strategy within each of these frameworks?

12 The movement away from a 'disposable consumer society' towards one that emphasizes creative recycling creates many opportunities for marketers. Can you identify some?

13 Conduct naturalistic observation at a local mall or shopping centre. Sit in a central location and observe the activities of mall staff and customers. Keep a log of the non-retailing activity you observe (special performances, exhibits, socializing, etc.). Does this activity enhance or detract from business conducted at the mall or shopping centre? As malls become more like high-tech game rooms, how valid is the criticism that shopping areas are only encouraging more loitering by teenage boys, who don't spend a lot in stores and simply scare away other customers?

14 Use the first five items from the eTailQ tool in Table 9.2 on p. 317 to compare and contrast six websites in two different product and service categories for their website design. Are there any other aspects of these websites' design which you might want to include in this comparison? Compare your extra items with the full range of eTailQ items (Table 2 in Wolfinbarger and Gilly 2003: 188-9, see n. 80 on p. 343).

15 Select three competing clothing stores in your area and conduct a store image study for each one. Ask a group of consumers to rate each store on a set of attributes and plot these ratings on the same graph. Based on your findings, are there any areas of competitive advantage or disadvantage you could bring to the attention of store management? (This technique was described in Chapter 5.)

16 Using Table 9.1 (p. 304) as a model, construct a person/situation segmentation matrix for a brand of perfume.

17 What applications of queuing theory can you find employed among local services? Interview consumers who are waiting in queues to determine how this experience affects their satisfaction with the service.

18 Discuss and critique the view that 'shoppers who blend store, mail order catalogues and websites spend more'.[209]

19 New interactive tools are being introduced that allow surfers on sites such as landsend.com to view apparel product selections on virtual models in full,

360-degree rotational view. In some cases, the viewer can modify the bodies, face, skin colouring and hairstyles of these models. In others, the consumer can project his or her *own* likeness into the space by scanning a photo into a 'makeover' program.[210] Visit **landsend.com** or another site that offers a personalized model. Surf around. Try on some clothes. How was your experience – how helpful was this model? When you shop for clothes online, would you rather see how they look on a body with dimensions the same as yours, or on a different body? What advice can you give website designers who are trying to personalize these shopping environments by creating life-like models to guide you through the site?

20 Choy and Loker (2004)[211] explored and classified internet sites supporting the wedding industry and the purchase of a wedding gown in their study of mass customization. They identified four major categories: marketing, browsing, advice and customizing. Choose another industry (e.g. mother and baby; travel; leisure; pets; music) and classify the websites according to their characteristics and strategies. What categories can you identify?

■ NOTES

1. 'Consumers hit at poor service', *Marketing* (5 December 1996): 4.
2. Laurette Dube and Bernd H. Schmitt, 'The Processing of Emotional and Cognitive Aspects of Product Usage in Satisfaction Judgments', in Rebecca H. Holman and Michael R. Solomon, eds, *Advances in Consumer Research* 18 (Provo, UT: Association for Consumer Research, 1991): 52–6; Lalita A. Manrai and Meryl P. Gardner, 'The Influence of Affect on Attributions for Product Failure', in ibid.: 249–54.
3. Peter J. Burke and Stephen L. Franzoi, 'Studying situations and identities using experimental sampling methodology', *American Sociological Review* 53 (August 1988): 559–68.
4. Kevin G. Celuch and Linda S. Showers, 'It's Time To Stress *Stress*: the Stress-Purchase/Consumption Relationship', in Holman and Solomon, eds, *Advances in Consumer Research* 18: 284–9; Lawrence R. Lepisto, J. Kathleen Stuenkel and Linda K. Anglin, 'Stress: An Ignored Situational Influence', in ibid.: 296–302.
5. See Eben Shapiro, 'Need a little fantasy? A bevy of new companies can help', *New York Times* (10 March 1991): F4.
6. John D. Mayer and Yvonne N. Gaschke, 'The experience and meta-experience of mood', *Journal of Personality and Social Psychology* 55 (July 1988): 102–11.
7. Meryl Paula Gardner, 'Mood states and consumer behavior: A critical review', *Journal of Consumer Research* 12 (December 1985): 281–300; Scott Dawson, Peter H. Bloch and Nancy M. Ridgway, 'Shopping motives, emotional states, and retail outcomes', *Journal of Retailing* 66 (Winter 1990): 408–27; Patricia A. Knowles, Stephen J. Grove and W. Jeffrey Burroughs, 'An experimental examination of mood states on retrieval and evaluation of advertisement and brand information', *Journal of the Academy of Marketing Science* 21 (April 1993): 135–43; Paul W. Miniard, Sunil Bhatla and Deepak Sirdeskmuhk, 'Mood as a determinant of postconsumption product evaluations: Mood effects and their dependency on the affective intensity of the consumption experience', *Journal of Consumer Psychology* 1 (1992) 2: 173–95; Mary T. Curren and Katrin R. Harich, 'Consumers' mood states: The mitigating influence of personal relevance on product evaluations', *Psychology and Marketing* 11(2) (March/April 1994): 91–107; Gerald J. Gorn, Marvin E. Goldberg and Kunal Basu, 'Mood, awareness, and product evaluation', *Journal of Consumer Psychology* 2(3) (1993): 237–56.
8. Gordon C. Bruner, 'Music, mood, and marketing', *Journal of Marketing* 54 (October 1990): 94–104; Basil G. Englis, 'Music Television and its Influences on Consumers, Consumer Culture, and the Transmission of Consumption Messages', in Holman and Solomon, eds, *Advances in Consumer Research* 18: 111–14; see also Steve Oakes, 'Examining the Relationships Between Background Musical Tempo and Perceived Duration Using Different Versions of a Radio Ad', in B. Dubois, T. Lowrey, L.J. Shrum and M. Vanhuele, eds, *European Advances in Consumer Research* 4 (Provo, UT: Association of Consumer Research, 1999): 40–4.
9. Marvin E. Goldberg and Gerald J. Gorn, 'Happy and sad TV programs: How they affect reactions to commercials', *Journal of Consumer Research* 14 (December 1987): 387–403; Gorn, Goldberg and Basu, 'Mood, awareness, and product evaluation': 237–56; Curren and Harich, 'Consumers' mood states'.
10. Pradeep Kakkar and Richard J. Lutz, 'Situational Influence on Consumer Behavior: A Review', in Harold H. Kassarjian and Thomas S. Robertson, eds, *Perspectives in Consumer Behavior*, 3rd edn (Glenview, IL: Scott, Foresman, 1981): 204–14.
11. Carolyn Turner Schenk and Rebecca H. Holman, 'A Sociological Approach to Brand Choice: The Concept of Situational Self-Image', in Jerry C. Olson, ed., *Advances in*

Consumer Research 7 (Ann Arbor, MI: Association for Consumer Research, 1980): 610–14.

12. Russell W. Belk, 'An exploratory assessment of situational effects in buyer behavior', *Journal of Marketing Research* 11 (May 1974): 156–63; U.N. Umesh and Joseph A. Cote, 'Influence of situational variables on brand-choice models', *Journal of Business Research* 16(2) (1988): 91–9; see also J. Wesley Hutchinson and Joseph W. Alba, 'Ignoring irrelevant information: Situational determinants of consumer learning', *Journal of Consumer Research* 18 (December 1991): 325–45.

13. Gordon Foxall, 'Science and interpretation in consumer research: A radical behaviorist perspective', *European Journal of Marketing* 29(9) (1995): 1–90; Gordon Foxall, 'The Consumer Situation as Interpretive Device', in Flemming Hansen, ed., *European Advances in Consumer Research* 2 (Provo, UT: Association for Consumer Research, 1995): 104–8.

14. Laura Bird, 'Grey poupon tones down Tory image', *Wall Street Journal* (22 July 1994): B2.

15. Peter R. Dickson, 'Person–situation: segmentation's missing link', *Journal of Marketing* 46 (Fall 1982): 56–64.

16. Bernard Dubois and Gilles Laurent, 'A Situational Approach to Brand Loyalty', in E. Arnould and L. Scott, eds, *Advances in Consumer Research* 26 (Provo, UT: Association for Consumer Research, 1999): 657–63.

17. Booz-Allen Hamilton's Digital Consumer Project and Nielsen/NetRatings reported in Laura Mazur, 'Web marketers must now adapt to the occasion', *Marketing* (29 May 2003): 16 (http://search.epnet.com/login.aspx?direct=true&db=buh&an=10029509).

18. Laura Mazur, 'Web marketers must now adapt to the occasion'.

19. Anja Stöhr, 'Air-Design: Exploring the Role of Scents in Retail Environments', in B. Englis and A. Olofsson, eds, *European Advances in Consumer Research* 3 (Provo, UT: Association for Consumer Research, 1998): 126–32.

20. Delphine Dion, 'A Theoretical and Empirical Study of Retail Crowding', in Dubois, Lowrey, Shrum and Vanhuele, eds, *European Advances in Consumer Research* 4: 51–7.

21. Daniel Stokols, 'On the distinction between density and crowding: Some implications for future research', *Psychological Review* 79 (1972): 275–7.

22. Carol Felker Kaufman, Paul M. Lane and Jay D. Lindquist, 'Exploring more than 24 hours a day: A preliminary investigation of polychronic time use', *Journal of Consumer Research* 18 (December 1991): 392–401.

23. Laurence P. Feldman and Jacob Hornik, 'The use of time: An integrated conceptual model', *Journal of Consumer Research* 7 (March 1981): 407–19; see also Michelle M. Bergadaa, 'The role of time in the action of the consumer', *Journal of Consumer Research* 17 (December 1990): 289–302.

24. Jean-Claude Usunier and Pierre Valette-Florence, 'Individual time orientation: A psychometric scale', *Time and Society* 3(2) (1994): 219–41.

25. June Cotte, S. Ratneshwar and David Glen Mick, 'The times of their lives: Phenomenological and metaphorical characteristics of consumer timestyles', *Journal of Consumer Research* 31 (September 2004): 333–45.

26. Ibid.

27. Robert J. Samuelson, 'Rediscovering the rat race', *Newsweek* (15 May 1989): 57.

28. Jared Sandberg, 'NoChores.com', *Newsweek* (30 August 1999): 30 (2).

29. Jack Neff, 'Dawn of the online icebox', *Advertising Age* (15 March 1999): 17.

30. 'Plugged in: Hong Kong embraces the Octopus Card', *The New York Times on the Web* (8 June 2002).

31. Kaufman, Lane and Lindquist, 'Exploring more than 24 hours a day'.

32. Quoted in 'Fast food? It just isn't fast enough anymore', *New York Times* (6 December 1989): A1.

33. John P. Robinson, 'Time squeeze', *Advertising Age* (February 1990): 30–3.

34. Agnès Durande-Moreau and Jean-Claude Usunier, 'Individual Time-Styles and Customer Satisfaction: The Case of the Waiting Experience', in *Marketing for an Expanding Europe*, Proceedings of the 25th EMAC Conference, ed. J. Berács, A. Bauer and J. Simon (Budapest: Budapest University of Economic Sciences, 1996): 371–90; see also Shirley Taylor, 'Waiting for service: The relationship between delays and evaluations of service', *Journal of Marketing* 58 (April 1994): 56–69.

35. Ad Pruyn and Ade Smidts, 'Customers' Reactions to Waiting: Effects of the Presence of "Fellow Sufferers" in the Waiting Room', in Arnould and Scott, eds, *Advances in Consumer Research* 26: 211–16.

36. Quoted in Gabriele Morello, 'Sicilian time', *Time and Society* 6(1) (1997): 55–69. However, Morello concludes that in spite of such indications of traditional time perceptions, modernization is showing up in changed paces and attitudes towards time also in Sicily.

37. David H. Maister, 'The Psychology of Waiting Lines', in John A. Czepiel, Michael R. Solomon and Carol F. Surprenant, eds, *The Service Encounter: Managing Employee/Customer Interaction in Service Businesses* (Lexington, MA: Lexington Books, 1985): 113–24.

38. A.T.H. Pruyn and A. Smidts, 'Customers' Evaluations of Queues: Three Exploratory Studies', in W.F. van Raaij and G. Bamossy, eds, *European Advances in Consumer Research* 1 (Provo, UT: Association for Consumer Research, 1993): 371–82.

39. Johan Anselmsson, 'Customer-Perceived Service Quality and Technology-Based Self-Service', doctoral dissertation, Lund University, 2001.

40. Robert J. Graham, 'The role of perception of time in consumer research', *Journal of Consumer Research* 7 (March 1981): 335–42.

41. Alan Zarembo, 'What if there weren't any clocks to watch?', *Newsweek* (30 June 1997): 14; based on research reported in Robert Levine, *A Geography of Time: The Temporal Misadventures of a Social Psychologist, or How Every Culture Keeps Time Just a Little Bit Differently* (New York: Basic Books, 1997).

42. See also Morello, 'Sicilian time'.

43. David Lewis and Darren Bridger, *The Soul of the New Consumer: Authenticity – What We Buy and Why in the New Economy* (London: Nicholas Brealey Publishing, 2000).

44. Sigmund Grønmo, 'Concepts of Time: Some Implications for Consumer Research', in Thomas K. Srull, ed., *Advances*

in Consumer Research 16 (Provo, UT: Association for Consumer Research 1989): 339–45.

45. Gabriele Morello and P. van der Reis, 'Attitudes Towards Time in Different Cultures: African Time and European Time', *Proceedings of the Third Symposium on Cross-Cultural Consumer and Business Studies* (Honolulu: University of Hawaii, 1990); Gabriele Morello, 'Our attitudes towards time', *Forum 96/2* (European Forum for Management Development, 1996): 48–51.

46. Gary Davies, 'What should time be?', *European Journal of Marketing* 28(8/9) (1994): 100–13.

47. Esther S. Page-Wood, Carol J. Kaufman and Paul M. Lane, 'The Art of Time', in Proceedings of the Academy of Marketing Science (1990).

48. Eric N. Berg, 'Fight on quick pizza delivery grows', *New York Times* (29 August 1989): D6.

49. Søren Askegaard and Tage Koed Madsen, 'The local and the global: Traits of homogeneity and heterogeneity in European food cultures', *International Business Review* 7(6) (1998): 549–68; for a thorough discussion of food culture, see Claude Fischler, *L'Homnivore* (Paris: Odile Jacob, 1990).

50. Mark J. Arnold and Kristy E. Reynolds, 'Hedonic shopping motivations', *Journal of Retailing* 79 (2003): 90–1.

51. Daniel Miller, *A Theory of Shopping* (Cambridge: Polity Press, 1998).

52. For a scale that was devised to assess these dimensions of the shopping experience, see Barry J. Babin, William R. Darden and Mitch Griffin, 'Work and/or fun: Measuring hedonic and utilitarian shopping value', *Journal of Consumer Research* 20 (March 1994): 644–56.

53. Ibid.

54. Adapted from Andrea Groeppel-Klein, Eva Thelen and Christoph Antretter, 'The Impact of Shopping Motives on Store Assessment', in Dubois, Lowrey, Shrum and Vanhuele, eds, *European Advances in Consumer Research* 4: 63–72.

55. Quoted in Robert C. Prus, *Making Sales: Influence as Interpersonal Accomplishment* (Newbury Park, CA: Sage Library of Social Research, Sage, 1989): 225.

56. Arnold and Reynolds, 'Hedonic shopping motivations': 77–95.

57. Ibid.: 80–1.

58. For a scale that was devised to assess these dimensions of the shopping experience, see Babin, Darden and Griffin, 'Work and/or fun: measuring hedonic and utilitarian shopping value'.

59. Cele Otnes and Mary Ann McGrath, 'Perceptions and realities of male shopping behavior,' *Journal of Retailing* 77 (Spring 2001): 111–37.

60. Arnold and Reynolds, 'Hedonic shopping motivations': 89–90.

61. Gregory P. Stone, 'City shoppers and urban identification: Observations on the social psychology of city life', *American Journal of Sociology* 60 (1954): 36–45; Danny Bellenger and Pradeep K. Korgaonkar, 'Profiling the recreational shopper', *Journal of Retailing* 56(3) (1980): 77–92.

62. Stephen Brown and Rhona Reid, 'Shoppers on the Verge of a Nervous Breakdown', in S. Brown and D. Turley, eds, *Consumer Research: Postcards from the Edge* (London: Routledge, 1997): 79–149.

63. Nina Gruen, 'The retail battleground: Solutions for today's shifting marketplace', *Journal of Property Management* (July–August 1989): 14.

64. 'Petrol selling: Pump action', *The Economist* (27 January 1996): 62.

65. Personal communication with a Finnish reviewer.

66. 'Slaget om Europa', *Jyllands Posten* (12 February 1997).

67. Arieh Goldman, 'The shopping style explanation for store loyalty', *Journal of Retailing* 53 (Winter 1977–8): 33–46, 94; Robert B. Settle and Pamela L. Alreck, 'Hyperchoice shapes the marketplace', *Marketing Communications* (May 1988): 15.

68. 'Kundekort som konkurrencevåben', *Export* 36 (6 September 1996): 4–6.

69. Some material in this section was adapted from Michael R. Solomon and Elnora W. Stuart, *Welcome to Marketing.Com: The Brave New World of E-Commerce* (Upper Saddle River, NJ: Prentice Hall, 2001).

70. Seema Williams, David M. Cooperstein, David E. Weisman and Thalika Oum, 'Post-web retail', *The Forrester Report*, Forrester Research, Inc., September 1999; Catherine Arnold, 'Across the pond', *Marketing News* (28 October 2002): 3.

71. Mikael Lundström, 'E-handel inget för svensson', *Info* 8 (2000): 52–4.

72. Rebecca K. Ratner, Barbara E. Kahn and Daniel Kahneman, 'Choosing less-preferred experiences for the sake of variety', *Journal of Consumer Research* 26 (June 1999): 1–15.

73. *Markedsføring* (25 November 2000): 18.

74. Ellen Sheng, 'Advertisers sharpen their targeting', *WSJ Online* (27 October 2004).

75. *Markedsføring* (25 September 2000): 22.

76. *Markedsføring* (9 November 2000): 14.

77. Jennifer Gilbert, 'Customer service crucial to online buyers', *Advertising Age* (13 September 1999): 52.

78. 'The grid layout is a rectangular arrangement of displays and long aisles that generally run parallel to one another. The freeform layout is a free-flowing and asymmetric arrangement of displays and aisles, employing a variety of different sizes, shapes and styles of display. In the racetrack/boutique layout, the sales floor is organized into individual, semi-separate areas, each built around a particular shopping theme': Adam P. Vrechopolous, Robert M. O'Keefe, Georgios I. Doukidis and George J. Siomkos, 'Virtual store layout: An experimental comparison in the context of grocery retail', *Journal of Retailing* 80 (2004): 13–22.

79. Ibid.

80. Mary Wolfinbarger and Mary C. Gilly, 'eTailQ: Dimensionalizing, measuring and predicting etail quality', *Journal of Retailing* 79 (2003): 183–98. Their article provides a useful managerial tool (eTailQ) for assessing the quality of virtual stores.

81. Datamonitor predicted that by the end of 2003 almost 60 million European consumers would bank online: Laura Mazur, 'Web marketers must now adapt to the occasion', *Marketing* (29 May 2003): 16 (http://search.epnet.com/login.aspx?direct-true&db-buh&an=10029509).

82. Bob Tedeschi, 'More e-commerce sites aim to add "Sticky" Content', *NYT Online* (9 August 2004).

83. Kevin J. O'Brien, 'German quiz shows thrive as contestants stay home', *NYT Online* (9 August 2004).

84. Chuan-Fong Shih, 'Conceptualizing consumer experiences in cyberspace', *European Journal of Marketing* 32(7/8) (1998): 655–63.

85. Quoted in Timothy L. O'Brien, 'Aided by internet, identity theft soars', *The New York Times on the Web* (3 April 2000).

86. Alka Varma Citrin, Donald E. Stern, Eric R. Spangenberg and Michael J. Clark, 'Consumer need for tactile input: An internet retailing challenge', *Journal of Business Research* 56 (2003): 915–22. See also Joann Peck and Terry L. Childers, 'Individual differences in haptic information processing: The need for touch scale', *Journal of Consumer Research* 30 (December 2003): 430–42, whose scale includes both instrumental and autotelic factors which differentiate between need for touch as part of the pre-purchase decision-making process, and the need for touch as an end in itself. The importance of touch (particularly as an end in itself) points to this as a potential barrier to the use of e-commerce by some consumers across all product groups.

87. Rita Choy and Suzanne Loker, 'Mass customization of wedding gowns: Design involvement on the internet', *Clothing and Textiles Research Journal* 22(1&2) (2004): 79–87.

88. *Markedsføring* (17 February 2000): 20.

89. Kortnery Stringer, 'Shoppers who blend store, catalog, web spend more', *The Wall Street Journal Online* (3 September 2004): A7.

90. Marc Gobé, *Emotional Branding: The New Paradigm for Connecting Brands to People* (New York: Allworth Press, 2001): xxv.

91. Ibid.

92. An excellent collection of articles on this topic is found in Pasi Falk and Colin Campbell, eds, *The Shopping Experience* (London: Sage, 1997).

93. C. Gardner and J. Sheppard, *Consuming Passion: The Rise of Retail Culture* (London: Unwin Hyman, 1989).

94. Stephen Brown, 'Sex 'n' Shopping', Working Paper 9501 (University of Stirling: Institute for Retail Studies, 1995); see also Stephen Brown, 'Consumption Behaviour in the Sex 'n' Shopping Novels of Judith Krantz: A Poststructuralist Perspective', in Kim P. Corfman and John G. Lynch, Jr., eds, *Advances in Consumer Research* 23 (Provo, UT: Association for Consumer Research, 1996): 43–8.

95. Véronique Aubert-Gamet, 'Twisting servicescapes: Diversion of the physical environment in a re-appropriation process', *International Journal of Service Industry Management* 8(1) (1997): 26–41.

96. Stephen Brown, *Postmodern Marketing* (London: Routledge, 1995), discussion on pp. 50ff.; Lars Thøger Christensen and Søren Askegaard, 'Flexibility in the marketing organization: The ultimate consumer orientation or Ford revisited?', *Marketing Today and for the 21st Century*, Proceedings of the XIV EMAC Conference, ed. Michelle Bergadàà (Cergy-Pontoise: ESSEC, 1995): 1507–14.

97. For a study of consumer shopping patterns in a mall that views the mall as an ecological habitat, see Peter N. Bloch, Nancy M. Ridgway and Scott A. Dawson, 'The shopping mall as consumer habitat', *Journal of Retailing* 70(1) (1994): 23–42.

98. Turo-Kimmo Lehtonen and Pasi Mäenpää, 'Shopping in the East Centre Mall', in Falk and Campbell, eds, *The Shopping Experience*: 136–65.

99. Quoted in Jacquelyn Bivins, 'Fun and mall games', *Stores* (August 1989): 35.

100. Sallie Hook, 'All the retail world's a stage: Consumers conditioned to entertainment in shopping environment', *Marketing News* 21 (31 July 1987): 16.

101. Stephen Brown, 'Marketing as multiplex: Screening postmodernism', *European Journal of Marketing* 28(8/9) (1994): 27–51.

102. David Chaney, 'The department store as a cultural form', *Theory, Culture and Society* 1(3) (1983): 22–31.

103. Cecilia Fredriksson, 'The Making of a Swedish Department Store Culture', in Falk and Campbell, eds, *The Shopping Experience*: 111–35.

104. 'ING uses the soft sell for online banking unit', *Wall Street Journal* (17 October 2000): A18.

105. Pauline Maclaran and Lorna Stevens, 'Romancing the Utopian Marketplace', in S. Brown, A.M. Doherty and B. Clarke, eds, *Romancing the Market* (London: Routledge, 1998): 172–86.

106. Patrick Hetzel, 'When Hyperreality, Reality, Fiction and Non-Reality are Brought Together: A Fragmented Vision of the Mall of America Through Personal Interpretation', in Englis and Olofsson, eds, *European Advances in Consumer Research* 3: 261–6; see also Fabian Csaba, 'Designing the Retail-Entertainment Complex: A Marketing Ethnography of the Mall of America', doctoral dissertation, Odense University, School of Business and Economics, 1998.

107. Millie Creighton, 'The Seed of Creative Lifestyle Shopping: Wrapping Consumerism in Japanese Store Layouts', in ed. John F. Sherry Jr., *Servicescapes: The Concept of Place in Contemporary Markets* (Lincolnwood, IL: NTC Business Books, 1998): 199–228.

108. 'Enticing Europe's shoppers: U.S. way of dressing and of retailing spreading fast', *New York Times* (24 April 1996): D1(2).

109. Robert V. Kozinets, John F. Sherry, Diana Storm, Adam Duhachek, Krittinee Nuttavuthisit and Benet DeBerry-Spence, 'Ludic agency and retail spectacle', *Journal of Consumer Research* 31 (December 2004): 658–72.

110. Patrick Hetzel and Veronique Aubert, 'Sales Area Design and Fashion Phenomena: A Semiotic Approach', in van Raaij and Bamossy, eds, *European Advances in Consumer Research* 1: 522–33.

111. Søren Askegaard and Güliz Ger, 'Product-Country Images as Stereotypes: A Comparative Analysis of the Image of Danish Food Products in Germany and Turkey', *MAPP Working Paper* 45 (Aarhus: The Aarhus School of Business, 1997).

112. Susan Spiggle and Murphy A. Sewall, 'A choice sets model of retail selection', *Journal of Marketing* 51 (April 1987): 97–111; William R. Darden and Barry J. Babin, 'The role of emotions in expanding the concept of retail personality', *Stores* 76 (April 1994) 4: RR7–RR8.

113. Most measures of store image are quite similar to other attitude measures, as discussed in Chapter 5. For an

excellent bibliography of store image studies, see Mary R. Zimmer and Linda L. Golden, 'Impressions of retail stores: A content analysis of consumer images,' *Journal of Retailing* 64 (Fall 1988): 265–93.

114. Ibid.

115. Spiggle and Sewall, 'A choice sets model of retail selection'.

116. Philip Kotler, 'Atmospherics as a marketing tool,' *Journal of Retailing* (Winter 1973–74): 10; Anna Mattila and Jochen Wirtz, 'Congruency of scent and music as a driver of in-store evaluations and behavior', *Journal of Retailing* 77 (Summer 2001): 273–89; J. Duncan Herrington, 'An Integrative Path Model of the Effects of Retail Environments on Shopper Behavior', in Robert L. King, ed., *Marketing: Toward the Twenty-First Century* (Richmond, VA: Southern Marketing Association, 1991): 58–62; see also Ann E. Schlosser, 'Applying the functional theory of attitudes to understanding the influence of store atmosphere on store inferences', *Journal of Consumer Psychology* 7(4) (1998): 345–69.

117. Fabian Csaba and Søren Askegaard, 'Malls and the Orchestration of the Shopping Experience in a Historical Perspective', in Arnould and Scott, eds, *Advances in Consumer Research* 26: 34–40.

118. Deborah Blumenthal, 'Scenic design for in-store try-ons', *New York Times* (9 April 1988): N9.

119. Charles S. Areni and David Kim, 'The influence of in-store lighting on consumers' examination of merchandise in a wine store', *International Journal of Research in Marketing* 11(2) (March 1994): 117–25.

120. Jean-Charles Chebat, Claire Gelinas Chebat and Dominique Vaillant, 'Environmental background music and in-store selling', *Journal of Business Research* 54 (2001): 115–23; Judy I. Alpert and Mark I. Alpert, 'Music influences on mood and purchase intentions', *Psychology and Marketing* 7 (Summer 1990): 109–34.

121. Brad Edmondson, 'Pass the meat loaf', *American Demographics* (January 1989): 19.

122. Dhruv Grewal, Julie Baker, Michael Levy and Glenn B. Voss, 'The effects of wait expectations and store atmosphere evaluations on patronage intentions in service-intensive retail store', *Journal of Retailing* 79 (2003): 259–68.

123. 'Through the looking glass', *Lifestyle Monitor* 16 (Fall/Winter 2002).

124. 'Butikken er en slagmark', *Berlingske Tidende* (15 July 1996): 3.

125. Jennifer Lach, 'Meet you in aisle three', *American Demographics* (April 1999): 41.

126. Marianne Meyer, 'Attention shoppers!', *Marketing and Media Decisions* 23 (May 1988): 67.

127. Ernest Beck, 'Diageo attempts to reinvent the bar in an effort to increase spirits sales', *The Wall Street Journal* (23 February 2001).

128. Easwar S. Iyer, 'Unplanned purchasing: Knowledge of shopping environment and time pressure', *Journal of Retailing* 65 (Spring 1989): 40–57; C. Whan Park, Easwar S. Iyer and Daniel C. Smith, 'The effects of situational factors on in-store grocery shopping', *Journal of Consumer Research* 15 (March 1989): 422–33.

129. Michael Wahl, 'Eye POPping persuasion', *Marketing Insights* (June 1989): 130.

130. 'Zipping down the aisles', *New York Times Magazine* (6 April 1997).

131. Peter McGoldrick, Erica J. Betts and Kathleen A. Keeling, 'Antecedents of Spontaneous Buying Behaviour During Temporary Markdowns', in Arnould and Scott, eds, *Advances in Consumer Research* 26: 26–33.

132. Cathy J. Cobb and Wayne D. Hoyer, 'Planned versus impulse purchase behavior', *Journal of Retailing* 62 (Winter 1986): 384–409; Easwar S. Iyer and Sucheta S. Ahlawat, 'Deviations from a Shopping Plan: When and Why Do Consumers Not Buy as Planned?', in Melanie Wallendorf and Paul Anderson, eds, *Advances in Consumer Research* 14 (Provo, UT: Association for Consumer Research, 1987): 246–9.

133. Andrea Groeppel-Klein, 'The Influence of the Dominance Perceived at the Point-of-Sale on the Price-Assessment', in Englis and Olofsson, eds, *European Advances in Consumer Research* 3: 304–11.

134. Dennis Desrochers, 'European consumers respond to spray samplers', *Global Cosmetic Industry* 171(16) (June 2003): 28.

135. Chairman-CEO A.G. Laffley, quoted in Jack Neff, 'P&G boosts design's role in marketing', *Advertising Age* (9 February 2004): 52.

136. Claudia Kotschka, 'VP design, strategy and innovation', quoted in ibid.

137. William Keenan, Jr., 'Point-of-purchase: From clutter to technoclutter', *Sales and Marketing Management* 141 (April 1989): 96.

138. *Markedsføring* 13 (1999): 24.

139. Meyer, 'Attention shoppers!'.

140. Cyndee Miller, 'Videocart spruces up for new tests', *Marketing News* (19 February 1990): 19; William E. Sheeline, 'User-friendly shopping carts', *Fortune* (5 December 1988): 9.

141. Bernard Swoboda, 'Multimedia Customer Information Systems at the Point of Sale: Selected Results of an Impact Analysis', in Englis and Olofsson, eds, *European Advances in Consumer Research* 3: 239–46.

142. 'Effective demands', *Marketing* (5 December 1996): 34–8.

143. 'A never-ending toy story', *Marketing* (5 December 1996): 33.

144. Erin White, 'Look up for new products in aisle 5: In-store TV advertising gains traction globally; Timely pitch at shoppers', *The Wall Street Journal Online* (23 March 2004): B11.

145. John P. Cortez, 'Media pioneers try to corral on-the-go consumers', *Advertising Age* (17 August 1992): 25.

146. Merissa Marr, 'Fox to pitch its movies at the mall as TV-ad costs escalate: Studio says new approach avoids broadcast clutter', *The Wall Street Journal Online* (15 July 2004): B6.

147. Cyndee Miller, 'MTV "Video Capsule" features sports for music retailers, corporate sponsors', *Marketing News* (3 February 1992): 5.

148. 'Dutch shop lets clients burn own CDs', *Wall Street Journal* (14 November 2000): B10.

149. Constance L. Hays, 'Wal-Mart is upgrading its vast in-store television network, the fifth-largest television network in the United States', *NYT Online* (21 February 2005).

150. Sally Beatty, 'Bank of America places ads in ATMs to offset expenses', *The Wall Street Journal Interactive Edition* (25 July 2002); David L. Margulus, 'Going to the A.T.M. for more than a fistful of twenties', *New York Times on the Web* (17 January 2002).

151. See Robert B. Cialdini, *Influence: Science and Practice*, 2nd edn (Glenview, IL: Scott, Foresman, 1988).

152. Richard P. Bagozzi, 'Marketing as exchange', *Journal of Marketing* 39 (October 1975): 32–9; Peter M. Blau, *Exchange and Power in Social Life* (New York: Wiley, 1964); Marjorie Caballero and Alan J. Resnik, 'The attraction paradigm in dyadic exchange', *Psychology and Marketing* 3(1) (1986): 17–34; George C. Homans, 'Social behavior as exchange', *American Journal of Sociology* 63 (1958): 597–606; Paul H. Schurr and Julie L. Ozanne, 'Influences on exchange processes: Buyers' preconceptions of a seller's trust-worthiness and bargaining toughness', *Journal of Consumer Research* 11 (March 1985): 939–53; Arch G. Woodside and J.W. Davenport, 'The effect of salesman similarity and expertise on consumer purchasing beha-vior', *Journal of Marketing Research* 8 (1974): 433–6.

153. Paul Busch and David T. Wilson, 'An experimental analysis of a salesman's expert and referent bases of social power in the buyer–seller dyad', *Journal of Marketing Research* 13 (February 1976): 3–11; John E. Swan, Fred Trawick Jr., David R. Rink and Jenny J. Roberts, 'Measuring dimensions of purchaser trust of industrial salespeople', *Journal of Personal Selling and Sales Management* 8 (May 1988): 1.

154. For a study in this area, see Peter H. Reingen and Jerome B. Kernan, 'Social perception and interpersonal influence: Some consequences of the physical attractiveness stereo-type in a personal selling setting', *Journal of Consumer Psychology* 2 (1993): 25–38.

155. Linda L. Price and Eric J. Arnould, 'Commercial friend-ships: Service provider–client relationships in context', *Journal of Marketing* 63 (October 1999): 38–56.

156. Mary Jo Bitner, Bernard H. Booms and Mary Stansfield Tetreault, 'The service encounter: Diagnosing favorable and unfavorable incidents', *Journal of Marketing* 54 (January 1990): 7–84; Robert C. Prus, *Making Sales* (Newbury Park, CA: Sage, 1989); Arch G. Woodside and James L. Taylor, 'Identity Negotiations in Buyer–Seller Interactions', in Elizabeth C. Hirschman and Morris B. Holbrook, eds, *Advances in Consumer Research* 12 (Provo, UT: Association for Consumer Research, 1985): 443–9.

157. Barry J. Babin, James S. Boles and William R. Darden, 'Salesperson stereotypes, consumer emotions, and their impact on information processing', *Journal of the Academy of Marketing Science* 23(2) (1995): 94–105; Gilbert A. Churchill Jr., Neil M. Ford, Steven W. Hartley and Orville C. Walker Jr., 'The determinants of salesperson perform-ance: A meta-analysis', *Journal of Marketing Research* 22 (May 1985): 103–18.

158. Siew Meng Leong, Paul S. Busch and Deborah Roedder John, 'Knowledge bases and salesperson effectiveness: A script-theoretic analysis', *Journal of Marketing Research* 26 (May 1989): 164; Harish Sujan, Mita Sujan and James R. Bettman, 'Knowledge structure differences between more effective and less effective salespeople', *Journal of Marketing Research* 25 (February 1988): 81–6; Robert Saxe and Barton Weitz, 'The SOCCO scale: A measure of the customer orientation of salespeople', *Journal of Marketing Research* 19 (August 1982): 343–51; David M. Szymanski, 'Determinants of selling effectiveness: The importance of declarative knowledge to the personal selling concept', *Journal of Marketing* 52 (January 1988): 64–77; Barton A. Weitz, 'Effectiveness in sales interactions: A contingency framework,' *Journal of Marketing* 45 (Winter 1981): 85–103.

159. Jagdish M. Sheth, 'Buyer–Seller Interaction. A Conceptual Framework,' in Beverlee B. Anderson, ed., *Advances in Consumer Research* 3 (Cincinnati, OH: Association for Consumer Research, 1976): 382–6; Kaylene C. Williams and Rosann L. Spiro, 'Communication style in the salesperson–customer dyad', *Journal of Marketing Research* 22 (November 1985): 434–42.

160. Marsha L. Richins, 'An analysis of consumer interaction styles in the marketplace,' *Journal of Consumer Research* 10 (June 1983): 73–82.

161. Rama Jayanti and Anita Jackson, 'Service Satisfaction: Investigation of Three Models', in Holman and Solomon, eds, *Advances in Consumer Research* 18: 603–10; David K. Tse, Franco M. Nicosia and Peter C. Wilton, 'Consumer satisfaction as a process', *Psychology and Marketing* 7 (Fall 1990): 177–93. For a treatment of satisfaction issues from a more interpretive perspective, see Susan Fournier and David Mick, 'Rediscovering satisfaction,' *Journal of Marketing* 63 (October 1999): 5–23.

162. Constance L. Hayes, 'Service takes a holiday', *New York Times* (23 December 1998): C1.

163. Eugene W. Anderson, Claes Fornell and Donald R. Lehmann, 'Customer satisfaction, market share, and profitability: Findings from Sweden', *Journal of Marketing* 58(3) (July 1994): 53–66.

164. Robert Jacobson and David A. Aaker, 'The strategic role of product quality', *Journal of Marketing* 51 (October 1987): 31–44; for a review of issues regarding the measurement of service quality, see J. Joseph Cronin Jr. and Steven A. Taylor, 'Measuring service quality: A reexamination and extension', *Journal of Marketing* 56 (July 1992): 55–68.

165. Anna Kirmani and Peter Wright, 'Money talks: Perceived advertising expense and expected product quality', *Journal of Consumer Research* 16 (December 1989): 344–53; Donald R. Lichtenstein and Scot Burton, 'The relation-ship between perceived and objective price-quality', *Journal of Marketing Research* 26 (November 1989): 429–43; Akshay R. Rao and Kent B. Monroe, 'The effect of price, brand name, and store name on buyers' perceptions of product quality: An integrative review', *Journal of Marketing Research* 26 (August 1989): 351–7.

166. Shelby Hunt, 'Post-transactional communication and dis-sonance reduction', *Journal of Marketing* 34 (January 1970): 46–51; Daniel E. Innis and H. Rao Unnava, 'The Usefulness of Product Warranties for Reputable and New Brands,' in Holman and Solomon, eds, *Advances in Consumer Research* 18: 317–22; Terence A. Shimp and William O. Bearden, 'Warranty and other extrinsic

cue effects on consumers' risk perceptions', *Journal of Consumer Research* 9 (June 1982): 38–46.

167. Morris Holbrook and Kim Corfman, 'Quality and Value in the Consumption Experience: Phaedrus Rides Again', in J. Jacoby and J.C. Olson, eds, *Perceived Quality: How Consumers View Stores and Merchandise* (Lexington, MA: D.C. Heath & Co., 1985): 31–57; Robert M. Pirsig, *Zen and the Art of Motorcycle Maintenance: An Inquiry into Values* (New York: Bantam Books, 1974).

168. Mia Stokmans, 'The Relation Between Postpurchase Evaluations and Consumption Experiences of Hedonic Products: A Case of Reading Fiction', in Englis and Olofsson, eds, *European Advances in Consumer Research* 3: 139–45.

169. Gilbert A. Churchill Jr. and Carol F. Surprenant, 'An investigation into the determinants of customer satisfaction', *Journal of Marketing Research* 19 (November 1983): 491–504; John E. Swan and I. Frederick Trawick, 'Disconfirmation of expectations and satisfaction with a retail service', *Journal of Retailing* 57 (Fall 1981): 49–67; Peter C. Wilton and David K. Tse, 'Models of consumer satisfaction formation: An extension', *Journal of Marketing Research* 25 (May 1988): 204–12; for a discussion of what may occur when customers evaluate a new service for which comparison standards do not yet exist, see Ann L. McGill and Dawn Iacobucci, 'The Role of Post-Experience Comparison Standards in the Evaluation of Unfamiliar Services,' in John F. Sherry Jr. and Brian Sternthal, eds, *Advances in Consumer Research* 19 (Provo, UT: Association for Consumer Research, 1992): 570–8; William Boulding, Ajay Kalra, Richard Staelin and Valarie A. Zeithaml, 'A dynamic process model of service quality: From expectations to behavioral intentions', *Journal of Marketing Research* 30 (February 1993): 7–27.

170. John W. Gamble, 'The expectations paradox: The more you offer customers, the closer you are to failure', *Marketing News* (14 March 1988): 38.

171. www.protest.net (accessed 17 June 2000).

172. Keith Naughton, 'Tired of smile-free service', *Newsweek* (6 March 2000): 44–5.

173. Jagdish N. Sheth and Banwari Mittal, 'A framework for managing customer expectations', *Journal of Market Focused Management* 1 (1996): 137–58.

174. Franz Bailom, Hans H. Hinterhuber, Kurt Matzler and Elmar Sauerwein, 'Das kano-modell der kundenzu-friedenheit', *Marketing ZFP* 2 (2nd quarter 1996): 117–26.

175. Marit G. Engeset, Kjell Grønhaug and Morten Heide, 'The impact of experience on customer satisfaction as measured in direct surveys', in *Marketing for an Expanding Europe*, Proceedings of the 25th EMAC Conference, ed. Berács, Bauer and Simon: 403–17.

176. Andreas Herrmann, Frank Huber and Christine Braunstein, 'A Regret Theory Approach to Assessing Customer Satisfaction when Alternatives are Considered', in Dubois, Lowrey, Shrum and Vanhuele, eds, *European Advances in Consumer Research* 4: 82–8.

177. Kjell Grønhaug and Alladi Venkatesh, 'Products and services in the perspectives of consumer socialisation', *European Journal of Marketing* 21(10) (1987); Folke Ölander, 'Consumer Satisfaction – A Sceptic's View', in H.K. Hunt, ed., *Conceptualization and Measurement of Consumer Satisfaction and Dissatisfaction* (Cambridge, MA: Marketing Science Institute, 1977): 453–88.

178. Mary C. Gilly and Betsy D. Gelb, 'Post-purchase consumer processes and the complaining consumer', *Journal of Consumer Research* 9 (December 1982): 323–8; Diane Halstead and Cornelia Droge, 'Consumer Attitudes Toward Complaining and the Prediction of Multiple Complaint Responses', in Holman and Solomon, eds, *Advances in Consumer Research* 18: 210–16; Jagdip Singh, 'Consumer complaint intentions and behavior: Definitional and taxonomical issues,' *Journal of Marketing* 52 (January 1988): 93–107.

179. Alan Andreasen and Arthur Best, 'Consumers complain – does business respond?', *Harvard Business Review* 55 (July/August 1977): 93–101.

180. Ingrid Martin, 'Expert–Novice Differences in Complaint Scripts', in Holman and Solomon, eds, *Advances in Consumer Research* 18: 225–31; Marsha L. Richins, 'A multivariate analysis of responses to dissatisfaction', *Journal of the Academy of Marketing Science* 15 (Fall 1987): 24–31.

181. John A. Schibrowsky and Richard S. Lapidus, 'Gaining a competitive advantage by analyzing aggregate complaints', *Journal of Consumer Marketing* 11 (1994) 1: 15–26.

182. Veronica Liljander, 'Consumer Satisfaction with Complaint Handling Following a Dissatisfactory Experience with Car Repair', in Dubois, Lowrey, Shrum and Vanhuele, eds, *European Advances in Consumer Research* 4: 270–5.

183. Tibbett L. Speer, 'They complain because they care', *American Demographics* (May 1996): 13–14.

184. 'Dunkin' donuts buys out critical web site', *The New York Times on the Web* (27 August 1999).

185. Quoted in Jan McCallum, 'I hate you, and millions know it', *BRW* (7 July 2000): 84.

186. S. McManis, 'An internet outlaw goes on record: Pleasant Hill student tells of his "Hacktivism"', *San Francisco Chronicle* (24 February 2002): A21.

187. Material adapted from a presentation by Glenn H. Mazur, QFD Institute, 2002.

188. Russell W. Belk, 'The Role of Possessions in Constructing and Maintaining a Sense of Past,' in Marvin E. Goldberg, Gerald Gorn and Richard W. Pollay, eds, *Advances in Consumer Research* 17 (Provo, UT: Association for Consumer Research, 1989): 669–76.

189. David E. Sanger, 'For a job well done, Japanese enshrine the chip', *New York Times* (11 December 1990): A4.

190. Jacob Jacoby, Carol K. Berning and Thomas F. Dietvorst, 'What about disposition?', *Journal of Marketing* 41 (April 1977): 22–8.

191. Mike Tharp, 'Tchaikovsky and toilet paper', *U.S. News and World Report* (December 1987): 62; B. Van Voorst, 'The recycling bottleneck', *Time* (14 September 1992): 52–4; Richard P. Bagozzi and Pratibha A. Dabholkar, 'Consumer recycling goals and their effect on decisions to recycle: A means–end chain analysis,' *Psychology and Marketing* 11 (July/August 1994): 313–40.

192. 'Finally, something at McDonald's you can actually eat', *UTNE Reader* (May/June 1997): 12.

193. Debra J. Dahab, James W. Gentry, and Wanru Su, 'New Ways to Reach Non-Recyclers: An Extension of the Model

of Reasoned Action to Recycling Behaviors' (paper presented at the meetings of the Association for Consumer Research, 1994).

194. Bagozzi and Dabholkar, 'Consumer recycling goals and their effect on decisions to recycle'; see also L.J. Shrum, Tina M. Lowrey and John A. McCarty, 'Recycling as a marketing problem: A framework for strategy development,' *Psychology and Marketing* 11 (July/August 1994): 393–416; Dahab, Gentry and Su, 'New Ways to Reach Non-Recyclers.'

195. John Markoff, 'Technology's toxic trash is sent to poor nations', *The New York Times on the Web* (25 February 2002); 'Recycling phones to charities, not landfills', *The New York Times on the Web* (26 October 2002).

196. 'Incentive schemes: Jam today', *The Economist* (12 April 1997): 67.

197. John F. Sherry Jr., 'A sociocultural analysis of a Midwestern American flea market', *Journal of Consumer Research* 17 (June 1990): 13–30.

198. Diane Crispell, 'Collecting memories', *American Demographics* (November 1988): 38–42.

199. John F. Sherry Jr., 'Dealers and dealing in a periodic market: Informal retailing in ethnographic perspective', *Journal of Retailing* 66 (Summer 1990): 174.

200. Alex Markels, 'Collectors shake, rattle and watch those bankrolls', *The New York Times on the Web* (13 October 2002).

201. Heather Won Tesoriero, 'Something old, something used: To quietly cut costs brides wear preowned', *The Wall Street Journal Online* (22 August 2003).

202. Saul Hansell, 'Meg Whitman and eBay, net survivors', *The New York Times on the Web* (5 May 2002).

203. Tina Kelly, 'Socks? With holes? I'll take it', *NYT Online* (16 March 2004).

204. Quoted in Stephanie Stoughton, 'Unemployed Americans turn to e-Bay to make money', *The Boston Globe* (16 October 2001).

205. However, see E.A. Greenleaf, 'Reserves, regret, and rejoicing in open English auctions', *Journal of Consumer Research* 31 (September 2004): 264–73 for a recent study of consumer behaviour within the context of English auctions, with specific reference to sellers' seeking to minimize regret and maximize rejoicing when setting reserve prices.

206. Allan J. Magrath, 'If used product sellers ever get organized, watch out', *Marketing News* (25 June 1990): 9; Kevin McCrohan and James D. Smith, 'Consumer participation in the informal economy', *Journal of the Academy of Marketing Science* 15 (Winter 1990): 62.

207. John Sutherland, 'The price of nostalgia', *Guardian G2* (28 March 2005): 5 (http://www.guardian.co.uk/g2/story/0,,1446610,00.html).

208. 'New kind of store getting more use out of used goods', *Montgomery Advertiser* (12 December 1996): 7A.

209. See Kortnery Stringer, 'Shoppers who blend store, catalog, web spend more', *The Wall Street Journal Online* (3 September 2004): A7 for a detailed discussion of these issues.

210. William Echison, 'Designers climb onto the virtual catwalk', *Business Week* (11 October 1999): 164.

211. Rita Choy and Suzanne Loker, 'Mass customization of wedding gowns: Design involvement on the internet', *Clothing and Textiles Research Journal* 22(1&2) (2004): 79–87.

GROUP INFLUENCE AND OPINION LEADERSHIP

Rich plays sport every day. The obsession that started with football has branched out into, at various times, cricket, tennis and squash. In fact, the need to play some sort of competitive sport means that days off become tedious, frustrating affairs. Rich will happily skip a lecture to play in a university football league, especially the 11-a-side league on a Wednesday afternoon, which Rich insists on keeping free. The original team that Rich played for has become his closest circle of friends, and they always celebrate an important victory with a heavy night out, with the importance of the health benefits of sport relegated to a poor second against the joys of a great team spirit.

Recently Rich decided he needed new football boots, since the ends of his trusty Pumas had both split open, letting in rain, mud and whatever else had gotten onto the football pitch. He has also got a bit sick of his mates telling him he looks like he is wearing tramp's shoes; in the university matches there was a certain amount of prestige to be upheld. Since he has had the Pumas so long, however, he feels he deserves some expensive boots.

Rich's mates don't have many positive things to say about Nike football boots. His friend Pete had bought the same boots as Thierry Henry wore, Nike Vapours, which were incredibly light. However, Pete found they did not offer him as much support as he wanted, so Rich decided Nike was probably out for him as well. He wanted to get some Puma boots but there wasn't a great variety. So that left Reebok or Adidas, but he knew that Reebok seemed primarily to be focused on basketball and American football, so their boots probably wouldn't suit him either. Adidas represented his final choice (there was no point even considering other brands which his mates would start ribbing him about). The next decision was whether or not to get screw-in studs or moulded studs. Screw-ins invariably fell out in Rich's experience however much you tightened them, whereas moulded studs stayed in and looked pretty flashy as well. However, Rich had seen fellow team-mates with moulded studs falling over constantly on wet, muddy pitches, and since English pitches were frequently muddy Rich decided he had to go for screw-ins, despite the fact he would have to buy a set of replacement studs. The only thing Rich had to do now was to buy the flashiest pair that none of his mates had so that he could impress them. After all, you want to stand out in the crowd, to be individual and different, but maybe not *too* different . . .

R.J.W. HOGG, Leeds University

■ INTRODUCTION

Football is central to Rich's identity as a sports-loving student, and his team-mates influence many of his buying decisions for sports kit. Humans are social animals. We all belong to groups, try to please others and pick up cues about how to behave by observing the actions of those around us. In fact, our desire to 'fit in' or to identify with desirable individuals or groups is the primary motivation for many of our purchases and activities. We often go to great lengths to please the members of a group whose acceptance we covet.

This chapter focuses on how other people, whether fellow footballers and team-mates, co-workers, friends and family or just casual acquaintances, influence our purchase decisions. It considers how our preferences are shaped by our group memberships, by our desire to please or be accepted by others, even by the actions of famous people whom we've never met. Finally, it explores why some people are more influential than others in affecting consumers' product preferences, and how marketers go about finding those people and enlisting their support in the persuasion process.

■ REFERENCE GROUPS

Rich doesn't model himself on *any* footballer – only the people with whom he really identifies can exert that kind of influence. For example, Rich primarily identifies with other sport enthusiasts, especially football players. The English Football League represents one of Rich's most important *reference groups*.

▶ A **reference group** is 'an actual or imaginary individual or group conceived of having significant relevance upon an individual's evaluations, aspirations, or behaviour'.[1] Reference groups influence consumers in three ways. These influences, *informational*, *utilitarian*, and *value-expressive*, are described in Table 10.1.

Types of reference groups

Although two or more people are normally required to form a group, the term *reference group* is often used a bit more loosely to describe *any* external influence that provides social cues.[2] The referent may be a cultural figure and have an impact on many people (the late Mother Teresa, or members of royal families, or football teams) or a person or group whose influence is confined to the consumer's immediate environment (Rich's various football teams, 5-a-side and 11-a-side). Reference groups that affect consumption can include parents, fellow football enthusiasts and team members, class mates, motorcycle or other leisure activity enthusiasts, a political party or even sports clubs such as Manchester United and bands such as U2.

Some groups and individuals exert a greater influence than others and affect a broader range of consumption decisions. For example, our parents may play a pivotal role in forming our values toward many important issues, such as attitudes about marriage ▶ or where to go to university. This type of influence is **normative influence** – that is, the reference group helps to set and enforce fundamental standards of conduct. In contrast, ▶ a Harley-Davidson club or Manchester United fan club might exert **comparative influence**, whereby decisions about specific brands or activities are affected.[3]

Formal vs. informal groups

A reference group can take the form of a large, formal organization that has a recognized structure, regular meeting times and officers. Or it can be small and informal, such as a group of friends or students living in a university hall of residence. Marketers tend to have more control over their influencing of formal groups because they are more easily identifiable and accessible.

Table 10.1 Three forms of reference group influence

Informational influence	The individual seeks information about various brands from an association of professionals or independent group of experts.
	The individual seeks information from those who work with the product as a profession.
	The individual seeks brand-related knowledge and experience (such as how Brand A's performance compares to Brand B's) from those friends, neighbours, relatives or work associates who have reliable information about the brands.
	The brand the individual selects is influenced by observing a seal of approval of an independent testing agency.
	The individual's observation of what experts do (such as observing the type of car that police drive or the brand of television that repairmen buy) influences his or her choice of a brand.
Utilitarian influence	So that he or she satisfies the expectation of fellow work associates, the individual's decision to purchase a particular brand is influenced by their preferences.
	The individual's decision to purchase a particular brand is influenced by the preferences of people with whom he or she has social interaction.
	The individual's decision to purchase a particular brand is influenced by the preferences of family members.
	The desire to satisfy the expectations that others have of him or her has an impact on the individual's brand choice.
Value-expressive influence	The individual feels that the purchase or use of a particular brand will enhance the image others have of him or her.
	The individual feels that those who purchase or use a particular brand possess the characteristics that he or she would like to have.
	The individual sometimes feels that it would be nice to be like the type of person that advertisements show using a particular brand.
	The individual feels that the people who purchase a particular brand are admired or respected by others.
	The individual feels that the purchase of a particular brand would help show others what he or she is or would like to be (such as an athlete, successful business person, good parent, etc.)

Source: Adapted from C. Whan Park and V. Parker Lessig, 'Students and housewives: Differences in susceptibility to reference group influence', *Journal of Consumer Research* 4 (September 1977): 102. Reprinted with permission of The University of Chicago Press.

In general, small, informal groups exert a more powerful influence on individual consumers. These groups tend to be more involved in our day-to-day lives and to be more important to us, because they are high in normative influence. Larger, formal groups tend to be more product- or activity-specific and thus are high in comparative influence.

multicultural dimensions

'Common man' or 'slice-of-life' depictions, which highlight 'real' people, are more realistic and thus more credible than celebrities or superstars. While we admire perfect people, it can be frustrating to compare ourselves with them and their actually using the product may seem improbable. By including people who are successful but not perfect, consumers' identification with them is often enhanced. This strategy has been successfully employed in the classic 'Dewar's Profiles', a series of ads describing the lifestyles of non-celebrity high achievers who happen to drink Dewar's Scotch Whisky. Since the strategy uses real people from many different walks of life, the company has expanded its ad campaigns to focus on accomplished people in different countries. For example, a Thai ad highlights a successful architect who lives in Bangkok, while a Spanish campaign features a 29-year-old flight instructor.[4]

This Marks and Spencer's advertising campaign used non celebrities to endorse its message, 'Exclusively For Everyone'.
The Advertising Archives

Membership vs. aspirational reference groups

Some reference groups consist of people the consumer actually knows; others are composed of people the consumer can either *identify with* or admire. Not surprisingly, many marketing efforts that specifically adopt a reference group appeal concentrate on highly visible, widely admired figures (such as well-known athletes). These **aspirational reference groups** comprise idealized figures such as successful business people, athletes or performers.[5]

Identificational reference groups

Since people tend to compare themselves with those who are similar, they are often swayed by knowing how people like themselves conduct their lives. For this reason,

Many products, especially those targeted at young people, are often touted as a way to take the inside track to popularity. This Brazilian shoe ad proclaims: 'Anyone who doesn't like them is a nerd'.

many promotional strategies include 'ordinary' people whose consumption activities provide informational social influence. For example, in the campaign for fish consumption discussed in Chapter 4, the endorsing actors performed as very ordinary people to underline the message that special fish dishes are not difficult to prepare and are not only for high-class gourmets.[6]

▶ The likelihood that people will become part of a consumer's **identificational membership reference group** is affected by several factors, including:

- *Propinquity:* As physical distance between people decreases and opportunities for interaction increase, relationships are more likely to form. Physical nearness is called *propinquity.* An early study on friendship patterns in a housing complex showed this factor's strong effects: residents were much more likely to be friends with the people next door than with those who lived only two doors away. Furthermore, people who lived next to a staircase had more friends than those at the ends of a corridor (presumably, they were more likely to 'bump into' people using the stairs).[7] Physical structure has a lot to do with who we get to know and how popular we are.

- *Mere exposure:* We come to like persons or things simply as a result of seeing them more often, which is known as the *mere exposure phenomenon.*[8] Greater frequency of contact, even if unintentional, may help to determine one's set of local referents. The same effect holds when evaluating works of art or even political candidates.[9] One study predicted 83 per cent of the winners of political primaries solely by the amount of media exposure given to candidates.[10]

- *Group cohesiveness:* The degree to which members of a group are attracted to each other and value their group membership is called *cohesiveness.* As the value of the group to the individual increases, so too does the likelihood that the group will guide consumption decisions. Smaller groups tend to be more cohesive because in larger groups the contributions of each member are usually less important or noticeable. By the same token, groups often try to restrict membership to a select few, which increases the value of membership to those who are admitted. Exclusivity of membership is a benefit often promoted by credit card companies, book clubs and so on, even though the actual membership base might be fairly large.

marketing opportunity

Members of reference groups have a huge influence on our tastes and desires, but connecting with like-minded people in the first place can be a challenge in today's hectic world. Numerous online matchmaking services have sprung up to search for that perfect date including sites such as Lava Life in the USA and uDate in the UK. One site called **Match.com** alone boasts over 3 million members worldwide. And once you find that perfect someone you can even check out his or her background by using sites like **repcheck.com** that provide reports about a person's reputation.[11]

Of course, if you're too shy even to meet prospective mates this way you can always try the Lovegety, a Japanese product. It works this way: Boy sees girl. Boy is too shy to talk to girl. Instead he flicks on his male Lovegety and sends out an infrared signal. If the girl's Lovegety is within 5 metres of his, it starts to chirp with delight. Depending on her interest, she can send back one of three responses: talk, karaoke and friend. Wow, nothing like a little romantic karaoke to set the mood.[12]

Positive vs. negative reference groups

Reference groups may exert either a positive or a negative influence on consumption behaviours. In most cases, consumers model their behaviour to be consistent with what they think the group expects of them. In some cases, though, consumers may try to distance themselves from other people or groups who function as *avoidance groups*. He or she may carefully study the dress or mannerisms of a disliked group and scrupulously avoid buying anything that might identify him or her with that group. Many consumers find it difficult to express what they want whereas they can quite clearly express what they do not want. In fact, some researchers suggest that the phenomenon of distaste is much more decisive for our consumption choices but harder to study than tastes, since our choices are quite obvious compared to all the non-selected alternatives.[13] For example, rebellious adolescents often resent parental influence and may deliberately do the opposite of what their parents would like as a way of making a statement about their independence. As Romeo and Juliet discovered, nothing makes a partner more attractive than a little parental opposition.

The motivation to distance oneself from a negative reference group can be as or more powerful than the desire to please a positive group.[14] That's why advertisements occasionally show an undesirable person using a competitor's product to subtly make the point that the target of the message can avoid winding up like *that* kind of person by staying away from the products he or she buys. As a once-popular book reminded us, 'Real men *don't* eat quiche!'[15] Today, others have adapted this avoidance group appeal to point out the ways we define ourselves by not consuming some products or services. For example, a T-shirt for sale on a computer-oriented website proudly proclaims, 'Real Men Don't Click Help'.

Virtual communities

In ancient times (that is, before the Web was widely accessible), most membership reference groups consisted of people who had face-to-face contact. Now, it's possible to share interests with people whom you've never met – and probably never will. Have you ever heard of the band Widespread Panic? No? Well, the band never had a music video on MTV or cracked the Billboard Top 200. But it was one of the top 40 touring bands in the USA. How did it get to be so successful? Simple – the group built a virtual community of fans and opened itself up to them. It enlisted listeners to help promote the group in exchange for free tickets and backstage passes. Then, it went virtual: the band allowed fans to send messages to its recording studio, and hard-core followers could find out vital information like what band members ate for lunch via regular updates on their website.[16]

A **virtual community of consumption** is a collection of people whose online interactions are based upon shared enthusiasm for and knowledge of a specific consumption activity. These anonymous groups grow up around an incredibly diverse set of interests – everything from Barbie dolls to fine wine.

Virtual communities come in many different forms:[17]

- *Multi-user dungeons (MUD)*. Originally, these were environments where players of fantasy games met. Now they refer to any computer-generated environment where people interact socially through the structured format of role- and game-playing. In a game called EverQuest, on any given night up to 50,000 people can be found roaming around a fantasy land in cyberspace. This is known as a 'massively multiplayer game', which combines the stunning graphics of advanced gaming with the social scene of a chat room. Players create a character as a virtual alter ego, which may be a wise elf or a back-stabbing rogue. The game is also the centre of an active social scene. Players can travel around in groups of six; in many cases they settle into a regular group and spend two to three hours each night online with the same people. One couple even held a virtual wedding while playing. The bride reported, 'We only had one death, a guest who was killed by the guards. It was a lot of fun.'[18] Realizing that the average online player logs 17 hours per week, firms like Sony, Microsoft and Sega are building their own virtual worlds to get a piece of the action. As one game company executive put it, 'This is not a genre of game but a break-through new medium. It provides a completely new social, collaborative shared experience. We're basically in the Internet community business.'[19]

- *Rooms, rings and lists*. These include internet relay chat (IRC), otherwise known as *chat rooms*. *Rings* are organizations of related home pages, and *lists* are groups of people on a single mailing list who share information.

- *Boards*. Online communities can be organized around interest-specific electronic bulletin boards. Active members read and post messages sorted by date and subject. There are boards devoted to musical groups, films, wine, cigars, cars, comic strips, even fast-food restaurants.

▶ - *Blogs*. The newest and fastest growing form of online community is the **weblog**, or *blog*. These online personal journals are building an avid following among internet users who like to dash off a few random thoughts, post them on a website and read similar musings by others. Although these sites are similar to web pages offered by Geocities and other free services, they employ a different technology that lets people upload a few sentences without going through the process of updating a website built with conventional home page software. For example, one site (**www.livejournal.com**) signed up 690,000 registered users in four years and added another 1,100 every day. Bloggers can fire off thoughts on a whim, click a button and quickly have them appear on a site. Weblogs frequently look like online diaries, with brief musings about the day's events, and perhaps a link or two of interest. A new blogger puts in his or her offering every
▶ 40 seconds, so this burgeoning **Blogosphere** (the name given to the universe of active weblogs) is starting to look like a force to be reckoned with. Already, one media giant is smelling blood: recognizing that many thousands of Brazilians are getting into blogging, **Globo.com** is licensing blogger software and is posting blogs from Brazilian *telenovela* (soap opera) stars like Boris, an 800-year-old vampire who wears armour and a horned helmet.[20]

Some communities are created by individuals whose web pages are hosted on sites like **geocities.com**. Others are sponsored by companies who want to give devotees of a product or a lifestyle a congenial place to 'meet'. This could, for example, be people who are fans of a specific product or a TV show. News Digital Media gives Bart Simpson fanatics free internet access at **simpson.com**. The site is intended to complement the TV show and to give fans a place to congregate.[21] Other than the more global sites at, for example, **geocities.com**, there is a proliferation of national community sites for specific

Role-playing computer games involve thousands of players worldwide in interactive, online communities.

consumer profiles. In Denmark, for example, there are sites for teenage girls (**surfergirl.dk**), for themes such as relationships (**lovefinder.dk**), or an extremely popular site for medical problems (**netdoktor.dk**).

Virtual communities are still a new phenomenon, but their impact on individuals' product preferences promises to be huge. These loyal consumers are essentially working together to form their tastes, evaluate product quality and even negotiate for better deals with producers. They place great weight on the judgements of their fellow members.

While consumption communities are largely a grass-roots phenomenon founded by consumers for other consumers, these community members can be reached by marketers – if they are careful not to alienate members by being too aggressive or 'commercial'. Using newsgroup archives and search engines, companies can create a detailed profile of any individual consumer who has posted information. Firms like Warner Brothers form communities with fans around the world. The company noticed that many fans of Bugs Bunny, Batman and the Tazmanian Devil were downloading images and sound clips onto their personal web pages and then selling ad space on those pages. Instead of suing its fans, Warner created an online community called ACME City that builds home pages for registered members. Many corporate-sponsored sites build home pages for new members and ask for nothing in return except personal information on a registration form. They can use this information to fine-tune the online experience by making advertising, contests and rewards programs more relevant.

marketing opportunity

Some online startups are profiting by creating websites that give people a forum for their opinions about product likes and dislikes. **Epinions.com** was started by several well-known Silicon Valley venture capitalists. This service both rewards and rates product reviewers, in hope of giving them enough incentive to provide useful opinions. Anyone can sign up to give advice on products that fit into the site's 12 categories, and shoppers can rate the reviews on a scale from not useful to very useful. To build credibility, and to eliminate suspicions that they are merely company shills (people posing as satisfied customers), advisers can build a page on the site with photos and personal information. Reviewers earn royalties of from $1 to $3 for every ten times their review is read, and their picture can be featured on the FrontPage if their reviews are widely read. According to one of the founders, the site relies on a 'web of trust' in which viewers and advisers tend to be matched up over time with people whose opinions they have come to trust: 'It mimics the way word-of-mouth works in the real world.' When a recommendation results in a sale, the company earns a referral fee from merchants.[22]

How do people get drawn into consumption communities? Internet users tend to progress from asocial information gathering ('lurkers' are surfers who like to watch but don't participate) to increasingly affiliative social activities. At first they will merely browse the site but later they may well be drawn into active participation.

The intensity of identification with a virtual community depends on two factors. The first is that the more central the activity is to a person's self-concept, the more likely he or she will be to pursue active membership in a community. The second is that the intensity of the social relationships the person forms with other members of the virtual community helps to determine the extent of their involvement. As Figure 10.1 shows, combining these two factors creates four distinct member types:

1 *Tourists* lack strong social ties to the group, and maintain only a passing interest in the activity.

2 *Minglers* maintain strong social ties, but are not very interested in the central consumption activity.

Figure 10.1 Virtual communities

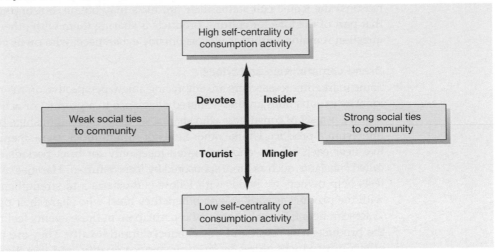

Source: Adapted from Robert V. Kozinets, 'E-tribalized marketing: the strategic implications of virtual communities of consumption', *European Management Journal* 17(3) (June 1999): 252–64.

3 *Devotees* express strong interest in the activity, but have few social attachments to the group.

4 *Insiders* exhibit both strong social ties and strong interest in the activity.

Devotees and insiders are the most important targets for marketers who wish to exploit communities for promotional purposes. They are the heavy users of virtual communities. And, by reinforcing usage, the community may upgrade tourists and minglers to insiders and devotees.[23] But marketers have only scratched the surface of this intriguing new virtual world.

Virtual consumption communities hold great promise, but there is also great potential for abuse if members can't trust that other visitors are behaving ethically. Many hard-core community members are sensitive to interference from companies, and react negatively when they suspect that another member may in fact be a marketer who wants to influence evaluations of products on the site.

More generally, e-commerce sites know that consumers give more weight to the opinions of real people, so they are finding ways to let these opinions be included on their websites. This trend of posting customer reviews was started by **Amazon.com** in 1995. Now, sellers of computers and other high-priced products post customer reviews.[24] A great idea – but in a highly publicized lawsuit Amazon was accused of charging publishers to post positive reviews on the site. The company had to offer refunds for all books it recommended and now Amazon tells customers when a publisher has paid for a prominent display on its site.[25]

A basic topic for discussion is: who owns the net? The outcome of a legal case against the music exchange service Napster, ruling that it was illegal to organize even non-profitable exchange of music files among its users, tends to point in the direction that cyberspace can be patented and owned. However, the reaction among hard-core virtual community people seems to be that there will always be ways of circumventing such attempts to stop the free flows of information within the virtual communities. A similar case is the so-called PotterWar, a website created as a protest against Warner Brothers, which holds the rights to Harry Potter related products. They threatened creators of sites such as **HarryPotterNetwork.net** with heavy lawsuits if control of the sites was not given to Warner. It turned out that most of the sites were owned by 12–15-year-olds without the slightest commercial interest. The problem for Warner Brothers and many other producers of cultural products is that on the one hand they like (for good pecuniary reasons) the iconic cult status their products may obtain, but on the other they neglect that part of the love for cultural products is sharing them with other devotees.[26] The big question remains, within as well as outside cyberspace: who owns culture?

Brand communities and tribes

▶ Some marketing researchers are embracing a new perspective on reference groups as they identify groups built around a shared allegiance to a product or activity. A **brand community** is a set of consumers who share a set of social relationships based upon usage or interest in a product. Unlike other kinds of communities, these members typically don't live near each other – and they often meet only for brief periods at organized events called *brandfests*, such as those sponsored by Jeep, Saturn or Harley-Davidson. These brandfests help owners to 'bond' with fellow enthusiasts and strengthen their identification with the product as well as with others they meet who share their passion.

Researchers find that people who participate in these events feel more positive about the products as a result and this enhances brand loyalty. They are more forgiving than others of product failures or lapses in service quality, and less likely to switch brands even if they learn that competing products are as good or better. Furthermore, these community members become emotionally involved in the company's welfare, and they often serve as brand missionaries by carrying its marketing message to others.[27]

▶ The notion of a **consumer tribe** is similar, because this refers to a group of people who share a lifestyle and who can identify with each other through a shared allegiance to an activity or a product. Although these tribes are often unstable and short-lived, at least for a time members identify with others through shared emotions, moral beliefs, styles of life, and of course the products they jointly consume as part of their tribal affiliation.

▶ The challenge of **tribal marketing** is to link one's product to the needs of a group as a whole. Many tribes devoted to activities like skateboarding or basketball are youth oriented, and we'll talk more about these in Chapter 13. However, there are also plenty of tribes with older members, such as car enthusiasts who gather to celebrate such cult products (see Chapter 4) as the Citroën and Mini Cooper in Europe and the Ford Mustang in the USA.[28]

▶ Other research has identified **communities of practice** as a potentially valuable way of understanding and interpreting group behaviour. Communities of practice are 'an aggregate of people who come together around mutual engagement in an endeavour'.[29] Developed from work in socio-linguistics, communities of practice are usually defined by three characteristics: 'mutual engagement; a joint enterprise; and a shared repertoire'.[30] A recent study of Bolton school girls showed how consumption symbols (e.g. Rockport shoes) could be combined with other social symbols (e.g. language) in order to create meanings related to group identity:[31] 'we are surrounded by stylistic material, and as long as we can position ourselves in relation to the sources of that material, and attribute meaning to it, we can use it'.[32]

When reference groups are important

Reference group influences are not equally powerful for all types of products and consumption activities. For example, products that are not very complex, that are low in perceived risk and that can be tried prior to purchase are less susceptible to personal influence.[33] In addition, the specific impact of reference groups may vary. At times they may determine the use of certain products rather than others (owning or not owning a computer, eating junk food versus health food), whereas at other times they may have specific effects on brand decisions within a product category (wearing Levi's jeans versus Diesel jeans, or smoking Marlboro cigarettes instead of a national brand).

Figure 10.2 Relative effects of reference groups

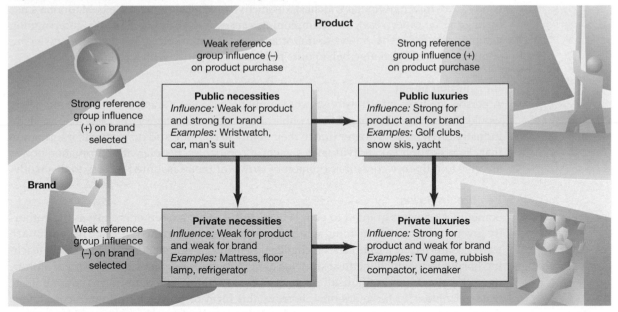

Source: Adapted from William O. Bearden and Michael J. Etzel, 'Reference group influence on product and brand purchase decisions', *Journal of Consumer Research* 9 (September 1982): 185. Reprinted with permission of The University of Chicago Press.

Two dimensions that influence the degree to which reference groups are important are whether the purchase is to be consumed publicly or privately and whether it is a luxury or a necessity. As a rule, reference group effects are more robust for purchases that are (1) luxuries rather than necessities (e.g. yachts), because products that are purchased with discretionary income are subject to individual tastes and preferences, whereas necessities do not offer this range of choices; and (2) socially conspicuous or visible to others (e.g. living room furniture or clothing), because consumers do not tend to be swayed as much by the opinions of others if their purchases will never be observed by anyone but themselves.[34] The relative effects of reference group influences on some specific product classes are shown in Figure 10.2. This obviously does not mean that a reference group cannot exert influence on the consumption of private necessities.

The power of reference groups

Why are reference groups so persuasive? The answer lies in the potential power they wield over us. **Social power** refers to 'the capacity to alter the actions of others'.[35] To the degree that you are able to make someone else do something, whether they do it willingly or not, you have power over that person. The following classification of *power bases* can help us to distinguish among the reasons why a person can exert power over another, the degree to which the influence is allowed voluntarily, and whether this influence will continue to have an effect in the absence of the power source.[36]

Referent power

If a person admires the qualities of a person or a group, he or she will try to imitate those qualities by copying the referent's behaviours (choice of clothing, cars, leisure activities) as a guide to forming consumption preferences, just as Rich's sporting friends and football team-mates affected his preferences. Prominent people in all walks of life can affect people's consumption behaviours by virtue of product endorsements (e.g. top model Cindy Crawford for Omega watches), distinctive fashion statements (e.g. Madonna's use of lingerie as outerwear), or championing causes (e.g. Brigitte Bardot's campaigning against fur). **Referent power** is important to many marketing strategies because consumers voluntarily change behaviours to please or identify with a referent.

Information power

A person can have **information power** simply because he or she knows something others would like to know. Editors of trade publications such as *Women's Wear Daily* in the fashion industry often possess power due to their ability to compile and disseminate information that can make or break individual designers or companies. People with information power are able to influence consumer opinion by virtue of their (assumed) access to the 'truth'.

Legitimate power

Sometimes power is granted to people by virtue of social agreements, such as the authority given to the police, Customs and Excise officers and the armed forces. The **legitimate power** conferred by a uniform is recognized in many consumer contexts, including teaching hospitals, in which medical students don white coats to enhance their aura of authority with patients, and organizations such as banks, where tellers' uniforms communicate trustworthiness.[37] Marketers may 'borrow' this form of power to influence consumers. For example, an ad featuring a model wearing a nurse's uniform can add an aura of legitimacy or authority to the presentation of the product as seen in TV advertising campaigns in the babies' nappy market.

Every cigarette we smoke makes fatty deposits stick in our arteries.

We'll help you give up before you clog up completely. bhf.org.uk

This anti-tobacco advertisement draws on the legitimate and expert power represented by The British Heart Foundation, and combines it with stark images of the effects which smoking has on arteries – and thus on our health – to create a strong anti-smoking message.
The Advertising Archives

Expert power

To attract the casual internet user, US Robotics signed up British physicist Stephen Hawking to endorse its modems. A company executive commented, 'We wanted to generate trust. So we found visionaries who use US Robotics technology, and we let them tell the consumer how it makes their lives more productive.' Hawking, who has Lou Gehrig's (motor neurone) disease and speaks via a synthesizer, said in one TV spot, 'My body may be stuck in this chair, but with the internet my mind can go to the end of the universe.'[38]

▶ **Expert power** such as that possessed by Hawking is derived from possessing specific knowledge about a content area; it helps to explain the weight many of us assign to reviews of restaurants, books, films, cars and so on by critics who specialize in evaluating products on our behalf.[39] This power base also underlies the appeal of television shows, where panels of authorities – often a mix of journalists and professional experts – discuss issues of interest to consumers.

Reward power

When a person or group has the means to provide positive reinforcement (see Chapter 3), that entity will have **reward power** over a consumer to the extent that this reinforcement is valued or desired. The reward may be tangible, as occurs when an employee is given a pay rise. Or, the reward may be intangible: social approval or acceptance is often what is exchanged in return for moulding one's behaviour to a group or buying the products expected of group members. However, this kind of power is perhaps wearing thin in advertising, since an over-exploitation of reward arguments has left such campaigns with little credibility. The Sprite soft drink campaign under the slogan 'Image is nothing, thirst is everything, obey your thirst' makes fun of other commercials' use of reward power by suggesting something seen as more basic, thirst. However, the slogan in itself paradoxically promises a reward in the form of an image – of somebody who does not fall for cheap tricks.[40]

Coercive power

While coercive power is often effective in the short term, it does not tend to produce permanent attitudinal or behavioural change. **Coercive power** refers to influencing a person by social or physical intimidation. Surveillance of some sort is usually required to make people do something they do not wish to do. Fortunately, coercive power is rarely employed in marketing situations, unless you count those annoying calls from telemarketers! However, elements of this power base are evident in fear appeals, intimidation in personal selling, and campaigns that emphasize the negative consequences that can occur if people do not use a product.

■ CONFORMITY

The early bohemians who lived in Paris around 1830 made a point of behaving differently from others. One flamboyant figure of the time became famous for walking a lobster on a leash through the Luxembourg Gardens (originally the grounds of the Luxembourg Palace). His friends drank wine from human skulls, cut their beards in strange shapes, and slept in tents on the floors of their garrets.[41]

In every age there are those who 'march to their own drummer'. However, most people tend to follow society's expectations regarding how they should act and look (with a little improvisation here and there, of course). **Conformity** refers to a change in beliefs or actions as a reaction to real or imagined group pressure. In order for a society to function, its members develop **norms**, or informal rules that govern behaviour. If such a system of agreements and rules did not evolve, chaos would result. Imagine the confusion if a simple norm such as sitting down to attend class did not exist.

marketing pitfall

Norms change slowly over time, but there is general agreement within a society about which ones should be obeyed, and we adjust our way of thinking to conform to these norms. A powerful example is the change in attitudes toward smoking since the 1960s, when this practice was first linked with health concerns such as cancer and emphysema. By the mid-1990s, some communities in the United States had outlawed smoking in public places. New York City did this in 2002. The Netherlands banned smoking from many public places in January 2004; Eire banned smoking in all public places in March 2004; Norway banned smoking in restaurants and bars in June 2004; and Scotland is proposing to introduce a ban from June 2006 (though this is being hotly contested). In October 2003 the French government raised the price of cigarettes by 20 per cent in an attempt to cut levels of smoking.[42]

Much of the motivation to begin smoking at an early age is due to peer pressure; the alluring advertising images of smokers as cool, sexy or mature help to convince many young people that beginning the habit is a path to social acceptance. Because the power of advertising to influence attitudes is widely recognized, some groups have tried to fight fire with fire by creating anti-smoking ads that depict smoking as an ugly habit that turns people off.

Are these ads effective? One study of non-smoking seventh graders examined their perceptions of smokers after being exposed to both cigarette ads and anti-smoking ads. Results were promising: the researchers found that those who saw the anti-smoking ads were more likely to rate smokers lower in terms of both personal appeal and common sense. These findings imply that it is possible to use advertising to debunk myths about the glamour of smoking, especially if used in tandem with other health education efforts.[43]

We conform in many small ways every day – even though we don't always realize it. Unspoken rules govern many aspects of consumption. In addition to norms regarding appropriate use of clothing and other personal items, we conform to rules that include gift-giving (we expect birthday presents from loved ones and get upset if they do not materialize), sex roles (men are often expected to pick up the bill on a first date) and personal hygiene (we are expected to shower or bathe regularly to avoid offending others).

Types of social influence

Just as the bases for social power can vary, so the process of social influence operates in several ways.[44] Sometimes a person is motivated to model the behaviour of others because this mimicry is believed to yield rewards such as social approval or money. At other times, the social influence process occurs simply because the person honestly does not *know* the correct way to respond and is using the behaviour of the other person or group as a cue to ensure that he or she is responding correctly.[45] **Normative social influence** occurs when a person conforms to meet the expectations of a person or group.

In contrast, **informational social influence** refers to conformity that occurs because the group's behaviour is taken as evidence of reality: if other people respond in a certain way in an ambiguous situation, we may mimic their behaviour because this appears to be the correct thing to do.[46]

Reasons for conformity

Conformity is not an automatic process, and many factors contribute to the likelihood that consumers will pattern their behaviour after others.[47] Among the factors that affect the likelihood of conformity are the following:

- *Cultural pressures:* Different cultures encourage conformity to a greater or lesser degree. The American slogan 'Do your own thing' in the 1960s reflected a movement away from conformity and towards individualism. In contrast, Japanese society is characterized by the dominance of collective well-being and group loyalty over individuals' needs. Most European societies are situated somewhere between these two, in this respect, 'extreme' cultures. In an analysis of the reading of a soft drinks TV commercial, Danish consumers stressed the group solidarity that they saw in the ad, an aspect not mentioned at all by the American sample.[48]

● *Fear of deviance:* The individual may have reason to believe that the group will apply *sanctions* to punish behaviour that differs from the group's. It is not unusual to observe adolescents shunning a peer who is 'different' or a corporation or university passing over a person for promotion because he or she is not a 'team player'.

● *Commitment:* The more a person is dedicated to a group and values membership in it, the more motivated he or she will be to follow the dictates of the group. Rock groupies and followers of religious sects may do anything that is asked of them, and terrorists (or martyrs and freedom fighters, depending on the perspective) may be willing to die for the good of their cause. According to the *principle of least interest,* the person or group that is least committed to staying in a relationship has the most power, because that party won't be susceptible to threatened rejection.[49]

● *Group unanimity, size, and expertise:* As groups gain in power, compliance increases. It is often harder to resist the demands of a large number of people than just a few, and this difficulty is compounded when the group members are perceived to know what they are talking about.

● *Susceptibility to interpersonal influence:* This trait refers to an individual's need to identify or enhance his or her image in the opinion of significant others. This enhancement process is often accompanied by the acquisition of products the person believes will impress his or her audience and by the tendency to learn about products by observing how others use them.[50] Consumers who are low on this trait have been called *role-relaxed;* they tend to be older, affluent and to have high self-confidence. Based on research identifying role-relaxed consumers, Subaru created a communications strategy to reach these people. In one commercial, a man is heard saying, 'I want a car . . . Don't tell me about wood panelling, about winning the respect of my neighbours. They're my neighbours. They're not my heroes.'

Social comparison: 'How am I doing?'

Informational social influence implies that sometimes we look to the behaviour of others to provide a yardstick about reality. **Social comparison theory** asserts that this process occurs as a way of increasing the stability of one's self-evaluation, especially when physical evidence is unavailable.[51] Social comparison even applies to choices for which there are no objectively correct answers. Such stylistic decisions as tastes in music and art are assumed to be a matter of individual choice, yet people often assume that some choices are 'better' or more 'correct' than others.[52] If you have ever been responsible for choosing the music to play at a party, you can probably appreciate the social pressure involved in choosing the right 'mix'.

Although people often like to compare their judgements and actions with those of others, they tend to be selective about precisely who they will use as benchmarks. Similarity between the consumer and others used for social comparison boosts confidence that the information is accurate and relevant (though we may find it more threatening to be outperformed by someone similar to ourselves).[53] We tend to value the views of obviously dissimilar others only when we are reasonably certain of our own.[54]

Social comparison theory has been used to explore the effects of advertising images on women's self-perceptions of their physical attractiveness and their levels of self-esteem.[55] Many early studies showed that social comparison, when studied in terms of

let's face it, firming the thighs
of a size 8 supermodel is no challenge.

There's not much point in testing a new firming lotion on size-eight
supermodel thighs, is there? That's why Dove's Firming range was tested on
ordinary women with real lives to live – and real, curvy thighs to firm.
After using Dove's nourishing and effective combination of moisturisers and
seaweed extracts, we asked if they'd go in front of the camera. What better
way to show the unretouched, unairbrushed results?

new Dove Firming Range

This Dove campaign entitled 'Real Beauty'
deliberately avoided ideal images of models,
and chose pictures of ordinary women
consumers to get its messages across.
The Advertising Archives

only self-evaluation, is likely to have a negative effect on self-esteem. However, the incorporation of the specific goal (self-evaluation; self-improvement; or self-enhancement[56]) suggests that social comparison can have either positive or negative effects on self-feelings depending on the goal for social comparison.[57] A recent study suggests that the direction of spontaneous social comparison and social evaluation processes may be determined by fairly subtle cues. Whereas most advertising research suggests that comparisons with idealized models lead to contrast, this study found evidence that comparisons can also lead to assimilation of standards into the self-evaluation.[58]

In general people tend to choose a *co-oriented peer*, or a person of equivalent standing, when performing social comparison. For example, a study of adult cosmetics users found that women were more likely to seek information about product choices from similar friends to reduce uncertainty and to trust the judgements of similar others.[59] The same effects have been found for evaluations of products as diverse as men's suits and coffee.[60]

Tactical requests

How do we increase the likelihood that a person will conform to our wishes? The way a request for compliance is phrased or structured can make a difference. One well-known sales tactic is known as the *foot-in-the-door technique*, where the consumer is first asked a small request and then is 'hit' for something bigger.[61] This term is adapted from door-to-door selling. Experienced salespeople know that they are much more likely to make a sale if they first convince a customer to let them into the house to deliver their sales pitch. Once the person has agreed to this small request, it is more difficult to refuse a larger one, since the consumer has legitimized the salesperson's presence by entering into a dialogue. The salesperson is no longer a threatening stranger at the door.

Other variations on this strategy include the *low-ball technique*, where a person is asked a small favour and is informed after agreeing to it that it will be very costly, or the *door-in-the-face technique*, where a person is first asked to do something extreme (a request that is usually refused) and is then asked to do something smaller. In each of these cases, people tend to go along with the smaller request, possibly because they feel guilty about denying the larger one.[62]

Group effects on individual behaviour

With more people in a group, it becomes less likely that any one member will be singled out for attention. People in larger groups, or those in situations where they are unlikely to be identified, tend to focus less attention on themselves, so normal restraints on behaviour are reduced. You may have observed that people sometimes behave more wildly at fancy dress parties, at hen or stag parties or partying on, for example, charter holidays, than they would normally do. This phenomenon is known as **de-individuation**. This is a process in which individual identities get submerged within a group and a special situation.

marketing pitfall

University parties sometimes illustrate the dark side of de-individuation when students are encouraged by their peers to consume almost superhuman volumes of alcohol in group settings. About 4.5 million young people in the United States are estimated to be alcohol-dependent or problem drinkers. Binge drinking among university students is reaching epidemic proportions. In a two-week period, 42 per cent of all college students engage in binge drinking (more than five drinks at a time) versus 33 per cent of their non-university counterparts. One in three students drinks primarily to get drunk, including 35 per cent of university women. For most, social pressure to abandon all inhibitions is the culprit.[63] Binge drinking is also increasingly recognized as a problem in the UK,[64] and not only among university students.[65]

Costumes hide our true identities and encourage deindividuation.
Alamy/Martin Dalton

Social loafing describes the phenomenon that people do not devote as much to a task when their contribution is part of a larger group effort.[66] Waitresses are painfully aware of social loafing: people who eat in groups tend to tip less per person than when they are eating alone.[67] For this reason, many restaurants automatically add on a fixed gratuity for groups of six or more.

There is some evidence that decisions made by groups differ from those that would be made by each individual. In many cases, group members show a greater willingness to consider riskier alternatives following group discussion than they would if members made their own decisions with no discussion. This change is known as the **risky shift**.[68] Several explanations have been advanced to explain this increased riskiness. One possibility is that something similar to social loafing occurs. As more people are involved in a decision, each individual is less accountable for the outcome, resulting in *diffusion of responsibility*.[69] The practice of placing blanks in at least one of the rifles used by a firing squad is one way of diffusing each soldier's responsibility for the death of a prisoner. Another explanation is termed the *value hypothesis*. In this case, riskiness is a culturally valued characteristic, and social pressures operate on individuals to conform to attributes valued by society.[70]

Evidence for the risky shift is mixed. A more general effect appears to be that group discussion tends to increase **decision polarization**. Whichever direction the group members were leaning towards before discussion began – whether towards a risky choice or towards a more conservative choice – becomes even more extreme in that direction after discussion. Group discussions regarding product purchases tend to create a risky shift for low-risk items, but they yield more conservative group decisions for high-risk products.[71]

Shopping patterns

Shopping behaviour even changes when people do it in groups. For example, people who shop with at least one other person tend to make more unplanned purchases, buy more and cover more areas of a store than those who go alone.[72] These effects are due to both normative and informational social influence. Group members may be convinced to buy something to gain the approval of the others, or they may simply be exposed to more products and stores by pooling information with the group. For these reasons, retailers are well advised to encourage group shopping activities.

marketing opportunity

The institution of home shopping parties, as epitomized by Tupperware, capitalizes on group pressure to boost sales.[73] A company representative makes a sales presentation to a group of people who have gathered in the home of a friend or acquaintance. This format is effective because of informational social influence: participants model the behaviour of others who can provide them with information about how to use certain products, especially since the home party is likely to be attended by a relatively homogeneous group (e.g. neighbourhood housewives) that serves as a valuable benchmark. Normative social influence also operates because actions are publicly observed. Pressures to conform may be particularly intense and may escalate as more and more group members begin to 'cave in' (this process is sometimes termed the *bandwagon effect*). In addition, de-individuation and/or the risky shift may be activated: as consumers get caught up in the group, they may find themselves willing to try new products they would not normally consider.

These same dynamics underlie the latest variation on the Tupperware **home shopping parties**' technique: the Botox party. The craze for Botox injections that paralyze facial nerves to reduce wrinkles (for three to six months anyway) is being fuelled by gatherings where dermatologists or plastic surgeons redefine the definition of house calls. For patients, mixing cocktail hour with cosmetic injections takes some of the anxiety out of the procedure. Egged on by the others at the party, as many as ten patients can be 'de-wrinkled' in an hour. An advertising executive who worked on the Botox marketing strategy explained that the membership reference group appeal is more effective than the traditional route of using a celebrity spokesperson to promote the injections in advertising: 'We think it's more persuasive to think of your next-door neighbour using it.'[74] The only hitch is that after you get the injections your face is so rigid that your friends can't tell if you're smiling.

Resistance to influence

Many people pride themselves on their independence, unique style, or ability to resist the best efforts of salespeople and advertisers to buy products.[75] Indeed, individuality should be encouraged by the marketing system: innovation creates change and demand for new products and styles.

Anti-conformity vs. independence

It is important to distinguish between *independence* and *anti-conformity*; in anti-conformity, defiance of the group is the actual object of behaviour.[76] Some people will go out of their way *not* to buy whatever happens to be in fashion. Indeed, they may spend a lot of time and effort to ensure that they will not be caught 'in style'. This behaviour is a bit of a paradox, because in order to be vigilant about not doing what is expected, one must always be aware of what is expected. In contrast, truly independent people are oblivious to what is expected; they 'march to their own drummers'.

Reactance and the need for uniqueness

People have a deep-seated need to preserve freedom of choice. When they are threatened with a loss of this freedom, they try to overcome this loss. This negative emotional state is termed **reactance**, and results when we are deprived of our freedom to choose.[77] This feeling can drive us to value forbidden things even if they wouldn't be that interesting to us otherwise. For example, efforts to censor books, television shows or rock music because some people find the content objectionable may result in an *increased* desire for these products by the public.[78] Similarly, extremely overbearing promotions that tell consumers they must or should use a product may lose customers in the long run, even those who were already loyal to the advertised brand! Reactance is more likely to occur when the perceived threat to one's freedom increases and as the threatened behaviour's importance to the consumer also increases.

If you have ever arrived at a party wearing the same outfit as someone else, you know how upsetting it can be, a reaction resulting from a search for uniqueness.[79] Consumers who have been led to believe they are not unique are more likely to try to compensate by increasing their creativity, or even to engage in unusual experiences. In fact, this is one explanation for the purchase of relatively obscure brands. People may try to establish a unique identity by deliberately *not* buying market leaders.

This desire to carve out a unique identity was the rationale behind Saab's shift from stressing engineering and safety in its marketing messages to appealing to people to 'find your own road'. According to a Saab executive, 'Research companies tell us we are moving into a period where people feel good about their choices because it fits their own self-concept rather than social conventions.'[80]

■ WORD-OF-MOUTH COMMUNICATION

Despite the abundance of formal means of communication (such as newspapers, magazines and television), much information about the world is conveyed by individuals on an informal basis.[81] If you think carefully about the content of your own conversations in the course of a normal day, you will probably agree that much of what you discuss with friends, family members or co-workers is product-related: whether you compliment someone on her dress and ask her where she bought it, recommend a new restaurant to a friend, or complain to your neighbour about the shoddy treatment you got at the bank, ▶ you are engaging in **word-of-mouth communication (WOM)**. Recall, for example, that Rich's choice of football boots was directly initiated by comments and suggestions from his friends and team-mates. This kind of communication can be an efficient marketing tool. When the film *The Blair Witch Project* became a big success, it was almost assured beforehand because of the pre-premiere WOM sparked by a good website and heavy exploitation of the blurring of reality and fiction.

Information obtained from those we know or talk to directly tends to be more reliable and trustworthy than that received through more formal channels and, unlike advertising, it is often backed up by social pressure to conform to these recommendations.[82] Another factor in the importance of WOM is the decline in people's faith in institutions. As traditional endorsers are becoming increasingly problematical to use, celebrities because they can be unreliable and classical authority figures because of the withering of their authority, and, indeed, as people are becoming more cynical about all sorts of commercial communications, they turn to sources which they feel are above commercial exploitation: friends and family.[83] The importance of personal, informal product communication to marketers is further underscored by one advertising executive, who stated, 'Today, 80 per cent of all buying decisions are influenced by someone's direct recommendations.'[84]

The dominance of WOM

In the 1950s communications theorists began to challenge the assumption that advertising is the primary determinant of purchases. It is now generally accepted that advertising is more effective at reinforcing existing product preferences than at creating new ones.[85] Studies in both industrial and consumer purchase settings underline the idea that while information from impersonal sources is important for creating brand awareness, word-of-mouth is relied upon in the later stages of evaluation and adoption.[86] The more positive information consumers get about a product from peers, the more likely they will be to adopt the product.[87]

The influence of others' opinions is at times even more powerful than one's own perceptions. In one study of furniture choices, consumers' estimates of how much their friends would like the furniture was a better predictor of purchase than their *own* evaluations.[88]

Factors encouraging WOM

Product-related conversations can be motivated by a number of factors:[89]

● A person might be highly involved with a type of product or activity and get pleasure in talking about it. Computer hackers, avid birdwatchers, football fans and 'fashion plates' seem to share the ability to steer a conversation toward their particular interests.

● A person might be knowledgeable about a product and use conversations as a way to let others know it. Thus, word-of-mouth communication sometimes enhances the ego of the individual who wants to impress others with their expertise.

● A person might initiate such a discussion out of genuine concern for someone else. We are often motivated to ensure that people we care about buy what is good for them, do not waste their money, and so on.

- One way to reduce uncertainty about the wisdom of a purchase is to talk about it. Talking gives the consumer an opportunity to generate more supporting arguments for the purchase and to garner support for this decision from others.

Most WOM campaigns happen spontaneously, as a product begins to develop a regional or a subcultural following, but occasionally a 'buzz' is created intentionally. For example, when launching a new brand of beer, called Black Sheep, bottles were distributed and maximum exposure to opinion leaders in the trade ensured in order to pave the way for a massive word-of-mouth effect, intended as the vehicle carrying the new brand towards success.[90] A similar *word-of-mouth advertising* technique was used when a group of opinion leaders, or 'influencers', was used to market services in the insurance market.[91]

Guerrilla marketing

To promote hip hop albums, Def Jam and other labels started building a buzz months before a release, leaking advance copies to DJs who put together 'mix tapes' to sell on the street. If the kids seemed to like a song, *street teams* then pushed it to club DJs. As the official release date neared, these groups of fans started slapping up posters around the inner city. They plastered telephone poles, sides of buildings and car windscreens with promotions announcing the release of new albums by artists such as Public Enemy, Jay-Z, DMX or L.L. Cool J.[92]

▶ These streetwise strategies started in the mid-1970s, when pioneering DJs promoted their parties through graffiti-style flyers. This type of grass-roots effort epitomizes **guerrilla marketing**, promotional strategies that use unconventional locations and intensive word-of-mouth campaigns to push products. As Ice Cube observed, 'Even though I'm an established artist, I still like to leak my music to a kid on the street and let him duplicate it for his homies before it hits radio.'[93]

Today, big companies are buying into guerrilla marketing strategies big time. Coca-Cola did it for a Sprite promotion, Nike did it to build interest in a new shoe model.[94] Upmarket fashion companies are adopting this strategy, in order to offer shoppers a different retailing experience compared with conventional retail outlets. Comme des Garçons Guerrilla Store opened in New York in February 2004: 'in the first example of provisional retailing by an established fashion house, the store plans to close in a year even if it is making money. All 20 stores that the Tokyo-based company plans to open by next year, including one in Brooklyn in September [2004], will adopt the same guerrilla strategy, disappearing after a year.'[95]

When RCA Records wanted to create a buzz around teen pop singer Christina Aguilera, they hired a team of young people to swarm the Web and chat about her on popular teen sites. They posted information casually, sometimes sounding like fans. Just before one of her albums debuted, RCA also hired a direct marketing company to email electronic postcards filled with song snippets and biographical information to 50,000 web addresses.[96] Guerrilla marketing delivers: the album quickly went to No. 1 in the charts.

In Singapore, the EMI Group PLC gave fans of Gorillaz, a popular rock group of four cartoon characters, the opportunity to exchange text messages over their mobile phones with the band member of their choice. Each member has a distinctive look and personality, and after a favourite character was selected its cartoon face was sent to the recipient's mobile phone. These phone numbers are, of course, a potential gold mine for EMI, as they'll allow the company to communicate with music fans at will. EMI chose Gorillaz because its fan base is young, hip and devoted. As the company's managing director observed, 'For a very cool band like Gorillaz, the last thing you want to do is go mainstream.' That explains why the text messages used in the promotion were distinctly anti-corporate: A typical one read, 'Greedy record company wants me 2 tell U 2 buy Gorillaz album. Record people suck. Buy or don't buy, up to you.'[97]

Viral marketing

Many students are big fans of hotmail, a free email service. But there's no such thing as a free lunch: hotmail inserts a small ad on every message sent, making each user a salesperson. The company had 5 million subscribers in its first year and continues to grow exponentially.[98] **Viral marketing** refers to the strategy of getting customers to sell a product on behalf of the company that creates it. This approach is particularly well suited to the Web, since emails circulate so easily. According to a study by Jupiter Communications, only 24 per cent of consumers say they learn about new websites in magazine or newspaper ads. Instead, they rely on friends and family for new site recommendations, so viral marketing is their main source of information about new sites.[99] The chief executive of **Gazooba.com**, a company that creates viral marketing promotions, observed that 'the return mail address of a friend is a brand that you trust'.[100] Obviously, given what was discussed above, there may be some ethical problems and limitations as to how much marketers can infiltrate what otherwise is a network of friends/fans, before this particular 'brand that you trust' is no longer trusted.

The film *A.I.* (Artificial Intelligence) launched an elaborate viral marketing campaign by listing a credit at the end of the film for Jeanine Salla, who was described as a 'sentient machine therapist'. Curious viewers who typed in her name into the Google search engine got back a list of web addresses and they eventually got drawn into a futuristic murder mystery where characters (including robots) from the film emailed and voice mailed them with clues. The campaign generated more than 3 million sessions, and 28 per cent of the visitors remained online for more than half an hour.[101]

Efficiency of WOM

Interpersonal transmissions can be quite rapid. The producers of *Batman* showed a trailer to 300 Batman fans months before its release to counteract widespread anger about the casting of Michael Keaton as the hero. The film-makers attribute the film's eventual huge success to the positive word-of-mouth that quickly spread following the screening.[102]

WOM is especially powerful in cases where the consumer is relatively unfamiliar with the product category. Such a situation would be expected in cases where the product is new (e.g. medication to prevent hair loss) or is technologically complex (e.g. DVD recorders). As one example, the strongest predictor of a person's intention to buy a residential solar water heating system was found to be the number of solar heating users the person knew.[103]

Negative WOM

Word-of-mouth is a two-edged sword that can cut both ways for marketers. Informal discussions among consumers can make or break a product or store. Furthermore, consumers weigh **negative word-of-mouth** more heavily than they do positive comments. According to one study, 90 per cent of unhappy customers will not do business with a company again. Each of these people is likely to share their grievance with at least nine other people, and 13 per cent of these disgruntled customers will go on to tell *more than 30* people of their negative experience.[104]

Especially when making a decision about trying a new product or service, the consumer is more likely to pay more attention to negative information than positive information and to relate news of this experience to others.[105] Some consumers may even use negative WOM in order to restore their own positive self-image, for example in cases where a product offering is judged not to have corresponded to the person's self. Instead of blaming oneself for a misjudgement which would harm self-images of rationality and being in control, negative WOM may be the outcome.[106] Negative WOM has been shown to reduce the credibility of a firm's advertising and to influence consumers' attitudes toward a product as well as their intention to buy it.[107] And negative WOM is even easier to spread online. Many dissatisfied customers and disgruntled former employees have been 'inspired' to create websites just to share their tales of woe with others. For example, a website for people to complain about the Dunkin' Donuts chain became so popular the company bought it in order to control the bad press it was getting. It grew out of a complaint by the original owner because he could not get skimmed milk for his coffee.[108]

tangled web

There is a long and 'honoured' tradition of people inventing fake stories to see who will swallow them – like the one in 1824 when a man convinced 300 New Yorkers to sign up for a construction project. He claimed that all the new building in the lower part of Manhattan (what is now the Wall Street area) was making the island bottom-heavy. As a result it needed to be sawn off and towed out to sea or all of New York City would tip over! During 2005 the Edinburgh branch of the prestigious fashion store Harvey Nichols found itself inundated with heavily pregnant women. The store did not stock any clothing for this group of consumers, so could not really account for this influx of customers. However, these women had heard that the store would give £500 (about 735 euros) to any woman whose labour started while they were in the store.[109]

The Web is a perfect medium for spreading rumours and hoaxes, and we can only guess how much damage that construction 'project' would cause today if construction crews were recruited via email! Modern day hoaxes abound; many of these are in the form of email chain letters promising instant riches if you pass the message on to ten friends.

Other hoaxes involve major corporations. A popular one promised that if you tried Microsoft products you would win a free trip to Disneyland. Nike received several hundred pairs of old trainers a day after the rumor spread that you would get a free pair of new shoes in exchange for your old, smelly ones (pity the delivery people who had to cart these packages to the company!). Procter & Gamble received more than 10,000 irate calls after a rumour began spreading on newsgroups that its Febreze fabric softener killed dogs. In a pre-emptive strike, the company registered numerous website names such as **febrezekillspet.com**, **febrezesucks.com**, and **ihateprocterandgamble.com** to be sure angry consumers didn't use them. The moral? Don't believe everything you click on.

Rumours

▶ A **rumour**, even if it has no basis in fact, can be a very dangerous thing. In the 1930s, 'professional rumourmongers' were hired to organize word-of-mouth campaigns to promote clients' products and criticize those of competitors.[110] As information is transmitted among consumers, it tends to change. The resulting message usually does not resemble the original at all.

Social scientists who study rumours have examined the process by which information gets distorted. The British psychologist Frederic Bartlett used the method of *serial reproduction* to examine this phenomenon. A subject is asked to reproduce a stimulus, such as a drawing or a story. Another subject is given this reproduction and asked to copy that, and so on. This technique is shown in Figure 10.3. Bartlett found that distortions almost inevitably follow a pattern: they tend to change from ambiguous forms to more conventional ones as subjects try to make them consistent with pre-existing schemas. This process, known as *assimilation,* is characterized by *levelling,* where details are omitted to simplify the structure, or *sharpening,* where prominent details are accentuated.

In general, people have been shown to prefer transmitting good news rather than bad, perhaps because they like to avoid unpleasantness or dislike arousing hostility. However, this reluctance does not appear to occur when companies are the topic of conversation. Corporations such as Procter & Gamble and McDonald's have been the subjects of rumours about their products, sometimes with marked effects on sales.

Figure 10.3 The transmission of misinformation. These drawings provide a classic example of the distortions that can occur as information is transmitted from person to person. As each person reproduces the figure, it gradually changes from an owl to a cat

Source: Kenneth J. Gergen and Mary Gergen, *Social Psychology* (New York: Harcourt Brace Jovanovich, 1981): p. 365. Adapted from F.C. Bartlett, *Remembering* (Cambridge: Cambridge University Press, 1932).

marketing pitfall

After a very successful launching of the combined shampoo and conditioner Wash&Go on the Danish market in January 1990, where the product reached a market share (value) of more than 20 per cent in September that same year, a negative rumour caused a severe blow to its parent company. First, hairdressers complained about problems with doing colourings and perms on clients using the new product. Procter & Gamble denied the complaint, but did not dispel the rumour and soon had to deal with a second rumour: that the use of the product caused significant loss of hair. Their market share fell from 20 to 5 per cent.[111]

Most rumours have some 'kernel of truth', and it is very important for the company facing the rumour to detect it. The silicon in Wash&Go actually did cause problems for certain perm or colouring products, but this was not immediately acknowledged. Instead, the denial of the first rumour without producing substantial factual documentation led to the spreading of the second rumour, perhaps as an attempt to 'get even with' the 'aggressive' marketer. Large foreign companies are often targets of such negative word-of-mouth.[112] Procter & Gamble first tried to ignore the rumour by denial, then to refute it with reference to their own research, a source of information which had little credibility and probably strengthened the rumour rather than weakened it. Only when they asked the state environmental agency to conduct independent tests could Procter & Gamble disprove the rumours and slowly begin to regain the lost market shares.[113]

The Google search engine finds many matches for key word searches. For instance, the elaborate viral marketing campaign for the film *A.I.* (Artificial Intelligence) was based around key word searches on Google for 'Jeanine Salla' (described on page 370).

Used with permission from Google, Inc.

Rumours are thought to reveal the underlying fears of a society. While rumours sometimes die out by themselves, in other instances a company may take direct action to counteract them. A French margarine was rumoured to contain contaminants, and the company addressed this in its advertising by referring to the story as 'The rumour that costs you dearly'.[114]

multicultural dimensions

Multinational firms are especially prone to damage from rumours, since they may have less control over product quality, content or word-of-mouth. Several marketers in Indonesia, including Nestlé, have been damaged by rumours that their foods contain pork, which is prohibited to the 160 million Muslim consumers in that country. Islamic preachers, or mullahs, responded to these rumours by warning consumers not to buy products that might be tainted with pork fat. Nestlé spent more than $250,000 on an ad campaign to counteract the rumours.[115] In another recent incident in the Middle East, the Egyptian subsidiary of Coca-Cola had to get an edict from Egypt's mufti (top religious authority) certifying that the familiar Coca-Cola script logo does not in fact say 'No Mohammed, No Mecca' in Arabic after a rumour spread about hidden messages. This problem echoed one experienced a few years earlier by Nike, which recalled 38,000 pairs of shoes because its flaming air logo resembled the Arabic script for Allah.[116]

■ OPINION LEADERSHIP

Although consumers get information from personal sources, they tend not to ask just *anyone* for advice about purchases. If you decide to buy a new stereo, you will most likely seek advice from a friend who knows a lot about sound systems. This friend may own a sophisticated system, or he or she may subscribe to specialized magazines such as *Stereo Review* and spend free time browsing through electronics stores. On the other hand, you may have another friend who has a reputation for being stylish and who spends *his* free time reading fashion and lifestyle magazines and shopping at trendy boutiques. While you might not bring up your stereo problem with him, you may take him with you to shop for a new wardrobe.

This so-called opinion leadership is an important influence on a brand's popularity in many categories. The market for sports accessories is among these, where both celebrity endorsements (see Chapter 6) and sponsorship are major marketing tools in order to form opinions. The American Gatorade sports drink company made its entrance on the British market on an exclusive opinion leadership basis, sponsoring sports events and professionals like the captain of the national cricket team, but without any major promotion of the product itself. This suspense strategy created curiosity, interest and enquiries, and probably pre-shaped a lot of opinion leaders' opinions about the product before its major launch in distribution outlets.[117]

The nature of opinion leadership

Everyone knows people who are knowledgeable about products and whose advice is taken seriously by others. These individuals are **opinion leaders**. An opinion leader is a person who is frequently able to influence others' attitudes or behaviours.[118] Some people's recommendations carry more weight than others.

Opinion leaders are extremely valuable information sources for a number of reasons:

- They are technically competent and thus convincing because they possess expert power.[119]

- They have pre-screened, evaluated and synthesized product information in an unbiased way, so they possess knowledge power.[120] Unlike commercial endorsers, opinion leaders do not represent the interests of one company. They are more credible because they have no 'axe to grind'.

Opinion leadership is a big factor in the marketing of athletic shoes. Many styles first become popular in the inner city and then spread by word-of-mouth.

Carl Schneider/Getty Images, Inc.

- They tend to be socially active and highly interconnected in their community.[121] They are likely to hold offices in community groups and clubs and to be active outside of the home. As a result, opinion leaders often have legitimate power by virtue of their social standing.

▶ - They tend to be similar to the consumer in terms of their values and beliefs, so they possess referent power. Note that although opinion leaders are set apart by their interest or expertise in a product category, they are more convincing to the extent that they are *homophilous* rather than *heterophilous*. **Homophily** refers to the degree that a pair of individuals is similar in terms of education, social status and beliefs.[122] Effective opinion leaders tend to be slightly higher in terms of status and educational attainment than those they influence but not so high as to be in a different social class.

- Opinion leaders are often among the first to buy new products, so they absorb much of the risk. This experience reduces uncertainty for others who are not as courageous. Furthermore, whereas company-sponsored communications tend to focus exclusively on the positive aspects of a product, the hands-on experience of opinion leaders makes them more likely to impart *both* positive and negative information about product performance.

Whereas individual behavioural and psychological traits are the most important in identifying opinion leaders, there are some indications that opinion leadership does not function the same way in different cultures. For example, there are cultural differences in how much people rely on impersonal vs. personal information. In a study of opinion leadership in 14 European countries plus the USA and Canada, the countries most characterized by the use of impersonal information seeking (from consumer magazines, etc.) were Denmark, Norway, Sweden and Finland, whereas the countries least characterized by impersonal information seeking were Italy, Portugal and Spain.[123]

The extent of an opinion leader's influence

When marketers and social scientists initially developed the concept of the opinion leader, it was assumed that certain influential people in a community would exert an overall impact on group members' attitudes. Later work, however, began to question the assumption that there is such a thing as a *generalized opinion leader*, somebody whose recommendations are sought for all types of purchases. Very few people are capable of being expert in a number of fields. Sociologists distinguish between those who are *monomorphic,* or expert in a limited field, and those who are *polymorphic*, or expert in several fields.[124] Even opinion leaders who are polymorphic, however, tend to concentrate on one broad domain, such as electronics or fashion.

Research on opinion leadership generally indicates that although opinion leaders do exist for multiple product categories, expertise tends to overlap across similar categories. It is rare to find a generalized opinion leader. An opinion leader for home appliances is likely to serve a similar function for home cleaners but not for cosmetics. In contrast, *a fashion opinion leader* whose primary influence is on clothing choices may also be consulted for recommendations on cosmetics purchases, but not necessarily on microwave ovens.[125]

Opinion leaders vs. other consumer types

Early conceptions of the opinion leader role also assumed a static process: the opinion leader absorbs information from the mass media and in turn transmits data to opinion receivers. This view has turned out to be overly simplified; it confuses the functions of several different types of consumers. Furthermore, research has shown some evidence that the flow of influence is not one-way but two-way, so that opinion leaders are influenced by the responses of their followers.[126] This would reflect a more complex communication situation as described by the interactive communication model discussed in Chapter 6.

Opinion leaders may or may not be purchasers of the products they recommend. Early purchasers are known as *innovators* (see Chapter 15). Opinion leaders who are also early purchasers have been termed **innovative communicators**. One study identified a number of characteristics of male university students who were innovative communicators for fashion products. These men were among the first to buy new fashions, and their fashion opinions were incorporated by other students into their own clothing purchases. Other characteristics included:[127]

- They were socially active.
- They were appearance-conscious and narcissistic (i.e., they were quite fond of themselves and self-centred).
- They were involved in rock culture.
- They were heavy magazine readers.
- They were likely to own more clothing, and a broader range of styles, than other students.
- Their intellectual interests were relatively limited.

Opinion leaders also are likely to be **opinion seekers**. They are generally more involved in a product category and actively search for information. As a result, they are more likely to talk about products with others and to solicit others' opinions as well.[128] Contrary to the static view of opinion leadership, most product-related conversation does not take place in a 'lecture' format in which one person does all of the talking. A lot of product-related conversation is prompted by the situation and occurs in the context of a casual interaction rather than as formal instruction.[129] One study, which found that opinion seeking is especially high for food products, revealed that two-thirds of opinion seekers also view themselves as opinion leaders.[130] This updated view of interpersonal product communication is contrasted with the traditional view in Figure 10.4.

The market maven

Consumers who are expert in a product category may not actively communicate with others, whereas other consumers may have a more general interest in being involved in product discussions. A consumer category called the **market maven** has been proposed to describe people who are actively involved in transmitting marketplace information of all types. Market mavens are not necessarily interested in certain products and may not

Figure 10.4 Updated opinion leadership model

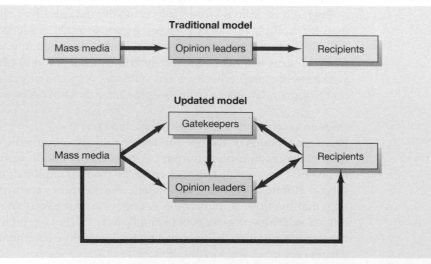

Figure 10.5 Scale items used to identify market mavens

> **1.** I like introducing new brands and products to my friends.
>
> **2.** I like helping people by providing them with information about many kinds of products.
>
> **3.** People ask me for information about products, places to shop, or sales.
>
> **4.** If someone asked me where to get the best buy on several types of products, I could tell him or her where to shop.
>
> **5.** My friends think of me as a good source of information when it comes to new products or sales.
>
> **6.** Think about a person who has information about a variety of products and likes to share this information with others. This person knows about new products, sales, stores, and so on, but does not necessarily feel he or she is an expert on one particular product. How well would you say this description fits you?

Source: Adapted from Lawrence Feick and Linda Price, 'The market maven: A diffuser of marketplace information', *Journal of Marketing* 51 (January 1987): 83-7.

necessarily be early purchasers of products; they're just into shopping and staying on top of what's happening in the marketplace. They come closer to the function of a generalized opinion leader because they tend to have a solid overall knowledge of how and where to procure products. A scale that has been used to identify market mavens is shown in Figure 10.5.[131]

The surrogate consumer

In addition to everyday consumers who are influential in influencing others' purchase decisions, a class of marketing intermediary called the **surrogate consumer** is an active player in many categories. A surrogate consumer is a person who is hired to provide input into purchase decisions. Unlike the opinion leader or market maven, the surrogate is usually compensated for his or her advice.

Interior designers, stockbrokers or professional shoppers can all be thought of as surrogate consumers. Whether or not they actually make the purchase on behalf of the consumer, surrogates' recommendations can be enormously influential. The consumer in essence relinquishes control over several or all decision-making functions, such as information search, evaluation of alternatives, or the actual purchase. For example, a client may commission an interior designer to update her house, and a broker may be entrusted to make crucial buy/sell decisions on behalf of investors. The involvement of surrogates in a wide range of purchase decisions tends to be overlooked by many marketers, who may be mis-targeting their communications to end-consumers instead of to the surrogates who are actually sifting through product information.[132]

Identifying opinion leaders

Because opinion leaders are so central to consumer decision-making, marketers are quite interested in identifying influential people for a product category. In fact, many ads are intended to reach these influentials rather than the average consumer, especially if the ads contain a lot of technical information.

Professional opinion leaders

Perhaps the easiest way to find opinion leaders is to target people who are paid to give expert opinions. *Professional opinion leaders* are people such as doctors or scientists who obtain specialized information from technical journals and other practitioners.

Marketers who are trying to gain consumer acceptance for their products sometimes find it easier to try to win over professional opinion leaders, who (they hope) will, in turn, recommend their products to customers. A case in point is the effort by Roc SA, maker of Europe's leading brand of hypoallergenic lotions, to break into the lucrative American market for skin-care products. Instead of competing head-to-head with the lavish consumer advertising of Revlon or Estée Lauder, the French company decided first to gain medical acceptance by winning over pharmacists and dermatologists. In 1994 the company began advertising in medical journals, and the product was distributed to dermatologists and to pharmacies patronized by patients of dermatologists. A free telephone number was established to provide interested consumers with the names of pharmacies carrying the range.[133]

Of course, this approach may backfire if it is carried to an extreme and compromises the credibility of professional opinion leaders. In several countries, the medical industry has a dubious reputation of 'bribing' doctors with invitations to product presentations disguised as conferences, often held in glamorous places.

Consumer opinion leaders

Since most opinion leaders are everyday consumers and are not formally included in marketing efforts, they are harder to find. A celebrity or an influential industry executive is by definition easy to locate. He or she has national or at least regional visibility or may be listed in published directories. In contrast, opinion leaders tend to operate at the local level and may influence five to ten consumers rather than an entire market segment. In some cases, companies have tried to identify influentials and involve them directly in their marketing efforts, hoping to create a 'ripple effect' as these consumers sing the company's praises to their friends. Many department stores, for instance, sponsor fashion panels, usually composed of adolescent girls, who provide input into fashion trends, participate in fashion shows and so on.

Because of the difficulties involved in identifying specific opinion leaders in a large market, most attempts to do so instead focus on exploratory studies where the characteristics of representative opinion leaders can be identified and then generalized to the larger market. This knowledge helps marketers target their product-related information to appropriate settings and media. For example, one attempt to identify financial opinion leaders found that these consumers were more likely to be involved in managing their own finances and tended to use a computer to do so. They were also more likely to follow their investments on a daily basis and to read books and watch television shows devoted to financial issues.[134]

The self-designating method

The most commonly used technique to identify opinion leaders is simply to ask individual consumers whether they consider themselves to be opinion leaders.

However, there are obvious problems with self-designation. While respondents who report a greater degree of interest in a product category are more likely to be opinion leaders, the results of surveys intended to identify *self-designated opinion leaders* must be viewed with some scepticism. Some people have a tendency to inflate their own importance and influence, whereas others who really are influential might not admit to this quality or be conscious of it.[135] Just because we transmit advice about products does not mean other people *take* that advice. For someone to be considered a bona fide opinion leader, his or her advice must actually be heard and heeded by opinion seekers. An alternative is to select certain group members (*key informants*) who in turn are asked to identify opinion leaders. The success of this approach hinges on locating those who have accurate knowledge of the group and on minimizing their response biases (the tendency to inflate one's own influence on the choices of others).

While the self-designating method is not as reliable as a more systematic analysis (in which individual claims of influence can be verified by asking others whether the person

Figure 10.6 A revised and updated version of the opinion leadership scale

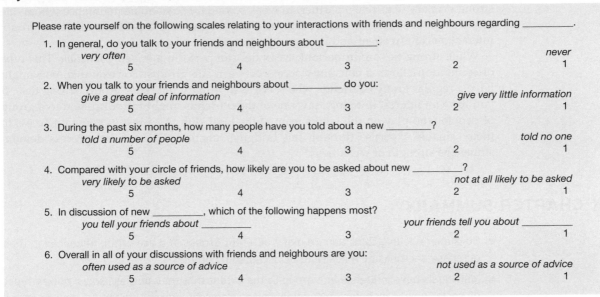

Please rate yourself on the following scales relating to your interactions with friends and neighbours regarding _____.

1. In general, do you talk to your friends and neighbours about _____:
   very often   *never*
       5   4   3   2   1

2. When you talk to your friends and neighbours about _____ do you:
   give a great deal of information   *give very little information*
       5   4   3   2   1

3. During the past six months, how many people have you told about a new _____?
   told a number of people   *told no one*
       5   4   3   2   1

4. Compared with your circle of friends, how likely are you to be asked about new _____?
   very likely to be asked   *not at all likely to be asked*
       5   4   3   2   1

5. In discussion of new _____, which of the following happens most?
   you tell your friends about _____   *your friends tell you about _____*
       5   4   3   2   1

6. Overall in all of your discussions with friends and neighbours are you:
   often used as a source of advice   *not used as a source of advice*
       5   4   3   2   1

Source: Adapted from Terry L. Childers, 'Assessment of the psychometric properties of an opinion leadership scale', *Journal of Marketing Research* 23 (May 1986): 184-8; and Leisa Reinecke Flynn, Ronald E. Goldsmith and Jacqueline K. Eastman, 'The King and Summers opinion leadership scale: revision and refinement', *Journal of Business Research* 31 (1994): 55-64.

is really influential), it does have the advantage of being easy to administer to a large group of potential opinion leaders. In some cases not all members of a community are surveyed. One of the original measurement scales developed for self-designation of opinion leaders is shown in Figure 10.6.

Sociometry

A web-based service has been created that is based on the popular play *Six Degrees of Separation*. The basic premise of the plot is that everyone on the planet is separated by only six other people. The website (**www.sixdegrees.com**) allows a person to register and provide names and email addresses of other people, so that when the user needs to network a connection is made with others in the database.

This site is a digital version of more conventional **sociometric methods**, which trace communication patterns among group members and allow researchers systematically to map out the interactions that take place among group members. By interviewing participants and asking them to whom they go for product information, researchers can identify those who tend to be sources of product-related information. This method is the most precise, but it is very hard and expensive to implement because it involves very close study of interaction patterns in small groups. For this reason, sociometric techniques are best applied in a closed, self-contained social setting, such as in hospitals, prisons, and army bases, where members are largely isolated from other social networks.

Many professionals and services marketers depend primarily on word-of-mouth to generate business. In many cases consumers recommend a service provider to a friend or fellow worker, and in other cases business people will make recommendations to their customers. For example, only 0.2 per cent of respondents in one study reported choosing a physician based on advertising. Advice from family and friends was the most widely used criterion.[136]

Sociometric analyses can be used to better understand *referral behaviour* and to locate strengths and weaknesses in terms of how one's reputation is communicated through a community.[137] *Network analysis* focuses on communication in social systems, considers the relations among people in a *referral network*, and measures the *tie strength* among them. Tie strength refers to the nature of the bond between people. It can range from strong primary (e.g., one's partner) to weak secondary (e.g., an acquaintance whom one rarely sees). A strong tie relationship may be thought of as a primary reference group; interactions are frequent and important to the individual.

While strong ties are important, weak ties can perform a *bridging function*. This type of connection allows a consumer access between sub-groups. For example, you might have a regular group of friends who serve as a primary reference group (strong ties). If you have an interest in tennis, say, one of these friends might introduce you to a group of people who play on the tennis team at the local club. As a result, you gain access to their valuable expertise through this bridging function. This referral process demonstrates the strength of weak ties.[138]

■ CHAPTER SUMMARY

- Consumers belong to or admire many different groups and are often influenced in their purchase decisions by a desire to be accepted by others.

- Individuals have influence in a group to the extent that they possess *social power*; types of social power include information power, referent power, legitimate power, expert power, reward power and coercive power.

- Brand communities unite consumers who share a common passion for a product. Brandfests organized by companies to encourage this kind of community can build brand loyalty and reinforce group membership.

- We conform to the desires of others for two basic reasons: (1) People who model their behaviour on others because they take others' behaviour as evidence of the correct way to act are conforming because of *informational social influence*, and (2) those who conform to satisfy the expectations of others or to be accepted by the group are affected by *normative social influence*.

- Group members often do things they would not do as individuals because their identities become merged with the group; they become de-individuated.

- Individuals or groups whose opinions or behaviour are particularly important to consumers are *reference groups*. Both formal and informal groups influence the individual's purchase decisions, although the impact of reference group influence is affected by such factors as the conspicuousness of the product and the relevance of the reference group for a particular purchase.

- The Web has greatly amplified consumers' abilities to be exposed to numerous reference groups. Virtual consumption communities are composed of people who are united by a common bond – enthusiasm about or knowledge of a specific product or service.

- *Opinion leaders* who are knowledgeable about a product and whose opinions are highly regarded tend to influence others' choices. Specific opinion leaders are somewhat hard to identify, but marketers who know their general characteristics can try to target them in their media and promotional strategies.

- Other influencers include *market mavens*, who have a general interest in marketplace activities, and *surrogate consumers*, who are compensated for their advice about purchases.

- Much of what we know about products comes about through word-of-mouth communication (WOM) rather than formal advertising. Product-related information tends to be exchanged in casual conversations. Guerrilla marketing strategies try to accelerate the WOM process by enlisting consumers to help spread the word.

- While word-of-mouth is often helpful for making consumers aware of products, it can also hurt companies when damaging product *rumours* or negative word-of-mouth occurs.

- Emerging marketing strategies try to leverage the potential of the Web to spread information from consumer to consumer extremely quickly. *Viral marketing* techniques enlist individuals to promote products, services, websites, etc. to others on behalf of companies. A new mode of online communication called blogging allows consumers to easily post their thoughts about products for others to see.

- Sociometric methods are used to trace referral patterns. This information can be used to identify opinion leaders and other influential consumers.

▶ KEY TERMS

Aspirational reference groups (p. 352)
Blogosphere (p. 355)
Brand community (p. 358)
Coercive power (p. 361)
Communities of practice (p. 358)
Comparative influence (p. 350)
Conformity (p. 361)
Consumer tribe (p. 358)
Decision polarization (p. 366)
De-individuation (p. 365)
Expert power (p. 361)
Guerrilla marketing (p. 369)
Home shopping parties (p. 366)
Homophily (p. 375)
Identificational membership reference group (p. 353)
Information power (p. 360)
Informational social influence (p. 362)
Innovative communicators (p. 376)
Legitimate power (p. 360)
Market maven (p. 376)
Negative word-of-mouth (p. 370)

Normative influence (p. 350)
Normative social influence (p. 362)
Norms (p. 361)
Opinion leaders (p. 374)
Opinion seekers (p. 376)
Reactance (p. 367)
Reference group (p. 350)
Referent power (p. 360)
Reward power (p. 361)
Risky shift (p. 366)
Rumour (p. 371)
Social comparison theory (p. 363)
Social power (p. 359)
Sociometric methods (p. 379)
Surrogate consumer (p. 377)
Tribal marketing (p. 358)
Viral marketing (p. 370)
Virtual community of consumption (p. 354)
Weblog (p. 355)
Word-of-mouth communication (WOM) (p. 368)

CONSUMER BEHAVIOUR CHALLENGE

1 Compare and contrast the five bases of power described in the text. Which are most likely to be relevant for marketing efforts?

2 Why is referent power an especially potent force for marketing appeals? What factors help to predict whether reference groups will or will not be a powerful influence on a person's purchase decisions?

3 Evaluate the strategic soundness of the concept of guerrilla marketing. For what types of product categories is this strategy most likely to be a success?

4 Discuss some factors that determine the amount of conformity likely to be observed among consumers.

5 Under what conditions are we more likely to engage in social comparison with dissimilar others versus similar others? How might this dimension be used in the design of marketing appeals?

6 Discuss some reasons for the effectiveness of home shopping parties as a selling tool. What other products might be sold this way?

7 Discuss some factors that influence whether membership groups will have a significant influence on a person's behaviour.

8 Why is word-of-mouth communication often more persuasive than advertising?

9 Is there such a thing as a generalized opinion leader? What is likely to determine if an opinion leader will be influential with regard to a specific product category?

10 The adoption of a certain brand of shoe or apparel by athletes can be a powerful influence on students and other fans. Should secondary school and university coaches be paid to determine what brand of athletic equipment their players will wear?

11 The power of unspoken social norms often becomes obvious only when these norms are violated. To witness this result first-hand, try one of the following: stand facing the back wall in a lift; serve dessert before the main course; offer to pay cash for dinner at a friend's home; wear pyjamas to class; or tell someone not to have a nice day.

12 Identify a set of avoidance groups for your peers. Can you identify any consumption decisions that are made with these groups in mind?

13 Identify fashion opinion leaders at your university or business school. Do they fit the profile discussed in the chapter?

14 Conduct a sociometric analysis within your hall of residence or neighbourhood. For a product category such as music or cars, ask each individual to identify other individuals with whom they share information. Systematically trace all of these avenues of communication, and identify opinion leaders by locating individuals who are repeatedly named as providing helpful information.

15 The strategy of *viral marketing* gets customers to sell a product to other customers on behalf of the company. That often means convincing your friends to climb on the bandwagon, and sometimes you get a small percentage return (or other reward) if they end up buying something.[139] Some might argue that means you're selling out your friends (or at least selling to your friends) in exchange for a marketing reward. Others might say you're just sharing the wealth with those you care about. Have you been involved in viral marketing by passing along names of your friends or sending them to a website such as **hotmail.com**? If so, what happened? How do you feel about this practice? Discuss the pros and cons of viral marketing.

■ NOTES

1. C. Whan Park and V. Parker Lessig, 'Students and housewives: Differences in susceptibility to reference group influence', *Journal of Consumer Research* 4 (September 1977): 102–10.

2. Kenneth J. Gergen and Mary Gergen, *Social Psychology* (New York: Harcourt Brace Jovanovich, 1981).

3. Harold H. Kelley, 'Two Functions of Reference Groups', in Harold Proshansky and Bernard Siedenberg, eds, *Basic Studies in Social Psychology* (New York: Holt, Rinehart & Winston, 1965): 210–14.

4. David Murrow, 'Dewar's profiles travel well', *Advertising Age* (14 August 1989): 28.

5. A. Benton Cocanougher and Grady D. Bruce, 'Socially distant reference groups and consumer aspirations', *Journal of Marketing Research* 8 (August 1971): 79–81.

6. 'Flere vil spise mere fisk', *Markedsføring* 18 (1996): 18.

7. L. Festinger, S. Schachter and K. Back, *Social Pressures in Informal Groups: A Study of Human Factors in Housing* (New York: Harper, 1950).

8. R.B. Zajonc, H.M. Markus and W. Wilson, 'Exposure effects and associative learning', *Journal of Experimental Social Psychology* 10 (1974): 248–63.

9. D.J. Stang, 'Methodological factors in mere exposure research', *Psychological Bulletin* 81 (1974): 1014–25; R.B. Zajonc, P. Shaver, C. Tavris and D. Van Kreveid, 'Exposure, satiation and stimulus discriminability', *Journal of Personality and Social Psychology* 21 (1972): 270–80.

10. J.E. Grush, K.L. McKeogh and R.F. Ahlering, 'Extrapolating laboratory exposure research to actual political elections', *Journal of Personality and Social Psychology* 36 (1978): 257–70.

11. www.repcheck.com, accessed 31 December 2002.

12. 'BT Openworld hooks up with uDate', *New Media Age* (5 December 2002); 'iVillage enters the dating arena with Match.Com', *New Media Age* (22 August 2002): 7; 'Virtual valentines?' Yahoo! Internet Life (1 February 2002); Jon Herskovitz, 'Japanese look for love', *Advertising Age International* (13 July 1998): 6.

13. Richard Wilk, 'A critique of desire: Distaste and dislike in consumer behavior', *Consumption, Culture and Markets* 1(2) (1997): 175–96; see also Pierre Bourdieu, *Distinction: A Social Critique of the Judgement of Taste* (London: Routledge, 1984); E.N. Banister and M.K. Hogg, 'Negative symbolic consumption and consumers' drive for self-esteem: The case of the fashion industry', *European Journal of Marketing* 7 (2004): 850–68; B.S. Turner and J. Edmunds, 'The distaste of taste: Bordieu, cultural capital and the Australian post-war elite', *Journal of Consumer Culture* 2(2) (2002): 219–40.

14. Basil G. Englis and Michael R. Solomon, 'To be and not to be: Reference group stereotyping and *The Clustering of America*', *Journal of Advertising* 24 (Spring 1995): 13–28; Michael R. Solomon and Basil G. Englis, 'I Am Not, Therefore I Am: The Role of Anti-Consumption in the Process of Self-Definition', Special Session at the Association for Consumer Research meetings, October 1996, Tucson, Arizona.

15. Bruce Feirstein, *Real Men Don't Eat Quiche* (New York: Pocket Books, 1982); www.auntiefashions.com, accessed 31 December 2002.

16. Greg Jaffe, 'No MTV for Widespread Panic, just loads of worshipful fans', *Wall Street Journal Interactive Edition* (17 February 1999).

17. This typology is adapted from material presented in Robert V. Kozinets, 'E-tribalized marketing: The strategic implications of virtual communities of consumption', *European Management Journal* 17(3) (June 1999): 252–64.

18. Tom Weber, 'Net's hottest game brings people closer', *Wall Street Journal Interactive Edition* (20 March 2000).

19. Quoted in Marc Gunther, 'The newest addiction', *Fortune* (2 August 1999): 122–4, at 123.

20. Bob Tedeschi, 'Is weblog technology here to stay or just another fad?', *The New York Times on the Web* (25 February 2002); Steven Levy, 'Living in the Blog-Osphere', *Newsweek* (26 August 2002): 42–4; David F. Gallagher, 'Free weblog service and a vampire, too', *The New York Times on the Web* (26 August 2002); David F. Gallagher, 'A site to pour out emotions, and just about anything else', *The New York Times on the Web* (5 September 2002).

21. Laurie J. Flynn, 'Free internet service for Simpsons fans', *New York Times on the Web* (24 January 2000).

22. Bob Tedeschi, 'Product reviews from anyone with an opinion', *New York Times on the Web* (25 October 1999).

23. Kozinets, 'E-tribalized marketing'.

24. Bob Tedeschi, 'Online retailers find that customer reviews build loyalty', *New York Times on the Web* (6 September 1999).

25. 'Bookseller offers refunds for advertised books', *Opelika-Auburn News* (11 February 1999): A11.

26. *Information* (14 February 2001): 2.

27. James H. McAlexander, John W. Schouten and Harold F. Koenig, 'Building brand community', *Journal of Marketing* 66 (January 2002): 38–54; Albert Muniz and Thomas O'Guinn, 'Brand community', *Journal of Consumer Research* (March 2001): 412–32.

28. Veronique Cova and Bernard Cova, 'Tribal aspects of postmodern consumption research: The case of French in-line roller skaters', *Journal of Consumer Behavior* 1 (June 2001): 67–76.

29. Penelope Eckert and Sally McConnell-Ginet, 'Think practically and look locally: Language and gender as community-based practice', *Annual Review of Anthropology* (1992): 461–90, at 464, cited in Emma Moore, 'Approaches to Identity: Lesson from Sociolinguistics', Seminar paper, Customer Research Academy, Manchester School of Management, UMIST, UK (22 April 2004): 2.

30. Etienne Wenger, *Communities of Practice: Learning, Meaning and Identity* (Cambridge: Cambridge University Press, 1998), cited in Moore 'Approaches to Identity'.

31. Emma Moore, 'Learning Style and Identity: A Sociolinguistic Analysis of a Bolton High School', unpublished Ph.D. dissertation, University of Manchester (2003).

32. Penelope Eckert, 'Constructing Meaning in Sociolinguistic Variation', paper presented at the Annual Meeting of the American Anthropological Association, New Orleans, USA (November 2002) (accessible at www.stanford.edu/~eckert/AAA02.pdf), cited in Moore 'Approaches to Identity': 3.

33. Jeffrey D. Ford and Elwood A. Ellis, 'A re-examination of group influence on member brand preference', *Journal of Marketing Research* 17 (February 1980): 125–32; Thomas S. Robertson, *Innovative Behavior and Communication* (New York: Holt, Rinehart & Winston, Inc., 1980): ch. 8.

34. William O. Bearden and Michael J. Etzel, 'Reference group influence on product and brand purchase decisions', *Journal of Consumer Research* 9 (1982): 183–94.

35. Gergen and Gergen, *Social Psychology*: 312.

36. J.R.P. French Jr. and B. Raven, 'The Bases of Social Power', in D. Cartwright, ed., *Studies in Social Power* (Ann Arbor, MI: Institute for Social Research, 1959): 150–67.

37. Michael R. Solomon, 'Packaging the service provider', *The Service Industries Journal* 5 (March 1985): 64–72.

38. Quoted in Tamar Charry, 'Advertising: Hawking, Wozniak pitch modems for U.S. robotics,' *The New York Times News Service* (5 February 1997).

39. Patricia M. West and Susan M. Broniarczyk, 'Integrating multiple opinions: The role of aspiration level on consumer response to critic consensus', *Journal of Consumer Research* 25 (June 1998): 38–51.

40. Lars Thøger Christensen and Søren Askegaard, 'Identities and images of products and organizations: A semiotic exercise', *European Journal of Marketing* 35(3/4) (2001): 292–315.

41. Luc Sante, 'Be different! (Like everyone else!)', *The New York Times Magazine* (17 October 1999).

42. BBC News, 'Smoking curbs: the global picture': http://news.bbc.co.uk/1/hi/world/4016477.stm (accessed 1 March 2005).

43. Cornelia Pechmann and S. Ratneshwar, 'The effects of antismoking and cigarette advertising on young adolescents' perceptions of peers who smoke', *Journal of Consumer Research* 21 (September 1994): 236–51.

44. See Robert B. Cialdini, *Influence: Science and Practice*, 2nd edn (New York: Scott, Foresman, 1988) for an excellent and entertaining treatment of this process.

45. For the seminal work on conformity and social influence, see Solomon E. Asch, 'Effects of Group Pressure Upon the Modification and Distortion of Judgments', in D. Cartwright and A. Zander, eds, *Group Dynamics* (New York: Harper & Row, 1953); Richard S. Crutchfield, 'Conformity and character', *American Psychologist* 10 (1955): 191–8; Muzafer Sherif, 'A study of some social factors in perception', *Archives of Psychology* 27 (1935): 187.

46. Robert E. Burnkrant and Alain Cousineau, 'Informational and normative social influence in buyer behavior', *Journal of Consumer Research* 2 (December 1975): 206–15.

47. For a study attempting to measure individual differences in proclivity to conformity, see William O. Bearden, Richard G. Netemeyer and Jesse E. Teel, 'Measurement of consumer susceptibility to interpersonal influence', *Journal of Consumer Research* 15 (March 1989): 473–81.

48. Douglas B. Holt, Søren Askegaard and Torsten Ringberg, '7ups and Downs', unpublished manuscript, Penn State University.

49. John W. Thibaut and Harold H. Kelley, *The Social Psychology of Groups* (New York: Wiley, 1959); W.W. Waller and R. Hill, *The Family, a Dynamic Interpretation* (New York: Dryden, 1951).

50. Bearden, Netemeyer and Teel, 'Measurement of consumer susceptibility to interpersonal influence'; Lynn R. Kahle, 'Observations: Role-relaxed consumers: A trend of the nineties', *Journal of Advertising Research* (March/April 1995): 66–71; Lynn R. Kahle and Aviv Shoham, 'Observations: Role-relaxed consumers: Empirical evidence', *Journal of Advertising Research* (May/June 1995): 59–62.

51. Leon Festinger, 'A theory of social comparison processes', *Human Relations* 7 (May 1954): 117–40.

52. Chester A. Insko, Sarah Drenan, Michael R. Solomon, Richard Smith and Terry J. Wade, 'Conformity as a function of the consistency of positive self-evaluation with being liked and being right', *Journal of Experimental Social Psychology* 19 (1983): 341–58.

53. Abraham Tesser, Murray Millar and Janet Moore, 'Some affective consequences of social comparison and reflection processes: The pain and pleasure of being close', *Journal of Personality and Social Psychology* 54(1) (1988): 49–61.

54. L. Wheeler, K.G. Shaver, R.A. Jones, G.R. Goethals, J. Cooper, J.E. Robinson, C.L. Gruder and K.W. Butzine, 'Factors determining the choice of a comparison other', *Journal of Experimental Social Psychology* 5 (1969): 219–32.

55. M.L. Richins, 'Social comparison and the idealized images of advertising', *Journal of Consumer Research* 18 (June 1991): 71–83; M.C. Martin and P.F. Kennedy, 'Advertising and social comparison: Consequences for female preadolescents and adolescents', *Psychology and Marketing* 10(6) (1993): 513–29; M.C. Martin and P.F. Kennedy, 'Social Comparison and the Beauty of Advertising Models: The Role of Motives in Comparison', in Chris T. Allen and Deborah Roedder John, eds, *Advances in Consumer Research* 21 (Provo, UT: Association for Consumer Research, 1994): 365–71; M.C. Martin and N.J. Gentry, 'Stuck in the model trap: The effects of beautiful models in ads on female pre-adolescents and adolescents', *Journal of Advertising* 26(2) (Summer 1997): 19–33.

56. See J.V. Wood, 'Theory and research concerning social comparisons of personal attributes', *Psychological Bulletin* 106 (September 1989): 231–48 for a detailed exposition of the evolving debates around the theory of social comparison.

57. Martin and Kennedy, 'Advertising and social comparison'; Martin and Kennedy, 'Social Comparison and the Beauty of Advertising Models'; Martin and Gentry, 'Stuck in the model trap'; Margaret K. Hogg, Margaret Bruce and Kerry Hough, 'Female images in advertising: The implications of social comparison for marketing', *International Journal of Advertising* 18(4) (1999): 445–73; Margaret K. Hogg and Aikaterini Fragou, 'Social comparison goals and the consumption of advertising: towards a more contingent view of young women's consumption of advertising', *Journal of Marketing Management* 19 (7–8) (September 2003): 749–80.

58. Michael Hafner, 'How dissimilar others may still resemble the self: Assimilation and contrast after social comparison', *Journal of Consumer Psychology* 14(1&2) (2004): 187–96.

59. George P. Moschis, 'Social comparison and informal group influence', *Journal of Marketing Research* 13 (August 1976): 237–44.

60. Burnkrant and Cousineau, 'Informational and normative social influence in buyer behavior'; M. Venkatesan, 'Experimental study of consumer behavior conformity and independence', *Journal of Marketing Research* 3 (November 1966): 384–7.

61. J.L. Freedman and S. Fraser, 'Compliance without pressure: The foot-in-the-door technique', *Journal of Personality and Social Psychology* 4 (1966): 195–202.

62. R.B. Cialdini, J.E. Vincent, S.K. Lewis, J. Catalan, D. Wheeler and B.L. Darby, 'Reciprocal concessions procedure for inducing compliance: The door-in-the-face effect', *Journal of Personality and Social Psychology* 31 (1975): 200–15.

63. J. Craig Andrews and Richard G. Netemeyer, 'Alcohol Warning Label Effects: Socialization, Addiction, and Public Policy Issues', in Ronald P. Hill, ed., *Marketing and Consumer Research in the Public Interest* (Thousand Oaks, CA: Sage, 1996): 153–75; 'National study finds increase in college binge drinking', *Alcoholism and Drug Abuse Weekly* (27 March 2000): 12–13; Emma Banister and Maria Piacentini, ' "Binge Drinking: Do They Mean Us?" Living Life to the Full in Students' Own Words', in C. Pechmann and L. Price, eds, *Advances in Consumer Research* 33 (forthcoming).

64. Maria Piacentini and Emma N. Banister, 'Getting hammered? . . . Students coping with alcohol', *Journal of Consumer Behaviour* 5(2) (Spring 2006).

65. BBC Online, http://www.bbc.co.uk/insideout/southeast/series2/nhs_binge_drinking_alcohol_abuse_drunk_alcoholism.shtml (17 February 2003); *Guardian*, http://society.guardian.co.uk/drugsandalcohol/story/0,8150,874700,00.html (14 January 2003).

66. B. Latane, K. Williams and S. Harkins, 'Many hands make light the work: The causes and consequences of social loafing', *Journal of Personality and Social Psychology* 37 (1979): 822–32.

67. S. Freeman, M. Walker, R. Borden and B. Latane, 'Diffusion of responsibility and restaurant tipping: Cheaper by the bunch', *Personality and Social Psychology Bulletin* 1 (1978): 584–7.

68. Nathan Kogan and Michael A. Wallach, *Risk Taking* (New York: Holt, Rinehart & Winston, 1964).

69. Nathan Kogan and Michael A. Wallach, 'Risky shift phenomenon in small decision-making groups: A test of the information exchange hypothesis', *Journal of Experimental Social Psychology* 3 (January 1967): 75–84; Kogan and Wallach, *Risk Taking*; Arch G. Woodside and M. Wayne DeLozier, 'Effects of word-of-mouth advertising on consumer risk taking', *Journal of Advertising* (Fall 1976): 12–19.

70. Roger Brown, *Social Psychology* (New York: The Free Press, 1965).

71. David L. Johnson and I.R. Andrews, 'Risky shift phenomenon tested with consumer product stimuli', *Journal of Personality and Social Psychology* 20 (1971): 382–5; see also Vithala R. Rao and Joel H. Steckel, 'A polarization model for describing group preferences,' *Journal of Consumer Research* 18 (June 1991): 108–18.

72. Donald H. Granbois, 'Improving the study of customer in-store behavior', *Journal of Marketing* 32 (October 1968): 28–32.

73. Len Strazewski, 'Tupperware locks in new strategy', *Advertising Age* (8 February 1988): 30.

74. Quoted in Melanie Wells, 'Smooth operator', *Forbes* (13 May 2002): 167–8.

75. Gergen and Gergen, *Social Psychology*.

76. L.J. Strickland, S. Messick and D.N. Jackson, 'Conformity, anticonformity and independence: Their dimensionality and generality', *Journal of Personality and Social Psychology* 16 (1970): 494–507.

77. Jack W. Brehm, *A Theory of Psychological Reactance* (New York: Academic Press, 1966).

78. R.D. Ashmore, V. Ramchandra and R. Jones, 'Censorship as an Attitude Change Induction', paper presented at meeting of Eastern Psychological Association, New York, 1971; R.A. Wicklund and J. Brehm, *Perspectives on Cognitive Dissonance* (Hillsdale, NJ: Erlbaum, 1976).

79. C.R. Snyder and H.L. Fromkin, *Uniqueness: The Human Pursuit of Difference* (New York: Plenum Press, 1980).

80. Quoted in Raymond Serafin, 'Non-conformity sparks Saab', *Advertising Age* (3 April 1995): 27.

81. See for instance the *Daily Princetonian*'s editorial about Thefacebook.com as 'possibly the biggest word-of-mouth trend to hit campus since St Ives Medicated Apricot Scrub found its ways into the women's bathroom', cited by Peter Applebome, 'On campus, hanging out by logging on', *NYT Online* (1 December 2004); see also note 99.

82. Johan Arndt, 'Role of product-related conversations in the diffusion of a new product', *Journal of Marketing Research* 4 (August 1967): 291–5.

83. ' "Word-of-mouth" to become true measure of ads', *Marketing* (9 February 1995): 7.

84. Quoted in Barbara B. Stern and Stephen J. Gould, 'The consumer as financial opinion leader', *Journal of Retail Banking* 10 (Summer 1988): 43–52.

85. Elihu Katz and Paul F. Lazarsfeld, *Personal Influence* (Glencoe, IL: Free Press, 1955).

86. John A. Martilla, 'Word-of-mouth communication in the industrial adoption process', *Journal of Marketing Research* 8 (March 1971): 173–8; see also Marsha L. Richins, 'Negative word-of-mouth by dissatisfied consumers: A pilot study', *Journal of Marketing* 47 (Winter 1983): 68–78.

87. Arndt, 'Role of product-related conversations in the diffusion of a new product'.

88. James H. Myers and Thomas S. Robertson, 'Dimensions of opinion leadership', *Journal of Marketing Research* 9 (February 1972): 41–6.

89. James F. Engel, Robert J. Kegerreis and Roger D. Blackwell, 'Word-of-mouth communication by the innovator', *Journal of Marketing* 33 (July 1969): 15–19.

90. 'Black sheep of the Theakston family', *Marketing* (3 December 1992): 24.

91. Kimberley Paterson, 'Giving a boost to word-of-mouth advertising', *Rough Notes Co. Inc.* (April 1999).

92. Sonia Murray, 'Street marketing does the trick', *Advertising Age* (20 March 2000): S12.

93. Quoted in 'Taking to the streets', *Newsweek* (2 November 1998): 70–3, at 71.

94. Constance L. Hays, 'Guerrilla marketing is going mainstream', *New York Times on the Web* (7 October 1999).

95. Cathy Horyn, 'A store made for right now: You shop until it's dropped' *NYT Online* (17 February 2004).

96. Wayne Friedman, 'Street marketing hits the internet', *Advertising Age* (1 May 2000): 32; Erin White, 'Online buzz helps album skyrocket to top of charts', *Wall Street Journal Interactive Edition* (5 October 1999).

97. Quoted in Gabriel Kahn, 'Virtual rock band corresponds with fans via text messaging', *The Wall Street Journal Online* (19 April 2002).

98. Jared Sandberg, 'The friendly virus', *Newsweek* (12 April 1999): 65–6.

99. See also for instance Thefacebook.com which was launched by five Harvard students and had attracted over 1 million students from 300 US universities within the space of ten months to sign up. Peter Applebome, 'On campus, hanging out by logging on', *NYT Online* (1 December 2004).

100. Karen J. Bannan, 'Marketers try infecting the internet', *New York Times on the Web* (22 March 2000).

101. Peter Landau, 'A.I. promotion', *Mediaweek* (12 November 2001).

102. Bill Barol, 'Batmania', *Newsweek* (26 June 1989): 70.

103. Dorothy Leonard-Barton, 'Experts as negative opinion leaders in the diffusion of a technological innovation', *Journal of Consumer Research* 11 (March 1985): 914–26.

104. Chip Walker, 'Word-of-mouth', *American Demographics* (July 1995): 38–44.

105. Richard J. Lutz, 'Changing brand attitudes through modification of cognitive structure', *Journal of Consumer Research* 1 (March 1975): 49–59; for some suggested remedies to bad publicity, see Mitch Griffin, Barry J. Babin and Jill S. Attaway, 'An Empirical Investigation of the Impact of Negative Public Publicity on Consumer Attitudes and Intentions', in Rebecca H. Holman and Michael R. Solomon, eds, *Advances in Consumer Research* 18 (Provo, UT: Association for Consumer Research, 1991): 334–41; Alice M. Tybout, Bobby J. Calder and Brian Sternthal, 'Using information processing theory to design marketing strategies', *Journal of Marketing Research* 18 (1981): 73–9; see also Russell N. Laczniak, Thomas E. DeCarlo and Sridhar N. Ramaswami, 'Consumers' responses to negative word-of-mouth communication: An attribution theory perspective,' *Journal of Consumer Psychology* 11(1) (2001): 57–74.

106. Gulden Asugman, 'An Evaluation of Negative Word-of-Mouth Research for New Extensions', in B. Englis and A. Olofsson, eds, *European Advances in Consumer Research* 3 (Provo, UT: Association for Consumer Research, 1998): 70–5.

107. Robert E. Smith and Christine A. Vogt, 'The effects of integrating advertising and negative word-of-mouth communications on message processing and response', *Journal of Consumer Psychology* 4(2) (1995): 133–51; Paula Fitzgerald Bone, 'Word-of-mouth effects on short-term and long-term product judgments', *Journal of Business Research* 32 (1995): 213–23.

108. 'Dunkin' donuts buys out critical web site', *The New York Times on the Web* (27 August 1999); for a discussion of ways to assess negative WOM online, see David M. Boush and Lynn R. Kahle, 'Evaluating negative information in online consumer discussions: From qualitative analysis to signal detection', *Journal of EuroMarketing* 11(2) (2001): 89–105.

109. Gerard Seenan, 'Shop till you drop at Harvey Nicks', *The Guardian* (26 March 2005) (http://www.guardian.co.uk/uk_news/story/0,,1445911,00.html).

110. Charles W. King and John O. Summers, 'Overlap of opinion leadership across consumer product categories', *Journal of Marketing Research* 7 (February 1970): 43–50.

111. Jan Møller Jensen, 'A Strategic Framework for Analysing Negative Rumors in the Market Place: The Case of Wash & Go in Denmark', in J. Sirgy, K.D. Bahn and T. Erem, eds, *World Marketing Congress* 6 (Istanbul: Proceedings of the Sixth Bi-Annual Conference of the Academy of Marketing Science, 1993): 559–63.

112. John F. Sherry Jr., 'Some Implications of Consumer Oral Tradition for Reactive Marketing', in Thomas Kinnear, ed., *Advances in Consumer Research* 11 (Ann Arbor, MI: Association for Consumer Research, 1984): 741–7.

113. Jensen, 'A strategic framework'.

114. John Leo, 'Psst! Wait 'Till you hear this: A scholar says rumors reveal our fears and desires', *Time* (16 March 1987): 76.

115. Sid Astbury, 'Pork rumors vex Indonesia', *Advertising Age* (16 February 1989): 36.

116. Mae Ghalwash, 'Squint hard, be creative in search for blasphemy in Coca-Cola logo', *Opelika-Auburn News* (22 May 2000): 2A.

117. 'Beware Yanks bearing drinks', *Marketing* (5 March 1992): 23–4.

118. Everett M. Rogers, *Diffusion of Innovations*, 3rd edn (New York: Free Press, 1983).

119. Leonard-Barton, 'Experts as negative opinion leaders in the diffusion of a technological innovation'; Rogers, *Diffusion of Innovations*.

120. Herbert Menzel, 'Interpersonal and Unplanned Communications: Indispensable or Obsolete?' in *Biomedical Innovation* (Cambridge, MA: MIT Press, 1981): 155–63.

121. Meera P. Venkatraman, 'Opinion leaders, adopters, and communicative adopters: A role analysis', *Psychology and Marketing* 6 (Spring 1989): 51–68.

122. Rogers, *Diffusion of Innovations*.

123. Niraj Dawar, Philip M. Parker and Lydia J. Price, 'A cross-cultural study of interpersonal information exchange', *Journal of International Business Studies* (3rd quarter 1996): 497–516.

124. Robert Merton, *Social Theory and Social Structure* (Glencoe, IL: Free Press, 1957).

125. King and Summers, 'Overlap of opinion leadership across consumer product categories'; see also Ronald E. Goldsmith, Jeanne R. Heitmeyer and Jon B. Freiden, 'Social values and fashion leadership', *Clothing and Textiles Research Journal* 10 (Fall 1991): 37–45; J.O. Summers, 'Identity of women's clothing fashion opinion leaders', *Journal of Marketing Research* 7 (1970): 178–85.

126. Gerrit Antonides and Gulden Asugman, 'The communication structure of consumer opinions', in Flemming Hansen, ed., *European Advances in Consumer Research* 2 (Provo, UT: Association for Consumer Research, 1995): 132–7.

127. Steven A. Baumgarten, 'The innovative communicator in the diffusion process,' *Journal of Marketing Research* 12 (February 1975): 12–18.

128. Laura J. Yale and Mary C. Gilly, 'Dyadic perceptions in personal source information search', *Journal of Business Research* 32 (1995): 225–37.

129. Russell W. Belk, 'Occurrence of Word-of-Mouth Buyer Behavior as a Function of Situation and Advertising Stimuli', in Fred C. Allvine, ed., *Combined Proceedings of the American Marketing Association series,* no. 33 (Chicago: American Marketing Association, 1971): 419–22.

130. Lawrence F. Feick, Linda L. Price and Robin A. Higie, 'People Who Use People: The Other Side of Opinion Leadership', in Richard J. Lutz, ed., *Advances in Consumer Research* 13 (Provo, UT: Association for Consumer Research, 1986): 301–5.

131. For discussion of the market maven construct, see Lawrence F. Feick and Linda L. Price, 'The market maven', *Managing* (July 1985): 10; scale items adapted from Lawrence F. Feick and Linda L. Price, 'The market maven: A diffuser of marketplace information', *Journal of Marketing* 51 (January 1987): 83–7.

132. Michael R. Solomon, 'The missing link: Surrogate consumers in the marketing chain', *Journal of Marketing* 50 (October 1986): 208–18.

133. Andra Adelson, 'A french skin-care line seeks to take America by first winning over pharmacists', *New York Times* (14 February 1994): D7.

134. Stern and Gould, 'The consumer as financial opinion leader'.

135. William R. Darden and Fred D. Reynolds, 'Predicting opinion leadership for men's apparel fashions', *Journal of Marketing Research* 1 (August 1972): 324–8. A modified version of the opinion leadership scale with improved reliability and validity can be found in Terry L. Childers, 'Assessment of the psychometric properties of an opinion leadership scale', *Journal of Marketing Research* 23 (May 1986): 184–8.

136. 'Referrals top ads as influence on patients' doctor selections', *Marketing News* (30 January 1987): 22.

137. Peter H. Reingen and Jerome B. Kernan, 'Analysis of referral networks in marketing: Methods and illustration', *Journal of Marketing Research* 23 (November 1986): 370–8.

138. Peter H. Reingen, Brian L. Foster, Jacqueline Johnson Brown and Stephen B. Seidman, 'Brand congruence in interpersonal relations: A social network analysis', *Journal of Consumer Research* 11 (December 1984): 771–83; see also James C. Ward and Peter H. Reingen, 'Sociocognitive analysis of group decision-making among consumers', *Journal of Consumer Research* 17 (December 1990): 245–62.

139. Thomas E. Weber, 'Viral marketing: Web's newest ploy may make you an unpopular friend', *The Wall Street Journal Interactive Edition* (13 September 1999).

'It's just being a student isn't it?' – The story of a young binge drinker

EMMA N. BANISTER and MARIA G. PIACENTINI, Department of Marketing, Lancaster University Management School, Lancaster, UK

CONTEXT

Alcohol is economically important in the UK with the value of the alcoholic drinks market estimated at more than £30 billion in 2004, providing employment for around 1 million people.[1] However, excessive alcohol consumption is recognized as an increasingly serious problem for Western countries and the public costs of alcohol are estimated at £20 billion per year, through health problems, lost productivity, crime and antisocial behaviour, and social harm including family breakdown.[2] Binge drinking is of particular concern in the UK and is prevalent among young people between the ages of 16 and 24. It is widely acknowledged that alcohol plays a key role in the lives of many undergraduate students with recent research suggesting that half the UK student population regularly binge drink. Despite increased financial hardship among the student population and widespread campaigns about the dangers of heavy drinking, students' alcohol expenditure was nearly £1 billion in 2004, £300 million more than on food.[3] Why is it that so many students choose to drink heavily? Melanie is a first year student at a British university. Here she talks about her social life at university and in particular focuses on her alcohol consumption.[4]

MELANIE'S STORY

'I know I perhaps drink too much but it's part of being a student isn't it? I don't drink much during the week . . . Well, apart from Mondays and Wednesdays, which are big student nights out. I tend to go out Monday, Wednesday, Friday and maybe Saturdays. Sometimes on a Sunday or Thursday I just go to a college bar but then I would just have an orange or a Diet Coke or something.

A typical night begins with anything up to two hours getting ready. Usually it will be more like an hour, but if it's a special occasion I will spend about two hours, making sure that everything is perfect – hair, nails, fake tan on my legs etc. I want to look my best! Sometimes we will have like a fashion show where all us girls parade our possible outfits to try and find something to wear. I don't have a good night if I don't feel good about myself at the start of the night. Also I enjoy this part of the evening, it's an important part of the run-up to going out – and usually we will have a few drinks as we get ready. Often this is something fairly cheap like Lambrini.[5] We tend to go out about half past eight.

We tend to budget for the night by taking out a certain amount and only spending to that limit. I usually take like £20 or £25 out. And when that is finished, then that's it. I think it is different for me, 'cos I tend to be known for being a bit of a "heavyweight",[6] so I tend to drink more than the others. Some of my friends only take £15 out, although I know lads who will go out with £30. We know the drink prices in all the local bars and clubs so we tend to go to different places depending on what we fancy drinking. Last night I had two doubles in Bar Sol, followed by a few shots in Sensations, three cocktails in Lounge, and then three bottles in Prohibition. It's quite a lot [laughs] but I feel fine today. I remember one night working out that I drank 30 units in one night. And then I found out the other day that the recommended amount for a bloke for a week is 21 units.[7]

Wednesday is our big night out. There's usually about 15 of us go out together. We go to the Cotton Cub, which is a cheesy[8] nightclub, where most people I know tend to go. It's a student night and most weeks it's a wild night out. All the sports clubs go (e.g. football, hockey, rugby etc.). So it is expected of you if you are a member of any sports teams. There are always loads of people there and everyone is really drunk. The night ends at 3am, but I tend to go home earlier if the music is a bit boring or if I've sobered up a bit. I usually conk out[9] on the bus on the way home.

Why do I drink so much? I guess I drink because I like it and I like what it does to me. For me, the signs of good nights out are people doing funny things, making you laugh, dancing all night, being "hyper". I can't imagine nights out without alcohol. I do know people who don't drink when they are broke or if they are trying to lose weight, but for me personally I would rather just not go out. I don't see the point of going out and not drinking. It's a waste of money if you are not going to get drunk, especially as soft drinks are just as expensive as alcoholic ones. I like the taste of drink, and I like trying lots of different drinks – like banana schnapps or something random. I do it to be different. People are always saying "what's that? Can I try it?"

I see myself as friendly, bubbly and fairly confident, but I can also be a bit shy in some situations. I think my character changes a bit with the drink though. Like sometimes I am a bit coy when I see someone who I have seen the night before when I have been really lively and stuff. Also I might get a bit more aggressive when I am drunk, like I can sometimes come across as a bit rude and a bit "off" when I have had a few. But, mostly I think alcohol has a good effect, I am much more upbeat and have more of a laugh.

I do sometimes wonder what I am doing to my health, because I know I drink too much and I know it isn't exactly good for you. When I get really drunk my memory sometimes goes and the next day I can't remember things. The day after a big session someone will be like "you did this, you were chatting to this guy" and I'm like "I don't remember". That's quite worrying. My friends are like, "you have to stop getting that drunk". I've learnt about the brain in my psychology classes and I know a little about what drink does to your brain, and I reckon I am really damaging myself.

My sister calls me a binge drinker. She works full time and doesn't drink at all during the week. But she does at the weekend. She tells me I shouldn't drink like I do, that I should drink steadily throughout the week. And I think, well surely it's worse if you're drinking every night. My mum gives me lots of advice, she says "just make sure that you've got your friends with you" and "make sure you have one alcoholic drink and one non-alcoholic drink". She knows I drink a lot, although probably not how much, because she has picked me up on a few occasions when I've had big nights out at home. I think my mum thinks that it's just a phase I am going through. It's just being a student isn't it?

Sometimes when I am on the bus or something I see other people in the same sort of drunken state that I regularly get in. Sometimes it is funny, but at other times I think it's pathetic, and I guess it does make me stop and think about myself and my own behaviour. But then I think you are only young once and you are only a student once, I won't have the opportunity to drink so much once I start working full time.'

QUESTIONS

1 Identify the consumer behaviour theories you could draw on to identify the function(s) that alcohol fulfils

for Melanie and the means by which she seeks to rationalize her high levels of alcohol consumption.

2 Identify the important reference groups mentioned by Melanie. What effect(s) do they have on her behaviour and why are some of these reference groups more influential than others?

3 Are there similar examples of alcohol abuse and binge drinking in your country? (if yes, answer (a), if no, answer (b).)

(a) Does your government have a strategy concerning alcohol reduction and what are its key aspects? Drawing on Melanie's story which policies do you think are most likely to prove effective for young people and students?

(b) If not, why do you think binge drinking is not a problem in your society? Are there any other examples of excessive consumption behaviours in your society?

4 Look at the material on the Portman Group website (**http://www.portmangroup.org.uk/**). Drawing on the case material, which campaigns (if any) do you think would be effective in influencing the drinking habits of your peer group? Why?

Notes

1. *Alcohol Harm Reduction Strategy For England, 2004*, Cabinet Office, Strategy Unit, http://www.strategy.gov.uk/output/Page3669.asp (accessed 29 April 2004).
2. Ibid.
3. Curtis, P. (2004), 'Students set to spend £1bn on alcohol', *The Education Guardian*, 23 August, http://education.guardian.co.uk/students/finance/story/0,12728,1289126,00.html (accessed 2 September 2004).
4. The name of this consumer is fictional as are the names of the venues (i.e. bars and club) and do not relate to existing places known by these names.
5. Lambrini is a brand of sparkling perry drink.
6. Meaning she can 'take' her drink well.
7. The current UK government guidelines for alcohol consumption are no more than 3-4 units per day for men and 2-3 units per day for women. However, there is a tendency by consumers to translate these guidelines into a weekly allowance.
8. Colloquialism meaning not cool and trendy. A cheesy nightclub would typically refer to a venue playing chart music rather than any particular specialist music type.
9. Meaning falls asleep.

Holiday decision-making: an adaptable and opportunistic ongoing process

ALAIN DECROP, University of Namur, Belgium

Consumers have traditionally been portrayed as rational and risk averse. As a consequence, consumer decision-making has been presented from a problem-solving or information processing perspective.[1] These models start from the assumption that any consumer need or desire creates a problem within the individual. The consumer undertakes to solve that problem by deciding a course of action in order to satisfy this need or desire. Decision-making typically entails five steps: need recognition, information search, evaluation of alternatives, product choice (purchase), and decision outcomes (post-purchase evaluation). An alternative view[2] has seen consumers' decision-making as a hierarchy of cognitive, affective and behavioural responses (i.e. the C-A-B sequence). Within the context of these two main approaches, existing models of holiday decision-making have seen it as: a rational process implying high involvement;[3] high risk perception;[4] extensive problem-solving and information search;[5] and a sequential evolution of plans which starts from the generic decision to go on holiday.[6]

The objective of this case is to show how consumer decision-making – within the context of going on holiday – may vary from these traditional tenets. We followed the holiday decision-making process of 27 Belgian households (singles, couples, families and groups of friends) over the course of a year. They were interviewed in-depth four times: three times before their summer holiday and once after it. Many interesting findings emerged which challenged traditional ways of understanding consumer decision-making.

Holiday decision-making proved to be an ongoing process which was not necessarily characterized by fixed sequential stages, and which did not stop once a decision had been made. Firstly, the generic decision about whether or not to go on holiday was not always the starting point; and sometimes this generic decision was irrelevant (for instance, in the case of regular holidaymakers). For example, a young family had two possible holiday plans. They had already decided on transportation (car), accommodation (camping), activities (beach and visits), and organization (by oneself). However, in April they still did not know whether or not they would go on holiday:

Anne (F, 41, family): *'Actually, it's not up to us to decide. There are administrative factors that stand in the way at the moment, and it is clear that if we're looking for a job, and he [her husband] finds a job starting on June 15th, it's not entirely appropriate to ask for holidays for the entire month of August! It would be a bit stupid to refuse a job on the grounds that you cannot go away on vacation this year. It is the second year where we do not have control over anything!'*

Secondly, there is seldom a linear (i.e. sequential and hierarchical) evolution of holiday plans. Situational factors, as well as levels of involvement, are responsible for many deviations and changes of mind. Daydreaming, nostalgia and anticipation are other important influences. Thirdly, final decisions and bookings are often made very late. There are a number of reasons for this, e.g. risk reduction, expectancy (situational variables), availability (opportunism), loyalty and personality. Finally, informants often expressed cognitive dissonance or post-decision regret, which they strove to reduce.

In the same way, information search is not always a well-defined stage in the holiday decision-making process. Information collection tends to be ongoing, and it does not stop when the holiday has been booked. Substantial amounts of information are gathered during and/or just after the holiday experience. Cognitive dissonance and prolonged involvement (hedonic consumption) are the major explanations for this. Moreover, information search is much less intensive and purposive than is usually assumed. A majority of holidaymakers could be described as low information searchers; they do not prepare their trip in much detail nor for a long time beforehand, rather they prefer serendipitous discoveries and the unexpected. When they were asked about whether or not they had already collected a lot of information about their forthcoming holiday in Tenerife in June, Vincent replied on behalf of a group of young friends:

Vincent (M, 26, friend party): *'No, it's on the spot. That's better unplanned, to decide on the day: "we'll go and visit this, we'll go and visit that". It's . . . Planning everything in advance is a bit annoying.'*

Interviewer: *'So you prefer the unexpected and to organize everything once you arrive?'*

Vincent: *'Yes, it's better . . . to say already, to see the images and everything. When you arrive, you no longer see it in the same way. You pass it by and you do not even inquire about it because you have read about it, you are . . . It's better to go without having seen anything. You go, you discover and you're more amazed because you're discovering that . . .'*

Searching for holiday information tends to be memory-based (internal) rather than stimulus-based (external). Information is often collected accidentally and passively. Moreover, when information is collected it is not always used and/or sometimes it is put aside for later on. Finally, information collection is a weak predictor of actual choice but rather indicates preferences. Of course, the extent of information collection depends on the holidaymaker's levels of involvement and risk aversion.

Informants found it difficult to say when they started thinking about their current holiday project(s). 'Ever since our last holiday ended' was a typical answer. This is another indication that holiday decision-making is an ongoing circular process: as one holiday ends, then planning starts for the next one. The time during and just after a holiday is particularly fruitful for nurturing other projects. In fact, it appears that most holidaymakers are involved in a number of holiday plans all at the same time. These involve different time horizons, different types of decision-making units, different formulas, and different types of decision-making processes.

In general, holiday decision-making seems to be adaptable (Payne, Bettman and Johnson 1993) and opportunistic (Wilson & Wilson 1988). Incidental learning seems to play a bigger role than intentional learning. This is different from most existing models which assume the existence of a (bounded) rational, problem-solving holidaymaker. Holiday decision-making often takes account of contextual contingencies, and is triggered off incidentally through information collection or opportunities:

Danièle (F, 44, family): *'Sometimes, we still want to go somewhere, and then the opportunity arises. Our parents tell us "oh, we are going to Spain, would you like to join us?" and we say "why not?" and off we go. The times when we have gone away with* Intersoc *as monitors, it was also because your brother-in-law said: "you really don't want to go? You know, I need leaders . . ." And that's how it was decided! Six months earlier we wouldn't have known we were going there.'*

Adaptability and opportunism are even more obvious when looking at holidaymakers' decision strategies. Overall, these strategies are adapted according to the situation and, more particularly, to the type of decision-making unit in which they are involved. Heuristics tend to be constructed on the spot rather than being planned *a priori*. Moreover, a substantial number of informants did not use any well-defined strategies in making their holiday decisions. Needs and desires were connected with choice solutions just because they were evoked at the same time. Finally, holidaymakers preferred simple decision rules although these might not necessarily be accurate. In line with Bettman, Johnson and Payne's (1991) general properties of choice heuristics, it seems that holidaymakers' decision strategies are characterized by a limited amount of processing, selective processing (the amount of processing is not consistent across alternatives or attributes), qualitative rather than quantitative reasoning, attribute-based and non-compensatory rules (as contrasted with alternative-based and compensatory), and the lack of an overall evaluation for each alternative.

Findings further indicate that emotional factors are particularly powerful in shaping holiday choices. Sometimes, people make their holiday decisions according to momentary moods or emotions. The sudden and unforeseen nature of choices is highlighted: a person chooses according to a *coup de tête* (sudden impulse), *coup de plaisir* (sudden pleasure), or *coup de cœur* (falling in love). This suggests that the affective choice mode (Mittal 1988) is more relevant than the traditional information processing mode (Bettman 1979) as far as a highly experiential product such as holidays is concerned. In the same way, Holbrook's (1984) C-E-V (consciousness, emotion, value) model may be more appropriate to account for holiday decision-making rather than the classical C-A-B model. This hedonic and experiential view of consumer behaviour focuses on product usage, and on the hedonic and symbolic dimensions of the product. It is especially relevant for particular categories of products such as novels, plays, sporting events or travel.

However, some systematic themes can be detected in holiday decision-making. Holiday plans (destinations) move from being dreams (preferences or ideal level) to reality (expectation level) as time elapses. There is a growing commitment to choice. Sometimes, the preferred aspects of a holiday are replaced by second choices or alternative solutions. While holidaymakers tend to be optimistic and idealistic at the outset of their holiday plans, they become more realistic over time. The objective intervention or subjective perception of contextual factors is the major reason for this shift. Contextual facilitators (e.g. occupation or the family situation) are first considered while contextual inhibitors (e.g. time or money budget) are taken into account later. Another interpretation of the shift from dream to reality is in terms of the FCB grid.[7] The 'feel-learn-do' and the 'feel-do-learn' sequences appear to be more salient than the traditional 'learn-feel-do' model in holiday decision-making. Moreover, holiday plans are instrumental (and dynamic) in achieving higher-order (and quite stable) goals. Major goals are satisfaction maximization (hedonism) and return on investment (utilitarianism). Finally, information accumulates in a natural, non-purposive way from one source to the other without much searching effort. Information collection becomes more important in the very last days just before a booking is made and during the holiday experience. Further, there is a shift from internal to external sources of information, and from general (destination) to more specific (practical) information.

In conclusion, holiday decision-making is not necessarily as rational and cognitive as it has often been assumed to be. It entails emotions, adaptability and opportunism to a large extent. There is not one process but a plurality of holiday decision-making processes.

QUESTIONS

1 Identify and discuss how holiday decision-making, as it was described in this case, is different from the traditional problem-solving approach to consumer decision-making.

2 Compare the information search process, as it was described here for holidays, with the search process that consumers might follow for another product category (e.g. a household appliance or a perfume).

3 What managerial implications (for tour operators or travel agents) would you draw from the findings that were presented in this case?

Sources

Ajzen, I. and M. Fishbein (1980), *Understanding Attitudes and Predicting Social Behavior* (Englewood Cliffs, NJ: Prentice Hall).

Bettman, J.R. (1979), *An Information Processing Theory of Consumer Choice* (Reading, MA: Addison-Wesley).

Bettman, J.R., E.J. Johnson and J.W. Payne (1991), 'Consumer Decision Making', in T.S. Robertson and H.H. Kassarjian, eds, *Handbook of Consumer Behavior* (Englewood Cliffs, NJ: Prentice Hall): 50–84.

Engel, J.F., D.T. Kollat and R.D. Blackwell (1973), *Consumer Behavior* (New York: Holt, Rinehart & Winston).

Fishbein, M. and I. Ajzen (1975), *Belief, Attitude, Intention and Behavior: An Introduction to Theory and Research* (Reading, MA: Addison Wesley).

Goodall, B. (1988), 'How Tourists Choose their Holidays: An Analytical Framework', in B. Goodall and G. Ashworth, eds, *Marketing in the Tourist Industry: The Promotion of Destination Regions* (London: Routledge): 1–17.

Holbrook, M.B. (1984), 'Emotion in the Consumption Experience: Toward a New Model of the Human Consumer', in R.A. Peterson, W.D. Hoyer and W.R. Wilson, eds, *The Role of Affect in Consumer Behavior: Emerging Theories and Applications* (Lexington, MA: Lexington Books): 17–52.

Howard, J.A. and J.N. Sheth (1969), *The Theory of Buyer Behavior* (New York: John Wiley & Sons).

Lavidge, R.J. and G.A. Steiner (1961), 'A model for predictive measurements of advertising effectiveness', *Journal of Marketing* 25 (October): 59–62.

Mansfeld, Y. (1992), 'Tourism: Towards a behavioural aproach. The choice of destination and its impact on spatial behaviour', *Progress in Planning* 38: 1–92.

Mathieson, A. and G. Wall (1982), *Tourism: Economic, Physical and Social Impacts* (Harlow: Longman).

Middleton, V.T. (1994), *Marketing in Travel and Tourism* (Oxford: Butterworth-Heinemann).

Mittal, B. (1988), 'The role of affective choice mode in the consumer purchase of expressive products', *Journal of Economic Psychology*, 9: 499–524.

Moutinho, L. (1987), 'Consumer behaviour in tourism', *European Journal of Marketing*, 21(10): 2–44.

Nicosia, F.M. (1966), *Consumer Decision Processes: Marketing and Advertising Implications* (Englewood Cliffs, NJ: Prentice Hall).

Payne, J.W., J.R. Bettman and E.J. Johnson (1993), *The Adaptive Decision Maker* (Cambridge: Cambridge University Press).

Um, S. and J.L. Crompton (1990), 'Attitude determinants in tourism destination choice', *Annals of Tourism Research* 17: 432–48.

van Raaij, W.F. and D.A. Francken (1984), 'Vacations decisions, activities and satisfaction', *Annals of Tourism Research* 11: 101–12.

Vaughn, R. (1980), 'How advertising works: A planning model', *Journal of Advertising Research* 20(5): 27–33.

Wilson, E.J. and D.T. Wilson (1988), ' "Degrees of freedom" in case research of behavioral theories of group buying', *Advances in Consumer Research* 15: 587–94.

Woodside, A.G. and S. Lysonski (1989), 'A general model of traveler destination choice', *Journal of Travel Research* 27 (Spring): 8–14.

Notes

1. See for instance: Nicosia 1966; Howard and Sheth 1969; Engel, Kollat and Blackwell 1973; Bettman 1979.
2. For example, Lavidge and Steiner 1961; Fishbein and Ajzen 1975; Ajzen and Fishbein 1980.
3. Moutinho 1987.
4. Goodall 1988.
5. Mathieson and Wall 1982; Middleton 1994.
6. Mansfeld 1992; Um and Crompton 1990; van Raaij and Francken 1984; Woodside and Lysonski 1989.
7. FCB = Foote, Cone and Belding: Vaughn, 1980.

From space to place: creating Utopian meanings in a festival marketplace

PAULINE MACLARAN, De Montfort University, Leicester, UK, and STEPHEN BROWN, University of Ulster, Northern Ireland

Places, such as retail centres, are much more than spatial coordinates or dots on a map. As places become intimately associated with life's events, they come to represent symbols of the experiences concerned. In other words, a space becomes a place when it becomes invested with meanings by those who use it. This case study shows how a retail space can come to hold very special meanings for consumers, and how these meanings may not necessarily be understood by the retail management.

Developed out of a beautiful eighteenth-century building, the Powerscourt Townhouse Centre opened as a festival marketplace in 1981, a short walk away from one of Dublin's busiest shopping areas, Grafton Street. The centre comprised three levels of retail outlets grouped around an enclosed courtyard. The majority of shops sold specialist merchandise, with jewellery, ladies' fashions, antiques and eating places predominating. Like its American and European counterparts (i.e. Harborplace, Baltimore and Covent Garden, London), Powerscourt offered an allegedly unique shopping environment, the 'Powerscourt Experience', as it was described on promotional material. Festival marketplaces provide an alternative to the uniformity of shopping centres which offer mass-produced goods via high street chains such as Next, Miss Selfridge, New Look and Zara. They typically occupy a refurbished building of acknowledged architectural merit, retail an eclectic mix of speciality goods and services, are tenanted by independent retailers rather than national chain stores, encourage recreational as opposed to utilitarian shopping activities, and adopt an essentially aesthetic ethos involving artworks, craft activities and designer goods.

On the ground floor in Powerscourt there was a central café where shoppers could pass the time chatting or people-watching. Surrounding this were small market stalls, selling an eclectic mix of products, from ice cream to bonsai trees. Rising up from the courtyard was a stage for cultural events with a grand piano to provide special recitals and enhance the centre's ambience. More exclusive shops, on the higher levels, proffered a range of designer jewellery, clothing, antiques and paintings. Its quirky mix of shops and entertainment gave Powerscourt a special ambience that consumers loved. Its combination of arts and crafts, and the sense that there was something for everyone, made it very different from other high street shopping. Many people came just to sit with friends over coffee or food in the many restaurants that were interspersed throughout the centre. Visually, a plethora of colourful signs, restaurant canopies and plant greenery greeted shoppers as they entered the courtyard. Powercourt's somewhat haphazard layout encouraged exploration and gave shoppers a sense of discovery. It was not unusual for some actually to lose their way as they wandered around the different floors.

During the 1990s, as many other retail innovations appeared in Dublin, Powerscourt lost some of its special appeal. Its retail mix became a little jaded as small shops came and went and parts of the centre had a rather run-down appearance. The management of the centre decided to carry out a major refurbishment that lasted well over a year and brought about radical changes to the ambience of the centre, which moved towards mainstream retailing. Smaller units were replaced with larger chain stores, such as FCUK and Karen Millen, the market-type stalls disappeared completely, and a minimalist design approach was applied throughout. The immediate hedonic impact that assailed consumers on entering the centre, the blaze of colours and smells from fruit and vegetables, largely evaporated. High wooden surrounds that demarked the new central restaurant area on the ground floor countermanded the soaring effect of superabundant space that used to strike consumers as they entered the centre.

There were strong emotional responses from consumers and retailers, many of whom were very disappointed with, and distressed by, this modernization. To understand how changes to a shopping centre could provoke such deep reactions it helps if we explore the meanings that consumers had created within such an environment. In the case of Powerscourt, these meanings had a very utopian content.

The concept of utopia comes from Sir Thomas More's renowned classic of 1516, about an imaginary land called Utopia. More's detailed description of this idyllic environment gave birth to a distinctive literary genre, one that describes diverse types of ideal communities where social harmony and perfection prevails. Spanning over 500 years and including well over 3,000 writings, utopian thinking has produced many varied, often conflicting visions of perfection. As time and space vary, so too does the conception of what constitutes the ideal life. Many now argue that the value of this body of work lies in the mental processes that it inspires, as a means to question existing reality. In drawing attention to the gap between what is and what could be, such literature continually inspires a critical but creative view of the world. Accordingly, the utopian impulse has been identified in the web of contemporary social life, in computer games, cults, communities and lifestyle magazines. In keeping with a postmodern world, the utopian imagination has itself become fragmented, dispersed throughout our daily lives and, most often, dispensed by the marketing system.

Commentators have increasingly alluded to the utopian qualities of shopping centres, both in terms of their physical layouts and the social activities that they contain. In Powerscourt there were three key utopian processes that underpinned the consumer experience therein:

- *Sensing displace*. The discovery of a utopia always involves some type of dislocation, a travelling between worlds, whether physical or temporal, in order to provide a setting in which to contrast and compare the present. There are several factors that contributed to Powerscourt being a displace. Many visitors came across the centre by chance because signage to the centre was minimal. This meant that often the centre was a serendipitous find that surprised and delighted. Consumers often 'stumbled' across it and this gave them a sense of exploration, and discovery that activated the utopian imagination. Regarded as a world apart, the centre evoked feelings of elsewhereness, a displacement from the present, and a distancing that was both spatial and temporal.

- *Creating playspace*. As a retail space, pre-refit Powerscourt was full of contradictions and underlying tensions that remained unresolved. Like More's Island of Utopia, it was neither the old world nor the new, neither eighteenth-century Georgian times, nor modern-day Ireland. Within the centre itself, furthermore, these tensions remained unresolved, playing against each other and underpinning the overall spatial arrangement. Retailers mixed styles unashamedly in Powerscourt to achieve the effect of a giant collage that greeted consumers as they entered the main courtyard.

With no uniformity to shop front design or signage, an array of different codes and references intermingled in an intriguingly idiosyncratic manner. This meant that consumers could weave their own personalized fantasies into their experiences there.

- *Performing artscape*. Powerscourt was at once a commercial space and a special place that evoked other, more elevated values, both in terms of its preservation of a historic building and the copious arts, crafts and antiques contained within. Above and beyond its intrinsic cultural capital, Powerscourt functioned as a form of stage-set for marketplace theatre and retail dramaturgy. With its grand piano on central stage, it evoked the feeling of drama about to unfold, a story about to be told. In highlighting the contrast with other, more utilitarian forms of shopping, this entertainment added to Powerscourt's exalted, extra-special nature, thereby enhancing its aspirational appeal, its utopian promise of perfectibility.

As the refurbishment took place, and the centre moved towards mainstream retailing, consumers complained that it could now be anywhere and that it had lost its special ambience that so strongly differentiated it from other high street shopping venues. After the refurbishment the environment no longer evoked the feelings encapsulated in the themes above. Many consumers were very angry at the changes, believing that a unique place had been sacrificed to the encroaching forces of globalization and, indeed, that a part of their heritage had been taken away. They blamed the management of the centre and dissatisfaction with the new minimalist look only served to increase their nostalgia for the 'old' Powerscourt which had once symbolized for them the antithesis of high street shopping.

This case study highlights how marketers and consumers are involved in joint cultural production of spaces and how marketers need to be aware of the important social role they play in the organization of such spaces. Their relationships with consumers are enhanced by judicious use of marketing activities within the spaces concerned. As this Powerscourt study demonstrates, when marketers overlook this social role their marketing activities may actually subvert, rather than support, consumers' interest in a particular space. In particular, it highlights the importance for management of understanding the meaning systems that consumers create around marketing phenomena and how these may be very powerful and enduring.

QUESTIONS

1 Compare and contrast a shopping centre with a festival marketplace in terms of how consumers experience each of these retail environments.

2 Discuss the reasons why consumers were disappointed with the refurbishment in Powerscourt.

3 Suggest alternative strategies that the Powerscourt management could have pursued when they carried out the refurbishment.

4 Think of some examples of other retail or service environments to which consumers may attach personalized meanings, e.g. pubs, restaurants, hairdressers and so forth. Then think of one that is a favourite of yours and discuss what it means to you.

Further reading

Maclaran, P. (2003), 'Allegorizing the Demise of a Utopian Retroscape: Every Piano Tells a Story', in S. Brown and J. Sherry, eds, *Time and the Market: Ecumenical Essays on the Rise of Retroscapes* (Chicago: ME Sharpe): 94-114.

Maclaran, P. and S. Brown (2001), 'The future perfect declined: Utopian studies and consumer research', *Journal of Marketing Management* 17(3-4): 367-90.

Maclaran, P. and S. Brown (2005), 'The center cannot hold: consuming the utopian marketplace', *Journal of Consumer Research*, September.

Maclaran, P., S. Brown and L. Stevens (1999), 'The Utopian Imagination: Spatial Play in a Festival Marketplace', in B. Dubois, T.M. Lowrey, L.J. Shrum and M. Vanhuele, eds, *European Advances in Consumer Research* 4 (Provo, UT: Association for Consumer Research): 304-9.

How second-hand consumption re-enchants and empowers the consumer's life

DOMINIQUE ROUX, Université Paris 12, France

Anne and Philippe first got to know each other in the Paris area in the 1980s. Now in their forties, they are married with two children aged 12 and 15. Anne works as a management controller for a leading French car manufacturer and Philippe as a telecom engineer.

When they met, they were both comfortably off middle-class junior managers. Because of Philippe's work, they moved for a short period to the north of France. During that time, they discovered the 'Grande Braderie' of Lille, an annual discount market dating back to the fairs of the Middle Ages, which attracts thousands of participants and exhibitors each year from the French-Belgian frontier area. They were astounded and quite won over in the course of a night spent bargain-hunting among the 70 kilometres of streets displaying goods of every imaginable kind. They also made a point at weekends of visiting the various second-hand sales that were advertised as taking place in the villages of the Lille region. Both practical and pleasurable, such occasions provided the opportunity to get to know the area, as well as for picking up decorative household knick-knacks, clothes or tools, according to their mood at the time. In this region, second-hand sales were such a common occurrence that it seemed quite natural to go there and wander around on the lookout for bargains.

Undoubtedly, the most striking memory Anne has of this period is of acquiring her wedding dress. She didn't want to buy it in a traditional shop, where the dresses all seemed the same – not necessarily unattractive, but banal. One Sunday they were in a charming village 10 kilometres from Lille, when Anne, without having planned on doing so, found herself standing in front of a market stall where, hanging from the sunshade, was an Empire-style wedding dress. Intrigued, she stared at it for a long time, admiring its pure straight lines, embellished by fine lace facing and pearls stitched to the bodice. She was irresistibly attracted to it, but, not daring to imagine she might be married in a dress bought at a flea market, she turned it over and over, disbelievingly. The stall-holder offered it to her for the equivalent of 15 euros, a price that seemed ridiculous, exciting and very appealing, in that the dress appeared to be in perfect condition. What's more, to Anne's experienced eye it looked to be her size. After asking Philippe's opinion – he found the idea rather amusing – she finally left with what she would later come to think of as a trophy. Years later, the famous 'flea-market wedding dress' had become something of a fetish object, to the extent that Anne had recounted 'the legend' to her daughters, promising to bequeath it to them when they got married.

The following year, with Philippe's training complete, the return to the Paris area left them feeling depressed. They were struck by the absence of second-hand markets, something they had not been aware of before they left. They also wondered why such events did not exist or seemed unknown in Paris. By way of compensation, during their holidays, they would have no hesitation in making a detour of several kilometres to rummage through a second-hand store signposted along a country road. Anne always managed to find some pieces of old lace, and Philippe antiquarian books.

When their first daughter was born, friends passed on to them baby clothes they had no further use for. Anne had also retrieved the clothes her mother had saved from her childhood, and which she was happy to see her daughter wearing.

Then, to their great surprise, two or three years later a number of second-hand markets made their appearance in the Paris area. Anne and Philippe were delighted by this development, and began to believe that the pleasures of their Lille years would again be part of their daily life. At the same time, second-hand stores started opening up here and there, and they would often make a tour of them at random. Anne especially liked looking for decorative items for the house, but more than anything, such places were like great caves, full of treasure. One would never know what one might find there. They were permeated with an antiquated atmosphere, and Anne loved the untidy profusion of abandoned objects. Sometimes pathetic but often touching, these fragments of personal histories seemed always to be part and parcel of the dust that covered them. Every now and then, in Paris, she would push open the door of a second-hand clothes shop, and admire the originality of the somewhat outdated dresses and beautifully-cut ladies' suits. The clothes were all different, each item unique. Clearly they had been worn very little. A woman had once loved them, then cast them aside. Anne found things there that she never saw in regular clothes shops, items that seemed attractive precisely because they weren't available through the standard distribution channels. By wearing these clothes, she too could feel herself to be unique and different. She would also buy lots of things for her children, pretty little outfits that were practically unworn.

Philippe, for his part, appreciated finding useful items. He often had a clear idea of what he was looking for. What was the point of rushing to the supermarket? he said. Second-hand markets and stores were full of things people no longer wanted and which were still in perfect working order. Why pay more, why buy at high prices when high quality goods were thrown out? Often the products sold at hypermarkets did not appear to be any more appealing or effective than others that had already been used and proved their worth. He was also particularly sensitive to waste, and to the consumption race that seemed to him to be as futile as it was harmful. His financial commitment to humanitarian causes – donations that he made every year to various charities – went hand in hand with respect for resources and a concern for the preservation of objects as much as with the labour that had produced them. It was by no means unusual for him, on the days allocated for the disposal of bulky objects, to collect various items of furniture, electrical equipment or computers from the Paris streets and pavements. He would salvage the components and test them out. He liked to say that from three discarded bikes he had reconstructed one for his daughter. He did this not out of necessity but through conviction, finding ridiculous all the waste and incompetence that led people to throw things away without even trying to repair them. Increasingly, Philippe has begun purchasing on the internet. Second-hand sales sites enable him to find out-of-print old books, which he collects, as well as CDs and DVDs.

Anne and Philippe were aware that they were increasingly avoiding the standard distribution channels. They still did their day-to-day shopping in hypermarkets, and bought certain products new for convenience, security or when appropriate. But very often they preferred to wait, compare and find better value for money or something more original. Their approach was in part one of economic calculation, but allied to the pleasure of being resourceful. This feeling of being smarter arose to some extent from the sense of making better buying choices for themselves and of using their resources intelligently, but also from the moral satisfaction of not contributing to overall wastage. At the age of 40, with a settled life and materially well-off, they did not feel they were changing the world, but rather were living in a different way in terms of consumption. The increase in the various channels of exchange between private individuals and second-hand goods in general gave them great pleasure, since it enabled them to re-enchant their life as consumers while reclaiming a whole domain of freedom.

QUESTIONS

1   What factors do consumers consider when comparing second-hand distribution channels, either favourably or unfavourably, with traditional channels?

2   Would you say that Anne and Philippe have the same motivations toward second-hand shopping? What distinguishes them or brings them together in terms of their profiles (e.g. attitudes; values; perceptions)?

3   Do certain alternative distribution channels seem to cater better for certain types of motivation rather than others? Which features of the different channels respond best to which orientations?

4   In what respects can second-hand exchanges between consumers be said to enhance their power? In your opinion does this constitute a long-term threat to traditional channels?

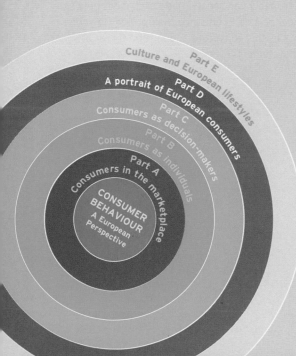

Part E
Culture and European lifestyles

Part D
A portrait of European consumers

Part C
Consumers as decision-makers

Part B
Consumers as individuals

Part A
Consumers in the marketplace

CONSUMER
BEHAVIOUR
A European
Perspective

A PORTRAIT OF EUROPEAN CONSUMERS

The chapters in this part consider some of the social influences that help to determine who we are, with an emphasis on the various subcultures to which we belong. Chapter 11 provides a discussion of family structures in Europe, and identifies the many instances in which our purchase decisions are made in conjunction with the family. Chapter 12 focuses on factors that define our social classes, and how membership in a social class exerts a strong influence on what we buy with the money we make. Chapter 13 discusses the strong influence that age has on our behaviour as consumers, with an emphasis on the bonds we share with others who were born at roughly the same time.

EUROPEAN FAMILY STRUCTURES AND HOUSEHOLD DECISION-MAKING

Saturday is the main shopping day, and Caleb is accompanying his mother to the supermarket. He doesn't usually go with her, and he suspects that Kymberly, his mum, would rather go without him. She spends less and gets home faster without him, she says. But he's going today anyway, partly to be sure that she picks out the right stuff for his eleventh birthday party. The Power Rangers tablecloth and biscuits were OK last year, but he's almost a teenager now and he plans to push heavily for the right food and decorations. He wants a party with the 'right atmosphere' – maybe some music by Coldplay or Mariah Carey. Even though these two artistes are really different he's seen a lot of them on TV, and his friends at school talk about both artistes all the time. If he could just get his mum to buy *both* CDs, he would have a better idea of which to play for 'setting the mood' at his party.

First, though, they have to get the family's regular shopping out of the way. Kymberly gets a little exasperated as Caleb and his little sister Riley argue over the best type of dog food to get for Baggins, their new puppy. Finally, at Kymberly's urging, they move on to the next aisle, where she quickly throws two cans of tuna fish into the trolley. She starts to move on, but from behind her she hears Caleb say: 'You're not really going to buy that brand, are you? Don't you know that they still use nets to catch their tuna and those nets kill hundreds of innocent dolphins every year!' This was news to Kymberly. After getting over her initial irritation at being told how to shop by a child who can't even tidy his room, she realizes that Caleb is making a lot of sense.

As she puts the offending cans back on the shelf, she remarks, 'Well, Caleb, I think I should send you to do the shopping from now on. Maybe I can get you to go shopping with your father too – sometimes I think he could use a little more common sense on those rare occasions when he steps into the supermarket.'

■ INTRODUCTION

Children are becoming a major force in persuading their parents to clean up their act when it comes to the environment. One study showed that one-third of parents have changed their shopping habits to be more environmentally conscious because of information they received from their children. Teenagers have been instrumental in projects ranging from home and school recycling to persuading tuna companies to stop buying tuna caught in nets that also trap dolphins. Many companies are becoming aware of young people's influence in everyday family buying decisions, and some are trying hard to convince 'green teens' that their products are environmentally friendly.[1]

Caleb's influence on Kymberly's choice of an environmentally safe product illustrates that many consumer decisions are made jointly. The individual decision-making process described in detail in Chapter 8 is, in many cases, too simplistic since more than one person may be involved in any stage of the problem-solving sequence, from initial problem recognition and information search to evaluation of alternatives and product choice. For example, the decision to get a pet is often made jointly by family members. The children may be instrumental in persuading their reluctant parents to get a dog or a cat, while the parents may be responsible for the information search to determine what breed to get or where to get it. Then, the entire family may be involved in selecting the puppy or kitten that will soon become another family member.

Whether they are choosing a can of tuna or buying a new multimedia entertainment system for the home, consumers commonly work together. This chapter examines issues related to *collective decision-making*, where more than one person is involved in the purchasing process for products or services that may be used by multiple consumers. We focus specifically on one of the most important organizations to which we all claim membership – the family unit. We'll consider how members of a family negotiate among themselves, and how important changes in the modern family structure are affecting this process. The chapter concludes by discussing how 'new employees' – children – learn to become consumers.

■ THE FAMILY

Constructing and deconstructing the family in Europe

While it might still be too early to draw definite conclusions, it's reasonable to speculate that historians will regard the period from the 1990s to 2005 as one of the most politically, socially and economically turbulent time-frames in modern history. Radical political and market changes throughout Western and Eastern Europe are reflections and outcomes of intense social change in European societies that have been under way since the 1950s. While the extent and pace of changes and the national perceptions of social change have differed from one country to another, it is clear that many of our social institutions have been altered over the past four decades, not least of which is the notion of 'family'. As of 1 May 2004 the population of the European Union stood at almost 454 million, the third largest population of any political entity after China (1,283 million) and India (1,041 million). While the ten newest EU member countries have more similarities than differences with the 'former 15' EU members in family structure, there are some important trends in age distributions, marriage patterns, employment, salary rates between men and women and ageing of the populations of our individual member states which will have a major impact on consumer consumption patterns of European families in the years to come.

Before moving on to a discussion of the forces that have changed our notions of family, and what these changes mean in terms of consumer behaviour, we need to spend a moment tackling the thorny question 'What is the family, and how do we gather data about it?' There is a great deal of family diversity throughout Europe, and the conceptualization of *family* is based on ideology, popular mythology and conventions that are firmly rooted in each country's historical, political, economic and cultural traditions. Certainly, European governments have had a strong history of requiring regular and up-to-date socio-demographic information on the behaviour of families (birth rates, fertility rates, divorce rates), and about family forms (size, structure and organization). This sort of information is an essential component in governments' policy-making processes.

Yet, despite a long history of international collaboration and the growing need for reliable information about demographic trends in Europe, by the mid-1990s data on households and families in the European Union were still far from comparable.[2] Attempts to standardize data collection methods across countries have had to deal with issues such as national political priorities and ideologies, the centralization and autonomy of the organizations responsible for data collection, and the reluctance of some governments to accept decisions taken at the supranational level. As an example of the problems of comparing families across Europe, consider the problem of dealing with the *age of children living at home*. In most EU member states, no age limit was applied during the 1991 census. However, in Denmark, Finland and Sweden, children were considered as part of the family up to the age of 18, and in Luxembourg to 25. France applied a limit of 25 years until 1982, but this was abolished for the 1991 census, which increased the proportion of lone-parent families by 35 per cent! Eurostat's 1991 census reported that the 'traditional family' (man, woman and children under one roof) made up just 54 per cent of the European population, while their 1996 report (using a new sampling frame and method) concluded that the traditional one-family household is still predominant throughout Europe, comprising 72 per cent of the population.[3] In today's Europe, increasing migration rates, falling fertility rates, and delaying marriage until later in life (or cohabitation instead of marriage) all influence the reporting and analyses of statistics used to paint a portrait of the European family. As Europe moves on into the new millennium, more standardized and comparable forms of data about the family will be collected.

marketing opportunity

Under the same roof: living arrangements in the European Union

Across Europe there is evidence that the family unit is changing and evolving:

● In 2001 there were five marriages per 1,000 inhabitants in EU-25, compared with almost eight in 1975.

● The average age at which people get married has increased, from 26 years for men in 1980 within the EU-15 countries, to over 30 years today. For women, the corresponding increase has been from 23 to 28 years.

● There is also a rise in the rate of marital breakdown in both the EU-15 countries and in the new member states. Looking at marriage cohorts of the EU-15 countries, the proportion of divorces is estimated at 15 per cent for marriages entered into in 1960. For those more recently married couples (1980) the proportion has doubled to 29 per cent. There are however, considerable differences between countries with more than 40 per cent of marriages (entered into post-1980) ending in divorce in Denmark, Finland, Sweden and the United Kingdom, compared with 15 per cent or less in the southern member states.

● The number of births outside marriage in the EU-15 countries continues to rise, which is largely a reflection of the growing popularity of cohabitation: from 6 per cent of all births in 1970 to almost 29 per cent in 2002. In Sweden and Estonia, more than half (56 per cent) of the children born in 2002 had unmarried parents. The proportion is around 40 per cent in several other countries (Denmark, France, Latvia, Finland, Slovenia, and the United Kingdom). In contrast, low levels (albeit increasing ones) are seen in many southern

European countries, including Greece (1.5 per cent in 1980 to 3.9 per cent in 2002), Italy (4.3 per cent to 10 per cent) and Spain (3.9 per cent to 19 per cent in 2002).

● There is a sharp increase in the number of children living with one adult, and a fall in the number of couples with children. In 2000, 10 per cent of children aged 0–14 years were living with just one adult in the EU-15 countries compared with 6 per cent in 1990. The overwhelming majority of these single parents are women.

● In 1961 there were 14 million one-person households in EU-15 countries. By 1995 this number had tripled to 42 million, and the estimate by Eurostat suggests a further increase to 62 million by 2025.

● Households are becoming smaller, with more people living alone at all ages. Within the EU-15 countries the absolute number of households will increase by 20 million by 2025, with an average size of 2.2 people per household.

● Results also suggest that there is a different pattern of living emerging between northern countries, and southern countries plus Ireland. In the Mediterranean countries and Ireland, children tend to live in the parental home until they are ready to form new, usually legalized, family units. Also, more than one generation share the same household. In northern countries, the transition from the parental home to forming a new family is less straightforward, with living alone and cohabitation periods in between.[4]

From both a statistical as well as a sociological perspective, 'family' is hard to nail down. However, one thing is certain – the concept of family will continue to exist and will manifest itself in varying forms over time and across countries throughout Europe. Figure 11.1 provides an overview of the many components which make up our notion of a European household.

Defining the modern family

Some experts have argued that as traditional family living arrangements have declined, people are placing even greater emphasis on the role of siblings, close friends and other relatives to provide companionship and social support.[5] In the US, some people are even

Figure 11.1 Components of the 'modern family'

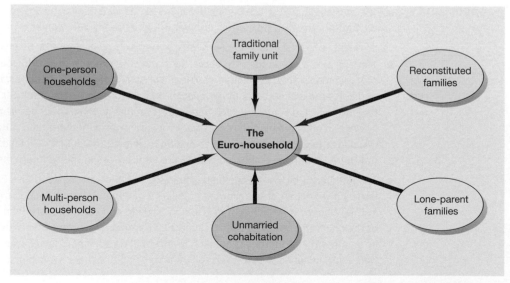

joining 'intentional families', groups of strangers who meet regularly for meals and who spend holidays together. Over 500 of these communities currently operate in the US.[6]

Many marketers have focused on the renewed interest in family life brought about by the more flexible definitions of what constitutes a family.[7] While families were indeed out of fashion in the 1960s and 1970s, being seen by some as an infringement of personal freedom, 90 per cent of the respondents in one recent survey confirmed that family life was one of the most important things to them.[8] In a radical departure from its old, 'affluent singles' days, half of the holidaymakers who stay at Club Med resorts now bring their families along.[9]

▶ The **extended family** was once the most common family unit. It consisted of three generations living together and often included not only the grandparents, but aunts,
▶ uncles and cousins. The **nuclear family**, a mother and a father and one or more children (perhaps with a dog thrown in for good measure), became the model family unit over time. However, many changes have occurred since the 1960s.

Just what is a household?

For statistical purposes, Eurostat has implemented the United Nation's definition of the family unit based on the 'conjugal family concept'. *The family* is defined in the narrow sense of a family nucleus as follows: 'The persons within a private or institutional household who are related as husband and wife or as parent and never-married child by blood or adoption.' Thus, a family nucleus comprises a married couple without children or a married couple with one or more never-married children of any age, or one parent with one or more never-married children of any age. The definition tries to take into account whenever possible, couples who report that they are living in consensual unions, regardless of whether they are legally married. Under the more recent European Community
▶ Household Panel, a **family household** is more broadly defined, as a 'shared residence and common housekeeping arangement'. Marketers are interested in both of these units, not only for their similarities, but as a way of understanding differences. Changes in consumers' family structures, such as cohabitation, delayed marriage and delayed childbirth, the return of mothers to the workforce and the upheaval caused by divorce, often represent opportunities for marketers as normal purchasing patterns become unfrozen and people make new choices about products and brands.[10]

Age of the family

As shown in the Marketing Opportunity above, since 1960 the EU has seen a trend of falling numbers of marriages and an increase in the number of divorces. Moreover, people are remarrying more often than they did before the 1960s, and men are more likely to form a new family than women. Couples marry youngest in Portugal and oldest in Denmark, and the greatest age difference between husbands and wives is to be found in Greece.

Overall, consumers aged between 35 and 44 were responsible for the largest increase in the number of households, growing by almost 40 per cent since 1980.[11] Half of all family householders fell into this age group in the year 2000. Figure 11.2 provides a breakdown of the EU population by household size. The key segment to change in the coming 20 years will be the significant increase in adults living alone – a segment which will increase to over 62 million households by 2025.[12]

Family size

Worldwide, surveys show that almost all women want smaller families than they did a decade ago. In 1980, the average European household contained 2.8 people, but today that number has slipped to 2.6 people. Furthermore, the current average number of children per woman is below the generational replacement threshold level, with a fertility rate for Europe of 1.44 children per woman in 1993 (compared to almost double this in

Figure 11.2 Population living in private households by household type, EU-25, 2002

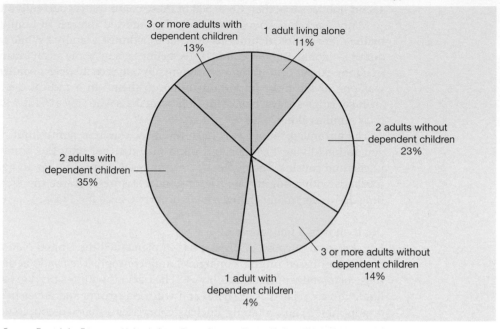

Source: Eurostat – European Union Labour Force Survey, Figure 13. Eurostat © European Communities, 2002.

1964). A UK study predicts that one in five women born in the 1960s–1980s will remain childless – a halving of the birth rate of their mother's generation.[13] Family size is dependent on such factors as educational level, the availability of birth control and religion. The ▶ **fertility rate** is determined by the number of births per year per 1,000 women of childbearing age. For several decades now fertility rates in the EU have remained clearly below replacement levels of 2.1, a trend which is reinforced by the enlargement of the EU to the EU-25. Among the new member states only Cyprus (1.57 children per woman) and Malta (1.51) are a little above the average for EU-15 (1.47).[14]

Marketers keep a close eye on the population's birth rate to gauge how the pattern of births will affect demand for products in the future. Even when a married couple does live with children, families are shrinking. The number of European households comprising one or two people is increasing (from 22 per cent to 26 per cent during 1980–90) and the number of households with four or more people is falling (from 34 per cent to 25 per cent during 1980–90).[15] The number of unmarried adults and one-person households is steadily rising (they now account for 26 per cent of European households, and are projected to be the fastest growing segment through to the year 2025). Some marketers are beginning to address the fact that this group is under-represented in advertising.[16] Gold Blend coffee built a very popular TV ad campaign around a romance between two single neighbours, while Procter & Gamble introduced Folger's Singles 'single-serve' coffee bags for people who live alone and don't need a full pot.[17] On the other hand, many singles report that they avoid buying single-size food portions or eating alone in restaurants since both remind them of their unattached status – they prefer takeaway food.[18]

Single men and women constitute quite different markets. More than half of single men are under the age of 35, while among people over age 65 women account for 80 per cent of one-person households. Despite single males' greater incomes, single women dominate many markets because of their spending patterns. Single women are more likely than single men to own a home, and they spend more on housing-related items and furniture. Single men, in contrast, spend more overall in restaurants and on cars. However, these spending patterns are also significantly affected by age: middle-aged single women, for example, spend *more* than their male counterparts on cars.[19]

Who's living at home?

In many cases the nuclear family is being transformed to resemble the old-fashioned extended family. Many adults are being forced to care for parents as well as for children. A growing trend in the United States and Europe is for middle-aged couples to be faced with the prospect of caring for both their children and their parents simultaneously. Americans spend on average 17 years caring for their children, but 18 years assisting elderly parents.[20] Middle-aged people have been termed *'the sandwich generation'*, because they must attend to those above and below them in age. The problem of caring for ageing parents became so acute in Singapore that the government established a Tribunal for the Maintenance of Parents in 1996. A new law now requires adult offspring to take care of their parents, a practice which traditionally is a priority in Asian cultures. Two hundred cases involving neglected parents were heard by the Tribunal in its first six months of operation.[21] As the population ages and life expectancies continue to climb in developed countries, the problem of allocating resources to the support of parents will only get worse.

Non-traditional family structures

The European Community Household Panel regards any occupied housing unit as a household, regardless of the relationships among people living there. Thus, one person living alone, three room-mates or two lovers all constitute households. Less traditional households will rapidly increase these if trends persist. One-parent households are increasing steadily throughout Europe (most common in the UK, Denmark and Belgium, least common in Greece). Although these households are in the majority of cases headed by women, there is also an increasing trend for fathers to take on this role.[22] In the United States, 10 million children live with a step-parent or with children who are not full brothers or sisters, and 24 per cent of all children live in one-parent families.[23]

marketing opportunity

Many people are extremely attached to pets, to the point where companion animals might be considered part of the family. Pets are seen by many as therapeutic, and often are assumed to share our emotions. Over 35 per cent of European households and over 42 per cent of American households own at least one pet.[24] Together, they spend over $30 billion a year on their pets (more than they spend on going to the cinema and home videos combined).[25] In France, there are twice as many dogs and cats as children![26]

The inclusion of pets as family members creates many marketing opportunities, ranging from bejewelled collars to professional dogwalkers. Listed below are worldwide samples of some recent attempts to cater to people's pet attachments.[27]

● Macy's department store opened a Petigree shop for dogs and cats. Says one employee, 'You can put your dog in a pink satin party dress or a 1920s flapper dress with fringe.' Other items include a wedding dress for dogs (for $100; the veil is extra), a $48 black dinner jacket or a $30 trench coat.

● A vet in Maryland offers holistic medicine for pets. He features natural foods, acupuncture and chiropractic massages. The vet also sells the 'Rodeo Drive Fragrance Collection' (named after a fashionable street in Beverly Hills), a set of spray colognes for dogs.

● A 25-minute video, *Doggie Adventure*, was produced for dogs. Shot with a camera balanced two feet off the ground, it takes viewers on a romp from a dog's perspective.

● Kennelwood Village, a day-care centre for dogs in St Louis, features a swimming pool (with a lifeguard on duty), tetherball tournaments and whirlpool therapy for arthritic canines.

● In the UK, pet insurance is a £100 million industry, with more than a million pets being covered by insurance policies.

● About 85 per cent of Swedish dogs carry health and life insurance.

Effects of family structure on consumption

A family's needs and expenditures are affected by such factors as the number of people (children and adults) in the family, their ages, and whether one, two or more adults are employed outside of the home.

Two important factors determining how a couple spend time and money are whether they have children and whether the woman works. Couples with children generally have higher expenses, and not just for the 'basics' such as food and utilities bills. Studies in the UK estimate that the costs of keeping a teenager 'in the style to which they aspire' run close to £66,000, and the costs of getting a child to the teen years is approaching £33,000.[28] In addition, a recently married couple make very different expenditures compared with people with young children, who in turn are quite different from a couple with children in college, and so on. Families with working mothers must often make allowances for such expenses as nursery care and a working wardrobe for the woman.

**multicultural
dimensions**

The Euro-housewife: considerable differences between EU member states

- The percentage of women aged between 25 and 59 who describe themselves as housewives varies considerably between member states. While the EU average is 33 per cent, it ranges from a high of 60 per cent in Ireland (Spain, Greece, Italy and Luxembourg are also high), to a mere 4 per cent in Denmark.

- Barely 6 per cent of women between 25 and 39 without children stay at home, compared with 36 per cent with one child under 5 and 52 per cent with at least two children under 5.

- EU-wide, only 7 per cent of today's housewives stopped working because of marriage – but this number peaked at 15 per cent in Greece and 14 per cent in Spain. However, 42 per cent stop because of children.

- Family obligations, such as housework, caring for children or others are the main reason why 84 per cent of housewives are not looking for work.

- Being a housewife is strongly related to the level of education. Housewives represent 45 per cent of EU women aged from 25 to 59 with lower secondary education, 26 per cent with upper secondary education, and only 13 per cent of women with higher educational levels.[29]

The family life cycle

Recognizing that family needs and expenditures change over time, the concept of the ▶ **family life cycle (FLC)** has been widely used by marketers. The FLC combines trends in income and family composition with the changes in demands placed upon this income. As we grow older, our preferences for products and activities tend to change. In many cases, our income levels tend to rise (at least until retirement), so that we can afford more as well. In addition, many purchases that must be made at an early age do not have to be repeated very often. For example, we tend to accumulate durable goods, such as furniture, and only replace them as necessary.

A life-cycle approach to the study of the family assumes that pivotal events alter role relationships and trigger new stages of life which modify our priorities. These events include the birth of a first child, the departure of the last child from the house, the death of a spouse, retirement of the principal wage earner and divorce.[30] Movement through these life stages is accompanied by significant changes in expenditures on leisure, food, durables and services, even after the figures have been adjusted to reflect changes in income.[31]

Table 11.1 The family life cycle: an updated view

	Age of head of household		
	Under 35	**35-64**	**Over 64**
One adult in household	Bachelor I	Bachelor II	Bachelor III
Two adults in household	Young couple	Childless couple	Older couple
Two adults plus children in household	Full nest I Full nest II	Delayed full nest Full nest III	

Source: Adapted from Mary C. Gilly and Ben M. Enis, 'Recycling the Family Life Cycle: A Proposal for Redefinition', in Andrew A. Mitchell, ed., *Advances in Consumer Research* 9 (Ann Arbor, MI: Association for Consumer Research, 1982): 274, Figure 1.

This focus on longitudinal changes in priorities is particularly valuable in predicting demand for specific product categories over time. For example, the money spent by a couple with no children on eating out and holidays will probably be diverted for quite different purchases after the birth of a child. While a number of models have been proposed to describe family life-cycle stages, their usefulness has been limited because in many cases they have failed to take into account such important social trends as the changing role of women, the acceleration of alternative lifestyles, childless and delayed-child marriages and single-parent households.

Four variables are necessary to describe these changes: age, marital status, the presence or absence of children in the home, and their ages. In addition, our definition of marital status (at least for analysis purposes) must be relaxed to include any couple living together who are in a long-term relationship. Thus, while room-mates might not be considered 'married', a man and a woman who have established a household would be, as would two homosexual men or women who have a similar understanding.

When these changes are considered, this approach allows us to identify a set of categories that include many more types of family situations.[32] These categories, which are listed in Table 11.1, are derived by dividing consumers into groups in terms of age, whether there is more than one adult present, and whether there are children. For example, a distinction is made between the consumption needs of people in the Full nest I category (where the youngest child is under 6), the Full nest II category (where the youngest child is over 6), the Full nest III category (where the youngest child is over 6 and the parents are middle-aged), and the Delayed full nest (where the parents are in their forties but the youngest child is under 6).

Life-cycle effects on buying

As might be expected, consumers classified into these categories show marked differences in consumption patterns. Young bachelors and newlyweds have the most 'modern' sex-role attitudes, are the most likely to exercise regularly, to go to pubs, concerts, the cinema and restaurants, and to go dancing; and they consume more alcohol. Families with young children are more likely to consume health foods such as fruit, juice and yogurt, while those made up of single parents and older children buy more junk foods. The monetary value of homes, cars and other durables is lowest for bachelors and single parents, but increases as people go through the full nest and childless couple stages. Perhaps reflecting the bounty of wedding gifts, newlyweds are the most likely to own appliances such as toasters, ovens and electric coffee grinders. Babysitter and day care usage is, of course, highest among single-parent and full nest households, while home maintenance services (e.g. lawnmowing) are most likely to be employed by older couples and bachelors.

The growth of these additional categories creates many opportunities for enterprising marketers. For example, divorced people undergo a process of transition to a new social role. This change is often accompanied by the disposal of possessions linked to the former role and the need to acquire a set of possessions that help to express the person's new identity as he or she experiments with new lifestyles.[33]

■ THE INTIMATE CORPORATION: FAMILY DECISION-MAKING

The decision process within a household unit in some ways resembles a business conference. Certain matters are put up for discussion, different members may have different priorities and agendas, and there may be power struggles to rival any tale of corporate intrigue. In just about every living situation, whether a conventional family, students sharing a house or apartment, or some other non-traditional arrangement, group members seem to take on different roles just as purchasing agents, engineers, account executives and others do within a company.

Household decisions

▶ Two basic types of decisions are made by families.[34] In a **consensual purchase decision**, the group agrees on the desired purchase, differing only in terms of how it will be achieved. In these circumstances, the family will probably engage in problem-solving and consider alternatives until the means for satisfying the group's goal is found. For example, a household considering adding a dog to the family but concerned about who will take care of it might draw up a chart assigning individuals to specific duties.

▶ Unfortunately, life is not always that easy. In an **accommodative purchase decision**, group members have different preferences or priorities and cannot agree on a purchase that will satisfy the minimum expectations of all involved. It is here that bargaining, coercion, compromise and the wielding of power are all likely to be used to achieve agreement on what to buy or who gets to use it. Family decisions are often characterized by an accommodative rather than a consensual decision. Conflict occurs when there is incomplete correspondence in family members' needs and preferences. While money is the most common source of conflict between marriage partners, television choices come a close second![35] Some specific factors determining the degree of family decision conflict include the following:[36]

- *Interpersonal need* (a person's level of investment in the group): a child in a family situation may care more about what his or her family buys for the house than a college student who is living in student accommodation.

- *Product involvement and utility* (the degree to which the product in question will be used or will satisfy a need): a family member who is an avid coffee drinker will obviously be more interested in the purchase of a new coffeemaker to replace a malfunctioning one than a similar expenditure for some other item.

- *Responsibility* (for procurement, maintenance, payment, and so on): people are more likely to have disagreements about a decision if it entails long-term consequences and commitments. For example, a family decision about getting a dog may involve conflict regarding who will be responsible for walking and feeding it.

- *Power* (or the degree to which one family member exerts influence over the others in making decisions): in traditional families, the husband tends to have more power than the wife, who in turn has more than the oldest child, and so on. In family decisions, conflict can arise when one person continually uses the power he or she has within the group to satisfy his or her priorities. For example, if Caleb believed that his mother was not very likely to buy him both CDs, he might be willing to resort to extreme tactics to influence her, such as throwing a temper tantrum or refusing to participate in family chores.

In general, decisions will involve conflict among family members to the extent that they are important or novel and/or if individuals have strong opinions about good and bad alternatives. The degree to which these factors generate conflict determines the type of decision the family will make.[37]

Sex roles and decision-making responsibilities

▶ Traditionally, some buying decisions, termed **autocratic decisions**, were made by one spouse. Men, for instance, often had sole responsibility for selecting a car, while most decorating choices fell to women. Other decisions, such as holiday destinations, were
▶ made jointly; these are known as **syncratic decisions**. According to a study conducted by Roper Starch Worldwide, wives tend to have the most say when buying groceries, children's toys, clothes and medicines. Syncratic decisions are common for cars, holidays, homes, appliances, furniture, home electronics, interior design and long-distance phone services. As the couple's education increases, more decisions are likely to be made together.[38]

Identifying the decision-maker

The nature of consumer decision-making within a particular product category is an important issue for marketers, so that they know who to target and whether or not they need to reach both spouses to influence a decision. For example, when market research in the 1950s indicated that women were playing a larger role in household purchasing decisions, lawnmower manufacturers began to emphasize the rotary mower over other power mowers. Rotary mowers, which conceal the cutting blades and engine, were often depicted being used by young women and smiling grandmothers to relieve fears of injuries.[39]

Researchers have paid special attention to which spouse plays the role of what has
▶ been called the **family financial officer (FFO)**, who keeps track of the family's bills and decides how any surplus funds will be spent. Among newlyweds, this role tends to be played jointly, and then over time one spouse or the other tends to take over these responsibilities.[40] Spouses usually exert significant influence on decision-making, even after one of them has died. An Irish study found that many widows claim to sense the continued presence of their dead husband, and to conduct 'conversations' with them about household matters.[41]

In traditional families (and especially those with low educational levels), women are primarily responsible for family financial management – the man makes it, and the woman spends it.[42] Each spouse 'specializes' in certain activities.[43] The pattern is different among families where spouses adhere to more modern sex-role norms. These couples believe that there should be more shared participation in family maintenance activities. In these cases, husbands assume more responsibility for laundering, house cleaning, day-to-day shopping, and so on, in addition to such traditionally 'male' tasks as home maintenance and waste removal.[44] Of course, cultural background is an important determinant of the dominance of the husband or wife. Husbands tend to be more dominant in decision-making among couples with a strong Mediterranean ethnic identification.[45] Even in northern Europe, the pattern of traditional 'male' and 'female' roles is still fairly strong.

Four factors appear to determine the degree to which decisions will be made jointly or by one or the other spouse:[46]

1 *Sex-role stereotypes*: Couples who believe in traditional sex-role stereotypes tend to make individual decisions for sex-typed products (i.e. those considered to be 'masculine' or 'feminine').

2 *Spousal resources*: The spouse who contributes more resources to the family has the greater influence.

3 *Experience*: Individual decisions are made more frequently when the couple has gained experience as a decision-making unit.

4 *Socio-economic status*: More joint decisions are made by middle-class families than in either higher- or lower-class families.

multicultural dimensions

Traditional sex roles are quite prevalent in Japan, where women have less power than in any other industrialized country. The contraceptive pill is banned, and a wife is legally prohibited from using a different surname from that of her husband. Fewer than one in ten Japanese managers are women, one of the lowest ratios in the world (women are twice as likely to be managers in Mexico or Zimbabwe).

However, something of a quiet revolution is happening in Japanese homes as some obedient spouses have had enough. Recently women have started to rebel against the inevitability of getting married young and staying at home with babies. The number of unmarried people over the age of 30 has doubled in the last 20 years.

For those who do marry, things are changing as well. Traditionally, a wife would wait up all night for a drunken husband to come home so she could kneel down with her forehead touching the floor and proclaim, 'Welcome home, honourable sir'. Now, she is more likely to lock him out of the house until he sobers up. Most Japanese men are given a budget by their wives for lunch, cigarettes and girlie magazines. One housewife noted, 'Your home is managed very well if you make your men feel that they're in control when they are in front of others, while in reality you're in control.'[47]

Men's attitudes towards family life are also changing. Japanese fathers spend so much time working that more than a quarter of children surveyed said their dads never take them for a walk or play games with them. Owing to long working hours, a typical Japanese father has only 36 minutes a day to spend with his children. About 60 per cent of Japanese men typically do not eat breakfast at home, and about 30 per cent regularly miss dinner. Now, balancing work and family is becoming a heated topic, especially as recession weakens the guarantee of lifetime employment and men are re-examining their priorities.[48] This change was reflected in some recent McDonald's advertising, which showed doting fathers helping children with their bikes. This would not be noteworthy in America, but got a lot of attention in a country where fathers typically are shown as corporate warriors or even as superheroes (for example, a popular advertising character is called PepsiMan).

A hit Japanese software product called 'Princess Maker' is intended to give men more involvement in family life. The player controls the activities, hobbies and clothing of a girl character he 'raises' from childhood. He names her, picks her birthday and even chooses her blood group, which some Japanese believe determines character traits. The girl's progress is monitored in categories including sexiness, strength and intelligence. Note: This bestselling program would probably not go down too well in the West, since this 'virtual daughter' can be programmed to dress in lingerie! If the player makes unwise choices about her activities, she appears in a slinky dress and he is notified that she is destined to be a bar hostess.[49]

Despite recent changes in decision-making responsibilities, women are still primarily
▶ responsible for the continuation of the family's **kin network system**: they perform the rituals intended to maintain ties among family members, both immediate and extended. This function includes such activities as coordinating visits among relatives, phoning and writing to family members, sending greetings cards, making social engagements, and so on.[50] This organizing role means that women often make important decisions about

the family's leisure activities, and are more likely to decide with whom the family will socialize.

With many women now working outside the home, men are participating more in housekeeping activities, but women continue to do the lion's share of household chores. Ironically, this even appears to be true when the woman's income actually exceeds her husband's![51] Overall, the degree to which a couple adhere to traditional sex-role norms determines how much their allocation of responsibilities will fall along familiar lines and how their consumer decision-making responsibilities will be allocated.

Heuristics in joint decision-making

The *synoptic ideal* calls for the husband and wife to take a common view and act as joint decision makers. According to this ideal, they would very thoughtfully weigh alternatives, assign to one another well-defined roles, and calmly make mutually beneficial consumer decisions. The couple would act rationally, analytically and use as much information as possible to maximize joint utility. In reality, however, spousal decision-making is often characterized by the use of influence or methods that are likely to reduce conflict. A couple 'reaches' rather than 'makes' a decision. This process has been described as 'muddling through'.[52]

One common technique for simplifying the decision-making process is the use of *heuristics* (see Chapter 8). Some decision-making patterns frequently observed when a couple makes decisions in buying a new house illustrate the use of heuristics:

- The couple's areas of common preference are based upon salient, objective dimensions rather than more subtle, hard-to-define cues. For example, a couple may easily agree on the number of bedrooms they need in the new home, but will have more difficulty achieving a common view of how the home should look.

- The couple agrees on a system of *task specialization*, where each is responsible for certain duties or decision areas and does not interfere in the other's. For many couples, these assignments are likely to be influenced by their perceived sex roles. For example, the wife may seek out houses in advance that meet their requirements, while the husband determines whether the couple can obtain a mortgage.

- Concessions are based on the intensity of each spouse's preferences. One spouse will yield to the influence of the other in many cases simply because his or her level of preference for a certain attribute is not particularly intense, where in other situations he or she will be willing to exert effort to obtain a favourable decision.[53] In cases where intense preferences for different attributes exist, rather than attempt to influence each other, spouses will 'trade off' a less-intense preference for a more strongly felt one. For example, a husband who is indifferent to kitchen design may yield to his wife, but expect that in turn he will be allowed to design his own garage workshop. It is interesting to note that many men apparently want to be very involved in making some decorating decisions and setting budgets – more than women want them to be. According to one survey, 70 per cent of male respondents felt the husband should be involved in decorating the family room, while only 51 per cent of wives wanted them to be.[54]

■ CHILDREN AS DECISION-MAKERS: CONSUMERS-IN-TRAINING

Anyone who has had the 'delightful' experience of supermarket shopping with one or more children knows that children often have a say in what their parents buy, especially for products like breakfast cereal.[55] In addition, children increasingly are being recognized as a potential market for traditionally adult products. For example, Kodak is putting a lot of promotional effort into encouraging children to become photographers. Most

Children begin making selections and purchases of products at an early age. By the time they reach their teens, the process of socialization and peer influence is well underway. Teenage girls and their horses are a clear example of this socialization process with respect to lifestyle choices and consumption behaviours.

Photo: Gary Bamossy

children nowadays own or have access to a digital camera, and taking photos is seen as a cool pursuit. Websites which will post photos and mail printed photos to children are flourishing, as children take more control of their own photo collections.

▶   **Parental yielding** occurs when a parental decision maker is influenced by a child's request and 'surrenders'. The likelihood of this occurring is partly dependent on the dynamics within a particular family – as we all know, parental styles range from permissive to strict, and they also vary in terms of the amount of responsibility children are given to make decisions.[56] The strategies children use to request purchases were documented in one study. While most children simply asked for things, other common tactics included saying they had seen it on television, saying that a sibling or friend had it, or bargaining by offering to do chores. Other actions were less innocuous; they included directly placing the object in the trolley and continuous whining – often a 'persuasive' behaviour![57]

multicultural dimensions

In a controversial effort to control the size of its population, The People's Republic of China offers many incentives for parents to have only one child. One by-product of this campaign is that some claim the country is producing a pampered generation of spoiled only children, who are called 'little emperors'. Parents are trying to give these offspring a rich childhood which they themselves didn't enjoy during the dark days of the Cultural Revolution. They are spending a very large portion of family income on toys, books and computers. Baby food, which didn't exist in China a couple of decades ago, is now a major budget item.[58]

Of course, the Chinese are not alone in viewing the child as a status symbol. Infant wear and other items for toddlers has become a $23 billion business in North America and Western Europe. Dual-career couples are waiting longer to start a family and thus are able to spend more on them – the number of women aged 30 or over when the first child is born has quadrupled since 1970, and the number of first children born to women over 40 has more than doubled. As a result, children's designer clothing is booming – Versace sells a $250 black motorcycle jacket for the junior James Dean, and Nicole Miller offers a $150 cocktail dress for the petite *femme fatale*.[59] And infants are not being left out: Ralph Lauren sells a cashmere blanket for $350, L.L. Bean, the direct marketer of outdoor gear, has added toddler snow suits to its catalogues, and Nike is marketing a line of toddler athletic wear.[60]

Children often play important roles in family consumer decision-making, and they are gaining responsibility as consumers in their own right. They continue to support the toy and sweet industries, of course, but now they also buy and/or influence the purchase of many other products as well. For better or for worse, the new generation is, as the bumper sticker proclaims, 'Born to Shop'. Shopping now ranks among the top seven interests and activities of America's children.[61] Over 80 per cent of young respondents in one survey said their primary wish was to have more money to buy things.[62] In the next section, we'll consider how children learn to make these choices.

Consumer socialization

Children do not spring from the womb with consumer skills already in memory. ▶ Consumer socialization has been defined as the process 'by which young people acquire skills, knowledge, and attitudes relevant to their functioning in the market-place'.[63] Where does this knowledge come from? Friends and teachers certainly participate in this process. For instance, children talk to one another about consumer products, and this tendency increases with age.[64] Especially for young children, though, the two primary socialization sources are the family and the media.

Influence of parents

Parents' influences in consumer socialization are both direct and indirect. They deliberately try to instil their own values about consumption in their children ('you're going to learn the value of the pound/euro'). Parents also determine the degree to which their children will be exposed to other information sources, such as television, salespeople and peers.[65] Grown-ups serve as significant models for observational learning (see Chapter 3). Children learn about consumption by watching their parents' behaviour and imitating it. This modelling is facilitated by marketers who package adult products in child versions.

The process of consumer socialization begins with infants, who accompany their parents to shops where they are initially exposed to marketing stimuli. Within the first two years of life, children begin to make requests for desired objects. As children learn to walk, they also begin to make their own selections when they are in shops. By the age of 5, most children are making purchases with the help of parents and grandparents, and by 8 most are making independent purchases and have become fully-fledged consumers.[66] The sequence of steps involved in turning children into consumers is summarized in Figure 11.3.

marketing pitfall

Three dimensions combine to produce different 'segments' of parental styles. Parents characterized by certain styles have been found to socialize their children differently.[67] 'Authoritarian parents', who are hostile, restrictive and emotionally uninvolved, do not have warm relationships with their children, are active in filtering the types of media to which their children are exposed, and tend to have negative views about advertising. 'Neglecting parents' also do not have warm relationships, but they are more detached from their children and exercise little control over what their children do. In contrast, 'indulgent parents' communicate more with their children about consumption-related matters and are less restrictive. They believe that children should be allowed to learn about the marketplace without much interference.

Figure 11.3 Five stages of consumer development by earliest age at onset and median age at onset

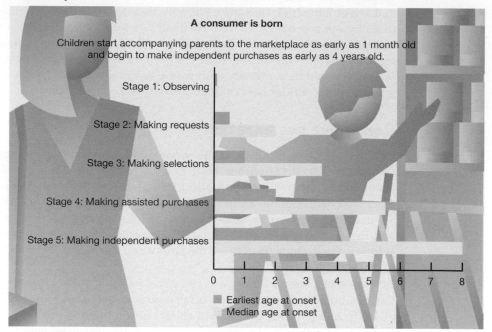

Source: Adapted from James U. McNeal and Chyon-Hwa Yeh, 'Born to shop', *American Demographics* (June 1993): 36.

European and global brands are part of the social expression of young children, as well as their parents!

The Advertising Archives

Girls playing with Lego.
Photo: Søren Askegaard

Influence of television: 'the electric babysitter'

It's no secret that children watch a lot of television. As a result, they are constantly bombarded with messages about consumption, both contained in commercials and in the programmes themselves. The medium teaches people about a culture's values and myths. The more a child is exposed to television, whether the programme is a local 'soap' or *Baywatch* the more he or she will accept the images depicted there as real.[68] In Britain, *Teletubbies* went a step further – it was made for viewers from 3 months to 2 years old. It's unclear if this show would succeed in the United States, since babies aren't seen as a lucrative market for advertising messages (yet!).[69]

In addition to the large volume of programming targeted directly at children, children also are exposed to idealized images of what it is like to be an adult. Since children over the age of 6 spend about a quarter of their television viewing during prime time, they are affected by programmes and commercials targeted at adults. For example, young girls exposed to adult lipstick commercials learn to associate lipstick with beauty.[70]

Sex-role socialization

Children pick up on the concept of gender identity at an earlier age than was previously believed – perhaps as young as age 1 or 2. By the age of 3, most children categorize driving a truck as masculine and cooking and cleaning as feminine.[71] Even cartoon characters who are portrayed as helpless are more likely to wear frilly or ruffled dresses.[72] Toy companies perpetuate these stereotypes by promoting gender-linked toys with commercials that reinforce sex-role expectations through their casting, emotional tone and copy.[73]

One function of child's play is to rehearse for adulthood. Children 'act out' different roles they might assume later in life and learn about the expectations others have of them. The toy industry provides the props children use to perform these roles.[74] Depending on which side of the debate you're on, these toys either reflect or teach children about what society expects of males versus females. While pre-school boys and girls do not exhibit many differences in toy preferences, after the age of 5 they part company: girls tend to stick with dolls, while boys gravitate towards 'action figures' and high-tech diversions. Industry critics charge that this is because the toy industry is dominated by males, while toy company executives counter that they are simply responding to children's natural preferences.[75]

Often 'traditional' sex roles are stressed in children's products; the same item may be designed and positioned differently for boys and girls. Huffy, for example, manufactures bicycles for both boys and girls. The boys' versions have names such as 'Sigma' and 'Vortex', and they are described as having 'maxed-out features that'll pump your pulse'. The girls' version is more demure. It is called 'Sweet Style', and comes in pink or purple. As a company executive described it in contrast to the boys' bikes, the girls' model 'is a fashion bike. It's not built for racing or jumping – just the look.'[76]

Cognitive development

The ability of children to make mature, 'adult' consumer decisions obviously increases with age (not that grown-ups always make mature decisions). Children can be segmented by age in terms of their **stage of cognitive development**, or ability to comprehend concepts of increasing complexity. Some recent evidence indicates that young children are able to learn consumption-related information surprisingly well, depending on the format in which the information is presented (for instance, learning is enhanced if a videotaped vignette is presented to small children repeatedly).[77]

The foremost proponent of the idea that children pass through distinct stages of **cognitive development** was the Swiss psychologist Jean Piaget, who believed that each stage is characterized by a certain cognitive structure the child uses to handle information.[78] In one classic demonstration of cognitive development, Piaget poured the contents of a short, squat glass of lemonade into a taller, thinner glass. Five-year-olds, who still believed that the shape of the glass determined its contents, thought this glass held more liquid than the first glass. They are in what Piaget termed a *preoperational stage of development*. In contrast, 6-year-olds tended to be unsure, but 7-year-olds knew the amount of lemonade had not changed.

Many developmental specialists no longer believe that children necessarily pass through these fixed stages at the same time. An alternative approach regards children as differing in information-processing capability, or the ability to store and retrieve information from memory (see Chapter 3). The following three segments have been identified by this approach:[79]

1 *Limited*: Below the age of 6, children do not employ storage and retrieval strategies.

2 *Cued*: Children between the ages of 6 and 12 employ these strategies, but only when prompted.

3 *Strategic*: Children aged 12 and older spontaneously employ storage and retrieval strategies.

This sequence of development underscores the notion that children do not think like adults, and they cannot be expected to use information in the same way. It also reminds us that they do not necessarily form the same conclusions as adults do when presented with product information. For example, children are not as likely to realize that something they see on television is not 'real', and as a result they are more vulnerable to persuasive messages.

Marketing research and children

Despite their buying power, relatively little real data on children's preferences or influences on spending patterns is available. Compared with adults, children are difficult subjects for market researchers. They tend to be unreliable reporters of their own behaviour, they have poor recall, and they often do not understand abstract questions.[80]

This problem is compounded in Europe, where some countries restrict marketers' ability to interview children.

Still, market research can pay off, and many companies, as well as a number of specialized firms, have been successful in researching some aspects of this segment.[81] After interviewing elementary school pupils, Campbell's Soup discovered that children like soup, but don't like to admit it because they associate it with 'nerds'. The company decided to reintroduce the Campbell kids in its advertising after a prolonged absence, but they are now slimmed down and more athletic to reflect an updated, 'un-nerdy' image.[82]

Product testing

A particularly helpful type of research with children is product testing. Young subjects can provide a valuable perspective on which products will succeed. One confectionery company has a Candy Tasters Club, composed of 1,200 kids aged 6 to 16, who evaluate its product ideas. For example, the group vetoed the idea of a Batman lollipop, claiming that the superhero was too macho to be sucked.[83] The Fisher-Price Company maintains a nursery known as the Playlab. Children are chosen from a waiting list of 4,000 to play with new toys, while staff members watch from behind a one-way mirror.[84] H.J. Heinz held a contest for children to create new ketchup bottle labels and received about 60,000 entries; Binney & Smith asked children to rename its Crayola crayons after personal heroes.[85]

Other techniques include ethnographic research, where researchers spend time with children or videotape them as they shop. The most successful interviewers are those who try not to be 'adultcentric' (i.e. as an adult authority figure who assumes that children's beliefs are just unreal fantasies); they act as a friend to the children and are willing to use a variety of projective techniques and props to get children to express themselves in their own terms.[86]

Message comprehension

Since children differ in their ability to process product-related information, many serious ethical issues are raised when advertisers try to appeal directly to them.[87] Children tend to accept what they see on television as real, and they do not necessarily understand the persuasive intent of commercials – that they are paid advertisements. Pre-school children may not have the ability to make any distinctions between programming and commercials.

Children's cognitive defences are not yet sufficiently developed to filter out commercial appeals, so in a sense altering their brand preferences may be likened to 'shooting fish in a barrel', as one critic put it.[88] Although some ads include a disclaimer, which is a disclosure intended to clarify a potentially misleading or deceptive statement, the evidence suggests that young children do not understand these either.[89] The Children's Advertising Review Unit (CARU) drew up guidelines for child-oriented websites after receiving complaints that children had difficulty distinguishing ads from content. These include clear identification of the sponsor and the right to cancel purchases made online.[90]

Children's level of understanding is especially hard to assess, since pre-schoolers are not very articulate. One way round this problem is to show pictures of children in different scenarios, and ask the subjects to point to the sketch that corresponds to what a commercial is trying to get them to do. The problem with children's processing of commercials has been exacerbated by television programming that essentially promotes toys (Transformers, for example). This format has been the target of a lot of criticism because it blurs the line between programming and commercials (much like 'infomercials' for adults, as described in Chapter 8).[91] Parents' groups object to such shows because, as one mother put it, the 'whole show is one big commercial'.[92]

CHAPTER SUMMARY

■ Many purchasing decisions are made by more than one person. Collective decision-making occurs whenever two or more people are involved in evaluating, selecting or using a product or service.

■ Demographics are statistics that measure a population's characteristics. Some of the most important of these relate to family structure, e.g. the birth rate, the marriage rate and the divorce rate. In Europe, collecting reliable and comparable data regarding the family unit has not always been a straightforward process.

■ A household is an occupied housing unit. The number and type of European households is changing in many ways, for example through delays in getting married and having children, and in the composition of family households, which increasingly are headed by a single parent. New perspectives on the family life cycle, which focuses on how people's needs change as they move through different stages in their lives, are forcing marketers to consider more seriously such consumer segments as homosexuals, divorcees and childless couples when they develop targeting strategies.

■ Families must be understood in terms of their decision-making dynamics. Spouses in particular have different priorities and exert varying amounts of influence in terms of effort and power. Children are also increasingly influential during a widening range of purchase decisions.

■ Children undergo a process of socialization, whereby they learn how to be consumers. Some of this knowledge is instilled by parents and friends, but a lot of it comes from exposure to mass media and advertising. Since children are in some cases so easily persuaded, the ethical aspects of marketing to them are hotly debated among consumers, academics and marketing practitioners.

▶ KEY TERMS

Accommodative purchase decision (p. 410)

Autocratic decisions (p. 411)

Cognitive development (p. 418)

Consensual purchase decision (p. 410)

Consumer socialization (p. 415)

Extended family (p. 405)

Family financial officer (FFO) (p. 411)

Family household (p. 405)

Family life cycle (FLC) (p. 408)

Fertility rate (p. 406)

Kin network system (p. 412)

Nuclear family (p. 405)

Parental yielding (p. 414)

Stage of cognitive development (p. 418)

Syncratic decisions (p. 411)

CONSUMER BEHAVIOUR CHALLENGE

1   Review a number of popular media which are published in countries in southern Europe as well as media targeted for northern European countries. How do the ads' depictions of *family* seem to differ by region? In what sorts of consumption situations do they seem highly similar? Why?

2 Do you think market research should be performed on children? Give the reasons for your answer. What do you think about the practice of companies and survey firms collecting public data (e.g. from marriage licences, birth records or even death announcements) to compile targeted mailing lists? State your opinion from both a consumer's and marketer's perspective.

3 Marketers have been criticized for donating products and services to educational institutions in exchange for free promotion. Is this a fair exchange, in your opinion, or should corporations be prohibited from attempting to influence youngsters in school?

4 For each of the following five product categories – groceries, cars, holidays, furniture and appliances – describe the ways in which you believe a married couple's choices would be affected if they had children.

5 In identifying and targeting newly divorced couples, do you think marketers are exploiting these couples' situations? Are there instances where you think marketers may actually be helpful to them? Support your answers with examples.

6 Arrange to interview two married couples, one younger and one older. Prepare a response form listing five product categories – groceries, furniture, appliances, holidays and cars – and ask each spouse to indicate, without consulting the other, whether purchases in each category are made by joint or unilateral decisions and to indicate whether the unilateral decisions are made by the husband or the wife. Compare each couples' responses for agreement between husbands and wives relative to who makes the decisions and compare both couples' overall responses for differences relative to the number of joint versus unilateral decisions. Report your findings and conclusions.

7 Collect ads for three different product categories in which the family is targeted. Find another set of ads for different brands of the same items in which the family is not featured. Prepare a report on the effectiveness of the approaches.

8 Observe the interactions between parents and children in the cereal section of a local supermarket. Prepare a report on the number of children who expressed preferences, how they expressed their preferences and how parents responded, including the number who purchased the child's choice.

9 Watch three hours of children's programming on commercial television stations and evaluate the marketing techniques used in the commercials in terms of the ethical issues raised in the final section of this chapter. Report your findings and conclusions.

10 Select a product category and, using the life-cycle stages given in the chapter, list the variables that will affect a purchase decision for the product by consumers in each stage of the cycle.

11 Consider three important changes in modern European family structure. For each, find an example of a marketer who has attempted to be conscious of this change as reflected in product communications, retailing innovations, or other aspects of the marketing mix. If possible, also try to find examples of marketers who have failed to keep up with these developments.

NOTES

1. Nancy Marx Better, 'Green teens', *The New York Times Magazine* (8 March 1992) 3: 44; Howard Schlossberg, 'Kids teach parents how to change their buying habits', *Marketing News* (1992): 8.

2. T. Eggerickx and F. Bégeot, 'Les recensements en Europe dans les années 1990. De la diversité des pratiques nationales à la comparabilité internationales des résulats', *Population* 41(2) (1993): 327–48. Standardization efforts continue. See *The Social Situation in the European Union*, an annual report commissioned by the European Council, and published by Eurostat.

3. F. Simoes-Casimiro and M.G. Calado-Lopes, 'Concepts and Typologies of Household and Family in the 1981 and 1991 Population Censuses in the Twelve Community Countries'. Unpublished report for Eurostat (Lisbon: Instituto Superior de Estatistica e Gescao de Informaçào, 1995); 'Gezinsleven binnen de EU onder druk', *Nederlandse Dagblad* (7 July 1995); 'Statistics in focus: population and social conditions', *Eurostat* (Luxembourg: Office for Official Publications of the European Communities, 2004).

4. 'Trends in households in the European Union: 1995–2025', *Eurostat, Statistics in Focus*, Theme 3-24/2003 (Luxembourg: Office for Official Publications of the European Communities, 2004).

5. Robert Boutilier, 'Diversity in family structures', *American Demographics Marketing Tools* (1993): 4–6; W. Bradford Fay, 'Families in the 1990s: Universal Values, Uncommon Experiences', *Marketing Research* 5 (Winter 1993) 1: 47.

6. Ellen Graham, 'Craving closer ties, strangers come together as family', *The Wall Street Journal* (4 March 1996): B1 (2).

7. David Cheal, 'The ritualization of family ties', *American Behavioral Scientist* 31 (July/August 1988): 632.

8. 'Women and men in the European Union: a statistical portrait' (Luxembourg: Office for Official Publications of the European Communities, 1996); 'Families come first', *Psychology Today* (September 1988): 11.

9. Christy Fisher, 'Kidding around making sense', *Advertising Age* (27 June 1994): 34.

10. Alan R. Andreasen, 'Life status changes and changes in consumer preferences and satisfaction', *Journal of Consumer Research* 11 (December 1984): 784–94; James H. McAlexander, John W. Schouten and Scott D. Roberts, 'Consumer behavior and divorce', *Research in Consumer Behavior* 6 (1993): 153–84.

11. 'Men and women in the European Union: a statistical portrait' (Luxembourg: Office for Official Publications of the European Communities, 1995); 'The big picture', *American Demographics* (March 1989): 22–7; Thomas G. Exter, 'Middle-aging households', *American Demographics* (July 1992): 63.

12. 'Trends in households in the European Union: 1995–2025'.

13. 'The population of the EU on 1 January, 1995', *Statistics in Focus. Population and Social Conditions*, no. 8 (Luxembourg: Office for Official Publications of the European Communities, 1995); Nicholas Timmins, 'One in five women to remain childless', *The Independent* (4 October 1995).

14. 'Trends in households in the European Union: 1995–2025': 14.

15. 'Men and women in the European Union: a statistical portrait': 72.

16. Peg Masterson, 'Agency notes rise of singles market', *Advertising Age* (9 August 1993): 17.

17. Christy Fisher, 'Census data may make ads more single minded', *Advertising Age* (20 July 1992): 2.

18. Calmetta Y. Coleman, 'The unseemly secrets of eating alone', *The Wall Street Journal* (6 July 1995): B1 (2).

19. Stephanie Shipp, 'How singles spend', *American Demographics* (April 1988): 22–7; Patricia Braus, 'Sex and the single spender', *American Demographics* (November 1993): 28–34.

20. 'Mothers bearing a second burden', *New York Times* (14 May 1989): 26.

21. Seth Mydans, 'A tribunal to get neglected parents smiling again', *The New York Times* (27 December 1996): A4.

22. 'Men and women in the European Union: a statistical portrait': 76.

23. 'Census paints a new picture of family life', *The New York Times* (30 August 1994): 22.

24. Diane Crispell, 'Pet projections', *American Demographics* (September 1994): 59.

25. Howard G. Chua-Eoan, 'Reigning cats and dogs', *Time* (16 August 1993): 50 (2); Patricia Braus, 'Cat beats dog, wins spot in house', *American Demographics* (September 1993): 24 (2).

26. Quoted in Youssef M. Ibrahim, 'French love for animals: Too fervent?', *New York Times* (2 February 1990): A5.

27. Woody Hochswender, 'The cat's meow', *New York Times* (16 May 1989): B7; Judann Dagnoli, 'Toothcare for terriers', *Advertising Age* (20 November 1989): 8; 'For fido, broccoli and yogurt', *New York Times* (16 April 1989); Chua-Eoan, 'Reigning cats and dogs'; William E. Schmidt, 'Right, then: Your policy covers Fido for therapy', *The New York Times* (15 May 1994): 4.

28. Gary Younge, 'Parents face a £66,000 bill', *The Guardian* (27 May 1996); Liz Hunt, 'The cost of growing: School-children need huge sums', *The Independent* (19 August 1996).

29. 'Trends in households in the European Union: 1995–2025'.

30. Mary C. Gilly and Ben M. Enis, 'Recycling the Family Life Cycle: A Proposal for Redefinition', in Andrew A. Mitchell, ed., *Advances in Consumer Research* 9 (Ann Arbor, MI: Association for Consumer Research, 1982): 271–6.

31. Charles M. Schaninger and William D. Danko, 'A conceptual and empirical comparison of alternative household life cycle models', *Journal of Consumer Research* 19 (March 1993): 580–94; Robert E. Wilkes, 'Household life-cycle stages, transitions, and product expenditures', *Journal of Consumer Research* 22 (1) (June 1995): 27–42.

32. These categories are an adapted version of an FLC model proposed by Gilly and Enis (1982). Based on a recent empirical comparison of several competing models, Schaninger and Danko found that this framework outperformed others, especially in terms of its treatment of non-conventional households, though they recommend

several improvements to this model as well. See Gilly and Enis, 'Recycling the family life cycle: a proposal for redefinition', in Mitchell, ed., *Advances in Consumer Research* 9; Schaninger and Danko, 'A conceptual and empirical comparison of alternate household life cycle markets'; Scott D. Roberts, Patricia K. Voli and KerenAmi Johnson, 'Beyond the Family Life Cycle: An Inventory of Variables for Defining the Family as a Consumption Unit', in Victoria L. Crittenden, ed., *Developments in Marketing Science* 15 (Coral Gables, FL: Academy of Marketing Science, 1992): 71–5.

33. James H. McAlexander, John W. Schouten and Scott D. Roberts, 'Consumer Behavior and Divorce', in *Research in Consumer Behavior* (Greenwich, CT: JAI Press, 1992); Michael R. Solomon, 'The role of products as social stimuli: A symbolic interactionism perspective', *Journal of Consumer Research* 10 (December 1983): 319–29; Melissa Martin Young, 'Disposition of Possession During Role Transitions', in Rebecca H. Holman and Michael R. Solomon, eds, *Advances in Consumer Research* 18 (Provo, UT: Association for Consumer Research, 1991): 33–9.

34. Harry L. Davis, 'Decision making within the household', *Journal of Consumer Research* 2 (March 1972): 241–60; Michael B. Menasco and David J. Curry, 'Utility and choice: An empirical study of wife/husband decision making', *Journal of Consumer Research* 16 (June 1989): 87–97; for a recent review, see Conway Lackman and John M. Lanasa, 'Family decision-making theory: An overview and assessment', *Psychology and Marketing* 10 (March/April 1993) 2: 81–94.

35. Shannon Dortch, 'Money and marital discord', *American Demographics* (October 1994): 11 (3).

36. Daniel Seymour and Greg Lessne, 'Spousal conflict arousal: Scale development', *Journal of Consumer Research* 11 (December 1984): 810–21.

37. For recent research on factors influencing how much influence adolescents exert in family decision-making, see Ellen Foxman, Patriya Tansuhaj and Karin M. Ekstrom, 'Family members' perceptions of adolescents' influence in family decision making', *Journal of Consumer Research* 15 (March 1989) 4: 482–91; Sharon E. Beatty and Salil Talpade, 'Adolescent influence in family decision making: A replication with extension', *Journal of Consumer Research* 21 (September 1994) 2: 332–41.

38. Diane Crispell, 'Dual-earner diversity', *American Demographics* (July 1995): 32–7.

39. Thomas Hine, *Populuxe* (New York: Alfred A. Knopf, 1986).

40. Robert Boutilier, *Targeting Families: Marketing To and Through the New Family* (Ithaca, NY: American Demographics Books, 1993).

41. Darach Turley, 'Dialogue with the departed', in F. Hansen, ed., *European Advances in Consumer Research* 2 (Provo, UT: Association for Consumer Research, 1995): 10–13.

42. Dennis L. Rosen and Donald H. Granbois, 'Determinants of role structure in family financial management', *Journal of Consumer Research* 10 (September 1983): 253–8.

43. Robert F. Bales, *Interaction Process Analysis: A Method for the Study of Small Groups* (Reading, MA: Addison-Wesley, 1950); for a cross-gender comparison of food shopping strategies, see Rosemary Polegato and Judith L. Zaichkowsky, 'Family food shopping: Strategies used by husbands and wives', *The Journal of Consumer Affairs* 28 (1994): 2.

44. Alma S. Baron, 'Working parents: Shifting traditional roles', *Business* 37 (January/March 1987): 36; William J. Qualls, 'Household decision behavior: The impact of husbands' and wives' sex role orientation', *Journal of Consumer Research* 14 (September 1987): 264–79; Charles M. Schaninger and W. Christian Buss, 'The relationship of sex role norms to household task allocation', *Psychology and Marketing* 2 (Summer 1985): 93–104.

45. Cynthia Webster, 'Effects of Hispanic ethnic identification on marital roles in the purchase decision process', *Journal of Consumer Research* 21 (September 1994) 2: 319–31; for a recent study that examined the effects of family depictions in advertising among Hispanic consumers, see Gary D. Gregory and James M. Munch, 'Cultural values in international advertising: an examination of familial norms and roles in Mexico', *Psychology and Marketing* 14(2) (March 1997): 99–120.

46. Gary L. Sullivan and P.J. O'Connor, 'The family purchase decision process: A cross-cultural review and framework for research', *Southwest Journal of Business and Economics* (Fall 1988): 43; Marilyn Lavin, 'Husband-dominant, wife-dominant, joint', *Journal of Consumer Marketing* 10 (1993) 3: 33–42; Nicholas Timmins, 'New man fails to survive into the nineties', *The Independent* (25 January 1996). See also Roger J. Baran, 'Patterns of Decision Making Influence for Selected Products and Services Among Husbands and Wives Living in the Czech Republic', in Hansen, ed., *European Advances in Consumer Research* 2; Jan Pahl, 'His money, her money: Recent research on financial organization in marriage', *Journal of Economic Psychology* 16 (1995): 361–76; Carole B. Burgoyne, 'Financial organization and decision-making within Western "households"', *Journal of Economic Psychology* 16 (1995): 421–30; Erich Kirchler, 'Spouses' joint purchase decisions: Determinants of influence tactics for muddling through the process', *Journal of Economic Psychology* 14 (1993): 405–38.

47. Quoted in Nicholas D. Kristof, 'Japan is a woman's world once the front door is shut', *The New York Times* (19 June 1996): A1 (2), p. A8.

48. Yumiko Ono, 'McDonald's doting dads strike a chord in Japan', *The WSJ Interactive Edition* (8 May 1997).

49. The Associated Press, 'Hit Japanese software lets players raise "daughter"', *Montgomery Advertiser* (7 April 1996): 14A.

50. Micaela DiLeonardo, 'The female world of cards and holidays: Women, families, and the work of kinship', *Signs* 12 (Spring 1942): 440–53.

51. Tony Bizjak, 'Chore wars rage on – even when wife earns the most', *The Sacramento Bee* (1 April 1993): A1 (3).

52. C. Whan Park, 'Joint decisions in home purchasing: A muddling through process', *Journal of Consumer Research* 9 (September 1982): 151–62; see also William J. Qualls and Françoise Jaffe, 'Measuring Conflict in Household Decision Behavior: Read My Lips and Read My Mind', in John F. Sherry Jr and Brian Sternthal, eds, *Advances in Consumer Research* 19 (Provo, UT: Association for Consumer Research, 1992).

53. Kim P. Corfman and Donald R. Lehmann, 'Models of co-operative group decision-making and relative influence: An experimental investigation of family purchase decisions', *Journal of Consumer Research* 14 (June 1987).

54. Alison M. Torrillo, 'Dens are men's territory', *American Demographics* (January 1995): 11 (2).

55. Charles Atkin, 'Observation of parent–child interaction in supermarket decision-making', *Journal of Marketing* 42 (October 1978).

56. Les Carlson, Ann Walsh, Russell N. Laczniak and Sanford Grossbart, 'Family communication patterns and marketplace motivations, attitudes, and behaviors of children and mothers', *Journal of Consumer Affairs* 28(1) (Summer 1994): 25–53; see also Roy L. Moore and George P. Moschis, 'The role of family communication in consumer learning', *Journal of Communication* 31 (Autumn 1981): 42–51.

57. Leslie Isler, Edward T. Popper and Scott Ward, 'Children's purchase requests and parental responses: Results from a diary study', *Journal of Advertising Research* 27 (October/November 1987).

58. Patrick E. Tyler, 'As a pampered generation grows up, Chinese worry', *The New York Times* (25 June 1996): A1, A6.

59. Robert Berner, 'Toddlers dress to the nine and designers rake it in', *The WSJ Interactive Edition* (27 May 1997).

60. Quoted in Lisa Gubernick and Marla Matzer, 'Babies as dolls', *Forbes* (27 February 1995): 78–82, at 79.

61. Horst H. Stipp, 'Children as consumers', *American Demographics* (February 1988): 27.

62. Melissa Turner, 'Kids' marketing clout man-sized', *Atlanta Journal* (18 February 1988): E10.

63. Scott Ward, 'Consumer Socialization', in Harold H. Kassarjian and Thomas S. Robertson, eds, *Perspectives in Consumer Behavior* (Glenville, IL: Scott, Foresman, 1980): 380.

64. Thomas Lipscomb, 'Indicators of materialism in children's free speech: Age and gender comparisons', *Journal of Consumer Marketing* (Fall 1988): 41–6.

65. George P. Moschis, 'The role of family communication in consumer socialization of children and adolescents', *Journal of Consumer Research* 11 (March 1985): 898–913.

66. James U. McNeal and Chyon-Hwa Yeh, 'Born to shop', *American Demographics* (June 1993): 34–9.

67. See Les Carlson, Sanford Grossbart and J. Kathleen Stuenkel, 'The role of parental socialization types on differential family communication patterns regarding consumption', *Journal of Consumer Psychology* 1 (1992) 1: 31–52.

68. See Patricia M. Greenfield, Emily Yut, Mabel Chung, Deborah Land, Holly Kreider, Maurice Pantoja and Kris Horsley, 'The program-length commercial: A study of the effects of television/toy tie-ins on imaginative play', *Psychology and Marketing* 7 (Winter 1990): 237–56 for a study on the effects of commercial programming on creative play.

69. Jill Goldsmith, 'Ga, ga, goo, goo, where's the remote? TV show targets tots', *Dow Jones Business News* (5 February 1997), accessed via *The Wall Street Journal Interactive Edition* (6 February 1997).

70. Gerald J. Gorn and Renee Florsheim, 'The effects of commercials for adult products on children', *Journal of Consumer Research* 11 (March 1985): 9, 62–7; for a study that assessed the impact of violent commercials on children, see V. Kanti Prasad and Lois J. Smith, 'Television commercials in violent programming: an experimental evaluation of their effects on children', *Journal of the Academy of Marketing Science* 22 (1994) 4: 340–51.

71. Glenn Collins, 'New studies on "girl toys" and "boy toys"', *New York Times* (13 February 1984): D1.

72. Susan B. Kaiser, 'Clothing and the social organization of gender perception: A developmental approach', *Clothing and Textiles Research Journal* 7 (Winter 1989): 46–56.

73. D.W. Rajecki, Jill Ann Dame, Kelly Jo Creek, P.J. Barrickman, Catherine A. Reid and Drew C. Appleby, 'Gender casting in television toy advertisements: Distributions, message content analysis, and evaluations', *Journal of Consumer Psychology* 2 (1993) 3: 307–27.

74. Lori Schwartz and William Markham, 'Sex stereotyping in children's toy advertisements', *Sex Roles* 12 (January 1985): 157–70.

75. Joseph Pereira, 'Oh boy! In toyland, you get more if you're male', *The Wall Street Journal* (23 September 1994): B1 (2); Joseph Pereira, 'Girls' favorite playthings: dolls, dolls, and dolls', *The Wall Street Journal* (23 September 1994): B1 (2).

76. Brad Edmondson, 'Snakes, snails, and puppy dogs' tails', *American Demographics* (October 1987): 18.

77. Laura A. Peracchio, 'How do young children learn to be consumers? A script-processing approach', *Journal of Consumer Research* 18 (March 1992): 4, 25–40; Laura A. Peracchio, 'Young children's processing of a televised narrative: Is a picture really worth a thousand words?', *Journal of Consumer Research* 20 (September 1993) 2: 281–93; see also M. Carole Macklin, 'The effects of an advertising retrieval cue on young children's memory and brand evaluations', *Psychology and Marketing* 11 (May/June 1994) 3: 291–311.

78. Jean Piaget, 'The child and modern physics', *Scientific American* 196 (1957) 3: 46–51; see also Kenneth D. Bahn, 'How and when do brand perceptions and preferences first form? A cognitive developmental investigation', *Journal of Consumer Research* 13 (December 1986): 382–93.

79. Deborah L. Roedder, 'Age differences in children's responses to television advertising: An information processing approach', *Journal of Consumer Research* 8 (September 1981): 1, 44–53; see also Deborah Roedder John and Ramnath Lakshmi-Ratan, 'Age differences in children's choice behavior: The impact of available alternatives', *Journal of Marketing Research* (29 May 1992): 216–26; Jennifer Gregan-Paxton and Deborah Roedder John, 'Are young children adaptive decision makers? A study of age differences in information search behavior', *Journal of Consumer Research* (1995).

80. Janet Simons, 'Youth marketing: children's clothes follow the latest fashion', *Advertising Age* (14 February 1985): 16.

81. Stipp, 'Children as consumers'; see Laura A. Peracchio, 'Designing research to reveal the young child's emerging competence', *Psychology and Marketing* 7 (Winter 1990): 257–76 for details regarding the design of research on children.

82. 'Kid power', *Forbes* (30 March 1987): 9–10.

83. Dena Kleiman, 'Candy to frighten your parents with', *New York Times* (23 August 1989): C1.

84. Laura Shapiro, 'Where little boys can play with nail polish', *Newsweek* (28 May 1990): 62.

85. Matt Murray, 'Marketers want kids' help and their parents' loyalty', *The WSJ Interactive Edition* (6 May 1997).

86. Cindy Clark, 'Putting Aside Adultcentrism: Child-Centered Ethnographic Research', unpublished manuscript (C.D. Clark Limited, 1991); Cindy Clark, 'Some Practical In's and Out's of Studying Children as Consumers', paper presented at the AMA Research Roundtable (March 1986).

87. Gary Armstrong and Merrie Brucks, 'Dealing with children's advertising: Public policy issues and alternatives', *Journal of Public Policy and Marketing* 7 (1988): 98–113.

88. Bonnie Reece, 'Children and shopping: Some public policy questions', *Journal of Public Policy and Marketing* (1986): 185–94.

89. Mary Ann Stutts and Garland G. Hunnicutt, 'Can young children understand disclaimers in television commercials?', *Journal of Advertising* 16 (Winter 1987): 41–6.

90. Ira Teinowitz, 'CARU to unveil guidelines for kid-focused web sites', *Ad Age* (21 April 1997): 8.

91. Steve Weinstein, 'Fight heats up against kids' TV "commershows"', *Marketing News* (9 October 1989): 2.

92. Alan Bunce, 'Are TV ads turning kids into consumers?', *Christian Science Monitor* (11 August 1988): 1.

INCOME AND SOCIAL CLASS

Finally, the big day has come! David is going home with Julia to meet her parents. David had been doing some contracting work at the publishing company where Julia works, and it was love at first sight. Even though David had attended the 'School of Hard Knocks' on the streets of Liverpool, while Julia studied Classics at Trinity College, Oxford, somehow they knew they could work things out despite their vastly different social backgrounds. Julia's been hinting that the Caldwells have money from *several* generations back, but David doesn't feel intimidated. After all, he knows plenty of guys from both Liverpool and London who have wheeled-and-dealed their way into six figures; he thinks he can handle one more big shot in a silk suit, flashing a roll of bills and showing off his expensive modern furniture with mirrors and gadgets everywhere you look.

When they arrive at the family estate 90 minutes outside London, David looks for a Rolls-Royce parked at the end of the long, tree-lined driveway, but he sees only a Jeep Cherokee – which, he decides, must belong to one of the servants. Once inside, David is surprised by how simply the house is decorated and by how understated everything seems. The hall floor is covered with a faded Oriental rug, and all the furniture looks really old – in fact, there doesn't seem to be a stick of new furniture anywhere, just a lot of antiques.

David is even more surprised when he meets Mr Caldwell. He had half-expected Julia's father to be wearing a tuxedo and holding a large glass of cognac like the people on *Lifestyles of the Rich and Famous*. In fact, David had put on his best Italian silk suit in anticipation and was wearing his large cubic zirconium ring so Mr Caldwell would know that he had money too. When Julia's father emerges from his study wearing an old rumpled cardigan and plimsolls, David realizes he's definitely not in the same world . . .

■ CONSUMER SPENDING AND ECONOMIC BEHAVIOUR

As David's eye-opening experience at the Caldwells' suggests, there are many ways to spend money, and a wide gulf exists between those who have it and those who don't. Perhaps an equally wide one exists between those who have had it for a long time and those who 'made it the hard way – by earning it!' This chapter begins by considering briefly how general economic conditions affect the way consumers allocate their money. Then, reflecting the adage 'The rich are different', it will explore how people who occupy different positions in society consume in very different ways. Whether a person is a skilled worker like David or a child of privilege like Julia, his or her social class has a profound impact on what he or she does with money and on how consumption choices reflect the person's 'place' in society.

As this chapter illustrates, these choices play another purpose as well. The specific products and services we buy are often intended to make sure *other* people know what our social standing is – or what we would like it to be. Products are frequently bought

▶ and displayed as markers of social class: they are valued as status symbols. Indeed, it is quite common for a product to be positioned on the basis of its (presumed) place in the social hierarchy. The chapter concludes with an assessment of the evolving natures of such status symbols, and it considers some reasons why status-driven products are not always accurate indicators of a consumer's true social standing.

▶ The field of behavioural economics, or economic psychology, is concerned with the 'human' side of economic decisions. Beginning with the pioneering work of the psychologist George Katona, this discipline studies how consumers' motives and their expectations about the future affect their current spending, and how these individual decisions add up to affect a society's economic well-being.[1]

Income patterns

Many Europeans would probably say that while they are comfortable, they don't earn enough money. In reality, the average European's standard of living continues to improve. Gross Domestic Product more than doubled and in some EU countries quadrupled between 1980 and 1995, although this boom was by no means shared equally among all consumer groups.[2] Individual income shifts were linked to two key factors: a shift in women's roles and increases in educational attainment.[3]

Woman's work

One reason for this increase in income is that there has also been a larger proportion of people of working age participating in the labour force. While men are more likely to have paid employment than women are, the greatest increases in paid employment in EU countries over the past decade have been among women. This steady increase in the numbers of working women is a primary cause of the increase in household incomes. Still, throughout the Union, women's average full-time earnings are less than men's, and 30 per cent of women in employment are working part-time, against only 6.5 per cent of men. Female part-time is particularly prevalent in The Netherlands, where it accounts for almost 75 per cent of female employment, and the United Kingdom (44 per cent).[4] In 2001, the average gross monthly wage of women working on a full-time basis was 76 per cent of the earnings of a man. In Belgium, Denmark, Luxembourg and Sweden, the average wages of women are equivalent to 84–85 per cent of men's. In Ireland, the Netherlands, and the UK, on the other hand, women's wages represent only 69–70 per cent of men's.[5] The differences in pay are particularly high among older workers, the highly skilled and those employed with supervisory job status. Men are not only more concentrated in higher paid sectors and occupations, but within these sectors and occupations they are also more likely than women to hold supervisory responsibilities and if

Figure 12.1 Difference between men's and women's annual average earnings as a percentage of men's annual average earnings, 2001

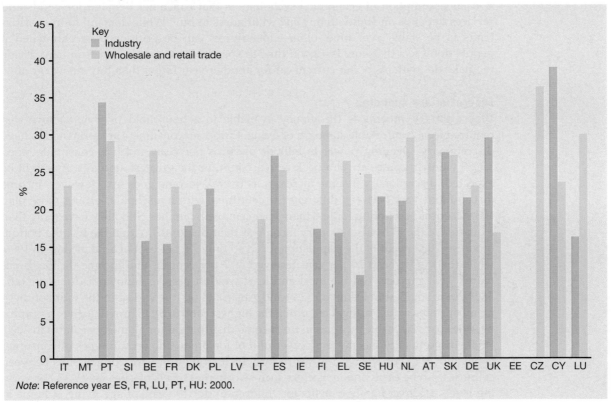

Note: Reference year ES, FR, LU, PT, HU: 2000.

Source: Based on *Eurostat, Harmonised Statistics on Earnings*, Figure 41 (Luxembourg: Office for Official Publications of the European Communities, 2004). © European Communities, 2004.

they do so the earnings are relatively higher.[6] Yet in spite of these increases in household income, women are more likely to be in part-time work, a situation which reflects the more traditional activities of caring for the household and children living at home – activities that are still seen as primarily their responsibility. As discussed in the previous chapter, family situation, the number and age of children living at home and the educational level of women heavily influence their employment activities.

Figure 12.1 shows the 'gender pay gap' between men and women in the EU-25 countries.

Yes, it pays to go to school!

Another factor that determines who gets a bigger slice of the pie is education. Although the expense of going to college often entails great sacrifice, it still pays in the long run. University and higher professional study graduates earn about 50 per cent more than those who have gone through secondary school only during the course of their lives. Close to half of the increase in consumer spending power during the past decade came from these more highly educated groups. Full-time employees with a tertiary education qualification earn on average considerably more than those who have completed upper secondary school (A-levels, *Baccalauréat*, Abitur, HBO or equivalent). In general, the trend is that the younger generation of Europeans is better qualified than the older generations. In 2002, 77 per cent of the younger generation aged 20–24 had completed at least upper secondary education (*Baccalauréat*, Abitur, HBO, apprenticeship) compared with only 55 per cent of people aged 50–64.[7]

To spend or not to spend, that is the question

A basic assumption of economic psychology is that consumer demand for goods and services depends on ability to buy *and* willingness to buy. While demand for necessities tends to be stable over time, other expenditures can be postponed or eliminated if people don't feel that now is a good time to spend.[8] For example, a person may decide to 'make do' with his or her current car for another year rather than buy a new car now.

Discretionary spending

▶ **Discretionary income** is the money available to a household over and above that required for a comfortable standard of living. European consumers are estimated to have discretionary spending power in billions of euros per year, and it is consumers aged 35–55 whose incomes are at a peak who account for the greatest amounts. As might be expected, discretionary income increases as overall income goes up. However, income distributions vary between different EU countries, with households earning more than 100,000 euros accounting for less than 5 per cent of all families. Still, they have more than a quarter of the EU's discretionary income at their disposal.[9] Within the EU, the bottom (poorest) 20 per cent of the population received only 7.6 per cent of total income in 1996, while the top (richest) 20 per cent received 39.3 per cent of total income (i.e. 5.2 times more). This gap between the most and least well-off persons (known as the *share ratio S80/S20*) is smallest in Denmark (2.9) and Austria (4.0). It is widest in the four southern member states, with Portugal recording the highest ratio (6.8). Figure 12.2 gives a graphic overview of disposable incomes in the income distribution for all member states in 2000. While discretionary income is a powerful tool for predicting certain types of consumer behaviour, it is not always a measure for which straightforward comparisons between countries can be easily made. Factors such as different levels of sales tax (VAT) or varying levels of direct family benefits for children under 19 years of age living at home in various EU countries account for differences in what constitutes true discretionary income.

Individual attitudes towards money

Many consumers are entertaining doubts about their individual and collective futures, and are anxious about holding on to what they have. A consumer's anxieties about money are not necessarily related to how much he or she actually has: acquiring and managing money is more a state of mind than of wallet. Money can have a variety of complex psychological meanings: it can be equated with success or failure, social acceptability, security, love or freedom.[10] Some clinical psychologists even specialize in treating money-related disorders, and report that people feel guilty about their success and deliberately make bad investments to ease this feeling! Other clinical conditions include atephobia (fear of being ruined), harpaxophobia (fear of becoming a victim of robbers), peniaphobia (fear of poverty) and aurophobia (fear of gold).[11] The Roper/Starch survey found that security was the attribute most closely linked to the meaning of money. Other significant associations included comfort, being able to help one's children, freedom and pleasure.[12]

Consumer confidence

▶ A consumer's beliefs about what the future holds is an indicator of **consumer confidence**, which reflects the extent to which people are optimistic or pessimistic about the future health of the economy and how they will fare in the future. These beliefs influence how much money a consumer will pump into the economy when making discretionary purchases.

Many businesses take forecasts about anticipated spending very seriously, and periodic surveys attempt to 'take the pulse' of the European consumer. The Henley Centre

Figure 12.2 Disposable income per capita across the EU-25, 2000

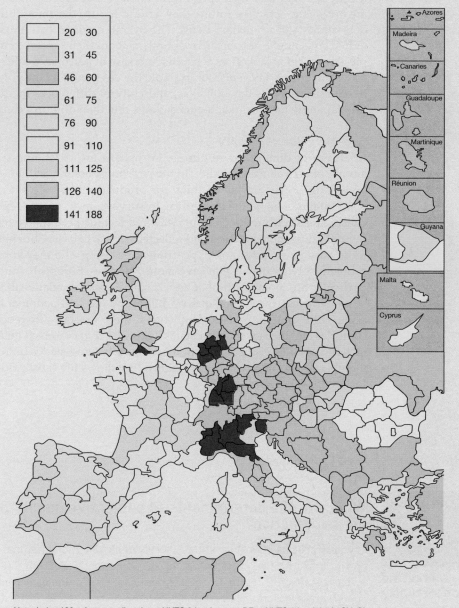

20	30
31	45
46	60
61	75
76	90
91	110
111	125
126	140
141	188

Note: Index 100 – Average all regions; NUTS 2 level except DE at NUTS 1 level: L, A, CY, SI: no data available.

Source: Eurostat, *Statistics in Focus*, Theme 3-7/2003 (Luxembourg: Office for Official Publications of the European Communities, 2004): 113, Map 2. © European Communities 2004.

conducts a survey of consumer confidence, as does Eurostat and the EuroMonitor. The following are the types of questions posed to consumers in these surveys:[13]

> *'My standard of living will change for the better over the next year.'*
>
> *'My quality of life will improve over the next year.'*
>
> *'I will have a lack of money when I retire.'*
>
> *'I spend too much of my income, and intend to spend less next year.'*
>
> *'I am concerned about the amount of free time I have.'*

When people are pessimistic about their prospects and about the state of the economy, they tend to cut back their spending and take on less debt. On the other hand, when they are optimistic about the future, they tend to reduce the amount they save, take on more debt and buy discretionary items. The overall **savings rate** thus is influenced by individual consumers' pessimism or optimism about their personal circumstances (for example, fear of being laid off vs. a sudden increase in personal wealth due to an inheritance), as well as by world events (for example the election of a new government or an international crisis such as the Gulf War) and cultural differences in attitudes towards saving (the Japanese have a much higher savings rate than do Europeans or Americans).[14]

Seeking value vs. quality

In an era of diminished resources, Europeans are redefining traditional relationships among price, value and quality. In the past (most notably in the 1980s), people seemed to be willing to pay almost anything for products and services. Consumers still claim to want quality – but at the right price. In surveys, most people report that they regret the conspicuous consumption of the 1980s and feel the need to live with less. The attitude of the 1990s was more practical and reflected a 'back to basics' orientation. People now want more hard news instead of 'hype' from advertising, and they appreciate ads that feature problem-solving tips or that save money or time. European youth (age range 12–24) in particular are more sceptical of advertising messages, relative to the total population.

Nonetheless, the general quality of life, and life satisfaction of European consumers is high, with some important distinctions: there are big differences between the EU-15 countries and the new member states with respect to perceived quality of life and life satisfaction. Also, levels of satisfaction are more heterogeneous among citizens of the new member states and in the EU-15. Figure 12.3 shows life satisfaction measures by country for the EU-25 countries.

marketing opportunity

What are the determinants of subjective quality of life and life satisfaction?

The abstract idea of what constitutes quality of life does not differ that much across Europe, and if there are differences, there is no clear divide between EU-15 countries and the new member states. The reason for this basic similarity is that the dominant concerns in all countries are income, family life and health. However, whereas abstract ideas of a good life are rather similar, actual determinants of life satisfaction are not:

● In many new member states, income satisfaction is of key importance for overall life satisfaction. Hence, improving income satisfaction is the best way to improve life satisfaction. In general, following income improvement, satisfaction with health and with family life also have a strong impact of how people evaluate their lives.

● In the EU-15 countries, income satisfaction matters less for life satisfaction. On the whole, satisfaction with family life and social life are the strongest determinants of subjective quality of life in these countries.

● The paramount importance of income in the East and its relative low importance in the West once again are linked with differences in economic development. Consumers in the new member states, at present, put greater emphasis on material demands, which are currently under-fulfilled in these countries to a large degree.[15]

Figure 12.3 Life satisfaction by country

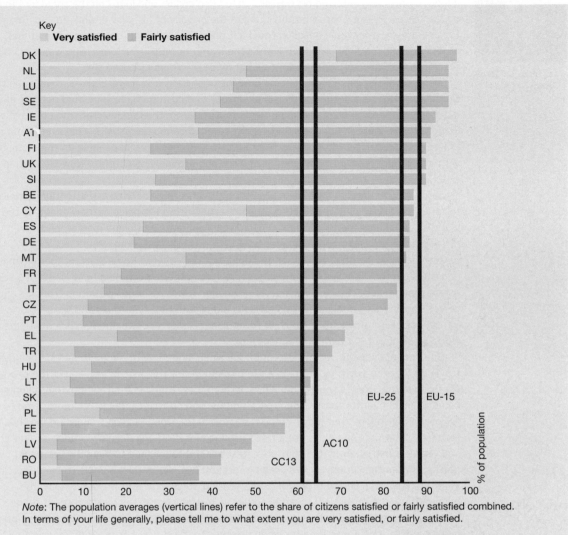

Note: The population averages (vertical lines) refer to the share of citizens satisfied or fairly satisfied combined. In terms of your life generally, please tell me to what extent you are very satisfied, or fairly satisfied.

Source: Eurostat, Statistics in Focus, Theme 3-24/2003 (Luxembourg: Office for Official Publications of the European Communities, 2004). © European Communities, 2004.

■ SOCIAL CLASS

All societies can be roughly divided into the haves and the have-nots (though sometimes 'having' is a question of degree). While social equality is a widely held value throughout Europe, the fact remains that some people seem to be more equal than others. As David's encounter with the Caldwells suggests, a consumer's standing in society, or **social class**, is determined by a complex set of variables, including income, family background and occupation.

The place one occupies in the social structure is not just an important determinant of *how much* money is spent. It also influences *how* it is spent. David was surprised that the Caldwells, who clearly had a lot of money, did not seem to flaunt it. This understated way of living is a hallmark of so-called 'old money'. People who have had it for a long time don't need to prove they've got it. In contrast, consumers who are relative newcomers to affluence might allocate the same amount of money very differently.

marketing opportunity

'Winston Churchill preferred his with starched linen collars and loops on the shoulders to hold up his braces. Prince Charles has his fitted in the privacy of his palace, while fashion mogul Ralph Lauren – who, you'd imagine, could get them for free at his own shop – sometimes orders dozens at a time. And then there's the rather eccentric customer who wants his to resemble Australian prisoner uniforms – but made of cream-coloured silk.

What all these people have in common – the politicians and powerbrokers, royals and the slightly offbeat – is a desire for the simple luxury of a custom-made shirt. And not just any old made-to-measure shirt: these garments must be from the famous craftsmen of Jermyn Street, whose shops in London's SW1 district cater to connoisseurs with a passion for fine tailoring and a perfect fit. At prices from £100 to £155 per shirt, depending on the cloth, and with a minimum order of between four and six, you probably can't afford to wear anything else.

Jermyn Street tailors have been practising the art of fine service and attention to detail for over a century – it's what their customers expect from the place acknowledged as the world's capital of made-to-measure shirts. 'We have created a unique market, and have attracted the top customers, who feel quite comfortable here', notes Paul Cuss, chief patternmaker at Turnbull and Asser, the holder of the coveted Royal Warrant for shirtmaking, and the shop that supplies Prince Charles . . . among others. According to Mr Cuss, 'It's very establishment, very clubby.' With its heavy wooden furniture, stuffed hunting trophies and velvet Hapsburgian smoking jackets for sale, along with ties, bathrobes and boxer shorts and a framed picture of Winston Churchill, Turnbull and Asser's cosy emporium is a gentlemen's world straight out of *Country Life* magazine.

One can imagine the Jermyn Street of old, when landed gentry and Etonian schoolboys travelled there to buy their shirts in a rite of passage for the aristocracy, and in the process established the street's reputation. While Jermyn Street thrives on tradition, their clients come from all over the world. The French and fashion-conscious Italians come for the 'tailored English look', but the shirtmakers admit to following fashion trends: among the serious solid whites and blues are a few shocking pink, lilac and dayglow orange samples.

Precise construction of the shirt also means that it takes time to have the garment finished. After measuring, there's a wait of around two weeks for a sample to be made. Then there's a trial period of washing and wearing, to see if the fit is right. Finally, the hand-cutters and sewers get to work, and in six to eight weeks the masterpiece is ready – and you can walk proudly down the street, knowing you've joined an exclusive club whose members say price doesn't matter when it comes to style.'[16]

A universal pecking order

In many animal species, a social organization develops whereby the most assertive or aggressive animals exert control over the others and have the first pick of food, living space and even mating partners. Chickens, for example, develop a clearly defined dominance–submission hierarchy. Within this hierarchy, each hen has a position in which she is submissive to all of the hens above her and dominates all of the ones below her (hence the origin of the term *pecking order*).[17]

People are no different. They also develop a pecking order where they are ranked in terms of their relative standing in society. This standing determines their access to such resources as education, housing and consumer goods. And people try to improve their ranking by moving up the social order whenever possible. This desire to improve one's lot, and often to let others know that one has done so, is at the core of many marketing strategies.

▶ While every culture has its social hierarchies, variations in terms of how explicit these distinctions are can be observed. Stratification of one sort or another is universal, even in societies that officially disdain such a process. For example, in China, a supposedly classless society, the children of top party officials, who are called *gaoganzidi*, irritate many Chinese. These offspring have a reputation for laziness, enjoying material pleasures and getting the best jobs by virtue of their family connections. They are thus a privileged class in a classless society.[18]

multicultural dimensions

'It is Saturday night in a club in central London. The crowd is enjoying the standard fare of nightclubs: the R&B music is loud enough to make conversation hard; the bar is doing a brisk trade in pricey drinks; and coming through the door is a steady stream of punters in designer-label plumage. Less standard is that each of these young people handing over the £10 entry fee is Asian. And, from door staff to promoter, so is nearly everyone else. This is Mumbai Rouge, self-styled 'hangout for the affluent Asian professional' and the self-assurance of the phrase is matched by the confidence of the clientele. Nightclubs are only part of it. Anyone mingling with the crowd when India play cricket at the Oval or shopping in areas with a large Asian population, such as Harrow or Slough or Wolverhampton, would find ample evidence of the optimism and material aspirations of young British Asians.

The Institute of Practitioners in Advertising reported last year that Asians in the UK were far more likely to own a personal computer or a DVD player than the population overall, and that 72 per cent had pay-TV at home, compared with 39 per cent of the UK population.

On other measures, too, Asians as a group seem an attractive target for businesses. They are increasing in numbers (2.3 m, according to the 2001 Census); younger than the white population overall; more likely to be found in big cities; and making important economic advances. According to the Cabinet Office, male workers of Indian origin went from earning an average 8 per cent less than their white counterparts in 1994 to earning 3 per cent more by 2000. Asians still find it more difficult to get jobs than whites, but the broad outline is of a group increasingly at home. Indeed, most of the Asian population is British-born and one, two or even three, generations removed from their countries of ancestral origin. While the first generation had to save money and establish themselves, their children and grandchildren have British roots and feel able to play hard.

Yet if the story of Asians in the UK has largely been one of integration, communications professionals have tended to put them in a niche or ignore them. In January 2003, just 2 per cent of advertising campaigns featured actors from ethnic minorities – despite blacks and Asians making up 8 per cent of the population. About five years ago, in an effort to correct this imbalance, marketing consultant Anjna Raheja coined the term 'brown pound'. 'It was intended', she says, 'to draw attention to the growing economic power of Asian – and black – consumers.' It has been widely used and may have helped to increase the proportion of advertisements featuring ethnic minorities to 7 per cent by November last year. But what seems to have filled the vacuum is a cliché. As Ms Raheja notes: 'There has been some trading in stereotypes.' An advertisement for the Halifax Building Society this year featured a Bollywood-style troupe singing about how personal loans were 'sweeter than chutney'. Similarly, Walkers Crisps' campaign for Chicken Tikka Masala crisps showed Gary Lineker, the TV presenter and former soccer player, marrying an Asian granny – and getting the keys to the cornershop.'[19]

Social class affects access to resources

Just as marketers try to carve society into groups for segmentation purposes, sociologists have developed ways to describe meaningful divisions of society in terms of people's relative social and economic resources. Some of these divisions involve political power, while others revolve around purely economic distinctions. Karl Marx felt that position in a society was determined by one's relationship to the *means of production*. Some people (the haves) control resources, and they use the labour of others to preserve their privileged positions. The have-nots lack control and depend on their own labour for survival, so these people have the most to gain by changing the system. Distinctions among people that entitle some to more than others are perpetuated by those who will benefit by doing so.[20]

The sociologist Max Weber showed that the rankings people develop are not one-dimensional. Some involve prestige or 'social honour' (he called these *status groups*), some rankings focus on power (or *party*), and some revolve around wealth and property (*class*).[21]

Social class affects taste and lifestyles

The term 'social class' is now used more generally to describe the overall rank of people in a society. People who are grouped within the same social class are approximately equal in terms of their social standing in the community. They work in roughly similar occupations, and they tend to have similar lifestyles by virtue of their income levels and common tastes. These people tend to socialize with one another and share many ideas and values regarding the way life should be lived.[22]

marketing pitfall

'Stemar gazes over the expansive new verandah of his summer cottage on a tranquil island off Norway's south-eastern coast, chatting on his cell phone. The 50-year-old Oslo accountant recently added a host of amenities such as hot running water to his *hytte*, as Norwegians call their rustic summer cabins. Now he plans to put in a paved road to his front door and a swimming pool in the garden. 'There's nothing wrong with a little comfort', says Stemar. Well, maybe not in other summer playgrounds such as France's Côte d'Azur, but here in austere Norway, the words 'comfort' and 'vacation' are not synonymous. Thanks to the recent oil boom, many Norwegians are spending their new-found wealth upgrading spartan summer chalets with tennis courts, jacuzzis and even helipads. But in a country where simplicity and frugality are cherished virtues, and egalitarianism is strong, the display of wealth and money is suspect. Some politicians have suggested bulldozing the houses of the wealthy if they block access to the sea, and trade union leaders have blasted a new breed of Norwegians who favour showy yachts and life in the fast lane, and who build fences around private property.

'The rich can be quite vulgar', grumbles Stemar's neighbour Brit, who demanded that he trim a metre or so off his verandah because she and her husband, Gustav, could see it from their cabin lower down the hill. Both teachers, Brit and Gustav are nearing retirement, and have a more traditional Norwegian view of how to spend their summer, and how to spend their money. At stake, many say, are Norwegian ideals of equality and social democracy. These dictate that all Norwegians should have the same quality of life and share the national wealth equally. Norwegians champion austerity because they haven't always been prosperous. Before oil was discovered about 20 years ago, only a few families were considered wealthy. This frugality is obvious even in the capital, Oslo. For all the new oil money, plus low inflation, the city isn't a brash 'Kuwait of the North'.

Summer chalets should reflect the spartan mood, diehards say, and vacation activities must be limited. Scraping down paint is popular, as is hammering down loose floorboards. So is swimming in lakes, fishing for supper and chopping wood. But not much else. As another neighbour, Aase, puts it: 'We like to, uh, sit here. I'd like the rich to stay away from here. They would ruin the neighbourhood.''[23]

Social class is as much a state of being as it is of having: as David saw, class is also a question of what one *does* with one's money and how one defines one's role in society. Although people may not like the idea that some members of society are better off or 'different' from others, most consumers do acknowledge the existence of different classes and the effect of class membership on consumption. As one wealthy woman observed when asked to define social class: 'I would suppose social class means where you went to school and how far. Your intelligence. Where you live . . . Where you send your children to school. The hobbies you have. Skiing, for example, is higher than the snowmobile . . . It can't be [just] money, because nobody ever knows that about you for sure.'[24]

Social stratification

In college, some students always seem to be more popular than others. They have access to many resources, such as special privileges, expensive cars, generous allowances or dates with other equally popular classmates. At work, some people are put on the fast track and are promoted to prestige jobs, given higher salaries and perhaps such perks as a parking space, a large office or the keys to the executive cloakroom.

In virtually every context, some people seem to be ranked higher than others. Patterns of social arrangements evolve whereby some members get more resources than others by virtue of their relative standing, power and/or control in the group.[25] The phenomenon of **social stratification** refers to this creation of artificial divisions in a society: 'those processes in a social system by which scarce and valuable resources are distributed unequally to status positions that become more or less permanently ranked in terms of the share of valuable resources each receives'.[26]

Achieved vs. ascribed status

If you recall groups you've belonged to, both large and small, you'll probably agree that in many instances some members seemed to get more than their fair share while others were not so lucky. Some of these resources may have gone to people who earned them through hard work or diligence. This allocation is due to *achieved status*. Other rewards may have been obtained because the person was lucky enough to be born rich or beautiful. Such good fortune reflects *ascribed status*.

Whether rewards go to the 'best and the brightest' or to someone who happens to be related to the boss, allocations are rarely equal within a social group. Most groups exhibit a structure, or status hierarchy, in which some members are somehow better off than others. They may have more authority or power, or they are simply more liked or respected.

Class structure around the world

Every society has some type of hierarchical class structure, where people's access to products and services is determined by their resources and social standing. Of course, the specific 'markers' of success depend on what is valued in each culture. For the Chinese, who are just beginning to experience the bounties of capitalism, one marker of success is hiring a bodyguard to protect oneself and one's newly acquired possessions![27]

Japan is a highly status-conscious society, where upmarket, designer labels are popular and new forms of status are always being sought. To the Japanese, owning a traditional rock garden, formerly a vehicle for leisure and tranquillity, has become a coveted item. Possession of a rock garden implies inherited wealth, since aristocrats traditionally were patrons of the arts. In addition, considerable assets are required to afford the necessary land in a country where property is extraordinarily expensive. The scarcity of land also helps to explain why the Japanese are fanatical golfers: since a golf course takes up so much space, membership of a golf club is extremely valuable.[28]

On the other side of the world from Japan, there is always England: England is also a class-conscious country, and, at least until recently, consumption patterns were preordained in terms of one's inherited position and family background. Members of the upper class were educated at public schools such as Eton and Harrow, and had a distinctive accent. Remnants of this rigid class structure can still be found. 'Hooray Henrys' (wealthy young men) play polo at Windsor and at the moment hereditary peers can still take their seat in the House of Lords.

The dominance of inherited wealth appears to be fading in Britain's traditionally aristocratic society. According to a survey, 86 of the 200 wealthiest people in England made their money the old-fashioned way: they earned it. Even the sanctity of the Royal Family, which epitomizes the aristocracy, has been diluted because of tabloid exposure and the antics of younger family members who have been transformed into celebrities more like rock stars than royalty.[29]

Social mobility

▶ To what degree do people tend to change their social class? In some traditional societies social class is very difficult to change, but in Europe, any man or woman can become prime minister. **Social mobility** refers to the 'passage of individuals from one social class to another'.[30]

This passage can be upward, downward or even horizontal. *Horizontal mobility* refers to movement from one position to another roughly equivalent in social status, like becoming a nurse instead of a junior school teacher. *Downward mobility* is, of course, not very desirable, but this pattern is unfortunately quite evident in recent years as redundant workers have been forced to join the dole queue or have joined the ranks of the homeless. In the United States, a conservative estimate is that 600,000 Americans are homeless on a given day.[31]

Despite that discouraging trend, demographics decree that there must be *upward mobility* in European society. The middle and upper classes reproduce less than the lower classes (an effect known as *differential fertility*), and they tend to restrict family size below replacement level. Therefore, so the reasoning goes, positions of higher status over time must be filled by those of lower status.[32] Overall, though, the offspring of blue-collar consumers tend also to be blue-collar while the offspring of white-collar consumers tend also to be white-collar.[33] People tend to improve their positions over time, but these increases are not usually dramatic enough to catapult them from one social class to another.

Components of social class

When we think about a person's social class, there are a number of pieces of information we can consider. Two major ones are occupation and income. A third important factor is educational attainment, which is strongly related to income and occupation.

Occupational prestige

In a system where (like it or not) a consumer is defined to a great extent by what he or she does for a living, *occupational prestige* is one way to evaluate the 'worth' of people. Hierarchies of occupational prestige tend to be quite stable over time, and they also tend to be similar in different societies. Similarities in occupational prestige have been found in countries as diverse as Brazil, Ghana, Guam, Japan and Turkey.[34]

A typical ranking includes a variety of professional and business occupations at the top (e.g. director of a large corporation, doctor or college lecturer), while those jobs hovering near the bottom include shoeshiner, unskilled labourer and dustman. Because a person's occupation tends to be strongly linked to his or her use of leisure time, allocation of family resources, political orientation and so on, this variable is often considered to be the single best indicator of social class.

Income

The distribution of wealth is of great interest to social scientists and to marketers, since it determines which groups have the greatest buying power and market potential. Wealth is by no means distributed evenly across the classes. While there is a more equitable distribution of wealth across European countries relative to Latin America, Asia and

America (the top fifth of the population in the United States controls about 75 per cent of all assets),[35] there is still a disportionate share of wealth controlled by a small segment of the European population. As we have seen, income per se is often not a very good indicator of social class, since the way money is spent is more telling. Still, people need money to allow them to obtain the goods and services that they need to express their tastes, so obviously income is still very important.

The relationship between income and social class

Although consumers tend to equate money with class, the precise relationship between other aspects of social class and income is not clear and has been the subject of debate among social scientists.[36] The two are by no means synonymous, which is why many people with a lot of money try to use it to improve their social class.

One problem is that even if a family increases household income by adding wage earners, each additional job is likely to be of lower status. For example, a housewife who gets a part-time job is not as likely to get one that is of equal or greater status than the primary wage earner's. In addition, the extra money earned may not be pooled for the common good of the family. Instead it may be used by the individual for his or her own personal spending. More money does not then result in increased status or changes in consumption patterns, since it tends to be devoted to buying more of the same rather than upgrading to higher-status products.[37]

The following general conclusions can be made regarding the relative value of social class (i.e. place of residence, occupation, cultural interests, etc.) vs. income in predicting consumer behaviour:

- Social class appears to be a better predictor of purchases that have symbolic aspects, but low-to-moderate prices (e.g. cosmetics, alcohol).

- Income is a better predictor of major expenditures that do not have status or symbolic aspects (e.g. major appliances).

- Social class and income data together are better predictors of purchases of expensive, symbolic products (e.g. cars, homes, luxury goods).[38]

Measurement of social class

Because social class is a complex concept which depends on a number of factors, not surprisingly it has proved difficult to measure. Early measures included the Index of Status Characteristics developed in the 1940s and the Index of Social Position developed by Hollingshead in the 1950s.[39] These indices used various combinations of individual characteristics (such as income, type of housing) to arrive at a label of class standing. The accuracy of these composites is still a subject of debate among researchers; one recent study claimed that for segmentation purposes, raw education and income measures work as well as composite status measures.[40]

Blue-collar workers with relatively high-income jobs still tend to view themselves as working class, even though their income levels may be equivalent to those of many white-collar workers.[41] This fact reinforces the idea that the labels 'working class' or 'middle class' are very subjective. Their meanings say at least as much about self-identity as they do about economic well-being.

Problems with measures of social class

Market researchers were among the first to propose that people from different social classes can be distinguished from each other in important ways. While some of these dimensions still exist, others have changed.[42] Unfortunately, many of these measures are badly dated and are not as valid today for a variety of reasons, four of which are discussed here.[43]

Most measures of social class were designed to accommodate the traditional nuclear family, with a male wage earner in the middle of his career and a female full-time home-maker. Such measures have trouble accounting for two-income families, young singles living alone, or households headed by women which are so prevalent in today's society (see Chapter 11).

Another problem with measuring social class is attributable to the increasing anonymity of our society. Earlier studies relied on the *reputational method*, where extensive interviewing was done within a community to determine the reputations and backgrounds of individuals. This information, coupled with the tracing of interaction patterns among people, provided a very comprehensive view of social standing within a community.

This approach is virtually impossible to implement in most communities today. One compromise is to interview individuals to obtain demographic data and to combine these data with the subjective impressions of the interviewer regarding the person's possessions and standard of living. An example of this approach appears in Figure 12.4. Note that the accuracy of this questionnaire relies largely on the interviewer's judgement,

Figure 12.4 Living room clusters and social class

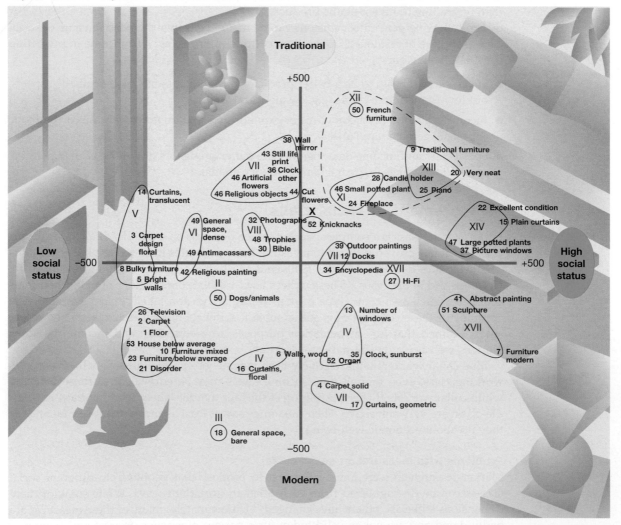

Source: Edward O. Laumann and James S. House, 'Living room styles and social attributes: The patterning of material artifacts in a modern urban community', *Sociology and Social Research* 54 (April 1970): 321–42.

especially regarding the quality of the respondent's neighbourhood. These impressions are in danger of being biased by the interviewer's own circumstances, which may affect his or her standard of comparison. This potential problem highlights the need for adequate training of interviewers, as well as for some attempt to cross-validate such data, possibly by employing multiple judges to rate the same area.

One problem with assigning people to a social class is that they may not be equal in their standing on all of the relevant dimensions. A person might come from a low-status ethnic group but have a high-status job, while another may live in a fashionable part of town but did not complete secondary school. The concept of **status crystallization** was developed to assess the impact of inconsistency on the self and social behaviour.[44] It was thought that since the rewards from each part of such an 'unbalanced' person's life would be variable and unpredictable, stress would result. People who exhibit such inconsistencies tend to be more receptive to social change than are those whose identities are more firmly rooted.

A related problem occurs when a person's social class standing creates expectations that are not met. Some people find themselves in the not unhappy position of making more money than is expected of those in their social class. This situation is known as an *overprivileged condition* and is usually defined as an income that is at least 25–30 per cent over the median for one's class.[45] In contrast, *underprivileged* consumers, who earn at least 15 per cent less than the median, must often devote their consumption priorities to sacrificing in order to maintain the appearance of living up to class expectations.

Lottery winners are examples of consumers who become overprivileged overnight. As attractive as winning is to many people, it has its problems. Consumers with a certain standard of living and level of expectations may have trouble adapting to sudden affluence and engage in flamboyant and irresponsible displays of wealth. Ironically, it is not unusual for lottery winners to report feelings of depression in the months after the win. They may have trouble adjusting to an unfamiliar world, and they frequently experience pressure from friends, relatives and business people to 'share the wealth'.

One New York winner who was featured prominently in the media is a case in point. He was employed as a mail porter until he won $5 million. After winning the lottery, he divorced his wife and married his girlfriend. She wore a $12,000 gown to the ceremony and the couple arrived in a horse-drawn carriage. Other purchases included a Cadillac with a Rolls-Royce grill and a $5,000 car phone. He later denied rumours that he was heavily in debt due to his extravagant spending.[46]

The traditional assumption is that husbands define a family's social class, while wives must live it. Women borrow their social status from their husbands.[47] Indeed, the evidence indicates that physically attractive women tend to 'marry up' to a greater extent than attractive men. Women trade the resource of sexual appeal, which historically has been one of the few assets they were allowed to possess, for the economic resources of men.[48] The accuracy of this assumption in today's world must be questioned. Many women now contribute equally to the family's well-being and work in positions of comparable or even greater status than their spouses. *Cosmopolitan* magazine offered this revelation: 'Women who've become liberated enough to marry any man they please, regardless of his social position, report how much more fun and spontaneous their relationships with men have become now that they no longer view men only in terms of their power symbols.'[49]

Employed women tend to average both their own and their husband's respective positions when estimating their own subjective status.[50] Nevertheless, a prospective spouse's social class is often an important 'product attribute' when evaluating alternatives in the interpersonal marketplace (as David and Julia were to find out). *Cosmopolitan* also discussed this dilemma, implying that social class differences are still an issue in the mating game: 'You've met the (almost) perfect man. You both adore Dashiell Hammett thrillers, Mozart, and tennis. He taught you to jet ski; you taught him the virtues of tofu

... The problem? You're an executive earning ninety-thousand dollars a year. He's a taxi driver ...'[51]

Problems with social class segmentation: a summary

Social class remains an important way to categorize consumers. Many marketing strategies do target different social classes. However, marketers have failed to use social class information as effectively as they could for the following reasons:

- They have ignored status inconsistency.
- They have ignored intergenerational mobility.
- They have ignored subjective social class (i.e. the class a consumer identifies with rather than the one he or she objectively belongs to).
- They have ignored consumers' aspirations to change their class standing.
- They have ignored the social status of working wives.

■ HOW SOCIAL CLASS AFFECTS PURCHASE DECISIONS

Different products and stores are perceived by consumers to be appropriate for certain social classes.[52] Working-class consumers tend to evaluate products in more utilitarian terms such as sturdiness or comfort rather than style or fashionability. They are less likely to experiment with new products or styles, such as modern furniture or coloured appliances.[53] In contrast, more affluent people tend to be concerned about appearance and body image, so they are more avid consumers of diet foods and drinks compared to people in small, working-class towns. These differences mean that the cola market, for example, can be segmented by social class.[54]

Class differences in worldview

A major social class difference involves the *worldview* of consumers. The world of the working class (including the lower-middle class) is more intimate and constricted. For example, working-class men are likely to name local sports figures as heroes and are less likely to take long holidays in out-of-the-way places.[55] Immediate needs, such as a new refrigerator or TV, tend to dictate buying behaviour for these consumers, while the higher classes tend to focus on more long-term goals, such as saving for college fees or retirement.[56]

Working-class consumers depend heavily on relatives for emotional support and tend to orient themselves in terms of the community rather than the world at large. They are more likely to be conservative and family oriented. Maintaining the appearance of one's home and property is a priority, regardless of the size of the house.

While they would like to have more in the way of material goods, working-class people do not necessarily envy those who rank above them in social standing.[57] The maintenance of a high-status lifestyle is sometimes not seen as worth the effort. As one blue-collar consumer commented: 'Life is very hectic for those people. There are more breakdowns and alcoholism. It must be very hard to sustain the status, the clothes, the parties that are expected. I don't think I'd want to take their place.'[58]

The blue-collar consumer quoted here may be right. While good things appear to go hand in hand with higher status and wealth, the picture is not that clear. The social scientist Emile Durkheim observed that suicide rates are much higher among the wealthy. He wrote in 1897, 'the possessors of most comfort suffer most'.[59] The quest for riches has the potential to result in depression, deviant behaviour and ruin. In fact, a survey of affluent American consumers (they made an average of $176,000 a year) supports this notion. Although these people are in the top 2.5 per cent income bracket in America, only 14 per cent said they are very well off.[60]

▶   The concept of a **taste culture**, which differentiates people in terms of their aesthetic and intellectual preferences, is helpful in understanding the important yet subtle distinctions in consumption choices among the social classes. Taste cultures largely reflect education (and are also income-related).[61] A distinction is often made between low-culture and high-culture groups (this is discussed in more detail in Chapter 16).

While such perspectives have met with criticism due to the implicit value judgements involved, they are valuable because they recognize the existence of groupings based on shared tastes in literature, art, home decoration and so on. In one of the classic studies of social differences in taste, researchers catalogued homeowners' possessions while asking more typical questions about income and occupation. Clusters of furnishings and decorative items which seemed to appear together with some regularity were identified, and different clusters were found depending on the consumer's social status. For example, religious objects, artificial flowers and still-life portraits tended to be found together in relatively lower-status living rooms, while a cluster containing abstract paintings, sculptures and modern furniture was more likely to appear in a higher-status home (see Figure 12.4).[62]

Another approach to social class focuses on differences in the types of *codes* (the ways meanings are expressed and interpreted by consumers) used within different social strata. Discovery of these codes is valuable to marketers, since this knowledge allows them to communicate to markets using concepts and terms most likely to be understood and appreciated by specific consumers.

▶   The nature of these codes varies among social classes. **Restricted codes** are dominant among the working class, while elaborated codes tend to be used by the middle and upper classes. Restricted codes focus on the content of objects, not on relationships

▶   among objects. **Elaborated codes**, in contrast, are more complex and depend upon a more sophisticated worldview. Some differences between these two general types of codes are provided in Table 12.1. As this table indicates, these code differences extend to the way consumers approach such basic concepts as time, social relationships and objects.

Marketing appeals that are constructed with these differences in mind will result in quite different messages. For example, a life insurance ad targeted at a lower-class person might depict in simple, straightforward terms a hard-working family man who feels good immediately after purchasing a policy. An upmarket appeal might depict a more affluent older couple surrounded by photos of their children and grandchildren and contain extensive copy emphasizing the satisfaction that comes from planning for the future and highlighting the benefits of a whole-life insurance policy.

Targeting the poor

While poor people obviously have less to spend than rich ones, they have the same basic needs as everyone else. Low-income families purchase such staples as milk, bread and tea at the same rates as average-income families. And minimum-wage level households spend a greater than average share on out-of-pocket health care costs, rent and food consumed at home. In 2001, certain household types in the EU-15 countries were more likely to be at risk of poverty: single parents with dependent children (these single parents are overwhelmingly female parents), young people living alone, old people living alone, and two-adult households with three or more dependent children.[63]

The unemployed do feel alienated in a consumer society, since they are unable to obtain many of the items that our culture tells us we 'need' to be successful. However, idealized advertising portrayals don't seem to appeal to low-end consumers who have been interviewed by researchers. Apparently, one way to preserve self-esteem is by placing oneself outside the culture of consumption and emphasizing the value of a simple

Table 12.1 Effects of restricted versus elaborated codes

	Restricted codes	Elaborated codes
General characteristics	Emphasize description and contents of objects Have implicit meanings (context dependent)	Emphasize analysis and interrelationships between objects, i.e. hierarchical organization and instrumental connections Have explicit meanings
Language	Use few qualifiers, i.e. few adjectives or adverbs Use concrete, descriptive, tangible symbolism	Have language rich in personal, individual qualifiers Use large vocabulary, complex conceptual hierarchy
Social relationships	Stress attributes of individuals over formal roles	Stress formal role structure, instrumental relationships
Time	Focus on present; have only general notion of future	Focus on instrumental relationship between present activities and future rewards
Physical space	Locate rooms, spaces in context of other rooms and places: e.g. 'front room', 'corner shop'	Identify rooms, spaces in terms of usage; formal ordering of spaces: e.g. 'dining room', 'financial district'
Implications for marketers	Stress inherent product quality, contents (or trustworthiness, goodness of 'real-type'), spokesperson Stress implicit fit of product with total lifestyle Use simple adjectives, descriptors	Stress differences, advantages vis-à-vis other products in terms of some autonomous evaluation criteria Stress product's instrumental ties to distant benefits Use complex adjectives, descriptors

Source: Adapted from Jeffrey F. Durgee, 'How Consumer Sub-Cultures Code Reality: A Look at Some Code Types', in Richard J. Lutz, ed., *Advances in Consumer Research* 13 (Provo, UT: Association for Consumer Research, 1986): 332.

way of life with less emphasis on materialism. In some cases, they enjoy the advertising as entertainment without actually yearning for the products; a comment by one 32-year-old British woman is typical: 'They're not aimed at me, definitely not. It's fine to look at them, but they're not aimed at me so in the main I just pass over them.'[64]

Some marketers are developing products and services for low-income consumers. These strategies may be obvious in some cases (or even bordering on the insulting), as when S.C. Johnson & Son, manufacturers of Raid insect spray, regularly hosts 'cockroach evictions' at inner-city housing developments. Other strategies raise important ethical issues, especially when marketers of so-called 'sin products' such as alcohol and tobacco single out what many feel is a vulnerable audience. For example, manufacturers of malt liquors and fortified wines concentrate their efforts in poor areas where they know their products sell best.

Targeting the rich

We live in an age where elite department stores sell Donna Karan and Calvin Klein Barbies, and Mattel's Pink Splendor Barbie comes complete with crystal jewellery and a bouffant gown sewn with 24-carat threads.[65] To dress that 'living doll', Victoria's Secret offers its Million Dollar Miracle Bra, with over 100 carats of real diamonds.[66] *Somebody* must be buying this stuff . . .

Many marketers try to target affluent markets. This practice often makes sense, since these consumers obviously have the resources to expend on costly products (often with higher profit margins). *The Robb Report*, a magazine targeted at the affluent (average reader income is $755,000), in 1996 estimated that 4.8 million American households had a net worth of at least $1 million, up 118 per cent from 1992. The magazine segments the wealthy into three markets: the marginally rich (household income $70,000–$99,999), the comfortably rich (income of $100,000–$249,000), and the super rich ($250,000+).[67]

However, it is a mistake to assume that everyone with a high income should be placed in the same market segment. As noted earlier, social class involves more than absolute income: it is also a way of life, and affluent consumers' interests and spending priorities are significantly affected by such factors as where they got their money, how they got it, and how long they have had it.[68] For example, the marginally rich tend to prefer sporting events to cultural activities, and are only half as likely as the super rich to frequent art galleries or the opera.[69]

The rich *are* different. But they are different from one another as well. Income alone is not a good predictor of consumer behaviour, which reminds us that the wealthy can be further segmented in terms of attitudes, values and preferences. For example, according to industry experts drivers in the luxury car market can be segmented as follows:

● Cadillac owners want to be chauffeured. They are not very attentive to styling details or the car's colour. Their primary interests are in comfort and the impression they make on others.

● Porsche owners prefer to drive themselves. They are more interested in performance than luxury. The colour red is a favourite.

● Jaguar owners are more austere. They are interested in elegance and prefer darker colours.

● Mercedes owners like to feel they are in control. They tend to prefer muted shades of tan, grey and silver.

multicultural dimensions

In a land where one-child families are the rule, Chinese parents spare few expenses when bringing up baby. They want to show off their pampered child and are eager to surround their 'little emperors' with status goods. To meet this need, foreign companies are rushing in, hawking the staples of Western baby care from disposable nappies to Disney cot sheets. These items are expensive luxuries in China, and plenty of families are splurging. Chinese families spend one-third to one-half of their disposable income on their children, according to industry estimates. The Disney Babies line of T-shirts, rattles and cot linens – all emblazoned with likenesses of baby Mickey Mouse and other familiar characters – are available in department stores in a dozen or so Chinese cities. These products are true extravagances: a Disney cotton T-shirt, for example, sells for the local equivalent of about $7.25-$8.45, compared to $1.20 for a Chinese-made shirt. But as a Disney spokesman observed, 'New parents are willing to pay the extra. Mickey is portrayed as fun and intelligent in China – characteristics parents want for their children.'[70]

Old money

When people have enough money for all intents and purposes to buy just about anything they want, ironically social distinctions no longer revolve around the amount of money they have. Instead, it appears to be important to consider *where* the money came from and *how* it is spent. The 'top out-of-sight class' (such as Julia's parents) live primarily on inherited money. People who have made vast amounts of money from their own labour do not tend to be included in this select group, though their flamboyant consumption patterns may represent an attempt to prove their wealth.[71] The mere presence of wealth is thus not sufficient to achieve social prominence. It must be accompanied by a family history of public service and philanthropy, which is often manifested in tangible markers that enable these donors to achieve a kind of immortality (e.g. Rockefeller University or the Whitney Museum).[72] 'Old money' consumers tend to make distinctions among themselves in terms of ancestry and lineage rather than wealth.[73] Old money people (like the Caldwells) are secure in their status. In a sense, they have been trained their whole lives to be rich.

The nouveaux riches

Other wealthy people do not know how to be rich. The Horatio Alger myth, where a person goes from 'rags to riches' through hard work and a bit of luck, is still a powerful force in Western society and, more recently, in Asian societies as well. Although many people do in fact become 'self-made millionaires', they often encounter a problem (although not the worst problem one could think of!) after they have become wealthy and have changed their social status: consumers who have achieved extreme wealth and have relatively recently become members of upper social classes are known as the *nouveaux riches*, a term that is sometimes used in a derogatory manner to describe newcomers to the world of wealth.

The *nouveau riche* phenomenon is also widespread in Russia and other eastern European countries, where the transition to capitalism has paved the way for a new class of wealthy consumers who are spending lavishly on luxury items. One study of wealthy Russians identified a group of 'super-spenders', who earn about $1,000 a month and spend as much on discretionary items as they do on rent. They would like to spend more money, but are frustrated by the lack of quality products and services available to them![74]

marketing opportunity

In a sixteenth-century fortress in Florence, the semi-annual Florence children's fashion show is on, and retail buyers from around the world are moving from one designer's booth to another, putting together their Spring lines. However, down in the basement, in an isolated booth, only buyers who have RSVP'd are allowed inside, and then only after entering a security code into a computer. Once in, they are served drinks in gold-rimmed goblets, and seated in gold chairs as they view video screens showing children playing and lounging in clothes that are elegant, understated, exquisitely detailed – and priced at hundreds of euros apiece. There are no actual clothes on display in the booth, nor order forms, nor any price lists. Such commercial touches are deemed *déclassé* by the creators of I Pinco Pallino.

'Definitely to my heart, our clothes are art,' says Stefano Cavalleri, the firm's 49-year-old founder. 'Extending our image is the key point, not selling more clothes.' But Pinco is indeed selling clothes. In a market where people have more money than ever and are always looking for new ways to spend it, Pinco is suddenly hot. These aren't children's clothes for everyone, not even among the rich. The target market: mothers who, in the words of the buyers thronging the Pinco booth, regard their children as 'fashion accessories'. The fashion house turns out some of the most expensive children's clothes available anywhere. A pale green organza dress embellished with hand-embroidered silk goes for 700 euros. Dressing a child in a complete Pinco ensemble – featuring jacket, handbag, shoes and hat in signature silks and laces with detailed embroidery and sequins – will run into well over 1,100 euros. Already selling his creations at only the most fashionable of department stores and boutiques in Europe and America, Mr Cavalleri is working on a plan to open a Pinco boutique on Manhattan's Upper East Side, where he vows to introduce New Yorkers to his 'fairy-tale world'.[75]

Alas, many *nouveaux riches* are plagued by *status anxiety*. They monitor the cultural environment to ensure that they are doing the 'right' thing, wearing the 'right' clothes, being seen in the 'right places', using the 'right' caterer, and so on.[76] Flamboyant consumption can thus be viewed as a form of symbolic self-completion, where the excessive display of symbols thought to denote 'class' is used to make up for an internal lack of assurance about the 'correct' way to behave.[77]

The 'Get Set'

While the possession of wealth is clearly an important dimension of affluence, this quality may be as much determined by attitudes towards consumption as it is by level of income. Some marketers have identified a consumer segment composed of well-off, but not rich, people who desire the best products and services, even though they may have to be more selective about those items they are able to buy. These consumers are realistic about what they can afford and prefer to sacrifice in some areas so that they can have the best in others. Various advertising and marketing research agencies have given this segment such labels as the *Influentials*, the *New Grown-Ups* and the *Get Set*.

While many upper-class brands tried in the past to downmarket themselves to attract the mass market, there are some indications that this strategy is reversing. Because of the Get Set's emphasis on quality, one scenario is that marketers will encourage the masses to 'buy up' into products associated with the upper classes, even if they are forced to buy less. A print campaign for Waterford Crystal exemplifies this approach. The theme line, 'Steadfast in a world of wavering standards', is calculated to appeal to consumers who desire authenticity and lasting value.[78]

■ STATUS SYMBOLS

People have a deep-seated tendency to evaluate themselves, their professional accomplishments, their material well-being and so on, in relation to others. The popular phrase 'keeping up with the Joneses' (in Japan it's 'keeping up with the Satos') refers to the comparison between one's standard of living and that of one's neighbours.

Satisfaction is a relative concept, however. We hold ourselves to a standard defined by others that is constantly changing. Unfortunately, a major motivation for the purchase and display of products is not to enjoy them, but rather to let others know that we can afford them. In other words, these products function as status symbols. The desire to accumulate these 'badges of achievement' is summarized by the slogan 'He who dies with the most toys, wins'. Status-seeking is a significant source of motivation to procure appropriate products and services that the user hopes will let others know that he or she has 'made it'.

Conspicuous consumption

The motivation to consume for the sake of consuming was first discussed by the social analyst Thorstein Veblen at the turn of the last century. Veblen felt that a major role of
▶ products was for **invidious distinction** – they are used to inspire envy in others through
▶ display of wealth or power. Veblen coined the term **conspicuous consumption** to refer to people's desire to provide prominent visible evidence of their ability to afford luxury goods. Veblen's work was motivated by the excesses of his time. He wrote in the era of the robber barons, where the likes of J.P. Morgan, Henry Clay Frick, William Vanderbilt and others were building massive financial empires and flaunting their wealth by throwing lavish parties. Some of these events of excess became legendary, as described in this account:

> there were tales, repeated in the newspapers, of dinners on horseback; of banquets for pet dogs; of hundred-dollar bills folded into guests' dinner napkins; of a hostess who attracted attention by seating a chimpanzee at her table; of centerpieces in which lightly clad living maidens swam in glass tanks, or emerged from huge pies; of parties at which cigars were ceremoniously lighted with flaming banknotes of large denominations.[79]

The trophy wife

This flaunting of one's possessions even extended to wives: Veblen criticized the 'decorative' role women were often forced to play as they were bestowed with expensive clothes, pretentious homes and a life of leisure as a way to advertise the wealth of their husbands – a sort of 'walking advertisement'. Such fashions as high-heeled shoes, tight corsets, billowing trains on dresses and elaborate hairstyles all conspired to ensure that wealthy women could barely move without assistance, much less perform manual labour. Similarly, the Chinese practice of foot-binding turned women into cripples who had to be carried from place to place.

The modern potlatch

Veblen was inspired by anthropological studies of the Kwakiutl Indians, who lived in the American Pacific Northwest. These Indians had a ceremony called a **potlatch**, a feast where the host showed off his wealth and gave extravagant presents to the guests. The more one gave away, the better one looked to the others. Sometimes, the host would use an even more radical strategy to flaunt his wealth. He would publicly destroy some of his property to demonstrate how much he had.

This ritual was also used as a social weapon: since guests were expected to reciprocate, a poorer rival could be humiliated by being invited to a lavish potlatch. The need to give away as much as the host, even though he could not afford it, would essentially force the hapless guest into bankruptcy. If this practice sounds 'primitive', think for a moment about many modern weddings. Parents commonly invest huge sums of money to throw a lavish party and compete with others for the distinction of giving their daughter the 'best' or most extravagant wedding, even if they have to save for 20 years to do so.

The leisure class

This process of conspicuous consumption was, for Veblen, most evident among what he termed the *leisure class*, people for whom productive work is taboo. In Marxist terms, this reflects a desire to link oneself to ownership or control of the means of production, rather than to the production itself. Any evidence that one actually has to work for a living is to be shunned, as suggested by the term the 'idle rich'.

Like the potlatch ritual, the desire to convince others that one has a surplus of resources creates the need for evidence of this abundance. Accordingly, priority is given to consumption activities that use up as many resources as possible in non-constructive pursuits. This *conspicuous waste* in turn shows others that one has the assets to spare. Veblen noted that 'we are told of certain Polynesian chiefs, who, under the stress of good form, preferred to starve rather than carry their food to their mouths with their own hands'.[80]

marketing opportunity

Consolidating for luxury

The luxury goods sector in Europe is in the midst of an important consolidation, as smaller groups find it increasingly difficult to compete with bigger rivals in terms of advertising spending, retail networks and production capacity. As a result, groups such as French luxury goods giant LVMH, Moet Hennessy and Gucci have been buying up smaller names over the past years. Perhaps the biggest 'fashion family' is LVMH, with its stable of fashion brands including Louis Vuitton, Christian Dior, Givenchy, Christian Lacroix, Celine, Loewe, Kenzo, Fendi and Emilio Pucci.

In an effort to take full control of production in order to maintain high standards of quality and to meet rigorous delivery schedules demanded by global retail customers, Giorgio Armani SpA recently established a joint venture with Italian menswear group Ermenegildo Zagna SpA to produce one of its menswear lines. As the wealthy become more attracted to yachting, the yachtmaker Swan has been bought by fashion house Leonardo Ferragamo to close the gap between high fashion and the high seas.[81]

The tanning salon industry may be said to owe its success to consumers' desire to pay for the illusion that they have idle time to soak up the sun.

The Advertising Archives

The death – and rebirth – of status symbols

While ostentatious products fell out of favour in the early part of the 1990s, later in the decade there was a resurgence of interest in luxury goods. European companies such as Hermes International, LVMH Hennesey Louis Vuitton and Baccarat enjoyed sales gains of between 13 and 16 per cent, as affluent consumers once again indulged their desires for the finer things in life. One market researcher termed this trend 'the pleasure revenge' – people were tired of buying moderately, eating low-fat foods and so on, and as a result sales boomed for self-indulgent products from fur coats to premium ice creams and caviar. As the Chairman of LVMH put it, 'The appetite for luxury is as strong as ever. The only difference is that in the 1980s, people would put a luxury trademark on anything. Today only the best sells.'[82]

Parody display

As the competition to accumulate status symbols escalates, sometimes the best tactic is to switch gears and go into reverse. One way to do this is to deliberately *avoid* status symbols – that is, to seek status by mocking it. This sophisticated form of conspicuous consumption has been termed **parody display**.[83] A good example of parody display is the home-furnishing style known as High Tech, which was in vogue in America a few years ago. This motif incorporated the use of industrial equipment (e.g. floors were covered with plates used on the decks of destroyers), and pipes and support beams were deliberately exposed.[84] This decorating strategy was intended to show that one is so witty and 'in the know' that status symbols aren't necessary. Hence, the popularity of old, torn blue jeans and 'utility' vehicles such as jeeps among the upper classes. 'True' status is thus shown by the adoption of product symbolism that is deliberately not fashionable.

CHAPTER SUMMARY

- The field of behavioural economics considers how consumers decide what to do with their money. In particular, *discretionary expenditures* are made only when people are able and willing to spend money on items above and beyond their basic needs. *Consumer confidence* – the state of mind consumers have about their own personal situation, as well as their feelings about their overall economic prospects – helps to determine whether they will purchase goods and services, take on debt or save their money.

- In the past ten years, consumers overall have been relatively pessimistic about their future prospects. A lower level of resources has caused a shift towards an emphasis on quality products that are reasonably priced. Consumers are less tolerant of exaggerated or vague product claims, and they are more sceptical about marketing activities. Consumers in their twenties are particularly sceptical about the economy and marketing targeted at their age group.

- A consumer's *social class* refers to his or her standing in society. It is determined by a number of factors, including education, occupation and income.

- Virtually all groups make distinctions among members in terms of relative superiority, power and access to valued resources. This *social stratification* creates a status hierarchy, where some goods are preferred over others and are used to categorize their owners' social class.

- While income is an important indicator of social class, the relationship is far from perfect since social class is also determined by such factors as place of residence, cultural interests and worldview.

- Purchase decisions are sometimes influenced by the desire to 'buy up' to a higher social class or to engage in the process of *conspicuous consumption*, where one's status is flaunted by the deliberate and non-constructive use of valuable resources. This spending pattern is a characteristic of the *nouveaux riches*, whose relatively recent acquisition of income, rather than ancestry or breeding, is responsible for their increased *social mobility*.

- Products are used as status symbols to communicate real or desired social class. *Parody display* occurs when consumers seek status by deliberately avoiding fashionable products.

▶ KEY TERMS

Behavioural economics (p. 428)
Conspicuous consumption (p. 447)
Consumer confidence (p. 430)
Discretionary income (p. 430)
Elaborated codes (p. 443)
Invidious distinction (p. 447)
Parody display (p. 449)
Potlatch (p. 448)
Restricted codes (p. 443)

Savings rate (p. 432)
Social class (p. 433)
Social hierarchies (p. 434)
Social mobility (p. 438)
Social stratification (p. 437)
Status crystallization (p. 441)
Status symbols (p. 428)
Taste culture (p. 443)

CONSUMER BEHAVIOUR CHALLENGE

1 The concepts *income* and *wealth* are measured in different ways throughout Europe, in spite of the standardization of currency that took place in 1999. Look through several recent issues of *Review of Income and Wealth* to get an idea of how these concepts differ across countries. For marketers, do you have any suggestions as to how to segment income groups for a European-wide strategy?

2 What are some of the obstacles to measuring social class in European society? Discuss some ways to get around these obstacles.

3 What consumption differences might you expect to observe between a family characterized as underprivileged vs. one whose income is average for its social class?

4 When is social class likely to be a better predictor of consumer behaviour than mere knowledge of a person's income?

5 How do you assign people to social classes, or do you at all? What consumption cues do you use (e.g. clothing, speech, cars, etc.) to determine social standing?

6 Thorstein Veblen argued that women were often used as a vehicle to display their husbands' wealth. Is this argument still valid today?

7 Given present environmental conditions and dwindling resources, what is the future of 'conspicuous waste'? Can the desire to impress others with affluence ever be eliminated? If not, can it take on a less dangerous form?

8 Some people argue that status symbols are dead. Do you agree?

9 Compile a list of occupations, and ask a sample of students who are studying a variety of subjects (both business and non-business) to rank the prestige of these jobs. Can you detect any differences in these rankings as a function of students' subjects?

10 Compile ads that depict consumers of different social classes. What generalizations can you make about the reality of these ads and about the media in which they appear?

11 Identify a current set of fraudulent status symbols, and construct profiles of consumers who are wearing or using these products. Are these profiles consistent with the images portrayed in each product's promotional messages?

12 The chapter observes that some marketers are finding 'greener pastures' by targeting low-income people. How ethical is it to single out consumers who cannot afford to waste their precious resources on discretionary items? Under what circumstances should this segmentation strategy be encouraged or discouraged?

NOTES

1. Fred van Raaij, 'Economic psychology', *Journal of Economic Psychology* 1 (1981): 1–24.
2. Peter S.H. Leeflang and W. Fred van Raaij, 'The changing consumer in the European Union: A meta-analysis', *International Journal of Research in Marketing* 12 (1995): 373–87.
3. Data in this section are adapted from Fabian Linden, *Consumer Affluence: The Next Wave* (New York: The Conference Board, Inc., 1994); 'Trends in households in the European Union: 1995–2025', *Eurostat, Statistics in Focus*, Theme 3–24/2003 (Luxembourg: Office for Official Publications of the European Communities, 2004).
4. 'Trends in households in the European Union: 1995–2025': 51.
5. 'Living conditions in Europe: Statistical pocketbook', Earnings and Income, *Eurostat* (Luxembourg: Office for Official Publications of the European Communities, 2000): 65.
6. 'Trends in households in the European Union: 1995–2025', 'Earnings of men and women': 80; see also Hugh Muir, 'Women in less than 10% of top jobs', *The Guardian* (5 January 2004), http://www.guardian.co.uk/gender/story/0,11812,1116127,00.html; Melissa Benn, 'Jobs for the Boys', *The Guardian* (5 January 2004).
7. 'Trends in households in the European Union: 1995–2025', 'Education and its outcomes': 44.
8. Christopher D. Carroll, 'How does future income affect current consumption?', *Quarterly Journal of Economics* 109 (February 1994) 1: 111–47.
9. 'Demographic statistics, 1997: Population and social conditions series', *Eurostat* (Luxembourg: Office for Official Publications of the European Communities, 1997). See also the Europa Server at: http://europa.eu.int.
10. Jose J.F. Medina, Joel Saegert and Alicia Gresham, 'Comparison of Mexican-American and Anglo-American attitudes toward money', *Journal of Consumer Affairs* 30(1) (1996): 124–45.
11. Kirk Johnson, 'Sit down. Breathe deeply. This is *really* scary stuff', *New York Times* (16 April 1995): F5. For a scale that measures consumer frugality, see John L. Lastovicka, Lance A. Bettencourt, Renee Shaw Hughner and Ronald J. Kuntze, 'Lifestyle of the tight and frugal: Theory and measurement', *Journal of Consumer Research* 26 (June 1999): 85–98.
12. Robert Sullivan, 'Americans and their money', *Worth* (June 1994): 60 (12).
13. 'Frontiers: Planning or consumer change in Europe 96/97', 2 (London: The Henley Centre, 1996).
14. George Katona, 'Consumer saving patterns', *Journal of Consumer Research* 1 (June 1974): 1–12.
15. 'Trends in households in the European Union: 1995–2025', 'What the EU citizens think about their living conditions': 127.
16. Ernest Beck, 'Why custom-made shirts are a cut above', *Wall Street Journal Europe* (4–5 April 1997): 8.
17. Floyd L. Ruch and Davidip G. Zimbardo, *Psychology and Life*, 8th edn (Glenview, IL: Scott, Foresman, 1971).
18. Louise Do Rosario, 'Privilege in China's classless society', *World Press Review* 33 (December 1986): 58.
19. Aditya Chakrabortty, 'Out with curry and Bollywood', *The Financial Times* (24 November 2004), http://news.ft.com/cms/s/54595ae4-3e4a-11d9-a9d7-00000e2511c8.html.
20. Jonathan H. Turner, *Sociology: Studying the Human System*, 2nd edn (Santa Monica, CA: Goodyear, 1981).
21. Ibid.
22. Richard P. Coleman, 'The continuing significance of social class to marketing', *Journal of Consumer Research* 10 (December 1983): 265–80; Turner, *Sociology*.
23. Ernest Beck, 'Cabin fever swirls around posh cottages on Norwegian coast', *Wall Street Journal Europe* (6 August 1997): 1.
24. Quoted by Richard P. Coleman and Lee Rainwater, *Standing in America: New Dimensions of Class* (New York: Basic Books, 1978): 89.
25. Ibid.
26. Turner, *Sociology*.
27. Nicholas D. Kristof, 'Women as bodyguards: In China, it's all the rage', *New York Times* (1 July 1993): A4.
28. James Sterngold, 'How do you define status? A new BMW in the drive. An old rock in the garden', *New York Times* (28 December 1989): C1.
29. Robin Knight, 'Just you move over, 'Enry 'Iggins: A new regard for profits and talent cracks Britain's old class system', *U.S. News & World Report* 106 (24 April 1989): 40.
30. Turner, *Sociology*: 260.
31. See Ronald Paul Hill and Mark Stamey, 'The homeless in America: An examination of possessions and consumption behaviors', *Journal of Consumer Research* 17 (December 1990): 303–21.
32. Joseph Kahl, *The American Class Structure* (New York: Holt, Rinehart & Winston, 1961).
33. Leonard Beeghley, *The Structure of Social Stratification in The United States*, 3rd edn (Allyn and Bacon, 2000).
34. Coleman and Rainwater, *Standing in America*: 220.
35. Turner, *Sociology*.
36. See Coleman, 'The continuing significance of social class to marketing'; Charles M. Schaninger, 'Social class versus income revisited: An empirical investigation', *Journal of Marketing Research* 18 (May 1981): 192–208.
37. Coleman, 'The continuing significance of social class to marketing'.
38. Bernard Dubois and Gilles Laurent, 'Is There a Euroconsumer for Luxury Goods?', in W. Fred van Raaij and Gary J. Bamossy, eds, *European Advances in Consumer Research* 1 (Provo, UT: Association for Consumer Research, 1993): 59–69; Bernard Dubois and Gilles Laurent, 'Luxury Possessions and Practices: An Empirical Scale', in F. Hansen, ed., *European Advances in Consumer Research* 2 (Provo, UT: Association for Consumer Research, 1995): 69–77; Bernard Dubois and Patrick Duquesne, 'The market for luxury goods: Income versus culture', *European Journal of Marketing* 27(1) (1993): 35–44.
39. August B. Hollingshead and Fredrick C. Redlich, *Social Class and Mental Illness: A Community Study* (New York: John Wiley, 1958).
40. John Mager and Lynn R. Kahle, 'Is the whole more than the sum of the parts? Re-evaluating social status in marketing', *Journal of Business Psychology*, in press.
41. R. Vanneman and F. C. Pampel, 'The American perception of class and status', *American Sociological Review* 42 (June 1977): 422–37.
42. Donald W. Hendon, Emelda L. Williams and Douglas E. Huffman, 'Social class system revisited', *Journal of Business Research* 17 (November 1988): 259.
43. Coleman, 'The continuing significance of social class to marketing'.

44. Gerhard E. Lenski, 'Status crystallization: A non-vertical dimension of social status', *American Sociological Review* 19 (August 1954): 405–12.

45. Richard P. Coleman, 'The Significance of Social Stratification in Selling', in *Marketing: A Maturing Discipline, Proceedings of the American Marketing Association 43rd National Conference*, ed. Martin L. Bell (Chicago: American Marketing Association, 1960): 171–84.

46. Melinda Beck and Richard Sandza, 'The lottery craze: Multimillion dollar prizes raise new concerns that the games prey on the poor', *Newsweek* (2 September 1985): 16; Rhoda E. McKinney, 'Has money spoiled the lottery millionaires?', *Ebony* (December 1988): 150.

47. E. Barth and W. Watson, 'Questionable assumptions in the theory of social stratification', *Pacific Sociological Review* 7 (Spring 1964): 10–16.

48. Zick Rubin, 'Do American women marry up?', *American Sociological Review* 33 (1968): 750–60.

49. Sue Browder, 'Don't be afraid to marry down', *Cosmopolitan* (June 1987): 236.

50. K.U. Ritter and L.L. Hargens, 'Occupational positions and class identifications of married working women: A test of the asymmetry hypothesis', *American Journal of Sociology* 80 (January 1975): 934–48.

51. Browder, 'Don't be afraid to marry down': 236.

52. J. Michael Munson and W. Austin Spivey, 'Product and brand-user stereotypes among social classes: Implications for advertising strategy', *Journal of Advertising Research* 21 (August 1981): 37–45.

53. Stuart U. Rich and Subhash C. Jain, 'Social class and life cycle as predictors of shopping behavior', *Journal of Marketing Research* 5 (February 1968): 41–9.

54. Thomas W. Osborn, 'Analytic techniques for opportunity marketing', *Marketing Communications* (September 1987): 49–63.

55. Coleman, 'The continuing significance of social class to marketing'.

56. Jeffrey F. Durgee, 'How Consumer Sub-Cultures Code Reality: A Look at Some Code Types', in Richard J. Lutz, ed., *Advances in Consumer Research* 13 (Provo, UT: Association for Consumer Research, 1986): 332–7.

57. David Halle, *America's Working Man: Work, Home, and Politics Among Blue-Collar Owners* (Chicago: University of Chicago Press, 1984); David Montgomery, 'America's working man', *Monthly Review* (1985): 1.

58. Quoted in Coleman and Rainwater, *Standing in America*: 139.

59. Durkheim (1958), quoted in Roger Brown, *Social Psychology* (New York: The Free Press, 1965).

60. Lenore Skenazy, 'Affluent, like masses, are flush with worries', *Advertising Age* (10 July 1989): 55.

61. Herbert J. Gans, 'Popular Culture in America: Social Problem in a Mass Society or Social Asset in a Pluralist Society?', in Howard S. Becker, ed., *Social Problems: A Modern Approach* (New York: Wiley, 1966); Helga Dittmar, 'Material possessions as stereotypes: Material images of different socio-economic groups', *Journal of Economic Psychology* 15 (1994): 561–85; Helga Dittmar and Lucy Pepper, 'To have is to be: Materialism and person perception in working class and middle class British adolescents', *Journal of Economic Psychology* 15 (1994): 233–5.

62. Edward O. Laumann and James S. House, 'Living room styles and social attributes: The patterning of material artifacts in a modern urban community', *Sociology and Social Research* 54 (April 1970): 321–42; see also Stephen S. Bell, Morris B. Holbrook and Michael R. Solomon, 'Combining esthetic and social value to explain preferences for product styles with the incorporation of personality and ensemble effects', *Journal of Social Behavior and Personality* (1991) 6: 243–74.

63. 'Trends in households in the European Union: 1995–2025' 'Low-income households': 70.

64. Quoted in Richard Elliott, 'How do the unemployed maintain their identity in a culture of consumption?', in Hansen, ed., *European Advances in Consumer Research* 2: 1–4, at 3.

65. Cyndee Miller, 'New Line of Barbie dolls targets big, rich kids', *Marketing News* (17 June 1996): 6.

66. Cyndee Miller, 'Baubles are back', *Marketing News* (14 April 1997): 1 (2).

67. Anita Sharpe, 'Magazines for the rich rake in readers', *Wall Street Journal* (16 February 1996): B1 (2).

68. 'Reading the Buyer's Mind', *U.S. News & World Report* (16 March 1987): 59.

69. Rebecca Piirto Heath, 'Life on easy street', *American Demographics* (April 1997): 33–8.

70. Quoted in 'Western companies compete to win business of Chinese babies', *Wall Street Journal Interactive Edition* (15 May 1998).

71. Paul Fussell, *Class: A Guide Through the American Status System* (New York: Summit Books, 1983): 29.

72. Elizabeth C. Hirschman, 'Secular immortality and the American ideology of affluence', *Journal of Consumer Research* 17 (June 1990): 31–42.

73. Coleman and Rainwater, *Standing in America*: 150.

74. M.H. Moore, 'Homing in on Russian "Super Spenders"', *Adweek* (28 February 1994): 14–16. See also: Carol Vogel, 'Fabergé collection bought by Russian for a return home', *The New York Times* (5 February 2004), http://www.nytimes.com/2004/02/05/arts/design/05FABE.html?th=&pagewanted=print&position.

75. Monica Langley, 'Italian firm fashions a look tailor-made for indulgent parents', *Wall Street Journal* (24 August 2000): A1.

76. Jason DeParle, 'Spy anxiety: The smart magazine that makes smart people nervous about their standing', *Washingtonian Monthly* (February 1989): 10.

77. For an examination of retailing issues related to the need for status, see Jacqueline Kilsheimer Eastman, Leisa Reinecke Flynn and Ronald E. Goldsmith, 'Shopping for status: The retail managerial implications', *Association of Marketing Theory and Practice* (Spring 1994): 125–30.

78. Dennis Rodkin, 'Wealthy attitude wins over healthy wallet: Consumers prove affluence is a state of mind', *Advertising Age* (9 July 1990): S4.

79. John Brooks, *Showing off in America* (Boston: Little, Brown, 1981): 13.

80. Thorstein Veblen, *The Theory of the Leisure Class* (1899; reprint, New York: New American Library, 1953): 45.

81. Teri Agins, 'Luxury match? LVMH targets Donna Karan', *Wall Street Journal* (19 December 2000): B1; Deborah Ball, 'High style on the high seas', *Wall Street Journal* (14 September 2000): B1; Deborah Ball, 'Italy's Finpart to acquire Cerruti, Gucci set to buy Zamasport Unit', *Wall Street Journal* (9 October 2000): B16.

82. Quoted in Miller, 'Baubles are back'; Elaine Underwood, 'Luxury's tide turns', *Brandweek* (7 March 1994): 18–22. See also Ball, 'Italy's Finpart to acquire Cerruti'.

83. Brooks, *Showing off in America*.

84. Ibid.: 31–2.

chapter 13

AGE SUBCULTURES

It's just a few months before winter weather really sets in, and Joost is lying on his bed 'channel surfing' on the TV and daydreaming about trying out his new ice-hockey skates on the frozen lakes near the flat where he and his father live in the suburbs of Amsterdam. His father tried to convince him to buy the classic 'hoge Noren' – black high-top touring skates with a long blade that have been 'classics' in Holland for decades, but Joost insisted on ice-hockey skates. His response was: 'Your skates are for middle-aged, old-fashioned skaters who are too serious about the whole thing. I want skates I can mess about in. Besides, these skates go well with my new Fila winter jacket.'

While Joost is switching from one channel to another, an advertisement for a skiing holiday comes on the screen and catches his limited attention. Images of 'extreme skiing' are mixed with scenes of young people sitting around a well-stocked breakfast table. Text appears at the bottom of the screen, instructing the viewer to go to the teletext page for more information. The entire advertisement lasts 15 seconds. Joost uses the remote control to switch to the teletext page, and scans the ski package offerings. Great! Ten days in Austria for just 415 euros. It includes round-trip bus transportation, twin rooms, half-board and nine days of ski passes. Before moving on to the next channel, he notes down the travel agent's website address. With the TV still on, he logs on to his computer and checks the website. He can book the trip on the Web. First, he needs to ask a few friends to see if they want to go during the Christmas break. Then he just needs his Dad's permission . . . and his credit card number.

■ AGE AND CONSUMER IDENTITY

The era in which a consumer grows up creates for that person a cultural bond with the millions of others born during the same time period. As we grow older, our needs and preferences change, often in unison with others who are close to our own age. For this reason, a consumer's age exerts a significant influence on his or her identity. All things being equal, we are more likely than not to have things in common with others of our own age. In this chapter, we'll explore some of the important characteristics of some key age groups, and consider how marketing strategies must be modified to appeal to diverse age subcultures.

Age cohorts: 'my generation'

▶ An **age cohort** consists of people of similar ages who have undergone similar experiences. They share many common memories about cultural heroes (e.g. Clint Eastwood vs. Brad Pitt, or Frank Sinatra vs. Kurt Cobain), important historical events (e.g. the 1968 student demonstrations in Paris vs. the fall of the Berlin Wall in 1989), and so on. Although there is no universally accepted way to divide people into age cohorts, each of us seems to have a pretty good idea of what we mean when we refer to 'my generation'.

Marketers often target products and services to one or more specific age cohorts. They recognize that the same offering will probably not appeal to people of different ages, nor will the language and images they use to reach them. In some cases separate campaigns are developed to attract consumers of different ages. For example, travel agencies throughout Europe target youth markets during the months of May and June for low-cost summer holidays to Mallorca, and then target middle-aged, more affluent consumers for the same destination during September and October. What differs in the two campaigns are the media used, the images portrayed and the prices offered.

Choosing for 'hockey'-style ice skates goes well beyond just product and price considerations. Review this chapter's opening consumer vignette for the more complete picture of the complex choice processes of teens.
Photo: Gary Bamossy

The appeal of nostalgia

Because consumers within an age group confront crucial life changes at roughly the same time, the values and symbolism used to appeal to them can evoke powerful feelings of nostalgia (see Chapter 3). Adults aged 30+ are particularly susceptible to this phenomenon.[1] However, young people as well as old are influenced by references to their past. In fact, research indicates that some people are more disposed to be nostalgic than others, regardless of age. A scale that has been used to measure the impact of nostalgia on individual consumers appears in Table 13.1.

Table 13.1 The nostalgia scale

Scale items
• They don't make 'em like they used to.
• Things used to be better in the good old days.
• Products are getting shoddier and shoddier.
• Technological change will ensure a brighter future (reverse coded).
• History involves a steady improvement in human welfare (reverse coded).
• We are experiencing a decline in the quality of life.
• Steady growth in GNP has brought increased human happiness (reverse coded).
• Modern business constantly builds a better tomorrow (reverse coded).

Note: Items are presented on a nine-point scale ranging from strong disagreement (1) to strong agreement (9), and responses are summed.

Source: Morris B. Holbrook and Robert M. Schindler, 'Age, sex, and attitude toward the past as predictors of consumers' aesthetic tastes for cultural products', *Journal of Marketing Research* 31 (August 1994): 416.

Chapter 3 noted that product sales can be dramatically affected by linking a brand to vivid memories and experiences, especially for items that are associated with childhood or adolescence. Vespa scooters, Hornby electric trains and the coupon 'saving points' from Douwe Egberts coffee are all examples of products that have managed to span two or more generations of loyal consumers, giving the brand a strong equity position in competitive and crowded markets.

Many advertising campaigns have played on the collective memories of consumers by using older celebrities to endorse their products, such as American Express's campaign which featured Eric Clapton and Lou Reed. In Japan, Ringo Starr (the Beatles' drummer) is used to help promote demand for apples. The target market is middle-aged consumers, and it doesn't hurt that, phonetically, 'Ringo' means *apple* in Japanese. To assess just how pervasive nostalgia is, pay attention to television commercials, and notice how often they are produced against a background of 'classic songs'. *Memories* magazine, which was founded to exploit the nostalgia boom, even offers advertisers a discount if they run old ads next to their current ones.

■ THE TEEN MARKET: IT TOTALLY RULES

With a spending capacity of more than 61 billion euros per year, the European youth market of teens is a powerful demographic and an important culture to understand intimately for businesses looking to grow and maintain relevancy in the future. In 1956, the label 'teenage' first entered the (American) vocabulary, as Frankie Lymon and the Teenagers became the first pop group to identify themselves with this new subculture. The concept of teenager is a fairly new cultural construction; throughout most of history a person simply made the transition from child to adult (often accompanied by some sort of ritual or ceremony, as we'll see in a later chapter). The magazine *Seventeen*, launched in 1944, was based on the revelation that young women didn't want to look just like their mothers. In the early 1960s, the teenage drama between rebellion and conformity began to unfold, pitting Elvis Presley with his greased hair and suggestive hip swivels against more 'parentally approved' types such as Cliff Richard. Now this rebellion is played out by being detached from the adult world, as exemplified by teen idols like hip-hop star Eminem or the confused, sullen teenagers appearing daily on Ricki Lake, Jerry Springer and other daytime talk shows which are broadcast on European satellite networks.[2]

Teen values and conflicts

As anyone who has been there knows, puberty and adolescence can be both the best of times and the worst of times. Many exciting changes happen as individuals leave the role of child and prepare to assume the role of adult. These changes create a lot of uncertainty about the self, and the need to belong and to find one's unique identity as a person becomes extremely important. At this age, choices of activities, friends and 'looks' are crucial to social acceptance. Teenagers actively search for cues from their peers and from advertising for the 'right' way to look and behave. Advertising geared to teenagers is typically action-oriented and depicts a group of 'in' teenagers using the product. Teenagers use products to express their identities, to explore the world and their new-found freedom in it, and also to rebel against the authority of their parents and other socializing agents. Joost's rejection of his father's suggestion to buy 'classic' skates, and his choice of ice-hockey skates which fashionably matched his Fila jacket, are mild expressions of these sorts of expressive consumption behaviours. Marketers often do their best to assist in this process. The range of consumer products targeted at teenagers (and particularly young ones) is greater than ever. Then again, so is teenagers' disposable income from part-time jobs and weekly pocket money.[3]

Teenagers in every culture grapple with fundamental developmental issues as they make the transition from childhood to adult. According to research by Saatchi & Saatchi, there are four themes of conflict common to all teens:

1 *Autonomy vs. belonging.* Teenagers need to acquire independence so they try to break away from their families. On the other hand, they need to attach themselves to a support structure, such as peers, to avoid being alone. A thriving internet subculture has developed to serve this purpose, as has text messaging via mobile phones.[4] The net (World Wide Web) has become the preferred method of communication for many young people, since its anonymity makes it easier to talk to people of the opposite sex, or of different ethnic and racial groups.[5]

2 *Rebellion vs. conformity.* Teenagers need to rebel against social standards of appearance and behaviour, yet they still need to fit in and be accepted by others. Cult products that cultivate a rebellious image are prized for this reason. Skeleteens, a line of natural soft drinks in flavours like Brain Wash, Black Lemonade and DOA, developed such a following thanks to its 'dangerous' mystique. This underground product was first discovered by California bikers in America, who were drawn to the images of skulls and crossbones on the labels.[6]

3 *Idealism vs. pragmatism.* Teenagers tend to view adults as hypocrites, while they see themselves as being sincere. They have to struggle to reconcile their view of how the world should be with the realities they perceive around them.

4 *Narcissism vs. intimacy.* Teenagers can be obsessed with their appearance and needs. On the other hand, they also feel the desire to connect with others on a meaningful level.[7]

Teenagers throughout history have had to cope with insecurity, parental authority and peer pressure. At the start of the new millennium, however, these issues are compounded by concerns about the environment, racism, AIDS and other pressing social problems. Today's teenagers often have to cope with additional family responsibilities as well, especially if they live in non-traditional families where they must take significant responsibility for shopping, cooking and housework. Marketers have a difficult time 'defining' the values of today's European teens, perhaps because they are living in such socially dynamic and demanding times. A study among 500 young opinion leaders aged 14–20 across 16 European countries suggests that this age group's credo should be: 'don't define us – we'll define ourselves'. Respondents were asked their opinions on a wide range of subjects, from new technology to family relationships, divorce, drugs, alcohol, politics, fashion, entertainment, sex and advertising. Some of the highlights of this study[8] are:

Teenagers in every culture grapple with personal and social issues as they make the transition from childhood to adulthood. What better way to work through issues than together, at the snack bar!

Photo: Gary Bamossy

- Living life to the 'fullest' is mandatory; ambition drives them, as does the fear of failure. Young eastern Europeans strongly believe that hard work will give them a high standard of living and education is their passport to this better life.

- They perceive the 'digitized' future as one that lacks warmth – something Europe's teenagers, a divorce-experienced generation, is actively seeking.

- New technology which allows for '24-hour commerce' will lead to further stress for this generation, and a blurring of home/office means they will work longer and harder than any previous generation.

- The phone at home is still a central method for teens to talk to each other, although mobile phones are quickly penetrating this group's social network.

- This is a very visually literate generation, with clear understanding of a commercial's aims. Clichés will not be tolerated, and will lead to immediate rejection, particularly in the Nordic countries. Only eastern European teens have yet to achieve this level of 'advertising cynicism'.

- This generation is both brand-aware and brand-dismissive. It represents an opportunity, but not a homogeneous market. The successful marketer will be aware that for these consumers, an aspirational quality is essential, that heritage is an advantage, and that nothing is forever.

multicultural dimensions

Teen rebellion is a new phenomenon in Japan, a country known for rigid conformity and constant pressure to succeed. Now more and more teenagers are questioning the rules. The drop-out rate among students in junior and senior high school increased by 20 per cent in a two-year period. More than 50 per cent of girls have had intercourse by their senior year of high school.[9]

Japanese youth are very style-conscious, and currently there are several niches or 'tribes', each with very well-defined looks and rules.[10] A popular look for Japanese girls is called the 'Gals': they are easily recognized by their bleached yellow hair, salon-tanned skin, chalk-white lipstick and 7-inch platform heels. Other groups include the Sports Clique (low-heeled Air Mocs and Gap clothing) and the Back-Harajuku Group (baggy sweatshirts, colourful jeans, sneakers (trainers) and long scarves).

To try to win the loyalty of young consumers in Japan, five big companies including Toyota, Matsushita and Asahi Breweries formed a marketing alliance. They are introducing a range of products, from beer to refrigerators, all with the same brand name of 'Will' (yes, Will). Critics are not sure the plan will work because these companies as of now do not have very modern images, so only time will tell if this ambitious plan Will or won't.[11]

Appealing to the teen market

Consumers in this age subculture have a number of needs, including experimentation, belonging, independence, responsibility and approval from others. Product usage is a significant medium to express these needs. Because they are so interested in many different products and have the resources to obtain them, the teen market is avidly courted by many marketers. Much of this money goes towards 'feel-good' products – cosmetics, posters and fast food – with the occasional body piercing thrown in as well.

Because today's teenagers were raised on TV and they tend to be much more canny than older generations, marketers must tread lightly when they try to reach them. This gadget-loving, fashion-conscious generation is also considered the most materialistic generation of youngsters in history. In the UK alone, this group has the fastest-rising spending power on the high street, between £600 million and £1 billion a year. They watch 22,000 TV adverts a year, receive about £11–12 (16–18 euros) spending allowance a week and are thought to have a direct influence on 60 per cent of all parental expenditure.[12] As Joost illustrated with his five minutes of information-gathering on TV, teletext and the internet, teenagers in Europe have increasingly complex media consumption habits, and are acknowledged as being more advertising-literate. In particular, the messages must be seen as authentic and not condescending. In spite of teenagers' more critical evaluation of television advertising, there is no doubt that TV adverts have a clear influence on their purchases.

Marketers view teenagers as 'consumers-in-training', since brand loyalty is developed during this age. A teenager who is committed to a brand may continue to purchase it for many years to come. Such loyalty creates a barrier to entry for other brands that were not chosen during these pivotal years. Thus, advertisers sometimes try to 'lock in' consumers to certain brands so that they will buy these brands in the future more or less automatically. As one teen magazine ad director observed, 'We . . . always say it's easier to start a habit than stop it.'[13]

marketing opportunity

Pre-teen girls are a major market unto themselves. Marketers use the term *tweens* to describe the 20+ million children aged 8–14 who spend $14 billion euros a year on clothes, CDs, films and other 'feel-good' products. Limited Too sells mostly to 10- and 11-year-old girls and now mails a catalogue directly to pre-teen girls rather than to their parents. Not surprising, since pre-teen girls buy over $4.5 billion of clothing a year. Limited Too is developing make-up products targeted at this age segment as well, featuring fragrances like Sugar Vanilla and Snow Musk.[14]

Tweens are 'between' childhood and adolescence and exhibit characteristics of both age groups.[15] As one tween commented, 'When we're alone we get weird and crazy and still act like kids. But in public we act cool, like teenagers.' This age group drove the success of films like *Titanic* and boy groups like 'N Sync – they account for about 9 per cent of all CD sales.[16] They like to talk on the phone and in chat rooms, they squeal and shout when the Backstreet Boys take the stage – and they've definitely got marketers' attention.

For example, Kodak made a $75 million, five-year commitment to convince tween girls to buy its single-use Kodak Max cameras. According to internal research, this segment is 50 per cent more likely than boys of the same age to own a camera. When girls were asked to name their most prized possession, 15 per cent said photographs, while only 4 per cent of their male counterparts put photos at the top of their lists. Kodak discovered that a majority of girls keep journals, collect quotes and maintain online bulletin boards, and the company is betting that this desire to share experiences with friends will turn into a picture-perfect marketing strategy.[17]

Shown here are two collages representing images of 'cool'. One collage was put together by a European and one by an American. Can you tell which is which? One person is male, the other female. Any predictions here?

Photo: Gary Bamossy

Teenagers also exert a strong influence on the purchase decisions of their parents (see Chapter 11).[18] In addition to providing 'helpful' advice to parents, teenagers are increasingly buying products on behalf of the family. As discussed in Chapter 11, mothers are most likely to return to the workforce (most often to part-time work) once the children in the household are at school and have become more independent.[19]

Researching the youth market

Research firms are coming up with innovative ways to tap the desires of teens, many of whom don't respond well to traditional survey techniques. Sometimes respondents are given a video camera and are asked to record a 'typical' day at school – along with play-by-play commentary to help interpret what's going on. Greenfield Consulting Group uses what it calls the 'teen-as-creative-director' technique. The firm gives teens camcorders and asks them to complete a two-part creative assignment that will be judged by their peers. A typical task is to create a video collage of the 'coolest/hippest/whatever-est' things they can find and write a song/poem/story that describes what 'cool/hip' is all about. After the teens complete their assignments, they present their work to each other at a focus group facility, judge the work collectively, and award cash prizes to the creators of the best video and song/poem/story.

A recent study asked young people in the United States and the Netherlands to write essays about what is 'cool' and 'uncool'.[20] The researchers found that being cool has several meanings, though there were a lot of similarities between the two cultures when kids use this term. Some of the common dimensions include having charisma, being in control and being a bit aloof. And many of the respondents agreed that being cool is a moving target: the harder you try to be cool, the more uncool you are! Some of their actual responses are listed here:

- 'Cool means being relaxed, to nonchalantly be the boss of every situation, and to radiate that' (Dutch female).
- 'Cool is the perception from others that you've got "something" which is macho, trendy, hip, etc.' (Dutch male).
- 'Cool has something stand-offish, and at the same time, attractive' (Dutch male).
- 'Being different, but not too different. Doing your own thing, and standing out, without looking desperate while you're doing it' (American male).
- 'When you are sitting on a terrace in summer, you see those machos walk by, you know, with their mobile [phones] and their sunglasses. I always think, "Oh please, come back to earth!" These guys only want to impress. That is just so uncool' (Dutch female).
- 'When a person thinks he is cool, he is absolutely uncool' (Dutch female).
- 'To be cool we have to make sure we measure up to it. We have to create an identity for ourselves that mirrors what we see in magazines, on TV, and with what we hear on our stereos' (American male).

■ BABY BUSTERS: 'GENERATION X'

The cohort of consumers between the ages of 18 and 29 consists of over 30 million Europeans who will be a powerful force in years to come. This group, which has been labelled 'Generation X', 'slackers' or 'busters', was profoundly affected by the economic downturn in the first part of the 1990s. So-called baby busters include many people, both in and out of higher education, whose tastes and priorities are beginning to be felt in fashion, popular culture, politics and marketing. While the percentage of Europeans aged 25–29 is high in terms of completing upper secondary education (71 per cent in

1999, compared with 50 per cent of persons aged 50–59), this group also has a large drop-out rate, with one in five Europeans between the ages of 18 and 24 leaving the education system without completing a qualification beyond lower secondary schooling.[21] Even the World Bank is sensitive to targeting this group of future policy-makers in a vernacular they can relate to. Their Public Service Advertisement for World Hunger Day, which was broadcast by MTV in North America and Europe, was very 'Gen-X'. Images flashed by of the globe, babies, food, war, fluorescent bananas and attractive young people gazing at the camera, backed by a beat with a jazz infusion and ending with words in distinctive type: 'The World Bank. Knowledge and resources for change'.[22]

Marketing to busters or marketing bust?

Although the income of this age cohort is below expectations, they still constitute a formidable market segment – partly because so many still live at home and have more discretionary income. Busters in their twenties are estimated to have an annual spending power of $125 billion, and their purchases are essential to the fortunes of such product categories as beer, fast food and cosmetics.

Because many busters have been doing the family shopping for a long time, marketers are finding that they are much more sophisticated about evaluating advertising and products. They are turned off by advertising that either contains a lot of hype or takes itself too seriously. They see advertising as a form of entertainment but are turned off by overcommercialization.[23] As the Vice-President of Marketing for MTV put it, 'You must let them know that you know who they are, that you understand their life experiences. You want them to feel you're talking directly to them.'[24]

Nike took a soft-sell approach to woo younger buyers of its athletic shoes. Its ads show little of the product, focusing instead on encouraging readers to improve themselves through exercise. Other ads make fun of advertising: an ad created for a Maybelline eye shadow depicts supermodel Christy Turlington coolly posing in a glamorous setting. She then suddenly appears on her living room couch, where she laughs and says 'Get over it'.

One of the more successful commercials created specifically for this group was from a bank! Qualitative market research by Midland Bank (now HSBC) showed that money was one of university students' major worries. Its series of TV ads featuring Sam, 'a new student', was humorous but avoided being patronizing. It also aimed to emphasize Midland's claim that it offered the best and cheapest deals. The message was reinforced by a no-nonsense PR campaign on student financing which received 25 editorial mentions in national publications. The success of the campaign took Midland to market leadership in this segment.[25]

Perhaps one reason why marketers' efforts to appeal to Xers with messages of alienation, cynicism and despair have not succeeded is that many people in their twenties aren't depressed after all! Generation Xers are quite a diverse group – they don't all wear reversed baseball caps and work in temporary, low-paid mindless jobs. Despite the birth of dozens of magazines catering to 'riot grrrls' and other angry Xers with names like *Axcess*, *Project X* and *KGB*, the most popular magazine for 20-something women is *Cosmopolitan*. What seems to make this age cohort the angriest is constantly being labelled as angry by the media![26]

The advertising agency Saatchi & Saatchi sent teams of psychologists and cultural anthropologists into the field to study the buster subculture. These researchers identified four key segments:

1 *Cynical disdainers*: The most pessimistic and sceptical about the world.
2 *Traditional materialists*: The most like baby boomers in their thirties and forties, these young people are upbeat, optimistic about the future, and actively striving for what they continue to view as the desire for material prosperity.

3 *Hippies revisited*: This group tends to espouse the non-materialistic values of the 1960s. Their priorities are expressed through music, retro fashion and a strong interest in spirituality.

4 *Fifties machos*: These consumers tend to be young conservatives. They believe in stereo-typed gender roles, are politically conservative and are the least accepting of multi-culturalism.[27]

marketing pitfall

'A name that is not just memorable but also quickly articulates a brand's personality is essential in the tobacco market, where marketing options have been increasingly curtailed. Now, as UK legislators ponder a clampdown on the promotion of alcoholic drink, especially when it appeals to young people, newcomer Easy Drinking Whisky Company is putting this to the test.

EDWC has created JMR, a brand aimed at 20-to-30-year-olds, a younger audience than whisky traditionally attracts. The brand's personal touch extends to light-hearted snapshots of the founders on all product labels. Packaging design eschews the traditional whisky imagery of dark colours, heathers and tweed in favour of contemporary graphics. The descriptive product names are also designed to distinguish JMR's three new whiskies – *Rich Spicey*, *Smooth Sweeter* and *Smokey Peaty* – away from traditional brand names. Smooth Sweeter is JMR's entry-level product, promising the easiest taste for the Scotch novice.

JMR is on sale in 220 Oddbins retail stores across the UK. In the UK, Oddbins is a natural fit as it is a youthful retail brand that encourages staff to make personal recommendations. Live events will also be essential to drive brand awareness internationally through product sampling. Without the budget to compete with established brands such as Glenfiddich, EDWC is relying on brand personality and publicising the ethos behind the business.

'Easy Drinking Whisky Company promotional strategy is that of challenging the approach to whisky distilling, marketing and promotion taken by established distilleries.' The company has set out to create whisky that is more accessible to people like the three founders – all in their early 30s – and to demystify malt whisky, which is currently positioned by the big distilleries as a drink for connoisseurs. Most whisky drinkers are aged 40-plus. EDWC is targeting 25-to-45-year-olds. The palate of younger drinkers naturally creates a preference for sweeter drinks such as alcopops.

Other reasons that younger people do not drink whisky include perceptions of it as a 'dad's drink', conventional malt whisky marketing that alienates younger consumers and a price that tends to be higher than 'easier' alternatives such as vodka. EDWC is pricing its whiskies below the market average. The company hopes its approach to advertising will keep JMR out of the line of sight of UK legislators now considering a further tightening of alcohol marketing regulation to combat excessive alcohol consumption, particularly among young adults and teenagers. Drinks industry observers, however, believe that a fine balancing act is required if drinkers aged 20 to 30 are to be won without the brand also appealing to teenagers.'[28]

■ BABY BOOMERS

▶ The **baby boomers** are the source of many fundamental cultural and economic changes. The reason: power in numbers. As the Second World War ended, they began to establish families and careers at a record pace. Imagine a large python that has swallowed a mouse: the mouse moves down the length of the python, creating a moving bulge as it goes. So it is with baby boomers. In 2003 there were 74 million elderly people aged 65 and over in the EU-25 countries, compared with only 38 million in 1960. The baby boomers' ageing, coupled with extended longevity, and the overall lower fertility levels in the EU means that the population will continue to grow older for the coming decades.[29]

Figure 13.1 Demographic trends by age group, EU-15, 1980–2020

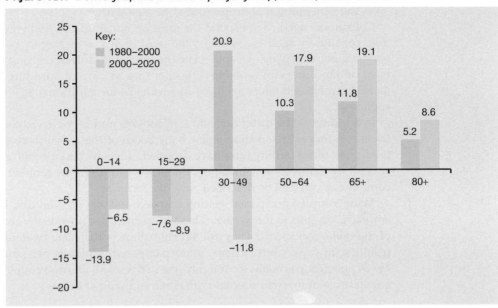

Source: Eurostat - *Demographic Statistics*, Figure 12, Eurostat © European Communities, and 1999-based demographic projections.

The cultural impact of boomers

Figure 13.1 shows the projections of the European population for both youth and boomers for a 60-year period. This increase in the proportion of older citizens and decrease in the proportion of youth is often referred to as the 'greying and de-greening' of the European population, a structural trend which has major implications for the marketing of goods and services.

As teenagers in the 1960s and 1970s, this generation created a revolution in style, politics and consumer attitudes. As they have aged, their collective will has been behind cultural events as diverse as the Paris student demonstrations and hippies in the 1960s and Thatcherism and yuppies in the 1980s. Now that they are older, they continue to influence popular culture in important ways.

Economic power: he who pays the piper, calls the tune

Because of the size and buying power of the boomer group over the last 20 years, marketers focused most of their attention on the youth market. The popular slogan at the time, 'Don't trust anyone over thirty', also meant that people over 30 had trouble finding products appropriate to their age groups. Times have changed, and again it is the baby boomers who have changed them. For example, boomers tend to have different emotional and psychological needs from those who came before them. Domain, a high-fashion furniture chain, found that its core boomer clientele is as concerned about self-improvement as it is about home decor. The company launched a series of in-store seminars dealing with themes like women's issues and how to start a business, and found its repeat business doubled.[30]

This 'mouse in the python' has moved into its mid-thirties to fifties, and this age group is now the one that exerts the most impact on consumption patterns. Most of the growth in the market will be accounted for by people who are moving into their peak earning years. As one commercial for VH1, the music-video network that caters to those who are a bit too old for MTV, pointed out, 'The generation that dropped acid to escape reality . . . is the generation that drops antacid to cope with it.'

Consumers aged 35–44 spend the most on housing, cars and entertainment. In addition, consumers aged 45–54 spend the most of any age category on food, clothing and personal pension plans. To appreciate the impact middle-aged consumers have and will have on the European economy, consider this: at current spending levels, a 1 per cent increase in householders aged 35–54 results in an additional $8.9 billion in consumer spending.

In addition to the direct demand for products and services created by this age group, these consumers are creating a new baby boom of their own to keep marketers busy in the future. Since fertility rates have dropped, this new boom is not as big as the one that created the baby boom generation: the new upsurge in the number of children born in comparison can best be described as a *baby boomlet*.

Many couples postponed getting married and having children because of the new emphasis on careers for women. These consumers are now beginning to hear the ticking of the biological 'clock'. They are having babies in their late twenties and early thirties, resulting in fewer (but perhaps more pampered) children per family. Couples in the 25–34 age group account for roughly one in five of all married couples in Europe, but for one in three of married couples with children living at home.

**marketing
opportunity**

Beer: a matter of taste, or age?

'In one of his rare rhetorical flourishes, former Prime Minister John Major once proclaimed that Britain would remain a land of 'dog lovers, invincible green suburbs, and warm beer'. Today, the dogs still roam the leafy suburbs, but warm ales, long a symbol of British beer-drinking habits, are no longer 'cool'.

'Drink ice cold' instructs the new bottle for Worthington ale, a venerable British beer. T&R Theakston Ltd, renowned for such traditional tipples as Old Peculier, is rolling out an ale called Cool Cask, served at 50 °F, compared with a typical 54 °–56 °F for traditional British ales. Far bolder, Guinness Ltd promotes an alternative version of its stout called Guinness Extra Cold, poured from the tap at 39 °F, about the same as US-style lagers. Partisans of traditional ales are appalled. 'You might as well just serve water', says Mick Lewis, 49 years old, and chairman of the North London branch of the Campaign for Real Ale, whose members drown their sorrows the old-fashioned way.

Beer marketers, however, see more future in people like Alec Skelton. This 29-year-old British lawyer, dapper in rectangular glasses and a sleek charcoal-grey suit, glides to the bar at the Old Bell, a 330-year-old pub on Fleet Street. The offerings include Brakspear and Timothy Taylor Landlord, two revered English ales, hand pumped from the cellar. Mr Skelton doesn't hesitate: he calls for a cold bottle of Budweiser. 'I like the cool, crisp taste', he says. He also likes the image. In his mind, ale stands for a 'slightly older generation, family, countryside', while Bud is hip and urban. The clincher, perhaps, is that Mr Skelton's father drinks ale, and even brews it at home.

In the past, British beer seemed warm only to foreigners. Usually, it was served at least a few degrees below room temperature, a habit formed in the days before refrigeration, when beer was stored in cellars. But the average temperature of beer in the UK has been falling gradually for decades. Why this national cooling? The British have been steadily switching from ale to lager, the cold, golden style of beer that predominates in most parts of the world. In 1960 lager accounted for just 1 per cent of the British beer market. In 2000, lager's share was 62 per cent – a testament to decades of heavy advertising for foreign brands such as Budweiser, Stella Artois and Foster's. Once young drinkers get used to cold beer, they often find their fathers' ale too warm to be refreshing.'[31]

■ THE GREY MARKET

The old widowed woman sits alone in her clean but sparsely furnished apartment, while the television blares out a soap opera. Each day, she slowly and painfully makes her way out of the apartment and goes to the corner shop to buy essentials, bread, milk and vegetables, always being careful to pick the least expensive offering. Most of the time she sits in her rocking chair, thinking sadly of her dead husband and the good times she used to have.

Is this the image you have of a typical elderly consumer? Until recently, many marketers did. As a result, they largely neglected the elderly in their feverish pursuit of the baby boomer market. But as our population ages and people are living longer and healthier lives, the game is rapidly changing. A lot of businesses are beginning to replace the old stereotype of the poor recluse. The newer, more accurate image is of an elderly person who is active, interested in what life has to offer, and is an enthusiastic consumer with the means and willingness to buy many goods and services.

Grey power: shattering stereotypes

By the year 2010, 20 per cent of Europeans will be 62 or older. This fastest-growing age segment can be explained by the ageing of 'boomers', an increase in awareness of healthy lifestyles and nutrition, coupled with improved medical diagnoses and treatment. Over the past 50 years, life expectancy of men and women has risen steadily: by around 10 years for each sex. Throughout the European Union, women live longer than men. In

Saga Magazine is the UK's biggest selling monthly magazine exclusively for people aged 50 and over.
Courtesy of Saga Magazine

1998 the life expectancy of women in the EU-15 countries was 81 years, while that for men was 75. Estimates are that the life expectancy of women and men may reach 84 and 78 years respectively by the year 2020.[32] Not only is this segment growing and living longer, but older adults have large amounts of discretionary income, since they typically have paid off their mortgage, and no longer have the expense of raising and educating children.

Most elderly people lead more active, multidimensional lives than we assume. Many engage in voluntary work, continue to work and/or are involved in daily care of a grandchild. Still, outdated images of mature consumers persist. In one survey, one-third of consumers over age 55 reported that they deliberately did *not* buy a product because of the way an elderly person was stereotyped in the product's advertising.[33]

Seniors' economic clout

There is abundant evidence that the economic health of elderly consumers is good and getting better. Some of the important areas that stand to benefit from the surging **grey market** include holidays, cars, home improvements, cruises and tourism, cosmetic surgery and skin treatments, health, finance and legal matters, and 'how-to' books for learning to cope with retirement.

It is crucial to remember that income alone does not capture the spending power of this group. As mentioned above, elderly consumers are no longer burdened with the financial obligations that drain the income of younger consumers. Elderly consumers are much more likely to own their home, have no mortgage or have a (low-cost or subsidized) rented house or apartment. Across Europe, approximately 50 per cent of pensioners' income still comes from state pensions, yet it is clear that older consumers are time-rich, and have a significant amount of discretionary income to spend.[34] The relatively high living standards of future retirees (the baby boomers) and the stability of public finances in different European states has led to an active discussion of pension reform plans throughout the European Union. Nonetheless, pensions will continue to play an important role in the discretionary incomes of Europe's retired population. Table 13.2 shows the amounts paid out in pensions as a percentage of final salary. As a final note on the two major demographic trends in Europe, let's link together the 'greying' and the 'de-greening' populations. Figure 13.2 shows the dependency ratio of the number of people in the EU-25 countries over the age of 65, relative to the number of people

Table 13.2 Amounts paid out in pensions as a percentage of final salary

Salary	20,000 euros	50,000 euros
Belgium	58%	45%
Finland	60%	59%
France	67%	51%
Germany	45%	43%
Greece	70%	48%
Ireland	53%	21%
Italy	78%	75%
The Netherlands	76%	31%
Portugal	74%	74%
Spain	94%	63%
UK	35%	14%
USA (for comparison)	71%	45%

Note: Different systems are not always directly comparable, as some base pensions on final salary, while others on average salary. Higher-income workers are treated differently, depending on country.

Sources: Fitch Investor Services; *Wall Street Journal* (30 October 2000): A21.

Figure 13.2 Old age dependency ratio

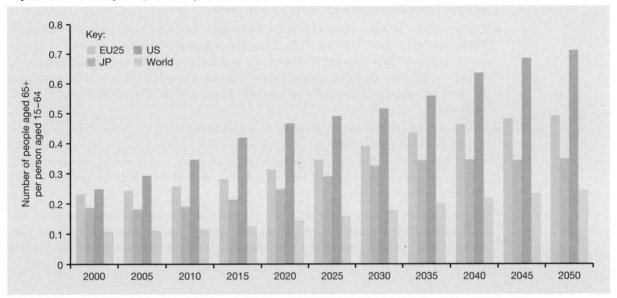

Source: For EU-15, Eurostat 2000 Demographic Projections (baseline scenario). For all other, UN World Population Prospects – 2002 Revision (Medium Var.).

aged 15–64 (those who are theoretically still employed).[35] While Japan (JP) faces the most critical scenario, the EU is also looking at a future with a greater percentage of the elderly, relative to a smaller percentage of younger people. This will have significant implications for social security payments, and the offerings of goods and services.

marketing opportunity

A few marketers are beginning to recognize the vast potential of the senior market and are designing products and services to cater to the specific needs of the elderly. A growing number of magazines are also being targeted to meet the interests of the older consumer. *Active Life*, *Saga Magazine*, *Mature Tymes* and *Plus* are all targeted at the 'over 50' market, although you wouldn't necessarily know it by the magazines, photos, advertising or articles! Most covers show vital, active 50-plussers, and the advertising focuses on quality of service, value for money and straightforward communications. With the exception of a few older faces promoting incontinence products, you're more likely to see consumers on mountain bikes than tending the garden.

Even companies that have relatively many 65-plussers as a target market don't feel the need to associate 'old' with their products or services. Advertisements for river and ocean cruises (which have a high percentage of older clientele throughout Europe) show busy discos and swimming pools dominated by 30–40-year-old clients, with a few wrinkle-free elderly in the photo. The accent to the elderly market is on product benefits, and not whether the product is best suited for a particular age group.[36]

Researchers have identified a set of key values that are relevant to older consumers. For marketing strategies to succeed, they should be related to one or more of these factors:[37]

● *Autonomy.* Mature consumers want to lead active lives and to be self-sufficient. Financial services and financial planning are increasing markets for the elderly segment, who have a strong need to remain independent. While companies are the largest purchasers of cars in the UK, the majority of private buyers are 'greys' – a further sign of their financial muscle and desire for autonomy.[38]

● *Connectedness.* Mature consumers value the bonds they have with friends and family. While the 'grey' don't relate well to their own age group (most elderly report feeling on average ten years younger than they are, and feel that 'other' elderly behave 'older' than they do), they do value information which communicates clear benefits to cohorts in their age group. Advertisements which avoid patronizing stereotypes are well received.

● *Altruism.* Mature consumers want to give something back to the world. Thrifty Car Rental found in a survey that over 40 per cent of older consumers would select a rental car company if it sponsored a programme that gives discounts to senior citizens' centres. Based on this research, the company launched its highly successful 'Give a Friend a Lift' programme.

● *Personal growth.* Mature consumers are very interested in trying new experiences and developing their potential. By installing user-friendly interactive touch-screen computer stations in European stores, GNC has found that older consumers have become better educated about health issues, and are loyal to the brand.[39]

Perceived age: you're only as old as you feel

The 'grey' market does not consist of a uniform segment of vigorous, happy, ready-to-spend consumers – nor is it a group of senile, economically marginalized, immobile people. In fact, research confirms the popular wisdom that age is more a state of mind than of body. A person's mental outlook and activity level has a lot more to do with his or her longevity and quality of life than does *chronological age*, or the actual number of years lived. In addition to these psychological dimensions of age, there are also cultural influences on what constitutes ageing, and perceptions of what is 'elderly' across different European markets.[40]

▶   A better yardstick to categorize the elderly is **perceived age**, or how old a person feels. Perceived age can be measured on several dimensions, including 'feel-age' (how old a person feels) and 'look-age' (how old a person looks).[41] The older consumers get, the younger they feel relative to actual age. For this reason, many marketers emphasize product benefits rather than age appropriateness in marketing campaigns, since many consumers will not relate to products targeted to their chronological age.[42]

marketing pitfall

Some marketing efforts targeted at the elderly have backfired because they reminded people of their age or presented their age group in an unflattering way. One of the more infamous blunders was committed by Heinz. A company analyst found that many elderly people were buying baby food because of the small portions and easy chewing consistency, so Heinz introduced a line of 'Senior Foods' made especially for denture wearers. Needless to say, the product failed. Consumers did not want to admit that they required strained foods (even to the supermarket cashier). They preferred to purchase baby foods, which they could pretend they were buying for a grandchild.

In Holland, a country where bicycles are an important mode of personal transportation, a specially designed 'elderly bicycle' was a resounding failure in spite of its competitive product benefits. While conventional marketing wisdom would suggest that a firm communicate its unique functional benefits to a target market, this wisdom backfired for the Dutch 'greys'. Positioning the bicycle as an easy-to-pedal 'senior bicycle' was met with a negative response, as the Dutch elderly who still ride a bicycle (a common sight in Holland!) feel too young to be riding a 'senior' bike.[43]

Segmenting seniors

The senior subculture represents an extremely large market: the number of Europeans aged 62 and over exceeds the entire population of Canada.[44] Because this group is so large, it is helpful to think of the mature market as consisting of four subsegments: an 'older' group (aged 55–64), an 'elderly' group (aged 65–74), an 'aged' group (aged 75–84) and finally a 'very old' group (85+).[45]

The elderly market is well suited for segmentation. Older consumers are easy to identify by age and stage in the family life cycle. Most receive social security benefits so they can be located without much effort, and many subscribe to one of the magazines targeted to the elderly, discussed earlier in this section. *Saga Magazine* in the UK has the largest circulation of any European magazine, with over 750,000 monthly readers. Selling holidays and insurance to the over-50s, the parent company also makes use of a database with over 4 million over-50s.

Several segmentation approaches begin with the premise that a major determinant of elderly marketplace behaviour is the way a person deals with being old.[46] *Social ageing theories* try to understand how society assigns people to different roles across the lifespan. For example, when someone retires he/she may reflect society's expectations for someone at this life stage – this is a major transition point when people exit from many relationships.[47] Some people become depressed, withdrawn and apathetic as they age, some are angry and resist the thought of ageing, and some appear to accept the new challenges and opportunities this period of life has to offer.

▶ Table 13.3 summarizes some selected findings from one current segmentation approach, called **gerontographics**, which divides the mature market into groups based on both level of physical well-being and social conditions, such as becoming a grandparent or losing a spouse.

Table 13.3 Gerontographics

Segment	55-plus	Profile	Marketing implications
Healthy indulgers	18%	Have experienced the fewest events related to ageing, such as retirement or widowhood, and are most likely to behave like younger consumers. Main focus is on enjoying life.	Looking for independent living and are good customers for discretionary services like home-cleaning and answering machines.
Healthy hermits	36%	React to life events like the death of a spouse by becoming withdrawn. Resent that they are expected to behave like old people.	Emphasize conformity. They want to know their appearance is socially acceptable, and tend to be comfortable with well-known brands.
Ailing outgoers	29%	Maintain positive self-esteem despite adverse life events. They accept limitations but are still determined to get the most out of life.	Have health problems that may require a special diet. Special menus and promotions will bring these people into restaurants seen as catering to their needs.
Frail recluses	17%	Have adjusted their lifestyles to accept old age, but have chosen to cope with negative events by becoming spiritually stronger.	Like to stay put in the same house where they raised their families. Good candidates for redecorating, also for emergency response systems.

Source: Adapted from George P. Moschis, 'Life stages of the mature market', *American Demographics* (September 1996): 44-50.

marketing pitfall

Many consumer products will encounter a more sympathetic reception from the elderly if products and the packages they come in are redesigned to be sensitive to physical limitations. While aesthetically appealing, packages are often awkward and difficult to manage, especially for those who are frail or arthritic. Also, many serving sizes are not geared to smaller families, widows or widowers and other people living alone, and coupons tend to be for family-sized products, rather than for single servings.

Older people may have difficulty with ring-pull cans and push-open milk cartons. Ziploc packages (self-sealing plastic bags) and clear plastic wrap are also difficult to handle. Packages need to be easy to read and should be made lighter and smaller. Finally, designers need to pay attention to contrasting colours. A slight yellowing of the eye's lens as one ages makes it harder to see background colours on packages. Discerning between blues, greens and violets becomes especially difficult. The closer identifying type colours are to the package's or advertisement's background colour, the less visibility and attention they will command.

In general, the elderly have been shown to respond positively to ads that provide an abundance of information. Unlike other age groups, these consumers are not usually amused, or persuaded, by imagery-oriented advertising. A more successful strategy involves the construction of advertising that depicts the aged as well-integrated, contributing members of society, with emphasis on them expanding their horizons rather than clinging precariously to life.

Some basic guidelines have been suggested for effective advertising to the elderly. These include the following:[48]

- Keep language simple.
- Use clear, bright pictures.
- Use action to attract attention.
- Speak clearly, and keep the word count low.
- Use a single sales message, and emphasize brand extensions to tap consumers' familiarity.
- Avoid extraneous stimuli (excessive pictures and graphics can detract from the message).

■ CHAPTER SUMMARY

- Europeans have many things in common with others merely because they are about the same age or live in the same country, or same part of the country. Consumers who grew up at the same time share many cultural memories, so they may respond to marketers' *nostalgia* appeals that remind them of these experiences.

- Important age cohorts include teenagers, 18–29-year-olds, baby boomers and the elderly. *Teenagers* are making a transition from childhood to adulthood, and their self-concepts tend to be unstable. They are receptive to products that help them to be accepted and enable them to assert their independence. Because many teenagers receive allowances, and/or earn pocket money but have few financial obligations, they are a particularly important segment for many non-essential or expressive products, ranging from chewing gum to hair gel, to clothing fashions and music. Because of changes in family structure, many teenagers are taking more responsibility for their families' day-to-day shopping and routine purchase decisions.

- *'Gen-Xers'*, consumers aged 18-29, are a difficult group for marketers to 'get a clear picture of'. They will be a powerful force in the years to come, whose tastes and priorities will be felt in fashion, popular culture, politics and marketing.

- *Baby boomers* are the most powerful age segment because of their size and economic clout. As this group has aged, its interests have changed and marketing priorities have changed as well. The needs and desires of baby boomers have a strong influence on demands for housing, childcare, cars, clothing and so on. Only a small proportion of boomers fit into an affluent, materialistic category.

- As the population ages, the needs of *elderly* consumers will also become increasingly influential. Many marketers traditionally ignored the elderly because of the stereotype that they are inactive and spend too little. This stereotype is no longer accurate. Most of the elderly are healthy, vigorous and interested in new products and experiences – and they have the income to purchase them. Marketing appeals to this age subculture should focus on consumers' self-concepts and perceived ages, which tend to be more youthful than their chronological ages. Marketers should emphasize the concrete benefits of products, since this group tends to be sceptical of vague, image-related promotions. Personalized service is of particular importance to this segment.

▶ KEY TERMS

Age cohort (p. 456)	**Gerontographics** (p. 471)
Baby boomers (p. 464)	**Grey market** (p. 468)
Generation X (p. 462)	**Perceived age** (p. 470)

CONSUMER BEHAVIOUR CHALLENGE

1 As Europe moves further into the process of creating a single market and single currency, citizens' attitudes regarding different aspects of this complex process are monitored in all countries. See the following website for the most recent survey findings: **http://europa.eu.int/en/comm/dg10/infcom/epo/eo.html**. What sorts of tentative conclusions can you make with respect to the influence that age has on attitudes towards single currency and other 'pan-European' efforts? What are the possible implications for the marketing of goods and services using a pan-European strategy?

2 Over the past few years, the Vatican has been involved in a variety of events aimed at developing a closer and stronger relationship with Europe's youth. At the invitation of the Pope, Bob Dylan (who was 50-something) gave a concert in 1997. Other Vatican-sponsored projects, such as World Youth Day, have enlisted French fashion designers (see Amy Barrett, 'John Paul II to share stage with marketers', *Wall Street Journal Europe*, 19 August 1997: 4). Do a literature and Web search to document the Vatican's activities that are targeted at youth. What goals do they seem to have in mind? What are the key segments? (Think in terms of age group segments, as well as geographic and cultural segmentation variables.) How successful a 'marketer' is the Vatican, in your opinion?

3 Below are a number of European retail websites. After reviewing the sites, give an analysis of target market and age segmentation strategies used by these firms.

www.waf.it.mall (a weekend of shopping in Florence?)
www.one4you.be (interested in beer from Belgium?)
www.bexley.fr ('trend-resistant' shoes – French classics)
www.demon.co.uk/mace/cacmall.html (desert plants, offered in a variety of languages)
www.creor.com (high-value jewellery from Italy, priced in dollars)
www.classicengland.co.uk (Anglophile heaven – historical newspapers, teapots, etc.)

4 Why did baby boomers have such an important impact on consumer culture in the second half of the twentieth century?

5 How has the baby boomlet changed attitudes towards child-rearing practices and created demand for different products and services?

6 Is it practical to assume that people aged 55 and older constitute one large consumer market? What are some approaches to further segmenting this age subculture?

7 What are some important variables to keep in mind when tailoring marketing strategies to the elderly?

8 Find good and bad examples of advertising targeted at elderly consumers. To what degree does advertising stereotype the elderly? What elements of ads or other promotions appear to determine their effectiveness in reaching and persuading this group?

■ NOTES

1. Bickley Townsend, 'Où sont les neiges d'antan?' ('Where are the snows of yesteryear?'), *American Demographics* (October 1988): 2.
2. Stephen Holden, 'After the war the time of the teen-ager', *New York Times* (7 May 1995): E4.
3. 'Same kids, more money', *Marketing* (29 June 1995): 37; see also the following websites for some overviews of allowances: http://www.kiplinger.com/drt.drthome.html and http://pages.prodigy.com/kidsmoney/.
4. Birgitte Tufte and Jeanetter Rasmussen, 'Children on the Net: State of the Art and Future Perspectives Regarding Danish Children's Use of the Internet' in Darach Turley and Stephen Brown, eds, *European Advances in Consumer Research: All Changed, Changed Utterly?* 6 (Valdosta, GA: Association for Consumer Research, 2003: 142–6; Anthony Patterson, Kim Cassidy and Steve Baron, 'Communication and Marketing in a Mobilized World: Diary Research on "Generation Txt"' in Turley and Brown, eds, *European Advances in Consumer Research*: 147–52; Hanman, Natalie, 'The kids are all writing', *The Guardian* (9 June 2005), http://www.guardian.co.uk/online/story/0,,1501803,00.html.
5. 'Same kids, more money'; Scott McCartney, 'Society's subcultures meet by modem', *Wall Street Journal* (8 December 1994): B1 (2).
6. Sara Olkon, 'Black soda with skulls on label isn't aimed at the Pepsi generation', *Wall Street Journal* (24 May 1995): B1.
7. Junu Bryan Kim, 'For savvy teens: Real life, real solutions', *Advertising Age* (23 August 1993): S1 (3pp.).
8. 'Hopes and fears: Young European opinion leaders', GfK, adapted from *Marketing Week* (25 June 1998) (study of 500 opinion leaders aged 14–20 from 16 western and eastern European countries).
9. Howard W. French, 'Vocation for dropouts is painting Tokyo red', *New York Times on the Web* (5 March 2000).
10. Yumiko Ono, 'They say that a Japanese gal is an individualist: Tall, tan, blond', *Wall Street Journal Interactive Edition* (19 November 1999).
11. Yumiko Ono, 'Meet a beer, a car, a refrigerator, and a fabric deodorizer, all named Will', *Wall Street Journal Interactive Edition* (8 October 1999).
12. Leslie de Chernatony, 'From red nose to Blue Tooth: Techno savvy tweens top retails' Christmas list', http://www.business.bham.ac.uk/bbs/static/images/cme_resources/Users/milesta/press%20release%20archive.pdf (accessed December 2004).
13. Ellen Goodman, 'The selling of teenage anxiety', *Washington Post* (24 November 1979).
14. Yumiko Ono, 'Limited Too will blitz preteens with catalogs of their very own', *Wall Street Journal Interactive Edition* (15 August 1998).
15. See the following set of recent articles researching how European children 'learn' to be consumers:

Emma N. Banister and Margaret K. Hogg, 'Consumer Social-isation and the Formation of Children's Likes and Dislikes'; Sarah Todd, 'Children and Money'; Maria Piacentini and Julie Tinson, 'Understanding Social Influences on Children's Food Choices; Elisabeth Götze, 'Perspectives on Intercultural Differences of Pre-school Children's Brand Knowledge and Brand Attitudes' all in in Turley and Brown, eds, *European Advances in Consumer Research*.

16. Quoted in Karen Springen, Ana Figueroa and Nicole Joseph-Goteiner, 'The truth about tweens', *Newsweek* (18 October 1999): 62–72, at 64.

17. Matthew Grimm, 'Snap it, girlfriend!', *American Demographics* (April 2000): 66–7.

18. Ellen R. Foxman, Patriya S. Tansuhaj and Karim M. Ekstrom, 'Family members' perceptions of adolescents' influence in family decision making', *Journal of Consumer Research* 15 (March 1989): 482–91.

19. 'Men and women in the European Union: A statistical portrait', *Eurostat* (Luxembourg: Office for Official Publications of the European Communities, 1995).

20. Gary J. Bamossy, Trinske Antonidies, Michael R. Solomon and Basil G. Englis, 'You're not Cool if You Have to Ask: Gender in the Social Construction of Coolness', paper presented at the Association for Consumer Research Gender Conference, Chicago, June 2000; Trinske Antonides, 'The Underlying Dimensions of Coolness', unpublished masters thesis, Vrije Universiteit, Amsterdam, 2000. See also this website on 'cool': http://www.pbs.org/wgbh/pages/frontline/shows/cool/.

21. 'Living Conditions in Europe: Statistical handbook', *Eurostat* (Luxembourg: Office for Official Publications of the European Communities, 2000): 29.

22. Deborah Klosky, 'World Bank ads target youths', *Wall Street Journal Europe* (7 October 1997): 4; Karen Ritchie, *Marketing to Generation X* (New York: Lexington Books, 1995); Rob Nelson, *Revolution X: Survival Guide for Our Generation* (New York: Penguin Books, 1994); for a 'Gen-X' website, see http://www.acent.net/in-mtl/v04n03/generax.htm; Laura Zinn, 'Move over, boomers', *Business Week* (14 December 1992): 7.

23. 'Generation next', *Marketing* (16 January 1997): 25.

24. Quoted in T.L. Stanley, 'Age of innocence . . . not', *PROMO* (February 1997): 28–33, at 30.

25. 'Generation next', 26.

26. Scott Donaton, 'The media wakes up to Generation X', *Advertising Age* (1 February 1993): 16 (2); Laura E. Keeton, 'New magazines aim to reach (and rechristen) Generation X', *Wall Street Journal* (17 October 1994): B1.

27. Faye Rice, 'Making generational marketing come of age', *Fortune* (26 June 1995): 110–14.

28. Meg Carter, 'Whiskey taste designed for a youthful palate', *Financial Times* (22 January 2004), http://news.ft.com/servlet/ContentServer?pagename=FT.com/StoryFT/FullStory&c=StoryFT&cid=1073281204097&p=1059480266913.

29. 'Trends in households in the European Union: 1995–2025' *Eurostat, Statistics in Focus*, Theme 3-24/2003 (Luxembourg: Office for Official Publications of the European Communities, 2004): 38.

30. Rice, 'Making generational marketing come of age'.

31. James Hagerty, 'Cooler heads prevail as Britain loses lust for warm, cloudy ales', *Wall Street Journal* (29 August 2000): A1.

32. 'Living conditions in Europe: Statistical handbook': 101.

33. 'Shades of grey', *Marketing* (24 April 1997); 'Baby boom generatie moet oud-zijn modieus maken' ['Baby boom generation has to make "old" in fashion'], *NRC Handelsblad* (2 May 1996): 7; Melinda Beck, 'Going for the gold', *Newsweek* (23 April 1990): 74.

34. 'Shades of grey'.

35. 'Trends in households in the European Union: 1995–2025': 93.

36. 'Shades of grey'; 'Baby boom generatie moet oud-zijn modieus maken'.

37. David B. Wolfe, 'Targeting the mature mind', *American Demographics* (March 1994): 32–6.

38. 'Shades of grey'.

39. Allyson Steward-Allen, 'Marketing in Europe to the consumer over age fifty', *Marketing News* 31(16) (4 August 1997): 18.

40. Gabriele Morello, 'Old is Gold, But What is Old?', ESO-MAR seminar on 'The Untapped Gold Mine: The Growing Importance of the Over-50s' (Amsterdam: ESOMAR, 1989); Gabriele Morello, 'Sicilian time', in *Time and Society* (London: Sage, 1997): 6(1): 55–69. See also 'Living conditions in Europe: Statistical handbook': 9–21.

41. Benny Barak and Leon G. Schiffman, 'Cognitive Age: A Nonchronological Age Variable', in Kent B. Monroe, ed., *Advances in Consumer Research* 8 (Provo, UT: Association for Consumer Research, 1981): 602–6.

42. David B. Wolfe, 'An ageless market', *American Demographics* (July 1987): 27–55.

43. 'Baby boom generatie moet oud-zijn modieus maken'.

44. 'Demographic statistics 1997', *Eurostat* (Luxembourg: Office for Official Publications of the European Communities, 1997); see also http://europa.eu.int (accessed 5 August 2005); Lenore Skenazy, 'These days, it's hip to be old', *Advertising Age* (15 February 1988).

45. This segmentation approach is based on the US population and follows William Lazer and Eric H. Shaw, 'How older Americans spend their money', *American Demographics* (September 1987): 36. See also 'Shades of grey' for a two-segment approach to the UK elderly market, and 'Living conditions in Europe: Statistical handbook': 9–21.

46. Ellen Day, Brian Davis, Rhonda Dove and Warren A. French, 'Reaching the senior citizen market(s)', *Journal of Advertising Research* (December/January 1987/88): 23–30; Warren A. French and Richard Fox, 'Segmenting the senior citizen market', *Journal of Consumer Marketing* 2 (1985): 61–74; Jeffrey G. Towle and Claude R. Martin Jr., 'The Elderly Consumer: One Segment or Many?', in Beverlee B. Anderson, ed., *Advances in Consumer Research* 3 (Provo, UT: Association for Consumer Research, 1976): 463.

47. Catherine A. Cole and Nadine N. Castellano, 'Consumer behavior', *Encyclopedia of Gerontology* 1 (1996): 329–39.

48. J. Ward, 'Marketers slow to catch age wave', *Advertising Age* (22 May 1989): S-1.

Consumption of gold and gold jewellery in Turkey

ÖZLEM SANDIKCI, Bilkent University, Ankara, Turkey, and
BURÇAK ERTIMUR, University of California, Irvine

Turkish consumers love gold and gold jewellery. While Turkey is not a major gold producing country, it constitutes one of the world's biggest gold consuming markets, ranked fifth in world demand. It is also the world's second biggest exporter of gold jewellery products after Italy. Gold jewellery is one of the fastest growing sectors in Turkey, with around 35,000 jewellers' shops scattered all over the country.

An important distinction must be made between consumption and investment demand for gold. Typically, gold bars and coins are treated as investment and jewellery as consumption items. However, the term jewellery refers to a wide range of products with different characteristics. In Western developed markets, gold jewellery is usually low carat and bought primarily for adornment purposes. In Asia and the Middle East, on the other hand, most gold jewellery is high carat, which can be easily converted back to raw gold. Thus, gold jewellery functions as both adornment and saving tools.

There are three forms of gold products in Turkey: gold bars, coins and jewellery. Gold bars are traded on the Istanbul Gold Exchange and used solely for investment. Gold coins and jewellery, however, serve multiple purposes. Gold coins, which are termed 'Republican coins' are available in five different sizes. Gold jewellery, on the other hand, comes in 14, 18 or 22-carat forms. The 14 and 18 carat items of jewellery are usually modern designs while the 22 carat jewellery is more highly valued for investment purposes. This gold jewellery includes plain bracelets - *ray bilezik* - which are among the most frequently purchased items for saving purposes. Most of the traditional designs, such as *Trabzon* and *Tel Kare*, are also 22 carat.

Turkish people use gold coins and jewellery for three different purposes: ornamentation, gift-giving and investment.

Gold jewellery adorns the bodies of many Turkish consumers. Factors such as design, size, carats and accompanying stones determine whether the jewellery is appropriate for day or night wear. Typically, smaller and simpler designs are preferred for daily use whereas larger items of gold jewellery with precious stones are worn at night and on special occasions. Moreover, women try to match the gold jewellery to the clothes they are wearing in order to convey a particular desired self-image. Some women state that they purchase new gold jewellery when they realize that they don't possess a design that suits a particular dress. For many, gold jewellery connotes ostentation, and they believe that women wear gold jewellery for social occasions in order to show off and impress others.

Although gold coins are typically purchased for investment purposes, they might be used for self-ornamentation as well. The most common example of this is *besi bir yerde* – a special type of necklace made out of coins. Since these necklaces are 22 carats of gold, they can easily be converted into money without any loss of value. Wearing these necklaces, however, seems to be a dying tradition, confined mostly to village women.

Gold jewellery and gold coins are also given as gifts on various occasions. In Turkey, it is customary to give gold jewellery or coins as gifts to women getting engaged or married, to newborn babies, and to boys who are being circumcised. In these contexts, the gift operates as an artefact marking the role transition and signifies the strength of the bond among family members and close friends. Gold can also be an appropriate gift item for celebrating occupational events such as retirement or promotion and personally symbolic days such as birthdays or wedding anniversaries. The choice between an item of jewellery and coins as a gift depends on three factors: the existence of a traditionally appropriate gift item for a particular occasion, the intimacy of the relationship, and the taste of the giver and the receiver. For example, if the gift is for a newborn baby, then it is always a gold coin. The decision, in this case, is about the size of the coin and ultimately depends on the intimacy of the relationship. Typically, the closer the relationship is, the bigger the size of the gold coin. However, when there is no clear norm about the type of gold gift, the selection is guided by a combination of factors. For example, when the gift is to be given to a woman getting married, gold jewellery is preferred if the relationship is close and the giver is knowledgeable about the taste of the recipient. If, however, the taste of the recipient is not known, gold coins, which are standard and non-personalized items, are given.

Both gold jewellery and coins can be purchased for investment purposes. Although gold offers no rate of return or dividend apart from the potential capital gain that may result if its market price rises, its high value and easy portability renders it a prominent saving tool. Jewellery items with less craftsmanship, such as plain bracelets, are preferred as they preserve their value better and can be more easily converted into money in times of need. Consumers from lower economic classes especially prefer plain designs so that they do not pay for the craftsmanship. Consumers from the higher income groups, on the other hand, tend to select crafted models, but they prefer items that do not contain stones. However, even when gold jewellery is purchased for investment reasons, aesthetic concerns are present. These items of gold jewellery are still used for adorning the body and worn by the owner in her daily life.

Gold coins also function as an investment tool, an alternative to foreign currency or deposit accounts. Especially in rural areas where access to a bank is limited, collecting gold coins is an attractive option. They can be stored at home, and during times of personal financial difficulty or political or economic turmoil they can easily be converted into cash. The practice of purchasing gold coins is also common in the cities. Many urban housewives engage in a social activity referred to as 'gold days'. Every two or four weeks, women meet at the house of one of the participants to drink afternoon tea and chat. Every time they meet, each brings a gold coin or money equivalent to a fraction of it. At the end of the day, the host gathers all the gold coins and money. Typically, drawing a name determines who will be the next host, and eventually all women have their turn to collect gold coins. The benefit of gold days is that they help women to save little amounts of money, and then receive a lump sum amount which they can either continue to save or spend for other needs.

QUESTIONS

1 What types of rituals is consumption of gold jewellery and coins a part of?

2 What kinds of utilitarian and symbolic motives might underlie the practice of giving gold jewellery and coins as gifts?

3 How might social class affect jewellery consumption?

4 What kind of messages do personal adornments communicate about self-identity?

Socially excluded? Low income consumers' grocery shopping behaviour[1]

SALLY HIBBERT, Nottingham University Business School, UK,
MARIA PIACENTINI, Department of Marketing, Lancaster University, UK, and
HAYA AL-DAJANI, Department of Marketing, University of Strathclyde, UK

Barimore is a housing estate in Scotland. It is approximately 6 kilometres from Newvale, the nearest town, and 12 kilometres from the city of Glasgow. The area has been classified as moderately deprived, based on measures of male unemployment, overcrowding, social class, car ownership and home ownership. In the past there were a number of food retailers based in the community but, over time, these have closed down due to the competitive pressures of major supermarkets and changing shopping habits. Yet none of the major supermarkets have opened stores near to the housing estate. The remaining local shops are not primarily food retailers and have a poor range of foodstuffs, which tend to be low quality (especially fruit and vegetables) and relatively expensive. There is a small supermarket and a number of small independent retailers approximately 1.5 kilometres from Barimore in Falton, which is a walkable distance for fit and healthy consumers but a bus journey away for those with limited mobility. There is a regular and reasonably reliable bus service to the community, but bus fares are perceived to be expensive and many people find it difficult to carry large amounts of shopping home on the bus, particularly people with disabilities, the elderly, those with small children or large families. As a result, some residents of Barimore feel that they have poor access to grocery stores and experience substantial constraints in acquiring the groceries that they need to provide adequately for their families.

Among the community, people have developed diverse shopping habits and some cope with their constraints better than others. Many people undertake a main grocery shopping trip to a major supermarket such as Asda or Tesco, discounters[2] such as Lidl or Aldi or a combination of these and specialist independent stores that offer them a satisfactory range of goods and enable them to get best value for money. Sometimes people struggle home from this shopping trip on the bus, others have an arrangement to get a lift home in a friend's, a family member's or a neighbour's car, but many people resort to taking a taxi. The latter option is expensive and has to be restricted but it is regarded as an unavoidable necessity. This main shopping trip is typically supplemented with numerous 'top-up' shopping trips, either to local retailers or to the nearest town – Newvale – where people might undertake other shopping tasks and pick up small amounts of groceries that they are able to carry home on the bus. This pattern of shopping suits these consumers from a convenience perspective. For some, it also fits in with the periodicity of their income: they do a 'big shop' when the money comes into the household, but as it starts to run out they spend small amounts to tide them over until the next pay day or social security payment.

On the whole, residents of Barimore who shop in this way are content that the constraints they face are not too severe and that they cope adequately with them. Alison's opinion, that the shopping options are reasonably satisfactory, is quite typical:

'we have the shops down there [in Falton], which is quite good, and there's two grocers, there's quite a selection really, but I think it's a stop gap for people, they have their weekly shopping, say, in Newvale.'

However there is, of course, some variability in how well people manage. The quote below highlights how Mary copes with the difficult task of meeting the needs and wants of a family of five, including three teenage boys, on a limited income. Mary purchases foodstuffs that meet her preferred standards immediately after receiving her benefit payment, but is obliged to make compromises in the period leading up to the next payment. Asked why she bought fruit and vegetables only 'sometimes', she explained that it was due to:

'Financial reasons. I can only get a giro [social security payment] once a fortnight so I've got to get what I want, because the second week comes along and I don't have any more money.'

Mary noted that while waiting for the next benefit payment she is restricted to shopping for 'bits' from local stores but, referring to the previous week when she had spent £50 on one such trip, she emphasized that this 'top up' shopping often works out as very expensive. By contrast, Lilly, an older woman whose family has grown up and left home, is illustrative of someone who is confident and has a strong sense of control despite difficult circumstances:

'Some of the things, I could shop for at Newvale you know, I'm very thrifty. I could tell you the price of a pound of onions in that shop and a pound of onions in that shop, they are a penny dearer so we'll go in that one, that's just me, I've always lived on a budget so I've always shopped on a budget.'

The relation of grocery shopping to the experience of disadvantage is not, therefore, simply explained in terms of income. An individual's ability to cope with their circumstances and develop strategies that best serve their needs and resources is an important factor. This is not, nevertheless, a simple problem of learning to manage on a budget. People who face problems of money 'running out', often find themselves in that position because of other family members. For instance, in families with older children, parents (generally the mother) are sometimes unable to keep sufficiently tight control over the family's consumption to be able to manage the task of providing food over the period that the income has to last.

In contrast to the pattern of shopping described above, some residents of Barimore – typically people living alone and people who have more severe mobility problems – do all of their shopping at local stores. These are the most constrained consumers. They are more dissatisfied with the groceries that they are able to buy and irritated by the poor value for money at local retailers but they do not see that they have any choice because they lack the resources needed to access better retail facilities. In many instances, these are older people who have benefited from better shopping facilities in the past.

Other Barimore residents, primarily those with a car and in paid employment, acquire nearly all of their groceries on a weekly shopping trip to a major supermarket, which is more resonant of contemporary shopping habits in the wider population.

Although grocery shopping tends to be a more functional task, there are often social and personal motives that influence shopping behaviour. One of the main reasons disadvantaged consumers cite for going shopping is to 'get out of the house'. Those who view grocery shopping excursions as having a leisure dimension include other types of activities in the shopping trip, such as visits to a café where they treat themselves to some form of refreshment, be it on their own or with a friend, partner or child. Penny, a mother with three young children, one of whom required a lot of medical care, enjoys shopping as a form of 'outing':

'sometimes when I take James [son] into town we go to a café for lunch for a wee treat, for something a bit different.'

People who shop at Barimore's community-based food co-operative[3] enjoy the opportunity for social interaction with other people who live in the community. John highlighted that this is particularly important for groups such as single mothers and the elderly. However, Anna comments that social interaction could be better facilitated:

'I think it should be more spread out. A lot of people like talking and meeting their friends, which is good and you get to know the people that are serving there. It could be set out better.'

Shopping is an important activity for disadvantaged consumers, as for everyone else; it is an important activity in acquiring the essential goods and services they need for their everyday life, but it is also a form of leisure and it affects people's sense of social in/exclusion in contemporary society. In particular, grocery shopping is important because of the implications for diet and health. A range of government and voluntary sector initiatives continue to seek to improve grocery shopping access for disadvantaged communities, and the related improvements in diet, but the challenge remains a substantial one.

QUESTIONS

1 What are the main constraints on residents of Barimore that influence their grocery shopping behaviour? How might restrictions differ for other low-income communities?

2 How do the constraints faced by consumers in Barimore influence their grocery shopping behaviour? What 'types' of shoppers are typical in this community?

3 The constraints experienced by consumers in this community vary in severity. Identify characteristics of consumers that experience the constraints more severely.

4 What public policy, voluntary sector and commercial initiatives might reduce the constraints experienced by the residents of Barimore in acquiring grocery shopping? What can individuals themselves do to cope better with the situation?

Notes

1. This case study draws on M. Piacentini, S.A. Hibbert and H. Al Dajani (2001), 'Diversity in deprivation: Exploring the grocery shopping behaviour of disadvantaged consumers', *International Review of Retail, Distribution and Consumer Research* 11(2): 141–58.

2. Discounters are 'no frills' retailers that offer a restricted range of products at low prices, sometimes selling only in bulk.

3. The community-based food co-operative is a local government funded retail initiative staffed by volunteers from Barimore. The co-op sells fruit and vegetables in Barimore's community centre twice a week.

Further reading

Alwitt, L.F. and T.D. Donley (1996), *The Low Income Consumer: Adjusting the Balance of Exchange* (London: Sage).

Klein, G., C. Whyley and N. O'Reilly (2004), *Paying More, Getting Less* (London: National Consumer Council).

Wrigley, N., D. Warm and B. Margetts (2002), 'Deprivation, diet and food retail access: Findings from the Leeds "Food Deserts" study', *Environment and Planning* 34: 151-80.

Scenes from the lives of Athenian mothers and daughters

KALIPSO KARANTINOU, Manchester Business School, UK

Michaela, Danae and Artemis live in Kifissia, a prosperous suburb in northern Athens with lovely apartment houses and villas, and elegant designer shops, within 30 minutes' drive of the centre of Athens and the upmarket shopping district of Kolonaki.

Michaela, at nearly two years old, already has very strong views about some aspects of consumption, particularly her clothing, which is chosen for her by her mother, Danae. She wears little T-shirts with trousers or dungarees for playtime in the morning; and dresses when going out to social gatherings and events. Michaela has already developed a sense for colour coordination and she has strong preferences with regard to her clothes (there are some clothes she refuses to wear and others that she cannot wait to put on). Sometimes in the mornings she checks her appearance in the mirror, looking closely at what she is wearing; she is also really delighted when someone compliments her on her outfits. As Michaela has got older she has been increasingly involved in choosing what to wear each day. Michaela is especially picky about her shoes and will not let anyone else choose which pair she wears. Each morning she stands in front of the cupboard where all her shoes are stored and picks out a pair herself; each time she chooses those that match her clothes. She particularly loves a pair of shoes that are identical to a pair her mother Danae owns; Michaela feels very proud each time they wear their matching shoes.

Michaela loves going to the park every day with her grandmother, Artemis – playing on the rides and in the sand. She has a favourite hat that she puts on to go to the park, a round pink and white one, which her father bought for her. Usually she ends the day completely worn out – and yet always surprises everyone by how much she revives after a good night's sleep and at seven o'clock every morning is always raring to go again – starting with breakfast of warm milk, followed at around nine o'clock by fruit (pears, bananas and strawberries are her favourite), orange juice and a piece of her favourite baby biscuit. She has her main meal around one o'clock, then a substantial snack (yogurt or baby porridge) at five o'clock and her milk at bedtime.

Michaela has already developed some strong preferences about food. There are some things that she just loves (fish, meat, brown bread, fresh salads, cooked vegetables, lentils, parmesan cheese, olive oil, baby porridge, yogurt) – and some things she is much less keen on (beans, eggs). Michaela has started to develop a real taste for Greek delicacies, and her grandmother's home-made moussaka, pastichio, oven lasagne (pasta with lots of different types of cheese, mushrooms and fresh cream) and pasticciada (spaghetti with red sauce and beef), are now some of her favourite dishes. However, she still has not developed a taste for feta cheese – and continues to pull a horrible face when she finds herself eating some by mistake. Michaela has a strong preference for certain brands or varieties of food, e.g. bananas and milk. She seems able to spot subtle differences in taste between the varieties, which makes her love one type and refuse to eat the others. Even though other members of the family cannot discern any difference, when shopping they choose these products according to her preferences.

Danae, a first-time mother in her late twenties, is a member of generation X. She worked hard after Michaela's birth to get fit again. Before Michaela was born she had read a lot about new babies, and after Michaela's arrival she continued to check with her paediatrician, the *Mother and Baby* book which she had come to rely on, her friends who were themselves young mothers, and her own mother, Artemis. She was very careful with Michaela's diet, as well as her own – and tried to make sure Michaela did not eat chocolates and sweet things. She had watched her own diet very carefully while she was pregnant. When she was expecting Michaela Danae had eaten fish twice a week and red meat regularly; drunk a litre of milk every day; and always eaten lots of fresh fruit and vegetables. She had avoided soft cheeses (because of fears of listeria); undercooked eggs; raw or undercooked meat (because of fears of salmonella) and some processed foods such as pâté, salami and proscuitto (which had always been one of her favourites). She had abstained from alcohol, cut down on coffee (allowing herself only one cup a day, which had at first been difficult to accept); cut out tea (because it prevented the absorption of iron) as well as biscuits and cakes; and had avoided parsley, raspberry tea and mango since they all seemed to be associated with miscarriage. She had continued to watch her diet carefully, especially in the first year whilst she was still breastfeeding Michaela. She didn't reintroduce alcohol into her diet until Michaela was fully weaned, and still only allows herself one cup of coffee a day. Danae and her husband also reduced to a minimum their own consumption of soft drinks, chips, toffees, cakes and chocolate. They both thought this was necessary to set Michaela a good example.

There had been many things to prepare and buy before Michaela was born – lots of little Babygros and outfits, as well as equipment, such as a cot, pram, baby carrier, baby bath, baby monitor and a buggy that turned into a car seat (which would be ideal for trips out). As first-time parents, Danae and her husband did not know what they would need once the baby arrived, and they ended up buying far more things than they needed, as they realized later on. They started by visiting two well-known large baby stores and getting their catalogues. It took a number of visits to both stores, while Danae was still pregnant, to tick off all the items on their (continuously expanding) shopping list.

One of Danae's pleasures, after Michaela was born, was going shopping for a new wardrobe for herself, and new clothes for Michaela. Even though she had managed to get back to her pre-pregnancy figure, Danae needed the reinvigoration and the self-pampering feeling that new clothes seem to bring. Managing to maintain her femininity along with her new image as a young mother was challenging but important to her. She also now needed two different sets of outfits. As a professional woman she needed a couple of new trouser suits with some tops for the office; and as a mother she needed lots of smart casual clothes which looked appropriate in the park as well as on the high street. For the first time in her life she discovered the advantages of in-wash stain removers to cope with the fruit juice stains which seemed to be attracted to her clothing whatever she did . . . and however careful she was.

Artemis is just about to celebrate her 50th birthday and is a baby boomer. She spends a lot of time with her granddaughter, Michaela, so she has also had to adjust her wardrobe to take account of days spent in the park and at the swimming pool with her. She recently bought a number of smart casual clothes and flat everyday shoes; she found this change to her wardrobe quite reinvigorating. Artemis is an 'empty nest parent'. She had missed Danae a lot when her daughter had first gone off to university abroad, but Artemis had had no real difficulty in filling her time. She had always been very active with charity and social work, and with more time to spare she was able to devote more time to these activities – she discovered she had a real knack for management and organization, and enjoyed running fund-raising and social events in Athens.

Artemis also absolutely loves throwing parties at home: she enjoys all the preparation that goes into it, organizing the house for guests, planning the menu and doing some of the cooking, if not all (depending on the number of guests each time). She and her husband frequently organize dinner parties for 4–8 guests but also quite a few big parties for 30–50 guests every year. Even now that caring for Michaela takes a lot of her time, she still enjoys them; they are just a bit more challenging to organize.

Artemis and her husband belong to a social club which meets each week. There are numerous social activities organized by the club every month (guest lectures, visits to exhibitions, visits to archaeological sites, etc.). They also love classical music and they enjoy going to Lyriki Skini (the Opera House), Megaro Moussikis (the concert hall) and Herodion in the summer (the ancient open theatre at the centre of Athens, directly below the Acropolis).

One of the things Artemis missed when Danae went away was going shopping with her daughter – one of their treats when they have a chance is to spend time together shopping. They love the shops in Kolonaki but they do most of their shopping in Kifissia and in the centre of Athens, such as in the busy Ermou street. When it comes to clothes, Artemis prefers to shop at a couple of stores she really likes, where they know her and she gets good personalized service. Still, she enjoys window shopping and does go to different stores for the odd item or for shoes and accessories.

Artemis does all her food shopping locally, working from a shopping list, but also responding to what foodstuffs are seasonal, fresh and available. There is an excellent market close to where she lives where she can buy fresh fruit and vegetables, as well as meat and fish. There is also a big supermarket close to home. They eat a lot of fish – usually grilled with herbs and served with salad. Fresh salads and cooked vegetables are always part of their daily menu.

A significant aspect of shopping activities for Artemis is gift shopping. Gift-giving is an important ritual in the Greek society and one that needs a big investment of time, effort and money. Artemis in principle enjoys buying gifts but sometimes gets a bit overwhelmed; there are quite a few gift-giving occasions every year: gifts are exchanged at Christmas; Easter; and also on birthdays and name-days (the feast day of a saint whose name one has). This makes choosing and giving gifts an all-year round activity and, due to the number of gifts that need to be bought each time, an activity that needs to be planned carefully.

QUESTIONS

1 Describe and assess the key consumer socialization factors identified in the case.

2 What intergenerational influences on consumer behaviour can you identify from this case study?

3 Compare and contrast the different sets of beliefs, motivations and values associated with baby boomer and generation X consumers, and their respective influences on patterns of consumption. Examine similar sets of consumers in your own country – identify and evaluate similarities and differences between baby boomer and generation X consumers in your society with the Greek examples given in the case.

4 Discuss the rituals and occasions associated with gift-giving in Greece. Compare these gift-giving rituals and occasions with your own country context.

Consuming across borders: four vignettes

RONAN DE KERVENOAEL, Graduate School of Management, Sabanci University, Istanbul, Turkey and JONATHAN ELMS, Department of Marketing, Lancaster University Management School, UK

The once unique products, images and perceptions of Paris and its small chic shops, the diamonds of Amsterdam, Belgian chocolate, Swiss watches, German cars and London's bespoke tailors, are becoming increasingly accessible to all European consumers. The economic, political, legislative and social harmonization among the EU member states has led to the ever-increasing mobility of inter-European travellers, with many migrants living and working abroad. For some this move is more long term than for others. Whatever their consumption patterns, choice and competition are being reshaped and reconstructed with the creation of a 'truly' European, or even 'global', consumer. In an attempt to illustrate this new type of shopper, we present four vignettes portraying the expansion and progression of the consumption process.[1] The first provides the example of a household from the UK choosing to live indefinitely in another European country. The second explores the impact of consumption patterns on 'weekenders', who represent an ever-growing segment of affluent consumers that is taking an ever-increasing number of short break holidays abroad every year. The third case is about the consumption patterns of an international student who is only staying for a limited period of time in the UK. The final vignette reflects on the consumption process of two foreign-born long-term residents of the UK.

VIGNETTE 1
Going native: Roger and Miriam

Over the past ten years a clear trend has emerged whereby increasing numbers of English households have decided to uproot and relocate to sunnier European climes. Like many, Roger and Miriam, now in their fifties, with their son finishing his postgraduate studies at university, decided to leave the doom and gloom of the UK for sunny Spain. Roger was a successful management consultant and Miriam was a homemaker. Having secured their pension position, they decided to make the most of the upbeat situation in the UK housing market by paying off their mortgage and downsizing, which would better suit their new lifestyle in retirement.

After many holidays and much deliberation, they finally decided to settle abroad, in the south of Spain on the Costa Blanca. Their original idea was to be close to an airport, not too far south because of fear of the intense summer heat, and not too close to other English families (in order to distance themselves from the cliché of 'Brits abroad'). Initially they didn't really consider issues such as language; local amenities such as hospitals, retail provision and leisure activities; the cost of living and potential job opportunities. It was very difficult for them to evaluate the extent to which they would need and use such services.

'Blinded by the sun' and the excitement of the new, they quickly bought a house, but resold it within their first year abroad. They then went on to buy what they really wanted, not what the Spanish estate agent thought they wanted: he had concentrated on a holiday home whereas they had wanted a property as a permanent home. Consumption of staple goods, such as groceries, was originally expensive as they tended to buy from familiar outlets and favourite brands. At this stage they felt that their lifestyle and consumption patterns were more enjoyable back in the UK. At home in England they could use the internet in English for many aspects of their daily consumption (e.g. food, banking, ticket reservations). In Spain they realized how big the language barrier was for them. With time, they went through a consumer resocialization process, learning anew about products, services, brands and places. At this point they started to realize the true potential of their new location. After about a year and a half, they realized that they had made the right choice. Rather than cutting links with their 'previous' lives, they successfully integrated aspects of their 'old' consumption patterns with the new. They still buy English newspapers, but also purchase local newspapers as well. They installed satellite TV so that they could keep up with news and programmes from the UK. They now feel much more settled, relying on their son, and a few 'holidays' back in the UK every year, to stock up on special treats and products for which there are no substitutes available locally.

VIGNETTE 2
The weekenders: Davina

A new generation of regular travellers has emerged as a result of the availability of cheap fares with low-cost airlines, combined with the opening of local airports which are convenient and offer an increasing number of routes for city-based and traditional holidays all year around. Davina, a widow in her late fifties, lives in a small town in the north of England. She enjoys travelling regularly, 6–8 times a year, with a close-knit group of friends. Davina is a member of the Women's Institute, has two daughters with their own families, is financially secure, has a permanent job as an office manager and owns her own house. As she is IT literate, she has the technical knowledge to access travel information and book flights and accommodation online in advance. She does not have a large budget but is well organized and benefits from the support of her close group of friends travelling with her (group prices). Davina enjoys culture and festivals, food and drink, fashion and meeting new people. She likes busy European capitals and short-break destinations. Davina feels that she deserves regular treats as she has worked hard all her life and now has only herself to take care of. She is aware that in the future, as she gets older, she will probably not be able to do as much so she really wants to enjoy life to the full while she still can.

While Davina can afford the costs of travel, she is restricted in terms of what souvenirs she can bring back. First of all, she does not speak any foreign languages and sometimes finds it difficult to get what she wants from shopkeepers. In addition, it is never the same spending in foreign currency as it seems like using 'Monopoly money'. Second, she is restricted by the small weight allowance of budget airlines across Europe, and has to remember to buy from Duty Free stores items that have been pre-ordered. What she really enjoys is bringing home stories and anecdotes that she can share with others. For example, she laughs at her behaviour or purchases in some situations and reflects that she would never do that at home (such as bargaining). She likes travelling with her close-knit group of friends as she feels the responsibility and stress of travelling is taken away from her.

VIGNETTE 3
Overseas student: Frederick

The British education system attracts an increasing number of overseas students. The UK has a long-established reputation as a multicultural society, with images of warm beer, fish and chips, bad food, the Royal Family, Manchester United and the Beatles. Fredrick is a student from Sweden studying Marketing. He comes from a small business school outside Stockholm. This is the first time that he has lived on his own outside the family home. He is only in the UK for one term. He lives on campus and arrived with two suitcases and without any private transport. Fredrick has a scholarship and also works in the local pub two evenings a week to help pay for his social life and learn more about the (in)famous British 'pub' culture. His room is a re-creation of his bedroom at home with photographs of friends and family and posters of Sweden.

As a student, Fredrick has come as much for the educational experience as he has for the consumption of what he refers to as 'quintessential Englishness'. He is, however, in constant contact with home and his close circle of friends. As he is not familiar with many types of stores and products available in the UK, he buys what he needs on a daily basis. He does not stockpile as he may have an opportunity to go out somewhere at short notice and his purchases are largely driven by the activities he undertakes. Fredrick borrows wherever possible from other 'local' friends so that he can take part in a variety of activities, e.g. squash racket, waterproof clothing, camping equipment.

Although his social life is important to him, he feels a certain responsibility to perform well so that his marks will be accepted by his Swedish university.

He does not spend much time in his room. He does not try to understand all the local products and brands, for example he always sends home for his usual medicines when he catches a cold. He compares prices and quality but does not purchase very often. He meets up regularly with other Swedes and goes with them to visit all the historical attractions. He likes trying local food specialities. As he is independent for the first time he is also keen to bring back home evidence of his own personal development.

VIGNETTE 4
Semi-permanent residency: Nathan and Leyla

With the enlargement of the EU and the Common Market, job opportunities are now available across the entire region. An increasing number of European expats now live all over the UK for medium-term periods. Nathan was born in the south of France, where he got his degree in Economics, and decided, once he had completed his undergraduate studies, that it was time to see the world. He registered for a Masters' degree in the UK and was subsequently offered a scholarship to do a Ph.D. Having established a social network of contacts within UK universities he was offered a short-term contract as a lecturer. He got married to a fellow overseas student (Leyla from Turkey) and they bought a house while they were expecting their first child. While they are still discovering many aspects of life in their new country (e.g. NHS, taxes, DIY, guarantees, white goods, credit cards) they are now very used to what to expect and how to get a good deal as they have now lived in the UK for nearly ten years. They are nearly perfectly fluent in the consumption patterns and practices of both their countries of origin and of the UK. They see themselves as demanding consumers, comparing both price and quality and taking advantage of all three countries' systems (e.g. running a continental car so that they do not have to have an MOT; also a continental car makes it more difficult to be traced for parking tickets). The patterns of consumption have adapted the longer they have stayed in the UK. They now regularly have takeaway meals and buy most of their everyday needs (clothes, poster art, furniture) through local retailers or online. They rely on a close group of UK friends for advice when they need it. Some specific purchases, mainly food, they delay until they have the opportunity to go home. They also do not hesitate to fly home for specific needs, such as visiting their own dentist. However, they are not engaged in the local community as much as they might be, and this leaves them feeling slightly outside of things when there are political campaigns or national debates (such as about the Iraq war). They also have problems because they always tend to think that the quality of all goods is better at home, for example, that clothes in France and Turkey really fit better, and that there is more choice. Leyla's size is smaller than the average UK size and she has problems finding things to fit every time she goes shopping for clothes. It is also harder to find clothes made from natural fibres in the UK. Nathan tries to re-create French home comforts by installing mixer taps for the kitchen sink, for example, rather than freezing or burning his hands each time he tries to rinse the plates when he is doing the washing up after dinner. Even after ten years he still find finds it hard to adapt to certain social norms. They both like drinking, but prefer drinking wine with food at a local restaurant rather than going to their local pub. They hope to leave one day and retire to a place the sun.

QUESTIONS

1 To what extent are we all 'global' consumers now?

2 Discuss the extent to which consumption patterns are culturally innate, and the extent to which they are (or can be) adapted through experiences of the host culture. Identify and evaluate the factors which influence the consumer resocialization processes experienced by these different groups of consumers.

3 To what extent is the consumption experience of place, culture and art becoming increasingly important within contemporary consumer culture?

4 Discuss the potential effect of global diasporas on consumer identity and self-concept.

Note

1. The vignettes were compiled from a series of short interviews conducted by the authors.

Further reading

Bengtsson, A., J. Ostberg and S. Askegaard (2001), 'Cross-border shopping in the European market: 1 litre of hard liquor, 20 litres of wines, 24 litre of beer, 400 cigarettes MAX 30 Kilo!', in European Advances in Consumer Research 5 Andrea Groppel-Klein and Franz-Rudolf Esch, eds (Provo, UT: Association for Consumer Research): 246–52.

Davies, A. and J. Fitchett (2004), '"Crossing culture": A multi-method enquiry into consumer behaviour and the experience of cultural transition', Journal of Consumer Behaviour 3(4): 315–30.

Thompson, CJ. and Z. Arsel (2004), 'The Starbucks Brandscape and consumers' (anticorporate) experiences of glocalization', Journal of Consumer Research 31(3): 631–43.

Thompson, C.J. and S.K. Tambyah (1999), 'Trying to be cosmopolitan', Journal of Consumer Research 26(3): 214–42.

DTI (2002): Cross border shopping.
http://www.dti.gov.uk/ccp/topics1/pdf1/ecomm2full.pdf

DTI (2002), Internet and cross border shopping.
http://www.dti.gov.uk/ccp/topics1/pdf1/ecomm2.pdf.

European Commission: Unlocking the potential of cross-border shopping in the EU: Commission publishes survey results.
http://europa.eu.int/comm/consumers/cons_int/safe_shop/fair_bus_pract/green_pap_comm/studies/index_en.htm.

House of Commons Library (2002): Research paper 02/40: Cross Border shopping and smuggling.
http://www.parliament.uk/commons/lib/research/rp2002/rp02-040.pdf.

Oasis, Information on public services, Irish Government: Consumer rights and cross-border shopping in the European Union.
http://www.oasis.gov.ie/consumer_affairs/consumer_rights_and_cross_border_shopping_in_the_european_union.html.

Advertising targeted towards children: are the legal controls effective? The case of Belgium

CLAUDE PECHEUX and CHRISTIAN DERBAIX, Consumer Behaviour Analysis Laboratory, Catholic University of Mons, Belgium

In February 2001, during its presidency of the European Community, Sweden argued in favour of a complete ban in the European Community on advertising targeted towards children. Although the Swedish position did not meet with the other EU members' approval, in Belgium it triggered off new debates about the need to control advertising directed at children. This issue is not new and advertising restrictions have already been implemented in some European countries. Two types of restrictions exist: those that control ad content (for example: children can only play a 'passive role' in ads for sweets in Finland) and those that restrict ad placement (ban on ads during children's programmes in Austria; ban on toy ads between 7 p.m. and 10 p.m. in Greece, etc.). In the Dutch-speaking part of Belgium, advertising was rapidly forbidden for five minutes before and five minutes after children's programmes (the so-called 'five minutes' rule). The French-speaking part of Belgium recently adopted the same measure. This raises the question: are such ad placement restrictions really efficient? If the objective of such measures is to avoid possible confusion between an ad and the surrounding or next programme (that may have very similar formats), it makes sense. However, from an ad effectiveness point of view, placement restrictions could be questioned. Indeed, is an advertisement more efficient if it appears during or around children's programmes rather than during or around family programmes, as suggested by the 'five minutes' rule (to the extent that children also watch family programmes)? In order to provide answers to these questions, two experiments were conducted.

STUDY 1

The first experiment focused on the affect (mood) generated by the programme and on its impact on the effectiveness of a TV ad. Two mood-generating TV programmes were selected: *The Flintstones* was chosen on the basis that it generated a positive mood, and a programme teaching children how to recycle plastic was selected as a neutral mood inducer. One hundred and eighty-one children aged from 8 to 12 participated in all sessions of the experiment (a prior session consisted of assessing participants' cognitive age, knowledge and enduring involvement in the test product class). For the main session, upon their arrival children had to take part in a mood-neutralizing task, followed by instructions which manipulated involvement in the ads (either high or low). One of the two programmes was then broadcast, and was interrupted by a string of commercials. A new advertisement for a new brand of biscuits targeted at children (but unknown to Belgian children) was used as the test ad.[1] It was placed first and last in a pod (collection) made of five ads targeted at children. Immediately after exposure to the ads, children had to complete measurement scales for ad attitude (Aad), brand attitude (Ab), brand beliefs, purchase intent and brand choice. In this research, the key constructs were all measured by multiple-item scales especially developed for children and recently published.

The results showed that programmes which generated positive affect (feelings) lead to more positive ad evaluations when compared with programmes that generated a neutral affect, although this was not true for brand evaluations. As far as the interaction effect is concerned, it means (see Figure 1) that the impact of positive affect (feelings) on ad evaluations is much clearer in the case of low felt involvement than in the case of high felt involvement. In other words, ad scores increase more when going from neutral to positive

Figure 1 Interaction between programme affect and felt involvement

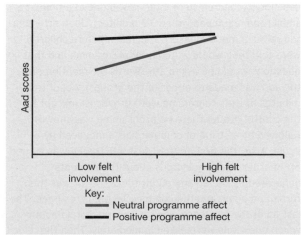

affect in the case of low felt involvement rather than in the case of high felt involvement.

Regressions were computed and showed that Aad was always a good predictor of Ab. The relationship between Aad and Ab is thus significant irrespective of the level of felt involvement. Additional and classic variables such as brand beliefs add nothing to the explanation of brand attitude when Aad is already in the model, even in the case of high felt involvement (whereas brand beliefs are usually highly significant among adults in the case of high felt involvement). In conclusion, the impact of Aad illustrates how affective variables and processes dominate among children exposed to commercials. This last result actually supports what others (Phelps and Hoy 1996; Derbaix and Bree 1997; Moore-Shay and Lutz 2000) have shown concerning the way children process and are persuaded by ads. This process is mainly affective, children 'reacting' to the ad and to its executional features, much more than analysing it.

STUDY 2

The second experiment aimed at achieving a better understanding of the role that programmes could play on ad effectiveness, when the programmes are varied along different dimensions. In that respect, two programme-related variables were used. The first one, 'programme liking',[2] is measured in this research by two items (dealing with the extent to which children liked/enjoyed the programme and to what extent they would like to watch it again). The second one is the target of the programme: the child versus the family. After a pre-study,[3] three programmes were selected: The Simpsons (a programme liked by children and targeted at them); Star Academy (a programme liked by children and targeted at the family); and the News (a programme not liked by children and targeted at the family[4]).

One hundred and twenty-six[5] children aged from 8 to 12 participated in the experiment which took place in schools (children were interviewed one at a time in a small room equipped with a TV monitor). Upon arrival in the room, a mood measure was taken before children were told they would watch a TV programme and that questions would be asked afterwards (no mention of the ads was made to either of the groups). About ten minutes of the programme were broadcast (except to the control group where no programme was shown) followed by a string of commercials announced by a jingle. After the first ad (first test ad), the TV was turned off in order to ask questions about the thoughts generated by the ad and ad attitude. The TV was then turned on again and the commercial break resumed. The last ad of the sequence was the second test ad about which questions were asked immediately. Then the children watched the second part of the programme, and this was followed by questions about the programme (programme liking and familiarity with this programme) and brand attitude. The children were then debriefed and thanked for their participation.

After some manipulation checks on programme liking, we compared the average scores obtained for both ad and brand attitude (for the two test ads). While the results do not show significant effects for brand attitudes (which may not be that surprising given the fact that the brands were known brands), interesting conclusions can be drawn for the ad attitude. Indeed, comparisons of means show that the ad evaluations are significantly more positive in the case of a programme not liked by children (the News) than in the case of the two programmes liked by children (Star Academy and The Simpsons). No significant difference is obtained, however, between these last two programmes.

Table 1 Study 2 – average aad

Group	Aad first ad	Aad last ad
Star Academy (liked) n = 35	16.66	18.00
Simpsons (liked) n = 32	16.66	17.94
News (disliked) n = 29	18.41	20.07
Control group n = 31	18.90	19.06

Aad scores range from 6 to 24.

What does this suggest? If we refer to the 'five minutes' rule implemented in Belgium, the results of Study 2 tend to suggest that such a rule is inefficient to the extent that it does not target the programmes around which the ads are the most efficient. Ads are indeed not more efficient in programmes targeted at children. They are more efficient around programmes that children do not like because in that particular case a contrast effect may operate between programmes and ads. Children seem to be 'relieved' to be watching something else.

QUESTIONS

1 Do you think that these two studies really answer the question about the relevancy of the 'five minutes' rule which was recently implemented in Belgium? Why?

2 Write down the design used in Study 2. What are the pros and cons of such a design?

3 What are the main arguments against and in favour of the Swedish position advocating a complete ban of advertising targeting children in the European Community?

4 Discuss the attitudes to advertising to children in your country.

Notes

1. The ad came from Switzerland where it was regularly aired.
2. And 'non weariness'.
3. About 40 children were interviewed about what they usually watched on TV and what they liked.
4. Even though children do not like the *News*, in many families children are in the room with their parents when the *News* is broadcast. Therefore, they are passively exposed to this programme.
5. After removing incomplete questionnaires.

Sources

Derbaix, Christian and Joël Bree (1997), 'The impact of children's affective reactions elicited by commercials on attitude toward the advertisement and the brand', *International Journal of Research in Marketing* 14(3): 207-29.

Moore-Shay, Elizabeth and Richard J. Lutz (2000), 'Children, advertising and product experiences: A multimethod inquiry', *Journal of Consumer Research* 27 (June): 31-48.

Phelps, Joseph E. and Mariea Grubbs Hoy (1996), 'The Aad-AB-PI relationship in children: The impact of brand familiarity and measurement timing', *Psychology and Marketing*, 13(1): 77-105.

Port wine: ruby, tawny, white and the premiums

CARLOS BRITO, University of Porto, Portugal

Port is a fortified wine named after Porto, the second-largest Portuguese city, from where it has traditionally been shipped. However, port begins its life in the Douro valley which starts some 100 km east of Porto (or Oporto in its anglicized form), and extends as far as the Spanish border. The valley is an administratively demarcated region where an estimated 30,000 farmers grow what is considered to be one of the great wines of the world.

The three most popular styles of port are ruby, tawny and white. The first is a young wine, somewhat full-bodied and fruity, with an open red colour. It is usually bottled after three years' ageing in wood and it is ready to drink immediately. It is usually consumed after dinner as a dessert wine. It goes very well with cheese, chocolate and dried fruits. Tawny is also a red wine but is aged longer than ruby. The wine becomes smoother, and acquires a brownish and lighter style. Tawny is considered the most 'versatile' of ports: it can be appreciated both as a dessert wine and as an aperitif (preferably chilled). In this case it goes very well with pâté, smoked ham and nuts. White port is, as its name suggests, made only with white grapes, and can be sweet or dry. After ageing usually 3–5 years in concrete vats, it is consumed chilled as an aperitif or summer drink. A good example is Portonic, a long drink made up of equal parts of white port and tonic water, served over ice with a slice of lemon.

Table 1 Average port prices in 2004

Types of Port	Average Price (euros/litre)
Standard port	
Ruby	3.50
Tawny	3.49
White	3.67
Special categories	
Vintage	17.83
LBV*	6.81
With indication of age	11.84

*LBV = Late Bottled Vintage

Source: Port and Douro Wines Institute.

In addition to these basic types, there are several special categories which correspond to the premium wines. Their prices are much higher than for a standard port. This is because their quality in terms of flavour and colour is better. However, there are also other reasons.

Firstly, the maturation process is longer and more complex, which tends to increase cost. Secondly, there are intangible aspects related to port: history and culture. In fact, a bottle of port not only includes wine in the strictest sense: it also embodies the history of port, which, in many respects, is linked to the history of Portugal over the past four centuries. And it also carries all of the social, cultural and geographical factors related to the environment of the Douro valley, a region that was declared a world heritage site by UNESCO. This means that when setting the price of port, especially premium ports, the shipping houses know that consumers value such intangible aspects.

Vintage, late bottled vintage and port with an indication of age are some of the best categories of port. The aristocrat of the wines is vintage port since it is produced with grapes of an outstanding year. It is bottled two years after the harvest and it matures in the bottle thereafter. Ten years is generally the absolute minimum, but 15 or 20 years might be needed. Vintage port and cheese are considered to have been created to be consumed together. An excellent example of this is the most classic and British combination: Stilton and Vintage.

Late bottled vintage (LBV) is also port of a single year but with a lower quality than vintage. It is bottled between the fourth and the sixth year after the harvest. New-style LBVs (which are becoming the majority) are filtered before bottling, and do not need further maturation in the bottle. Enjoy it during a meal, for example, with roasted duck or as a dessert wine with a wide range of chocolate of different textures.

Port with an indication of age can be 10, 20 or 30 years old or, rarely, over 40 years old. These ages, it should be noted, are average ages, and the old wines in the blend gain enormously from being refreshed by the addition of younger wine. These wines are aged in the cask and should not be further aged in the bottle. Ten-year-old port is fresh and fruity; the older ports are progressively nuttier, with less overt fruit. These ports are particularly pleasant when accompanying fresh fruit, light puddings, ice creams and not very rich cakes. They are also splendid as a digestive after coffee, when one enjoys the contentment that follows a good meal.

PORT TRADE

Although port is produced in the Douro valley, only a very small amount is shipped from there. In fact, almost all port produced in the valley is transported during the spring following the vintage to Porto where shippers' lodges are located. On arriving there, the wine is analysed in laboratories, tasted and classified. Then it matures for at least three years before being ready for commercialization.

There are dozens of shipping houses. Some of them are descendants of old British families established in Porto in the early seventeenth century. Croft (est. 1678), Warre & Co. (est. 1670) and Taylor, Fladgate & Yeatman (est. 1692) are examples of firms over 300 years old. Alongside the houses owned by the British families, there are important Portuguese-owned companies such as Real Companhia Velha and Ferreira. Some multinationals related to the drinks business have also taken a position in the sector. This is the case with Gran Cruz, owned by the multinational Martiniquaise, and Cockburn, owned by Allied Lyons.

Traditionally, nationality differences have been connected with distinct market orientations. In general, the Portuguese sector has dominated the home market along with very strong positions in France and Belgium. On the other hand, the British shippers have dominated the after-dinner segment, where quality and brand prestige are important factors in consumers' preferences. The United Kingdom is the largest market for premium ports, though in recent years this segment has grown considerably in some other countries such as the United States and Canada.

THE MARKETS

Although port is shipped to more than 100 countries, its sales are highly concentrated in just a few markets. The top three (France, Portugal and the United Kingdom) account for more than 50 per cent of total sales.

Each market has its own characteristics, and it is interesting to note that the top three countries are representative of distinct patterns of consumer behaviour.

France is the leading market. In 2004 it accounted for almost a quarter of total sales of port. Its profile is very typical: consumers are in general interested in cheap and young ports, and have little or no brand loyalty. Most trade is conducted via distributors who retail under their

Table 2 Port trade in 2004

Markets	Sales		Price
	10^3 euros	%	Euros/litre
France	92,525	23.1	3.50
Portugal	62,476	15.6	4.82
United Kingdom	55,270	13.8	5.14
Netherlands	50,624	12.7	3.31
Belgium	39,694	9.9	3.68
USA	29,861	7.5	7.88
Canada	18,986	4.7	8.39
Germany	9,822	2.5	3.75
Denmark	6,846	1.7	4.82
Spain	5,672	1.4	4.45
Others	28,248	7.1	4.51
Total	400,024	100.0	4.31

Source: Port and Douro Wines Institute.

own labels. In general, price is the critical factor in securing contracts. For the shipping house, this means uncertainty about orders, low profit margins, and minimal influence over the market.

In contrast to France, the United Kingdom, the third top market, is the largest market for premium ports. Special categories of port represent the majority of the total volume consumed there. Although vintage is considered to be the symbol of the British market, consumers are now moving towards lighter ports such as old tawny. For this reason, most shippers have launched new types of port in this segment – e.g. Cockburn's Special Reserve Tawny, Graham's 40-year-old tawny, and Croft's Distinction. But even these more standard ports have, in general, very good quality. As a result, their price is higher than the average price of standard ports shipped to France. Nevertheless, a significant part of port distributed in the UK is under the purchasers' own label, which reduces, to some extent, the shippers' control over the market.

Portugal, the second leading market accounting for 15.6 per cent of total sales, is neither a low quality nor a premium market. Consumers tend to prefer standard quality ports, particularly tawny and white port. Shippers' well-known brands have had a major impact on consumer preferences, although recent cases of heavy advertising and aggressive discounts have also succeeded in influencing consumer preferences.

Each market for port has its own different characteristics. One of the idiosyncrasies of the Portuguese market has to do with the reasons for buying port. A significant part of buying is for gift-giving inasmuch as it is common to give a bottle of port on special occasions such as anniversaries, parties and, especially, at Christmas. This fact has important consequences. Almost every family has at least one bottle of port at home – but did not buy it. Rather, it was given by someone else. This means that for a majority of consumers, the port they drink was chosen by someone else. Marketing strategies are affected by this fact. For instance, bottles, cases and labels are designed to take into account that in most instances port is bought as a gift. A good example of this is the form of the exterior packaging. Quite often bottles of port are sold inside a wooden or paper box. In addition to being a protective covering, its objective is to create promotional value since consumers tend to pay more for the appearance and prestige of better packages. But there is another interesting aspect. Square cases are more valued than round cases – because it is easier to wrap a square case.

France, Portugal and the United Kingdom are just three out of dozens of markets for port. In each one, consumer behaviour is different. This is undoubtedly one of the major challenges faced by the companies that produce and trade port: a great product but with many offerings.

QUESTIONS

1 What are the factors which influence product evaluation and choice in this case study?

2 Assume you are a marketing manager for the Portuguese market of a large port shipping house. Suggest some guidelines for an ad to promote a standard white port.

3 Use the port wine case to illustrate the concept of glocalization.

4 Discuss how you might market port in your own country.

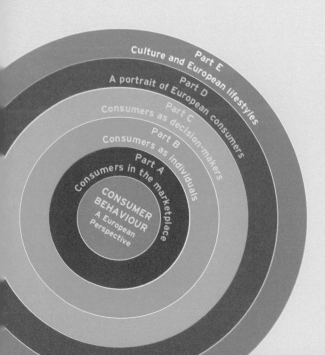

Part E
Culture and European lifestyles

Part D
A portrait of European consumers

Part C
Consumers as decision-makers

Part B
Consumers as individuals

Part A
Consumers in the marketplace

CONSUMER
BEHAVIOUR
A European
Perspective

CULTURE AND EUROPEAN LIFESTYLES

The final part of this book considers consumers as members of a broad cultural system. Chapter 14 starts this part by examining some of the basic building blocks of culture and consumption, and shows how consumer behaviours and culture are constantly interacting with each other. Chapter 15 looks at the production of culture, and how the 'gatekeepers' of culture help shape our sense of fashion and consumer culture. Chapter 16 focuses on the importance of understanding consumers' lifestyles throughout Europe, and illustrates the lifestyle concept and its marketing applications with a discussion of food, drink and cars. Finally, in Chapter 17 we look at some new perspectives on consumers' behaviour, including environmentalism, postmodernism and globalization. We try to place our western European consumer behaviour into the larger context of the global marketplace. These reflections on social changes in consumption bring our study of consumer behaviour into the new millennium.

CULTURE AND CONSUMER BEHAVIOUR

It's Thursday night, 7.30. Sean puts down the phone after speaking with Colum, his study partner in his consumer behaviour class. The weekly night out for the Irish marketing students has begun! Sean has just spent the summer months travelling in Europe. He was always amazed, and delighted, to find a place claiming to be an Irish pub - regardless of how unauthentic the place was, an Irish pub always sold Guinness, a true symbol of Ireland, he reflected. Sean had begun to drink when he started university. Initially, bottled beers straight from the fridge had been his preference. However, now that he's in his third year and a more sophisticated, travelled and rounded person, he feels that those beers were just a little too - well, fashionable. He has thus recently begun to drink Guinness. His dad, uncle and grandad, in fact most of the older men he knows, drink Guinness. That day in consumer behaviour the lecturer had discussed the 'Guinness Time' TV commercial which had been run the previous year. It featured a young man doing a crazy dance around a settling pint of Guinness. The young man saved his most crazed expression for the point when he took his first sip. The lecturer had pointed out that the objectives of the ad were to associate Guinness with fun - an important reason why young people drink alcohol - and to encourage them to be patient with the stout, as a good pint takes a number of minutes to settle.[1]

Sean has arranged to meet his friends in the local pub at 8.30. They will order 'three pints of the finest black stuff' and then have their own Guinness ritual. To begin, they watch it being poured and then look for the rising rings of the head - the best indication of a good pint. Once settled, a small top-up, and then ready for action. But they always wait and study their glasses before taking the first mouthful together - what a thing of beauty!

DAMIEN MCLOUGHLIN, University College, Dublin, Ireland

■ CULTURE AND CONSUMPTION

Consumption choices cannot be understood without considering the cultural context in which they are made: culture is the 'prism' through which people view products and try to make sense of their own and other people's consumer behaviour.

Sean's beer-drinking reflects his desire to associate with and dissociate from (with help from the media and marketers) a certain style, attitude and trendiness. Being an Irishman, his attachment to Guinness has a very different meaning in his world than it would have in, for example, trendy circles in continental cities, where Guinness may be associated with the very fashionability that Sean tries to avoid.

Indeed, it is quite common for cultures to modify symbols identified with other cultures and present these to a new audience. As this occurs, these cultural products undergo a process of **co-optation**, where their original meanings are transformed and often trivialized by outsiders. In this case, an Irish beer was to a large extent divorced from its original connection with the Irish traditional working class or rurality and is now used as a trendy way of consuming 'Irishness' abroad (but without the rural or lower-class aspect).[2]

This chapter considers how the culture in which we live creates the meaning of every-day products and how these meanings move through a society to consumers. As Figure 14.1 shows, meaning transfer is largely accomplished by such marketing vehicles as the advertising and fashion industries, which associate products with symbolic qualities. These goods, in turn, impart their meanings to consumers through different forms of ritual and are used to create and sustain consumer identities.

This chapter deals mainly with the way cultural values and symbols are expressed in goods and how consumers appropriate these symbols through consumption rituals. The next chapter will then take a closer look at fashion and other change processes in consumer culture. The first part of this chapter reviews what is meant by culture and how cultural priorities are identified and expressed. These social guidelines often take the form of *values*, which have already been discussed in Chapter 4. The second part considers the role of myths and rituals in shaping the cultural meaning of consumer products and consumption activities. The chapter concludes by exploring the concepts of the sacred and the profane and their relevance for consumer behaviour.

Culture, a concept crucial to the understanding of consumer behaviour, may be thought of as the collective memory of a society. Culture is the accumulation of shared

Figure 14.1 The movement of meaning

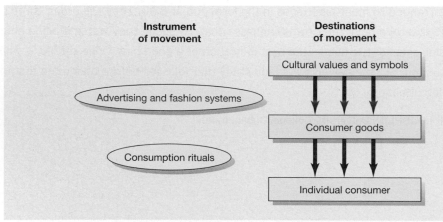

Source: Adapted from Grant McCracken, 'Culture and consumption: A theoretical account of the structure and movement of the cultural meaning of consumer goods', *Journal of Consumer Research* 13 (June 1986): 72. Reprinted with permission of The University of Chicago Press.

meanings, rituals, norms and traditions among the members of an organization or society. It is what defines a human community, its individuals, its social organizations, as well as its economic and political systems. It includes both abstract ideas, such as values and ethics, and the material objects and services, such as cars, clothing, food, art and sports, that are produced or valued by a group of people. Thus, individual consumers and groups of consumers are but part of culture, and culture is the overall system within which other systems are organized. This is a relatively new idea. Until recently, many researchers treated culture as a sort of variable that would explain differences in what they saw as the central dimension in society: economic behaviour. However, in our post-industrial society it has become increasingly evident that the principles of economy are themselves expressions of a specific kind of culture. Figure 14.2 provides an overview of this evolving approach to the relationship between culture and economy, indicating the all-encompassing influence that culture has on consumers.

Ironically, the effects of culture on consumer behaviour are so powerful and far-reaching that this importance is sometimes difficult to grasp or appreciate. We are surrounded by a lot of practices, from seemingly insignificant behaviours like pressing the start button of our Walkman to larger movements like flying to an exotic honeymoon in Thailand. What is important is that these practices have meaning to us, that we know how to interpret them. Culture is basically this interpretation system which we use to understand all those daily or extraordinary **signifying practices**[3] around us. Culture as a concept is like a fish immersed in water – we do not always appreciate this power until we encounter a different environment, where suddenly many of the assumptions we had taken for granted about the clothes we wear, the food we eat, the way we address others and so on no longer seem to apply. The effect of encountering such differences can be so great that the term 'culture shock' is not an exaggeration.

Figure 14.2 Relationship between culture and economy

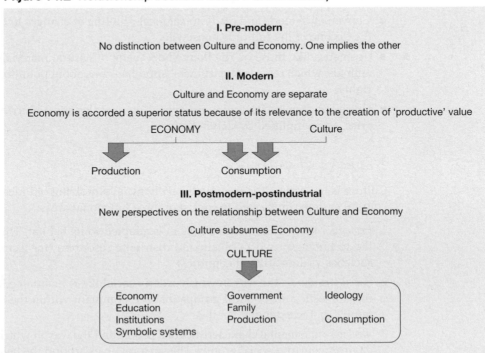

Source: Alladi Venkatesh, 'Ethnoconsumerism. A New Paradigm to Study Cultural and Cross-Cultural Consumer Behavior', in J.A. Costa and G. Bamossy, eds, *Marketing in a Multicultural World* (Thousand Oaks, CA: Sage, 1995).

The importance of these cultural expectations is only discovered when they are violated. For example, while on tour in New Zealand, the Spice Girls created a stir among New Zealand's Maoris by performing a war dance only men are supposed to do. A tribal official indignantly stated, 'It is not acceptable in our culture, and especially by girlie pop stars from another culture.'[4] Sensitivity to cultural issues, whether by rock stars or by brand managers, can only come by understanding these underlying dimensions – and that is the goal of this chapter.

Consumer behaviour and culture: a two-way street

A consumer's culture determines the overall priorities he or she attaches to different activities and products. It also determines the success or failure of specific products and services. A product that provides benefits consistent with those desired by members of a culture at any point in time has a much better chance of attaining acceptance in the marketplace. It may be difficult to guess the success or failure of certain products. Some years ago, the American business magazine *Forbes* predicted the imminent bankruptcy of the Danish stereo manufacturer Bang & Olufsen, and advised everybody to sell off their stocks in the company. In addition, they mocked the company's new product as a ghetto blaster, with the difference that the price was $3,000 and not $300. The product was the new 'on-the-wall' stereo with automatic sliding doors – the product was an instant success and the value of Bang & Olufsen stocks multiplied by 40![5] Here was a product that was launched when the time was right – something that *Forbes* overlooked.

The relationship between consumer behaviour and culture is a two-way street. On the one hand, products and services that resonate with the priorities of a culture at any given time have a much better chance of being accepted by consumers. On the other hand, the study of new products and innovations in product design successfully produced by a culture at any point in time provides a window on the dominant cultural ideals of that period. Consider, for example, some products that reflect underlying cultural processes at the time they were introduced:

- Convenience foods and ready-to-eat meals, hinting at changes in family structure and the decline of the full-time housewife.
- Cosmetics like those of The Body Shop, made of natural materials and not tested on animals, which reflected consumers' apprehensions about pollution, waste and animal rights.
- Unisex fragrances, indicating new views on sex roles and a blurring of gender boundaries, as exemplified by Calvin Klein.

Aspects of culture

Culture is not static. It is continually evolving, synthesizing old ideas with new ones. A cultural system can be said to consist of three functional areas:[6]

1 *Ecology* – the way in which a system is adapted to its habitat. This area is shaped by the technology used to obtain and distribute resources (for example, industrialized societies vs. less affluent countries).

2 *Social structure* – the way in which orderly social life is maintained. This area includes the domestic and political groups that are dominant within the culture (the nuclear family vs. the extended family).

3 *Ideology* – the mental characteristics of a people and the way in which they relate to their environment and social groups. This area revolves around the belief that members of a society possess a common **worldview**. They share certain ideas about principles of order and fairness. They also share an **ethos**, or a set of moral and aesthetic principles.

Oh my dog!

L'Eau de toilette

pour chien par

Dog Generation.

Testée sous contrôle
vétérinaire et
dermatologique.

Innocuité olfactive
et cutanée.

D.O.G
GENERATION
PARIS
www.doggeneration.com

Contemporary ads blur the lines
between subjects in this D.O.G. ad,
and play upon the brand's name. Is
this an ad that is well received in
your country's culture?

Corbis/Sygma

How cultures vary

Although every culture is different, a lot of research has aimed at reducing the cultural
variation to simpler principles. Cultures differ in their emphasis on individualism vs.
collectivism. In **collectivist cultures**, people subordinate their personal goals to those
of a stable in-group. By contrast, consumers in **individualist cultures** attach more
importance to personal goals, and people are more likely to change memberships when
the demands of the group (e.g. workplace, church, etc.) become too costly. A Dutch
researcher on culture, Geert Hofstede, has proposed this and three other dimensions, the
relation to differences in social power, handling of uncertainty and risk, and the degree
of masculine and feminine values, to account for much of this variability.[7] However,
Hofstede's and similar approaches have been much criticized. The four dimensions do
not account for the differences in the meaning and the role of the concepts in each culture. That each culture has to cope with problems of power, risk and uncertainty, gender
roles and the relationship between the individual and society is obvious. But that the
solutions to these problems are reducible to different levels on one and the same scale is
dubious, to say the least. For example, it is difficult to assume that concepts such as 'risk'
or 'masculine' would mean the same in all cultures.

Although we must be able to compare behaviour across cultures by using general concepts, we must do so by initially understanding and analysing every culture, and hence
every consumer culture, on the basis of its own premises, an approach known as **ethnoconsumerism**.[8] In Figure 14.3 the principles of an ethnoconsumerist methodology are
depicted. Note how central the notions of cultural categories and cultural practices are
to this approach to studying consumption. To illustrate the contribution of such an
approach to the study of consumer behaviour, consider a classic study of the meanings

Figure 14.3 Principles for an ethnoconsumerist approach to studying consumption

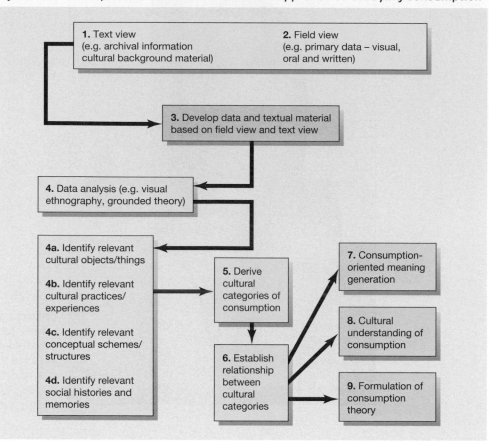

Source: Laurie Meamber and Alladi Venkatesh, 'Ethnoconsumerist Methodology for Cultural and Cross-Cultural Consumer Research', in R. Elliott and S. Beckmann, eds, *Interpretive Consumer Research* (Copenhagen: Copenhagen Business School Press, 2000): 87–108.

and roles of the Italian scooter in the Italian and British market contexts. Whereas in Italy the scooter was mainly positioned as a symbol of the new, modern and liberated Italian woman, epitomized in the Italian superstar actresses of the 1950s, the scooter in Britain became caught in a cultural clash between the more 'masculine' heavy industry and the blue-collar jobs expressed in subcultural terms among the 'rockers' and their motorcycles, and the more white-collar youth subculture of the 'mods', heavily engaged in conspicuous consumption activities. The latter adopted the scooter as their prime symbol and dominant mode of transport.[9] Even a simple thing like drinking a cup of coffee does not hold the same meaning in different cultures.[10]

Rules for behaviour

Values, as we saw in Chapter 4, are very general principles for judging between good and bad goals, etc. They form the core principles of every culture. From these flow norms, or rules, dictating what is right or wrong, acceptable or unacceptable. Some norms, called *enacted norms*, are explicitly decided upon, such as the rule that a green traffic light means 'go' and a red one means 'stop'. Many norms, however, are much more subtle. These *crescive norms* are embedded in a culture and are only discovered through interaction with other members of that culture. Crescive norms include the following:[11]

▶ ● A **custom** is a norm handed down from the past that controls basic behaviours, such as division of labour in a household or the practice of particular ceremonies.

▶ ● **Mores** are customs with a strong moral overtone. Mores often involve a taboo, or forbidden behaviour, such as incest or cannibalism. Violation of mores often meets with strong censure from other members of a society.

▶ ● **Conventions** are norms regarding the conduct of everyday life. These rules deal with the subtleties of consumer behaviour, including the 'correct' way to furnish one's house, wear one's clothes, host a dinner party, and so on.

All three types of crescive norms may operate to define a culturally appropriate behaviour. For example, mores may tell us what kind of food it is permissible to eat. Note that mores vary across cultures, so eating a dog may be taboo in Europe, while Hindus would shun beaf steak and Muslims avoid pork products. Custom dictates the appropriate hour at which the meal should be served. Conventions tell us how to eat the meal, including such details as the utensils to be used, table etiquette, and even the appropriate apparel to be worn at dinner time.

We often take these conventions for granted, assuming that they are the 'right' things to do (again, until we are exposed to a different culture!). And it is good to remember that much of what we know about these norms is learned *vicariously* (see Chapter 3), as we observe the behaviours of actors and actresses in films and TV series, but also television commercials, print ads and other popular culture media. In the long run, marketers have a great deal to do with influencing consumers' enculturation!

■ MYTHS AND RITUALS

Every culture develops stories and practices that help its members to make sense of the world. When we examine these activities in other cultures, they often seem strange or even unfathomable. Yet our *own* cultural practices appear quite normal – even though a visitor may find them equally bizarre!

It works like magic!

To appreciate how so-called 'primitive' belief systems which some may consider irrational or superstitious continue to influence our supposedly 'modern', rational society, consider the avid interest of many Western consumers in magic. Marketers of health foods, anti-ageing cosmetics, exercise programmes and gambling casinos often imply that their offerings have 'magical' properties that will ward off sickness, old age, poverty or just plain bad luck. People by the millions play their 'lucky numbers' in the lottery, carry lucky charms to ward off 'the evil eye', or have 'lucky' clothing or other products which they believe will bring them good fortune. Often consumers construct marketplace mythologies to serve multiple and sometimes competing ideological agendas – this is particularly true in the product categories which consumers use to deal with issues of health, healing and well-being.[12]

An interest in the occult tends to be popular, perhaps even more so when members of a society feel overwhelmed or powerless – magical remedies simplify our lives by giving us 'easy' answers. Marketing efforts are replete with more or less open references to magical practices.[13] And it is not just a matter of fooling consumers: magic is an active part also of our modern lives. Customers at river-rafting trips in America speak about the magical capacities of the river to transform their lives, heal psychological wounds and bring out the best in people.[14] Even a computer is regarded with awe by many consumers as a sort of 'electronic magician', with the ability to solve our problems (or in other cases to make data magically disappear!).[15] This section will discuss myths and rituals, two aspects of culture common to all societies, from the ancients to the modern world.

Myths

▶ Every society possesses a set of myths that define that culture. A **myth** is a story containing symbolic elements that expresses the shared emotions and ideals of a culture. The story may feature some kind of conflict between two opposing forces, and its outcome serves as a moral guide. In this way, a myth reduces anxiety because it provides consumers with guidelines about their world.

An understanding of cultural myths is important to marketers, who in some cases (most likely unconsciously) pattern their strategy along a mythic structure.[16] Consider, for example, the way that a company like McDonald's takes on 'mythical' qualities.[17] The golden arches are a universally recognized symbol, one that is virtually synonymous with American culture. Not only do they signify the possibility for the whole world symbolically to consume a bite of Americana and modernity, but they also offer sanctuary to Americans around the world, who know exactly what to expect once they enter. Basic struggles involving good vs. evil are played out in the fantasy world created by McDonald's advertising, as when Ronald McDonald confounds the Hamburglar. McDonald's even has a 'seminary' (Hamburger University) where inductees go to learn appropriate behaviours and be initiated into the culture. But of course, one of the most fundamental myths of the Western world is the myth of the 'exotic Other' which is basically different from ourselves, expressed by Kipling in his 'East is East and West is West, and never the twain shall meet'. This is reflected in consumer behaviour in the attraction to and collection of exotic goods such as Oriental carpets.[18]

The functions and structure of myths

Myths serve four interrelated functions in a culture:[19]

1 *Metaphysical* – they help to explain the origins of existence.

2 *Cosmological* – they emphasize that all components of the universe are part of a single picture.

3 *Sociological* – they maintain social order by authorizing a social code to be followed by members of a culture.

4 *Psychological* – they provide models for personal conduct.

Myths can be analysed by examining their underlying structures, a technique pioneered by the anthropologist Claude Lévi-Strauss. Lévi-Strauss noted that many stories involve *binary opposition*, where two opposing ends of some dimension are represented (good vs. evil, nature vs. technology). Characters and products often appear in advertisements to be defined by what they *are not* rather than by what they *are* (for example, this is *not* a product for those who feel old, *not* an experience for the frightened, *not* music for the meek, etc.).

Recall from the discussion of Freudian theory in Chapter 4 that the ego functions as a kind of 'referee' between the opposing needs of the id and the superego. In a similar fashion, the conflict between mythical opposing forces is sometimes resolved by a *mediating figure*, who can link the opposites by sharing characteristics of each. For example, many myths contain animals that have human abilities (e.g. a talking snake) to bridge the gap between humanity and nature, just as cars (technology) are often given animal names (nature) like Jaguar or Mustang.

Myths are found everywhere in modern popular culture. While we generally equate myths with the ancient Greeks or Romans, modern myths are embodied in many aspects of popular culture, including comic books, films, holidays and even commercials.

Comic book superheroes demonstrate how myths can be communicated to consumers
▶ of all ages. Indeed, some of these fictional figures represent a **monomyth**, a myth that is common to many cultures.[20] The most prevalent monomyth involves a hero who emerges from the everyday world with supernatural powers and wins a decisive victory

over evil forces. He then returns with the power to bestow good things on his fellow men. This basic theme can be found in such classic heroes as Lancelot, Hercules and Ulysses. The success of the Disney movie *Hercules* reminds us that these stories are timeless and appeal to people through the ages.

Comic book heroes are familiar to most consumers, and they are viewed as more credible and effective than celebrity endorsers. Film spin-offs and licensing deals aside, comic books are a multi-million dollar industry. The American version of the monomyth is best epitomized by Superman, a Christ-like figure who renounces worldly temptations and restores harmony to his community. Heroes such as Superman are sometimes used to endow a product, store or service with desirable attributes. This imagery is sometimes borrowed by marketers – PepsiCo tried to enhance its position in the Japanese market by using a figure called 'Pepsiman', a muscle-bound caricature of an American superhero in a skin-tight uniform, to promote the drink. Pepsiman even appears in a Sega game called *Fighting Vipers*.[21]

But there are many other, less obvious, mythological figures surrounding us. For example, the role of Einstein as a mythological figure, and one that is used for giving meaning to and promoting certain consumable objects such as films or posters, or in advertisements as a sort of indirect endorsement, has been studied by consumer researchers.[22]

Many blockbuster films and hit TV programmes draw directly on mythic themes. While dramatic special effects or attractive stars certainly don't hurt, a number of these films perhaps owe their success to their presentation of characters and plot structures that follow mythic patterns. Examples of these mythic blockbusters include:[23]

- *The Big Blue*. The sea is the offspring of many myths. Its inaccessibility and depth have always inspired humans to create imagery about this other world. The film depicts the search for a lost symbiosis between man and nature, where the only person with real access to this must give up his human life to become one with the purity and the graciousness of the sea, symbolized by the dolphins.

- *E.T.: The Extraterrestrial*. E.T. represents a familiar myth involving Messianic visitation. The gentle creature from another world visits Earth and performs miracles (e.g. reviving a dying flower). His 'disciples' are local children, who help him combat the forces of modern technology and an unbelieving secular society. The metaphysical function of myth is served by teaching that the humans chosen by God are pure and unselfish.

- *Easy Rider*. This 1969 cult film can be seen as the forerunner of the much-beloved road movie genre that has been among the most popular in recent decades, and which got its definitive feminist version with *Thelma and Louise*. These films feature myths of freedom and rebelliousness against the banalities of daily life (as expressed in one of the theme songs from *Easy Rider*, Steppenwolf's 'Born to be Wild'), which are recycled in a lot of commercial contexts. For instance, in a commercial for Ford's Cougar (another wild animal!) model, Dennis Hopper (anno 1998) driving a Cougar raced with himself riding a motorbike in the original *Easy Rider* film.[24]

- *Jaws*. This and films constructed around similar themes draw on myths of the beast, representing the wild, dangerous, untamed nature that is culture's (human being's) enemy. Such myths are known from Christianity and other religious mythologies, such as Norse mythology (the Midgaard Snake, the Fenris Wolf), and have played a central role in the way the Western world has regarded nature over the centuries.

Commercials as myths

Commercials can be analysed in terms of the underlying cultural themes they represent. For example, commercials for various food products ask consumers to 'remember' the mythical good old days when products were wholesome and natural. The mythical theme of the underdog prevailing over the stronger foe (i.e. David and Goliath) has been

This Spanish ad melds modern-day athletes with mythical figures.

Canal/ACB-Contrapunto BBDO Ad Agency

used by the car rental firm Avis in a now classic campaign where they stated 'We're only no. 2, we try harder'. Other figures from mythical narratives have been used by advertisers, such as the villain (a brand teasing its competitors), the hero (the brand in control) or the helper (the brand that helps you accomplish something).[25]

Rituals

▶ A ritual is a set of multiple, symbolic behaviours that occur in a fixed sequence and that tend to be repeated periodically.[26] Although bizarre tribal ceremonies, perhaps involving animal or virgin sacrifice, may come to mind when people think of rituals, in reality many contemporary consumer activities are ritualistic. Four major types of rituals are possession rituals, exchange rituals, grooming rituals and divestment rituals.[27] Below, we shall take a closer look at some of these.

Rituals can occur at a variety of levels, as noted in Table 14.1. Some of the rituals described are specifically American, but the US Super Bowl may be compared to the English FA Cup Final or the traditional ski jump competition in Austria on the first day of the new year. Some rituals affirm broad cultural or religious values, like the differences in the ritual of tea-drinking in Great Britain and France. Whereas tea seems a sensuous and mystical drink to the French, the drinking of coffee is regarded as having a more functional purpose. For the British, tea is a daily drink and coffee is seen more as a drink to express oneself.[28]

The ritual of going to a café with a selection of coffee opportunities was unknown outside the most metropolitan areas of the United States until recent times. No longer. The Starbucks Corporation has experienced phenomenal success by turning the coffee break into a cultural event that for many has assumed almost cult-like status. The average Starbucks customer visits 18 times a month, and 10 per cent of the clientele stops by twice

Table 14.1 Types of ritual experience

Primary behaviour source	Ritual type	Examples
Cosmology	Religious	Baptism, meditation, mass
Cultural values	Rites of passage Cultural	Graduation, marriage Festivals, holidays (Valentine's Day), Super Bowl
Group learning	Civic Group Family	Parades, elections, trials Business negotiations, office luncheons Mealtimes, bedtimes, birthdays, Mother's Day, Christmas
Individual aims and emotions	Personal	Grooming, household rituals

Source: Dennis W. Rook, 'The ritual dimension of consumer behavior', *Journal of Consumer Research* 12 (December 1985): 251–64. Reprinted with permission of The University of Chicago Press.

a day.[29] Starbucks has opened shops in Paris, in competition with the city's 2,000 traditional cafés and 31 Columbus Café outlets, in order to try and introduce the 'to go' coffee culture among Parisians. Preliminary results for Columbus Café for 2003 indicate that revenue was over 8 million euros.[30] The UK market for on-the-go food and drinks is predicted to grow by 262 million euros to 20.1 billion euros by 2008.

Gift giving has long been a cultural trait among the Japanese. In recent years, it has become popular within the context of a westernised Christmas season in Japan.

Getty Images/Taxi/Gen Nishino

Ritual artefacts

▶ Many businesses owe their livelihoods to their ability to supply ritual artefacts, or items used in the performance of rituals, to consumers. Birthday candles, diplomas, specialized foods and beverages (e.g. wedding cakes, ceremonial wine, or even sausages at the stadium), trophies and plaques, band costumes, greetings cards and retirement watches are all used in consumer rituals. In addition, consumers often employ a ritual script, which identifies the artefacts, the sequence in which they are used and who uses them. The proliferation of 'manners and style' books in recent years bears witness to the renewed interest in rituals after the belief of the beat generation that they could abolish ritual behaviour and just act 'normal' and be 'natural'. Of course, such behaviour required a whole new set of rituals . . .

But rituals are not restricted to the special occasions described above. Daily life is full of ritualized behaviour. Wearing a tie on certain occasions can be seen as a ritual, for example. The significance attached to rituals will vary across cultures (Valentine's Day is slowly gaining popularity in several European countries, and in the Middle East),[31] and will often be a mixture of private and public (generally shared) symbolism.[32]

Grooming rituals

Whether brushing one's hair 100 strokes a day or talking to oneself in the mirror, virtually all consumers undergo private grooming rituals. These are sequences of behaviours that aid in the transition from the private self to the public self or back again. These rituals serve various purposes, ranging from inspiring confidence before confronting the world to cleansing the body of dirt and other profane materials. Traditionally a female market, the grooming sector for men is a booming business. For example, Unilever has opened a new chain of barbershops in the UK that also offer facial treatments and manicures on top of the shaves and beard trims. The adaptation to the male market is almost perfect: the waiting rooms feature PlayStations and personal CD players instead of glossy magazines.[33]

When consumers talk about their grooming rituals, some of the dominant themes that emerge from these stories reflect the almost mystical qualities attributed to grooming products and behaviours. Many people emphasize a before-and-after phenomenon, where the person feels magically transformed after using certain products (similar to the Cinderella myth).[34]

Two sets of binary oppositions that are expressed in personal rituals are *private/public* and *work/leisure*. Many beauty rituals, for instance, reflect a transformation from a natural state to the social world (as when a woman 'puts on her face') or vice versa. In these daily rituals, women reaffirm the value placed by their culture on personal beauty and the quest for eternal youth.[35] This focus is obvious in ads for Oil of Olay beauty cleanser, which proclaim: 'And so your day begins. The Ritual of Oil of Olay'. Similarly, the bath is viewed as a sacred, cleansing time, a way to wash away the sins of the profane world.[36]

Gift-giving rituals

The promotion of appropriate gifts for every conceivable holiday and occasion provides an excellent example of the influence consumer rituals can exert on marketing phenom-
▶ ena. In the gift-giving ritual, consumers procure the perfect object (artefact), meticulously remove the price tag (symbolically changing the item from a commodity to a unique good), carefully wrap it and deliver it to the recipient.[37]

Gift-giving used to be viewed by researchers primarily as a form of economic exchange, where the giver transfers an item of value to a recipient, who in turn is somehow obliged to reciprocate. However, gift-giving is interpreted increasingly as a symbolic exchange, where the giver is motivated by acknowledging the social bonds between people.[38] These might then be seen as more economic and reciprocal but may also be guided by unselfish factors, such as love or admiration, without expectations of anything in return. Some

Table 14.2 Effects of gift-giving on social relationships

Relational effect	Description	Example
Strengthening	Gift-giving improves the quality of a relationship	An unexpected gift such as one given in a romantic situation
Affirmation	Gift-giving validates the positive quality of a relationship	Usually occurs on ritualized occasions such as birthdays
Negligible effect	Gift-giving has a minimal effect on perceptions of relationship quality	Non-formal gift occasions and those where the gift may be perceived as charity or too good for the current state of the relationship
Negative confirmation	Gift-giving validates a negative quality of a relationship between the gift-giver and the receiver	The selection of gift is inappropriate, indicating a lack of knowledge of the receiver. Alternatively the gift is viewed as a method of controlling the receiver
Weakening	Gift-giving harms the quality of the the relationship between giver and receiver	When there are 'strings attached' or gift is perceived as a bribe, a sign of disrespect or offensive
Severing	Gift-giving harms the relationship between the giver and the receiver to the extent that the relationship is dissolved	When the gift forms part of a larger problem, such as a threatening relationship. Or when a relationship is severed through the receipt of a 'parting' gift

Source: Adapted from Julie A. Ruth, Cele C. Otnes and Frederic F. Brunel, 'Gift receipt and the reformulation of interpersonal relationships', *Journal of Consumer Research* 25 (March 1999): 385–402, Table 1, p. 389.

research indicates that gift-giving evolves as a form of social expression: it is more exchange-oriented (instrumental) in the early stages of a relationship, but becomes more altruistic as the relationship develops.[39] One set of researchers identified multiple ways in which giving a gift can affect a relationship.[40] These are listed in Table 14.2.

Every culture prescribes certain occasions and ceremonies for giving gifts, whether for personal or professional reasons. The giving of birthday presents alone is a major undertaking. Business gifts are an important component in defining professional relationships, and great care is often taken to ensure that the appropriate gifts are purchased.

multicultural dimensions

The importance of gift-giving rituals is underscored by considering Japanese customs, where the wrapping of a gift is as important (if not more so) than the gift itself. The economic value of a gift is secondary to its symbolic meaning.[41] To the Japanese, gifts are viewed as an important aspect of one's duty to others in one's social group. Giving is a moral imperative (known as *giri*).

Highly ritualized gift-giving occurs during the giving of both household/personal gifts and company/professional gifts. Each Japanese has a well-defined set of relatives and friends with whom he or she shares reciprocal gift-giving obligations (*kosai*).[42]

Personal gifts are given on social occasions, such as at funerals, to people who are hospitalized, to mark movements from one stage of life to another (such as weddings, birthdays) and as greetings (when one is meeting a visitor). Company gifts are given to commemorate the anniversary of a corporation's founding or the opening of a new building, as well as being a routine part of doing business, as when rewards are given at trade meetings to announce new products.

Some of the items most desired by Japanese consumers to receive as gifts include gift coupons, beer and soap.[43] In keeping with the Japanese emphasis on saving face, presents are not opened in front of the giver, so that it will not be necessary to hide one's possible disappointment with the present.

The gift-giving ritual can be broken down into three distinct stages.[44] During *gestation*, the giver is motivated by an event to procure a gift. This event may be either *structural* (i.e. prescribed by the culture, as when people buy Christmas presents), or *emergent* (i.e. the decision is more personal and idiosyncratic). The second stage is *presentation*, or the process of gift exchange. The recipient responds to the gift (either appropriately or not), and the donor evaluates this response.

In the third stage, known as *reformulation*, the bonds between the giver and receiver are adjusted (either looser or tighter) to reflect the new relationship that emerges after the exchange is complete. Negativity can arise if the recipient feels the gift is inappropriate or of inferior quality. The donor may feel the response to the gift was inadequate or insincere or a violation of the reciprocity norm, which obliges people to return the gesture of a gift with one of equal value.[45] Both participants may feel resentful for being 'forced' to participate in the ritual.[46]

Self-gifts

People commonly find (or devise) reasons to give themselves something; they 'treat' themselves. Consumers purchase **self-gifts** as a way to regulate their behaviour. This ritual provides a socially acceptable way of rewarding themselves for good deeds, consoling themselves after negative events or motivating themselves to accomplish some goal.[47] Figure 14.4 is a projective stimulus similar to ones used in research on self-gifting. Consumers are asked to tell a story based on a picture such as this, and their responses are analysed to discover the reasons people view as legitimate for rewarding themselves with self-gifts. For example, one recurring story that might emerge is that the woman in the picture had a particularly gruelling day at work and needed a pick-me-up in the form

Figure 14.4 Projective drawing to study the motivations underlying the giving of self-gifts

Source: Based on David G. Mick, Michelle DeMoss and Ronald J. Faber, 'Latent Motivations and Meanings of Self-Gifts: Implications for Retail Management' (research report, Center for Retailing Education and Research, University of Florida, 1990).

of a new fragrance. This theme could then be incorporated into a promotional campaign for a perfume. With the growing evidence of hedonic motives for consumption in recent decades, self-gifts may represent an increasingly important part of the overall consumption pattern.

Holiday rituals

Holidays are important rituals in both senses of the word. Going on holiday was one of the most widespread rituals and tourism one of the biggest industries of the late twentieth century, and the trend looks set to continue.[48] On holidays consumers step back from their everyday lives and perform ritualistic behaviours unique to those times.[49] For example, going to Disneyland in Paris may mean a ritualized return to the memories of our own dreams of a totally free (of obligations, duties and responsibilities) fantasy land of play.[50] Holiday occasions are filled with ritual artefacts and scripts and are increasingly cast as a time for giving gifts by enterprising marketers. Holidays also often mean big business to hotels, restaurants, travel agents and so on.

For many businesses Christmas is the single most important season. Concerning the holidays of celebrations, most such holidays are based on a myth, and often a real (Guy Fawkes) or imaginary (Cupid on Valentine's Day) character is at the centre of the story. These holidays persist because their basic elements appeal to deep-seated patterns in the functioning of culture.[51]

The Christmas holiday is bursting with myths and rituals, from adventures at the North Pole to those that occur under the mistletoe. One of the most important holiday rituals involves Santa Claus, or an equivalent mythical figure, eagerly awaited by children the world over. Unlike Christ, this person is a champion of materialism. Perhaps it is no coincidence, then, that he appears in stores and shopping centres – secular temples of consumption. Whatever the origins of Santa Claus, the myth surrounding him serves the purpose of socializing children by teaching them to expect a reward when they are good and that members of society get what they deserve. Needless to say, Christmas, Santa Claus and other attached rituals and figures change when they enter into other cultural settings. Some of the transformations of Santa Claus in a Japanese context include a figure called 'Uncle Chimney', Santa Claus as a stand-in for the newborn Christ and Santa Claus crucified at the entrance of one department store with the words 'Happy Shopping' written above his head.[52] What does this tell us about the globalization process?

On Valentine's Day, standards regarding sex and love are relaxed or altered as people express feelings that may be hidden during the rest of the year. In addition to cards, a variety of gifts are exchanged, many of which are touted by marketers to represent aphrodisiacs or other sexually related symbols. It seems as if many people in consumer societies are always on the lookout for new rituals to fill their lives. This ritual was once virtually unknown in Scandinavia but is slowly becoming part of their consumption environment.[53] Also, the American ritual of celebrating Hallowe'en is now becoming fashionable in Europe, where the French in particular have adopted it as an occasion for festivities, dancing and the chance to show off new fashions.[54]

Rites of passage

What does a dance for recently divorced people have in common with 'college initiation ceremonies'? Both are examples of modern **rites of passage**, or special times marked by a change in social status. Every society, both primitive and modern, sets aside times where such changes occur. Some of these changes may occur as a natural part of consumers' life cycles (puberty or death), while others are more individual in nature (divorce and re-entering the dating market). As we saw with some of the other rituals, there seems to be a renewed interest in transition rites. They are increasingly becoming consumption objects in themselves as well as occasions for consumption. In order to satisfy the 'need' for rituals, not only do we import new ones from abroad, as we have seen, but in times of globalization many cultures also experience a renewed interest in the old rituals that have traditionally framed the cultural identity.[55]

Some marketers attempt to reach consumers on occasions in which their products can enhance a transition from one stage of life to another.[56] A series of Volkswagen ads underlined the role of the car in the freedom of women who were leaving their husbands or boyfriends.

Stages of role transition Much like the metamorphosis of a caterpillar into a butterfly, consumers' rites of passage consist of three phases.[57] The first stage, *separation*, occurs when the individual is detached from his or her original group or status (for example, the first-year university student leaves home). *Liminality* is the middle stage, where the person is literally in between statuses (the new arrival on campus tries to work out what is happening during orientation week). The last stage, *aggregation*, takes place when the person re-enters society after the rite of passage is complete (the student returns home for the Christmas holiday as a 'real university student'). Rites of passage mark many consumer activities, as exemplified by confirmation or other rites of going from the world of the child to the world of the adult. A similar transitional state can be observed when people are prepared for certain occupational roles. For example, athletes and fashion models typically undergo a 'seasoning' process. They are removed from their normal surroundings (athletes are taken to training camps, while young models are often moved to Paris or Milan), indoctrinated into a new subculture and then returned to the real world in their new roles.

The final passage: marketing death The rites of passage associated with death support an entire industry. Death themes are replete in marketing.[58] Survivors must make expensive purchase decisions, often at short notice and driven by emotional and superstitious concerns. Funeral ceremonies help the living to organize their relationships with the deceased, and action tends to be tightly scripted down to the costumes (the ritual black attire, black ribbons for mourners, the body in its best suit) and specific behaviours (sending condolence cards or holding a wake). (However, more and more seem to emphasize a certain personal touch to commemorate the individuality of the deceased.) Mourners 'pay their last respects', and seating during the ceremony is usually dictated by mourners' closeness to the individual. Even the cortège is accorded special status by other motorists, who recognize its separate, sacred nature by not overtaking as it proceeds to the cemetery.[59]

■ SACRED AND PROFANE CONSUMPTION

As we saw when considering the structure of myths, many types of consumer activity involve the demarcation, or binary opposition, of boundaries, such as good vs. bad, male vs. female – or even 'regular' vs. 'low-fat'. One of the most important of these sets of boundaries is the distinction between the sacred and the profane. **Sacred consumption** involves objects and events that are 'set apart' from normal activities, and are treated with some degree of respect or awe. They may or may not be associated with religion, but most religious items and events tend to be regarded as sacred. **Profane consumption** involves consumer objects and events that are ordinary, everyday objects and events that do not share the 'specialness' of sacred ones. (Note that profane does not mean vulgar or obscene in this context.)

Domains of sacred consumption

Sacred consumption events permeate many aspects of consumers' experiences. We find ways to 'set apart' a variety of places, people and events. In this section, we'll consider some examples of ways that 'ordinary' consumption is sometimes not so ordinary after all.

Sacred places are revered, not only in 'real life' but also in advertising, since they are immediately recognizable, highly visible and normally connote positive values. The present mythologies of the grandeur of antiquity and more generally myths attached to sacred places of world heritage are used here in a humorous (but also sacrilegious?) way for maximum attention and mind-provocation.

Sacred places

Sacred places have been 'set apart' by a society because they have religious or mystical significance (e.g. Bethlehem, Mecca, Stonehenge) or because they commemorate some aspect of a country's heritage (e.g. the Kremlin, Versailles, the Colosseum in Rome). Remember that in many cases the sacredness of these places is due to the property of contamination – that is, something sacred happened on that spot, so the place itself takes on sacred qualities. Tourism is one of the most common and rapidly spreading forms of consuming the sacred.[60]

Other places are created from the profane world and imbued with sacred qualities. When Ajax, the local football team of Amsterdam, moved from their old stadium, De Meern, to a larger, more modern stadium (De Arena), the turf from the old stadium was carefully lifted from the ground and sold to a local churchyard. The churchyard offers the turf to fans willing to pay a premium price to be buried under authentic Ajax turf!

Even the modern shopping centre can be regarded as a secular 'cathedral of consumption', a special place where community members come to practise shopping rituals.[61] Theme parks are a form of mass-produced fantasy that takes on aspects of sacredness. In particular, the various Disneylands are destinations for pilgrimages from consumers around the globe. Disneyland displays many characteristics of more traditional sacred places, especially for Americans, but Europeans too may consider these parks the quintessence of America. It is even regarded by some as the epitome of child(ish) happiness. A trip to the park is the most common 'last wish' for terminally-ill children.[62]

In many cultures, the home is a particularly sacred place. It represents a crucial distinction between the harsh, external world and consumers' 'inner space'. In northern and western Europe the home is a place where you entertain guests (in southern Europe it is more common to go out), and fortunes are spent each year on interior decorators and home furnishings; the home is thus a central part of consumers' identities.[63] But even here there are vast differences between, for example, the dominant traditionalist style of British homes and the modernist style of Danish homes.[64] Consumers all over the world go to great lengths to create a special environment that allows them to create the quality of homeliness. This effect is created by personalizing the home as much as possible, using such devices as door wreaths, mantel arrangements and a 'memory wall' for family photos.[65] Even public places, like various types of cafés and bars, strive for a home-like atmosphere which shelters customers from the harshness of the outside world.

Sacred people

People themselves can be sacred, when they are idolized and set apart from the masses. Souvenirs, memorabilia and even mundane items touched or used by sacred people take on special meanings and acquire value in their own right. Indeed, many businesses thrive on consumers' desire for products associated with famous people. There is a thriving market for celebrity autographs, and objects once owned by celebrities, whether Princess Diana's gowns or John Lennon's guitars, are often sold at auction for astronomical prices. A store called 'A Star is Worn' sells items donated by celebrities – a black bra autographed by Cher sold for $575. As one observer commented about the store's patrons, 'They want something that belonged to the stars, as if the stars have gone into sainthood and the people want their shrouds.'[66] More recently, the UK firm of ASOS (AsSeenOnScreen) has started a thriving online business targeted at 18–30-year-olds (primarily female) which offers for sale products that are identical to products that are seen in television shows. The company owners got the idea after reading an article reporting that the broadcasters of *Friends* (the television show) received over 28,000 telephone calls enquiring about a lamp that had appeared in one of the character's apartment.[67]

Sacred events

Many consumers' activities have taken on a special status. Public events in particular resemble sacred, religious ceremonies, as exemplified by the playing of the national anthems before a game or the reverential lighting of matches and lighters at the end of a rock concert.[68]

For many people, the world of sport is sacred and almost assumes the status of a religion. The roots of modern sports events can be found in ancient religious rites, such as fertility festivals (e.g. the original Olympics).[69] Indeed, it is not uncommon for teams to join in prayer prior to a game. The sports pages are like the Scriptures (and we describe ardent fans as reading them 'religiously'), the stadium is a house of worship, and the fans are members of the congregation. After the first Scottish victory in many years in a football match against England at Wembley Stadium, Scottish fans tore down the goals to bring pieces back home as sacred relics. Indeed, grass from stadiums of important matches, like World Cup finals, has been sold in small portions at large prices.

Devotees engage in group activities, such as tailgate parties (eating and drinking in the car park prior to the event) and the 'Mexican Wave', where (resembling a revival meeting) participants on cue join the wave-like motion as it makes its way around the stadium. The athletes that fans come to see are godlike; they are reputed to have almost superhuman powers (especially football stars in southern Europe and Latin America). Athletes are central figures in a common cultural myth, the hero tale. As exemplified by mythologies of the barefoot Olympic marathon winner (Abebe Bikila from Ethiopia, 1960), or of boxing heroes (legally) fighting their way out of poverty and misery, often the person must prove him- or herself under strenuous circumstances. Victory is achieved only through sheer force of will. Of course, sports heroes are popular endorsers in commercials, but only a few of these sports personalities 'travel' very well, since sports heroes tend to be first and foremost national heroes. However, a few people are known worldwide, at least within the key target for the ads, so that they can be used in international campaigns.

If sport is one domain that is becoming increasingly sacred (see the section on sacralization below), then the traditionally sacred realm of fine arts is considered by some in danger of desacralization. In a sale of a publishing company of classical music, various representatives voiced the fear that a takeover by one of the giants such as Sony, Polygram or EMI would mean the introduction of a market logic that would destroy its opportunities to continue to sponsor unknown artists and make long-term investments in them. It is argued that classical music is not a product that can be handled by any marketer, but requires special attention and a willingness to accept financial losses in order to secure artistic openness and creativity.[70] Such reactions (as justified as they may be) indicate that artists and managers conceive of themselves as dealing with sacred objects that cannot be subjugated to what is conceived as the profane legitimacy of the market.[71] Indeed, art and marketing is the subject of study for more and more marketing and consumer researchers, for example in considering art as a kind of service.[72] Famous film directors make commercial campaigns and music videos (and music video-makers turn into great film directors), while commercial film-makers celebrate each other with their own sets of prizes for creativity. And consider 'art placement': one artist proposed a series of films featuring a mysterious 'Mr Who' engaging in a lot of daily consumption activities and used clippings from commercials to portray Mr Who's consumer universe.[73] Art and marketing, in short, are becoming increasingly blurred.[74]

Tourism is another example of a sacred, non-ordinary experience of extreme importance to marketers. When people travel on holiday, they occupy sacred time and space. The tourist is continually in search of 'authentic' experiences which differ from his or her normal world (think of Club Med's motto, 'The antidote to civilization').[75] This travelling experience involves binary oppositions between work and leisure and being 'at home' vs. 'away'. Norms regarding appropriate behaviour are modified as tourists scramble for illicit experiences they would not dream of engaging in at home.

The desire of travellers to capture these sacred experiences in objects forms the bedrock of the souvenir industry, which may be said to be in the business of selling sacred memories. Whether a personalized matchbook from a wedding or a little piece of the Berlin Wall, souvenirs represent a tangible piece of the consumer's sacred experience.[76]

In addition to personal mementoes, such as ticket stubs saved from a favourite concert, the following are other types of sacred souvenir icons:[77]

- Local products (such as goose liver from Périgord or Scotch whisky).
- Pictorial images (postcards).
- 'Piece of the rock' (seashells, pine cones). Sometimes this can be problematic, however. For example it is forbidden to bring home corals and seashells from a lot of diving places around the earth, in order to prevent tourists from 'tearing down' the coral reef. But temptations are great. Even at Nobel Prize dinners approximately 100 of the noble guests each year cannot resist bringing home something, typically a coffee spoon, as a souvenir.[78]
- Symbolic shorthand in the form of literal representations of the site (a miniature Little Mermaid or Eiffel Tower).
- Markers (Hard Rock Café T-shirts).

From sacred to profane, and back again

Just to make life interesting, in recent times many consumer activities have moved from one sphere to the other. Some things that were formerly regarded as sacred have moved into the realm of the profane, while other, everyday phenomena are now regarded as sacred.[79] Both these processes are relevant to our understanding of contemporary consumer behaviour.

Desacralization

▶ **Desacralization** occurs when a sacred item or symbol is removed from its special place or is duplicated in mass quantities, becoming profane as a result. For example, souvenir reproductions of sacred monuments such as the Leaning Tower of Pisa or the Eiffel Tower, 'pop' artworks of the *Mona Lisa* or adaptations of important symbols such as the Union Jack by clothing designers, tend to eliminate their special aspects by turning them into inauthentic commodities, produced mechanically and representing relatively little value.[80]

Religion itself has to some extent been desacralized. Religious symbols, such as stylized crosses or New Age crystals, have moved into the mainstream of fashion jewellery.[81]

marketing pitfall

'Brand new Dolce & Gabbana rosary beads. These are becoming increasingly sought after. The item is brand new with all of the original tags and box. The authenticity hologram, and the serial number are integral – Jesus is on a cross. Virgin Mary is in the middle of the necklace and at the end a metal Dolce & Gabbana tag. Fabulous necklaces. Worn by super stars like David Beckham, Britney Spears also seen on BONO U2.'[82]

Rosary beads as a style statement, not a prayer ritual, are hot fashion with celebrities, again. In the mid-1980s, Madonna, who was brought up a Catholic, raised eyebrows and launched a fashion craze by wearing crucifixes and rosaries with corsets. Eventually, the look became 'cheesy' and faded away. But, like many '80s trends, rosaries 'are cool again' with celebs. Britney Spears and Marlon Wayans have been spotted by paparazzi wearing rosary beads with several chains and necklaces, and David Beckham, Soccer's hunky Brit was photographed for the cover of the July 2004 issue of *Vanity Fair*. He brought along his own rosary beads by Dolce & Gabbana, the favourite designers of Beckham and wife Victoria 'Posh Spice' Beckham.[83] Sales of rosary beads have been very strong across the UK and Italy in the past years, and this has not gone unnoticed by officials of the Catholic Church. In the UK, one Father pointed out that while this fashion trend is 'not doing wicked things and leading us astray, I am sorry that people are wearing them as fashion accessories and are not mindful of their religious significance'.[84] As an accessory line for men, rosaries have been very successfully promoted by Dolce & Gabanna. The significant difference in wearing the rosaries is that men adorn themselves with rosaries as necklaces, rather than carrying them in their hand, which is the more traditional use. Having rosaries displayed in a stylish context of a high fashion store window alongside other fashion items such as shirts and sunglasses serves to move the rosary beads from one (religious) meaning to another (commercial and fashionable) context.[85]

Religious holidays, particularly Christmas, are regarded by many (and criticized by some) as having been transformed into secular, materialistic occasions devoid of their original sacred significance. Benetton, the Italian clothing manufacturer, has been at the forefront in creating vivid (and often controversial) messages that expose us to our cultural categories and prejudices, but at times they have touched upon the issue of desacralization.[86]

Even the clergy are increasingly adopting secular marketing techniques. Especially in the United States, televangelists rely upon the power of television, a secular medium, to convey their messages. The Catholic Church generated a major controversy after it hired a prominent public relations firm to promote its anti-abortion campaign.[87] Nonetheless, many religious groups have taken the secular route, and are now using marketing techniques to increase the number of believers. A Danish bishop addressed a number of major food producing companies for a joint venture in profiling Pentecost as a holiday season equally as important as Christmas and Easter.[88] The question is whether the use of marketing changes the 'product' or 'service' of the churches?[89]

multicultural dimensions

The American 'market for religious belief' with its televangelists and its heavy promotion of various churches and sects is a very exotic experience for many Europeans. The ad depicted on page 518 for a Minneapolis church to help recruit worshippers is typical of the American trend towards secular practices being observed by many organized religions. It even uses a pun (on the curing of a headache?) to pass on the message of salvation.

Religious symbols have become fashion symbols for many. Celebrity users, such as Madonna, have speeded up the transition, moving the original meaning of sacred objects to a popular culture context, where the meaning is no longer religious, but is, instead, associated with secular goods.

Corbis/Neal Preston

Sacralization

▶ **Sacralization** occurs when objects, events and even people take on sacred meaning to a culture or to specific groups within a culture. For example, events like the Cannes Film Festival or Wimbledon and people like Elvis Presley or Princess Diana have become sacralized to some consumers.

Objectification occurs when sacred qualities are attributed to mundane items. One way that this process can occur is through *contamination*, where objects associated with sacred events or people become sacred in their own right. This explains the desire by many fans for items belonging to, or even touched by, famous people. One standard procedure through which objects become sacralized occurs when they become included in the collection of a museum.

In addition to museum exhibits displaying rare objects, even mundane, inexpensive things may be set apart in private *collections*, where they are transformed from profane items to sacred ones. An item is sacralized as soon as it enters a collection, and it takes on special significance to the collector that, in some cases, may be hard to comprehend

▶ by the outsider. **Collecting** refers to the systematic acquisition of a particular object or set of objects, and this widespread activity can be distinguished from hoarding, which is merely unsystematic collecting.[90] Collecting typically involves both rational and emotional components, since collectors are fixed by their objects, but they also carefully organize and exhibit them.[91]

Name an item, and the odds are that a group of collectors are lusting after it. The contents of collections range from various popular culture memorabilia, rare books and autographs, to Barbie dolls, tea bags, lawnmowers and even junk mail.[92] The 1,200 members of the American McDonald's Collectors' Club collect 'prizes' like sandwich wrappers and Happy Meal trinkets – rare ones like the 1987 Potato Head Kids Toys sell for $25.[93] Consumers are often ferociously attached to their collections; this passion is exemplified by the comment made in one study by a woman who collects teddy bears: 'If my house ever burns down, I won't cry over my furniture, I'll cry over the bears.'[94]

The ad for the Episcopal church discussed in the multicultural dimensions box on p. 516.

Church Ad Project, 1021 Diffley, Eagen, MN 55123

Some consumer researchers feel that collectors are motivated to acquire their 'prizes' in order to gratify a high level of materialism in a socially acceptable manner. By systematically amassing a collection, the collector is allowed to 'worship' material objects without feeling guilty or petty. Another perspective is that collecting is an aesthetic experience: for many collectors the pleasure emanates from being involved in creating the collection, rather than from passively admiring the items one has scavenged or bought. Whatever the motivation, hard-core collectors often devote a great deal of time and energy to maintaining and expanding their collections, so for many this activity becomes a central component of their extended selves (see Chapter 7).[95]

marketing opportunity

Make your brand a collectable, and enhance your exposure and your brand loyalty. Certain products and brands become cult objects for devoted collectors. In the early 1990s, 'Swatch fever' infected many people. The company made more than 500 different models, some of which were special editions designed by artists. Collectors' interest made a formerly mundane product into a rare piece of art (e.g. a 'Jelly Fish' that originally sold for $30 was sold at auction for $17,000). Although thousands of people still collect the watches, the frenzy began to fade by around 1993.[96] Some collectors' items are more stable. One of the corporations exploiting this opportunity to its fullest is the Coca-Cola Company. With the plethora of Coca-Cola collectables, a lot of devoted and often highly specialized collectors have been created all over the world. They appear as 'spokespersons' for the brand when they account for their sometimes fabulous collections in the media, and they create a lot of extra and extremely positive exposure for the brand. As one researcher noted: 'These are brand owners. Coca-Cola is theirs.'[97]

■ CONSUMER SOCIETY – MATERIAL CULTURE

New books and art exhibitions witness the increasing importance of branding and advertising in our societies.[98] In 2000, it was announced that Huntington Beach, a Los Angeles suburb, had made Coca-Cola the official drink of the community. For $600,000 per year the company will exclude Pepsi and other soft drinks from official buildings and put up drink dispensers and advertisements all over the city. The city council initiated the deal, saying it was an alternative to higher taxes.[99]

▶ Many people use the notion of the **consumer society** in order to describe the current type of social organization in the developed world. This is not only because we live in a world full of things, which we obviously do. Almost 24 hours a day we are surrounded by consumer objects, and lots of leisurely activities we engage in can also be characterized as consumption. But the most decisive step in the construction of consumer society is the new role of consumption activities. In most of the modern time period, it has been people's role in a production context that has been decisive for our social identity. The impact of our self-consciousness as workers, farmers, professors, artisans, etc. cannot be underestimated. But in recent decades we have seen a trend towards an increasing role for consumption patterns and style in people's identity formation. With the increase in consumption possibilities and the multiplication of styles and fashions, consumption has to some extent been cut off from its old connections to those production-defined roles. The plethora of goods and their varieties in range and styles has to a still higher degree made consumption choices statements about our personality, our values, aspirations, sympathies and antipathies, and our way of handling social relations.

Modern consumer culture is thus characterized by consumption-based identities, but other related features of a consumer society include many of the other topics discussed in this book: more and more aspects of human interaction available through the market, shopping as leisure activity combined with the variety of shopping possibilities including the new 'temples of consumption', the shopping centres, easier access to credit, the growing attention to brand images and the communicative aspects of product and packaging as well as the pervasiveness of promotion, the increasing political organization of consumers in groups with a variety of purposes and the sheer impossibility of not being a consumer and still participating in ordinary social life.[100] Things do matter.[101]

However, not all is well in consumer society. Many critics have attacked consumer society for a variety of reasons: that it erodes cultural differences, that it creates superficial and inauthentic forms of social interaction and that it inspires competition and individualism rather than solidarity and community. Whereas most of these assertions may not bear close scrutiny,[102] consumer society in general does represent some serious challenges for our future development, not least in terms of the pressure on the environment. While we will address environmental issues and consumption in the final chapter, the pressure of consumer society is not only felt on the environment but also on

▶ the individual consumer, sometimes with negative outcomes. **Consumer addiction** is a physiological and/or psychological dependency on products or services. While most people equate addiction with drugs, virtually any product or service can be seen as relieving some problem or satisfying some need to the point where reliance on it becomes extreme. In some cases, it is fairly safe to say that the consumer, not unlike a drug addict, has little or no control over consumption. The products, whether alcohol, cigarettes, chocolate or diet colas, control the consumer. Even the act of shopping itself is an addictive experience for some consumers.[103]

■ CHAPTER SUMMARY

- ■ A society's *culture* includes its values, ethics and the material objects produced by its people. It is the accumulation of *shared meanings* and traditions among members of a society. A culture can be described in terms of ecology (the way people adapt to their habitat), its social structure and its ideology (including people's moral and aesthetic principles). This chapter describes some aspects of culture and focuses on how cultural meanings are created and transmitted across members of a society.

- Members of a culture share a system of *beliefs* and *practices*, including *values*. The process of learning the values of one's culture is called enculturation. Each culture can be described by a set of core values. Values can be identified by several methods, though it is often difficult to apply these results directly to marketing campaigns due to their generality.

- *Myths* are stories containing symbolic elements that express the shared ideals of a culture. Many myths involve some binary opposition, where values are defined in terms of what they are and what they are not (e.g. nature vs. technology). Modern myths are transmitted through advertising, films and other media.

- A *ritual* is a set of multiple, symbolic behaviours which occur in a fixed sequence and tend to be repeated periodically. Rituals are related to many consumption activities which occur in popular culture. These include holiday observances, gift-giving and grooming.

- A *rite of passage* is a special kind of ritual which involves the transition from one role to another. These passages typically entail the need to acquire products and services, called ritual artefacts, to facilitate the transition. Modern rites of passage include graduations, initiation ceremonies, weddings and funerals.

- Consumer activities can be divided into *sacred* and *profane* domains. Sacred phenomena are 'set apart' from everyday activities or products. People, events or objects can become sacralized. *Objectification* occurs when sacred qualities are ascribed to products or items owned by sacred people. *Sacralization* occurs when formerly sacred objects or activities become part of the everyday, as when 'one-of-a-kind' works of art are reproduced in large quantities. *Desacralization* occurs when objects that previously were considered sacred become commercialized and integrated into popular culture.

- *Collecting* is one of the most common ways of experiencing sacred consumption in daily life. It is simultaneously one of the domains where consumption and passions are most heavily intertwined.

- The importance of consumption for understanding social interactions is now so big that we have begun to talk about our own societies as *consumer societies*, indicating that consumption might well be the single most important social activity.

▶ KEY TERMS

Collecting (p. 517)

Collectivist cultures (p. 501)

Consumer addiction (p. 519)

Consumer society (p. 519)

Conventions (p. 503)

Co-optation (p. 498)

Culture (p. 498)

Custom (p. 502)

Desacralization (p. 515)

Ethnoconsumerism (p. 501)

Ethos (p. 500)

Gift-giving ritual (p. 508)

Individualist cultures (p. 501)

Monomyth (p. 504)

Mores (p. 503)

Myth (p. 504)

Profane consumption (p. 512)

Rites of passage (p. 511)

Ritual (p. 506)

Ritual artefacts (p. 508)

Sacralization (p. 517)

Sacred consumption (p. 512)

Self-gifts (p. 510)

Signifying practices (p. 499)

Worldview (p. 500)

CONSUMER BEHAVIOUR CHALLENGE

1 Culture can be thought of as a society's personality. If your culture were a person, could you describe its personality traits?

2 What is the difference between an enacted norm and a crescive norm? Identify the set of crescive norms operating when a man and woman in your culture go out for dinner on a first date. What products and services are affected by these norms?

3 How do the consumer decisions involved in gift-giving differ from other purchase decisions?

4 The chapter argues that not all gift-giving is positive. In what ways can this ritual be unpleasant or negative?

5 Construct a ritual script for a wedding in your culture. How many artefacts can you list that are contained in this script?

6 What are some of the major motivations for the purchase of self-gifts? Discuss some marketing implications of these.

7 Describe the three stages of the rite of passage associated with graduating from university.

8 Identify the ritualized aspects of various kinds of sports that are employed in advertising.

9 Some people have raised objections to the commercial exploitation of cultural figures. For example, in the United States many consumers deplored the profits that film-makers and business people made from films such as *Malcolm X* (e.g. by selling a 'Malcolm X' air freshener). Others argued that this commercialization merely helps to educate consumers about what such people stood for, and is inevitable in our society. What do you think?

10 Interview two or three of your fellow students about collecting, talking about either their own collections or a collection of somebody they know of. Use concepts about the sacred to analyse the responses.

■ NOTES

1. According to tradition, the slow pour takes exactly 119.5 seconds as the bartender holds the glass at a 45-degree angle, fills it three-quarters full, lets it settle and tops it off with its signature creamy head. When Guinness tried to introduce *FastPour*, an ultrasound technology that dispenses the dark brew in just 25 seconds, to make the pull faster and thus increase the number of drinks staff can pour on a busy night, the brewer had to scrap the system when drinkers resisted the innovation. Note: Diageo (which owns Guinness) hasn't given up and is experimenting with other techniques in markets where this ritual isn't so inbred. A system under test in Tokyo called *Guinness Surger* is intended for bars that are too small to accommodate kegs. It lets a bartender pour a pint from a bottle, place the glass on a special plate, and zap it with ultrasound waves that generate the characteristic head. See See Dennis W. Rook, 'The ritual dimension of consumer behavior', *Journal of Consumer Research* 12

(December 1985): 251–64; Mary A. Stansfield Tetreault and Robert E. Kleine III, 'Ritual, Ritualized Behavior, and Habit: Refinements and Extensions of the Consumption Ritual Construct', in Marvin Goldberg, Gerald Gorn, and Richard W. Pollay, eds, *Advances in Consumer Research* 17 (Provo, UT: Association for Consumer Research, 1990): 31–8; Deborah Ball, 'British drinkers of Guinness say they'd rather take it slow', *The Wall Street Journal on the Web* (22 May 2003).

2. See, e.g., A. Fuat Firat, 'Consumer Culture or Culture Consumed', in Janeen A. Costa and G. Bamossy, eds, *Marketing in a Multicultural World: Ethnicity, Nationalism, and Cultural Identity* (Thousand Oaks, CA: Sage, 1995): 105–25.

3. Paul du Gay, Stuart Hall, Linda Janes, Hugh MacKay and Keith Negus, *Doing Cultural Studies: The Story of the Sony Walkman* (London: Sage, 1997).

4. 'Spice Girls dance into culture clash', *Montgomery Advertiser* (29 April 1997): 2A.

5. Personal communication with Jens Bernsen, 29 October 1997.

6. Clifford Geertz, *The Interpretation of Cultures* (New York: Basic Books, 1973); Marvin Harris, *Culture, People and Nature* (New York: Crowell, 1971); John F. Sherry Jr., 'The Cultural Perspective in Consumer Research', in Richard J. Lutz, ed., *Advances in Consumer Research* 13 (Provo, UT: Association for Consumer Research, 1986): 573–5.

7. Geert Hofstede, *Culture's Consequences* (Beverly Hills, CA: Sage, 1980); see also Laura M. Milner, Dale Fodness and Mark W. Speece, 'Hofstede's Research on Cross-Cultural Work-Related Values: Implications for Consumer Behavior', in W.F. van Raaij and G. Bamossy, eds, *European Advances in Consumer Research* 1 (Provo, UT: Association for Consumer Research, 1993): 70–6.

8. Alladi Venkatesh, 'Ethnoconsumerism: A Proposal for a New Paradigm to Study Cross Cultural Consumer Behavior', in Costa and Bamossy, eds, *Marketing in a Multicultural World*: 26–67.

9. Dick Hebdige, 'Object as Image: The Italian Scooter Cycle', in J.B. Schor and D.B. Holt, eds, *The Consumer Society Reader* (New York: The New Press, 2000): 117–54.

10. Brad Weiss, 'Coffee Breaks and Coffee Connections: The Lived Experience of a Commodity in Tanzanian and European Worlds', in D. Howes, ed., *Cross-Cultural Consumption* (London: Routledge, 1996): 93–105.

11. George J. McCall and J.L. Simmons, *Social Psychology: A Sociological Approach* (New York: The Free Press, 1982).

12. Craig J. Thompson, 'Marketplace mythology and discourses of power', *Journal of Consumer Research* 31 (June 2004): 162–80. The author formulates the construct of marketplace mythology to explore how cultural myths are used to create marketplace mythologies that serve multiple and often competing ideological agendas. He develops his arguments within the context of the natural health market. While this market is positioned as alternative to mainstream scientific medicine, both practitioners' and consumers' quest for scientific support to validate their holistic healing treatments generate a fundamental paradox. This paper examines the mythic constructions of nature, technology, and science and their relations to both natural health's marketplace mythology of holistic well-being and key competitive forces.

13. Eric Arnould, Cele Otnes and Linda Price, 'Magic in the Marketing Age', in S. Brown, A.M. Doherty and B. Clarke, eds, *Proceedings of the Marketing Illuminations Spectacular* (Belfast: University of Ulster, 1997): 167–78.

14. Eric Arnould and Linda Price, 'River magic: Extraordinary experience and the extended service encounter', *Journal of Consumer Research* 20 (June 1993): 24–45.

15. Molly O'Neill, 'As life gets more complex, magic casts a wider spell', *New York Times* (13 June 1994): A1 (2).

16. Douglas B. Holt and Craig J. Thompson, 'Man-of-Action heroes: the pursuit of heroic masculinity in everyday consumption', *Journal of Consumer Research* 31 (September 2004): 425–40.

17. Conrad Phillip Kottak, 'Anthropological Analysis of Mass Enculturation', in Conrad P. Kottak, ed., *Researching American Culture* (Ann Arbor, MI: University of Michigan Press, 1982): 40–74.

18. Güliz Ger and Fabian Csaba, 'Flying Carpets: The Production and Consumption of Tradition and Mystique', in S. Hoch and R. Meyer, eds, *Advances in Consumer Research* 27 (Provo, UT: Association for Consumer Research, 2000): 132–7.

19. Joseph Campbell, *Myths, Dreams, and Religion* (New York: E.P. Dutton, 1970).

20. Jeffrey S. Lang and Patrick Trimble, 'Whatever happened to the man of tomorrow? An examination of the American monomyth and the comic book superhero', *Journal of Popular Culture* 22 (Winter 1988): 157.

21. Yumiko Ono, 'PepsiCo's "American" superhero in Japanese ads is alien to U.S.', *Wall Street Journal Interactive Edition* (23 May 1997).

22. James Fitchett, Douglas Brownlie and Michael Saren, 'On the Cultural Location of Consumption: The Case of Einstein as a Commodity', in *Marketing for an Expanding Europe*, Proceedings of the 25th EMAC Conference, ed. J. Berács, A. Bauer and J. Simon (Budapest: Budapest University of Economic Sciences, 1996): 435–53; James Fitchett and Michael Saren, 'Consuming Einstein: The Nine Billion Names of the Commodity', in Brown, Doherty and Clarke, eds, *Proceedings of the Marketing Illuminations Spectacular*: 252–63.

23. Elizabeth C. Hirschman, 'Movies as Myths: An Interpretation of Motion Picture Mythology', in Jean Umiker-Sebeok, ed., *Marketing and Semiotics: New Directions in the Study of Signs for Sale* (Berlin: Mouton de Guyter, 1987): 335–74.

24. *Markedsføring* 1 (1999): 18.

25. Benoît Heilbrunn, 'My Brand the Hero? A Semiotic Analysis of the Consumer-Brand Relationship', in M. Lambkin et al., eds, *European Perspectives on Consumer Behaviour* (London: Prentice-Hall, 1998): 370–401.

26. See Rook, 'The ritual dimension of consumer behavior' Tetreault and Kleine, 'Ritual, ritualized behavior, and habit'.

27. Grant McCracken, *Consumption and Culture* (Bloomington, IN: Indiana University Press).

28. 'The skill of the chase', *Marketing Week* (30 April 1993): 38–40.

29. Bill McDowell, 'Starbucks is ground zero in today's coffee culture', *Advertising Age* (9 December 1996): 1 (2 pp.). For a discussion of the act of coffee drinking as ritual, see Susan Fournier and Julie L. Yao, 'Reviving Brand Loyalty: A Reconceptualization within the Framework of Consumer–Brand Relationships', working paper 96–039, Harvard Business School, 1996.

30. Ariane Bernard, 'New American beachhead in France: Starbucks', *New York Times* (16 January 2004); Helen Jung, 'Lattes for all: Starbucks plans global expansion', *The Associated Press* (20 April 2003), http://www.globalexchange.org/campaigns/fairtrade/coffee/662.html.

31. Farnaz Fassisi, 'As authorities frown, Valentine's Day finds place in Iran's heart' *The Wall Street Journal* (12 February 2004), http://online.wsj.com/article/0,,SB107654405884327601,00.html?mod=home%5Fpage%5Fone%5Fus.

32. Robert Grafton Small, 'Consumption and significance: Everyday life in a brand-new second-hand bow tie', *European Journal of Marketing* 27(8) (1993): 38–45.

33. 'Lynx to create chain of male grooming stores', *Marketing* (24 August 2000): 5.

34. Dennis W. Rook and Sidney J. Levy, 'Psychosocial Themes in Consumer Grooming Rituals', in Richard P. Bagozzi and Alice M. Tybout, eds, *Advances in Consumer Research* 10 (Provo, UT: Association for Consumer Research, 1983): 329–33.

35. Diane Barthel, *Putting on Appearances: Gender and Attractiveness* (Philadelphia: Temple University Press, 1988).

36. Quoted in ibid.

37. Russell W. Belk, Melanie Wallendorf and John Sherry Jr., 'The sacred and the profane in consumer behavior: Theodicy on the odyssey', *Journal of Consumer Research* 16 (June 1989): 1–38.

38. M. Tina Lowrey, Cele C. Otnes and Julie A. Ruth, 'Social influences on dyadic giving over time: A taxonomy from the giver's perspective,' *Journal of Consumer Research* 30 (March 2004): 547–58.

39. Russell W. Belk and Gregory S. Coon, 'Gift giving as agapic love: An alternative to the exchange paradigm based on dating experiences', *Journal of Consumer Research* 20 (December 1993) 3: 393–417.

40. Julie A. Ruth, Cele C. Otnes and Frederic F. Brunel, 'Gift receipt and the reformulation of interpersonal relationships', *Journal of Consumer Research* 25 (March 1999) 385–402.

41. Colin Camerer, 'Gifts as economic signals and social symbols', *American Journal of Sociology* 94 (Supplement 1988): 5180–214.

42. Robert T. Green and Dana L. Alden, 'Functional equivalence in cross-cultural consumer behavior: Gift giving in Japan and the United States', *Psychology and Marketing* 5 (Summer 1988): 155–68.

43. Hiroshi Tanaka and Miki Iwamura, 'Gift Selection Strategy of Japanese Seasonal Gift Purchasers: An Explorative Study', paper presented at the Association for Consumer Research, Boston, October 1994.

44. John F. Sherry Jr., 'Gift giving in anthropological perspective', *Journal of Consumer Research* 10 (September 1983): 157–68.

45. Daniel Goleman, 'What's under the tree? Clues to a relationship', *New York Times* (19 December 1989): C1.

46. John F. Sherry Jr., Mary Ann McGrath and Sidney J. Levy, 'The dark side of the gift', *Journal of Business Research* 28(3) (1993): 225–45.

47. David Glen Mick and Michelle DeMoss, 'Self-gifts: Phenomenological insights from four contexts', *Journal of Consumer Research* 17 (December 1990): 327; John F. Sherry Jr., Mary Ann McGrath and Sidney J. Levy, 'Egocentric Consumption: Anatomy of Gifts Given to the Self', in John F. Sherry Jr., ed., *Contemporary Marketing and Consumer Behavior: An Anthropological Sourcebook* (Thousand Oaks, CA: Sage, 1995).

48. On tourism as a central part of modern life, see John Urry, *The Tourist Gaze: Leisure and Travel in Contemporary Societies* (London: Sage, 1990), and John Urry, *Consuming Places* (London: Routledge, 1995). Scandinavians (or those who read Swedish!) may also consult Tom Odell, ed., *Nonstop! Turist i upplevelsesindustrialismen* (Lund: Historiska Media, 1999).

49. See, for example, Russell W. Belk, 'Halloween: An Evolving American Consumption Ritual', in Pollay, Gorn and Goldberg, eds, *Advances in Consumer Research* 17: 508–17; Melanie Wallendorf and Eric J. Arnould, 'We gather together: The consumption rituals of Thanksgiving Day', *Journal of Consumer Research* 18 (June 1991): 13–31.

50. Marc Augé, 'Un ethnologue à Euro Disneyland', *Le Monde Diplomatique* (September 1994).

51. Bruno Bettelheim, *The Uses of Enchantment: The Meaning and Importance of Fairy Tales* (New York: Alfred A. Knopf, 1976).

52. Brian Moeran and Lise Skov, 'Cinderella Christmas: Kitsch, Consumerism and Youth in Japan', in D. Miller, ed., *Unwrapping Christmas* (Oxford: Oxford University Press, 1993): 105–33.

53. *Markedsføring* 1 (1999): 4.

54. Anne Swardson, 'Trick or treat? In Paris, it's dress, dance, eat', *International Herald Tribune* (31 October 1996): 2.

55. Tuba Ustuner, Güliz Ger and Douglas B. Holt, 'Consuming Ritual: Reframing the Turkish Henna-Night Ceremony', in Hoch and Meyer, eds, *Advances in Consumer Research* 27: 209–14.

56. Michael R. Solomon and Punam Anand, 'Ritual Costumes and Status Transition: The Female Business Suit as Totemic Emblem', in Elizabeth C. Hirschman and Morris Holbrook, eds, *Advances in Consumer Research* 12 (Washington, DC: Association for Consumer Research, 1985): 315–18.

57. Arnold Van Gennep, *The Rites of Passage*, trans. Maika B. Vizedom and Gabrielle L. Caffee (London: Routledge & Kegan Paul, 1960; orig. published 1908); Solomon and Anand, 'Ritual costumes and status transition'.

58. Stephanie O'Donohoe and Darach Turley, 'Dealing with Death: Art, Mortality and the Marketplace', in S. Brown and A. Patterson, eds, *Imagining Marketing, Art, Aesthetics, and the Avant-Garde* (London: Routledge, 2001): 86–106.

59. Walter W. Whitaker III, 'The Contemporary American Funeral Ritual', in Ray B. Browne, ed., *Rites and*

Ceremonies in Popular Culture (Bowling Green, OH: Bowling Green University Popular Press, 1980): 316–25.

60. On sacredness in tourism, see, e.g., Urry, *The Tourist Gaze*, and Urry, *Consuming Places*.

61. Robert V. Kozinets, John F. Sherry Jr., Diana Storm, Adam Duhachek, Krittinee Nuttavuthisit and Benet DeBerry-Spence, 'Ludic agency and retail spectacle', *Journal of Consumer Research* 31 (December 2004): 658–72.

62. Kottak, 'Anthropological analysis of mass enculturation': 40–74.

63. Gerry Pratt, 'The House as an Expression of Social Worlds', in James S. Duncan, ed., *Housing and Identity: Cross-Cultural Perspectives* (London: Croom Helm, 1981): 135–79; Michael R. Solomon, 'The role of the surrogate consumer in service delivery', *Service Industries Journal* 7 (July 1987): 292–307.

64. Malene Djursaa and Simon Ulrik Kragh, 'Syntax and Creolization in Cross-Cultural Readings of Rooms', in B. Dubois, T. Lowrey, L.J. Shrum and M. Vanhuele, eds, *European Advances in Consumer Research* 4 (Provo, UT: Association for Consumer Research, 1999): 293–303.

65. Grant McCracken, '"Homeyness": A Cultural Account of One Constellation of Goods and Meanings', in Elizabeth C. Hirschman, ed., *Interpretive Consumer Research* (Provo, UT: Association for Consumer Research, 1989): 168–84.

66. James Hirsch, 'Taking celebrity worship to new depths', *New York Times* (9 November 1988): C1.

67. Lisa Urquhart, 'A star is worn as on-line retailer grows up', *Financial Times* (22 October 2004), http://news.ft.com/cms/s/341eec5a-23c7-11d9-aee5-00000e2511c8,dwp_uuid=43da3afc-1308-11d9-b869-00000e2511c8.html.

68. Emile Durkheim, *The Elementary Forms of the Religious Life* (New York: Free Press, 1915).

69. Susan Birrell, 'Sports as ritual: Interpretations from Durkheim to Goffman', *Social Forces* 60 (1981) 2: 354–76; Daniel Q. Voigt, 'American Sporting Rituals', in Browne, ed., *Rites and Ceremonies in Popular Culture*: 125–40.

70. 'Sale of UK publisher of classical music strikes a sour note', *Wall Street Journal Europe* (9 September 1997): 1, 4.

71. Søren Askegaard, 'Marketing, the performing arts, and social change: Beyond the legitimacy crisis', *Consumption, Markets and Culture* 3(1) (1999): 1–25.

72. Simona Botti, 'What Role for Marketing in the Arts? An Analysis of Art Consumption and Artistic Value', in Y. Evrard, W. Hoyer and A. Strazzieri, eds, *Proceedings of the Third International Research Seminar on Marketing Communications and Consumer Behavior* (Aix-en-Provence: IAE, 1999).

73. *Markedsføring* 2 (1999): 10.

74. Brown and Patterson, eds, *Imagining Marketing, Art, Aesthetics, and the Avant-Garde*.

75. Urry, *The Tourist Gaze*.

76. Belk et al., 'The sacred and the profane in consumer behavior'.

77. Beverly Gordon, 'The souvenir: Messenger of the extraordinary', *Journal of Popular Culture* 20 (1986) 3: 135–46.

78. 'Even at the dinner for the Nobel prizes, they steal the spoons', *Wall Street Journal* (7 December 2000): A1, A16.

79. Belk et al., 'The sacred and the profane in consumer behavior'.

80. Ibid.

81. Deborah Hofmann, 'In jewelry, choices sacred and profane, ancient and new', *New York Times* (7 May 1989).

82. Promotional text from 'First fashion' webpage, an online company specializing in the sale of handbags, wallets and accessories from top fashion design houses, http://www.1stinfashion.com/ProductDetails.aspx?productID=3078 (accessed 5 August 2005).

83. Karen Thomas, 'Rosary's second coming', *USA Today* (July 2004), http://www.usatoday.com/life/people/2004-06-17-rosaries_x.htm.

84. 'Church fears rosary fashion craze', *BBC News* (29 October 2004), http://news.bbc.co.uk/1/hi/business/3964667.stm.

85. For an interesting display of rosaries as fashion, see Dolce & Gabbana's website: http://www.dolcegabbana.it/ (accessed 5 August 2005). Gary Bamossy is grateful to Diego Rinallo and Stefania Borghini of Bocconi University, Milan, for their helpful insights on the discussion of rosaries as fashion.

86. Roberto Grandi, 'Benetton's Advertising: A Case History of Postmodern Communication', unpublished manuscript, Center for Modern Culture and Media, University of Bologna, 1994; Shawn Tully, 'Teens: The most global market of all', *Fortune* (16 May 1994): 90–7.

87. Quoted in 'Public relations firm to present anti-abortion effort to bishops', *New York Times* (14 August 1990): A12.

88. *Markedsføring* 4 (1999): 8.

89. Per Østergaard, 'The Broadened Concept of Marketing as a Manifestation of the Postmodern Condition', in *Marketing Theory and Applications*, Proceedings of the AMA Winter Educators Conference 4, R. Varandarajan and B. Jaworski, eds (Chicago: American Marketing Association, 1993): 234–9.

90. Dan L. Sherrell, Alvin C. Burns and Melodie R. Phillips, 'Fixed Consumption Behavior: The Case of Enduring Acquisition in a Product Category', in Robert L. King, ed., *Developments in Marketing Science* 14 (1991): 36–40.

91. Russell W. Belk, 'Acquiring, Possessing, and Collecting: Fundamental Processes in Consumer Behavior', in Ronald F. Bushard and Shelby D. Hunt, eds, *Marketing Theory: Philosophy of Science Perspectives* (Chicago: AMA, 1982): 185–90.

92. For an extensive bibliography on collecting, see Russell W. Belk, *Collecting in a Consumer Culture* (London: Routledge, 1995), or Russell W. Belk, Melanie Wallendorf, John F. Sherry Jr. and Morris B. Holbrook, 'Collecting in a Consumer Culture', in Russell W. Belk, ed., *Highways and Buyways* (Provo, UT: Association for Consumer Research, 1991): 178–215. See also Janine Romina Lovatt, 'The People's Show Festival 1994: A Survey', in S. Pearce, ed., *Experiencing Material Culture in the Western World* (London: Leicester University Press, 1997): 196–254; Werner Muensterberg, *Collecting: An Unruly Passion* (Princeton, NJ: Princeton University Press, 1994); Melanie Wallendorf and Eric J. Arnould, '"My favorite things": A cross-cultural inquiry into object attachment, possessiveness, and social linkage', *Journal of Consumer Research* 14 (March 1988): 531–47.

93. Calmetta Y. Coleman, 'Just any old thing from McDonald's can be a collectible', *Wall Street Journal* (29 March 1995): B1 (2).

94. Quoted in Ruth Ann Smith, 'Collecting as Consumption: A Grounded Theory of Collecting Behavior', unpublished manuscript, Virginia Polytechnic Institute and State University, 1994: 14.

95. See Belk, *Collecting in a Consumer Culture*.

96. 'A feeding frenzy for Swatches', *New York Times* (29 August 1991): C3; Patricia Leigh Brown, 'Fueling a frenzy: Swatch', *New York Times* (10 May 1992): 1, 9; Mary M. Long and Leon G. Schiffman, 'Swatch fever: An allegory for understanding the paradox of collecting', *Psychology and Marketing* 14 (August 1997) 5: 495–509.

97. Jan Slater, 'Collecting the Real Thing: A Case Study Exploration of Brand Loyalty Enhancement Among Coca-Cola Brand Collectors', in Hoch and Meyer, eds, *Advances in Consumer Research* 27: 202–8.

98. Jane Pavitt, 'The art of marketing', *Marketing* (19 October 2000).

99. *Markedsføring* 7 (1999): 12.

100. Celia Lury, *Consumer Culture* (New Brunswick, NJ: Rutgers University Press, 1996). Another excellent book on the rise of consumer culture is Don Slater, *Consumer Culture and Modernity* (Cambridge: Polity Press, 1997).

101. Daniel Miller, 'Why Some Things Matter', in D. Miller, ed., *Material Cultures: Why Some Things Matter* (London: UCL Books, 1998): 3–21.

102. Daniel Miller, 'Consumption as the Vanguard of History', in D. Miller, ed., *Acknowledging Consumption* (London: Routledge, 1995): 1–57; see also Cornelia Dröge, Roger Calantone, Madhu Agrawal and Robert Mackay, 'The consumption culture and its critiques: A framework for analysis', *Journal of Macromarketing* (Fall 1993): 32–45.

103. Richard Elliott, 'Addictive consumption: Function and fragmentation in postmodernity', *Journal of Consumer Policy* 17 (1994): 159–79; Thomas C. O'Guinn and Ronald J. Faber, 'Compulsive buying: A phenomenological exploration', *Journal of Consumer Research* 16 (1989): 147–57.

CULTURAL CHANGE PROCESSES

15

Joost and Lieke are riding the Intercity train from Amsterdam to Nijmegen after a fun day of shopping in Amsterdam with friends. Lieke takes out a small electronic device from her bag. 'What's that?' Joost asks. 'It's the new J.K. Rowling novel – *Harry Potter and the Half-Blood Prince*,' Lieke answers. 'What?' Joost is surprised. 'You mean that this is a book?' 'Well, not exactly,' says Lieke, 'it's an e-book. It has software that lets me download novels and other things and read them like I would read a book – no scrolling the text and all that. I got the download at Boekhandel Atheneum a few hours ago, and I wanted to start reading on the train ride home.' 'Argh!' Joost gives Lieke a look of bewilderment as Lieke puts in her iPod ear pieces and listens to the newest Coldplay album that she legally downloaded from the internet and settles in to 'read' her electronic version of Harry Potter. Joost thinks to himself that this electronic book gadget and Lieke's iPod are perfect examples of brand offerings from mainstream marketing companies that he so loves to avoid. Lieke notices the look of mild contempt on Joost's face and says, 'It's just getting started, but they expect e-books to cover 10 per cent of the book market in a few years.' Joost doesn't reply. Instead he digs out his old 256 KB MP3, and starts listening to his alternative electronic music from Aphex Twin that he downloaded for free from the internet. Never mind that their record label, Warp, accepts all major credit cards on their website . . .

■ INTRODUCTION

The Rolling Stones. Miniskirts. Kipper ties. Fast food. High-tech furniture. New architecture. James Bond. We inhabit a world brimming with different styles and possibilities. The food we eat, the cars we drive, the clothes we wear, the places we live and work, the music we listen to – all are influenced by the ebb and flow of popular culture and fashion. Consumers may at times feel overwhelmed by the sheer choice in the marketplace. A person trying to decide on something as routine as what to have for lunch has many hundreds of alternatives from which to choose. Despite this seeming abundance, however, the options available to consumers at any point in time actually represent only a *small fraction* of the total set of possibilities. In this chapter, we shall follow marketers and cultural gatekeepers' attempts to set their marks on which possibilities get the most attention and which trends and tendencies become victorious in the battle for a place in our minds as consumers. We will take a closer look at processes of change driving the ever-changing styles of consumption we are presented with. And, referring back to Figure 14.1, we will look at how fashions and consumption styles spread within and among societies.

Even though most of the consumers we have been dealing with in this book may live in Western middle-class areas each with their national and local characteristics, they are often able to 'connect' symbolically with millions of other young consumers by relating to styles that originated far away – even though the original meanings of those styles may have little relevance to them. The spread of fashions in consumption is just one example of what happens when the meanings created by some members of a culture are interpreted and produced for mass consumption.

Take the example of rap music. Baggy jeans and outfits featuring gold vinyl skirts, huge gold chains and bejewelled baseball caps which used to be seen only on the streets of impoverished urban areas are being adapted by haute couture fashion designers for the catwalks of Manhattan and Paris. In addition, a high proportion of people who buy recordings of rap music are white. How did rap music and fashions, which began as forms of expression in the black urban subculture, make it to mainstream America and the rest of the world? A brief chronology is given in Table 15.1.

Table 15.1 The mainstreaming of popular music and fashion

Date	Event
1968	Bronx DJ Kool Herc invents hip hop.
1973-8	Urban block parties feature break-dancing and graffiti.
1979	A small record company named Sugar Hill becomes the first rap label.
1980	Manhattan art galleries feature graffiti artists.
1981	Blondie's song 'Rapture' hits number one in the charts.
1985	Columbia Records buys the Def Jam label.
1988	MTV begins *Yo! MTV Raps*, featuring Fab 5 Freddy.
1990	Hollywood gets into the act with the hip-hop film *House Party*; Ice-T's rap album is a big hit on college radio stations; amid controversy, white rapper Vanilla Ice hits the big time; NBC launches a new sitcom, *Fresh Prince of Bel Air*.
1991	Mattel introduces its Hammer doll (a likeness of the rap star Hammer, formerly known as M.C. Hammer); designer Karl Lagerfeld shows shiny vinyl raincoats and chain belts in his Chanel collection; designer Charlotte Neuville sells gold vinyl suits with matching baseball caps for $800; Isaac Mizrahi features wide-brimmed caps and takeoffs on African medallions; Bloomingdale's launches Anne Klein's rap-inspired clothing line by featuring a rap performance in its Manhattan store.
1992	Rappers start to abandon this look, turning to low-fitting baggy jeans, sometimes worn backwards; white rapper Marky Mark appears in a national campaign wearing Calvin Klein underwear, exposed

Table 15.1 (cont'd)

Date	Event
	above his hip-hugging pants; composer Quincy Jones launches *Vibe* magazine and it wins over many white readers.[1]
1993	Hip-hop fashions and slang continue to cross over into mainstream consumer culture. An outdoor ad for Coca-Cola proclaims, 'Get Yours 24-7'. The company is confident that many viewers in its target market will know that the phrase is urban slang for 'always' (24 hours a day, 7 days a week).[2]
1994	The (late) Italian designer Versace pushes oversized overalls favoured by urban youngsters. In one ad, he asks, 'Overalls with an oversize look, something like what rappers and homeboys wear. Why not a sophisticated version?'[3]
1996	Tommy Hilfiger, a designer who was the darling of the preppie set, turns hip hop. He gives free wardrobes to rap artists such as Grand Puba and Chef Raekwon, and in return finds his name mentioned in rap songs – the ultimate endorsement. The September 1996 issue of *Rolling Stone* features the Fugees, several band members prominently display the Hilfiger logo. In the same year the designer uses rap stars Method Man and Treach of Naughty by Nature as runway models. Hilfiger's new Tommy Girl perfume plays on his name but also is a reference to the New York hip-hop record label Tommy Boy.[4]
1997	Coca-Cola features rapper LL Cool J in a commercial that debuts in the middle of the sitcom *In the House*, a TV show starring the singer.[5]
1998	In their battle with Dockers for an increased share of the khaki market, Gap launches its first global advertising campaign. One of the commercials 'Khakis Groove' includes a hip-hop dance performance set to music by Bill Mason.[6]
1999	Rapper turned entrepreneur Sean (Puffy) Combs introduces an upscale line of menswear he calls 'urban high fashion'. New companies FUBU, Mecca and Enyce attain financial success in the multibillion-dollar industry.[7] Lauryn Hill and the Fugees sing at a party sponsored by upscale Italian clothier Emporio Armani and she proclaims, 'We just wanna thank Armani for giving a few kids from the ghetto some great suits.'[8]
2000	360hip-hop.com, a Web-based community dedicated to the hip-hop culture, is launched. In addition to promoting the hip-hop lifestyle, the site allows consumers to purchase clothing and music online while watching video interviews with such artists as Will Smith and Busta Rymes.[9]
2001	Hip-hop dancing becomes the rage among China's youth, who refer to it as *jiew*, or street dancing.[10]
2002-3	Toy manufacturers mimic the hip-hop practice of using the letter 'Z' instead of the letter 'S' in names. This trend started with the 1991 film *Boyz N The Hood* (a title that was itself borrowed from a 1989 song by the rap group N.W.A.). It caught on with other hip-hop terms like 'skillz', 'gangstaz' and 'playaz'. Musical artists including 504 Boyz, Kidz Bop Kidz, Xzibit, the Youngbloodz and Smilez incorporated the popular 'Z' into their names. During the 2002 Christmas season, Target created a children's section called 'Kool Toyz', where parents can buy dolls with names like Bratz (Girlz and Boyz), Diva Starz and Trophy Tailz – and a doll's house to put them in called Dinky Digz. They can find a toy called Scannerz, a karaoke machine named Loud Lipz, and Marble Moovz, a toddlers' marble set. There's more, including Rescue Rigz, ControlBotz, 4Wheelerz and the American Patriotz action figures.[11]
2004-5	The global fast-food chain McDonald's offers to pay rappers 4.15 euros every time a song is played which drops the name of the 'Big-Mac'. Artists who have 'referenced' well-known products include Jay-Z, 50 Cent and Snoop Dogg. Among the happy beneficiaries have been brands such as Courvoisier, Gucci, Dom Perignon, Bently and Porsche.[12] Hip Hop and rappers are also part of the growing fusion of music and sports, with rap artists busting a move into a field formerly dominated by pro athletes and celebrities. Rappers 50 Cent, Snoop Dog and Xzibit, have their own signature shoes through Reebok Pony and Da Da footware. Missy Elliott has teamed with Adidas to sell her own Respect Me line of trainers, jackets and bags. The casual shoe segments (used more for fashion than sports) they endorse have emerged as the fastest growing piece of the $17 billion athletic footwear market. Casual shoe sales grew 24.5 per cent in 2004, compared with less than 5 per cent for athletic shoes.[13] Even electronic gadgetry has been targeted by rap artists. 50 Cent has broken into the digital music hardware scene with his new 'G-Unit' MP3 Watch. The 256 MB version boasts a price of 405 euros! While the watch does not have any cutting edge features, it is clearly a price which is targeted to the high end of MP3 players.[14]

Figure 15.1 The culture production process

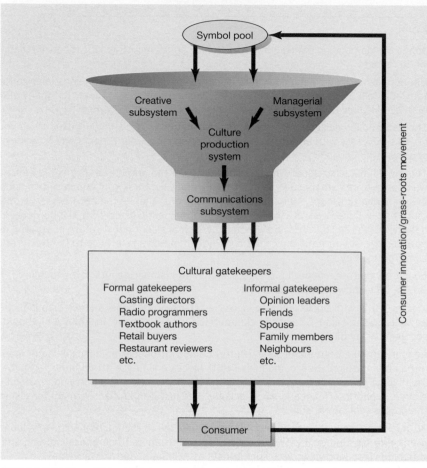

Source: Adapted from Michael R. Solomon, 'Building Up and Breaking Down: The Impact of Cultural Sorting on Symbolic Consumption', in J. Sheth and E.C. Hirschman, eds, *Research in Consumer Behavior* (Greenwich, CT: JAI Press, 1988): 325–51.

Cultural selection

The selection of certain alternatives over others – whether cars, dresses, computers, recording artists, political candidates, religions or even scientific methodologies – is the culmination of a complex filtration process resembling a funnel, as depicted in Figure 15.1. Many possibilities initially compete for adoption, and these are steadily narrowed down as they make their way down the path from conception to consumption in a process of **cultural selection**.

The internet has made the spotting and selection of the various trends and changes in society, the symbol pool, easier. New trend-watching services can be paid for scouring the world for new possibilities in colours, fabrics, designs or combinations. They can access pictures from runways of great fashion shows, look at store decorations from H&M or Banana Republic, or look at photos of cool London/Paris/Amsterdam/Berlin youngsters sporting the latest rebellious twist to the clothing companies' standard offerings. Even though the subscription to these services is costly, many companies think they are well worth their price, because they save in business trips and other types of costly trend-spotting fieldwork.[15]

Our tastes and product preferences are not formed in a vacuum. Choices are driven by the images presented to us in mass media, our observations of those around us, and even by our desires to live in the fantasy worlds created by marketers. These options are constantly evolving and changing. A clothing style or type of cuisine that is 'hot' one year may be 'out' the next.

Culture production systems

No single designer, company or advertising agency is solely responsible for creating popular culture. Every product, whether a hit record, a car or a new fashion, requires the input of many different participants. The set of individuals and organizations responsible for creating and marketing a cultural product is a **cultural production system (CPS)**.[16]

The nature of these systems helps to determine the types of product that eventually emerge from them. Factors such as the number and diversity of competing systems and the amount of innovation versus conformity that is encouraged are important. For example, an analysis of the Country & Western music industry has shown that the hit records it produces tend to be similar to one another during periods when it is dominated by a few large companies, whereas there is more diversity when a greater number of producers are competing within the same market.[17]

The different members of a culture production system may not necessarily be aware of or appreciate the roles played by other members, yet many diverse agents work together to create popular culture.[18] Each member does his or her best to anticipate which particular images will be most attractive to a consumer market. Of course, those who are able to forecast consumers' tastes consistently will be successful over time.

Components of a CPS

A culture production system has three major subsystems: (1) a *creative subsystem* responsible for generating new symbols and/or products; (2) a *managerial subsystem* responsible for selecting, making tangible, mass-producing and managing the distribution of new symbols and/or products; and (3) a *communications subsystem* responsible for giving meaning to the new product and providing it with a symbolic set of attributes that are communicated to consumers.

An example of the three components of a culture production system for a record would be (1) a singer (e.g. Missy Elliott, a creative subsystem); (2) a company (e.g. Atlantic Records, which manufactures and distributes Madonna's records, a managerial subsystem); and (3) the advertising and publicity agencies hired to promote the albums (a communications subsystem). Table 15.2 illustrates some of the many *cultural specialists*, operating in different subsystems, who are required to create a hit CD.

Cultural gatekeepers

Many judges or 'tastemakers' influence the products that are eventually offered to consumers. These judges, or **cultural gatekeepers**, are responsible for filtering the overflow of information and materials intended for consumers. Gatekeepers include film, restaurant and car reviewers, interior designers, disc jockeys, retail buyers and magazine editors. Collectively, this set of agents is known as the *throughput sector*.[19]

Speaking the language of beauty

A recent study of cultural gatekeepers in the fashion and beauty industry illustrates how some cultural 'products' (in this case, fashion models) are selected and championed over other stylistic possibilities.[20] Editors at such women's magazines as *Cosmopolitan*, *Marie Claire*, *Depêche Mode* and *Elle* play an important role in selecting the specific variations of beauty that will appear in the pages of these 'bibles of fashion'. These images, in turn, will be relied on by millions of readers to decide what 'look' they would like to adopt – and, of course, which particular products and services (such as hairstyles, cosmetics, clothing styles, exercise programmes) they will need to attain these images.

Table 15.2 Cultural specialists in the music industry

Specialist	Functions
Songwriter(s)	Compose music and lyrics; must reconcile artistic preferences with estimates of what will succeed in the marketplace
Performer(s)	Interpret music and lyrics; may be formed spontaneously, or may be packaged by an agent to appeal to a predetermined market (e.g. Elton John or Green Day)
Teachers and coaches	Develop and refine performers' talents
Agent	Represent performers to record companies
A&R (artist & repertoire) executive	Acquire artists for the record label
Publicists, image consultants, designers, stylists	Create an image for the group that is transmitted to the buying public
Recording technicians, producers	Create a recording to be sold
Marketing executives	Make strategic decisions regarding performer's appearances, ticket pricing, promotional strategies, and so on
Video director	Interpret the song visually to create a music video that will help to promote the record
Music reviewers	Evaluate the merits of a recording for listeners
Disc jockeys, radio programme directors	Decide which records will be given airplay and/or placed in the radio stations' regular rotations
Record shop owner	Decide which of the many records produced will be stocked and/or promoted heavily in the retail environment

In this study, decision makers at a group of influential magazines identified a small set of 'looks' that characterize many of the diverse fashion models they evaluate on a daily basis – what is more, though each editor was studied independently, overall respondents exhibited a very high level of agreement among themselves regarding what the 'looks' are, what they are called, which are more or less desirable *and* which they expect to be paired with specific product advertisements. This research suggests that cultural gate-keepers tend to rely on the same underlying cultural ideals and priorities when making the selections that in turn get passed down the channel of distribution for consideration by consumers.

High culture and popular culture

Do Beethoven and Björk have anything in common? While both the famous composer and the Icelandic singer are associated with music, many would argue that the similarity stops here. Culture production systems create many diverse kinds of products, but some basic distinctions can be offered regarding their characteristics.

Arts and crafts

▶ One distinction can be made between arts and crafts.[21] An **art product** is viewed prim-
▶ arily as an object of aesthetic contemplation without any functional value. A **craft product**, in contrast, is admired because of the beauty with which it performs some function (e.g. a ceramic ashtray or hand-carved fishing lures). A piece of art is original, subtle and

valuable, and is associated with the elite of society. A craft tends to follow a formula that permits rapid production. According to this framework, elite culture is produced in a purely aesthetic context and is judged by reference to recognized classics. It is high culture – 'serious art'.[22]

High art vs. low art

The distinction between high and low culture is not as clear as it may first appear. In addition to the possible class bias that drives such a distinction (i.e. we assume that the rich have culture while the poor do not), high and low culture are blending together in interesting ways. Popular culture reflects the world around us; these phenomena touch rich and poor. In many places in Europe, advertising is widely appreciated as an art form and the TV/cinema commercials have their own Cannes festival. In France and Great Britain certain advertising executives are public figures in their respective countries. For over ten years, Europeans in different countries have paid relatively high entrance fees to watch an all-night programme in a cinema consisting of nothing but television commercials.[23]

The arts are big business. All cultural products that are transmitted by mass media become a part of popular culture.[24] Classical recordings are marketed in much the same way as Top-40 albums,[25] and museums use mass-marketing techniques to sell their wares. The Parisian museums even run a satellite gift shop at the Charles de Gaulle airport.

Marketers often incorporate high art imagery to promote products. They may sponsor artistic events to build public goodwill or feature works of art on shopping bags.[26] When observers from Toyota watched customers in luxury car showrooms, the company found that these consumers tended to view a car as an art object. This theme was then used in an ad for the Lexus with the caption: 'Until now, the only fine arts we supported were sculpture, painting and music'.[27]

Cultural formulae

Mass culture, in contrast, churns out products specifically for a mass market. These products aim to please the average taste of an undifferentiated audience and are predictable because they follow certain patterns. As illustrated in Table 15.3 many popular art forms,

This advertisement demonstrates the adaptation of famous paintings ('high art') to sell products ('low art').

Used with permission of Robson Brown Advertising, Newcastle upon Tyne, England

Table 15.3 Cultural formulae in public artforms

Artform/genre	Classic western	Science fiction	Hard-boiled detective	Family sitcom
Time	1800s	Future	Present	Any time
Location	Edge of civilization	Space	City	Suburbs
Protagonist	Cowboy (lone individual)	Astronaut	Detective	Father (figure)
Heroine	Schoolmistress	Spacegirl	Damsel in distress	Mother (figure)
Villain	Outlaws, killers	Aliens	Killer	Boss, neighbour
Secondary characters	Townsfolk, Indians	Technicians in spacecraft	Police, underworld	Children, dogs
Plot	Restore law and order	Repel aliens	Find killer	Solve problem
Theme	Justice	Triumph of humanity	Pursuit and discovery	Chaos and confusion
Costume	Cowboy hat, boots, etc.	High-tech uniforms	Raincoat	Normal clothes
Locomotion	Horse	Spaceship	Beat-up car	Family estate car
Weaponry	Sixgun, rifle	Rayguns	Pistol, fists	Insults

Source: Arthur A. Berger, *Signs in Contemporary Culture: An Introduction to Semiotics* (New York: Longman, 1984): 86. Copyright © 1984. Reissued 1989 by Sheffield Publishing Company, Salem, WI. Reprinted with permission of the publisher.

▶ such as detective stories or science fiction, generally follow a **cultural formula**, where certain roles and props often occur consistently.[28] Computer programs even allow users to 'write' their own romances by systematically varying certain set elements of the story. Romance novels are an extreme case of a cultural formula. The romance novel and other formulae reflect the consumer society by the way consumption events and different brands play a role in the story and in the construction of the different atmospheres described.[29]

Reliance on these formulae also leads to a *recycling* of images, as members of the creative subsystem reach back through time for inspiration. Thus, young people in Britain watch retro channels like Granada Plus and UK Gold broadcasting classic decades-old soaps, and old themes are recycled for new soap series. Designers modify styles from Victorian England or colonial Africa, DJs sample sound bits from old songs and combine them in new ways, and The Gap runs ads featuring now-dead celebrities including Humphrey Bogart, Gene Kelly and Pablo Picasso dressed in khaki trousers.[30] With easy access to VCRs, CD burners, digital cameras and imaging software, virtually anyone can 'remix' the past.[31]

Artists and companies in the popular music or film industry may be more guided by ideas of what could make a 'hit' than by any wish for artistic expression. And creators of aesthetic products are increasingly adapting conventional marketing methods to fine-tune their mass-market offerings. In the United States, market research is used, for example, to test audience reactions to film concepts. Although testing cannot account for such intangibles as acting quality or cinematography, it can determine if the basic themes of the film strike a responsive chord in the target audience. This type of research is most appropriate for blockbuster films, which usually follow one of the formulae described earlier. In some cases research is combined with publicity, as when the producers of the film *Men in Black*, featuring Will Smith, showed the first 12 minutes of the film to an advance audience and then let them meet the stars to create a pre-release buzz.[32]

Even the content of films is sometimes influenced by this consumer research. Typically, free invitations to pre-screenings are handed out in shopping centres and cinemas. Attendees are asked a few questions about the film, then some are selected to participate in focus groups. Although groups' reactions usually result in only minor editing changes,

This Werther's Original ad illustrates how a mass produced product (sweets) can be portrayed as a link between generations, and evoke a strong emotional link too.

The Advertising Archives

occasionally more drastic effects result. When initial reaction to the ending of the film *Fatal Attraction* was negative, Paramount Pictures spent an additional $1.3 million to shoot a new one.[33] Of course, this feedback isn't always accurate – before the megahit *E.T.: The Extra-Terrestrial* was released, consumer research indicated that no one over the age of four would go to see the film![34]

Reality engineering

Let us take a short trip to a cosy corner of the United States. The village of Riverside, Georgia has a colourful history. You can look at the sepia photographs showing the town in the nineteenth century, or read excerpts from period novels lauding the settlement's cosmopolitan flair. You'll also discover that the town was used as a Union garrison during the American Civil War. There's only one hitch: Riverside didn't exist until 1998. The account of nineteenth-century Riverside is a clever fabrication created to promote a new housing and commercial development. The story 'is a figment of our imagination', acknowledges the developer.[35]

Like Riverside, many of the environments in which we find ourselves, whether shopping centres, sports stadiums or theme parks, are composed at least partly of images and characters drawn from products, marketing campaigns or the mass media. **Reality engineering** occurs as elements of popular culture are appropriated by marketers and converted to vehicles for promotional strategies.[36] These elements include sensory and spatial aspects of everyday existence, whether in the form of products appearing in films, scents pumped into offices and shops, advertising hoardings, theme parks, video monitors attached to shopping trolleys, and so on.

The people of Disney Corporation are probably the best worldwide-known reality engineers, through their theme parks in California and Florida, and their newer parks in Japan and Europe. Disneyland-Paris got off to a problematic start when it opened in 1991. Fewer visitors and especially too few clients for the hotel and congress facilities created economic problems. But the conceptualization of the park was changed, made less American and more European, and now the park is drawing huge crowds. Also other consumption facilities and housing areas have been created around it, including a giant shopping centre where one of the streets will be a recreation of a 'typical street' of one of the local villages.[37] But other themed environments like the Asterix park, future parks or artificially created tropical environments are becoming increasingly popular for shorter holidays throughout Europe. The British-owned chain Center Parcs now has 14 villages in Europe – five in the Netherlands, four in the UK, two each in Belgium and France, and one in Germany – all of them built on the concept of constructing a happy and safe environment for the confirmation of family values – a life 'in brackets' away from the risks and hassles of the 'real society'.[38]

The Lost City, a new resort in South Africa, blurs the boundaries even further; it has created a 'fake' Africa for affluent guests. The complex is drought-proof and disease-proof, and it features a three-storey water slide, an 'ocean' with a panic button that will stop the wave motion on command, and a nightly volcanic eruption complete with 'non-allergenic' smoke.[39] The melding of marketing activity with popular culture is evident in other contexts as well. A British coffee ad recently borrowed the words from the Beatles' song 'A Day in the Life' and went so far as to include a shot of John Lennon's signature round-framed glasses sitting on a table. The British Boy Scouts announced that they would begin accepting corporate sponsorships for merit badges.

multicultural dimensions

One of the most controversial intersections between marketing and society occurs when companies provide 'educational materials' to schools. In the United States, many firms, including such companies as Nike and Nintendo, provide free book covers covered with ads. Almost 40 per cent of secondary schools in the United States start the day with a 'video feed' from Channel One, which exposes students to commercials in the classroom in exchange for educational programming. Similarly, an internet company called ZapMe! gives client schools free computers and internet connections as well as a network of 11,000 educational sites in exchange for a promise to use the computers at least four hours a day. Commercials run continuously on the lower left-hand quarter of the screen, and the company has permission to monitor the students' browsing habits, breaking down the data by age, sex, and zip code. In a few cases companies are contracting with schools to run focus groups with their students during the school day in order to get reactions to new product ideas. Coca-Cola signed a ten year $8 million exclusive beverage contract with the Colorado Springs, Colorado school system. In some schools 9-year-olds practise maths by counting Tootsie Rolls (a brand of sweets), and use reading software that sports logos from KMart, Coke, Pepsi and Cap'n Crunch cereal.

Corporate involvement with schools is hardly new - in the 1920s Ivory Soap sponsored soap-carving competitions for students. But, the level of intrusion is sharply increasing as companies scramble to compensate for the decrease in children's viewership of television on Saturday mornings and weekday afternoons and find themselves competing with videos and computer games for their attention. Many educators argue that these materials are a godsend for resource-poor schools that otherwise would have hardly any other way to communicate with students. What do you think?[40]

Nor is this a purely American phenomenon any longer. The Danish consumer 'ombudsman' attacked a new series of mathematics books for primary schools for including references to brand names. The publishers defended themselves with the argument that it was to provide more realistic cases for the school children.

Marketing sometimes seems to exert a self-fulfilling prophecy on popular culture. As commercial influences on popular culture increase, marketer-created symbols make their way into our daily lives to a greater degree. Historical analyses of plays, best-selling novels and the lyrics of hit songs, for example, clearly show large increases in the use of brand names over time.[41]

Reality engineering is accelerating due to the current popularity of product place-ments by marketers. It is quite common to see real brands prominently displayed or to hear them discussed in films and on television. In many cases, these 'plugs' are no accid-ent. **Product placement** refers to the insertion of specific products and/or the use of brand names in film and TV scripts. Today most major releases are brimming with real products. Directors like to incorporate branded props because they contribute to the film's realism. When Stephen Spielberg did the film *Minority Report* he used such brands as Nokia, Lexus, Pepsi, Guinness, Reebok and American Express to lend familiarity to the plot's futuristic settings. Lexus even created a new sports car model called the Maglev just for the film.[42]

Some researchers claim that product placement can aid in consumer decision-making because the familiarity of these props creates a sense of cultural belonging while gener-ating feelings of emotional security.[43] One recent study found that consumers are more persuaded by embedded products when they are consistent with the plot.[44] On the other hand, a majority of consumers polled believe the line between advertising and program-ming is becoming too fuzzy and distracting (though, as might be expected, concerns about this blurring of boundaries rose steadily with the age of respondents).[45] For better or worse products are popping up everywhere:

- Although IBM sells a lot more computers, Apples are seen in many more TV shows and films such as *Mission Impossible* and *Independence Day*. Producers like to use the Apple because its image is more hip. But Apple will only let that happen if the brand is identified onscreen.[46]

- Philip Morris paid to place Marlboro cigarettes and signs in *Superman* movies and doled out $350,000 to have Lark cigarettes featured in the James Bond film *Licence to Kill*.[47]

- The American hit reality show *Survivor* portrayed the adventures of 16 people stranded on a desert island near Borneo for 39 days. They battled for a chance to wear Reeboks, drink Budweiser, and sleep in a Pontiac Aztec sport-utility vehicle.[48]

Product placement has been an American phenomenon – until recently. Now, mar-keters in other countries are discovering the value of placing their brand messages wherever they can.[49] In France, cafés are turning table tops into advertising space for United Airlines, Swatch watches and other companies. Although some patrons decry the invasion of such commercialism into the 'sacred' French practice of lounging at bistros, the owner of a firm that is supplying the ads observes, 'We want to make cafés more interesting places for people to visit.'[50] *Sacre bleu!*

In China, product placement is emerging as a new way to get noticed. Most com-mercials on Chinese state-run TV play back-to-back in ten-minute segments, making it difficult for any one 30-second ad to attract attention. So, enterprising marketers are embedding product messages in the shows instead. A soap opera called *Love Talks* fea-tures such products as Maybelline lipstick, Motorola mobile phones and Ponds Vaseline Intensive Care lotion.[51]

In India, the booming Bombay film industry (known as Bollywood) is discovering the potential of films to expose viewers to brand names (Indian cinema attracts huge local audiences, even in villages where television is not available). Coca-Cola paid to have its local soft drink, Thums Up, prominently featured in a Hindi-language remake of the Quentin Tarantino classic *Reservoir Dogs*. Just in case the audience misses the placements, in one scene just before bullets start flying a group of slickly dressed gangsters flash each other the thumbs-up sign.[52]

Media images significantly influence consumers' perceptions of reality, affecting viewers' notions about such issues as dating behaviour, racial stereotypes and occupa-tional status.[53] Studies of the **cultivation hypothesis**, which relates to media's ability to shape consumers' perceptions of reality, have shown that heavy television viewers tend to overestimate the degree of affluence in the country, and these effects also extend to such areas as perceptions of the amount of violence in one's culture.[54] Also, the depiction of consumer environments in programmes and advertisements may lead to further marginalization of, for example, unemployed people, who cannot afford to buy into the depicted lifestyle,[55] or to outright addicted consumers, who cannot refrain from constantly buying various goods, although they may not use these at all.

■ THE DIFFUSION OF INNOVATIONS

▶ New products and styles termed innovations constantly enter the market. An **innovation** is any product or service that is perceived to be new by consumers. These new products or services occur in both consumer and industrial settings. Innovations may take the form of a clothing or fashion accessory style (such as Jean-Paul Gaultier's skirts for men, or Dolce & Gabbana's rosary beads necklaces for men), a new manufacturing technique, or a novel way to deliver a service. If an innovation is successful (most are not), it spreads through the population. First it is bought and/or used by only a few people, and then more and more consumers decide to adopt it, until, in some cases, it seems that almost everyone has bought or tried the innovation. Diffusion of innovations refers to the process whereby a new product, service or idea spreads through a population. There is a tendency for technical goods especially to diffuse more rapidly these days. Sixteen per cent of the Swedish population possessed a mobile phone in 1994 – six years later, in 2000, the number was 80 per cent. Likewise, the number of Swedes with internet access was 74 per cent in 2004, up from 55 per cent in 2000.[56]

Adopting innovations

A consumer's adoption of an innovation may resemble the decision-making sequence discussed in Chapter 8. The person moves through the stages of awareness, information search, evaluation, trial and adoption, although the relative importance of each stage may differ depending on how much is already known about a product,[57] as well as on cultural factors that may affect people's willingness to try new things.[58] A study of 11 European countries found that consumers in individualistic cultures are more innovative than consumers in collective cultures.[59]

However, even within the same culture, not all people adopt an innovation at the same rate. Some do so quite rapidly, and others never do at all. Consumers can be placed into approximate categories based upon the likelihood of adopting an innovation. The categories of adopters, shown in Figure 15.2, can be related to phases of the product life-cycle concept used widely by marketing strategists.

As can be seen in Figure 15.2, roughly one-sixth of the population (innovators and early adopters) is very quick to adopt new products, and one-sixth of the people (laggards) is very slow. The other two-thirds are somewhere in the middle, and these majority adopters represent the mainstream public. In some cases people deliberately wait before adopting an innovation because they assume that its technological qualities will be improved or that its price will fall after it has been on the market.[60] Keep in mind that the proportion of consumers falling into each category is an estimate; the actual size of each depends upon such factors as the complexity of the product, its cost and other product-related factors, but possibly also varies from country to country.

Even though innovators represent only 2.5 per cent of the population, marketers are always interested in identifying them. According to standard theory, these are the brave souls who are always on the lookout for novel developments and will be the first to try a new offering. Just as generalized opinion leaders do not appear to exist, innovators

Figure 15.2 Types of adopter

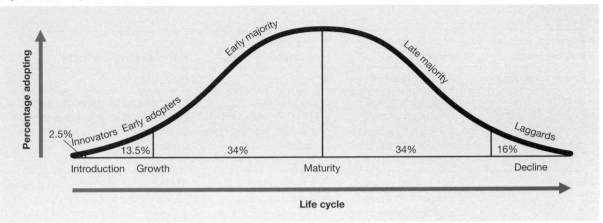

tend to be category-specific. A person who is an innovator in one area may even be a laggard in another. For example, someone who prides himself on being at the cutting edge of fashion may have no conception of new developments in recording technology and stereo equipment.

Despite this qualification, some generalizations can be offered regarding the profile of innovators.[61] Not surprisingly they tend to have more favourable attitudes towards taking risks. They are also, at least in an American context, likely to have higher educational and income levels and to be socially active. However, in a European study of the fashion and clothing market, the same correlation between socio-demographic variables and innovative or early adopting behaviour could not be found.[62] On the other hand, a Spanish study, perhaps not surprisingly, concluded that innovators tend to be younger and, more interestingly, that publicity and advertisement would have the biggest influence on product adoption in the early years of commercialization of a product, whereas word-of-mouth and other non-producer controlled information becomes more important thereafter.[63]

▶ **Early adopters** share many of the same characteristics as innovators, but an important difference is their degree of concern for social acceptance, especially with regard to expressive products such as clothing, cosmetics and so on. Generally speaking, an early adopter is receptive to new styles because he or she is involved in the product category and also places high value on being in fashion. The universality of the dichotomy of innovators and adopters has been challenged by research pertaining to health foods, suggesting that (1) three groups can be distinguished, namely innovators, more-involved adopters and less-involved adopters, and (2) there is not a big difference between the purchase rate of new products between innovators and adopters; rather the difference lies in the kind of innovations tried and the approach to trying new products.[64] Table 15.4 gives a brief description of the different types of consumers and their approach to new product trials.

Types of innovations

Innovations can contain a technological level and involve some functional change (for example, car air bags) or be of a more intangible kind, communicating a new social meaning (like a new hairstyle). However, contrary to what much literature states,[65] both are symbolic in the sense that one refers to symbols of technical performance and safety and the other to less tangible symbols, such as courage and individuality. Both types refer to symbols of progress.[66] New products, services and ideas have characteristics that

Table 15.4 Decision styles of market segments based on adoption, innovation and personal involvement

Adoption decision process stage	Less-involved adopters	Innovators	More-involved adopters
Problem recognition	Passive, reactive	Active	Proactive
Search	Minimal, confined to resolution of minor anomalies caused by current consumption patterns	Superficial but extensively based within and across product class boundaries	Extensive within relevant product category; assiduous exploration of all possible solutions within that framework
Evaluation	Meticulous, rational, slow and cautious; objective appraisal using tried and tested criteria	Quick, impulsive, based on currently accepted criteria; personal and subjective	Careful, confined to considerations raised by the relevant product category: but executed confidently and (for the adopter) briskly within that frame of reference
Decision	Conservative selection within known range of products, continuous innovations preferred	Radical: easily attracted to discontinuously new product class and able to choose quickly within it. Frequent trial, followed by abandonment	Careful selection within a product field that has become familiar through deliberation, vicarious trial, and sound and prudent pre-purchase comparative evaluation
Post-purchase evaluation	Meticulous, tendency to brand loyalty if item performs well	Less loyal; constantly seeking novel experiences through purchase and consumption innovations	Loyal if satisfied but willing to try innovations within the prescribed frame of reference; perhaps tends towards dynamically-continuous

Source: Gordon R. Foxall and Seema Bhate, 'Cognitive style and personal involvement as explicators of innovative purchasing of health food brands', *European Journal of Marketing* 27(2)(1993): 5-16. Used with permission.

determine the degree to which they will probably diffuse. Innovations that are more novel may be less likely to diffuse, since they require bigger changes in people's lifestyles and thus more effort. On the other hand, most innovations are close to being of the 'me too' kind, and thus do not necessarily possess qualities that would persuade the consumer to shift from existing product types. In any case, it should be noted that in spite of all the good intentions of the marketing concept to ensure that there is a market before the product is developed, the failure rate of new products is as high as ever, if not higher.[67]

Behavioural demands of innovations

Innovations can be categorized in terms of the degree to which they demand changes in behaviour from adopters. Three major types of innovation have been identified, though these three categories are not absolutes. They refer, in a relative sense, to the amount of disruption or change they bring to people's lives.

▶ A **continuous innovation** refers to a modification of an existing product, as when a breakfast cereal is introduced in a sugar-coated version, or Levi's promoted 'shrink-to-fit' jeans. This type of change may be used to set one brand apart from its competitors. Most product innovations are evolutionary rather than revolutionary. Small changes are made to position the product, add line extensions or merely to alleviate consumer boredom.

Consumers may be lured to the new product, but adoption represents only minor changes in consumption habits, since innovation perhaps adds to the product's convenience or to the range of choices available. A typewriter company, for example, many years ago modified the shape of its product to make it more user friendly. One simple change was the curving of the tops of the keys, a convention that was carried over on today's computer keyboards. One of the reasons for the change was that secretaries with long fingernails had complained about the difficulty of typing on the flat surfaces.

▶ A **dynamically continuous innovation** is a more pronounced change in an existing product, as represented by self-focusing cameras or touch-tone telephones. These innovations have a modest impact on the way people do things, creating some behavioural changes, although the touch-tone telephone is an expression of a larger innovation involving many discontinuous renewals of daily life: the digitalization of communication. When introduced, the IBM electric typewriter, which used a 'golf ball' rather than individual keys, enabled typists to change the typeface of manuscripts simply by replacing one ball with another.

▶ A **discontinuous innovation** creates major changes in the way we live. Major inventions, such as the aeroplane, the car, the computer and television have radically changed modern lifestyles, although, as can be seen from these examples, major changes normally take some time from the point of introduction. The personal computer has, in many cases, supplanted the typewriter, and it has created the phenomenon of 'telecommuters' by allowing many people to work from their homes. Of course, the cycle continues, as new innovations like new versions of software are constantly being made; dynamically continuous innovations such as the keyboard 'mouse' compete for adoption; and discontinuous innovations like wristwatch personal computers loom on the horizon.

marketing opportunity

These years, the new interactive communication technologies provide a lot of opportunities for product innovations. Electrolux, the large Swedish appliance producer, is currently testing household reactions and changes in consumer lifestyles in 50 Danish homes following the installment of the world's first intelligent refrigerator, the Electrolux Screenfridge. In collaboration with an Ericsson subsidiary, the company has developed this new communication center of the home, with built-in touch screen on the refrigerator door that provides perpetual access to broadband communication technology (including automated shopping lists), internet, TV and radio. Even more 'intelligent features' are being developed for the product. Says one young mother from one of the test households: 'I enjoy the on-line internet access in the kitchen, as it is the place we spend most of our time. I believe I'll use the Screenfridge for everyday information, like looking up phone numbers, finding bus schedules or getting dinner ideas. I know I'll also try internet food shopping; with two children it would be great to have the groceries delivered to the home.'[68]

Prerequisites for successful adoption

Regardless of how much behavioural change is demanded by an innovation, several factors are desirable for a new product to succeed:[69]

● *Compatibility*. The innovation should be compatible with consumers' lifestyles. As an illustration, a manufacturer of personal care products tried unsuccessfully several years ago to introduce a hair remover cream for men as a substitute for razors and shaving cream. This formulation was similar to that used widely by women to remove hair from their legs. Although the product was simple and convenient to use, it failed because men were not interested in a product they perceived to be too feminine and thus threatening to their masculine self-concepts.

● *Trialability*. Since an unknown is accompanied by high perceived risk, people are more likely to adopt an innovation if they can experiment with it prior to making a commitment. To reduce this risk, companies often choose the expensive strategies of distributing free 'trial-size' samples of new products. For example, the Swedish coffee brand Gevalia has distributed free samples targeted especially at young people, because there is some evidence that fewer young people are drinking coffee, and those that do, begin later in life.

A cultural emphasis on science in the late 1950s affected product designs, as seen in the design of cars with large tail fins (to resemble rockets).

Corbis/R. Gates

- *Complexity*. The product should be low in complexity. A product that is easier to understand and use will often be preferred to a competitor. This strategy requires less effort from the consumer, and it also lowers perceived risk. Manufacturers of DVD players, for example, have put a lot of effort into simplifying usage (such as on-screen programming) to encourage adoption.

- *Observability*. An innovation that is easily observable is more likely to spread, since this quality makes it more likely that other potential adopters will become aware of its existence. The rapid proliferation of 'bum bags' (pouches worn around the waist in lieu of wallets or purses) was due to their high visibility. It was easy for others to see the convenience offered.

- *Relative advantage*. Most importantly, the product should offer relative advantage over alternatives. The consumer must believe that its use will provide a benefit other products cannot offer. For example, the success of many environmentally friendly product alternatives may be due to the fact that, once consumers have been convinced about the environmental advantages of the product, it is a clear and easily understandable advantage compared to competing products.

The social context of innovations

One critical but relatively little researched aspect is the importance of the social context of product adoption behaviour.[70] This is linked to the importance of visibility of the product innovation as well as the influence of the reference group which is seen as related to the new product. For example, Western products are admired in many contexts in Asia and Africa, or the marketizing economies of Eastern Europe, for the sole reason of being linked to the status of the Western world, which is seen as 'better', more 'developed' and generally of a higher status.[71] Likewise, in Europe the association of new products with the American way of life will have a significant impact on the adopting behaviour of various groups in society but will differ in different European countries.

Another aspect of the social dimension of innovation is the pitfall of being caught up in too many continuous innovations due to an ever finer market segmentation and customization approach. This may take resources away from more strategic considerations of changing 'the way things are done'.[72] For example, a British bank had created such a complex structure of financial services and accounts, as well as charges attached to these services, that customers began to complain about waiting time and lack of understanding of their own financial affairs. The bank simplified the structure to one account type and a much simpler charge system and successfully made this a unique selling proposition in a market dominated by more complex offerings.[73]

■ THE FASHION SYSTEM

▶ The **fashion system** consists of all those people and organizations involved in creating symbolic meanings and transferring these meanings to cultural goods. Although people tend to equate fashion with clothing, be it haute couture or street wear, it is important to keep in mind that fashion processes affect *all* types of cultural phenomena from the more mundane (what do you think of high fashion nappy bags in unisex style?[74]) to high art, including music, art, architecture and even science (i.e. certain research topics and scientists are 'hot' at any point in time). Even business practices are subject to the fashion process; they evolve and change depending on which management techniques are in vogue, such as total quality management or 'the learning organization'.

Fashion can be thought of as a *code*, or language, that helps us to decipher these meanings.[75] However, fashion seems to be *context-dependent* to a larger extent than language. That is, the same item can be interpreted differently by different consumers and in different situations.[76] The meaning of many products is *undercoded* – that is, there is no one precise meaning, but rather plenty of room for interpretation among perceivers.

▶ At the outset, it may be helpful to distinguish among some confusing terms. **Fashion** is the process of social diffusion by which a new style is adopted by some group(s) of consumers. In contrast, *a fashion* (or style) refers to a particular combination of attributes. And, to be *in fashion* means that this combination is currently positively evaluated by some reference group. Thus, the term *Danish Modern* refers to particular characteristics of furniture design (i.e. a fashion in interior design); it does not necessarily imply that Danish Modern is a fashion that is currently desired by consumers.[77]

Cultural categories

▶ The meaning that does get imparted to products reflects underlying **cultural categories**, which correspond to the basic ways we characterize the world.[78] Our culture makes distinctions between different times, between leisure and work, between genders and so on. The fashion system provides us with products that signify these categories. For example, the clothing industry gives us clothing to denote certain times (evening wear, resort wear), it differentiates between leisure clothes and work clothes, and it promotes masculine, feminine or unisex styles.

Interdependence among product meanings

These cultural categories affect many different products and styles. As a result, it is common to find that dominant aspects of a culture at any point in time tend to be reflected in the design and marketing of very different products. This concept is hard to grasp, since on the surface a clothing style, say, has little in common with a piece of furniture or with a car. However, an overriding concern with a value such as achievement or environmentalism can determine the types of product likely to be accepted by consumers at any point in time. These underlying or latent themes then surface in various aspects of design. A few examples of this interdependence will help to demonstrate how a dominant fashion motif reverberates across industries.

● Costumes worn by political figures or film and rock stars can affect the fortunes of the apparel and accessory industries. The appearance in a film of the actor Clark Gable not wearing a vest (unusual at that time) dealt a severe setback to the men's apparel industry, while Jackie Kennedy's famous 'pillbox' hat prompted a rush for hats by women in the 1960s. Other cross-category effects include the craze for ripped sweatshirts instigated by the film *Flashdance* or the singer Madonna's legitimization of lingerie as an acceptable outerwear clothing style.

● Some years ago, the Louvre in Paris was remodelled to include a controversial glass pyramid at the entrance designed by the architect I.M. Pei. Shortly thereafter, several designers unveiled pyramid-shaped clothing at Paris fashion shows.[79]

● In the 1950s and 1960s, much of the Western world was preoccupied with science and technology. This concern with 'space-age' mastery was fuelled by the Russians' launching of the Sputnik satellite, which prompted fears that the West (and here, most importantly the United States) was falling behind in the technology race. The theme of technical mastery of nature and of futuristic design became a motif that cropped up in many aspects of popular culture – from car designs with prominent tailfins to high-tech kitchen styles.

Collective selection

Fashions tend to sweep through countries; it seems that all of a sudden 'everyone' is doing the same thing or wearing the same styles. Some sociologists view fashion as a form of *collective behaviour*, or a wave of social conformity. How do so many people get tuned in to the same phenomenon at once, as happened with hip-hop styles?

Remember that creative subsystems within a culture production system attempt to anticipate the tastes of the buying public. Despite their unique talents, members of this subsystem are also members of mass culture. Like the fashion magazine editors discussed earlier, cultural gatekeepers are drawing from a common set of ideas and symbols, and are influenced by the same cultural phenomena as the eventual consumers of their products.

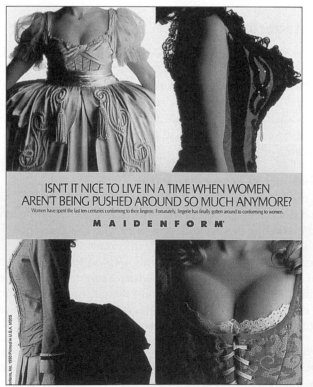

This ad for Maidenform illustrates that fashions have accentuated different parts of the female anatomy throughout history.

Copyright © 1994 by Maidenform, Inc.

▶ The process by which certain symbolic alternatives are chosen over others has been termed **collective selection**.[80] As with the creative subsystem, members of the managerial and communications subsystems also seem to develop a common frame of mind. Although products within each category must compete for acceptance in the marketplace, they can usually be characterized by their adherence to a dominant theme or motif – be it the grunge look, sixties nostalgia, Danish Modern or nouvelle cuisine.

Behavioural science perspectives on fashion

Fashion is a very complex process which operates on many levels. At one extreme, it is a macro, societal phenomenon affecting many people simultaneously. At the other, it exerts a very personal effect on individual behaviour. A consumer's purchase decisions are often motivated by his or her desire to be in fashion. Fashion products are aesthetic objects, and their origins are rooted in art and history. For this reason, there are many perspectives on the origin and diffusion of fashion. Although these cannot be described in detail here, some major approaches can be briefly summarized.[81]

Psychological models of fashion

Many psychological factors help to explain why people are motivated to be in fashion. These include conformity, variety-seeking, personal creativity and sexual attraction. For example, many consumers seem to have a 'need for uniqueness': they want to be different, but not too different.[82] For this reason, people often conform to the basic outlines of a fashion, but try to improvize and make a personal statement within these guidelines.

▶ One of the earliest theories of fashion proposed that 'shifting **erogenous zones**' (sexually arousing areas of the body) accounted for fashion changes. Different parts of the female body are the focus of sexual interest, and clothing styles change to highlight or hide these parts. For example, people in the Victorian era found shoulders exciting, a 'well-turned ankle' was important at the beginning of the twentieth century, while the back was the centre of attention in the 1930s.

While these shifts may be due to boredom, some have speculated that there are deeper reasons for changes in focus; body areas symbolically reflect social values. In medieval times, for example, a rounded belly was desirable. This preference was most likely a reflection of the fact that multiple pregnancies were necessary to maintain population growth in an age when infant mortality was high. Interest in the female leg in the 1920s and 1930s coincided with women's new mobility and independence, while the exposure of breasts in the 1970s signalled a renewed interest in breastfeeding.[83] Breasts were de-emphasized in the 1980s as women concentrated on careers, but some analysts have theorized that a larger bust size is now more popular as women try to combine professional activity with child-rearing. Now, some suggest that the current prevalence of the exposed midriff reflects the premium our society places on fitness.[84] It's important to note that until very recently the study of fashion focused almost exclusively on its impact on women. It is to be hoped that this concentration will broaden as scholars and practitioners begin to appreciate that men are affected by many of the same fashion influences.

Psychological research suggests that it is possible to distinguish between two different personality types, respectively more or less sensitive to the opinion of their social surroundings (also called high and low self-monitors). The high self-monitors have been demonstrated to stress the brand of a consumer good (specifically clothing) more than low self-monitors, who are on the other hand more positive to functional product attributes.[85]

Economic models of fashion

Economists approach fashion in terms of the model of supply and demand. Items that are in limited supply have high value, while those readily available are less desirable. Rare items command respect and prestige.

▶   Veblen's notion of **conspicuous consumption** proposed that the wealthy consume to display their prosperity, for example by wearing expensive (and at times impractical) clothing. The functioning of conspicuous consumption seems more complex in today's society, since wealthy consumers often engage in *parody display*, where they deliberately adopt formerly low status or inexpensive products, such as jeeps or jeans. On the other hand, new hierarchies develop between generic jeans signalling a traditional, work-oriented, classless or lower-class environment, and designer jeans expressing an urban, upmarket, class-distinctive and more contemporary lifestyle.[86] Other factors also influence the demand curve for fashion-related products. These include a *prestige-exclusivity effect*, where high prices still create high demand, and a *snob effect*, where lower prices actually reduce demand ('only a cheapskate would pay so little for that!').[87]

Sociological models of fashion

The collective selection model discussed previously is an example of a sociological approach to fashion. In addition, much attention has been focused on the relationship between product adoption and class structure.

▶   The **trickle-down theory**, first proposed in 1904 by Georg Simmel, has been one of the most influential approaches to understanding fashion. It states that there are two conflicting forces that drive fashion change. First, subordinate groups try to adopt the status symbols of the groups above them as they attempt to climb up the ladder of social mobility. Dominant styles thus originate with the upper classes and *trickle down* to those below. However, this is where the second force comes into play: those people in the superordinate groups are constantly looking below them on the ladder to ensure that they are not imitated. They respond to the attempts of lower classes to 'impersonate' them by adopting even *newer* fashions. These two processes create a self-perpetuating cycle of change – the engine that drives fashion.[88]

The trickle-down theory was quite useful for understanding the process of fashion changes when applied to a society with a stable class structure, which permitted the easy

Some people argue that consumers are at the mercy of fashion designers. What do you think?
Diesel S.p.A.

identification of lower- versus upper-class consumers. This task is not so easy in modern times. In contemporary Western society, then, this approach must be modified to account for new developments in mass culture.[89]

- A perspective based on class structure cannot account for the wide range of styles that are simultaneously made available in our society. Modern consumers have a much greater degree of individualized choice than in the past because of advances in technology and distribution. Just as an adolescent is almost instantly aware of the latest style trends by watching MTV, *elite fashion* has been largely replaced by *mass fashion*, since media exposure permits many groups to become aware of a style at the same time.

- Consumers tend to be more influenced by opinion leaders who are similar to them. As a result each social group has its own fashion innovators who determine fashion trends. It is often more accurate to speak of a *trickle-across effect*, where fashions diffuse horizontally among members of the same social group.[90]

- Anybody who has been on a skiing holiday will have noticed the *subcultural fashions* demonstrated among the skiers. In fact, more and more consumption-based subcultures, sailing enthusiasts for instance, adopt their own fashions in order to reinforce their community feeling and distinguish themselves from outsiders.[91]

- Finally, current fashions often originate with the lower classes and *trickle up*. Grassroots innovators typically are people who lack prestige in the dominant culture (like urban youth). Since they are less concerned with maintaining the status quo, they are more free to innovate and take risks.[92] Whatever the direction of the trickling, one thing is sure: that fashion is always a complex process of variation, of imitation and differentiation, of adoptions and rejections in relation to one's social surroundings.[93]

This blurring of origins of fashion has been attributed to the condition of postmodernity when there is no fashion, only fashions, and no rules, only choices,[94] and where the norms and rules can no longer be dictated solely from the haute couture or other cultural gatekeepers but where the individual allows him- or herself more freedom in creating a personal look by mixing elements from different styles.[95] This obviously has the consequence that the relatively linear models of fashion cycles discussed below become less able to predict actual fashion developments.[96]

A French researcher followed the development in the editorial content of a French fashion magazine since 1945. It turned out that the content became more global and less 'French' over the years, but also that the magazine gradually shifted away from a dictate of one certain fashion style at each point in time to an approach in the 1990s where several styles were promoted in each issue and consumers were invited to mix and match and create their own personal style independently of high fashion.[97] A similar blurring of high and low fashion was demonstrated by a prize-winning campaign, where a charity organization used former international top model Renee Toft Simonsen for promoting clothes from their second-hand shops.[98] Neither she nor the agency got any payment for their participation.

The fashion system, then, is becoming increasingly complex. Brands may be very significant to consumers and they may be less ashamed to admit that than previously but they are less committed to any one brand over a longer period. The fashion industry is trying to compensate for this by overexposing their brands, putting the brand name very conspicuously all over clothing, bags, accessories, etc. in order to get a maximum of exposure out of the 'catch'.[99] The fashion industry is also exploring the individual styles for new market opportunities and new meanings of fashion goods for wider distribution.[100] Even those trying to rebel against fashion dictates by turning to ugliness as a motif for their choice of 'look' cannot escape. Ugliness in a variety of forms is becoming increasingly fashionable; as one consumer said: 'these shoes were so ugly I just had to have them'.[101] The ugly and disgusting seems to form a specific trend in certain companies' marketing strategies.[102]

marketing pitfall

A *knock-off* is a style that has been deliberately copied and modified, often with the intent to sell to a larger or different market. Haute couture clothing styles presented by top designers in Paris and elsewhere are commonly 'knocked off' by other designers and sold to the mass market. The Web is making it easier than ever for firms to copy these designs – in some cases so quickly that their pirated styles appear in stores at the same time as the originals. Wildcatters such as First View have set up websites to show designers' latest creations, sometimes revealing everything from a new collection. Things have become so bad that The House of Chanel requires photographers to sign contracts promising their shots will not be distributed on the internet.[103] But, isn't imitation the sincerest form of flattery?

Cycles of fashion adoption

In 1997, a little digital animal swept across the planet. After enjoying considerable success in Japan in 1996 with about 3 million units sold, it spread throughout the world during 1997 where the population by the summer had increased to a total of 7 million with approximately twice that number in back orders. The Tamagochi, as it is known, is an electronic pet that must be nurtured, played with and taken care of just as a living being. Failure to do so means it will weaken and show signs of maltreatment until it eventually dies. That is, in the Japanese version it dies. This unhappy ending did not appeal to Americans who therefore created their own version where it flies off to another planet if not treated well. Needless to say, the Japanese 'authentic' versions quickly became collectors' items (see the discussion of collections in the previous chapter). Today, many consumers might not know what a Tamagochi is, but anybody with children will know what a Pokémon is.

The stories of the Tamagochi or the Pokémon show how quickly a consumer craze can catch on globally. Although the longevity of a particular style can range from a month to a century, fashions tend to flow in a predictable sequence. The **fashion life cycle** is quite similar to the more familiar product life cycle. An item or idea progresses through basic stages from birth to death, as shown in Figure 15.3.

Variations in fashion life cycles

The diffusion process discussed earlier in this chapter is intimately related to the popularity of fashion-related items. To illustrate how this process works, consider how the

Figure 15.3 A normal fashion cycle

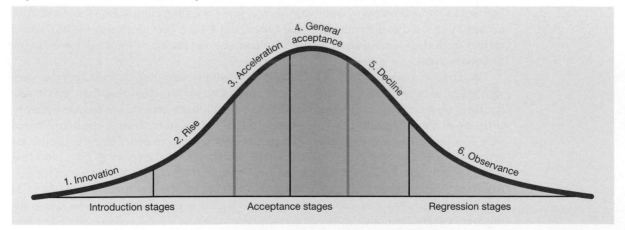

Source: Susan Kaiser, *The Social Psychology of Clothing* (New York: Macmillan, 1985). Reprinted with permission.

▶ **fashion acceptance cycle** works in the popular music business. In the *introduction stage*, a song is listened to by a small number of music innovators. It may be played in clubs or on 'cutting-edge' radio stations, which is exactly how 'grunge rock' groups such as Nirvana got their start. During the *acceptance stage*, the song enjoys increased social visibility and acceptance by large segments of the population. A record may get wide airplay on 'Top-40' stations, steadily rising up the charts 'like a bullet'. This process may of course be supported or even generated by marketing efforts from the record company.

In the *regression stage*, the item reaches a state of social saturation as it becomes overused, and eventually it sinks into decline and obsolescence as new songs rise to take its place. A hit record may be played once an hour on a Top-40 station for several weeks. At some point, though, people tend to get sick of it and focus their attention on newer releases. The former hit record eventually winds up in the discount rack at the local record store.

Not everybody shares the same musical tastes. Nor, as we discussed above, is everybody necessarily influenced by the same fashion in clothing anymore. As society may become more characterized by lifestyles than by generalizable consumption patterns spreading through social classes as in the class-based fashion models, the social groups in question may consist more of a particular lifestyle than actual social classes. For example, one may distinguish generally between the more risk-prone and the more prudent fashion consumers, and each of these two groups have their own independent fashion cycles that do not necessarily influence the other groups.[104]

Figure 15.4 illustrates that fashions are characterized by slow acceptance at the beginning, which (if the fashion is to 'make it') rapidly accelerates and then tapers off. Different classes of fashion can be identified by considering the relative length of the fashion acceptance cycle. While many fashions exhibit a moderate cycle, taking several years to work their way through the stages of acceptance and decline, others are extremely long-lived or short-lived.

Figure 15.4 Comparison of the acceptance cycle of fads, fashions and classics

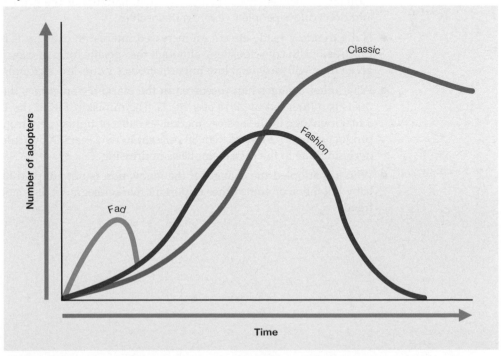

Source: Susan Kaiser, *The Social Psychology of Clothing* (New York: Macmillan, 1985). Reprinted with permission.

▶   A **classic** is a fashion with an extremely long acceptance cycle. It is in a sense 'anti-fashion', since it guarantees stability and low risk to the purchaser for a long period of time. Keds sneakers, classic so-called 'tennis shoes' introduced in the United States in 1917, have been successful because they appeal to those who are turned off by the high-fashion, trendy appeal of L.A. Gear, Reebok and others. When consumers in focus groups were asked to project what kind of building Keds would be, a common response was a country house with a white picket fence. In other words, the shoes are seen as a stable, classic product. In contrast, Nikes were often described as steel-and-glass skyscrapers, reflecting their more modernistic image.[105]

▶   A **fad** is a very short-lived fashion. Fads are usually adopted by relatively few people. Adopters may all belong to a common subculture, and the fad 'trickles across' members but rarely breaks out of that specific group.[106] Some key characteristics of fads include:

- The fad is non-utilitarian – that is, it does not perform any explicit purpose function.

- The fad is often adopted on impulse; people do not undergo stages of rational decision-making before joining in.

- The fad diffuses rapidly, gains quick acceptance, and is short-lived.

Distinguishing beforehand between fads or more lasting tendencies of change is not easy, and many consulting agencies make a living out of being trend-spotters. However, here are a few points that may be helpful in distinguishing short-lived fads from longer-lasting innovations:[107]

- Does it fit with basic lifestyle changes? If a new hairstyle is hard to care for, this innovation will not be consistent with women's increasing time demands. On the other hand, the movement to shorter-term holidays is more likely to last because this innovation makes trip planning easier for harried consumers.

- What are the benefits? The switch to leaner meats and cuts came about because these meats are perceived as healthier, so a real benefit is evident.

- Can it be personalized? Enduring trends tend to accommodate a desire for individuality, whereas styles such as mohawk haircuts or the grunge look are inflexible and don't allow people to express themselves.

- Is it a trend or a side effect? An increased interest in exercise is part of a basic trend towards health consciousness, although the specific form of exercise that is 'in' at any given time will vary (e.g. low-impact aerobics vs. in-line skating).

- What other changes have occurred in the market? Sometimes the popularity of products is influenced by *carry-over effects*. The miniskirt fad in the 1960s brought about a major change in the hosiery market, as sales of tights grew from 10 per cent of this product category to more than 80 per cent in two years. Now, sales of these items are declining due to the casual emphasis in dressing.

- Who has adopted the change? If the innovation is not adopted by working mothers, baby boomers, or some other important market segment, it is not likely to become a trend.

■ CHAPTER SUMMARY

■ The styles prevalent in a culture at any point in time often reflect underlying political and social conditions. The set of agents responsible for creating stylistic alternatives is termed a culture production system. Factors such as the types of people involved in this system and the amount of competition by alternative product forms influence the choices that eventually make their way to the marketplace for consideration by end consumers.

■ Culture is often described in terms of high (or elite) forms and low (or popular) forms. Products of popular culture tend to follow a cultural formula and contain predictable components. On the other hand, these distinctions are blurring in modern society as imagery from 'high art' is increasingly being incorporated into marketing efforts and marketed products (or even marketing products like advertisements) are treated and evaluated as high art.

■ The *diffusion of innovations* refers to the process whereby a new product, service or idea spreads through a population. A consumer's decision to adopt a new item depends on his or her personal characteristics (if he or she is inclined to try new things) and on the characteristics of the item. Products sometimes stand a better chance of being adopted if they demand relatively little change in behaviour from consumers and are compatible with current practices. They are also more likely to diffuse if they can be tested prior to purchase, if they are not complex, if their use is visible to others, and, most importantly, if they provide a relative advantage vis-à-vis existing products.

■ The fashion system includes everyone involved in the creation and transference of symbolic meanings. Meanings that express common cultural categories (for instance, gender distinctions) are conveyed by many different products. New styles tend to be adopted by many people simultaneously in a process known as collective selection. Perspectives on motivations for adopting new styles include psychological, economic and sociological models of fashion.

■ Fashions tend to follow cycles that resemble the product life cycle. The two extremes of fashion adoption, classics and fads, can be distinguished in terms of the length of this cycle.

▶ KEY TERMS

Art product (p. 532)
Classic (p. 550)
Collective selection (p. 545)
Conspicuous consumption (p. 546)
Continuous innovation (p. 540)
Craft product (p. 532)
Cultivation hypothesis (p. 537)
Cultural categories (p. 543)
Cultural formula (p. 534)
Cultural gatekeepers (p. 531)
Cultural production system (CPS) (p. 531)
Cultural selection (p. 530)
Discontinuous innovation (p. 541)

Dynamically continuous innovation (p. 541)
Early adopters (p. 539)
Erogenous zones (p. 545)
Fad (p. 550)
Fashion (p. 543)
Fashion acceptance cycle (p. 549)
Fashion life cycle (p. 548)
Fashion system (p. 543)
Innovation (p. 538)
Product placement (p. 537)
Reality engineering (p. 535)
Trickle-down theory (p. 546)

CONSUMER BEHAVIOUR CHALLENGE

1 Construct a 'biography' of a product, tracing its progress from the time it was introduced. How long did it take to diffuse to the mass market? Do the same consumers use the product now as those who first adopted it? What are its future prospects – is it destined for obsolescence? Would you characterize the product as either a classic or a fad?

2 Some consumers complain that they are 'at the mercy' of designers: they are forced to buy whatever styles are in fashion because nothing else is available. Do you agree that there is such a thing as a 'designer conspiracy'?

3 What is the basic difference between a fad, a fashion and a classic? Provide examples of each.

4 What is the difference between an art and a craft? Where would you characterize advertising within this framework?

5 Think about some innovative products that you can remember, but which disappeared. Try to reflect on the reasons why these innovations failed.

6 Then try to remember some successful innovations. What characteristics made them successful? Do the successes and failures fit with the criteria mentioned in this chapter?

7 The chapter mentions some instances where market research findings influenced artistic decisions, as when a film ending was reshot to accommodate consumers' preferences. Many people would oppose this use of consumer research, claiming that books, films, records or other artistic endeavours should not be designed merely to conform to what people want to read, see or hear. What do you think?

8 Many are claiming a more individualistic style of fashion these years. Discuss whether individualism in style and fashion has actually increased or whether we are being conformist in new ways.

■ NOTES

1. Nina Darnton, 'Where the homegirls are', *Newsweek* (17 June 1991): 60; 'The idea chain', *Newsweek* (5 October 1992): 32.
2. Cyndee Miller, 'X marks the lucrative spot, but some advertisers can't hit target', *Marketing News* (2 August 1993): 1.
3. Ad appeared in *Elle* (September 1994).
4. Marc Spiegler, 'Marketing street culture: Bringing hip-hop style to the mainstream', *American Demographics* (November 1996): 23–7; Joshua Levine, 'Badass sells', *Forbes* (21 April 1997): 142–8.
5. Jeff Jensen, 'Hip, wholesome image makes a marketing star of rap's LL Cool J', *Advertising Age* (25 August 1997): 1.
6. Alice Z. Cuneo, 'Gap's 1st global ads confront dockers on a khaki battlefield', *Advertising Age* (20 April 1998): 3–5.
7. Jancee Dunn, 'How hip-hop style bum-rushed the mall', *Rolling Stone* (18 March 1999): 54–9.
8. Quoted in Teri Agins, 'The rare art of "gilt by association": How Armani got stars to be billboards', *The Wall Street Journal Interactive Edition* (14 September 1999).

9. Eryn Brown, 'From rap to retail: Wiring the hip-hop nation', *Fortune* (17 April 2000): 530.

10. Martin Fackler, 'Hip hop invading China', *The Birmingham News* (15 February 2002): D1.

11. Maureen Tkacik, ' "Z" zips into the zeitgeist, subbing for "S" in hot slang', *The Wall Street Journal Interactive Edition* (4 January 2003); Maureen Tkacik, 'Slang from the 'hood now sells toyz in target', *The Wall Street Journal Interactive Edition* (30 December 2002).

12. 'Return of the Mac – coming soon' (29 March 2005), http://news.bbc.co.uk/2/hi/business/4389751.stm.

13. Michael McCarthy, 'Rappers sample athletes' turf', *USA Today* (5 July 2005), http://www.usatoday.com/sports/2005-07-04-rap-endorsements_x.htm.

14. J.D. Biersdorfer, 'MP3 watch from 50 Cent (the price is a bit higher)', *New York Times* (14 July 2004), http://www.nytimes.com/2005/07/14/technology/circuits/14watch.html?ex=1278993600&en=4a067b6cc70ec100&ei=5088&partner=rssnyt&emc=rss.

15. Teri Agins, 'To track fickle fashion, apparel firms go online', *The Wall Street Journal* (11 May 2000): B1.

16. Richard A. Peterson, 'The Production of Culture: A Prolegomenon', in Richard A. Peterson, ed., *The Production of Culture*, Sage Contemporary Social Science Issues (Beverly Hills, CA: Sage, 1976) 33: 7–22.

17. Richard A. Peterson and D.G. Berger, 'Entrepreneurship in organizations: Evidence from the popular music industry', *Administrative Science Quarterly* 16 (1971): 97–107.

18. Elizabeth C. Hirschman, 'Resource exchange in the production and distribution of a motion picture', *Empirical Studies of the Arts* 8 (1990) 1: 31–51; Michael R. Solomon, 'Building Up and Breaking Down: The Impact of Cultural Sorting on Symbolic Consumption', in J. Sheth and E.C. Hirschman, eds, *Research in Consumer Behavior* (Greenwich, CT: JAI Press, 1988): 325–51.

19. See Paul M. Hirsch, 'Processing fads and fashions: An organizational set analysis of cultural industry systems', *American Journal of Sociology* 77 (1972) 4: 639–59; Russell Lynes, *The Tastemakers* (New York: Harper & Brothers, 1954); Michael R. Solomon, 'The missing link: Surrogate consumers in the marketing chain', *Journal of Marketing* 50 (October 1986): 208–19.

20. Michael R. Solomon, Richard Ashmore and Laura Longo, 'The beauty match-up hypothesis: Congruence between types of beauty and product images in advertising', *Journal of Advertising* 21 (December 1992): 23–34.

21. Howard S. Becker, 'Arts and crafts', *American Journal of Sociology* 83 (January 1987): 862–89.

22. Herbert J. Gans, 'Popular Culture in America: Social Problem in a Mass Society or Social Asset in a Pluralist Society?', in Howard S. Becker, ed., *Social Problems: A Modern Approach* (New York: Wiley, 1966).

23. Peter S. Green, 'Moviegoers devour ads', *Advertising Age* (26 June 1989): 36.

24. Michael R. Real, *Mass-Mediated Culture* (Englewood Cliffs, NJ: Prentice-Hall, 1977).

25. For some websites that show 'Top-40' music sales in Europe and North America, see: http://top40-charts.com/, and http://www.bbc.co.uk/radio1/chart/singles.shtml (accessed 5 August 2005).

26. Annetta Miller, 'Shopping bags imitate art: Seen the sacks? Now visit the museum exhibit', *Newsweek* (23 January 1989): 44.

27. Kim Foltz, 'New species for study: Consumers in action', *New York Times* (18 December 1989): A1.

28. Arthur A. Berger, *Signs in Contemporary Culture: An Introduction to Semiotics* (New York: Longman, 1984).

29. Stephen Brown, 'Psycho shopper: A comparative literary analysis of "the dark side"', in Flemming Hansen, ed., *European Advances in Consumer Research* 2 (Provo, UT: Association for Consumer Research, 1995): 96–103; Stephen Brown, 'Consumption Behaviour in the Sex'n'Shopping Novels of Judith Krantz: A Post-structuralist Perspective', in J. Lynch and K. Corfman, eds, *Advances in Consumer Research* 23 (Provo, UT: Association for Consumer Research, 1996): 96–103.

30. Randall Frost, 'Staying power: Surviving the limelight', http://www.brandchannel.com/features_effect.asp?pf_id=215#more (accessed 5 August 2005), and Jonathan Guthrie, 'Why using a dead celebrity sells', *Financial Times* (26 April 2005), http://news.ft.com/cms/s/f93e84d2-b675-11d9-aebd-00000e2511c8.html.

31. Michiko Kakutani, 'Art is easier the 2d time around,' *The New York Times* (30 October 1994): E4. See also Stephen Brown, *Retro-Marketing* (London: Routledge, 2001).

32. Nigel Andrews, 'Filming a blockbuster is one thing; striking gold is another', *Financial Times*, accessed via Simon & Schuster College Newslink (20 January 1998).

33. Helene Diamond, 'Lights, camera . . . research!', *Marketing News* (11 September 1989): 10.

34. Nigel Andrews, 'Filming a blockbuster is one thing; striking gold is another'.

35. 'A brand-new development creates a colorful history', *The Wall Street Journal Interactive Edition* (18 February 1998).

36. Michael R. Solomon and Basil G. Englis, 'Reality engineering: Blurring the boundaries between marketing and popular culture', *Journal of Current Issues and Research in Advertising* 16 (Fall 1994) 2: 1–17.

37. 'Hollywood-sur-brie', *Le nouvel observateur* (14 November 1996): 18–19.

38. 'Les "mondes artificiels" attirent toujours plus de vacanciers', *Le Monde* (22–23 December 1996); see also John Urry, 'Cultural change and contemporary holiday making', *Theory, Culture, and Society* 5(1) (1988).

39. Bill Keller, 'For rich tourists (and not too African)', *New York Times* (3 December 1992) 2: A1.

40. Suzanne Alexander Ryan, 'Companies teach all sorts of lessons with educational tools they give away', *The Wall Street Journal* (19 April 1994): B1 (2); Cyndee Miller, 'Marketers find a seat in the classroom', *Marketing News* (20 June 1994): 2.

41. T. Bettina Cornwell and Bruce Keillor, 'Contemporary Literature and the Embedded Consumer Culture: The Case of Updike's Rabbit', in Roger J. Kruez and Mary Sue MacNealy, eds, *Empirical Approaches to Literature and Aesthetics: Advances in Discourse Processes* 52 (Norwood, NJ: Ablex Publishing Corporation, 1996): 559–72; Monroe

Friedman, 'The changing language of a consumer society: Brand name usage in popular American novels in the postwar era', *Journal of Consumer Research* 11 (March 1985): 927–37; Monroe Friedman, 'Commercial influences in the lyrics of popular American music of the postwar era', *Journal of Consumer Affairs* 20 (Winter 1986): 193.

42. Wayne Friedman, ' "Minority report" stars Lexus, Nokia', *Advertising Age* (17 June 2002): 41.

43. Denise E. DeLorme and Leonard N. Reid, 'Moviegoers' experiences and interpretations of brands in films revisited', *Journal of Advertising* 28(2) (1999): 71–90.

44. Cristel Antonia Russell, 'Investigating the effectiveness of product placement in television shows: The role of modality and plot connection congruence on brand memory and attitude', *Journal of Consumer Research* 29 (December 2002): 306–18.

45. Claire Atkinson, 'Ad intrusion up, say consumers', *Advertising Age* (6 January 2003): 1.

46. Jennifer Tanaka and Marc Peyser, 'The apples of their eyes', *Newsweek* (30 November 1998): 58.

47. Nancy Marsden, 'Lighting up the big screen', *San Francisco Examiner* (4 August 1998).

48. Joe Flint, 'Sponsors get a role in CBS reality show', *The Wall Street Journal Interactive Edition* (13 January 2000).

49. Stephen J. Gould, Pola B. Gupta and Sonja Grabner-Kräuter, 'Product placements in movies: A cross-cultural analysis of Austrian, French and American consumers' attitudes toward this emerging, international promotional medium', *Journal of Advertising* 29 (Winter 2000): 41–58.

50. Sarah Ellison, 'French cafés now serve up logos du jour with au laits', *The Wall Street Journal Interactive Edition* (2 June 2000).

51. Peter Wonacott, 'Chinese TV is an eager medium for (lots of) product placement', *The Wall Street Journal Interactive Edition* (26 January 2000).

52. Gabriel Kahn, 'Product placement booms in new Bollywood films', *The Wall Street Journal Interactive Edition* (30 August 2002).

53. George Gerbner, Larry Gross, Nancy Signorielli and Michael Morgan, 'Aging with television: Images on television drama and conceptions of social reality', *Journal of Communication* 30 (1980): 37–47.

54. Stephen Fox and William Philber, 'Television viewing and the perception of affluence', *Sociological Quarterly* 19 (1978): 103–12; W. James Potter, 'Three strategies for elaborating the cultivation hypothesis', *Journalism Quarterly* 65 (Winter 1988): 930–9; Gabriel Weimann, 'Images of life in America: The impact of American T.V. in Israel', *International Journal of Intercultural Relations* 8 (1984): 185–97.

55. Stephanie O'Donohue, 'On the Outside Looking In: Advertising Experiences Among Young Unemployed Adults', in Flemming Hansen, ed., *European Advances in Consumer Research* 2 (Provo, UT: Association for Consumer Research): 264–72; Richard Elliott, 'How Do the Unemployed Maintain Their Identity in a Culture of Consumption?', in Hansen, ed., *European Advances in Consumer Research* 2: 273–6.

56. 'Mobilen har blivit en vardagspryl', *Info*, 9 (2000): 52–4; Internet Usage in the European Union, 2005, http://www.internetworldstats.com/stats4.htm#eu.

57. Susan B. Kaiser, *The Social Psychology of Clothing* (New York: Macmillan, 1985); Thomas S. Robertson, *Innovative Behavior and Communication* (New York: Holt, Rhinehart & Winston, 1971).

58. Eric J. Arnould, 'Toward a broadened theory of preference formation and the diffusion of innovations: Cases from Zinder Province, Niger Republic', *Journal of Consumer Research* 16 (September 1989): 239–67.

59. Jan-Benedict E.M. Steenkamp, Frenkel ter Hofstede and Michel Wedel, 'A cross-national investigation into the individual and national cultural antecedents of consumer innovativeness', *Journal of Marketing* 63(2) (1999): 55–69.

60. Susan L. Holak, Donald R. Lehmann and Farena Sultan, 'The role of expectations in the adoption of innovative consumer durables: Some preliminary evidence', *Journal of Retailing* 63 (Fall 1987): 243–59.

61. Hubert Gatignon and Thomas S. Robertson, 'A propositional inventory for new diffusion research', *Journal of Consumer Research* 11 (March 1985): 849–67.

62. Frank Huber, 'Ein konzept zur ermittlung und bearbeitung des frühkaufersegments im bekleidungsmarkt', *Marketing ZFP* 2 (2nd Quarter 1995): 110–21.

63. Eva Martinez, Yolanda Polo and Carlos Flavián, 'The acceptance and diffusion of new consumer durables: Differences between first and last adopters', *Journal of Consumer Marketing* 15(4) (1998): 323–42.

64. Gordon R. Foxall and Seema Bhate, 'Cognitive style and personal involvement as explicators of innovative purchasing of health food brands', *European Journal of Marketing* 27(2) (1993): 5–16.

65. Elizabeth C. Hirschman, 'Symbolism and Technology as Sources of the Generation of Innovations', in Andrew Mitchell, ed., *Advances in Consumer Research* 9 (Provo, UT: Association for Consumer Research, 1982): 537–41.

66. Søren Askegaard and A. Fuat Firat, 'Towards a Critique of Material Culture, Consumption and Markets', in Susan M. Pearce, ed., *Experiencing Material Culture in the Western World* (London: Leicester University Press, 1997): 114–39.

67. Stephen Brown, *Postmodern Marketing* (London: Routledge, 1995).

68. Erik Kruse, 'New Product Development and Design: The Kitchen of the Future, the Refrigerator with the Internet Screen and Household-Consumer Contexts', paper presented at the Association for Consumer Research Conference (Salt Lake City, UT: 16–19 October 2000). See also www.kitchengate.dk.

69. Everett M. Rogers, *Diffusion of Innovations*, 3rd edn (New York: Free Press, 1983).

70. Robert J. Fisher and Linda L. Price, 'An investigation into the social context of early adoption behavior', *Journal of Consumer Research* 19 (December 1992): 477–86.

71. Güliz Ger and Russell W. Belk, 'I'd like to buy the world a Coke: Consumptionscapes of the "less affluent world" ', *Journal of Consumer Policy* 19 (1996): 271–304; Robin A. Coulter, Linda L. Price and Lawrence Feick, 'Rethinking the origins of involvement and brand commitment: Insights from postsocialist Central Europe' *Journal of Consumer Research* 30 (September 2003): 151–69.

72. W. Chan Kim and Renée Mauborgne, 'Value innovation: The strategic logic of high growth', *Harvard Business Review* (January–February 1997): 103–12.

73. 'Dare to be different', *Marketing* (13 February 1997): 22–3.

74. 'Diaper bag double take', *Discount Merchandiser* (March 2000).

75. Umberto Eco, *A Theory of Semiotics* (Bloomington, IN: Indiana University Press, 1979).

76. Fred Davis, 'Clothing and Fashion as Communication', in Michael R. Solomon, ed., *The Psychology of Fashion* (Lexington, MA: Lexington Books, 1985): 15–28.

77. Melanie Wallendorf, 'The Formation of Aesthetic Criteria Through Social Structures and Social Institutions', in Jerry C. Olson, ed., *Advances in Consumer Research* 7 (Ann Arbor, MI: Association for Consumer Research, 1980): 3–6.

78. Grant McCracken, 'Culture and consumption: A theoretical account of the structure and movement of the cultural meaning of consumer goods', *Journal of Consumer Research* 13 (June 1986): 71–84.

79. 'The eternal triangle', *Art in America* (February 1989): 23.

80. Herbert Blumer, *Symbolic Interactionism: Perspective and Method* (Englewood Cliffs, NJ: Prentice-Hall, 1969); Howard S. Becker, 'Art as collective action', *American Sociological Review* 39 (December 1973); Richard A. Peterson, 'Revitalizing the culture concept', *Annual Review of Sociology* 5 (1979): 137–66.

81. For more details, see Kaiser, *The Social Psychology of Clothing*; George B. Sproles, 'Behavioral Science Theories of Fashion', in Solomon, ed., *The Psychology of Fashion*: 55–70.

82. C.R. Snyder and Howard L. Fromkin, *Uniqueness: The Human Pursuit of Difference* (New York: Plenum Press, 1980).

83. Alison Lurie, *The Language of Clothes* (New York: Random House, 1981).

84. Linda Dyett, 'Desperately seeking skin', *Psychology Today* (May/June 1996): 14.

85. Susan Auty and Richard Elliott, 'Social Identity and the Meaning of Fashion Brands', B. Englis and A. Olofsson, eds, *European Advances in Consumer Research* 3 (Provo, UT: Association for Consumer Research, 1998): 1–10.

86. John Fiske, *Understanding Popular Culture* (Boston: Unwin Hyman, 1989): especially 1–21.

87. Harvey Leibenstein, *Beyond Economic Man: A New Foundation for Microeconomics* (Cambridge, MA: Harvard University Press, 1976).

88. Georg Simmel, 'Fashion', *International Quarterly* 10 (1904): 130–55.

89. Grant D. McCracken, 'The Trickle-Down Theory Rehabilitated', in Solomon, ed., *The Psychology of Fashion*: 39–54.

90. Charles W. King, 'Fashion Adoption: A Rebuttal to the "Trickle-Down" Theory', in Stephen A. Greyser, ed., *Toward Scientific Marketing* (Chicago: American Marketing Association, 1963): 108–25.

91. Gillian Hogg, Suzanne Horne and David Carmichael, 'Fun, Fashion, or Just Plain Sailing? The Consumption of Clothing in the Sailing Community', in B. Dubois, T. Lowrey, L.J. Shrum and M. Vanhuele, eds, *European Advances in Consumer Research* 4 (Provo, UT: Association for Consumer Research, 1999): 336–40.

92. Alf H. Walle, 'Grassroots innovation', *Marketing Insights* (Summer 1990): 44–51.

93. Patrick Hetzel, 'The Role of Fashion and Design in a Postmodern Society: What Challenges for Firms?', in M.J. Baker, ed., *Perspectives on Marketing Management* 4 (London: John Wiley & Sons, 1994): 97–118.

94. Stuart and Elizabeth Ewen, cited in Mike Featherstone, *Consumer Culture and Postmodernism* (London: Sage, 1993): 83.

95. Patrick Hetzel, 'The role of fashion and design in a postmodern society: what challenges for firms?'

96. Anne F. Jensen, 'Acknowledging and Consuming Fashion in the Era after "Good Taste" – From the Beautiful to the Hideous', Doctoral Dissertations from the Faculty of Social Science, no. 40 (Odense: University of Southern Denmark, 1999).

97. Patrick Hetzel, 'A Socio-Semiotic Analysis of the Media/Consumer Relationships in the Production of Fashion Systems: The Case of the "Elle-France" Magazine', in Englis and Olofsson, eds, *European Advances in Consumer Research* 3: 104–7.

98. 'Topmodel i genbrugstøj', *Fyens Stiftstidende, Erhverv* (1 November 2000): 1.

99. 'Panik i mode-fabrikken', Intervju med Alladi Venkatesh, *Dagens Nyheter* (27 June 2000): B1.

100. Don Slater, *Consumer Culture and Modernity* (Cambridge: Polity Press, 1997).

101. Anne F. Jensen and Søren Askegaard, 'In Pursuit of Ugliness. Searching for a Fashion Concept in the Era After Good Taste', Working Paper in Marketing, no. 17 (Odense: Odense University, 1998).

102. Anonymous, 'FCUK Consumer Research: On Disgust, Revulsion and Other Forms of Offensive Advertising', paper submitted to the 2001 Association for Consumer Research European Conference (Berlin, 20–23 June).

103. Robin Givhan, 'Designers caught in a tangled web', *The Washington Post* (5 April 1997): C1 (2 pp).

104. Anne F. Jensen and Per Østergaard, 'Dressing for Security or Risk? An Exploratory Study of Two Different Ways of Consuming Fashion', in Englis and Olofsson, eds, *European Advances in Consumer Research* 3: 98–103.

105. Anthony Ramirez, 'The pedestrian sneaker makes a comeback', *New York Times* (14 October 1990): F17.

106. B.E. Aguirre, E.L. Quarantelli and Jorge L. Mendoza, 'The collective behavior of fads: The characteristics, effects, and career of streaking', *American Sociological Review* (August 1989): 569.

107. Martin G. Letscher, 'How to tell fads from trends', *American Demographics* (December 1994): 38–45.

LIFESTYLES AND
EUROPEAN CULTURES

Margaret and Karin are both executives in an advertising agency. After a particularly gruelling week, they are looking forward to a well-deserved weekend off. Margaret is enthusiastically telling Karin about her plans. Since she won't have to get up early in the morning, she's going to sleep late in her new apartment. Then she's planning to go window-shopping and maybe meet some friends for lunch in one of the cafés where she knows that some of them will be. Then she'll go back and rest in the afternoon until it's time to join her friend Anna to go to the new techno and rave place, which she heard about the other day. There, they'll dance their hearts out all night.

Karin just chuckles to herself: while Margaret's wasting her time in bed in the city, *she's* going to get up early to join a tour to a nearby bird sanctuary organized by the environmental group of which she's a member. She has heard that it will also be possible to see some rare orchids. By four o'clock, she plans to be comfortably planted in front of the computer in order to write an open letter to the municipal authorities concerning the current debate on whether to stop using pesticides in public parks and along the roadsides. Then she'll just sit back and relax, perhaps watch a rented video of one of the good films she missed due to lack of time . . .

Karin is sometimes amazed at how different she is from Margaret, though both think of themselves as sophisticated and in touch with the times. They also earn the same salary and do almost the same things at work all week long. How can their tastes be so different at the weekend? Oh well, Karin sighs to herself, that's why they make chocolate *and* vanilla.

■ LIFESTYLES AND CONSUMPTION CHOICES

Karin and Margaret strongly resemble one another demographically. They were both raised in middle-class households, have similar educational backgrounds, are about the same age and they share the same occupation and income. However, as their leisure choices show, it would be a mistake to assume that their consumption choices are similar as well. Karin and Margaret each choose products, services and activities that help them define a unique *lifestyle*. This chapter first explores how marketers approach the issue of lifestyle and then how they use information about these consumption choices to tailor products and communications to individual lifestyle segments. It then considers how lifestyle choices are affected by where people live, and it considers some issues that occur when firms attempt to market their products in unfamiliar cultures.

Lifestyle: who we are, what we do

In traditional societies, which place a high value on a collective mentality, consumption options are largely dictated by class, caste, village or family. In a modern consumer society, however, people are freer to select the products, services and activities that define themselves and, in turn, create a social identity that is communicated to others. One's choice of goods and services makes a statement about who one is and about the types of people with whom one wishes to identify – as well as those from whom we wish to maintain some distance!

▶   **Lifestyle** refers to a pattern of consumption reflecting a person's choices of how he or she spends time and money, but in many cases it also refers to the attitudes and values attached to these behavioural patterns. Many of the factors discussed in this book, such as a person's self-concept, reference group and social class, are used as 'raw ingredients' to fashion a unique lifestyle. In an economic sense, one's lifestyle represents the way one has elected to allocate income, both in terms of relative allocations to different products and services and to specific alternatives within these categories.[1] Other distinctions describe consumers in terms of their broad patterns of consumption, such as those that differentiate between consumers in terms of how proportions of their income are allocated to various sectors of consumption. Often, these allocations create a new kind of status system based less on income than on accessibility to information about goods and how these goods function as social markers.[2]

Lifestyles may be considered as group identities. Marketers use demographic and economic approaches in tracking changes in broad societal priorities, but these approaches do not begin to embrace the symbolic nuances that separate lifestyle groups. Lifestyle is more than the allocation of discretionary income. It is a statement about who one is in society and who one is not. Group identities, whether of hobbyists, athletes, or drug users, take their form based on acts of expressive symbolism. The self-definitions of group members are derived from the common symbol system to which the group is dedicated. Such self-definitions have been described by a number of terms, including *lifestyle, public taste, consumer group, symbolic community* and *status culture*.[3]

Each lifestyle is (somewhat) unique. Patterns of consumption based on lifestyles are often composed of many ingredients that are shared by others in similar social and economic circumstances. Still, each person provides a unique 'twist' to this pattern which allows him or her to inject some individuality into a chosen lifestyle. For example, a 'typical' student (if there is such a thing) may dress much like his or her friends, go to the same places and like the same foods, yet still indulge a passion for running marathons, stamp collecting or community service, activities which make him or her unique.

Lifestyles don't last forever, and are not set in stone; unlike deep-seated values, people's tastes and preferences evolve over time, so that consumption patterns that were viewed favourably at one point in time may be laughed at or sneered at a few years later.

If you don't believe that, simply think back to what you, your friends and your family were wearing, doing and eating five or ten years ago: where *did* you find those clothes? Because people's attitudes regarding physical fitness, social activism, sex roles for men and women, the importance of home life and family, and many other things, do change, it is vital for marketers to monitor the social landscape continually to try to anticipate where these changes will lead. Empty nesters, for instance, who are adults whose children have left home, represent an increasingly attractive market, especially for food, drink and personal care. In terms of disposable income, the UK, Holland and Germany have particularly wealthy empty nesters.[4] As the article in the Marketing opportunity box shows, changing patterns of earnings and consumption challenges our assumptions about traditional consumer responsibilities and roles.

marketing opportunity

'It is difficult to schedule an interview with Joanna Public these days – she simply doesn't have the time. Busy enjoying her youth, advancing her career and spending her large disposable income, she represents the most influential sector in modern British society. Once it was middle-aged Joe Public senior who wielded the power, followed by his fresh-faced son, Joe Public junior. Now it's Joanna and her 10 million twenty-to-thirtysomething girl friends who are the new darlings of the retailers and politicians who want their money and their votes. Joanna's value to the economy is immense: she not only chooses the larger purchases for herself and her partner but also decides where they eat, how they decorate their home and what they wear.

According to a recent 'Project Home' study conducted by Allegra Strategies, a UK consumer retail and lifestyle consultancy, women have always controlled the high street but in the past five years they have completely dominated it. Allegra's Project Home research suggests that not only do Joanna and her pals now make up eight out of 10 customers in homeware shops, but the most successful stores are those that have 'feminised' to appeal to their tastes: selling a carefully packaged lifestyle, instead of individual products, in an environment that is attractive, relaxing and sexy. Study results conclude that young women now drive the decisions on what to buy and, unlike older women, it is she, and not her boyfriend or husband, who decides how much to spend.

We all know Joanna: the university-educated professional who is having too much fun socialising and spending the £24,500 she earns each year to have children. Women in this group are key shoppers and are increasingly emancipated in exercising that power. They control their own budgets and will go on to control household budgets.

Patrick Gray of Experian, the consumer research organisation, agrees on the need to understand how important Joanna will be as she ages: 'If retailers win Joanna over now, she will probably become the decision-maker in the household and use similar brand values when it comes to buying for her children and partner.' So successful have retailers been in attracting Joanna that, according to Experian, she spent 18 per cent more on clothing, footwear and accessories in 2004 than in 2003.

'This is extraordinary considering that women in Britain still earn just 82 per cent of the wages that men do; one of the lowest figures in Europe, while for part-time workers, the pay gap has actually widened in the past year – part-time women now earn 41 per cent less than part-time men,' said Will Galgey, director of the Henley Centre market research company. 'Despite this, women's borrowing doubled between 1996 and 2001, with the average woman in debt owing more than 13 times her monthly income and more likely than men to possess store cards with outrageously high interest rates.''[5]

■ LIFESTYLE MARKETING

The lifestyle concept is one of the most widely used in modern marketing activities. It provides a way to understand consumers' everyday needs and wants, and a mechanism to allow a product or service to be positioned in terms of how it will allow a person to pursue a desired lifestyle. A **lifestyle marketing perspective** recognizes that people are increasingly conscious about the fact that we all sort ourselves and each other into groups on the basis of the things we/they like to do, how we/they like to spend our/their leisure time and how we/they choose to spend disposable income.[6] These choices in turn create opportunities for market segmentation strategies that recognize the potency of a consumer's chosen lifestyle in determining both the types of products purchased and the specific brands more likely to appeal to a designated lifestyle segment.

Products are the building blocks of lifestyles

To study lifestyles is to appreciate the profoundness of the superficial, as one lifestyle analyst has put it.[7] According to a German survey of 291 of the biggest marketing research and advertising agencies, 68 per cent of them used lifestyle research of some kind, mostly for the sectors of food, cosmetics, cars, drinks and fashion and clothing.[8] Consumers often choose products, services and activities over others because they are associated with a certain lifestyle. For this reason, lifestyle marketing strategies attempt to position a product by fitting it into an existing pattern of consumption. That explains why cool restaurants, bars, and hotels like the Buddha Bar and Man Ray in Paris (as well as the Standard Hotel in Los Angeles and the Sunset Beach hotel/restaurant in New York's Hamptons) are branching out by selling CDs featuring the music playing on site. Aspiring lounge lizards can recreate the 'insider' experience without leaving home.[9]

Because a goal of lifestyle marketing is to provide consumers with opportunities to pursue their chosen ways to enjoy their lives and express their social identities, a key aspect of this strategy is to focus on product usage in desirable social settings (see Chapter 10). The goal of associating a product with a social situation is a long-standing one for advertisers, whether the product is included in a round of golf, a family dinner or a night at a glamorous club surrounded by the hip-hop elite or sporting and football stars.[10] Thus people, products and settings are combined to express a certain consumption style, as shown in Figure 16.1.

Product complementarity

The adoption of a lifestyle marketing perspective implies that we must look at *patterns* of behaviour to understand consumers. We can get a clearer picture of how people use products to define lifestyles by examining how they make choices in a variety of product

Figure 16.1 Linking products to lifestyle

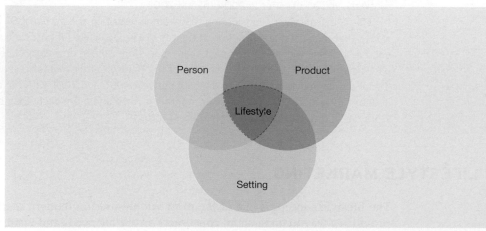

This ad illustrates how a product offering can be highly complementary to the lifestyle of the decision maker – in this case, the wife.

S, C, P, F . . . , Patricia Luján, Carlitos. Photo: Biel Capllonch

categories. Indeed, many products and services do seem to 'go together', usually because they tend to be selected by the same types of people. In many cases, products do not seem to 'make sense' if unaccompanied by companion products (e.g. fast food and paper plates, or a suit and tie) or are incongruous in the presence of others (e.g. a big, upholstered chair in a high-tech office or the IKEA ad, shown above). Therefore, an important part of lifestyle marketing is to identify the *set* of products and services that seems to be linked in consumers' minds to a specific lifestyle. As one study noted, 'all goods carry meaning, but none by itself. . . . The meaning is in the relations between all the goods, just as music is in the relations marked out by the sounds and not in any one note.'[11]

▶   **Product complementarity** occurs when the symbolic meanings of different products are related to each other.[12] Bacardi rum and Coca-Cola have for some time advertised their products together. And, research evidence suggests that even a relatively unattractive product becomes more appealing when evaluated with other, liked products.[13] Some marketers have gone as far as putting their brands on the same product, a phenomenon known as *co-branding*.[14] For example, in various European countries one product variant of Häagen-Dazs ice cream was co-branded with Bailey's Irish Cream liqueur. The German car maker Porsche has teamed up with Canada's Fairmont Hotels & Resorts chain to appeal to one another's customers. Fairmont's best-known properties are its Regal Hotel on San Francisco's Nob Hill and New York's Plaza Hotel, but the chain wants to spread its cachet to other lesser-known properties. In turn, Porsche figures Fairmont's upmarket clientele is the perfect market for its upgraded Boxster convertible and new Cayenne sport-utility vehicle.[15] A more recent venture has been Courvoisier's entry into the world of fashion with the parent company Allied Domecq (the world's second-largest spirits company) launching a collection of luxury sportswear for men and women in its 'Atelier Courvoisier' collection, and planning similar extensions for its other brands (such as Stolichnaya vodka and Malibu coconut rum).[16] Most often, though, consumers themselves, inspired by opinion leaders and other parts of the culture production system (see Chapters 10, 14 and 15), will construct the product complement-arities themselves.

▶   These sets of products, termed **consumption constellations**, are used by consumers to define, communicate and perform social roles.[17] For example, the (American) 'yuppie' of the 1980s was defined by such products as a Rolex watch, BMW car, Gucci briefcase, a squash racket, fresh pesto, white wine and brie. The yuppie culture eventually spread to Europe and somewhat similar constellations could be found for what were called 'Sloane Rangers' in the United Kingdom and 'Bon Chic Bon Genre' in France. While people today take pains to avoid being classified as yuppies, this social role had a major influence on defining cultural values and consumption priorities in the 1980s.[18] Sometimes these constellations do actually take the form of anti-constellations from the very beginning, at least for some consumer segments. That is, people define their own style more in terms of what they are not, through a set of non-choices (due to lack of affordability, accessibility or availability) or anti-choices (due to abandonment, avoidance or aversion) of products and/or brands.[19] What positive and/or negative consumption constellations might characterize you and your friends today?

Psychographics

As Margaret and Karin's lifestyle choices demonstrated, consumers can share the same demographic characteristics and still be very different people. For this reason, marketers need a way to 'breathe life' into demographic data to identify, understand and target consumer segments that will share a set of preferences for their products and services. Chapter 7 discussed some of the important differences in consumers' self-concepts and personalities that play a big role in determining product choices. When personality variables are combined with knowledge of lifestyle preferences, marketers have a tool

▶   with which to view consumer segments. This tool is known as **psychographics**, which involves the description of consumers based mainly on such psychological and social psychological factors as values, beliefs and attitudes, and is used to explain why these consumers have a propensity to consume certain products or brands, use certain services, devote time to certain activities and use certain media.[20]

Psychographic research was first developed in the 1960s and 1970s to address the shortcomings of two other types of consumer research: motivational research and quantitative survey research. *Motivational research*, which involves intensive personal interviews and projective tests, yields a lot of information about individual consumers. The information gathered, however, was often idiosyncratic and deemed not very useful or reliable.[21] At the other extreme, *quantitative survey research*, or large-scale demographic surveys, yields only a little information about a lot of people. As some researchers observed, 'The marketing manager who wanted to know why people ate the com-petitor's cornflakes was told "32 per cent of the respondents said *taste*, 21 per cent said *flavour*, 15 per cent said *texture*, 10 per cent said *price*, and 22 per cent said *don't know* or *no answer*".'[22]

In many applications, the term 'psychographics' is used interchangeably with 'lifestyle' to denote the separation of consumers into categories based on differences in choices of consumption activities and product usage. While there are many psycho-graphic variables that can be used to segment consumers, they all share the underlying principle of going beyond surface characteristics to understand consumers' motivations for purchasing and using products. Demographics allows us to describe *who* buys, but psychographics helps us understand *why* they buy.

Conducting a psychographic analysis

Some early attempts at lifestyle segmentation 'borrowed' standard psychological scales (often used to measure pathology or personality disturbances) and tried to relate scores on these tests to product usage. As might be expected, such efforts were largely disappointing (see Chapter 7). These tests were never intended to be related to everyday consumption activities and yielded little in the way of explanation for purchase behaviours. The technique is more effective when the variables included are more closely related to actual consumer behaviours. If you want to understand purchases of household cleaning products, you are better off asking people about their attitudes towards household cleanliness than testing for personality disorders.

Psychographic studies can take several different forms:

- *A lifestyle profile* looks for items that differentiate between users and non-users of a product.
- *A product-specific profile* identifies a target group and then profiles these consumers on product-relevant dimensions.
- *A general lifestyle segmentation* places a large sample of respondents into homogeneous groups based on similarities of their overall preferences.
- *A product-specific segmentation* tailors questions to a product category

AIOs

Most contemporary psychographic research attempts to group consumers according to some combination of three categories of variables – activities, interests and opinions – which are known as **AIOs**. Using data from large samples, marketers create profiles of customers who resemble each other in terms of their activities and patterns of product usage.[24] The dimensions used to assess lifestyle are listed in Table 16.1.

To group consumers into common AIO categories, respondents are given a long list of statements and are asked to indicate how much they agree with each one. Lifestyle is thus teased out by discovering how people spend their time, what they find interesting and important and how they view themselves and the world around them, as well as demographic information.

Typically, the first step in conducting a psychographic analysis is to determine which lifestyle segments are producing the bulk of customers for a particular product. Researchers attempt to determine who uses the brand and try to isolate heavy, moderate and light users. They also look for patterns of usage and attitudes towards the product. In some cases, just a few lifestyle segments account for the majority of brand users.[25]

Table 16.1 Lifestyle dimensions

Activities	Interests	Opinions	Demographics
Work	Family	Themselves	Age
Hobbies	Home	Social issues	Education
Social events	Job	Politics	Income
Holiday	Community	Business	Occupation
Entertainment	Recreation	Economics	Family size
Club membership	Fashion	Education	Dwelling
Community	Food	Products	Geography
Shopping	Media	Future	City size
Sports	Achievements	Culture	Stage in life cycle

Source: William D. Wells and Douglas J. Tigert, 'Activities, interests and opinions', *Journal of Advertising Research* 11 (August 1971): 27-35.

After the heavy users are identified and understood, the brand's relationship to them is considered. Heavy users may have quite different reasons for using the product; they can be further subdivided in terms of the *benefits* they derive from using the product or service. For instance, marketers at the beginning of the walking shoe craze assumed that purchasers were basically burned-out joggers. Subsequent psychographic research showed that there were actually several different groups of 'walkers', ranging from those who walk to get to work to those who walk for fun. This realization resulted in shoes aimed at different segments.

Uses of psychographic segmentation

Psychographic segmentation can be used in a variety of ways.

- *To define the target market.* This information allows the marketer to go beyond simple demographic or product usage descriptions (such as, middle-aged men or frequent users).

- *To create a new view of the market.* Sometimes marketers create their strategies with a 'typical' customer in mind. This stereotype may not be correct because the actual customer may not match these assumptions. For example, marketers of a facial cream for women were surprised to find their key market was composed of older, widowed women rather than the younger, more sociable women to whom they were pitching their appeals.

- *To position the product.* Psychographic information can allow the marketer to emphasize features of the product that fit in with a person's lifestyle. Products targeted at people whose lifestyle profiles show a high need to be around other people might focus on the product's ability to help meet this social need.

- *To communicate product attributes better.* Psychographic information can offer very useful input to advertising creatives who must communicate something about the product. The artist or writer obtains a much richer mental image of the target consumer than that obtained through dry statistics, and this insight improves his or her ability to 'talk' to that consumer.

- *To develop overall strategy.* Understanding how a product fits, or does not fit, into consumers' lifestyles allows the marketer to identify new product opportunities, chart media strategies and create environments most consistent and harmonious with these consumption patterns. For example, inexpensive airline tickets have become very popular in Germany, with intra-country fares often lower than the price of a train ticket. The increase in flights has sparked concern of environmental worries among 'the Greens', even though the Greens are one of the market segments most likely to book the low fare airline tickets. Research has shown that conflicting values (in this case, low fares vs. air pollution) can be addressed in promotions by better understanding the motives that cause the tensions.[26]

- *To market social and political issues.* Psychographic segmentation can be an important tool in political campaigns and can also be employed to find similarities among types of consumers who engage in destructive behaviours, such as drug use or excessive gambling. A psychographic study of men aged 18 to 24 who drink and drive highlighted the potential for this perspective to help in the eradication of harmful behaviours. Researchers divided this segment into four groups: 'good timers', 'well adjusted', 'nerds', and 'problem kids'. They found that one group in particular – 'good timers' – is more likely to believe that it is fun to be drunk, that the chances of having an accident while driving drunk are low, and that drinking increases one's appeal to the opposite sex. Because the study showed that this group is also the most likely to drink at rock concerts and parties, is most likely to watch MTV, and tends to listen to album-oriented rock radio stations, reaching 'good timers' with a prevention campaign was made easier because messages targeted to this segment could be placed where these drinkers were most likely to see and hear them.[27]

Lifestyle segmentation typologies

Marketers are constantly on the lookout for new insights that will allow them to identify and reach groups of consumers that are united by a common lifestyle. To meet this need, many research companies and advertising agencies have developed their own *segmentation typologies* which divide people into segments. Respondents answer a battery of questions that allow the researchers to cluster them into a set of distinct lifestyle groups. The questions usually include a mixture of AIOs, plus other items relating to their perceptions of specific brands, favourite celebrities, media preferences and so on. These systems are usually sold to companies wanting to learn more about their customers and potential customers.

At least at a superficial level, many of these typologies are fairly similar to one another, in that a typical typology breaks up the population into roughly 5–10 segments. Each cluster is given a descriptive name, and a profile of the 'typical' member is provided to the client. Lifestyle categories in this system include such segments as 'avant guardians' (interested in change), 'pontificators' (traditionalists, very British), 'chameleons' (follow the crowd) and 'sleepwalkers' (contented underachievers). Unfortunately, it is often difficult to compare or evaluate different typologies, since the methods and data used to devise these systems are frequently *proprietary* – this means that the information is developed and owned by the company, and the company feels that it would not be desirable to release this information to outsiders.

Lifestyle analyses are widely used in Europe. For example, one British company recently unveiled ConsumerBank, a database with 240 pieces of information on each of 40 million consumers.[28] Increasingly sophisticated efforts are being made to develop lifestyle typologies that transcend national borders. Many of these systems have been developed to understand European buying habits, and in particular to determine if it is possible to identify 'Euro-consumers', who share the same lifestyle orientations despite living in, say, France rather than Italy. These studies have had mixed success, with most researchers reporting that people in each nation still have a lot of idiosyncrasies that make it difficult to group them together.[29] Below we will provide some examples of such international lifestyle segmentation efforts.

RISC

Since 1978, the Paris-based Research Institute on Social Change (RISC) has conducted international measurements of lifestyles and sociocultural change in more than 40 countries, including most European countries. The long-term measurement of the social climate across many countries makes it possible to give more qualified guesses and anticipations of future change. It makes it possible to see signs of change in one country before it eventually spreads to other countries. For example, concern for the environment appeared in Sweden in the early 1970s, then in Germany in the late 1970s, in France at the beginning of the 1980s and in Spain in the early 1990s.[30]

The values and attitudes questions are the foundation of the measurement of 'trends', defined as the degree of agreement or disagreement with a set of attitudes that have been selected to define this trend. Based on statistical analysis of the respondents' scores on each trend, each individual is located in a virtual space described by three axes, representing the three most discriminating dimensions in the data material. The vertical axis (Exploration/Stability) separates people motivated by change, creativity, volatility and openness from people motivated by stability, familiarity, tradition and structure. The horizontal axis (Social/Individual) distinguishes people oriented towards collective

Figure 16.2 The ten RISC segments

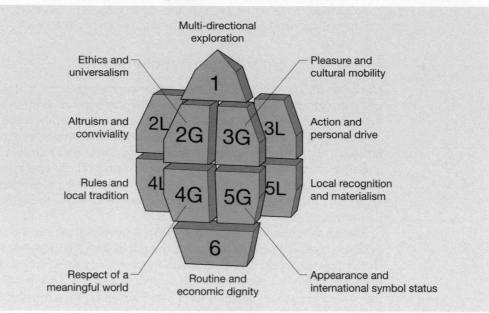

Source: RISC Methodology (Paris: RISC International, 1997): 14.

needs from people oriented more towards satisfaction of individual needs. The third axis (Global/Local) indicates a distance between people who are comfortable with broad and unfamiliar environments, multiple loose connections and large-scale networking from people preferring close-knit relationships and a desire for the elements of life to be connected in a predictable manner. The population is then divided into ten segments referring to their position in this virtual space. Figure 16.2 illustrates the ten segments (G for global, L for Local (behind)) and their main life aspirations.

Each of the 40 trends can also be located in the space according to the gravity point of the people who scored highest on the particular trend. Trends that are related to exploration will thus be located near the top of the map, individualism trends to the right, locality trends are smaller because they are at the back, and so on. While the position of the trends tends not to vary greatly, the percentage of various populations (countries, age groups, heavy users of a brand) supporting each trend will differ greatly. In the example in Figure 16.3, the indices are for the United Kingdom as compared to the European total. Darker colours indicate the trends that are more important in Britain as compared to the European average: cultural mobility, expanding vitality, narrow bounds, law and leaders, social recognition, well-being and epicurism (a quality-of-life orientation towards 'the finer things' in life).

The use of RISC typically involves identifying users of a brand and understanding those users better; it is also used to monitor changes in the profiles of users over time. Furthermore, potential target groups, the product benefits and the kind of communication that would attract and reach them can be indicated by systems such as RISC. In the example in Figure 16.4 we see the lifestyle profiling of German car brand B (approximately 21 per cent of the population) and car brand M (approximately 19 per cent) as their first, second or third choice if they were going to buy a new car. Car brand B has a strong profile, individual and experimental, with both global and local orientations. Car brand M, in contrast, has a more uniform profile, with evidence of popularity across all segments of the population. However, there is a very strong presence in cell 1, the group that is most interested in new designs, technologies and functions.

Figure 16.3 Trend map of the UK

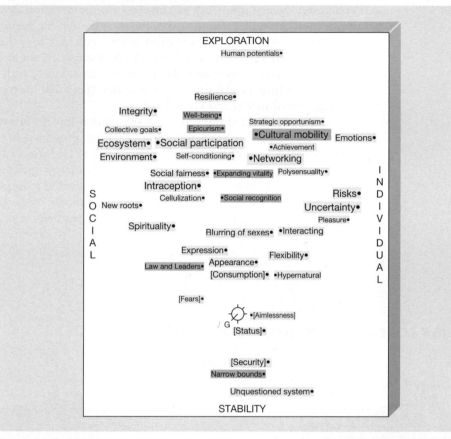

Source: RISC Methodology (Paris: RISC International, 1997).

Figure 16.4 Choice of brand for the next new car, Germany, brand B/brand M, 1995

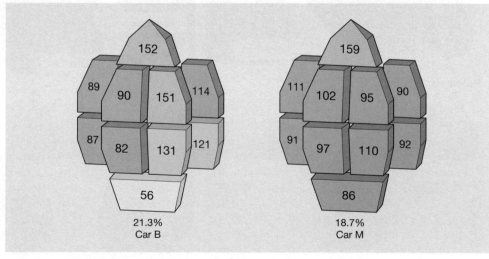

Source: RISC Methodology (Paris: RISC International, 1997).

CCA socio-styles

A Paris-based agency, the CCA (Centre de Communication Avancé), introduced a European lifestyle typology in the early 1990s. Although the mapping principle of this lifestyle typology is similar to that of most other typologies, they use a somewhat different methodological approach since their questionnaires are not attitude-based, but use a variety of question formats and also projective techniques, such as various scenario descriptions of future social forms or consumption types that the respondent must relate to, or suggestive drawings and vignettes.[31]

The CCA study divided the European population into 16 lifestyles, regrouped into 6 so-called 'mentalities'. The resulting lifestyle map, presented in the usual suggestive vignette format, is seen in Figure 16.5. One of the advantages of this system was that the 16 individual lifestyles could be gathered in other larger groups rather than just the mentalities to form marketing segments specifically adapted to a specific product sector. So some lifestyles would be grouped to form food segments, others to form car segments. In terms of innovative approaches used for lifestyle segmentation, this is probably one of the more interesting ones.[32]

Figure 16.5 CCA Eurostyles, 16 lifestyles in 6 mentalities

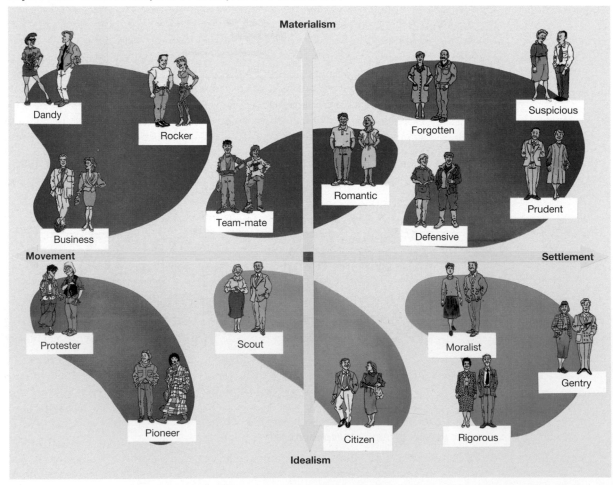

Source: CCA, Paris, 1990.

Figure 16.6 A theoretically based lifestyle model

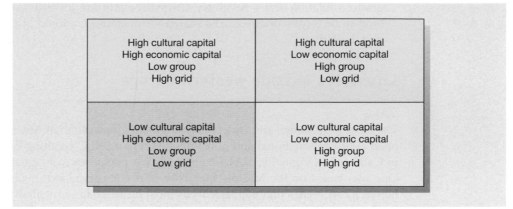

High cultural capital High economic capital Low group High grid	High cultural capital Low economic capital High group Low grid
Low cultural capital High economic capital Low group Low grid	Low cultural capital Low economic capital High group High grid

Source: Adapted from Henrik Dahl, *Hvis din nabo var en bil* (Copenhagen: Akademisk forlag, 1997).

Towards a theoretically based lifestyle approach?

One leading French sociologist, Pierre Bourdieu, proposed a lifestyle concept that is closely linked to social class. In a major empirical study, he tried to demonstrate how people's tastes and lifestyles in French society are dependent on what he named **habitus** (systems of classification of phenomena adopted from our socialization processes) and our economic and cultural capital.[33] He distinguished between various forms of capital that the individual can use as assets to construct his or her lifestyle, tastes and consumption patterns. This approach has been applied within American consumer research to distinguish between consumer tastes among various social groupings.[34] More recently, an attempt has been made to translate Bourdieu's terms into a relatively simple lifestyle categorization scheme. Based on Bourdieu's notions of economic capital (income and wealth) and cultural capital (education plus the ability to distinguish between cultural styles and categories) combined with Mary Douglas's grid-group theory,[35] four different but fundamental consumer types are proposed. This model, depicted in Figure 16.6, has so far been applied only in Denmark, but since it has a strong theoretical base it is likely to function in other countries as well.

The distinction between grid and group refers to an individual's relation to his or her own social group and to the general social system (or grid). So the model distinguishes between people with high and low group identification and a more or less affirmative (high and low) relation to the organization of society (the grid). The model ends up with the following segments:

- *1st quadrant*: Professional, career-oriented people, with higher education and income, and with a rather individualistic attitude and an unproblematic relation to the social organization (they are responsible for much of it anyway). Their search for meaning is characterized by ambition for power and wealth.

- *2nd quadrant*: Well-educated intellectuals with less well-paid career opportunities (many university professors here), with a high degree of identification with their professional group, but with a critical attitude towards society. Their search for meaning lies in the realization of their own intellectual ideals.

- *3rd quadrant*: Relatively wealthy people, with low education or not so culturally interested (the stereotypical self-made (wo)man). They do not show any particular interest, neither on a group level nor on a social level, and they may even tend to consider the rest of society (and everything strange) as relatively hostile.

● *4th quadrant*: Low on both types of capital, money and education, but with strong group affiliation and a relatively affirmative attitude towards society, these people tend to be locally oriented. The search for meaning is rooted in their daily activities and daily lives.[36]

Lifestyles outside western Europe

VALS

▶ The most well-known and widely used segmentation system in America is **VALS**, developed at SRI International and now operated out of SRI Consulting Business Intelligence in California. Originally, VALS combined two perspectives to create lifestyle clusters. One was based on the Maslow hierarchy of needs (discussed in Chapter 4). Maslow's hierarchy stipulates that people's needs must be satisfied sequentially – that is, companionship is not a priority until physical needs are met, and so on. The second perspective was based on the distinction made by the sociologist David Riesman between *inner-directed* people, who value personal expression and individual taste, and *outer-directed* people, who tend to be swayed by the behaviour and reactions of others.

Responding to criticisms of the VALS model, as well as to changing social values, the developers decided to update the system.

Increasing social diversity made social values less effective as predictors of consumer behaviour. The current VALS system measures consumer behaviour on the basis of psychological dimensions, which are more resilient in periods of social change, and key demographics.

The current VALS system divides US adults into eight groups determined both by psychological characteristics and 'resources', which include such factors as income, education, energy levels and eagerness to buy. In the VALS structure, groups are arrayed vertically by resources and horizontally by self-orientation, as shown in Figure 16.7. Actualizers are at the top of the figure because they have the highest level of resources. Actualizers are successful, sophisticated, take-charge people. They are open to change and enjoy self-discovery. The next three groups also have sufficient resources but differ in their self-orientations:[37]

● *Fulfilleds* are satisfied, reflective and comfortable. They tend to be practical and value functionality.

● *Achievers* are career-oriented and prefer predictability over risk or self-discovery.

● *Experiencers* are impulsive, young and enjoy offbeat or risky experiences.

The next three groups have fewer resources but also differ in their self-orientation:

● *Believers* have strong principles and favour proven brands.

● *Strivers* are trendy, approval-seeking and resource-constrained, favour stylish products and emulate the purchases of people with greater material wealth.

● *Makers* are action-oriented and tend to focus their energies on self-sufficiency. They are more likely than other groups to work on their cars, can their own vegetables, or build their own houses.

Strugglers are at the bottom of the resource ladder. They are most concerned with meeting the needs of the moment.

Other international lifestyle segmentations

Japanese culture values conformity; one way to refer to the desire to fit in is *hitonami consciousness*, which translates as 'aligning oneself with other people'. Despite this overall emphasis, there is a growing segment of Japanese consumers who are swimming against

Figure 16.7 VALS 2 segmentation system

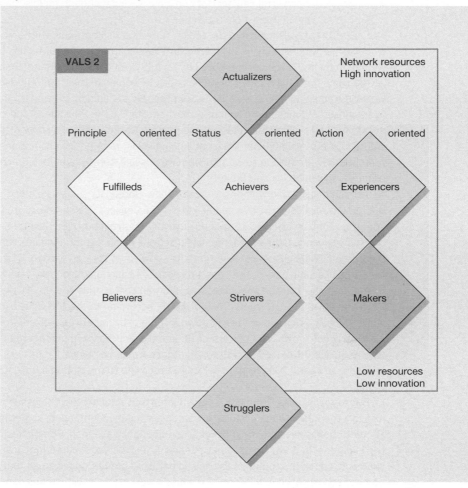

the tide. These people have been called 'life designers' to reflect their interest in crafting their own lifestyle patterns. One Japanese segmentation scheme divides consumers into 'tribes' and includes among others the 'crystal tribe' (which prefers well-known brands), 'my home tribe' (family oriented) and 'impulse buyer tribe'.[38]

multicultural dimensions

'The surging popularity of HBO's hit series *Sex and the City* among single, working women in Asia has spawned a cross-marketing bonanza. 'The series speaks for everything that is in the minds of most women,' declares Bunyapattra Boribalbureephun, a single, 30-year-old public-relations consultant who lives in Bangkok. Sporting a skin-baring gown and Chanel jewelry as she sips champagne at a 'Shoes in the City' fashion show at Bangkok's elite Central Department Store, Ms Boribalbureephun insists the show has real resonance. 'Carrie's being a fashion chameleon and self-assured inspires me the most,' she says of the show's lead character, Carrie Bradshaw, played by Sarah Jessica Parker. The Shoes in the City night, one in a three-day whirl of themed fashion shows, public mall displays and invitation-only cocktail parties, was the first in a series of such events that will be co-hosted by HBO and retail companies in top malls in Bangkok and Manila throughout August. The target market: fans like Ms Boribalbureephun, who live for each episode. The show has a tremendous resonance with a small but powerful segment of consumers - independent, middle-class working women - that has proved an irresistible attraction for retailers.

Part of the show's appeal in the region reflects a demographic shift among women in Asia, who are marrying and giving birth later. In Thailand, the number of babies being born to women in their 20s will decline 25% between 1990 and 2010, estimates Asian Demographics. At the same time, the number of babies born to women in their 30s will rise 1%. Single, working women in their 20s and 30s are precisely the kind of consumers that companies like Johnson & Johnson are trying to reach. In Manila, the Philippines, the company is using events in Manila which take place in the upscale Rockwell Mall, to show off a new black-colored Carefree panty liner launched in Manila last month. The promotional event managers feel that they are talking to women who are upscale, trendy, and fashion conscious about the products shown in *Sex and the City*.

Though many Asian women follow the show closely, its sexually explicit content is often out of step with conservative middle-class Asia. Censors in Malaysia, a predominately Muslim country, routinely ask HBO to snip out the more outrageous bits. Even in Singapore, where the show is banned, the characters wield serious fashion clout. Singaporeans evade censors by ordering DVDs online and watching the show when they go abroad. It is so widely followed that it has become part of the consciousness of fashionable Singaporeans.

In China, the average annual income in urban centers has soared 315 per cent between 1990 and 2000 to 6,317 yuan ($763 or €821), according to the *China Statistical Yearbook*. And while Chinese officials don't break down income growth between sexes, women's slice of the pie clearly has grown. The portion of the female work force in managerial positions doubled to 6.1% in 2000 from 2.9% in 1990, and those women employed in professional or technical jobs rose to nearly 23% from 17 per cent, according to the National Bureau of Statistics of China.

But to really understand how sophisticated and complex the Chinese woman has become, just talk to a Chinese man. 'Modern women are independent, open, sometimes wasteful, never stingy to themselves,' wrote a 50-year-old Shanghainese man. Companies have taken note of the evolution. In 1998, for example, Procter & Gamble Co.'s marketing strategy for Rejoice shampoo, one of the country's top-selling hair-care brands, pulled an ad that featured an airline hostess and replaced it with one of a woman working as an airline mechanical engineer. The change was driven by consumer surveys that showed women had become more career-focused. Since then, women again have raised the bar, and Rejoice has tried to keep pace. The latest ad for Rejoice Refresh shampoo, running now on Chinese TV, features a girl playing beach volleyball. 'You find a lot of these girls in China,' says Mr Cheng. 'They're very demanding, they want to be better, but they also want to fulfill other aspirations. Previously, that was career fulfillment, but these days it's "I would also like myself to become a more beautiful lady".'

A key driver of this new attitude, besides rising incomes, is the dramatic change in the retail landscape itself: Women are more focused on fashion because there is simply more fashion available to them. The offerings have increased dramatically. For example, shampoo for women has always been offered, but consumers used to have three or five to choose from. Today, there are over 300 brands from which to choose. At the same time, quality has gone up and price has come down.

During this period of rapid change, the income gap between women and men actually has grown. Urban Chinese women make about 63% of what men make for similar work, more than seven percentage points lower than in 1990, according to a survey last year by the All China Women Federation. Nonetheless, women's attitudes are evolving at a breakneck pace. One-quarter of urban, unmarried woman say they want to marry but not have kids, according to a survey conducted by Sinofile Information Services. An additional 11% of unmarried women say they would prefer to stay single. 'The traditional archetypes in China were the ingenue and the caregiver. Marketers can explore newly evolving archetypes: woman as hero, woman as lover, woman as creator, explorer.'[39]

As countries in *eastern Europe* convert to free market economies, many marketers are exploring ways to segment these increasingly consumption-oriented societies. Some Western products such as Marlboro cigarettes and McDonald's are already firmly entrenched in Russia. The D'Arcy Masius Benton & Bowles Advertising Agency, which has offices in Moscow and St Petersburg, conducted a psychographic study of Russian consumers, and has proclaimed that the country's 150 million consumers can be divided into five segments, including 'Cossacks' (status-seeking nationalists who drive BMWs, smoke Dunhill cigarettes and drink Rémy Martin cognac), 'Kuptsi' (merchants who value practical products and tend to drive Volkswagens, smoke Chesterfields and drink Stolichnaya vodka) and 'Russian Souls' (passive consumers who drive Lada cars, smoke Marlboros and drink Smirnoff).[40]

The value of lifestyle typologies

Generally, lifestyle analyses of consumers are exciting because they seek to provide a sort of complete sociological view of the market and its segments and trends, but their general character is their biggest weakness, since the underlying assumption – that these general segments have relatively homogeneous patterns of consumer behaviour – is far from proven.[41] One needs only to consider the index numbers in Figure 16.4 to realize that the predictive power of this typology is not extraordinary. Add to this the generally weak theoretical foundation and the problems of reliability and validity linked to the large-scale questionnaires and to the operationalization of complex social processes in simple variables, and it is understandable why some marketers see lifestyles more as a way of 'thinking the market' and as an input to creative strategies than as descriptions of segments defined by their consumer behaviour.[42]

One attempt to overcome the problem of generally defined segments is the introduction of sectorial lifestyles, an idea proposed by the CCA in the 1980s. The principle behind sectorial lifestyles is that only variables (attitudes, behaviour, etc.) that are considered relevant to a specific domain of consumption are included in the survey. The lifestyles defined on the basis of such an approach thus pertain to this specific sector of consumption only. Later in this chapter, we shall discuss an example of such a sectorial lifestyle system: food-related lifestyles.

■ GEOGRAPHIC INFLUENCES ON LIFESTYLES

The consumption patterns of different countries' regions have been shaped by unique climates, cultural influences and resources. These national and regional differences can exert a major impact on consumers' lifestyles, since many of our preferences in foods, entertainment and so on are dictated by local customs and the availability of some diversions rather than others. The lifestyles of people in each country and each region differ in a variety of ways, some quite subtle and some quite noticeable, some easy to explain and some not so obvious. Needless to say, between northern and southern Italy, northern and southern Germany, Paris and Provence, London and Scotland there may be large differences in terms of consumption patterns and lifestyles and, consequently, in marketing and marketing research practices.[43]

Regional consumption differences: the macro-level

In some cases, it may make sense to distinguish between larger regions comprising several countries. For example, many companies operating in Europe consider Scandinavia (Denmark, Norway and Sweden) or the Benelux (Belgium, the Netherlands and Luxembourg) to be more or less one market due to the perceived similarities between the countries. That there are relative similarities between these countries is a matter of fact, but

McDonald's hamburgers are only part of the offering to consumers in China. The restaurants' western styling and western food are as much of an attraction as the hamburgers themselves.

Corbis/Michael S. Yamashinka

marketers should beware of overestimating the homogeneity of such macro-regions. Portraits of macro-regions can be drawn with rough strokes only with a very big brush. In the following section we will look at a couple of examples of such macro-regions in Europe.

Such regions are taken increasingly seriously by marketers. In the wake of the construction of the bridge over the strait of Øresund linking Copenhagen in Denmark with Malmö in the southern part of Sweden, the potential for a whole new region of education, research, shopping and other kinds of interaction has been created.[44] As a consequence, a regional dairy producer introduced what may well be the first-ever deliberately transnational regional product – a fermented yogurt-type product specifically designed and tested to span the variations in taste found in the Swedish and Danish markets. The product, named after the strait, comes with complete text in Swedish and Danish and features a person bathing in the water that separates but now (re)connects the two regions.

Since food consumption is traditionally linked to geographical conditions such as climate, or distance from the sea or mountains, another study hypothesized the importance of local or regional patterns of consumption across national borders compared to national consumption patterns.[45] The results of an analysis of 138 food-related variables from 15 countries, however, showed that national or linguistic borders seem more significant in defining patterns of food consumption. Figure 16.8 illustrates the 12 general food cultures in Europe suggested by this study. To list a few of the defining characteristics of some of the food cultures, the French/French–Swiss, Wallonian and Italian clusters are characterized by, among other things, the importance of sensory pleasure and the high consumption of red wine; the Germanic cluster of countries by a high degree of health consciousness; the Portuguese and Greek food cultures by relatively traditional eating patterns with a fascination for new 'global' food; the Norwegian and Danish food cultures by their openness to convenience products (and, for the Danes, also the love of beer); and the British and Irish for their extraordinary desire for sweets and tea. One large Dutch travel firm has even developed and promoted a resort hotel in Turkey where all the rooms are done in 'Amsterdam style' and, of course, the hotel's menu consists of Dutch favourites.[46]

Interestingly, it is predominantly in the centre of Europe that food cultures exhibit overlapping national borders (France–Switzerland; Germany–Switzerland–Austria; the

Figure 16.8 Twelve possible European food cultures?

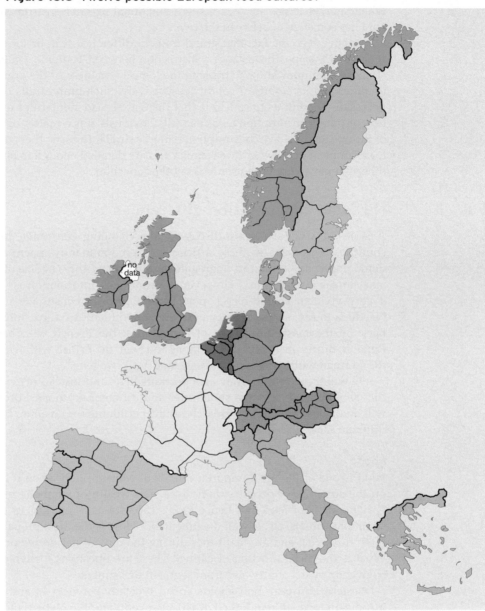

Source: Søren Askegaard and Tage Koed Madsen, 'The local and the global: Exploring traits of homogeneity and heterogeneity in European food cultures', *International Business Review* 7(6) (1998).

Netherlands–Flanders), the only exception being the British–Irish food culture. The more geographically peripheral countries (Scandinavia, Iberia, Italy and Greece) show 'national food cultures'. Is this due to more exchange and interrelationship historically among the people in the 'crossroads of Europe'? Or is it language that decides basic cultural patterns? If so, this would confirm the famous Whorf–Sapir hypothesis that language is not only a means for expressing culture but actually creates it by instituting certain schemes of classification of events, things and people. The fact that the food cultures defined in this study exactly follow linguistic lines of division (with the exception of there being two French-speaking clusters) could point in that direction. Or it could reflect the simple fact that the language of the questionnaire is very decisive for the response pattern. If the latter is the case, then it would be a strong criticism of the way in which marketers use surveys as a cross-national research instrument.[47] The truth probably lies somewhere between the two.

We have seen the fact that grand traits of differences can be located between certain regions in Europe, for instance a distinction between Teutonic, Gallic and Anglo-Saxon styles of communicating,[48] stressing the logical strictness of the argument, its rhetorical qualities and its empirical validity respectively. Such grand traits of similarities do not necessarily permit us to conclude that there are broad similarities in the food consumption or other consumption areas as well. Obviously it is a matter of scope. Certain parts of Europe tend to have consumption patterns similar to each other compared with China, for example. But whether these similarities are detailed enough to be useful to marketers other than in a very broad sense is another question.

National consumption differences

A series of articles recently discussed 'the changing consumer' in various European countries. The focus in these articles was predominantly macro-oriented changes in demography and economy, aggregate family expenditures or size of distribution outlets and similar information.[49] However relevant such information is, it does not provide a very vivid 'flesh-and-blood' portrait of European consumers in various countries. Needless to say, such portraits are extremely difficult to draw unless one wants to fall back on the most simple use of stereotypes: the French with baguette, cheese and Renault; the Spanish with paella, tapas and Seat; the British with tea, biscuits and Rover; the German with sauerkraut, sausage and Volkswagen.

We will try to refrain from such portraits here, and instead provide a set of examples that should illustrate some similarities and differences among European countries. We will do that by referring to research results pertaining to consumer behaviour from three different market sectors.

Food

Food is one of the most important fields of consumption when it comes to the impact on the structure of people's daily lives. The wealth of symbolic meanings attached to various kinds of food and hence food's capacity as a 'marker' of certain roles, status, situations, rituals, etc. is well documented.[50] How is the meal prepared and eaten? How often do we eat and at what times during the day? What do we drink with the meals? What is the social function of eating? These are questions for which the answers vary from country to country and from segment to segment.

Western European households spend typically between 14 and 17 per cent of their income on food, although the UK (10.1 per cent) and the Netherlands (11.0 per cent) are exceptions to this rule.[51] How this sum is spent varies greatly from country to country, depending on local production and local culinary patterns. The per capita consumption of different food products in European countries varies several hundred per cent in all categories. For example, the consumption of fresh fish in Spain and Portugal is about ten times that of Austria or the UK, and the consumption of pork in Denmark about ten times that of France. The consumption of potatoes is high in Ireland, but it is actually higher in Greece, and by far the lowest in Italy, which consumes approximately four times more pasta per inhabitant than the Swiss, who are the second most avid consumers of pasta in the European market.[52] There is evidence that Britons are eating out more. They spent an average of £312 (460 euros) per person a year in 2004; and this is forecast to rise to £356 (525 euros) by 2009. This compares with Italians (who spent £295 (435 euros)) and the French (£249 (367 euros)) per head in 2004. This also indicates a trend away from home-cooked meals, and by 2008 it is estimated that '3 billion extra breakfasts, lunches and evening meals will be consumed out-of-home relative to 2003 in the UK . . . Consumers

Table 16.2 Food-related lifestyle segments in four countries

	France %	Germany %	UK %	Denmark %
Uninvolved	18	21	9	11
Careless		11	27	23
Rational	35	26	33	11
Moderate	16			
Ecological moderate				20
Conservative	13	18	19	11
Adventurous		24	12	25
Hedonistic	18			

Source: Adapted from Karen Brunsø, Klaus G. Grunert and Lone Bredahl, 'An Analysis of National and Cross-National Consumer Segments Using the Food-Related Lifestyle Instrument in Denmark, France, Germany and Great Britain', MAPP Working Paper 35 (Aarhus: The Aarhus School of Business, January 1996).

now want to maximize their time and going out in the week allows them the chance to socialize without the hassle of cooking.'[53]

A group of researchers developed a food-related lifestyle instrument based on means–end theory (see Chapter 4).[54] The instrument includes attitude statements concerning five different domains: quality aspects, ways of shopping, cooking methods, consumption situations and purchasing motives. Tests of its cross-cultural validity showed reasonable results, at least within north-western Europe.[55] An application of the food-related lifestyle model in four European countries between 1993 and 1995 suggested that certain segments are found in all countries, some are found in three countries and some only in one country. The size of the segments, however, varies significantly, as seen in Table 16.2. These differences may shed some light on the differences between the national food cultures in question.

The 'uninvolved' segment (predominantly in Germany and France) have little interest in food, do not attach importance to quality, tend to nibble and graze rather than eat 'real meals' and use convenience products and fast food more than the average. Single males with a low education level are over-represented in this segment. The 'careless' segment (predominantly in the UK and Denmark) are spontaneous food shoppers, tempted by new products. They are attracted by convenience foods, are younger, single and have relatively high incomes. The 'rational consumers' segment (predominantly in France and the UK) are very interested in food and are careful planners of both dinner and shopping. They try to maximize the quality/price ratio of their purchases, and get self-fulfilment from cooking. They tend to be female, with families, working part-time. The 'conservative' segment (predominantly the UK and Germany) consider cooking a woman's task. They plan their meals and shopping, eat at fixed hours and seek security in their eating behaviour by sticking to traditions. They are older, rural and with lower income and education. The 'adventurous' segment (predominantly Denmark and Germany) like to try new (exotic) recipes and products, they go for quality products and often shop in specialized stores. The whole family takes part in the cooking, and the social aspects of eating are considered very important. They are generally well-educated families with double incomes and children.

Apart from the relative distributions of the segments, two of the segments found may tell us something specific about the national consumption environments. In Denmark the 'ecologically moderate' (moderately involved in food, highly involved in environmentally friendly produce) indicate the strength of the market share of ecological produce

(35 per cent increase in sales volume in 1996). The hedonists in France are a little less adventurous than segments of that name in other countries beyond the scope of this study, but they are more focused on the sensory pleasure of eating, indicating a gastronomic sophistication. For example, it has been suggested that French consumers have more sophisticated purchasing behaviour for beef than consumers in Germany, the UK and Spain.[56] An important emerging concern across European societies revolves around attitudes to genetically modified foods, for example, Danish health authorities opposed the introduction of fortified cereals by Kellogg's onto the Danish market. Under recent European rules, genetically modified ingredients have to be identified on the labels of all food products.[57] Organics represent the fastest-growing segment of natural food and drinks. Between 2002 and 2007 the European organics market is expected to see a compound annual growth rate of 10.6 per cent, reaching $16 billion in 2007.[58]

Research such as this food-related lifestyle study may be taken as evidence that it is easier to define segments across countries and cultures based on psychological rather than behavioural variables. This would seem to be the case, since similar motivations may result in very different kinds of behaviour, which are influenced by Europe's varying cultural norms and habits.

Trends in tastes and foods are tracked by companies concerned with new product development or new product extension. Recent research by Mintel showed that 'the world is getting spicier'. 2005 saw the launch of lavender-flavoured custard or crème anglaise; ice cream with a hint of green tea; Unilever's Magnum chilli ice cream and innovations such as Nestlé's apple crumble-filled chocolate bars and Douwe Egberts' sugar lumps flavoured with amaretto, chocolate or 'Irish cream'.[59] Another important growing trend is the adoption of 'new age beverages' (herb or juice based drinks or iced tea and coffee) in Europe. This market has seen value growth at 10.2 per cent a year from 1996 to 2001, while volumes have grown by 9.7 per cent. European tastes remain conservative, and iced tea currently holds the largest market share. However, 'new age beverage sales differ radically across the continent. Eastern Europe has not yet caught "new age fever", and there is little penetration. In the rest of Europe, wide variations exist – Sweden's market was worth $12.1 million in 2002 for example, but neighbouring Finland sold three times that figure . . . Switzerland has the largest new age beverages sector in Europe, accounting for almost a quarter of the market . . . in consumption terms, the average European drank 6.46 litres of new age beverages in 2001, whilst the average Swiss drank 107.48 litres . . . carbonates still hold the largest share in Europe, representing over 40% of the soft drinks market . . . [whilst] bottled water [is] the second largest sector of the European soft drinks market.'[60]

Global trends can be seen in changing patterns of product-related consumption; for instance, Starbucks has opened shops in Paris, in competition with the city's 2,000 traditional cafés and 31 Columbus Café outlets, in order to try and introduce the ''to go' coffee culture among Parisians . . . 'We were told the French would never drink coffee out of paper cups', said Philippe Bloch co-president of Columbus Café, 'wouldn't take them to go, wouldn't drink anything other than espresso, and certainly not coffee beverages with a high added value like cappuccino or iced coffees. And that is not true.'' Preliminary results for Columbus Café for 2003 indicate that revenue was over 8 million euros.[61] The UK market for on-the-go food and drinks is predicted to grow by 262 million euros to 20.1 billion euros by 2008. 'In the face of lengthening working hours, increased commuting time and delays, consumers are increasingly making use of their time in transit to eat and drink, in an attempt to use what many view as lost time.'[62] There is evidence that eating trends are moving away from meals towards snacking. Across Europe the number of meals that people eat is forecast to decline at the rate of 0.2 per cent per year between 2003 and 2008, while snacking is forecast to rise by 0.7 per cent: 'the trend is particularly clear in . . . Spain'.[63] In Britain about one in five (22 per cent) eating occasions are 'on the go' which compares with a European average of about one

Figure 16.9 What are people eating?

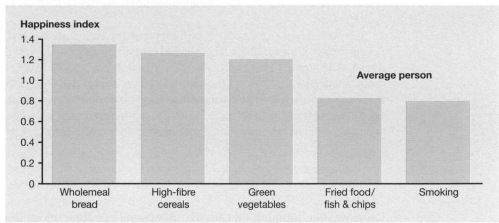

Source: Ed Crooks and Dan Roberts, 'How to be happy', *Financial Times*, 27/28 December 2003.

in six (15 per cent). 'The overriding need for convenience means that health takes a back seat in consumer's food and drink choices. British consumers eat healthily only 31% of the time when on-the-go – compared to 44% of the Swedes and 43% of the Dutch.'[64]

The other key global trend is changing styles of consumption, with the growing adoption of American-style eating habits being blamed for the increasing incidence of obesity. British consumers have been described as the 'waddling snack kings of Europe . . . They eat 10 billion bags of crisps a year, more than the rest of Europe put together . . . consumption stands at 7.2 kg a year or up to three bags of crisps a week for every man, woman and child in Britain, and is growing by 3 per cent a year. Italy, by contrast, consumes 1 kg per person per year.'[65] There's also some evidence that this 'unhealthy' eating is negatively correlated (not a causality claim) to an individual's subjective rating of 'happiness': Figure 16.9 shows survey results of Europeans' eating behaviours, correlated with their self rating of happiness (where a measure of 1 is the average happiness rating). Those respondents eating relatively 'healthy' foods self-rate themselves as happier, relative to those who eat fried food/fish and chips, and those who smoke. Does this sound like you? Do you have an explanation for this study's findings?[66]

marketing pitfall

Lifestyle trends: American patterns of eating spreading out

'*Krispy Kreme* arrived in Britain this month at the food section of Harrods, just a quick sashay away from pricey bonbons and minitubs of pâté. It is another example of how familiar American-style eating habits, and their bulging consequences, have become in Britain and most other European countries. While Americans have a reputation for tilting the scale more than any other people in the world – and in fact they do – Europeans are fast catching up.

In Britain the percentage of obese adults is three times what it was just two decades ago, the fastest-growing rate in Western Europe. An estimated 21 percent of men and 23.5 percent of women are now considered obese here, compared with 27 percent of men and 34 percent of women in America. The definition does not cover people regarded as merely overweight and is based on a body mass formula that factors in weight, height, sex and age.

The trend is similar across Europe. Sedentary lifestyles are part of the reason, experts say. So is an environment where adults and children alike are bombarded with commercials for yummy, sugary foods. But most of all, Europeans are eating differently: they are eating more like Americans. Fast-food restaurants and jumbo American-style portions have barreled across borders and oceans. Fatty foods are not only plentiful but often cheaper than fresh, healthful food.

The rates of obesity for children in Britain have tripled in just 10 years. Nearly 1 in 5 of all 15-year-olds in Britain is obese, according to recent figures from the Health Development Agency. The figure is 1 in 10 for 6-year-olds. International Obesity Task Force, a research group affiliated with the World Health Organization, argues that 'There is a high risk that these children are going to die before their parents.' In one survey of parts of southern Italy, cited in a report by the task force, 36 percent of the 9-year-olds were obese or overweight. In Spain the figure for overweight or obese children and adolescents reaches 27 percent.'[67]

Drink

Drinking, like eating, is an activity full of symbolic dimensions linked to gender, class, lifestyle, situations and rituals.[68] The drinking cultures in Europe differ highly in terms of what is drunk, how and when. One of the most obvious differences in the European drinking pattern is the distinction between beer cultures and wine cultures. Countries such as Germany, Belgium, Austria, Denmark and Ireland have the highest per capita consumption of beer, whereas Italy, France, Portugal and Luxembourg lead the way in wine consumption.[69] To explain such huge differences, it has been argued that in some of these countries, such as Germany, France and Italy, consumption of beer and wine is so interwoven in daily lifestyles and the cultural fabric that it is hard to imagine those cultures without them. Economic and public policy factors are also important, and reflect attitudes towards alcohol in government institutions. In countries such as Finland, Norway and Sweden, alcoholic beverages stronger than 'light beer' (around 2 per cent alcohol) are sold only in state monopolies and are heavily taxed. Hence, the figures in Table 16.3 may be understated by up to 30 per cent due to legal and illegal duty-free imports and home production.[70]

It has been suggested that we should distinguish between two kinds of drinking traditions in Europe. Multidimensional drinking patterns characterize drinking that occurs in connection with other social activities. Examples would be wine with meals in southern Europe, or beer and wine festivals in Germany. Drinking in these countries is traditionally not related to excess or to special occasions only. On the other hand, uni-dimensional drinking patterns occur in countries where moderate continuous drinking linked to daily social activities is replaced by occasional drinking (weekends or holidays only) but is characterized by people drinking excessively.[71]

Other major variations in drink consumption patterns are revealed by statistics. Carbonated drinks are most popular in Great Britain, Ireland and Denmark, whereas mineral water consumption is especially high in France, Belgium and Italy. The Germans, Dutch, Finns and Greeks consume most spirits among western Europeans, while Italians have the lowest consumption level of such drinks.[72] Obviously, statistics of this kind do not reveal much about the types of product consumed, nor about the consumption situations. For example, schnapps may account for the spirits consumption in Germany, ouzo in Greece, genever in the Netherlands and vodka in Finland. Furthermore, the commonness of various consumption situations for such drinks varies across countries and among lifestyles. Wine may be used at religious ceremonies or at dinner each evening, beer on the beach or in a bar after working hours, carbonated drinks after sports or for children's birthday parties, and so on. What kinds of various rituals involving drinking can you think of in your country? Does your country have rituals related to the drinking of non-alcoholic beverages, such as coffee and tea?

European drinking patterns seem to indicate that increasing health consciousness leads to a trend in drinking lower alcohol content beverages. This may also be due to

Table 16.3 Beer and wine consumption per capita in 19 countries

Ranked in order of per capita consumption in 1991 (wine in litres)			Ranked in order of per capita consumption in 1991 (beer in litres)		
Rank	Country	1991	Rank	Country	1991
1	France	66.8	1	Germany	142.7
2	Portugal	62.0	2	Denmark	125.9
3	Luxembourg	60.3	3	Austria	123.7
4	Italy	56.8	4	Ireland	123.0
5	Switzerland	48.7	5	Luxembourg	116.1
6	Spain	34.3	6	Belgium	111.3
7	Austria	33.7	7	United Kingdom	106.2
8	Greece	32.4	8	Netherlands	88.5
9	Germany	24.9	9	USA	87.4
10	Belgium	23.9	10	Finland	85.3
11	Denmark	22.0	11	Spain	70.9
12	Netherlands	15.3	12	Switzerland	70.1
13	Sweden	12.3	13	Portugal	67.4
14	United Kingdom	11.5	14	Sweden	59.3
15	Finland	7.4	15	Norway	52.8
16	USA	7.2	16	France	40.5
17	Norway	6.9	17	Greece	40.0
18	Ireland	4.6	18	Iceland	24.2
19	Iceland	4.4	19	Italy	22.5

Source: Adapted from David Smith and J. Robert Skalnik, 'Changing Patterns in the Consumption of Alcoholic Beverages in Europe and the United States', in Flemming Hansen, ed., *European Advances in Consumer Research 2* (Provo, UT: Association for Consumer Research, 1995): 343–55. Used with permission.

increasingly blurred borders between multidimensional and unidimensional drinking patterns. In general, drinking patterns are becoming more similar across Europe. Traditional wine-drinking countries show the largest increase in beer consumption over time, while an increase in wine-drinking is occurring in traditional beer-drinking countries.[73]

Cars

The car is a third highly symbolic good with a great deal of cultural significance attached to it. Again, consumption differs among European countries for various reasons, such as local infrastructure, local production facilities, taxation or traditions. For instance, the percentage of families owning two cars is highest in Italy (41 per cent), France (30 per cent), the UK (29 per cent) and western Germany (26 per cent). The numbers reflect, among many other factors, the power and importance of local car industries to shape conditions so that car ownership is feasible. But industry efforts to facilitate car ownership only help to explain a general 'car culture' in these countries. The reasons for a low number of families having two cars may vary from relative poverty (Greece, Portugal, Spain) to small distances (the Netherlands) and high taxation (Denmark).[74]

In the car market, as in many other markets, the discussion continues as to whether it makes sense to segment consumers across countries. One argument for segmentation which cuts across countries is that the benefits of private car ownership are strongly felt, regardless of the differing driving habits and transport circumstances in different countries. Thus, in principle, all car consumers should be found in one of the basic proposed categories: pleasure-seekers, image-seekers and functionality-seekers.

The German car manufacturer BMW has argued that although their customers' demographic and economic profiles are quite similar, they do not operate within a standard

European consumer market and standardized marketing activities.[75] This is due to two reasons: first, they argue that the differences in size of the various segments are so great that it makes no sense to target the same segment in various countries; but secondly, and more importantly, they argue that they have discovered variations between the *benefits ultimately sought* by car drivers in different countries.

As a consequence of a study conducted in Italy, France, the Netherlands, Switzerland and Austria, BMW can break purchase criteria down into three levels: criteria that are important in *all* countries, criteria that are important to all motorists in *one* country, and criteria that are important to *some consumers in all* countries. On the pan-European level the following criteria were detected: reliability, safety, quality and advanced technology. These are thus necessary minimum requirements to be considered as a potential supplier. On the national level, the following set of differences was detected. In the Netherlands, much importance is attached to the car's overall integrity rather than to qualities such as interior design. Furthermore, the reputation of the brand turned out to be very important for the Dutch. In France, special importance was attached to the self-confidence provided by the car and to its road-holding abilities. Both Austrian and Swiss customers were very demanding, but, unlike the Austrians, the Swiss wanted a car to be discreet while Austrians placed importance on a car as a prestigious status symbol. Finally, the Italians looked for a car that accorded with their personal style and with dynamic driving capacities. In general, the study's conclusions were that BMW drivers are more demanding in terms of styling, exclusiveness, driving dynamics and advanced technology than average European drivers, but that, within this segment, special importance was attached to different dimensions across different countries. In the five countries studied, BMW discovered a total of seven common segments whose names speak more or less for themselves: the unpretentious car fan (18 per cent); the prestige-oriented sporty driver (25 per cent); the hedonist (9 per cent); the utilitarian thinker (13 per cent); the traditionalist (17 per cent); the prestige-oriented achiever (10 per cent); and the understatement buyer (9 per cent). However, as shown in Figure 16.10, the size of each of the segments varies considerably in each country. The country-specific results indicate that different models appeal to different segments in different countries. For example, it could be types 6 and

Figure 16.10 Distribution of car segments in five European countries

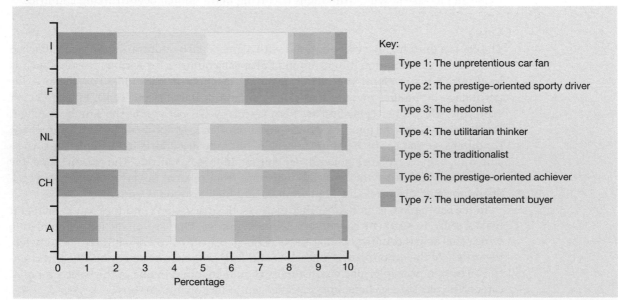

Source: Horst Kern, Hans-Christian Wagner and Roswitha Harris, 'European aspects of a global brand: The BMW case', *Marketing and Research Today* (February 1990): 47–57. Used with permission.

2 in Austria whereas it could be types 1 and 4 in Switzerland. The case of BMW is a good combination of pan-European and country-specific approaches to analysing consumer behaviour.

marketing opportunity

Big cars, small cars, sporty cars, practical cars, sleek cars, family cars . . .

'Diversity is the name of the game at 75th International Motor Show in Geneva. With the huge emphasis placed on catering to as many consumers as possible, today's variety means the show's 80,000 square meters (861,000 square feet) of floor space at the PalExpo are filled with a mind-boggling range of vehicles designed for every conceivable life style. 'The trend is going toward versatility and a lot of variety,' said Yves Dubreil, vice president-deputy director of vehicle engineering at Renault. 'It used to be that car brands had a straightforward range that went from small to big. It reflected social status. The bigger the car I had, the more important or rich I was.'

'Cars are no longer an indication of a driver's social status, instead, they make a statement about a person's lifestyle. And there are a lot of different lifestyles.' For the sociable soul, there's the cavernous and friendly Renault Grand Espace. For the more dynamic, there's the sporty Ferrari F430 Spyder or the Mazda MX-5, both making their world premieres in Geneva. The adventurous can take control of the 4x4 new Jeep Grand Cherokee, an off-roader actually produced in Austria, or the top-of-the-range Mercedes M-Class SUV. The business tycoon can slip into the sleek, newly redesigned BMW 3-Series or the Mercedes CLK, which also underwent a stunning facelift.

'You spend a lot of time in your car; you want it suited to you,' said Fabio Capano, director of product communication for Toyota Motor Marketing Europe. 'You also want it tailored to all of your modern-day needs.' This means today's vehicles must meet mobile phone, music, entertainment, navigational and informational demands.

'Bluetooth, a hands-free option for your phone, having your mobile phone reception switch over to reception from your car antenna, a place to recharge your mobile phone, a navigational screen where you can also look at all your phone numbers and your address book: you want a car that features or adapts to the latest electronic possibilities,' Dubreil said. 'It's one of our major concerns today.'

Cars are now being built so well that they can last at least 10-12 years, but electronic technology evolves much faster than that, and allowing for swapping out components requires a great deal of forethought, he added. Some car makes, such as Toyota, Renault and Lexus, already offer bluetooth options, but other companies are less willing to make costly additions today for tomorrow's unknown.

'We want to keep Chevrolet as affordable as possible, an entry-level car,' said Eric Neve, manager of Motorsports Europe for Chevrolet. 'We won't install capabilities for a technical accessory if there's only a slight possibility it's coming up in future years.' But the relationship between car makers and the electronics business is getting tighter. Accepting the widely respected Deutsche Industrie Normen, car makers from around the world use universal dimensions for electronic accessories so consumers can change radios, CD players and navigational aids unhampered. This also applies to hidden electronic devices, such as air bags. That, however, gives electronics suppliers a certain amount of power over the automotive industry.

'It's an interesting debate because the car industry relies heavily on electronics suppliers,' Neve said. 'You don't want them dictating what's available or else all the cars would be the same. There are only a few big suppliers – Delphi, Bosch, Siemens – but you still want your car to be a Chevrolet and not something simply off the shelf. We have some power to demand certain things, of course. When a supplier talks to Chevrolet, it's a potential 1.3 million cars a year. It's the power of volume.''[76]

European advertising preferences and regulations

Consumers in different countries are accustomed to different forms of advertising. In many cases, advertising content is regulated by the government. For example, tobacco advertising in Denmark is not allowed to depict young people, and Swedish tobacco advertising targeted at end-users must not show any people at all. The European Commission in Brussels has taken initiatives to impose even stricter controls on advertising, introducing among other things a total ban on tobacco advertising in Europe.

In Germany, pricing is controlled, and special sales can be held only for a particular reason, such as going out of business or the end of the season. Advertising also focuses more on the provision of factual information rather than on the aggressive hard sell. Indeed, it is illegal to mention the names of competitors.[77] Unlike the Anglo-Saxon advertising culture, comparative advertising is banned in most Latin and Germanic countries in Europe.

But the differences among European countries are not restricted to the legal area. There are also differences concerning which type of television advertising spots and print ads will work best in various European countries. A comparative study of French and German TV spots revealed a distinct profile of the ads in these two countries. French TV ads tended to have less product information, to have a less direct way of communicating about socially sensitive topics, to rely more on non-verbal and implicit communication types and to present women in a more seductive and sexually alluring manner.[78] The same differences concerning the general image of French communication as seductive and imaginative vs. a more factual and sober German style were confirmed when looking at other types of communication such as television news programmes and news magazines. Another study of all ads sent out on a couple of TV channels in each country confirmed this difference, stressing the more frequent use of puns and the more rapid and personalized rhythm of the French ads, although no difference in information level was found.[79] Surprisingly, in the latter study not one single common ad was sampled in Germany and France. It seems that the use of pan-European advertising is still limited.

One possible explanation for this difference may be due to the distinction between ▶ ▶ **low-context** and **high-context cultures**.[80] In a high-context culture, messages tend to be more implicit and built into the communication context, whereas communication in low-context cultures tends to be more explicit, specific and direct. France, according to this perspective of classifying culture, is relatively high-context compared with Germany, which belongs among the most low-context cultures in the world.

In comparison, the British have a more favourable attitude to advertising than either the French or the Germans. They tend to think of advertising as a humorous and entertaining part of daily life, and have less concerns about its manipulative capacities.[81] Indeed, the British ads may be funnier. One study found a relatively big difference between the degree to which humour is used in televised advertising. Humour was used in 88.8 per cent of British ads compared to 74.5 per cent in France and only 61 per cent in Germany. And in a sample of internationally used ads, the share of humorous ads dropped to 32.2 per cent.[82] It seems that humour is still a very national thing. Or maybe there are other explanations? These findings are supported by another source which concluded that, relative to Americans, the British tended to regard advertising as a form of entertainment. Compared with the United States, British television commercials also contained less information.[83] One advertising executive stated outright that from watching a sample reel of German and British car ads respectively, it would be evident that the German ones would be much more rational and the British ones much more emotional.[84]

Not only do attitudes about ads vary across Europe, the same can be said for preferences of media. For example, in France outdoor posters are a highly developed and popular medium for creative campaigns. Cinema advertising is also enjoyable to the

French. In the UK, adverts in daily newspapers are more important compared with other European countries, and in Germany the radio medium is more important than elsewhere.[85] But the use of various media is difficult to compare among countries due to variations in the regulation of media use: interrupting programmes with advertising is not permitted in Scandinavian countries, for example, and is not practised on German public TV channels.

Cultural differences may influence actual reader comprehension of a certain advertisement. Most of these studies have concluded that ads, like other pictures or communications, are understood culturally, and that readership is so different that a standardized execution of the ad becomes problematic.[86] When two different TV spots (called 'Hitchhiker' and 'Quackers') for the chocolate bar KitKat were tested in six different countries, the consumers (all younger people) showed significant differences in what they retained as the main idea of the ad and the main product characteristic (see Table 16.4).[87]

The variations could be explained by different factors such as relative familiarity with the product concept (in Italy), the small size of the product in relation to local competitors (the Netherlands), popularity of English-style humour (Germany) and the prevailing advertising style in the country (France). Another study comparing Danish and American readings of international ads has detected similar variations in readership due to cultural backgrounds. For example, an ad for a lemon-flavoured soft drink featuring young people enjoying themselves on a beach was interpreted by the Danes as showing the strength of the community and by Americans as showing individual freedom.[88] It

Table 16.4 Differences in message decoding of two ads in six European countries

	Main idea		
	Hitchhiker		**Quackers**
Belgium	Product for young people		You can share it
England		A break with KitKat	
Holland	Product for young people		A break with KitKat
Italy		Product quality	
Germany	To relax		A break with KitKat
France	'Magic effect'		To relax

© Copyright GfK
Source: ESOMAR, Madrid, 1992.

	Main product characteristics		
	Hitchhiker		**Quackers**
Belgium	Good product		Crispy bar
England	Chocolate bar with wafer		A snack
Holland		Little	
Italy		Good product	
Germany	Relax with KitKat		Chocolate bar
France	Crispy bar		Good product

© Copyright GfK
Source: ESOMAR, Madrid, 1992.

Source: J. Andrew Davison and Erik Grab, 'The contributions of advertising testing to the development of effective international advertising: The KitKat case study', *Marketing and Research Today* (February 1993): 15-24. Used with permission.

is probably safe to conclude that, although there are often certain similarities in the way ads are understood across cultures, the readership tends to focus on different themes in different countries.[89]

A recent worldwide study by Leo Burnett found that women are 'underserved by our [advertising] industry, at least in terms of being approached with advertising that motivates and moves them in ways they find relevant and meaningful . . . they're tuning out ads that don't present women in realistic and believable ways'.[90] Their research suggested that 'changing perceptions of money, sex, humor, emotion and authenticity' meant that advertisers were having increasing difficulty in reaching this key group which is responsible for up to 80 per cent of consumer decision-making.[91]

multicultural dimensions

The internet is bringing new cultural differences to the marketplace. The Scandinavians are those who have the highest home-internet linkage frequency in Europe, but the sales leaders by far in terms of turnover are Germany and the UK. These two countries alone account for about 55 per cent of the e-commerce turnover in Europe (Germany 30 per cent and the UK 25 per cent). It takes France, Italy, the Netherlands and Sweden combined just to reach the turnover level of the UK. Also, there are big differences in user profiles. The UK is heavily over-represented among the group of 12–17-year-old Europeans who surf the net, whereas the Germans are very under-represented. On the other hand, relatively more French (21–34 years) and Germans (age group 25–34 only) surf the internet compared to the British. For the EU-25, market penetration of the internet is high (47%), relative to much of the world, and relative to non-EU-25 European countries (16%). Sweden (73%), Denmark (69%), and the Netherlands (66%) lead the EU-25 in market usage.[92]

Regional consumption differences: the micro-level

Geodemography

▶ The term **geodemography** refers to analytical techniques that combine data on consumer expenditures and other socio-economic factors with geographic information about the areas in which people live in order to identify consumers who share common consumption patterns.

Geodemography is based on the assumption that 'birds of a feather flock together' – that people who have similar needs and tastes tend to live near one another. Given this, it should be possible to locate 'pockets' of like-minded people who can then be reached more economically by direct mail and other methods. Important dimensions in differentiating between neighbourhoods, suburbs, inner-city areas or towns are factors such as income level, ethnic background and demographics (most notably age). Geographic information is increasingly being combined with other data to paint an even more complete picture of the consumer. Several marketing research ventures now employ
▶ **single-source data** where information about a person's actual purchasing history is combined with geodemographic data, thus allowing marketers to learn even more about the types of marketing strategies that motivate some people to respond.

■ ETHNIC AND RELIGIOUS SUBCULTURES

Sevgi, waking up early on Saturday morning, braces herself for a long day of errands and chores. As usual, her mother expects her to do the shopping while she is at work, and then help prepare the food for the big family get-together tonight. Of course, her older brother would never be asked to do the shopping or help out in the kitchen – these are women's jobs.

Family gatherings make a lot of work, and Sevgi wishes that her mother would use prepared foods once in a while, especially on a Saturday when Sevgi has errands of her own to do. But no, her mother insists on preparing most of her food from scratch; she rarely uses any convenience products, to ensure that the meals she serves are of the highest quality.

Resigned, Sevgi watches TRTint on the family's cable-TV while she's getting dressed, and then she heads down to the local newsagent in 'De Pijp' to buy a magazine – there are dozens of Turkish magazines and newspapers for sale and she likes to pick up new ones occasionally. Then Sevgi buys the grocery items her mother wants; the Islamic *halal* butcher is a long-time family friend and already has the cuts of lamb prepared for her. The vendors at the open air stalls in the Albert Cuyp Market where she and her mother shop all the time know her, and provide her with choice quality olives and vegetables. One quick stop at the local sweetshop to pick up the family's favourite *drop* (liquorice) and she's almost done. With any luck, she'll have a few minutes to stop at the music shop and pick up the latest Black Eyed Peas CD. She really liked their music on Bob Geldof's Live8 concert worldwide telecast. She'll listen to it in the kitchen while she chops, peels and stirs. Sevgi smiles to herself: despite a busy day preparing the house and meal for the family party, she feels that Amsterdam is a great place to live.

Subcultures and consumer identity

Yes, Sevgi lives in Amsterdam, not Istanbul. However, this consumer vignette could just as easily have taken place in London, Berlin, Stockholm, Marseilles or thousands of other cities throughout Europe. There are well over 25 million Europeans who belong to an ethnic sub-group, and in several European countries such as France, Belgium and Germany, they collectively account for around 10 per cent of the total population. In the UK, the ethnic communities represented are forecast to double in population to over 6 million within the next 30 years.[93]

Turkish consumers have much in common with members of other racial and ethnic groups who live in Europe. These groups of consumers observe the same national holidays, their expenditures are affected by the country's economic health and they may join together in rooting for their host country's national team in the football World Cup. Nevertheless, while European residency (and in most cases European citizenship) provides the raw material for some consumption decisions, others profoundly affect (see Figure 16.11) and are profoundly affected by the enormous variations in the social fabric of the country where they live.

Consumers' lifestyles are affected by group memberships *within* the society at large. ▶ These groups are known as **subcultures**, whose members share beliefs and common experiences that set them apart from others. While subcultural group memberships often have a significant impact on consumer behaviour, some subcultural identifications are more powerful than others. Every consumer belongs to many subcultures. These memberships can be based on similarities in age (major subcultural consumer groups based on age have already been discussed in Chapter 13), race or ethnic background, place of residence, or even a strong identification with an activity or art form. Whether 'Dead Heads', 'Netizens', or skinheads, each group exhibits its own unique set of norms, vocabulary and product insignias (such as the British Lonsdale sports and fashion clothier, whose sweatshirts signify white racists to many youths in the Netherlands[94]). These 'communities' can even gel around fictional characters and events. Many devotees of *Star Trek*, for example, immerse themselves in a make-believe world of starships, phasers, and Vulcan mind melds.[95] Our subcultures often play a key role in defining the extended self (see Chapter 7) and typically command fierce loyalty.

Figure 16.11 Ethnic food service outlets per million population in major European cities

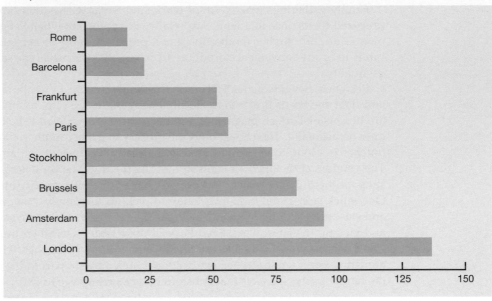

Source: Adapted from Datamonitor, *Wall Street Journal Europe* (9 December 1997): 4.

Ethnic and racial subcultures

Ethnic and religious identity is a significant component of a consumer's self-concept. An ► **ethnic** or **racial subculture** consists of a self-perpetuating group of consumers who are held together by common cultural and/or genetic ties, and is identified both by its members and by others as being a distinguishable category.[96]

In some countries, such as Japan, ethnicity is almost synonymous with the dominant culture, since most citizens claims the same homogeneous cultural ties (although Japan has sizeable minority populations, most notably people of Korean ancestry). In heterogeneous societies like those found in Europe, many different cultures are represented, and consumers may expend great effort to keep their subcultural identification from being submerged into the mainstream of the dominant society.

Ethnicity and marketing strategies

Although some companies may feel uncomfortable at the notion that people's racial and ethnic differences should be explicitly taken into account when formulating marketing strategies, the reality is that these subcultural memberships are frequently paramount in shaping people's needs and wants. Membership of these groups is often predictive of such consumer variables as level and type of media exposure, food preferences, the wearing of distinctive apparel, political behaviour, leisure activities and even willingness to try new products.

Furthermore, research evidence indicates that members of minority groups are more likely to find an advertising spokesperson from their own group to be more trustworthy, and this enhanced credibility in turn translates into more positive brand attitudes.[97] In addition, the way marketing messages should be structured depends on subcultural differences in how meanings are communicated. As discussed earlier in this chapter, sociologists make a distinction between *high-context cultures* and *low-context cultures*. In a high-context culture, group members tend to be tightly knit, and they are likely to infer meanings that go beyond the spoken word. Symbols and gestures, rather than words, carry much of the weight of the message. Many minority cultures are high-context and have strong oral traditions, so perceivers will be more sensitive to nuances in advertisements that go beyond the message copy.[98]

'To be or not to be: that is the answer'

One important way to distinguish between members of a subculture is to consider the extent to which they retain a sense of identification with their country of origin vs. their host country. **Acculturation** refers to the process of movement and adaptation to one country's cultural environment by a person from another country.[99] The nature of this transition process is affected by many factors. Individual differences, such as whether the person speaks the host country language, influence how difficult the adjustment will be.

The person's contacts with **acculturation agents** – people and institutions that teach the ways of a culture – are also crucial. Some of these agents are aligned with the *culture of origin* (in Sevgi's case, Turkey). These include family, friends, the mosque, local businesses and Turkish-language media that keep the consumer in touch with his or her country of origin. Other agents are associated with the *culture of immigration* (in this case, the Netherlands), and help the consumer to learn how to navigate in the new environment. These include state schools and Dutch-language media.

As immigrants adapt to their new surroundings, several processes come into play. *Movement* refers to the factors motivating people to uproot themselves physically from one location and go to another. Although many ethnic members throughout Europe are second generation (born in the country where they live), their parents are more likely to have been the first to arrive in the new country. On arrival, immigrants encounter a need for *translation*. This means attempting to master a set of rules for operating in the new environment, whether learning how to decipher a different currency or understanding the social meanings of unfamiliar clothing styles. This cultural learning leads to a process of *adaptation*, where new consumption patterns are formed.

As consumers undergo acculturation, several things happen. Many immigrants undergo (at least to some extent) *assimilation*, where they adopt products that are identified with the mainstream culture. At the same time, there is an attempt at *maintenance* of practices associated with the culture of origin. Immigrants stay in touch with people in their country, and many continue to eat ethnic foods and read ethnic newspapers. Their continued identification with their home culture may cause *resistance*, as they resent the pressure to submerge their identities and take on new roles. Figure 16.12 provides an overview of the processes involved in consumer acculturation.

These processes illustrate that ethnicity is a fluid concept, and that the boundaries of a subculture are constantly being recreated. An *ethnic pluralism* perspective argues that ethnic groups differ from the mainstream in varying degrees, and that adaptation to the larger society occurs selectively. Research evidence argues against the notion that assimilation necessarily involves losing identification with the person's original ethnic group. For example, Sevgi feels comfortable in expressing her 'Turkishness' in a variety of consumption-related ways: the magazines she buys, the TV programmes on the Turkish network she chooses to watch, her choice of ethnically appropriate gifts for events such as weddings and *bayram* (religious holidays).[100] Alternatively, she has no problems at all in expressing consumption behaviours of the mainstream culture – she loves eating *drop* (Dutch liquorice), buys 'Western' music and has her favourite outfits for going out to the cinema and clubs. The best indicator of ethnic assimilation, these researchers argue, is the extent to which members of an ethnic group have social interactions with members of other groups in comparison with their own.[101]

Figure 16.12 A model of consumer acculturation

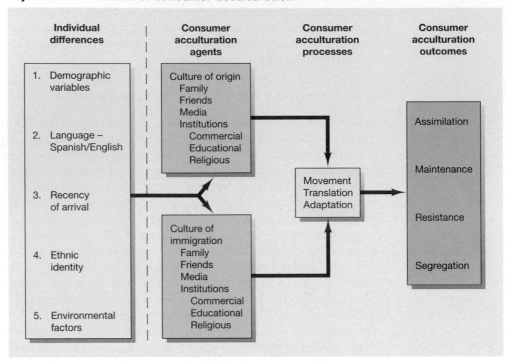

Source: Adapted from Lisa Peñaloza, '*Atravesando fronteras*/border crossings: A critical ethnographic exploration of the consumer acculturation of Mexican immigrants', *Journal of Consumer Research* 21 (June 1994): 32–54.

The impact of religion on consumption

Religion per se has not been studied extensively in marketing, possibly because it is seen as a taboo subject. The very low-key or non-existent approach by large multinational or pan-European companies reflects the same sort of caution that these companies have in targeting ethnic groups – companies are having to decide whether religiously or ethnically-tailored programmes foster greater brand loyalty or whether any advantage is outweighed by the risks of misreading the target market and causing offence. Without question, the most successful companies targeting and serving both ethnic and religious segments are small businesses, whose managers and owners are often members of the group.[102] However, the little evidence that has been accumulated indicates that religious affiliation has the *potential* to be a valuable predictor of consumer behaviour.[103] Religious subcultures have been shown to exert an impact on such consumer variables as personality, attitudes towards sexuality, birth rates and household formation, income and political attitudes.

Putting together descriptive demographic profiles of Europe's major religious groups is not an exact science. For example, French law prohibits any question on religion in national censuses, although with an estimated 4–5 million Muslim inhabitants France undoubtedly has the biggest Islamic community in western Europe. As a faith, Islam is now second only to Roman Catholicism in France.[104] Similar problems with taking a census are found in the UK. Britain's 1.6 million-strong Muslim population is small, but has the fastest growth rate of all religions in the country. The thousand or so existing mosques are likely to be converted warehouses, churches or community halls. The hundreds of new mosques being built feature traditional Islamic domes and minarets – a trend which signals the growing economic vitality of British Muslims, as well as local authorities' growing acceptance of mosques.[105] While Islam is the fastest-growing religion in Europe, it is difficult to generalize about Muslims beyond belief in the teachings of the Koran, identifying holidays and periods of fasting such as Ramadan, and certain dietary restrictions. Coming from more than 120 countries and a variety of ethnic groups (Blacks, Asians, Arabs, Europeans), they are like many groups of consumers in Europe – diverse in their celebrations of consumption habits.

Christianity has dominated the history and cultural development of Europe, and has played an important role in the shaping of the European continent. While the many denominations of Christians make it the largest religious grouping in Europe (roughly 600 million), active membership is on the decline, with fewer and fewer adults attending services on any given Sunday.[106] In response to this trend, the Vatican has been involved in a variety of events aimed at developing closer and more active relationships with Europe's youth. Enlisting French fashion designers for World Youth Day, having Bob Dylan perform at a Vatican-sponsored rock concert, and having Easter Mass and information about the Vatican on a website are recent attempts to get youth involved with the church.[107] Divided roughly into the more Protestant North and the predominantly Catholic South, Christianity still makes up the majority religion in Europe in terms of claimed membership. Its major holidays of Easter and Christmas and celebrations such as 'Carnival' (*Faschung* in Germany) are celebrated or observed to such an extent that large industries such as travel and retailing rely on these seasons as the times of the year when they earn the most revenues.

marketing pitfall

There are mixed feelings in the Catholic community about the spread of religious imagery in popular culture. On the one hand, the Vatican museum opened its first boutique outside Vatican walls, and is now selling silk ties and scarves designed for the Vatican by Salvatore Ferragamo.[108] On the other hand, an ad in a Danish campaign for the French car manufacturer Renault had to be withdrawn after protests from the Catholic community. The ad described a dialogue during confession between a Catholic priest and a repenting man. The man's sins can be atoned for by reciting Ave Marias until he confesses to having scratched the paint of the priest's new Renault – at which point the priest shouts 'heathen' and orders the man to pay a substantial penalty to the church.[109]

■ EURO-CONSUMERS: DO THEY EXIST?

A number of trends seem to be valid for all western European markets.[110] These include:

- a tendency to more unevenly distributed income;
- an increasing number of older people;
- a decrease in household size;
- a growing proportion of immigrants;
- increase in environmental concern and consumption of 'green' products;
- relatively increasing consumption of services compared to durable goods.

In spite of these common trends, there are, as we have seen, big differences in the local contexts in which these trends are found as well as differences in the degree to which the trend is significant in each individual country.

Many European managers expect an increase in the importance of Euro-brands and Euro-consumers.[111] However, *why* and *when* companies should or could adopt pan-European strategies or not remains a complex matter. One study suggested 21 influencing factors on pan-European marketing standardization, including management characteristics, firm characteristics, industry characteristics and government character-istics, but not market characteristics![112]

We believe that consumer behaviour analysis must play an important role in the decision to standardize or adapt marketing strategies. All consumers will differ to some extent in what they buy, why they buy, who makes the purchase decision, how they buy, when they buy and where they buy.[113] Some of these differences may be explained at the lifestyle level and less so on the national level, and some are very obviously related to national or regional differences. It is also obvious that some differences are disappearing, due to the increasingly international supply of goods and the increasing international-ization of the retailing system in Europe.[114] However, not even the fact that similar goods are bought in similar stores across European countries permits us to confirm the existence of the Euro-consumer. Product usage and knowledge, and to a certain extent imagery, may be relatively shared among Europeans, but as soon as one takes the con-texts of acquisition, consumption and disposal into account, the actual role and meaning of the product in daily life becomes coloured by the local culture. No lifestyle survey has yet demonstrated a truly European profile in any of the lifestyles; European segments continue to be defined in rather abstract common denominators.

It is often asserted that segments such as international business people, or younger people mainly influenced by trends from MTV and other 'global youth culture' phe-nomena, are especially prone to standardized marketing. European managers are people who tend to be prime consumers of pan-European media, like business magazines or CNN (in hotel rooms).[115] So there may be a tendency to a higher degree of international-ization among younger, wealthier and more educated people. The question is how deep the similarity really is. A study of consumption of luxury goods in five major European markets concluded that the pan-European consumer of luxury brands is between 35 and 49 years old, lives in a major city, has a high income and a university education, and occupies a managerial job. On the other hand, there were big differences between the various countries in the level of brand awareness and purchase level, and the degree of significance of socio-economic factors for purchase of luxury brands. For example, Spain and Italy are strongly segmented due to socio-economic differences, while in France, the UK and Germany these socio-economic differences are less useful in explaining luxury consumption. The level of purchase and awareness was found to be high in France, the UK and Italy, and low in Germany and Spain. The most 'mature' market for luxury brands was France, the UK and a narrow Italian segment, whereas the rest of the Italians lacked the money, the Germans lacked the motivation and the Spanish lacked both.[116]

In general, the absence of the Euro-consumer does not mean that Svensson of Sweden, Smith of the UK, Smit of Holland, Simón of Spain and Schultz of Germany cannot have more in common in certain aspects than they have with their compatriots. But it means that these similarities can be analysed and understood only with methods that are also able to take the differences into consideration. Hence the call for an understanding of the new cultural units that make up today's marketplace of international lifestyles, global issues, national rituals and local habits.[117]

■ CHAPTER SUMMARY

- ■ A consumer's *lifestyle* refers to the ways he or she chooses to spend time and money and how his or her values, attitudes and tastes are reflected by consumption choices. Lifestyle research is useful to track societal consumption preferences and also to posi-tion specific products and services to different segments.

- ■ Marketers segment by lifestyle differences, often by grouping consumers in terms of their *AIOs* (activities, interests and opinions).

- *Psychographic techniques* attempt to classify consumers in terms of psychological, subjective variables in addition to observable characteristics (demographics). A variety of systems, such as RISC, have been developed to identify consumer 'types' and to differentiate them in terms of their brand or product preferences, media usage, leisure time activities, and attitudes towards such broad issues as politics and religion.

- Interrelated sets of products and activities are associated with social roles to form *consumption constellations*. People often purchase a product or service because it is associated with a constellation which, in turn, is linked to a lifestyle they find desirable.

- Where one comes from is often a significant determinant of lifestyle. Many marketers recognize national or regional differences in product preferences, and develop different versions of their products for different markets.

- Because a consumer's culture exerts such a big influence on his or her lifestyle choices, marketers must learn as much as possible about differences in cultural norms and preferences when marketing in more than one country. One important issue is the extent to which marketing strategies must be tailored to each culture, rather than standardized across cultures.

- A set of techniques called *geodemography* analyses consumption patterns using geographical and demographic data, and identifies clusters of consumers who exhibit similar psychographic characteristics.

- Consumers identify with many groups that share common characteristics and identities. These large groups that exist within a society are called *subcultures*, and membership in them often gives marketers a valuable clue about individuals' consumption decisions. A large component of a person's identity is determined by his or her ethnic origins, racial identity and religious background. The growing numbers of people who claim multi-ethnic backgrounds are beginning to blur the traditional distinctions drawn among these subcultures.

- Recently, several minority groups have caught the attention of marketers as their economic power has grown. Segmenting consumers by their *ethnicity* can be effective, but care must be taken not to rely on inaccurate (and sometimes offensive) ethnic stereotypes.

- Because a consumer's culture exerts such a major influence on his or her lifestyle choices, marketers must learn as much as possible about differences in cultural norms and preferences when marketing in more than one country.

- Given that we, as consumers, must take part in many activities that reflect our local cultures, Euro-consumers as an overall segment do not exist. The existence of a Euro-consumer is at best limited to certain segments of the population, the young and the (international) managerial class, and to certain situations.

▶ KEY TERMS

Acculturation (p. 589)
Acculturation agents (p. 589)
AIOs (p. 563)
Consumption constellations (p. 562)
Ethnic subculture (p. 588)
Geodemography (p. 586)
Habitus (p. 569)
High-context culture (p. 564)
Lifestyle (p. 558)

Lifestyle marketing perspective (p. 560)
Low-context culture (p. 584)
Product complementarity (p. 561)
Psychographics (p. 562)
Racial subculture (p. 588)
Single-source data (p. 586)
Subcultures (p. 587)
VALS (p. 570)

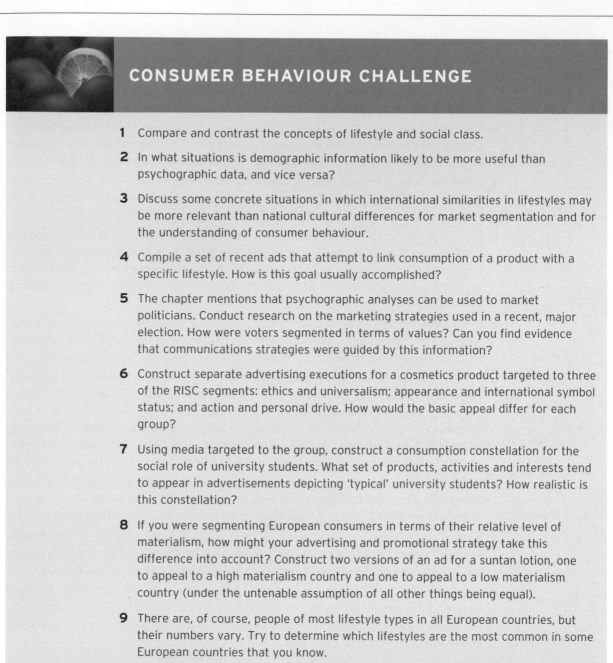

CONSUMER BEHAVIOUR CHALLENGE

1 Compare and contrast the concepts of lifestyle and social class.

2 In what situations is demographic information likely to be more useful than psychographic data, and vice versa?

3 Discuss some concrete situations in which international similarities in lifestyles may be more relevant than national cultural differences for market segmentation and for the understanding of consumer behaviour.

4 Compile a set of recent ads that attempt to link consumption of a product with a specific lifestyle. How is this goal usually accomplished?

5 The chapter mentions that psychographic analyses can be used to market politicians. Conduct research on the marketing strategies used in a recent, major election. How were voters segmented in terms of values? Can you find evidence that communications strategies were guided by this information?

6 Construct separate advertising executions for a cosmetics product targeted to three of the RISC segments: ethics and universalism; appearance and international symbol status; and action and personal drive. How would the basic appeal differ for each group?

7 Using media targeted to the group, construct a consumption constellation for the social role of university students. What set of products, activities and interests tend to appear in advertisements depicting 'typical' university students? How realistic is this constellation?

8 If you were segmenting European consumers in terms of their relative level of materialism, how might your advertising and promotional strategy take this difference into account? Construct two versions of an ad for a suntan lotion, one to appeal to a high materialism country and one to appeal to a low materialism country (under the untenable assumption of all other things being equal).

9 There are, of course, people of most lifestyle types in all European countries, but their numbers vary. Try to determine which lifestyles are the most common in some European countries that you know.

10 If you have access to foreign TV channels, try to compare the advertising in the ones from your own country with the foreign ones. Are the styles different? Are the predominant products different? Is the use of a certain style of advertisement for a certain type of product similar or dissimilar?

11 Extreme sports. Chat rooms. Vegetarianism. Can you predict what will be 'hot' in the near future? Identify a lifestyle trend that is just surfacing in your universe. Describe this trend in detail, and justify your prediction. What specific styles and/or products are part of this trend?

12 Locate one or more consumers (perhaps family members) who have emigrated from another country. Interview them about how they adapted to their host culture. In particular, what changes did they make in their consumption practices over time?

13 Religious symbolism is being used increasingly in advertising, even though some people object to this practice. For example, the French fashion house Marithe and François Girbaud used a poster of well-dressed women posed in a version of Leonardo da Vinci's *The Last Supper*: the poster was banned in Milan.[118] In another example, a French Volkswagen ad for the relaunch of the Golf showed a modern version of *The Last Supper* with the tag line, 'Let us rejoice, my friends, for a new Golf has been born'.[119] A group of clergy in France sued the company and the ad had to be removed from 10,000 hoardings. One of the bishops involved in the suit said, 'Advertising experts have told us that ads aim for the sacred in order to shock, because using sex does not work any more.' Do you agree? Should religion be used to market products? Do you find this strategy effective or offensive? When and where is this appropriate, if at all?

■ NOTES

1. Pierre Valette-Florence, *Les styles de vie* (Paris: Nathan, 1994); Benjamin Zablocki and Rosabeth Moss Kanter, 'The differentiation of life-styles', *Annual Review of Sociology* (1976): 269–97.

2. Mary T. Douglas and Baron C. Isherwood, *The World of Goods* (New York: Basic Books, 1979).

3. Richard A. Peterson, 'Revitalizing the culture concept', *Annual Review of Sociology* 5 (1979): 137–66.

4. MarketWatch: Global Roundup Market Snapshots, 'Empty nesters: UK consumers have the most left to spend', Datamonitor Report DMCM1090 'empty nesters' (October 2004) www.datamonitor.com: 40.

5. Amelia Hill and Anushka Asthana, 'She's young, gifted, and ahead of you at the till', *The Observer* (2 January 2005), http://observer.guardian.co.uk/uk_news/story/0,6903,1382042,00.html.

6. Søren Askegaard, 'Livsstilsundersøgelser: henimod et teoretisk fundament', doctoral dissertation, School of Business and Economics: Odense University, 1993.

7. Henrik Dahl, *Hvis din nabo var en bil* (Copenhagen: Akademisk Forlag, 1997).

8. Thomas Drieseberg, 'Lebensstile in der marktforschung – eine empirische bestandsaufnahme', *Soziologie – Planung und Analyse* 5 (1992): 18–26.

9. Julia Cosgrove, 'Campari and CD?', *Business Week* (1 July 2002): 14.

10. William Leiss, Stephen Kline and Sut Jhally, *Social Communication in Advertising* (Toronto: Methuen, 1986).

11. Douglas and Isherwood, *The World of Goods*: 72–3.

12. Michael R. Solomon, 'The role of products as social stimuli: A symbolic interactionism perspective', *Journal of Consumer Research* 10 (December 1983): 319–29.

13. Christopher K. Hsee and France Leclerc, 'Will products look more attractive when presented separately or together?', *Journal of Consumer Research* 25 (September 1998): 175–86.

14. Anders Bengtsson, *Consumers and Mixed-Brands: On the Polysemy of Brand Meaning*, doctoral dissertation, Lund: Lund Business Press; Anders Bengtsson, 'Unnoticed Relationships: Do Consumers Experience Co-branded Products?', in Susan Broniarczyk and Kent Nakamoto, eds, *Advances in Consumer Research* 29 (Provo, UT: Association for Consumer Research, 2002): 521–7.

15. Christina Binkley, 'Fairmont and Porsche team up in luxury cross-marketing deal', *The Wall Street Journal Online* (8 October 2002).

16. Vanessa O'Connell, 'Courvoisier to launch clothing line: Luxury sportswear plans to transform liquor label into lush lifestyle brand', *The Wall Street Journal Online* (13 February 2004).

17. Michael R. Solomon and Henry Assael, 'The Forest or the Trees? A Gestalt Approach to Symbolic Consumption', in Jean Umiker-Sebeok, ed., *Marketing and Semiotics: New Directions in the Study of Signs for Sale* (Berlin: Mouton de Gruyter, 1988): 189–218; Michael R. Solomon, 'Mapping product constellations: A social categorization approach to symbolic consumption', *Psychology and Marketing* 5(3) (1988): 233–58; see also Stephen C. Cosmas, 'Life styles and consumption patterns', *Journal of Consumer Research* 8(4) (March 1982): 453–5.

18. Russell W. Belk, 'Yuppies as Arbiters of the Emerging Consumption Style', in Richard J. Lutz, ed., *Advances in Consumer Research* 13 (Provo, UT: Association for Consumer Research, 1986): 514–19.

19. Margaret Hogg, 'Anti-Constellations: Conceptualization and Content', in B. Englis and A. Olofsson, eds, *European Advances in Consumer Research* 3 (Provo, UT: Association for Consumer Research, 1998): 44–9.

20. Askegaard, 'Livsstilsundersøgelser: henimod et teoretisk fundament': 103–5.

21. Bill Schlackman, 'An Historical Perspective', in S. Robson and A. Foster, eds, *Qualitative Research in Action* (London: Edward Arnold, 1989): 15–23.

22. William D. Wells and Douglas J. Tigert, 'Activities, interests, and opinions', *Journal of Advertising Research* 11 (August 1971): 27.

23. Piirto Heath, 'Psychographics: "Q'est-ce que c'est"?', *American Demographics* (November 1995).

24. Alfred S. Boote, 'Psychographics: Mind over matter', *American Demographics* (April 1980): 26–9; William D. Wells, 'Psychographics: A critical review', *Journal of Marketing Research* 12 (May 1975): 196–213.

25. Joseph T. Plummer, 'The concept and application of life style segmentation', *Journal of Marketing* 38 (January 1974): 33–7.

26. J.E. Burroughs and A. Rindfleisch, 'Materialism and well-being: a conflicting values perspective', *Journal of Consumer Research* 29(3): 348–70; Hugh Williamson, 'All the rage in Germany: Cheap flights', *Financial Times* (26 March 2004), http://news.ft.com/servlet/Content Server?pagename=FT.com/StoryFT/FullStory&c= StoryFT&cid=1079419851116&p=1079419860606.

27. John L. Lastovicka, John P. Murry, Erich A. Joachimsthaler, Gurav Bhalla and Jim Scheurich, 'A lifestyle typology to model young male drinking and driving', *Journal of Consumer Research* 14 (September 1987): 257–63.

28. 'CMT "Lifestyle" launch', *Marketing* (3 February 1994): 4.

29. Valerie Latham, 'Do Euroconsumers exist?', *Marketing* (24 June 1993): 3.

30. Internal document, RISC.

31. Bernard Cathelat, *Socio-Styles-Système* (Paris: Editions d'organisation, 1990).

32. Askegaard, 'Livsstilsundersøgelser: henimod et teoretisk fundament': 67–77.

33. Pierre Bourdieu, *La distinction: critique social du jugement* (Paris: Editions de Minuit, 1979; Eng. trans. 1984).

34. Douglas B. Holt, 'Does cultural capital structure American consumption?', *Journal of Consumer Research* 25 (June 1998): 1–25.

35. Mary Douglas, *Natural Symbols* (New York: Random House, 1973).

36. Dahl, *Hvis din nabo var en bil*: 55–81.

37. Martha Farnsworth Riche, 'VALS 2', *American Demographics* (July 1989): 25.

38. Leiss et al., *Social Communication in Advertising*.

39. Cris Prystay, 'Marketers to Chinese women offer more room to be vain', *The Wall Street Journal* (30 May 2002); Cris Prystay and Montira Narkvichien, 'Sex and the City singles out Asian women for marketers', *The Wall Street Journal* (8 August 2002).

40. Stuart Elliott, 'Sampling tastes of a changing Russia', *New York Times* (1 April 1992) 2: D1.

41. Valette-Florence, *Les styles de vie*.

42. Askegaard, 'Livsstilsundersøgelser: henimod et teoretisk fundament'.

43. 'Going it alone', *Marketing News* (11 September 2000).

44. Per Olof Berg, Anders Linde-Laursen and Orvar Löfgren, eds, *Invoking a Transnational Metropolis* (Lund: Studentlitteratur, 2000).

45. Søren Askegaard and Tage Koed Madsen, 'The local and the global: Patterns of homogeneity and heterogeneity in European food cultures', *International Business Review* 7(6) (1998): 549–68.

46. Pieter van Erven Dorens, 'Hollandse hap aan Turkse kust' (Dutch bit on the Turkish coast), *Reiskrant* (4 January 2005), http://reiskrant.nl/reiskrant/reisnieuws/16943671/Hollandse_hap_in_Turks_hotel.html.

47. See discussions in the following: Alladi Venkatesh, 'Ethnoconsumerism: A New Paradigm to Study Cultural and Cross-Cultural Consumer Behaviour', in Janeen A. Costa and G. Bamossy, eds, *Marketing in a Multicultural World* (Thousand Oaks, CA: Sage, 1995): 26–67; Jean-Claude Usunier, *Marketing Across Cultures*, 3rd edn (London: Prentice-Hall, 2000); Askegaard and Madsen, 'The local and the global: Patterns of homogeneity and heterogeneity in European food cultures'; Klaus Grunert, Suzanne Grunert and Sharon Beatty, 'Cross-cultural research on consumer values', *Marketing and Research Today* 17 (1989): 30–9.

48. Usunier, *Marketing Across Cultures*.

49. Peter S.H. Leeflang and W. Fred van Raaij, 'The changing consumer in the European Union: A "meta-analysis"', *International Journal of Research in Marketing* 12(5) (1996): 373–87.

50. See among many sources: M. Douglas, 'Food as a system of classification', in *In the Active Voice* (London: Routledge & Kegan Paul, 1982): 82–124; P. Farb and G. Armelagos, *Consuming Passions: The Anthropology of Eating* (Boston: Houghton Mifflin, 1980); P. Fieldhouse, *Food and Nutrition: Customs and Culture* (London: Croom Helm, 1986); C. Fischler, *L'Homnivore* (Paris: Ed. Odile Jacob, 1990); A. Warde, *Consumption, Food, and Taste* (London: Sage, 1997).

51. Euromonitor, *European Marketing Data and Statistics* (1997): 6, 254.

52. Ibid.: 328–31.

53. Datamonitor Press Release, 'Death of the home-cooked meal?' (27 January 2005), http://www.datamonitor.com/~376a33171d1c48d3b229cbf476ed44e0.

54. Klaus G. Grunert, Karen Brunsø and Søren Bisp, 'Food-Related Lifestyle: Development of a Cross-Culturally Valid Instrument for Market Surveillance', in L. Kahle and L. Chiagouris, eds, *Values, Lifestyles and Psychographics* (Mahwah, NJ: Lawrence Erlbaum Associates, 1997): 337–54.

55. See, however, Søren Askegaard and Karen Brunsø, 'Food-related lifestyle in Singapore: Preliminary testing of a western European research instrument in Southeast Asia', *Journal of Euromarketing* 7(4) (1999): 65–86.

56. Klaus G. Grunert, 'What's in a Steak? A Cross-Cultural Study on the Quality Perception of Beef', MAPP Working Paper 39 (Aarhus: The Aarhus School of Business, 1996).

57. Deborah Ball, Sarah Ellison, Janet Adamy and Geoffrey A. Fowler, 'Recipes without borders? Big food marketers adjust levels of fat and sodium to fit regulations, tastes', *The Wall Street Journal* (18 August 2004): B1.

58. MarketWatch: Global Round-up, 'Organic food and drink: European spend to reach $16 billion in 2007', Datamonitor Report DMCM1079 'Natural and fresh food and drinks' (May 2004) www.datamonitor.com: 37.

59. Lois Rogers, 'Hint of chilli hots up the ice cream market', *The Sunday Times Britain*, TimesOnline (27 March 2005) http://www.timesonline.co.uk/article/0,,2087-1543261,00.html.

60. MarketWatch: Drinks, Datamonitor (April 2003) www.datamonitor.com (related research: Datamonitor Report DMCM0351: The European Soft Drinks Market to 2006).

61. Ariane Bernard, 'New American beachhead in France: Starbucks', *New York Times* (16 January 2004).

62. MarketWatch: Global Round-up: Drinks Market Snapshots: Datamonitor Report DMCM0684, 'People on the move 2003', (March 2004) www.datamonitor.com: 33.

63. MarketWatch: Food Market Snapshots, 'Eating trends: snacking set for 0.7 per cent annual rise in Europe', Datamonitor Report DMCM1086, 'Mealtime behaviors and occasions 2004' (November 2004) www.datamonitor.com: 61.

64. Dominik Nosalik, MarketWatch: Global Round-up: Food Feature Analysis: 'Increase in eating "on-the-go" jeopardizes health', Datamonitor (January 2004) www.datamonitor.com: 62.

65. Lois Rogers, 'We are the waddling snack kings of Europe', *Sunday Times Online* (6 March 2005), http://www.timesonline.co.uk/article?0,,2087-1512641,00.html.

66. Ed Crooks and Simon Briscoe, 'How to be happy', *Financial Times* (27/28 December 2003), http://news.ft.com/servlet/ContentServer?pagename=FT.com/StoryFT/FullStory&c=StoryFT&cid=1071251776881&p=1012571727088.

67. Lizette Alvarez, 'U.S. eating habits, and Europeans, are spreading visibly', *New York Times* (31 October 2003).

68. Mary Douglas, ed., *Constructive Drinking: Perspectives on Drink from Anthropology* (Cambridge: Cambridge University Press, 1987).

69. David Smith and J. Robert Skalnik, 'Changing Patterns in the Consumption of Alcoholic Beverages in Europe and the United States', in Flemming Hansen, ed., *European Advances in Consumer Research* 2 (Provo, UT: Association for Consumer Research, 1995): 343–55.

70. Ibid.

71. Pekka Sulkunen, 'Drinking Patterns and the Level of Alcohol Consumption: An International Overview', in R.J. Gibbins et al., eds, *Research Advances in Alcohol and Drug Problems* 3 (New York: John Wiley, 2000).

72. Euromonitor, *European Marketing Data and Statistics*: 334.

73. Smith and Skalnik, 'Changing Patterns in the Consumption of Alcoholic Beverages in Europe and the United States'.

74. Yves Marbeau, 'Eurodemographics? Nearly there!', *Marketing and Research Today* (March 1992): 47–57.

75. Horst Kern, Hans-Christian Wagner and Roswitha Harris, 'European aspects of a global brand: The BMW case', *Marketing and Research Today* (February 1990): 47–57.

76. Erica Bulman, 'Bigger not always better: size of cars no longer a reflection of social status', FT.COM (3 March 2005), http://search.ft.com/search/article.html?id=050303006359.

77. Matthias D. Kindler, Ellen Day and Mary R. Zimmer, 'A Cross-Cultural Comparison of Magazine Advertising in West Germany and the U.S.', unpublished manuscript, University of Georgia, Athens, 1990.

78. Michael Schroeder, 'Germany – France: Different Advertising Styles – Different Communication Concepts', in W.F. van Raaij and G. Bamossy, eds, *European Advances in Consumer Research* 1 (Provo, UT: Association for Consumer Research, 1993): 77–83.

79. Björn Walliser and Fabienne Moreau, 'Comparaison du style français et allemand de la publicité télévisée', *Cahiers du CESAG* 98 1/11 (1998).

80. Edward T. Hall, *Beyond Culture* (New York: Doubleday, 1976).

81. Hans Heyder, Karl Georg Musiol and Klaus Peters, 'Advertising in Europe – attitudes towards advertising in certain key East and West European countries', *Marketing and Research Today* (March 1992): 58–68.

82. Ullrich Appelbaum and Chris Halliburton, 'How to develop international advertising campaigns that work: The example of the European food and beverage sector', *International Journal of Advertising* 12(3) (1993): 223–41.

83. Marc G. Weinberger and Harlan E. Spotts, 'A situational view of information content in TV advertising in the U.S. and U.K.', *Journal of Marketing* 53 (January 1989): 89–94; see also Abhilasha Mehta, 'Global markets and standardized advertising: Is it happening? An analysis of common brands in USA and UK', in *Proceedings of the 1992 Conference of the American Academy of Advertising* (1992): 170.

84. 'Abroadminded', *Marketing* (24 April 1997): 20–1.

85. Heyder, Musiol and Peters, 'Advertising in Europe'.

86. Wendelin G. Müller, 'Die Standardisierbarkeit internationaler Werbung: Kulturen verlangen Adaptionen', *Marketing ZFP* 3 (3rd Quarter 1996): 179–90.

87. J. Andrew Davison and Erik Grab, 'The contributions of advertising testing to the development of effective international advertising: The KitKat case study', *Marketing and Research Today* (February 1993): 15–24.

88. Douglas B. Holt, Søren Askegaard and Torsten Ringberg, '7Ups and downs: cross cultural differences in the reading profile of advertising' (in press).

89. Eduardo Camargo, 'The Measurement of Meaning: Sherlock Holmes in Pursuit of the Marlboro Man', in Umiker-Sebeok, ed., *Marketing and Semiotics*: 463–83.

90. Cheryl Berman quoted in 'Leo Burnett discovers ads aimed at women fall short on five counts', Leo Burnett Press Release (24 June 2004), http://www.leoburnett.com/news/press_releases/2004/prjul09–13743.asp.

91. Ibid.

92. Source: mmxi Europe, www.mmxieurope.com/data/metrixcentral; Internet Usage in the European Union, 2005, http://www.internetworldstats.com/stats4.htm#eu.

93. Demographic Statistics 1997: Population and Social Conditions Series (Luxembourg: Office for Official Publications of the European Communities, 1997); 'Colour Blind', *Marketing Week* (21 June 1996): 38–40.

94. 'Groninger discotheken verbieden omstreden kleding (Groningen disco forbids controversial clothing), *De Telegraaf* (11 January 2005), http://www2.telegraaf.nl/binnenland/17132161/Groninger_discotheken_verbieden_omstreden_kleding.html.

95. Erik Davis, 'tlhIngan Hol Dajatlh'a' (Do You Speak Klingon?)', *Utne Reader* (March/April 1994): 122–29; additional material provided by personal communication, Prof. Robert V. Kozinets, Northwestern University, October 1997; and adapted from Philip Kotler, Gary Armstrong, Peggy H. Cunningham and Robert Warren, *Principles of Marketing*, 3rd Canadian edn (Scarborough, Ontario: Prentice Hall Canada, 1997): 96.

96. See Frederik Barth, *Ethnic Groups and Boundaries: The Social Organization of Culture Difference* (London: Allen & Unwin, 1969); D. Bell, 'Ethnicity and Social Change', in N. Glazer and D.P. Moynihan, eds, *Ethnicity: Theory and*

Experience (Cambridge, MA: Harvard University Press, 1975): 141–74; D.L. Horowitz, 'Ethnic Identity', in ibid.: 109–40; J. Kotkin, *Tribes* (New York: Random House, 1993); Venkatesh, 'Ethnoconsumerism'; Michel Laroche, Annamma Joy, Michael Hui and Chankon Kim, 'An Examination of Ethnicity Measures: Convergent Validity and Cross-Cultural Equivalence', in Rebecca H. Holman and Michael R. Solomon, eds, *Advances in Consumer Research* 18 (Provo, UT: Association for Consumer Research, 1991): 150–7; Melanie Wallendorf and Michael Reilly, 'Ethnic migration, assimilation, and consumption', *Journal of Consumer Research* 10 (December 1983). 292–302; Milton J. Yinger, 'Ethnicity', *Annual Review of Sociology* 11 (1985): 151–80.

97. Rohit Desphandé and Douglas M. Stayman, 'A tale of two cities: distinctiveness theory and advertising effectiveness', *Journal of Marketing Research* 31 (February 1994): 57–64; Stephen Riggins, 'The Media Imperative: Ethnic Minority Survival in the Age of Mass Communication', in S.H. Riggins, ed., *Ethnic Minority Media: An International Perspective* (London: Sage, 1992): 1–22.

98. Steve Rabin, 'How to sell across cultures', *American Demographics* (March 1994): 56–7.

99. See Lisa Peñaloza, '*Atravesando fronteras*/border crossings: A critical ethnographic exploration of the consumer acculturation of Mexican immigrants', *Journal of Consumer Research* 21(1) (June 1994): 32–54.

100. Gokcen Coskuner and Ozlem Sandikci, 'New Clothing: Meanings and Practices', in Barbara E. Kahn and Mary Frances Luce, eds, *Advances in Consumer Research* 31 (Valdosta, GA: Association for Consumer Research, 2004): 285–90.

101. A. Fuat Firat, 'Consumer Culture or Culture Consumed?', in Costa and Bamossy, eds, *Marketing in a Multicultural World*: 105–25; Michael Laroche, Chankon Kim, Michael K. Hui and Annamma Joy, 'An empirical study of multidimensional ethnic change: The case of the French Canadians in Quebec', *Journal of Cross-Cultural Psychology* 27(1) (January 1996): 114–31.

102. Elizabeth C. Hirschman, 'Religious Affiliation and Consumption Processes: An Initial Paradigm', in *Research in Marketing* (Greenwich, CT: JAI Press, 1983): 131–70.

103. See, for example, Nejet Delener, 'The effects of religious factors on perceived risk in durable goods purchase decisions', *Journal of Consumer Marketing* 7 (Summer 1990): 27–38.

104. 'The Muslims in France: Rejecting their ancestors the Gauls', *The Economist* (16 November 1996): 113–14.

105. Clare Garner, 'Builders answer Islam's growing call to prayer', *The Independent* (4 February 1997): 7.

106. Madeline Bunting, 'Churchgoing bottoms out', *The Guardian* (10 August 1996): 2; 'Catholic Church loses mass appeal', *The Guardian* (30 January 1996): 4; 'België is niet langer katholiek (Belgium is no longer Catholic)', *Trouw* (19 September 1996); Madeline Bunting, 'Revolving door throws doubt on evangelical churches' revival', *The Guardian* (28 August 1996); for a comprehensive website on the world's religions and their populations, see: http://www.adherents.com/Religions_By_Adherents.html.

107. Amy Barrett, 'John Paul II to share stage with marketers', *Wall Street Journal Europe* (19 August 1997): 4; see also www.mix.it/rai/papa.

108. 'Vatican opens boutique outside walls', *Montgomery Advertiser* (10 June 1996): 4A.

109. *Markedsføring* 10 (1996): 22.

110. Leeflang and van Raaij, 'The changing consumer in the European Union: A "Meta-Analysis" '.

111. Massoud Saghafi and Donald Sciglimpaglia, 'Marketing in an Integrated Europe', in M. Bergadaà, ed., *Marketing Today and for the 21st Century* 1 (ESSEC: Proceedings of the 24th EMAC Conference, 1995): 1069–76.

112. Fred van Eenennaam, 'Standardization of International Marketing Processes in a Pan-European Context: Some Research Hypotheses', in Bergadaà, ed., *Marketing Today and for the 21st Century* 2: 1221–41.

113. Vern Terpstra and Kenneth David, *The Cultural Environment of International Business*, 2nd edn (Cincinnati: Southwestern, 1985).

114. André Tordjman, 'European Retailing: Convergences, Differences, and Perspectives', in P.J. McGoldrick and G. Davies, eds, *International Retailing: Trends and Strategies* (London: Pitman, 1995): 17–50.

115. 'Abroadminded'.

116. Bernard Dubois and Gilles Laurent, 'Is There a Euroconsumer for Luxury Goods?', in van Raaij and Bamossy, eds, *European Advances in Consumer Research* 1: 58–69.

117. Susan P. Douglas and C. Samuel Craig, 'The changing dynamic of consumer behavior: Implications for cross-cultural research', *International Journal of Research in Marketing* 14 (1997): 379–95.

118. Sophie Arie, 'Supper is off: Milan bans Da Vinci parody', *The Guardian* (4 February 2005): 15.

119. Claudia Penteado, 'Brazilian ad irks Church', *Advertising Age* (23 March 2000): 11.

NEW TIMES, NEW CONSUMERS

Six weeks before St Valentine's Day, called Lovers' Day in Turkey, Ayşe starts planning for that special romantic evening. She remembers that last year she and her husband could not find a table in any restaurant in Ankara, all hotels and restaurants had been fully booked and florists had run out of red roses. So she acts early and makes a reservation for two at a good restaurant. She starts window shopping for a gift that she would like to receive. She sees a St Valentine's Day Swatch that she really likes. Two weeks before Lovers' Day she starts asking her husband what he is thinking of getting her. She takes him to the shopping centre and shows him the St Valentine's Day Swatch and tells him that she'd like that *very* much. On Lovers' Day Ayşe's husband remembers that he has not yet bought anything, goes to get the St Valentine's Day Swatch – only to discover that the shop has run out of them. Instead he buys a much more expensive Swatch. When he comes home, he finds his wife, dressed up ready to go out for dinner. Excited, she closes her eyes and puts her arm forward, confident that he will put a watch around her wrist. And he does. But when she opens her eyes and sees that it is not the St Valentine's Day Swatch, she is upset – and furious. She bursts into tears; they have an argument; and Ayşe goes to the bedroom and takes off her nice clothes. They spend the evening at home, in separate rooms, not talking to each other. Some Lovers' Day, she thinks.

Later, Ayşe tells the story to her friends, some of whom think it's very funny . . .

GÜLIZ GER, Bilkent University, Ankara

■ INTRODUCTION

The opening vignette illustrates one of the processes related to changes in consumer societies that are discussed in this chapter, globalization. Lovers' Day started to be celebrated in Turkey about a decade ago, first by exchanging cards among school friends. It has become more widespread in the last few years, mostly among the urban middle class who now exchange gifts and make a special evening of it. St Valentine's Day, appropriated as Lovers' Day, is taking root among married and unmarried couples in this Muslim country where traditional norms of respectability did not allow dating – dating is not what 'nice' girls were supposed to do, and many from conservative or lower-middle-class families still frown on it. As well as globalization, we will take a closer look at two other tendencies that may be profoundly changing the way we consume and behave in the marketplace, namely environmentalism and political consumption on the one hand and postmodernism on the other.

■ ENVIRONMENTALISM: SAVING THE PLANET WITH A SHOPPING BASKET

The environmental issue has gained a lot of momentum in recent years. The environmental concerns of the general public endure in spite of a certain backlash and disbelief in the flourishing 'green marketing' strategies in the 1990s.[1] There is a growing awareness that rather short-sighted lifestyles in all parts of the world lead to the depletion of energy sources, pollution, deterioration of soil fertility, reductions in biodiversity and climate change. One example has been the exponential growth of cheap flights in Europe, which have changed patterns of travelling and patterns of consumption – but are also provoking an increasingly lively debate about the environmental costs involved (see more details regarding the consumer concerns around these cheap flights in Chapter 16). And there is also an awareness that consumption patterns play a direct or an indirect role in all of these problems.[2]

Furthermore, there is a growing awareness that a 'greener consumer society' need not be one of joylessness and abstention and need not be in total opposition to the current system of production and marketing. The fashion clothing manufacturer EDUN, launched by, among others, U2's Bono, positions itself as a fashion clothing line promoting respect for the people who make its products, the place where those people work, the materials used, and the consumer – all of EDUN's retail outlets are on the high end, with a lifestyle orientation that matches up with EDUN's intended image of fairness, thoughtfulness and the total environment.[3] But it all started some decades ago with the encouragement to recycle . . .

Recycling

▶ The issue of product disposition and recycling is doubly vital because of its enormous public policy implications. We live in a throwaway society, which creates problems for the environment and also results in a great deal of unfortunate waste. Training consumers to recycle has become a priority in many countries. Japan recycles about 40 per cent of its waste, and this relatively high rate of compliance is partly due to the social value the Japanese place on recycling: citizens are encouraged by waste disposal lorries which periodically rumble through the streets playing classical music or children's songs.[4] In Europe in 1999 a network was established in Vienna to provide a repair and service centre. This network has grown to include 43 companies which now repair everything from leather gloves to dishwashers. During 2004, 73,000 items were repaired for over 4,400 customers.[5] Companies continue to search for ways to use resources more efficiently, often at the prompting of activist consumer groups. For example, McDonald's restaurants bowed to pressure by eliminating the use of styrofoam packages, and its outlets in Europe experimented with edible breakfast dishes made of maize.[6] Even in China, the waste problem is taken more seriously, as hundreds of restaurants have started washing and recycling chopsticks, and the government is planning to put a tax on disposable chopsticks.[7]

Several studies have examined the relevant goals consumers have to recycle. One used a means–end chain analysis of the type described in Chapter 4 to identify how specific instrumental goals are linked to more abstract terminal values. The most important lower-order goals identified were: 'avoid filling up landfills', 'reduce waste', 'reuse materials' and 'save the environment'. These were linked to the terminal values of: 'promote health/avoid sickness', 'achieve life-sustaining ends' and 'provide for future generations'. Another study reported that the perceived effort involved in recycling was the best predictor of whether people would go to the trouble – this pragmatic dimension outweighed general attitudes towards recycling and the environment in predicting intention to recycle.[8] Yet another (European) study concluded, among other things, that one major motivating factor for recycling was a high perceived effectiveness of the action, that is, whether the consumer thinks it makes a difference if he or she recycles.[9] By applying such techniques to the study of recycling and other product disposal behaviours, it will be easier for social marketers to design advertising copy and other messages that tap into the underlying values that will motivate people to increase environmentally responsible behaviour.[10]

Even taking into account the difficulties in measurement, statistics reveal that the production of waste differs enormously among the countries of Europe. In the late 1980s, the yearly municipal solid waste per capita in western European countries ranged from 231 kg in Portugal to 608 kg in Finland. As a comparison, the corresponding figure in the United States was 864 kg. The different levels of waste generation are due to differences in general income level and to differences in consumption styles.[11]

Waste management also differs among countries. Different types of recycling programmes in Denmark encourage people to cut down on household waste and recycle as much as possible, as the municipal waste management systems charge consumers according to weight or volume of the household waste.[12] The Danish model of waste management, which stresses local responsibility for source separation programmes, is now marketed globally through onsite visits and video cassettes.[13] In Germany, producers are required by law to be responsible for the redistribution and recycling of used products.[14] In addition to recycling, other disposal programmes have caught the authorities' interest. In several European countries, including Spain, Italy, France and Denmark, economic incentives have been offered by the state to encourage car owners to replace their old car with a newer one, in order to reduce air pollution and increase road safety.[15] The advent of the expanded European Community in January 2004 saw the introduction of a European Union Directive WEEE: Directive on Waste Electrical and Electronic Equipment, alongside the initiative ROHS (Reduction of use of certain hazardous substances), due to come into force in January 2006. 'These directives seek to set in place the means by which companies recycle electrical and electronic products and to eliminate the uses of some toxic materials . . . a major concern is to reduce the release of toxic materials into the environment during product disposal; some of the routes include leaching into watercourses, if products are dumped, or into the atmosphere, if assemblies are incinerated . . . companies that have carefully studied design for dismantling have reported that the insights they've gained can lead to substantial economies in manufacturing'.[16] Graham Prophet goes on to examine the importance of brand image: 'in the fiercely competitive world of consumer product sales, it is one more battleground where the right image might give you an edge'.[17] Showing environmental responsibility and sustainability as integral to the production and sales of goods could add an important

This ad recalls the refrain from a song 'Ten green bottles' to emphasize its message about recycling bottles and glass.
Corbis/Mike R. Whittle; Ecoscene

dimension to the brand image of products and services, and thus influence consumer attitudes, especially amongst the younger generation of consumers.

Recycling has proved to be only the beginning of a more profound process, taking into consideration not only recyclability but also environmental issues connected to the production process. Concern for the environment, or **environmentalism**, is no longer confined to recycling but applies to all aspects of the production and consumption processes and is affecting marketing strategies for products ranging from nappies to fast food. For example, Ecover, a highly environmentally conscious Belgian producer of detergents and cleaning products, appealed to consumers' environmental concerns in a tongue-in-cheek way by recycling its competitors' old TV commercials. The company used five black-and-white commercials from the 1950s and superimposed a colour picture of its brand over the competing brand while a voice-over explained that the old commercial had been recycled.[18] It has been argued that environmental concern is gradually becoming a new universal value, not in its militant form but as a more tacit precondition for the degree of acceptability of products.[19] One commentator expressed it in a paradox: 'Environmentalism means that we will no longer have ecological milk. We will have milk and industrial milk.' This might also lead to more sensitivity towards various kinds of natural products and products from smaller, independent producers. Different consumer groups are thus increasing pressure on producers to demonstrate that they are producing in such a way as to preserve nature and resources rather than exploit them.

Certain retail chains in Europe have been pioneering environmentally friendly policies. Migros, the largest Swiss retail chain, has cut down on packaging material, increased its use of train transportation, and introduced various forms of non-toxic, well-insulated stores to cut energy consumption, etc. Tengelmann of Germany (chlorine-free products, milk-dispensing machines for recyclable milk containers), Otto, the world's largest mail-order company (environmental friendliness as corporate culture, collaborations with the Worldwide Fund for Nature), Sainsbury's (recycled plastic bags, a 'Penny Back Scheme' donating refunded pennies to charity), Tesco (comprehensive labelling, healthy eating programme and organically grown produce) and Co-op of the UK are among the pion-eering retailers for environmental issues.[20]

There are obvious differences among various European countries concerning the role of environmentalism. It is a politically more important issue in such countries as Germany, Denmark and Sweden. A study of the relative importance of environmental concern in car purchases ranked Germany first, followed by the UK, France and Spain.[21]

Environmentalist attitudes and behaviours have proved hard to predict. Some have argued that the trend is waning since an organization such as Greenpeace has experi-enced a decline in membership. Others have concluded that while attitudes are 'green', actual behaviour is less likely to change. This was the conclusion of one 1991 study of Danish consumers.[22] Since then, the demand for ecological produce in the dairy, egg and vegetable sectors has exploded, in Denmark as in many other countries. One major indication that environmentalism is becoming a (more or less) global value and is not just a passing fad is the role that concern for the environment plays in youth-oriented media such as MTV and, not least, in school curricula.[23]

Many consumer studies have tried to establish a distinct value profile for environmentally-oriented consumers,[24] discussing, for example, whether they are more individually or socially oriented.[25] Values such as 'close relationships to others' and 'social justice' have been identified as being associated with a higher degree of environ-mentally conscious attitudes and behaviour.[26]

An environmentally related issue such as the use of growth hormones in milk and beef is a major problem in trade negotiations between Europe and the United States. Some argue by references to scientific data stating that there is no risk,[27] but others maintain that it is a matter of production and consumption ethics more than of actual risks to consumers.

The debate over the risks concerning growth hormones in beef has been over-shadowed by the problems relating to the spreading of BSE (or Mad Cow Disease) which created a general distrust of British beef when the disease was first detected in 1996, both in Britain and abroad.[28] Since then, the disease has spread to other European countries, creating a virtual consumer flight from beef in certain countries, notably Germany and Italy (where sales dropped 30 per cent nationwide).[29] Even in Sweden, where no cases of BSE have been detected, 41 per cent of consumers have become doubtful whether they should eat beef and 11 per cent have begun to eat less. Two per cent stopped eating beef altogether.[30] The latest food scare in the UK involved an illegal cancer-causing dye, Sudan 1. Adulterated chilli powder was imported from Asia, and used in the production of Worcestershire sauce, which was subsequently added to a range of products so that there were over 30 contaminated foods which were then re-exported across Europe (e.g. to Malta, Spain, Greece, Italy, Austria, Switzerland, France, Belgium, the Netherlands and Denmark) and to American markets (such as, the USA, Canada, Bermuda, Bahamas, Antigua and Grenada).[31] Such food scares have led to a growing distrust in modern industrial production methods, especially within the food industry, following the logic expressed by many consumers that 'when you make the poor cows into cannibals just for profitability, things are bound to go wrong'.

marketing pitfall

National news: product recalls rise sharply

'A sharp rise in recalls of dangerous or faulty products - dramatically illustrated by last month's Sudan 1 dye alert which sparked Britain's most sweeping food recall - is hitting businesses across Europe.

The number of recalls has increased by 175 per cent in a year following the introduction of a European Union product safety directive, according to PwC, the professional services firm. It expects this expensive trend to continue and predicts a rise in insurance claims filed as a result.

Premier Foods, WM Morrison, Boots, Mitsubishi Motors and Coca-Cola have all been involved in high-profile recalls.

The advertising costs alone of pulling a single product line are estimated at £100,000 by the CBI. The total bill can top seven figures and demands for compensation can pass down the supply chain from retailers to wholesalers to manufacturers and their suppliers.

Toys, skincare products, food-making equipment and garden sheds were among items withdrawn in EU states during the year to February 2005 surveyed by PwC. Some 373 product recalls were reported in total. Recalls occurred at the rate of 11 a week in February, compared with four in the same month in 2004.

Most products were pulled on regulators' orders in member states rather than voluntarily by companies. The EU directive is designed to improve consumer protection and increase transparency in the reporting of recalls.

As part of its implementation of the EU directive, however, the government also plans to move from the current voluntary system on withdrawal to one where, as a last resort, companies could be forced to pull products.

Companies will also be compelled to keep more information on product origins and any customer complaints, and to notify enforcement bodies if problems arise.

Businesses continuing to sell unsafe products would be liable to fines and directors to prison sentences.

The regulations will cover second-hand and antique products as well as products provided as part of a service, such as children's high-chairs used in restaurants. The CBI is generally supportive of the changes but believes that businesses should not have to pay enforcement costs in all cases, including if alerts prove unfounded.

It said: 'We believe this is inequitable and the general rule that the loser pays should apply' The employers' body also wants to see a central notification body for product recalls. For UK companies trading in several EU states, there is the issue of ensuring that regulators in different countries have been made aware of any recalls.

Businesses have until the end of the month to lobby the Department of Trade and Industry about the new rules.

Experts warn that there appear to be inconsistencies in how different countries report recalls. Large markets such as Italy and the Netherlands do not appear in PwC's top 10 of most active recallers, which is headed by Hungary and Spain. The UK was seventh.

Graeme Berry, a director at PwC, said it was too early to identify clear national differences but forecast a rise in companies trying to protect themselves.

Companies can take out liability policies against claims for damage or injury to people or property resulting from faulty, dangerous or contaminated products. There is a further market in insurance designed to cover the costs of operational recalls ranging from publicity to supply chain investigation, destruction of faulty stock, lost profits or the marketing needed to offset damage to the company's brand.

Mr Berry said: 'Recall insurance is a product that will feature much more commonly in the future as general understanding of the risks, and general appetite among underwriters, increases.'

Although recalls are most common in children's, food and drugs sectors, they have also hit industrial suppliers.'[32]

▶ It has been suggested that we live in a **risk society**, where our ways of producing goods are increasingly producing just as many and even more 'bads' or risks,[33] risks that the consumer will have to take into account in his or her decision-making. Another field where such unknown risks have made consumers sceptical about the benefits suggested to them by the industry is that of genetically manipulated organisms (GMO). One fear

The advertising emphasizes the organic nature of Sunsweet's range of juices, using 'organic' both as a name for the product range and also including references to organic in the advertising copy.

The Advertising Archives

expressed by consumers in a study of acceptance or rejection of GMO foods in Sweden and Denmark was of too great a concentration of power in a few giant corporations dominating both research and industry.[34] Thus, what is at stake on the consumer level, disregarding the international economic interests involved, seems to be the confrontation of an economic vs. a moral logic.

Similar results were found for several European countries in a cross-national study. Testing consumer attitudes and purchase intentions regarding GMO foods, it was concluded that an overall rejection of the technology as such was found in Denmark, Germany, Great Britain and Italy, although a slightly less negative attitude was found in Italy (mainly because consumers said that they knew less about GMO).[35] In connection with this study, various types of information material were also tested, some more informational, some more emotional, in order to estimate the potential of informational campaigns in changing negative attitudes. But whatever information was given to the consumers, it only made their attitude *more* negative. Thus, any cue that reminded the consumers about the fact that the product contained or had used GMO in the production process immediately turned the consumers against the product even if the cues were positive, something which points to the deep-seated nature of this scepticism among European consumers. The introduction of the European wide General Products Safety Directive[36] has helped to heighten European consumers' awareness of product safety generally, and has established standards and policies to protect consumer health and safety.[37]

Corporate social responsibility

Parallel to changing consumer attitudes towards environmentalism and sustainability can be traced changing attitudes among companies and businesses as they recognize the changing nature of their customer. **Corporate social responsibility (CSR)** has become increasingly prominent in companies' provision of and stakeholders' approaches to buying goods and services. CSR addresses two kinds of commercial responsibility: 'commercial responsibilities (that is running their businesses successfully) and social responsibilities (that is their role in society and the community)'.[38] CSR Europe, established in 1995 by the then EC president, Jacques Delors 'is the leading European business network for corporate social responsibility with over 60 leading multinational corporations as members . . . [committed to helping] companies integrate CSR into the way they do business every day'.[39] CSR Europe commissioned MORI (Market and Opinion Research International) to undertake the first ever European survey of consumers' attitudes towards CSR in September 2000. Twelve thousand participants were interviewed across 12 European countries (Belgium, Denmark, France, Finland, Germany, Great Britain, Italy, Netherlands, Portugal, Spain, Sweden and Switzerland): '70% of European consumers say that a company's commitment to corporate social responsibility is important when buying a product or service, and 1 in 5 would be very willing to pay more for products that are socially environmentally responsible. . . . The research strongly implies – in line with previous studies – that the public's key priority for companies is a demonstration of corporate citizenship [e.g. quality and service; human health and safety; being open and honest] rather than just charitable or community giving.'[40] In turn the study also identified 'the active conscious consumer' or 'socially responsible activists' (SR activists) who were defined 'as those people how have participated in 5 or more socially responsible activities in the last twelve months. Across Europe more than a quarter are activists. In Switzerland, Sweden and Belgium the proportion rises to two in five. In contrast, only around one in ten could be classified in this way in Germany, France, Portugal and Italy. The top ranking activities across Europe are recycling household waste, followed by giving money to good causes. Each has been done by more than half the public in the last twelve months. Around two in five have also bought a product or service because of its links with good causes, or a product labeled as social, ethical or environmental. Similar proportions have bought organic food and given voluntary help to a good cause.'[41]

The political consumer

The discussion above points to an increasing awareness of the political and moral consequences of consumption choices among many consumers. This means that the green consumer is gradually being followed by, or perhaps is turning into, the **political consumer**.[42] The political consumer uses his or her buying pattern as a weapon against companies he or she doesn't like and in support of the companies that reflect values similar to the consumer's own. This consumer type selects products according to the company's ethical behaviour, which includes respect for human rights, animal protection, environmental friendliness and support for various benevolent causes. The political consumer is supported by such agencies as the Vancouver-based Adbusters,[43] which engages in twisting campaigns from major companies that, for some reason, have come under their spotlight for immoral or harmful behaviour. For example, they made a spoof on the well-known Coca-Cola polar bear campaign by depicting a family of bears on a tiny ice floe, with the sign 'Enjoy Climate Change' written in that well-known type from the Coca-Cola logo, thereby protesting against the company's use of ozone-harming gases in its vending machines.[44] This kind of 'peaceful' rebelliousness against what is seen as control over our minds and imagination by major companies is called *culture*

This Adbusters campaign against exploitation of cheap labour in Indonesia highlights the role of the major corporation, Nike, and uses its logo and line 'to be all you can be' to create individual awareness of the global impact of big corporations (and individual consumer choice of running shoe) on newly emerging economies and their labour forces.

Courtesy of www.adbusters.org

jamming.[45] Vigilante marketing is also emerging where new ads and ideas for campaigns appear without either client or agency involvement. These are often generated by free-lances, fans or agencies looking for work.[46]

Not all companies are on the defensive, though. Companies such as The Body Shop are founded on the idea of natural and non-animal-tested products and a maximum of environmental concern. But their concerns are becoming directed towards a broader array of social values. They took up the debate over beauty ideals by introducing 'Ruby', a Barbie lookalike doll but one with considerably rounder forms, in order to fight the tyranny of thinness and the impossible body ideal of the supermodels which are also endorsed by Barbie's shape. The reaction was predictable: Mattel Inc., the producers of Barbie, took out an injunction against The Body Shop because Ruby's face was too like Barbie's.

Many other companies are now working proactively to avoid the sort of trouble Shell ran into in Denmark, the Netherlands and Germany with the Brent Spar case,[47] or the difficulties French exporters experienced in the wake of nuclear testing in 1996. Just to mention a few cases, the mineral water company Ramlösa, together with the Red Cross in Scandinavia, campaigned for clean water acts in the Third World under the slogan 'Water for Life',[48] and British Telecom ran a campaign underlining its work for elderly and disabled people.[49] The two brewery giants Heineken and Carlsberg both withdrew plans for large-scale investments in Myanmar (Burma) after consumers' protests against what was seen as direct support for the repressive military government there.

There is a risk that the political consumer may become an even more moralizing, polit-ically correct consumer, as has occurred in the political and cultural climate of the United

There are **3 billion** women who **don't** look like **supermodels** and **only 8** who **do.**

The Body Shop's Ruby, a Barbie lookalike doll but with considerably rounder forms, introduced in order to fight the tyranny of thinness and impossible body ideal of the supermodels which are reinforced by Barbie's shape.

The Advertising Archives

States. In fact, some British consumer groups have taken action against the companies that screened commercials during the TV broadcast of the controversial film *The Last Temptation of Christ*.[50] The question is: where is the dividing line between morality and moralizing?

Consumer boycotts

As we have seen, we live in a period when many consumers are becoming increasingly aware that their consumption pattern is part of a global political and economic system, to the extent that they become political consumers. Sometimes a negative experience can trigger an organized and devastating response, as when a consumer group organizes a *boycott* of a company's products. These efforts can include protests against everything from investing in a politically undesirable country (as when Carlsberg withdrew their investments from Myanmar, as mentioned above, or when Shell was accused of tolerating pollution and political repression of the people of the Ogoni region of Nigeria) to efforts to discourage consumption of products from certain companies or countries (as during the boycott of French wines and other products during the nuclear testing in the Pacific in 1996, an action which was especially strongly felt in the Netherlands and in the Scandinavian countries). In the United States, the inclusion of obscene or inflammatory song lyrics have led to boycott threats, as when law enforcement organizations threatened to boycott Time Warner after it distributed a rap song by Ice-T entitled 'Cop Killer'.

Boycotts are not always effective – studies show that normally only a limited percentage of a country's consumers participate in them. However, those who do are disproportionately vocal and well educated, so they are a group companies especially don't want to alienate. The negative PR that arises from media coverage of the boycott may be problematic for the company in the long run, since competitors may gain relative advantages. After the boycott of French wines in Denmark had calmed down, French wines had lost 20 per cent of the market share. However, that was not seen as the biggest problem, since the general impression was that consumers could be persuaded to switch back to French wines. But many supermarket shelves had been reorganized in order to give more space to Italian and Spanish wines, and this was considered a more serious problem.[51]

One increasingly popular solution used by marketers is to set up a joint task force with the boycotting organization to try to iron out the problem. In the United States, McDonald's used this approach with the Environmental Defense Fund, which was concerned about its use of such things as polystyrene containers, bleached paper and antibiotics in food. The company agreed to test a composting programme, to switch to plain brown bags and to eliminate the use of antibiotics in such products as poultry.[52]

Lately, much of consumers' political resistance to the behaviour of companies and marketers has been related to the processes of globalization. The global marketplace has been accused of being based on unfair trade principles and of eroding cultural and social patterns around the world, favouring the rich countries and cultures of the western world at the expense of the rest of the world's populations and cultures. Demonstrations at the gatherings of the World Trade Organization have attracted much media attention, as has the action led by a French cheese producer against the construction of a McDonald's restaurant in his home town in southern France. The target was not so much McDonald's per se as the processes it represents, sometimes called *McDonaldization*,[53] the cultural erosion and the withering of quality standards for cheap, large-scale production. Consequently, the activists behind this formed an organization the name of which translates into something like 'farmers against lousy food'.[54] This and other organizations, like ATTAC, questioning the benefits of what they perceive as an uncontrolled global market, have enjoyed considerable success recently. Hence, we will take a closer look at some aspects of globalization, consumption and marketing.

■ GLOBAL MARKETING AND CULTURE

Learning about the practices of other cultures is more than just interesting – it is an essential task for any company that wishes to expand its horizons and become part of the international or global marketplace at the beginning of the new millennium. In this section, we'll consider some of the issues confronting marketers who seek to use a global marketing approach. We'll also consider the consequences of the 'Americanization' or 'Westernization' of global culture, as marketers continue to export Western popular culture to a globe of increasingly affluent consumers, many of whom are eagerly waiting to replace their traditional products and practices with the offerings of Benetton, Levi's, McDonald's, Nestlé and Unilever.

Think globally, act locally

As corporations increasingly find themselves competing in many markets around the world, the debate has intensified regarding the necessity of developing separate marketing plans for each culture. A lively debate has ensued regarding the need to 'fit in' to the local culture. Let's briefly consider each viewpoint.

Adopting a standardized strategy

Proponents of a standardized marketing strategy argue that many cultures, especially those of relatively industrialized countries, have become so homogenized that the same approach will work throughout the world. By developing one approach for multiple markets, a company can benefit from economies of scale, since it does not have to incur the substantial time and expense of developing a separate strategy for each culture.[55] This viewpoint represents an **etic perspective**, which focuses on commonalities across cultures. An etic approach to a culture is objective and analytical: it reflects impressions of a culture as viewed by outsiders, which assume that there are common, general categories and measurements which are valid for all cultures under consideration.

This advert for HSBC illustrates how a global company uses a local message to signify its relevance to the consumer marketplace in different countries.

The Advertising Archives

Adopting a localized strategy

▶ On the other hand, many marketers choose to study and analyse a culture using an **emic perspective**, which focuses on variations within a culture. This approach assumes that each culture is unique, with its own value system, conventions and regulations. This per-
▶ spective argues that each country has a **national character**, a distinctive set of behaviour and personality characteristics.[56] An effective strategy must be tailored to the sensibilities and needs of each specific culture. An emic approach to a culture is subjective and experiential: it attempts to explain a culture as it is experienced by insiders.

Given the sizeable variations in tastes within a relatively homogeneous country like the United States, it is hardly surprising that people around the world have developed their own preferences. Unlike Americans, for example, Europeans favour plain chocolate over milk chocolate, which they regard as suitable only for children. Whisky is considered a 'classy' drink in France and Italy, but not in England. Crocodile bags are popular in Asia and Europe, but not in the United States. Americans' favourite tie colours are red and blue, while the Japanese prefer olive, brown and bronze. Even global brands are perceived differently across markets. In the Netherlands and the UK, Heineken beer is positioned (and perceived) as a middle-priced, mainstream beer, while in the United States and the rest of Europe it is perceived (and priced) as a premium beer. Alternatively, Budweiser beer (the American brand, not the original Czech brand) has a very middle-priced and mainstream position in the United States, yet is a premium-priced beer in Europe and South America.[57]

Superstitions and cultural sensitivities

Marketers must be aware of a culture's norms regarding such sensitive topics as taboos and sexuality. For example, the Japanese are superstitious about the number four. *Shi*, the Japanese word for four, also means death. For this reason, in Japan Tiffany sells glassware and china in sets of five.

The consequences of ignoring these issues became evident during the 1994 soccer World Cup, when both McDonald's and Coca-Cola made the mistake of reprinting the Saudi Arabian flag, which includes sacred words from the Koran, on disposable packaging used in promotions. Despite their delight at having a Saudi team in contention for the cup, and the satisfaction with Coca-Cola sponsoring the team, Muslims around the world protested at this borrowing of sacred imagery, and both companies had to scramble to rectify the situation.[58]

Cultures vary sharply in the degree to which references to sex and bodily functions are permitted. Many American consumers would blush at much European advertising, where sexuality is much more explicit. This dimension is particularly interesting in Japan, which is a culture of contradictions. On the one hand, the Japanese are publicly shy and polite. On the other hand, sexuality plays a significant role in this society. *Manga*, the extremely popular Japanese comic books which comprise a billion-dollar industry, stress themes of sex and violence. Nudity is quite commonplace in Japanese advertising and general media.[59]

In contrast, a controversy in India illustrates problems that can arise in a more conservative culture. The government-run television network rejected a spot for KamaSutra condoms which showed a couple sitting on a bed playing chess. As the woman sweeps the pieces off the board, she mouths the word 'Check' while he mouths the word 'Mate'. The tagline reads, 'For the pleasure of making love'.[60]

marketing opportunity

Let's talk about (selling) sex

'Sex is big business. Yet, oddly enough, the companies whose business is founded on the sexual activities of ordinary people know very little about what goes on in the bedroom. Certain facts which companies in other industries take for granted – such as the size of the market, product trends, market dynamics – are not available to companies that operate in and around the sex business.

Since Alfred Kinsey's work about sexual behaviour contributed to the sexual revolution that took place in the 1950s and 1960s, there would appear to be – at least in the west – a second sexual revolution. Sex has always been a good way for companies to sell their products, whether these are cars or clothing. Yet now a host of companies that trade on sex in some way – from high-street retailers to drugs companies – are experiencing a dramatic growth in their business.

For example, the women's lingerie market is now estimated to be worth $30 bn a year, according to just-style.com, a leading research company. Euromonitor, another research group, estimates that the US market for women's underwear is worth $11 bn.

The subject of sex remains controversial, however. Only last year, Boots, the UK's high street chemist, reversed its initial plan to stock sex aids such as vibrators on its shelves.

Companies and other interested groups have endeavoured to fill the knowledge gap about sexual behaviour. But, here again, the research has been skewed to address particular interests. For example, pharmaceutical companies have invested huge sums in the development of drugs for tackling sexual malfunction and disease. Bringing Viagra to market is thought to have cost Pfizer between $500 m and $1 bn in research and development, typical of the cost of launching a new drug – a sum that is far greater than that spent on conventional sex research. All told, it means that the picture of people's sexual behaviour remains an unfinished jigsaw puzzle. It also means that the business opportunities – together with any wider social, health and emotional consequences – will be harder to establish.

Given the remarkable paucity of evidence about people's sexual behaviour, it would appear that corporate strategy is based more on guess work than hard facts. As yet this does not seem to have impeded the development of companies that put sex at the core of their business. Many, indeed, are fast becoming mainstream.

Beate Uhse, Europe's only quoted retailer of sex products, which is based in Germany, has 200 sex shops in nine countries. Last year it saw sales rise by 30 per cent – having opened outlets at motorway service stations.

Ann Summers, the UK's leading "passion and fashion" retailer, has 110 high street stores, together with other outlets in Ireland and Spain. SSL, the manufacturer of the Durex condom range and other sex aids, has seen sales of its market-leading contraceptives rise steadily in recent years.

Meanwhile, Marks & Spencer, a traditional provider of underwear to Britain's middle classes, now stocks the clothing of Agent Provocateur, a lingerie company.

In the pharmaceutical industry, companies such as Pfizer, Lilly and Bayer have found new business opportunities by devising drugs that deal not only with disease but also dysfunction. This year, sales of drugs such as Viagra and Cialis, which deal with erectile dysfunction, are expected to be around $2.25 bn, having quadrupled in the past seven years, according to Datamonitor, a consultancy.'[61]

Does global marketing work?

So, after briefly considering some of the many differences one encounters across cultures globally, the often voiced question still remains: does global marketing work? Given the growth of global brands and global marketing strategies over the past few decades, the practical answer has to be 'yes'. But this doesn't add much in terms of insights for managers. Perhaps the more appropriate question is, *when* and *why* does it work?

Although the argument for a homogeneous world culture is appealing in principle, in practice it has met with mixed results. We have discussed how one reason for the difficulties of using a global marketing approach is that consumers in different countries have different conventions and customs, which may mean that they simply do not use products in the same way. Kellogg's, for example, discovered that in Brazil big breakfasts are not traditional – cereal is more commonly eaten as a dry snack.

Some large corporations, such as Coca-Cola, have been successful in crafting a single, international image. Still, even Coca-Cola must make minor modifications to the way it presents itself in each culture. Although Coke commercials are largely standardized, local agencies are permitted to edit them to highlight close-ups of local faces.[62] Says one executive: 'Coca-Cola is a *multi-local* company.'[63]

Starbucks represents another major US corporation which has exported its imagery abroad. A recent study examined 'consumers' experiences of glocalization and global brands' hegemonic influences upon local markets as well as consumer tastes and practices within the context of the Starbucks brandscape'.[64] The authors argued that Starbucks represented an example of a **hegemonic brandscape**, i.e. 'a cultural system of service-scapes that are linked together and structured by discursive, symbolic and competitive relationships to a dominant (market driving) experiential brand'.[65]

As the world's borders seem to shrink due to advances in communications, many companies continue to develop global advertising campaigns. In some cases they are encountering obstacles to acceptance, especially in less-developed countries or in those areas, such as central and eastern Europe, that are only just beginning to embrace Western-style materialism as a way of life.[66]

To maximize the chances of success for these multicultural efforts, marketers must locate consumers in different countries who nonetheless share a common worldview. This is more likely to be the case among people whose frame of reference is relatively more international or cosmopolitan, and/or who receive much of their information about the world from sources that incorporate a worldwide perspective.

Who is likely to fall into this category? The same two segments that were candidates for pan-European marketing: (1) affluent people who are 'global citizens' and who are exposed to ideas from around the world through their travels, business contacts and media experiences, and as a result share common tastes. For example, one study when it was carried out found that, with the exceptions of musical taste and food consumption, the new elite in Zimbabwe to a high degree emulated the consumption tastes and styles of the UK and the USA;[67] (2) young people whose tastes in music and fashion are strongly influenced by international pop culture broadcasting many of the same images and sounds to multiple countries.[68]

marketing pitfall

The language barrier is one problem confronting marketers who wish to break into foreign markets. One technique that is used to avoid this problem is where a translated ad is retranslated into the original language by a different interpreter to catch errors. Some specific translation obstacles that have been encountered around the world include the following:[69]

- Wrigley's Spearmint Gum reads as 'Shark's sperm' in some east European countries.
- When Vauxhall launched its Nova model in Spain, it realized that the name meant 'doesn't go' in Spanish.
- Also in Spain, Mitsubishi discovered that its four-wheel-drive model Pajero would be known as 'Wanker'.
- When Rolls-Royce introduced its Silver Mist model in Germany, it found that the word 'mist' is translated as 'excrement'. Similarly, Sunbeam's hair curling iron, called the Mist-Stick, translated as 'manure wand'. To add insult to injury, Vicks is German slang for sexual intercourse, so that the company's name had to be changed to Wicks in this market.

The Coca-Cola invasion: exporting Western lifestyles

The allure of western consumer culture has spread throughout the world, as people in other societies slowly but surely fall under the spell of far-reaching advertising campaigns, contact with tourists and the desire to form attachments with other parts of the world. This attraction sometimes results in bizarre permutations of products and services, as they are modified to be compatible with local customs. Consider these events:[70]

- In Peru, Indian boys can be found carrying rocks painted to look like transistor radios.
- In Papua New Guinea, some tribesmen put Chivas Regal wrappers on their drums and wear Pentel pens through their noses, instead of traditional nose bones.
- Bana tribesmen in the remote highlands of Kako, Ethiopia, pay to watch *Pluto the Circus Dog* on a Viewmaster.
- When a Swazi princess marries a Zulu king, she wears red touraco wing feathers around her forehead and a cape of windowbird feathers and oxtails. He is wrapped in a leopard skin. All is recorded on a Kodak movie camera while the band plays 'The Sound of Music'.
- In addition to traditional gifts of cloth, food and cosmetics, Nigerian Hausa brides receive cheap quartz watches although they cannot tell the time.

'I'd like to buy the world a Coke'

As indicated by these examples, many formerly isolated cultures now incorporate Western objects into their traditional practices. In the process, the meanings of these objects are transformed and adapted to local tastes (at times in seemingly bizarre ways). Sometimes the process enriches local cultures, sometimes it produces painful stresses and strains the local fabric.

The West (and especially the United States) is a *net exporter* of popular culture. Western symbols in the form of images, words and products have diffused throughout

As this Swedish ad for Wrangler jeans shows, products associated with the 'authentic' American West are in demand around the world.
The Advertising Archives

the world. This influence is eagerly sought by many consumers, who have learned to equate Western lifestyles in general and the English language in particular with modernization and sophistication. As a result, people around the world are being exposed to a blizzard of Western products that are attempting to become part of local lifestyles.

For example, American-inspired TV game shows are popular around the world: *Geh Aufs Ganze* (*Let's Make a Deal*) is one of Germany's top shows. Although *The Dating Game* went off the air in the United States in 1989, it is now seen in ten foreign countries and emerged top in its time slot in Poland, Finland and (when it was shown) England, where it's called *Blind Date*. In Singapore a cult has formed around locally produced broadcasts of *The $25,000 Pyramid*, while in France *Le Juste Prix* (*The Price is Right*) attracts almost half the country's viewers. Not everyone in these countries is happy with the Western influence – producers of *The Dating Game* in Turkey received death threats from Muslim fundamentalists.[71]

The American appeal is so strong that some non-US companies go out of their way to create an American image. A British ad for Blistex lip cream, for example, includes a fictional woman named 'Miss Idaho Lovely Lips' who claims Blistex is 'America's best-selling lip cream'.[72] Recent attempts by American marketers to 'invade' other countries include:

- Kellogg's is trying to carve out a market for breakfast cereal in India, even though currently only about 3 per cent of Indian households eat such products. Most middle-class Indians eat a traditional hot breakfast which includes such dishes as *chapatis* (unleavened bread) and *dosas* (a fried pancake), but the company is confident that it can entice them to make the switch to Corn Flakes, Froot Loops and other American delicacies.[73] However, India has proved quite a difficult market to change, even for powerful multinational companies.[74]

- The National Basketball Association is fast becoming the first truly global sports league. Nearly $500 million of licensed merchandise was sold *outside* the United States in 1996. A survey of 28,000 teenagers in 45 countries conducted by the DMB&B advertising agency found that Michael Jordan is by far the world's favourite athlete. In China, his Chicago Bulls team (translated as 'The Red Oxen') is virtually everyone's favourite.[75]

- The British are avid tea-drinkers, but how will they react to American-style iced tea? US companies like Snapple are hoping they can convince the British that iced tea is more than hot tea that's gone cold. These firms may have some way to go, based on the reactions of one British construction worker who tried canned iced tea for the first time: 'It was bloody awful.'[76]

- Pizza Hut is invading, of all places, Italy. The country that invented pizza will be exposed to the American mass-produced version, quite a different dish from the local pizza, which is often served on porcelain dishes and eaten with a knife and fork. On the other hand, one of Pizza Hut's top performing restaurants is now located in Paris, a centre of fine cuisine, so only time will tell if Italians will embrace pizza 'American-style'.[77]

Globalization is often identified with Americanization – and American foreign policy (e.g. over Afghanistan and Iraq) can therefore affect consumer attitudes to American products.[78] Younger European consumers (18–35) seem more positively predisposed towards US goods than older consumers (aged 35+). Recent research (based on a poll of 1,000 people in nine countries) suggests that 'young adults in several European countries are more inclined to have a taste for American goods than older people in their countries . . .

1 A third of those between the age of 18 and 24 in France said they would prefer to buy US goods if the price and quality were the same. Only about one in 10 of those 35 and older felt that way.

2 Six in 10 of those from 18–24 in Britain said they would prefer to buy American goods if the price and quality were the same, almost twice the number of those 35 and over who felt that way.

3 A third of those from 18–24 in Italy said they would prefer to buy American goods compared with one in 10 of those 35 and over.'[79]

The West invades Asia

Although a third of the world's countries have a per capita GNP of less than $500, people around the world now have access to Western media, where they can watch reruns of shows like *Lifestyles of the Rich and Famous* and *Dallas*, idealized tributes to the opulence of Western lifestyles. To illustrate the impact of this imagery around the world, it is interesting to compare its impact in two very different Asian countries.

Consider how the material expectations of consumers in the People's Republic of China have escalated. Twenty years ago, the Chinese strove to attain what they called the 'three bigs': bikes, sewing machines and wristwatches. This wish list was later modified to become the 'new big six', adding refrigerators, washing machines and televisions. At the last count, the ideal is now the 'eight new things'. The list now includes *colour* televisions, cameras and video recorders.[80] Chinese women are starting to demand Western cosmetics costing up to a quarter of their salaries, ignoring domestically produced competitors. As one Chinese executive noted, 'Some women even buy a cosmetic just because it has foreign words on the package.'[81]

In contrast to China, the Japanese have already become accustomed to a bounty of consumer goods. Still, the Japanese are particularly enthusiastic borrowers of Western culture. American music and films are especially popular, perhaps because they are the best way to experience US lifestyles and popular culture. They have even recreated an entire Dutch village (complete with real Dutch people who 'perform' daily), which is one of Japan's top honeymoon destinations.

The Japanese often use Western words as a shorthand for anything new and exciting, even if they do not understand their meaning. The resulting phenomenon is known as 'Japlish',[82] where new Western-sounding words are merged with Japanese. Cars are given names like Fairlady, Gloria and Bongo Wagon. Consumers buy *deodoranto* (deodorant) and *appuru pai* (apple pie). Ads urge shoppers to *stoppu rukku* (stop and look), and products are claimed to be *yuniku* (unique).[83] Coca-Cola cans say 'I feel Coke and sound special', and a company called Cream Soda sells products with the slogan 'Too old to die, too young to be happy'.[84] Other Japanese products with English names include Mouth Pet (breath freshener), Pocari Sweat ('refreshment water'), Armpit (electric razor), Brown Gross Foam (hair-colouring mousse), Virgin Pink Special (skin cream), Cow Brand (beauty soap) and Mymorning Water (canned water).[85] For an interesting and revealing website which features dozens of well known Western celebrities doing commercials for Japanese media, spend some time at Japander![86]

Emerging consumer cultures in transitional economies

In the early 1980s the American TV show *Dallas* was broadcast by the Romanian communist government to show the decadence of Western capitalism. The strategy backfired, and instead the devious (but rich!) J.R. became a revered icon in parts of eastern Europe and the Middle East – to the extent that a tourist attraction outside Bucharest includes a big white log gate that announces (in English) the name: 'South Fork Ranch'.[87] Western 'decadence' appears to be infectious.[88]

Mainland China is one of the newest markets opening up to Western business and culture. When McDonald's opened in China in the early 1990s, their new Beijing restaurant became their largest outlet in the world with more than 700 seats and 1,000 employees. Hong Kong Disneyland opened their $1.8 billion park in September 2005. They expect to attract 5.6 million visitors in their first year, drawing a third of these from mainland China (http://money.cnn.com/2005/09/11/news/international/disney_hk.reut/).

Getty Images/M.N. Chan

After the collapse of communism, eastern Europeans emerged from a long winter of deprivation into a springtime of abundance. The picture is not all rosy, however, since attaining consumer goods is not easy for many in transitional economies, where the economic system is still 'neither fish nor fowl', and governments ranging from China to Romania struggle with the difficult adaptation from a controlled, centralized economy to a free market system. These problems stem from such factors as the unequal distribution of income among citizens, as well as striking rural–urban differences in expectations and values. The key aspect of a transitional economy is the rapid change required in social, political and economic dimensions as the populace is suddenly exposed to global communications and external market pressures.[89]

The newest members of the EU-25 countries are already aware of the challenges and opportunities that face them. Table 17.1 provides an overview of these new member countries, and a summary of some of their aspirations as citizens and consumers in the enlarged European Union.

Some of the consequences of the transition to capitalism include a loss of confidence and pride in the local culture, as well as alienation, frustration and an increase in stress as leisure time is sacrificed to work ever harder to buy consumer goods. The yearning for the trappings of Western material culture is perhaps most evident in parts of eastern Europe, where citizens who threw off the shackles of communism now have direct access to coveted consumer goods from the United States and western Europe – if they can afford them. One analyst observed, 'as former subjects of the Soviet empire dream it, the American dream has very little to do with liberty and justice for all and a great deal to do with soap operas and the Sears Catalogue'.[90] But consumers regularly have found themselves in situations where their real income and their employment security have gone down. Typically, the share of income used on basics such as food has risen, so for a large part of the population the question is how much wealth and happiness consumer society has brought, at least in the short term.[91] This frustrating situation, and the lack of experience with 'real capitalism', has made too many consumers an easy prey for hustlers, who persuade them to invest their money in pyramid games and dubious investment companies. This does not just happen in small side streets. One Russian investment company gave free metro tickets to all Muscovites and advertised heavily on TV. For those who knew what advertising was about, this was a sign of economic potency, while those who did not took it as some kind of officially approved encouragement from the state. Both resulted in a lot of confidence in the firm. Unfortunately, the whole thing ended in political scandal and enormous losses for the consumers-turned-investors.[92]

In 1990 more than 60 countries had a GNP of *less* than $10 billion. In contrast, more than 135 transnational companies had revenues greater than that figure. The dominance of these marketing powerhouses has helped to create a *globalized consumption ethic*. As people the world over are increasingly surrounded by goods and tempting images of them, a material lifestyle becomes more important to attain. Shopping evolves from being a weary, task-oriented struggle to locate even basic necessities to being a leisure activity, where possessing consumer goods becomes a mechanism to display one's status – often at great personal sacrifice. In Turkey one researcher met a rural consumer, a mother who deprived her child of nutritious milk from the family's cow and instead sold it in order to be able to buy sweets for her child because 'what is good for city kids is also good for my child'.[93] As the global consumption ethic spreads, the products wished for in different cultures become homogenized – Christmas is now celebrated among some urbanites in Muslim Turkey, even though gift-giving (even on birthdays) is not customary in many parts of that country.

In some cases, the meanings of these desired products are adapted to local customs and needs. In Turkey some urban women use ovens to dry clothes and dishwashers to wash muddy spinach. The process of creolization occurs when foreign influences are absorbed and integrated with local meanings – just as modern Christianity incorporated

Table 17.1 The new Europeans: demographics and attitudes towards EU membership

	Poland	Czech Republic	Hungary	Slovakia	Slovenia
Population (millions)	38.2	10.2	10	5.4	2
GDP per capita	42.90%	2.90%	55.30%	49.1	69.7
Unemployment rate	19.10%	8.00%	5.90%	16.60%	6.40%
Hourly labour cost	€4.48	€3.9	€3.8	€3.1	€9.0
Internet usage rate	23%	26%	16%	16%	38%
Mobile telephone usage rate	36%	84%	68%	54%	77%
Higher education rate	12.2%	11.80%	14.10%	10.80%	14.80%
% household spending on food	19.9%	18.80%	19.40%	22.10%	17.20%
% household spending on housing	24.6%	22.80%	18.40%	23.10%	20.00%
Meaning of the EU	Freedom of movement Euro Peace	Freedom of movement Euro Peace	Freedom of movement within the EU Peace Euro	Freedom of movement Euro Economic prosperity	Euro Freedom of movement Peace
Meaning of EU citizenship	Right to work in the EU Right to emigrate Access to education	Right to work in the EU Access to education Right to emigrate	Right to work in the EU Access to education Right to emigrate	Right to work in the EU Access to education Right to emigrate	The right to work in the EU Access to healthcare and social welfare Access to education
Main fears of enlargement	Cost of accession Problem for farmers Increase in organized crime	Problems for farmers Cost of accession Increase in organized crime	Problems for farmers Cost of accession Transferred jobs	Increase in organized crime Cost of accession Problems for farmers	Increase in organized crime Problems for farmers Cost of accession

	Cyprus	Malta	Estonia	Latvia	Lithuania
Population (millions)	0.7	0.4	1.3	2.3	3.4
GDP per capita	78.0	69.2	42.2	36.6	41.4
Unemployment rate	4.70%	8.80%	9.50%	10.50%	11.70%
Hourly labour cost	€10.7	€7.5	€3.0	€2.4	€2.7
Internet usage rate	29%	21%	33%	13%	14%
Mobile telephone usage rate	58%	70%	65%	39%	47%
Higher education rate	30%	8.80%	29.70%	19.60%	21.90%
% household spending on food	19.60%	20.40%	22.90%	25.5%	30.70%
% household spending on housing	7.70%	5.9%	21.00%	16.10%	14.00%
Meaning of the EU	Economic prosperity Freedom of movement Peace	Freedom of movement Stronger say in the world Economic prosperity	Freedom of movement Euro Bureaucracy	Freedom of movement Social protection Economic prosperity	Freedom of movement Euro Economic prosperity
Meaning of EU citizenship	Right to emigrate Right to work in the EU Access to education	Right to work in the EU Access to education Right to emigrate	Right to work in the EU Access to education Right to emigrate	Right to work in the EU Access to education	Right to work in the EU Access to education Right to emigrate
Main fears of enlargement	Increase in organized crime Transferred jobs Cost of accession	Transferred jobs Loss of power Increase in organized crime	Increase in organized crime End of national currency Cost of accession	Increase in organized crime Problems for farmers Cost of accession	Increase in organized crime Cost of accession Problems for farmers

Source: Stephen Brown, *Postmodern Marketing* (London: Routledge, 1995). Table 4.2, page 120.

Consumption of global products and symbols: Japanese motorcyclists with 'chopped' bikes, jackets, jeans and that 'rebel' look.

Harley Davidson, Inc.

the pagan Christmas tree into its own rituals. Thus, a traditional clothing style such as a *bilum* worn in Papua New Guinea may be combined with Western items like Mickey Mouse shirts or baseball caps.[94] These processes make it unlikely that global homogenization will overwhelm local cultures, but rather that there will be multiple consumer cultures, each blending global icons such as Nike's pervasive 'swoosh' with indigenous products and meanings.

Consumer resistance: back to the roots?

Despite the proliferation of Western culture around the world, there are signs that this invasion is slowing. Japanese consumers are beginning to show signs of waning interest in foreign products as the health of their country's economy declines. Some of the latest 'hot' products in Japan now include green tea and *yukata*, traditional printed cotton robes donned after the evening bath.[95] Several locally made products are catching on in parts of eastern Europe due to their lower prices and improved quality, combined with the perceptions that sometimes the imported products are inferior versions. Some Muslims are rejecting Western symbols as they adhere to a green Islamic philosophy which includes using natural, traditional products.[96]

Some critics in other countries deplore the creeping Americanization of their cultures. Debates continue in many countries on the imposition of quotas that limit American television programming.[97] The conflict created by exporting American culture was brought to a head in trade negotiations in the WTO (the global trade agreement), which deadlocked over the export of American films to Europe (the US share of the European cinema market is about 75 per cent). As one French official put it, 'French films are the cinema of creation. American films are products of marketing.'[98]

In Europe the French have been the most outspoken opponents of creeping Americanization. They have even tried to ban the use of such 'Franglish' terms as *le drugstore*, *le fast food* and even *le marketing*, though this effort was ruled unconstitutional.[99] The French debate over cultural contamination was brought to a head by the 1991 opening of EuroDisney in a Paris suburb. In addition to the usual attractions, hotels with names like The Hotel New York, The Newport Bay Club and The Hotel Cheyenne attempt to recreate regions of America. The park seems to have rebounded after a shaky start, including renaming it Disneyland Paris since EuroDisney somehow seemed incompatible. But some Europeans have been less than enthusiastic about the cultural messages being sent by the Disney organization. One French critic described the theme park as 'a horror made of cardboard, plastic and appalling colours – a construction of hardened chewing gum and idiotic folklore taken straight out of a comic book written for obese Americans'.[100]

There is also evidence of changing attitudes among women worldwide, in this case in relation to advertising. Research conducted in seven countries suggested changing perceptions of how marketers used money, sex, humour, emotion and authenticity in their marketing communications. Leo Burnett Worldwide Chairman and CEO, Linda Wolf, has argued that 'Women around the world are changing in significant ways . . . their evolving perspectives . . . must be addressed by advertisers if they want to truly connect with women [who make] . . . upwards of 80 per cent of all buying decisions'.[101] Along with Wolf, Cheryl Berman, Chairman and Chief Executive Officer of Leo Burnett USA, argued that advertisers must:[102]

1 *'Follow the money*: Acknowledge how women's new financial strength is affecting their buying habits in many key categories.

2 *Try a new position*: Sex sells, but it has to be approached with a distinctly female point of view.

3 *Use emotion carefully*: Women will turn off advertising that tries to portray emotion without truly evoking emotion.

4 *Make it funny*: Women would welcome more humour in commercials directed at them.

5 *Make it real*: Present women with authentic characters and situations that they can relate to in real ways.'

Globalization: not a one-way street

▶ Based on these discussions, we are now able to reflect a little more on the notion of **globalization**. An anthropological study of developments in the British food culture revealed four different types of consumption practices that are currently shaping the way local and foreign products and practices enter into the British way of creating a self-identity through food.[103] The *global food* culture, represented mainly by American fast food, indicates a willingness either to buy into the particular context of Americana, or quite the opposite, to join a wave of globally uniform consumption patterns that are found everywhere and therefore belong nowhere in particular. *Expatriate food* refers to the search for authentic meals and products from other cultures – a 'real Tuscany evening for you and your partner'. Thus it also depends on global knowledge of food cultures, but focuses on the differences between local food cultures. Thirdly, *nostalgia food* represents a search for local authenticity – Stilton cheese, sticky toffee puddings – from the cultural heritage, which is threatened by the internationalization of British cooking patterns. The study quotes the *Sunday Times*: 'Having shamefully neglected our own traditional dishes for 40 years, we now have a flashy, meretricious cuisine based, for the most part, on ersatz imitations of Mediterranean food.'[104] Finally, *creolization* of food involves blending various traditions into new ones, such as Chinese dishes omitting ingredients considered unappetizing in Western culture, Mexican food with less chilli, or Indianized versions of sandwiches. This creolization, or 'localizing' of foods, is found in many European countries. In the Netherlands, Indonesian food has been adapted to fit the tastes of the mainstream culture, just as Turkish sandwiches have been modified in Germany.[105] These trends probably exist in all European countries but vary in importance and in their influence and outcomes in terms of eating behaviour.

It is interesting to note that all four are related to globalization trends, but only global food leads to a tendency to standardize consumption patterns. The typology is also interesting because, in a fairly comprehensible way, it illuminates that globalization is much more than McDonaldized homogenization. And we may see these tendencies as relevant for all types of consumption, not just for consumption of food. So whether we look at retailing, interior decoration, tourism or musical tastes, we may find at least these four tendencies, taking the notion of globalization beyond the interpretation of it as homogenization. It also includes the increasing awareness of other styles and tastes, and the search for 'exotic authenticity', as well as the incorporation of this 'exoticism' into local habits and consumption styles. And finally, the exposure to all this 'otherness' often makes consumers more aware of their own cultural roots, and the tastes and consumption styles that they would define as 'our own'. All these offers of old and new, strange and familiar, authentic and creolized, tend to coexist in the marketplace. Therefore, it is not so strange that some authors discuss globalization more in terms of fragmentation than in terms of homogenization.[106] Fragmentation is also a key aspect of the postmodern view on consumers and consumption, to which we shall now turn.

marketing pitfall

Cigarettes are among the most successful of Western exports. Asian consumers alone spend $90 billion a year on cigarettes, and Western tobacco manufacturers continue to push relentlessly into these markets. Cigarette advertising, often depicting glamorous Western models and settings, is found just about everywhere, on hoardings, buses, shop fronts and clothing, and many major sports and cultural events are sponsored by tobacco companies. Some companies even hand out cigarettes and gifts in amusement areas, often to pre-teens.

A few countries have taken steps to counteract this form of Westernization. Singapore bans all promotions that mention a product's name. Hong Kong has prohibited cigarette ads from appearing on radio and TV. Japan and South Korea do not allow ads to appear in women's magazines. Industry executives argue that they are simply competing in markets that do little to discourage smoking (e.g. Japan issues health warnings like 'Please don't smoke too much'), often against heavily subsidized local brands with names like Long Life (Taiwan). The warnings and restrictions are likely to increase, however: smoking-related deaths have now overtaken communicable diseases for the 'honour' of being Asia's No. 1 killer.[107]

■ POSTMODERNISM?

Many of the themes mentioned earlier in this part of the book, such as the globalization process, reality engineering or the blurring of the fashion picture, have been linked to larger social processes dominating the last part of the twentieth century. One proposed ▶ summary term for these processes is **postmodernism** – one of the most widely discussed and disputed terms in consumer research in the past few years.[108]

Postmodernists argue that we live in a modern era where we share beliefs in certain central values of modernism and industrialism. Examples of these values include the benefits of economic growth and industrial production, and the infallibility of science. In opposition, postmodernism questions the search for universal truths and values, and ▶ the existence of objective knowledge.[109] Thus a keyword is **pluralism**, indicating the co-existence of various truths, styles and fashions. Consumers (and producers) are relatively free to combine elements from different styles and domains to create their own personal expression.

There have been several attempts to sum up features of postmodernism and their implications for marketing and consumer behaviour.[110] Together with pluralism, one European researcher has suggested that postmodernism can be described by six key features:[111]

▶ ● **Fragmentation**. The splitting up of what used to be simpler and more mass oriented, exemplified by the ever-growing product ranges and brand extensions in more and
▶ more specialized variations. An alternative form of brand extension is **retro branding** conceptualized as 'the revival or relaunch of a brand from a prior historical period that differs from nostalgic brands by the element of updating'.[112] Even within the retailing environment we experience the proliferation of outlets within the concentration of bigger outlets (shopping centres). Such specialized and stylized outlets often carry an in-depth assortment of a very narrow product range, such as teas or ties. The advertising media have also become fragmented, with increasingly specialized TV channels, magazines, radio stations and websites for placing one's advertising.

▶ ● **De-differentiation**. Postmodernists are interested in the blurring of distinctions between hierarchies such as 'high and low culture', or 'politics and show business'. Examples would be the use of artistic works in advertising and the celebration of advertising as artistic works. Companies such as Coca-Cola, Nike and Guinness have their own museums. Another clear example is the blurring of advertisements and TV programmes, wherein more and more TV programmes feature advertising for themselves (in order to increase viewer ratings) and TV commercials look like 'real' programming, as in the ongoing soap opera with a couple spun around the coffee brand Gold Blend. The blurring of gender categories also refers to this aspect of postmodernism.

▶ ● **Hyperreality**. The spreading of simulations and the loss of the sense of the 'real' and the 'authentic', as in the cases of re-engineered environments discussed earlier in this chapter, or in shopping centres simulating ancient Rome (The Forum in Las Vegas) or a Parisian street (West Edmonton Mall, Canada). Finally, products can be hyperreal to the extent that they simulate something else: for instance, sugarless sugar, fat-free fat (olestra) or the butter replacement brand I Can't Believe It's Not Butter! In fact, it has been argued that marketing may be the most important contributor to the creation of hyperreality, since the essence of marketing and particularly advertising is to create a simulated reality by resignifying words, situations and brands.[113]

marketing pitfall

Sometimes companies may fall victim to their own hyperreality. It is the dream of many producers to create a strong brand with a solid position in cultural life. But as they do so, their brand images are incorporated into the general cultural sign system, and the company loses control over the signs attached to the brand name. For example, the name 'Barbie' today is much more than a brand name – it has almost become a name for a personality type. When a Danish pop group, Aqua, enjoyed a huge success with the song 'Barbie', which contained lyrics alluding to the sex life of this hyperreal personality (e.g. 'you can dress my hair, undress me everywhere'), Mattel Inc. was not amused. They sued the pop group for abuse of the Barbie name and for destroying the pure and positive image of Barbie's world created through a long range of expensive campaigns. This is yet another example of the blurring of marketing and popular culture, and the question is: can you patent culture?[114]

▶ ● **Chronology**. This refers to the consumer's search for the authentic and a preoccupation with the past – like real or authentic Chinese or Italian foods or the search for one's nostalgic roots in foods (or other consumer goods) as we 'used to know it'.[115] Likewise, the increase in the 'no-nonsense' formats of various advertising campaigns may be seen as a return to a simpler, less contrived period of the past. Retro brands are of relevance here as well because 'these revived brands invoke brand heritage which triggers personal and communal nostalgia'.[116] What appeals to consumers here

The seventeenth-century Danish landmark of the 'round tower' of Copenhagen has been recreated (in a slightly smaller version) in the simulated Danish environment of Solvang, California, founded as a 'little Denmark' by Danish immigrants in the nineteenth century, but gradually becoming more of a hyperreal theme park under the influence of marketing in the postwar period. The tower in Solvang houses a local pizza restaurant: Tower Pizza, of course!

Photo: Søren Askegaard

is that in a period of accelerating change, the stability of the good old days remains comforting.

▶ ● **Pastiche**. The playful and ironic mixing of existing categories and styles is typical of pastiche. An example would be one advertisement doing a parody of another or making references to slogans or other elements borrowed from other campaigns. Pastiche also involves self-referentiality (the advertisement recognizes itself as being an ad, by showing (mock) scenes from its own creative process). Table 17.2 provides a set of examples of such parodies and self-referentialities from British advertising. Self-referentiality may create hyperreality, as when a British ad for the Yellow Pages featuring an author searching for a retail store where he could find a copy of his own old book about fly-fishing actually led to the writing of such a book. Needless to say, when the book was launched, the advertisement was re-run![117]

Other pastiches flourish, as when we see deliberate blurring of styles such as advertisements borrowing from films, or films and TV programmes borrowing from the advertisement style, all of it done 'tongue-in-cheek'. A British ad for cream depicted a Mona Lisa looking first to one side, then to the other, then drawing out an éclair (cake with cream), which she would bite, followed by the pay-off line: 'Naughty but nice'.[118] Indeed, one discussion of postmodernism and its impact on marketing was in itself a pastiche using a lot of cinematic metaphors and changed film titles to structure its chapters.[119]

▶ ● **Anti-foundationalism**. This last feature of postmodern marketing efforts refers not to parody but to an outright 'anti-campaign campaign' – for example, campaigns encouraging the receiver of the message *not* to take notice of the message since somebody is trying to seduce and take advantage of him or her. Other examples include anti-product products like 'death brand cigarettes', Jolt Cola ('with all the caffeine and twice the sugar'[120]) or the Icelandic Aquavit brand's appropriation of its own nickname 'black death', complete with new labels including skulls. Finally, there's

Table 17.2 A few examples of pastiche in British advertising

Category	Content	Examples
	Parody	
Direct	One advertisement parodies another	Carling Black Label (lager) spoof of Levi's (jeans) celebrated 'launderette' sequence
Indirect	Advert 'appropriates' byline/icon etc. of another	Do It All (DIY superstores) advertised 'the united colors of Do It All' (Benetton)
	Self-referentiality	
Direct	Adverts about advertising (set in soap advertising agency; adverts for forthcoming ads, etc.)	Next 'instalment' of advertising operas (Renault 21 family; Gold Blend couple, etc.) advertised beforehand
Indirect	Retransmission of old adverts that have acquired new meanings in the interim, or stylistic evocation of old ads	Repeat showings of 'I'm going well, I'm going Shell' series featuring Bing Crosby, etc. Once innovative, now quaint

'anti-fashion' – consumers' claims that they search for certain types of ugliness when buying shoes and clothing in order to construct a very personal and ostentatious style (sound like anyone you know?).[121] The green movement and the political consumer discussed above, as well as groups involved in movements of voluntary simplicity (particularly active in the United States) or the like, can be seen as anti-foundational in their rejection of standard products in favour of alternative choices which they perceive as less harmful to the natural and human environments.

Postmodernism has also been attached to such themes as the ability of readers to see through the hype of advertising.[122] This may suggest that we are becoming more skilled consumers and readers/interpreters of advertising, recognizing ads as hyperreal persuasion or seduction attempts which do not intend to reflect our own daily experiences. This skilled readership may have sparked various of the tendencies to anti-ads or pastiches discussed above. Younger consumers especially may be prone to detect and enjoy the self-referentiality or intertextuality of advertising.[123]

Another process attached to postmodernism is the greater significance of the aesthetics of everyday life, referring to the tendency to focus more and more on the design and appearance of goods or objects. According to this view, the style and imagery attached to consumer objects becomes of primary importance when judging your purchase. Indeed, some may argue that the consumer lifestyle in itself becomes a kind of work of art. More and more people act as if they are the main character in the film about their own life, and their activities and styles have to be selected carefully in order to meet the quality and excitement criteria of this personally staged biography.[124]

Certain postmodernists stress the liberatory aspects of postmodernism – that consumers are free to play with symbols and create their own constellations of products and lifestyles from available elements while being less concerned with norms and standards. Since there is an inherent scepticism in postmodernism, a postmodernist attitude is also a critical attitude.[125] Others point to the fact that the refusal to accept, indeed to *care* about, values, may lead to passivity and political degeneration of societies[126] and to the inherent contradictions within the positions taken by postmodernists.[127] Whether one sees the 'postmodern consumer' as a critical and creative person, or as a passive, entertainment-seeking 'couch potato', the changes in marketing and consumption referred to in the postmodern framework are fundamental for understanding changes in our European markets as we move further into the twenty-first century.

Self-parody is one approach to communication in our postmodern era.
The Advertising Archives

■ CHAPTER SUMMARY

■ The *green movement* is a common denominator in the trend towards increased attention to the environmental impact of human activities. In terms of consumption, this has broadened the scope of enviromental judgement from recycling of scarce resources to attention to the whole production and distribution process.

■ The green movement may be an indication of an even broader trend towards more conscious reflection on the ethical aspects of consumption. The *political consumer* 'votes with his/her shopping basket' in an attempt to influence companies to care for the natural as well as the human environment, adding issues such as human rights to the set of dimensions that influence purchases.

■ Followers of an *etic perspective* believe that the same universal messages will be appreciated by people in many cultures. Believers in an *emic perspective* argue that individual cultures are too unique to permit such standardization: marketers instead must adapt their approaches to be consistent with local values and practices. Attempts at global marketing have met with mixed success: in many cases this approach is more likely to work if the messages appeal to basic values and/or if the target markets consist of consumers who are more internationally rather than locally oriented.

- The Western world is a net exporter of popular culture. Consumers around the world have eagerly adopted Western products, especially entertainment vehicles and items that are linked symbolically to a uniquely Western lifestyle (e.g. Marlboro, Levi's, BMW, Nestlé). Despite or because of the continuing 'Americanization' or 'Westernization' of cultures in the world, some consumers are alarmed by this influence, and are instead emphasizing a return to local products and customs.

- Postmodernism involves processes of social change in an era, where the 'grand truths' of modernism such as scientific knowledge or the progressiveness of economic growth are no longer taken for granted. Postmodernism includes social processes such as fragmentation, de-differentiation, hyperreality, chronology, pastiche and anti-foundationalism.

▶ KEY TERMS

Anti-foundationalism (p. 623)

Chronology (p. 622)

Corporate social responsibility
  (CRS) (p. 606)

Creolization (p. 617)

De-differentiation (p. 622)

Emic perspective (p. 610)

Environmentalism (p. 602)

Etic perspective (p. 609)

Fragmentation (p. 622)

Globalization (p. 620)

Hegemonic brandscapes (p. 612)

Hyperreality (p. 622)

National character (p. 610)

Pastiche (p. 623)

Pluralism (p. 621)

Political consumer (p. 606)

Postmodernism (p. 621)

Recycling (p. 600)

Retro branding (p. 622)

Risk society (p. 604)

Transitional economies (p. 617)

CONSUMER BEHAVIOUR CHALLENGE

1 In your opinion, in which areas have environmental issues had the biggest impact on consumer behaviour? Why do you think that is the case?

2 Is the 'political consumer' a fad or a new and growing challenge for marketers and producers? Discuss.

3 Go to your local supermarket to check the selection of ecological products. How are they presented in the store? What does that say about the way these products are regarded?

4 Try to provide an estimate about how often environmental issues are mentioned in advertising. Are these messages credible? Why, or why not?

5 What do you think about boycotts as consumers' response to what is perceived as companies' unethical behaviour?

6 Identify and assess the importance of corporate social responsibility for companies, consumers and government policy.

7 What role does the globalization process play in your personal consumption profile? After reflecting on that, take a walk in your nearest shopping area and look for signs of the global and the local. What is from 'somewhere else'? What is distinctively local? Are there mixtures, or are these two domains separate? Can you identify any *hegemonic brandscapes*?

8 Try to collect advertisements that reflect the postmodern features of fragmentation, de-differentiation, hyperreality, chronology, pastiche and anti-foundationalism.

9 Reflect on your and your friends' consumption patterns in the same light. What do you see?

■ NOTES

1. Andrew Crane, 'Facing the backlash: Green marketing and strategic reorientation in the 1990s', *Journal of Strategic Marketing* 8 (2000): 277–96.

2. John Thøgersen, 'Making Ends Meet: A Synthesis of Research on Consumer Behaviour and the Environment', Working Paper 99–1 (The Aarhus School of Business: Department of Marketing, 1999).

3. James Fitchett and Andrea Prothero, 'Contradictions and Opportunities for a Green Commodity', in E. Arnould and L. Scott, eds, *Advances in Consumer Research* 26 (Provo, UT: Association for Consumer Research, 1999): 272–5; see EDUN's website for an overview of their total ecological approach to manufacturing through to marketing: http://edun.ie/(accessed 2 July 2005).

4. Mike Tharp, 'Tchaikovsky and toilet paper', *U.S. News and World Report* (December 1987): 62; B. Van Voorst, 'The recycling bottleneck', *Time* (14 September 1992): 52–4; Richard P. Bagozzi and Pratibha A. Dabholkar, 'Consumer recycling goals and their effect on decisions to recycle: A means–end chain analysis', *Psychology and Marketing* 11 (July/August 1994) 4: 313–40.

5. 'Companies in Austria set up repair/reuse network for old appliances', *Business Emmaus* 26(6) (Nov/Dec 2004): 4.

6. 'Finally, something at McDonald's you can actually eat', *Utne Reader* (May–June 1997): 12.

7. Philip Pan, 'Chop shoo-ey', *Washington Post* (30 January 2001); 'China promotes recycling economy', *Xinhua News Agency* (1 November 2004), http://www.china.org.cn/english/2004/Nov/110857.htm.

8. Debra J. Dahab, James W. Gentry and Wanru Su, 'New Ways to Reach Non-Recyclers: An Extension of the Model of Reasoned Action to Recycling Behaviors', in Frank Kardes and Mita Sujan, eds, *Advances in Consumer Research* 22 (Provo, UT: Association for Consumer Research, 1994): 251–6.

9. Rik G.M. Pieters, 'Changing garbage disposal patterns of consumers: Motivation, ability, and performance', *Journal of Public Policy and Marketing* 10(2) (1991): 59–76.

10. Bagozzi and Dabholkar, 'Consumer recycling goals and their effect on decisions to recycle'; see also L.J. Shrum, Tina M. Lowrey and John A. McCarty, 'Recycling as a marketing problem: A framework for strategy development', *Psychology and Marketing* 11(4) (July/August 1994): 393–416.

11. John Thøgersen, 'Wasteful Food Consumption: Trends in Food and Packaging Waste', in W.F. van Raaij and G. Bamossy, eds, *European Advances in Consumer Research* 1 (Provo, UT: Association for Consumer Research, 1993): 434–9.

12. Suzanne C. Grunert, 'Antecedents of Source Separation Behaviour: A Comparison of Two Danish Municipalities', in *Marketing for an Expanding Europe*, Proceedings of the 25th EMAC Conference, ed. J. Berács, A. Bauer and J. Simon (Budapest: Budapest University of Economic Sciences, 1996): 525–37.

13. 'Global markedsføring af danske miljøløsninger', *Markedsføring* 8 (1995): 12.

14. Manfred Kirchgeorg, 'Kreislaufwirtschaft – neue herausforderungen für das marketing', *Marketing ZFP* 4 (4th Quarter 1995): 232–48.

15. Timothy Aeppel, 'From license plates to fashion plates', *Wall Street Journal* (21 September 1994): B1 (2).

16. Graham Prophet, 'Make and break: designing for the big crunch' EDN Comment in *EDN Europe* 49(1) (January 2004): 25, www.edn.com.

17. Ibid.

18. *Advertising Age* (2 May 1992).

19. Giampaolo Fabris, 'Consumer studies: new perspectives', *Marketing and Research Today* (June 1990): 67–73.

20. Walter Hopfenbeck, *The Green Management Revolution: Lessons in Environmental Excellence* (Englewood Cliffs,

NJ: Prentice-Hall, 1993); for an up-to-date look at recycling of steel products and packaging, see: http://www.apeal.org/Contents/Base05.html.

21. Armin Herker, 'Eine Erklärung des Umweltbewußten Konsumentenverhaltens', *Marketing ZFP* 3 (3rd Quarter, 1995): 149–61.

22. Suzanne C. Grunert, 'Everybody Seems Concerned About the Environment: But Is This Concern Reflected in (Danish) Consumers' Food Choice?', in van Raaij and Bamossy, eds, *European Advances in Consumer Research* 1: 428–33.

23. Carolyn Strong, 'A Preliminary Investigation: A Step Towards an Understanding of Children as Environmentally Conscious Consumers', in *Marketing for an Expanding Europe*: 2139–49.

24. Paul M.W. Hackett, 'Consumers' Environmental Concern Values: Understanding the Structure of Contemporary Green Worldviews', in van Raaij and Bamossy, eds, *European Advances in Consumer Research* 1: 416–27.

25. Jean-Luc Gianneloni, 'The Combined Effect of Age, Level of Education and Personal Values on the Attitude Towards the Protection of the Environment', in *Marketing Today and for the 21st Century*, Proceedings of the 24th EMAC Conference, ed. Michelle Bergadaà (Cergy-Pontoise: ESSEC, 1995): 373–89.

26. Suzanne C. Grunert and Kai Kristensen, 'The Green Consumer: Some Danish Evidence', *in Marketing for Europe – Marketing for the Future*, Proceedings of the 21st EMAC Conference, ed. K.G. Grunert and D. Fuglede (Aarhus: The Aarhus School of Business, 1992): 525–39.

27. J. Robert Skalnik, Patricia Skalnik and David Smith, 'Growth Hormones in Milk-Producing Cows: For the Consumer, Much Ado About Nothing . . . Perhaps', in Flemming Hansen, ed., *European Advances in Consumer Research* 2 (Provo, UT: Association for Consumer Research, 1995): 201–3.

28. Andrew P. Smith, James A. Young and Jan Gibson, 'How now, mad-cow? Consumer confidence and source credibility during the 1996 BSE scare', *European Journal of Marketing* 33(11/12) (1999): 1107–22.

29. 'Mad-cow scare pulls Italy's head from the sand', *Wall Street Journal* (17 January 2001): A21.

30. SIFO survey, reported in *Aftonbladet* (5 February 2001): 8–9.

31. 'Anatomy of a food scare', *The Guardian* (26 February 2005): 12.

32. Carlos Grande, 'National news: Product recalls rise sharply', *Financial Times* (21 March 2005).

33. Ulrich Beck, *Risk Society* (London: Sage Publications, 1992).

34. Karin Ekström and Søren Askegaard, 'Daily Consumption in Risk Society: The Case of Genetically Modified Foods', in S. Hoch and R. Meyer, eds, *Advances in Consumer Research* 27 (Provo, UT: Association for Consumer Research, 2000): 237–43.

35. Lone Bredahl, 'Determinants of Consumer Attitudes and Purchase Intentions with Regard to Genetically Modified Foods – Results from a Cross-National Survey', MAPP Working Paper no. 69 (Aarhus: The Aarhus School of Business, 2000).

36. For a broad and current overview of ongoing consumer protection issues in the EU, see: http://europa.eu.int/comm/consumers/index_en.htm.

37. Klaus Grunert, 'Consumers' Attitudes to Genetically Modified Foods', research presentation, Lund University, 8 March 2001.

38. MORI, 'Stakeholder dialogue: consumer attitude' (November 2000), http://www.csreurope.org/whatwedo/consumerattitudes_page408.aspx.

39. CSR Europe website, http://www.csreurope.org (accessed 15 March 2005).

40. MORI, 'Stakeholder dialogue: consumer attitudes'.

41. Ibid.

42. Bente Halkier, 'Consequences of the politicization of consumption: The example of environmentally friendly consumption practices', *Journal of Environmental Policy and Planning* 1 (1999): 25–41.

43. http://www.adbusters.org/home/ (accessed 30 July 2005).

44. www.cokespotlight.org; see also www.adbusters.org and www.corpspotlight.org (accessed 30 July 2005).

45. Kalle Lasn, 'Culture Jamming', in J.B. Schor and D.B. Holt, eds, *The Consumer Society Reader* (New York: The New Press, 2000): 414–32.

46. Nat Ives, 'Advertising: Unauthorized campaigns used by unauthorized creators become a trend', *New York Times* (23 December 2004); see www.gomotron.com and www.MadisonAveNew.com for posting suggestions for companies such as Coca-Cola, Mitsubishi Motors, North American and Alltel (accessed 30 July 2005).

47. 'Oil and troubled waters', *Marketing* (29 June 1995): 13.

48. 'Vand for livet – et unikt kampagnesamarbejde', *Markedsføring* 5 (1996): 2.

49. 'BT pushes community role', *Marketing* (12 December 1996): 9.

50. 'Crossing the moral minefield', *Marketing* (22 June 1995): 11.

51. 'Bordeaux vil generobre den tabte hyldeplads', *Markedsføring* 12 (1996): 6.

52. Marcus Mabry, 'Do Boycotts Work?', *Newsweek* 3 (6 July 1992): 35; 'McDonald's antibiotic project: No more playing chicken with antibiotics', retrieved 16 July 2005 at: http://www.environmentaldefense.org/partnership_project.cfm?subnav=project_fullstory&projectID=1.

53. George Ritzer, *The McDonaldization of Society* (Thousand Oaks, CA: Pine Forge Press, 1993); George Ritzer, *The McDonaldization Thesis* (Thousand Oaks, CA: Pine Forge Press, 1998).

54. José Bové and François Dufour, *Le monde n'est pas une marchandise. Des paysans contre la malbouffe* (Paris: La Découverte, 2000).

55. Theodore Levitt, *The Marketing Imagination* (New York: The Free Press, 1983).

56. Terry Clark, 'International marketing and national character: A review and proposal for an integrative theory', *Journal of Marketing* 54 (October 1990): 66–79.

57. Julie Skur Hill and Joseph M. Winski, 'Goodbye global ads: Global village is fantasy land for marketers', *Advertising Age* (16 November 1987): 22; Margaret K. Hogg and Maria H. Savolainen, 'Symbolic Consumption

and the Situational Self', in Basil Englis and Anna Olofsson, eds, *European Advances in Consumer Research* 3 (Provo, UT: Association for Consumer Research, 1998).

58. 'Packaging draws protest', *Marketing News* (4 July 1994): 1.

59. Laurel Anderson Hudson and Marsha Wadkins, 'Japanese popular art as text: Advertising's clues to understanding the consumer', *International Journal of Research in Marketing* 4 (1988): 259–72; see also *Manga*'s English language website about Japanese animation (amine) at: http://www.manga.com/ (accessed 30 July 2005).

60. David Alexander, 'Condom controversy: Suggestive KamaSutra ads arouse India', *Advertising Age International* (27 April 1992): 1–12.

61. Simon Briscoe, 'Companies that use basic instinct', *Financial Times* (25 February 2005), http://news.ft.com/cms/s/3afde698-8691-11d9-8075-00000e2511c8.html.

62. Hill and Winski, 'Goodbye global ads'.

63. Søren Askegaard and Fabian Csaba, 'The Good, the Bad and the Jolly: Taste, Image and the Symbolic Resistance to the Coca-Colonization of Denmark', in S. Brown and A. Patterson, eds, *Imagining Marketing* (London: Routledge, 2001): 124–240.

64. Craig J. Thompson and Zeynep Arsel, 'The Starbucks brandscape and consumers' (anticorporate) experiences of glocalization', *Journal of Consumer Research* 31 (December 2004): 631–42.

65. Ibid.: 632.

66. See, for example, Russell W. Belk and Güliz Ger, 'Problems of Marketization in Romania and Turkey', *Research in Consumer Behavior* 7 (Greenwich, CT: JAI Press, 1994): 123–55.

67. Russell W. Belk, 'Consumption Patterns of the New Elite in Zimbabwe', paper presented at the Association for Consumer Research Conference, Salt Lake City, 16–19 October 2000.

68. See also Ulf Hannerz, 'Cosmopolitans and Locals in World Culture', in Mike Featherstone, ed., *Global Culture* (London: Sage, 1990): 237–52.

69. 'Abroadminded', *Marketing* (24 April 1997): 20–1.

70. Eric J. Arnould and Richard R. Wilk, 'Why Do the Natives Wear Adidas? Anthropological Approaches to Consumer Research', in Elisabeth C. Hirschman and Morris B. Holbrook, eds, *Advances in Consumer Research* 12 (Provo, UT: Association for Consumer Research, 1985): 748–52.

71. Robert LaFranco, 'Long-lived kitsch', *Forbes* (26 February 1996): 68.

72. Dana Milbank, 'Made in America becomes a boast in Europe', *Wall Street Journal* (19 January 1994): B1 (2).

73. Suman Dubey, 'Kellogg invites India's middle class to breakfast of ready-to-eat cereal', *Wall Street Journal* (29 August 1994): B3B.

74. Giana Eckhardt and Humaira Mahi, 'Globalization and the Consumer in Emerging Markets: India Will Survive', paper presented at the Association for Consumer Research Conference, Salt Lake City, 16–19 October 2000.

75. 'They all want to be like Mike', *Fortune* (21 July 1997): 51–3.

76. Tara Parker-Pope, 'Will the British warm up to iced tea? Some big marketers are counting on it', *Wall Street Journal* (22 August 1994): B1 (2).

77. John Tagliabue, 'Proud palaces of Italian cuisine await Pizza Hut', *New York Times* (1 September 1994): A4.

78. For a scholarly and provocative discussion on 'Brand America', and the impacts that American marketing practices have on the rest of the world, see: Johny K. Johansson, *In Your Face: How American Marketing Excess Fuels Anti-Americanism* (Upper Saddle River, NJ: Financial Times Prentice Hall, 2004).

79. Will Lester, 'Poll: Young adults in EU like U.S. goods', Associated Press, AP online (22 February 2005), http://search.ft.com/search/article.html?id=050222009366. For the market research report see Ipsos News Center 'Opinion around the world: Nine-country AP/IPSOS poll: Buy American? Global publics question U.S. export of consumer goods and democracy' (23 February 2005), http://www.ipsos-na.com/news/pressrelease.cfm?id=2568. See also: 'The global brand scorecard: The 100 top brands', *Business Week* (2 August 2004): 69–71.

80. David K. Tse, Russell W. Belk and Nan Zhou, 'Becoming a consumer society: A longitudinal and cross-cultural content analysis of print ads from Hong Kong, the People's Republic of China, and Taiwan', *Journal of Consumer Research* 15 (March 1989): 457–72; see also Annamma Joy, 'Marketing in modern China: An evolutionary perspective', *CJAS* (June 1990): 55–67, for a review of changes in Chinese marketing practices since the economic reforms of 1978.

81. Quoted in Sheryl WuDunn, 'Cosmetics from the West help to change the face of China', *New York Times* (6 May 1990): 16.

82. See: http://www.tokyotales.com/japlish/ (accessed 30 July 2005).

83. John F. Sherry Jr. and Eduardo G. Camargo, ' "May your life be marvelous": English language labeling and the semiotics of Japanese promotion', *Journal of Consumer Research* 14 (September 1987): 174–88.

84. Bill Bryson, 'A taste for scrambled English', *New York Times* (22 July 1990): 10; Rose A. Horowitz, 'California beach culture rides wave of popularity in Japan', *Journal of Commerce* (3 August 1989): 17; Elaine Lafferty, 'American casual seizes Japan: Teenagers go for N.F.L. hats, Batman and the California Look', *Time* (13 November 1989): 106.

85. Lucy Howard and Gregory Cerio, 'Goofy Goods', *Newsweek* (15 August 1994): 8.

86. http://www.japander.com/japander/zz.htm (accessed 30 July 2005).

87. Prof. Russell Belk, University of Utah, personal communication, 25 July 1997.

88. Material in this section adapted from Güliz Ger and Russell W. Belk, 'I'd like to buy the world a coke: Consumptionscapes of the "less affluent world" ', *Journal of Consumer Policy* 19(3) (1996): 271–304; Russell W. Belk, 'Romanian Consumer Desires and Feelings of Deservingness', in Lavinia Stan, ed., *Romania in Transition* (Hanover, NH: Dartmouth Press, 1997): 191–208; see also Güliz Ger, 'Human development and humane consumption: Well being beyond the good life', *Journal of Public Policy and Marketing* 16(1) (1997): 110–25.

89. Prof. Güliz Ger, Bilkent University, Turkey, personal communication, 25 July 1997.

90. Erazim Kohák, 'Ashes, ashes . . . Central Europe after forty years', *Daedalus* 121 (Spring 1992): 197–215, at 219, quoted in Belk, 'Romanian Consumer Desires and Feelings of Deservingness'.

91. Elena Milanova, 'Consumer Behavior in an Economy of Distress', in Arnould and Scott, eds, *Advances in Consumer Research* 26: 424–30.

92. Natasha Tolstikova, 'MMM as a Phenomenon of the Russian Consumer Culture', in B. Dubois, T. Lowrey, L.J. Shrum and M. Vanhuele, eds, *European Advances in Consumer Research* 4 (Provo, UT: Association for Consumer Research, 1999): 208–15.

93. Güliz Ger, 'The positive and negative effects of marketing on socioeconomic development: The Turkish case', *Journal of Consumer Policy* 15 (1992): 229–54.

94. This example courtesy of Prof. Russell Belk, University of Utah, personal communication, 25 July 1997.

95. Jennifer Cody, 'Now marketers in Japan stress the local angle', *Wall Street Journal* (23 February 1994): B1 (2).

96. Ger and Belk, 'I'd like to buy the world a coke: Consumptionscapes of the "less affluent world"'.

97. Steven Greenhouse, 'The television Europeans love, and love to hate', *New York Times* (13 August 1989): 24.

98. Charles Goldsmith and Charles Fleming, 'Film industry in Europe seeks wider audience', *Wall Street Journal* (6 December 1993): B1 (2).

99. Sherry and Camargo, 'May your life be marvelous'; 'French council eases language ban', *New York Times* (31 July 1994): 12.

100. Quoted in Alan Riding, 'Only the French elite scorn Mickey's debut', *New York Times* (1992) 2: A1.

101. 'Leo Burnett discovers ads aimed at women fall short on five counts', Cannes, France (24 June 2004), Leo Burnett press release, http://www.leoburnett.com/news/press_releases/200/prjul09-13743.asp.

102. Ibid.

103. Allison James, 'Cooking the Books: Global or Local Identities in Contemporary British Food Cultures?', in David Howes, ed., *Cross-Cultural Consumption* (London: Routledge, 1996): 77–92.

104. Ibid.: 89.

105. Ayse S. Caglar, 'McDöner Kebap and the Social Positioning Struggle of German Turks', in J.A. Arnold and G.J. Bamossy, eds, *Marketing in a Multicultural World: Ethnicity, Nationalism, and Cultural Identity* (London: Sage, 1995): 209–30.

106. A. Fuat Firat, 'Globalization of fragmentation – a framework for understanding contemporary global markets', *Journal of International Marketing* 5(2) (1997): 77–86.

107. Mike Levin, 'U.S. tobacco firms push eagerly into Asian market', *Marketing News* (21 January 1991) 2: 2.

108. Two special issues of *International Journal of Research in Marketing* 10(3) (1993) and 11(4) (1994), both edited by A. Fuat Firat, John F. Sherry Jr. and Alladi Venkatesh, have been decisive for the introduction of themes of postmodernism in marketing and consumer research.

109. Craig J. Thompson, 'Modern truth and postmodern incredulity: A hermeneutic deconstruction of the metanarrative of "scientific truth" in marketing research', *International Journal of Research in Marketing* 10(3) (1993): 325–38.

110. See, for example, A. Fuat Firat and Alladi Venkatesh, 'Postmodernity: The age of marketing', *International Journal of Research in Marketing* 10(3) (1993): 227–49; James Ogilvy, 'This postmodern business', *Marketing and Research Today* (February 1990): 4–22; W. Fred van Raaij, 'Postmodern consumption', *Journal of Economic Psychology* 14 (1993): 541–63.

111. Stephen Brown, *Postmodern Marketing* (London: Routledge, 1995): 106ff.

112. Stephen Brown, Robert V. Kozinets and John F. Sherry Jr., 'Teaching old brands new tricks: Retro branding and the revival of brand meaning', *Journal of Marketing* 67 (July 2003): 19–33.

113. Fuat Firat and Venkatesh, 'Postmodernity: The age of marketing'.

114. Eric Arnould and Søren Askegaard, 'HyperCulture: The Next Stage in the Globalization of Consumption', paper presented at the 1997 Annual Association for Consumer Research Conference in Denver, Colorado, 16–19 October.

115. See James, 'Cooking the Books'.

116. Brown, Kozinets and Sherry Jr., 'Teaching old brands new tricks'.

117. Brown, *Postmodern Marketing*.

118. Judith Williamson, *Consuming Passions: The Dynamics of Popular Culture* (London: Marion Boyars, 1988).

119. Stephen Brown, 'Marketing as multiplex: Screening postmodernism', *European Journal of Marketing* 28(8/9) (1994): 27–51.

120. Brown, *Postmodern Marketing*.

121. Anne F. Jensen and Søren Askegaard, *In Pursuit of Ugliness: On the Complexity of the Fashion Concept After the Era of Good Taste*, Working Paper in Marketing no. 14 (Odense University: School of Business and Economics, 1997).

122. Richard Elliott, Susan Eccles and Michelle Hodgson, 'Re-coding gender representations: Women, cleaning products, and advertising's "New Man"', *International Journal of Research in Marketing* 10(3) (1993): 311–24.

123. Stephanie O'Donohoe, 'Raiding the postmodern pantry: Advertising intertextuality and the young adult audience', *European Journal of Marketing* 31(3/4) (1997): 234–53.

124. Mike Featherstone, *Consumer Culture and Postmodernism* (London: Sage, 1991).

125. A. Fuat Firat and Alladi Venkatesh, 'Liberatory Postmodernism and the Reenchantment of Consumption', *Journal of Consumer Research* 22 (December 1995): 239–67.

126. Dominique Bouchet, 'Rails without ties: The social imaginary and postmodern culture. Can postmodern consumption replace modern questioning?', *International Journal of Research in Marketing* 11(4) (1993): 405–22.

127. Brown, 'Marketing as multiplex: Screening postmodernism'.

Consumption and immigration: the distribution of the Halal brand in Spain

CARLOS BALLESTEROS, CARMELINA VELA, LAURA SIERRA Universidad
Pontificia Comillas, Madrid, Spain

Zahara has the same problem every time she goes to the supermarket. In addition to the difficulty which faces all housewives in drawing up a shopping list, she has to spend half her precious time checking the labels on the products she wishes to buy. Just as if she were buying pharmaceuticals, this mother of a Muslim family must scrutinize the labels of all the food products she purchases to ensure that nothing that is considered as *Haram* (forbidden) by her religion will end up on her dinner table. For the 700,000 Muslims living in Spain, this is not an easy task. The religious restrictions imposed on the consumption of foodstuffs means that in many cases the consumption of even everyday items can represent a challenge to their spiritual beliefs.

Islam teaches that before eating meat, a good Muslim must be sure that the animal has been sacrificed without suffering and under certain conditions. These conditions are difficult to verify when you don't live in a Muslim country. However, some organizations have responded to the significant opportunity represented by some 25 million consumers throughout the EU. They have begun providing products produced in accordance with religious regulations, aimed specifically at this market. Thus, for Zahara and her family, it is becoming much easier to buy foodstuffs which conform to their religious beliefs.

THE ENVIRONMENT: THE IMMIGRANT POPULATION IN SPAIN

At the beginning of the twentieth century, Spain was a population exporter. A large number of Spaniards left the country, travelling to the north of Europe and Latin America for political and economic reasons. Today, history has reversed itself. Spain has become a receiver of population with an immigrant community of approximately 5 per cent. Immigration has significant social and economic repercussions, modifying the character of the host country. The market is transformed through the appearance of new and diverse needs of new multicultural communities.

It is difficult to gather accurate information regarding this phenomenon. The most reliable information is probably that of the Municipal Register. Between 1992 and 2000 the growth in immigration was fairly steady.

Figure 1 Growth in immigration, in thousands of persons

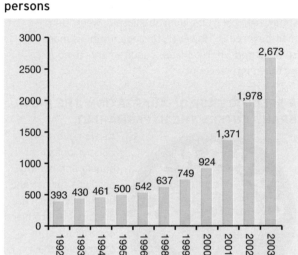

Source: INE, *Evolución de los extranjeros residentes. España en Cifras 2003-04*, www.ine.es, online publications (date of publication 02.04, (May 20, 2004)).

From 2000 onwards this growth may be described as exponential, as demonstrated by Figure 1.

The Municipal Register gives a total of 2,672,596 immigrants in 2003, which is almost double the figure of the previous year. The largest percentage of immigrants come from Ecuador, followed by Morocco, Colombia, the UK, Romania, Germany and Argentina, as shown in Table 1.

Table 1 Immigrants by nationality

Nationality	Number	Percentage of total foreign population
Ecuadorians	390,297	14.65
Moroccans	378,974	14.23
Colombians	244,684	9.18
British	161,507	6.06
Rumanians	137,347	5.16
Germans	130,232	4.89
Argentines	109,445	4.11

Source: INE, *Explotación estadística del Padrón. January 1, 2003*, www.ine.es (accessed May 2004).

The supermarkets, hypermarkets and other distribution companies are adapting some of their product lines to meet the gastronomic needs of the immigrant population. In Spain, a change is occurring among the large food distribution companies. They are beginning to note the increased demand for foreign products. A report of the Vth Semana de Alimentación, held in Madrid in October 2003, revealed that the Spanish Ibero-American food market had a turnover of some 25 million euros. Demand grew in particular for basic food products such as corn flour, cane sugar, tropical fruits, guayaba-based sweets and malt beverages. However, this adaptation is more complicated when religious requirements need to be taken into account.

A SPECIFIC CASE OF ADAPTATION: THE *HALAL* BRAND ENTERS THE HYPERMARKET

Junta Islamica

® As we have seen, Zahara looks for quality and healthy products for her and her family which are prepared or produced according to the precepts of the Koran without this becoming an additional economic burden. For Zahara, it is essential to know the process from the slaughterhouse to the supermarket, what is now known as the 'traceability system'. Muslims are often doubtful about the origins of food, particularly as it is difficult to find the necessary information regarding the origin of meat and how and by whom it was sacrificed.

However, it has become increasingly easy to find these products. Alcampo, Carrefour and Eroski, three of the principal food distributors in Spain, have recently started stocking items bearing the *Halal Guarantee* in their product lines (June 2004), particularly in those cities with significant Muslim communities. This introduction, which has not been associated with price increases, was also accompanied during the early months by free consumer information in order to familiarize consumers with the brand. Some of the most prominent meat producers in Spain, such as El Pozo or Casademont, now include this type of guarantee with some of their products.

The *Halal Guarantee* is a brand created by the Halal Institute of the Islamic Council of Spain in order to identify those products which meet the conditions

required by Islamic law. Thus, in addition to fresh meat, it controls the production process of other manufactured food products: dairy products, biscuits, prepared meats, products containing lactic acids, and even non-alcoholic beer. This brand has been regulated by law for more than 15 years. In Spain there are approximately 60 Spanish companies whose products now bear this quality guarantee.

The two sectors where this label principally applies are:

1   Food producers and/or processors or beverage companies. In this case, the *Halal* label guarantees that

   ● products are free of any substance or ingredient which may be forbidden (*Haram*), or any component derived from a forbidden animal;

   ● if a product is produced, manufactured and/or stored, the tools or machinery used are in accordance with the stipulations of Islamic law as well as Spanish health regulations;

   ● these food products do not come into contact with substances or products which are forbidden during their production, manufacture, processing, storage or transport;

   ● in the case of fresh meats, the animals have been sacrificed in accordance with Islamic law;

   ● in the case of beverages, these do not contain alcohol.

2   Service sector establishments. In this case it signifies that they meet the conditions required by Muslims in terms of food, places dedicated to prayer and facilities necessary to perform ablutions.

However, Zahara and her family may be the victims of false guarantees or possible fraud. While the Islamic Institute is the only entity officially authorized by the Spanish government to provide this guarantee (Spain is the only European country with a certifying institution), many products are sold with a *Halal* label which was not granted by the Institute. At certain times of the year, many North African immigrants cross Spain from Belgium, Holland or France, en route to their countries of origin on the so-called Ruta del Estrecho, and this has been the source of some problems.

In August 2004, the Institute sued a well-known chain of service stations 'for the illegitimate use of the *Halal* label and for consumer fraud'. It also sought the removal of the signs announcing the sale of *Halal* products in its service stations, specifically those on the 'Route' mentioned above. According to the company, it was not offering food produced or prepared by Spanish companies according to the precepts of the Koran but selling products from various countries and for this reason they were not eligible for the guarantee label. A simple case of unfair competition? A monopolistic drive by the Institute? A fraud by producers trying to sell something as pure which in fact isn't?

The truth is that many places sell a wide range of products bearing the *Halal* label (whether official or not). For Zahara and her family and the rest of the Muslim community resident in Spain (and by extension, in Europe), it is becoming easier to find foodstuffs which meet their religious beliefs, values and consumption habits.

QUESTIONS

1 Investigate if a case similar to that of Zahara has occurred in your community. Are there cultures and groups that require special products because of their beliefs?

2 Consider the repercussions on consumption caused by religious norms in other religions such as Judaism, Christianity, Buddhism, Sikhism, Hinduism.

3 Reflect on the future of immigration in Spain (or another country) and the consequences this may have on sectors other than the food industry e.g. banking and money transfers to other countries, holidays, customs of dress, and opinions on advertising.

4 Do you believe that a company should anticipate the specific needs of an immigrant community or should it wait until their number becomes significant?

5 Debate the issues around acculturation, and the flow of influences between immigrant and host communities.

6 What new consumption trends or situations may arise out of the second or third generation of immigrants as compared to the first?

Black youth identity in Britain: acculturation, consumption, hip hop and self-identity

ANDREW LINDRIDGE, Manchester Business School, UK and
KAMALDEEP DHILLON, Institute of Psychiatry, King's College London, UK

BACKGROUND

I'm in the Benz on Monday, the BM on Tuesday
Range on Wednesday, Thursday I'm in the Hooptay
Porsche on Friday, I do things my way
Vipe or Vette, I tear up the highway[1]

The lyrics of the black[2] American singer 50 Cents (whose mother was an immigrant to the USA from the Caribbean) singing about the cars he drives demonstrates the importance of symbolic and conspicuous consumption in emphasizing success and wealth. This case study briefly explores hip-hop music and symbolic consumption amongst ethnic minorities, particularly in relation to the construction of black identity amongst black youths in Britain.

INTRODUCTION

The advent of hip-hop music in the United States has been widely seen as the only original musical genre to appear in the past 30 years. Originating in the South Bronx, New York, in the late 1970s, hip hop represents a cultural movement with specific styles of dance, fashion, graffiti art and music (rap).[3] Hip-hop music captures the daily experiences within the US black community in New York, and has been seen as providing a way to confront and challenge the racism they experience in everyday life. Some African-Caribbean groups within the British black community have also used hip-hop music in order to express their experiences of life in Britain.

Andrea Levy's prize-winning novel *Small Island* shows the degrees of prejudice encountered by Caribbean immigrants into Britain after the Second World War. A consequence of African-Caribbean people's experiences of racism in Britain may be reflected in their limited opportunities to utilize Britain's economic wealth, compared with other ethnic groups, such as immigrants from the Indian subcontinent. In twenty-first-century Britain, 49 per cent of African-Caribbean households are classified as low income (Stationery Office 2004). An African-Caribbean school student is four times more likely to be excluded from school; by 16, they are the lowest performing ethnic group, which is in stark contrast to their performance at 11, when they are the highest achieving ethnic group on leaving primary

school. Christian (2002) argues that a consequence of racism is that to be black and British demands a double consciousness. This point can be linked to debates about acculturation where members of a minority community seek to negotiate their relationships with the dominant societal groups, and strive to achieve access to wider opportunities.

ACCULTURATION, CULTURE, CONSUMPTION AND HIP HOP

Acculturation represents a multifaceted and ongoing process where the continual interactions between the minority and dominant ethnic group iteratively affect cultural attitudes, behaviours and values across society. An important aspect of the acculturation process is often the need for individuals to demonstrate success in life, either to the dominant societal group or to their own ethnic group. This behaviour is consistent with consumer acculturation theories that argue that products imbued with cultural meaning are deliberately consumed by ethnic minorities to demonstrate their cultural adaptation, i.e. acculturation. However, an alternative consumer acculturation perspective is that ethnic minority individuals who demonstrate conspicuous consumption often do so in order to show their sense of rejection from the dominant society. This rejection may arise from experiences of racism often culminating in poor academic performance, inability to obtain well-paid jobs and struggles to establish a self-identity that is both recognized and valued by their own ethnic group and others. The ethnic minority person's sense of rejection may then be represented by the consumption of products that differentiates them from the dominant group and highlights their differences. A consumption act potentially reflects their perceived sense of rejection and demonstrates their inability and/or unwillingness to conform to the dominant societal culture.

One example of how acculturation and consumption affects African-Caribbean black identity in Britain (and its related cultural values) can be seen in music and poetry. These art forms provide important opportunities to represent the experiences and relate the narratives of ethnicity and difference. Black youths living in Britain may, therefore, use hip-hop culture as a way of supporting cultural identity in everyday settings and to authenticate a wider sense of their black identity. Music is one way of facilitating the formation of subcultural groups and networks for young African-Caribbeans living in Britain, as well as the maintenance and enhancement of personal identities. Consumption of key products can convey clearly determined cultural meanings, such as group belonging, as well as success and wealth in a hostile society. Hip hop has become a particular pop culture phenomenon because it uses brands within its lyrics as a means of demonstrating success and wealth to others, without necessarily wanting their approval. For example, the American Top 40 in 2003 contained hip-hop (rap) songs that had brand references for Mercedes-Benz cars (112 times), Gucci (47 times), Burberry (42 times), Hennessy Cognac (35 times) and Nike (26 times). The hip-hop (rap) artist most likely to sing about brands in 2003 was 50 Cents who mentioned 31 different brands compared with the second highest artist, Lil' Kim, who mentioned only 15 different brands.

Considered then within the wider debates about acculturation, culture and racism, some African-Caribbean youths in Britain may use hip hop in order to create part of the cultural context for black identity. Wearing the same brands as their favourite hip-hop artists may provide a means of identifying themselves with black role models, and also reflect a deliberate and conscious effort to assert their individual and group differences from both their own ethnic group and the dominant societal culture.

QUESTIONS

1 To what extent would you agree that products can be imbued with cultural meanings? What brands or products do you think are imbued with which specific cultural meanings?

2 The case study argued that when ethnic minorities experience racism, during the acculturation process, they may feel excluded from society. A consequence of this exclusion may be a desire to consume products that emphasize their difference. Is this argument still valid considering the worldwide success of hip-hop culture and rap music?

3 Do you think that hip-hop culture and rap music's focus on brands has more to do with general youth attitudes and behaviours regarding using brands to demonstrate a sense of belonging to reference groups rather than as a cultural statement about racism?

Notes

1. 'Poor Lil Rich' from the album *Get Rich or Die Tryin* by the artist 50 Cents who is singing about a variety of car brands in these lines: Mercedes-Benz, BMW, Range Rover (from Land Rover), 'Hooptay' means an old car that has been customized at large cost to make it distinctive, Porsche, Viper (from Dodge) and Corvette (from General Motors).
2. The term 'Black' was used in the 1960s during the Civil Rights Movement in the USA.
3. Rap is the musical culmination of hip-hop culture.

Sources

Christian, M. (2002), *Black Identity in the 20th Century: Expressions of the US and UK African Diaspora* (London: Hanshib Publications).
Stationery Office (2004), *Census 2001* (London: The Stationery Office).

Further reading

Hughes, A. (2002), *Hip-Hop Economy* (Black Enterprise): 32, 70–6.
Peñaloza, L. (1994), '*Atravesando fronteras*/border crossings: A critical ethnographic exploration of the consumer acculturation of Mexican immigrants', *Journal of Consumer Research* 21: 32-54.

Brand building on Holy Mount Athos: consumer perceptions of speciality wine brands

APHRODITE PANAGIOTALIDES,
Evangelos Tsantalis SA, Halkidiki, Greece

INTRODUCTION

In 2002, Evangelos Tsantalis SA, the leading Greek winery in terms of both Greek market and export market sales, commissioned market research to investigate the relative position of its Agioritikos wine brand in the Greek market. Agioritikos had been in the market for almost 30 years and had inevitably reached maturity.

The aim of the research was to investigate consumer attitudes towards the brand and to detect possible directions for development of this and other brands from the Mount Athos Vineyards.

THE AGIORITIKOS VALUES

Agioritikos was the first 'topikos oinos' (regional wine) of Greece, a category initiated in 1981 with the accession of Greece to the EEC. The Greek appellation system is built according to the French system and this category corresponds to the French Vin de Pays.

Topikoi oinoi (regional wines) are a special category of table wine, a level above the 'common' table wine and a level below OPAP (VQPRD) wines. Like OPAP wines, *topikoi oinoi* originate from specific vineyard areas and grape varieties, but there is greater flexibility in terms of both geographical area and grape varieties permitted by law. The ability to mention variety, vineyard area and vintage year on *topikoi oinoi* labels (something not allowed for table wines) also offers more value to the consumer.

Apart from instilling a new wine category, Agioritikos wine embodies an entire cultural system, tightly interwoven with the Greek Orthodox religion. Holy Mountain or Mount Athos ('Agion Oros' in Greek, hence the name 'Agioritikos') is the third finger of the Halkidiki peninsula in Northern Greece. The history of Mount Athos is very rich and for more than 1,000 years closely related to the Orthodox Church. Mount Athos is an independent monastic community, a unique place of great natural beauty, dedicated to prayer, obedience and meditation. Here lie 20 monasteries, 12 monastic villages and 700 small communities of Christian Orthodox monks in steep, impervious rocks and hills.

Wine has always been an integral part of life on Mount Athos and vine cultivation one of the most important occupations of the monks. A notable winemaking tradition exists that has lasted throughout the centuries and has made the Mount Athos wine renowned.

Many dignitaries visit Mount Athos to speak with the monks about intellectual or worldly matters, to seek their precious advice and to soak up the inimitable beauty of the unspoilt nature, away from modern civilization. Prince Charles is a regular visitor and has made many donations to the Vatopedi Monastery of Mount Athos.

The Agioritikos wine therefore carries all the strengths of its holy origins, of the 'unspoilt' ecosystem of Mount Athos, as well as the famous viticultural and winemaking tradition of the monks of Mount Athos, who have been making wine both as part of their religious duties (for use in Holy Communion) and to drink with their meals. Evangelos Tsantalis is the only winery allowed to cultivate vineyards on Mount Athos and bring the Mount Athos wine to the 'outside world', a very important USP for the winery.

So consumers bought Agioritikos as a treat, to drink on special occasions, to entertain at home or in restaurants. It was considered a status symbol that reflected the exalted status of Mount Athos.

The bottle, in the shape of a flask, echoes the flasks used by the monks to carry water or wine to the fields or when travelling.

The label is printed on a beige parchment-like paper in Byzantine-style lettering and carries the insignia of the Saint Panteleimon Monastery, where the Mount Athos Vineyards are situated. At a time when branded Greek wine was a rarity, Agioritikos was a real category leader.

MARKET SURVEY RESULTS

But let us see how far these values coincide with today's consumer perceptions of the Agioritikos brand. The following general associations (in no particular order) were recorded for the Agioritikos wine during the market survey:

- Delicious, soft, pleasant, refreshing wine
- For a festive occasion
- With good food
- Traditional wine
- Mount Athos
- Well-known brand
- Fun, party, dance, celebration
- Invigoration
- Relaxation
- Euphoria
- Escape
- Quality

The basic parameters of Agioritikos' identity according to the survey were:

Product
- A product of consistent quality
- Worth its money
- Easily drunk
- Pleasant wine

Price
- Not expensive

Bottle
- Stands out
- Has been around for a long time – habit
- Characteristic ('only Agioritikos has a shape')

Tsantali winery
- Has been in the market for years
- Traditional
- Strong brand – Tsantali is a strong name in the world of wine – 'Guarantee'
- Distinctive packaging
- Affordable quality
- 'Honest' wines

Reasons for acceptance
- 'Good price/quality ratio'
- 'Popular'
- 'Good taste'
- 'Tsantali is a winery with more than a century of history – quality guarantee'
- Familiarity: 'the wine you know'

Reasons for rejection
- 'Common'
- 'You get bored with it' – 'there are so many other choices'
- 'It has aged; it hasn't been renewed for a long time'.

Occasions to use

Agioritikos is consumed:

- with 'parea' (close friends)
- in tavernas or nightclubs
- often at club functions

but not consumed:

- in upmarket restaurants
- with romantic company
- with acquaintances (as opposed to friends)
- alone

THE AGIORITIKOS VALUES IN TODAY'S WINE MARKET ENVIRONMENT

Social and individual modes of wine consumption

To understand the Agioritikos values for the present-day consumer, one must first understand that all wines should achieve a careful balance between their social and individual values of consumption, where individual values are presently on an upward trend.

Taking the instance where wine is consumed in a *social* context, we have the notions of status and social acceptance linked to a 'successful' wine choice. The consumer enters an attractive role in which perhaps they feel they do not belong, that of the wine connoisseur, and acts out this role during a business meal or social dinner. We also have the notions of the 'parea' (circle of friends), a vital component of Greek society, companionship and communication within the parea, even 'emancipation' through the parea.

On an *individual* level, wine is a reward after a hard day at work, i.e. a taste of something different, something healthy or luxurious, or a means of stress relief and relaxation. Wine in Greece (as opposed to 'hard' alcohol) is considered 'pure' and 'natural' and 'good for the health'.

And then there is wine as a simple thing, a habit, i.e. wine for *everyday* consumption, with normal meals. Let's not forget that traditionally wine is consumed in Greece at the table, with food, on an everyday basis.

Discussion of survey results

In the last decade small, 'boutique' wineries have emerged capturing sales from established brands, by conveying an image of luxury and uniqueness. Agioritikos, which embodied these values in the past, has in the process experienced declining sales.

In terms of *social* values of consumption, these boutique wines are seen to offer more status value, higher quality, more attention to detail and more know-how. In terms of *individual* values of perception, boutique wines are believed to exude an air of sophistication and luxury. This is a general consumer perception problem for quality wines from large producers.

Agioritikos has therefore found itself stuck in the middle among:

1 more expensive (boutique) wines from small producers;

2 wines of the same level – also from large producers. Newer wines that are therefore seen to be more unusual belong here;

3 cheaper 'mass production' wines, which have a price advantage.

The survey suggested that the Tsantali winery needs to remind those consumers, who are growingly sceptical of the Agioritikos brand, of the brand values: 'uniqueness and authenticity of Mount Athos', 'parea', 'affordable luxury'. Tsantali need to promote the reasons that explain and justify the unique quality of Agioritikos and to reassure these customers of their choice.

There are also consumers, however, for whom Agioritikos still represents 'stability', 'timeless value', 'quality', a 'classic', 'traditional' choice. The survey found that for these consumers a possible packaging change of the bottle and/or the label would alienate the wine from its core values of heritage and tradition. Such a change was seen by the consumers to show lack of consistency: if Agioritikos were to be bottled in a standard 'Bordeaux' bottle, it would not be recognizable any more and some might even view it with scepticism, as a sign of lesser quality. These consumers stated that the wine's packaging should remain as it is, with the possible inclusion of extra information in the form of a neck tag.

EVANGELOS TSANTALIS' MARKETING STRATEGY FOR THE AGIORITIKOS BRAND

The marketing strategy Evangelos Tsantalis SA chose to follow was to bring to market contemporary brands conveying 'limited release' values, in other words to introduce more focus into its product offering. The vineyard site of Mount Athos, with its holiness, purity and uniqueness, was ideally placed to convey such distinct attributes.

The company's board decided to focus its new product development on the Mount Athos Vineyards and bring to market two product ranges:

● 'Mount Athos Vineyards Red', 'Mount Athos Vineyards White': an entry-level offer;

● 'Metoxi' and 'Chromitsa', red and white wine respectively, as a limited-release duo of flagship wines, only available through specialized wine shops at premium prices.

Thus the Mount Athos Vineyards play the role of a boutique winery within the large Evangelos Tsantalis winery. What the Agioritikos wine used to offer in terms of peerless prestige and sophistication, and which came under threat from the boutique wineries, is now offered by the new brands from Mount Athos.

The graphic design of the labels of the Mount Athos wines is especially strong, while the Tsantali brand name is downplayed on the label. The company is hoping that the new brands will be seen to embody added value, to convey quality and reward on an emotional level and thus to add a layer of complexity that will appeal to the more discerning consumer.

The Agioritikos wine is still part of the Tsantali portfolio, targeting the more traditional consumer and also the Greek communities abroad, who have a nostalgic attitude towards their homeland. This is a very large and important market for Tsantali, who sell a lot of Agioritikos wine to the Greek restaurants and Greek delicatessen stores abroad, mainly in Germany and the United States.

QUESTIONS

1 What proposals would you make to the Marketing Manager of Evangelos Tsantalis SA regarding the Agioritikos wine, the 'new' brands from Mount Athos and any further new product development from Mount Athos?

2 Discuss how lifestyle choices are determined by status, role-playing and show-off issues.

3 What is the role of heritage and tradition in modern product choices? Are the emotional factors embodied by artisanal products strong enough to instigate purchase?

4 How can a company capitalize on tradition and an established image, yet move ahead?

5 How can wineries bypass the hurdles of generational marketing ('I don't want to drink what my parents' drink')?

6 How can 'historical' brands ward off competition?

7 What branding opportunities arise from changing demographics: ageing population; increasing disposable income; growing interest in wine and culture; bias towards higher quality and price?

Sandra: an illustration of addictive consumption

SUSAN ECCLES, Department of Marketing,
Lancaster University Management School, Lancaster, UK

Superficially, an addictive consumer in the retail environment looks no different from any other consumer – 'people see a smart, well-dressed woman, not a hopeless addict'. Unlike many other addictive behaviours, there are no physical signs; no obviously bizarre actions; no unsociable behaviour that would give rise to comment from staff or other customers. To most of us, we would see someone immersed in, and enjoying, the same activity as many other consumers. Away from the retail environment, another picture emerges of someone who feels guilty, hides or never uses her purchases, and soon feels the familiar craving and anticipation that only another shopping trip can alleviate. However, it would be misleading to present all these women as profoundly unhappy, or in urgent need of medical supervision. Many of them lead reasonably satisfactory lives, fulfil their roles as wives, mothers, daughters and employees, and it is only their addiction to consumption that marks them out as 'different'.

Sandra is 58 years old, twice divorced and now married to Nick, who is 15 years her junior. Her son committed suicide some 13 years ago, but she has a married daughter and grandson. She lives in a spacious modern house in the north of England. She works full-time as an administrator, but is due to retire soon. She is not in debt but has spent several thousand pounds of her own savings over the past few years to pay off credit cards and loans. She tends to buy goods in phases – a week buying handbags, a few days buying blouses and so on. Sandra is extremely energetic and she does not appear to need (or get) much sleep. She is very smartly dressed and presented, and her house is tastefully decorated and furnished. She describes herself as:

'...a very, very fussy shopper. I go into the shop and I've got to have a sweater. I weigh them all up; I measure them all out; I can't make up my mind about three of the same colour. I bring them all home and try them on until 2 a.m. or 3 a.m. in the morning, until I find the one that is just right. Then, when I've found the right one, I have to go back the next morning and buy one of every colour in that. Then, they are forgotten. Probably just hung up in the wardrobe and never worn.'

She describes these phases of buying particular items as 'missions':

'When I knew I was going to retire, I went off sick for a couple of days . . . I thought, "What will I wear?" I've got forty to fifty work suits, but that was my next mission – something to wear in the house. So I bought tracksuits, indoor and outdoor; Reebok trainers, lightweight and silky; polo shirts in every colour, so that I could have one a day, and I never wear them. I'll be like a tramp in jeans in the house or my old trousers but they are there, so that when I get out of bed I could think, "That is what I could put on". Bags next. I love leather bags. . . .'

And she goes on to describe her handbag mission. Apart from the purchases themselves, Sandra finds the whole experience of going to the shops exciting and describes the experience:

'I just love the feeling of excitement and wonderment as I go into the shopping mall. I love the buzz of people; the colour and displays; the whole atmosphere. I can just soak up that feeling at the beginning of my shopping trip – it's almost as if I say to myself "OK, you're at home now, you can relax and enjoy yourself".'

Sandra considers herself to be a very discerning shopper ('I do surveys on things, like which will wash the best') and will check each item to make sure it is perfect (has no snags or marks) and that the fit and cut are just right. She has a real 'eye' for colour and design, and can tell almost at a glance whether an item will match up with other clothes in her wardrobe. She admits:

'I will spend hours both in the shops and at home considering and comparing different items – invariably, buying more than one and, on many occasions, worrying at night about something I have seen that day in the shops but not bought.'

On these occasions, she will arrive late for work in order to go back to the shop as soon as it opens the next day. Sandra is not secretive about her shopping behaviour:

'I don't think I necessarily boast about my purchases, but I do feel a great pride when I find that "perfect outfit" – even though I may have spent several days searching for it and it ends up, along with most of my other *purchases either in the loft or hanging unworn in one of my four double wardrobes!'*

She feels she is seen as a 'canny shopper' by others (akin to the 'market maven' described by Feick and Price 1985) who often turn to her for advice on where to shop or how to coordinate an outfit. However, she goes shopping virtually daily:

'I get withdrawal symptoms and feel depressed if I don't go to the shops. I tried staying in on a Saturday last week and went for a long walk with Nick. We got back at 4.20 p.m. and I was sweating. I thought, "I have to go in to town" and I thought, "Well, what am I looking for? I don't need anything" but I can always see something.'

About shopping generally, Sandra is quite adamant about its importance in her life:

'If ever there was anyone born to shop, it must be me! I have to say it's the most important thing in my life and gives me a real sense of purpose. Although I hate the fact that I can't break the habit, if I'm really honest, I don't want to – what else could I do that would give me so much pleasure and satisfaction?'

It would be unfair to say that Sandra has had a particularly charmed or easy life. She was one of five children, and her father was in the Second World War while her mother worked in a local mill. Although she won a scholarship to the high school, her family was too poor to afford the full school uniform – a source of great embarrassment to the young Sandra. She does admit that she wanted her children to have the material things she never had, and has had to cope with the suicide of her only son when he was 19 years old. She does, however, come across as a person who has coped with the ups and downs of life, and is generous with her time to others, offering a sympathetic and supportive ear to those who need to talk. She is smart, articulate, intelligent and meticulous. She perceives herself as a skilled shopper – *'I get so much pleasure out of it'* even though *'I know it is a problem'*.

Sandra was accompanied on one of her shopping trips, and the behaviour she describes is evident in her actions. Her energy, determination and sense of 'mission' are quite exhausting to experience – but the very genuine pleasure and satisfaction she gains from making just the right decision and purchase is quite obvious.

QUESTIONS

1 Do you think the behaviour of Sandra (and other addictive consumers) is deviant and/or abnormal? Why, or why not?

2 Identify some of the reasons why consumers such as Sandra may become addicted to the consumption

experience. How does this inform us about the consumption behaviour and patterns of more 'mainstream' consumers?

3 To what extent does marketing and advertising influence the behaviour of consumers like Sandra, and should marketers be more ethical and responsible in their practices?

Sources
Feick, L.F. and L.L. Price (1985), 'The market maven', *Managing* 2 (July): 10-14.

Further reading
Baumeister, R., T. Heatherton and D. Tice (1994), *Losing Control: How and Why People Fail at Self-Regulation* (San Diego: Academic Press).

Csikszentmihalyi, M. (1988), 'The Flow Experience and Its Significance for Human Psychology', in M. Csikszentmihalyi and I. Csikszentmihalyi, eds, *Optimal Experience: Psychological Studies of Flow in Consciousness* (Cambridge: Cambridge University Press): 36-59.

d'Astous, A. and S. Tremblay (1989), 'The Compulsive Side of Normal Consumers: An Empirical Study', in G. Avlonitis, N. Papavasiliou and A. Kouremenos, eds, *Marketing Thought and Practice in the 1990s*, 1: 657-69.

Eccles, S. (2002), 'The lived experiences of women as addictive consumers', *Journal of Research for Consumers* 4 (A Web-based interdisciplinary journal) www.cambridgemedia.com.au/sites/jorc/academic/academic_article.asp?ArticleID=17, vol 4.

Eccles, S. and H. Woodruffe-Burton (2000), 'Off to the Shops: Why Do we Really Go Shopping?', in M. Catterall, P. Maclaran and L. Stevens, eds, *Marketing and Feminism: Current Issues and Research* (London: Routledge): (183-201).

Elliott, R. (1994), 'Addictive consumption: Function and fragmentation in postmodernity', *Journal of Consumer Policy* 17(2): 159-79.

Elliott R., S. Eccles and K. Gournay (1996), 'Man management? Women and the use of debt to control personal relationships', *Journal of Marketing Management*, 12(7): 657-69.

Elliott R., S. Eccles and K. Gournay (1996), 'Revenge, existential choice and addictive consumption', *Psychology and Marketing* 13(8): 753-68.

Faber, R.J. and T.C. O'Guinn (1992), 'A clinical screener for compulsive buying', *Journal of Consumer Research* 19: 459-69.

Faber, R.J., T.C. O'Guinn and R. Krych (1987), 'Compulsive consumption', *Advances in Consumer Research* 14: 132-5.

O'Guinn, T.C. and R.J. Faber (1989), 'Compulsive buying: A phenomenological exploration', *Journal of Consumer Research* 16(2): 147-57.

Orford, J. (1992), *Excessive Appetites: A Psychological View of Addictions* (Chichester: John Wiley & Sons).

Scherhorn, G. (1990), 'The addictive trait in buying behavior', *Journal of Consumer Policy* 13: 33-51.

Scherhorn, G., L.A. Reisch and G. Raab (1990), 'Addictive buying in West Germany: An empirical study', *Journal of Consumer Policy* 13: 355-87.

Glass collectors in consumer culture

KARIN M. EKSTRÖM Centre for Consumer Science (CFK), Goteborg, Sweden

It is Saturday morning and Sven is driving his Volvo on his way to a meeting arranged by an association of glass collectors in the south of Sweden. He is cheerfully singing some old Abba tunes as he drives along. His wife, Anna, looks at him and smiles happily when he sings for the fifth time 'I have a dream'. She knows his dream is to have a big collection of glass from the 1920s. Anna has been really looking forward to this weekend trip, because it represents an adventure that is miles away from the mundane routines of the week. Sven is also thinking about the meeting; there will be a researcher there talking about collecting as a consumption phenomena. He wonders what she is going to say: maybe that he is crazy, or just passionately involved in collecting. He was surprised that there is research in this area at all, but why not? Things are important in people's lives and there are plenty of collectors around. Sven is really looking forward to meeting Björn who regularly attends these meetings.

Björn has a very interesting collection and also knows a great deal about glass. Sven is going to ask him about a bowl he bought at an auction a couple of weeks ago. It is a fantastic bowl, the glass really shimmers, but it does not have signature. Perhaps Björn knows who the designer is. Sven paid quite a lot for it. He thinks it is designed by a Simon Gate in the 1920s, but even if it isn't, it is OK, because he really likes it. It complements the other items in their collection and Anna likes it as well.

As he drives into the parking lot, the mobile phone rings. It is Olle, another collector, who is calling to see if they are on the way. He is worried about the icy November roads and says that he really is looking forward to the dinner tonight. He also asks if they want to take a walk to the Cathedral of Växjö on Sunday morning to see the recently created triptych by glass artist Bertil Vallien.

The collecting club which has gathered in the auditorium represents a group of glass enthusiasts. They listen attentively to the researcher, Dr Karolina Svensson, who starts out by saying that collecting is a widespread activity among consumers in their everyday lives, and this is particularly true among children. Stamps, coins, porcelain figures and cuddly animals are examples of common collections. However, collecting embraces not only material things, but can also involve ideas and experiences such as visits to mountain peaks or islands. Collecting is different from accumulating and hoarding (Belk et al. 1988). A common definition is: 'the process of actively, selectively, and passionately acquiring and possessing things removed from ordinary use and perceived as part of a set of non-identical objects or experiences' (Belk 1995a: 67). The researcher continues her talk on collecting, describing how it reflects many aspects of contemporary consumer culture (e.g. Belk et al. 1991). A collector devotes a lot of resources such as time, money and skills to define and develop his/her individual collection. Exchange, which involves both acquisition and divestment of things, takes place in flea markets, collectors' markets, antique shops and over the internet. Collecting is widespread as it involves both consumption and production phenomena. Collecting represents consumption in that collectable items are acquired, displayed and disposed of, often involving different rituals (e.g. McCracken 1988) related to acquisition, possession and divestment. The collector produces and redefines his/her collection over time by adding, displaying and divesting items. Also, the collector produces him/herself as a collector and relates him/herself to other collectors and collections. In a postmodern society, consumption and production should not be considered as juxtapositions of opposites, but rather as something which is iterative and interchangeable (e.g. Firat and Venkatesh 1995).

Anna whispers to Sven that this all sounds a bit too complex. He nods. The researcher says that individuals creatively construct their own meanings of collecting. It is important to understand not only what a collector does to his/her collection, but what a collection does to the collector. She cites Corrigan (1997: 48) who writes: 'It becomes hard to know whether you are collecting French clocks, or they are collecting you – there is a tight connection between the individual subject and the object.' The audience of glass collectors is laughing. Karolina Svensson thinks that maybe they recognize the strong connections between themselves and their collections.

She continues to present different motives for collecting such as curiosity, interest, nostalgia and memories about times which have passed, status, a way to express power and control, but also social interaction. Sven thinks that for him and Anna it is about interest in glass, the design, the craft involved, the beauty, but also social interaction. Maybe he is more involved in the technical details of how glass is produced than Anna, but she shares the interest in design and really likes visiting glass studios, glass factories, glass exhibitions at museums as well as going to the auctions and collectors' markets regularly. He looks at the collectors who are gathered at the meeting today, wondering what is driving their collecting interest. Well, he knows for sure that for Ulf it is nostalgia. Ulf's collection consists of glass from the glass factory near where he grew up. His father used to work in the glass factory, but it was really only when he grew up that Ulf discovered the beauty of glass and became a collector, focusing on glass from the place where and the period when he grew up. Erik, in the back row, collects drinking glasses, for example, glögg glasses. He loves to bring them out for Christmas and crayfish parties and thinks it is important to use them and not just have them shut away neatly in cupboards. They remind him of parties during his childhood.

The researcher says that collecting can express stability in a turbulent world. Collections can express values or something which is important for a collector's identity. To lose a collection can involve losing part of your identity. Sven thinks that it is good that he installed a burglar alarm recently. Now he does not have to worry about being away for the weekend. Karolina Svensson continues by saying that the degree of goal orientation differs among collectors. Sven thinks of Rune and Ingrid, sitting next to him, who have visited auctions every week for the past 20 years looking for glass. Also, the rituals vary among collectors. While some collectors only want the perfect glass, others are willing to buy something with a chip. Rituals regarding the cleaning of glass and dusting also differ. The researcher explains that collections can be displayed in different ways such as vertical/horizontal, and structured/unstructured (Belk et al. 1988). Vertical display means that the collection is often gathered in a cupboard or on a shelf, while horizontal display means that the collection is spread or scattered around, for example all over the house. The structured/unstructured dimension has to do with aspects of order, balance, and symmetry as opposed to entropy, collative properties and disarray (Belk et al. 1988). Anna whispers to Sven that their collection is displayed horizontally and Sven laughs quietly.

The researcher continues by saying that even though collecting has accelerated in the twentieth century (e.g.

Belk et al. 1991), there is a long history of collecting (e.g. Belk 1995a; Pearce 1995). Some reasons why collecting has increased during the last century are rising real incomes, broadened conceptualization of collectables, accelerated production of identical objects in series or sets, and the reduced age at which old things are perceived as being worth preserving (Belk et al. 1991). Over the years, certain companies have started to mass-merchandise 'collectables' to consumers, for example dolls and coffee cups. They thereby reinforce the social and economic significance of collecting by prepackaging the experience for consumers (Belk et al. 1991). Also, ordinary companies have started to recognize that consumers often buy things for collecting, and therefore have started marketing things as collectables or including promotional collectables in their standard packages (such as breakfast cereals). Karolina Svensson points out that income can be a barrier to what consumers can afford to collect and can therefore be excluding. For example, poorer families may not be able to afford to buy commercial collectables aimed at children. Collecting can involve passionate consumption while the negative aspects can involve addiction and selfishness (Belk 1995a). Collecting which becomes addictive or compulsive can harm both the collector and his/her family financially as well as psychologically (Belk 1995b).

The researcher explains how fears about completing a collection can be avoided by upgrading the standards for the collection, branching into related areas of collecting, or by starting a completely new collection (Belk et al. 1991). It is the process rather than the end which is of interest to the collector. Sven thinks about Arne who is sitting in the first row. His glass collection can never be completed. No one knows how many items were produced of the glass he collects and they lack signatures. Karolina Svensson ends by saying that collectors represent a variety of personalities, people with different experiences and backgrounds. Sven feels happy, the researcher has helped him justify his behaviour to himself: he is not crazy and he is proud of their collection. Karolina Svensson says that collectors develop expertise, become knowledgeable and preserve history. By studying collecting over time, it is possible to recognize how the meanings of things change during different historical periods. Sven and Anna smile and look at each other; it sounds as if their big leisure activity isn't so bad after all, even though they sometimes feel that they spend a little too much money. On the other hand, they do not smoke and they watch their spending carefully when it comes to food and clothes.

QUESTIONS

1 Discuss the ways in which collecting represents symbolic consumption.

2 Give examples of companies which consider collecting in their marketing strategies. Can you identify factors which make them successful and unsuccessful?

3 Interview a collector and try to identify the process of collecting, and also the different rituals related to his/her collecting behaviour(s).

4 Discuss the benefits and problems of collecting in our society.

Sources

Belk, Russell W. (1988), 'Possessions and the extended self', *Journal of Consumer Research* 15, September: 139-68.

Belk, Russell W. (1995a), *Collecting in a Consumer Society* (London: Routledge).

Belk, Russell W. (1995b), 'Collecting as luxury consumption: Effects on individuals and households', *Journal of Economic Psychology* 16: 477-90.

Belk, Russell W., Melanie Wallendorf, John Sherry, Morris Holbrook and Scott Roberts (1988), 'Collectors and Collecting', in *Advances in Consumer Research* 15, Michael J. Houston, ed. (Provo, UT: Association for Consumer Research): 548-53.

Belk, Russell W., Melanie Wallendorf, John F. Sherry Jr. and Morris B. Holbrook (1991), 'Collecting in a Consumer Culture', in *Highways and Buyways*, Russell W. Belk, ed. (Provo, UT: Association for Consumer Research).

Corrigan, Peter (1997), *The Sociology of Consumption: An Introduction* (London: Sage).

Firat, A. Fuat and Alladi Venkatesh (1995), 'Liberatory postmodernism and the reenchantment of consumption', *Journal of Consumer Research* 22, December: 239-67.

McCracken, Grant (1988), *Culture and Consumption* (Bloomington, IN: University Press).

Pearce, Susan M. (1995), *On Collecting: An investigation into collecting in the European Tradition* (London: Routledge).

Adapt or die? Developments in the British funeral industry

DARACH TURLEY, Dublin City University, Eire and
STEPHANIE O'DONOHOE, University of Edinburgh, Scotland

Six Foot Under, the American gothic tragicomedy about a caring but dysfunctional family who run an independent funeral home, has registered impressive ratings on many European TV networks. This superior soap opera has not only been an impressive recruitment tool for an industry not previously associated with glamour and sexiness; it has also lifted the veil on practices shrouded in mystery, fear and distaste. One of the key storylines in the first two series was the family's steadfast refusal to be wooed or bullied into selling out to a large profit-hungry conglomerate. Such a theme would no doubt resonate with many British funeral directors; the UK market – worth over £1 billion a year – has been characterized as a 'cottage industry', since 60 per cent of the market is controlled by private, local firms. The co-operative movement accounts for 25 per cent, and the remaining 15 per cent is controlled by corporate groups. The market is likely to become more consolidated, however, as venture capitalists enter it. Currently, over 600,000 funerals take place each year, at an average cost of around £1,600 (about 2,400 euros) but this number is set to rise in the next decade as baby boomers enter old age.

One of the most significant developments in the UK market was the creation of Dignity Caring Funeral Services in 1994, when Houston-based Service Corporation International (SCI) acquired two regional funeral groups accounting for 12.7 per cent of the UK market. SCI has been called the McDeath of the funeral industry. Owning over 1,200 funeral homes in seven countries, it has grown by acquiring established family-owned funeral homes. Although it standardizes operations where possible, it encourages family members to stay on in the business as employees, and those businesses continue to trade under the original names. Not all private businesses have been tempted to join the SCI fold: as Guy Thompson, an independent funeral operator in Fort Worth, Texas, declared 'a funeral home is more than an inventory, more than its list of clients, more than a profit-making business. A funeral home is an institution that serves the community.'

No stranger to controversy, SCI has been the subject of many lawsuits for restraint of trade, monopolistic practices, and distressing events surrounding the preparation and treatment of human remains. In the UK, its acquisitions attracted the attention of the Competition Commission, which insisted that the company dispose of funeral homes in areas where it dominated the market. More controversy was to come over SCI's working practices. The UK funeral industry has traditionally been characterized by a 'no sell' or 'low sell' approach, but this was not the SCI way; a BBC television exposé in 1996 drew attention to internal SCI documentation concerning its strategies to increase the average spend on funerals (and coffins) and engage in more aggressive selling. Two years later, a Channel 4 documentary caused outrage when it showed staff in one of the company's funeral homes treating the dead disrespectfully. SCI's presence in the UK market is now much reduced; a £220 million management buyout of Dignity took place in 2002, although SCI retained a 20 per cent share of the company. Over 500 funeral directors now work for Dignity, which is the UK's largest provider of funeral plans. Reflecting standard SCI practice, although it has streamlined and standardized its literature, logo, and corporate colours, the Dignity brand is not emphasized; its funeral homes retain their original name to capitalize on local reputation: as the Dignity website puts it, it 'has funeral directors in towns and cities across the country who have served their local communities for generations'.

Co-operative Funeralcare (formerly the Co-operative Group's Funeral Service) is the other major force in the UK market, performing over 85,000 funerals a year through more than 500 branches in the UK. As its website emphasizes, it is part of the Co-operative movement, and thus 'caring for others and concern for the community are at the heart of everything we do'. In recent years, it has sought to update the funeral experience and ensure its services resonate with contemporary consumer requirements. It developed a new design concept for its funeral homes to make them lighter, brighter and more welcoming than the traditional model, associated with 'mahogany furniture, aspidistra plants, a ticking grandfather clock, a musty smell and an elderly gentleman out of a Dickens novel', as one independent undertaker put it. Seeking to provide more choice, knowledge and support to bereaved customers, it established a public panel, Funeralcare Forum, to examine ways of improving funeral experiences. Members of the panel were drawn from various charities working with dying and bereaved people, and the Forum also commissioned research to understand British people's attitudes to death and funerals.

Co-operative Funeralcare also appointed a design company to develop integrated marketing materials, spanning newspaper and radio advertising, display material, classified advertising, direct mail, an information pack and website. Seeking to differentiate the brand by focusing on 'local people giving extraordinary care', promotional material features stories of staff uncovering little details about the deceased which helped bereaved customers create a personally meaningful funeral.

CRITICISMS OF THE FUNERAL INDUSTRY

As the Director General of Fair Trading has noted, 'the bereaved are at their most vulnerable as consumers and need protection from the effects of unfair competition and aggressive sales techniques'. A number of reports indicated that the interests of bereaved consumers have not always been well served. A 2001 report by the Office of Fair Trading (OFT) noted that funeral directors are not subject to any registration, licensing or control, and the absence of compulsory professional qualifications. There was no single code of practice, and compliance with the various codes was 'patchy' and inadequately monitored. Although 96 per cent of the 400 bereaved respondents surveyed expressed satisfaction with the funeral they had organized, many people did not know what to expect in the first place. They felt under pressure to act quickly, spent little time thinking about their purchase and were reluctant to shop around. The OFT recommended that funeral businesses should be more open about their charges, details of their ownership and the options available to consumers.

Several subsequent reports indicate little progress. A 2002 *Which?* report drew on a mystery shopping exercise in 25 funeral homes – including independent, Co-op and Dignity businesses. While most funeral directors were helpful and considerate, a few were tactless and insensitive, and the quality of information and advice was sometimes poor. Enormous differences in price, service levels and code compliance were found. No one tried to pressure the researchers into buying expensive, unsuitable coffins, but some commented disparagingly on the cheapest options. Similarly, the Citizens Advice Service has provided evidence of a continuing lack of information on choice, costs and sources of financial assistance.

It appears that funeral directors are not the only ones causing problems for bereaved consumers; research by the Funeralcare Forum indicates that families have been poorly served by crematoria, which set vastly inconsistent (and often unreasonably short) time slots for example, and by the lack of standard regulations across burial authorities concerning headstone size, material, inscriptions and mementoes.

THE TREND TOWARDS PERSONALIZATION

One development facing both individual and conglomerate funeral directors in the UK is growing consumer disillusion with standardized, conveyer-belt funeral and burial ceremonies. This development may be attributed in part to an ageing population: at the beginning of the twentieth century two-thirds of all deaths were due to infectious diseases where people died young and relatively quickly. Nowadays, the same proportion die from long-term degenerative ailments associated with old age, meaning that they will have both the time and the ability to arrange their own rituals of departure and disposal. The move towards personalization may also reflect a more general desire on the part of consumers to individualize and personalize marketplace offerings. Very often, this trend results in moving away from the commercially specified, commodified product or service and returning to some original, more authentic and wholesome version. There are signs that this mood is filtering through to the funeral industry too. Dissatisfied with what are seen as tired, depersonalized generic funeral rituals, both those planning ahead for their funerals and bereaved survivors are looking to play a more active role in the style and format of the final farewell. A report commissioned by Co-operative Funeralcare found 'growing enthusiasm for personal, custom-made ceremonies that owe less and less to religion'. Even within the more traditional funeral ceremony there are signs that mourners desire more involvement, coupled with greater flexibility and less anonymity in the way it is conducted. For example, goods and possessions that were intimately associated with the dead person – part of their extended self – or that symbolized their goals or accomplishments feature prominently in many services. Most ceremonies now include some appreciation of the deceased spoken by a close relative or friend. Indeed, responding to growing demand for advice on writing eulogies, Co-operative Funeralcare published a guide called *Well-Chosen Words*, containing examples of tributes to both public and private figures.

The personalizing imperative is also evident in the choice of funeral music. In 2002, the Co-operative

Group's Funeral Service reported increasing demand for popular music, with the top three songs being Bette Midler's 'Wind Beneath My Wings', Celine Dion's 'My Heart Will Go On', and Whitney Houston's 'I Will Always Love You'. A sense of gallows humour is evident in other less common choices, such as 'Firestarter' by The Prodigy, 'Another One Bites the Dust' by Queen, and 'Wake Me Up Before You Go-Go' by Wham! In March 2005, 45,000 Europeans were asked what music they would like to be played at their funeral. The top two choices were Queen's 'The Show Must Go On' and Led Zeppelin's 'Stairway to Heaven'. Mozart's *Requiem* was the only piece of classical music featuring in the top ten, causing *The Times* newspaper to print an editorial bemoaning the departure from the dirge in funerals.

The break with tradition can also be seen in new ways of disposal. At present there are over 100 woodland and nature reserve burial sites dotted around the UK countryside. Clients are welcome to visit and select their preferred burial site while still well and in full health. The manicured and managed rows of headstones in traditional cemeteries have given way to woodlands and meadows. Families can use whichever mode of transport they wish to bring the remains to the site. Any type of coffin, casket or shroud is acceptable provided it is biodegradable. Headstones and plaques have been replaced by wooden notices that will disintegrate over time. There is a strong preference at these sites for burial and the ceremony itself tends to be of the 'designer' variety, tailored to the life, loves and achievements of the deceased. For those who have been cremated, there is still great potential for personalization. Many people have their ashes scattered in a favourite place, like a football ground, river, or site of significant memories.

QUESTIONS

1 Many consumer advocacy groups have expressed concern over the vulnerability of bereaved consumers to commercial exploitation. To what extent do you feel this concern is justified?

2 What are the barriers to an overtly commercial approach to providing funeral services in the UK?

3 In Chapter 14 it was noted that rituals usually involve both symbolic behaviours and artefacts. What would you consider to be the principal symbolic behaviours and artefacts in contemporary British funerals? Are there any of these elements that are 'new', any others that seem to be diminishing in importance?

4 How do developments within the UK funeral industry reflect changing consumer demographics, values and lifestyles?

5 Researching the needs or experiences of bereaved consumers calls for great sensitivity on the part of the researcher. What considerations should be taken into account in order to conduct ethical research in this area?

Sources

Ahmed, K. (1998), 'Funeral firm tries to ban TV exposé', The *Guardian* (12 May): 7.

Consumers Association (2002); *Which? Online Report on Funeral Directors* (March), www.which.co.uk.

Dwek, R. (1999), 'Death and the salesmen', *Marketing Business* (March): 12–15.

Gardner, S. (2004), 'Stiff competition: making a living with death', www.brandchannel.com/features (12 April).

Godwin, P. and S. Boseley (1996), 'Have a nice death', *The Guardian* (27 February).

Hudson, S. (2004), 'Fending off McDeath', *Fort Worth Weekly Online* (24 November) www.fwweekly.com/isues/2004-11-24/feature.asp.

Marsh, S. (2005), 'Hymns? We're playing Angels instead', *The Times* (10 March).

Office of Fair Trading (2001) Funerals: a report of the OFT inquiry into the funerals industry, July, http://www.oft.gov.uk/NR/rdonlyres/3D07A9EC-F0CB-4531-AIAF-03309C09F560/0/report2.pdf.

Toomey, Christine (2000), 'DIY Funerals', *Sunday Times Magazine* (29 October)

http://bifd.org.uk: British Institute of Funeral Directors
www.funeralcare.co-op.co.uk
http://nafd.org.uk: National Association of Funeral Directors
http://ww7.investorrelations.co.uk/dignity/index.jsp: Dignity Website

GLOSSARY

Absolute threshold the minimum amount of stimulation that can be detected on a sensory channel (p. 46)

Accommodative purchase decision the process to achieve agreement among a group whose members have different preferences or priorities (p. 410)

Acculturation the process of learning the beliefs and behaviours endorsed by another culture (pp. 115, 589)

Acculturation agents friends, family, local businesses and other reference groups which facilitate the learning of cultural norms (p. 589)

Activation models of memory approaches to memory stressing different levels of processing that occur and activate some aspects of memory rather than others, depending on the nature of the processing task (p. 74)

Actual self a person's realistic appraisal of his or her qualities (p. 210)

Adaptation the process that occurs when a sensation becomes so familiar that it is no longer the focus of attention (p. 48)

Affect the way a consumer feels about an attitude object (p. 140)

Age cohort a group of consumers of the same approximate age who have undergone similar experiences (p. 456)

Agentic goals goals that stress self-assertion and mastery and are associated with males (p. 216)

AIOs (Activities, Interests and Opinions) the psychographic variables used by researchers in grouping consumers (p. 563)

Androgyny the possession of both masculine and feminine traits (p. 217)

Anti-foundationalism an anti-campaign campaign encouraging the consumer not to take notice of a message (p. 623)

Art product a creation viewed primarily as an object of aesthetic contemplation without any functional value (p. 532)

Atmospherics the use of space and physical features in store design to evoke certain effects in buyers (p. 323)

Attention the assignment of cognitive capacity to selected stimuli (p. 48)

Attitude a lasting, general evaluation of people (including oneself), objects or issues (p. 138)

Attitude object (A$_o$) anything towards which one has an attitude (p. 138)

Attitude towards the act of buying (A$_{act}$) the perceived consequences of a purchase (p. 156)

Attitude towards the advertisement (A$_{ad}$) a predisposition to respond favourably to a particular advertising stimulus during an exposure situation (p. 144)

Autocratic decisions purchase decisions that are made exclusively by one spouse (p. 411)

Baby boomers a large cohort of people born between 1946 and 1964 who are the source of many important cultural and economic changes (p. 464)

Balance theory considers relations among elements a person might perceive as belonging together and people's tendency to change relations among elements in order to make them consistent or balanced (p. 149)

Behaviour a consumer's actions with regard to an attitude object (p. 140)

Behavioural economics the study of the behavioural determinants of economic decisions (p. 428)

Behavioural influence perspective the view that consumer decisions are learned responses to environmental cues (p. 260)

Behavioural learning theories the perspectives on learning that assume that learning takes place as the result of responses to external events (p. 62)

Binary opposition a defining structural characteristic where two opposing ends of a dimension are presented (p. 504)

Body cathexis a person's feelings about aspects of his or her body (p. 223)

Body image a consumer's subjective evaluation of his or her physical appearance (p. 223)

Brand equity a brand that has strong positive associations and consequently commands a lot of loyalty (p. 67)

Brand loyalty a pattern of repeat product purchases accompanied by an underlying positive attitude towards the brand (p. 289)

Chronology the consumer's search for the authentic and a preoccupation with the past (p. 622)

Classic a fashion with an extremely long acceptance cycle (p. 550)

Classical conditioning the learning that occurs when a stimulus eliciting a response is paired with another stimulus which initially does not elicit a response on its own but will cause a similar response over time because of its association with the first stimulus (p. 63)

Cognition the beliefs a consumer has about an attitude object (p. 140)

Cognitive development the ability to comprehend concepts of increasing complexity as a person ages (p. 418)

Cognitive learning the learning that occurs as a result of internal mental processes (p. 66)

Cognitive structure the factual knowledge or set of beliefs about a product and the way these are organized (p. 275)

Collecting the accumulation of rare or mundane and inexpensive objects, which transforms profane items into sacred ones (p. 517)

Collective selection the process whereby certain symbolic alternatives tend to be chosen jointly in preference to others by members of a group (p. 545)

Collectivist culture a cultural orientation which encourages people to subordinate their personal goals to those of a stable in-group (p. 501)

Communal goals goals that stress affiliation and the fostering of harmonious relations and are associated with females (p. 216)

Communications model a framework specifying that a number of elements are necessary for communication to be achieved including a source, message, medium, receivers and feedback (p. 168)

Comparative influence the process whereby a reference group influences decisions about specific brands or activities (p. 350)

Compatibility a prerequisite for a product's adoption; the product should fit the consumer's lifestyle (p. 485)

Compensatory decision rules allow information about attributes of competing products to be averaged; poor standing on one attribute may be offset by good standing on another (p. 291)

Complexity ease of understanding and use of a product; greater ease lowers the effort and perceived risk in adoption (p. 485)

Conformity a change in beliefs or actions as a reaction to real or perceived group pressure (p. 361)

Consensual purchase decision a decision in which the group agrees on the desired purchase and differs only in terms of how it will be achieved (p. 410)

Conspicuous consumption the purchase and prominent display of luxury goods as evidence of the consumer's ability to afford them (pp. 447, 546)

Consumer addiction a physiological and/or psychological dependency on products or services (p. 519)

Consumer behaviour the processes involved when individuals or groups select, purchase, use or dispose of products, services, ideas or experiences to satisfy needs or desires (p. 5)

Consumer confidence the state of mind of consumers relative to their optimism or pessimism about economic decisions; people tend to make more discretionary purchases when their confidence in the economy is high (p. 430)

Consumer satisfaction/dissatisfaction (CS/D) the overall attitude a person has about a product after it has been purchased (p. 328)

Consumer socialization the process by which people acquire skills that enable them to function in the marketplace (p. 415)

Consumption constellations a set of products and activities used by consumers to define, communicate and perform social roles (p. 562)

Continuous innovation a product change or new product that requires relatively little adaptation in the consumer's behaviour (p. 540)

Convention norms regarding the conduct of everyday life (p. 503)

Co-optation a cultural process where the original meaning of a product or other symbol associated with a subculture is modified by members of mainstream culture (p. 498)

Craft product a creation valued because of the beauty with which it performs some function; this type of product tends to follow a formula that permits rapid production; it is easier to understand than an art product (p. 532)

Creolization the blending of various eating traditions with new ones to make national food tastes fit the tastes of mainstream culture (p. 617)

Cultivation hypothesis a perspective emphasizing media's ability to distort consumers' perceptions of reality (p. 537)

Cultural categories the grouping of ideas and values that reflect the basic ways members of society characterize the world (p. 543)

Cultural formula where certain roles and props often occur consistently in many popular art forms, such as detective stories or science fiction (p. 534)

Cultural gatekeepers individuals who are responsible for determining the types of message and symbolism to which members of mass culture are exposed (p. 531)

Cultural selection the process where some alternatives are selected in preference to those selected by cultural gatekeepers (p. 530)

Culture the values, ethics, rituals, traditions, material objects and services produced or valued by members of society (p. 498)

Culture production system (CPS) the set of individuals or organizations responsible for creating and marketing a cultural product (p. 531)

Custom a norm that is derived from a traditional way of doing something (p. 502)

Database marketing involves tracking consumers' buying habits and crafting products and information tailored to people's wants and needs (p. 14)

De-differentiation the blurring of distinctions between hierarchies such as high and low cultures or politics and show business (p. 622)

De-individuation the process whereby individual identities are submerged within a group, reducing inhibitions against socially inappropriate behaviour (p. 365)

Demographics the observable measurements of a population's characteristics, such as birth rates, age distribution or income (p. 9)

Desacralization the process that occurs when a sacred item or symbol is removed or is duplicated in mass quantities and as a result becomes profane (p. 515)

Desire to wish or long for consumer goods which contribute to the formation of consumers' self-image; also refers to the sociogenic nature of needs (p. 103)

Differential threshold the ability of a sensory system to detect changes or differences among stimuli (p. 46)

Discontinuous innovation a product change or new product that requires a significant amount of adaptation of behaviour by the adopter (p. 541)

Discretionary income the money available to an individual or household over and above that required for maintaining a standard of living (p. 430)

Drive theory focuses on the desire to satisfy a biological need in order to reduce physiological arousal (p. 92)

Dynamically continuous innovation a product change or new product that requires a moderate amount of adaptation of behaviour by the adopter (p. 541)

Early adopters people receptive to new styles because they are involved in the product category and place high value on being fashionable (p. 539)

Ego the system that mediates between the id and the superego (p. 101)

Ego involvement the importance of a product to a consumer's self-concept (p. 109)

Elaborated codes the ways of expressing and interpreting meanings that are complex and depend on a sophisticated worldview; they tend to be used by the middle and upper classes (p. 443)

Elaboration likelihood model (ELM) the approach that one of two routes to persuasion (central vs. peripheral) will be followed, depending on the personal relevance of a message; the route taken determines the relative importance of message contents vs. other characteristics, such as source attractiveness (p. 196)

Emic perspective an approach to studying cultures that stresses the unique aspects of each culture (p. 610)

Encoding the process in which information from short-term memory is entered into long-term memory in recognizable form (p. 72)

Enculturation the process of learning the beliefs and behaviours endorsed by one's own culture (p. 115)

Environmentalism a general concern for the environment as it is affected by all aspects of production and consumption processes (p. 602)

Erogenous zones areas of the body considered by members of a culture to be foci of sexual attractiveness (p. 545)

Ethnic subculture a self-perpetuating group of consumers held together by common cultural ties (p. 588)

Ethnoconsumerism the understanding and analysis of each culture, including consumer culture, on the basis of its own premises (p. 501)

Ethos a set of moral, aesthetic and evaluative principles (p. 500)

Etic perspective an approach to studying culture that stresses the commonalities across cultures (p. 609)

Evaluative criteria the dimensions used by consumers to compare competing product alternatives (p. 277)

Evoked set those products already in memory plus those prominent in the retail environment that are actively considered during a consumer's choice process (pp. 74, 273)

Exchange the process whereby two or more organizations or people give and receive something of value (p. 7)

Exchange theory the perspective that every interaction involves an exchange of value (p. 327)

Expectancy disconfirmation model the perspective that consumers form beliefs about product performance based on prior experience with the product and/or communications about the product that imply a certain level of quality; their actual satisfaction depends on the degree to which performance is consistent with these expectations (p. 329)

Expectancy theory the perspective that behaviour is largely 'pulled' by expectations of achieving desirable 'outcomes' or positive incentives, rather than 'pushed' from within (p. 93)

Experiential perspective an approach stressing the gestalt or totality of the product or service experience, focusing on consumers' affective responses in the marketplace (p. 260)

Exposure an initial stage of perception where some sensations come within range of consumers' sensory receptors (p. 47)

Extended family traditional family structure where several generations and/or relatives such as aunts, uncles and cousins live together (p. 405)

Extended problem-solving an elaborate decision-making process often initiated by a motive that's fairly central to the self-concept and accompanied by perceived risk; the consumer tries to collect as much information as possible and carefully weighs product alternatives (p. 261)

Extended self the definition of self created by the external objects with which one surrounds oneself (p. 214)

Extinction the process whereby learned connections between a stimulus and response are eroded so that the response is no longer reinforced (p. 63)

Fad a short-lived fashion (p. 550)

Family financial officer (FFO) the family member who is in charge of making financial decisions (p. 411)

Family household a housing unit containing at least two people who are related by blood or marriage (p. 405)

Family life cycle (FLC) a classification scheme that segments consumers in terms of changes in income and family composition and the changes in demands placed on this income (p. 408)

Fantasy a self-induced shift in consciousness, often focusing on an unattainable or improbable goal; sometimes fantasy is a way of compensating for a lack of external stimulation or for dissatisfaction with the actual self (p. 210)

Fashion the process of social diffusion by which a new style is adopted by a group or groups of consumers (p. 543)

Fashion acceptance cycle the diffusion process of a style through three stages: introduction, acceptance and regression (p. 549)

Fashion life cycle the 'career' or stages in the life of a fashion as it progresses from launch to obsolescence (p. 548)

Fashion system those people or organizations involved in creating symbolic meanings and transferring these meanings to cultural goods (p. 543)

Fear appeal an attempt to change attitudes or behaviour through the use of threats or by the highlighting of negative consequences of non-compliance with the request (p. 191)

Fertility rate a rate determined by the number of births per year per 1,000 women of child-bearing age (p. 406)

Figure-ground principle the gestalt principle whereby one part of a stimulus configuration dominates a situation while other aspects recede into the background (p. 52)

Foot-in-the-door technique based on the observation that a consumer is more likely to comply with a request if he or she has first agreed to comply with a smaller request (p. 149)

Fragmentation the splitting up of what used to be simple and mass-oriented, exemplified by ever-growing product ranges and brand extensions (p. 622)

Frequency marketing a marketing technique that reinforces regular purchasers by giving them prizes with values that increase along with the amount purchased (p. 70)

Functional theory of attitudes a pragmatic approach that focuses on how attitudes facilitate social behaviour; attitudes exist because they serve some function for the person (p. 139)

Generation X (Gen-Xers or baby busters) the cohort of consumers aged 18–29, who were profoundly affected by the economic recession of the early 1990s (p. 462)

Geodemography techniques that combine consumer demographic information with geographic consumption patterns to permit precise targeting of consumers with specific characteristics (p. 586)

Gerontographics a research tool which divides the mature market into groups based on level of physical well-being and social conditions (p. 471)

Gestalt psychology a school of thought that maintains people derive meaning from the totality of a set of stimuli rather than from an individual stimulus (p. 51)

Gift-giving ritual the events involved in the selection, presentation, acceptance and interpretation of a gift (p. 508)

Goal a consumer's desired end-state (p. 90)

Grey market term used to describe the phenomenon of a fast-growing segment of consumers aged 62 or older (p. 468)

Habitual decision-making the consumption choices that are made out of habit, without additional information search or deliberation among products (p. 262)

Habitus systems of classification of phenomena adopted from our socialization processes (p. 569)

Hedonic consumption the multisensory, fantasy and emotional aspects of consumers' interactions with products (p. 39)

Heuristics the mental rules of thumb that lead to a speedy decision (p. 280)

Hierarchy of effects a fixed sequence of steps that occurs during attitude formation; this sequence varies depending on such factors as the consumer's level of involvement with the attitude object (p. 140)

High-context culture group members tend to be tightly knit and messages and meanings are implicit and built into the communication context (p. 564)

Homeostasis the state of being where the body is in physiological balance; goal-oriented behaviour attempts to reduce or eliminate an unpleasant motivational state and returns to a balanced one (p. 92)

Hyperreality a phenomenon associated with modern advertising in which what is initially stimulation or hype becomes real (p. 55, 622)

Icon a sign that resembles the product in some culturally meaningful way (p. 53)

Id the system oriented to immediate gratification (p. 100)

Ideal of beauty a model, or exemplar, of appearance valued by a culture (p. 224)

Ideal self a person's conception of how he or she would like to be (p. 210)

Impulse buying a process that occurs when the consumer experiences a sudden urge to purchase an item that he or she cannot resist (p. 324)

Individualist culture a cultural orientation that encourages people to attach more importance to personal goals than to group goals; values such as personal enjoyment and freedom are stressed (p. 501)

Inertia the process whereby purchase decisions are made out of habit because the consumer lacks the motivation to consider alternatives (pp. 106, 289)

Information power power given simply because one knows something others would like to know (p. 360)

Information search the process whereby a consumer searches for appropriate information to make a reasonable decision (p. 265)

Informational social influence the conformity that occurs because the group's behaviour is taken as evidence about reality (p. 362)

Innovative communicators opinion leaders who are also early purchasers (p. 376)

Instrumental values those goals that are endorsed because they are needed to achieve desired end-states or terminal values (p. 118)

Interactionist a perspective on human communication which relies on three basic premises about communication, i.e. the meaning of things, ideas and actions (p. 169)

Interference a process whereby additional learned information displaces earlier information resulting in memory loss for the item learned previously (p. 78)

Interpretant the meaning derived from a symbol (p. 53)

Interpretation the process whereby meanings are assigned to stimuli (p. 50)

Interpretivism a research perspective that produces a 'thick' description of a consumer's subjective experiences and stresses the importance of the individual's social construction of reality (p. 26)

Invidious distinction the display of wealth or power to inspire envy in others (p. 447)

Involvement the motivation to process product-related information (p. 105)

ISO standards a set of quality criteria developed in 1987 to regulate product quality by the International Standards Organization (p. 329)

JND (just noticeable difference) the minimum change in a stimulus that can be detected by a perceiver (p. 46)

Kin network system the rituals intended to maintain ties among family members, both immediate and extended (p. 412)

Knowledge structures organized systems of concepts relating to brands, stores and other concepts (p. 74)

Laddering a technique for uncovering consumers' associations between specific attributes and general consequences (p. 119)

Lateral cycling a process where already purchased objects are sold to others or exchanged for other items (p. 336)

Latitudes of acceptance and rejection formed around an attitude standard; ideas that fall within a latitude will be favourably received, while those falling outside this zone will not (p. 149)

Learning a relatively permanent change in a behaviour as a result of experience (p. 62)

Lifestyle a set of shared values or tastes exhibited by a group of consumers especially as these are reflected in consumption patterns (p. 558)

Lifestyle marketing perspective a perspective that recognizes that people are increasingly conscious that we sort ourselves and each other into groups on the basis of the things we/they like to do and how we/they spend our/their disposable income (p. 560)

Limited problem-solving a problem-solving process in which consumers are not motivated to search for information or evaluate rigorously each alternative; instead they use simple decision rules to arrive at a purchase decision (p. 262)

Long-term memory the system that allows us to retain information for a long period (p. 74)

Looking-glass self the process of imagining the reaction of others towards oneself (p. 211)

LOV (list of values) a scale developed to isolate values with more direct marketing applications (p. 118)

Low-context culture messages tend to be more explicit, specific and direct (p. 584)

Market beliefs the specific beliefs of decision rules pertaining to marketplace phenomena (p. 281)

Market maven a person who often serves as a source of information about marketplace activities (p. 376)

Materialism the importance consumers attach to worldly possessions (p. 125)

Means-end chain a research approach that assumes that very specific product attributes are linked at levels of increasing abstraction to terminal values (p. 119)

MECCAs (Means-end Conceptualization of the Components of Advertising Strategy) a research approach in which researchers generate a map depicting relationships between functional product or service attributes and terminal values and then use this information to develop advertising strategy (p. 121)

Memory a process of acquiring information and storing it over time (p. 72)

Metaphor the use of an explicit comparison between a product and some other person, place or thing (p. 194)

Monomyth a myth with basic characteristics that are found in many cultures (p. 504)

Mores norms with strong moral overtones (p. 503)

Motivation an internal state that activates goal-oriented behaviour (p. 90)

Motivational research a qualitative research approach based on psychoanalytical (Freudian) interpretations with a heavy emphasis on unconscious motives for consumption (p. 101)

Multi-attribute attitude models those models that assume that a consumer's attitude (evaluation) of an attitude object depends on the beliefs he or she has about several or many attributes of the object; the use of a multiattribute model implies that an attitude towards a product or brand can be predicted by identifying these specific beliefs and combining them to derive a measure of the consumer's overall attitude (p. 151)

Myth a story containing symbolic elements which expresses the shared emotion and ideals of a culture (p. 504)

National character a distinctive set of behaviour and personality characteristics that describe a country's people or culture (p. 610)

Negative reinforcement the process whereby a negative reward weakens responses to stimuli so that inappropriate behaviour is avoided in the future (p. 64)

Non-compensatory decision rules a set of simple rules used to evaluate competing alternatives; a brand with a low standing on one relevant attribute is eliminated from the consumer's choice set (p. 290)

Normative influence the process in which a reference group helps to set and enforce basic standards of conduct (p. 350)

Normative social influence the conformity that occurs when a person alters his or her behaviour to meet the expectations of a person or group (p. 362)

Norms the informal rules that govern what is right and wrong (p. 361)

Nostalgia a bittersweet emotion when the past is viewed with sadness and longing; many 'classic' products appeal to consumers' memories of their younger days (p. 78)

Nuclear family a contemporary living arrangement composed of a married couple and their children (p. 405)

Object a semiotic term, the product that is the focus of the message (p. 53)

Observability the visibility of a product (p. 542)

Observational learning the process in which people learn by watching the actions of others and noting the reinforcements they receive for their behaviours (p. 66)

Operant conditioning the process by which the individual learns to perform behaviours that produce positive outcomes and to avoid those that yield negative outcomes (p. 64)

Opinion leaders those people who are knowledgeable about products and who are frequently able to influence others' attitudes or behaviours with regard to a product category (p. 374)

Opinion seekers usually opinion leaders who are also involved in a product category and actively search for information (p. 376)

Paradigm a widely accepted view or model of phenomena being studied. The perspective that regards people as *rational information processors* is currently the dominant paradigm, though this approach is now being challenged by a new wave of research that emphasizes the frequently subjective nature of consumer decision-making (p. 26)

Parental yielding the process that occurs when a parental decision-maker is influenced by a child's product request (p. 414)

Parody display the deliberate avoidance of widely used status symbols, whereby the person seeks status by mocking it (p. 449)

Pastiche the playful and ironic mixing of existing categories and styles (p. 623)

Perceived age how old a person feels rather than his or her chronological age (p. 470)

Perceived risk the belief that use of a product has potentially negative consequences, either physical or social (p. 271)

Perception the process by which stimuli are selected, organized or interpreted (p. 36)

Perceptual selectivity the process in which people attend to only a small portion of the stimuli to which they are exposed (p. 47)

Persuasion an active attempt to change attitudes (p. 166)

Pluralism the coexistence of various styles, truths and fashions (p. 621)

Point-of-purchase stimuli (POP) the promotional materials that are deployed in shops or other outlets to influence consumers; decisions at the time products are purchased (p. 326)

Political consumer the political consumer uses his or her buying pattern as a weapon against or support for companies which share the person's own values (p. 606)

Popular culture the music, films, sports, books, celebrities and other forms of entertainment consumed by the mass market (p. 14)

Positive reinforcement the process whereby rewards provided by the environment strengthen response to stimuli (p. 64)

Positivism a research perspective that relies on the principles of the 'scientific method' and assumes that a single reality exists; events in the world can be objectively measured; and the causes of behaviour can be identified, manipulated and predicted (p. 26)

Postmodernism a theory that questions the search for universal truths and values and the existence of objective knowledge (p. 621)

Potlatch a Kwakiutl Indian feast at which the host displays his wealth and gives extravagant gifts (p. 448)

Priming the process in which certain properties of a stimulus are more likely to evoke a schema than others (p. 50)

Principle of closure implies that consumers tend to perceive an incomplete picture as complete (p. 51)

Principle of cognitive consistency the belief that consumers value harmony among their thoughts, feelings and behaviours and that they are motivated to maintain uniformity among these elements (p. 146)

Principle of similarity the gestalt principle that describes how consumers tend to group objects that share similar physical characteristics (p. 52)

Problem recognition the process that occurs whenever the consumer sees a significant difference between his or her current state and some desired or ideal state; this recognition initiates the decision-making process (p. 263)

Product complementarity the view that products in different functional categories have symbolic meanings that are related to one another (p. 561)

Product placement the process of obtaining exposure for a product by arranging for it to be inserted into a film, television programme or some other medium (p. 537)

Profane consumption the process of consuming objects and events that are ordinary or of the everyday world (p. 512)

Psychographics the use of psychological, sociological and anthropological factors to construct market segments (pp. 9, 562)

Punishment the process or outcome that occurs when a response is followed by unpleasant events (p. 64)

Racial subculture a self-perpetuating group held together by ties of common culture and/or genetics, identified by its members and others as a distinguishable category (p. 588)

Rational perspective a view of the consumer as a careful, analytical decision-maker who tries to maximize utility in purchase decisions (p. 259)

Reactance a boomerang effect that may occur when consumers are threatened with a loss of freedom of choice; they respond by doing the opposite of the behaviour advocated in a persuasive message (p. 367)

Reality engineering the process whereby elements of popular culture are appropriated by marketers and become integrated into marketing strategies (e.g. product placement) (p. 535)

Recycling the re-use of resources in order to protect the environment (p. 600)

Reference group an actual or imaginary individual or group which has a significant effect on an individual's evaluations, aspirations or behaviour (p. 350)

Referent power the power of prominent people to affect others' consumption behaviours by virtue of product endorsements, distinctive fashion statements or championing causes (p. 360)

Relationship marketing the strategic perspective that stresses the long-term, human side of buyer/seller interactions (p. 13)

Relative advantage the belief that a product's use will provide a benefit other products cannot offer (p. 542)

Resonance a literary device, frequently used in advertising, which uses a play on words to communicate a product benefit (p. 195)

Response bias a form of contamination in survey research where some factor, such as the desire to make a good impression on the experimenter, leads respondents to modify their true answers (p. 82)

Restricted codes the ways of expressing and interpreting meanings that focus on the content of objects and tend to be used by the working class (p. 443)

Retrieval the process whereby desired information is accessed from long-term memory (p. 72)

RISC (Research Institute on Social Change) an organization that conducts international measurements of socio-cultural change in more than 40 countries (p. 565)

Risky shift group members show a greater willingness to consider riskier alternatives following group discussions than they would if each member made his or her own decision without prior discussion (p. 366)

Rites of passage sacred times marked by a change in social status (p. 511)

Ritual a set of multiple, symbolic behaviours that occur in fixed sequence and that tend to be repeated periodically (p. 506)

Ritual artefacts items or consumer goods used in the performance of rituals (p. 508)

Role theory the perspective that much of consumer behaviour resembles action in a play (p. 6)

Rumour a word-of-mouth campaign to promote one product and criticize its competitors (p. 371)

Sacralization a process that occurs when ordinary objects, events or people take on sacred meaning to a culture or to specific groups within a culture (p. 517)

Sacred consumption the process of consuming objects and events that are set apart from normal life and treated with some degree of respect or awe (p. 512)

Savings rate the amount of money saved for later use influenced by consumers' pessimism or optimism about their personal circumstances and perceptions of the economy (p. 432)

Schema an organized collection of beliefs and feelings represented in a cognitive category (pp. 37, 76)

Self-concept the attitude a person holds to him- or herself (p. 208)

Self-gifts the products or services bought by consumers for their own use as a reward or consolation (p. 510)

Self-image congruence models the approaches based on the prediction that products will be chosen when their attributes match some aspect of the self (p. 213)

Self-perception theory an alternative explanation of dissonance effects; it assumes that people use observations of their own behaviour to infer their attitudes towards an object (p. 148)

Semiotics a field of study that examines the correspondence between a sign and the meaning(s) it conveys (p. 52)

Sensation the immediate response of sensory receptors to such basic stimuli as light, colour and sound (p. 36)

Sensory memory the temporary storage of information received from the senses (p. 73)

Sex-typed traits characteristics that are stereotypically associated with one sex or another (p. 216)

Shopping orientation a consumer's general attitudes and motivations regarding the act of shopping (p. 313)

Short-term memory the system that allows us to retain information for a short period (p. 73)

Sign the sensory imagery that represents the intended meanings of the object (p. 53)

Signifying practices practices that have meaning to individuals, who know how to interpret them, thanks to the understanding of culture as the interpreting system (p. 499)

Single-source data a compilation of information that includes different aspects of consumption and demographic data for a common consumer segment (p. 586)

Sleeper effect the process whereby differences in attitude change between positive and negative sources seem to diminish over time (p. 173)

Social class the overall rank of people in society; people who are grouped within the same social class are approximately equal in terms of their social standing, occupations and lifestyles (p. 433)

Social comparison theory the perspective that people compare their outcomes with others as a way to increase the stability of their own self-evaluation, especially when physical evidence is unavailable (p. 363)

Social hierarchy a ranking of social desirability in terms of consumers' access to such resources as money, education and luxury goods (p. 434)

Social judgement theory the perspective that people assimilate new information about attitude objects in the light of what they already know or feel; the initial attitude as a frame of reference and new information are categorized in terms of this standard (p. 149)

Social marketing the promotion of causes and ideas (social products), such as energy conservation, charities and population control (p. 19)

Social mobility the movement of individuals from one social class to another (p. 438)

Social stratification the process in a social system by which scarce and valuable resources are distributed unequally to status positions which become more or less permanently ranked in terms of the share of valuable resources each receives (p. 437)

Sociometric methods the techniques for measuring group dynamics that involve tracing of communication patterns in and among groups (p. 379)

Source attractiveness the dimensions of a communicator which increase his or her persuasiveness; these include expertise and attractiveness (p. 176)

Source credibility a communication source's perceived expertise, objectivity or trustworthiness (p. 173)

Stage of cognitive development segmentation of children by age or their ability to comprehend concepts of increasing complexity (p. 418)

Status crystallization the extent to which different indicators of a person's status are consistent with one another (p. 441)

Status symbols products that are purchased and displayed to signal membership in a desirable social class (p. 428)

Stimulus discrimination the process that occurs when behaviour caused by two stimuli is different as when consumers learn to differentiate a brand from its competitors (p. 64)

Stimulus generalization the process that occurs when the behaviour caused by a reaction to one stimulus occurs in the presence of other, similar stimuli (p. 63)

Storage the process that occurs when knowledge entered in long-term memory is integrated with what is already in memory and 'warehoused' until needed (p. 72)

Store gestalt consumers' global evaluation of a store (p. 323)

Store image the 'personality' of a shop composed of attributes such as location, merchandise suitability and the knowledge and congeniality of the sales staff (p. 322)

Subculture a group whose members share beliefs and common experiences that set them apart from the members of the main culture (p. 587)

Superego the system that internalizes society's rules which works to prevent the id from seeking selfish gratification (p. 101)

Surrogate consumer a professional who is retained to evaluate and/or make purchases on behalf of a consumer (p. 377)

Symbolic interactionism a sociological approach stressing that relationships with people play a large part in forming the self; people live in a symbolic environment and the meaning attached to any situation or object is determined by a person's interpretation of those symbols (p. 210)

Symbolic self-completion theory the perspective that people who have an incomplete self-definition in some context will compensate by acquiring symbols associated with a desired social identity (p. 213)

Syncratic decisions purchase decisions that are made jointly by spouses (p. 411)

Taste culture a group of consumers who share aesthetic and intellectual preferences (p. 443)

Terminal values end-states desired by members of a culture (p. 118)

Theory of cognitive dissonance   a theory based on the premise that people have a need for order and consistency in their lives and that a state of tension is created when beliefs or behaviours conflict with one another (p. 95)

Theory of reasoned action   a version of the Fishbein multi-attitude theory that considers such factors as social pressure and the attitude towards the act of buying a product rather than attitudes towards just the product itself (p. 155)

Time style   determined by an individual's priorities, it incorporates such dimensions as economic time, past or future orientation, time submissiveness and time anxiety (p. 306)

Transitional economies   countries that are in the process of transforming their economic system from a controlled, centralized system to a free market one (p. 617)

Trialability   the likelihood of experimenting with an innovation prior to making a commitment (p. 541)

Trickle-down theory   the perspective that fashions spread as a result of status symbols associated with the upper classes trickling down to the other social classes as these consumers try to emulate those with higher status (p. 546)

Two-factor theory   the perspective that two separate psychological processes are operating when a person is repeatedly exposed to an ad; repetition increases familiarity and thus reduces uncertainty about the product, but over time boredom increases with each exposure and at some point the level of boredom begins to exceed the amount of uncertainty reduced, resulting in wear-out (p. 184)

Uses and gratifications theory   argues that consumers are an active, goal-directed audience who draw on mass media as a resource to satisfy needs (p. 169)

Value   a belief that some condition is preferable to its opposite (p. 113)

Value system   a culture's ranking of the relative importance of values (p. 114)

Values and Lifestyles (VALS)   a psychographic segmentation system used to categorize consumers into clusters (p. 570)

Want   the particular form of consumption chosen to satisfy a need (p. 92)

Word-of-mouth communication (WOM)   the information transmitted by individual consumers on an informal basis (p. 368)

Worldview   the ideas shared by members of a culture about principles of order and fairness (p. 500)

INDEXES

■ AUTHOR INDEX

■ PRODUCT/COMPANY/NAME INDEX

■ SUBJECT INDEX

Bold page numbers indicate terms emboldened in text or defined in **glossary**.